ENCYCLOPEDIA OF
U.S. Labor and Working-Class History

ENCYCLOPEDIA OF
U.S. Labor and Working-Class History

VOLUME 2
G–N
INDEX

Eric Arnesen

EDITOR

Routledge
Taylor & Francis Group
New York   London

Routledge is an imprint of the
Taylor & Francis Group, an informa business

Routledge
Taylor & Francis Group
270 Madison Avenue
New York, NY 10016

Routledge
Taylor & Francis Group
2 Park Square
Milton Park, Abingdon
Oxon OX14 4RN

Printed in the United States of America on acid-free paper
10 9 8 7 6 5 4 3 2 1

International Standard Book Number-10: 0-415-96826-7 (Hardcover)
International Standard Book Number-13: 978-0-415-96826-3 (Hardcover)

Library of Congress Cataloging-in-Publication Data

Arnesen, Eric.
    Encyclopedia of U.S. labor and working-class history / Eric Arneson.
        p. cm.
    Includes bibliographical references and index.
    ISBN 0-415-96826-7
    1. Labor--United States--History--Encyclopedias. 2. Working class--United States--History--Encyclopedias. 3. Industrial relations--United States--History--Encyclopedias. I. Title. II. Title: Encyclopedia of United States labor and working-class history.

HD8066.A78 2006
331.0973'03--dc22   2006048640

Visit the Taylor & Francis Web site at
http://www.taylorandfrancis.com

and the Routledge Web site at
http://www.routledge-ny.com

CONTENTS

ASSOCIATE EDITORS

CONTRIBUTORS

María Graciela Abarca
University of Buenos Aires, Argentina

Ellen S. Aiken
University of Colorado

Lindsey Allen
Independent Scholar

Edie Ambrose
Xavier University

David M. Anderson
Louisiana Tech University

Ronald Applegate
Cornell University

Eric Arnesen
University of Illinois at Chicago

Andrew Arnold
Kutztown University of Pennsylvania

Dexter Arnold
University of Cincinnati

Steve Ashby
University of Indiana

Carl L. Bankston, III
Tulane University

Lucy G. Barber
National Archives and Records Administration

James R. Barrett
University of Illinois at Urbana-Champaign

Kathleen M. Barry
University of Cambridge, UK

Rachel A. Batch
Widener University

Beth Thompkins Bates
Wayne State University

Joshua Beaty
College of William and Mary

Mildred Allen Beik
Independent Scholar

Evan P. Bennett
Independent Scholar

Michael J. Bennett
Independent Scholar

Julie Berebitsky
University of the South

Timothy A. Berg
McHenry County College, Illinois

Aaron Max Berkowitz
University of Illinois at Chicago

Matthew S. R. Bewig
University of Florida

Mary H. Blewett
University of Massachusetts at Lowell

Kevin Boyle
Ohio State University

Lauren H. Braun
University of Illinois at Chicago

Douglas Bristol
University of Southern Mississippi

David Brody
University of California at Davis (emeritus)

Jamie L. Bronstein
New Mexico State University

Edwin L. Brown
University of Alabama at Birmingham

CONTRIBUTORS

Victoria Bissell Brown
Grinnell College

David Brundage
University of California at Santa Cruz

Emily Brunner
University of Chicago

Robert Bruno
University of Illinois at Urbana-Champaign

Nicholas Buchanan
Massachusetts Institute of Technology

Peter H. Buckingham
Linfield College

Stephen Burwood
State University of New York at Geneseo

Robert Bussell
University of Oregon

Jenny Carson
University of Toronto

Theresa A. Case
University of Houston

Kenneth M. Casebeer
University of Miami Law School

James G. Cassedy
National Archives and Records Administration

Marisa Chappell
Oregon State University

Robert W. Cherney
San Francisco State University

Daniel Clark
Oakland University

Catherine Clinton
Independent Scholar

Andrew Wender Cohen
Syracuse University

Peter Cole
Western Illinois University

Stephen Cole
Notre Dame de Namur University

Timothy C. Coogan
LaGuardia Community College, New York

Axel B. Corlu
Binghamton University, State University of New York

Seth Cotlar
Willamette University

Evan Matthew Daniel
Tamiment Library/Robert F. Wagner Labor Archives, New York University

Catharine Christie Dann
College of William and Mary

Colin Davis
University of Alabama at Birmingham

G. V. Davis
Marshall University

Greta de Jong
University of Nevada at Reno

John D'Emilio
University of Illinois at Chicago

Dennis A. Deslippe
Australian National University

Anthony DeStefanis
College of William and Mary

Ileen A. DeVault
Cornell University

Victor G. Devinatz
Illinois State University

Steven Deyle
University of California at Davis

Steven Dike-Wilhelm
University of Colorado

Brian Dolinar
Claremont Graduate University

Colleen Doody
DePaul University

Gregory Downey
University of Wisconsin at Madison

Michael V. Doyle
Skidmore College

Alan Draper
St. Lawrence University

Philip Jacques Dreyfus
San Francisco State University

Melvyn Dubofsky
Binghamton University, State University of New York

Douglas R. Egerton
Le Moyne College

Kathleen L. Endres
University of Akron

Beth English
Princeton University

John Enyeart
Bucknell University

Steve Estes
Sonoma State University

Candace Falk
University of California at Berkeley

Rosemary Feurer
Northern Illinois University

Lisa Michelle Fine
Michigan State University

Leon Fink
University of Illinois at Chicago

Michael W. Fitzgerald
St. Olaf College

John H. Flores
University of Illinois at Chicago

Mary E. Fredrickson
Miami University of Ohio

Joshua B. Freeman
Graduate Center, City University of New York

John D. French
Woodrow Wilson International Center for Scholars

Daniel Geary
University of California at Berkeley

Gregory Geddes
Binghamton University, State University of New York

Erik S. Gellman
Northwestern University

Gene C. Gerard
Tarrant County College, Texas

Kristin Geraty
Indiana University

Larry G. Gerber
Auburn University

Heidi Scott Giusto
Duke University

Lawrence B. Glickman
University of South Carolina

Susan M. Glisson
University of Mississippi

Chad Alan Goldberg
University of Wisconsin

Steve Golin
Bloomfield College

Risa L. Goluboff
University of Virginia

Elliott J. Gorn
Brown University

Thomas M. Grace
Cornell University

George N. Green
University of Texas at Arlington

Jean-Denis Grèze
Independent Scholar

James Green
University of Massachusetts at Boston

Brian Greenberg
Monmouth College

Richard A. Greenwald
Drew University

CONTRIBUTORS

John Grider
University of Colorado

Andrew Gyory
Independent Scholar

Pamela Hackbart-Dean
Georgia State University

Greg Hall
Western Illinois University

Daniel Harper
University of Illinois

Kenneth J. Heineman
Ohio University

John Heinz
Chicago Maritime Society

Jeffrey Helgeson
University of Illinois at Chicago

Danielle Hidalgo
Independent Scholar

Frank Tobias Higbie
University of Illinois at Urbana-Champaign

Matthew Hild
Georgia State University

Adam J. Hodges
University of Houston at Clear Lake

Sean Holmes
Brunel University, United Kingdom

Michael Honey
University of Washington-Tacoma

Adam Howard
University of Florida

Tera Hunter
Carnegie Mellon University

Maurice Isserman
Hamilton College

Maurice Jackson
Georgetown University

Catherine O. Jacquet
University of Illinois at Chicago

Elizabeth Jameson
University of Calgary

Robert F. Jefferson
Xavier University

Richard J. Jensen
University of Nevada at Las Vegas (emeritus)

John B. Jentz
Raynor Memorial Libraries, Marquette University

Edward P. Johanningsmeier
Independent Scholar

Robert D. Johnston
University of Illinois at Chicago

Gwen Hoerr Jordan
University of Wisconsin at Madison

Yevette Richards Jordan
George Mason University

Lisa Kannenberg
The College of Saint Rose

Anthony Kaye
Pennsylvania State University

Brian Kelly
Queens University Belfast, Northern Ireland

Kevin Kenny
Boston College

Andrew E. Kersten
University of Wisconsin at Green Bay

Lionel Kimble, Jr.
Chicago State University

Marta M. Knight
California State University at Sacramento

Steven D. Koczak
New York State Senate Research Service

David Koistinen
American University of Beirut, Lebanon

James C. Kollros
St. Xavier University

Robert Korstad
Duke University

Molly Ladd-Taylor
York University

Clarence Lang
University of Illinois at Urbana-Champaign

Jennifer Langdon-Teclaw
University of Illinois at Chicago

R. Todd Laugen
Metropolitan State College of Denver

Bruce Laurie
University of Massachusetts, Amherst

Mark Lause
University of Cincinnati

John Leggett
Rutgers University

Steven Leikin
San Francisco State University

Karen Leroux
Drake University

Steven C. Levi
Independent Scholar and Author

Alex Lichtenstein
Rice University

Robbie Lieberman
Southern Illinois University

Joseph Lipari
University of Illinois at Chicago

Rebecca S. Lowen
Independent Scholar

Stephanie Luce
University of Massachusetts at Amherst

Jennifer Luff
Service Employees International Union

John M. Lund
Keene State College, University of New Hampshire

Brigid Lusk
Northern Illinois University

John F. Lyons
Joliet College

Robert Macieski
University of New Hampshire

Nancy MacLean
Northwestern University

Anastasia Mann
Princeton University

Geoff Mann
Simon Fraser University

Wendi N. Manuel-Scott
George Mason University

Kathleen Mapes
State University of New York at Geneseo

Sharon Mastracci
University of Illinois at Chicago

Joseph A. McCartin
Georgetown University

John Thomas McGuire
State University of New York at Cortland

Elizabeth McKillen
University of Maine at Orono

Robert C. McMath, Jr.
University of Arkansas

Eden Medina
Indiana University

Ronald Mendel
University of Northampton, United Kingdom

Timothy Messer-Kruse
University of Toledo

Jack Metzgar
Roosevelt University

Steven Meyer
University of Wisconsin at Milwaukee

Gregory M. Miller
University of Toledo

Heather Lee Miller
Historical Research Associates, Inc.

James A. Miller
George Washington University

CONTRIBUTORS

Timothy Minchin
La Trobe University

Samuel Mitrani
University of Illinois at Chicago

Marian Mollin
Virginia Polytechnic Institute and State University

Scott Molloy
University of Rhode Island

Paul D. Moreno
Hillsdale College

Alexander Morrow
University of Oregon

Scott Nelson
College of William and Mary

Caryn E. Neumann
Ohio State University

Mitchell Newton-Matza
Lexington College

Bruce Nissen
Florida International University

Mark A. Noon
Bloomsburg University of Pennsylvania

Stephen H. Norwood
University of Oklahoma

Kathleen Banks Nutter
Smith College

Kathryn J. Oberdeck
University of Illinois at Urbana-Champaign

Edward T. O'Donnell
College of the Holy Cross

Richard Oestricher
University of Pittsburgh

Brigid O'Farrell
Stanford University

Amy C. Offner
Dollars and Sense *Magazine*

John S. Olszowka
Mercyhurst College

Colleen O'Neill
Utah State University

Liesl Miller Orenic
Dominican University

Annelise Orleck
Dartmouth College

Merideth Oyen
Georgetown University

David Palmer
Flinders University, Australia

Karen Pastorello
Tompkins Cortland Community College, New York

Barry Pateman
University of California-Berkeley

Brad Paul
National Policy and Advocacy Council on Homelessness (NPACH)

Ruth Percy
University of Toronto

Michael Perman
University of Illinois at Chicago

Jean Pfaelzer
University of Delaware

Lori Pierce
DePaul University

Michael Cain Pierce
University of Arkansas

Jerald Podair
Lawrence University

Kevin Noble Powers
Georgetown University

David Purcell
University of Cincinnati

Peter Rachleff
Macalester College

Bruno Ramirez
University of Montreal, Canada

Scott E. Randolph
Purdue University

Padma Rangaswamy
South Asian American Policy and Research Institute

David C. Ranney
University of Illinois at Chicago (emeritus)

Gerda W. Ray
University of Missouri at St. Louis

Jonathan Rees
Colorado State University at Pueblo

Steven A. Reich
James Madison University

David M. Reimers
New York University (emeritus)

Ester Reiter
Atkinson College, York University

Rachel R. Reynolds
Drexel University

Christopher Rhomberg
Yale University

Lawrence Richards
University of Richmond

Elizabeth Ricketts
Indiana University of Pennsylvania

Steven A. Riess
Northeastern Illinois University

Howard Rock
Florida International University

John C. Rodrigue
Louisiana State University

Marc S. Rodriguez
University of Notre Dame

Donald W. Rogers
Central Connecticut State University and Housatonic Community College

Gerald Ronning
Albright College

Margaret Rose
University of California at Santa Barbara

Sarah F. Rose
University of Illinois at Chicago

John J. Rosen
University of Illinois at Chicago

Doug Rossinow
Metropolitan State University

Kate Rousmaniere
Miami University

Margaret C. Rung
Roosevelt University

Jason Russell
York University

John Russell
Georgia State University

Francis Ryan
Moravian College

Joseph C. Santora
Essex County College

Ralph Scharnau
Northeast Iowa Community College, Peosta

Ronald W. Schatz
Wesleyan University

Michael Schiavone
Flinders University, Australia

Kevin E. Schmiesing
Acton Institute

Dorothee Schneider
University of Illinois at Urbana-Champaign

Katrin Schultheiss
University of Illinois at Chicago

Rima Lunin Schultz
University of Illinois at Chicago

Carlos A. Schwantes
University of Missouri at St. Louis

CONTRIBUTORS

James Searing
University of Illinois at Chicago

Karin A. Shapiro
Duke University

Paul Siegel
Independent Scholar

Michael W. Simpson
University of Wisconsin at Madison

Joseph E. Slater
University of Toledo

Eric Richard Smith
University of Illinois at Chicago

Michael Spear
City University of New York

Robyn Ceanne Spencer
Pennsylvania State University

Sarah Stage
Arizona State University, West Campus

Howard R. Stanger
Canisius College

Richard Stott
George Washington University

David O. Stowell
Keene State College, University of New Hampshire

Shelton Stromquist
University of Iowa

Thomas Summerhill
Michigan State University

Paul Michel Taillon
University of Auckland, New Zealand

Vanessa Tait
University of California at Berkeley

Clarence Taylor
Baruch College, City University of New York

Kieran W. Taylor
University of North Carolina at Chapel Hill

Michael M. Topp
University of Texas at El Paso

Frank Towers
University of Northern Colorado

Martin Tuohy
National Archives and Records Administration, Great Lakes Branch

Mary C. Tuominen
Denison University

Joseph M. Turrini
Auburn University

Emily E. LaBarbera Twarog
University of Illinois at Chicago

William E. Van Vugt
Calvin College

Susannah Walker
Virginia Wesleyan University

Wilson J. Warren
Western Michigan University

Peter Way
Bowling Green State University

John Weber
College of William and Mary

Edmund F. Wehrle
Eastern Illinois University

Carl R. Weinberg
Indiana University

Robert E. Weir
Mount Holyoke College

Virginia Wright Wexman
University of Illinois at Chicago

Carmen Teresa Whalen
Williams College

Jeannie M. Whayne
University of Arkansas

John White
Independent Scholar

Marcus Widenor
University of Oregon

John Fabian Witt
Columbia University

David Witwer
Lycoming College

Kenneth C. Wolensky
Pennsylvania Historical and Museum Commission

James Wolfinger
Northwestern University

Chris Wonderlich
University of Illinois at Chicago

John Chi-Kit Wong
Washington State University

Robert H. Woodrum
Clark Atlanta University

Gerald Zahavi
State University of New York at Albany

Minna P. Ziskind
University of Pennsylvania

David A. Zonderman
North Carolina State University

ALPHABETICAL LIST OF ENTRIES

THEMATIC LIST OF ENTRIES

Concepts and Developments

Abolitionism
Affirmative Action
American Exceptionalism
American Standard of Living
Anarchism
Anticommunism
Apprenticeship
Arbitration
Artisans
Arts and Crafts Movement
Assembly Line Production
Blacklists
Boycotts
Capital Flight
Catholic Church
Central Labor Unions
Child Care
Child Labor
Civil Rights
Cold War
Collective Bargaining
Company Towns
Convict Labor in the New South
Cooperation
Coxey's Army
Culture, Working-Class
De-Industrialization
Disfranchisement
"Don't Buy Where You Can't Work" Campaigns
Dorr War
Dual Unionism
Education, Labor
Emancipation and Reconstruction
Environmentalism
Family Wage
Film
Five Dollar Day
Foreign Policy
Fourierism

Free-Soilism
Gender
Globalization
Gold Rush
Great Migration
Great Society/War on Poverty (1960s)
Historiography of American Labor History
Hoboes
Housework
Immigration Restriction
Indentured Servitude
Industrial Democracy
Industrial Unionism
Injunctions
Labor Day
Labor Republicanism
Labor Theory of Value
Living Wage
Living Wage Campaigns
Maquiladoras
May Day
Migrant Farmworkers
Music
New Left
New South
New York City Fiscal Crisis (1970s)
No-Strike Pledge
Novels, Poetry, Drama
Operation Dixie
Organized Crime
Pattern Bargaining
Peonage
Philadelphia Plan
Plumb Plan
Politics and Labor, Nineteenth Century
Portal-to-Portal Pay
Protocol of Peace
Racketeering and RICO
Rosie the Riveter
Sacco and Vanzetti
Sexual Harassment
Sharecropping and Tenancy

Legal Cases, Acts, and Legislation

Management

Racial and Ethnic Categories of Workers

African-Americans
Africans (Twentieth Century)
Central Americans
Croatians
Cubans
English Workers
Finns
French-Canadians
Germans
Guatemalans
Irish
Italians
Jamaicans
Jews
Mexican and Mexican American Workers
Native Americans
Puerto Ricans
South Asians
Southeast Asians

Regions

Borders: Mexico/U.S.
California
Hawaii
Midwest
Pacific Northwest
South
Southwest

Strikes

A. E. Staley Strike (1995)
Actors' Strike (1919)
Anthracite Coal Strike (1902)
Anti-Rent Wars (New York)
Atlanta Washerwomen's Strike (1881)
Bacon's Rebellion
Bisbee Deportation/Copper Strike (1917)
Bogalusa Labor Conflict of 1919
C&O Canal Workers Strike (1834)
Chicago Teamsters Strike (1905)
Chinese Laborers' Strike on the Transcontinental
  Railroad (1867)
Cripple Creek Strikes
Delano Grape Strike (1965–1970)
Elaine, Arkansas Massacre (1919)

Gastonia Strike (1929)
Great Upheaval
Haymarket Affair (1886)
Homestead Strike (1892)
J.P. Stevens Campaign (1963–1980)
Japanese Strike in Hawai'i (1909)
Journeymen Carpenters Strike in New York (1833)
Kohler Strike (1954)
Lawrence Strike (1912)
Lord Dunmore's Proclamation
Louisiana Sugar Strike (1887)
Lowell Turnouts (1834, 1836)
Ludlow Massacre (1914)
Lynn Shoe Strike (1860)
Memorial Day Massacre (1937)
Memphis Sanitation Strike (1968)
New Orleans General Strike (1892)
New York City Hospital Strike (1959)
Oakland General Strike (1946)
Ocean Hill-Brownsville Strikes (1968)
Oxnard Strike (1903)
P-9 Strike
Paterson (NJ) Silk Strike (1913)
Phelps Dodge Copper Strike (1983–1984)
Philadelphia Journeymen Cordwainers Strike (1806)
Philadelphia Printers Strike (1786)
Philadelphia Transit Strike (1944)
Pittston Coal Strike (1989–1990)
Postal Strike (1970)
Professional Air Traffic Controllers Organization
  Strike (1981)
Pueblo Revolt (1680)
Pullman Strike and Boycott (1894)
Railroad Shopmen's Strike (1922)
Railroad Strikes (1877)
Rock Springs, Wyoming, Strike of 1885
San Joaquin Valley Cotton Strike (1933)
Scottsboro Case
Sit-Down Strikes (1937)
Steel Strike (1959)
Strike Wave (1919)
Tennessee Convict Uprising (1891–1892)
Tompkins Square Riot (1874)
United Parcel Service Strike (1997)
Uprising of the 20,000 (1909)
West Virginia Mine War (1920–1921)
Wheatland Strike/Riot (1913)

Trade Unions

Agricultural Workers Organization
Air Line Pilots' Association

THEMATIC LIST OF ENTRIES

INTRODUCTION

At the dawn of the twenty-first century, the scholarly field of labor history is a large, sophisticated, and diverse one. Prior to the 1960s, economists, political scientists, and historians largely took individual trade unions and the labor movement as the subjects of their academic investigations. Since the 1960s, however, the emergence of the "new labor history" has broadened the investigative lens considerably, embracing countless topics that earlier scholars might not even recognize as belonging to their field. Trade unions and labor movements continue, of course, to be legitimate subjects of exploration, but labor history has come to embrace much more. Initially concerned with grassroots activism, the experiences of the rank and file, and working-class communities and their cultures, the "new labor history"—which by 2006 is no longer very new—is deeply concerned with politics, law, race, ethnicity, gender, law, and migration. The sheer heterogeneity of America's working classes now stands at the heart of much of the field. Historians clearly recognize that just as there was no single working class possessing shared interests, so too was there no single working-class identity, culture, or ideology.

Today, a large and growing number of labor historians and labor studies scholars have produced a large and rich body of literature on a vast array of subjects. The Labor and Working-Class History Association and the Labor Studies Association boast hundreds of members, the field publishes multiple journals, articles on labor's past regularly find their way into non-labor oriented journals, and the themes explored by labor historians are routinely covered in U.S. history textbooks. To a significant extent, labor history, long considered by its practitioners to be a vital component of the larger drama of American history, is recognized as such by the larger field of American historians as well.

The *Encyclopedia of U.S. Labor and Working-Class History* builds upon the past several generations of scholarship to explore numerous dimensions of the working-class past. Its conception of what constitutes labor history is expansive and capacious, its sense of the borders between different fields porous. While attentive to the field's traditional focus on skilled craft and semi-skilled manufacturing workers, it devotes considerable attention to occupations that have only more recently attracted scholarly attention, such as longshoring, domestic service, prostitution, nursing, teaching, hair styling, computer programming, sleeping car portering, housework, and agriculture. It erodes the artificial boundaries between labor history and African-American history, treating the subjects of slavery, the slave trade, slave rebellions, and abolitionism, for instance, as integral to the recounting of the history of American labor. The heterogeneity of the working class is a central theme, with the *Encyclopedia* providing extensive coverage of race and gender divisions and the experiences of a multitude of immigrant groups.

How to Use This Book

Organization

The *Encyclopedia of U.S. Labor and Working-Class History* is organized in a straightforward and easy to use **A to Z format**. Users will find a number of useful features accompanying the entries, including **References and Further Reading** and **See Also** suggestions for easy cross-referencing. The volumes each include a thematic list of entries, in addition to an alphabetical list of entries and a **thorough, analytical index**.

Illustrations

The *Encyclopedia* includes 78 illustrations. These photographs, culled from the archives of the Library of Congress, accompany specific entries, and depict strikes, union meetings, workers, and influential leaders.

INTRODUCTION

Thematic Coverage

The *Encyclopedia of U.S. Labor and Working-Class History* features 662 independent entries ranging in length from 500 to 6,000 words. The topics covered fall into 11 broad categories:

Concepts and Developments: Entries included in this category look in depth at central concepts, ideas, and broad developments in the history of American workers. American exceptionalism, sexual harassment, music, affirmative action, syndicalism, strikebreaking, living wage campaigns, immigration restriction, indentured servitude, and the historiography of labor history are only a few of the subjects treated in this broad-ranging category.

Government Agencies and Committees: Entries falling into this category examine government agencies affecting labor. Among the many covered are the Fair Employment Practice Committee, the LaFollette Civil Liberties Committee, the U.S. Women's Bureau, and the Federal Bureau of Investigation.

Individuals: Entries in this category cover a diverse set of figures intimately involved in labor relations and working-class life over the past two and a half centuries. Familiar figures like Walter Reuther, Jimmy Hoffa, George Meany, and A. Philip Randolph will be found in this section. But the list of key figures includes a host of less familiar names, including labor poet George Lippard, community activist Saul Alinsky, settlement house leaders Florence Kelley and Jane Addams, the mythic figure John Henry, labor troubadour Joe Hill, African-American labor activists Richard L. Davis, Willard Townsend, and Maida Springer, anarchist Lucy Parsons, and labor journalist John Swinton.

Legal Cases, Acts, and Legislation: This category focuses on laws and court cases affecting labor relations and working-class life. Examples in this group include the Chinese Exclusion Acts, the Civil Rights Act of 1964, Aid to Families with Dependent Children (AFDC), the Immigration and Nationality Act of 1965, and the North American Free Trade Agreement.

Management: Business organizations and programs (such as labor-management cooperation, welfare capitalism, and the National Right to Work Committee) are examined in this category.

Organizations: Organizations that are not unions, but nonetheless were working-class associations or bodies that dealt with working-class issues, compose another category. The Socialist Party of America, the Colored Farmers' Alliance, the Populist Party, and the March on Washington Movement fall into this category.

Periods: Lengthy chronological entries provide broad coverage of the principal contours of the evolution of labor systems and labor relations from the colonial era to the present. The period covered in each essay (the colonial era, the antebellum era, the Gilded Age and Progressive Era, the 1940s, and 1980 to the present, for example) conforms to an established periodizaiton or logical block of time corresponding to key developments.

Racial and Ethnic Categories of Workers: Racial and ethnic/immigration groups constitute another category of entries, with coverage of a wide range of groups including the Irish, Mexican and Mexican Americans, French Canadians, and recent immigrants from Southeast and South Asia and Central America.

Regions: Key geographical regions with a defined historical scholarship (including the South, the Pacific Northwest, the Southwest, and California) are explored in this category of entries.

Strikes: Strikes and labor-related conflicts represent a significant group of entries. Well-known events such as the Pullman Strike of 1894, the 1912 Lawrence Textile Strike, the 1937 Memorial Day Massacre, and the J.P. Stevens campaign are examined, as are many lesser known conflicts including the 1881 Atlanta Washerwomen's Strike, the 1919 Bogalusa, Louisiana strike, and the 1891–1892 Tennessee Convict Uprising.

Trade Unions: Numerous entries explore the history of trade unions in the nineteenth and twentieth centuries. While commonly recognized and major unions and union federations such as the United Steelworkers of America, the Knights of Labor, the International Brotherhood of Teamsters, and the Industrial Workers of the World are covered, so too are unions that are not household names, such as the Stockyards Labor Council, the International Fur and Leather Workers Union, and the United Hatters', Cap and Millinery Workers' International Union. Particular attention is paid to unions and labor associations composed of non-white workers and women, including the Brotherhood of Sleeping Car Porters, the United Farm Workers of America, the Southern Tenant Farmers Union, the Women's Trade Union League, and the Coalition of Labor Union Women.

A total of 298 scholars in the United States and Europe have contributed to the *Encyclopedia*. These individuals are specialists in their fields and bring to the project a vast wealth of knowledge and expertise. They share no historiographical or political perspective, and each has approached their subjects as she or he saw fit. Indeed, the interpretations offered are those of the authors and, at times, similar topics are explored from different or even conflicting interpretive positions.

Acknowledgments

Since the actual labor that goes into creating an encyclopedia of this sort is vast and collective, numerous people necessarily contributed significant to bringing this project to fruition. The five associate editors—Leon Fink, Cindy Hahamovitch, Tera Hunter, Bruce Laurie, and Joseph McCartin—are all superb scholars of labor's past who devoted considerable time and energy to conceptualizing the volume, identifying potential authors, and reading, editing, and engaging the arguments of the hundreds of entries in this volume. Without their editorial care and expertise, this project would have been impossible to complete. At Routledge, Mark L. Georgiev helped shape the project in its early stages, while Kristen Holt oversaw the massive logistical operation of contacting authors, answering queries, and shepherding the project through the editorial process. Closer to home, fellow historian Katrin Schultheiss provided her usual and invaluable intellectual support and guidance throughout the project's life, while our children Rachel, Samuel, and William patiently, and sometimes not so patiently, endured my continual thinking-out-loud about the project and countless of its individual subjects. While their interests remained largely fixed on baseball, soccer, and children's fiction—they provided no editorial support but did occasionally ask good questions—I suspect that they learned something about the history of labor and the craft of history in the process. I look forward to the day when they too can use and learn from the *Encyclopedia*.

Eric Arnesen

G

GARMENT INDUSTRY

The production of clothes from the Colonial Era up until the early nineteenth century was small-scale and largely home-based. Clothes were made to order and fitted for an individual. Given the prevalence of this mode of production, there were few demands for the industrialization of the production process. Indeed in many households, clothes were made by family members. Those who could afford to hired artisan tailors and dressmakers to make them an entire garment from start to finish. These skilled tailors and tailoresses tended to be native-born Americans or German and British immigrants, with immigrant groups represented to a lesser degree. Some tailors traveled from house to house in search of work carrying their tools with them. Other tailors and dressmakers worked from workshops, usually in, or connected to their homes, and employed journeymen and apprentices. The master craftsperson was thus a manufacturer, a teacher, and a retailer. Even at this early date, New York City was the largest center of clothing production and remained so up until the late twentieth century, although increasingly garments were also produced in other locations.

Both tailors of men's clothing and their apprentices were male, although the assistance of female family members was often called for during the finishing process or when the workload was especially heavy. Dressmaking was one of the few craft trades open to women in this period, largely because it was considered improper for men to engage in the physical contact with women involved in fitting a dress. This concern carried over into the twentieth century, and women continued to remain a large proportion of workers in the custom-made dress trade.

The garment trade in the United States expanded following the introduction of a protective tariff in 1816, which allowed American garment producers to capture the market in ready-made clothing for southern slaves, heretofore dominated by English companies. Ready-made garments—those not made to order and of a lesser quality than those worn by whites—relied more heavily on unskilled labor. The expansion of the ready-made trade catering to Americans of all races and classes beginning in the nineteenth century produced significant changes to the garment industry.

In the first half of the nineteenth century, ready-made garments became increasingly popular among a broader spectrum of the male population; accordingly the men's clothing industry underwent considerable change. The growth in ready-made clothing that was designed to fit an average person, as opposed to measured to fit a specific individual, meant that the manufacturing process could be standardized, greater numbers of semi- and unskilled workers could be employed, and production could be expanded. Although there remained a custom-made trade for the middle and upper classes, increasingly production of ready-made clothes moved out of the small-scale workshop, away from the guidance of an artisan tailor, and into the factory, where the manufacturer replaced the artisan. The first recorded factory was established in New York in 1831 (Boston and

New Bedford, Massachusetts, became other centers of clothing manufacture by the mid-nineteenth century).

Unlike in the factories of the late nineteenth or twentieth centuries, garments were not actually assembled in these early plants. Clothes were designed and cut in factories, but the cut fabric was sent out to be sewed by individuals who worked in their homes in what was known as "home work." Because of the labor-intensive nature of the garment industry, coupled with the general lack of equipment necessary, clothes were assembled in workers' living spaces. This meant that workers paid for lighting and heating in addition to the purchase of needles and thread, which continued even once production had moved to factories. Manufacturers thus increased their profit margin while workers turned their homes into production centers. Despite such exploitation some workers, particularly married women with children, preferred home work because it with them to engage in wage labor while attending to their domestic responsibilities, namely, childcare.

The Garment Industry in the Late Nineteenth Century

The demand for uniforms during the Civil War (1861–1865) further encouraged the development of the ready-made trade in the men's garment industry. At the same time, changing fashions facilitated the development and growth of the women's ready-made trade. Largely because of women's fashions, it was not until the post-Civil War years that the women's garment industry adopted ready-made techniques on a large scale, although cloaks (originally meaning capes or coats but increasingly including suits) had been made *en mass* before the 1860s. Home work was less prevalent in the women's garment trade and inside shops, in which the majority of a garment was made in one establishment employing girls and young women, dominated until the 1880s. However, conditions in these shops were poor. A study in Boston (the center of the cloak industry at this time) in 1871 recorded that workers were crammed into upper floor rooms with poor ventilation, often with no toilets or drinking water. These girls and women usually worked for 10 hours a day, but as they were paid by the piece, they often took work home with them to finish late into the night. After the 1880s, the women's ready-made garment trade became more like the men's. More male workers were employed, suits were made in larger quantities, and contracting was introduced.

By the 1880s, garment centers had developed throughout and beyond the Northeast. Important centers included Chicago, Philadelphia, Cleveland, Detroit, Baltimore, Milwaukee, Rochester, St. Louis, Cincinnati, Louisville, and Syracuse. Manufacturers built larger factories; there was greater standardization of sizes, styles, and processes; and the manufacturing process was subject to a greater subdivision of tasks. Subcontractors began to distribute the cut cloth to be sewn as manufacturers expanded and could no longer handle all the orders themselves. As fashions changed more frequently and orders were put in at the last minute, manufacturers were precluded from producing year round and stockpiling. In addition to poor working conditions, workers were thus faced with seasonal slow downs or unemployment in the production of both men's and women's clothes. The men's garment trade peaked between January and March and then fell off until November. The women's had two distinct peaks in the spring and fall. In between these months, many workers were unemployed. Some found casual work, while many women returned to their domestic commitments.

This expansion of the garment industry in the 1880s and 1890s occurred at the same time as waves of European immigrants were arriving in the United States. The makeup of the workforce changed as people from Eastern Europe (the majority of whom were Jewish) arrived, replacing a workforce that was largely of Irish and German descent. New immigrants, some of whom had worked as skilled tailors in Europe, provided an abundant cheap-labor supply and thus assisted in the expansion of the industry but were habitually exploited. Many immigrants found work through ethnic networks, and the dominance of immigrants in the garment trade meant that the ability to speak English was not necessarily a requirement. This was especially true when the employer was an immigrant entrepreneur who had moved from the workforce to a subcontracting or management position.

Sweatshops became endemic around the late nineteenth century (not just in the United States but in Europe, too) as demand for, and production of, ready-made clothing increased. Sweatshop conditions occurred in factories as well as in people's homes. Sweatshops were characterized by long hours for low wages in poor conditions. Deductions were often made for thread and needles; mistakes had to be paid for by the worker; rooms were often badly lit, were too hot in the summer and too cold in the winter, and were poorly ventilated. Both women and men worked in such conditions and at times child labor was used, especially by workers who worked in their own homes where clothing manufacture could involve the whole family.

Garment workers parading on May Day, New York, New York. Library of Congress, Prints & Photographs Division [LC-USZ62-41871].

The 1892 Tenement House Act in New York, although difficult to enforce, encouraged a move from production in homes to factories. Inside-shops thus grew, particularly in the newer garment centers, such as Chicago, which produced 17% of goods in the men's garment trade (to New York's 40%) by 1909. Factory production was more inclined to standardization of products and the division of the production process into multiple semi- or unskilled tasks. The subdivision of the work process entailed dividing a single skilled job into multiple tasks. The individual tasks tended to involve less skill, although there was no inherent necessity for them to do so. For example the task system that had long been practiced in Europe and was brought to the United States by immigrants in the late nineteenth century maintained skill levels but encouraged specialization. The incentive on the part of the employer to deskill the individual tasks was twofold. Lower wages could be paid to semi- and unskilled workers, and by paying piece rates (based on the number of items completed) instead of weekly rates (based on the number of hours worked), workers were encouraged to increase their own production levels in order to earn a decent wage.

Closely connected to this was the fact that the deskilled, subdivisional system afforded the employer greater control over the workers for s/he was less reliant on skilled workers who were of more limited supply.

Processes of mechanization were closely connected to subdivision and the move to factories; indeed they often happened hand in hand. The mechanization of the garment industry began in the 1850s when the first viable sewing machines were marketed. (Elias Howe invented the sewing machine in 1846.) Singer became the pre-eminent manufacturer, increasing its output from 810 machines in 1853 to 21,000 a decade later and 232,000 by 1873. Within 4 years 87,000 had been sold in the United States. Sewing machines were put to use in both small-scale workshops, larger scale factories, and by individuals at home as prices fell in the interwar years. Other machines included the band-knife, also introduced in the 1850s; the buttonhole machine that in the 1880s could sew six buttonholes a minute; and Dearborn's blind-stitch machine for felling hems that was first introduced in 1900 and was improved 2 years later so that it could be used for padding collars and lapels.

In factories workers used electrical sewing machines, edge-pressers, collar- and lapel-padding machines, and felling machines, all of which led to a further growth in semi- and unskilled jobs in the trade. For example at a Hart, Schaffner, and Marx factory in Chicago, 150 separate operations were involved in the manufacture of a coat. Such machines could also lead to rationalization and thus a loss of skilled positions. Skilled positions (such as cutting and pressing) tended to be occupied by male workers, while women were employed as machine operators and finishers (for example buttonholers), which were perceived to require less skill. This gendered division of labor was not unique to the garment industry. However the discourse surrounding clothing production was more readily able to draw on contemporary gender discourses that perceived domestic chores, including sewing, to be women's work. Constructing sewing as something women could do naturally meant that it was not considered an acquired skill and thus had neither high payment nor status.

Unionization at the Turn of the Twentieth Century

The large number of immigrants arriving in the United States looking for work and the lack of union organization in the garment trades facilitated these poor conditions. Small groups of workers working in a multitude of locations across a city were incredibly difficult to organize, and although attempts were sporadically made to challenge single issues, it was not until the turn of the twentieth century that nationwide unions had any strength. One of the first significant protests occurred in New York in the summer of 1883. Seven hundred cloak makers and dressmakers, half of them women, struck in what New York newspapers named the "Emigrants' Strike." Although the Cloak and Dressmakers' Association was formed out of the strike, it was short lived, as was common at the time.

Until 1891 in the men's garment trade and 1900 in the women's, there were no national garment workers' unions although workers often organized on a city or state basis. National unions were needed in both sectors of the industry, for increasingly manufacturers looked to other cities when faced with a strike to get their garments made. Without nationwide unions, there was no way of limiting this, and thus workers' power was considerably limited. In the last half of the nineteenth century, numerous unions representing the range of workers in the garment industry sprung up sporadically, often around strikes,

at times affiliating with the national federation the Knights of Labor. The workers who organized with the Knights tended to be the more skilled and more educated, which by the late nineteenth century, were the minority in the garment industry.

The first nationwide garment union was the United Garment Workers (UGW), founded in New York in 1891 to organize the men's garment industry. The first elected leaders were American-born workers who supported the American Federation of Labor's (AFL) pure and simple unionism, while the majority of union members were immigrant workers who were often sympathetic to socialism and anarchism. Although the leadership remained male-dominated, the UGW claimed to do a better job of organizing women workers than many of the previous local unions. Nevertheless women still remained excluded from the union executive, and the union demonstrated limited commitment to their organization.

The Garment Industry and Garment Unions in the Twentieth Century

The structure of the industry as established by the early twentieth century changed little in the next century. It remained a labor-intensive, low-technology trade reliant on cheap labor. Immigrant workers remained an important factor, although the immigrant groups changed. As competition from imported goods in the later twentieth century increased, American companies looked for cheaper production methods, including relocating within the United States and then going overseas in search of even cheaper labor markets.

Although the work process remained the same and manufacturers were reluctant to improve working conditions, they were increasingly pushed to do so as garment trade unions grew stronger. Cloak makers, who were among the most skilled in the women's garment trade, founded the International Ladies' Garment Workers' Union (ILGWU) in 1900. The ILGWU got off to an inauspicious start with only 11 delegates from seven local unions, all of whom were Jewish and from the East Coast, attending the founding convention. However a strike of children's cloak makers in New York in 1907 helped to revitalize the union. The 1909 Uprising of the Twenty Thousand, in which thousands of shirtwaist workers, many of whom were women, walked out in New York, galvanized the ILGWU's position. Following the Great Revolt, another strike in 1910 in New York that saw 60,000 workers on strike, the ILGWU demonstrated its potential power in securing an unprecedented agreement known as the Protocol of Peace that secured wage and hour standards and allowed for the impartial arbitration of disputes and a joint commission to address workplace health concerns.

Workers in the men's garment industry inspired by the New York protests also began to challenge the standards in their sector of the industry. In Chicago in the winter of 1910–1911, a general strike in the men's garment industry peaked with 40,000 workers out. The strike began when 18-year-old Hannah Shapiro, a Ukrainian Jewish immigrant who worked at Shop 5 of Hart, Schaffner, and Marx, led her coworkers out in protest of reduced wages, and soon spread across the city. As in the Uprising of the Twenty Thousand, women thus played an important role in the Chicago strike, although also as in New York, the public voice of the strike all too quickly became male. Nevertheless both the Uprising of the Twenty Thousand and the Chicago strike demonstrated the potential of cross-class alliances that were the foundations of the women's labor movement. The Women's Trade Union League in both cases played an important role in organizing soup kitchens, negotiating with city officials and employers, and using their role in the public eye to draw attention to the plight of working women.

The 1910–1911 Chicago strike sowed seeds of dissent within the men's garment trade unions. Unhappy with the role of the UGW leadership in December 1914, Chicago workers led a group of delegates at the UGW convention in Nashville, Tennessee, out of the convention to form a rump session that became the Amalgamated Clothing Workers of America (ACWA). It organized workers on a quasi-industrial basis and thus was more welcoming to semi- and unskilled workers, many of whom were immigrants and women. Women played a central role in work protests and were an increasing constituent of the membership, but they remained marginal among union officials. Although Dorothy Jacobs Bellanca became the first female vice-president of a major trade union (the ACWA) in July 1916 at the age of 21 and Fannia Cohn became organizing secretary of the ILGWU General Education Committee in the same year and then educational director 2 years later, they remained the only women on the executive committees of the two leading garment unions.

Because the ACWA claimed jurisdiction over the same group of workers as the UGW, it was perceived to be a dual union by the American Federation of Labor (AFL) and thus was not issued a charter. Nevertheless the ACWA had rapid success. By 1916, it had a national membership of 48,000, and this had jumped to 138,000 just 3 years later. Moreover the ACWA secured a landmark agreement with Hart,

Schaffner, and Marx in 1919 that secured a 44-hour week, and New York's manufacturers soon followed.

The Great Depression caused decreased production and increased unemployment in the garment industry. In 1934, the production value of garments produced in Chicago was only 30% of what it had been in 1929; in Rochester, New York, it was only 28%. As union membership dropped, employers shattered the wage and hour standards that the ILGWU and ACWA had secured in the 1920s. Nevertheless the ILGWU and the ACWA capitalized on Section 7a of the New Deal's National Industrial Recovery Act (June 1933) that gave workers the right to join unions and to engage in collective bargaining. In particular they tried, with varied success, to organize the newer garment centers, such as Puerto Rico and Los Angeles. By 1924, the latter was already the fourth largest center of garment production in the United States. Also in the 1930s, both the ILGWU and the ACWA as advocates of industrial unionism were highly influential in the formation in November 1935 of the Committee for Industrial Organization (CIO—later the Congress of Industrial Organizations).

After World War II the trend that had begun in the 1920s of garment manufacturers relocating in search of higher profit margins was accentuated. Often this meant moving from a union stronghold to the non-unionized South or West. Thus the garment industry declined in the Northeast and Pennsylvania. The West, especially California, and the South, especially North Carolina, benefited. The former became the center of the bourgeoning sportswear industry. Immigrants still made up a large proportion of the workforce, but instead of being eastern European Jews and Italians, by the 1960s the dominant groups were southeast Asians and Hispanics. (Workers from these ethnic groups were also an increasingly important component of the workforce in such cities as New York.) This was true of other areas garment manufacturers moved to. For example Miami's garment industry was boosted in the late 1960s by New York-based companies leaving a union stronghold to relocate in Florida and employing members of the Cuban immigrant community, which was unorganized and at least initially relatively passive. The ILGWU and ACWA (which merged with the Textile Workers' Union of America in 1976 to form the Amalgamated Clothing and Textile Workers' Union [ACTWU]) continued to try to organize these new garment centers.

By 1989, Los Angeles had surpassed New York as the largest U.S. garment-producing center. Many workers were undocumented, and employers used this against them if they protested low wages or poor conditions. The industry remained seasonal, as it had been since the nineteenth century. Work peaked in March, declined in the summer before picking up again in the fall, then dropped off again in January to begin the cycle again. Surveys in the 1990s revealed extensive violation of laws regulating health and safety, wages, hours, and homework, but with a declining number of government inspectors, there was little that could be done to enforce such regulations.

As the twentieth century came to a close, imported garments increasingly threatened the American-based industry. By the late 1990s, more than 60% of garments sold in the United States were imported, mostly from Asian countries. The first large wave of Asian imports in the 1960s forced American companies to look for cheaper production methods. Item 807 of the U.S. Tariff Schedule (1963) facilitated the move to overseas production. Under this ordinance cut garments could be shipped overseas for assembly and when re-imported to the United States; U.S. duties were paid on only the difference in value that low-cost assembly had added. In 1983, the Reagan administration further encouraged such processes with the creation of the Caribbean Basin Initiative that extended special trade rights to 22 countries. Although more work was available in these overseas locations, investigations in the late twentieth century revealed that real wages in the garment industry declined in the countries chosen for relocation.

Despite advances in the technology of clothing manufacture and the textiles involved and decades of stability in the garment trade, unions' highly exploitative sweatshop conditions still remained at the turn of the twenty-first century. In August 1995, the Department of Labor raided a compound in El Monte (a middle-class suburb of Los Angeles) and uncovered a sweatshop where 72 undocumented workers from Thailand worked behind barbed-wire fences earning around $1.60 an hour. The clothes they made were destined for such well-known stores as Macy's, Filene's, and J. C. Penny's. Indeed across the Los Angeles area at the turn of the twenty-first century, conditions were remarkably similar to those a hundred years earlier. The largest garment center in the country may have moved from the East to the West Coast and the immigrant groups employed shifted from eastern and southern Europeans to Central Americans and southeast Asians, but workers, a majority of whom are women, still worked in sweatshop conditions with little organization or protection. Trade unions widened their campaign base in the 1990s as they had in the 1910s. They found support on U.S. college campuses with the formation of United Students against Sweatshops in 1998. However companies continued to resist the unionized shop. Indeed some companies responded to attempts by the

United Needletrades, Industrial and Textile Employees (UNITE—founded in 1995 from the merger of the ILGWU and ACTWU) to organize in California by moving production to Mexico.

RUTH PERCY

References and Further Reading

Argesinger, Jo Anne E. *Making the Amalgamated: Gender, Ethnicity, and Class in the Baltimore Clothing Industry, 1899–1939.* Baltimore, MD: Johns Hopkins University Press, 1999.

Bender, Daniel E. *Sweated Work, Weak Bodies: Anti-Sweatshop Campaigns and Languages of Labor.* New Brunswick, NJ: Rutgers University Press, 2004.

Budish, J. M., and George Soule. *The New Unionism in the Clothing Industry.* New York: Harcourt, Brace and Howe, 1920.

Fraser, Steven. *Labor Will Rule: Sidney Hillman and the Rise of American Labor.* New York: The Free Press, 1991.

Green, Nancy L. *Ready-to-Wear and Ready-to-Work: A Century of Industry and Immigrants in Parish and New York.* Durham, NC: Duke University Press, 1997.

Rosen, Ellen Israel. *Making Sweatshops: The Globalization of the U.S. Apparel Industry.* Berkeley: University of California Press, 2002.

Ross, Andrew, ed. *No Sweat: Fashion, Free Trade, and the Rights of Garment Workers.* New York: Verso, 1997.

Seidman, Joel. *The Needle Trades.* New York: Farrar and Rinehart, 1942.

Tyler, Gus. *Look for the Union Label: A History of the International Ladies' Garment Workers' Union.* Armonk, NY: M. E. Sharpe, 1995.

See also **Amalgamated Clothing Workers of America/ UNITE; Cohn, Fannia; Hillman, Sidney; International Ladies' Garment Workers' Union; Lemlich, Clara Shavelson; Nestor, Agnes; Newman, Pauline M.; Pessota, Rose; Protocol of Peace; Schneiderman, Rose; Triangle Shirtwaist Fire; United Garment Workers**

GARVEY, MARCUS (AUGUST 17, 1887– JUNE 10, 1940)
Black Nationalist

Jamaican native Marcus Garvey led the first mass movement among African-Americans in the United States. Garvey's short-lived and ultimately unsuccessful effort to stoke black nationalism into a Back-to-Africa movement provided a dramatic episode in the Harlem Renaissance of the 1920s.

Garvey was born in Jamaica and received an elementary education there. He was trained as a printer,

Convention address by Hon. Marcus Garvey delivering constitution for Negro rights. Library of Congress, Prints & Photographs Division, NYWT & S Collection [LC-USZ62-109628].

became a foreman, and led a printers' strike in Kingston in 1907. The strike failed and probably permanently soured Garvey on collective labor action. He was blacklisted and worked in Costa Rica and Panama before settling in London and returning to work as a printer in 1912. In London he studied the works of Booker T. Washington and admired his philosophy of racial self-help. He also met Duse Mohhamend Ali, who was working toward self-determination for Egyptians. Garvey wrote for Ali's magazine and began to imagine a program of racial solidarity among blacks of the Diaspora, who would return to and redeem Africa.

After a brief return to Jamaica, Garvey moved to the United States and settled in Harlem in 1916. With war raging in Europe and the United States torn over whether to join it or not, this was a particularly exciting time and place to be. Booker T. Washington, widely regarded as the premier race leader, had just died, and the National Association for the Advancement of Colored People (NAACP), formed by many of Washington's rivals, was beginning to grow into the nation's principal civil rights organization. Hundreds of thousands of southern blacks were migrating into northern cities, attracted by industrial jobs and less formal segregation and pushed by poor cotton crops and southern racism, in what was known as the Great Migration. This migration continued into the 1920s, especially when Congress made permanent the wartime interruption of European immigration. Garvey established the Universal Negro Improvement and Conservation Association and African Communities' League, usually called the Universal Negro Improvement Association (UNIA). He published a newspaper (the *Negro World*) and launched a number of business ventures, the most important of which was the Black Star steamship line, which would show that blacks could be successful entrepreneurs and aid in the return of African-Americans to Africa. He was a flamboyant orator and showman, dressed in imperial regalia as he led his crusade. Many of his detractors, most particularly W. E. B. Du Bois at the NAACP, regarded him as a vulgar charlatan, and his methods did smack of those of the rising European dictators of the interwar years.

Like Booker T. Washington and most black leaders of the period, Garvey was largely hostile to organized labor. He was impressed at the power that the American Federation of Labor (AFL) had acquired during World War I and urged black Americans to organize their own unions. He warned black workers to steer clear of white unions, either of Communists or what he called the American Federation of White Workers or Laborers. He urged blacks to undercut white unions by working for lower wages. As a racial separatist who wanted to build a separate black economy, he was especially hostile to the white and light-skinned socialists and integrationists in the NAACP. He went so far as to praise the Ku Klux Klan for "their honesty of purpose toward the Negro. They are better friends of my race, for telling us what they are, and what they mean, thereby giving us a chance to stir for ourselves." His supporters mailed a severed hand to union leader A. Philip Randolph as a threat in response to his criticism of Garvey.

In the early 1920s, the *Negro World* had 50 thousand subscribers; and there were perhaps as many dues-paying members of the UNIA. But Garvey's business methods proved to be his undoing. The Black Star Line was a fiasco, and Garvey was indicted for mail fraud related to its finances in 1922. He was convicted and began a 5-year prison sentence in 1925, continuing to run the UNIA from his Atlanta cell. President Coolidge commuted his sentence in 1927, and the U.S. deported Garvey. After unsuccessfully trying to revive the UNIA in Jamaica, he moved back to London in 1935, where he died 5 years later.

For all his failings, the charismatic Garvey obviously struck an important chord among African-Americans. He was able to claim a mass appeal and legitimacy as a race leader that few have been able to match. His emphasis on separatism and racial pride tapped into a persistent African-American sentiment that marked Booker T. Washington before him and the Black Power militants of the 1960s. Many of his critics perhaps let their aversion to his tone and style obscure their similarities. Du Bois for example embraced economic separatism and self-help in the 1930s and ended up returning to Africa himself. At the very least Garvey signaled a new consciousness among black Americans as they urbanized and moved North in the interwar years.

PAUL D. MORENO

References and Further Reading

Cronon, Edmund David. *Black Moses: The Story of Marcus Garvey and the Universal Negro Improvement Association*. Madison: University of Wisconsin Press, 1955.
Hill, Robert A. *The Marcus Garvey and Universal Negro Improvement Papers*. 9 vols. Berkeley: University of California Press, 1983–1995.
Jacques-Garvey, Amy, ed. *Philosophy and Opinions of Marcus Garvey*. 2 vols. New York: Atheneum, 1969.
Stein, Judith. *The World of Marcus Garvey: Race and Class in Modern Society*. Baton Rouge: Louisiana State University Press, 1985.

GASTONIA STRIKE (1929)

The violent strike at the Loray mill in Gastonia, North Carolina, that began in April 1929 stood out in the wave of unrest that swept the southern textile industry in the late 1920s and early 1930s because of the leadership role played by the Communist-led National Textile Workers' Union (NTWU). Unions of any sort were uncommon in the South at the time, so it seemed particularly incongruous that a Communist union might make headway in the region. But in the early days of the strike, thousands of white, pro-segregation, God-fearing cotton mill workers attended strike rallies organized by labor activists who stood for atheism and racial equality in addition to promoting the interests of industrial workers.

Since the 1870s, Gastonia had grown considerably along with the rise of the southern cotton textile industry. Thousands of impoverished farmers from the Piedmont and southern Appalachia had fled to industrial centers like Gastonia looking for a chance to escape from debt. Boosters in Gastonia promoted their English-speaking, hardworking, cheap, and faithful work force. Mill owners emphasized their paternal oversight of company-owned villages, including their support of churches. While the Loray mill had been constructed largely with local capital, in 1919 it was purchased by the Jenckes Spinning Company of Rhode Island, which merged with the Manville Company, also of Rhode Island, in 1923. This was part of the long-term but rapidly escalating transition of the textile industry from the North to the South, where labor costs offered a competitive advantage.

The 1929 strike in Gastonia arose from the same combination of pressures and grievances that had already produced serious textile labor conflicts in Henderson, North Carolina, in 1927 and earlier in 1929 in Elizabethton, Tennessee. Most significantly the market for textiles had been erratic at best during the 1920s. Following the exhaustion of the wartime economic boom, textiles slumped into serious depression in 1921 and had experienced only a few months of prosperity at a time since then. Cotton prices, the largest factor in the cost of production, were unpredictable throughout the decade, largely because of the boll weevil. Having only limited control of their circumstances, mill owners, including those at Loray,

Strike's on—they put away the spools. Library of Congress, Prints & Photographs Division, NYWT & S Collection [LC-USZ62-109628].

were forced to economize by increasing the pace of work and adding more tasks to each employee's routine.

At the Loray mill, a new superintendent in 1927 had to contend with declining markets for his main product, fabrics used in the production of automobile tires. The auto industry was slumping, and tire manufacturers were developing their own textile mills. In response the Loray superintendent cut the work force from 3,500 to 2,200 while maintaining the same level of production. In many cases workloads doubled. In addition workers suffered from two 10% wage cuts and arbitrary power exerted by supervisors. Weavers at Loray walked out briefly in protest in May 1928. The superintendent was replaced in late 1928, and his successor eased the stretch-out and invested more in community welfare programs. But mill workers were obviously exhausted and angry well before the much larger 1929 strike.

Triggering the Strike

In March 1929, representatives of the NTWU entered Gastonia, hoping to organize southern textiles as a stepping stone toward a Communist United States. The Loray strike, claimed the NTWU, would lead to

a general strike in Gaston County, followed by an uprising of the entire southern textile labor force. The NTWU's lead organizer, Fred Beal, found Loray workers ripe for a strike but worried about adequate organization and preparation. After several union supporters were fired, Beal called a meeting for March 30 that was attended by nearly 1,000 people. Two days later virtually the entire Loray workforce went on strike. The NTWU helped formulate the workers' list of demands, which for the most part emphasized basic trade union concerns like recognition of the union, a minimum weekly wage, a 40-hour week, ending the stretch-out and speed-up, and improved cleanliness and sanitation in both the mill and village. These demands hardly distinguished the NTWU from the more ideologically conservative United Textile Workers (UTW), affiliated with the American Federation of Labor (AFL). But the NTWU lambasted the UTW for its inability to lead successful strikes in Henderson and Elizabethton, not to mention an earlier failure in Gastonia in 1919. Ironically civic boosters praised the absent UTW in 1929 but offered only firm resistance to any sort of unionism before, during, and after.

Although NTWU organizers in Gastonia were sensitive to local concerns, top Communist party officials demanded advocacy of racial equality and atheism. Given the long-term segregation of textile jobs, very few Loray workers were black, and all of them were confined to menial jobs. When the NTWU tried to organize local blacks to demand equal opportunities in the mill and equal membership in the union, few turned out for fear of white reprisal. White Loray workers seemed to tolerate union calls for racial equality as long as the NTWU fought harder for their demands. Local Communist organizers strategically played down the union's atheism as well. Town leaders however trumpeted the evils of an organization that would promote race mixing and abolish churches.

The strike's fate was sealed however by the force of the state. On April 2, pickets at the Loray mill scuffled with local authorities at the plant gate, prompting the governor to send the National Guard to restore order, which was defined as assuring that the plant could operate. This show of force resulted in dozens of arrests of strikers and an opportunity for strike-breakers to enter the plant with military protection. Many strikers were among those willing to cross the picket lines. Within two weeks the strike was effectively over, and within a month, only some 200 die-hards continued to hold out. It is impossible to know exactly why the strike crumbled so quickly, but Beal's concern about lack of preparation appears to have been well-placed. The NTWU had nowhere near the resources necessary either to replace the strikers' paychecks or to offer even minimal relief. Moreover the company threatened to evict rebellious workers. Continued striking appeared likely to lead to hunger and homelessness if not incarceration as well.

Bloody Aftermath

The Loray strike made its mark however because of events that occurred well after the strike was essentially broken. After their headquarters was burned, holdout strikers and their NTWU backers organized themselves in a tent colony outside the company's jurisdiction and continued to agitate for their demands. On June 7, the "bitter enders" held a rally and marched toward the mill. On the way they were turned back by Gastonia police, some of whom demanded to search the new union headquarters in the tent colony. A major fight ensued, shots were fired, and a striker and four police officers were wounded. No one knows who fired the shots, but one of the officers, Police Chief Orville Aderholt, died the following day. This set in motion a wave of repression against strikers and NTWU organizers, with most strike leaders arrested for murder before they could be lynched.

The first prosecution of the defendants ended in a mistrial because after authorities brought a life-size wax model of Aderholt into the courtroom, a juror suffered an emotional breakdown. The suspension of legal proceedings served as a green light to many anti-union activists in Gastonia. Some remaining NTWU organizers were kidnapped and beaten, while others were taken out of the county and jailed elsewhere. The tent colony was attacked to the point that it had to be abandoned. In this wave of repression, the NTWU officially called off the strike but not before a group of union supporters traveling in a truck were attacked with gunfire by vigilantes. In this altercation a single mother of five, Ella May Wiggins, who was known as a feisty woman and as the strike's balladeer, was shot to death. Despite dozens of eyewitnesses, no one was ever convicted of Wiggins's murder.

Those accused of killing the police chief however were convicted after a second trial. The prosecution emphasized atheism more than evidence, and the jury deliberated for less than an hour. The NTWU defendants however skipped bail and escaped to the Soviet Union. After becoming disillusioned with life under communism, Fred Beal returned to the United States and was ultimately sent back to Gastonia to serve his sentence. Four years later, Beal was paroled by the governor.

The Gastonia strike received national attention because of its violence and the presence of Communists in such an unlikely location. Much of the later attention to the conflict has centered on the Communist leadership and the subsequent trials that convicted Aderholt's alleged killers and exonerated Wiggins's. The conditions of labor for the thousands of textile workers however worsened throughout the 1930s. The speedup, stretch-out, and arbitrary power of management continued to be the millhands' primary complaint and would be at the core of their unsuccessful participation in the General Textile Strike of 1934.

DANIEL CLARK

References and Further Reading

Daniel, Clete. *Culture of Misfortune: An Interpretive History of Textile Unionism in the United States*. Ithaca, NY: ILR Press, 2001.

Hall, Jacquelyn Dowd, James Leloudis, Robert Korstad, Mary Murphy, Lu Ann Jones, and Christopher Daly. *Like a Family: The Making of a Southern Cotton Mill World*. Chapel Hill: University of North Carolina Press, 1987.

Marshall, F. Ray. *Labor in the South*. Cambridge, MA: Harvard University Press, 1967.

Mitchell, George Sinclair. *Textile Unionism in the South*. Chapel Hill: University of North Carolina Press, 1931.

Pope, Liston. *Millhands and Preachers: A Study of Gastonia*. New Haven, CT: Yale University Press, 1942.

Salmond, John. *Gastonia 1929: The Story of the Loray Mill Strike*. Chapel Hill: University of North Carolina Press, 1995.

Tipppett, Tom. *When Southern Labor Stirs.* New York: Jonathan Cape and Harrison Smith, 1931.

See also **American Federation of Labor; General Textile Strike of 1934; National Textile Workers' Union; Textiles; United Textile Workers**

GENDER

Most human societies have allocated different tasks to men and women. The ways in which tasks are allocated, however, varies widely over time and across cultures. Both sexual difference and social constructions of masculinity and femininity have influenced the kinds of work that women and men historically have performed. Labor thus is marked by gender, a term that refers not only to sexual difference, but to the social and historical meanings societies ascribe to sexual difference and to the power relations those meanings produce.

Gendered Divisions of Labor

Gendered divisions of labor are not natural, that is, they are not necessarily linked to sex differences. They have instead emerged in response to particular historical developments and have shifted over time. Although the labor of both men and women has been equally important to the survival and prosperity of human societies, male and female work roles have not always held equal value. For much of American history, the labor of men has held higher value than that of women. Women's political and social status and the value accorded to women's work are linked. In general women's status tends to be higher when they contribute substantially to the economy, control the fruits of their labor, and receive public recognition for their contributions. Women's status also tends to be higher where there is no clear distinction between public and private and no sharply defined class structure.

There is nothing fixed about the relationship between sexual difference and the ways in which societies allocate labor. Archeological evidence indicates that early humans probably did not link work roles closely to sex differences and that women hunted along with men. Foraging societies that subsisted on a combination of gathering available vegetation and hunting both small and large game animals would gain no survival benefit by assigning either of these tasks exclusively to men or women, and anthropological evidence gleaned from foraging societies in the

recent past indicates that hunting is not entirely incompatible with pregnancy, childbirth, and child-rearing. The tendency for women to spend less time producing food and more time nursing and caring for children may have arisen in part from improved hunting technologies that boosted infant survival rates. Eventually the development of agriculture gave rise to new sets of tasks that more closely matched the rhythms of childcare.

In precontact Native American societies, farming and hunting complemented one another. Among the matriarchal Iroquois, women farmed and so provided the most abundant and stable source of food. They controlled food distribution. Men hunted, but they also cleared the fields so that women could plant. Iroquois men and women held relatively equal status. Although Iroquois men ran tribal political organizations, women had the power to nominate council elders and depose chiefs. Among Pueblo societies, men cultivated the cornfields, but women owned the corn and controlled the processing and distribution of corn meal. Women built the houses and acted as household heads, while men's status was tied to hunting, warfare, and religion. Hunting and warfare tended to increase male power and status, but they produced gross gender inequality only in societies where women lacked power based on their contributions to the economy. The fact that Iroquois and Pueblo women could divorce their spouses as easily as could men serves as a measure of women's relative equality in both cultures.

Intruding European cultures changed the division of labor within Native American societies in ways that marginalized women's economic contributions, limited their political influence, and reduced their social status. French traders for example were interested primarily in acquiring furs supplied by the Native American men of the Great Lakes region, not in the small game, tools, utensils, or clothing that women produced. Moreover as the items women produced became more readily available through trade, women's contribution to community subsistence became less important. Women's work came to revolve narrowly around preparing furs for trade. Although women's work was vital to the fur trade, women did not produce furs, nor did they control the price and distribution of furs. Before the Spanish colonized New Mexico, Pueblo women controlled their households and the distribution of the meat their husbands provided through hunting. Franciscan priests intervened directly to change the work roles of Pueblo women and men. As priests began converting the Pueblo peoples to Catholicism, they encouraged men to assert authority within the household and put households and property in the hands of men rather than women.

English colonists brought to the new world social, political, and religious structures that subordinated women within both church and state. Married women had no independent legal status, no voice in public affairs, and no status within their own households. Households were patriarchal; women had no control over household affairs, property, or children. Northern rural families divided labor between field work and home work, with men generally performing the former and women the latter. However men's and women's work roles tended to complement each other, and their tasks sometimes overlapped. Women had primary responsibility for the production of cloth, for example, but men assembled looms, planted flax, and sheared sheep. During the height of the growing season and at harvest time, women helped in the fields and performed some of the same tasks as boys, such as hoeing, haying, and husking corn. There were other tasks women could have performed but did not. For example they did not drive cattle to market nor carry grain to the mill, as boys did. Women's work, though varied, remained centered on household and farmstead.

Although men held broader political rights and economic responsibilities than did women and men's work held higher status, households were the basic units of economic production, and women were essential to their operation. Women's economic activities and the autonomy those activities fostered contrasted sharply with their legal and political status. As historian Laurel Thatcher Ulrich has demonstrated, northern colonial women participated in and managed a largely invisible economy that brought income into the household. They kept their own accounts, contracted for work, and paid their own bills. Within this circumscribed, female network, women contributed substantially to household economies and controlled what they produced and earned as they traded and sold goods like butter and cheese and generated income from such activities as spinning, weaving, and midwifery.

As in rural economies, women's domestic labor remained critical to the functioning of urban households, but urban economies provided work opportunities for colonial women that rural economies did not. Although shop keeping and other mercantile activities were largely male occupations, both married and unmarried women in towns took in lodgers, ran taverns, and kept shops. Still women's opportunities remained far more restricted than those of men, since women were far less likely to acquire specialized training in a craft or skill. Unmarried women could enter into male-dominated occupations more easily than married women whose domestic tasks kept them from pursuing other work. Unmarried women could

exchange credit and debt, own and rent property, and control their own money. Married women could however keep accounts and act as "deputy husbands" in a spouse's absence, and many widows continued family businesses after the death of a husband. In urban as in rural economies, single women developed mutually beneficial economic networks, and urban women's contributions to local economies gave them a degree of status and autonomy.

Early Industrial Capitalism and Gendered Divisions of Labor

As commerce expanded in the early 1800s, distinctions between men's and women's work grew sharper. The example of the New England shoemaking industry suggests that the development of a more rigid sexual division of labor resulted from a conscious decision on the part of male shoemakers to expand production and yet protect the status of their craft. In order to increase production, male artisans assigned wives, daughters, and female household help the task of shoe binding, or sewing shoe uppers. Artisans then separated shoe binding from knowledge of the rest of the craft. Women were excluded from apprenticeships, thereby ensuring that they would remain subordinate to men in the production process and reserving the artisan training system for men. This sexual division of labor carried over into the early factory system. By excluding women from certain jobs, men protected their positions as skilled workers; built worker solidarity grounded in a mutualistic, masculine identity; and maintained greater control over the workplace. As merchant manufacturers began to replace artisans as employers, shoe binders divided into two groups. Married women still worked at home in the out-work system, earning the lowest wage in the shoemaking industry. Young, mostly single women worked in the factory system, where their work remained limited to shoe binding. As men's and women's work roles grew more distinct, the complementarity that had characterized pre-industrial labor gave way to labor competition between men and women.

The slave labor system, on the other hand, tended to blur gendered divisions of labor. Slave men and women labored together in the fields. Although slave men generally were expected to perform the heaviest work, women also performed hard labor and were similarly punished if their work came up short. Within their own quarters however, slave families preserved a gendered division of labor that resembled that of white rural families. Men hunted, fished, and trapped during off-work hours; and women cooked, sewed, and cared for children. The work that African-American men and women performed for their families was of necessity cooperative. They relied on kin networks as well as on nuclear families to maintain households under the slave system.

Class-Based Constructions of Gender

Although class structure remained relatively fluid in the early stages of industrial capitalism, clear class distinctions gradually emerged and with them class-based constructions of gender. During the 1840s and 1850s, as the number of self-employed workers fell and the ranks of wage workers swelled with the arrival of large numbers of immigrants, skilled workers lost ground both to mechanization and labor competition. Decreasing wages and the presence of a slave labor system in the South led northern industrial workers to characterize their condition as "wage slavery." Masculinity stood at the core of working-class formation. In the North a distinctive working-class construction of manhood emerged that rested on workingmen's ability to control work rules and the pace of production, to command respect from the bosses, and to earn a family wage, that is, a wage sufficient to support a family of dependents so that women and children would not have to become wage earners themselves. The family wage ideal thus emerged as a response to specific industrial conditions. It also developed within the presence of a powerful, middle-class ideology defining male and female gender roles and as a reflection of working-class masculinity.

Middle-class constructions of manhood rested on the image of the self-made man and emphasized independence, self-sufficiency, and the ability to provide for one's family. As entrepreneurial and managerial positions developed in commercial centers, middle-class men's productive work moved away from the household while middle-class women remained in the domestic sphere. As consumer goods became more readily available to middle-class women, they performed less productive work and more reproductive work. The "cult of true womanhood" elevated middle-class women's status as wives and mothers and gave them greater moral authority within the household, but the labor they performed as housekeepers and child minders became less visible and less valued.

Working-class men whose wages and status were declining saw in the middle-class model of domesticity a means to raise wage rates, resist industrial capitalism, and shore up working-class masculinity. They argued that an industrial system that pushed wages down and so forced wives and children into the labor market threatened to degrade working-class women. The wives and daughters of the well-to-do would, they pointed out, no more associate with factory girls than they would slaves. Workingmen argued that not only would their wives and children suffer if they were forced to enter the labor market in order to supplement the family income, but that their own status as workingmen would be degraded as well if their wives and daughters were forced to become factory girls.

Factory girls themselves had a different view. As the textile industry developed in the 1820s, young, single women from rural areas began to migrate to factory towns like Lowell, Massachusetts, to work in textile mills. Drawn by the promise of both economic and cultural opportunities, they entered the workforce in large numbers during the 1830s. Sensitive to middle-class prescriptions of womanhood, factory owners tried to reproduce the domesticity that presumably protected true womanhood by lodging women in company-managed boarding houses, enforcing strict moral standards, and closely monitoring their activities. Factory girls resisted company control, asserted their independence, and upheld the dignity of labor. The female work culture gave rise to a version of class consciousness that reflected women's experiences as workers and that challenged both the cult of domesticity and capitalist labor relations.

The Lynn shoe workers strike of 1860 demonstrates the ways in which workingmen's and women's interests diverged. When the strike began, male shoe workers asked for workingwomen's support. They hoped to organize female shoe binders as an auxiliary force to encourage community support and to boycott uncooperative shoe bosses. Yet male artisans remained committed to the family wage. They were not prepared to acknowledge or fight for the interests of female factory operatives. For their part the factory operatives opposed a strike strategy whose only goal was to raise men's wages. They began to organize female shoe workers, asking married women who worked at home to join them in striking for higher wages. Such a gender-based coalition would have protected the wages of both married outworkers and single factory operatives. Male workers opposed this alliance, fearing that higher wages for factory operatives would encourage wives to enter factory work rather than stay at home. Male shoe workers persuaded their wives that joining the factory girls would alienate the bosses, result in less home work, and hurt men's chances to win a family wage. The home workers rejected the strategy of the factory girls, supporting higher wages for men instead.

Home workers who put family interests above their individual interests as wage earners weakened the position of female shoe binders relative to employers. Male artisans who defined women primarily as family members rather than acknowledging their interests as workers largely excluded them from the process of class formation and thus weakened the ability of the working class to challenge industrial capitalism. In the process of resisting capitalist intrusion into their craft, men and women shoe workers debated not just the place of women in the shoe industry, but the meanings of womanhood and manhood.

Labor, Gender, and Relations of Power

Working-class men's ambivalence toward female workers continued through the late nineteenth and into the twentieth century. In 1869, the newly formed Knights of Labor declared its support for equal rights for all workers regardless of race or gender but at first excluded women from membership. When a group of female shoemakers in Philadelphia won a strike in 1881, formed a labor organization, and sought admission into the Knights of Labor, the national organization was forced to stand by its principles and admit them to the union. Women subsequently joined in large numbers, particularly in the shoemaking, textile, and clothing industries. By the mid-1880s, women constituted 10% of Knights of Labor membership. Despite opposition from some male members of the order, women served as union organizers and proved to be active, even militant, unionists. In 1888, female organizers called on the Knights of Labor either to uphold the principle of equal pay for equal work or admit that it was a mockery and eliminate the statement supporting an equal pay policy from their platform.

As the Knights of Labor faltered in the 1890s, the American Federation of Labor (AFL) took its place and grew to include 4 million workers by 1920. During that same period, the proportion of women in the workforce increased rapidly. In a competitive labor market, male unionists understood the threat that unorganized female workers posed. Trade unionists repeatedly affirmed a commitment to unionize female workers and support equal pay for equal work but did so largely in order to protect male wage rates. Unionists continued to pursue the family wage, arguing that women's contribution to the home and their duties as mothers were so valuable that they ought not to be in the workforce at all and that employers' exploitation of mostly unskilled, female workers constituted a capitalist assault on the working-class family. As the pragmatic, craft-based AFL came to dominate the labor movement, antagonism toward female workers grew among some affiliates, and a discourse that centered on male privilege developed. An article appearing in the July 5, 1893, issue of the *Coast Seamen's Journal* commented that women were mentally and physically incapable of achieving great things, but they were capable of making it impossible for men to be what nature intended them to be, that is the providers and protectors of women and children. The author argued that the labor movement's principal responsibility was to ensure that every man had a chance to earn enough to provide for a wife and family. Ignoring any wage-earning aspirations that female workers might have had themselves, he wrote that once male workers earned a family wage, the issue of women in industry and in the union would cease to exist. Such rhetoric bore little relation to reality. The family wage, had workers succeeded in getting it, would have benefited only women in stable marriages. It did no good for single, divorced, or abandoned women whose interests would have been better served by access to high-paying jobs that offered opportunities for advancement. In the end keeping women out of the workforce proved impossible. Most women working for wages in the early 1900s were single, and they often supported mothers and younger siblings with their pay. Only 3.3% of female industrial workers were organized into trade unions. Because unskilled women could not count on trade unions to work on their behalf for higher wages or better working conditions, working-class women sought the help of middle-class reformers and legislators to address the problems of organizing female workers and improving working conditions.

In 1903, middle-class reformers and working-women founded the National Women's Trade Union League (NWTUL), a national labor organization dedicated to unionizing female workers in order to obtain better working conditions and higher wages. Many if not most middle-class women involved in labor reform remained convinced that women's place was in the home, but they realized that women who worked had to do so in order to support themselves and their families. Given the necessity of women's work, middle-class reformers committed themselves to improving working conditions and wage rates. Middle-class women did not however support strikes as a means of achieving those goals. Rather they supported state intervention in the form of minimum wage laws and protective labor legislation. States began to enact laws regulating the conditions and hours for workers in the early twentieth century. The Supreme Court at first struck down such legislation on the grounds that it denied workers the right to make their own employment contracts. However in *Muller v. Oregon* (1908) the Court sustained protective legislation for women on the grounds that their "physical structure" and "maternal functions" placed them at a disadvantage. In the Court's estimation, women could not work so long or so hard as men and requiring them to do so endangered the health and well being of the nation's future citizens. But passing protective labor legislation could hurt as well as help working women. While it shielded women from some of the worst abuses of early twentieth-century industrial capitalism, it also excluded them from a number of highly skilled, highly paid occupations that required night work or that were deemed too physically taxing for women. As historian Alice Kessler-Harris has pointed out, because protective legislation divided workers into those who could and could not perform certain work roles, it is responsible in part for institutionalizing women's subordinate position in the labor force. Protective legislation drew fire from groups like the Women's League for Equal Opportunity, which lobbied against night work laws and the 54-hour workweek for women. The chief opponent of protective legislation was the National Woman's party (NWP), the nation's most militant suffrage organization. In 1921, the NWP proposed an equal rights amendment to the Constitution of the United States that read: "No political, civil or legal disabilities or inequalities on account of sex nor on account of marriage, unless applying equally to both sexes, shall exist within the United States or any territory thereof." The proposed amendment sparked a battle between groups like the NWTUL, which believed that it would worsen conditions for workingwomen, and groups that believed effective union organization would do more for women than protective labor legislation. A new style of unionism that had taken shape during the pre-World War I period of Socialist party activism gave the latter groups some hope that they were right. The new unionism fostered a sense of working-class solidarity that was absent in the craft unions of the AFL. These new unions enrolled female members, offered social programs for workingwomen, and won wage increases and shorter working hours. The new unions however remained as male-dominated as the old. Women were permitted greater involvement at lower levels of organization, but men monopolized all union offices and male leaders did not trust female organizers nor allow women to handle strikes. Limited job opportunities, protective labor legislation, and varying levels of exclusion from labor union participation isolated women from the mainstream of the labor movement and marginalized women within sex-segregated jobs.

Labor and Gender in the Twentieth Century

The number of workingwomen increased steadily over the course of the twentieth century, but they remained in sex-segregated jobs. In 1910, 51% of single women worked for wages, but until World War II, about 90% of all working women filled only 10 different occupations. These occupations included secretarial work, retail sales, telephone switchboard operation, and teaching. Black women, who had far fewer opportunities than did whites, remained employed mostly in agricultural or domestic work. Sex-segregation contributed to the assignment of low wages and status to these jobs even when those jobs previously had been filled by men.

During World War II, new opportunities opened up for women. War work made women aware of job possibilities they had not previously considered, but Kessler-Harris has argued that women's wartime experience reflected continuity as well as change. The inroads women made into higher paying, male-dominated occupations continued an earlier trend of working women to seek better wages, higher status, and greater job satisfaction. The war provided women some of what they sought. Patriotic rhetoric suggested that war work took precedence over home responsibilities, handing those women who aspired to work outside the home a compelling reason to do so. Black women, older women, and professional women all took advantage of the wartime labor shortage to enter well-paying jobs. Black women's gains were most dramatic. About 20% of black women who previously had been limited to low-paying domestic service jobs before the war found higher paying positions. By the end of the war, the number of black women working as factory operatives and in clerical, sales, and professional work had increased substantially.

Still the gains women made were limited by the view that they were temporary workers. During the war employers refused to integrate women into training programs that might provide access to skills beyond those essential for their immediate tasks. Management believed that additional training would be a wasted investment for temporary help. Women pressed for pay equal to that of male workers, and unions fought to maintain wage levels during the war in order to protect men's wages, but most women were forced to return to lower paying, sex-segregated jobs. After the war women's participation in the work force dropped by the same percentage as it had risen to meet wartime labor shortages, indicating that most of the women who remained in the workforce after the war would have been working for wages anyway.

But by 1950, the overall rate of women's participation in the workforce had risen to 32%, a net gain of 16% from 1940–1950.

The publicity accorded female workers in war industries during World War II made it clear to Americans that women could do men's work but whether or not they wanted to was a different matter. The shop floor represented a stronghold of male culture, a world away from family responsibilities and feminine influences. When women did invade the male culture of the shop floor, as they did occasionally before the war and more permanently beginning in the 1970s, they met with derision, hostility, and sexual harassment. The gap between the jobs women were interested in and capable of performing and the limitations imposed by a return to the prewar, sex-segregated labor market fueled second-wave feminism. The women's movement of the 1960s challenged both the sex-segregated labor market and the gender-based wage differential. From 1960–1970, the number of women in skilled, male-dominated trades had risen by 80%. By 1970, more than 40% of married women worked for wages. Women's wage rates however remained only 59% of those for men. The tension between the rising participation of women in the workforce and consistently low wage rates prompted demands for legislation to address gender inequalities in the workplace. As more and more women from all classes and levels of education entered into the workforce, gendered divisions of labor became less rigid and the sex-segregated labor market began to break down, though not so fast nor so fully as women hoped. Many male jobs opened up to women, but less rigid gender-based divisions of labor also offered broader opportunities for men drawn to traditionally female occupations like nursing or for fathers who wanted to take a more active role in child rearing by staying home with their children part-time. Comparing men's and women's work roles in the late twentieth and early twenty-first century to those in earlier periods of American history demonstrates the degree to which gendered divisions of labor, gender constructions, and gender-based relations of power have shifted and evolved over time.

Gender and Labor History

Human labor—its allocation, organization, and valuation—has always been marked by gender and so have analyses of labor history and working-class formation. Through the 1960s, labor historians focused on formal institutions of power, such as trade unions, and on male labor leaders and organizations and so excluded women from labor history. Labor historians have relied on male experiences and changes in workingmen's status in order to periodize labor history and working-class formation. As labor historians shifted from studying men who held formal positions of power to ordinary union members and unorganized workers, they began to look at workers and work cultures and at how race and ethnicity shaped working-class experiences. At the same time, the fields of women's history and feminist theory were developing, and working-class historians began incorporating perspectives on women and families in their analyses.

But the incorporation of women's experiences and perspectives in working-class histories did not in and of itself make for a gendered analysis of labor history. As Joan Scott pointed out, E. P. Thompson's pathbreaking study of working-class formation, *The Making of the English Working Class*, included the stories of individual women but still constructed class as a masculine identity. Thompson associated working-class consciousness and class formation with the politics of male workers and focused on women's domestic experience even when women as workers, not wives, constituted the subject of his narrative. His concern was to assess capitalism's impact on male workers, not to assess the reasons for women's lower status and lower value in the labor market.

The development of feminist theory and gendered interpretations of workers' experiences have expanded, enriched, complicated, and fundamentally changed labor and working-class history. Using gender as a category of analysis has opened the field up to new questions and new ways of thinking by redefining the terms worker and workplace, highlighting gendered divisions within working-class households, on the shop floor, and in the labor movement; and challenging the notion that a unified set of class interests exists. Feminist historians have asked how divisions of labor based on sex led to women's lower status and lower value in the labor market. Attending to social constructions of gender has raised questions about when and why working-class men and women supported family-wage ideology, why craft unions excluded women, and how employers used gender ideology to divide the working class. Analyzing relations of gender has illuminated the ways in which men and women used particular gender constructions and ideologies to promote their own interests, their families' interests, and working-class interests. Viewing shop floor and factory as gendered spaces has yielded insight into how male and female work cultures have fostered worker solidarity and challenged employers for control over the workplace. The scholarship that has emerged from using gender as a category of analysis amply demonstrates how gender was embedded in daily work practices and class relations and offers historians a fresh and fruitful perspective on labor history.

ELLEN S. AIKEN

References and Further Reading

Baron, Ava. *Work Engendered.* Ithaca, NY: Cornell University Press, 1991.
Blewett, Mary. "Conflict among Lynn's Shoemakers." In *Major Problems in the History of American Workers,* edited by Eileen Boris and Nelson Lichtenstein. Lexington, MA: D. C. Heath and Company, 1991.
Bonvillain, Nancy. *Women and Men: Cultural Constructs of Gender.* Upper Saddle River, N J: Prentice-Hall, 2001.
Brettell, Caroline B., and Carolyn F. Sargent. *Gender in Cross-Cultural Perspective.* 4th ed. Upper Saddle River, NJ: Prentice Hall, 2005.
Cobble, Dorothy Sue. *The Other Women's Movement: Workplace Justice and Social Rights in Modern America.* Princeton, NJ: Princeton University Press, 2003.
Foner, Philip S. *Women and the American Labor Movement: From Colonial Times to the Eve of World War I.* New York: The Free Press, 1979.
Frader, Laura Levine. "Gender and Labor in World History." In *A Companion to Gender History,* edited by Teresa A. Meade and Merry E. Wiesner-Hanks. Malden, MA: Blackwell Publishing Ltd., 2004.
Gutiérrez, Ramón A. *When Jesus Came, the Corn Mothers Went Away.* Stanford, CA: Stanford University Press, 1991.
Horowitz, Roger, ed. *Boys and Their Toys? Masculinity, Technology, and Class in America.* New York: Routledge, 2001.
Kessler-Harris, Alice. "The Labor Movement's Failure to Organize Women." In *Major Problems in the History of American Workers,* edited by Eileen Boris and Nelson Lichtenstein. Lexington, MA: D. C. Heath and Company, 1991.
———. *Out to Work.* Oxford: Oxford University Press, 1983, 2003.
Main, Gloria L. "Gender, Work, and Wages in Colonial New England." In *Major Problems in American Women's History,* edited by Mary Beth Norton and Ruth M. Alexander. Boston: Houghton Mifflin, 2003.
Scott, Joan Wallach. *Gender and the Politics of History.* New York: Columbia University Press, 1988.
Ulrich, Laurel Thatcher. *A Midwife's Tale.* New York: Vintage Books, 1990.
Wulf, Karin. *Not All Wives: Women of Colonial Philadelphia.* Ithaca, NY: Cornell University Press, 2000.

GENERAL WORKERS' LEAGUE

Various associations of *émigré* German craftsmen and radicals adopted the name *Arbeiterbund* (Workers League or Labor league) in the years before the Civil War. These were largely the work of revolutionary-minded German artisans who had been active overseas before immigrating to the United States, although conditions for immigrant labor in the United States sustained the organizations. Their presence had a major impact on the American workers' movement at a formative period in its history.

German Workers' Associations and the Workers' Revolution

The cooperationist goals, conspiratorial means, and insurrectionist tactics of the nineteenth-century French revolutionary associations may have been even more appealing to the relatively transient German artisans. Auguste Blanqui's *Société des Familles* and *Société des Saisons* inspired the 1834 formation of the *Bund der Geaechteten* (the League of the Proscribed, or Outlaws), which reorganized 2 years later as the *Bund der Gerechten* (the League of the Just).

The group embraced a German version of an emergent socialist ideology, specifically that of Wilhelm Weitling (1808–1871), a Magdeburg tailor, whose numerous works include, most famously, his *Garantien der Harmonie und Freiheit* (1842). The league also sought to foster ideas of international labor solidarity through broader educational societies. Its general socialist ideas and its broad orientation drew Karl Marx and Friedrich Engels into the group. In 1847, it adopted a new name, the *Bund der Kommunisten* (Communist league), on behalf of which Marx and Engels wrote their famous *Manifesto.* Some of these generally migratory workers found their way to the United States, and the numbers would become a legion with the defeat of the 1848–1849 revolutionary upheavals.

General Workers' League

A former member of the league, Hermann Kriege (1820–1850), came to the United States, and then launched a newspaper to promote revolutionary and socialist ideas. In 1845, he founded the *Association der Social-Reformer* (the Social Reform association) in New York City, and it spread to Newark, Cincinnati, Milwaukee, Philadelphia, Chicago, and St. Louis. The group embraced American land reform radicalism, but Kriege gave his deepest loyalties to the Democratic party. Kriege returned to Germany for

511

the 1848 revolutionary upheavals but returned a less ambitious and more conservative figure.

Weitling's immigration to the United States was permanent. In 1850, as American workers were forming citywide industrial congresses and other bodies, Weitling helped unite 2,400 German artisans in New York into a *Centralkommission der veringten Gewerbe* (Central Commission of the United Trades). Riding the tide of a strike movement and inspired by the cooperative vision of continental socialism, it mobilized 4,500 members in 1,700 trades, inspiring similar bodies in Baltimore, St. Louis, and other cities.

Weitling and others eager to establish a national coordinating body called the October 1850 convention that founded the *Allgemeiner Arbeiterbund* (General Workers' league). The group gained sometimes large affiliates in Baltimore, Buffalo, Cincinnati, Detroit, Dubuque, Louisville, Maysville, Newark, Philadelphia, Pittsburgh, Rochester, St. Louis, Trenton, and Williamsburg, as well as New York City. English-speaking radicals at the New York City Industrial Congress also established American Labor leagues, presumably cooperative bodies inspired by their German comrades.

However this *Arbeiterbund* did not pursue the earlier successes in the trades but pursued cooperative agitation and invested much effort in launching a socialist society at Communia in Iowa. Local associations, calling themselves a *Verein* or a *Gemeide,* surely attained a greater influence on labor activism in those years. Finally the organization seemed even more utopian against the background of the explosive agitation over slavery. By 1852, this *Arbeiterbund* went into decline.

The American Workers' League

In that year a handful of veteran radicals started a tiny *Proletariarbund,* partly to fill the void left by the orientation of the *Arbeiterbund.* Its primary leader was Joseph Weydemeyer (1818–1866), a veteran of the Prussian artillery as well as the Communist league and the 1848 revolutions. It proclaimed labor solidarity, human equality, hostility to slavery, and opposition to all capitalist parties.

By March 1853, the ideas of Weydemeyer's *Proletariarbund* proved sufficient to draw some 800 workers from the New York area to a convention that launched a new *Amerikanische Arbeiterbund.* It briefly drew together many of the local *Arbeiterverein,* established a *Frauenverein* for women, and restated the radical egalitarianism of its predecessor.

The organization gained some support in German-speaking communities across the country, but was overshadowed by the existence of the much broader *Sozialistischer Turnerbund.* A revolutionary republican gymnastic and theatrical club in Germany, the Turners in the United States were explicitly in favor of abolishing classes.

Then, too, from 1854–1858, a loose federation of émigré groups evolved in New York uniting German socialists with French, Italian, Hungarian, Polish, Cuban, and other radicals. They formed a general Universal Democratic Republican Society, then an ongoing convention of liberal societies that celebrated revolutionary anniversaries beneath socialist slogans and red flags.

Communist Club and International Ties

The Panic of 1857 led to massive demonstrations by the unemployed and the final phase of antebellum German workers' organization. The nationalists, largely still looking for a revival of the republicanism of 1848 launched another *Allgemeiner Arbeiterbund von Nord-Amerika,* but it never revived the promises of its namesakes.

That same year, Friedrich Albert Sorge (1828–1906), a veteran of the earlier efforts by both Weydemeyer and Weitling, took the initiative in launching a tiny local *Kommunist Klub* that revived the militant egalitarianism and socialist vision of the earlier groups. By July 1858, the group helped form an American section of the international association. Although largely dominated by the old republican nationalism of 1848, the group became the most immediate forerunner on both sides of the Atlantic of the International Workingmen's Association, the "first international" formed in 1864.

By 1858, however, Weydemeyer had moved into the Midwest, ultimately to St. Louis. He and much of the antebellum German workers movement were consumed by the Union war effort in the Civil War.

MARK LAUSE

References and Further Reading

Levine, Bruce. *The Spirit of 1848: German Immigrants, Labor Conflicts, and the Coming of the Civil War.* Urbana: University of Illinois Press, 1992.
Wittke, Carl. *Utopian Communist: A Biography of Wilhelm Weitling, Nineteenth-Century Reformer.* Baton Rouge: Louisiana State University Press, 1950.

See also **Germans**

GEORGE, HENRY (1839–1897)
Political Economist, Reformer

A self-taught political economist, Henry George wrote one of the most powerful and widely read critiques of the late nineteenth-century industrial United States. Published in 1879, *Progress and Poverty: An Inquiry into the Cause of Industrial Depressions and of Increase of Want with Increase of Wealth,* argued that the growing inequities between social classes in the Gilded Age threatened American democracy. It went on to become the best-selling book on political economy in the nineteenth century and launched George as a prominent social reformer with an international following.

Henry George was born in Philadelphia on September 2, 1839, the son of Catherine (Vallance) George and Richard George, a publisher of religious books. Disinterested in formal schooling, he quit at age 13 to serve as a foremast boy on a 1-year journey aboard a ship. On his return in 1856, he worked briefly as an apprentice printer before striking out for San Francisco to prospect for gold. After years trying his hand at many different jobs, often living in extreme poverty, he eventually embarked on an uneven career as a journalist, writing for and editing numerous San Francisco papers. In 1861, he married Annie Fox, with whom he had four children.

By the mid-1870s, George became increasingly interested in questions of political economy and social justice, especially as he experienced personal poverty and witnessed growing labor unrest in California during the depression of 1873–1877. Despite his lack of formal education, George read widely, especially the classics of political economy. He was also an evangelical Christian who came to view his reform impulse in almost messianic terms and laced much of his writing with biblical references.

Fundamentally George was worried about the deleterious effects of industrial capitalism on American democracy. Why, he wondered, were the many indisputable benefits of industrial progress accompanied by an increase in the number of people living in poverty? Could the defining features of the nation's republican ideals and institutions—liberty, equality, and opportunity—endure in a society increasingly dominated by large corporations and powerful millionaires like Jay Gould and William K. Vanderbilt?

Deeply troubled by these questions and committed to answering them, George began writing *Progress and Poverty* in 1877 and completed it 2 years later. Land monopoly, explained George, caused modern industrial society to produce "an increase of want with [an] increase of wealth." Real estate speculators and land monopolists, he asserted, siphoned off a major portion of the wealth created not by them but rather by the collective labors of the community. Monopolists grew rich on these unearned profits while a growing number of society's producers toiled in poverty with little opportunity for advancement: Hence, the growth of poverty amid progress.

The solution, asserted George, was for the government to appropriate these profits through a uniform land value tax or what his supporters eventually took to calling the "single tax." With the rewards of speculation eliminated, undeveloped land and resources held by speculators would be made available to those seeking to develop them. Economic opportunity would once again flourish, and poverty would decline. Tax revenues would rise, allowing for the construction of parks, schools, libraries, and other institutions dedicated to public benefit.

George offered his readers this vision of a future utopia but also one of apocalyptic horror should society fail to heed his warning. "This association of poverty with progress," he wrote at the beginning of his book, "is the great enigma of our times.... It is the riddle which the Sphinx of Fate puts to our civilization, and which not to answer is to be destroyed." If unchecked by radical reform, *laissez faire* industrial capitalism would ultimately destroy the American republic.

While radical in many respects, especially for his challenge to private property rights, George was not a socialist. In many ways he offered his single-tax program as an alternative to both *laissez faire* economics and socialism.

Initially *Progress and Poverty* drew almost no attention from readers and critics. Undaunted George decided in 1880 to move to New York City to raise his profile and draw attention to his book. There he met influential people and delivered lectures to reform-minded groups. He also joined the Land league, an Irish nationalist organization dedicated not only to winning Ireland's independence from Great Britain, but to abolishing the landlord system that left most of the Irish people in poverty. Although not Irish, George joined the cause because he saw the Irish struggle against land monopoly as a test case for his single-tax reform. In 1881–1882, he traveled to Ireland as a special correspondent for the *Irish World* (New York), reporting on the progress of the struggle for land reform. Before long working-class Irish Americans were some of George's greatest admirers.

Indeed working-class Americans of all ethnicities emerged as George's strongest base of support in those early years. As one labor leader put it, *Progress and Poverty* taught them that "poverty is an artificial condition of man's invention," and not an inevitable aspect of human existence. "Workingmen and women, learning all this,...commenced to wrestle with their chains."

Progress and Poverty also attracted a wide readership among intellectuals and middle-class reformers in the United States and Great Britain. His tours of Ireland and Britain in 1881–1882, 1884, and 1885 brought him into contact with many prominent figures, such as Herbert Spencer. He later became a correspondent with Leo Tolstoy, who admired his writings on land reform.

From 1883–1886, George continued to write and lecture on the ideas expressed in *Progress and Poverty*. In 1883, he agreed to write a series of articles on social problems for *Frank Leslie's Weekly*, one of the most popular journals of the day. These were eventually collected into book form and published as *Social Problems* (1883). By this time George had also become a staunch proponent of free trade, a highly contentious issue in the Gilded Age, eventually publishing *Protection or Free Trade; An Examination of the Tariff Question, with Especial Regard to the Interests of Labor* (1886).

In 1886, a year of unprecedented labor unrest, workers in New York City nominated George as the United Labor party candidate for mayor. George conducted a spirited campaign in a race that drew national attention. On election day, George outpolled the republican candidate, the 27-year-old Theodore Roosevelt but lost narrowly to Democrat Abram Hewitt. George and his supporters hoped this strong showing was the sign of greater things to come, perhaps even the establishment of a national reform or labor party and a presidential campaign in 1888. But infighting, some of it generated by George's decision to purge the movement of socialists, led to the collapse of the United Labor party in 1887.

For the rest of his career, George found his strongest base of supporters among middle-class reformers. By 1889, they had established 131 single-tax clubs across the country to promote his ideas. In 1890, George went on a world tour, delivering lectures and meeting land reform advocates. By the mid-1890s, single-tax clubs sprang up in Great Britain, Canada, Ireland, Australia, Denmark, and Hungary. He suffered a stroke in late-1891 and curtailed his travels in favor of writing. He started writing the *Science of Political Economy*, a book not published until after his death in 1897. In 1892, he published *A Perplexed Philosopher*, a book in which he vented his ire at the British political economist Herbert Spencer for turning against land reform. Over the next few years, George opened his Manhattan house as a salon for progressive-minded people to meet and talk.

In 1897, New York City reformers again turned to George to run for mayor as a candidate of the Thomas Jefferson party. In poor health, George died five days before the election. Running in his place, his son, Henry George, Jr., still managed to garner 5% of the vote.

The influence of *Progress and Poverty* extended far beyond the life of its author, shaping the consciousness of many prominent late-nineteenth- and early-twentieth-century reformers, including Jacob A. Riis, Ignatius Donnelly, Fr. John A. Ryan, and Robert LaFollette. The book is still in print, and Henry George schools and single-tax organizations operate in at least 22 countries.

EDWARD T. O'DONNELL

References and Further Reading

Adelson, Robert V., ed. *The Critics of Henry George: A Centenary Appraisal of Their Strictures on Progress and Poverty*. 1979.
Barker, Charles Albro. *Henry George*. Oxford, 1955.
O'Donnell, Edward T. *The Talisman of a Lost Hope: Henry George and Gilded Age America*. New York: Columbia University Press, 2000.

GERMANS

Germans have played a distinctive and substantial role in American labor history, particularly during the peak of the American industrial revolution in the last-third of the nineteenth century. This period coincided with the highest wave of German immigration to the United States as well as with intense political ferment and organizational innovation within labor circles in Germany. Thus large in number, German immigrants also brought with them political ideas and organizational models that figured prominently in the history of American workers even when the volume of German immigration subsided after the turn of the century.

Germans and the International Reach of German Culture

There are Germanic peoples spread throughout central Europe; and they have never been encompassed within the boundaries of one nation state to the extent of the English, French, and Spanish. Today most German-speaking people are included in the three nations of Germany, Austria, and Switzerland; but there are pockets of ethnic Germans in northern Italy, the Czech Republic, Hungary, Romania, and Russia. Small remnants of their former selves, most of these enclaves derive from the Austro-Hungarian Empire that dominated central Europe for centuries before it was broken up after World War I. This multi-ethnic empire made German the most common language of business and government for much of central Europe. Thus the German language, and through it German culture, had a considerably wider reach than the German nation founded by Otto von Bismarck in 1871 that people today typically equate with Germany and the Germans.

Migration patterns reinforced this extensive influence, particularly for working people. European journeymen, including those from Scandinavia, traditionally wandered before settling down in one city. German was the most useful language for both traveling and learning a trade within central Europe. It even served workers well in the United States. Samuel Gompers, the most important American labor leader before the 1930s, was of Dutch and Jewish extraction; but he grew up in London and New York City, where he worked in a small cigar-making firm whose workers spoke mainly German. In the 1870s, a Swedish cigar maker translated the *Communist Manifesto* for the young Gompers, who was so interested in German socialism that he taught himself the language so he could read German labor thinkers.

Founding a German Nation and Exporting *Émigrés*

Germans were late in founding a nation state in comparison to the English, French, and Americans. The efforts of Germans to build a nation in the nineteenth century profoundly influenced the emigrants who left and thus their role in American labor history as well.

Since Germanic people were so dispersed, they lacked a common culture and in many respects, a common language because they spoke so many dialects. Even within the area united by Bismarck, there were 39 separate states and free cities. In the late eighteenth and early nineteenth centuries, German intellectuals tried to standardize the language and build a more unified culture as the first step in building a nation. They also created numerous voluntary organizations to promote cultural unity and patriotism. This combination of cultural and political goals was evident in the popular Turner societies, which

were designed to form the citizens of the new German republic through physical exercise, primarily gymnastics, cultural activities, and political action. The ubiquitous mutual benefit societies, whose main goal was providing insurance, also sometimes pursued similar cultural and political activities. Familiar with such groups, German immigrants, especially artisans, brought with them to the United States organizational models and experience useful for promoting the culture and politics needed by labor movements. *Émigrés* informed by the efforts to found a German nation were particularly important carriers of these traditions.

In the midnineteenth century Germans made two attempts to found a modern nation state in the area roughly between Switzerland and Austria to the south and the Baltic Sea to the north. In 1848, a wave of popular uprisings swept Europe, and their one unifying characteristic was opposition to monarchy and aristocracy. Opinion about a desirable new order ranged from conservative constitutional monarchies to radical republics. Within the numerous contemporary German states, artisans—particularly journeymen—took part in these revolutions, pushing the revolutionaries toward re-ordering society and the economy, not simply the political order. Yet the established powers counterattacked and crushed the revolutions, inaugurating a reactionary period in European history and sending waves of political refugees abroad, including to the United States.

Known as the "48ers" in American history, these political *émigrés* quickly assumed leadership positions in the German immigrant communities already established in American cities. The skills at organizing and agitation they had honed in Germany served them well in the United States amid the political ferment of the 1850s. For the 48ers the Civil War was a second chance to fight and defeat aristocracy, this time in the form of southern slaveholders. They enthusiastically led their followers, many of whom were German craftsmen, in support to the North and the Republican party. During the war the 48ers and their allies advocated emancipation sooner than mainstream Republicans, and during Reconstruction, they pushed for the radical transformation of the southern social and political order. They were usually friendly to the numerous unions that emerged in the North during the war, and some of them helped lead the movement for an 8-hour workday afterward. Although not typically workers themselves, the 48ers helped integrate working-class German immigrants into American politics; and they gave German-based labor organizations energy and a distinct political direction.

While Americans were preoccupied with the Civil War and Reconstruction, Bismarck led Prussia into a series of military conflicts that resulted in the founding of the Second Empire in 1871, following the decisive defeat of France in the Franco-Prussian War. At the same time Ferdinand Lassalle organized the first German labor movement.

His movement was rooted in a network of social and political clubs appealing mainly to craftsmen and lower level professionals, not in labor unions, principally because there were so few unions within the German states at the time. Industrialization, and consequently unions, had not advanced in Germany so far as in Great Britain or in the northern United States; and in addition Lassalle's political movement fit into the ferment created by Bismarck's nation building politics. Strong unions did emerge in Germany as did a core of Marxist labor leaders. Both provoked intense debates in the late 1860s and 1870s about the role of unions and political parties within the labor movement as well as about how labor should address Bismarck's reactionary monarchy. These debates produced the vital German labor thought that so impressed Gompers. Many of the debaters themselves fled to the United States when Bismarck's government passed the Antisocialist Laws, which were in force from 1878–1890.

This whole period from the mid-1860s through the 1880s sent a stream of German labor and political *émigrés* to the United States comparable in size and influence to the previous generation of 48ers, although the newcomers tended to be more radical and more embedded in labor organizations and culture. In 1869, such *émigrés* as Fredrich A. Sorge helped found the International Workingmen's Association, as the American branch of the First Communist International. They were prominent in subsequent labor initiatives like the Workingmen's party of the United States as well as in the anarchist labor movement that played such a large role in the Haymarket Affair of 1886. The same wave of exiles helped found and maintain a web of unions, Turner societies, newspapers, political clubs, and mutual benefit societies that sustained German-language labor movements within New York, Brooklyn, Philadelphia, Buffalo, Chicago, Cleveland, St. Louis, Cincinnati, and Milwaukee. The existence of such movements illustrated the unusually large role of German immigrants in the workforces and economies of American industrial cities, particularly those in the Midwest. German-language labor movements by no means encompassed all or even most German workers in these cities, but they enlivened and emboldened Germans who belonged to English-language unions and political parties. The culture sustained by these movements also inspired German workers in smaller cities.

The Mass Migrations

The 48ers and the post-Civil War labor *émigrés* were numerically tiny elements in a massive international migration of Europeans in the second-half of the nineteenth century. People from the area encompassed in Bismarck's Reich constituted the largest national element in this European exodus, and the highpoints of German emigration mirrored those of all Europeans. With the advent of the twentieth century, the patterns of German and European emigration diverged.

From 1840–1900, people from Ireland, Scandinavia, and central Europe dominated the European emigration. After 1900, the origins of the emigrants shifted to the east toward Russia and south toward Italy and the Mediterranean. In the nineteenth century there were three waves of European immigrants arriving in the United States, peaking in the mid-1850s, the late 1860s, and the mid-1880s. The third wave was the largest and the second the smallest, though still very substantial. The volume of emigration from the area defined by Bismarck's Reich corresponded exactly to these three larger waves from Europe, with the peak years for the Germans being 1854, 1869, and 1882. During the whole 60-year period, Germans always constituted from a quarter to a third of all the foreign-born in the United States.

The Germans settled disproportionately in the mid-Atlantic and midwestern states where the contemporary growth of American industry was concentrated. The Midwest also offered enough available farmland to attract a substantial proportion of the Germans to the countryside. Nonetheless the strong demand from industry attracted even more to urban areas: In 1890, two-fifths of Germans lived in cities, almost double the figure for native-born Americans.

Both the geographic origins and kinds of people leaving Germany changed substantially from 1840–1900. Those leaving before the Civil War came largely from the Rhine River valley, that is, from west central and southwestern Germany. Economic dislocation and political turmoil prompted people to leave, and the Rhine offered convenient transportation to international ports in Holland. The emigrants tended to be peasants and artisans who, while desperate at the time, were not economically destitute. They had the resources to make an international journey; and they often traveled in families, intending to settle permanently in the United States. When they did so, they created German enclaves in both the countryside and cities that became models for defining ethnic culture in America.

The relatively small excess of men over women in mid-nineteenth-century German districts illustrated the intent of the people to settle and create communities. In contrast when immigrants planned to work and then leave, as in mining camps, men dramatically outnumbered women. German women in cities entered the labor market in smaller proportions than did women of many other nationalities, preferring to contribute to their families' income by taking in boarders or helping out in family-owned shops or businesses. The proportion of German women entering the labor market in the United States did increase toward the end of the nineteenth century; and they showed a growing preference for factory work, particularly in the garment industry, over domestic service, which originally had been their most typical occupational choice. Women also began to take a more prominent role in the labor movement.

After the Civil War the origins of the emigrants began to shift to the north and east within Germany, encompassing larger German port and industrial cities as well as vast East Prussian agricultural areas dominated by large noble landowners known as *Junkers*. Thus more and more emigrants were both experienced urban workers and impoverished rural laborers, who did not have the resources to set themselves up on farms in the United States. These trends among the German emigrants reflected the advancing industrial revolution within Germany and the expansion of a transatlantic labor market using innovations in transportation and communication, such as steamships and the telegraph. Thus a higher proportion of the post-Civil War German emigrants followed leads in an international labor market in pursuit of wage labor rather than a farm or their own workshop, which were increasingly unlikely objectives given the development of the American economy. The experienced urban workers among them, women included, were more likely to emigrate by themselves rather than with families. In the twentieth century practically all German emigrants were workers of this type.

By the early twentieth century, the German industrial revolution had developed so extensively that Germany itself was importing workers, commonly Poles from the East. The era of mass German emigration was over, since most German migrants went to their own country's burgeoning industrial cities. Meanwhile new waves of immigrants were arriving in the United States from eastern and southern Europe, making the first decade of the twentieth century the highpoint of European immigration to this country, although this time the Germans did not mirror the larger trend. While German immigration remained significant after 1900, it was modest by former standards.

From German Immigrants to German-American Workers

The diversity, volume, and timing of German immigration in the second-half of the nineteenth century accentuated the impact of Germans on American labor history. German immigrants came from a huge European region encompassing an extensive range of economic development, from backward rural areas to advanced industrial cities. Experienced urban workers combined with the post-Civil War *émigrés* to provide leadership to Germans new to both cities and the labor market. The Germans also came in huge numbers comparable only to the Irish at the time. This mixture of quantity with diversity created the possibility for German-speaking labor movements within the United States. The possibilities for such movements were enhanced by the success of German entrepreneurs in dominating whole economic sectors in American cities, such as brewing and distilling, baking, tailoring, and furniture making.

The timing of the German mass migration was as important as its diversity and scale. The highest German waves coincided with the most dramatic and traumatic phase of American industrialization when everyone, whether immigrant or native-born American, was trying to understand and build a place for him/herself in a modern industrial society. Anyone with a viable model or cogent idea at least got a hearing. Because of this ferment, Germans were able to make an unusual contribution toward defining the shape of American labor institutions by adapting their experiences and traditions to American conditions. This process required both imagination and sacrifice.

Social-Democratic politics could not perform the same unifying role in the United States as it had in Germany, where it functioned as a cultural and political touchstone for defining and unifying the German industrial working class. In the different American political culture, Social-Democratic politics could not even unite German immigrant workers, much less link them in a larger movement with other immigrants and native-born Americans. At the same time in the United States, the German models of union organization and cultural institution building became especially important even as Germans provided the largest constituency for various socialist political parties as well as for the anarchist movement of the 1880s. Thus Germans contributed mightily not only to the American left but also to defining and sustaining bureaucratically organized craft unions and business unionism generally.

The twentieth century brought a profound crisis to Germans in the United States, and not only because the German mass migrations were over. The corporate reorganization period in the United States from 1898–1904 not only set up the model for the new corporate economy but also weakened the German-dominated sectors of the U.S. urban economy. Caught up in a new economic order and lacking a sustaining stream of immigrants, German labor movements were no longer viable. For all Germans, not only workers, the early twentieth century posed the fundamental problem of how to be first of all American but of a distinctive German cast. Ethnic folk culture provided one option, but there were others that did not rely on the German language or distinctive cultural markers. Among them was "municipal socialism," the American term for Social-Democratic politics, which became prominent during the Progressive Era, particularly in midwestern cities. Another such option was building craft unions, usually with substantial benefits and often with left-leaning politics, within the American Federation of Labor (AFL). The anti-German patriotic feeling unleashed by World War I made these options for being a German-American worker even more important because they were less visibly German.

JOHN B. JENTZ

References and Further Reading

Gjerde, Jon. "Prescriptions and Perceptions of Labor and Family among Ethnic Groups in the Nineteenth-Century American Middle West." In *German-American Immigration and Ethnicity in Comparative Perspective*, edited by Wolfgang Helbich and Walter D. Kamphoefner. Madison, WI: Max Kade Institute for German-American Studies, 2004.

Harzig, Christiane. "The Role of German Women in the German-American Working-Class Movement in Late Nineteenth-Century New York." *Journal of American Ethnic History* 8, 2 (1989): 87–107.

———. "Creating a Community: German-American Women in Chicago." In *Peasant Maids—City Women: From the European Countryside to Urban America*, edited by Christiane Harzig. Ithaca, NY and London: Cornell University Press, 1997.

Hoerder, Dirk, and Jörg Nagler, eds. *People in Transit: German Migrations in Comparative Perspective, 1820–1930.* New York: Cambridge University Press/German Historical Institute, 1995.

———. "Migration in the Atlantic Economies: Regional European Origins and Worldwide Expansion" and "From Migrants to Ethnics: Acculturation in a Societal Framework." In *European Migrants: Global and Local Perspectives*, edited by Dirk Hoerder and Leslie Page Moch. Boston, MA: Northeastern University Press, 1996.

Jentz, John B., and Hartmut Keil. "From Immigrants to Urban Workers: Chicago's German Poor in the Gilded Age and Progressive Era, 1883–1908." *Vierteljahrschrift für Sozial- und Wirtschaftsgeschichte* 68, 1 (1981): 52–97.

Keil, Hartmut, and John B. Jentz, eds. *German Workers in Industrial Chicago, 1850–1910.* DeKalb, IL: Northern Illinois University Press, 1983.

———. *German Workers in Chicago: A Documentary History of Working-Class Culture from 1850 to World War I.* Urbana and Chicago: University of Illinois Press, 1988.

———. *German Workers' Culture in the United States 1850 to 1920.* Washington, DC and London, UK: Smithsonian Institution Press, 1988.

Levine, Bruce. *The Spirit of 1848: German Immigrants, Labor Conflict, and the Coming of the Civil War.* Urbana and Chicago: University of Illinois Press, 1992.

Nadel, Stanley. *Little Germany: Ethnicity, Religion, and Class in New York City, 1845–80.* Urbana and Chicago: University of Illinois Press, 1990.

Sartorius von Walterhausen, August. *August Sartorius von Waltershausen: The Workers' Movement in the United States, 1879–1885*, edited by David Montgomery and Marcel van der Linden. Cambridge, UK: Cambridge University Press, 1998 (essays originally published in the 1880s).

Schneider, Dorothee. *Trade Unions and Community: The German Working Class in New York City, 1870–1900.* Urbana and Chicago: University of Illinois Press, 1994.

Sombart, Werner. "Why Is There No Socialism in the United States?" In *Economic Life in the Modern Age*, edited by Nico Stehr and Reiner Grundmann. New Brunswick, NJ: Transaction Publishers, 2001 (originally published 1906).

See also **Anarchism; Bakery and Confectionary Workers Union; Berger, Victor L.; Central Labor Unions; Craft Unionism; Gompers, Samuel; Haymarket Affair; Immigration and Nationality Act of 1965; International Cigar Makers Union; International Workingmen's Association; Marx, Karl; Socialist Labor Party; Sorge, Friedrich; Spies, August Smith; Strasser, Adolph; United Brewery Workers**

GI BILL

Signed by Franklin D. Roosevelt in June of 1944, the GI Bill, or Serviceman's Readjustment Act of 1944 (SRA), delivered a cornucopia of benefits to 7.8 million veterans of World War II at a cost of $77 billion. Hailed as an expression of the nation's gratitude to those who had rendered military service during the war, the GI Bill was just as fundamentally a labor-market intervention designed to prevent a postwar depression. Most Americans recognized that barring some external stimulus, when hostilities ended and the military discharged 16 million American servicemen into the civilian economy, the number of workers would far exceed the available jobs. The specter of idle, hungry workers waiting in endless lines for government handouts struck fear in the hearts of a population that had grown accustomed to the high wages and creature comforts made possible by the booming wartime economy.

At first glance the GI Bill appeared to offer something to every veteran of the Second World War. Qualifying veterans received federally backed, low-interest loan guarantees for housing, businesses, and farms; tuition for education and vocational training, as well as unemployment and self-employment subsidies and services. The education and training benefit for which the GI Bill is best-known offered veterans one year of full-time training at colleges, trade schools, and business and agriculture programs in addition to time equal to their military service, for a maximum of 48 months. Federal subsidies reaching $500 a year flowed through the Veterans' Administration to universities and trade schools. So enthusiastic was the response that by 1947 veterans comprised 49% of college students. Many were the first in their families to seek higher education. At Rutgers College in New Jersey, the influx of ex-GIs swelled enrollment from 750 in September 1945 to 4,200 2 years later and set the stage for an explosive expansion in facilities. Less academically oriented veterans who qualified might get seed loans to start farms or businesses. Still others (59%) cashed in on a special unemployment fund, claiming $20 a week for up to one year. Not only did the GI Bill launch the careers of a generation of doctors, lawyers, teachers, academics, and businessmen, it also birthed a generation of skilled laborers.

A central premise of the GI Bill, namely, that the federal government had a responsibility to take an expansive role in the postwar economy, came straight out of the New Deal. The National Resources Planning Board (NRPB) had been conceived by Harold Eckes in 1933 to coordinate the efforts of the Public Works Administration. Once the war began, its focus shifted to attaining full employment after the war. In 1943, the NRPB released two pamphlets detailing its vision of postwar social provision. In *After the War—Full Employment*, Alvin H. Hansen, the nation's leading Keynesian and a member of the Harvard Economics Department, advocated aggressive deficit spending and an increase in personal and corporate income tax to allow the federal government to continue after the war to prime the demand side of the economic equation. In *Security, Work, and Relief Policies*, members of the NRPB proposed a range of social supports administered by the Federal Security Administration to meet the employment, housing, and educational needs of all Americans. The report endorsed federal programs to put money into the hands of the poor through expanded unemployment insurance, general assistance, and a massive, ongoing public works' program, as a means to stimulate the economy.

To many on the labor-left, the prospect of universal social security seemed not just morally desirable, but fiscally sound as well as politically realistic. Organized labor—represented by the newly swelled ranks of the Congress of Industrial Organizations (CIO), the American Federation of Labor (AFL) and independent unions—welcomed the NRPB reports. The Socialist party and the National Farmers Union also endorsed the plans. Champions of the rights of the disenfranchised, among them Clark Foreman of the Southern Conference for Human Welfare and Lester Granger of the National Urban League, likewise cheered the proposals as overdue amendments to such New Deal programs as the National Labor Relations Act and the Social Security Act. Written in the 1930s to the specifications of southern Democrats and a handful of Republicans whose support was necessary, these programs had excluded many of the nation's poorest citizens, leaving as much as one-third of the African-American labor force, as well as a wide swath of white workers, without any safety net. Essentially the NRPB proposed demobilization of the armed forces as a double opportunity: to remedy gaps in New Deal social provision and set the economy on stable footing.

Critics derided these postwar plans as pie-eyed and worse. To the *Wall Street Journal*, the postwar proposals looked like "a halfway house to socialism!" Congressional conservatives like Senator Robert Taft of Ohio jeered that the plans for full employment had been hatched in a den of Marxism. Editors at the *New York Times* fanned the flames encircling the NRPB, condemning the proposals as "Bismarkian." Altogether the response revealed that the fragile consensus that had held through the late 1930s would not survive the challenge of postwar planning. Results of the midterm elections of 1942 had only emboldened the anti-New Deal cohort in Congress. Midwestern voters in particular had elected Republican candidates committed to the return of private enterprise as the engine of a healthy economy. Their ascendancy meant that FDR lacked the political capital, if he ever had the will, to effectuate the NRPB's ambitious plans. Weeks after the group released its reports, Congress cut off its funding. Plucked from their New Deal roots, postwar plans grew energetically, but in a decidedly different direction.

Having kicked the NRPB to the curb, conservatives in Congress turned to the American Legion, the nation's largest veterans group, for its vision of postwar federal planning. Founded in 1919 by veterans of World War I descended from some of the nation's oldest families (including Teddy Roosevelt, Jr.), the American Legion gained national attention in its first year of existence in a lethal face-off with the Wobblies in Centralia, Washington. It was a fitting *entrée*, since the legion, whose members—unlike its leadership—were mainly middle-class white men living outside the nation's cities, maintained close ties to the Chamber of Commerce and the National Association of Manufacturers and would develop a track record of support for immigration quotas, veteran bonuses, racial segregation, strike breaking, and loyalty oaths through the next several decades.

Congressman John E. Rankin of Mississippi introduced a legion-authored version of a GI Bill of Rights in the House. Rankin's endorsement alone spoke volumes about the limits of the proposal. Chairman of the House World War Veterans' Committee and a southern Democrat *par excellence*, Rankin mingled his support for the rights of veterans with outspoken racism, anti-Semitism, and antipapism. Just as he and other southern Democrats had left their mark on federal legislation during the 1930s, crafting policy palatable to white southern interests because it excluded the mostly African-American domestic and agricultural workforce, Rankin and his colleagues insisted that postwar veteran legislation likewise accommodate the racist political economy of the South.

Like the bulwarks of the welfare state that preceded it, the GI Bill emerged race and gender neutral on its face. But both the design and implementation of the law guaranteed *de facto* discrimination. Rankin, and his Senate counterpart, Missouri Democrat Bennett Champ Clark, a founder of the American Legion, insisted on an omnibus bill that combined the bill's diverse features (concerning housing, education, unemployment insurance, and so forth) into a single provision and vested loose administration of the funds in the Veterans' Administration (VA) under General Omar Bradley, a reliable ally.

From the perspective of Republicans and southern Democrats, the genius of the bill hinged on local control of federal funds. Since the federal government guaranteed only loans and reimbursed tuition, veterans had to apply to local, typically white-run institutions. Loan applicants who lacked collateral or credit encountered grim odds. The VA offered no hope, hewing as it did to the segregationist policies of the Federal Housing Authority, which mandated that, "properties shall continue to be occupied by the same social and racial classes." Institutionalized racism also limited the ability of veterans of color to access the education provision of the GI Bill. Of the South's 647 colleges and universities after World War II, only 102 admitted blacks. Theoretically the situation improved as one moved north. Yet in 1946, 46 African-American students joined nine thousand white coeds in classes at the University of Pennsylvania—making it among the least restrictive schools in the Ivy League.

But some of the problems associated with the GI Bill ran deeper than discriminatory implementation. Even if bankers and college administrators had treated all veterans fairly, beneficiaries of the legislation would still have been disproportionately male and white because on balance, most veterans fit this demographic. Under the guidance of Director General Louis Hershey, the Selective Service Administration had enlisted Americans in numbers disproportionate to their representation in the population. For example women's participation in the military topped out at 2%. For African-American males, generations of inadequate health care and education compounded by discriminatory draft boards that conspired to keep their numbers down. Since only half of young black males, as compared to three-fourths of whites in the same age bracket, entered the armed forces during the war, even in the absence of racism, proportionately fewer African-Americans would have qualified for benefits.

Arguably women workers paid the highest price when the legion's version of the GI Bill edged out plans for a broader entitlement. Administrators at the Bureau of Labor Statistics (BLS) described the "imbalance between wartime additions to the labor force and industry's normal demand for women workers." Absent a federal plan for full employment, corporations righted the imbalance themselves, turning out their female wartime hires in droves. Anecdotal evidence on this point abounds. At the Federated Press, a leftist news service in New York City, journalist Betty Goldstein (later Betty Freidan) lost her job to a veteran. Records from the U.S. Employment Service (USES) confirm that along with the Veterans' Re-employment Act of 1946, the GI Bill shunted women workers, especially those in manufacturing, to the end of the job queue or into lesser-paid, pink-collar jobs. From July of 1945 to April of 1946, nearly 3.5 million women exited the labor force, while almost 3.8 million men (re-) entered.

According to popular wisdom, women had joined the workforce "for the duration" and looked forward to leaving their jobs when it had ended. Of course millions of women already worked for a wage before the war, and a survey by the Women's Bureau suggested that 75% wished or needed to do so after the war. Even in the midst of the longest strike wave in American history, management and unions colluded with the federal government to force women workers out. They greeted the flurry of pink slips as a return to normal labor market conditions—not as evidence that the GI Bill had boosted some workers over others.

Through the mid-to-late 1940s and across the spectrum of the labor-left, a smattering of organizations condemned the clusivity of the GI Bill as anathema to American ideals. Progressive and Communist veterans bored into the American Legion, by then over one million members strong, hoping to weigh in on postwar plans—before being expelled. At the University of Chicago, social scientist St. Clair Drake founded the United Negro and Allied Veterans. Goals of the group, including "protection of lives and property of veterans in the Deep South," and "enforcement of federal laws governing Negro rights and benefits," spoke volumes about the status of many black veterans. Declaring themselves "citizens first, veterans, second," diverse veterans, including cartoonist Bill Mauldin and civil rights pioneer Medgar Evers, joined chapters of the American Veterans' Committee (AVC). Members of the AVC picketed the offices of Metropolitan Life, principal backer of the Levittown developments constructed across the country for the benefit of white veterans. Before being neutralized by anticommunism, many of these groups pressed federal lawmakers to expand on a universal scale the benefits the GI Bill had enshrined for some veterans.

Despite its partiality, fans of the GI Bill have always drowned out its critics. Many veterans did use the provision as a bridge to a more comfortable existence. But because of the way the law was written, many other veterans and nonveterans could not. In relative terms their position actually worsened as a result. It is even possible that the broad entitlements outlined in the GI Bill actually undercut efforts to win universal opportunity and equality of citizenship. Today the 1944 GI Bill is remembered not as an entitlement program, but rather as a patriotic gesture. The effect perpetuates the belief that when at midcentury a generation of white men stepped into coveted jobs, schools, and neighborhoods, they did so by merit alone rather than by explicit design.

ANASTASIA MANN

References and Further Reading

Brinkley, Alan. *The End of Reform: New Deal Liberalism in Recession and War*. New York: Knopf, 1995.
Dalfiume, Richard M. *Desegregation of the Armed Forces: Fighting on Two Fronts, 1939–1953*. Columbia: University of Missouri Press, 1969.
Mann, Anastasia. "All for One, but Most for Some: Veteran Politics and the Shaping of the Welfare State during the World War II Era." Ph.D. dissertation. Northwestern University, 2003.
Milkman, Ruth. *Gender at Work: The Dynamics of Job Segregation by Sex during World War II*. Urbana: University of Illinois Press, 1987.
Ross, Davis R.B. *Preparing for Ulyees: Politics and Veterans during World War II*. New Haven, CT: Yale University Press, 1969.

Cases and Statutes Cited

Servicemen's Readjustment Act of 1944, P.L. 346.

GILDED AGE

The Gilded Age, referring to the years from the 1870s to the end of the nineteenth century, constituted a formative period in American labor history. These years witnessed very rapid economic development, urbanization, and the growth of immigration. The period also saw the growing social polarization of American society, expressed not only in socio-economic segregation in cities and the growth of both poverty and great wealth, but also in bitter and often violent strikes that punctuated the period. Finally the era saw the emergence of key labor institutions like the American Federation of Labor (AFL) and the national trade unions, the growth and then decline of an alternative model of labor organizing, the Order of the Knights of Labor (KOL). The central paradox of the Gilded Age, the extremely rapid economic growth and generation of wealth on the one hand and the growth of social inequality and poverty on the other hand, was effectively summed up in the title of a widely read 1879 book by the social reformer Henry George: *Progress and Poverty*.

Economic and Technological Change

By the end of the Gilded Age, the United States had become the leading industrial nation in the world, decisively overtaking its rivals, England, France, and Germany. American factories, mines, and mills turned out products on a scale that would have been incomprehensible to an earlier generation, while new inventions, like the telephone, typewriter, and electric lighting, reshaped American life. In 1890, for the first time in American history, the value of manufactured goods overtook that of agricultural products.

The U.S. economic growth in this period was based in part on its vast natural resources. Farmland provided food for a growing urban workforce, while extensive coal reserves, iron deposits, and mineral resources supplied the raw materials to feed mills and factories. Federal policies, such as banking acts (which established a stable currency), high tariffs (which gave protection from foreign competition to infant industries), and large federal loans and land grants to railroad companies, also provided important spurs to industrialization.

A massive surge of railroad construction lay at the center of American economic growth in this period. From 1873–1893 over 100,000 miles of track were laid, giving the United States the most extensive transportation system in the world. Railroad building stimulated industrialization directly by generating a huge demand for iron, steel, coal, and lumber and indirectly by linking the diverse regions of the country into a vast national market, thus offering potentially huge profits to industrialists who could provide this market with manufacturing goods.

Improvements were also made in the quality of rail transportation. By the end of the 1880s, all the nation's railroads maintained a standard gauge, permitting cars to be transferred easily between tracks owned by separate companies. Such technological improvements as the Westinghouse air brake allowed trains to move more safely at faster speeds, though accidents, especially in cities, left many urban residents injured or dead each year and engendered much hostility to the railroads. Railroad companies even divided the nation into its present time zones to increase the regularity of service.

By increasing the speed of transportation and the quantity of goods that could be shipped, these developments helped set off a revolution in industry by encouraging manufacturers to adopt techniques of mass production. In the new steel industry for example, manufacturers introduced the most important invention of the period, the Bessemer converter, which increased the speed of steel production dramatically and allowed the output of steel to one-half million tons in 1877 to nearly five million tons in 1892. By the end of the nineteenth century, the United States was the greatest steel-producing nation in the world. The output of copper and crude oil increased dramatically as well. Steelmaker Andrew Carnegie captured the rapid pace of change dramatically in 1885 when he observed: "the Republic thunders past with the rush of the express."

The Gilded Age was a period of tremendous inventiveness. By the 1890s, there were over 300,000 telephones, which Alexander Graham Bell had invented in the 1870s, in use around the country. Thomas Edison, who produced his first electric lamp in 1879, was manufacturing over a million light bulbs a year by 1890. But most industries that gained prominence in this period produced capital goods rather than consumer goods like telephones and lights. Though the pre-Civil War phase of industrialization had revolved around such consumer industries as clothing and shoes, this phase was based on manufactured goods that would be used by other industries—above all the railroad.

But for all its impressiveness, economic growth in the Gilded Age was marked by profound uncertainty. While the years from the end of the Civil War to 1873 were tenuously prosperous, the so-called Panic of that year threw the nation's entire financial system into chaos and led to 4 years of the most severe depression the nation had yet seen. An upswing in the late 1870s brought a return of good times, but this was followed by another (less severe) depression that lasted from 1882–1885. Worse than either of these downturns was the depression of 1893–1897, which scarred towns and cities across the nation with massive unemployment and sharply falling wages. For workers this newly prominent "business cycle," a pattern of several years of rapid economic growth followed by several years of economic downturn accompanied by widespread unemployment and declining wages, became a source of tremendous concern.

Many U.S. workers toiled in the factories and workshops of the Midwest and the Northeast, the industrial heart of the nation in these years. It was the economic core stretching from Massachusetts and Maryland in the east to Illinois, southern Wisconsin, and eastern Missouri in the west that felt the greatest impact of industrialization. The scale of the workplace also changed dramatically. In the 1870s, only a handful of factories that employed over 500 workers existed in the country. Manufacturing took place mainly in small and medium plants. By 1900, there were over 1,000 American factories that employed over 500 workers. In Pennsylvania there were three steel-making facilities that employed over 8,000 workers.

The period was marked by the dramatic growth of big business in a number of sectors of the economy but most notably on the railroads. The railroad network created a national market, and the railroads themselves became the nation's first truly large business, employing thousands of people and pioneering new organizational structures in the process. Large business organizations also emerged in iron and steel, the electrical industry, oil drilling and refining, and farm machinery manufacture. Huge enterprises like the Pennsylvania Railroad, Standard Oil, and International Harvester not only became household names, but also began to exert tremendous political power in the nation.

Not every part of the nation was affected equally by these changes. In the South for instance, while important manufacturing cities like Atlanta and the new steel center of Birmingham emerged and while large coal-mining and lumbering operations became important, much of the economy still turned on agriculture, where black and white sharecroppers and tenant farmers eked out a meager living on the land. Cotton, so central to the early phase of American industrialization, remained dominant in the region even if slavery no longer existed. New Orleans, the South's great city, developed as the port of this region, with a variety of black and white workers laboring on the city's docks and in its warehouses. So, too, in the Far West, extractive industries like lumbering and mining remained critical in these years. Along with the rapid growth of farming on the Great Plains and on the Pacific Coast, this increased the population of the region significantly, while not leading to the kind of great industrial cities that emerged in the East and Midwest.

In global terms this was a very significant period. In the last-quarter of the nineteenth century, a true world economy came into being. International trade grew rapidly along with the movement of both people and capital across national borders. Food and raw materials of various sorts produced around the globe found their way to the industrializing economies of Europe and North America. All of this was inextricably connected to developments in the United States and particularly to the heavily immigrant composition of its growing working class.

The Working Class: Composition and Conditions

Not surprisingly given this rapid economic expansion, the size of the American labor force grew dramatically over these years. This growing labor force was made up partly by the movement of those Americans from agriculture to industry. Though agriculture expanded dramatically in the late nineteenth century, especially on the Great Plains, millions of black and white rural Americans sought jobs in rapidly growing cities or found industrial wage work (coal mining, railroad building and track maintenance, lumbering) in rural areas. But massive immigration from Asia, Mexico, and especially in these years, Europe was one of the most important facts of the whole period. From 1870–1900, nearly 12 million immigrants entered the United States. By 1900, 10.4 million American residents were foreign-born, representing 13.6% of the total population. The working class was even more heavily immigrant than the population as a whole.

At the beginning of this period, immigrants from northern and western Europe (particularly Germany, Scandinavia, Britain, and Ireland) tended to dominate the flow. Especially after 1890, immigrants from southern and eastern Europe (Italy, Russia, and the Austro-Hungarian empire) grew important, a trend that would reach a peak in the early years of the twentieth century. Though less significant in total numbers, migrants from Mexico played a critical role in the Southwest, constituting an important part of the labor force in mining and smelting, railroad maintenance, and large-scale agriculture. Immigration from China, which had been crucial to the California economy in the 1860s and 1870s and to the completion of the first transcontinental railroad in 1869, was curtailed by the Chinese Exclusion Act of 1882. A product of an intensely xenophobic anti-Chinese movement, the act led to an increase in immigration from Japan, while also tracing the shape of restrictive immigration legislation that would be widely adopted in the twentieth century.

The high levels of immigration in this period made the American working class the most ethnically and racially diverse in the world. A similar diversity could be found in workers' labor conditions and standards of living. For the working class as a whole, steadily falling prices and advancing wages from the 1870s to the 1890s led to an important rise in standards of living. Yet there remained a wide gulf in the living standards of different groups among workers, particularly between highly skilled workers whose wages allowed them to live in some comfort and those of less skilled and prosperous urban or rural workers.

But life for even the relatively prosperous workers remained extremely precarious in this era. The absence of pensions, compensation for on-the-job injuries, or any form of unemployment insurance meant that workers lived in constant fear of injury or layoffs. The length of the working week (60 hours or more for many) and the intensity of work was also a source of dissatisfaction for many workers. But perhaps most galling was the obvious disdain with which middle-class and upper-class Americans viewed the working class. This disdain reflected important shifts in the larger ideological context within which the labor movement operated.

Ideological and Legal Context

The Gilded Age was among other things a period of significant ideological change. In earlier periods many American writers and politicians had expressed concern about the potential of economic growth to produce social inequality, monopolistic abuses of economic power, and political corruption. Though such concerns did not entirely vanish in this era, they were supplanted by an emphasis on the links between economic growth and upward social mobility: American capitalism was increasingly praised as paving the way for the self-made man. This linkage made the otherwise troubling rise of large-scale industrial capitalism seem fully compatible with American democracy.

This ideological shift was reflected in rulings by state and federal courts (including the U.S. Supreme Court) that gave business important new rights while providing a major challenge to workers and the labor movement. In particular the courts increasingly moved to a position that allowed no room for state laws (including for instance maximum-hour laws) that tried to regulate business. Workers' rights by contrast were limited to nothing more than "liberty of contract" and "ownership of the capacity to labor." The due protection clause of the Fourteenth Amendment, originally designed to enable the federal government to overturn state laws that violated the rights of citizens, was transformed in a series of court decisions to emphasize the rights of corporations.

This trend culminated in 1905 when in the *Lochner v. New York* case, the Supreme Court overturned a state law that limited the working hours of bakers, declaring that the law "interfered with the right of contract between employer and employee" and thus violated individual freedom. But even in the Gilded Age, the trend in the law was increasingly clear and sharply limited the ability of the labor movement to achieve some of its most important objectives.

Strikes and Conflict

The rapid pace of economic change along with the deep social inequality characteristic of this period led to considerable labor conflict. In some famous strikes, workers went down in defeat, though in many local strikes, especially in the building and metal trades, worker gains were not uncommon. There were notable peaks in strike activity during these years (particularly 1885–1886 and 1892–1895), but beyond this Gilded Age, strikes demonstrated a clear pattern over time: Strikes became more organized and more likely to be coordinated by unions. And one particular type of strike, the sympathy strike, in which a group of workers went out in support of another group, was particularly prominent in this era.

The period in addition was marked by several very large strikes that focused the attention of much of the nation on what was called the "labor question." In July 1877, wage cuts on the Baltimore and Ohio Railroad triggered a walkout by railroad workers in Martinsburg, West Virginia, and wage cuts by the Pennsylvania Railroad triggered a nationwide railroad strike that spread across the entire nation. After the Philadelphia militia fired on strikers in Pittsburgh, killing 20 people, railroad workers, supported by local ironworkers and other city residents, responded by up setting fire to the property of the Pennsylvania Railroad there. Spreading to cities as far away as Galveston, Texas, and San Francisco, the strike remained peaceful and orderly in some localities. In St. Louis for example, a general strike, drawing support from both black and white working-class residents, virtually shut down the city for several days. But it in others localities, such as Chicago, the actions of heavily armed police and eventually troops in working-class districts, led to tremendous violence. In San Francisco white working-class racism came to the fore as a crowd meeting to discuss action against the railroads ended up rampaging through the city's Chinatown, burning buildings and killing several residents. The strike, which lasted two weeks, came to an end only with the introduction of federal troops on the side of the railroads.

The rapid growth of the KOL (see the following paragraphs) and the revival of trade unions in the late 1870s and early 1880s prepared the stage for another period of intense class conflict in the middle years of this decade. The trigger this time was the demand for the 8-hour day. Coordinated especially by trade unionists through the Federation of Organized Trade and Labor Unions, a lobbying body they established in 1881, the movement first took the form of campaigning for state laws that mandated the 8-hour day. But the ineffectiveness of laws that were passed led many workers to turn to direct action. A series of large demonstrations and strikes across the nation that began on May 1, 1886, won shorter hours for many workers while generating considerable fear among middle- and upper-class Americans. When Chicago police moved to break up an 8-hour meeting in Haymarket Square, a bomb thrown into the ranks of the police (and killing one officer) focused middle-class fears on the threat of anarchism. The execution the following year of four men (all radical leaders but none of them implicated convincingly in the actual murder of the police officer) won much enthusiastic support from the middle-class press while convincing many in the labor movement that a grievous miscarriage of justice had been perpetrated.

The 1890s saw industrial conflict on an even larger scale. In 1892, steel maker Andrew Carnegie, determined to break the power of the local Amalgamated Iron and Steel Workers' lodge at his giant steelworks in Homestead, Pennsylvania, initiated a massive lockout of the union workers that led to months of conflict, occasioned by gun battles between workers and Pinkerton detectives. This bitter conflict ended in November of that year with a complete victory for Carnegie, who was now on the road to achieving a completely nonunion operation.

Not all industrial conflicts ended this way. On the New Orleans docks, a dynamic center of biracial unionism in spite of the racism of many white workers and the segregation of blacks and whites off the job, a struggle of African-American teamsters and white packers and scale men for shorter hours culminated in a successful general strike in 1892 that gave union workers one of their most significant victories in the nineteenth century. But in the wake of the depression that began the following years, it became much more difficult for workers to win strikes or improve their position, a point most clearly visible in the great Pullman strike and boycott of 1894.

The background of this conflict was the rapid growth of the American Railway Union (ARU), an industrial union led by Eugene V. Debs that embraced workers from a wide variety of different railroad occupations across the country. At its convention in June 1894, workers then on strike at the Pullman Car Company's manufacturing operations in Illinois asked the ARU to support them by refusing to handle Pullman cars (luxury sleeping cars) on tracks anywhere in the country. The convention agreed, and the Pullman boycott (essentially a large-scale sympathy strike) ensued. By early July a strike of massive proportions had spread across much of the Midwest and West, leading to equally massive intervention by the federal government. An injunction was handed down against the strikers, Debs was imprisoned, and armed troops across the nation (along with a declaration of martial law in Chicago) brought defeat to the Pullman workers and eventually destruction to the new ARU.

Labor Organizations

Underneath and related to the intense industrial conflict of this era, many workers were attempting to build labor organizations to improve their position. In the early 1870s, several groups of workers, especially anthracite (hard) coal miners and coopers, had some notable successes in building such unions, though these were mainly wiped out by the depression of the middle years of the decade. In the mid-1880s, which saw the nineteenth-century peak of membership in labor organizations (with nearly a million members of trade unions or KOL assemblies in 1886), dock workers, meatpacking workers, bituminous (soft) coal miners, and iron and steel workers also made

important strides, joined by railroad workers and workers in the building trades in the early 1890s. Building and maintaining such unions though necessitated a constant struggle, not only with employers, but with fellow workers, for it involved asserting a mutuality and solidarity in the face of the individualism that was at the center of the ideology of the period.

In addition to unions representing workers in particular occupations, there were also efforts to bring workers across occupational lines into larger umbrella organizations. The National Labor Union, in the Civil War era, had been an important example of such an organization, but the NLU collapsed in the early 1870s. Building on the traditions of the NLU, but much more significant during this period was an organization called the Noble and Holy Order of the KOL, which, in membership terms, was the largest labor organization in the nineteenth century. Much more than a labor union or federation of unions, the KOL represented a truly massive expression of working-class opposition to the social inequality and political corruption of the Gilded Age. In its heyday in the mid-1880s, the Knights expounded a cooperative and mutualistic philosophy that ran counter to the individualism and materialism that dominated the era.

Founded by Uriah Stephens and a small group of his fellow garment cutters in Philadelphia in 1869, the Knights were at first closer to a secret fraternal society than a labor organization. But as one of the few organizations of workers to survive the depression of the 1870s, the order put aside its secrecy in 1878 and embarked on the building of a national labor reform movement. Led now by Terence V. Powderly, a former machinist and the mayor of Scranton, Pennsylvania, the Knights sought to create an organization that would encompass all members of what they called the "producing classes." In fact the Knights did organize across lines of skill, gender, religion, and nationality. Female factory and mill workers for example, though excluded from the order in the 1870s, forced Powderly and other leaders of the KOL to recognize their right to join following a successful 1881 strike by female shoemakers in Philadelphia. By the mid-1880s, women constituted one-tenth of the KOL membership, and female organizers like Leonora Barry and Elizabeth Rodgers were highly visible leaders of the order.

Race proved to be a greater hurdle. In the Far West in fact the organization expressed racial animosities openly, often spearheading the powerful white working-class movement against Chinese immigrants in this region. The KOL leaders praised the 1882 Chinese Exclusion Act as a victory for American workers. During the 1880s, members of the KOL participated in San Francisco boycotts of Chinese-made cigars and in a race riot in Rock Springs, Wyoming, that left 28 Chinese workers dead.

The Knights' relationship to African-American workers however was quite different. In spite of considerable white working-class hostility to African-Americans, the KOL both admitted and attracted many southern African-American members, numbering approximately 60,000 by the summer of 1886. The order's national convention of that year, held in Richmond, Virginia, asserted the willingness of the organization to organize southern African-American workers despite the intense opposition from southern elites. African-American Knights continued to face discrimination within the organization, and a true biracial unionism never emerged, but the order continued to represent a vehicle for the expression of African-American working-class aspirations through the entire decade of the 1880s.

The Knights were also actively involved in American politics. Though they never established a political party of their own, members of the KOL were full participants in an explosion of independent working-class political activity that spread across the nation in the years from 1885–1888. But beginning the middle of the decade, employers, supported by the government and the press, resisted further union growth and broke strikes, weakening the order in fundamental ways. The Haymarket incident and the antiradical sentiment that followed on its heels also hurt the order despite Powderly's strong opposition to anarchism. Finally the KOL experienced serious internal divisions as many members shifted their allegiance to unions affiliated with the new American Federation of Labor (AFL). As a result the order's membership fell from a peak of 700,000 in 1886 to just 200,000 in 1890; by the turn of the century, it was all but dead.

As the Knights declined however national unions of a variety of workers, particularly cigar makers, carpenters, iron molders, iron and steel workers, printers and coal miners, continued to grow. The growing strength of these new national unions, and more particularly, the jurisdictional disputes that erupted between these unions and the KOL, led them to establish the AFL in December 1886. Building on the foundations of the earlier Federation of Organized Trades and Labor Unions (by now virtually dead), the AFL differed from the Knights in asserting the fundamental right of each national union to control its trade. Led by Samuel Gompers, a cigar maker and former socialist, Adolph Strasser, and Peter J. McGuire, the AFL set an agenda of building new national unions and mobilizing workers in a new campaign for the 8-hour day. Gompers and other AFL leaders urged workers (especially skilled craftsmen who were the federation's main constituency) to avoid what they saw as "utopian" movements to abolish the wages system.

While the AFL was much smaller through this period than the Knights had been, the willingness of highly skilled craftsmen to use the strike (and especially the sympathy strike) to achieve their ends made the AFL and the national unions the dynamic center of the labor movement by the opening years of the 1890s. The depression and bitterly fought strikes of this decade weakened the organization in the years from 1893–1897. But as economic growth returned in the years after the end of the depression, the AFL was positioned to grow, and trade union membership grew dramatically in the years from 1897–1904. Important victories in bituminous coal mining (1898) and the metal trades (1901) increased the appeal of the AFL, though these would also help trigger the anti-union open-shop drive that dominated the first part of the Progressive Era.

DAVID BRUNDAGE

References and Further Reading

Arnesen, Eric. *Waterfront Workers of New Orleans: Race, Class, and Politics, 1863–1923*. New York: Oxford University Press, 1991.

Avrich, Paul. *The Haymarket Tragedy*. Princeton, NJ: Princeton University Press, 1984.

Brody, David. *Steelworkers in America: The Nonunion Era*. Cambridge, MA: Harvard University Press, 1960.

Cohen, Nancy. *The Reconstruction of American Liberalism, 1865–1914*. Chapel Hill: University of North Carolina Press, 2002.

Dubofsky, Melvyn. *Industrialism and the American Worker, 1865–1920*. 3rd ed. Wheeling, IL: Harlan Davidson, 1996.

Dubofsky, Melvyn. *The State and Labor in Modern America*. Chapel Hill: University of North Carolina Press, 1994.

Fink, Leon. *In Search of the Working Class: Essays in American Labor History and Political Culture*. Urbana: University of Illinois Press, 1994.

———. *Workingmen's Democracy: the Knights of Labor and American Politics*. Urbana: University of Illinois Press, 1983.

Gutman, Herbert G. *Work, Culture, and Society in Industrializing America: Essays in American Working-Class and Social History*. New York: Knopf, 1976.

Laurie, Bruce. *Artisans into Workers: Labor in Nineteenth-Century America*. New York: Hill and Wang, 1989.

Levine, Susan. *Labor's True Woman: Carpet Weavers, Industrialization, and Labor Reform in the Gilded Age*. Philadelphia, PA: Temple University Press, 1984.

Montgomery, David. *The Fall of the House of Labor: The Workplace, the State, and American Labor Activism, 1865–1925*. Cambridge, UK: Cambridge University Press, 1987.

Oestreicher, Richard. *Solidarity and Fragmentation: Working People and Class Consciousness in Detroit, 1875–1900*. Urbana: University of Illinois Press, 1986.

Rachleff, Peter J. *Black Labor in the South: Richmond, Virginia, 1865–1890*. Philadelphia, PA: Temple University Press, 1984.

Salvatore, Nick. *Eugene V. Debs: Citizen and Socialist*. Urbana: University of Illinois Press, 1982.

Saxton, Alexander. *The Indispensable Enemy: Labor and the Anti-Chinese Movement in California*. Berkeley: University of California Press, 1971.

GLOBALIZATION

The U.S. labor history has been marked by shifts in the manner in which global capitalism organizes itself to accumulate and distribute profits. Such shifts result in historic periods that are not only economic but also political. A shift to a new period presents unique challenges to workers attempting to organize themselves. The phenomenon known as globalization represents the most recent period in these terms.

Viewed as a system for the accumulation and distribution of capitalist profit, globalization has a number of dimensions. Central to this system is a high mobility of capital achieved through an extensive worldwide credit system and the development of new technologies. The technologies include the ability to break up the production of goods into small parts and produce each part in a different location. Globalization has also been institutionalized through such supranational institutions as the World Bank, the International Monetary Fund (IMF), the World Trade Organization (WTO), and the North American Free Trade Agreement (NAFTA). Changes in domestic laws that include economic policies; privatization; the elimination of barriers to foreign goods, services, and capital; and deregulation of business are also part of the institutionalization of globalization. Most importantly for labor, globalization involves a search for "flexible labor markets" that are defined in terms of the reduction of many high-wage jobs, elimination of costly benefits, the eradication of many work rules, and the removal of barriers to part-time and temporary labor. Because this system represents an historic shift, a proper understanding of globalization requires that we trace its development over time.

The Historical Context of Globalization

The industrial revolution represented a shift that led to the formation of the earliest U.S. labor unions. In the early twentieth century, another shift occurred that was generated by a new form of production process that included huge factories with assembly lines that engaged in mass production. This so-called "Fordist" period led to a new form of labor organization based on entire industries. In the U.S. this shift initially generated the organization of the International Workers of the World (IWW) and later the Congress of Industrial Organizations (CIO).

The economic crisis of the 1930s and the growth of mass-production industries led to a high degree of labor union militancy. That militancy resulted in concessions from the government, which passed legislation to sanction the right to organize and bargain collectively (Wagner Act of 1935). The militancy subsided during World War II but picked up again thereafter. It was at this point that there was a distinct shift to a new period that would enable Fordism to become a global system. This shift was initiated at a conference attended by representatives of 44 nations in Bretton Woods, New Hampshire, in July of 1944.

The Bretton Woods Conference resulted in an agreement that was to govern global capitalism until 1971. It put the United States. in a position to be the dominant player in world commerce through its role in the rebuilding of Europe and Japan in the wake of the destruction of World War II. The key features of the system included making the U.S. dollar the international medium of exchange, with its value relative to other currencies fixed and redeemable in gold. The World Bank was established to offer loans largely for the rebuilding of Europe, and the IMF offered short-term loans that enabled nations to avoid inflationary pressures that could interfere with the reconstruction process. A protocol, called the General Agreement on Tariffs and Trade (GATT), was also established to avoid trade wars.

Initially the need for postwar rebuilding and the Bretton Woods Agreement created a huge demand for U.S. products. But the system needed two things for it to sustain itself. One was the ability of the United States to extract cheap resources from the developing world. A challenge from the growing Soviet Union undermined this ability and became the context for the Cold War and U.S. foreign policy from 1945 to 1991, when the Soviet Union collapsed. The second need was for continuity in the U.S. production process, which required an end to militant trade unionism and unpredictable strikes. As a result the U.S. government essentially offered labor a share of the profits of the postwar system in return for support for U.S. foreign policy and some guarantee that production would not be disrupted by untimely strikes. This was the context for the Taft-Hartley Act of 1947 that limited organized labor's tactics. The deal also led to the merger of the American Federation of Labor (AFL) with the more militant CIO in 1955 and the expulsion of some of the more militant union leaders throughout the 1950s. The AFL-CIO also established overseas institutes that supported U.S. foreign policy objectives in many developing nations.

In return labor received concessions of its own through a strong alliance with the Democratic party. The larger labor unions negotiated long-term contracts that often tied wages to productivity. Unions disciplined their members to eliminate work stoppages during the term of the contract. These contracts were protected by the government, and there was an informal yet universally honored agreement that workers engaged in legal strikes would not be replaced. Furthermore government economic policy emphasized employment growth. The Employment Act of 1946 called for policies to promote "maximum employment, production and purchasing power."

The Birth of Globalization

In the 1960s and 1970s, a number of forces combined to unravel the Bretton Woods system. For one thing the postwar rebuilding process was complete, and Europe, Japan, and the Soviet Union all emerged as serious challengers to U.S. economic dominance. Wars of national liberation in colonies and the emergence of a nonaligned nations' movement in the developing world undermined easy access to cheap natural resources. The loss of the Vietnam War in 1975 confirmed the decline of U.S. hegemony in the developing world. Domestically during the 1960s, the Civil Rights movement challenged the fact that people of color had often been left out of the benefits of the old Bretton Woods system.

These forces began to manifest themselves both economically and politically. Economically there were wide-spread economic crises throughout the world. In the United States in the early-to-middle 1970s, this took the particularly virulent form of "stagflation," a previously unknown phenomenon of simultaneous high unemployment and high inflation. In 1971, a run on the dollar, whose value was guaranteed in gold under the Bretton Woods Agreement, caused President Nixon unilaterally to cancel that guarantee by not honoring demands for gold for dollars. In 1973, President Nixon unilaterally announced that the exchange rates of all currencies would fluctuate and be determined by supply and demand. This action canceled a central tenant of the Bretton Woods system. In 1974, a cartel of oil-producing nations (OPEC) restricted oil output of its members, thus driving up the global price of oil. This act fueled global inflation, adding to the growing economic crisis. A second such "oil shock" occurred in 1979, deepening the crisis even further.

Inside the United States, the growing antiwar movement and the civil rights movements were gaining momentum at the very time that the post-World War II prosperity period was ending. In some of the major industries like auto and steel, caucuses within unions were forming, demanding equal treatment for people of color and women and in some cases, an end to the blanket support unions were giving to U.S. foreign policy.

Meanwhile beneath the radar screen of most working people, there were other developments under way that were paving the way for the major political and economic shift now known as globalization. One was the flow of dollars in the form of loans to the developing world. The U.S. government and those of other developed nations began to try to win spheres of influence in the increasingly independent-minded developing world by giving loans—often propping up regimes that were friendly to the West. In addition with the collapse of the gold standard and floating currencies, many banks were caught with a glut of dollars, which were loaned out with abandon to developing nations. As a result debt in the developing world began to skyrocket. From 1973–1984, debt in developing nations increased from $100 billion to over $900 billion. But in 1982, the global economic crisis was pressing hard on the developing world, and there began a series of major debt defaults that included Mexico, Brazil, Argentina, and India, as well as such smaller nations as Ghana, Zaire, Bangladesh, and Somalia.

In the face of global debt default, the IMF stepped in offering 10-year "bridge loans" that would enable these nations to pay their debts. But in return the IMF imposed what became known as structural adjustment programs (SAPs) that required these nations to open up their economies to foreign goods and capital and to restructure their economies to emphasize production for export markets. The SAPs also included internal economic policies that emphasized inflation reduction, such as tight money, social spending cuts, and wide-scale privatization. The World Bank followed suit by offering long-term development loans with similar strings attached. In addition associations of lenders—both governments and banks—played a role in monitoring compliance with these terms. Over time economic policies of many developed nations were fully under the control of the United States and other developed nations as well as their banks.

Another important development going on behind the scenes on the world stage were a series of informal meetings and funded research projects that were being carried on by global elites and their governments to attempt to formalize and further institutionalize the emerging world order. One of the most significant forums was the Organization for Economic Cooperation and Development (OECD), which consists of government officials of the richest nations of the world. A series of reports by the OECD beginning in 1977, led by U.S. economist and presidential advisor Paul McCracken, spelled out the goal of "labor market flexibility." The so-called McCracken Commission traced the world's economic woes to the lack of such flexibility and set out a series of policy goals that included reduction in excessive wages, benefits and work rules, and an end to barriers to the use of part-time and temporary labor. The McCracken report and a series of other reports by OECD and other elite associations, such as the Trilateral Commission, began to spell out a broad policy alternative to the Bretton Woods system. These initiatives were followed by some clear policy shifts in the United States that clearly ran counter to the Bretton Woods era deal with labor.

In 1978, the Humphrey-Hawkins Full Employment and Balanced Growth Act was passed, reaffirming the priorities of the 1946 Full Employment Act. But 2 years later the U.S. Federal Reserve Bank effectively nullified this act of Congress by pushing up interest rates to halt inflation even though it meant that unemployment would soar to nearly 10%. From that point forward, U.S. economic policy shifted from one that emphasized fighting unemployment to a priority on lowering inflation even at the expense of employment and job growth. A second policy shift that ended the Bretton Woods era labor policy came when President Reagan fired striking air controllers in 1982 and announced that they would be permanently replaced. This act sent a signal to employers that it was now politically acceptable to replace striking workers. And employers took that signal and began using permanent replacement workers to break strikes.

Globalization in Practice

The shifts in domestic economic policy are not solely aimed at organized labor. They also reflect the key role that finance plays in the emerging phenomenon of globalization. As noted earlier, high capital mobility is central to the definition of globalization itself. Debt is one aspect of this. Not only is debt a mechanism to regulate and control economic policies in the developing world that are favorable to mobile capital, it has become a major industry. Since the spike in debt of developing nations to $900 billion in 1984, that

debt now stands at approximately $2.5 trillion. But debt is not limited to the developing world. Within the United States debt has become a key way to prop up standards of living. In 1949, U.S. household debt as a percentage of personal income was 29.5%. By 1979, it was up to 63%, and only half of that was due to mortgages. By 1989, that percentage was up to 76%, and today it is over 90%. Similarly credit card debt has spiked during this period. Not only has the business of making loans expanded, but debt itself has become a commodity. Various kinds of debt are now packaged and sold in global capital markets, their price being a function of how much return can be realized by collection and sales of debt. A secondary market for debt has expanded rapidly during this period in which speculators buy debt instruments in anticipation of its value at some specified future date. One measure of this growth is the relative importance of such financial futures contracts at the Chicago Board of Trade (CBOT). While in 1975 such contracts comprised only 1.5% of CBOT business, today they are over 80%.

The biggest risk to creditors in a system where there is strong political control over the economic policies of debtor nations and where there is a strong secondary market for debt itself is inflation, because it lowers the value of dollar-denominated financial assets. That is why domestic economic policies in the United States place such a priority on keeping inflation rates low even at the expense of employment. But capital mobility is also a key part of globalization in other ways. The structural adjustment policies that accompany debt open economies to foreign investors who not only invest in plants and equipment, but also in foreign stocks and bonds. Such portfolio investment represents over a third of capital flows into the developing world. It now averages about $47 billion a year, up from only $5 billion two decades ago. These trends combined with technological developments in process, transportation, and telecommunication technologies make it possible for large corporations to pursue a search for flexible labor markets all over the globe. The production of goods can be broken into pieces and carried out in different locations, with final assembly at a different location altogether. These same forces have also enabled service industries to source workers globally. The growth of such information technology workers as programmers in India is but one example.

In the U.S. these developments have led to a sharp decline in manufacturing jobs and more recently in selected service industries. During the 1990s, 1.5 million manufacturing jobs were lost in the United States. From 2000–2003, another 3 million jobs have disappeared, many due to the 2001 recession, but manufacturing job loss continued throughout the so-called "jobless recovery." Service jobs are just beginning to leave the country, so there is still a net growth. But highly skilled computer programmer jobs and entry-level call center and telephone operator jobs are already leaving the country. Estimates of the number of service jobs in the United States that are at risk range from 3 to over 14 million. These trends are not confined to the United States. A number of countries that initially benefited from the movement of production jobs are themselves experiencing rapid job dislocations. Globalized agricultural markets and SAP-imposed trade policies have led to the decline of agriculture jobs in countries like Mexico and India. At the same time many of the factory assembly jobs in Mexico's *maquiladora* sector (see References) that came from the United States have left for Bangladesh and China. And India is also experiencing the dislocation of many of its textile and apparel jobs.

In the United States the fact of capital mobility and the present political and policy climate that are also part of globalization have encouraged employers to use more aggressive tactics toward organized labor. A study of union-organizing efforts found that from 1992–1995, over half the employers surveyed had used the threat of closing and/or moving production during union-organizing drives. The average annual number of organizing efforts has declined from about 300,000 in the mid-1970s to less than 100,000 by the mid-1990s. The percentage of private-sector U.S. workers in unions is now under 9%, down from over 40% in the 1940s. The percentage has fallen more than five points in the last decade alone.

Meanwhile the institutionalization of globalization has continued over that same decade. Beyond the continuation and expansion of the SAPs by the IMF and World Bank, there have been a series of so-called trade agreements that have further strengthened the programs embedded in the SAPs. These agreements include the lowering of barriers to trade, but more importantly, they have opened many nations to a regulation-free form of capital mobility. The largest such agreement involved replacing the Bretton Woods era GATT with the WTO in 1995, which enforces a broad array of global rules that bind more than one hundred nations. The NAFTA between the United States, Canada, and Mexico, which contains even more stringent rules, went into effect in 1994. In addition there have been dozens of bilateral and multilateral agreements including nations in Africa and Latin America.

There have also been continuing changes in U.S. domestic policy that reinforce the policy trends discussed earlier. Changes in welfare and job-training legislation have encouraged a movement of workers into nonunion employment where wages are below federal poverty standards and benefits nonexistent. These jobs are often in the temporary help industry, representing a successful effort to establish flexible labor markets in the United States. Recent changes in labor legislation allow replacement workers hired during a strike to decertify the union if a strike lasts more than a year. Appointments to labor relations' boards that hear complaints about violations of labor law have further weakened organized labor.

Historically a shift to a new period has meant a response from labor. And that response is well under way, although it is far from complete. The challenge yet to be met is how to organize in a climate where firms can replace striking workers, decertify their unions, and take production of goods and services out of the country. Organized labor has begun to meet the challenge by opposing further institutionalization of globalization. While many major trade agreements and SAPs have gone forward over labor's efforts to stop them, there have been some successes as well, and nationally the form of globalization has become a political issue. Organized labor has also eliminated its old overseas institutes and formed coalitions with labor unions in other nations to stop SAPs and trade agreements and also to present internationalist alternatives. Finally there have been efforts to ally with community organizations and other nongovernmental organizations around issues of economic and social justice—to broaden the constituency of the unions beyond their own membership base.

DAVID C. RANNEY

References and Further Reading

Brofenbrenner, Kate. "Final Report: The Effects of Plant Closing or Threat of Plant Closing on the Right of Workers to Organize." Submitted to the Labour Secretariat of the North American Commission for Labor Cooperation. Ithaca: New York State School of Industrial and Labor Relations, Cornell University, 1996.

Chossudovsky, Michel. *The Globalization of Poverty: The Impact of the IMF and World Bank Reforms.* London: Zed Books, 1998.

Dicken, Peter. *Global Shift: Transforming the World Economy.* 3rd ed. New York: The Guilford Press, 1998.

Epstein, Gerald, Julie Graham, and Jessica Nembhard. *Creating a New World Economy: Forces of Change.* Philadelphia, PA: Temple University Press, 1993.

Hemispheric Social Alliance. *Lessons From NAFTA: The High Cost of "Free Trade."* Toronto: Canadian Centre for Policy Alternatives, 2003.

McCracken, Paul, et al. *Towards Full Employment and Price Stability: A Report to the OECD by a Group of Independent Experts.* Paris: OECD, 1977.

Ranney, David C. *Global Decisions, Local Collisions: Urban Life in the New World Order.* Philadelphia, PA: Temple University Press, 2003.

See also **American Federation of Labor-Congress of Industrial Organizations; Civil Rights; Maquiladoras; Taft-Hartley Act**

GOLD RUSH

The discovery of gold in California commenced the greatest of the American mineral rushes and provided the model for all future precious metal strikes in the United States. In January 1848, one week before the signing of the Treaty of Guadalupe-Hidalgo formally ended the Mexican-American War and ceded California to the United States, gold was discovered on the American River. Slowly word spread back East and then around the world. In the spring of 1849, thousands of men set off by boat and the Overland Trail for the western slopes of the Sierra Nevada Mountains. In the 1850 census, three-quarters of California's population of 85,000 were American-born; fewer than 1,000 of the Americans were blacks. The largest foreign-born delegations were from Mexico, England, Germany, France, China, and Chile. The forty-niners were of varying social background. The adventurers, as the press dubbed them, were, in an oft-repeated phrase, "of all classes of men." Passenger lists of ships heading for California from American ports show that the majority were skilled and semiskilled manual workers. The expense of the journey was too high for laborers to come. There were also large contingents of nonmanual workers and farmers. While ethnically and occupationally the miners were diverse, in one respect those who came to the West Coast were remarkably uniform—they were overwhelmingly male. Ninety-three percent of California's population was male; almost three-quarters were males aged 20–40.

The gold was found mostly in placers, deposits of sand and gravel along the banks of rivers and creeks. Placer mining was hard, muddy, work. The period in which miners could profit by individually panning gold was short, and by 1849 most worked in groups. Typically one or two men would dig gravel from the riverbank and place it in a sieved device known as a cradle; another man would rock the cradle as a third poured water into it to separate the gold from the rock. The physical labor mining demanded tended to blur the line that separated social classes in the East. All were now manual workers—the eastern notion that "hand work" was undignified was discarded. Miners of middle-class background often abandoned the tenets of respectable society and drank, gambled, and brawled in ways eastern workers would have found familiar. A potent solidarity resulted. Miners stuck closely together. It was almost unheard of for companions to desert each other, and injured or sick gold hunters were tenderly cared for by other forty-niners.

Membership in the fraternity of miners was open only to whites. Occasionally native-born Americans opposed all other groups in the mines, including French and German immigrants, but usually it was the color line that mattered. Stories of exceptional solicitude to fellow white miners in diaries and reminiscences are interspersed with accounts of savagery to people of color. Mexicans, "greasers" in miners' parlance, and Chileans, were targets of white miners' wrath. Although Chileans had been the first to mine a promising stretch of the Calaveras River, in December 1849 white miners forced them to leave, precipitating a violent confrontation the press called "the Chilean War." In the struggle a Chilean and two Americans were killed. In retaliation the American miners took the Chileans involved into custody, executed three by firing squad, and cut off the ears of three others. Though the numbers of Chinese miners were small in the early rush, they were targets of ferocious prejudice, foreshadowing later anti-Chinese activities by white California workers.

Over 400 million dollars worth of gold was extracted in California from 1849–1855. Making $10 or even $15 a day was common in 1849, huge sums by eastern standards. But supplies were extraordinarily expensive, and it was difficult to accumulate much money. Only a very few struck it rich. By 1850, easily worked deposits were becoming scarce. Miners began to build dams to divert rivers and then dig up the riverbed. This required larger groups of men and considerable capital. "To get gold, you must employ gold," the expression went. In 1851, there were said to be 10 dams on the Feather River, each costing around $8,000. Mining was becoming a business, and investment companies formed in California and the East. In addition to river mining, entrepreneurs turned to hydraulic mining in which a powerful stream of water was aimed at a hillside and the muddy runoff directed into a sluice to separate the gold. Underground mining operations were begun. The shift that had taken several decades in the East from small groups of men working by hand to large capitalized operations with many employees was accomplished in California in a few years. The days of the independent prospector clearly were over; "mining is now reduced to a system," one disgusted adventurer wrote. Many of the forty-niners returned East or decided to try their hand at prospecting elsewhere in the West.

Mining companies in the mid-1850s began hiring workers for three or four dollars a day. Given the high living expenses, employees often did little better than break even. Bosses increasingly turned to immigrants to work at such wages. Chinese were hired in growing numbers, as were Irish and Germans. Almost everywhere mining was carried on in the United States there were Cornish miners, and the Golden State was no exception. The 1860 census showed 82,000 men employed in mining in California, making it by far the largest occupation in the state. Those dissatisfied with wages or working conditions usually simply quit to find a better job either in another mine or in another occupation; it was only in the 1870s that the first miners' unions were formed in California. The amount of gold dug peaked in 1852, after that it declined fairly quickly before leveling off in the mid-1860s. By 1880, there were still 37,000 miners in California, exceeded only by the number of laborers.

RICHARD STOTT

References and Further Reading

Johnson, Susan. *Roaring Camp: The Social World of the California Gold Rush*. New York: Norton, 2000.

Paul, Rodman W. *California Gold: The Beginning of Mining in the Far West*. Lincoln: University of Nebraska Press, 1947.

Rohrbough, Malcom J. *Days of Gold: The California Gold Rush and the American Nation*. Berkeley: University of California Press, 1997.

GOLDMAN, EMMA (JUNE 27, 1869– MAY 14, 1940)
Anarchist

Emma Goldman, the anarchist writer and lecturer for freedom in all realms of life and champion of the cause of the oppressed—like many American anarchists—had a complex and paradoxical relationship to labor. On the one hand, she supported the rights of labor, but on the other, she believed that even the 8-hour workday was a concession to a capitalist system, the lifeblood of which was largely dependent on the exploitation of the working class.

Goldman was catapulted into political action as a young garment worker and recent *émigré* to Rochester, New York, from Kovno, Lithuania, in the aftermath of the dramatic trial and execution of the anarchists blamed for the violence that erupted at a labor demonstration at Chicago's Haymarket Square. Determined to give voice to those who had been silenced, she moved to the Lower East Side radical enclave of New York City in 1890. The Russian Jewish immigrant found her first

constituency with non–English-speaking immigrant workers—especially German anarchist militants and clusters of Jewish and Italian anarchists. Goldman searched for a place within the American Left and strongly identified with those who simultaneously supported the rights of labor, were impatient with gradualism, and believed that the power structure of the labor unions themselves bred corruption. Goldman herself had worked in garment factories and like most militant anarchists was a member of the International Working People's Association (IWPA, known as the Black International), a federation of loose-knit autonomous groups of mostly German workers (a group—reconstituted as the IWMA— that she rejoined in 1922 on leaving Russia and with whom she continued to be affiliated when she worked with the anarchists during the Spanish civil war from 1936–1938). She believed that labor agitation at the workplace, on the streets, at public meetings, and demonstrations was integral as a strategy for a complete transformation of society.

Emma Goldman on a street car. Library of Congress, Prints & Photographs Division [LC-B2-4215-16].

Although Goldman supported militant labor unions' efforts to win their demands, she was critical of the union structure itself, viewing it as a bargaining agent that ultimately rigidified the antagonistic dichotomy between workers and bosses. In her lectures, she encouraged workers to question the various hierarchies within their unions: and to recognize the divisive impact of the distinctions among the trades, the practice of ethnic and racial exclusion, and the generalized insensitivity to the plight of the unemployed not only among unions but in a culture that celebrated "labor's day" in times of tremendous unemployment. She worked closely with the unemployed movements of 1893, 1908, and 1914—and even went to jail for 10 months (1893–1894) for addressing a crowd of demonstrators ostensibly with the call: "You demand bread, and if you cannot acquire it through peaceful means you will get it by force. Unite and take it by force, if you cannot take it peacefully." Goldman characterized this incident in her autobiography as a punishment for encouraging the poor to take food from the palaces of the rich as their sacred right. Ever the gadfly, she had no qualms about riding the strength of an organized movement nor playing devil's advocate; the conscience, the truth-teller, the thorn in the side of liberals and of some union reformers, Goldman was ever-ready to push it further to the left. In her acceptance of the fact that work was basic to life she argued that "everyone should do that which he likes best, not merely a thing he is compelled to do to earn his daily bread" (in an interview with Nellie Bly, 17 September 1893). Though she never officially became a member of any union in the United States, the horrific work conditions and brutal reprisals against organizers and strikers outraged Goldman and prompted her to devote a great part of her life to raising awareness of the plight of labor. Many moderate union negotiators publicly distanced themselves from Goldman and the anarchists even though they appear to have sanctioned militant activists who boldly practiced direct action tactics—like work slowdowns or even the use of dynamite—to bolster the union's ability to flex their muscles on the bargaining table. Still Goldman maintained close ties to various labor organizers and consistently rallied support and legal defense funds for strikers.

Support for Industrial and Trade Union Labor Struggles

Among the many unions she spoke before—in the years from 1891–1901—were the American Labor Union in Newark, New Jersey; the Glass Blowers' Union in Monaca, Pennsylvania; the Brewers' and Malters' Union, the Painters and Decorators' Union, and the Scandinavian Painters' Union in Chicago, Illinois; and the United Labor League in Philadelphia, Pennsylvania. In spite of ideological differences and sporadic tensions, Goldman marched in the 1891 May Day parade with the Working Women's Society of the United Hebrew Trade (UHT) Organization. But when in 1892 Alexander Berkman, her closest comrade, shot and stabbed steel magnate Henry Clay Frick as a symbolic act of labor retaliation for his role in the Homestead Plant Pinkerton's shooting of locked-out striking workers, the UHT chose not to come to his defense. Berkman was sentenced to 22 years in prison, during which time Goldman worked almost incessantly to build ties to as many unions as she could rally across the country and in Europe to lobby for the commutation of Berkman's sentence (who was released after 14 years when a law applying to corrupt politicians inadvertently was applicable to his case). Among the unions that joined her campaign were the United Mine Workers, who passed a resolution in 1900 demanding Berkman's release, and some smaller unions, including the Central Labor Union and the Brewers' Union. After 14 years, Goldman's (and others') efforts on Berkman's behalf succeeded—and he was released.

Her agitation for Berkman's release included working with delegates from the American Federation of Labor (AFL) even though she was critical of its policies with the focus on trade unions of skilled workers, its exclusion of many new immigrants, and its general aversion to anarchists. Goldman was especially reproachful of its president, Samuel Gompers, whom she labeled "the great mogul of the American Federation of Labor," characterizing him as the epitome of conciliatory leadership ("Letters from a Tour," *Sturmvogel* 15 December 1897–February 1898). Even with her various complaints, her behind-the-scenes lobbying effectively prompted the drafting of a resolution at the 1896 AFL conference to the Pennsylvania Board of Pardons condemning Berkman's sentence as excessive and moved Gompers himself to write to Senator Boise Penrose requesting that he intercede on Berkman's behalf.

Those Central Labor Unions that had considerable numbers of anarchists in their ranks opened their doors to Goldman, especially in Boston, Massachusetts, and in Detroit, Michigan. Genuinely committed to labor, in spite of her critique of the shortcomings of the union movement, she spoke out about the all-too-common brutality of her times against striking workers, emphasizing incidents like the horrific Hazelton–Latimer massacre of 1897 to expose the bitterness of the battle. Her lectures included "The Struggle between Capital and Labor," "Cooperation, an Important Factor in the Industrial Struggle," "The Failure of So-Called Free Unions," and "The Right to Be Lazy." She delivered her talk on "The Effect of the War on the Workers" in England in 1900, as part of a general critique of England's role in the Boer War. During her time in Paris in 1900, as she awaited the commencement of the banned International Revolutionary Congress of the Working Peoples where she attended several secret meetings, she was impressed with syndicalist ideas emerging from the French labor movement. By 1907, when she attended the Anarchist Congress in Amsterdam, anarchists were engaged in formal discussions about the incorporation of syndicalist tactics into anarchist practice along with their more general debate about the efficacy of individual and collective action; Goldman spoke in favor of the complementarities of both strategies. In 1913, in Goldman's pamphlet on the possibilities and influences of Syndicalism, she contrasted, as she did all through her life the young and relatively underdeveloped American labor movement to the sophistication and power of its European counterparts.

In 1901, just after the assassination attempt on President McKinley by a man who claimed to be an anarchist influenced by Goldman's ideas, she found herself devastatingly isolated from most of the labor movement. Most unions and radicals distanced themselves from anyone associated however wrongly with the act. Restrictive anti-anarchist laws that followed, intended to further isolate anarchists, actually created a free-speech advocacy link between radicals and middle-class liberals that was in some ways a greater force than either had experienced before. Goldman's power to articulate these issues and to reach the American public on the issue of free speech became an extraordinary asset to the ongoing battle for free expression and the right to organize at the workplace.

Goldman's fight for free speech also included voicing the desire to free people from the prison of conventional mores—especially the public's fear of unharnessed sexuality. The ongoing cultural war was often perceived as, or manipulated by conservatives to appear to be, more threatening than the challenges of labor unrest or even of the raging ideological political battles—including the anarchist critique of government—to the fragile stability of the social order. Goldman defined anarchism as a philosophy that advocated the possibility of a harmonious social order outside the bounds of law and government; it included free speech, sexual freedom, birth control; a critique of the nuclear family, prisons, war, the economy, church, schools; and a response to "the call of labor" in her bold assertion of labor's right to defend itself. Goldman supported and spread information

about labor struggles in the United States. and abroad in her magazine *Mother Earth* (from 1906 until it was banned in 1917). In its very first year of publication in 1906, she wrote about "The Idaho Outrage"—in which Western Federation of Miners' militant union officials Haywood, Moyer, and Pettibone were extradited from Colorado and charged with the murder of ex-Idaho governor Frank Steunenberg. She collected money for their defense at her meetings, wrote an obituary for Pettibone in 1908, and by 1913, befriended Bill Haywood. A reading of the "Fund Appeals" in *Mother Earth* along with the documents that track Goldman's collections at meetings include an impressive range of labor defense funds, including the Aberdeen Free Speech Fund (1911), the Alexander Aldamas Defense Fund (1912–1913), the Wheatland Case (1913), the Colorado War Fund (a 1914 collection to purchase arms for striking workers in and around Ludlow), the Free Speech Fight (Everett, 1916), and the Ingmar Defense Committee (March 1916).

Wobblies and Anarchists

Although some historiography associates anarchists and anarchism with the Industrial Workers of the World (IWW), Goldman's particular relationship to the IWW was far from unreservedly enthusiastic. From her perspective the IWW seemed to have begun as a predominantly socialist union in 1905, and although Goldman adhered to its advocacy of the inclusion of all workers, she detested its hierarchy—often considering the IWW a front for socialists engaged in a factional fight to gain power. Unlike some anarchists who did join the IWW, Goldman stayed clear of any formal organizational ties—a decision she held to even in 1908 when the IWW abandoned its actual support for mainstream political movements (although the organization debated the issue for years). Not until 1909, when the IWW's active and often violent direct-action free speech fights spread across the West Coast, did Goldman offer her public support. She went to San Diego in 1912 to join the IWW Free Speech Fight with her manager, Ben Reitman. Vigilantes dragged him into the desert, covered him in tar and sage brush, and the police promptly escorted her out of town. Her brush with mob violence against the Wobblies was an indelibly horrific experience that in the end made her remarkably effective in speaking out against the rampant brutality against those who dared to organize labor.

Her tendency toward sectarianism on labor issues was muted and in many ways, countered by responsibilities to her journal, which was created in part to offer a space for information and support of movements that meshed with her anarchist principles and strategies for change. Thus while she voiced her support for the IWW free speech fights in San Diego, Goldman also opened the pages of *Mother Earth* to an article about the Butte, Montana, labor struggles by William Z. Foster, who was then associated with the short-lived Syndicalist League of North America. This group (which included the anarchists Jay Fox and Lucy Parsons, who left the IWW with the intention of revolutionizing the AFL from the inside) practiced the French tactic of working within the existing union structure. They identified themselves as a militant minority within the AFL and adhered to the strategy of "boring from within" rather than working in a separate union like the IWW. Later in 1915 and 1916, Goldman opposed the IWW's movement toward centralization within the organization. But Goldman herself who never engaged in the micro-factions within the unions also began to express a comradely loyalty to the IWW, in part because it was becoming clear that the government had redirected much of its suspicions and violence away from anarchists toward the Wobblies. This phenomenon, symbolized by the murder of Joe Hill, was a travesty of justice to which she added her voice in a chorus of outrage and continued to support both IWW-led strikes and their retaliatory actions.

Intellectual Proletarians, Women, Theater, and a New Rapprochement with Industrial Labor

Goldman's definition of workers and of class oppression extended beyond the parameters of the industrial labor force to what she labeled in her 1914 lecture and essay "the intellectual proletarians"—writers, artists, professionals—whose material privilege often masked the weakening effect of the system on them. However she saw the potential in this stratum to hold to a vision beyond basic needs and to go to the people as the Narodnaya Volya group of Russia had before them. Such a rapprochement with labor could be expressed in action and in their common template for a more just world. In part influenced by the ambiance and literature of the Russian revolution and by her own experience as a woman, Goldman also saw the potential of women, especially middle-class American women, as an eventual force of liberation—not on the basis of their fight for suffrage but for their remarkable attunement to internal oppression, which held its own universality. As her audiences expanded

beyond her immigrant anarchist circles, she rode the wave of the woman's movement and as she had in the labor movement, tried to move them further to the left. Her ideas on the power of women and of the middle class made her an anomaly to most union activists—whose struggle for labor justice was often so all-consuming that it was difficult to reach farther than their more immediate economic goals.

But Goldman believed that the struggle for freedom extended beyond material necessities. She hoped to bring her ideas on cultural issues, including the social significance of modern drama, not only to those who traditionally frequented the theater, but also at least once to workers on lunch break deep within a mine shaft. She sometimes used the characters in plays, especially those in the works of Henrik Ibsen, to underscore the value of single heroic acts—whether expressed in interpersonal relations or in public actions. In so doing she reinforced the strength and potential of the people who attended her lectures, no matter where they fell on the social hierarchy of power and money.

She referred to the power of the theater to affect change as the dynamite capable of bringing down the old and of building toward the new. And yet the metaphor of dynamite had other ramifications in Goldman's political lexicon. Believing that American workers were in the midst of a vicious social war, with institutional force from industry, government, and police virtually relentless, Goldman asserted both overtly and covertly that the right of retaliation, of using force against force was a necessary strategy—borne both of desperation, hope, and the desire for self-respect.

Supporting Militancy

Regardless of their guilt or innocence, she supported the McNamara brothers after the 1910 *Los Angeles Times* explosion—a position she articulated in her 1914 essay "Self-Defense for Labor." The suspected suppliers of dynamite for the McNamaras, Matthew Schmidt and David Caplan, benefited from Goldman's efforts on their behalf: She harbored Schmidt and raised funds within and outside the unions for both Caplan and Schmidt when they were arrested. And yet it is important to note that of the hundreds of fund appeals to help those in battle with the law over their militant actions, hers was not a blanket support; all of her efforts were connected first and foremost to labor's right to defend itself and to actions she perceived that would in some way further the anarchist cause.

In July 1916, when Goldman planned to lecture in San Francisco on "Preparedness: The Road to Universal Slaughter," a bomb went off at the Preparedness Day parade. Militants within the San Francisco labor movement were prime suspects. The Antipreparedness Movement was not only in defense of the young working-class men who were sure to be drafted into military service for World War I, but it was a union-initiated movement that also feared that the influx of an armament industry would break the strength of the city's renowned closed shop. Although Goldman was less acquainted with union activists imprisoned in relation to the bombing than her comrade Alexander Berkman, she did know some of the local union organizers. While others hesitated, unsure about associating with the act and fearful of reprisals, Goldman and Berkman quickly mounted a campaign on both the East and West coasts to raise funds and support from unions for the arrested suspects in the Preparedness Day bombing. By August they had revived the International Workers Defense League, and by December 1916, Goldman addressed a large crowd on the subject at a rally in New York City's Carnegie Hall sponsored by the UHT. When Berkman was threatened with extradition from New York to San Francisco as a suspect in the bombing because of his close association with the militant unionists, the UHT joined a support committee—and not only published the pamphlet "They Want to Hang Alexander Berkman," but also donated over a thousand dollars to his defense.

At this time Goldman's interest in helping labor activists close to the IWW who had become targets for arrests culminated in the formation of the League for the Amnesty of Political Prisoners—a group whose manifesto was published in the March 1918 issue of the IWW paper, *Labor Defender*. In part for their work in linking issues of labor with the anticonscription sentiments that were growing as the United States prepared to enter the First World War, both Goldman and Berkman were arrested in New York in 1917 and ultimately deported to Russia in 1919.

Conclusion

Although she never abandoned her commitment to the working class—and documented her own dreadful experiences in New York's garment factories in her autobiography *Living My Life*—she was never a Mother Jones or an Elizabeth Gurley Flynn. Goldman was a propagandist, an articulator of challenging ideas, an arouser of consciousness, more than a day-to-day organizer or operative in a larger structure—even if that structure for change was a union that held within it a template of the concerns and practices of the society she hoped to create.

Some of her rigidity with regard to unions and to cynicism about progressive labor laws eased over the years. When Goldman was allowed back into the United States for a 90-day visit in 1934, she modified her blanket critique of legal reform by applauding President Franklin Delano Roosevelt's plan for social security in the United States, which she viewed as a positive change, within the limits of government, a bold expression of sympathy with, and interest in, protecting the nation's workers. And from 1936–1938, during her many visits to Spain to work with the Spanish anarchists, she allied herself fully with their union movement: In this case to the CNT-FAI anarchist labor federation—an act of allegiance to a union that had no precedent in her relation to the union movement in the United States. This anarchist workers' federation supplied the unifying vision and promise that felt more in synchrony with what she referred to as her beautiful ideal."

When Goldman died in 1940, unions from across the globe sent their respects. A Communist newspaper in the United States accused her of being an agent of the government because of her vocal critique of the Soviet experiment (specifically her strong opposition to the submergence of the Soviets and unions into the Bolshevik system and the loss of free speech that culminated in the brutal attack by the Red Army on the Kronstadt sailors who demanded union and Soviet autonomy). She was ultimately lauded for being true to her belief in the power of critical thinking, in questioning authority and ingrained assumptions—and even for her critique of unions struggling for the same justice to which she devoted her life.

CANDACE FALK and BARRY PATEMAN

References and Further Reading

Emma Goldman Papers. University of California Berkeley web site. http://sunsite.berkeley.edu/Goldman (1995–).

Falk, Candace; Barry Pateman, and Jessica Moran, eds. *Emma Goldman: A Documentary History of the American Years, 1890–1919.* 4 vols. Berkeley: University of California Press, 2003–2009. Vol. 3: *Light and Shadows. 1910–1916. forthcoming,* Vol. 4. *The War Years. 1917–1919. forthcoming.*

Falk, Candace, Ronald J. Zboray, et al. eds. *Emma Goldman Papers: A Microfilm Edition.* 69 reels, Alexandria, VA: Chadwyck-Healey, 1991–1993.

Falk, Candace, Stephen Cole, et al. eds. *Emma Goldman: A Guide to her Life and Documentary Sources.* Alexandria, VA: Chadwyck-Healey, 1995.

Goldman, Emma. *Living My Life*. 2 vols. New York: Knopf, 1931. Reprint, New York: Dover Publications, 1970.

See also **Berkman, Alexander; Foster, William Z.; Haymarket Affair (1886); Haywood, William D. "Big Bill"; Hill, Joe; Industrial Workers of the World; Syndicalism**

GOMPERS v. BUCK'S STOVE AND RANGE CO. (1911)

Although it did not establish a significant precedent within labor law, *Gompers v. Buck's Stove and Range Co.* was arguably the most highly publicized court case involving unions during the Progressive Era. American Federation of Labor (AFL) leader Samuel Gompers was threatened with jail; the case figured prominently in the 1908 presidential election; and many citizens believed that free speech for unionists and the successful incorporation of workers into the polity were gravely threatened. In the end the outcome of the case was anticlimactic, but it nevertheless galvanized significant changes within the labor movement.

The case began at almost the same time that labor suffered a significant blow to its ability to conduct secondary boycotts in *Loewe v. Lawlor* (better known as the Danbury Hatters case). Indeed the same bitterly anti-union organization, the American Anti-Boycott Association (AABA), instigated both *Loewe* and *Gompers*. In the latter case however, the players were much more prominent.

Buck's Stove and Range was a powerful St. Louis firm; its chief executive, James Van Cleave, was also president of the National Association of Manufactures. In 1906, Van Cleave refused to adhere to a union-employer agreement that effectively standardized wages and hours throughout the stove industry. The AFL retaliated by placing Van Cleave's company on its We Don't Patronize list.

Van Cleave had long been spoiling for a fight with unions. With the aid of the AABA, he sought an injunction to prevent AFL leaders from carrying out their boycott. He won a temporary injunction that did not technically prevent the boycott but prevented any written or oral communication that might spread it.

Despite the threat it represented, Gompers embraced this opportunity as an affront to labor's rights. The AFL leader had been preparing an offensive against the organization's enemies, hoping to strictly limit or even outlaw the labor injunction. Such a campaign might not only strengthen organized labor, but at a time of considerable socialist opposition

to his moderate policies, cement Gompers's position within the AFL.

Gompers and his lawyer Alton Parker (the 1904 Democratic presidential nominee and a president of the American Bar Association) formulated a strategy that would garner maximum public support. The AFL formally dropped Buck's Stove from its boycott list but continued to speak out against Van Cleave as unfair. This was still a conscious violation of the injunction, but for many it turned the case into a clean free speech issue.

In July 1908, Gompers, AFL Vice-President John Mitchell, and AFL Secretary Frank Morrison were held in contempt. Gompers, worried that the very existence of the AFL might be in danger, scrambled to gain as many progressive allies as possible. In a historic turn, the AFL repudiated its nonpartisanship and latched on to the Democratic party for protection from rapacious capitalists and especially tyrannical judges.

Republicans, recognizing a possible public relations disaster in their generally antilabor stance, maneuvered to ensure that the case would not be heard until after the 1908 presidential election. Soon thereafter, reckless and corrupt judge Daniel Thew Wright of the District Court for the District of Columbia shocked the nation by sentencing Gompers to a year in jail on the contempt charges (Morrison received a six-month sentence; Mitchell, nine months). Appellate decisions upheld Wright, although bail allowed the three unionists to stay out of prison.

By the time the cases (one on the legality of the injunction and one on the contempt charges) were combined and reached the Supreme Court in 1911, an unexpected twist stole much of the episode's thunder. Van Cleave had died the previous year, and his successor at Buck's Stove quickly settled the boycott—which had been having a devastating effect on the company. The injunction issue was thus rendered legally moot. In turn the court overturned the contempt charges against Gompers and his colleagues on a technicality. Judge Wright forced a tragicomic coda to the case when he sought to institute criminal, as opposed to the previous civil, proceedings against the AFL leaders, but the Supreme Court rebuked him again in 1914 in the case of *Gompers v. U.S.*

Labor celebrated a victory in these two cases, but their legal triumphs were actually quite narrow. Instead the AFL's greatest achievement in *Buck's Stove* flowed from the political vindication that came from its defense of free speech. With labor's increasing legitimacy came a newfound political power that then mildly blossomed during the administration of Woodrow Wilson.

Robert D. Johnston

References and Further Reading

Ernst, Daniel R. *Lawyers against Labor: From Individual Rights to Corporate Liberalism.* Urbana: University of Illinois Press, 1995.
Greene, Julie. *Pure and Simple Politics: The American Federation of Labor and Political Activism, 1881–1917.* New York: Cambridge University Press, 1998.

Cases and Statutes Cited

Gompers v. Buck's Stove and Range Co. 221 U.S. 418 (1911)
Gompers v. U.S. 233 U.S. 604 (1914)
Loewe v. Lawlor 208 U.S. 274 (1908)

See also **American Federation of Labor; Gompers, Samuel**

GOMPERS, SAMUEL (1850–1924)
Founder, American Federation of Labor

Labor leader a voter—Samuel Gompers, president of the American Federation of Labor, casting his ballot in his home district. Library of Congress, Prints & Photographs Division [LC-USZ62-117862].

Samuel Gompers, founder and president of the American Federation of Labor (AFL) for 37 years, was both extraordinary and exemplary of many skilled workers during the late nineteenth and early twentieth centuries. Born into a family of Dutch Jewish immigrants in London in 1850, Gompers attended four years of school before leaving formal education to join his father on the benches of a cigar shop at the age of 10. In 1863, the entire Gompers family used the Cigar Makers' Society of England's emigration fund to immigrate to New York City. Arriving at the New York City docks in the midst of the Draft Riot of July 1863, the Gompers family settled into a typical immigrant existence in New York. The Gompers men, including young Sam, soon found employment as cigar makers and joined the U.S. cigar makers' union. At the age of 17, Gompers married Sophia Julian, who proceeded to give birth to at least nine children.

Like many other young immigrants, the teenaged Sam Gompers quickly became immersed in New York City's immigrant, intellectual, and fraternal life. From 1863–1880, Gompers belonged to, and participated in, the early Cigar Makers' International Union (CMIU), the Ancient Order of Foresters, the Independent Order of Odd Fellows, the Knights of Labor, the International Workingmen's Association, Felix Adler's Ethical Culture Society, the debating club at Cooper Union, and many others. Though Gompers generally eschewed organized religion, his Jewish background gave him another level on which to identify with the Jewish immigrants pouring into Manhattan's industries at the time. From this mix of influences, Gompers began to develop his ideas about the best form and function possible for unions.

The young Gompers quickly became active in the CMIU, both locally and nationally. During the 1870s, he managed the union's aggressive campaign to abolish tenement house cigar making in New York City, ultimately achieved through the passage of state legislation making such production illegal. Gompers carried the insights and skills he had gained in the anti-tenement-house fight in the CMIU into the new attempt at a national organization of unions, the Federation of Organized Trades and Labor Unions (FOTLU), in 1881 becoming the head of FOTLU's legislative branch.

In 1886, Gompers attended the Ohio meeting that transformed FOTLU into the AFL. Based in large part on his reputation as head of FOTLU's only effective branch, the assembled union delegates elected Gompers to the presidency of the new organization.

He would be re-elected to that position every year except one up until his death in 1924.

Gompers often spoke of the lessons he learned from one of his early coworkers and mentors, Ferdinand Laurrell. In his autobiography, Gompers wrote, "Time and again, under the lure of new ideas, I went to Laurrell with glowing enthusiasm. Laurrell would gently say, 'Study your union card, Sam, and if the idea doesn't square with that, it isn't true.' My trade union card came to be my standard in all new problems" (*Seventy Years of Life and Labor: An Autobiography,* 1925). Throughout his life, Gompers used this concept to make decisions about both his own actions and those of other unions and their leaders.

Gompers brought his experiences in the CMIU into the AFL and based many of his early actions and decisions in that organization on his old mentor's advice. Throughout his years in leadership of the AFL, he would stress the importance of the autonomy of individual national unions and their need to focus on economic goals and fiscal stability. From his own union experiences, Gompers truly believed in the efficacy of craft unionism, the organization of workers along occupational lines, the establishment of a system of dues and corresponding benefits, and the necessity for union leaders to maintain control over the actions of their members and therefore over the payment of such things as strike benefits. Along with these principles came Gompers's defense of the autonomy and jurisdictions of the individual national unions. In this view the AFL itself was supposed to be a helpful support for national unions and those workers hoping to establish such unions. In return Gompers expected those unions and their members to demonstrate the kind of careful self-discipline he himself had learned in the CMIU.

In the early years of the AFL, Gompers and his fellow AFL officers succeeded in large part in carrying out this vision of American unionism. Faced with an economy still dependent on the skills of a minority of workers within the working class, the ideals of craft unionism worked to protect and maintain unions for these workers who could afford craft union dues. Gompers also believed in the early years that this basic structure of unionism could simply be extended to workers in other less-skilled occupations. Unskilled laborers, semiskilled factory workers, women, African-Americans, and immigrants could all achieve successful organization if they just followed the pattern set by the skilled-craft unions. This required first and foremost that these workers be prepared to keep up the payment of regular dues to their union and that they then accept the control of the union over fiscal disbursements. While Gompers could at times express sympathy with those workers who could not afford to pay dues at the level paid by skilled workers, his sympathy often ended with the belief that they simply could not be "good union members of good unions." Without financial stability and tight fiscal discipline, the craft unions of Gompers's vision would not survive.

Gompers's early years in New York also set the roots of his attitudes about strike mediation and negotiations. Tied closely to his conception of union self-discipline, Gompers believed that the most constructive resolutions of strikes came out of a bilateral discussion of the workers' interests. The presentation and debate of strike issues would create greater understanding by both sides. The resulting compromises and agreements provided what Gompers believed to be the most lasting conclusions to strikes, contributing to an increasingly solid base for future union demands and negotiations. Accordingly Gompers spent considerable amounts of time presenting himself as a mediator for unions in strike situations. Whether he was dealing with garment workers in New York or workers elsewhere, Gompers would attempt to set forward strikers' demands to employers in as rational a manner as possible. Once Gompers or some other union leader successfully worked out a compromise, Gompers expected union members to understand the importance of union stability and ratify the agreement accordingly. Later in the AFL's history, Gompers would carry this concept over into his dealings with the National Civic Federation when he became one of the first union leaders to join this national organization, which sought to mediate labor disputes before they erupted into open conflict.

At the fourteenth annual convention of the AFL in 1894, the always-simmering debates over socialism within the organization boiled over into open and often rancorous disputation. In the heated political atmosphere of the preceding year, the 1893 convention had asked member unions to vote on a detailed "political programme" for the national organization, the platform of which included Plank 10, calling for "the collective ownership by the people of all means of production and distribution." Gompers led the charge against the programme and particularly Plank 10 at the 1894 convention, contributing to the ultimate defeat of both. The other planks of the programme were ratified, leaving the organization with a range of issues to address but without an official political stance. In the aftermath of the two-day-long debate, the convention voted to replace Gompers with John McBride of the United Mine Workers as president of the AFL.

Gompers's one-year hiatus from the presidency ultimately led to several important changes in the AFL itself. Gompers would spend the year traveling both internationally to meet with various European trade union leaders and nationally to continue to support U.S. workers' organizing efforts. His meetings with British and other European unionists provided Gompers with additional examples of the benefits of constructive craft unionism and the drawbacks of irresponsible socialism. Travel throughout the United States and in particular, a long southern swing on behalf of the United Garment Workers, reinforced Gompers's basic beliefs about union organization: Organization along craft or trade lines coupled with the financial responsibility and organizational self-discipline of both workers and their unions. Throughout his life Gompers would not waver from these concepts. Neither would he countenance vacillations on the part of the AFL itself. In many ways this marks the beginning of his growing conservatism over questions of union structure and form.

During Gompers's sabbatical year, as he called it, McBride moved the AFL's headquarters to Indianapolis, Indiana, far from Gompers's original base in New York. When the AFL re-elected Gompers to its presidency at the convention of 1895, Gompers temporarily moved to Indianapolis to take back the office. He did not move his family from New York City at this time, believing that this first year back with the AFL would prove the organization's fate. On re-election again in 1896, Gompers, firm now in his conviction that the AFL had chosen to follow his vision of trade unionism, moved the headquarters to Washington, D.C., in 1897. In so doing Gompers affirmed his belief in the endurance of the AFL as an actor, both economically and politically, on the national stage.

Biographer Bernard Mandel suggested that "Gompers's trade union policy for the twentieth century marked the end of the A.F. of L.'s youthful militancy and the beginning of its conservative middle age" (B. Mandel, *Samuel Gompers, A Biography*, 1963). When Gompers moved the AFL headquarters (and his family) to Washington in 1897, he himself was 47 years old, the father of six, and the leader of the most powerful organization of workers in the country. Gompers had more than 30 years' experience in the union movement by this time. His future efforts on behalf of the AFL and its members would continue to be based on these early experiences. Fewer and fewer men would be able to shake him in his beliefs.

The years immediately preceding the AFL's move to Washington had seen a growing number of judicial moves against the union movement. In Gompers's first years in Washington, legal decisions became increasingly important in his work. Gompers had been wary of employers' use of injunctions dating from the early 1890s. In fact this wariness had led him to oppose the passage of the Sherman Anti-Trust Act in 1890. Despite many unionists' support for the act, Gompers insisted that it was written in such a way that it would be used against unions. He had then had to grapple with the invocation of the act against unions time and time again. In Gompers's eyes, the entire legal system became suspect. In the early twentieth century, Gompers would become entangled in two key court cases: That of the Danbury Hatters and that of Buck's Stove and Range Co. In both cases national business organizations provoked and supported the lawsuits. Both cases also would ultimately land in the Supreme Court. These cases as well as his own legal liabilities in each helped convince Gompers that the AFL had to enter politics in order to obtain relief from the power of injunctions.

On March 21, 1906, Gompers and other AFL representatives presented an eight-point Bill of Grievances to President Theodore Roosevelt, the speaker of the house, and the president *pro tem* of the Senate. All three politicians immediately rejected its consideration. Prepared for this reaction, the AFL threw itself into political activity. While they did not desert completely their previous nonpartisan stance, Gompers and other union leaders began to take a much stronger political stand than they had previously. Gompers had already stated his opinion that the unions should "Reward [their] friends and punish [their] enemies." This basic belief would now be carried out with much more vigor. In the summer of 1908, Gompers would appear before the platform committees of both the Republican and Democratic national conventions, failing to influence the Republican party but succeeding in gaining some support from the Democrats.

Unlike the political programme of 12 years earlier, the 1906 Bill of Grievances contained no overtly socialist points. Gompers assured friends and colleagues that economic activities remained the prime purpose of the labor movement and that these political demands would never detract from the efforts of constructive trade unionism. The AFL's entrance into the political arena in 1906 provided a model for union voluntarism, or careful nonpartisan political participation. Rather than highlighting the AFL's long and tortured relationship with socialists, the 1906 Bill of Grievances represented more its newfound points of complicity with the Progressive movement of the time. Ultimately this political move would lead Gompers to endorse Woodrow Wilson for president in 1914 and thereby ensure Gompers's ultimate involvement in World War I planning and execution.

At the same time that Gompers and the AFL were becoming increasingly involved in politics, a new labor organization was creating new problems for the craft union movement. The Industrial Workers of the World (IWW), established in 1905, contained many of the ideas (and individuals) from the Left that Gompers had come to hate most heatedly. On top of calling for an end to capitalism and advocating sabotage and violence if necessary, the IWW also threatened to organize less-skilled workers into unions, embodying the antithesis of Gompers's constructive craft unions. Garnering considerable publicity through their innovative tactics, the IWW quickly became widely known and discussed. Gompers probably felt personally threatened by the IWW's new tactics and publicity. The IWW's penchant for violence in language if nothing else as well as its pacifist stance toward World War I would soon place the organization even more at odds with Gompers and the AFL. Newly linked with a sitting U.S. president, Gompers would support the U.S. efforts in the war and encourage AFL unions and their members to cooperate with war efforts both military and industrial. Mirroring President Wilson's path into the world war, Gompers moved through neutrality to preparedness and finally endorsed the United States becoming a belligerent in the war. Through cooperation with the war efforts, Gompers expected the AFL to gain respect from all sides: The public, government, and businesses. He would advise the White House on labor conflicts in the United States during the war, oppose the Bolshevik revolution in Russia, and travel through the war zone in Europe.

Did Gompers feel that his cooperation with the war effort had been worth the effort? While he would continue to defend his wartime work, the events of the immediate postwar years belie his generally rosy view. The War Labor Board was discontinued after the war ended, and the new Communist Party U.S.A. would soon become a hotbed of dual unionism. In 1924, Gompers supported Robert La Follette's independent campaign for president as a protest against the established parties' continued spurning of the AFL's support. By the end of the war in 1919, Gompers was 69 years old. His vision was failing and his hearing weakening. His wife suffered a stroke that year, dying in May of 1920. Gompers then married a divorcee some 30 years his junior in 1921. By all accounts, she made his life miserable for his remaining years.

Gompers would continue to run the AFL, refusing to let any but his closest friends and employees know of his weakening health. In November 1924, Gompers presided over every session of the Forty-Fourth Annual Convention of the AFL in El Paso, Texas, his last. For months he had been declining from kidney problems and a weakening heart. He knew this would be his final convention. William Green read Gompers's prepared statement for him at the convention's opening. In this statement, Gompers reminded delegates that he had been with the AFL since its beginnings in 1881 and urged them to remain committed to his vision of craft unionism. On adjournment the entire convention went to Mexico City for the inauguration of the first labor President in North America and the ensuing Pan American Federation of Labor meeting. On December 8, Gompers took to his bed. He was then rushed back to San Antonio, Texas, where he died on December 13. He was buried in Tarrytown, New York, on December 18, 1924.

ILEEN A. DEVAULT

References and Further Reading

Gompers, Samuel. *Seventy Years of Life and Labor: An Autobiography*. New York: E. P. Dutton, 1925.
Kaufman, Stuart Bruce. *Samuel Gompers and the Origins of the American Federation of Labor, 1848–1896*. Westport, CT: Greenwood Press, 1965.
Livesay, Harold G. *Samuel Gompers and Organized Labor in America*. Boston, MA: Little, Brown, and Co., 1978.
Mandel, Bernard. *Samuel Gompers, A Biography*. Yellow Springs, OH: Antioch Press, 1963. Salvatore, Nick, ed. *Seventy Years of Life and Labor: An Autobiography*. Ithaca, NY: ILR Press, 1984.
The Samuel Gompers Papers. 9 vols. Urbana-Champaign, IL: University of Illinois Press, 1986-.

See also **American Federation of Labor; American Federation of Labor-Congress of Industrial Organizations; Craft Unionism; Industrial Workers of the World**

GRADUATE TEACHING ASSISTANTS

Graduate teaching assistants (TAs), along with other forms of contingent academic labor, such as adjunct or part-time instructors, have become increasingly important in the modern university. According to the American Association of University Professors, the number of graduate students who also serve as classroom instructors rose by 35% from 1975 to 2000. As the number of graduate students employed as teaching assistants and instructors has grown, a movement in favor of organizing TAs into unions has arisen. While the earliest TA union was founded in the late sixties at the University of Wisconsin-Madison (UWM), this phenomenon did not become common until the 1990s. Today academia is one of the few areas of union growth, and the movement to organize graduate students has led to jurisdictional disputes, especially between the American Federation of Teachers (AFT) and the United Auto Workers (UAW).

The first graduate teaching assistant union, the Teaching Assistants' Association (TAA) at UWM was originally founded in 1966 as an outgrowth of antiwar and New Left activism on campus. It slowly evolved into a union throughout the late sixties, and in 1970, the TAA led a successful four-week strike in order to pressure the university into bargaining with them in good faith. The major issues that motivated the TAA were a desire to ensure job security and complaints over teaching conditions, particularly workload and class size. Despite the success of the TAA, graduate teaching assistants at other universities did not follow the example of the UWM students.

Beginning in the late 1980s and early 1990s however, a series of unions were formed at state universities across the country. This increase in academic unionization paralleled both the unprecedented growth in the number of graduate student instructors and the increasingly tight academic labor market. In addition the fact that unionization campaigns on academic campuses were much more likely to succeed than the national average encouraged a number of unions without a history of academic organizing to encourage the unionization of TAs. With the decline of unionization in their traditional industries, such unions as the UAW, the Communications Workers of America (CWA), and the United Electrical, Radio, and Machine Workers of America (UE) all became involved in TA organizing drives. These drives have been largely successful, and as of 2003, TA unions existed at around 25 public university campuses, representing almost 40,000 graduate students.

The success of TA organizing on public universities was not paralleled on private university campuses however. Private universities fall under the jurisdiction of the National Labor Relations Board (NLRB), which held until 2000 that graduate teaching assistants were primarily students rather than employees and that therefore they were not entitled to unionization. However in 2000, the NLRB ruled in favor of the right of graduate students at New York University (NYU) to organize a union of teaching and research assistants. This ruling seemed to throw the door open for further unionization of teaching assistants on private campuses. However in 2003, a new NLRB, led by three Republicans appointed by President George W. Bush, reversed its earlier decision, ruling that graduate teaching assistants at Brown University were not primarily employees and thus were not entitled to union representation. The board based this decision primarily on the 25-year precedent that preceded the NYU decision and had consistently denied TAs at private universities union recognition.

Despite the general lack of success of organizing efforts on private campuses, TA unionization is a growth industry for unions. Surprisingly the UAW is the largest player in the graduate employee union movement, with over 40% of the TA union members belonging to the autoworkers' union as of 2003. This has led to some criticism of the UAW by others within the labor movement and has opened TA unionization efforts to criticism from the outside as well. The movement of some unions, especially UAW and the United Steelworkers of America, away from their traditional bases into such sectors as retail and academia has drawn criticism from the unions that traditionally served those areas. And these sorts of jurisdictional disputes have on at least one occasion sparked contentious organizing drives between the UAW and AFT on the same campus. More importantly perhaps the image of the UAW as a blue-collar, mass-production union has been used against it during a number of TA organizing drives. Some have attributed its loss at Cornell in 2003 to, among other things, the fear that the autoworkers' union would not be as effective in an academic environment as a more traditional teaching union, such as the AFT.

AARON MAX BERKOWITZ

See also **American Federation of Teachers**

GREAT DEPRESSION: 1930s
The Initial Impact of the Economic Collapse

In the American popular imagination, the Great Depression began on Black Tuesday, October 29, 1929, when the stock market crashed. Indeed that dramatic event marks a fitting end to the Roaring Twenties, a decade remembered for its frenetic embrace of modernity and all its material and cultural products. But for American working people, the beginning of the Great Depression is much harder to pinpoint. Beneath the glittering surface of the 1920s prosperity lay a deep vein of poverty affecting entire regions and large numbers of people. The working people associated with the so-called "sick industries"—agriculture, mining, textiles—never did participate in the good times. But the overall magnitude of the crisis as it unfolded after the Crash made misery nearly universal for working people. As the economy collapsed, the unemployment spike was stunning: From 3.2% in 1929 to 24.9% in 1933. Seesawing throughout the 1930s, unemployment still never fell below 14%. Workers who were lucky enough to hold on to their jobs frequently took sharp pay cuts; in 1933—87% of businesses reported that they had lowered wages since 1929 by an average of 18%, and many more had reduced hours.

The aggregate statistics on unemployment hide a great deal of variation by region, by industry, by such demographic factors as gender, race, and ethnicity. Southerners for example sometimes claim that they never even noticed the Depression; they had been poor so long it looked normal. Per capita income in the South was already just 50% of the national average in 1929. But it got even worse: Income from cotton, still the backbone of the southern economy, fell by more than two-thirds by 1932. Sharecroppers and tenant farmers were devastated, with black farmers doubly so. By 1933, over 12,000 black sharecroppers had been forced off the land, and a new urban migration was underway. In the region's chief industry, textiles, extreme competition from the mid-1920s on drove down prices and deep wage cuts became endemic.

The heavy-industry belt of the Northeast and Midwest took a major hit. The Depression arrived a little later in this sector, with sharpest contractions occurring after 1930. By 1932, unemployment in Chicago was 40%; on Minnesota's Mesabi Range, an astonishing 70% of the iron miners were out of work. New England textile workers shared the fate of their southern brethren. The electrical industry fell in slow motion; General Electric (GE) workers for example first lost the perks of welfare capitalism, then saw wages and hours spread thin; then half of them lost their jobs. Steel and auto were laid low. In Detroit unemployment stood at nearly 50%. Midwestern farmers suffered, too. In Wisconsin dairy farmers striking for higher prices ambushed their neighbors on country roads, dumping milk into the dirt. And farmers on the Plains saw their prices fall first and then their topsoil take off in the wind, settling eventually in such unlikely places as downtown Memphis and the decks of ships at sea.

The legacy of racism intensified the troubles of minority populations. In California xenophobia ratcheted up as jobs became scarce. Mexican and Mexican-American farm workers were pushed out to make way for white migrants from the distressed South and Plains states, and hundreds of thousands were deported and repatriated against their will. Further up the coast, recent Filipino immigrants, technically U.S. citizens as colonial subjects, were reclassified as aliens in 1934 and pressured to repatriate. African-Americans nationwide once again found themselves first out the door and last in line for relief.

Women's experience was complex. The service industries where most women work were less severely affected than heavy industry, and in fact by the end of the 1930s, that sector had expanded and with it the numbers of women employed. In some respects the very rigidity of the sexual division of labor preserved women's jobs. Seldom were men, however desperate, willing to take women's work. An exception was teaching, where women's share of jobs fell from 85% to 78% over the decade. Still women's already too-low wages were cut, and job scarcity created enormous cultural pressures on women to leave the workforce and cede their jobs to breadwinners. The pressure was particularly hard on married women. Many municipalities and businesses fired women with employed husbands. At its 1931 convention, the American Federation of Labor (AFL) re-affirmed its conviction that women's proper place was in the home and declared that employment preference should be given to those on whom others depended, a seemingly gender-neutral category that nevertheless signaled men. Work relief programs as they developed in the mid-1930s were constructed with the male breadwinner as model; few programs were designed for women and those that were reinforced traditional women's roles by emphasizing domestic occupations like housekeeping and sewing. Minority women were additionally disadvantaged by New Deal programs—Social Security and the Fair Labor Standards Act, for example—that excluded agricultural and domestic workers.

The Early Response to the Crisis

American institutions and the political establishment were singularly unprepared to cope effectively with a crisis of this magnitude. Among industrialized nations, the United States was notably resistant to the notion of the state's responsibility for social provision. Veterans' pensions constituted the sole legitimate entitlement of any kind. In the face of mounting unemployment, no federal or state program existed to provide relief or in any way aid the unemployed. A handful of large corporations had instituted private unemployment programs, but they were few and their benefits meager. General Electric, for example, had installed a program based on mandatory employee contributions partially matched by the company; the plan carried GE workers through the harsh winter of 1931 but crashed that April.

The lack of government assistance reflected the widespread notion, especially popular in elite circles, that poverty, whatever the cause, was most likely an individual moral failure, not the byproduct of a flawed system. President Herbert Hoover, though not quite so callous or naive, nevertheless believed staunchly that direct relief by the federal government would corrode the moral fiber of free individuals. Hoover believed that the proper sphere for such activities was local government and the voluntary contributions of private individuals. The face-to-face interaction of benefactor and recipient could weed out the slackers from the worthy poor. Relief tended to be in kind rather than in cash and frequently had some small, meaningless, manual task attached as a moral tonic. As the logical outgrowth of this orientation, breadlines and soup kitchens became the relief form of choice, ubiquitous in cities, run by private charities and individuals and agencies of local government. But such sources were overextended and rapidly exhausted. Still Hoover resisted calls for relief until the final months of his administration when he signed the Emergency Relief and Construction Act that allocated $300 million for loans to states.

At the beginning of the crisis, radicals on the Left were the only groups actually taking action to aid the desperate. The Communist Party, USA (CPUSA) was first to act; even before the market crash, Communists were organizing in the cities among the poor and unemployed, so by 1930, when unemployment began to become a mass phenomenon, the party was well-positioned to respond. On March 6, 1930, the CPUSA organized unemployed demonstrations in major cities that mobilized several hundred thousand marchers, much to the party's surprise. The size and energy of the demonstrations put the problem on the national radar scope for the first time and inspired the Communists to create a national organization, the Unemployed Councils of the USA. At the national level, the council lobbied, organized petition drives, and staged two national hunger marches. But the councils' greatest impact remained at the local level, where they responded to the particular local grievances of the unemployed. Local councils intervened to assist relief applicants for example and to pressure local officials for more adequate relief without the humiliation of intrusive investigations. When relief took the form of jobs, the councils agitated for better compensation and working conditions. But their most dramatic and popular actions were eviction protests. Council members vigorously and physically resisted police attempts to enforce eviction orders, mobilizing whole neighborhoods very effectively.

Other Left groups were slower to respond but eventually as successful as the Communists. The sclerotic Socialist party did nothing until stung into action by the young activists of their League for Industrial Democracy (LID). The LID was quite successful though less confrontational than the Communists, favoring negotiation over the more flamboyant and disruptive council tactics. The socialists, like the Communists, were attentive to the particular distress of minorities; both groups were interracial in composition and leadership and worked to raise awareness about the higher rate of unemployment among African-Americans and persistent discrimination in relief programs as they developed.

The third major radical group addressing unemployment were followers of A. J. Muste. The Musteites crafted what they called an American approach to the problem, wedding self-help and patriotic appeals to form the Unemployed Citizens' League. The league, whose first incarnation was the vigorously effective Seattle Unemployed Citizens' League, grew particularly well in small cities and towns, notably in the mining towns of Pennsylvania and West Virginia and steel towns of Ohio, where the main street values of patriotism and self-help resonated strongly.

With the beginning of the New Deal and the advent of federal relief programs in 1933, and especially the extensive work programs of the Works Progress Administration (WPA) in 1935, the orientation of radical unemployed activism changed. The New Deal Administration became the focus of unemployed workers' hopes and expectations, and as attention shifted from local to national, the unemployed groups did likewise. And they began to cooperate with each other across the factional lines that ordinarily divided them. The CPUSA's inauguration of the Popular Front did much to foster cooperation, and in 1935, the three groups merged to create the Workers' Alliance. The alliance began to function more on the national level, as a pressure group attempting to influence policy formation, particularly working toward enactment of federal unemployment insurance.

The radical response to unemployment was a critical contribution to the federal programs that eventually emerged. The radicals defended the rights and dignity of working people as citizens, defined the problem as systemic, and insisted that the federal government take on the responsibility for social provision. Their ideas and orientation influenced the leftish wing of the New Deal relief administration and the shape of programs that they designed. Many of the unemployed activists took their new skills and moved on into other arenas, especially the industrial union drives that erupted in the late 1930s.

The New Deal

Franklin D. Roosevelt's energetic attack on the massive problems created by the Depression presented a vivid contrast to Hoover's cautious restraint. Roosevelt took office in March 1932; within the first three months, the famous 100 Days, the New Deal

Administration had crafted and launched relatively bold initiatives to provide temporary relief to the suffering citizenry and stabilize the reeling economy. Among the agencies created to provide relief to poor and working people were the Federal Emergency Relief Administration (FERA), the Civil Works' Administration (CWA), and the Civilian Conservation Corps (CCC), and finally the Works' Progress Administration (WPA). The New Deal's initial programs to stabilize agriculture and industry, the Agricultural Adjustment Administration (AAA) and the National Recovery Administration (NRA), also inaugurated programs that deeply affected farm and factory labor.

Roosevelt's relief programs were structured as federal-state collaborations, with the money flowing from the federal spigot but distributed by the states. This arrangement was intended to secure state-level political support and to give states discretion in identifying and addressing needs, but it also opened the door to distortions. Southern administrators for example were often able to sustain discriminatory policies, a two-tiered approach, that entrenched racial inequality. New Deal relief policy also favored work over direct relief, a nod to the cultural predisposition to distrust the able-bodied unemployed. But New Deal work relief was not the degrading, punitive "make work" of traditional relief but rather socially useful projects that restored pride and won widespread public acclaim.

The FERA, enacted May 12, 1933, was primarily a direct-relief program providing one federal dollar for each three put up by the states, a provision necessarily waived often due to the insolvency of the states. The CWA was a short-term experiment in public works created in the fall of 1933 and intended to help the unemployed survive the winter. An ambitious project headed by Harry Hopkins, the CWA put 3.5 million workers on jobs in the first six weeks. In its short lifespan, the CWA workers constructed over 500,000 miles of roads and began many construction projects later completed by the WPA. In addition the agency created projects to address needs of women workers—sewing, of course—and white-collar workers. The CWA was quite popular despite the brevity of its existence and functioned as a precursor to the much-larger WPA.

Young people were disproportionately affected by the crisis, and the CCC was for them or at least the males among them. The CCC had the dual purpose of taking care of young men and repairing the devastation resulting from a century of unregulated environmental exploitation by industry and agriculture. The young men were paid $30 per month, with $25 sent directly to their families, to provide for their support. At its peak the CCC enrolled 500,000 young men who lived in camps and performed a dazzling array of tasks. They built roads and campsites in parks, planted millions of trees, fought forest fires, built irrigation systems, fought soil erosion. Like most New Deal programs however the CCC had its racist dimension. Young blacks were allowed to enroll in the corps but into segregated units and unlike white youth who often traveled far from their homes to work, for instance, on western projects, the black youths were kept primarily in the South. They were also subjected to a quota system rather than admitted according to need.

The most famous and controversial initiative was the WPA, enacted by executive order on May 6, 1935. The WPA was an election-year project truly massive in scale, averaging over two million workers on the monthly payroll for the entire 6 years of its existence. The WPA supported a diverse range of occupations from the typical construction worker to artists and writers. The bulk of the projects were aimed at reconstructing and completing the national infrastructure. The WPA workers constructed over 500,000 miles of roads, like the beautiful Blue Ridge Parkway that snakes over the Appalachian peaks from Virginia to Georgia, and numerous public buildings, including 85,000 courthouses, 5,900 schools, and over 1,000 airports.

Roosevelt's programs to stabilize agriculture and industry also had tremendous impact, by no means all positive, on working people, particularly in the South. There the AAA moved to aid farmers by creating mechanisms like production control subsidies, price supports, and credit that would keep farmers on the land and limit agricultural output until commodity prices recovered. Local committees administering the program allowed landlords to pocket the allocations, giving them the capital to begin mechanization, while putting tenant's land into the acreage-reduction scheme. Displaced sharecroppers and tenant farmers migrated to the cities where New Deal relief kept them afloat until harvest time when their labor was again in demand. It was a sweet deal for landowners—not so good for already-impoverished sharecroppers and tenants. Thousands migrated from the region.

Organized Labor and the New Deal

The labor movement was at low ebb when the Depression began. A decade of open-shop repression had vitiated the gains made during WWI, and in 1929, the craft unions of the AFL could claim only 3.6 million members, 11% of the nonagricultural labor force. By 1941, membership had grown to 10.5 million, nearly 28% of the workforce. The stunning growth is indicative of a remarkable decade in U.S. labor history. In the course of the Depression, the U.S. labor movement was transformed structurally and demographically, augmenting the craft union structure of the AFL with a new industrial unionism embodied in the Congress of Industrial Organizations (CIO) that embraced the multitudes of unskilled and semiskilled operatives, many of them ethnic, and racial minorities and women, who populated the vast mass-production industries. Labor also transcended the AFL's traditional distrust of political engagement during the decade. From the federation's founding in 1886, the state had been little more than an engine of repression; by 1941, for better or worse, organized labor had become a vital element in the Democratic party's New Deal coalition. And finally the movement came out of the Depression thoroughly enmeshed in a new, state-regulated labor relations regime.

Labor's change of fortune began with passage of the Norris-LaGuardia Act, signed by Hoover in 1932, which addressed some of the more egregious anti-union practices of the modern era. The act outlawed the infamous "yellow dog" contracts that required workers to eschew unions as a condition of employment, and it restricted the use of the hated federal injunctions that had been used promiscuously against strikes and boycotts. Norris-LaGuardia was very important but quickly eclipsed by the passage of Roosevelt's industrial recovery program, the National Industrial Recovery Act (NIRA) passed on June 16, 1933, that set up the National Recovery Administration. The NIRA required that industries write codes to govern all elements of the production process, from wages and prices to market shares, as a means of eliminating the cutthroat competition that had undermined prices. The act also mandated that certain new rights be extended to workers.

Section 7(a) established workers' right to bargain collectively with their employers through representatives of their own choosing, opening the door to union organization as a means of improving workers' wages and consumer power. Workers all over the nation responded with what employers considered unseemly enthusiasm, organizing in droves and petitioning for AFL charters. In the year following the NIRA passage, the AFL signed nearly one million new members.

But the AFL could not or would not adapt to the very different organizational needs of the disparate workforces of mass industries, so they cut skilled workers from the new unions, annexed them to appropriate craft unions, and generally neglected the remaining unskilled and semiskilled workers whose occupations fell outside traditional craft jurisdictions.

In the process they undermined workers' strength in the industrial workplace.

By late 1934, employers' refusal to recognize their employees' unions plus the ineffective response of the AFL had exposed the flaws of Section 7(a) and discredited AFL leadership. Heightened expectations met massive obstacles, and frustration erupted in strikes across the nation involving 1.5 million workers, including the Textile Strike of 1934, the largest strike in U.S. history, and an astonishing outburst from the long-oppressed "lintheads" of the South. The 1934 strikes were an accurate barometer of rising working-class anger after years of comparative passivity, and the active leadership of radicals in many of the struggles once again raised red flags in the centers of power, from corporate boardrooms to Washington, D.C.

Within the AFL key leaders sympathetic to the desire for industrial organization began to push hard for the federation to adapt to the new form. Chief among them were John L. Lewis of the United Mine Workers (UMW), Sidney Hillman of the Amalgamated Clothing Workers of America (ACWA), and David Dubinsky of the International Ladies' Garment Workers' Union (ILGWU). All three headed unions that were industrial in structure, and they were thus inclined to respond favorably to the demand for industrial organization raised by workers in the industrial core. Together they launched the Committee for Industrial Organizations on November 9, 1935, and began to issue industrial union charters. The committee stayed within the AFL until November 1938, when it left and formed a rival federation of industrial unions, the Congress of Industrial Organizations (CIO).

In May 1935, the NIRA was ruled unconstitutional by the Supreme Court, and Section 7(a) expired. But employers' refusal to abide by its labor provisions had inspired Senator Robert Wagner (Democrat-NY) to develop a new bill to remedy the weaknesses of Section 7(a). The National Labor Relations Act, known as the Wagner Act, was passed July 5, 1935, and reaffirmed by the Supreme Court in 1937. Wagner was much tougher and more explicit in its advocacy of workers' right to organize. The act expanded worker protections, outlawed key employer antiunion practices, and created a three-member National Labor Relations Board (NLRB) with meaningful enforcement power. Most importantly the act established mechanisms for conducting representation elections and required that employers bargain with winning unions.

Armed with this new weapon, and in the very favorable political climate created with Roosevelt's landslide re-election in 1936, the CIO went to town, fielding a veritable army of skilled and dedicated organizers, many of them Communists. The CIO launched dramatic campaigns from 1936–1937 that succeeded in organizing the heart of the industrial core. The autoworkers' victories in the winter and spring of 1936–1937 truly energized the movement.

The critical event was the famous six-week sit-down strike conducted by auto workers in Flint, Michigan, against General Motors, the largest and most profitable U.S. corporation. The autoworkers' stunning victory there came to symbolize CIO solidarity and militancy, galvanizing not only autoworkers but all labor. By the end of the decade, workers in auto, steel, rubber, the electrical industry, and many more had organized industrial unions and affiliated with the CIO. In an era when the stress of hard times easily divided people, the CIO formed unions that were inclusive, organizing all workers in a given industry regardless of race, ethnicity, or sex or skill. Stung by the CIO's success, the AFL began to compete vigorously, and in the end the established federation outdid the CIO, emerging from the Depression nearly twice the size of the younger organization.

Legacy of the Great Depression

Roosevelt's programs did much to alleviate the distress despite their flaws and limitations, but the New Deal is not generally credited with ending the Great Depression. That honor goes to World War II. By 1939, war in Europe prompted rearmament in the United States, and American workers went back to work. Much had changed. Though much of the New Deal was intended to be temporary, some legislation had established permanent changes that benefited working people. The Fair Labor Standards Act of 1938 established minimum wages, maximum hours, and new standards governing child labor. The Social Security Act provided some measure of old-age security and a system of unemployment compensation. Both acts typically discriminated against minorities but still established the framework for a minimal system of social provision that continued to improve for the next four decades until rolled back in the Reagan revolution. Unions, existing tenuously on the borders of legitimacy at the beginning of the Great Depression, had achieved a degree of institutional stability that was to be solidified through the war years. The state was now an active agent in the new, regulated regime of labor-management relations. The "rule of law" was introduced into the workplace.

LISA KANNENBERG

References and Further Reading

Bernstein, Irving. *Turbulent Years: A History of the American Worker, 1933–1941*. Boston: Houghton Mifflin, 1970.

Buhle, Mary Jo, Paul Buhle, and Dan Georgakas. *Encyclopedia of the American Left*. Urbana, IL: University of Illinois Press, 1992.

Cohen, Lizabeth. *Making a New Deal: Industrial Workers in Chicago, 1919–1939*. New York: Cambridge University Press, 1990.

Derber, Milton, and Edwin Young, eds. *Labor and the New Deal*. Madison, WI: University of Wisconsin Press, 1957.

Dubofsky, Melvin, and Stephen Burwood, eds. *Women and Minorities during the Great Depression*. Philadelphia, PA: Taylor and Francis, 1990.

Faue, Elizabeth. *Community of Suffering and Struggle: Women, Men, and the Labor Movement in Minneapolis, 1915–1945*. Chapel Hill, NC: University of North Carolina Press, 1991.

Fine, Sidney. *Sit-Down: The General Motors Strike of 1936–1937*. Ann Arbor, MI: University of Michigan Press, 1970.

Gerstle, Gary, and Steve Fraser, eds. *The Rise and Fall of the New Deal Order*. Princeton, NJ: Princeton University Press, 1989

Gordon, Colin. *New Deals: Business, Labor, and Politics in America, 1920–1935*. New York: Cambridge University Press, 1994.

Kelley, Robin D. G. *Hammer and Hoe: Alabama Communists during the Great Depression*. Chapel Hill, NC: University of North Carolina Press, 1990.

Lowitt, Richard, and Maurine Beasley, eds. *One-Third of a Nation: Lorena Hickok Reports on the Great Depression*. Urbana, IL: University of Illinois Press, 1983.

McElvaine, Robert S. *The Great Depression: America, 1929–1941*. New York: Times Books, 1984.

Rose, Nancy. *Put to Work: Relief Programs in the Great Depression*. New York: Monthly Review Press, 1994.

Scharf, Lois. *To Work and to Wed: Female Employment, Feminism, and the Great Depression*. Westport, CT: Greenwood Press, 1980.

Vargas, Zaragosa. *Labor Rights Are Civil Rights: Mexican-American Workers in the Twentieth Century*. Princeton, NJ: Princeton University Press, 2005.

GREAT MIGRATION

The Great Migration of the World War I era witnessed the geographical relocation of 450,000 to 500,000 African-Americans from the states of the South to industrial cities in the North; during the 1920s, another wave of migration brought an additional 700,000 black southerners to northern cities. While African-Americans had never been stationary, the scale of the Great Migration was unprecedented. As such it was accompanied by considerable public scrutiny and at times, social conflict. African-Americans, like their white counterparts, discussed and debated the causes, character, and impact of the movement of so many people; unlike their white counterparts, they tended to understand and even celebrate the movement as a decisive move toward a better life despite the obstacles to advancement that blacks encountered in the North.

If the movement of southern blacks "came as a surprise, to North and South alike," as the white periodical, the *Contemporary Review*, put it in 1918, "its causes were of long standing." African-Americans' reasons for migrating were straightforward. So-called "push factors" prompting the decision to leave the South included grinding poverty, widespread antiblack violence, the denial of political rights (capped by a wave of disfranchisement laws and constitutional provisions), the lack of educational and other opportunities, and the day-to-day humiliations that the system of white supremacy and Jim Crow imposed on black southerners. As largely rural sharecroppers, southern blacks were often mired in debt and poverty, exercising little control or influence in the economic realm. The outbreak of World War I in 1914 cut off the European market for southern cotton exports, contributing to an agricultural depression, while flooding and a growing boll weevil infestation of southern cotton crops initially hurt southern farmers and sharecroppers. Economic, social, and political conditions in the South then convinced many southern blacks to undertake the risky move of re-establishing their lives in the North.

While the magnitude of the World War I era migration was unprecedented, black mobility was not. Within the South a steady stream of African-Americans migrated to southern cities and more often engaged in local geographical moves in search of better economic opportunities. The need to earn cash led many black southerners to embrace a strategy of seasonal migration that took black men to timber, railroad construction, or turpentine camps or to brickyards or coal mines, where they engaged in wage labor for brief periods of time before returning to their families in rural communities. For their part, some black women engaged in limited migration to work as domestic servants or washerwomen. In some instances spontaneous or organized campaigns promoted the migration of black southerners. Following the final collapse of Reconstruction, as many as 25,000 former slaves from Louisiana, Texas, and Mississippi took part in what contemporaries referred to as an exodus to Kansas in 1879–1880, despite fierce opposition from both black leaders and white elites. Known as "exodusters," these people made explicit their desire to escape from political and economic violence and seek opportunities outside of the South. Over a decade later in the 1890s, tens of thousands of southern blacks made their way to the Oklahoma Territory when the federal government opened the region to non-Indian settlers.

One of the strongest obstacles to black migration to the North in the pre-World War I decades was an absence of jobs open to black workers there. Northern businessmen shared much of the racial prejudice of southern businessmen and planters. With an alternative labor supply in the form of significant numbers of eastern and southern European immigrants, northern businessmen erected and maintained racial barriers to employment that relegated the relatively small number of northern blacks to unskilled jobs in industry or to domestic service or other service jobs, moves endorsed by skilled white workers. When the start of World War I in 1914 led to a dramatic reduction of immigration from Europe however, the northern employment situation for blacks in the North slowly changed. Labor shortages led employers to begin hiring small but growing numbers of black workers by 1915–1916; when the military draft and voluntary enlistments heightened the labor shortage in 1917 and 1918, employers increasingly turned to black labor, particularly southern black migrants, as a solution. For the first time, the industrial sector of the North—including packinghouses, steel mills, and automobile plants—began hiring thousands of black male (and in the case of packinghouses, female) workers, while black women found jobs in lumber and railroad yards and numerous smaller factories. The new availability of work in the North constituted a powerful "pull factor" drawing southern blacks to the region.

Southern blacks learned of these new opportunities from a variety of sources. Labor agents representing several railroad companies (including the Erie, Pennsylvania, and Union Pacific railroads) actively recruited black men for jobs laying or repairing railroad track in the North and West. While many historians have argued that labor agents played only a minor role in spurring migration, southern whites were convinced that agents were stirring up trouble and contributing to a labor famine in their region. Accordingly municipalities and state governments passed laws to restrict or ban labor recruiting, and local police departments harassed agents and migrants alike. More important in promoting the migration process were northern African-American newspapers like the *Chicago Defender*, which publicized abundant job openings in the North, condemned southern racial practices, and portrayed the North in positive terms as a land of hope and promise. Although white officials sometimes sought to prevent their distribution in the South, black newspapers made their way into countless black homes. Finally black southerners who successfully established new homes in the North communicated through letters to, and return visits with, their relatives and friends left behind, reinforcing the clear message that migration North led to social and political advancement and economic prosperity.

Conditions for African-Americans in the North in many ways represented a sharp improvement over those in the South; blacks could often vote without harassment and could participate in a wide range of rich cultural, religious, and fraternal organizations, for instance. Yet migrants encountered considerable racial hostility and discrimination in their new homes. Skilled white workers, many of whose unions had long barred African-Americans from membership, resented the arrival of so many potential black competitors; in some cases, they refused to work with blacks or resorted to work stoppages to block their introduction into previously all-white labor forces. Striking white workers in East St. Louis, Illinois, took out their fury on black migrants during a bitter labor conflict in July 1917. Although no precise figures are available, contemporaries estimated that from 40 to 200 blacks were killed by white rioters, while 6,000 blacks were driven from their homes. Described by the National Association for the Advancement of Colored People (NAACP) as the "massacre of East St. Louis," the organization blamed white trade unionists for the violence and condemned the city police and state militia for doing little to protect those under attack. "Mr. President, Why Not Make America Safe for Democracy?" read the NAACP's protest signs during a silent march of 10,000 demonstrating against the violence.

Conflicts over employment were not the only source of racial discord during the era of the Great Migration, for housing issues proved contentious as well. Housing markets were often highly segregated, with blacks relegated to specific geographical sections of cities and to markedly inferior housing stock. Black efforts to move into better white neighborhoods were almost uniformly met with opposition and even violence.

In the aftermath of World War I, whites across the country expressed hostility to black wartime gains and in some cases, vowed to roll back the clock. The year 1919 witnessed a massive strike wave affecting many of the country's industrial centers, the repression of newly formed chapters of the NAACP, and a rise in racial violence. (There were approximately 76 lynchings of black Americans that year.) During the summer of 1919, brutal race riots occurred in many cities, including Washington, D.C. and Chicago, where whites, led by street gangs, spent five days assaulting black Chicagoans. In Elaine, Arkansas, planters unleashed a reign of terror against sharecroppers who had organized the Progressive Farmers' and Household Union, killing a minimum of 25 people (and possibly several hundred) and arresting many other participants.

The vehemence of the white reaction can be attributed in part to resentment of black advances and evidence of a new disposition among black Americans. The migration itself disquieted southern white planters who feared a loss of control over their black labor force. Although few southern whites honestly admitted to the brutality of their labor and racial systems that prompted black departures, African-Americans often did not hesitate to point out inequality or identify oppression as a source of the migration. Some even described the outflow of southern blacks as "a silent protest" against southern oppression or as a "Great American Protest" against "the unbearable living conditions" in the South.

That new disposition also manifested itself in a new willingness by blacks to challenge racial inequalities directly. Even before the war, white observers had detected a "growing race consciousness" among northern blacks. By the war years, talk of the emergence of the "new Negro" was common. African-American socialists A. Philip Randolph and Chandler Owen began publishing the *Messenger* magazine during the war, a journal that harshly attacked American racial practices, capitalism, participation in the war, and moderate black leaders too willing to compromise. While few blacks adopted such a radical stance, many did reveal what black government official George Edmund Haynes described in 1919 as "a new consciousness." Howard University's Alain Locke concluded that the "younger generation is vibrant with a new psychology; the new spirit is awake in the masses" (*The New Negro,* 1983). What this meant in practice was a growing willingness on the part of many African-Americans to engage in more direct protest and to insist on citizenship rights. Although the rise of Marcus Garvey's short-lived Universal Negro Improvement Association is often viewed as the primary vehicle for black protest in this era, it had considerable company in many other quarters. The NAACP, initially a middle-class organization, grew tremendously during the war years, attracting many working-class black members in the South. By the end of the war, the association could boast of 90,000 members, up from only 6,000 or so in 1914. The black club women's movement also grew considerably in these years, undertaking social-uplift programs, lobbying efforts, and the campaign for women's suffrage. Even trade unionism attracted a growing number of black participants in these years despite the movement's often-hostile stance toward African-Americans. The wartime and postwar Stockyards Labor Council in Chicago and the United Mine Workers of America in Alabama, which welcomed blacks as members, may have been interracial exceptions to the broader rule of white union hostility, but thousands of black workers joined all-black unions to pursue their own agendas and protect their own interests. Gulf Coast longshoremen, Florida phosphate workers, Mobile commercial laundry workers, Birmingham district coal miners, southern domestic workers, timber workers in Louisiana and East Texas, and railroad firemen, brakemen, Pullman porters, dining car waiters, and freight handlers formed or joined union locals (usually all-black) during the war.

The postwar "racial counterrevolution" halted and in many cases wiped out many if not all of the wartime black advances. Southern NAACP chapters were driven out of existence, many black (and white) unions were destroyed, and local challenges to the racial order were met with white violence. But try as they might, whites could not fully reestablish the prewar racial status quo. Black migrants lost economic ground in the industrial sector immediately after the war, but they retained their foothold in the dynamic core of the nation's economy. During the 1920s, migration again picked up, ultimately surpassing that of the war years. Black communities in the North, particularly Harlem in New York and Chicago, expanded dramatically in size, offering a modicum of cultural and political independence and creating the foundation for a new black politics in the 1930s and 1940s, characterized by a new grassroots militancy that would itself establish the groundwork for the emergence of the modern civil rights movement that ultimately brought down the Jim Crow order.

ERIC ARNESEN

References and Further Reading

Arnesen, Eric. *Black Protest and the Great Migration: A Brief History with Documents*. Boston, MA: Bedford/St. Martin's, 2002.

Clark-Lewis, Elizabeth. *Living in, Living out: African-American Domestics in Washington, D.C., 1910–1940*. New York: Kodansha International, 1994.

Cohen, William. *At Freedom's Edge: Black Mobility and the Southern White Quest for Racial Control 1861–1915*. Baton Rouge: Louisiana State University Press, 1991.

Gottlieb, Peter. *Making Their Own Way: Southern Blacks' Migration to Pittsburgh, 1916–30*. Urbana: University of Illinois Press, 1987.

Grossman, James. *Land of Hope: Chicago, Black Southerners, and the Great Migration*. Chicago, IL: University of Chicago Press, 1989.

Harrison, Alferdteen, ed. *Black Exodus: The Great Migration from the American South*. Jackson: University Press of Mississippi, 1991.

Henry, Florette. *Black Migration: Movement North, 1900–1920*. Garden City, New York: Anchor Books, 1976.

Kirby, Jack Temple. "The Southern Exodus, 1910–1960: A Primer for Historians." *Journal of Southern History* 49, 4 (November 1983): 585–600.

Locke, Alain, ed. *The New Negro*. New York: Atheneum, 1980. (Reprint)

Painter, Nell Irvin. *Exodusters: Black Migration to Kansas after Reconstruction*. New York: W. W. Norton & Company, 1986. (Reprint)

Phillips, Kimberly L. *Alabama North: African-American Migrants, Community, and Working-Class Activism in Cleveland, 1915–45*. Urbana: University of Illinois Press, 1999.

Reich, Steven A. "Soldiers of Democracy: Black Texans and the Fight for Citizenship, 1917–1921." *Journal of American History* 82, 4 (March 1996): 1490–1498.

Rudwick, Elliot. *Race Riot at East St. Louis, July 2, 1917*. Urbana: University of Illinois Press, 1982. (Reprint)

Sernett, Milton C. *Bound for the Promised Land: African American Religion and the Great Migration*. Durham, NC: Duke University Press, 1997.

Stein, Judith. *The World of Marcus Garvey: Race and Class in Modern Society*. Baton Rouge: Louisiana State University Press, 1986.

See also **Disfranchisement; Elaine, Arkansas Massacre (1919); National Association for the Advancement of Colored People; Randolph, A. Philip; Sharecropping and Tenancy; South; Stockyards Labor Council; World War I**

GREAT SOCIETY/WAR ON POVERTY (1960s)

In the era of the 1960s, the U.S. government sought to tackle the vexing phenomenon of substantial poverty within the world's wealthiest society. *The Other America*, written by democratic socialist Michael Harrington and published to wide attention in 1962, shocked Americans by informing them that a great deal of poverty remained amid the general affluence of American society. At least 20% of the U.S. population fell below the U.S. government's official poverty line in the early 1960s. At a time of rising liberalism and surging idealism, poverty became a prominent item on the nation's agenda for action. At the high tide of this liberal idealism, during the presidency of Lyndon B. Johnson (1963–1969), the ambition to reduce poverty levels was enfolded in the far broader agenda of social improvement that went by the name "the Great Society." Antipoverty efforts, like other elements in the Great Society that mainly benefited the middle class, persisted through the 1960s and most of the 1970s under both Democratic and Republican administrations in Washington.

By 1970, the national poverty rate had fallen to less than 13%, and this trend continued for several years. Although the Great Society and specifically the War on Poverty would become controversial in the ensuing decade, the achievements of these programs were substantial. So why did these programs stir such controversy? Part of the explanation is political. Although the organized labor movement was a key element in the Democratic party coalition led by presidents John F. Kennedy (1961–1963) and Johnson, its concerns—and more broadly, those of the working class as a whole—were not much taken into account in developing these programs. This lack of connection set the stage for rightist efforts to detach labor from the Great Society coalition.

From Kennedy to Nixon

Kennedy was aware of the stir caused by Harrington's book, but he already had authorized an antipoverty initiative by 1962. Embodied in the Area Development Act of 1961, Kennedy's effort sought to address the widespread privation that afflicted Appalachia. Kennedy had witnessed this poverty first-hand while campaigning in the Democratic presidential primary race in West Virginia in 1960. Addressing Appalachian poverty through a governmental program carried little political risk—something that was surely taken into account by the hardheaded pragmatists and politicos of the Kennedy administration—as this was largely white poverty. The specter of technically driven unemployment also began to loom large at this time. In response Kennedy signed into law the Manpower Development and Retraining Act (MDTA) in 1962. This act provided matching funds to state governments that financed programs to teach marketable skills to workers rendered jobless by automation. The MDTA was not presented as part of a poverty policy, but its focus soon shifted from those thrown out of work by automation to young men, especially African-Americans, who had never had good jobs in the first place.

When Johnson became president following Kennedy's assassination, he took Kennedy's antipoverty effort much further. In his January 1964 state-of-the-union address, he declared "unconditional war on poverty" in America. This marked the rhetorical high point of liberal hopes to eliminate the contradiction of "want amid plenty." As had Kennedy, Johnson presented unemployment and poverty as two distinct problems. Johnson's war on poverty included a wide array of programs, including job training, legal assistance for the poor, and support for early childhood education, known as Head Start. In later years critics of the War on Poverty often conflated it with the Great Society. But the Great Society programs were distinct

from the War on Poverty. They aimed to benefit the broad middle class and included an astonishing array of initiatives, among them the improvement and beautification of America's highways, the creation of public television, the large-scale sponsorship of the arts, and federal aid to elementary and higher education. Some of the Great Society programs did benefit the poor in particular. The most important such instance was Medicare, the program created in 1965 that provides medical care to all elderly Americans regardless of income or wealth. Medicaid, created at the same time as Medicare, offered health coverage to the poor of all ages. But the quality of Medicaid varied from state to state because the federal government allowed the states to administer the program and set benefit levels, and it pegged its own contributions to what the individual states were willing to spend.

Less than a decade after Johnson's stated commitment to eradicate poverty, most of his antipoverty program was gone, and the War on Poverty was routinely scorned by those on the right (as well as some in the center) as the embodiment of misguided 1960s-era big government. Yet paradoxically Johnson's successor, President Richard M. Nixon (1969–1974), continued to increase government spending to alleviate poverty even as he shut down Johnson's program. Nixon approved a large expansion of the food stamp program, and at his most ambitious, he proposed guaranteeing a minimum income to all American families. This Family Assistance Plan was defeated in Congress after it was attacked both from the right (for the usual reasons) and from the left (for its parsimony).

When discussing 1960s antipoverty efforts, commentators often paint with a broad brush, portraying these efforts simply as a series of handouts to the poor. Such portrayals are inaccurate. In fact there were three different types of antipoverty programs in existence in the 1960s. One type was indeed public assistance or welfare, mainly in the form of Aid to Families with Dependent Children (AFDC), which was first created as Aid to Dependent Children in the 1930s. Its caseload grew more than threefold from 1960–1975; most of this growth occurred under Nixon, not under Johnson. A second type was the War on Poverty, administered through the Office of Economic Opportunity (OEO). It was composed not of welfare programs but of service programs designed to help the poor gain decent positions within the productive economy. As the OEO slogan put it, the government was offering a "hand up not a handout." The third type was social insurance, composed of universal or entitlement programs that provided benefits to rich and poor alike. The main entitlement programs were Medicare, created in 1965, and Social Security, which was created in the 1930s and augmented under Johnson and Nixon.

Structural Unemployment or a Culture of Poverty?

In the 1960s, two ideas dominated analyses of poverty: "Structural unemployment," which focused on economic factors, and the "culture of poverty," which focused on the behavior and attitudes of the poor. Harrington popularized both ideas in *The Other America*; both concepts at that time were associated with the political left. Structural unemployment was not the result of the regular downturns in a capitalist economy. Rather it was created through changes in economic geography that placed certain populations that at one time had had access to employment outside the region of good opportunities. Generating economic growth would thus not solve the problem of structural unemployment; targeted governmental efforts were required. Despite the widespread awareness of the existence of structural unemployment in the United States, this concept became the orphan of the War on Poverty.

The culture of poverty theory saw the poor as trapped by hopelessness. Prolonged deprivation had left them dispirited and apathetic, incapable of envisioning a better life and thus unable to take action to improve their own lot. While conservatives tended to view poverty as impervious to government-administered cures, liberals intended the service programs of the War on Poverty to break down the culture of poverty. The OEO, under the leadership of Sargent Shriver, was charged not just with helping prepare the poor for productive work, but also with involving the poor in finding their own, local solutions to their problems; this was the purpose of the Community Action Program (CAP). Some hoped that CAP, by bringing the poor into the political process, would give them a sense of empowerment and agency and in this way undermine the culture of poverty. But CAP proved highly controversial in ways that its planners had not envisioned. City governments found themselves besieged by militant activists demanding better and more costly services for the poor. The chieftains of local political machines, some of them allied both with the national Democratic party and with labor unions, were appalled to find that the people making trouble for them were sometimes supported by CAP funds. When these political bosses complained about CAP to the White House, there was little doubt that

their unhappiness would count for more than the opinions of social scientists, poverty advocates, and the poor themselves. This political conflict helped to dim Johnson's enthusiasm for OEO early in its history.

Jobs or Job Training?

From the start leftist critics viewed the War on Poverty as a halfway measure at best. They were likely to point out that from 1964–1967, OEO spent only $6.2 billion, less than 1% of the gross national product in those years, to address the problems of one-fifth of the population. They also were disappointed with Johnson's unwillingness to consider large-scale job creation through New Deal-style public-works programs, or the redistribution of income (by taxing the well-off and giving cash payments to the poor). To Johnson such approaches were politically impossible. He did not fear criticism from his left so much as attacks from his political right. In this apprehension Johnson was at least partly correct, since Nixon and his conservatives allies did dismantle OEO as soon as they had the opportunity.

Antipoverty policy debates in the 1960s first intersected with the concerns of the labor movement during the early months of the Johnson administration when various government appointees worked at Johnson's behest to develop proposals quickly for his consideration. Few of the key players in this process had links to organized labor, and for the most part, they did not think about antipoverty policy in terms of a job's policy. The exception was Johnson's secretary of labor, Willard Wirtz. He pressed the idea that job creation was the best antipoverty policy, echoing views that had been expressed earlier by Kennedy's first secretary of labor, Arthur Goldberg. While Wirtz advocated a public-works program to expand government employment, he did not see this as the only method for reducing poverty. But he thought it should be part of the policy mix, establishing the federal government as the "employer of last resort."

Johnson's response to this proposal is highly instructive: He was coldly silent. He was a "budget hawk" and had no intention of spending large sums of money on the War on Poverty. Johnson also had no appetite for a confrontation with private businesses, which since the 1930s had fiercely opposed big public-works projects, viewing them as competition for workers, which would drive up wages. The job-creation idea was dropped, never coming back into policy discussion at high levels. Job training would be the dominant theme in the employment dimension of the War on Poverty. Johnson administration officials proposed involving the craft unions, which ran their own apprenticeship systems, in job-training efforts aimed at young male African-Americans, whose unemployment rate was especially high and whose representation in the craft unions, especially the building trades, was very low. This linkage between the craft unions and the War on Poverty's job-training program created considerable friction. Two important elements in the Democratic party's political coalition became locked in bitter conflict, ultimately damaging the fortunes of that party.

Conflict with the Trade Unions

After the rioting by young African-Americans in the Watts neighborhood of Los Angeles in 1965, the Johnson administration felt a more urgent need to address the problem of joblessness among the black urban population. Government requirements for nondiscriminatory hiring by government contractors, which affected construction trade unions, were tightened. This effort dovetailed with the War on Poverty's job-training emphasis, since the government sought voluntary cooperation from the lily-white building trades in job-training programs that would bring young black men into the trades. The craft unions in general sought to fend off any infringement on their members' control over entry into the unions. The building trades had an especially stark history of keeping African-Americans out, as civil rights leaders pointed out forcefully and often. When Johnson's efforts to bring change with a minimum of coercion brought paltry dividends, threats of tougher action—with specific hiring goals and timetables (which the union described as quotas)—followed.

When Nixon became president, he made good on those lingering threats. In 1969, his secretary of labor, George Schultz, announced the implementation of the Philadelphia plan, which mandated hiring goals and timetables for government construction contracts around the country. The new, tougher policy resulted in a significant increase in the representation of people of color in the skilled trades in the 1970s. The policy also provided Nixon with a political dividend by worsening the conflict between skilled white labor and African-Americans, a traditional social cleavage that already had worked to Nixon's advantage in the 1968 election. Even though Nixon was aiding black workers in this instance, his hostility to other elements in the civil rights agenda helped him reap the benefits of the growing "white backlash" of the era.

Increased Assistance, Declining Poverty

Despite criticism on all sides of the alleged ineffectiveness of the War on Poverty, it is sensible to see the decline in poverty in the 1960s and 1970s as the result of three factors: Antipoverty efforts; the expansion of universal entitlement programs; and the unusually high levels of overall economic growth that characterized the mid-to-late 1960s and early 1970s.

Poor relief grew enormously during Nixon's presidency through the expansion of food stamps and other programs. Why the numbers of people drawing AFDC payments grew so much during the 1960s and 1970s is a matter of interpretation. Most scholars attribute the growth to a new assertiveness among the poor who, influenced by the civil rights and other movements of the 1960s, claimed the governmental assistance to which they were entitled but for which many poor Americans in earlier decades had been too intimidated to apply. Some of the stigma traditionally attached to welfare had dissipated in the 1960s, a development that commentators on the right lamented and those on the left viewed positively.

In the 1980s and 1990s, the expansion of government support for the poor that had occurred under Presidents Kennedy, Johnson, and Nixon came under serious and successful attack. Just as poverty rates had declined in the era of the 1960s when poor relief had been increased, so poverty rates rose in the 1980s and 1990s as government policy toward the poor became stingier. Great Society entitlement programs, which tied the fate of the poor to that of the middle class to some degree, were less vulnerable to attack.

DOUG ROSSINOW and REBECCA S. LOWEN

References and Further Reading

Berkowitz, Edward D. *America's Welfare State: From Roosevelt to Reagan.* Baltimore: The Johns Hopkins University Press, 1991.
Davis, Martha F. *Brutal Need: Lawyers and the Welfare Rights Movement, 1960–1973.* New Haven, CT: Yale University Press, 1993.
Katz, Michael. *The Undeserving Poor: From the War on Poverty to the War on Welfare.* New York: Pantheon Books, 1989.
Matusow, Allen J. *The Unraveling of America: Liberalism in the 1960s.* New York: Harper & Row, 1984.

O'Connor, Alice. *Poverty Knowledge: Social Science, Social Policy, and the Poor in Twentieth-Century U.S. History.* Princeton, NJ: Princeton University Press, 2001.

Patterson, James T. *America's War on Poverty, 1900–1994.* Cambridge, MA: Harvard University Press, 1994.

Piven, Frances F., and Richard Cloward. *Regulating the Poor: The Functions of Public Welfare.* New York: Random House, 1971.

Quadagno, Jill. *The Color of Welfare: How Racism Killed the War on Poverty.* New York: Oxford University Press, 1994.

See also **Aid to Families with Dependent Children (AFDC); Welfare Rights**

GREAT UPHEAVAL

"Great upheaval" is a term used by historians to describe an upsurge in labor and political activism beginning in mid-1885. Historians differ on when it ended, with some opting for as early as 1888 and others as late as 1890. The Great Upheaval represented a serious challenge to the emerging hegemony of industrial and investment capitalism. For a brief moment, it appeared possible that capitalism itself could be supplanted by (or have to compete with) alternative economic systems. In the end capitalism prevailed but in compromised forms that ultimately blunted some of its harshest aspects.

The great upheaval is an analytical construct that emerged from the "new social history" of the 1960s and 1970s. Earlier histories often neglected the narratives of working people, immigrants, women, and minorities in favor of political narratives that saw power as a top-heavy process in which decisions filtered down to largely passive masses. The "bottom-up" focus of the new social history altered such interpretations and forced historians to pay more attention to factors like race, class, ethnicity, and gender. This led to a serious re-evaluation of the 1880s, which had traditionally been viewed as a conservative period. In older narratives the 1886 Haymarket riot in Chicago stood as an aberration that was quickly and effortlessly subdued. By looking at local politics, reform movements, labor unions, and immigrant associations, social historians reinterpreted the 1880s as a restive period that produced serious challenges to the elites who dominated political, social, cultural, and economic life after the Civil War.

The term great upheaval is sometimes applied to the cataclysmic 1877 railroad strikes, but most historians now restrict it to the mid-to-late 1880s and see 1877 as part of an overall pattern of discontent that reached its fullest expression a decade later. Nearly all historians agree that the Knights of Labor's (KOL) unexpected strike victory over Jay Gould's Southwestern rail system in August 1885 was the opening salvo of the great upheaval. The KOL's triumph gave hope to dispirited workers at a key moment in time.

Labor organizations struggled after the Civil War. Various labor congresses produced manifestos that were more sound than fury, 8-hour leagues met with little success, and the National Labor Union failed to materialize as the potent nationwide labor federation its founders had hoped. It, like many trade unions, perished in the aftermath of the severe Panic of 1873, an economic downturn that stretched into 1878. The railroad strikes of 1877 ended in a rout for capital, which, coupled with hysteria over arrests of alleged Molly Maguires in 1876, contributed to a general repression of labor and reform organizations. Third-party attempts, like the Greenback-Labor party, which hoped to fuse the concerns of farmers, urban workers, and monetary reformers, generated local success in the late 1870s but also faltered as national movements. The KOL, founded in 1869, had just over 28,000 members in 1880, hardly enough to challenge the power structure. The Federation of Organized Trade and Labor Unions (FOTLU) formed in 1881 but was practically moribund by 1884, due in part to another recession in 1882–1883.

By the 1870s, it was clear that new forms of capitalism based on industrial output, speculation, and investment were supplanting older forms of wealth based on land, rent, agricultural production, and proprietorships. The logic of new capitalist schemes was even harsher than that of older paternalist models. Most workers toiled long hours, often under dangerous conditions, for poverty-level wages. Moreover the ideology of social Darwinism justified both rapacious capitalism and poverty by positing business success as an expression of a survival-of-the-fittest biological imperative and impoverishment as a personal, moral failing. Mark Twain and Charles Dudley Warner called the period of ruthless capitalist speculation the Gilded Age, a label that stuck.

Gilded Age speculators and captains of industry faced a serious challenge in the mid-to-late 1880s. Capitalism, though ascendant, was still viewed with suspicion by many Americans. During the great upheaval the very logic of wage earning was attacked. Agrarian reformers associated with farmers' alliances and many urban workers appealed to older ideals of an independent yeomanry, thus renewing calls for land reform. Groups like the KOL set up cooperative production and retail enterprises in which the price of goods was determined by the labor theory of value, not the profit motive, and called for an end to the wage systems. Various socialist and anarchist organizations also called for an end to capitalism, some advocating the use of violence if necessary. Even many trade unions, on the rise again after 1884, called for the ultimate abolition of wages, all the while seeking to raise them in the short term.

Gilded Age social and cultural norms were also challenged. Women's suffrage and feminist groups gained momentum, temperance groups won new members, and African-American leaders lobbied for civil rights. Within religious institutions, early adherents of the Social Gospel movement began to challenge social Darwinists and denounce the hypocrisy of well-heeled congregants who repressed laborers. On a less salutary note, reformers often also demanded immigration restriction, especially of the Chinese.

The KOL's dramatic victory over Jay Gould gave hope to millions. Gould, who once bragged he could hire half of the working class to kill the other half, was the epitome of a robber baron. As the principal stockholder of Western Union, he crushed the KOL and telegraphers' union in an 1882 strike. He was also the architect of the sprawling Southwestern Railway system, a conglomerate that controlled thousands of miles of track and individual rail lines in the Midwest and Southwest. Gould was known as a brutal employer, even by the Gilded Age's debased standards. The KOL workers along Gould's lines fought off wage cuts in 1884, then endured a May through August strike in 1885 that forced Gould to capitulate. When the details of the settlement were released in September, working people rushed to join the Knights under what proved to be the illusory assumption that if Gould could be defeated, labor could prevail against any foe.

The KOL saw its membership surge from fewer than 112,000 to between 729,000 and a million in a single year. Many workers who had never before been union members joined the organization, including increasing numbers of African-Americans and women. So many workers rushed to join the KOL that it was forced to declare a moratorium against chartering new locals until existing applications were processed, a task it never completed. Both Knights and workers outside the organization took matters into their own hands, with 1886 seeing an upsurge of strikes; whereas 1885 saw 645 strikes idling 159,000 workers, in 1886 more than 407,000 workers walked off in 1,436 separate work stoppages. For the next 10 years, there were more than a thousand strikes each year except for 1888. Many of these involved the KOL, even though the KOL officially opposed strikes except as a last resort. The general tenor of the times was such that the KOL's leaders were unable to control the zeal of their own rank-and-file, a situation that ultimately crippled the organization.

The most infamous moment of the great upheaval occurred in Chicago in early May 1886. A nationwide strike had been called for May 1—the inaugural International Workers' Day—in which workers would walk away from their jobs in a show of strength designed to foist the 8-hour day on recalcitrant employers. May Day was actually a bust as a national movement, since the KOL and several trade unions refused to sanction an event organized largely by anarchists and Marxists. Rather than the millions organizers hoped would protest, fewer than 300,000 actually struck on May 1. About one-fifth of the total took to the streets of Chicago, where the 8-hour protest coincided with an ongoing strike against the McCormick Harvester works. When police killed two workers on May 1, a protest in Haymarket Square was called for May 4. As the last speaker was finishing his speech, police cordoned off the area and began advancing on the crowd when a bomb was hurled, and the police opened fire. Seven officers and four protestors died, and more than 50 were wounded.

The Haymarket bombing and the subsequent arrest of eight anarchists touched off demands by elites to repress radicals, but it galvanized labor groups and reformers just as fervently as it did the Gilded Age power structure. Millions decried the arrest, trial, and conviction of the anarchists as a travesty of justice, and massive protests erupted in the United States, Canada, and Europe. The ballot box became another focal point to express dissatisfaction. Third parties proliferated in advance of state and local elections, the most-famous being the United Labor party, which put forth single-tax architect Henry George as its candidate for New York City's mayor. George finished a close second in New York, but across the United States, numerous working-men's candidates won local races. Knights of Labor candidates were elected in at least 58 different towns and cities and wielded significant political power in large cities like Milwaukee and Richmond, and in smaller towns like Rochester, New Hampshire, and Rutland, Vermont.

Trade unions were also revitalized by the great upheaval. In December 1886, Samuel Gompers and Adolph Strasser reorganized the FOTLU as the American Federation of Labor (AFL), an umbrella organization that saw the strike as a primary weapon in the struggle between capital and labor. Given the rise of the AFL and the reconstituted membership of the KOL, 1887 was destined to be a strike-plagued year. Many workers embarked on job stoppages heedless of warning signs that the 1885 victory over Gould would prove difficult to duplicate. The KOL was already reeling from losses in the Chicago stockyards and in a second strike against Gould in 1886.

Strikes in 1887 by New England shoemakers, New York and New Jersey dockworkers, and Reading Railroad employees all ended badly and touched off bitter battles between the KOL and trade unions with each accusing the other of betrayal.

Although incompetence and broken solidarity played a role in lost strikes, their overall significance has been exaggerated. In truth organized labor underestimated the power of capitalist foes and failed to anticipate the strength of the backlash it launched to counter the great upheaval. Four of the Haymarket men were hanged in November 1887, and labor was already on the defensive by 1888, the year Edward Bellamy's novel *Looking Backward* inspired the birth of the quasi-socialist Nationalist movement. A strike loss by rail workers on the Chicago, Burlington & Quincy line proved traumatic. By then the KOL was in steep decline, and the AFL proved more adroit at winning jurisdictional battles against the Knights than in defeating employers.

Moreover capital proved itself better organized than labor. Many of labor's 1886 electoral victories were undone from 1887–1890, due in part to well-funded oppositional campaigns. Republicans and Democrats often put forth fusion candidates to avoid vote splitting and where necessary, even used gerrymandering processes to isolate labor's ballot box potential. Capitalists did not hesitate to use heavy-handed tactics when political maneuvers failed. The use of labor spies, scabs, and Pinkerton detectives was commonplace in workplaces where unions appeared strong. The KOL was especially vulnerable, since it represented more workers in mass-production industries controlled by wealthy investors than the AFL, whose skilled workers tended to be found in smaller workshops. Equally at risk were ideological radicals, especially anarchists who found themselves frequent victims of repression.

By 1890, the year the lost New York Central strike eviscerated what was left of the KOL's presence in the urban United States, the great upheaval was largely a spent force. Labor's dreams of jettisoning the wage system gave way to the AFL's focus on pure-and-simple unionism, a strategy that confined itself largely to negotiations over wages, hours, and working conditions. The 1890s was a particularly brutal period in American labor relations in which the full blunt of the capitalist backlash played itself out in dramatic strikes, such as Homestead (1892) and Pullman (1894), and in exercises of raw power like the Lattimer massacre (1897).

Although it is tempting to view the great upheaval as a failure, such a conclusion is overly pessimistic. It was a turning point in history in which sincere alternatives to competitive capitalism were put forth but failed. Nonetheless turning points seldom yield simplistic either/or results, and the great upheaval was no exception. The events of the 1880s, followed by the unsettled and violent 1890s, led many Americans, especially among the rising middle classes, to embrace the cause of social reform, repudiate *laissez faire* business practices, and battle against corruption. In retrospect the great upheaval was both the swan song of social Darwinism and a precursor of the Progressive Era.

ROBERT E. WEIR

References and Further Reading

Fink, Leon. *Workingmen's Democracy: The Knights of Labor and American Politics*. Urbana: Univ. of Illinois Press, 1983.

Laurie, Bruce. *Artisans into Workers: Labor in Nineteenth-Century America*. New York: Hill and Wang, 1989.

Weir, Robert. *Beyond Labor's Veil: The Culture of the Knights of Labor*. University Park, PA: Penn State Univ. Press, 1996.

GREENBACK-LABOR PARTY

The Greenback-Labor party (GLP) was the first nationally organized third-party movement since the close of the Civil War that combined various local electoral coalitions, some of which were labor parties.

Origins

What came to be called "greenbackism" was rooted in antebellum labor reform ideology. Albert Brisbane, Josiah Warren, William B. Greene, and, especially, Edward N. Kellogg advocated the exchange of value through a paper medium. By the 1850s, they argued that the manipulation of the money supply, coupled to cooperation, might transform the social order.

Far more broadly though, the federal government financed the Civil War in part through the printing of paper "greenbacks." Wartime spending and the inflation that resulted helped farmers minimize indebtedness, fueled business investments, and contributed to employment and in parts of the work force, prosperity. After the war reform-minded leaders of the Democrats, nationally the minority party, were eager to focus on new issues like "the Ohio idea" that the government should continue to print limited amounts of paper money.

Greenbackers

Postwar labor reformers took up the issue along with the demand for a legislated 8-hour workday. By 1868, adherents of the National Labor Union (NLU) formed state labor reform parties in New England and, in 1871 moved the NLU to call for a new party. In February 1872, the National Labor Reform Party (NLRP) convened in Columbus, adopted a remarkably uninspiring platform centered on the reform Democratic position on paper money and nominated Illinois Democrat David Davis in an effort to influence his nomination by that party. When Davis declined, a delegated interim committee of the NLRP simply endorsed the straight-out Democratic candidate, who received so few votes that it is doubtful the ranks of the NLU followed the endorsement.

The Panic of 1873 politicized the mass organizations of midwestern farmers, like the Patrons of Husbandry or the Grange. Illinois farmers built a Peoples' Antimonopolist party, and a similar Independent party formed in Indiana. By 1874, such parties formed in Missouri, Michigan, Nebraska, Iowa, Minnesota, Kansas, and Wisconsin. While these insurgents had been divided on paper money, on June 10, 1874, the original two state parties held coordinated state conventions that adopted paper money. A November 25 convention in Indianapolis united the new insurgents with former NLRP groups from Connecticut, Illinois, New York, Ohio, Pennsylvania, and West Virginia. Although NLRP leaders favoring a broader platform met in Harrisburg on March 3, 1875, the meeting generated little interest. The new organization called itself the Independent party or the National party (as opposed to the state parties), but the press called it the Greenback party.

Congressional passage of the Specie Resumption Act (1875) authorizing the elimination of greenbacks by 1879 threatened further economic hardships and seemed to offer the insurgents a common grievance just as the Kansas-Nebraska Act a generation before inspired the rise of the Republican party. The nominating convention that gathered on May 15, 1876, in Indianapolis was as dominated as the former NLRP by large delegations from Ohio and Illinois urging a nomination to influence the Democrats. Under the urging of a small New York group, the convention named the aged Jacksonian Peter Cooper and California Senator Newton Booth, the latter later declining and being replaced by Samuel F. Cary of Ohio. Once more, the Democrats were not interested, and the official count gave Cooper only 81,740 votes.

Laborites

After the NLRP debacle of 1872, the more radical participants turned to the International Workingmen's Association, which self-fragmented along ethnic lines in short order. In 1874, various suspended sections combined with a Newark labor party to launch the Social Democratic Workingmen's Party of North America, which merged with some midwestern organizations in 1876 to form the Workingmen's Party of the United States (WPUS).

The brutal and bipartisan repression of the railroad strike of 1877 inspired a wave of mass working-class protest votes. The railroads announced yet another round of pay cuts that July, and their desperate employees walked out, detonating what became a national general strike. The federal authorities, often over the objection of local officials, sent troops to break the strike.

After this workers' organizations grew quickly. Most remarkably, the Knights of Labor abandoned secrecy in 1882 and began absorbing trade unions and other workers' associations. Sometimes in conjunction with the socialists and sometimes in competition with them, local labor parties contended for office. From New Haven to St. Louis, Milwaukee to Covington, workers began electing socialist and labor nominees to office. In other places they became Greenbackers or formed a natural alliance with other insurgents.

The GLP

On February 22, 1878, a small convention in a bitterly cold Toledo schoolhouse united the Greenbackers with representatives of many of these local independent labor groups. This was what called itself the GLP.

A number of important groups remained aloof. The Union Greenback Clubs declined to merge into the GLP. The socialists ignored the development and transformed their WPUS into the Socialistic Labor party (SLP) at the end of 1877. In the South a number of independent splinters from the Democrats took place with the triumph of white "redeemer" Democratic governments, with Virginia's Readjusters' party in the forefront. The Workingmen's party of California remained focused on the exclusion of the Chinese, who were vilified for having brought down wages and standards of living. Finally an association of freethinkers launched a National Liberal party.

The GLP assumed the same community functions in places as those of the Grange. The party gained some serious pockets of strength outside the Midwest, offering a real possibility for a fusionist strategy. When the GLP elected officials in parts of Republican New England, Democrats offered fusion. So, too, where the GLP gained ground in northern Alabama, fusion with the Republicans offered a greater opportunity for victory.

The GLP Strength

The off-year national election of 1878 produced what was proportionately the largest third-party movement in U.S. history not to result in the displacement of a major party. From 802,000 to 852,000 votes went to exclusively Greenback, Independent, Independent Greenback, or National candidates, with another 25,000 divided between the socialists and prohibitionists. Those running with either Democratic endorsements or no Democratic opposition got another 303,400, with another 217,000 going to insurgents who seemed to have Republican support. Independent Democrats running against Democratic candidates had another 150,000 and independent Republicans over 18,000. This totaled an insurgent vote of between about 1,000,000 and counting the results of fusion, 1,600,000. The numbers sufficed to elect 22 independents to Congress, including future members of the Bellamy socialist clubs, Reverend Gilbert Delamatyr of Indiana, and James Baird Weaver of Iowa, and the St. Louis labor reformer, Nicholas Ford.

In June 1880, a national convention at Chicago expanded the GLP platform. Among other things it endorsed woman suffrage and adopted the SLP's resolution: "We declare that land, air, and water are the grand gifts of nature to all mankind, and the law or custom of society that allows any person to monopolize more of these gifts of nature than he has a right to, we earnestly condemn and demand shall be abolished." The party nominated Republican Weaver for president and the elderly Texan Barzalai J. Chambers for vice-president. The candidate actively stumped the country, campaigning not only against a monopoly over the money supply, but over land and the means of transportation as well. Weaver also became the first American presidential candidate to defend without qualification the rights of all workers to organize.

Despite its promise, the national campaign faltered and failed on the strategy of fusion. Officeholders in Maine hoped to retain their positions through an alliance with the Democrats even though such a coalition would be disastrous in Alabama. Weaver warned against the strategy and found himself marginalized, misreported, and then rendered invisible in the nation's press. Fusion in Maine, adopted in spite of his protests, eventually reclassified the 65,310 ballots cast for mostly GLP electors into officially Democratic votes. The official national totals gave Weaver-Chambers a mere 306,867 votes, a radical falling-off from the 1878 numbers.

Legacy

After 1880, the focus of political insurgency shifted from the Midwest and its currency issue. The National Antimonopoly party in 1884 and the Union Labor party in 1888 pre-empted the remnants of the GLP, which opted merely to endorse the candidates of other parties.

The labor attitude to the Populists after 1890 radically colored the memory of the GLP. Now organized by the American Federation of Labor rather than the Knights, workers remained far more skeptical of the Populists than they had been of the GLP. For ostensibly different reasons, the organized socialists similarly kept their distance.

MARK LAUSE

References and Further Reading

Destler, Chester M. *American Radicalism, 1865–1901*. New London: Connecticut College, 1946.

Lause, Mark A. *The Civil War's Last Campaign: James B. Weaver, the Greenback-Labor Party and the Politics of Race and Section*. Lanham, MD: University Press of America, 2001.

Montgomery, David. *Beyond Equality*. New York: Alfred A. Knopf, 1967.

Ritter, Gretchen. *Goldbugs and Greenbacks: the Antimonopoly Tradition and the Politics of Finance in America, 1865–1900*. Cambridge and New York: Cambridge University Press, 1997.

See also **Antebellum Era; Brisbane, Albert; Civil War and Reconstruction; Green, William**

GUATEMALANS

The first large wave of Guatemalan immigrant workers in the United States occurred in the early 1980s, when many *campesinos* (peasants)—as well as liberal and progressive professionals—were driven from their homes by the violence of Guatemala's 36-year civil war between a right-wing military dictatorship in charge of the country since a U.S.-led coup in 1954 and a Marxist-led guerrilla army. Altogether the violence of that war, cresting in the period from

1978–1982 with the razing of entire Mayan villages deemed too sympathetic to the insurgency, left some 200,000 casualties and nearly one million displaced persons. Many of the latter would find their way to the United States, particularly the West Coast, Texas, and Florida, where they initially found work alongside Mexicans and other Central Americans as agricultural laborers. Soon they were drawn to more urban, industrial employment as well, particularly food processing, construction, landscaping, and ultimately, low-wage service jobs. By the early 1990s, as the civil war wound down toward an eventual formal peace agreement between government and guerrilla factions in 1996, the earlier stream of war refugees gave way to a chain migration of economic refugees (from a land with nearly 40% unemployment) drawing on family and village ties. Both groups of migrants fled by foot, bus, and van rides across Mexico, crossed the border of Texas or Arizona, then generally headed west to pick crops in California and/or east to do the same in Florida. From these initial ports of entry, they engaged in secondary migrations to find work. Kansas, Georgia, Alabama, North Carolina, Colorado, as well as Toronto, British Columbia, and even Prince Edward Island, Canada, all reported significant clusters of new Guatemalan arrivals by 2000. By 2002, an estimated 1.2 million Guatemalans were living in the United States.

For a brief time the Guatemalans actually possessed a special employment advantage under U.S. immigration and refugee law, even over other Latin American laborers. Beginning in the fall of 1986, the Immigration Reform and Control Act (IRCA) affected would-be immigrants in important ways. On the one hand IRCA implemented a generous legalization program for some two million undocumented immigrants who had arrived prior to 1982; on the other hand it both beefed up border surveillance and established tough new sanctions for employers who hired more recent, illegal aliens. While throwing a new obstacle in the way of undocumented Mexicans and others, the new rules left a slight window ajar for Guatemalans and other *émigrés* from war-torn Central America in the form of appeals for asylum under the Refugee Act of 1980. To be sure the initial opening was not very inviting; less than 1% of Guatemalans for example who filed for asylum from June 1983 to September 1986 were granted protection. Especially after the Immigration and Nationalization Service (INS) entered into a settlement agreement with advocates for both Salvadoran and Guatemalan asylum applicants in *ABC v. Thornburgh* in 1991, the INS not only guaranteed due process under more lenient guidelines (that is, "without consideration of nationality") for future claimants but agreed to re-adjudicate the claims of every Salvadoran and Guatemalan applicant who had previously been denied relief. In the wake of ABC, a tide of Guatemalan asylum applications poured in; given the huge backlog of such applications, applicants (and their employers) could count not only on an initial, temporary work permit but also on regular annual renewals pending a distant asylum hearing. This welcome mat was withdrawn when new restrictions were announced with the Illegal Immigration Reform and Immigration Restriction Act (IIRAIRA), authorizing the "expedited removal" of "inadmissible aliens," in 1997. Though softened in impact by administrative mandates for a few years, the events of 9/11 led to strict enforcement of IIRAIRA provisions and generally a new climate of fear and insecurity among the still largely undocumented Guatemalan working-class in the United States.

While largely unorganized and situated in decidedly nonunion areas of the U.S. labor force, in selective cases, Guatemalan immigrants have displayed a capacity to blend informal community ties with labor union mobilization. The rise of a newly powerful Los Angeles labor movement in the 1990s—including the Service Employees International Unions's (SEIU's) Justice for Janitors campaign, the Hotel and Restaurant Employee's New Otani drive, and other efforts led by drywallers, house framers, and tortilla makers—found political refugees from the previous decade's struggles in Guatemala and El Salvador taking important grassroots roles. In Morganton, North Carolina, a location otherwise remote from union influence, for example, the Case Farms poultry plant, with some 80% Guatemalan workforce, witnessed nearly a decade-long unionizing campaign. Winning a National Labor Relations Board (NLRB) representation election in 1995 but failing thereafter to secure a collective-bargaining contract, this laboring community effort devolved into a Worker Rights Center, struggling at once for work place protections and better immigration laws.

LEON FINK

References and Further Reading

Davis, Mike. *Magical Realism: Latinos Re-invent the U.S. City.* New York: Verso, 2000.

Fink, Leon. *The Maya of Morganton: Work and Community in the Nuevo New South.* Chapel Hill: University of North Carolina Press, 2003.

Loucky, James, and Moors, Marilyn M. *The Maya Diaspora: Guatemalan Roots, New American Lives.* Philadelphia, PA: Temple University Press, 2000.

GUTMAN, HERBERT (1928–1985)
Historian

Born the son of left-wing, Jewish immigrant parents in Queens, New York, Herbert G. Gutman became one of two leading voices (the other is David Montgomery) of what became known as the new labor history—effectively an intellectual renaissance in the field—that began in the late 1960s. Perhaps best known for his essays that highlighted the roles of ordinary workers in previously little-examined industrial communities of the Gilded Age, Gutman had established a reputation as one of the nation's premier historians of African-American as well as labor and social history before his untimely death from a heart attack in 1985.

Gutman's intellectual interests developed both from his training and his reactions to the world around him. A product of New York City public schools, he advanced from Queens College, where he studied history alongside his journalism major, to Columbia University, where his emergent social history interests met the disinterest of his advisor, Richard Hofstadter, to the University of Wisconsin, where left-wing heterodoxy flourished and where he began a widespread set of inquiries about American working-class history, culminating in a 1959 Ph.D. dissertation, inelegantly titled, "Social and Economic Structure and Depression: American Labor in 1873 and 1874." Professionally Gutman moved from Fairleigh Dickenson College to the State University of New York at Buffalo to the University of Rochester and finally to appointments at both the City College of New York and the Graduate Center of the City University of New York.

As a historian Gutman's literary legacy is several-fold. Though for years avid readers searched for his essays either in relatively obscure state historical journals or pressed friends for unpublished copy circulating only in manuscript form, two significant anthologies now facilitate access to Gutman's work: *Work, Culture, and Society in Industrializing America: Essays in American Working-Class and Social History* and the posthumous collection edited and supplemented with a fine introduction [on which this entry heavily relies] by Ira Berlin, *Power & Culture: Essays on the American Working Class.* In addition those who wish to appreciate, and reckon with, Gutman's work and characteristic method should read *The Black Family in Slavery and Freedom, 1750–1925* and *Slavery and the Numbers Game: A Critique of "Time on the Cross."* Finally his influence is palpably evident in the two-volume textbook that was initiated under his direction on the American Social History Project,

Who Built America? Working People and the Nation's Economy, Politics, Culture, and Society.

For most readers the first hint of new directions in the field of labor history arrived with Gutman's "The Workers' Search for Power: Labor in the Gilded Age," in *The Gilded Age: A Reappraisal.* Previously labor history, with its disciplinary origins rooted in the institutional economics of the Progressive Era, had focused almost entirely on labor unions and their leaders. Now Gutman focused attention on the lives, and willed self-activity, of ordinary working people, both at their workplaces and in the larger social, religious, and political life of their communities. Distilling the evidence from the several case studies of his dissertation, Gutman emphasized the public skepticism with which the small-town United States greeted industrial capitalism as well as the effectiveness of alliances hatched between workers and shopkeepers to keep corporate power at bay. The seeming openness of the political system to alternative trajectories at a key moment in the modernization of American life challenged assumptions about a unified, liberal American ideology common to the postwar consensus school of American historiography. That Gutman's discoveries occurred just as domestic contemporary politics themselves became embroiled in the conflicts of the civil rights, student, and antiwar movements lent outside fuel to the fires of a conflict-oriented school of social history. Publication of the British neo-Marxist E. P. Thompson's *The Making of the English Working-Class* in 1964 lent inside support—and an inspiring model—to the same cause.

Both Gutman's skills as a social historian of *histoire totale* and his preoccupation with the puzzle of U.S. class consciousness (or what many have called the problem of "American exceptionalism") are on display in many of his signature articles, such as "Labor in the Land of Lincoln: Coal Miners on the Prairie," written in 1966–1967 and published posthumously in the Berlin-edited anthology. The themes of town building, immigration, class structure, social mobility, standards of living, women's place in community protests, racial divisions, and class and ethnic structure all receive extended treatment even as the author follows two Scottish-born miners, John James and Daniel McLaughlin, through a narrative focusing on labor conflict and political organization. Though Gutman convincingly documents the strength of local, immigrant-based worker solidarity in the union stronghold of Braidwood, Illinois, across the 1860s and 1870s, he also uncovers patterns that would frustrate such solidarity over the long haul. The nearby town of Streator, for one, failed to maintain the strike discipline of the Braidwood miners. For another erstwhile union stalwart John James moved up the ranks in area coal companies and ended up as anti-union mine superintendent. Long after he had written the Braidwood manuscript, Gutman, in a 1982 address to the Organization of American Historians, implicitly returned to such dilemmas. He identified a "central tension in all dependent groups over time" as that "between individualist (utilitarian) and collective (mutualist) ways of dealing with, and sometimes over-coming, dependence and inequality."

Gutman's single most influential argument for labor and social historians was likely that contained in his 1973 *American Historical Review* essay, "Work, Culture, and Society in Industrializing America, 1815–1919." The result of his own assimilation of the cultural Marxism and cultural anthropology, Gutman here emphasized the continuous cultural clash of a largely rural and immigrant-derived work-ing class with the discipline imposed by the factory system. At once upholding the integrity of pre-indus-trial traditions and insisting on the peculiarities of an American working class continually re-made by great immigrations and internal migrations, he countered the dominant notion of immigration historians (as centrally defined by the work of Oscar Handlin) that immigration necessitated an immediate breakdown of old values in order to assimilate to consensual American norms.

The emphasis on cultural persistence and resis-tance, as particularly transmitted through family ties, central to "Work, Culture, and Society," also fundamentally informed Gutman's next great re-search project on the history of the black family in slavery and freedom. Provoked by the contemporary debates that tied the 1960s-era wave of urban crime and violence to the pathology or breakdown of African-American family in slavery, Gutman extend-ed an initial critique of the Moynihan Report into a far-reaching empirical probe. His own late

nineteenth-century data on multiple urban sites, for example, indicated that the great majority of black workers lived in nuclear families with both parents present. Now with an extensive sweep of plantation records, he documented the thick and very African-influenced bonds of kinship that sustained the enslaved peoples during their greatest trials. The post-Civil War determination to reunite families broken by slave sale attains an heroic centrality in Gutman's work. Overall, he argued, the family functioned as a central agent of resistance, and class formation, within the African-American community. Such emphasis on lower-class agency helped to spark a long-running argument (one might better say feud) with Gutman's former Roches-ter colleague, slavery historian Eugene D. Genovese. Though both drew heavily on Marxist influences, the latter's top-down emphasis on ruling-class hegemony proved inimical to Gutman's core emphasis on, and sympathies with, ordinary working people. In any case, their disagreements for a time fueled insightful but also painfully vitriolic exchanges over the direction of American social history.

LEON FINK

References and Further Reading

American Social History Project. *Who Built America? Working People and the Nation's Economy, Politics, Culture, and Society.* 2 vols. New York: Pantheon, 1989, 1992.
Gutman. Herbert G. *The Black Family in Slavery and Free-dom, 1750–1925.* New York: Pantheon, 1976.
———. *Power & Culture: Essays on the American Working Class,* edited by Ira Berlin. New York: Pantheon, 1987.
———. *Work, Culture, and Society in Industrializing Amer-ica: Essays in American Working-Class and Social His-tory.* New York: Knopf, 1976.
———. *Slavery and the Numbers Game: A Critique of "Time on the Cross."* Urbana: University of Illinois Press, 1975.

See also **Historiography of American Labor History**

H

H-2 PROGRAM

Named for a provision of the 1952 Immigration and Nationality Act (McCarran-Walter Act) that permitted the temporary admittance of foreign workers, the H-2 Program allows U.S. agricultural producers to import foreign laborers to work in the fields on a seasonal basis. Growers who wish to participate first must demonstrate that they are unable to hire sufficient domestic workers, as certified by the U.S. Department of Labor. Upon receiving certification, growers' organizations may contract directly with foreign governments to import workers on a temporary basis. The program requires that growers pay for workers' transportation to the work site and back (which can be recouped if the worker does not work the entire season), provide free housing for workers, pay a minimum wage called an Adverse Effect Wage Rate (AEWR) designed to ensure that imported labor does not depress wages for domestic workers in the same industry in a given region, and offer workers employment for at least three fourths of the workdays covered by the contract. Meanwhile, laborers who enter the United States via the program—sometimes called H-2 workers—must work where assigned by the sponsoring growers' association and are expected to return to their home countries once their contract expires. On the surface, the program appears to satisfy the needs of growers in need of a stable, but temporary, labor force; U.S. government officials hoping to stem the tide of illegal immigration; foreign governments seeking to supply their citizens with access to jobs; and workers hoping to avoid the pitfalls of immigrating illegally. In reality, however, the program has never fully pleased its participants.

The modern H-2 Program—also referred to as the H-2A Temporary Agricultural Worker Program to reflect the distinction between temporary agricultural workers and other temporary workers created by the 1986 Immigration Reform and Control Act (IRCA)—has its roots in the World War II experience. Wartime exigencies created labor shortages in many agricultural regions. In August 1942, Congress established the Mexican Labor Program in response to demands from western growers for access to more labor. The Bracero Program, as it came to be known, permitted the recruitment of Mexican citizens to work on U.S. farms on a temporary basis. All told, the wartime program—which lasted until 1947—brought nearly 220,000 Mexican workers to work in U.S. agriculture. In 1943, Congress created a similar British West Indies (BWI) Labor Program in response to pressure from eastern growers eager to obtain foreign workers. The program provided for the recruitment of workers from Jamaica, the Bahamas, the British Virgin Islands, and Barbados, but unlike braceros, BWI workers could work in industries other than agriculture. Most of the roughly 70,000 workers who came between 1943 and 1947, however, worked on farms from New England to Florida. In 1947, when unable to justify the program as a wartime necessity, federal authorities gave growers' organizations the authority to contract directly with foreign governments to import workers.

In 1951, citing a critical shortage of agricultural workers, Congress formally re-established the Mexican

Labor Program by passing what came to be known as Public Law 78. From 1951 to 1964, when abuses led Congress to bring the program to an end, hundreds of thousands of temporary Mexican workers came to the United States through the program each year. At the request of East Coast growers, Congress left BWI workers out of this program and instead permitted these workers through a provision in the 1952 Immigration and Nationality Act. Chapter 1, section 101, paragraph H, part 2—hence the shorthand of H-2—of the law allowed for temporary admission of aliens into the United States "to perform other temporary services or labor, if unemployed persons capable of performing such services or labor cannot be found in this country." Unlike Public Law 78, which provided for formal agreements between the U.S. and Mexican governments as to the conditions under which workers might be imported, this law provided broad approval for U.S. employers to import workers under conditions to be determined by the attorney general in consultation with the Department of Labor. Modeled after European "guest worker" programs established to allow for the temporary admission of workers for postwar reconstruction work, the H-2 provision codified a special class of nonimmigrant workers in U.S. immigration law for the first time.

U.S. agricultural interests, many of whom had been importing workers all along following the end of the wartime program, stepped up use of the imported labor after passage of the law. East Coast apple and Florida sugarcane growers, especially, came to depend less on native migrant workers—the traditional source of seasonal farm labor along the eastern seaboard—and more on imported Caribbean guest workers. Throughout the 1960s and 1970s, tens of thousands of Jamaicans and Bahamians came to the United States on temporary visas to pick apples and cut sugarcane. While the use of H-2 workers appeared to be declining in the 1970s and 1980s, agreements made in the early 1990s between U.S. growers and the Mexican government, which at first had refused to allow its citizens to participate in the program because of the abuses of the Bracero Program, once again expanded the program. In 1999, roughly 96% of the more than 28,000 visas issued for the program went to Mexican citizens. By this time, tobacco growers, who hired roughly 42% of the H-2 workers, had replaced sugarcane and apple growers as the greatest employer of imported foreign labor, although H-2 workers continue to be employed in a diverse number of agricultural enterprises, from picking strawberries in Florida to herding sheep in Wyoming.

Despite its increasing popularity, the H-2 Program has created a number of problems and encountered criticism from a number of sectors, even from those who are generally supportive of its work. Growers complain that the program's regulations, especially its Adverse Effect Wage Rate, create an undue burden and have called for reductions in government oversight. Farmworker advocates, meanwhile, have responded that growers have benefited from the program by both eliminating the need to offer higher wages to attract local workers and preventing the movement of H-2 workers from one farm to another, effectively working around the laws of supply and demand that guide labor markets. At the same time, workers have reported numerous instances of employer misconduct, including, among other things, failure to pay the AEWR, failure to provide livable housing, and violence against workers. At the same time, critics of illegal immigration have noted that, despite the program's promise of stemming the flood of immigrants entering the United States illegally, it has instead provided a conduit for increased illegal immigration. A 2001 study of H-2 workers in North Carolina, for example, found that upwards of 40% of workers left their assigned job sites before finishing their contracts, an act that made their very presence in the country illegal.

It is expected that use of the H-2 Program will grow further in the coming years. While H-2 workers make up only a small percentage of farmworkers at the present time, an increasing number of U.S. agricultural producers have expressed interest in participating in the program. In addition, an increasing number of elected officials have voiced support for expansion of the program as a way of providing a stable agricultural labor force without the pressure of illegal immigration. If the program expands, it is a certainty that temporary workers will become a permanent feature of American agricultural production.

EVAN P. BENNETT

References and Further Reading

Briggs, Vernon M. Jr. "Guestworker Programs: Lessons from the Past and Warnings for the Future." Center for Immigration Studies *Backgrounder*. March 2004.

Hahamovitch, Cindy. "Creating Perfect Immigrants: Guestworkers of the World in Historical Perspective." *Labor History* 44, no. 1 (2003): 69–94.

———. "'In America Life Is Given Away': Jamaican Farmworkers and the Making of Agricultural Immigration Policy." In *The Countryside in the Age of the Modern State: Political Histories of Rural America*, edited by Catherine McNichol Stock and Robert D. Johnston. Ithaca, NY: Cornell University Press, 2001, pp. 134–160.

Rasmussen, Wayne D. *A History of the Emergency Farm Labor Supply Program, 1943–1947*. Washington DC: U.S. Department of Agriculture, 1951.

Wasem, Ruth Ellen, and Geoffrey K. Colliver. "Immigration of Agricultural Guest Workers: Policy, Trends, and

Legislative Issues." Congressional Research Service Report RL30852, February 15, 2001, www.ncseonline. org/NLE/CRSreports/Agriculture/ag-102.cfm.
Yeoman, Barry. "Silence in the Fields." *Mother Jones* 26, no. 1 (2001): 40–47.

Statutes Cited

Immigration and Nationality Act, Act of June 27, 1952, 66 Stat. 163
Immigration Reform and Control Act of 1986, Act of Nov. 6. 1986, 100 Stat. 359

See also **McCarran-Walter Act (1952)**

HALEY, MARGARET (1861–1939)
Founder, Chicago Teachers' Federation

Margaret Angela Haley was the founding leader of the Chicago Teachers' Federation, the first teachers' association to affiliate with organized labor. As the Federation's paid business representative for 40 years, Haley organized over half of the city's women elementary teachers into a powerful political unit, while promoting teachers' activism around the country. An advocate for women teachers' rights as workers and for educational reform, Haley was both a charismatic local union leader and a nationally known educational and political activist.

Margaret Haley was born in Joliet, Illinois, to Irish immigrant parents. Her father had labored with other Irish workers in the construction of the Illinois and Michigan canal and was a member of the Knights of Labor and the Irish National Land League. Haley began teaching in rural Illinois schools as a teenager and later moved with her family to Chicago, where for 16 years she taught elementary school in the heart of the Stockyards district. During that time, she studied progressive education at the Illinois Normal School, where she read Henry George's *Progress and Poverty*; the Cook County Normal School, where she studied under the progressive teacher educator Francis Parker; and Catholic summer schools for teachers, where she learned about liberal Catholic social movements.

Haley began her political activism in a Catholic women's fraternal insurance organization, where she led a revolt against an authoritarian leader. In 1898, she joined the recently founded Chicago Teachers' Federation, which organized to advocate for improved pensions and salaries. The Federation represented only women elementary teachers, who comprised the great majority of the Chicago teaching force and who worked under a separate salary scale from predominately male administrative and secondary school staff. In 1900, Haley left the classroom to become the paid business representative, lobbyist, and administrative leader of the Federation, a position she held until her death in 1939. Catherine Goggin, a founding member of the Federation, shared leadership with Haley until her death in 1916.

Haley shaped the nascent women's organization into a powerful political force. Drawing on her observations of the Chicago labor movement, Haley argued that public school teachers had the right to shape their own working conditions, and she developed professional supports and education for teachers with representative councils, classes on progressive education, a regular news bulletin, and monthly membership meetings. Early on, Haley recognized that disenfranchised women teachers' demand for improved salaries carried little weight with the elected officials who controlled the public purse. Supported by John Fitzpatrick of the Chicago Federation of Labor (CFL), Haley convinced her membership that affiliation with labor was the only way that women teachers could gain political leverage. This was a difficult sell because it went against the public perception that women teachers were middle-class professionals who should be above the belligerent masculine politics of industrial labor unions. Furthermore, many male unionists suspected that women workers would dilute the labor movement. In 1902, the Federation affiliated with the CFL. For over a decade, the Chicago Teachers' Federation played an active role in the CFL, as well as the Illinois State Federation of Labor, the American Federation of Labor, and the Women's Trade Union League.

In 1916, Haley joined the Federation with seven other teachers' organizations to form a national unit, the American Federation of Teachers. As the oldest and largest of the groups, the Chicago Federation was designated Local 1. This affiliation was short-lived, however, when the Chicago Board of Education enacted a series of regulations that effectivly prohibited its teachers from membership in labor unions. In 1917, the Federation withdrew from all of its local, state, and national labor affiliations.

Haley's vision of teacher organization reached beyond bread-and-butter issues to a wide range of social and educational reforms. First among these was her advocacy of school finance reform. An advocate of Henry George's single tax, Haley argued for the enforcement of taxation laws on private corporations, and she lobbied against private interests' contributing to the curriculum, funding, and management of public schools. Haley's most celebrated accomplishment within the Federation was her investigation and successful legal challenge of corporate tax deductions that had lowered Chicago school board income so that teachers were denied a long-promised raise. Haley led the legal battle of the widely publicized "tax case" between 1900 and 1904, and it led her to work for other municipal reform movements including electoral reform, municipal ownership of basic utilities, and women's suffrage.

Haley argued that teacher unions should advocate for democratic practices in educational management and that women teacher union members should be key players in educational policy making. Haley traversed the country to promote political activism among the nation's predominately female teaching force, pressuring the powerful, administrator-dominated National Education Association to include the representation of women teachers. In her 1904 speech before that group, "Why Teachers Should Organize," she argued not only for the organization of protective unions for teachers, but also for an expanded notion of teacher professionalism that included the democratic participation of teachers in school management. Haley fought against powerful textbook companies' influence on the curriculum, objected to vocational education, which she believed narrowed the opportunities of working-class students, and led campaigns against what she called the "factoryization" of education through economic restrictions, standardized curriculum, and centralized leadership.

Haley was a charismatic leader and a dynamic speaker, who strategically played off of her appearance as a petite middle-aged Irish school marm in her campaigns for fiscal equity and teachers' rights. She was an expert at maneuvering high-profile political figures to support her cause. Yet she was also known for her stubbornness and inability to compromise, and she resisted changes in the city's teaching force, ignoring the needs of the increasing number of male and African-American teachers. The Federation declined in power and prestige through the 1920s and refused to join with the more inclusive Chicago Teachers' Union in 1937.

As a woman who played a central role in labor, civic, and educational politics, Haley was an extraordinary figure in American history. She is unique as a woman labor leader who made the unprecedented link between progressive education and teachers' working conditions, arguing that the two were interdependent.

KATE ROUSMANIERE

References and Further Reading

Reid, Robert L., ed. *Battleground: The Autobiography of Margaret A. Haley*. Urbana: University of Illinois Press, 1982.

Rousmaniere, Kate. *Citizen Teacher: The Life and Leadership of Margaret Haley*. Albany, NY: SUNY Press, 2005.

See also **Chicago Teachers' Federation**

HAMILTON, ALICE (FEBRUARY 27, 1869–SEPTEMBER 22, 1970)
Physician

A physician and leading expert in the field of industrial toxicology, the study of work-related illnesses and the dangerous effects of industrial metals and chemical compounds on workers, Alice Hamilton became one of the most important advocates for federal regulation of the workplace for workers' health and safety. Her studies of lead poisoning in enamel workers, carbon monoxide poisoning in steelworkers, mercury poisoning in hatters, and "dead fingers" syndrome among laborers using jackhammers raised awareness and led to major improvements in the work environment that saved countless lives. Her death in 1970 at the age of 101 came just three months before the passage of the Occupational Safety and Health Act (OSHA).

Hamilton was also a social activist for women's and workers' rights, and an internationalist who worked for peace and human rights on a global scale. Her progressive views were shaped by her experiences as a resident of Hull-House, the social settlement founded by Jane Addams and where Hamilton was a resident for four decades.

Born in New York City to Montgomery Hamilton and Gertrude (Pond) Hamilton, the second of four daughters, she was raised in her father's hometown of Fort Wayne, Indiana, where Hamiltons had been founders. Her father, a Princeton graduate unsuccessful in business, was an intellectual who provided his daughters with opportunities for critical thinking and delved into theological and philosophical subjects. Her mother was less analytical but passionate about issues of social justice, speaking out against the lynching of African-Americans, child labor, and cruelty to prisoners. Willing to think outside Victorian conventions, she impressed upon Alice her belief that every woman had a right to privacy. Alice and her sisters were tutored at home in languages, history, and literature, and received a superior education.

Following Hamilton tradition, the four sisters attended Miss Porter's School in Framington, Connecticut. Returning to Indiana, and to the reality that she would need to be self-supporting, her biographer Barbara Sicherman writes that Hamilton selected medicine because it was the only profession open to women that would allow her to be both independent and useful. Lacking a rigorous science background, Hamilton was tutored in physics and math before she entered Fort Wayne College of Medicine, which prepared her for study at the University of Michigan. She interned at hospitals in Minneapolis and Boston (1893–1894) and then returned to Ann Arbor in 1895 to assist in the bacteriology laboratory of her former professor, F. G. Novy. Hamilton next studied in Leipzig and Munich. She did postgraduate work at Johns Hopkins Medical School.

In the fall of 1897, she became a professor of pathology at the Woman's Medical School at Northwestern University in Chicago and also a resident at Hull-House. The settlement's involvement with the antisweatshop movement radicalized her. "At Hull-House one got into the labor movement as a matter of course, without realizing how or when," Hamilton explained (*Exploring the Dangerous Trades*, p. 80). Soon she was volunteering for the early morning [strike] picket "because the police were much less in evidence then" and she was "in mortal fear" of being dragged about if arrested (p. 82). She began to investigate the work and living conditions in the neighborhood realizing that labor unions were so caught up in efforts to safeguard wages that nothing was being done about industrial hygiene.

In 1902, she accepted a position at the new Memorial Institute for Infectious Diseases in Chicago. Hamilton adapted the Hull-House method of social investigation to her interest in public health issues. Just as Florence Kelley had investigated the sweatshop system and mapped household wages in the neighborhood, Hamilton investigated the incidents of typhoid and tuberculosis. She wrote articles and gave popular lectures to disseminate her findings and soon was appointed to public health committees.

In 1908, Hamilton was appointed to the Illinois Commission on Occupational Diseases, the first state to have such a commission. Hamilton's findings, published in 1910, led to Illinois establishing laws requiring job-related safety measures. As a result, the U.S. Bureau of Labor asked Hamilton to do a federal survey of occupational diseases in 1911. Hamilton continued her investigations for the bureau, but maintained her residency at Hull-House, and her independence. She became a pacifist and joined Jane Addams in the 1915 Women's Peace Conference at The Hague. Both she and Addams found time just 10 days prior to their journey abroad to testify at hearings in Springfield, Illinois, on child labor.

In 1919, Hamilton became an assistant professor of industrial medicine at Harvard University Medical School, the first woman appointed to its faculty. She asked for a six-month annual contract so she could maintain her connections with Hull-House and the freedom to pursue her own work. Hamilton began to publicize the dangers of the new industrial poisons that she discovered as new processes proliferated following World War I. Her book *Industrial Poisons in the United States* (1925) was the first American text on the subject and established her as one of the two leading authorities in the world. She instigated the U.S. surgeon general to call national conferences on tetraethyl lead (1925) and radium (1928).

Deeply disturbed by the conservative backlash in the 1920s, Hamilton protested the treatment of aliens and restrictive immigration laws. She joined the campaign to obtain commutation of the death sentence for Sacco and Vanzetti.

After her retirement from Harvard in 1935, Hamilton became a consultant in the Division of Labor Standards of the Department of Labor. In 1943, she wrote her autobiography, *Exploring the Dangerous Trades*. She served as president of the National Consumers' League (1944–1949) and remained a respected advisor to Hull-House. As an anti-Cold War liberal protesting the infringements on civil liberties at home, she was considered "dangerous" by the House Un-American Activities Committee in 1949. The FBI kept an active file on Alice Hamilton through the 1960s; she protested the war in Vietnam in 1963.

RIMA LUNIN SCHULTZ

Selected Works

Exploring the Dangerous Trades (1943)
Industrial Poisons in the United States (1925)
Industrial Toxicology (1934; revised edition 1949)
The International Congress of Women and Its Results, with Jane Addams and Emily Balch (1916)

References and Further Reading

Barbara Sicherman. *Alice Hamilton: A Life in Letters* (1984).
———. "Hamilton, Alice." In *Women Building Chicago 1790–1990: A Biographical Dictionary*, edited by Rima Lunin Schultz and Adele Hast. Bloomington: Indiana University Press, 2001.
———. "Working It Out: Gender, Profession, and Reform in the Progressive Era." In *Gender, Class, Race, and Reform in the Progressive Era*, edited by Noralee Frankel and Nancy S. Dye. Lexington: University Press of Kentucky, 1991, pp. 127–147.

HAPGOOD, POWERS (1899–1949)
Socialist Party Activist

Powers Hapgood was an important figure in the industrial union movement and the Socialist Party who won widespread recognition as a crusader for industrial democracy, civil liberties, and social justice during the first half of the twentieth century. His political odyssey was representative of an important historical relationship: connections between reform-minded elements of the middle class and the working class that provided vital support for the growth of the labor movement during the Progressive Era and the New Deal. Hapgood also wrestled with many of the key issues that have historically challenged the American labor movement and was a rare public voice that questioned the direction of industrial unionism and liberal politics at the outset of the Cold War.

Born into one of the Progressive Era's most prominent liberal families (his uncles were leading muckraking journalists and his father ran an Indiana company that won widespread praise as a model of industrial democracy and workers' control), Powers Hapgood was deeply influenced by familial commitments to service, sacrifice, and social responsibility. Following graduation from Harvard in 1920, he worked in coal mines, where he encountered class-conscious workers with an almost religious faith in their union, the United Mine Workers of America (UMWA), and a work culture rooted in values of self-reliance and solidarity that he found lacking within the middle class. He also discovered a mentor in John Brophy, a Pennsylvania UMWA leader whose advocacy of a "larger program" for the union based on public ownership of the mines, aggressive organizing, and workers education became the foundation for Hapgood's own brand of labor politics. Hapgood's prominent role in a bitter 1922 miners' strike in western Pennsylvania won him respect from workers and public recognition from liberals. It also led to his becoming a trusted interpreter of working-class struggles to middle-class audiences.

However, Hapgood's hopes of rising to a position of leadership in the union were dashed following the strike when he openly challenged the powerful UMWA president, John L. Lewis. Lewis contended that as a perpetually besieged institution, unions could not afford the luxury of democracy, while Hapgood insisted that democratic unionism was essential to provide workers the opportunity for civic participation and present industrial democracy as a legitimate alternative to corporate capitalism. This conviction, fundamental to Hapgood's vision for the labor movement, led him to manage John Brophy's unsuccessful bid for the UMWA presidency in 1926. In retaliation, John L. Lewis had Hapgood expelled from the union.

Hapgood spent the next decade on the political margins. Recruited to join the Communist Party (CP), he rejected its invitation because he doubted the party's democratic commitments. Instead, he became a leader within the Socialist Party but in contrast to many anti-Communist leftists, continued to defend the CP's legitimacy within the labor movement. Hapgood persisted in his quest to nurture industrial democracy by supporting insurgent efforts against John L. Lewis, seeking to extend workers' control within his father's company and aiding an interracial tenant farmers union in the southern United States. Demoralized by the failures of these efforts, Hapgood decided to submerge his qualms about centralized, top-down labor leadership and became one of the first three organizers hired by John L. Lewis in 1935 to help direct the Committee for Industrial Organization's (CIO) efforts to organize workers in America's mass production industries.

Hapgood emerged as one of Lewis's most trusted lieutenants, joining with other CIO organizers to provide critical strategic support that helped rubber workers in Akron, Ohio, and auto workers in Flint, Michigan, win some of the fledgling organization's most significant victories over powerful corporate opposition. Yet by the beginning of World War II, Hapgood feared that the democratic spirit of industrial unionism was being blunted by the growing centralization of union leadership and the new legalistic system that was emerging to govern industrial relations. In a personal effort to reclaim the CIO's early promise, Hapgood, now serving as a union leader in Indiana, aggressively sought to organize African-American workers and pressed the labor movement to combat discrimination within its own ranks. He also foresaw that Cold War-inspired attacks on the Communist Party would have a chilling effect on liberal politics and fought for the rights of Communists, a stance that eventually cost him his job, with a CIO bent on purging its ranks of CP-leaning unions.

Hapgood's premature death in 1949 cut short his efforts to recast labor and liberalism. His career remains significant, however, as an example of the social empathy and personal commitment that made cross-class alliances such a powerful political force during the first half of the twentieth century.

ROBERT BUSSEL

References and Further Reading

Bussel, Robert. *From Harvard to the Ranks of Labor: Powers Hapgood and the American Working Class*. University Park: Penn State Press, 1999.

———. "'A Love of Unionism and Industrial Democracy': Rose Pesotta, Powers Hapgood, and the Industrial Union Movement, 1933–1949." *Labor History* 38, nos. 2–3 (Spring-Summer 1997): 203–229.

See also **Brophy, John; United Mine Workers of America**

HARRINGTON, MICHAEL (1928–1989)
Socialist Intellectual

Michael Harrington was the best-known American socialist of his generation, and as such was one of the few prominent intellectuals in the 1960s, 1970s, and 1980s to identify himself as a strong supporter of the labor movement.

Harrington was born in St. Louis on February 24, 1928, into a staunchly Democratic, middle-class Irish-Catholic family. He was educated in the city's parochial schools and its elite Jesuit-run St. Louis University High, before going off for higher education at Holy Cross College in Worcester, Massachusetts, at the age of 16. He graduated from Holy Cross three years later, enrolling for a year in Yale Law School (where he made law review but decided against a career as a lawyer). In 1948–1949, he attended the University of Chicago, where he received his master's degree in English. He moved to New York City at the end of 1949, intending to become a writer.

With the outbreak of the Korean War in the summer of 1950, Harrington's life underwent a dramatic transformation. A crisis of faith and conscience led him in 1951 to join the radical pacifist Catholic Worker movement, a group founded and led by Dorothy Day. Harrington spent the next two years living amongst and caring for the poor in the Worker's "House of Hospitality" on New York's Lower East Side.

In time, Harrington grew disenchanted with the Catholic Worker's other-worldliness, feeling that the movement was putting the spiritual perfection of its adherents before the larger goal of changing society for the better. As his Catholicism waned, he was drawn to socialist doctrine, joining the Young People's Socialist League (YPSL) in 1952 and helping found the even more radical Young Socialist League (YSL) in 1954, which functioned as the youth affiliate of Max Shachtman's Independent Socialist League

(ISL). He worked for a time as executive secretary of the Workers Defense League (WDL), a left-wing legal advocacy organization, but increasingly supported himself as a freelance writer, contributing frequently to publications like *Dissent*, *Commentary*, and *Commonweal* magazines.

For much of the 1950s, Harrington's political activities were bound by the musty confines of radical sectarianism. In the later years of the decade, however, he was drawn into some of the early civil rights protests through his association with the black radical activist Bayard Rustin. In 1959, the ISL merged with the Socialist Party (SP)/Social Democratic Federation led by Norman Thomas, and the following year Harrington became editor of the SP's newspaper, *New America*. He also coedited a collection of essays with radical journalist Paul Jacobs on the contemporary labor movement, *Labor in a Free Society*, published in 1959, his first book.

It was Harrington's second book, *The Other America: Poverty in the United States*, published in 1962 by Macmillan, that would make him famous as "the man who discovered poverty." Making extensive use of U.S. Census data, Harrington argued in *The Other America* that a quarter to a third of the American population lived below the officially defined poverty level. An expanding economy was not enough, Harrington believed, to lift this "other America" out of poverty, for they were bound to their condition by a "culture of poverty." The poor were "people who lack education and skill, who have bad health, poor housing, low levels of aspiration and high levels of mental distress.... Each disability is the more intense because it exists within a web of disabilities." The book, which went on to sell over a million copies, helped inspire President Lyndon Johnson's War on Poverty. Harrington was invited to take part in some of the early strategy sessions in Washington to draw up the legislation that would become the Economic Opportunity Act of 1964.

In the 1960s, Harrington forged ties with leading figures in the labor movement, including United Auto Workers president Walter Reuther. He also worked closely with leading civil rights activists, including Martin Luther King Jr., and would help with the planning for King's Poor People's March on Washington in 1968, before King's assassination.

Harrington's political dream was to bring together a great coalition of labor, the poor, and civil rights, liberal, and student activists that he would refer to as "the left wing of the possible." But this dream was shattered by the explosive conflicts over the war in Vietnam and racial separatism of the later 1960s. Younger left-wing activists were dismayed by

Harrington's reluctance to break with the Johnson White House on the issue of the war in Vietnam. And they were mystified by his allegiance to the labor movement, discredited in their eyes by AFL-CIO president George Meany's belligerently prowar views. Harrington's support in 1968 for the United Federation of Teachers in the conflict over community control of schools in New York's Ocean Hill-Brownsville school district alienated many younger activists and intellectuals whom he looked to as natural allies.

Harrington also found himself increasingly at odds with many of his SP comrades, who reacted to the controversies of the 1960s by turning rightward, some of them becoming influential figures within the neo-conservative movement. When the Socialist Party refused to back George McGovern against Richard Nixon in the 1972 presidential campaign, Harrington decided he could no longer remain a member of the party; the following year he led a split which resulted in the founding of the Democratic Socialist Organizing Committee (DSOC), with Harrington as its chair.

DSOC and its successor organization, Democratic Socialists of America (DSA), enjoyed modest successes in the 1970s and 1980s, growing to a peak of about 5,000 members and enjoying close ties with the UAW and other liberally inclined unions. Harrington continued to publish extensively (writing 16 books on political topics before his death in 1989) and enjoyed a reputation as an eloquent public speaker. He also joined the political science department at Queens College and became a member of its American Federation of Teachers local.

MAURICE ISSERMAN

References and Further Reading

Harrington, Michael. *Fragments of the Century*. New York: Saturday Review Press, 1973.
Isserman, Maurice. *The Other American: The Life of Michael Harrington*. New York: Public Affairs Press, 2000.

HARVARD UNION OF CLERICAL AND TECHNICAL WORKERS

The Harvard Union of Clerical and Technical Workers (HUCTW), organized in 1988, represents 4,800 workers at Harvard University. The union's members are 70% women, and HUCTW has developed what its leaders call a "feminine model" of unionism. This model takes the union to be a vehicle not only for winning economic gains, but for building a community at work and promoting worker participation in a wide variety of workplace decisions. It pursues these goals through direct, person-to-person contact among members and a program of labor-management cooperation or "jointness" with the university administration.

Organizing the Union, 1973–1988

HUCTW won legal recognition in 1988 after an organizing drive that lasted nearly 15 years and faced strong opposition from Harvard. Sympathetically chronicled in works by the journalist John Hoerr and the economist Richard W. Hurd, the drive began in 1973 among research assistants in the Harvard Medical Area, which comprises Harvard Medical School and the Harvard School of Public Health. The drive was fueled by young, female workers frustrated by sexist treatment, a lack of career mobility, and low pay. Many workers, inspired by the women's movement, saw the union drive as an expression of feminism. The campaign took place alongside a wave of union organizing among women office workers and public-sector workers during the 1970s and 1980s.

Led by the research assistants Leslie Sullivan and Kristine Rondeau, both of whom eventually left their lab jobs to work as full-time organizers, the Medical Area workers held two unsuccessful union elections in 1977 and 1981. After the 1981 election, the National Labor Relations Board (NLRB), at Harvard's behest, ruled that the Medical Area was not an appropriate bargaining unit and that the workers needed to organize all of the university's 3,500 clerical and technical workers—a task considered nearly impossible. Rondeau launched a universitywide organizing drive in 1984, and the union won the election on May 17, 1988, in a close vote of 1,530 to 1,486. Harvard recognized HUCTW in November 1988 after an unsuccessful NLRB challenge.

The organizing drive was a grassroots affair that involved workers, students, and faculty. On campus, HUCTW was known for its creativity and sense of humor. Workers organized actions such as Hollywood-style bus tours of administrators' homes, and rallies featured parodic songs by the union's singing group, the Pipets.

Harvard conducted sophisticated anti-union campaigns before each election, using captive-audience meetings, one-on-one meetings between workers and supervisors, and a barrage of anti-union letters. Harvard's president, Derek Bok, a labor law scholar considered sympathetic to unions, sent anti-union letters to every worker in 1977 and 1988. During the 1981

Washington School for Secretaries. Students at Washington School for Secretaries at typewriters. Library of Congress, Prints & Photographs Division, Theodor Horydczak Collection [LC-H824-T-1215-003].

election, Harvard stationed armed guards around the voting site.

HUCTW's national affiliation changed twice during the organizing drive. In 1974, it affiliated with the industrial union District 65 because of its interest in women workers and its willingness to let the Harvard workers direct their own drive. District 65 affiliated with the United Automobile Workers (UAW) in 1979, and the organizers developed conflicts with that union's organizing model. They ran the campaign independently from 1984 to 1987, when they affiliated with the American Federation of State, County, and Municipal Employees (AFSCME).

"Women's Way of Organizing"

HUCTW developed an unusual organizing philosophy, which Rondeau has since promoted as "women's way of organizing." Whereas most unions conduct rapid organizing drives to limit the development of employers' anti-union campaigns, HUCTW slowly met workers one-on-one and focused on building relationships in the workplace. They used no literature, believing that it could become an easy but ineffective substitute for person-to-person contact. Organizers did not ask workers to sign union cards until the last stages of the campaign, maintaining that card signing did not build commitment to the union but should be the culmination of an organizing process that developed that commitment. Relationship building was not simply a tactic; organizers believed that women wanted a community at work and that creating one should be a central function of a union. This unorthodox approach caused the 1984 break with the UAW. By contrast, it impressed AFSCME, which later sent HUCTW staff to organize workers nationwide.

HUCTW's leaders maintained that organizing around specific concerns—low pay, sexist treatment, or anything else—invited the employer to quickly fix those problems to defuse the organizing effort. Instead, HUCTW organized around the idea that workers should be able to participate in decision making about their jobs. By "participation," HUCTW's leaders meant labor-management cooperation in determining workplace policies. Their philosophy of "jointness" or "codetermination" between workers and management found expression in an early slogan, "It's not anti-Harvard to be pro-union." Union leaders maintained that they wanted Harvard to function well and that they could help it do so if they had an institutional voice. According to HUCTW, there was no necessary opposition of interests between workers and management.

During the drive, the workers' energy and Harvard's hostility partially obscured the union leaders' commitment to labor-management cooperation. Many saw the union as jocularly confrontational because its public actions freely poked fun at Harvard. However, organizers did not promote anger at Harvard or position the union as the university's opponent.

HUCTW's leaders maintained that their nonoppositional approach came from the natural inclinations of women workers, who they believed were averse to aggression and conflict. The union's philosophy of "jointness" also had roots in the UAW, whose leadership had helped make labor-management cooperation the ascendant model in the automobile industry during the 1980s.

A minority of HUCTW members has consistently opposed jointness, however, arguing that it reflects not gender difference but a conciliatory political orientation. These members have maintained that women workers as much as men have conflicts with employers that are based on their opposing interests. They have run opposition candidates in union elections, winning up to 40% of the vote.

Jointness has proved contentious not only within HUCTW but in the U.S. labor movement as a whole. HUCTW, like the leadership of the UAW, has occupied a place at one end of a national debate about whether labor-management co-operation is a strategy for worker empowerment or a cooptive program for cultivating consent in the workplace. Elsewhere in the labor movement, jointness gave rise to mass rank-and-file opposition, most notably the 1980s New Directions movement within the UAW.

Jointness in Action, 1989–2004

HUCTW's contracts have produced strong gains in pay and benefits, with the average member salary rising from $20,000 in 1989 to nearly $36,000 in 2004, and the top of the pay scale reaching above $60,000 in 2004. HUCTW has also won strong family-oriented benefits, including generous maternity and paternity leave, subsidies for child care and after-school enrichment, domestic partner benefits, and flexible scheduling.

HUCTW's commitment to jointness has made its accomplishments dependent on the attitudes and interests of administrators. Between 1989 and 1991, Bok chose the Harvard economist John Dunlop to oversee relations with HUCTW. Dunlop, an architect of postwar industrial relations in the United States, had become an advocate of labor-management cooperation, which he believed could contain industrial conflicts that might otherwise destabilize the U.S. economy. Dunlop and Rondeau led the 1989 negotiations that produced HUCTW's unusual first contract. The contract provided significant economic gains, but in a departure from traditional labor practice, did not contain a grievance procedure, job classifications, seniority provisions, or rules governing transfers, promotions, or layoffs. HUCTW's leaders explained that they did not want a workplace governed by rigid rules, but one in which workers and managers creatively solved problems using moral reasoning.

The contract replaced the traditional grievance procedure with a "problem-solving procedure" in which workers first aimed to resolve conflicts with their supervisors and, failing that, turned to labor-management "problem-solving teams" to negotiate solutions. The contract also created joint councils and committees to discuss policy issues on an ongoing basis. HUCTW leaders argued that the problem-solving process and joint bodies allowed workers to address a broader range of issues than would a grievance procedure, which is designed to enforce only written contract provisions. The sociologist Susan C. Eaton argued in 1996 that joint processes helped HUCTW members change their relationships with supervisors, faculty, and students. However, she suggested that they were not effective at changing workplace policies. At best, they let workers decide how to implement managerial objectives.

The labor-management relationship ruptured in 1991, when Bok resigned and Neil Rudenstine became president. Rudenstine's administration took an adversarial stance toward HUCTW; in response, the union became more oppositional. Between 1992 and 1998, a large minority of joint councils did not function because of managerial hostility. HUCTW negotiated three contracts amid protracted conflicts, most significantly a successful fight from 1995 to 1997 to defend part-time workers' health benefits. The union also won financial support and internal hiring preferences for laid-off workers. In retrospect, HUCTW leaders express pride in their victories but lament the existence of conflict and describe this period as unproductive.

In 1999, a different group of administrators assumed responsibility for relations with HUCTW, and both sides renounced labor-management conflict. In 1999, HUCTW won membership for 1,000 workers whom Harvard had deliberately misclassified as contingent or managerial employees. Contracts ratified in 2001 and 2004 created new training and education programs to provide job skills and liberal arts education during work time. The contracts also created "New Work Systems at Harvard," a project to restructure jobs much as the "team concept" restructured auto assembly beginning in the 1970s. The project aims to train workers in a variety of skills and organize them into teams that function with minimal managerial supervision. The team concept, associated with the idea of jointness, has been hotly debated in the labor movement since the 1970s. HUCTW leaders maintain that teams give workers independence; New Directions members argued that they were co-optive.

In addition to its contract campaigns, HUCTW conducts a high level of internal organizing using one-on-one meetings. In 2004, women constituted 14 of HUCTW's 15 executive board members and three quarters of its 190 area representatives and joint council members. HUCTW staff have also successfully organized, and represent, workers at the University of Massachusetts-Memorial Hospital in Worcester, Massachusetts, and are organizing clerical and technical workers at Tufts University.

AMY C. OFFNER

References and Further Reading

Eaton, Susan C. "'The Customer Is Always Interesting': Unionized Harvard Clericals Renegotiate Work Relationships." In *Working in the Service Society*, edited by Cameron Lynne Macdonald and Carmen Sirianni. Philadelphia: Temple University Press, 1996, pp. 291–332.

Hoerr, John. *We Can't Eat Prestige: The Women Who Organized Harvard*. Philadelphia: Temple University Press, 1997.

Hurd, Richard W. "Organizing and Representing Clerical Workers: The Harvard Model." In *Women and Unions: Forging a Partnership*, edited by Dorothy Sue Cobble. Ithaca, NY: ILR Press, 1993, pp. 316–336.

Parker, Mike. "Industrial Relations Myth and Shop-Floor Reality: The 'Team Concept' in the Auto Industry." In *Industrial Democracy in America: The Ambiguous Promise*, edited by Nelson Lichtenstein and Howell John Harris. New York and Cambridge, England: Woodrow Wilson Center Press and Cambridge University Press, 1993, pp. 249–274.

See also **American Federation of State, County, and Municipal Employees (AFSCME); Clerical Work and Office Work; Coalition of Labor Union Women; Dunlop Commission; Gender; Industrial Democracy**

HAWAII

Known to Portuguese as *terra nova*, "new land," or Chinese as *tan heung shan*, "the fragrant sandalwood hills," workers migrated to the islands of Hawaii throughout the nineteenth and twentieth centuries in search of new possibilities. Work on the sugar plantations and other industries in Hawaii undoubtedly provided opportunities for many immigrants, but for all, the work was long, arduous, and poorly paid. Indeed, the gap between working-class expectation and experience frames much of the restive history of labor in Hawaii. Over the last two hundred years, Hawaii's working class has negotiated the rapid transition between indigenous community, colonial plantation economy, transpacific hub for people and commodities, and destination for tropical tourism.

The Emerging Plantation Economy

Prior to contact with European and American traders, work and production in the Hawaiian Islands were largely self-sufficient and shaped by kin networks and the powerful Polynesian monarchy. Migrating north from the Marquesas Islands to Hawaii between 500 AD to 700 AD, Polynesians imported crops like taro, sweet potatoes, and most notably, sugarcane. Along with these important food crops, settlers also brought sophisticated techniques of cultivation and technologies for oceanic transportation. Early anthropological accounts suggest the centrality of agricultural life. The significant imprint of agricultural work, for example, was evident in the social stratification, the geographic dispersal of villages, and even the naming of children. Hawaiians also maintained a vast knowledge of trade routes in the Pacific Ocean, exchanging goods like sandalwood throughout Oceania.

Contact with North America and Europe had significant implications for the conduct of trade, work, and production in Hawaii. Europeans' "discovery" of the islands in 1778 instantly established Hawaii as an important resupply point for Pacific whaling vessels. In turn, Polynesian natives "discovered" new markets for their wares, which led to a boom in the sandalwood trade to Asia. Despite these changes, the native economy remained largely intact for much of the late eighteenth and early nineteenth centuries under indigenous control. The establishment of Hawaii's first sugar plantation, in Koloa, Kauai, and the advent of large-scale private land ownership, known as the "Great *Mahele*" in 1848, transformed the social and economic conditions of Hawaii. For agricultural capitalists, like Koloa's operator William Hooper and his financiers, Ladd and Company, sugarcane was "to serve as an entering wedge" that would split the indigenous economy, opening the way for modern agricultural capitalism. The reticence or open resistance of the *maka'aianana*, or planter/worker class, to new systems of work and labor was evident in the consistent complaints of managers about native indolence, laziness, or irregular attendance in the fields. Increasingly unsatisfied, workers staged the first labor strike in 1841 over low wages and payment methods. Given the inconsistent labor supply, landowners' lack of expertise, and insufficient capital investment, early attempts to establish large-scale sugar production were quite unsuccessful, but they foreshadowed the future to come.

Unable to satisfy their enormous appetite for labor in the islands, sugar planters looked abroad for workers. Thousands of contract laborers from China arrived in 1852 under the newly established Master's and Servant's Act. When the global flow of coolie laborers dwindled, groups like the Planter's Labor and Supply Company, founded in 1882 and the predecessor to the Hawaiian Sugar Planters' Association, began to recruit heavily in Japan. Pushed off their land by conflict, drawn by the exaggerated promises of labor recruiters, and following previously established networks of migration, contract laborers believed Hawaii held promise. The migration of workers eventually brought nearly 46,000 Chinese and 180,000 Japanese to the islands. These two foundational populations would later be supplemented by 66,000 Filipinos, as well as workers from Portugal, Norway, Sweden, and Korea. The importation of labor and the subsequent explosion of sugar production in the islands, from 3 million pounds in 1850 to 24 million pounds in 1875, established Hawaii as a significant hub in the network of oceanic trade and helped cement the United States' presence in the Pacific.

Life on the Plantation

Hawaii's new residents struggled to create opportunity and develop a sense of community, despite the strenuous conditions of life in plantation work camps. Workdays in the sugarcane fields were long and difficult. Few tasks on the plantation were mechanized, and workers were strictly supervised by foremen, known as *lunas*, from the early morning to around 8:00 p.m. Plantations were largely a male homosocial world, until the turn of the century when contract laborers increasingly came to Hawaii as permanent settlers rather than sojourners. After *pau hana*, "quitting time," workers participated in community organizations, familial groups, and formed mutual aid societies, like the Japanese *tanomoshi*. Immigrants also

maintained many of their cultural practices, celebrating important religious and national holidays or preparing traditional foods.

To maintain order and ensure productivity on plantations, landowners employed a variety of methods, ranging from benevolent paternalism to heavy-handed repression. Nearly all aspects of the Hawaiian economy were consolidated within the hands of five companies, commonly referred to as the Big Five, which allowed landowners a tremendous degree of control in the islands. Moreover, plantation owners often insisted on racial segregation in work camps to discourage interracial solidarity. Planters offered workers free housing, medical care, and recreation, a package of benefits known as the perquisite system. In exchange, bosses demanded obedience to the plantation system, high productivity, and justified paying low wages. When these perquisites failed to satisfy workers' demands, plantation owners openly relied upon violence. Instances of physical abuse were not uncommon, and organized protests were often violently suppressed, as in the case of the lynching of a Japanese worker in 1899, the mass arrest of Filipino strike organizers in 1924, or the infamous Hilo Massacre in 1938, when police shot 50 unarmed demonstrating workers.

Resistance and Organization

Throughout the late nineteenth and early twentieth centuries, workers in Hawaii acted to improve the difficult conditions of plantation life, though often in hidden and unorganized ways. Much to the chagrin of their supervisors, fieldworkers regularly attempted to assert control over their work schedules through diffuse methods like absenteeism and foot dragging. Workers also endowed cultural practices like singing, poetry, and language with political meaning. Japanese work songs, known as *hole hole bushi*, or the common language among fieldworkers, pidgin, provided a medium for messages of working-class resistance and often reflected experiences of hardship and race and gender discrimination. Instances of organized resistance did occur. Chinese workers staged several work stoppages in 1891 and 1899, and Japanese workers conducted large-scale labor actions involving more than one thousand strikers in 1900, 1906, and 1909. Ethnic and racial divisions, however, consistently proved to be the greatest roadblock to successful labor organizing. The first multiplantation strike on the island of Oahu in 1920 united more than 12,000 Japanese, Chinese, and Filipino workers within the Hawaii Laborers' Association and suggested the power of interracial unity. But after five months, the strike came to an end due to the unwavering strength of plantation owners and a growing racial schism between the Japanese and Filipino leadership.

For Hawaii's workers, the 1930s and 1940s marked the beginning of successful long-term labor organizing. In 1935, after carefully monitoring the spread of industrial unionism along the Pacific coast of the United States, a group of longshoremen in Honolulu applied for a charter to the International Longshoremen's Association, the progenitor of the International Longshore and Warehouse Union (ILWU). In 1937, backed by the organizing strength and experience of the ILWU, fieldworkers on sugarcane and pineapple plantations fought for union recognition. Despite the impediment of World War II, the union grew rapidly during the 1940s and eventually represented more than 30,000 agricultural workers by 1946. The distinctiveness of labor and the working-class relations in Hawaii was evident throughout the ILWU's organizing campaign. The ILWU relied upon its prior experience organizing multi-ethnic working-class communities and workers. In addition to its traditional repertoire of tactics, in preparation for the "Great Sugar Strike" in August of 1946, the union developed a number of distinct strategies, such as organizing and lobbying in workers' native communities in the Philippines and Japan and forming multinational and global alliances with other sugar workers. By the end of the decade, the ILWU's campaign to organize Hawaii had been so successful that by some accounts, nearly one in eight working Hawaiians were represented by the union.

The 1940s also marked the beginning of labor's enduring impact on the islands' politics. For the first 40 years of territorial governance, the Big Five and a landed elite held firm control over Hawaiian politics. Political enfranchisement, public education, and most notably, the new power of organized labor began to undercut this oligarchy. Under pressure from labor unions, the National Labor Relations Board (NLRB) recognized the right of many plantation workers in the territory to organize unions in 1945. Originally excluded from this decision, fieldworkers won the right to collectively bargain later that year when the ILWU secured passage of the "Little Wagner Act," the first recognition of its kind in the United States. With momentum from these victories and backed by the power of labor unions, the Democratic Party swept statewide elections in 1954, instituting a progressive tax system in 1957, a sweeping land reform bill in 1959, and later, significant environmental protections and a comprehensive health insurance plan. Legislation in 1970 allowed public employees to collectively bargain, opening the door for groups like the Hawaiian School Teachers Association, the American Federation of State, County, and Municipal Employees (AFSCME), and the Hawaiian Nurses Association.

Challenges to Hawaiian Labor

Despite organized labor's overwhelming political successes, however, charges of a communist conspiracy stunted the power of organized labor and particularly the ILWU. Throughout the 1950s, the Federal Bureau of Investigation conducted numerous interviews with labor activists, and 66 residents were called before the House Un-American Activities Committee (HUAC) in April 1950. Many refused to testify and were indicted for contempt, earning them the title "the reluctant 39." When several ILWU members, namely Ichiro Izuka and Jack Kawano, publicly broke with the Union and provided federal investigators with details about communist activities in the islands, anticommunist groups, such as Imua, leveled strident claims against labor activists like Jack Hall, Bob McElrath, David Thompson, Levi Kealoha, and Tadashi Ogawa. In the most infamous incident, seven labor leaders were convicted and imprisoned for several months under provisions of the Smith Act for conspiring to teach the overthrow of the U.S. government. Despite the strength and vigor of the "red hunt" in the islands, the memory of labor's strike victories in the late 1940s and more recently in 1951 and 1952 remained strong. Working-class Hawaiians demonstrated their support for Hall and others, staging protests and work stoppages. In 1958, anticommunist organizations lost support and faded from public politics.

Since 1950, tourism has been the most dominant force of change for Hawaii's working class. Prompted by local calls for economic diversification and fueled by low-cost air travel, service sector jobs exploded in the late 1950s and 1960s. Meanwhile, union jobs in the sugar industry declined precipitously, from a peak in 1940 of 35,000 jobs to just 17,000 in 1957. Organized labor struggled to keep apace with rapid economic change. Several jurisdictional disputes in the grocery and retail sectors broke out between the ILWU and AFL-CIO in 1958 and 1959. To lessen the impact of the decline in sugarcane, unions sponsored job-training programs to help displaced workers transition from plantation work to the burgeoning tourist industry. Many workers have found new jobs in the service industry, but the struggle for union control has been difficult. In December 1970, ILWU workers organized the longest strike of hotel workers, 75 days. Other unions, such as Local 5 of the Hotel Workers' union (Hotel Employees and Restaurant Employees, HERE), have confronted large hotel chains' reliance upon nonunion labor, leading work stoppages in 1952, 1966, and a large strike of 7,500 workers in 1990.

Although tourism has largely replaced the agricultural economy, the early experience of plantation work has left an indelible mark upon the islands. Hawaii's population remains tremendously diverse, and unlike many other states, working-class organizations continue to influence the character of Hawaii's social, economic, and political life.

ALEXANDER MORROW

References and Further Reading

Beechert, Edward. *Working in Hawaii: A Labor History.* Honolulu: University of Hawaii Press, 1985.

Center for Labor Education and Research. "CLEAR Timeline of Hawai'i Labor History." http://homepages.uhwo. hawaii.edu/\~clear/Timeline.html.

Fuchs, Lawrence. *Hawaii Pono: A Social History.* New York City: Harcourt and Brace & World, Inc., 1961.

Okihiro, Gary. *Cane Fires: The Anti-Japanese Movement in Hawaii, 1865–1945.* Philadelphia: Temple University Press, 1991.

Takaki, Ronald. *Pau Hana: Plantation Life and Labor in Hawaii, 1835–1920.* Honolulu: University of Hawaii Press, 1983.

See also **Hawaii Laborers' Association; Japanese Strike in Hawai'i (1909)**

HAWAII LABORERS' ASSOCIATION

The Hawaii Laborers' Association (HLA) was founded in 1919 as the Japanese Federation of Labor or the Federation of Japanese Labor. The Association and the strike it initiated in 1920, often referred to as the "dual strike," are notable in the history of labor in Hawai'i because both represent the first effort on the part of Japanese and Filipino workers to organize across ethnic lines for the common good of sugar plantation workers. The dual strike was the first strike in Hawaiian history in which the two largest groups of workers attempted to work together to press for their demands. When the Hawaii Sugar Planters' Association (HSPA) and local politicians accused workers of being agents for the Japanese government during a strike on the sugar plantations of O'ahu, the Japanese Federation of Labor changed its name to the Hawaii Laborers' Association to symbolize its commitment to higher wages and better working conditions for all sugar plantation laborers.

The Japanese Federation of Labor was an umbrella organization founded by delegates from local labor associations in the Islands' plantation communities. These smaller organizations formed in the wake of a 1909 strike to protect the interest of plantation workers. In spite of the vast distances between plantation towns, they were able to stay organized by taking advantage of an existing network of community organizations. In smaller plantation towns, they often used religious organizations such as the Young Buddhist Association to meet and discuss the labor situation on the plantations. In 1919, representatives from these organizations met in Honolulu to discuss the economic situation of plantation workers. In the face of rising costs driven by wartime inflation and stagnating wages, Hawai'i's sugar workers demanded a raise in pay from 77 cents to $1.25 per day. In a formal petition to the HSPA, they articulated their demands: in addition to a raise, they asked for an eight-hour workday, paid maternity leave, and better health care and recreational facilities.

Filipino workers also began to organize in 1919. The Philippines became the newest source of labor for the plantations after the United States restricted Japanese immigration under the terms of the 1908 Gentleman's Agreement. As a protectorate of the United States, the Philippines offered plantation owners easy access to a large labor force. In the decade between 1909 and 1919, the number of Japanese workers on sugar plantations had declined from approximately 64% to 44% percent. During the same decade, the number of Filipino workers increased from a few hundred to nearly 10,000 workers, about 20% of the total workforce.

Because Filipinos had not been in the islands very long, they lacked the social networks of community organizations that facilitated labor organizing. However, they were led by a charismatic union organizer named Pablo Manlapit. Manlapit, who had arrived in Hawai'i from the Philippines in 1918, organized the Filipino Labor Union, which formed a loose affiliation with the Japanese Federation of Labor. Manlapit was to act as a go-between for the Japanese Federation and the Filipino workers. However, language and cultural differences impeded smooth cooperation between the two groups.

After the HSPA rejected the demands for higher wages, the Japanese Federation set out to plan its strike. Having learned from previous experience, the Japanese workers had planned to strike in the spring of 1920 as the sugar cane was ripening in the field and ready for harvest. It was thought that if their profits were rotting in the fields, sugar plantations owners would be more likely to negotiate. In addition, by not striking right away, they allowed themselves the several months it would take to raise the money for a strike fund to support workers and their families for the duration.

Filipino workers, however, jumped the gun and walked off several O'ahu plantations in January of 1920. This forced the hand of the Japanese Federation and a general strike was called for February, long before they were ready. Although they attempted to present a united front, there was no question that Japanese and Filipino workers and union leaders were at odds with one another over strike tactics, money, and the duration of the strike.

As it had in the past, the HSPA refused to negotiate and used its control over local politics, government, and media to undermine the workers, their union, and turn public opinion against them. Using spies and speculation, the HSPA fueled the ember of anti-Japanese sentiment by suggesting that the union was acting on the orders of the Japanese government. Through rumormongering in the press, they accused Federation officials of taking advantage of innocent workers in order to "Japanize" the islands. In response to these constant attacks, in April of 1920, the Federation changed its name to the Hawaii Laborers' Association to signal their independence from any foreign government and to deflect the accusation of "racialism."

The Japanese and Filipino workers also used publicity to attempt to encourage public support for the strike. On April 3rd they organized a "77 cents parade" through the streets of Honolulu, timed to coincide with the local celebration of the one hundredth anniversary of the arrival of Protestant missionaries in Hawai'i. Even as the local Protestant community was celebrating the triumph of Christianity in Hawai'i, women and children marched in Honolulu carrying picket signs that said, "God has created us equal" and "My Papa 77 cents a day. My Mama 58 cents a day."

As effective as their strategies were, the strike was broken after six months by the HSPA. Even local religious leaders had failed to bring the HSPA to the table. Once the strike was over, the HSPA and the local government worked to abolish the union by prosecuting its leadership. After the strike, 21 leaders of the Hawaii Laborers' Association were charged with conspiracy in the bombing of the house of a plantation translator named Sakamaki. Although there was little physical evidence to link the men to the crime, 15 were convicted and served from four to 10 years in prison. Upon their release, many returned to Japan.

The Hawaii Laborers' Association did not survive much beyond the strike of 1920 due to the organized strength and control of the HSPA. The strike and the Association were, however, influential in future labor organizing and demonstrated both the need and potential for cross-racial union organizations in Hawai'i.

LORI PIERCE

References and Further Reading

Beechert, Edward D. *Working in Hawai'i: A Labor History*. Honolulu: University of Hawai'i Press, 1985.
Duus, Masayo U. *The Japanese Conspiracy: The Oahu Strike of 1920*. Berkeley: University of California Press, 1999.
Okihiro, Gary. *Cane Fires: The Anti-Japanese Movement in Hawai'i 1865–1945*. Philadelphia: Temple University Press, 1991.
Reinecke, John E. *Feigned Necessity: Hawaii's Attempt to Obtain Chinese Contract Labor 1921–1923*. San Francisco: Chinese Materials Center, Inc., 1979.

See also **Japanese Strike in Hawai'i (1909)**

HAYMARKET AFFAIR (1886)

On May 4, 1886, at about 10:30 p.m., a protest rally near Chicago's Haymarket Square was about to end when six columns of police (176 officers in all) marched to the rally site on Desplaines Street and ordered the meeting's participants to disperse. The rally had been called by the city's anarchists, who were organized into the International Working People's Association, a group composed mainly of German and Bohemian immigrant workers. The purpose of the May 4 meeting was to protest an event that took place the night before when Chicago police intervened to stop strikes from assaulting strikebreakers leaving the McCormick harvester works on the South Side. In the fighting that ensued, the police shot and killed four strikers.

The city's leading anarchist organizer, August Spies, had opened the Haymarket meeting calling for a peaceful protest, though he had at many other times told workers to arm themselves and prepare to use dynamite bombs if and when the police and militia attacked. Like the other main speakers that night, Albert Parsons and Samuel Fielden, Spies was a visionary who believed that the workers' struggle for power would lead to a social revolution that would be violent because the ruling class would use all of its forces to put down any uprising or revolt.

Sam Fielden, the last speaker of the evening, did not call upon the crowd to attack the police, but he did say that workers should "throttle" and "kill the law." Hearing these words, plainclothes policemen reported to their commander, Chief Inspector John Bonfield, that Fielden was making incendiary remarks.

Although the mayor of Chicago, Carter H. Harrison, had told Bonfield that the rally was peaceful and that he should send police reserves home, the chief still decided to march on the rally and to disperse the small crowd that remained.

When the police arrived, Fielden objected to the command to disperse, saying, "But we are peaceful." Then he reluctantly agreed to end the meeting. Just then, a bomb was thrown into the police ranks; it exploded with terrific force. Wild gunfire erupted from the police revolvers, and according to police witnesses, firing came from the crowd as well, although this fact was disputed by many other eyewitnesses. One police officer died within minutes of the explosion, and six others died later from their wounds, although it is not clear how many were killed by the bomb fragments or by bullets, and it is not clear how many of the gunshots came from the police officers' own revolvers, though many probably did. At least 60 officers were wounded, along with unknown numbers of civilian bystanders (at least three of them were confirmed dead as a result of police gunfire).

The Haymarket bombing created hysteria in Chicago and across the nation, and led to the nation's first red scare. The *Chicago Tribune* blamed the mayor for allowing free speech for the anarchists and insisted that the government deport them and exclude any other "foreign savages who might come to America with their dynamite bombs and anarchic purposes."

In the aftermath of the bombing, Chicago police arrested scores of workers suspected of being anarchists, raided homes and offices without warrants, and stopped all public meetings. Immigrants were intimidated by the red scare and scapegoating that followed; it was a time when newspapers and public officials created a terrifying image of the European immigrant as a potential anarchist murderer—an image that endured in the popular imagination.

The red scare also had a chilling effect on the insurgent labor movement of the time, one that had propelled more than 300,000 workers into the streets on May 1, 1886, in a mass strike for the eight-hour day. Chicago was the epicenter of a storm of strikes that had been building for nearly two months, as skilled and unskilled, native and foreign-born men and women joined together in what they thought of as a freedom movement to gain precious hours of "their own time" from employers who arbitrarily insisted on at least 10 hours' work five days a week plus at least a half day on Saturday. Indeed, thousands of workers had already gained shorter hours in April as a result of strikes and demands on employers, including some by workers who demanded an eight-hour day with no reduction in pay.

There were political tensions in the strike movement, especially in Chicago where a strong anarchist-led body, the Central Labor Union, opposed the city's mainstream Trades and Labor Assembly. The former group, composed mainly of German and Czech

The Anarchist Riot in Chicago—A Dynamite Bomb Exploding Among the Police [McCormick Strike, Haymarket Square]. Library of Congress, Prints & Photographs Division [LC-USZ62-796].

immigrants, saw the eight-hour reform as a means of uniting workers toward a more revolutionary end, whereas the city's craft unions, led by American, Irish, and English moderates, regarded shorter hours as an end in itself. Tensions also existed between the anarchists and the reform leaders of the Knights of Labor. Some Chicago Knights shared the fears of their national leader, Terence V. Powderly, that a mass strike for eight hours would heighten class conflict and lead to violence.

However, as of May 3 the strikers had remained unified, and their strikes had remained nonviolent. This peaceful period ended that night when the police killed the strikers at the McCormick works, an event that led directly to the Haymarket rally on May 4 and to the violence that followed there.

Within a few days after the bombing, most of the eight-hour strikes had ended, as many trade unionists, like Samuel Gompers of the Federation of Organized Trades and Labor Unions, blamed the Haymarket bombing and its aftermath for killing the shorter hours movement. There were other reasons the movement receded, notably the actions of aggressive employer associations and the ambivalent attitudes of many union officials, but the Haymarket bombing nevertheless marked a turning point in labor history, one that signaled the rapid decline of the Knights of Labor in most cities and industries.

The trial of the eight Chicago anarchists indicted for the bombing began in Chicago on June 22, 1886. At the time, few outside the anarchist movement displayed any sympathy toward the defendants, who were assumed by the press to be guilty and worthy of hanging. The trial was a sensational affair that lasted most of the summer and attracted international attention. Then, as the proceedings wore on, more and more trade unionists and other citizens began to worry that the jury seemed to be packed with jurors who were biased against the defendants when the prosecution produced only circumstantial evidence that the accused anarchists were directly responsible for the bombing. Indeed, none of the anarchists were actually charged with throwing the lethal hand grenade; the prosecution charged them as accessories to murder because the anarchists had allegedly conspired with the bomber and abetted the bombing with their words and actions. Even sympathetic observers realized, however, that whatever the weaknesses in the state's case, the jury would find the defendants guilty.

Still, many observers were shocked when the jury members joined the announcement of their guilty verdict with a death sentence for all seven anarchists they had tried: August Spies, Michael Schwab, George Engel, Adolph Fischer, and Louis Lingg (all German-born workers), Samuel Fielden (an Englishman employed as a teamster), Oscar Neebe, and Albert Parsons (both American-born tradesmen).

All of these men had been active and effective union organizers and eight-hour strike leaders as well as dedicated anarchist agitators and propagandists. Indeed, August Spies and Albert Parsons had become nationally known figures in labor and radical movements of the time. Spies, the publisher of the nation's largest anarchist newspaper, *Chicagoer Arbeiter Zetiung*, was an author of the historic Pittsburg Manifesto, a revolutionary document issued in 1883 by socialist militants who had given up on electoral politics and the gradual overthrow of capitalism; and Albert Parsons was a legendary speaker and organizer much in demand as an orator and agitator.

Soon after the verdict was rendered in the Haymarket case, many labor union members, especially immigrants, began to feel that the anarchists had been tried and sentenced to death, not for the bombing, but for their militant words and actions on behalf of the working class. The anarchists' lawyers appealed for a new trial, complaining that the proceedings and the jury were blatantly biased against their clients. However, in October 1886, the judge who tried the case, Joseph E. Gary, sentenced three defendants (Fielden, Schwab, and Neebe) to 15 years in prison and condemned the other five men to death on the gallows. Before Gary issued his final edict, the anarchists delivered highly charged speeches to the court that would later be published, translated, and disseminated in many nations.

During the legal appeal of the death sentence to the Illinois and national supreme courts in 1887, concern and sympathy for the condemned men grew across the United States and in Europe, culminating in a massive petition campaign in November aimed at the governor of Illinois, Richard J. Oglesby, who was asked to commute the anarchists' sentences to life imprisonment. Workers, especially union members, generated most of the support for clemency, but the campaign attracted a few noted writers like the muckraker Henry Demarest Lloyd as well as many leading citizens of Chicago, including some who feared that executing the anarchists would make them martyrs to the revolutionary cause.

Scores of people descended upon the Illinois State capitol in Springfield as the execution date approached in November 1887. Governor Oglesby accepted petitions for clemency signed by thousands of citizens and heard many appeals, including an especially powerful argument for clemency made by Samuel Gompers, president of the newly formed American Federation of Labor, who also feared that the executions would confer martyrdom on the five condemned revolutionaries, who would be remembered as heroes who died fighting for freedom of speech.

As the governor pondered his decision, one of the anarchists, Louis Lingg, reportedly exploded a small dynamite cap concealed in a cigar in an apparent attempt to commit suicide. As Lingg lay dying, Governor Oglesby announced his decision that Spies, Parsons, Engel, and Fischer would be executed on November 11, as ordered by the court.

After the hangings took place on that day, long known to anarchists as "Black Friday," an intensely emotional reaction followed among workers, especially immigrants, and among anarchists and socialists in Europe. A few noted Americans like the writer William Dean Howells also expressed dismay over what the famous novelist called a "judicial murder" in Chicago.

The Haymarket case refused to die in the public imagination, especially in Chicago, where some citizens were haunted by the fear that a grave injustice had been done. The feelings of regret surfaced in June 1893 when an impressive monument was unveiled at the grave of the five anarchists in Waldheim Cemetery, outside of Chicago, and when the governor of Illinois, a Democrat of German birth named John Peter Altgeld, pardoned the three surviving anarchists serving time in prison. Altgeld's famous pardon included an expression of outrage over what the governor regarded as the injustice of the anarchists' 1886 trial.

In the late 1890s, the anarchists, now regarded by socialists and anarchists as the Haymarket martyrs, seemed to fade from view as radical and labor movements declined during the ensuing depression and the repression the followed the defeat of the Pullman boycott of 1894. And yet, the memory of the Haymarket anarchists proved to be remarkably resilient, especially in Spain and Italy, where the celebration of May Day as the international workers' holiday after 1890 was used to recall the sacrifice of Chicago revolutionaries who were remembered as having died for the eight-hour day. This memory endured even longer in Latin America, especially in Mexico where May 1 was known as the "day of the Chicago martyrs."

The memory of the Haymarket martyrs was also revived in the United States when socialists and anarchists celebrated May Day in the years between 1907 and 1917; it reappeared in 1937 after the Memorial Day massacre in Chicago, when police killed 10 unarmed picketers and the newspapers blamed it all on a Communist-inspired riot; and it resurfaced during and after the centennial on May 1, 1986, when a stream of plays, songs, poems, posters, documentaries, and historical essays retold the unforgettable Haymarket story.

JAMES GREEN

References and Further Reading

Avrich, Paul. *The Haymarket Tragedy*. Princeton, NJ: Princeton University Press, 1984.
Foner, Philip S., ed. *The Autobiographies of the Haymarket Anarchists*. New York: Humanities Press, 1969.
Green, James. *Death in the Haymarket: A Story of Chicago, the First Labor Movement, and the Bombing That Divided Gilded Age America*. New York: Pantheon, 2006.
————. "Globalization of Memory: The Enduring Remembrance of the Haymarket Martyrs around the World." *Labor: Studies of Working-Class History in the Americas* 2, no. 4 (2005): 5–15.
Nelson, Bruce C. *Beyond the Martyrs: A Social History of Chicago's Anarchists, 1870–1900*. New Brunswick, NJ: Rutgers University Press, 1988.
Parsons, Lucy, ed. *Famous Speeches of the Eight Chicago Anarchists in Court*. 1910. Reprint, New York: Arno Press, 1969.
Perrier, Hubert, Catherine Collomp, Michel Cordillot, and Marianne Debouzy. "The 'Social Revolution' in America? European Reactions to the Great Upheaval and the Haymarket Affair." *International Labor and Working-Class History* 29, no. 3 (1986): 38–52.
Roediger, David, and Franklin Rosemont, eds. *The Haymarket Scrapbook*. Chicago: Charles H. Kerr, 1986.
Smith, Carl N. "Cataclysm and Cultural Consciousness: Chicago and the Haymarket Trial." *Chicago History* 15, no. 3 (1986): 36–52.
————. "The Dramas of Haymarket." A Web Site of the Chicago Historical Society. www.chicagohistory.org/dramas/overview/over.htm.

HAYWOOD, WILLIAM D. "BIG BILL" (1869–1929)
Cofounder, Industrial Workers of the World

Perhaps the best-known member of the Industrial Workers of the World (IWW), William D. "Big Bill" Haywood cofounded and helped run the legendary union, the pre-eminent radical organization of its time. Previously, Haywood had been a leader of the militant Western Federation of Miners (WFM) and the Socialist Party. He still is recalled for his commanding presence, speaking style, and leadership.

Born in Utah Territory in 1869, Haywood grew up in a working-class family. Haywood first worked in a mine at the age of nine, the same age at which he lost one of his eyes (in a boyhood accident); his one-eyed visage later contributed to his imposing persona.

From 15, he worked in a series of mines—following the boom-and-bust industry. Along the way, he married and fathered two daughters; his wife became an invalid from difficulties in labor, and they drifted apart.

The WFM was at the forefront of Gilded Age labor strife, resisting increasingly powerful mining corporations in the Rocky Mountain West. Haywood joined the WFM in 1896 when working in Silver City, Idaho, moved up the ranks of local leadership, and relocated to Denver in 1902 to help lead the union. The 40,000-strong WFM became steadily more militant, violent, and leftist in response to intense corporate and governmental attacks.

This struggle expanded when Frank Steunenberg, a former governor of Idaho and noted anti-unionist, was murdered in 1905. Haywood, along with two other WFM leaders, was accused of the crime. The murderer confessed but claimed that Haywood and the others had hired him. Thus began the era's most celebrated case, ending in the acquittal of all three—primarily because the prosecution provided no evidence to corroborate the murderer's testimony.

That same year, 1905, Haywood helped found the IWW. Many socialists and radical unionists believed that the American Federation of Labor (AFL) was far too conservative. By contrast, the IWW—with Haywood chairing what he termed a "Continental Congress of the Working Class"—was committed to organizing all workers (regardless of their craft, gender, nationality, or race) in industrial unions and overthrowing capitalism. Haywood came to such radical notions from his own experiences as a miner, unionist, and organizer. As Haywood reportedly said, "I've never read Marx but I've got the marks of capitalism all over me."

Haywood became an IWW leader, especially during the period from 1912 to 1918. For years Haywood had struggled within the Socialist Party, but in 1913, he largely abandoned it for the more job-focused Wobblies. One of his most famous battles was the 1912 "Bread and Roses" textile strike in Lawrence, Massachusetts. After the first group of leaders was arrested on bogus murder charges, Haywood and Elizabeth Gurley Flynn led the 25,000 workers, mostly immigrant women, to a stunning victory. In 1913, while leading 30,000 striking silk workers in Paterson, New Jersey, Haywood captivated another group. New York City's bohemians, denizens of Greenwich Village, were enthralled by Haywood, who they said was a true working-class hero. He was known to them for his many quotable sayings,

W.D. Haywood leads Lowell strike parade. Library of Congress, Prints & Photographs Division [LC-DIG-ggbain-10357].

including his quote that the IWW is "socialism with its working clothes on."

With Haywood at the helm from 1914 to 1917, the IWW dramatically expanded. The IWW organized workers in war-related industries that experienced intense labor shortages (thereby giving workers more power). The 1910s experienced a surge in unionism and radicalism, not just in the States but in nations worldwide. Though many Wobblies argued that working-class men did all of the fighting and dying in all armies, the IWW, true to its anarchist leanings, left support of or opposition to the war to its members' consciences. Nevertheless, the IWW was widely considered to be an antiwar organization.

The IWW's radicalism and power made it a target, resulting in federal raids on IWW offices nationwide in September 1917. The following year, one hundred Wobblies were defendants in what became the longest trial in U.S. history. After four months, the jury came back in under an hour, finding all the defendants guilty on all counts. Haywood was sentenced to 20 years in a federal penitentiary. The Wobblies claimed they were tried on their beliefs—and no evidence of a planned general strike to undermine the nation's war effort ever has been uncovered.

After serving a year in Leavenworth, Haywood was freed temporarily in 1921 pending appeal, jumped bail, and fled to the Soviet Union. Haywood's actions were highly controversial among Wobblies, many believing he had abandoned the struggle. Haywood did not see the point in remaining in a capitalist jail, when he could join the world's first nation to overthrow capitalism. Moreover, Haywood was in failing health, his diabetes and ulcer having worsened dramatically while jailed.

Haywood's decade in the Soviet Union was troubling. He contributed little to his newly adopted home. Haywood could not return to his beloved homeland, did not speak Russian, and became an alcoholic. He died in 1928. Half of his ashes were placed inside the Kremlin's walls; the other half went to Chicago's famed Waldheim Cemetery, where the Haymarket Martyrs are buried. His memoir, *Bill Haywood's Book*, likely ghostwritten, was released in 1929.

Big Bill Haywood's life is typical and atypical of working-class Americans of his time. Like many poor boys, he had little formal education, instead entering the workforce. Subsequently, he experienced the insecurities, hard work, and dangers of such an existence. Like millions of others, he joined a union because he believed that he was powerless to protect his interests otherwise. Like hundreds of thousands, unionism and corporate hostility further radicalized him. He looms large over American labor history.

PETER COLE

References and Further Reading

Carlson, Peter. *Roughneck: The Life and Times of Big Bill Haywood.* New York: 1983.
Dubofsky, Melvyn. *"Big Bill" Haywood.* New York: St. Martin's Press, 1987.
———. *We Shall Be All: A History of the Industrial Workers of the World.* 2nd ed. Urbana: University of Illinois Press, 1988.
Foner, Philip S. *History of the Labor Movement in the United States.* Vol. 4: *The Industrial Workers of the World, 1905–1917.* New York: International Publishers, 1965.
Haywood, William D. *Bill Haywood's Book: The Autobiography of William D. Haywood.* New York: International Publishers, 1929.

See also **American Federation of Labor; Flynn, Elizabeth Gurley; Industrial Workers of the World**

HEIGHTON, WILLIAM (1801–1873)

William Heighton's career as an activist cleaves into two stages, one as a labor radical and one as an antislavery advocate. Born in 1801 in the village of Oundle in Northamptonshire, England, Heighton emigrated with his family around the War of 1812, settling in Philadelphia, where he married (Ann Beckley) and plied his trade of shoemaking in order to support a growing family. Little was heard from him until the second half of the 1820s, when he steered the Quaker City's struggling workers in a new direction.

The deterioration of the crafts attendant upon the acceleration of the market revolution plus the influence of political economists turned Heighton by the mid-1820s toward Anglo-American radicalism. Though he was familiar with the work of Thomas Paine, Heighton was especially impressed with the more recent writings of David Ricardo as well as John Gray, the primitive socialist who argued that working-class poverty stemmed from economic exploitation and political oppression, not simply the latter, as earlier radicals believed. In 1827, Heighton became the city's leading labor activist, delivering the first of three major addresses over the next two years, which were printed in pamphlet form and widely distributed within the city and to other urban centers. His spring and fall speeches in 1827 were hardhitting polemics based on the labor theory of value along with a comprehensive plan for economic reconstruction and working-class organization. Heighton depicted an economic landscape populated by "producers," and "accumulators," or the many and the few. The former group, which consisted of working people, farmers, and others working with their hands, were the creators of wealth; the latter, which consisted of bankers, merchants, and manufacturers, were among the nonmanual workers who appropriated the wealth created by producers. Accumulators prevailed in the political arena as well as in the economy because they had seized control of the political machinery in the wake of the Revolution. They maintained power by keeping producers ignorant generally and unaware of their own economic interests.

Heighton's remedial plan caught on. Between his two addresses, he had worked with a committee of comrades to draft the constitution and bylaws of what would become the Mechanics' Union of Trade Associations (MUTA). In January 1828, shortly after his second address, delegates from about nine trade unions ratified the new document, formally launching the nation's (and arguably the world's) first citywide organization of trade unions. Some members of the MUTA's leadership, including Heighton, doubled as the editorial committee of the *Mechanics' Free Press* (*MFP*), the union's official organ, which appeared in January 1828. Not long afterward, a meeting of the MUTA gave rise to nominating committees, which became known as the Working Men's Party, the first labor party in the nation. The Working Men got off to a rough start in 1828 but drew enough interest in 1829 to hold the balance of power; they ran even better in 1830 but lost the balance of power and disappeared entirely after the 1831 campaign. The new party faced the same obstacles that would hinder political insurgencies for the rest of the antebellum era, including thin resources and weak organization. In addition, the Democratic Party in the city of Philadelphia proved to be rather more flexible than its counterparts elsewhere, making room for working-class insurgents and selectively borrowing from their agenda.

Heighton took the 1830 election very hard, denouncing the "blindness" and "sappiness" of working people and leaving the city in a huff (*MFP*, October 29, 1830, and March 2, 1831). He wound up in rural Salem County, New Jersey, possibly with the idea of starting life anew. He remarried in the mid-1850s following the death of his first wife in the 1840s, and in the early 1860s he set aside his shoemaker's kit to pursue farming. He seems to have eschewed labor activism but retained his animus for the Protestant clergy (they were accumulators who also kept workers in darkness). He also took a growing interest in land reform, a nostrum in the 1840s that attracted a good number of labor advocates from the 1830s. In addition, the rusticated radical established a name among abolitionists, though it is not known when he became concerned about slavery (having published a single antislavery piece in the *MFP*) or if he joined the American Anti-Slavery Society or its New Jersey affiliate. By the Civil War, he was known well enough in abolitionist circles to be asked to contribute a short essay in 1865 for a book being prepared by George L. Stearns, the Medford, Massachusetts, linseed manufacturer and radical abolitionist who a decade earlier had been a member of the "Secret Six" who supported John Brown in Kansas and then in Virginia. In a letter he called his "political daguerrotype," Heighton argued that if "you wish to uproot slavery, break up the land monopoly" of the Old South. Otherwise, the "barbarous land-barons," in the region would "vent their spleen on the innocent and helpless freedmen" (Stearns, p. 43).

The one-time labor radical and autodidact and now radical abolitionist found himself in the eminent company of Wendell Phillips and Frederick Douglass. He had come a long way since leaving behind the labor movement. Future scholars would do well to chart that course.

BRUCE LAURIE

References and Further Reading

Arky, Lewis H. "The Mechanics' Union of Trade Associations and the Formation of the Philadelphia Working-Men's Movement." *Pennsylvania Magazine of History and Biography* 76 (April 1952): 142–176.

———. "The Mechanics' Union of Trade Associations and the Formation of the Philadelphia Working-Men's Movement." Ph.D. diss. University of Pennsylvania, 1952.

Foner, Philip S., ed. *William Heighton: Pioneer Labor Leader of Jacksonian Philadelphia*. New York: International Publishers, 1991.

Foster, A. Kristen. *Moral Visions and Material Ambitions: Philadelphia Struggles to Define the Republic, 1776–1836*. Lanham, MD: Lexington Books, 2004.

Harris, David J. *Socialist Origins in the United States: American Forerunners of Marx, 1817–1832*. Assen, Netherlands: Van Gorcum, 1968.

Heighton, William. *An Address Delivered before the Mechanics and Working Classes Generally, of the City and County of Philadelphia...by the "Unlettered Mechanic."* Philadelphia: The Mechanics' Delegation, 1827.

———. *An Address to the Members of Trade Societies, and to the Working Classes Generally...Together with a Suggestion and Outlines of a Plan, by Which They May Gradually and Indefinitely Improve Their Condition. By a Fellow-Laborer.* Philadelphia: By the Author, 1827.

———. *The Principles of Aristocratic Legislation, Developed in an Address, Delivered to the Working Peoples of the District of Southwark, and the Townships of Moyamensing and Passyunk*. Philadelphia: J. Coates, Jr., 1828.

Laurie, Bruce. *Working People of Philadelphia, 1800–1850*. Philadelphia: Temple University Press, 1980.

Mechanics' Free Press. Philadelphia, 1828–1831.

Schultz, Ronald. *The Republic of Labor: Philadelphia Artisans and the Politics of Class, 1780–1830*. New York: Oxford Univ. Press, 1993.

Stearns, George L., ed. *The Equality of All Men before the Law Claimed and Defended*. Boston: George C. Rand and Avery, 1865.

Young America. New York. Nov. 5, 1845.

See also **Mechanics' Union of Trade Associations of Philadelphia**

HENRY, JOHN

The story of John Henry follows from a song. John Henry was a giant—a powerful black man who worked on a tunneling gang on the Chesapeake & Ohio (C&O) railroad. He drove a "nine-pound hammer" into a steel chisel, hitting it so hard that "every time he brought his hammer down, you could see the steel going through." As the chisel buried itself into the side of the mountain, John Henry sang to match the beat:

> Ain't no hammer
> in these mountains,
> rings like mine,
> rings like mine.

The tunneling gang worked to pierce a million-year-old mountain in western Virginia that separated the east from the west. But the task seemed impossible. When John Henry first saw it, he feared he would fail. "The rock was so tall and John Henry so small that he laid down his hammer and he cried." Progress was slow, and the work was perilous. An inventor came up to the mountainside with a steam drill, which he declared was faster than any tunneling gang. John Henry challenged the steam drill to a race. The steam drill hammered on one side, John Henry on the other. John Henry sang while he hammered. His buddy had a stack of chisels, replacing each one as the tip dulled. John Henry and his hammer moved like a blur.

While the steam drill was powerful, John Henry was a "mighty, mighty man." At the end of the contest, John Henry "drove in fourteen feet, the steam drill only made nine." Then, just as John Henry finished, "his head spinning 'round," he fell. He knew where he was going, and asked for a cool drink of water before he died. Such a powerful man was John Henry, such an important man, that they took him to the White House and buried him in the sand. Even the steam engines paid their respects to the grave of John Henry, for "every locomotive come a roarin' by, said yonder lies a steel-drivin' man."

If a hundred people saw a contest between a hammer man and a steam drill in the early 1870s, there are more than a hundred versions of the song, the ballad of John Henry. By the 1880s, white men in the Appalachian Mountains knew it as a "Negro banjo pickers' melody." By the 1930s, it was so popular in the mountains of Virginia and Kentucky that the earliest country musicians, including Fiddlin' John Carson and the Skillet Lickers, had versions of the song. Every blues musician in eastern Virginia and along the Mississippi River could play it. In the middle 1930s, the folklorists Guy Johnson and Louis Chappell, with a small regiment of graduate students, traveled around the South to find the traces of John Henry. They discovered contradictory versions of the John Henry legend, placing him in North Carolina, Virginia, West Virginia, Alabama, Texas, and Jamaica. The folklorists and their students followed the story as well as they could, published their results, and moved on. There was something here: the Chesapeake & Ohio railroad *was* built through the mountains of western Virginia between 1870 and 1872. Steam drills had been tried there. Men and women knew of the many lives lost building those tunnels. But the records were lost, and the stories were contradictory.

By the 1920s, the song had become an anthem among members of the Harlem Renaissance, the American Communist Party, and white textile mill workers in the American South. For Communists, the John Henry ballad seemed to express exactly the Communist Party's view of black workers' struggles. Finally, in the 1960s, as black power activists became interested in his story, John Henry became more expressly a symbol of the battle against white power structures, while for musicians at the Newport Folk Festival he represented their opposition to new technologies like electric guitars and amplifiers. In the 1960s, John Henry became the focus of an event in West Virginia called the John Henry Folk Festival, a celebration organized by Ed Cabbell, an African-American musician, schoolteacher, and self-made expert on the story of John Henry. Cabbell's festival has gained new popularity due to the novel *John Henry Days* by Colson Whitehead, who visited the festival and explored how the story of John Henry's life could be shaped for commercial exploitation, appeal to jazz musicians, and become a kind of anthem for the epidemic of crack cocaine.

Scott Nelson has argued that John Henry was an actual person, a convict from the Virginia Penitentiary who participated in the construction of the Lewis Tunnel on the Chesapeake & Ohio Railroad. That tunnel was built between 1871 and 1873, and Nelson has demonstrated that John Henry, the convict, was shipped to the mountains to work on the railroad beginning in 1868, and that steam drills were used at the Lewis Tunnel site between 1872 and 1873 alongside the convicts from the penitentiary. Nearly two hundred workers died in the construction of this tunnel and were apparently all returned to the Virginia Penitentiary because of a stipulation in the employment contract that the C&O had to pay a $100 fine "for each prisoner not returned." The bodies appeared to have been returned, only to be buried in the sand next to the old white house of the Virginia penitentiary. This, according to Nelson, accounts for the final verse of many of the songs:

They took John Henry to the White House,
And buried him in the san'
And every locomotive comes roarin' by,
Says there lies a steel drivin' man,
Says there lies a steel drivin' man.

These bodies were only recently discovered, in 1992, when contractors dug up the grounds of the penitentiary to make room for new construction.

SCOTT NELSON

References and Further Reading

Cohen, Norm. *Long Steel Rail: The Railroad in American Folksong*. Urbana, University of Illinois Press, 2000.
Chappell, Louis W. *John Henry: A Folk-lore Study*. 1933. Reprint, Port Washington, NY: Kennikat Press, 1968.
Johnson, Guy B. *John Henry: Tracking Down a Negro Legend*. Chapel Hill: University of North Carolina Press, 1929.
Nelson, Scott R. "Who Was John Henry? Railroad Construction, Southern Folklore, and the Birth of Rock and Roll." *Labor: Studies of Working-Class History in the Americas* 2 (2005): 53–79.
Williams, Brett (1983). *John Henry: A Bio-Bibliography*. Westport, CT: Greenwood Press.

HERSTEIN, LILLIAN (APRIL 12, 1886– AUGUST 9, 1983)
Union Activist

Lillian Herstein, whom *Life* magazine described as "the most important woman in the American labor movement" in 1937, was a public schoolteacher, union activist, advocate of workers' education, and candidate for national political office. Herstein was born on April 12, 1886, on the west side of Chicago, the youngest of six children. Her Jewish parents, Wolf and Cipe, emigrated from Lithuania, then part of Tsarist Russia, to the United States shortly after the American Civil War. Her family owned a bookstore in Chicago. She attended Northwestern University, where she gained a degree in Latin and Greek and obtained an M.A. from the University of Chicago in 1924. After graduating from Northwestern University in 1907, Herstein, like many college-educated women at the time, became a schoolteacher. She taught in

high schools in Franklin Grove, Illinois, and Mount Vernon, Indiana, before entering the Chicago public school system in 1912. She initially taught in high schools and then in junior colleges for the rest of her career in Chicago. Like most women teachers of her generation, Herstein never married.

Influenced by her sister Gusta, a sales clerk who was active in the labor movement, and by the reform work of Margaret Haley and the Chicago Teachers' Federation, Herstein became a union activist. She joined the newly formed Federation of Women High School Teachers in 1914, a local affiliate of the American Federation of Teachers (AFT). Herstein represented her union in the Chicago Federation of Labor (CFL) and was for 25 years the only woman on the executive board of the CFL. She became active in the Chicago branch of the Women's Trade Union League. The League, formed in 1903, set out to organize women into unions, to establish workers', education programs, and to bring about legislation for shorter hours and protection for women. The organization was one in which schoolteachers like Lillian Herstein, middle-class reformers like Jane Addams of Hull-House and Mary McDowell of the University of Chicago settlement house, and labor leaders like Agnes Nestor worked together.

In addition to teaching in the Chicago public schools for 36 years, Herstein spent her evenings, weekends, and summers active in workers' education. In the 1920s and 1930s, Herstein taught English and public speaking at the Chicago Labor College run by the CFL and the Chicago Women's Trade Union League. She also taught at the University of Wisconsin, the University of Chicago, and the Bryn Mawr Summer School for Women Workers in Industry. Herstein went on to head the Chicago Works Progress Administration workers' education program in the 1930s.

To pursue her belief in democracy and social justice, Herstein became active in local and national progressive politics. She joined the Labor Party after World War I and then participated in the Farmer Labor Party, formed in 1920, which sought, unsuccessfully, to become a third-party alternative to the two major parties. In 1932, Herstein ran unsuccessfully for Congress in Illinois on the Progressive Party ticket, calling for old-age pensions and unemployment insurance. In 1936, she supported the re-election of President Franklin Roosevelt and directed the speaker's bureau of Labor's Non-Partisan League in Illinois, an organization formed to help win the re-election of Roosevelt. In the summer of 1937, President Roosevelt picked Herstein to serve on the U.S. delegation that attended the International Labor Organization (ILO) meeting in Geneva, Switzerland.

In the late 1930s, Herstein became active in the Chicago Teachers' Union (CTU), formed in 1937 by a merger of Herstein's union, the Federation of Women High School Teachers, and three other teacher unions. Chicago public schoolteachers had suffered from nonpayment of salaries in the early years of the Depression and from pay cuts throughout the 1930s. Nearly two thirds of the Chicago public schoolteachers joined the CTU, led by the high school teacher John M. Fewkes, making it the largest teachers union in the country. Herstein saw the union as a vehicle for reforming the public schools and in particular removing the political influence of Mayor Edward J. Kelly and the Democratic machine from the school system. She served on the executive committee of the CTU, participated in the work of the American Federation of Teachers, and ran for president of the AFT in 1938 but lost to Jerome Davis.

Herstein became disillusioned with the CFL and the CTU in the late 1930s. John Fitzpatrick, the leader of the CFL, moved the Federation closer to the Chicago Democratic political machine led by Mayor Kelly, and became more authoritarian in running the organization. The CTU became dominated by John M. Fewkes and his supporters, who wanted to eschew the social reformism of Herstein and embrace bread-and-butter unionism. In January 1940, Lillian Herstein resigned from the executive board of the CTU, accusing Fewkes of not consulting with the rest of the leadership. When she retired from teaching at the age of 65 in 1951, Fewkes unceremoniously removed her as CTU representative from the CFL.

During World War II, Herstein devoted herself to the war effort. She became a member of the War Production Board in 1942 as its woman's consultant on the West Coast and helped obtain child care and other facilities for women workers until the end of the war. When the war ended, Herstein returned to Chicago and helped expose the corruption and patronage that blighted the public school system and joined the campaign to remove Mayor Kelly from office. In December 1946, Kelly announced he would not run for re-election, and his supporters who ran the public schools at his behest resigned their posts.

After her retirement from teaching, Herstein worked for the Jewish Labor Committee, formed in New York in 1934, which opposed anti-Semitism and racism. The committee later became very involved with race relations in the United States, and she became a member of the Chicago Commission on Human Relations, initially formed in 1943 as the Mayor's Committee on Race Relations, and campaigned to racially integrate the building trades. Herstein continued to teach for local unions, wrote for labor journals, and campaigned for reform politicians against the Chicago Democratic machine. Herstein died on August 9, 1983.

JOHN F. LYONS

References and Further Reading

Balanoff, Elizabeth. Interview with Lillian Herstein, 1970–1971. Oral History Project in Labor History, Roosevelt University Archives, Chicago.

Balanoff, Elizabeth. "Lillian Herstein." In *Women Building Chicago, 1790–1990: A Biographical Dictionary*, edited by Rima Lunin Schultz and Adele Hast. Bloomington and Indianapolis: Indiana University Press, 2001, pp. 387–391.

Engelbrecht, Lester E. "Lillian Herstein: Teacher and Activist." *Labor's Heritage* 1 (April 1989): 66–75.

O'Farrell, Brigid, and Joyce L. Kornbluh, eds. *Rocking the Boat: Union Women's Voices, 1915–1975*. New Brunswick, NJ: Rutgers University Press, 1996.

See also **Addams, Jane; Hull-House Settlement (1889–1963); Nestor, Agnes; Women's Trade Union League**

HIGGINS, MONSIGNOR GEORGE G. (1916–2002)
Catholic Labor Activist

Beginning in the early twentieth century, a number of Catholic clergy became active in and on behalf of American labor unions. For 60 years, Monsignor George G. Higgins exemplified the ideal of the "labor priest." His strong public presence and his status as an official in the Catholic Church's bureaucracy lent credence to the view among Catholics and others that the Church was friendly toward the goals of organized labor. Similarly, his vigorous participation in the labor movement promoted the same idea among union officials and members. In this way, Higgins exerted significant influence on the character of the relationship between labor and the Church in the United States—a relationship considerably more confrontational in many other national contexts.

A native of Chicago, Higgins was ordained a priest for that archdiocese in 1940. He obtained master's and doctoral degrees in economics and political science from the Catholic University of America in Washington, DC, where he wrote his dissertation on "Voluntarism in Organized Labor in the U.S., 1930–1940." In Washington, he became involved with the Social Action Department of the National

Catholic Welfare Conference (NCWC), the national organization of the United States Roman Catholic bishops. Through the Catholic University and the NCWC, he became acquainted with and influenced by key figures in American Catholic social reform, including Bishop Francis Haas, Father Raymond McGowan, and Monsignor John A. Ryan.

Following completion of his studies in 1944, Higgins joined the staff of the Social Action Department, eventually succeeding Ryan and McGowan as its head and as author of the weekly column, "The Yardstick." Higgins retired from the bishops' conference in 1980 and concluded his career by teaching theology at the Catholic University. At his death, he was widely lauded by officials in both organized labor and the Church.

Higgins was an ardent supporter of organized labor, writing, speaking, and frequently acting in favor of workers' demands. His syndicated column and occasional articles appeared throughout the Catholic press, and his lecture engagements included the first Congress of Solidarity in Poland. He led prayers at innumerable rallies and strikes.

As the head of the bishops' social policy arm, Higgins played an important role as liaison between the Church and labor unions. He knew personally most of the major labor figures of the time, including Walter Reuther, Philip Murray, and George Meany. He supported the merger of the AFL and CIO and delivered the invocation at the first joint meeting of the new conglomerate in 1955.

He was appointed by the bishops to a committee charged with mediating the late-1960s dispute between César Chávez's United Farm Workers (UFW) and California grape owners, and was instrumental in bringing Church support to Chávez. When the Teamsters sought a separate arrangement with lettuce growers, Higgins opposed the action and defended the UFW. "My involvement in the farm labor problem has given me greater satisfaction than almost anything else I have done," he wrote later. Chávez, for his part, said in 1980, "I doubt that anybody has done as much for us as Monsignor Higgins has."

He also sought to influence labor in a fashion consistent with Catholic morality by, for example, arguing against unions' taking of positions in favor of abortion rights and by denouncing union corruption and racism. He supported congressional committees formed to investigate union abuses in the 1950s. "Unions cannot count on the support of the Church," he wrote in 1977, "when they discriminate against blacks, Hispanics, or other minority groups, when they engage in unjustified strikes, when they resort to violence, racketeering, or other lawless practices."

Yet Higgins insisted that the majority of American unions were not guilty of such offenses: "In general they are on the side of the angels . . . and are deserving of the support [of the Church]." Many Catholics, however, contested Higgins's vocal advocacy of union activity. During the UFW struggle, the vicar general of the Diocese of Monterey addressed a letter to all the priests in the country, criticizing Chávez and denouncing the "poorly informed churchmen" who supported him.

While defending organized labor against conservatives in the Church, Higgins had simultaneously to justify the Church's role in the labor movement against critics on the left who viewed Higgins and his allies, such as the Association of Catholic Trade Unionists, as harmfully conservative forces within American labor.

The popularity of Higgins's positions waned with the decline in union membership in the 1980s and 1990s. The labor priest model of Catholic engagement of social questions was increasingly beleaguered by criticism from various directions: conservative, communitarian, and socialist. Higgins recognized the decline in the power of unions and their popularity in the Church in his 1992 autobiography, but he remained optimistic about the future of organized labor.

KEVIN E. SCHMIESING

Selected Work

Higgins, Msgr. George G., with William Bole. *Organized Labor and the Church: Reflections of a "Labor Priest."* New York: Paulist Press, 1993.

References and Further Reading

Costello, Gerald M. *Without Fear or Favor: George Higgins on the Record.* Mystic, CT: Twenty-Third Publications, 1984.

O'Brien, John J. *George G. Higgins and the Quest for Worker Justice: The Evolution of Catholic Social Thought in America.* Lanham, MD: Rowman and Littlefield, 2005.

See also **Catholic Church**

HIGHLANDER FOLK SCHOOL/ HIGHLANDER RESEARCH AND EDUCATION CENTER

The Highlander Folk School stands as a beacon of social activism in Appalachia and the American South. Yet the school's origins were hardly propitious. Miles Horton, the school's founder and leading light for much of the twentieth century, established

Highlander during the midst of the Great Depression and in one of the poorest counties of the nation. Started in 1932 in the Grundy County, Tennessee, town of Monteagle, Highlander ultimately served as a meeting place and training ground for local and national leaders in the union movement, the civil rights movement, and the Appalachian Alliance. Though the school was sometimes compartmentalized into its various iterations, Horton insisted that Highlander was one school, simply targeting different groups over the first 75 years of its existence—CIO organizers in the 1930s and 40s, civil rights leaders during the 1950s and 60s, and Appalachian activists during the 1970s, 1980s and 1990s. Thousands of grassroots activists have attended Highlander's training workshops and residential programs, as have scores of national leaders, such as Eleanor Roosevelt, Martin Luther King Jr., Rosa Parks, Pete Seeger, Fannie Lou Hammer, Ralph Abernathy, Woody Guthrie, Andrew Young, Julian Bond, Stokely Carmichael, Septima Clark, and Esau Jenkins.

Horton envisioned Highlander as a center for social change where education would lie at the heart of the school's mission. The education would not involve traditional learning, where teachers impart knowledge to their students. Rather, Horton believed that knowledge resides in the experiences of people, that people know what their problems are and through discussion can come to viable solutions. To the extent that Highlander staff "taught," they did so through analogy, peer teaching, and storytelling. Horton was convinced that grassroots leadership entailed drawing on one's own experiences and learning to make collective decisions in seeking solutions. Horton knew, though, that experiences constituted nothing more than the raw material of learning. As he told Bill Moyers in a PBS documentary, "You only learn from the experiences you learn from," and "An experience you don't learn from is just a happening."

Workshops at Highlander followed a standard pattern. Small groups of roughly 25 to 30 people from specific institutions or movements came together to tackle fundamentally transformative issues, not simply to engage with smaller infrastructural issues. In his edited collection *Teaching for Social Justice*, William Ayers noted that workshop attendees collectively probed which problems needed solutions, what they needed to learn in order to resolve their predicament, and how group members would implement the decisions on their return to their respective communities (Ayers, p. 154). The curriculum was always based on the experiences that the students brought with them, their awareness of the problems facing their communities, and the relationship of that problem to conflict. They might, as Horton

commented in his autobiography, "have been opposed by mine owners or government, prevented from eating in some restaurants or denied their fare share of public resources" (Horton, p. 148). During workshops, Highlander staff generally re-inforced notions that working people deserved more than what they were getting, be it union recognition, more pay, better working conditions, political rights, or improved educational facilities for their communities. The staff further encouraged participants to assert control over the processes through which they could achieve these objectives.

In addition to community workshops, Highlander ran a variety of other programs. Some involved more intensive residential programs that lasted from six weeks to two months. Students came from unions and cooperatives and were expected to return to their communities better able to deal with the problems of their organizations. Other initiatives took Highlander's regular staff out into the field in outreach programs. Highlander's former students and other schools involved in leadership training drew on the Highlander staff to help with educational programs. Throughout all these activities, Highlander and its staff saw themselves as instruments to empower people.

Cultural activities like dance, drama, and especially music formed an integral part of the Highlander program. Horton believed that these cultural forms nourished the soul, created camaraderie, fostered determination, and developed pride in Appalachian and southern culture. In his autobiography, Horton credits his first wife and trained pianist, Zilphia Johnson Horton, for invigorating the cultural curriculum at Highlander. After learning the church hymn, "I'll Overcome Someday," from members of a South Carolina Congress of Industrial Organizations (CIO) Food and Tobacco Workers Union in the mid-1940s, she reworked it into the influential activist song, "We Shall Overcome" (Horton, pp. 77–78). Other singer-songwriters, like Pete Seeger, Guy Carawan, and Leadbelly, popularized songs like "No More Mourning" and "Bourgeois Blues" in a wide range of labor and civil rights settings.

Horton told Bill Moyers in his PBS interview that one measures people not just by their friends, but also by their enemies—that one needed "good, healthy enemies." By this measure, Horton was a remarkably successful man. In the words of Bill Moyers, who wrote the preface to his autobiography, Horton had been "beaten up, locked up, put upon and railed against by racists, toughs, demagogues and governors" (Horton, p. ix). The animus that Horton and his social project evoked also confronted Highlander as an institution. As the civil right movement gathered steam in the late 1950s, Highlander came under increasing attack. Unhappy with the ideas emanating from the institution, the governors of Georgia and Arkansas accused Highlander of being a communist training center where blacks and whites met as social equals. Without warning, the Internal Revenue Service revoked the school's tax-exempt status, and on July 31, 1959, Tennessee state troopers arrived at Highlander to search for evidence that would justify closure of the school. They ostensibly found three such rationales—that Highlander sold liquor without a license, that Horton operated the school for personal gain, and that the school was nonracial. Only the last charge had a basis in reality, but since Grundy County was dry, the presence of any intoxicating spirits provided a ready pretext for the state to padlock the doors and ultimately to revoke the school's charter and liquidate its property. Anticipating the failure of their appeals to these charges, Horton applied for a new charter, which he received in August 1961. The school re-opened as the Highlander Research and Education Center, based temporarily in Knoxville. A little more than a decade later, on February 11, 1972, Highlander moved yet again—this time to New Market, Tennessee, 25 miles east of Knoxville, on a farm in the foothills of the Smoky Mountains. As Horton reflected in a 1959 *Chicago Defender* article, recounted by Frank Adams, "You can padlock a building. But you can't padlock an idea. Highlander is an idea. You can't kill it and you can't close it in....It will grow wherever people take it" (Adams and Horton, p. 133).

KARIN A. SHAPIRO

References and Further Reading

Adams, Frank, with Myles Horton. *Unearthing Seeds of Fire: The Idea of Highlander.* Winston-Salem, NC: John F. Blair, 1975.

Ayers, William. "A Dream That Keeps on Growing: Myles Horton and Highlander." In *Teaching for Social Justice: A Democracy and Education Reader,* edited by William Ayers, Jean Ann Hunt, and Therese Quinn. New York: The New Press and Teachers College Press, 1998, pp. 150–156.

Glen, John. *Highlander: No Ordinary School.* Knoxville: University of Tennessee Press, 1996.

Horton, Aimee Isgrig. *The Highlander Folk School: A History of Its Major Programs.* New York: Carlson Publishing, 1989.

Horton, Myles, with Judith Kohl and Herbert Kohl. *The Long Haul: An Autobiography.* New York: Doubleday, 1990.

Horton, Myles, with Bill Moyers. *The Adventures of a Radical Hillbilly.* Video. Public Broadcasting System, 1981.

See also **Horton, Myles**

HILL, JOE (1879–1915)
Songwriter

Undeniably one of the most well-known, yet nevertheless mysterious, figures in U.S. labor history, Joe Hill was a celebrated songwriter who became, in death, a legend. Hill was recognized for writing many of the songs in the *Little Red Song Book*, published by the Industrial Workers of the World (IWW) sometime around 1904, although it is not possible to date the first publication exactly. His fame only grew after he was arrested for murder and executed. In subsequent decades, his status has become truly mythic, for the life he lived, the songs he wrote, the manner in which he died, and the many songs and stories that encircled him.

Curiously, precious little is known about a man whose fame is so great. Born in Gävle, Sweden, in 1879, Joel Hagglünd grew up quite poor in a very large Lutheran family. Like many poor, young Scandinavians, he moved to the United States in 1902, eventually anglicizing his name to Joseph Hillstrom and then Joe Hill. He moved frequently, joining the large migratory working class in America. Hill worked a variety of trades including longshoreman, logger, machinist, sailor, and musician. There are large gaps in our knowledge of Hill's whereabouts and activities for significant stretches of time, sometimes entire years.

Hill very much saw himself as steeped in the class struggle, in an era of intensifying industrial capitalism. The American West, relatively new to this powerful system, saw its land, resources, and peoples transformed and often destroyed. Like many others, he became increasingly hostile to capitalism, instead believing that a system that shared the wealth with those who produced it was far preferable. Around 1910, he joined the revolutionary, anticapitalist Industrial Workers of the World, nicknamed the Wobblies, and committed his life to the organization. He participated in strikes in British Columbia, the revolution in Mexico, and Wobbly organizing drives across the West.

Hill's fame was a result of his songwriting abilities, which he wielded for unionism and revolution. Hill became the leading folk labor troubadour, despite his status as a non-native speaker of English. Like many folksingers, Hill borrowed his melodies from popular songs of his day, so that anyone who might want to sing along would only need to learn the lyrics. As he made his way across the West, he wrote many songs for the famous IWW *Little Red Song Book*, which a worker could fit in his shirt pocket, cost a quarter, and was an important Wobbly organizing tool. Among his many songs, some of the most famous include: "The Preacher and the Slave," which attacked missionary Christians for promising people who suffered hope in an afterlife, thereby making them quiescent in this life; "Casey Jones, the Union Scab," which assailed craft unions for putting their narrow interests above those of the entire working class; and "There Is Power in a Union."

The impact of his songs was immense. The IWW is an important part of American history and culture not because of its large membership. Rather, the IWW was influential for the powerful ideals that it stood for, its members' commitment to the cause, and the colorful methods through which the union spread its gospel. Where many movements are serious to a fault, the IWW was playful, humorous, and willing to poke fun at itself. The IWW used popular culture, including music and cartoon, to deliver its message. Hill's songs were central to this effort.

Hill is known for not only his songs but also his still controversial demise. In 1914, a Salt Lake City area grocer was killed. Hill was convicted of the murder and sentenced to die. Hill steadfastly maintained his innocence, yet never produced a convincing alibi. Some have charged the state with not providing a fair trial. Others have suggested that Hill was set up because he was a radical Wobbly. While in jail, Hill remained in the public eye, receiving numerous visitors and supporters. One fellow Wobbly, Elizabeth Gurley Flynn, became the recipient of a Hill-penned song that earned her the nickname, "The Rebel Girl." Hill's case became a national cause célèbre, taken up not just by radicals but the mainstream American Federation of Labor and many liberals.

Hill always saw himself as a member of the rank and file, an ordinary, if militant, workingman. When asked, while sitting in jail, about his own background, he demurred by calling himself a "citizen of the world" and "from a planet called earth." Maintaining his innocence to the end, Hill was executed by firing squad. Famously, Hill penned his oft-cited "Last Will" and even more legendary final advice, "Don't mourn, organize." Per his request, his ashes were scattered in every state save Utah and across the globe.

The legend of Joe Hill lives on, appropriately, in songs and books about him. In 1936, Earl Robinson and Alfred Hayes published the song "Joe Hill," with its introduction, "I dreamed I saw Joe Hill last night." The song describes a conversation between the singer and the spirit of Hill, who continually insists "I never died," presumably as long as the ideas he espoused still are cherished. This song struck a chord with the American public, particularly as sung by the noted African-American radical Paul Robeson, whose baritone defined the song through the 1950s. Hill remained in the limelight when the highly respected author Wallace Stegner wrote a novel in 1950 about the life of Joe Hill, in which Stegner contended Hill was guilty. In 1969, Joan Baez sang an elegiac version of "Joe Hill" at Woodstock and recorded it the following year, bringing the song to a new generation. The passion with which he is remembered is testimony to his ongoing importance.

PETER COLE

References and Further Reading

Dubofsky, Melvyn. *We Shall Be All: A History of the Industrial Workers of the World.* 2nd ed. Urbana: University of Illinois Press, 1988.

Industrial Workers of the World. IWW Songs—to Fan the Flames of Discontent. Chicago: Charles H. Kerr, 1923.

Rosemont, Franklin. *Joe Hill: The IWW & the Making of a Revolutionary Workingclass Counterculture.* Chicago: Charles H. Kerr, 2003.

Smith, Gibbs M. *Joe Hill.* Salt Lake City, UT: Gibbs M. Smith, 1969. www.pbs.org/JoeHill.

HILLMAN, BESSIE ABRAMOWITZ (MAY 15, 1889?–DECEMBER 28, 1970)
Feminist and Labor Activist

Bessie Abramowitz Hillman reigned as one of the leading twentieth-century labor feminists for over 60 years. As a young immigrant woman in Chicago, Hillman led a massive strike that laid the foundation for the birth of the Amalgamated Clothing Workers of America (ACWA), the largest men's garment workers' union in the country. Following her marriage to the union's first president, Sidney Hillman, Bessie defied cultural dictates by continuing to organize and educate union workers even after the birth of her children. In 1946, Hillman was elected an ACWA vice president and spent the last 25 years of her life advocating for workers' rights.

Bas Sheva (Bessie) Abramowitz, the fourth daughter of Emanuel Abramowitz and Sarah Rabinowitz, was born during Passover in the tiny *shtetl* of Linoveh, Belarus. Her father was self-employed as a commission agent, buying wholesale commodities from the trains passing through the station near the Abramowitz home and selling them to peasants in the countryside. Sarah supplemented the family income by renting rooms to boarders. Bessie's parents hired a private tutor to educate their children at home.

In 1905, motivated by the probability of an arranged marriage to a local boy, Abramowitz decided to immigrate to America in the company of two cousins. Within days after arriving in New York, 16-year-old Abramowitz traveled to Chicago to stay with distant relatives who owned a boardinghouse. She took a job as a button sewer, hand finishing men's pants. Appalled by the sweatshop conditions, she organized and participated in a number of walkouts. In 1910, after obtaining work with Chicago's largest men's clothing firm, Hart, Schaffner and Marx (HSM), Abramowitz led a small group of women out the door of HSM Shop No. 5 and onto the streets of Chicago. At first, most workers laughed at the young immigrant women. But within three weeks, workers in other shops joined them. Margaret Dreier Robins, the president of the Women's Trade Union League (WTUL), donated thousands of dollars to the strikers and became a principal negotiator along with John Fitzpatrick, the president of the Chicago Federation of Labor. Eventually, even the men came out and the strikers' ranks swelled to almost 40,000, shutting down the entire industry.

Only the Hart, Schaffner and Marx workers won substantial gains, including the right to organize and the establishment of an arbitration board that set the precedent for collective bargaining in the industry. The majority of workers returned to their jobs in February 1911 after enduring frigid temperatures, police brutality, and near starvation without any concessions. Yet, the establishment of arbitration machinery, the cross-class alliances built between supportive progressive reformers and immigrant strikers, and the emergence of a core of strike leaders in the industry were extremely important developments. During the strike, Abramowitz met both Jane Addams, who became a mentor to her, and her future husband, Sidney Hillman, who became the first president of the Amalgamated Clothing Workers Union that was born during the 1910 Chicago Garment Workers Strike.

When the ACWA was officially founded in 1914, Bessie Abramowitz became the first woman elected to the General Executive Board. She served as a union officer until her May 3, 1916, marriage, when she relocated to New York. Bessie Abramowitz Hillman remained active in the union after the births of her two daughters, Philoine, born in 1917, and Selma, born in 1921.

During the Depression, Hillman played an instrumental part in the campaign to organize the runaway shops. These shops, which manufactured primarily shirts, left New York and other metropolitan areas to escape union jurisdiction. After the shops reopened in the rural regions of the northeastern states, the union sent organizers out to bring the workers into the union throughout the mid-1930s. Between 1937 and 1939, Bessie Hillman helped to organize the laundry workers in New York and became the first educational director for the laundry workers. Working closely with black workers for the first time in her life inspired Hillman to work on behalf of the civil rights movement. Labor rights and civil rights became synonymous in Hillman's mind for the rest of her life.

When World War II broke out, Franklin Roosevelt appointed Sidney Hillman to the Office of Production Management in Washington. Bessie stayed behind in New York to head the Amalgamated's War Activities Department, coordinating food, book, and blood drives for the troops overseas. Bessie Hillman helped to abolish the national Red Cross's blood segregation policy. The Hillmans had a personal stake in the war. Bessie Hillman lost 17 immediate family members as a result of the Nazi atrocities in Europe. Exhausted and disappointed when he was passed by for a position when the administration restructured its wartime agencies, Sidney suffered his fourth and final heart attack within a year after the war ended.

As she struggled to overcome the loss of her husband, in 1946, Bessie was re-elected to the General Executive Board as a vice president. Although she had finally achieved her rightful place in the union she helped to found, due to restrictions placed on women in the male-dominated ACWA, she found it impossible to act as she would have liked. Male union leaders assigned Hillman, the lone national female leader of a union where women composed the majority of workers, to ceremonial duties.

Bessie Hillman mounted intense campaigns for civil rights and for women's rights throughout the 1950s and 1960s. At the first Industrial Union Conference for women trade union leaders in 1961, Hillman berated the male-dominated hierarchies prevalent in trade unions, including her own. Token representation and lack of leadership positions was no longer acceptable to women unionists. Articulating her labor feminist agenda, she pressed for working women's full rights as workers, as union members, and as citizens.

In 1961, the President's Commission on the Status of Women chairperson Eleanor Roosevelt invited Hillman to serve on the Protective Labor Legislation Committee. Bessie used this national venue to continue to seek protective laws for women workers. In 1963, the commission published its report, *American Women*, and helped to lobby for the passage of the Equal Pay Act the same year. Hillman worked to expand the opportunities for women and minority workers. In the last year of her life, she traveled to Puerto Rico to help organize men's garment workers, and when no other union would, Hillman and the ACWA organized the production workers at Xerox Company in Rochester, New York. Bessie Hillman died in New York on December 28, 1970.

KAREN PASTORELLO

References and Further Reading

Bessie Abramowitz's papers are contained in the Records of the Amalgamated Clothing Workers of America at the Kheel Labor Management Documentation Center, Martin P. Catherwood Library, Cornell University.

Hillman, Bessie Abramowitz. "Gifted Women in Trade Unions." In *American Women: the Changing Image*, edited by Beverly Benner Cassara. Boston: Beacon Press, 1962.

Weiler, N. Sue. "The Uprising in Chicago: The Men's Garment Workers Strike, 1910–1911." In *A Needle, a Bobbin, a Strike*, edited by Joan Jensen and Sue Davidson. Philadelphia: Temple University Press, 1984, pp. 114–145.

See also **Amalgamated Clothing Workers of America**

HILLMAN, SIDNEY (MARCH 23, 1887– JULY 10, 1946)
Founder, Amalgamated Clothing Workers of America

Sidney Hillman came out of Czarist Russia to help found the largest union of men's garment workers in the United States at the age of 27. During Hillman's 32-year tenure (1914–1946), the Amalgamated Clothing Workers of America (ACWA) grew to one quarter of a million members. Under Hillman's hand, the labor movement was transformed by the introduction of industrial democracy that promised workers social and economic justice replete with full citizenship rights both on and off the shop floor. Hillman came of age just as the United States emerged in the international arena as an industrial power. Progressive reformers were among the first to recognize Hillman's talents as a premier mediator who could skillfully negotiate on behalf of labor with the owners of industry and government officials. He devised a strategy for a "new unionism" that accepted the principles of modern management in return for greater union control in the workplace. Consequently, Hillman's major accomplishments included the implementation of collective bargaining practices throughout the clothing industry. Sidney Hillman encouraged the union's rank and file to participate in the organization's educational activities and in the political arena to elect representatives sympathetic to labor interests. Hillman helped to create a new working-class conscious among garment workers that demanded improved living and working conditions for all workers.

Sidney Hillman was born into a Russian Jewish family in Zagare, Lithuania, a small town in the Russian Pale of Settlement on March 23, 1887. His parents, Schmuel Hillman, a merchant, and Judith Paikin, the owner of a small grocery store, expected him to continue the rabbinical family tradition by attending yeshiva. However, Hillman cut his religious training short to take a job where his contemporaries exposed him to the Jewish enlightenment movement (*Haskala*) as well as to the classic works of Darwin, Marx, Mill, and Spencer. At the age of 15, Hillman joined the General Jewish Workers Union, the Bund, and was jailed twice for his part in demonstrations during the Russian Revolution of 1905. The months he spent in prison strengthened his Marxist convictions, thus rendering him a "half-intellectual" in an increasingly secular culture.

After his second release from prison, Hillman fled to the home of his wealthy uncle in Manchester, England, where two of his three brothers were already staying. In 1907, Hillman arrived in New York, migrating soon afterward to Chicago, where one of his former Bund comrades had a pharmacy practice. Hillman worked in the warehouse, as a stock clerk and finally as a package wrapper at Sears before being hired as an apprentice cutter at Hart, Schaffner and Marx (HSM), the largest men's clothing firm in Chicago. While Hart, Schaffner and Marx had a reputation for modern Prussian-style management, it was no less oppressive as far as wages and hours than a small sweatshop.

On September 22, 1910, a group of young women who were frustrated by a series of arbitrary wage cuts walked off their jobs at Hart, Schaffner and Marx Shop Number 5. Hillman's future wife, 18-year-old Bessie Abramowitz, led the strike. Three weeks later, the male workers, including Sidney Hillman, who at first made fun of the mostly immigrant women strikers, joined them in the streets of Chicago. Workers from other shops swelled the strike ranks to almost 40,000. The workers who participated in the conflict endured an extremely harsh winter and police brutality. Due to the refusal of the xenophobic United Garment Workers (UGW), the only men's clothing union in existence at the time to support the strikers, and staunch employer resistance, only the Hart, Schaffner and Marx workers won strike concessions. The 30,000 workers in the other shops stayed on the picket lines until February, many eventually losing their jobs, while the HSM employees returned to their jobs with the guarantee of union recognition and the establishment of an arbitration board.

Despite the mixed results spelling defeat for the workers outside the HSM shops, the strike proved pivotal for the men's garment workers. Hillman emerged as a leader and benefited immensely from the friendship of the labor lawyer Clarence Darrow. Over the next few years, both Darrow and John E. Williams, the first chairman of the Board of Arbitration under the HSM agreement, became important mentors to Hillman, schooling him in English and in the art of industrial mediation. The Board of Arbitration provided for in the strike agreement marked the beginning of a collective bargaining process in the men's clothing industry. Hillman and the other young strike leaders also made important connections to the Chicago reform community that unconditionally supported the strikers, including Hull-House residents Jane Addams, Ellen Gates Starr, and Grace Abbott; the Women's Trade Union League president Margaret Dreier Robins; the progressive lawyer Harold Ickes; and the Chicago Federation of Labor (CFL) president John Fitzpatrick. The solidarity built among the diverse ethnic groups of men's garment workers in Chicago laid the foundation for the Amalgamated Clothing Workers of America. Hillman impressed all who observed him in action, earning a reputation as the leading labor statesman of his generation.

Following the strike, Hillman served as a business agent for the reconfigured Local 39 and also helped to organize workers in other Chicago shops. In 1914, he accepted an invitation from the International Ladies Garment Workers' Union (ILGWU) to move to New York to administer its Protocol of Peace, the system for arbitrating grievances in the women's clothing industry. While in New York, Hillman spent some time with Louis Brandeis, a progressive lawyer who had helped the strikers in the 1910 Chicago Strike and was committed to the employment of arbitration mechanisms to achieve industrial peace. Several months later, Hillman received a telegram from a group of insurgent workers attending the UGW's convention in Nashville, enlisting him as the new president of the union they were in the process of establishing. After some hesitation, Hillman accepted the presidency in December 1914 and returned to Chicago to help get the Amalgamated Clothing Workers off the ground and to marry in 1916 Bessie Abramowitz. The Hillmans relocated to New York so that Sidney could work at the union's headquarters. Sidney Hillman devoted his early union years to organizing the many ethnicities in the leading garment centers of Chicago, New York, Baltimore, Philadelphia, and Rochester.

During World War I, Hillman worked to facilitate arbitration agreements guaranteeing collective bargaining practices in the military uniform industry. He extended his influence outside the labor movement, working closely with influential progressive leaders in and around the government including Florence Kelley, the secretary of the National Consumer's League, and Felix Frankfurter and Walter Lippman, both officials in the secretary of war's office.

In the postwar years, the ACWA embraced Hillman's vision for "new unionism," which combined the concepts of scientific management and worker cooperation. True to the ACWA slogan, "To touch the worker from cradle to grave," the union introduced social welfare benefits such as unemployment insurance for Chicago workers, and cooperative housing projects and banks in New York. Although offering an alternative to the welfare capitalist practices of some of the nation's largest corporations, the union faced a number of challenges during the 1920s that threatened its very existence. In the aftermath of the red scare, unions—particularly those with ties to Russia like the ACWA, led primarily by Russian Jewish immigrants who supported the Russian Revolution from abroad—were suspect. Sidney Hillman successfully battled the anti-union sentiment prevalent in American society. He defeated extortion attempts from union racketeers and power coups by a small group of leftists within the union. Hillman successfully purged the corrupt elements within the union's ranks by the end of the decade. He also encouraged the development of educational and cultural programs to forge a sense of solidarity among the diverse unionists. Programs that offered English and citizenship classes proved popular among immigrant workers. Gradually, separate foreign language locals were dissolved and replaced with locals based on job types.

The economic decline that began in the late 1920s spiraled out of control by the early 1930s, exacting a high price for the Amalgamated. The stock market crash of 1929 and the Great Depression that followed virtually decimated the ACWA. Membership declined from 177,000 in 1920 to fewer than 110,000 by 1929. In the midst of the unfavorable political and economic climate, Hillman's 1931 proposal before the United States Senate Committee seeking the establishment of a national economic council representing agriculture, labor, and industry fell flat. Franklin Delano Roosevelt's election to the presidency marked the dawn of a new day for labor. Sidney Hillman recognized the opportunity for increased government responsibility and participation in the lives of the workers in the overtures the new president made to labor.

During his administration, Franklin Roosevelt amassed a national coalition of reformers, manufacturers, and labor leaders that included Sidney Hillman. With remarkable speed, Hillman ascended from the margins of American society to a government insider instrumental in shaping labor policy. Roosevelt named Hillman to the Labor Advisory Board of the National Recovery Administration (NRA) in 1933 and to the Industrial Recovery Board in 1934. Closer to the center of power, Sidney Hillman fortified labor's position by successfully advocating for the enactment of codes to standardize wages in the clothing industry. When the United States Supreme Court declared the National Industrial Recovery Act, with its provision for workers' rights to bargain collectively with their employers through representatives of their own choosing unconstitutional, Hillman helped to draft the Wagner Act. The 1935 passage of the National Labor Relations (or Wagner) Act guaranteed labor's right to organize and established collective bargaining practices as the foundation for industrial relations. The act also established the National Labor Relations Board (NLRB) to help protect workers' rights by ensuring that they were free to choose to be represented by unions. Hillman also lobbied for the passage of the Fair Labor Standards Act in 1938, which provided minimum wage and maximum hour regulations for many American workers.

By the mid-1930s, Hillman attempted to solidify the ACWA's place in the labor arena by affiliating with the American Federation of Labor (AFL) in 1933. But the Amalgamated was expelled from the AFL three years later. Due to the defeat of the industrial union resolutions at the 1935 AFL convention, Hillman became a founding member in the Committee for Industrial Organization (CIO). In 1938, the CIO held its first official convention and changed its name to the Congress of Industrial Organizations. Sidney Hillman became a CIO vice president. As the ACWA regained its strength, it supported the campaign for industrial unionism in the automobile, rubber, steel, and textile industries. In 1937, Hillman also helped to launch the Textile Workers Organizing Committee, which eventually became the Textile Workers Union of America. The rise of these new unions and the emergence of a new national organization, the CIO, marked the dawn of a new day for the labor movement.

Throughout the late 1930s, as labor and politics intertwined, Hillman established himself as a political entity. He made valiant efforts to coalesce the labor movement's varied political interests into a single association that would rally behind Roosevelt. In 1936, Hillman played a vital part in the founding of Labor's Non-Partisan League (LNPL). Roosevelt's re-election that same year represented a triumph for labor. As they worked to organize the industrial masses, Hillman and other CIO leaders hoped that someday labor could shepherd its own independent party.

During the war years, labor continued to make substantial strides under Hillman's guidance. As a member of the National Defense Advisory Commission (NDAC), he insisted that all government defense contractors obey labor laws and abide by a maximum 40-hour workweek. He encouraged the government to withdraw contracts from companies found to be in violation of existing legislation. In 1941, he achieved unprecedented power when FDR promoted him to the position of associate director of the Office of Production Management (which replaced the NDAC), where he was charged with guaranteeing a reliable supply of workers for the war effort. Yet 1941 marked a turbulent and strike-prone year for American workers that forced Hillman's hand and marked the decline of his influence in the Roosevelt administration. Appointed to the Labor Division of the War Production Board in 1942, he devised a plan for sweeping social and economic reform that ensured union security but failed to win the president over. In April 1942, FDR created the War Manpower Commission, bypassing the Amalgamated president and appointing the former governor of Indiana, Paul McNutt, to lead the agency instead. With his health impaired by the pressure of national defense work and worried about his family in war-torn Eastern Europe, Hillman suffered a major heart attack in the early summer of 1942 that left him hospitalized for months.

Out of a government post, nonetheless Hillman remained committed to Roosevelt and loyal to the Democratic Party. He created the CIO's Political Action Committee (PAC) in mid-1943 and immediately became its chairperson. He spent the remainder of the war years enlisting the CIO's political machinery in Roosevelt's name. The 1944 election elevated Hillman to the national spotlight when Republicans tried to discredit Roosevelt in the press by suggesting that the United States government was in the hands of a foreign-born Jew in the person of Sidney Hillman. The Republicans tried to create the impression that Hillman wielded unscrupulous power over the presidential administration. *The New York Times* reported that when the Democratic Party leaders asked for an endorsement of the vice presidential nominee, FDR supposedly replied, "Clear it with Sidney." Despite the negative publicity, Hillman was able to swing the labor vote to elect Roosevelt to an unprecedented fourth term. As World War II came to an end, Hillman allied with the British Trade Union leader Sir Walter Citrine to create the World Federation of Trade Unions, an organization that sought an official advisory position in the postwar arena. Much to Hillman's dismay, as the victor nations scrambled to oversee the rebuilding of Europe, the organization and its goals were not taken seriously.

The intensity with which Hillman performed his work exacted an overwhelming personal toll. In the months following the war's end, the Hillmans learned that they had lost 17 immediate family members to Hitler's wrath. Exhausted, Sidney Hillman succumbed to his fourth heart attack at the age of 59 and died at his Point Lookout cottage on Long Island on July 10, 1946. In the struggle to establish a more egalitarian society, Hillman left a legacy of landmark labor legislation that continues to protect workers' rights and improve their living standards. He is remembered with a number of health centers honoring his name and with the annual presentations of the Sidney Hillman Foundation, established in 1950, which makes annual awards for excellence in media and publishing exemplified by the ideals of Sidney Hillman.

KAREN PASTORELLO

References and Further Reading

The Amalgamated Clothing Workers of America. *To Promote the General Welfare: The Story of the Amalgamated.* New York: The Amalgamated Clothing Workers of America, 1950.

The Amalgamated Joint Boards and Local Unions in New York. *The Book of the Amalgamated in New York, 1914–1940.* New York: The Amalgamated Joint Boards and Local Unions in New York, 1940.

Fraser, Steven. *Labor Will Rule: Sidney Hillman and the Rise of American Labor.* Ithaca, NY: Cornell University Press, 1993.

Fraser, Steven. "Sidney Hillman: Labor's Machiavelli." In *Labor Leaders in America,* edited by Melvyn Dubofsky and Warren Van Tine. Urbana: University of Illinois Press, 1987.

Josephson, Matthew. *Sidney Hillman: Statesman of American Labor.* New York: Doubleday & Company, 1952.

Soule, George. *Sidney Hillman: Labor Statesman.* New York: Macmillan, 1939.

HISTORIOGRAPHY OF AMERICAN LABOR HISTORY

For nearly three quarters of a century, between the 1880s and the 1950s, the writing of labor history remained primarily the province of academic labor economists and a handful of amateur historians linked to specific trade unions and left-wing political parties. Sociologists also wrote numerous contemporary studies of working-class communities that drew upon knowledge of the past to illuminate the present. Before the end of World War II, however, few professionally trained, academic historians ventured into the field of labor history.

Because economists and partisans dominated the writing of labor history at first, it was usually written to promote specific public policies or special causes. Most of the amateur labor historians wrote on behalf of their unions or political parties, and enjoyed little readership beyond their own organizational circles. The labor economists had a different agenda. Nearly all of them, beginning with perhaps the first of the breed, Richard Ely, a professor of economics at the University of Wisconsin, advocated trade unionism and collective bargaining. They acted as social reformers and many of them were among the most prominent figures in the progressive movement of the early twentieth century, pioneers of the "Wisconsin idea," and of such concepts as workers' compensation, unemployment insurance, and social security. Their interest in public policy and their dual role as policy makers shaped the labor history that they wrote.

Labor history as a field of scholarship can best be said to begin with the work of John R. Commons, a protégé of Ely and the lead author of the first multivolume history of labor in the United States. Commons orchestrated not one but two massive multivolume works devoted to labor history. He edited an 11-volume documentary history of U.S. industrial society from the colonial times to 1880 that covered nearly every aspect of labor history, including the place of indentured servitude and slavery. The 11 volumes provided a foundation for the narrative labor history written by Commons, his students, and those influenced by the "Wisconsin school" of labor history. Commons's four-volume history of labor in the United States, published between 1918 and 1935, defined and dominated the field for decades. Commons himself wrote only brief introductions to two of the four volumes; the remainder of the first two narrative volumes carried the story of labor from colonial times to 1896, and the third volume, a collection of essays on structural rather than historical aspects of the subject, was written entirely by students and faculty associates of Commons. The fourth and perhaps most famous volume in the series, a history of American labor from 1896 to 1932, was the work of Selig Perlman and Philip Taft, two of Commons's more notable former students, and themselves leading long-term scholars of American labor history.

The Commons volumes shared a teleological quality, presenting the history of labor as the unfolding of a tale in which working people shed their individualistic behaviors and aspirations in order to accept their place as a permanent, dependent wage-earning class that could best serve its own interests by uniting collectively in responsible trade unions that bargained with employers about how to distribute equitably the wealth created by capitalist enterprises. Selig Perlman, the most intellectually ambitious of Commons's students, provided a theoretical framework for the history he and other labor economists wrote. Perlman asserted that workers shared a scarcity consciousness that led them to stress job control and to create unions that regulated access to jobs through strict conditions of apprenticeship, rigid rules for union membership, and closed-shop agreements with employers. For Perlman, the American Federation of Labor (AFL) craft unions that practiced job control through tightly controlled memberships and closed shops reflected the scarcity consciousness and core beliefs of American workers. Inclusive unions that admitted all workers, promoted class conflict, and sought the abolition of capitalism were, for Perlman, the product of the fevered imaginations of intellectuals that had no purchase among ordinary workers.

Nearly all the labor history written between 1918 and the 1950s shared some part of the Commons-Perlman approach. The economics department at The Johns Hopkins University and the university's press, for example, published a series of books that examined historically how trade unions regulated the labor market, restricted their memberships, exercised their labor market power through strikes, boycotts, and union labels, and engaged in contract bargaining with employers. Robert F. Hoxie and Norman Ware, two labor economists who wrote partly outside the Commons-Perlman framework, in their histories of organized labor between 1860 and 1918, nevertheless treated labor movement opponents of job-conscious AFL-style craft unionism, whether the Knights of Labor or the Industrial Workers of the World (IWW), as utopians whose visions lacked deep resonance among most workers and who were doomed to fail. Almost without exception, all the books written about labor history focused on the stories of individual unions, union federations, famous strikes, and routinized collective bargaining between unions and managements.

Even the most notable dissenter from the Commons-Perlman school, Philip S. Foner, a historian not an economist, wrote a multivolume history of labor in the United States and a myriad of separate studies that scarcely varied from the narrative model developed by the Wisconsin school. For Foner, like Commons, Perlman, Taft, and all the labor economists, labor history was primarily the story of trade unionists, strikes, bargaining with employers, union politics and lobbying, material factors that could be measured and quantified and not cultural factors that fell outside the sphere of union institutions and that eluded easy measurement. Foner followed the original script but reversed its heroes and judgments. For him, the AFL, while an advance over the utopian Knights of Labor, represented a setback for the mass of working people. Its leaders were men who neglected or oppressed African-Americans, Asians, and even southern and eastern European immigrants, women, and common laborers. They collaborated with employers rather than battling them; they disciplined their followers rather than encouraging them to wage class conflict; and they made peace with capitalism rather than overthrowing it. Foner had his own teleology. In his narrative, labor history must lead ineluctably to the rejection of job-conscious unionism, the triumph of socialism (communism after November 1917), and the end of capitalism.

A French historian of labor, Georges Haupt, captured precisely the limitations of the interpretive model built by such scholars as Commons, Perlman, and Foner. Their history, he wrote, "narrows the dimensions of the workers world and encloses it within a framework that is fixed and congealed. It does not focus on the working class itself but on its organizational and ideological representations." Such studies, the Frenchman concluded, "affect at the very most a small circle of partisans or lovers of historical detail."

Toward a New Labor History

Although most histories of labor continued to be written by labor economists or by Marxist-oriented scholars like Foner and to focus primarily on white male workers, their unions, and their struggles, a number of sociologists, some influenced by Marxism, began to write about different aspects of the working-class experience. Even Commons and Perlman hinted at a more capacious version of labor history. Perlman noted that the history of unions reflected workers' constant adaptation to their environment, both material and mental, through which they struggled not as "a class-conscious proletariat" but as American citizens with their own ideal of liberty. Here Perlman presaged the concept of "republican citizenship" that evolved into a staple of 1980s new labor history. Another Commons disciple expressed sentiments that decades later might better be associated with the ideas of Herbert Gutman, who some credit as the founding father of the "new labor history." Alluding to the "great migration" of African-Americans north during World War I, the Commons team member noted, "their manner of living and their modes of thinking had to be recast. The readjustment from the modus vivendi of agricultural peasants to that of industrial wage earners involved as great changes in their lives as in those of European peasant immigrants to the United States" (Commons, vol. 3, p. 44).

Other scholars, however, seized such kernels of scholarly complexity and turned them into more expansive portrayals of labor history. Vera Shlakman and Caroline Ware treated the world of women workers in the New England textile industry, most of whom lived their daily lives beyond the reach of trade unions or other institutionalized manifestations of the labor movement. Shlakman and Ware probed the factors that moved women into textile towns and factories, how their experiences as full-time wage workers shaped their daily lives outside the factory as well as within its gates, and the particular kind of female culture these workers created. Other observers and scholars wrote a series of books that dissected the lives and cultures of southern textile workers, most of whom entered the mills as family units. Although many of these studies were inspired by a series of strikes that swept across the Southern Piedmont between 1928 and 1934, the vast majority of mill families remained beyond the reach of unions. For most of them, religion and the church occupied a far more vital and influential part of their daily lives than trade unionism, as the study by the sociologist Liston Pope, *Millhands and Preachers*, attested. Sterling Spero and Abram Harris wrote the first general history of African-American workers in the industrial age, and Horace Cayton and George S. Mitchell described in their *Black Workers and the New Unions* how the labor upheaval of the 1930s transformed the relationship between African-American workers in mass-production industry and unions, turning it from one founded on mutual antipathy and despair to one based on cooperation and hope. The Yale sociologist E. W. Bakke published two books that portrayed the daily lives, family relations, cultural values, political practices, and search for work by the unemployed in Depression-era New Haven. Alfred Winslow Jones did much the same for the rubber workers of Akron, Ohio, using opinion-sampling methods to uncover how that city's industrial workers felt about such issues as corporate power, private property rights, religion, education, and politics. Had any historians paid attention to such scholarship in the 1930s and 1940s, they might have sensed a whole new way of writing the history of labor in the United States.

When historians, as distinguished from labor economists, industrial relations mavens, and sociologists, finally turned their attention to labor history in the late 1940s and 1950s, they concentrated on the staple agenda of traditional U.S. history. The big question asked by historians writing about workers was, did labor support Andrew Jackson? They questioned Arthur Schlesinger Jr.'s re-interpretation of Jacksonian Democracy, which claimed that the political movement drew its strongest support among workers in the nation's eastern seaboard and interior cities, not among western farmers and frontiersmen. Most of the historians who asked the question answered in the negative and even doubted that workers in the Jacksonian era thought of themselves as a class and behaved as one. One of the young historians who joined the debate, Richard Hofstadter, later one of the nation's most distinguished scholars, would forever remain linked to the "consensus school" of historical interpretation and to the notion that the United States was fundamentally a one-class, middle-class society. Alone among that group of historians, Edward Pessen continued to write books and articles about labor history, though that was never his primary interest.

What later came to be known as the "new labor history" emerged without proclamations, publicity, or even awareness that such a subfield existed. The three names most commonly associated with the creation of the "new labor history"—David Brody, Herbert Gutman, and David Montgomery—became linked to labor history only after its invention as a subfield of history. Indeed, the book that in some ways marked the birth of a new labor history, Irving Bernstein's *The Lean Years* (1959), remained the work of an industrial relations scholar. A year later, when David Brody's *Steelworkers in America: The Non-union Era* appeared, reviewers failed to stress its contribution to labor history. Instead, they treated the book largely as an addition to the growing body of literature on the impact of industrialization and immigration on the modernization of the United States. Only with hindsight can Brody's book be characterized as the opening salvo in the historians' emerging critique of the Commons-Perlman version of labor history. What made Brody's book notable was its emphasis on a nonunion labor force and its comparison of the cultures and behaviors of immigrant common laborers and U.S.-born skilled workers. Brody highlighted the aspects of working-class experience that Commons, Perlman, et al. neglected; he opened the pathways that other historians of labor would soon follow.

Yet nearly a decade passed before the sort of history that Brody wrote in 1960 had a real impact on professional history in the United States. During that time, omens of what later were characterized as the "new labor history" appeared. Most important perhaps were a brilliant essay and an epic book by the English historian Edward P. Thompson. His essay on the "moral economy of the premodern workers" and his larger book, *The Making of the English Working Class*, altered how historians came to understand and to write labor history. Thompson ended the sway of mechanical Marxists and nuts-and-bolts labor economists by endowing ordinary working people with nonmaterial customs, traditions, and beliefs, many of religious origin, that enabled them to resist their superiors and to act as their own historical agents in the making of a working class. Slowly at first and rapidly thereafter, historians of the United States would try to apply Thompson's methods and concepts to the history of American workers. Little noticed at that time, a young American historian had been publishing articles in minor state historical journals that paralleled some of Thompson's concerns and findings. That young scholar, Herbert Gutman, studied theretofore obscure events in labor history: strikes and riots in small railroad-dominated communities, a demonstration by unemployed workers in New York City, a comparison of a strike-torn coal-mining community and an iron enterprise-dominated city, and industrial conflict and social mobility in Paterson, New Jersey. In those articles, Gutman illustrated how workers viewed their world as well as the traditions and values that governed their behavior.

As the 1960s drew to an end, labor history still seemed to be peripheral to U.S. history's dominant concerns. Reviewers treated the eminent labor historian David Montgomery's first book *Beyond Equality* (1967) more as a re-interpretation of civil war and reconstruction historiography than as a venture in the writing of labor history. And they deemed Melvyn Dubofsky's first book, *When Workers Organize* (1968), as primarily a contribution to the historiography of Progressivism. But then in a paper delivered in 1969 and published a year later, David Brody announced the coming of age of labor history, an event he associated with the publication of two books in 1969: Irving Bernstein's *Turbulent Years* and Melvyn Dubofsky's *We Shall Be All*. Soon Brody and others heralded a "new labor history" that they distinguished from the old history associated with Commons and Perlman. The "old" had limited itself to the story of unionized workers for whom AFL-style craft qua business unionism represented the sine qua non of labor history in the United States. The "new" took as its province the entire working class, the vast majority outside of unions as well as the unionized minority; it treated neither the AFL nor business unionism as the be-all and end-all for organized labor and its history; it preferred contingency to determinism, and it treated workers as active citizens who made their own history.

Not only did the field of labor history flourish in the 1970s, but its practitioners also won greater respect within the larger discipline of history. Gutman, whose scholarship had appeared previously in peripheral journals or had remained unpublished, now found his work published in U.S. history's two primary scholarly journals of record: the *American Historical Review* and the *Journal of American History*. In 1975, one of the most respected trade publishers released a collection of Gutman's major published and unpublished essays and articles under the title *Work, Culture, and Society in Industrializing America*. Allan Dawley won the Bancroft Prize in History for his book on the shoe workers of Lynn, Massachusetts, and by the end of the decade a bequest from the family of the late Philip Taft established a Taft Prize for the best book published annually in labor history.

A burgeoning series of community studies, meantime, sought to determine the realities of occupational and social mobility across the mid- and late- nineteenth century, the most famous of which were Stephen Thernstrom's dissections of mobility among working people in Newburyport and Boston, Massachusetts. Other community studies challenged the "consensus school" of history, seeking to prove that a process of proletarianization in which artisans were separated from their tools of production created a distinct working class conscious of its subordinate position and determined to change it through collective action. Unlike the Commons-Perlman interpretation, which tightly linked class and trade unionism, the "new labor history" portrayed class consciousness as manifested in oppositional cultural, ideological, and religious ways that built on historical traditions and customs. Many of these younger labor historians saw themselves as disciples of E. P. Thompson and as scholars who had uncovered "the making of the American working class."

If anything, the myriad of community studies, a stream that never slackened, led to confusion as much as to enlightenment. Rather than revealing a working class conscious of its own interests, such studies disclosed a working class fractured along lines of ethnicity (national origins), race, and gender. Instead of attesting to the "making of an American working class," the new labor history revealed many working classes in a constant state of decomposition and recomposition. David Brody and David Montgomery sought to bring a measure of order out of the scholarly chaos in separate essay collections that focused on the workplace as the site of a collective job consciousness (in Brody's case) and of a workers' control ethic based on the autonomy and manliness of the skilled worker (in Montgomery's). Yet, when workers returned to their neighborhoods from their places of labor, they separated themselves on the basis of ethnicity, race, religion, and even politics. The more that was written and published about labor history, the more diffuse the subject grew. In 1984, the older and the younger practitioners of the "new labor history" met in a conference funded by the National Endowment for the Humanities, at which they discussed how to bring synthesis to the field. That conference, which gathered at Northern Illinois University, went about its business in a metaphorical and literal fog. Rather than establishing the basis for a new synthesis in American labor history, the conferees further fractured the field by raising the subjects of gender and patriarchy. Now, not only did labor historians have to contend with workers divided by ethnicity, race, and religion, but they also had to recognize that Montgomery's manly craftsman and Brody's job-conscious trade unionist were but a part of a working class that must perforce include its women. After such scholars as Alice Kessler Harris and Mari Jo Buhle laid down the challenge at the 1984 conference to treat gender as a vital aspect of labor history, historians have written a flood of books and articles on women workers, women and the labor movement, and masculinity as a central characteristic of the male worker.

The large, new body of scholarship about gender has clarified how women's work, career, and life trajectories differed from those of men. It attempted to explain how women and their work were marginalized by men and their unions as well as in most of the extant literature about the history of labor. Its practitioners interrogated the concept of skilled labor, suggesting that gender (masculinity), not knowledge acquired through years of training, created skill. They argued that concepts of masculinity and femininity defined nearly all aspects of work and the differential beliefs and behaviors of male and female workers and union members. Several gender scholars even credited the labor movement's hyper-masculinity with the movement's Pyrrhic victories and too-frequent blatant failures. Yet many of the interpretations and conclusions drawn by the historians of gender rested more on putative theories and assertions than on careful analysis or firm evidence. Indeed, much of the scholarship on gender and labor could be read to re-inforce prevailing beliefs in the field of labor history rather than to transform core knowledge in the field. In fact, one might argue that gender scholarship has served more to add to our knowledge of labor history than to reconceptualize how we perceive and comprehend the subject.

Goodbye to the New Labor History

As the twentieth century drew to its close, there was little new about writing "history from below," giving voice to the heretofore inarticulate, perceiving the diversity of working people, or introducing gender as a category of historical analysis. Not only had labor history created a valued place for itself in the larger discipline, it had become as diverse as the people and institutions that it studied. Labor economists and industrial relations authorities continued to write institutional histories of trade unions, labor markets, and collective bargaining. Sanford Jacoby, for example, wrote two of the finest books on the subject of corporate labor policies: *Employing Bureaucracy* and *Modern Manors*. Historians published books and articles about the rise and fall of trade unions and labor federations, among which the most notable might have been Robert Zieger's massive history of the Congress of Industrial Organizations, which delineated the lives of such labor leaders as John L. Lewis, Sidney Hillman, Walter Reuther, Jimmy Hoffa, and Samuel Gompers. Radical movements and industrial conflicts also remained essential parts of labor's story. Historians as well as sociologists persisted in studying local communities, and for them, as well as for many other scholars of labor, ethnicity, race, and gender remained vital parts of labor's history.

Two sets of scholars, however, dismissed the "new labor history" as old. One group, influenced by poststructuralism and postmodernism, rejected labor history's emphasis on measurable or quantifiable data, its focus on the material aspects of everyday life, and its acceptance at face value of the languages of trade unionism and working-class radicalism. These scholars became associated with what was known as the "linguistic turn" in labor history, a movement that borrowed from linguistic scholars, literary critics, and philosophers and that treated language rather than material factors as the source of human consciousness, including class consciousness. Language, rather than the forces and relations of production, constructed cultural meanings. Language thus created whatever sense of class existed. Hence, cultural studies rather than labor history held the key to understanding the working-class experience. Scholars attracted to the "linguistic turn" have been heavily involved in rewriting the history of gender, as attested to most notably by Joan Scott's leading role and by the stress on language and culture in the writings of Alice Kessler Harris, Nan Enstad, and Elizabeth Faue, among others.

A second group, associated most closely with the writings of David Roediger, insisted that the key to opening the hidden history of American workers was the concept of "whiteness." For them, "whiteness" and American citizenship acted as synonymous terms. Those workers defined as white occupied a privileged position causing each generation of new immigrant workers to struggle to define themselves as white, a possibility denied to those of African, Asian, and Native American (thus many Hispanics) origins. Thus, race had to be as much about being white as being black, brown, red, or yellow. Like the scholars and historians who took the "linguistic turn," the historians of whiteness focused more on language and cultural practices, both of which they read in particular ways, than on hard, or measurable, archival and documentary evidence to prove that Caucasian workers treasured their white skins and the privileges it conveyed. Because most of the scholars of whiteness, Matthew Frye Jacobson and others as well as Roediger, rely for their evidence mostly on language, which can be read in multiple ways and malleable cultural concepts, their findings have been subject to withering criticisms, most notably by Eric Arnesen and Peter Kolchin.

Yet another group of scholars unwilling to jettison either the old or the new labor history set as its agenda the internationalization of U.S. labor history. Aware that the history of workers in the United States has its own peculiarities, these historians insist that there is little exceptional about the American experience. From early on in the nineteenth century, capital and labor circled the globe. In the heyday of industrialization (1870s–1920s), the labor force in the United States was overwhelmingly immigrant in composition, composed in the main of working people who carried with them traditions and customs as well as concepts about worker movements that originated in their lands of origin. And such immigrant workers, as countless new studies have proved, rarely broke their links to their original home places, continuing to communicate with those who remained behind. The late twentieth century saw this process repeated on an even grander geographical stage, with capital circulating around the world more rapidly than ever and peoples from all continents moving in search of jobs and income. For a new generation of American labor historians, then, transnational capital, worker, and labor movements became the subject of their research and writing.

If labor history at the start of the twenty-first century no longer carried the freighted charge it had when its "newer" version was invented in the 1960s, it was well rid of that burden. Its practitioners have indeed restored voice to the previously inarticulate, turned those at the bottom of society into historical subjects with will and agency, and portrayed working people in all their ethnic, racial, gendered, and cultural diversity. They have continued to write solid institutional histories and substantial biographies; add more and more working-class communities to our knowledge base; broaden substantially our understanding of nonwhite workers; explore how gender has governed the behavior of workers; interrogate the language and cultural practices of working people; and probe the ever-changing relationship among workers, the state, and the law. Labor history has become a movable feast.

MELVYN DUBOFSKY

References and Further Reading

Baron, Ava, ed. *Work Engendered: Toward a New History of American Labor*. Ithaca, NY: Cornell University Press, 1991.

Brody, David. *In Labor's Cause: Main Themes on the History of the American Worker*. New York: Oxford University Press, 1993.

———, "The Old Labor History and the New." *Labor History* 20 (Winter 1979): 111–126.

Commons, John R. *History of Labor in the United States*, 4 volumes. New York: The Macmillan Company, 1918–1935.

Dubofsky, Melvyn. "Give Us That Old-Time Labor History: Philip S. Foner and the American Worker." *Labor History* 26 (1985): 118–137.

———. *Hard Work: The Making of Labor History*. Urbana: The University of Illinois Press, 2000.

Fink, Leon. *In Search of the Working Class: Essays in American Labor History and Political Culture*. Urbana: University of Illinois Press, 1994.

Foner, Philip S. *History of the Labor Movement in the United States*, 8 volumes. New York: International Publishers, 1947–2000.

Gutman, Herbert G. *Work, Culture, and Society in Industrializing America: Essays in American Working-Class and Social History*. New York: Knopf, 1976.

"ILWCH Roundtable: What Next for Labor and Working-Class History?" *International Labor and Working-Class History* 46 (Fall 1994): 7–92.

Jacoby, Sanford. *Modern Manors: Welfare Capitalism since the New Deal*. Princeton, NJ: Princeton University Press, 1997.

Montgomery, David. *The Fall of the House of Labor: The Workplace, the State, and American Labor Activism, 1865–1925*. New York: Cambridge University Press, 1987.

———. "To Study the People." *Labor History* 21 (Fall 1980): 485–512.

Moody, J. Carroll, and Alice Kessler-Harris, eds. *American Labor History: The Problems of Synthesis*. DeKalb, IL: Northern Illinois University Press, 1989.

Perlman, Selig. *A Theory of the Labor Movement*. New York: Macmillan, 1928.

Roediger, David. *The Wages of Whiteness: Race and the Making of the American Working Class*. New York: Verso, 1999.

Taft, Philip. *Organized Labor in American History*. New York: Harper & Row, 1964.

Zieger, Robert. *The CIO, 1935–1955*. Chapel Hill: The University of North Carolina Press, 1995.

HITCHMAN COAL & COKE COMPANY v. MITCHELL (1916)

At the turn of the twentieth century, labor unions were influencing the free market competition among coal operators in the United States. Nonunion companies in the South that paid their workers under union wages were outselling companies from the Midwest that employed union miners. The union operators that comprised the Central Competitive Field sought the assistance of the United Mine Workers (UMW) to standardize miners' wages to even the competition. Nonunion operators fiercely resisted the UMW's subsequent organizing campaigns in southern mines, generating a number of lawsuits. The definitive case that emerged out of this conflict was from West Virginia.

The lawsuit filed by the Hitchman Coal & Coke Company (HCCC) in 1907 against the United Mine Workers (UMW) executives was based on a history of volatile relations between the company and the union. In 1902, the HCCC opened a mine in Marshall County, West Virginia. Though it initially hired only nonunion miners, within a year, the UMW successfully organized the workers. That year and again in 1904, the miners went on strike over wages. Both strikes settled after several weeks, with the Company reporting significant financial losses after each strike. In 1906, the Hitchman miners went on strike again, this time in support of a strike called by the UMW over wage disputes by other regional miners. The HCCC responded aggressively.

The HCCC determined to transform its mine into a nonunion workplace. It re-opened and hired only those miners who professed they were not union members and agreed to keep the mine nonunion. These accords, commonly called yellow-dog contracts, included discharge as a penalty for violation. When UMW organizers attempted to persuade the new Hitchman miners to secretly join the union in violation of the yellow-dog contracts, the HCCC secured an injunction against UMW President John Mitchell and other executives barring them from soliciting the miners and initiating a strike.

In 1917, the United States Supreme Court upheld the legality of the yellow-dog contracts and the injunction. The majority held that the same liberty that allowed workers to form unions allowed other workers to agree not to form unions. It acknowledged that workers had a right to unionize, but asserted it was not an absolute right, insisting that it must be balanced against the company's conflicting property right to compete in the free market. Only Justice Brandeis's dissent drew on the emerging Progressive legal theories that rejected the classical reasoning that privileged employers' right to compete over labor's right to organize and strike.

In 1931, Congress negated the holding in *Hitchman* by passing the Norris-LaGuardia Act, which outlawed yellow-dog contracts, validated labor's right to form unions, and prohibited federal courts from issuing injunctions against unions engaged in peaceful activities. The Supreme Court upheld the Act in 1938. The Act, however, did not settle the issue of whether laborers could establish a closed shop. Though the National Labor Relations Act (1935) did permit employees and employers who were covered by the Act to jointly agree to hire only union workers, the Taft-Hartley Act (1947) effectively outlawed the closed shop, supporting an employee's right to work and not join a union. Yellow-dog contracts, nonetheless, remained illegal.

GWEN HOERR JORDAN

References and Further Reading

Ernst, Daniel R. *Lawyers against Labor: From Individual Rights to Corporate Liberalism*. Urbana: University of Illinois Press, 1995.

Horowitz, Morton. *The Transformation of American Law, 1870–1960*. New York: Oxford University Press, 1992.

Ross, William G. *A Muted Fury: Populists, Progressives, and the Labor Unions Confront the Courts, 1890–1937*. Princeton, NJ: Princeton University Press, 1994.

Cases and Statutes Cited

Hitchman Coal & Coke v. Mitchell, 245 U.S. 229 (1917)

NLRB v. Jones & Laughlin Steel Corp., 301 U.S. 1 (1937)

United States Supreme Court in Lauf v. Shinner, 303 U.S. 323 (1938)

HOBOES

Hoboes were migrant workers—primarily men—who stole rides on freight trains to move about the country in search of work, from the time the economic crisis of the 1870s created the first wave of mass unemployment. They found their jobs in the highly seasonal occupations of the West: crop harvesting, logging, mining, and especially railroad construction and maintenance. During the winter slack season, they made temporary homes in the transient districts of Chicago, Minneapolis, Kansas City, Spokane, Denver, Seattle, and

Meal time at the homeless men's bureau (for unatttached men). Library of Congress, Prints & Photographs Division, FSA/OWI Collection [LC-USF34-010131-D].

Oakland. By the mid-1920s, this seasonal migration was in decline, but the Great Depression swelled the ranks of the hoboes and created a new lore of poverty, travel, and rebellion. A small number of people continued to "ride the rails" throughout the twentieth century, but poor workers increasingly favored travel by automobile.

The exact origins of the term "hobo" are not known, but the most likely guess is that it was a modification of a greeting among western railroad workers—"Ho, Boy!" Another possible origin is "hoe boy," indicating an agricultural laborer. In the early twentieth century, the term "hobo" was frequently invoked as part of a hierarchy of vagrant workers. "Hoboes" were said to be those who traveled to find work, "tramps" were those who worked to support their travels, and "bums" were those who neither worked nor traveled. However, seasonal migrant laborers were just as likely to be known by varied occupational designations: harvest hand, lumberjack, and gandy dancer (railroad worker), to name a few.

Popular opinion associated hoboes with various social ills: crime, alcoholism, prostitution, and, more covertly, homosexuality. The seasonal workforce had its share of outcasts, dangerous criminals, and lost souls, but in the aggregate was a cross-section of working-class men in North America. As the labor economist William Leiserson wrote in 1916, "practically every wage earner" was in the migrant labor pool at one time or another. The result was a wide personal familiarity with the excitement of hoboing, as well as with the deprivation, physical strain, and exploitation of seasonal labor. With the growth of transient districts in Chicago, Minneapolis, and the West Coast towns, the world of migrant workers became linked with that of nonconformist artists, radicals, and sexual minorities. These districts fostered the popular unease with migrant culture but also offered an opportunity for voyeuristic nonmigrants to dabble in the wild world of the outcast.

Between 1915 and 1924, the Industrial Workers of the World (IWW) made significant gains organizing migrant workers, especially in timber, wheat harvesting, and oil pipeline construction. In 1915, the organization formed the Agricultural Workers Organization (AWO) with the goal of unionizing the wheat harvest of the Great Plains. This annual work event drew upwards of 100,000 people to the wheat belt, where they worked a succession of jobs following the harvest northward from Oklahoma to Canada. The AWO (renamed the Agricultural Workers Industrial Union, AWIU, in 1917) quickly became the largest and wealthiest union within the IWW organization. Following its members into other seasonal trades, the union funded organizing drives among lumberjacks in the upper Midwest and the Pacific Northwest, iron miners in northern Minnesota, and oil workers in the southern Great Plains.

This success drew the ire of employers and law enforcement officials, and the AWIU was almost completely suppressed between 1917 and 1919, with most of the organizers in jail. The union enjoyed a brief resurgence that ended with the IWW's factional split in 1924. By that time the seasonal labor market was in decline due to mechanization in wheat harvesting and construction, as well as a general decline in railroad building, and a shift toward automobile travel over trains.

The IWW drew many of its most memorable songs from these hobo workers, including *Hallelujah, I'm a Bum, The Big Rock Candy Mountain* (by Haywire Mac McClintock), and *The Preacher and the Slave* and *The Rebel Girl* (by Joe Hill). Their irreverent lyrics lampooned the religious missionaries and celebrated travel as much as they did the movement. Other activists learned to identify with the hobo world, even if their connections were scant. Although he was a commercial artist by training, Ralph Chaplin, the author of *Solidarity Forever*, highlighted his own youthful experiences in the harvest labor force. During the 1930s, country and western artists popularized the hobo song tradition, although with the exception of Woody Guthrie, most were not politically inflected.

FRANK TOBIAS HIGBIE

References and Further Reading

DePastino, Todd. *Citizen Hobo: How a Century of Homelessness Shaped America.* Chicago: University of Chicago Press, 2003.

Higbie, Frank Tobias. *Indispensable Outcasts: Hobo Workers and Community in the American Midwest, 1880–1930.* Urbana: University of Illinois Press, 2003.

Kornbluh, Joyce. *Rebel Voices: An IWW Anthology.* Chicago: Charles H. Kerr Co., 1998.

HOFFA, JAMES P. (1941–)
International Brotherhood of Teamsters

James P. Hoffa assumed the leadership of the International Brotherhood of Teamsters on March 3, 1999. As general president, Hoffa attempted to reverse the decline in membership in one of the nation's oldest and most influential labor unions. The Teamsters union had been plagued by corruption, mob

influence, internal divisiveness, and ineffective leadership. Son of James R. Hoffa, a former general president of the International Brotherhood of Teamsters who disappeared mysteriously in 1975, Hoffa aimed to rejuvenate the union's membership rolls, its public image, and political influence through stronger grassroots organizing. During his term as president, Hoffa led the highly controversial move to split from the American Federation of Labor-Congress of Industrial Organizations (AFL-CIO), ending the union's 50-year association.

Background

Born on May 19, 1941, in Detroit, Hoffa entered the labor force as a teenager in Michigan and Alaska, working as a loader, driver, and operator of heavy equipment. At the age of 18, Hoffa earned his first union card and was inducted into the Teamsters by his father. In high school, he played football and graduated with honors. In 1963, Hoffa attended Michigan State University, where he continued to play football and earned a degree in economics. He received a law degree in 1966 and the following year worked in the Michigan State Senate through a Ford Foundation Fellowship. Between 1968 and 1993, Hoffa practiced labor law, specializing in workers' compensation and Social Security cases, gaining increasing visibility in the union while representing Teamsters Joint Councils and union chapters. President George W. Bush appointed Hoffa to the Council on the 21st Century Workforce in 2002. Hoffa also held a seat on the Secretary of Energy's advisory board that same year.

Hoffa's first attempt at running for general president of the Teamsters was foiled by Ron Carey in 1996. Hoffa won his second bid for general president of the union in 1998 after Carey, accused of money laundering, was barred from running again. Vowing to boost membership in the Teamsters, Hoffa set out on a rigorous plan to rid the union of corruption and its association with organized crime. Hoffa claimed that years of internal strife and ineffective leadership, combined with the effects of a growing global economy, had contributed not only to a decline in Teamster membership, but to labor's influence on the whole.

General President of the International Brotherhood of Teamsters

Upon taking office, Hoffa set several goals for the union, including strict fiscal reform and budgetary accountability. He increased efforts in fighting unfair trade practices, specifically with nations such as Japan, Korea, and China, nations whose habit of dumping cheap goods into the American market hurt American workers. While he acknowledged that some aspects of globalization were unavoidable, Hoffa insisted the United States needed to insulate its strong, robust economy from the detrimental effects of outsourcing labor and importing cheap foreign goods. He advocated for stricter health and safety regulations, increased Teamster contract negotiations, and stronger enforcement of existing agreements. Although crediting the government in combating years of corruption, Hoffa concluded that such oversight had become unnecessarily oppressive and was no longer needed. Hoffa's term as general president can be characterized as one of increasing the union's self-determination, with a focus on building a strong membership base, thereby increasing its influence through support of local, state, and federal members' political aspirations. Hoffa achieved many of his goals for the union in the first few years of his presidency. The union's membership rolls increased, yet still remained below the 2 million members enrolled during his father's term as president. For the first time in 10 years, the Teamsters organization achieved a balanced budget. The Teamsters continued to fight for labor concessions, most notably for America West Airlines customer service representatives in 2005.

Controversial Split with the AFL-CIO

Hoffa's initial reforms, ambitious in scope and successful, were accompanied by heated controversy. In July 2005, and after 50 years of affiliation, the Teamsters' General Executive Board decided to end the Teamsters' membership within the powerful bloc of AFL-CIO-affiliated unions. In statements to the AFL-CIO president John J. Sweeney and to the Teamsters' union, Hoffa cited the AFL-CIO's focus on political influence over politicians as a major reason for the split. He accused AFL-CIO leadership of throwing money at politicians with no personal investment or experience in labor issues. He countered that the Teamsters would be more effective politically through increased membership and political involvement. He argued that labor could only become more effective through encouraging more union members to enter the political arena. In a sense, Hoffa was urging a return to labor's grassroots political activism reminiscent of his father's era.

The Teamsters and the Service Employees International Union (SEIU) alone took approximately one

third of the AFL-CIO bloc's members with them. The AFL-CIO leader John J. Sweeney accused the Teamsters and other unions involved in the split of dividing the labor movement and creating a favorable environment for those who seek to reverse worker gains. Sweeney warned that splintering the larger bloc of unions would open the door for corruption and the return of mob influence on the local level, weakening labor's influence in the workplace and at all political levels. Despite the split with AFL-CIO over the vision for labor's future, Hoffa insisted that the Teamsters would continue to support other unions' activism. To emphasize this, Hoffa pushed for a Teamsters partnership with the Communications Workers of America (CWA) in 2005.

"Change to Win" Federation

Hoffa's Teamsters and the Service Employee's International Union's exit from the AFL-CIO culminated in the formation of a new federation of unions including the United Brotherhood of Carpenters and Joiners of America, the United Food and Commercial Workers' Union (UFCW), UNITE-HERE (a union representing hotel, restaurant, and garment workers), United Farm Workers of America (UFW), and the Laborers International Union of North America (LIUNA). Under the moniker of "Change to Win," the new bloc of unions issued a statement vowing to vigorously pursue and implement strategies to organize workers in the private sector.

MARTA M. KNIGHT

References and Further Reading

Edsall, Thomas B. "Two Top Unions Split from AFL-CIO. Others Are Expected to Follow Teamsters." *Washington Post*, July 26, 2005, p. A1.
Greenhouse, Steven. "Democrats Concerned by Prospect of a Labor Schism." *New York Times*, July 24, 2005, p. 19.
Hoffa, James P., and C. Thomas Keegel, eds. *100 Years of Teamsters Legacy: A Strong Legacy, a Powerful Future.* Washington, DC: DeLancey Publishing, 2003.
International Brotherhood of Teamsters. "Biography of General President James P. Hoffa." www.teamster.org/about/hoffa/hoffabio.htm.
International Brotherhood of Teamsters. "The Change to Win Coalition Statement." http://www.teamsters.org/05news/PDF/20050725disaffiliationltr2.pdf. 2005–.
International Brotherhood of Teamsters. "Statement of James P. Hoffa on the Teamsters' Disaffiliation with the AFL-CIO." http://www.teamsters.org/05news/PDF/20050725disaffiliationltr2.pdf. 2005–.
United States Congress. House Committee on Education and the Workforce, Subcommittee on Oversight and

Investigations. *The International Brotherhood of Teamsters One Year after the Election of James P. Hoffa: Hearing before the Subcommittee on Oversight and Investigations of the Committee on Education and the Workforce, House of Representatives, One Hundred Sixth Congress, Second Session, Hearing Held in Washington, DC, March 28, 2000*. Washington, DC: U.S. Government Printing Office, 2000.

See also **Hoffa, James R.; International Brotherhood of Teamsters**

HOFFA, JAMES R. (1913–1975?)
President, International Brotherhood of Teamsters

One of the most notorious and controversial U.S. labor leaders in the twentieth century, James Riddle Hoffa began as a local union leader in Detroit in the 1930s and served as president of the International Brotherhood of Teamsters (IBT) from 1957 to 1971. During his career, he used aggressive organizing tactics to promote the union's growth while at the same time working to centralize its operations. Gains in wages and benefits during his tenure made him popular with the membership, but allegations of organized crime ties and corruption made him infamous with the general public. He came to symbolize for many Americans in the post-WWII era the problem of union corruption.

Hoffa's origins lay in the small-town Midwest. He was born in 1913 in southern Indiana, the son of a coal prospector of German-American heritage. His father's death in 1920 left his mother struggling to support four children by running a home laundry. In 1924, when Hoffa was 11 years old, the family sought better opportunities by relocating to Detroit. In an effort to supplement the meager wages his mother earned at an auto parts factory, Hoffa left school after completing the ninth grade to work as a stock boy in a dry goods store.

His first involvement with union organizing began in his late teen years. In the early days of the Great Depression, in 1930, the 17-year-old Hoffa took a job at a loading dock and warehouse run by the Kroger grocery store line. Although the 32 cents an hour Hoffa earned at Kroger's was a relatively good wage, he and the other employees there resented their working conditions. The men were paid only for time spent unloading freight, and usually they spent half their workday on-site waiting around to be assigned work. In addition, the supervisor, whom they nicknamed "the Little Bastard," verbally abused his employees and often fired them for capricious reasons. Hoffa helped organize his fellow employees and led a job action, which they timed to coincide with a shipment of fresh strawberries; the danger of having the whole shipment spoil placed extra pressure on the company to come to terms with the strikers. The job action succeeded, and the company agreed to many of the workers' demands. Hoffa was elected vice president of the local union that emerged in the warehouse.

He began working for Teamsters Local 299 in Detroit in 1935 and within a decade became one of the IBT's most important leaders in the Midwest. When he began with the IBT, its local affiliates in Detroit were small, struggling organizations. Hoffa worked alongside older, local Teamster leaders, such as Owen "Bert" Brennan and Albert Squires, seeking to organize both trucking and affiliated warehouse workers. Detroit newspapers described the frequent use of violence in these organizing campaigns. According to these reports, employers were threatened, businesses were bombed, and nonunion drivers assaulted. These activities brought Hoffa his first criminal conviction. In 1940, Hoffa pleaded no contest to a charge of violating the Sherman Anti-Trust Act by helping to set up a cartel of union-organized carting firms that would control Detroit's waste paper hauling. The indictment included an allegation that one of the businesses that had refused to go along with this cartel had been bombed. These aggressive tactics, however, did bring results. The first major organizing breakthroughs came in the carhaul industry, firms that transported new cars from the factories out to the various dealerships. Later victories in local cartage and warehouse work brought in more members, and the two locals with whom Hoffa was most identified, Local 299 and its affiliated warehouse local, Local 337, grew dramatically. In 1937, the two locals combined had about 2,000 members, and by 1950, they had more than 20,000.

In this period, Hoffa was strongly influenced by his contact with the Minneapolis Teamster leader Farrell Dobbs, who was a Trotskyist socialist. Building on a dramatic victory over employers in Minneapolis in 1934, Dobbs had begun to create a regionwide organizing and bargaining structure in the upper Midwest. From Dobbs's campaigns Hoffa came to see how the newly emerged intercity trucking industry allowed the Teamsters Union to engage in a kind of leapfrog organizing. Unionized warehouse workers in one city could refuse to handle freight from nonunion trucks coming from another city, forcing those trucking companies to agree to a union contract. At the same time, unionized drivers could refuse to deliver to a nonunion warehouse, forcing the warehouse employer to come to terms. Harnessing such tactics required the Teamsters to move away from the union's traditional localism and to create new regional levels of union governance, such as the North Central District Drivers Council, created in 1937 at Dobbs's urging. In such regionwide organizing, the union developed larger collective bargaining units, eventually creating a standard contract for Midwestern trucking industry employees in 12 states.

When Dobbs left the Teamsters in 1939, Hoffa became the leading force in the Midwestern Teamsters organization, pushing for regional centralization. He assumed Dobbs's post as the negotiating chairman of the Central States Drivers Council, the regional organization that had emerged out of the earlier North Central District Drivers Council. In the 1940s, Hoffa drew on the union's strength in the upper Midwest to organize trucking operations in the South. Using the leapfrog organizing technique, Hoffa wielded the threat of secondary boycotts to force southern nonunion trucking firms to sign collective bargaining agreements with the Teamsters. Hoffa then organized those employers into regional bargaining units, whose contracts were timed to expire at the same time as the Central States Drivers Council. By the end of the decade, the contract terms for union truck drivers from Louisiana to Minnesota were exactly the same. Hoffa had managed not only to breach the walls of the anti-union South, but had also won significant wage gains for southern truck company employees.

During this same period, Hoffa fought a number of jurisdictional battles in Detroit, and these inter-union struggles helped earn him a reputation for violence and ruthlessness. A series of violent feuds took place throughout the late 1930s and early 1940s, in which the Detroit Teamsters struggled against several unions, including the Brewery Workers Union, the Retail Clerks, and the Dairy Workers. Over the course of these conflicts, the staff of the Detroit Teamsters Joint Council, including Hoffa, became known for their affinity for street fighting. One of the most bitter and violent conflicts involved a Congress of Industrial Organizations (CIO) affiliate, the United Construction Workers Organizing Committee (UCWOC), formed in 1939 at the behest of John L. Lewis and directed by his brother Dennie Lewis. In September 1941, UCWOC launched a campaign directed at the heart of the jurisdiction of Hoffa's Local 299; UCWOC dispatched its organizers to sign up carhaul drivers. The Detroit Teamsters responded by fielding teams of their own organizers, who attacked UCWOC's people on sight. The resulting street battles marked a high point in Detroit's jurisdictional battles in this era, and some accounts have claimed that Hoffa turned to a local Mafia leader, Santo Perrone, for support in this conflict.

Hoffa's reputation for fiercely defending the union's jurisdiction, as well as his organizing triumphs, helped speed his ascent up the ranks of the IBT hierarchy. The Teamster president Daniel Tobin appointed Hoffa an International Trustee in 1944, and he was elected to that position by the union's convention in 1947. Five years later, at the fairly young age of 39, he was elected to one of the union's International Vice President posts, making him a member of the IBT's General Executive Board, its ruling body. In addition, he held a number of significant local and regional posts.

His real base of power, however, lay in his work with the interstate trucking industry, where he had long served as the chief negotiator for the Central States Drivers Council. Through his leadership role there, he had played a pivotal part in organizing and bargaining with trucking employers throughout the Midwest, the South, and increasingly the East Coast as well. Gains achieved in wages and benefits drew him support from the Teamster rank and file in the trucking locals. At the same time, the expansion of the collective bargaining unit, which included more and more locals under one standard contract, gave Hoffa, who helped administer that contract, the ability to reward local officials who supported him and punish those who did not.

Having accumulated a strong following, Hoffa was poised to take advantage of the opportunity that emerged in 1957 when Dave Beck, Tobin's successor as president of the IBT, chose not to run for re-election. The U.S. Senate's McClellan Committee had held well-publicized hearings into union corruption in early 1957 that focused on charges of malfeasance involving Beck. The scandal that emerged badly damaged Beck's reputation, and his support within the union evaporated. Hoffa's prominence in the union made him a front-runner to succeed Beck, but in his effort to do so, Hoffa faced bitter opposition from the McClellan Committee. The Committee's chief counsel, Robert Kennedy, helped set up an FBI sting operation in early 1957 that appeared to catch Hoffa in the act of bribing a member of the Committee's staff for inside information on its investigations. When Hoffa won an acquittal at trial on those charges, the McClellan Committee responded by holding two sets of public hearings in the months leading up to the IBT Convention (where the election of national officers would take place) in an effort to discredit Hoffa in the eyes of the union's delegates. Those hearings raised allegations of Hoffa's links with organized crime figures and of his improper involvement in a real estate development deal. The Committee also publicized a very lucrative truck leasing agreement between Hoffa's wife and a Teamster employer, an arrangement that amounted to an illicit gratuity for the Detroit Teamster leader.

The hearings made Hoffa a notorious figure, but they did not destroy his political position within the IBT. Neither in 1957, nor over the course of the next two years of repeated hearings on Hoffa, could the committee ever prove that Hoffa had taken an outright bribe to betray the interests of his members. Nor could it demonstrate that he had personally profited from any act of malfeasance involving union funds. To the extent that the McClellan Committee clearly had launched a crusade to end Hoffa's career, he could depict himself as the victim of a conspiracy by anti-union congressmen who disliked him for his vigorous efforts on behalf of his members. His support within the union was far from unanimous, but his opponents were a divided minority who faced difficult institutional barriers.

Meanwhile, the ability of Hoffa to survive the McClellan Committee hearings further increased his notoriety, and his case was used by many political figures to justify the need for stronger regulation of unions. The Landrum-Griffin Act, passed in 1959, was described by its supporters as a law that would respond to the threat posed by Hoffa and his type of union leader.

Hoffa's tenure as president of the IBT was marked both by his success in creating a national trucking contract and by his willingness to abet corrupt local leaders. In the face of stiff opposition from local unions that rejected the loss of autonomy it would bring, Hoffa gradually brought together all of the different regions and in 1964 signed the National Master Freight Agreement (NMFA). Covering workers involved in trucking and warehouses, Hoffa's NMFA created a standard set of wages and benefits all across the country. The achievement marked the high-water mark of his efforts to create a more centralized union. It also demonstrated his dedication to improving the working conditions of Teamsters in the freight industry. At the same time, however, Hoffa displayed an apparent indifference to other IBT members trapped in locals that were controlled by corrupt local leaders, many of whom had ties to organized crime. In Chicago's Local 777, for example, insurgents challenged their union's corrupt leader, Joseph Glimco, a reputed capo in the Chicago Mafia. They denounced Glimco's misuse of union funds and the local's failure to protect their working conditions. Hoffa reacted to their complaints by offering Glimco every possible form of support, and he responded in similar ways to other local reform efforts.

His support for individuals such as Glimco was usually seen as evidence of his close ties to organized crime. An illegal FBI wiretap in the early 1960s indicated that Hoffa communicated almost daily with a Detroit Mafia figure named Anthony Giacalone. He had similar long-term relationships with organized crime figures in New York and Chicago. The precise nature of his relationship with organized crime remains unclear, but clearly he facilitated particular kinds of corruption within the union. By protecting mob-connected local leaders such as Glimco, he allowed them to exploit vulnerable local members and extort employers. Hoffa also abetted the efforts of organized crime groups to profit from the financial decisions of various Teamster benefit and pension funds. Loans made by the Central States Pension Fund, for instance, often required the applicant to make a kickback to an organized crime sponsor with ties to the Teamsters.

Under the leadership of Attorney General Robert Kennedy, the Justice Department mounted a campaign to win a criminal conviction against Hoffa. The Department's efforts succeeded in 1964 when Hoffa was convicted of witness tampering and mail fraud. While appealing his convictions, Hoffa arranged for the creation of a new IBT post, a general vice president, who could function as a caretaker during his prison sentence. His goal was to maintain control of the union even during his jail sentence. At the IBT's 1966 convention, Hoffa supported the election to that post of one of his most trusted and seemingly least ambitious associates, Frank Fitzsimmons. Then, having exhausted his appeals, Hoffa began serving his 13-year prison sentence in 1967.

He disappeared four years after his release from prison in 1971. Hoping that it would improve his chances for parole, he resigned the union presidency in June 1971. Six months later, Richard Nixon granted him a presidential commutation that released him from jail. The conditions of that commutation barred Hoffa from any involvement in union affairs until 1980, but he soon began talking about running once again for the IBT's top post, possibly in 1976, when the next election was scheduled. Those plans may have been the cause of his death. Most accounts conclude that he was murdered at the behest of the Mafia in order to stop him from re-assuming leadership of the Teamsters. According to this theory, organized crime groups had found it easier to work with his successor, Fitzsimmons. On the day he disappeared, in July 1975, he had been scheduled to meet with the Detroit Mafia figure Giacalone. Hoffa's body has never been found, and to this date the investigation into his disappearance remains an open case.

DAVID WITWER

References and Further Reading

Brill, Steven. *The Teamsters*. New York: Simon and Schuster, 1978.

Fraley, Oscar, and James Hoffa. *Hoffa: The Real Story by James R. Hoffa As Told by Oscar Fraley*. New York: Stein and Day Publishers, 1975.

James, Ralph, and Estelle Dinnerstein James. *Hoffa and the Teamsters: A Study of Union Power*. Princeton, NJ: D. Van Nostrand Company, Inc., 1965.

Kennedy, Robert. *The Enemy Within*. New York: Harper & Brothers, 1960.

Moldea, Dan E. *The Hoffa Wars: Teamsters, Rebels, Politicians, and the Mob*. New York: Charter Books, 1978.

Mollenhoff, Clark. *Tentacles of Power: The Story of Jimmy Hoffa*. Cleveland: The World Publishing Company, 1965.

Romer, Sam. *The International Brotherhood of Teamsters: Its Government and Structure*. New York: John Wiley and Sons, Inc., 1962.

Russell, Thaddeus. *Out of the Jungle: Jimmy Hoffa and the Remaking of the American Working Class*. New York: A. A. Knopf, 2001.

Sheridan, Walter. *The Fall and Rise of Jimmy Hoffa*. New York: Saturday Review Press, 1972.

Sloane, Arthur A. *Hoffa*. Cambridge, MA: The MIT Press, 1991.

Velie, Lester. *Why Jimmy Hoffa Had to Die*. New York: Reader's Digest Press, 1977.

Witwer, David. *Corruption and Reform in the Teamsters Union*. Chicago: University of Illinois Press, 2003.

See also **Beck, David; Fitzsimmons, Frank E.; Hoffa, James P.; International Brotherhood of Teamsters; McClellan Committee Hearings; Organized Crime; Tobin, Daniel J.**

HOME CLUB

Home Club is the name of a loosely confederated band of dissidents within the Knights of Labor (KOL) from 1882 to 1890. Some scholars doubt the existence of such a group, and others feel its influence has been exaggerated, but the Home Club was powerful enough to shape KOL policy between 1885 through 1888. It was not a unified conspiracy, rather a lightening rod around which disgruntled Knights could strike at the KOL administration, especially its international leader, Terence V. Powderly.

The term "Home Club" derives from a plan to purchase a retirement home for aged Knights, credited to Victor Drury, a French-born KOL radical. It is not clear whether Drury was serious about said plan, or if it was a smokescreen to disguise plots against the KOL's central administration that focused on disputes over secrecy, ideological discord, and personality clashes. Some of these reflected contradictions inherent within the KOL from its 1869 inception.

The KOL was originally modeled on fraternal organizations, and it employed secretive, quasi-Masonic ritual practices. Secrecy both protected members from employer backlash and regulated the worthiness of members. Early on it was forbidden even to write or utter the organization's name publicly. This worked as long as the KOL was a small body whose membership was largely confined to Pennsylvania, but as the organization grew, ritual secrecy proved less practical. Discussion of altering secret practices emerged at the KOL's first national convention in 1878, the year Powderly succeeded the founder, Uriah Stephens, as head of the organization. Powderly, like many Knights, was a Roman Catholic who faced church sanctions due to the Vatican's prohibition against secret societies.

After years of debate, the KOL became a public organization on January 1, 1882, though its ritual remained a guarded secret. The decision to modify secrecy angered the traditionalists, many of whom accused Powderly of subverting the order's values. Brooklyn Assembly 1562 simply refused to abide by the decision. That same Brooklyn local was also the center of ideological and structural disputes that rocked the KOL.

As the KOL expanded into larger cities, it encountered a hodgepodge of ideology. Older Knights were mainly liberals, Greenbackers, or mild socialists, but New York City was a hotbed of more radical ideals. The KOL's dispute over secrecy coincided with a regional struggle between Marxian and Lassallean socialism. After 1882, most Greater New York locals were under the auspices of District Assembly 49 (DA 49). Local 1562 was composed of a large number of doctrinaire Marxists, several of whom precipitated a boycott against the Duryea Starch Company that was deemed without merit by the KOL's executive board. Key members, including Theodore Cuno and P. J. McGuire, were suspended from the KOL.

District 49 decided to make 1562's travails a cause célèbre, even though its leadership was composed mostly of Lassallean socialists and anarchists who rejected the Marxian precept that trade unions were latent revolutionary cells from which a new society could be formed. Instead, they called for independent political action and denounced trade unions as reactionary bodies that guarded the interests of skilled workers at the expense of class unity. This was a potentially explosive situation for the KOL, which contained both single-trade locals and "mixed" assemblies containing workers of various trades. Led by Victor Drury, an ex-Marxist convert to anarchism,

DA 49 launched a convoluted plan in which it appeared to champion suspended Marxists while, in fact, isolating them. The goal was to discredit the KOL's central administration, which Drury felt was too conservative and too sympathetic to trade unions. Plots and counterplots swirled from 1882 to mid-1886, with Powderly and others devoting enormous time and resources to combating the Home Club. Those efforts were hampered by the Home Club's successful cooptation of the secrecy issue. Drury and his New York allies actively recruited disgruntled Knights on behalf of the Home Club.

This meant that there was widespread discontent within the KOL at precisely the point in which it encountered a membership surge. Between 1885 and 1886, the KOL's official membership increased by nearly 700%, due largely to enthusiasm following the order's dramatic strike victory over the railroad baron Jay Gould. So many members poured into the KOL that it called a moratorium against new assemblies in March 1886 so that overstretched administrators could process applications. The KOL also convened a special assembly in late May to address the order's growing pains, including a spate of unauthorized strikes. That convention appointed six "auxiliary" members to the KOL's executive board, four of whom were critical of Powderly's administration. This gave anti-administration forces nine of the KOL's top 14 administrative posts.

That convention also investigated allegations of a Home Club conspiracy. Powderly surprisingly sided with a report that whitewashed the Home Club and decided to cooperate with the new executive board. He perhaps realized that the Home Club's base was too diffuse and bargained that he could divide it along ideological lines. Given that the special assembly convened just three weeks after the Haymarket explosion in Chicago, Powderly may also have decided to wait for the radical climate to cool before moving against dissidents.

In the interim, rejuvenated trade unions arose to challenge KOL supremacy, and Home Club Lassalleans steered the executive board toward an anti-trade union stance that divided the Knights. Trade-union supporters within the KOL, like Thomas Barry, Joseph Buchanan, P. J. McGuire, George McNeill, and John Morrison, made lurid charges about the Home Club and Powderly that further divided the Knights. The KOL soon found itself losing members nearly as fast as it gained them in the halcyon days of early 1886.

Despite a second whitewashed report in November 1886, the Home Club was on the defensive by early 1887, in part because the prostrike policy it endorsed in defiance of official KOL policy led to a series of ill-advised job actions that ended in defeat. Nonetheless, leaders like Drury and James Quinn proved adroit at transforming the Home Club from an ideological clique to one that drew upon general discontent. By late 1887, Powderly denounced the Home Club, though malcontents accused him of coddling it. Drury re-organized his inner circle as The Class and renewed recruitment efforts and deflected anger toward Powderly. At the 1887 convention, Powderly's supporters once again attacked critics with more ardor than the Home Club.

By mid-1888, however, the Drury-led coterie had overplayed its hand. A bruising fight within District 49 isolated most of the Home Club old guard, and the fall convention saw a repudiation of Home Club anti-trade union policies, as well as a Drury proposal to return the KOL to secrecy. By then, though, the damage was done. Trade unions denounced the Knights, the order continued to hemorrhage members, and the secretary-treasurer, John Hayes, originally a Home Club appointee, began to wrest power from Powderly. By 1890, most of the Home Club inner circle had been purged from the KOL. Ironically, doctrinaire Marxists, including Cuno, regained control of District 49. They, in coalition with agrarian radicals, ousted Powderly in 1893.

Although one can be skeptical of how much power the Home Club formally held, its influence on the KOL was enormous. In the early 1880s, it consumed organizational time and resources that could have been devoted to more productive enterprises, and its influence on strike and trade-union policies between 1885 and 1888 proved disastrous. The Home Club stands as an unfortunate example of how a small group can disrupt large organizations.

ROBERT E. WEIR

References and Further Reading

Fink, Leon. *Workingmen's Democracy: The Knights of Labor and American Politics*. Urbana: University of Illinois, 1983.

Phelan, Craig. "The Warp of Fancy: The Knights of Labor and the Home Club Takeover Myth." *Labor History* 40:3 (August 1999): 283–300.

Weir, Robert. *Knights Unhorsed: Internal Conflict in a Gilded Age Social Movement*. Detroit: Wayne State, 2000.

See also **Knights of Labor**

HOME ECONOMICS

Home economics traces its roots to the nineteenth-century work of Catharine Beecher, whose *Treatise on Domestic Economy*, first published in 1841, offered practical advice to women on cooking, family, health, infant care, and children's education, along with observations on proper home management. Schools of cookery, like the one managed by Fannie Merritt Farmer in Boston in the 1890s, also served as precursors to the home economics movement.

The home economics movement took shape during a decade of conferences held at Lake Placid, New York, from 1899 to 1908. Organized by Ellen Richards, the Lake Placid conferences brought together several disparate groups that ultimately united to form the American Home Economics Association in 1909. Richards, a chemist trained at Vassar and the Massachusetts Institute of Technology, led the domestic science faction that emphasized nutrition and sanitation along with training in institutional management. The household arts faction promoted instruction in cooking, sewing, and textiles. Proponents of domestic economy hearkened back to Catharine Beecher and focused on the housewife and her problems, particularly the difficulty in obtaining domestic servants.

Ellen H. Richards, who chaired the first Lake Placid meeting in the summer of 1899, acted as the "engineer" of the home economics movement. She sought to professionalize and upgrade home economics to provide a career path for college-educated women trained in science and to facilitate their employment in academics, social service, and industry. Her emphasis on rigorous research in the natural and social sciences led her protégées to become some of the most successful career women of their day. Among them was Marion Talbot, who parlayed her training in home economics at Wellesley College into a career in university administration at the University of Chicago. Early advocates of home economics sought to move women into public life, not to confine them to the kitchen. Home economics, which extended its domain into "municipal housekeeping," fed directly into the broader movement for social reform called for by its contemporaries in the Progressive Movement.

Ellen Richards's attempts to establish home economics in the prestigious Seven Sister schools of the East ran up against the opposition of M. Carey Thomas, the president of Bryn Mawr, who dismissed home economics as too gendered to be intellectually rigorous. Instead, home economics took hold in the co-educational land grant colleges in the Midwest and West. In some cases, male administrators used home economics to segregate women students. Iowa State launched the first home economics department in 1873, and similar departments soon followed in Kansas, Illinois, Florida, and California.

In 1914, the Smith-Lever Act, designed to improve life in rural America, provided funds for home economics through the Cooperative Extension Service of the Department of Agriculture. Under the direction of Martha Van Rensselaer, the College of Home Economics at Cornell University in Ithaca, New York, played a leading role in training home demonstration agents to work with farm women. In 1917, the Smith-Hughes Act funded home economics training on the college level for primary and secondary school teachers, making teacher training the central mission of collegiate home economics. While both measures provided needed funding for home economics, in the long run they proved a mixed blessing for the field: Smith-Lever tied home economics to rural life at the moment when the country was becoming increasingly urban, and Smith-Hughes promoted vocational training at a time when many colleges and universities increasingly valued research over teaching.

In times of national crisis, home economists used their professional training to advantage. During World War I, home economists helped the nation stretch its food resources, and in the depression of the 1930s, home economics advised women how to "make over and make do." But the reform ethos of the home economics movement lost steam with the demise of progressivism in the 1920s. Emphasis in the field gradually shifted to the individual home and family. In the 1920s, home economists entered business, running test kitchens and serving as mediators between their employers and female consumers. At the same time, self-styled experts like Christine Frederick (not a trained home economist) urged women to adopt scientific management in the kitchen, exhorting them give up the goal of a career and "come into the home."

In the long run, home economics, like nursing and other gendered professions, could never escape negative gender stereotypes. In the academy, not even a scientist of the stature of Agnes Fay Morgan at the University of California, Berkeley, could sustain her department. In 1955, a year after Morgan retired, Berkeley voted to dump its home economics department, leaving a more gender neutral "nutritional sciences" graduate program.

By the 1960s, home economics found itself increasingly beleaguered. In 1968, the Carnegie Corporation funded a study of the field, published under the title *The Changing Mission of Home Economics*. The author, Earl J. McGrath, confessed that he went into the study believing the field should be discontinued. Instead, he recommended its expansion. Nevertheless, universities continued to eliminate home economics or to hire male administrators, who quickly abandoned the gendered title in favor of terms like human development or human ecology. At the same time, a new generation of women who associated "home ec" with aprons and white sauce, attacked the field as part and parcel of the feminine mystique Betty Friedan lambasted in her 1963 best seller. The feminist Robin Morgan, invited to speak to the American Home Economics Association (AHEA) in 1973, announced, "I am here addressing the enemy," ignoring the reality that home economics had for decades provided careers for women and had served as the only bastion for women scholars in academia prior to the advent of women's studies. Indeed, Cornell University offered one of the first women's studies courses in the nation under the auspices of its College of Human Ecology.

In the ensuing decades, home economics struggled to redefine its mission and to escape the gendered stereotype of "stitching and stirring." In 1994, the AHEA voted to change its name to the American Association of Family and Consumer Sciences (AAFCS). Today the organization defines its mission as "improving individual, family, and community well-being; impacting the development, delivery, and evaluation of consumer goods and services; influencing the creation of public policy, and shaping social change."

SARAH STAGE

References and Further Reading

American Association of Family & Consumer Sciences Web Site. www.aafcs.org.
Brown, Marjorie M. *Philosophical Studies of Home Economics in the United States*, vols. 1 and 2. East Lansing: College of Human Ecology, Michigan State University, 1985 and 1993.
Nerad, Maresi. *The Academic Kitchen: A Social History of Gender Stratification at the University of California, Berkeley.* Buffalo, NY: SUNY Press, 1999.
Rossiter, Margaret. *Women Scientists in America: Before Affirmative Action, 1940–1972.* Baltimore: Johns Hopkins University Press, 1995.
———. *Women Scientists in America: Struggles and Strategies to 1940.* Baltimore: Johns Hopkins University Press, 1982.
Stage, Sarah, and Virginia Vincenti, eds. *Rethinking Women and Home Economics: Women and the History of a Profession.* Ithaca, NY: Cornell University Press, 1997.

HOMESTEAD STRIKE (1892)

The episode that most late nineteenth-century Americans associated with the Homestead Strike of 1892 was a bloody battle that took place between three hundred Pinkerton detectives and thousands of citizens of Homestead, Pennsylvania, on July 6, a confrontation that culminated in the community's violent retribution against the surrendering Pinkertons, Yet, as the historian Paul Krause has emphasized, to focus on the bloodshed of July 6 ignores the broader context for the conflict that was in fact decades old between, on the one hand, workers committed to protecting a "competence," or minimum standard of living, and on the other hand, industrialists dedicated to the primacy of the laws of supply and demand.

By the mid-nineteenth century, iron producers saw the Bessemer converter as the key to overcoming the workplace controls exercised by skilled workers, particularly puddlers, who carried on a long tradition of carefully and deliberately turning pig iron into wrought iron. The Bessemer process promised to make the work of puddlers irrelevant and to allow ironmasters a much freer hand in setting the terms and conditions of work for all mill employees. The process also created steel, a malleable metal that made possible the most important symbols and motors of industrial and national growth—a sprawling system of railroads, immense bridges and skyscrapers, and, for the U.S. Navy, battleship armor. Andrew Carnegie and other ironmasters saw progress in the new technology, but to steelworkers, these changes threatened to undermine their power and rights. Their relative independence, which, in their view, guarded the American republic against tyranny, was by the 1870s fast succumbing to the awesome political and economic influence of large-scale corporations.

The first salvo in the 1892 strike was fired nearly 20 years earlier in the 1874–1875 lockout of iron and steelworkers in the Pittsburgh area, where the factory town of Homestead was located. The lockout commenced after the puddlers' union, the Sons of Vulcan, rejected Pittsburgh manufacturers' call to tie their baseline wage to market prices for iron. The puddlers won, but with victory came their realization that they must renounce their traditional exclusiveness, as manufacturers had played on divisions of race and skill among steelworkers during the conflict, and the Bessemer process threatened the puddlers' entire occupation. In search of protection, the Vulcans cooperated with skilled metalworkers in forming the Amalgamated Association of Iron and Steel Workers (AAISW). In 1881, the AAISW opened its doors to skilled black workers, although, as the historian Dennis C. Dickerson has observed, most white unionists did so begrudgingly. Many steelworkers also joined the Knights of Labor (KOL).

Besides the issue of a "fair day's wages," the other chief issue animating steelworkers' labor activism involved the anti-union measures that metal makers took in the wake of the Great Strike of 1877, especially the ironclad agreement, which barred employees from union membership. While the historian Harold C. Livesay has characterized Carnegie's pre-1892 labor policies as an exception to this anti-union trend, in fact Carnegie aggressively sought to

The Homestead riot / drawn by W.P. Snyder after a photograph by Dabbs, Pittsburg. Library of Congress, Prints & Photographs Division [LC-USZ62-126046].

eliminate the influence of the AAISW and KOL in his mills. Certainly, in the wake of the 1886 labor unrest, Carnegie publicly expressed sympathy with unionism and criticized the practice of hiring strikebreakers to fill the places of strikers. Yet in 1887, he used Pinkertons and strikebreakers to defeat the AAISW and KOL at his Edgar Thomson Steel Works when workers refused his demand for wage cuts, a longer workday, and a reduction in the workforce. Carnegie then moved to implement these same changes at his Homestead Steel Works, which he had acquired in 1883. In 1886, he installed open-hearth furnaces, which effectively destroyed what little relevance puddlers held at the plant and reduced the skilled labor force. In May 1889, he announced that employees must accept a 25% wage reduction, a 12-hour day, and a three-year ironclad agreement.

In 1889, Homesteaders succeeded, as they had before. They united to physically eject strikebreakers from the town, who were mostly black, Southern European, and East Europeans, and turned back deputies sent to assume control of the mills. The company's inability to fill orders weakened Carnegie's hand. In the end, he was forced to sign a three-year contract with the AAISW. The AAISW had also won a strike against the mill's previous owners in 1882. Geography can in part explain these victories: outsiders had limited access to the town, so citizens were more easily able to defend it from strikebreakers. Second, Homestead's AAISW lodges, in contrast to the national union, granted membership to the unskilled and maintained amicable relations with the KOL. Despite the strong nativist sentiment of some of the town's citizens and the close association between ethnicity and skill, East Europeans, "old" immigrants, and native-born focused on their shared religious and political traditions in opposing mill owners' power. However, Homesteaders' strength in 1889 was illusory. Its union victories were isolated ones. Elsewhere in western Pennsylvania, the AAISW and KOL were unable to reverse a precipitous decline in labor's fortunes in the steel mills, mines, and the voting booth during the 1880s. Much was at stake, then, as Homesteaders well knew, in the 1892 conflict.

With the 1889 agreement set to expire on June 30, 1892, Carnegie turned to gaining full control over his Homestead workforce. In January, he ordered a survey of wage rates in Pittsburgh's steel mills, which found some skilled Homestead workers earning significantly more than their counterparts in Pittsburgh. Publicly, Carnegie's officials made much of these findings and the larger problem of a saturated steel market in explaining the call for wage cuts. They also claimed that the introduction of new technology had lightened the loads of skilled workers. In reality, Carnegie's foremost concern was unionism, as he made clear in his instructions to company officials.

In negotiating the new wage scales, Carnegie's representatives stalled repeatedly and insisted on impossible terms, such as a proposal that the contract end in the winter rather than the summer. The change was crucial. The collective power of steelworkers was weakest in the winter, when unemployment and the cost of living were highest. On the issue of wages, Homestead unionists objected to the notion that market forces rather than custom should govern workers' baseline income. They also viewed with alarm the company's proposition that it might reduce wage scales in any department that saw technological improvement. Contrary to company arguments that the plan would negatively affect only a small minority of workers, potentially, nearly all were at risk.

Henry Clay Frick, the chief of operations at Homestead, gave union leaders until June 24 to accept these terms. Once the deadline passed, Frick oversaw the construction of watchtowers and a barbed wire-topped fence on the steelwork's premises. He also sent for the Pinkerton agents and on June 29, ordered a lockout of the entire workforce. The AAISW Advisory Committee worked with local authorities in governing the town during the conflict, preventing damage to mills and blocking the entrance of strikebreakers. Despite strikers' orderliness, Frick succeeded in acquiring the county sheriff's aid in regaining the company's physical control of the steelworks. The Advisory Committee warned the sheriff that the arrival of nonunion men would bring violence. When a force of deputies arrived, townspeople showed them the unharmed mills and the way out of town. The next morning, when the Pinkertons attempted their well-known landing, Homestead's bitter, exhausted, desperate, but determined steelworkers, their families, and neighbors were waiting for them.

Ironically, most of the Pinkerton agents were unaware that the purpose of their journey was to assist in the lockout. They arrived heavily armed in company-owned barges, the *Iron Mountain* and the *Monongahela*. Town scouts warned of the Pinkertons' approach in the predawn hours of July 6. The mass of men, women, and children who filled the river's shoreline in front of the company's mills paid little heed to the strike committee's prohibition of violence, and despite the plea of the strike leader, Hugh O'Donnell, to turn back, the Pinkerton's commander, the zealous Frederick H. Heinde, ordered his men to disembark. A fight quickly broke out between Homesteaders and the agents; someone—it is unclear who—fired the first shots, and the two sides frantically exchanged a barrage of bullets. As the number of dead and wounded workers mounted, events escalated. Some workers unleashed a cannon against the Pinkertons, while others repeatedly attempted to sink the barges. Homesteaders insisted that they would accept surrender only on condition that the agents face charges for the murder of workers killed in the melee. The Pinkerton agents agreed, but despite the strike committee's promise of protection, once on shore they endured a punishing march through crowds of vengeful bystanders, one the widow of a killed striker, who beat them unmercifully. While no Pinkerton died at the hands of the crowd, the press described the violence in lurid terms and characterized the townspeople's revenge upon the Pinkertons as the actions of an irrational, savage mob.

On same day that the Pinkertons suffered the crowd's outraged assaults, Carnegie was vacationing in his native Scotland, quite purposely avoiding direct involvement in the clash that he knew Frick's tactics would inevitably bring. He had entrusted the handling of the lockout to Frick and instructed him to not back down. When reporters finally located Carnegie, he gave Frick his full support. Carnegie privately regretted his manager's handling of the strike, probably because he recognized almost immediately that the hostilities at Homestead belied his public professions of admiration for workers and trade unions. More indirectly and gradually, Carnegie admitted his own culpability as Frick's supervisor and sponsor. That acknowledgment came after years of public criticism of not Frick, but Carnegie, for his hypocrisy and spineless retreat across the Atlantic while a subordinate did his dirty work.

For his part, Frick almost certainly understood that the induction of a private army to secure the mills for strikebreakers would provoke townspeople to violence and thus the state to intervene on the company's behalf. On July 12, 8,500 state militiamen descended on Homestead and enforced martial law for over three months. Within weeks, Frick, too, fell victim to violence. On July 23, anarchist Alexander Berkman badly wounded him in an assassination attempt. The attack, and the ensuing association of the strike with it, further splintered the AAISW leadership. Less than three weeks later, 1,700 strikebreakers were running the mills at full capacity. On November 17, several hundred of the strikers returned to work, signaling the end of the lockout.

Labor repression, not labor reform, followed the Homestead debacle. While 13 states, including Pennsylvania, banned the use of nonresidents (that is, Pinkertons) as deputies, companies continued to employ private guards and local police officers to defeat striking or locked-out workers. In Homestead, the state made examples of strike participants and supporters. When a young soldier expressed glee at the news of Frick's brush with death, the militia's commander had him hung by his thumbs and dishonorably discharged. Carnegie's chief counsel, Philander Chase Knox (a Republican lawyer who went on to a career in national politics), aggressively pushed to convict over one hundred strikers of riot, murder, and conspiracy. Most eventually gained acquittal, but many who could not make bail were jailed during the long process, and a few were found guilty on questionable grounds and served time in prison. Knox also sought to bring treason charges against Advisory Committee members. While this legally groundless offensive failed, it demoralized labor activists and, as with the other legal charges, depleted strikers of energy and funds.

Although Carnegie's reputation deteriorated due to the lockout, the new management system that he imposed at Homestead helped make possible the spectacular rise of the Carnegie Steel Company, a consolidation of his various steel enterprises that formed in the midst of the strike on July 1, 1892. The new system was union-free. Ethnic and racial antagonisms among steelworkers, which amalgamation had tempered, quickly and violently came to the foreground. Not until the 1930s would unionism again make significant inroads in the steel industry.

THERESA CASE

References and Further Reading

Dickerson, Dennis C. "Black Sons of Vulcan, 1875–1916." In *Out of the Crucible: Black Steelworkers in Western Pennsylvania, 1875–1980*. Albany: State University of New York Press, 1986.
Krause, Paul: *The Battle for Homestead, 1880–1892: Politics, Culture, and Steel*. Pittsburgh, PA: University of Pittsburgh Press, 1992.
Livesay, Harold C. *Andrew Carnegie and the Rise of Big Business*, 2nd ed. New York: Longman, 2000.

See also **Steel and Iron**

HORTON, MYLES (1905–1990)
Founder, Highlander Folk School

Born in the southwest Tennessee town of Savannah in 1905, Myles Horton dedicated his life to the attainment of social justice for southerners, both black and white. In 1932, he founded the Highlander Folk School in Monteagle, Tennessee—an adult education center that brought pride and dignity to the people of Appalachia and that eventually helped to mold the leaderships of both southern unions and the civil rights movement.

Horton's early consciousness was powerfully shaped by experiences on farms and in mining and mill towns, along with a steady diet of Christian teachings. According to William Ayers, Horton once quipped, "I always liked the idea of Christianity, only problem was I never saw anyone practice it" (Ayers, p. 151). If Horton berated southern Christians for failing to act on their professed ideals, he nonetheless observed in his autobiography, *The Long Haul*, that he took to heart his mother's exhortation that "God is love, and therefore you love your neighbors" (Horton, *The Long Haul*, p. 7). In the opening pages of his autobiography, he further noted the pervasive influence of this simple tenet in his thinking and social practices. "If you believe people are of worth," Horton reflected, "you can't treat anybody inhumanely, and that means you not only have to love and respect people, but you have to think in terms of building a society that people can profit most from, and that kind of society has to work on the principle of love" (Horton, *The Long Haul*, pp. 6–7). Horton recognized that such idealism was easy to mouth. He would spend his life learning, studying, and teaching how to bring it alive in social practice.

Horton further honed his social philosophy by studying and discussing his ideas with some of the foremost social critics of his day. Starting his university education at Cumberland University in Lebanon, Tennessee, he continued it at the Union Theological Seminary in New York and at the University of Chicago. Between his junior and senior years at Cumberland, he spent the summer directing a Presbyterian vacation Bible school program in the town of Ozone, nestled in the Cumberland region of the east Tennessee mountains. When it became clear to him that the church hosting him was not meeting the needs of its congregants—people from mining and logging communities that were past their heydays—Horton instituted communitywide meetings where these working people could share their problems and seek joint solutions. Topics for discussion included how to build sanitary privies, test for typhoid in the wells, and restore denuded forests. Congregants pooled their knowledge and sought additional information and assistance from county officials. This experience of relying on communal expertise would serve as a model for Horton's approach at the Highlander Folk School, which in turn came to form the basis of twentieth-century social activism in many southern communities.

Horton coupled his Christian beliefs and formative experiences in Ozone with intensive reading and intellectual discussions with the likes of Reinhold Niebuhr (the Union Theological Seminarian and socialist who related Christian faith to modern politics), Robert Parks (the University of Chicago sociologist who coined the phrase "human ecology" to understand the vitality of society), John Dewey (the Columbia University philosophy professor who believed that the skills and knowledge that students learned be integrated fully into their lives as persons, citizens, and human beings), and Jane Addams (the social reformer and founder of Chicago's Hull-House Settlement). As William Ayers notes, all of these mentors helped Horton develop his ideas about a school for life, where people could solve problems together in an informal setting, and where experience would be the main teacher (Ayers, p. 153).

From Horton's founding of the Highlander Folk School on the eve of the New Deal, to his death in 1990 as the Soviet Union collapsed and America's commitment to deregulation gathered steam, he worked to translate his philosophy into practice. (Horton officially retired in 1973 but continued to live and work at Highlander.) During the early years, he focused Highlander's resources on improving the lives of Appalachian timber, mill, and mine workers. Later, Horton and the institution he led established programs on citizenship, school desegregation, and voter education. This work earned Horton wide admiration from social activists and community members. But he increasingly attracted critical attention from local, state, and federal officials. In the 1950s and early 1960s, he faced a series of trumped-up charges, including allegations that he promoted the sale and consumption of intoxicating liquor, and that he aided and abetted the Communist Party. This later charge had an ironic twist to it, since Horton was never a member of the Communist Party and eventually broke with the Congress of Industrial Organizations (CIO) partly over this issue. Of one charge, though, Horton stood proudly guilty—of operating a school that blacks and whites attended together. Once asked how he got blacks and whites to eat together in the segregated South, he responded, in words heard by

Rosa Parks and recorded by William Ayers, "All I did was put food on the table and ring the bell"(Ayers, p. 155). Horton's most significant legacies are a still-vibrant institution—the Highlander Research and Education Center (renamed in 1961)—and the powerful idea that oppressed people in America can effectively challenge their oppression through peer learning and collective action.

KARIN A. SHAPIRO

References and Further Reading

Adams, Frank, with Myles Horton. *Unearthing Seeds of Fire: The Idea of Highlander.* Winston-Salem, NC: John F. Blair, 1975.

Ayers, William. "A Dream That Keeps on Growing: Myles Horton and Highlander." In *Teaching for Social Justice: A Democracy and Education Reader,* edited by William Ayers, Jean Ann Hunt, and Therese Quinn. New York: The New Press and Teachers College Press, 1998, pp. 150–156.

Horton, Myles, with Bill Moyers. *The Adventures of a Radical Hillbilly.* Video. Public Broadcasting System, 1981.

Horton, Myles, with Judith Kohl and Herbert Kohl. *The Long Haul: An Autobiography.* New York: Doubleday, 1990.

Jacobs, Dale, ed. *The Myles Horton Reader: Education for Social Change.* Tennessee: Knoxville: University of Tennessee Press, 2003.

See also **Highlander Folk School/Highlander Research and Education Center**

HOTEL AND RESTAURANT EMPLOYEES INTERNATIONAL UNION

The Hotel Employees and Restaurant Employees International Union (HERE) has long represented groups that, until recently, were relatively rare in the labor movement: low-wage and often female service workers. Founded by food servers and bartenders, HERE expanded to include various hotel staff and, more recently, casino workers. Over the past century, the union has been wracked by internal conflicts and government probes into corruption, among other challenges. But HERE survived and still provides union representation for workers in the vast and growing hospitality industries.

Early Years

As early as 1866, waiters and bartenders in Chicago organized a union. By the 1880s, several such unions had formed and joined the Knights of Labor, but the relationship was a strained one (the formally anti-alcohol Knights wanted to exclude bartenders). By the late 1880s, waiters and barmen began affiliating with the new American Federation of Labor (AFL). On April 24, 1891, the AFL chartered the Waiters and Bartenders National Union, the original incarnation of HERE.

HERE suffered the first of many internal power struggles in the late 1890s, between factions led by Chicago-based, politically ambitious William C. Pomeroy and the St. Louis-based, bureaucratically scrupulous Jere L. Sullivan. By 1899, Sullivan triumphed and, with AFL backing, went on to serve for nearly three decades as the union's all-powerful secretary-treasurer (early presidents were essentially figureheads).

Over the course of the next few decades, HERE directed its energy to organizing bartenders, following the AFL craft model of representing only better-paid, skilled workers. The bartenders seemed a better bet to Sullivan than the other elite of the culinary world, the polyglot, high-turnover cooks and the low-wage, mostly foreign-born workers who staffed dining rooms and hotels. HERE was quite successful in organizing bartenders, particularly in working-class taverns. Within just a few years, a majority of the 20,000-plus male bartenders in the United States were unionized. The International did much less, however, in the large urban hotels and restaurants that, as of 1900, employed more than 300,000 workers. Still, the union grew quickly thanks to various local organizing efforts across the country. By 1904, HERE hit an early peak of 50,000 members and more than 500 locals.

Prohibition and a New Era of Growth

Prohibition devastated HERE. The Eighteenth Amendment's ban on liquor sales in 1920 quickly cost the union a third of its membership. The employer open-shop drives of the 1920s contributed to the decline, and the bartender-dominated union failed to take advantage of growth elsewhere, such as in the cafeteria trade. Concern grew throughout HERE over Sullivan's narrow approach to organizing, and in 1927, President Edward Flore (1911–1945) spearheaded a movement to dethrone him. Sullivan's death the next year enabled Flore to re-organize the union, shifting power permanently from the secretary-treasurer's to the president's office. Flore turned to the West Coast locals, traditionally more radical and inclusive, for help in broadening HERE's base.

By the 1930s, amid the Great Depression and the historic rise of industrial unionism in the United States, HERE adopted mixed craft- and industrial-style organizing and enrolled bellhops, maids, bus-boys, and other lower-level hotel and restaurant workers across the country. The union's membership nearly doubled in 1933, the first year New Deal legislation encouraged unionization. Widespread strikes in 1936 and 1937 brought further growth, as did economic mobilization for World War II. By 1940, membership topped 200,000, and by 1950, 400,000. At mid-century, HERE achieved its highest rate of unionization, when a quarter of all hotel and restaurant workers were organized.

Women, especially waitresses, grew more prominent in HERE in these years. In 1900, 50 Seattle waitresses, led by Alice Lord, had formed Local 240, the first waitresses' local in HERE. Additional waitress-only locals soon appeared in several Midwestern cities. As Prohibition devastated the bartending craft, it hastened the feminization of table service, and by the end of the 1920s, waitresses were a fifth of the HERE membership. Though more mixed-sex locals opened to them, waitresses' separate locals grew increasingly powerful, with around 40,000 of HERE's members by the late 1940s. Women in various trades composed 45% of the union's entire membership by 1950.

In the 1930s and 1940s, too, racial barriers in the union began to recede. Segregated locals became less common, and the particularly virulent hostility reserved for Asian culinary workers declined. HERE made little effort, however, to combat the engrained patterns of racial discrimination in culinary work.

Postwar Challenges

Into the postwar decades, HERE for the most part stagnated, maintaining a membership of 400,000 to 500,000, while the hotel and restaurant workforce grew into several millions. Under presidents Hugo Ernst (1945–1954) and Ed S. Miller (1954–1973), HERE won better working conditions, wage increases, and health and pension plans for many members after World War II. Particularly important were hour reductions in an industry with longer working days and weeks than most. The union found some new frontiers, such as Miami Beach's resorts in the 1950s, the small but high-profile Playboy Bunny workforce in the later 1960s, and Las Vegas, where HERE claimed 10,000 members by the 1980s. But aside from such bright spots, HERE could not keep up in the expanding hospitality industry. Growth was concentrated in the hard-to-unionize Sunbelt and suburbs, and the increasing number of part-timers also made new organizing difficult.

As total membership began to tumble in the 1970s, HERE underwent significant re-organization. A court determined in 1972 that the Civil Rights Act of 1964, which forbade sex discrimination in employment, rendered HERE's sex-segregated locals illegal. So ended seven decades of separate organizing by waitresses. The International soon decided to eliminate all craft-based distinctions as well. HERE thereafter was composed of amalgamated city locals containing workers from all hotel and restaurant trades.

Centralization of locals—and thus of power in the union—piqued federal interest in suspected mob influence over HERE. The government launched an official probe in 1976 of the union's alleged infiltration by organized crime. Mob involvement with some of the locals dated back to the era of Al Capone, but authorities believed it was spreading under the president, Edward T. Hanley (1973–1998). In 1986, a federal commission on organized crime named HERE among the nation's four most corrupt unions. Various investigations resulted in trusteeships for the large Atlantic City and New York City locals and a federal watchdog for the International from 1995 to 2000.

By the early twenty-first century, HERE's membership had fallen to 260,000, half its peak. But the union had a new president, John W. Wilhelm, renowned for his organizing skills, and in Las Vegas, one of the fastest-growing private-sector locals in the United States, with 50,000 members. In mid-2004, HERE joined with UNITE, the Union of Needletrades, Industrial and Textile Employees, to form UNITE HERE, representing more than 450,000 workers throughout North America. UNITE was itself the product of an earlier merger in 1995 of two other of the nation's oldest unions, the International Ladies' Garment Workers' Union (ILGWU) and the Amalgamated Clothing and Textile Workers Union (ACTWU). The UNITE-HERE merger brought together unions that historically represented many immigrants and women—and still do. Purged of corruption and proud of its racially diverse and majority female membership, HERE had come a long way from its early days as a bartenders' craft union.

KATHLEEN M. BARRY

References and Further Reading

Cobble, Dorothy Sue. *Dishing It Out: Waitresses and Their Unions in the Twentieth Century*. Urbana: University of Illinois Press, 1991.
Josephson, Matthew. *Union House, Union Bar: The History of the Hotel and Restaurant Employees and Bartenders International Union, AFL-CIO*. New York: Random House, 1956.
UNITE HERE Web Site. "Our History." www.unitehere. org. 2006– .

See also **Waitressing and Waiting/Food Service**

HOUSE UN-AMERICAN ACTIVITIES COMMITTEE/DIES COMMITTEE

The House Committee on Un-American Activities (HUAC) was established as a permanent committee of the House of Representatives in 1946. Its predecessor, the Dies Committee (named after its chairman, Representative Martin Dies, a Texas Democrat), was founded in 1938 and initially focused its investigations on the Ku Klux Klan and American Nazi sympathizers. During World War II, the Dies Committee turned its attention toward Communist subversion within the New Deal. After the beginning of the Cold War, HUAC began to focus almost exclusively on investigating the influence of domestic Communists in various institutions, such as government agencies, labor unions, and Hollywood.

HUAC's most memorable hearings involved claims that domestic Communists were engaged in espionage within the United States government. The most contentious of these hearings involved Alger Hiss, a high-ranking State Department employee who was accused by a former Communist, Whitaker Chambers, of having been a spy for the Soviet Union. Hiss denied the charges but was later found guilty of perjury for having denied under oath that he was a spy. While Hiss maintained his innocence until his death and claims of his innocence remain popular among certain segments of the American left, a growing scholarly consensus has arisen, based largely on declassified American and Soviet intelligence reports, that Hiss was indeed guilty of espionage.

The committee also investigated Communist infiltration of the labor movement, particularly within the Congress of Industrial Organizations (CIO). Its investigations turned up over two hundred CIO organizers who were alleged to be members of the Communist Party USA (CPUSA), and played an important role in strengthening the anti-Communist forces within the labor federation, which eventually purged 11 Communist-led unions by 1950. The most frequently cited HUAC investigation into labor, though, was the 1947 investigation of Communist subversion in the film industry, led by the committee's second chairman, John Parnell Thomas, a New Jersey Republican. This investigation became infamous when 10 members of the Screen Writer's Guild, the union representing writers in motion pictures and television, were cited for contempt of Congress because they refused to answer questions at HUAC hearings. In response to these citations, the Hollywood film studios set up a blacklist to prevent known or suspected Communists from working under their own name or with screen credits. Some estimates have placed the number of blacklisted artists at over three hundred.

HUAC has been the recipient of considerable criticism, both from contemporaries and from later scholars. It has been accused of making wild and unfounded accusations against individuals, engaging in witch hunts, and selecting its targets out of partisanship. Much of this criticism is undoubtedly correct, and much of the committee's rhetoric was extreme and incendiary. Nevertheless, recent revelations from both American intelligence decrypts and newly opened Soviet archives have made some of the committee's claims more plausible. In particular, many of those accused of having worked as Soviet spies during the New Deal and World War II eras appear to have engaged in espionage.

During the 1960s, HUAC became considerably less influential and was widely criticized by large segments of the mainstream of American opinion. In 1969, it changed its name to the Committee on Internal Security and was eventually abolished by the post-Watergate Congress in 1975.

AARON MAX BERKOWITZ

References and Further Reading

Powers, Richard Gid. *Not without Honor: The History of American Anti-Communism.* New Haven, CT: Yale University Press, 1998.
Schrecker, Ellen. *Many Are the Crimes: McCarthyism in America.* Princeton, NJ: Princeton University Press, 1998.

HOUSEWORK

In pre-industrial America, housework was divided between men, women, and children. There was a sexual division of labor, though its development sometimes seems mysterious. For example, men made cider and mead, but women made beer, ale, and wine. Women made and mended cloth clothing, while men worked with leather. Women and men both carried out tasks that required brute strength. Men chopped and hauled wood and also pounded and hauled corn. But women did laundry, a long and grueling task with pre-industrial tools, and also made soap. There were also a number of tasks that both men and women performed, such as weaving, milking cows, and paring potatoes. The work of both men and women was focused on the home. However, households were still tied to the market economy, because there were always some goods and services each could not produce and had to barter for, but the pre-industrial home was much more self-sufficient than its successor.

The historian Laurel Thatcher Ulrich has pointed out that the colonial American household did indeed rely on significant amounts of trade, and while the world of women was in some ways circumscribed by the borders of the family land, they were expected to seek out commerce that would benefit the home. Colonial women were manufacturers, agriculturalists, and traders—and the poorer the household, the more blurred the line between male and female work. Account books from the period often make trade appear as a male province, dominated as they were by both the names of men and the produce of their manufacture. But Ulrich has identified complex webs of barter and borrowing that women engaged in that composed a sort of informal, usually unrecorded, economy that was essential to the success of households. Her notion of the wife as "deputy husband" indicates that women were expected to do the work of men if necessary, although many tasks were normally gender specific. In colonial America, women were expected to accept a broad, and sometimes quite flexible, responsibility for the well-being of their families.

The historian Jeanne Boydston has argued that the early nineteenth century saw a shift from a gendered division of labor to a gendered definition of labor. As industrialization lured men outside the household and into the wage economy, the wage itself began to define legitimate work. This cultural devaluation of the household economy made the work of many women less visible just as the demands upon them were increasing. To make up for the often low wages paid to their husbands, wives had to be careful consumers and often avoided the marketplace if household production was possible. The industrial revolution that provided both the mass-produced goods and the wages for modern consumers to spend on them did not simply transform women into buyers and men into earners. Women built home furnishings and practiced cooking economies, for example, that made households viable, and they did so with decreasing help from men and children. The industrialization of the home during the latter half of the nineteenth century made up for this shortfall of human labor to some degree, but this transformation also produced new family demands on women while according them little recognition as workers. Like men toiling in factories, women houseworkers also became machine tenders, but the household had already been effectively removed from the cultural definition of work.

The historian Ruth Schwartz Cowan has argued that men increasingly left the household economy for wage work over the course of the nineteenth century because industrial-era household technologies made men's work redundant, increased the load carried by women, and necessitated a cash income. She used the iron stove to illustrate these dramatic changes. This innovation became the first widely owned "consumer durable" and made an extraordinary impact on the standard of living, relegating the open hearth to the past. The iron stove did not require the expensive services of a mason to install, used less fuel, and could be placed centrally in a room to heat its occupants while cooking their food. Men had spent a lot of time chopping and hauling wood in the era of the open hearth, but these stoves required coal, so that household responsibility was eliminated. However, the stove meant more work for women, who did the cooking. The stove greatly increased the cook's control over heat and made it possible to work with multiple dishes simultaneously, and because of more efficient fuel, they could do so for a longer period. Cooking became more of an art, and family expectations rose along with houseworker preparation time.

Men had other tasks replaced as well. The cheap availability of fine white flour made baking bread more complex for women than it had been with meal, but it meant that men no longer had to haul and pound grain. The mass production of shoes and the rise of the meatpacking industry meant that men no longer needed to work leather or butcher animals at home either. But obtaining coal, flour, shoes, and meat now required a regular supply of money. This trend only increased as households, over the course of the twentieth century, became wired to an array of complex technological systems: electricity, central heating, the telephone, running water, sewage disposal, and so on. A break in the supply of money would spell disaster for the household, so someone needed to bring in that money full-time. Men assumed this role, in part, because so much of their housework had been made technologically obsolete. They went out to bring home wages, and the work environments of men and women often greatly diverged.

Cowan's assertion that the home underwent thorough industrialization raises a number of important observations. Houseworkers of the industrial era were much more isolated than many of their counterparts in the wage economy and were usually engaged in a much wider variety of tasks. They were also, of course, unpaid and therefore had far less autonomy and power in a cash economy. However, the productivity of both industrial houseworkers and industrial wage workers often relied on complex machinery they could not make or repair. Thus, many workers both inside and outside the home were alienated from the tools that made their labor possible. These tools relied on nonhuman sources of energy, such as petroleum or electricity, and thus were often part of large and complex technological systems even further beyond their control. Yet, houseworkers have adopted machinery eagerly because it has usually raised the standard of living of their families and has made some tasks, such as laundry, far less grueling.

Americans tend to believe that the household, in the industrial era, became a unit of consumption and virtually ceased being a unit of production. While elements of the production of food, clothing, and health care have been removed from the home, others still remain. Also, examples abound to indicate that technological change has invented new types and standards of household production. The production of transportation services made possible by near universal access to the automobile by the mid-twentieth century was a major addition to housework. Pre-industrial households used to consume transportation services. Peddlers came to the door; retailers and service providers delivered and made house calls, but no longer. Delivery work shifted from seller to buyer, and thus houseworkers shifted from consumers to producers of transportation services. New standards, from the iron stove on, also created more work. Indoor plumbing made much higher hygiene standards possible and thus increased family expectations of the production of cleanliness by houseworkers. The historian Susan Strasser has noted that the impact of the automatic washer on doing laundry may have been to restructure, rather than reduce, the time required. As the process became far less arduous, families expected it to happen more often and to include clothing that previously would not have been deemed soiled enough to require washing. The evolution of the automatic dryer and synthetic fabrics yet further increased expectations, even as these innovations lessened hanging and ironing labor.

One study of families that had a comfortable standard of living in 1912 revealed that houseworkers toiled 56 hours per week. Subtract servants and add at least periodic wage or piecework employment, and the burdens on working-class women appear heavy indeed. In 1965, a study found that affluent houseworkers devoted 55 hours per week to household and child-care labor and their working-class counterparts devoted just two hours less. Thus, the workload for affluent houseworkers remained consistently high during the industrial era, though their households became thoroughly industrialized. Affluent women were also more likely to be working a "double day" in the latter half of the twentieth century, which working-class women had long known, while fulfilling housework expectations elevated by technological advances and doing so with considerably less servant labor. The basis of the economy shifted away from industry and toward services during this period, decreasing, but by no means bringing into equilibrium, the proportion and types of paid work coded as masculine and transforming the educational possibilities of women. These opportunities, where actually gained, were often hard won through movements such as the National Organization for Women, which pressured the government to expand and protect the economic rights of women during the 1960s and after. Even as women streamed in to the paid labor force in the latter half of the twentieth century, the cultural construction of housework as a full-time endeavor for women proved persistent. The industrialized household immeasurably improved the standard of living in the United States and made many crucial tasks less physically demanding for houseworkers, while also creating new types and standards of work and increasingly embedding it in ever more complex economic and technological systems.

ADAM J. HODGES

References and Further Reading

Boydston, Jeanne. *Home and Work: Housework, Wages, and the Ideology of Labor in the Early Republic*. Oxford: Oxford University Press, 1990.

Cowan, Ruth. *More Work for Mother: The Ironies of Household Technology from the Open Hearth to the Microwave*. New York: Basic, 1983.

Kessler-Harris, Alice. *In Pursuit of Equity: Women, Men, and the Quest for Economic Citizenship in Twentieth-Century America*. Oxford: Oxford University Press, 2001.

Matthews, Glenna. *"Just a Housewife": The Rise and Fall of Domesticity in America*. Oxford: Oxford University Press, 1987.

Strasser, Susan. *Never Done: A History of American Housework*. New York: Pantheon, 1982.

Ulrich, Laurel Thatcher. *Good Wives: Image and Reality in the Lives of Women in Northern New England: 1650–1750*. New York: Knopf, 1980.

HUDSON, HOSEA (1898–1989)

Hudson was born in Wilkes County, Georgia, and raised by his grandmother, Mrs. Julia Smith, a sharecropper. In 1917, he married Sophie Scruggs and continued work as a sharecropper until 1923, when at the age of 25 he become an iron molder, working in steel foundries in Georgia and Alabama. Their son, Hosea Jr., was born in 1920. In 1924, they moved to Birmingham and he began work as an iron molder. He worked at the Stockham Pipe and Fitting Plant in Birmingham, Alabama, from 1927 to 1932.

Unemployed in the late Depression days of the early New Deal era, he worked with the Alabama Welfare Department and after that the Federal Works Project Administration (WPA) in 1933 and 1938. Here he helped to organize the unemployed in Birmingham through mass mobilizations and demonstrations.

Returning to the steel industry, he worked at the Wallwork Foundry, which belonged to the Tennessee Coal and Iron Railroad Company, from 1937 to 1938, the Alabama Foundry Company from 1939 to 1942, and the Flakley Foundry Company from 1942 to 1947.

In 1931, Hudson joined the Communist Party USA (CPUSA). The Party was organized on the club, cell, or unit level, and he soon become a leader of his primary unit. His first task was to organize workers at the Stockham Foundry, but when his Party membership was discovered by the owners, he was fired in 1932.

He became active in the Scottsboro Case in 1931, joining the worldwide campaign to free nine young black men falsely accused of raping two white women in Alabama. In 1932, he became active in the Unemployed Councils, where he became involved in neighborhood initiatives to keep landlords from evicting tenants. If the landlords refused, the Council would put the tenants back in the buildings and, in case of cold weather, would take apart empty buildings for firewood.

Realizing his organizational abilities, the Central Committee of the CPUSA brought him to its national Training School in New York City in 1934. Here Hudson spent 10 weeks studying Marxist economics and social theory. He also learned more about trade union history and leadership skills and saw how he could relate theory to practice and vice versa. He was then sent by the Party to Atlanta, where he organized under the pseudonym Larry Brown.

Returning to Birmingham in 1937, his next job was at the Tennessee Coal and Iron Railroad Company, where he was assigned to the hot and oppressive Wallwork Foundry. He joined the United Steelworkers of America union (USWA), which did not have a Local 1489 at another plant. He soon became its recording secretary.

Elected as a delegate to the Southern Negro Youth Congress's (SNYC) second convention in 1938, he met its early leaders, among them James E. Jackson Jr., Edward Strong, and Louis Burnham. When the SNYC established its national headquarters in Birmingham, in 1939, Hudson worked closely with it leaders and with Esther Cooper Jackson, who later became its executive director. There Jackson and her husband James, who was a Southern Region coordinator of the Communist Party, held daily sessions

HUERTA, DOLORES C.

with Hudson, helping him further develop his reading and writing skills.

Finding himself unemployed again in 1938, Hudson plunged into his new work with the WPA. He then became vice president of Local 1 of the Workers Alliance Union of the Birmingham and Jefferson County locals of the WPA. Working successfully to bring more worker projects and unemployment aid to Jefferson County (Birmingham), he soon became vice president of the Jefferson County Industrial Union Council.

Following that, he began work at the Jackson Foundry of the Flakley Foundry Company, where he organized Local 2815 of the USWA and became president of the local. He also found the Right to Vote Club of Birmingham. He held other various union positions within the Birmingham Industrial Council and the USWA from 1940 until 1947. In 1945, he continued his work in the mass movement as vice president of the Alabama People's Education Association.

Identified by the *Birmingham Post* as a member of the National Committee of the CPUSA in late 1947, he was expelled from the union and fired from his job at the Jackson Foundry. He also was banned from work in any other foundries, where he had for years worked as a molder in the beginning years of the McCarthy–Truman Cold War era. His marriage of 30 years ended in 1946.

Hudson developed extensive contacts with many groups during these Birmingham years. He organized black workers within the confines of the Congress of Industrial Organizations (CIO). He also played a role in fighting for black voting rights throughout the South. Blessed with a strong bass baritone voice, he also sang with church choirs and barbershop quartets and was best known for his rendition of the song, "I Just Want to Be a Leader."

Hudson attempted to continue his political work by organizing the United Political Action Committee, but like many Communists during the period, Hudson was finally forced "underground" in 1950. From 1951 until 1953, he worked as CP liaison to Party units in the South. He also lived and worked as a mason and other odd jobs under various pseudonyms in Birmingham until Eugene "Bill" Connor, the infamous Birmingham police commissioner, using the Klu Klux Klan and police, tracked Hudson down and forced him to leave the city for good under threat of death. Finally, in 1954, he moved north to New York and took odd jobs, the last being as a janitor in a restaurant.

In 1962, he married his second wife, Virginia Marson, and in 1965, he retired from the restaurant. They moved first to Newark, New Jersey, and then settled in Atlantic City. His wife died in 1971, and he moved to Florida in 1984.

In the early 1970s, Hudson served as an adjunct professor at the Antioch College's Washington campus, and in 1972, he published his autobiography, *Black Worker in the Deep South*. Richard Arrington, the first African-American mayor of Birmingham, gave Hudson the keys to the city on February 26, 1980, which was also proclaimed Hosea Hudson Day. He wore the key around his neck on public occasions. He was a founding member of the Coalition of Black Trade Unionists.

Hudson moved to Florida in 1984 and remained there until his death at 91.

MAURICE JACKSON

References and Further Reading

Hudson, Hosea. *Black Worker in the Deep South.* New York: International Publishers, 1972.
Painter, Nell Irvin. *The Narrative of Hosea Hudson: His Life as a Communist in the South.* New York: W.W. Norton, 1994.

HUERTA, DOLORES C. (APRIL 10, 1930–)
Cofounder, United Farm Workers of America

Dolores Huerta is the cofounder of the United Farm Workers of America (UFW), AFL-CIO, and the most prominent Chicana labor leader of her generation in the United States. For over 50 years, she has tenaciously devoted herself to the struggle for unionization of farm workers and dignity and justice for agricultural laborers, Mexican-Americans, immigrants, and women. Huerta's unwavering dedication to social change is celebrated in song, murals, newspaper articles, and magazines, through honors and awards, and in the lives of tens of thousands of union members and supporters. Still active and organizing, she is recognized as one of the foremost women in the U.S. labor movement, Mexican-American groups, progressive politics, and feminist circles.

A nationally admired labor leader, political activist, and supporter of women's rights, Huerta was born in the small mining town of Dawson in northern New Mexico. She was the second child and only daughter of Juan Fernández and Alicia Cháves Fernández. Her father was a miner, a fieldworker, and after the couple divorced, a union activist and briefly a member of the New Mexico state legislature. After her divorce,

621

Alicia Fernández moved her family to Stockton, California. As a single parent during the Great Depression, she experienced difficulty supporting her young family. While she worked at a cannery at night and as a waitress during the day, Huerta's grandfather watched the children. During the 1940s, her family's circumstances improved. Huerta's mother, who had remarried, owned and operated a restaurant and hotel that catered to a multiethnic clientele. While Huerta and her brothers and stepsister helped run the establishment, their mother instilled in them an ethic of community service and encouraged their participation in a variety of social activities. Reflecting opportunities made possible by her emerging middle-class lifestyle, Huerta took violin, piano, and dance lessons. She also sang in the church choir and was an active Girl Scout.

Prodded by parental ambitions, Huerta excelled in school. After her high school graduation, she enrolled at Delta Community College, briefly interrupting her studies for her first, short marriage in 1950 to Ralph Head. Soon divorced with two daughters, she returned to school to prepare for a teaching career. Frustrated with her inability to help her students with their urgent needs of hunger and poverty, Huerta yearned for a more direct way to deal with social injustice and inequality.

Social and Labor Activism

She soon discovered an outlet for her desire for social change in the new wave of labor, civic, and political activism then sweeping the country after World War II. She joined the Agricultural Workers Association (AWA) founded by her local parish priest in Stockton, California. It later merged with the AFL-CIO-sponsored Agricultural Workers Organizing Committee (AWOC). Huerta won election as the secretary-treasurer of the group. Frustrated by the leadership and its policies, she eventually left. The postwar organization that would dramatically alter her life was the Community Service Organization (CSO), a Mexican-American self-help association that spread throughout the Southwest. The group asserted that grassroots organizing held the key to improving the conditions of the poor and politically disenfranchised barrio residents throughout California. A preferred strategy was the house meeting. The CSO recruited volunteers to teach citizenship classes, initiate voter registration drives in Mexican-American neighborhoods, and press for improved services in their communities. Because Huerta was outspoken, passionate, and determined,

the organization's leaders asked her to join the staff to advocate for CSO initiatives in Sacramento. Here she gained valuable experience as an organizer, activist, and lobbyist. During her tenure, she successfully lobbied for bills, including landmark legislation that allowed farm laborers to receive public assistance, retirement benefits, and disability and unemployment insurance, regardless of citizenship status. She also labored to end the Bracero (guest worker) program. Most significantly, she worked with César Chávez. The two were very different in temperament and had a contentious relationship throughout their association, but they shared an abiding commitment to social justice. Discouraged by the CSO's unwillingness to embrace the organization of farmworkers, the pair left to found the National Farm Workers Association (NFWA), the precursor to the United Farm Workers of America (UFW), in Delano in 1962.

Undaunted by her estrangement from her second husband, Ventura Huerta, and the responsibility of raising her family of seven children, Huerta threw herself into the organizing effort. She remained in Stockton for several years to organize workers in the agricultural valleys of northern California before Chávez successfully prevailed upon her to move her family to Delano and to work directly with him. Despite the long tradition of male dominance in the labor movement, Huerta was the first vice president and maintained a highly visible profile. As second in command to Chávez, she exerted a direct influence on guiding the union. In the pivotal 1965 Delano grape strike initiated by AWOC and joined by the NFWA, she devised strategy and inspired workers with her determination and courage. Eventually, the two organizations merged into the United Farm Workers Organizing Committee (UFWOC). The only woman on the executive board, Huerta took charge of negotiations and secured the first contract with Schenley Wine Company. Her tenacity and unconventional tactics extracted major concessions from wineries, such as pay raises, pesticide regulations, paid holidays and vacations, unemployment benefits, sanitation facilities, clean drinking water, health benefits, and eventually pensions. In addition, the union hiring hall replaced the exploitive labor contractor system. This collective bargaining agreement challenged the traditional power relations between farm laborers and corporate agriculture. It served as the model for contracts with other wineries such as Almaden, Gallo, Paul Masson, Christian Brothers, Franzia, and Novitiate.

When table grape growers refused to bargain, the union resorted to the nonviolent boycott. Huerta became a prominent figure in 1968 as director of the boycott in New York City, the primary distribution point for grapes, and then the East Coast director. Supported by a vibrant civil rights movement, she mobilized unions, political activists, ethnic and racial associations, students, religious supporters, environmentalists, and concerned consumers on behalf of "*La Causa*," the farmworkers' cause. In New York, Huerta also became aware of the growing feminist movement through her contacts with Gloria Steinem and other women's activists. Consequently, Huerta began to incorporate a feminist critique into her human rights' philosophy and sexual harassment clauses into her negotiations. Her passionate defense of farmworkers' rights provided a compelling model for women, encouraging them to move beyond traditional roles to join picket lines, marches, and boycotts across the nation despite their own personal reservations and over objections of unsupportive fathers or husbands. After five years of striking, the growing power of this cross-cultural and cross-class grassroots coalition finally forced Coachella and Delano table grape producers to negotiate the historic contracts of 1970.

Even before the union could fully savor its victory, it immediately confronted the lettuce, Gallo wine, and table grape boycotts of the 1970s. It was during this decade that the union ceased to be the United Farm Workers Organizing Committee (UFWOC) and became the United Farm Workers of America, or UFW. As in previous campaigns, Huerta's charisma, energy, organizing skills, frenetic travel calendar, and prodigious speaking schedule renewed the national boycott. Huerta juggled her union responsibilities with growing family demands as she began her unconventional liaison with Richard Chávez, brother of César Chávez, which produced four more children. Frequent separations from her large family did not deter her from her number one priority, the union. Unlike her male colleagues, Huerta's domestic arrangements departed from conventional expectations and drew criticism and comments from coworkers and observers in the media. She brushed off such concerns and focused on her work. Nevertheless, her constant travel, organizing, and publicizing contributed to the passage of the Agricultural Labor Relations Act (ALRA) in 1975, the first law to recognize the collective bargaining rights of farm laborers in California. This legislation raised expectations that the turmoil in the fields would come to an end.

The struggle between agribusiness and the UFW did not stop, but assumed a new legal dimension. The emphasis moved to elections in the fields and political organizing to protect the new legislation. As part of this effort, Huerta headed the union's Citizenship Participation Day Department (CPD), the political arm of the UFW, as she fought to defend the law

in Sacramento. In the 1980s, Huerta directed her energies to another ambitious initiative, the founding of Radio Campesina, the union's radio station (KUFW). This resource would become vital as the union faced an increasing conservative challenge from Republican administrations, including the Reagan presidency and the election of California Governor George Deukmejian, both allies of agribusiness.

Like other unions during this inhospitable political environment, the UFW lost hard-won contracts and experienced a declining membership. Huerta filled her schedule with speaking engagements, fund-raising, and publicizing the renewed boycotts of the 1980s. Appearing before state and congressional committees, she offered impassioned testimony on a variety of issues, including pesticides, the health problems of fieldworkers, Hispanic issues, and immigration policy. The 1985 Immigration Act she lobbied for provided amnesty and citizenship for over one million farmworkers who had lived, worked, and paid taxes in the United States. Her energy and commitment seemed boundless.

Huerta's loyalty to the farmworkers movement claimed a personal toll—family sacrifices, more than 20 arrests, and a life-threatening injury during a 1988 peaceful protest against the presidential candidacy of George H. W. Bush in San Francisco. Clubbed by a police officer, Huerta collapsed on the picket line. She was rushed to the hospital with broken ribs, and her spleen was removed in emergency surgery. A legal suit forced the police department to revise its rules regarding crowd control and police discipline. The court issued an $825,000 financial judgment as a consequence of her personal injury.

During her convalescence, Huerta took a leave from the union to work on the Fund for the Feminist Majority's Feminization of Power Campaign. While crisscrossing the country recruiting and encouraging Latinas to run for office, she was stunned by the premature death of her longtime collaborator, César Chávez, in 1993. Huerta returned to the union. With Chávez's untimely death, she became the revered elder. Always in demand as a speaker, she addressed a wide variety of labor, women's, political, student, and community groups, assigning her honorariums to the union. She contributed to organizing campaigns, even returning to the strenuous demands of the bargaining table to pressure strawberry, tomato, and mushroom growers.

Later Political Activism

In 2000, the 70-year-old Huerta reluctantly decided to cut back on her union activities. That year, she chose not to seek re-election to the union's Executive Board as secretary-treasurer. Her "retirement" did not mean abandoning her advocacy of labor, political, and women's issues. As the union's first vice president emeritus, she continued to speak on behalf of farmworkers, participated in the presidential campaign of Al Gore, and steadfastly supported women's rights. Toward the end of the campaign, she was suddenly stricken with an abdominal aneurysm that required surgery and massive blood transfusions. Confounding the medical community, but not those familiar with her fighting spirit, she recovered. After recuperating, she established the Dolores Huerta Foundation to train community leaders to advocate for immigrants, women, and children. Still drawn to politics, the Kerry/Edwards campaign appointed her to head up *Mujeres con Kerry* (Women with Kerry) in 2004.

Huerta's dedication to social change has been commemorated in murals and ballads; schools and parks have been named after her; and she has won numerous honors. The California State Senate awarded her the Outstanding Labor Leader Award in 1984. In 1993, she was inducted into the National Women's Hall of Fame. President Bill Clinton bestowed the Eleanor Roosevelt Award upon her in 1998.

A tireless activist for farmworkers, Mexican-Americans, women, and social justice, Huerta created an inspiring and unforgettable legacy to the labor, civil rights, and women's movements of the twentieth century. She steadfastly clung to her conviction that agricultural laborers, a workforce dismissed by the largely white leadership of mainstream unions as unorganizable, could be unionized. Proud of her Chicana heritage, she roused multiple generations of Mexican-Americans to fight for their rights. Rejecting mid-twentieth century ideals of femininity, she ignored conventional expectations for women and for Mexican-American women, in particular. For women, and especially Chicanas and Mexicanas, she has blazed a pioneering trail. Surmounting gender, ethnic, and class expectations, she has provided a powerful example and role model in the struggle for a decent standard of living, equality, and justice.

MARGARET ROSE

References and Further Reading

Levy, Jacques. *Cesar Chavez: Autobiography of La Causa.* New York: W. W. Norton & Company, Inc, 1975.
Majka, Linda C., and Theo J. Majka. *Farm Workers, Agribusiness, and the State.* Philadelphia: Temple University Press, 1982.
———. "Traditional and Non-traditional Patterns of Female Activism in the United Farm Workers of America, 1962 to 1980." *Frontiers* 11, no. 1 (March 1990): 26–32.
Rose, Margaret. "César Chávez and Dolores Huerta: Partners in 'La Causa.'" In *César Chávez: A Brief Biography with Documents,* edited by Richard Etulain. Boston: Bedford/St. Martin's, 2002.
———. "Dolores Huerta: The United Farm Workers Union." In *The Human Tradition in American Labor History,* edited by Eric Arnesen. Wilmington, DE: Scholarly Resources Inc, 2004, pp. 211–229.
———. "From the Fields to the Picket Line: Huelga Women and the Boycott, 1965–1975." *Labor History* 31, no. 3 (Summer 1990): 271–293.
———. "Gender and Civic Activism in Mexican American Barrios: The Community Service Organization, 1947–1962." In *Not June Cleaver: Women and Gender in Postwar America, 1945–1960,* edited by Joanne Meyerowitz. Philadelphia: Temple University Press, 1994, pp. 177–200.
———. "'Woman Power Will Stop Those Grapes': Chicana Organizers and Middle-Class Female Supporters in the Farm Workers' Grape Boycott in Philadelphia, 1969–1970." *Journal of Women's History* 7, no. 4 (Winter 1995): 6–36.

See also **Chávez, César Estrada; Delano Grape Strike (1965–1970); United Farm Workers of America**

HULL-HOUSE SETTLEMENT (1889–1963)

Jane Addams and Ellen Gates Starr, founders and residents, established Hull-House, Chicago's first settlement on September 18, 1889, as a protest against the widening gap between the haves and the have-nots in the industrial districts of modern cities. As residents, they took no salaries but paid their own expenses, choosing to live among working-class families and to learn about their needs. Instead of imposing solutions, Addams and Starr sought to work with their neighbors to improve urban life and were committed to sharing their cultural and educational advantages. After renting the once fashionable house built by the realtor Charles J. Hull in 1856, they decorated it as if it were their own home, with paintings, sculpture, and books, and invited their neighbors to social evenings, classes, and lectures.

Settlements proliferated in the 1890s, a period of labor unrest. Soon after opening Hull-House, daily experiences in the neighborhood focused Starr and Addams, and the other residents who soon joined them, on the labor struggle, and they allied themselves with labor leaders and reformers in the antisweatshop movement. Residents collected and publicized data about sweatshop conditions, demanded new laws to regulate the workplace and keep children in school, and encouraged their neighbors to organize themselves into unions. Highly politicized by life in the Nineteenth Ward of Chicago's Near West Side, an industrial neighborhood just west of the city's downtown, Hull-House residents began to advocate for public health reforms, construction of playgrounds and recreation centers, and improved affordable housing and better sanitation. Responsive to the needs of immigrants and their children, they redefined the nature of programs and educational curricula for public schools. These initiatives were fully expressed in the Progressive Party platform of 1912 that was developed in large part by settlement leaders. At the Bull Moose convention held in Chicago, Jane Addams seconded the nomination of Theodore Roosevelt as candidate for president of the United States.

Over the years, Hull-House welcomed reformers and radicals, socialists, communists, anarchists, and trade unionists as residents; there were also a significant number of young professionals from the fields of business, law, and medicine. Artists and writers, university people, social workers and college graduates in search of meaning in their lives also came to live at the settlement for periods of six months, one or two years, or in some cases for decades.

Some historians emphasize the social control features of settlement house initiatives, arguing that middle- and upper-middle-class residents hoped to assimilate immigrants into American middle-class values about family life and social behavior. Others question the motivation of the settlement movement in expanding the role of the state, especially arguing that the maternalist values of settlement leaders, who were predominantly women, led eventually to a two-tiered social welfare system in the United States that disadvantaged working-class women and minorities and attempted to enforce middle-class behavior and mores. Historians have also critiqued the race policies of social settlements, pointing out that these associations rarely resulted in interracial programs.

Hull-House and Gender

The overwhelming majority of residents at Hull-House were single women. Among these, a small group spent their adult lives at Hull-House. Many others, including Florence Kelley, Mary Kenney, Julia C. Lathrop, Grace Abbott, and Alice Hamilton, were leaders in the women's political culture of the late nineteenth and early twentieth century. Alliances forged at Hull-House linked social activist women in national and international networks. For many women, Hull-House and other settlements provided a new kind of social space in between a traditional domestic sphere and a new civic or professional life. Hull-House included male residents, too, but the settlement's leaders were women. Hull-House was a privately funded settlement for most of the association's 74-year history on Halsted Street. Money came primarily from reform-minded women. Louise deKoven Bowen was the single largest contributor to the settlement, and after she was appointed treasurer of Hull-House Association in 1907, she assumed much of the responsibility for fund-raising. Other major donors were Mary Rozet Smith, Addams's companion, and Helen Culver, heir to the Hull property. The wealthy male philanthropists Charles Hutchinson, Edward B. Butler, and Julius Rosenwald also contributed to Hull-House, but the settlement was never their major philanthropic focus as it became for Smith and Bowen. The settlement was incorporated as the Hull-House Association (HHA) in 1895, with Addams, John Dewey, Helen Culver, Allen B. Pond, and Mary Rozet Smith serving as trustees. Pond was the architect for the 12 additional settlement buildings. Educator and philosopher John Dewey was active at Hull-House during his tenure at the University of Chicago. The board of trustees remained small (less than 10) during Jane Addams's tenure as head resident and president. She remained in these positions until her death in May 1935, never receiving a salary and using her own inheritance to sustain the enterprise.

The almost unconditional support she received from the close-knit and small group of women donors who shared her political agenda was a major reason why Jane Addams could risk taking unpopular positions. She was also empowered by the independent status of Hull-House, one of the few settlements in the country that was not affiliated with either a religious body or a university.

After Addams's death, the Hull-House resident Adena Miller Rich served as head resident (1935–1937), refusing to accept any compensation in an effort to continue the original settlement tradition. Charlotte Carr (1937–1942) became the first paid director, and with her tenure during the New Deal came a greater reliance on public funding, a change that the HHA had resisted until almost the end of the 1920s. Professionalism in the field of social work as well as increased public funding and a full-time salaried director contributed to the demise of the settlement as a co-operative, resident-based community based on volunteerism.

Hull-House as a Social Center

Hull-House programs grew at a rapid pace as settlement residents became more familiar with the needs of the neighborhood. By 1907, the settlement was a complex of 13 buildings, 12 additional edifices having been constructed by architects Pond & Pond as new programs and services were added and space for a growing number of women and men residents was provided. Services for children included a kindergarten, nursery, well-baby clinic, public gymnasium, and playground. In 1907, Hull-House residents founded the Juvenile Protective Association (JPA), and in 1908, they established the Immigrants' Protective League (IPL). Both the IPL and the JPA were housed in the settlement's buildings and had their own boards and staff who worked closely with Hull-House. The settlement included a branch of the public library, a post office, and a cooperative boardinghouse for young workingwomen, the Jane Club. It acted as a liaison with city charities and social service agencies. Numerous social and recreational clubs attracted both children and adults. Educational programs for adults included college extension classes, lecture series, and vocational training. The arts were addressed through a rigorous Music School program, classes in visual and craft arts, sponsorship of theater groups and productions, exhibits, dance classes, and a collection of artwork for loan to club members. Many activities were geared toward neighborhood immigrants. Hull-House sponsored ethnic festivals and social events, and offered English and citizenship classes. By 1907, the settlement reported that nine thousand people attended classes or participated in activities.

Using the Performing and Visual Arts to Create Community

Addams and Starr, who had met while attending the Rockford Female Seminary in Rockford, Illinois, were influenced by Toynbee Hall, the East London settlement started in 1884 by Oxford graduates. They first put into place programs and activities that reflected their reading of John Ruskin, William Morris, and T. F. Horsfall, following the theory that it was essential that working people should have the opportunity to express themselves through the arts. It is not surprising that well-educated women who were disturbed by the seeming isolation and alienation of the working classes initially would turn to high culture as a means to bridge the class gap. The Shakespeare classes, the Plato Club, and the college-extension courses they offered appealed to the American-born clerks and schoolteachers of German and Irish descent, who still remained in the neighborhood that was rapidly being populated by newly arrived immigrants from southern and eastern Europe. Later,

Addams and residents Enella Benedict, head of the Art School, Eleanor Smith, director of the Music School, and Laura Dainty Pelham and Edith de Nancrede, of the Drama department, realized that the performing and visual arts could be vehicles for intercultural and cross-class activities. Theatrical and musical events where neighborhood children and adults performed for audiences that included the settlement's wealthy patrons, for example, created opportunities for privileged Chicagoans to learn firsthand about immigrant and working-class people. At the same time, pageants and holiday celebrations brought together neighbors from different cultural backgrounds.

As successive groups of European immigrants and migrants from the southern United States arrived in the Hull-House neighborhood, residents adapted the performing arts programs as ways of bringing children and adults of different races, ethnicities, and religions into social contact. Reproductions of European art and sculpture initially decorated the settlement's interior space, and the first new building added to the Hull home included art galleries and studios and a lending library where books and art reproductions could be borrowed. The Labor Museum that opened in 1900 also privileged European crafts. With the founding of the Hull-House Kilns in 1927, the settlement acknowledged the migrations of Mexicans. The Kilns were incorporated as a business, a reflection of the fact that Hull-House had become a major institution in the neighborhood and an employer of local crafts people in its industrial shops. Artists from Mexico were employed, but the directors of the kilns were Americans with connections to the School of the Art Institute of Chicago, and the paid workers were Mexicans from the neighborhood whose primary roles were to produce ceramic dishes that were sold in downtown Chicago shops. There were also opportunities to produce individual art pieces.

During the New Deal era, Hull-House increased its staff with federally funded workers and introduced a department of Workers' Education. Cultural differences in the neighborhood were decentered as shared working-class interests informed creative expressions in the visual and performing arts. Art exhibits included the work of Chicago-area African-American artists, and efforts to integrate programs and staff to reflect the changing demography of the neighborhood had mixed results. With the loss of federal funding during World War II and its aftermath, Hull-House resumed its Eurocentric emphases, as illustrated by the presence of a Latvian theater group in the 1950s.

Support of Labor Organization

The arrival of Florence Kelley brought labor issues to the center. Taking leadership of the antisweatshop campaign, Kelley and her allies were successful in obtaining passage of the first Factory Inspection Act in Illinois in 1893; this legislation also had provisions for reduction of hours for women workers (the eight-hour day clause) and compulsory school attendance for children through the age of 14. Appointed chief factory inspector, Kelley located her office in the settlement house.

Hull-House invited workers interested in organizing new unions to meet in its facilities and, when the new unions engaged in strikes, became sympathetic allies, providing bail money, contributing to the fund for striking workers' families, and protesting the anti-union politics of the employers. Chicago branches of the Women's Union Label League and the Women's Trade Union League met there. During the economic depression of 1893–1894, Hull-House opened a Model Lodging House for unemployed women and funded it through a cooperative arrangement with the Chicago Woman's Club. With the assistance of Hull-House, Mary Kenney and a group of women workers formed the Jane Club, a co-operative and self-governing boarding club. A house was built in the Hull-House complex for the club's use.

Sociological Investigation and Advocacy

The belief that an enlightened citizenry could be mobilized for reform causes was part of the Progressive Era's faith in the efficacy of social science investigation to produce solutions for society's problems. *Hull House Maps & Papers* (*HHM&P*) (1895) is the first study of its kind in the United States and directly influenced subsequent social surveys that also emanated from settlement houses rather than from universities. *HHM&P* condemn the sweating system in the garment trades and argue that only those workers who organized themselves into trade unions were able to improve their status. In subsequent studies—23 different investigations were conducted between 1892 and 1933—Hull-House residents explored child labor, tenement conditions, ethnic groups, infant mortality, midwifery, cocaine use, and the causes and prevention of truancy. Many of their findings were published in the *American Journal of Sociology*. They used this information to lobby for reforms.

Departure

The Hull-House neighborhood continued to change demographically. In 1938, the Jane Addams Homes, the city's first public housing development, was built southwest of the settlement. In the 1950s, parts of the neighborhood were razed for industrial use and to accommodate two expressways. Hull-House's director, Russell Ballard (1943–1963), advocated for community participation in the redevelopment of the old neighborhood, but by the 1950s, settlement houses no longer were in the vanguard of reform. There were discussions about the future of Hull-House.

In 1961, the Hull-House neighborhood was selected as the site for a new urban campus for the University of Illinois, and plans initially proposed the demolition of the 13-building settlement complex and the whole neighborhood that surrounded it. The plan provoked considerable protest from the neighborhood and generated a campaign to save some of the original Hull-House buildings. Two buildings were saved: the original Hull home and the Residents' Dining Hall building. The social service functions of the HHA moved to other Chicago sites in 1963. In 1967, the Jane Addams Hull-House Museum opened in the two remaining structures that had been saved and restored.

RIMA LUNIN SCHULTZ

References and Further Reading

Addams, Jane. *Twenty Years at Hull-House: With Autobiographical Notes.* New York: Macmillan Co., 1910.

Bryan, Mary Lynn McCree, and Allen F. Davis, eds. *One Hundred Years at Hull-House.* Revised, expanded edition of *Eighty Years at Hull-House*, 1969. Bloomington: Indiana University Press, 1990.

Carson, Minna. *Settlement Folk: Social Thought and the American Settlement Movement, 1885–1930.* Chicago: University of Chicago Press, 1990.

Davis, Allen F. *Spearheads for Reform: The Social Settlements and the Progressive Movement, 1890–1914.* New York: Oxford University Press, 1967.

Horowitz, Helen L. "Hull House as Women's Space." *Chicago History* 12 (1983): 40–55.

Jackson, Shannon. *Lines of Activity: Performance, Historiography, Hull-House Domesticity.* Ann Arbor: University of Michigan Press, 2000.

Lasch-Quinn, Elisabeth. *Black Neighbors: Race and the Limits of Reform in the American Settlement House Movement, 1890–1945.* Chapel Hill: The University of North Carolina Press, 1993.

Lissak, Rivka Shpak. *Pluralism and Progressives: Hull House and the New Immigrants, 1890–1919.* Chicago: University of Chicago Press, 1989.

Schultz, Rima Lunin, ed. "Urban Experience in Chicago: Hull-House and Its Neighborhoods, 1889–1963." www.uic.edu/jaddams/hull/urbanexp.

Sklar, Kathryn Kish. "Hull House in the 1890s: A Community of Women Reformers." *Signs: Journal of Women in Culture and Society* 10 (Summer): 658–677.
———."Who Funded Hull House." In *Lady Bountiful Revisited: Women, Philanthropy, and Power*, edited by Kathleen McCarthy. New Brunswick, NJ: Rutgers University Press, 1990.
Stebner, Eleanor J. *The Women of Hull House: A Study of Spirituality, Vocation, and Friendship.* Albany: State University of New York Press, 1997.
Trolander, Judith Ann. *Settlement Houses and the Great Depression.* Detroit: Wayne State University Press, 1975.

See also **Addams, Jane**

HUTCHESON, WILLIAM L. (1874–1953) President, United Brotherhood of Carpenters and Joiners (UBCJ), 1915–1951

Having experienced long periods of unemployment and witnessed failed organizing campaigns as a young itinerate carpenter, William L. Hutcheson developed a firm belief in business principles and the importance of centralized organization and strong leadership to the American labor movement. His style of leadership is usually described as business unionism, and his policies were often criticized as conservative and undemocratic. Nevertheless, he fought hard to preserve his union's jurisdictional claims and powerful position within the labor movement. He was among the most prominent labor leaders in the twentieth century.

Soon after becoming the general president of the UBCJ upon the death of the president, James Kirby, in 1915, Hutcheson intervened in a wage dispute between the New York District Council and the Building Trades Employers' Association. When locals called a strike without the approval of the national organization, he negotiated a settlement with the Employers' Association, and the UBCJ General Executive Board suspended and re-organized 61 locals. Because of the New York locals' tradition of independence, Hutcheson's decisive actions made it clear that powerful local unions and autonomous district councils would be closely monitored under his leadership.

Throughout his career, Hutcheson steadfastly opposed the concept of industrial unionism. For the leaders of the Carpenters union, the prospect of industrial unions raised the specter of jurisdictional losses and internal discord. Since 1914, the UBCJ had adhered to a policy of craft industrialism. In short, this meant that although the union claimed jurisdiction over the entire woodworking industry, it preferred not to organize all workers. Instead, the Brotherhood preferred to police the industry in the interests of preserving the carpenters' craft interests. In the 1920s, Hutcheson promptly expelled suspected agitators in response to Communists' attempts to infiltrate the UBCJ. When debates within the American Federation of Labor (AFL) over chartering industrial unions began in 1933, Hutcheson was a leading opponent. The split within the AFL, which led to the creation of the Congress of Industrial Organizations (CIO), was famously underscored in 1935 when Hutcheson and the United Mine Workers (UMW) president John Lewis engaged in a fistfight on the AFL convention floor. The UBCJ and the CIO continued their battles in jurisdictional disputes and remained bitter rivals for the remainder of Hutcheson's career.

Hutcheson rejected third-party political movements and argued that labor stood to gain more as a nonpartisan political pressure group. During World War I, for example, he was successful in achieving all of the Carpenters major wartime labor demands through his co-operation in the creation of the National War Labor Board. Throughout his career, Hutcheson sought to achieve gains for labor through the Republican Party. GOP principles meshed well with Hutcheson's conservatism, which generally tolerated only minimal governmental intervention in the economy. Within the labor movement, he warned rank-and-file members that the government could take away just as quickly as it could give to labor. He retreated slightly from this stance during the Great Depression and supported public works projects and unemployment insurance, but he opposed President Roosevelt in each of his elections.

Over the course of his career, Hutcheson became the dominant labor figure within the Republican Party. He turned down offers to serve as secretary of labor under presidents Harding, Coolidge, and Hoover, but advised each on labor issues. In addition to serving as a delegate to several Republican conventions, he was a regular visitor at the White House during Hoover's administration, and in 1944, he was considered as a potential vice presidential candidate. Despite his own conservatism, Hutcheson considered himself a liberalizing force within the Republican Party.

Hutcheson continued to support the Republican Party after passage of the Taft-Hartley Act in 1947, but he devoted much of the remainder of his career to fighting antilabor legislation. According to his biographer, Hutcheson helped influence President Truman to veto the Taft-Hartley Act, and in 1948, the Carpenters union joined the rest of the labor movement in campaigning against congressmen who had voted for the bill. Although he felt betrayed by Robert Taft and other conservative party members, Hutcheson remained a Republican and continued to advocate a nonpartisan policy for labor even when the AFL came out in support of the Democratic presidential candidate, Adlai Stevenson, in 1952.

Suffering from health problems, Hutcheson resigned his post as president in 1951 at the age of 77. He was succeeded by his son, Maurice, who held the office until 1972. After a brief stay at the union's retirement home in Lakeland, Florida (which he had been instrumental in establishing), Hutcheson returned to the Midwest, where he died on October 20, 1953.

JOHN J. ROSEN

References and Further Reading

Christie, Robert A. *Empire in Wood: A History of the Carpenters' Union*. Ithaca, NY: Cornell University Press, 1956.

Galenson, Walter. *The United Brotherhood of Carpenters: The First Hundred Years*. Cambridge, MA: Harvard University Press, 1983.

Raddock, Maxwell C. *Portrait of an American Leader: William L. Hutcheson*. New York: American Institute of Social Science, Inc., 1995.

See also **United Brotherhood of Carpenters and Joiners of America**

I

ILLINOIS WOMAN'S ALLIANCE

The Illinois Woman's Alliance (IWA) was formed in November 1888 as a cross-class and interracial coalition of 25 diverse women's organizations. Two prior decades of successful political organization by Chicago women around issues of women's rights and the protection of women and children had prepared the way for the IWA. Middle-class and elite women had enlarged the scope of their organizations to incorporate labor issues, and during the same period, women workers had formed labor unions and had affiliated with the men's Trade and Labor Assembly of Chicago.

The immediate incident leading to the IWA's formation was journalist Nell Nelson's "City Slave Girls," a shocking expose of conditions in Chicago's sweatshop, which appeared in the Chicago *Times.* Chicago had a tenement and workshop inspection law on the books that had been enacted in 1879 in response to the revelation that garments were being produced in tenement rooms where men, women, and children lay sick with diphtheria, measles, smallpox, tuberculosis, and other diseases that could be transmitted to purchasers of the garments. The inspection law was not enforced.

The IWA had 25 affiliates ranging from representatives of the Knights of Labor to the Chicago Woman's Club and the Prudence Crandall Club, one of the first African-American women's clubs in Chicago. At its peak the IWA could fill the city council chambers with 500 women. The IWA members included socialists, dress reformers, spiritualists, temperance advocates, and clubwomen.

Elizabeth Morgan, Caroline Huling, Corrine Stubbs Brown, and Fannie Barrier Williams all were IWA officers and represent a cross section of the women's movement in Chicago in the late nineteenth century. Morgan, British-born socialist, in 1888 helped found the Ladies' Federal Labor Union, No. 2703. It was affiliated with the American Federation of Labor (AFL) and adopted the Knights of Labor principle of treating housewives as producers. Morgan represented the Ladies' Federal and the larger Trade and Labor Assembly of Chicago in the IWA. Corrine Brown, a schoolteacher for 13 years and a principal for six before she married Frank Brown, a Chicago banker, was a member of the Socialist Labor party. She was both a leading clubwoman and the head of the Ladies' Federal Union No. 2703. Brown and Morgan issued the call for the formation of the IWA. Caroline Huling, the daughter of a newspaper publisher with political connections in New York State, was an early convert to France E. Willard's Women's Christian Temperance Union and a leader in the Cook County Equal Suffrage Association. She edited a short-lived suffrage newspaper, and in March 1888 was a delegate to the first International Council of Women. Fannie Williams, raised in Brockport, New York, taught school before she married S. Laing Williams, a black lawyer, and settled in Chicago. A member of Chicago's black elite, Williams authored newspaper and magazine articles, founded the Prudence Crandall Club, a literary society of upper-class African-American women and, after heated debate, was voted a member of the CWC.

The IWA slogan, "Justice to Children—Loyalty to Women," reflected the potential conflict inherent in the coalition as traditionalist women advocated moral reforms while feminists attempted to expand the authority and power of women in society. There were also disagreements between trade unionist women who resisted political solutions to economic problems initially and middle-class reformers who sought an expanded role of the state in these matters. The national solution of the race question in 1896 into acceptance of a system of segregated women's organizations meant that the interracial coalition achieved by the IWA would be an anomalous event, not the beginnings of a social transformation.

The balance of power of the coalition shifted when in 1892, Hull-House resident Florence Kelley became the leading figure of the antisweatshop movement. Kelley was a strong advocate of political solutions and with Corrine Brown and the IWA, lobbied successfully for the passage of a state factory inspection system and was appointed the first chief factory inspector. For the next 3 years, Kelley enforced the act's chief clauses. The 1893 act outlawed the labor of children under 14 years of age; it regulated the labor of children age 14–16; it banned the production of garments in tenements. It prohibited the employment of women and minors for more than 8 hours a day, a clause that made the Illinois act the most advanced in the United States.

The Illinois Manufacturers' Association (IMA) immediately challenged the 8-hour clause in the courts. In a surprising move that was condemned by members of the Trade and Labor Assembly and by many middle-class members of the IWA, the alliance passed a resolution in 1894 condemning the 8-hour clause. Accused of being the action of an antilabor group that had acted without a quorum, IWA stalwarts held another meeting and endorsed the controversial clause. There were charges that political and religious influences were at work in the IWA, steering the alliance away from its original prolabor stance. The IWA delegates to the Trade and Labor Assembly complained that the alliance had refused to pass a resolution in support of the Pullman strikers and had instead expressed its disapproval of strikes as a means to settle labor troubles. The IWA appeared to be on the brink of dissolution. Three years later the IWA still held meetings, but its officers did not include leading socialists or trade unionists or the leading clubwomen who had supported factory inspection legislation, including the 8-hour clause, and the alliance's agenda instead focused on more traditional women's issues, including the care and disposition of dependent children in state and county institutions. The Illinois Supreme Court had ruled in 1895 that the 8-hour clause was unconstitutional because it violated women's right to contract their labor on any terms set by their employer. The IWA however had demonstrated the power of a coalition that crossed the boundaries of class and race.

RIMA LUNIN SCHULTZ

References and Further Reading

Buhle, Mari Jo. *Women and American Socialism, 1870–1920*. 1981.
Scharnu, Ralph. "Elizabeth Morgan, Crusader for Labor Reform." *Labor History* (Summer 1973).
Schultz, Rima Lunin, and Adele Hast, eds. *Women Building Chicago 1790–1990: A Biographical Dictionary*. 2001.
Sklar, Kathryn Kish. *Florence Kelley and The Nation's Work: The Rise of Women's Political Culture, 1830–1900*. 1995.
Tax, Meredith. *The Rising of the Women: Feminist Solidarity and Class Conflict, 1880–1917*. 1980.

IMMIGRATION AND NATIONALITY ACT OF 1965

The national origins system set in place during the 1920s began to unravel during World War II, although the specific quotas were not replaced until 1965. During World War II, as a gesture to America's ally China, Congress repealed the Chinese Restriction acts, dating to 1882. The lawmakers, with the support of the Roosevelt administration, granted China a quota of only 105 annually and gave Chinese immigrants the right to become U.S. citizens. In 1946, India and the Philippines were also given quotas. The McCarran-Walter Act of 1952 granted all Asian countries small quotas. Japan was given the largest number: 185. Most nations received only 100 slots. The 1952 law also repealed a ban on naturalization for Asian immigrants. At that time the largest group of Asian immigrants in the United States was the over 70,000 Japanese who could now become United States citizens, and most did so.

These modifications responded to the changing post-1945 world and the United States' new role in that world. Foreign policy became part of immigration law because the United States did not wish its immigration laws to be explicitly racist. In a similar manner Congress agreed to admit 110,000 war brides (mostly English and German but 6,000 Chinese women as well) without regard for quotas and some other minor aspects of immigration law.

Congress and postwar presidents also wanted to admit many Europeans who were displaced because of the war and the outbreak of the Cold War, even though many lived in countries with small national-origins quotas, sometimes the minimum of 100. Congress responded to the refugee crisis by passing the Displaced Persons acts of 1948 and 1950. These laws allowed 400,000 persons to come to the United States regardless of their small allotments. The legislation allowed individual countries to mortgage their future quotas; in some cases this procedure mortgaged individual national allotments for over 100 years.

The McCarran-Walter Immigration Act of 1952 might have opened the door for limited Asian immigration, but it kept the Johnson-Reed system of national origins for Europeans. However the next year President Dwight Eisenhower asked Congress to admit another 200,000 persons regardless of the quotas, and the legislators agreed. Then by the parole power, Eisenhower admitted over 35,000 refugees fleeing the failed Hungarian revolution of 1956, and Congress sanctioned the president's action by enacting legislation allowing them to become immigrants. Still other refugees were granted entrance by special laws during the 1950s. When Fidel Castro seized power in Cuba and Cubans began to flee to the United States, once again President Eisenhower and later presidents admitted them. In 1961, President John F. Kennedy followed a similar pattern when he paroled into the United States 14,000 Chinese who had fled to Hong Kong.

Western Hemisphere nations had no quotas, but few immigrants came during World War II. Congress did authorize the importation of temporary Mexican workers, known as *braceros*, during the war. This program continued after 1945, lasting until 1964. Some of the *braceros* returned after their terms expired, becoming regular immigrants or undocumented aliens. Thus immigration from Mexico and the Western Hemisphere began to grow, running to roughly 120,000 annually in the early 1960s. These nonquota immigrants coupled with the various refugees from Europe and Asia meant that from 1945 to the early 1960s two-thirds of all immigrants entered as nonquota migrants.

Passage of the Immigration and Nationality (Hart-Celler) Act of 1965

Clearly the 1920s system was not working as intended. Moreover fear of immigrants had lessened during the 1950s and 1960s. Both Presidents Harry S. Truman and Dwight Eisenhower proposed substantial alterations for immigration policy, but neither president proposed scrapping the national origins quotas entirely. However President John F. Kennedy

went further and suggested a plan to end national origins quotas but without a large increase in immigration. After Kennedy's assassination, President Lyndon Johnson took up the call for immigration reform.

The liberal climate of the 1960s produced the Civil Rights acts of 1964 and 1965, Medicare, the War on Poverty, and other Great Society programs. With this climate it seemed that immigration reform would pass easily. The overwhelming victory of President Johnson in 1964 over Republican Barry Goldwater and a huge democratic majority in Congress reinforced the possibility of legislating new immigration policy.

In spite of the growing support for immigration reform, the president and other political leaders did not believe that substantial increases in immigration would pass. Thus proposed legislation liberalized immigration law but only cautiously. In the first place the total places enacted for the Eastern Hemisphere were only 170,000. The Johnson-Reed Act of 1924 used a figure of 150,000, which had been increased by several thousand after World War II. Thus the new system for the Eastern Hemisphere would have added only about 15,000 slots more than the current figure.

Spouses and minor children of U.S. citizens had been exempt from the quotas since 1924, and Congress added parents of U.S. citizens to the exempt list. The total of exempt persons was estimated to be only 50,000 or so, but the actual figures went over 300,000 during some years of the 1990s, a number that the framers of the 1965 law had not projected.

The main liberalization of the Hart-Celler Act was to give all nations the identical quota. Now Asian nations would have the same allotment (20,000 annually) as Great Britain and Germany, the countries favored under the Johnson-Reed Immigration Act.

This liberalization was not expected to be major, for Congress created a seven-category preference system to determine who would be permitted under the quotas. The Johnson-Reed Act had preferences for occupations and family members, but of course these had to fit within the national origins quotas. The preferences of the Hart-Celler Act were geared toward family unification, which accounted for 74% of the slots. The largest preference (24%) was for brothers and sisters of U.S. citizens, which prompted some observers to call the new law the "brothers and sisters act." The second largest preference was for spouses and minor children of permanent resident aliens (immigrants). The preferences aimed at aiding those nations, mostly European, with backlogs for family unification. Italy and Greece were expected to take advantage of the new system because they had backlogs of persons wanting to join family members already in the United States. They did so in the immediate years after the 1965 act went into effect. Italy for example, whose old quota was under 6,000, averaged over 25,000 for the first years after the new law went into effect.

Two preferences were set aside for those with special skills needed in the United States. These categories amounted to 20% under the preference system and were not expected to have a significant impact on employment, which helped to win support of organized labor. In the end these two categories were very important for Asian immigrants, for many possessed the desired skills. For example Asians, especially Chinese, Filipinos, Koreans, and Indians, entered as medical professionals. Once established they could use the family preferences to build a network of new immigration, thus making possible the large number of Asian immigrants by the 1980s. In part Asians could use the new system so effectively because the pressure for emigration in Europe lessened after the 1960s. The economies of Western Europe had recovered from World War II, and some nations, such as Germany, were importing temporary workers, and not sending many persons to the United States.

Congress also recognized that the large number of refugees from Europe, Asia, and the Middle East arriving after 1945 were admitted on an *ad hoc* basis, either by presidential use of the parole power or by special legislation. To remedy this situation, the lawmakers set aside the last preference for refugees, amounting to 10,200 places. This figure quickly proved inadequate and later forced Congress to revise and increase programs for refugees.

What of the Western Hemisphere? Key senators were alarmed by the growing number of Latinos entering the United States after the 1950s. These senators, with some support in the House of Representatives, persuaded the Johnson administration to accept for the first time a limit for the Western Hemisphere, amounting to 120,000 persons, a figure approximately equal to the number of newcomers from Canada, the Caribbean, and Latin America in the early 1960s. As was the case with the Eastern Hemisphere, spouses, minor children, and parents of U.S. citizens were exempt from the ceiling. In establishing this limit, Congress made the law more restrictive than the Johnson-Reed Immigration Act of 1924. Under the Hart-Celler Act the Western Hemisphere nations did not have preference categories, nor did they have national limits of 20,000, which proved to be an advantage for Mexico, the nation with the largest flow of immigrants to the United States in the early 1960s. However in the 1970s Congress gave the Western Hemisphere the same preferences as the Eastern Hemisphere, and in 1979 lawmakers created a worldwide uniform system by combining the two hemispheres.

As finally developed, the new immigration acts abolished the discrimination of national origins, replacing it with a total of 290,000 immigrants, with spouses, minor children, and parents of U.S. citizens being exempt. It was projected that the worldwide system would permit approximately 350,000 new immigrants to enter annually. Yet by the 1990s, immigration was averaging one million annually. Clearly other changes were required after the 1970s to make such large increases possible. The Hart-Celler Act had begun the process of liberalization of American immigration policy.

DAVID M. REIMERS

References and Further Reading

Daniels, Roger. *Guarding the Golden Door: American Immigration Policy and Immigrants since 1882*. New York: Hill and Wang, 2004.

Dinnerstein, Leonard. *America and the Survivors of the Holocaust*. New York: Columbia University Press, 1982.

Graham, Otis L., Jr. *Unguarded Gates: A History of America's Immigration Crisis*. Lanham, MD: Rowman and Littlefield Publishers, Inc., 2004.

Johnson, Kevin R. *The "Huddled Masses" Myth: Immigration and Civil Rights*. Philadelphia, PA: Temple University Press, 2004.

King, Desmond. *Making Americans: Immigration, Race, and the Origins of the Diverse Democracy*. Cambridge, MA: Harvard University Press, 2000.

Loescher, Gil, and John Scanlon. *Calculated Kindness: Refugees and America's Half-Open Door, 1945 to the Present*. New York: Free Press, 1986.

Reimers, David M. *Still the Golden Door: The Third World Comes to America*. 2nd ed. New York: Columbia University Press, 1992.

Tichenor, Daniel J. *Dividing Lines: The Politics of Immigration Control in America*. Princeton, NJ: Princeton University Press, 2002.

Vialet, Joyce. *U.S. Immigration Law and Policy, 1953–1979*. Washington, DC: Government Printing Office, 1979.

IMMIGRATION RESTRICTION

In spite of the importance of immigration to the U.S. national identity, the question of immigration has been a complicated one. The founding generation expressed a great deal of ambivalence toward immigration. Many were concerned that perhaps immigrants would not be able to adopt the American ideals of individual liberty and republican principles that were undergirding the new nation. This concern however was moderated by the sense that the United States had a special mission as a place of asylum.

Perhaps even more important, the founding fathers and the generations that succeeded them realized that immigrants—whether coming as indentured servants or independent individuals—would play an important role in building the nation characterized by a perennial labor shortage and what seemed like boundless land to the West yet to be conquered.

Considering the important role of immigration in the nation's founding, it might at first seem a bit surprising that the framers of the Constitution paid little attention to it. In fact the Constitution addresses the issue of immigration only once in its provisions, barring Congress from limiting the "migration or importation" of persons until 1808. Just as the framers left questions of immigration largely unaddressed, they also said little about the issue of naturalization, instead providing Congress with the power to "establish a uniform rule of naturalization." As such in 1790, the nations' first Congress responded by passing the Naturalization Act of 1790. This act stipulated that in order to become a naturalized citizen, immigrants had to have resided in the United States for 2 years and that one had to also pledge loyalty to the ideals embodied in the Constitution. Equally revealing the act also required that prospective citizens be "free white persons." Both substantively and symbolically, these stipulations demonstrated the importance of the idea of freedom and the notion of volitional citizenship—that partaking in shared republican ideals made disparate persons a people. However the "free white persons" clauses reaffirmed that only those who were white could truly be free, thereby racializing citizenship and reaffirming racial hierarchies.

Although the nation's first naturalization policy was exclusive and racist, Congress did nothing to try to limit the number of immigrants, even those not considered white. Nearly a century would pass before Congress would attempt to seriously limit who could come to the United States. The fact that Congress did not pass any meaningful restrictive legislation until the last quarter of the nineteenth century however does not mean that all residents viewed immigration positively. During the 1830s, 1840s, and 1850s, restrictionists looked for ways to limit the influence of Irish and Catholic immigrants. The creation of the American party in 1851 provided an institutional base for all those who hoped to redefine the nation's political community by dramatically increasing the number of years required for naturalization and limiting the rights of alien residents. However the historically easy pathway of naturalization open to free and white immigrants meant that by the early nineteenth century, many immigrant/ethnic communities had already

amassed political strength that the Whigs and the Jeffersonian Democrats of the 1830s and 1840s, or the Republicans of the 1850s and 1860s, could not easily ignore.

Recognizing the nation's need for labor, during the 1860s Congress, rather than restrict immigration, took steps to try to attract immigrant laborers to come to the United States. In 1862, Congress passed the Homestead Act providing 160 acres of land to those willing to toil on it for 5 years. Both citizens and aliens were eligible to apply. Two years later Congress passed an act to encourage immigration, which provided funds to overseas consular officials to publicize land and labor opportunities in the United States. This act also included a clause allowing businesses to pay the fare for European laborers who were willing to sign a 1-year labor contract. (This section was repealed in 1868 due to the political pressure of labor groups who feared that the incoming immigrants would be held in semiservitude and undermine the wages and rights of laboring men.)

Race and Labor Restrictions

The relative openness that characterized U.S. immigration policy began to change during the 1870s and 1880s. At the behest of western congressmen, who feared the influence of Chinese immigrants, in 1875 Congress passed the Page Law. This law banned "coolie labor" by making it illegal to bring in Asian immigrants without their voluntary consent. This act also excluded prostitutes from coming into the United States, a rather poorly veiled attempt to limit Chinese women from entering at all. Though western nativists celebrated the passage of the Page Law, they were far from satisfied. Just a year later they helped to spearhead the creation of a Joint Special Committee to Investigate Chinese Immigration. Charged with the task of assessing the "character and extent" as well as effect of Chinese immigration on the United States, the commission interviewed over one hundred witnesses (most prorestrictionists) and established a fact-finding mission. In spite of the public face of impartiality, the special commission merely repeated the racist charges made by westerners for decades—that Chinese immigrants undermined white labor and that Chinese immigrants could not assimilate into American culture politically, socially, racially, or economically. Largely adopting the report's findings, in 1880 both Democrats and Republicans pledged to place immigration restrictions on Chinese immigration, transforming the question of Chinese immigration and Chinese-American labor into a national rather than just a regional issue.

In 1882, Congress answered calls to limit Chinese immigration by passing the Chinese Exclusion Act, the most significant piece of immigration legislation since the nation's first Congress limited naturalization to free white persons. The Chinese Exclusion Act stipulated that Chinese laborers would be barred from coming into the United States for 20 years, a term that was changed to 10 years due to the pressure of President Chester Arthur, who was concerned about treaty obligations. (Chinese merchants and students were exempted from these restrictions.) Chinese laborers already in the United States who wished to travel outside the United States would need to attain certificates or face the prospect of being denied entry on trying to return. In addition to excluding future Chinese laborers and circumscribing the movement of Chinese laborers already in the United States, the act also made it easier to deport Chinese immigrants from the United States. It also stipulated that no state government could naturalize them.

It took just 6 years for Congress to revise the Chinese Exclusion Act, making it even more difficult for Chinese immigrants already in the United States. The Scott Act of 1888 revoked the right of Chinese laborers to travel outside the United States and gain reentry regardless of whether they had certificates allowing them to do so. Furthermore the Scott Act explicitly stated that Chinese merchants attempting to come into the United States would have to prove their exempted status by demonstrating the possession of $1,000 worth of property. (This represented an attempt to make it more difficult for Chinese laborers to come into the United States under the merchant status.) Finally in 1892, the year the original Chinese Exclusion Act was scheduled to expire, Congress passed the Geary Act. This act made permanent the prohibitions of Chinese laborers coming into the United States. It also stipulated that Chinese aliens in the United States had to carry certificates of residence, proving that they had been in the United States before 1882.

The original Chinese Exclusion Act marked an important turning point in U.S. immigration and labor law. First it linked race and class exclusions, thereby codifying popular assumptions that certain races were "unfree" laborers who undermined white workingmen and the republican ideals of the nation. The legislation also had a less apparent but nonetheless important effect—its enforcement required the building of an administrative immigration bureaucracy.

The issues of open immigration, labor, and race continued to garner public concern throughout the late nineteenth century. While western nativists campaigned to exclude Chinese immigrants, labor groups spearheaded efforts to limit U.S. businesses' access to contract laborers. Led by the Knights of Labor (KOL), laboring groups throughout the nation began to call for a general contract labor law that would make it illegal for U.S. companies to recruit foreign workers abroad. The reasoning behind the demand for a contract labor law was based on the assumption that those workers coming in with contracts were not really free workers but rather semi-enslaved workers. The KOL officials and supporters also believed that U.S. corporations recruited immigrant workers to break strikes, undermine wages, lower the standard of living, and defuse the political power of American workers.

In 1885, Congress responded to demands for a contract labor law by passing the Foran Act, also known as the Contract Labor Act. This act represented the KOL's most important legislative victory. The act invalidated all contracts made to import alien workers and empowered the federal government to deport any workers who had come to the United States after having been contracted to work while still overseas. Corporations that violated the act faced the prospect of fines up to $1,000. In spite of the celebration of the Foran Act as a labor victory, it did little to impede the mass migration of immigrant workers into the United States or to uphold the wages and standard of living of workers already here.

Expanding Restrictions

Although the Foran Act did little to restrict immigration, this does not mean that the federal government abandoned its efforts to regulate immigration. In 1891, Congress passed the Immigrant Act of 1891, mandating the creation of a new federal bureaucracy—the Immigration Bureau—to coordinate and oversee the nation's borders and screening of potential immigrants. With the creation of the Immigration Bureau the federal government took over from states and private agencies the power to determine who would be allowed into the United States. Equally important the 1891 legislation expanded the kinds of restrictions established with Foran by specifically excluding certain persons from entering the United States, including polygamists and those with contagious diseases. This act also made it easier for the Immigration Bureau to deport persons likely to become a public charge. The last provision, which came to be known as LPC, reflected the assumption that only those immigrants who could be self-supporting workers should be admitted into the United States.

The new restrictions laid out in the 1891 law did little to stop the growing numbers of immigrants coming into the United States: Millions of southern and eastern Europeans immigrated to the United States from 1890 to the early 1920s. The arrival of these immigrants on American shores and the essential role that they played in the booming industrial economy assured that immigration and labor would be two of the most important political issues of the late nineteenth and early twentieth centuries. On one hand these newest immigrants faced charges that they represented a docile, dependent, and servile labor force that embodied the worst abuses and effects of American capitalism. On the other hand nativists insisted that these very same immigrants were anarchists and socialists bringing in radical foreign ideals that would tear asunder the democratic fabric of the nation, both figuratively and literally.

Though these two charges—the one that immigrants were docile and the other that they were radical revolutionaries—might at first appear contradictory, nativists had no trouble making both claims at once. What wedded these two visions was the assumption that the newest immigrants were racially inferior. Labor organizations, which had often called for restricting immigration, were now joined by a host of patriotic and academic societies looking for ways to ferret out the undesirable immigrants. Whether motivated primarily by racial, social, political, or economic concerns (and most often a combination of all), these nativists insisted that southern and eastern Europeans represented a cheap immigrant labor force, which undermined the nation's economy and political ideals. (The fact that the nation suffered numerous economic recessions and depressions in this era did much to reinforce the assumption that immigrants were undermining the nation's economy.) Armed with the new science of eugenics and new allies in academic and political circles, the movement to restrict immigration into the United States gained greater strength and respectability.

As concern about the influence of the newest immigrants on the U.S. economy and society mounted, Congress created the Dillingham Commission in 1908 to study the issue of immigration, labor, and race and to come up with possible solutions. Supported with a significant budget and staffed by hundreds of expert social scientists, the commission produced a 42-volume report. The report compared and contrasted the nation's old (British, German, Irish, and so forth) immigrants with the newest arrivals, characterizing the former in a positive light while calling into question the influences of the latter immigrants on the nation's economy, social structure, political institutions, and racial makeup. In fact southern and eastern European immigrants were most often portrayed as an unskilled labor force of men and women who caused innumerable economic, social, political, and racial problems for the nation. As such the commission recommended that Congress pass a literacy test, increase the head tax, and begin to restrict immigration based on the prospective immigrant's national origins.

It took a number of years for all of the commission's recommendations to be put into place, but by the middle of the 1920s, all of the restrictions had been instituted. After many years of trying to pass a literacy clause, in 1917 Congress finally succeeded in doing so over the veto of President Woodrow Wilson. Four years later and after concern that the number of immigrants from southern and eastern Europe would increase dramatically now that World War I was over, Congress passed a Temporary Emergency Act to limit the number of immigrants coming into the United States to 387,803 a year. Rather than dole out these slots on a first-come basis, the act created a proportional representation quota system whereby the number of immigrants from any particular nation entering the United States could not be more than 3% of the immigrants already in the United States based on the 1910 census. In 1924 Congress agreed on a more permanent solution, further decreasing the number of immigrants to 186,437 a year and revising the quota system so that the number of immigrants allowed into the United States each year would be based on a percentage of immigrants already in the United States in 1890 rather than 1910, further decreasing the numbers of southern and eastern European immigrants who would be allowed to immigrate to the United States. This act also stipulated that only immigrants who could become naturalized citizens— which at this point included only those who were white and those of African descent—could immigrate to the United States at all, effectively barring all Asian immigrants from coming to the United States. Though the 1924 National Origins Act did not explicitly exclude laborers like the Chinese Exclusion Act, in practice it had a similar effect: Limit the number of supposedly racially inferior immigrants whom the nativists charged had begun to undermine the nation economically, socially, and politically.

Immigration Exceptions

In spite of the broad scope of the National Origins Act, it did include one very important exception—the

Western Hemisphere. The history of immigration policy toward the Western Hemisphere, and Mexico in particular, followed a very different trajectory than the one the United States was developing toward Asia and Europe. In 1911, the Dillingham Commission even lauded Mexican immigrants as a migratory and temporary workforce that would help to meet the needs of U.S. agriculture without changing the demographic profile of the United States. During World War I, the U.S. secretary of labor invoked a provision of the Immigration Act of 1917 to allow U.S. agricultural interests to recruit agricultural workers at the Canadian and Mexican borders by waiving head taxes, literacy tests, and contract labor laws. To make sure that these workers would return to their home country, the U.S. Department of Labor fingerprinted and photographed the incoming workers and withheld part of their wages. This program formally ended in 1921.

The relatively porous border between the United States and Mexico did not go unnoticed. Shortly after Congress succeeded in passing immigration restrictions with respect to European immigrants, it turned its attention to the issue of Mexican immigration. Many of the nation's leading restrictions were concerned that the nation had closed the front door while leaving the back door completely open. In response during the latter half of the 1920s, both the Senate and the House hosted numerous hearings and entertained a variety of bills that would have restricted immigration from the Western Hemisphere or Mexico alone. The restrictionists who wanted to restrict Mexican immigration made both racial and economic arguments, insisting that the Mexican immigrants who came to the United States undermined the racial foundations of the nation, which the just recently passed National Origins Act was supposed to protect, and undermined white workingmen and farmers who could not compete with the low wages and low standard of living of Mexican immigrants. Since many Mexican immigrants toiled in agriculture, these restrictionists also insisted that Mexican immigration led to the downfall of family farms and the rise of large corporate landed estates. These restrictionists however faced an equally well-organized and vocal contingent of antirestrictionists from the Southwest and Midwest who claimed that Mexicans were integral to the future of American agriculture. These antirestrictionists attempted to quell the race fears of restrictionists by claiming that Mexicans had a homing instinct that drew them back home. The issue, they insisted, was not one of immigration but rather a labor question. With the back-room influence of the U.S. State Department, which feared the diplomatic fallout if the United States restricted immigration

from the Western Hemisphere, the antirestrictionists prevailed.

The failure of Congress to pass a restrictive act to exclude Mexican immigrants however does not mean that the issue of Mexican immigration was simply ignored. In fact the United States turned to administrative means to try to monitor the number of immigrants coming into the United States, relying on a newly created border patrol and implementation of head taxes and LPC clauses to suit the needs of American agriculture. The underlying assumption of these administrative means of regulating Mexican immigration was the idea that Mexicans were not really immigrants but workers who could be allowed in when needed and propelled to leave when no longer necessary. This is perhaps best reflected during the Great Depression when municipal and state authorities, often working hand-in-hand with Mexican consular officials in the United States, repatriated thousands of Mexican immigrants to Mexico. Though the program began as a voluntary repatriation campaign whereby Mexican nationals wishing to return home would be provided transportation, it soon evolved into a coercive program as various U.S. officials pressured many Mexicans out of the United States.

The perception of Mexican immigrants as workers who could be imported and exported as need be was further codified in the Emergency Labor Importation Program, which began in 1942 as an emergency wartime measure and extended until 1964, years after the conflict had ended. This program, which became known as the *Bracero* program, was a bilateral agreement between Mexico and the United States, in which the former agreed to provide workers as long as the United States ensured wages, working conditions, and living standards. In practice U.S. officials did little to enforce the provisions of the program, and Mexican officials often found themselves powerless to force their northern neighbor to abide by the initial agreement. The program was finally disbanded in 1964 due to pressure from a public anxious about Mexican immigration as well as labor and civil rights groups who pointed to labor and civil rights violations.

A year after the disbanding of the *Bracero* program, Congress passed the Immigration Act of 1965, which abolished the national quota system, limited immigration worldwide to 290,000 a year, and created a maximum ceiling of 20,000 immigrants per country. In addition to creating a more equitable system for admissions, the 1965 legislation created a seven-category preference system of admissions, privileging family reunification while also reserving some slots for immigrants with special work skills.

The history of labor and immigration restriction can be characterized as *laissez faire* until the 1880s, when fault lines based on race and labor emerged. The restrictions on Chinese workers and contract labor extended the racialized and economic ideals embodied in the nation's first naturalization policy—that one had to be a free white person. Over the course of the late nineteenth and early twentieth centuries, Congress expanded the restricted categories, barring almost all Asian immigrants in 1917 and making sure that fewer southern and eastern European immigrants would come in 1921 and 1924. The most important exception to these widening restrictions was the Western Hemisphere, and Mexico in particular. The unwillingness of Congress to include the Western Hemisphere or Mexico in the national origins restrictions however was based on the idea that Mexican immigrants were not really immigrants at all but merely workers who would return to Mexico one day. Not only until 1965 did the United States abandon the racially influenced national origins and adopt a more egalitarian immigration policy.

KATHLEEN MAPES

References and Further Reading

Cardoso, Lawrence. *Mexican Emigration to the United States, 1897–1931: Socio-Economic Patterns*. Tucson: University of Arizona Press, 1987.
Collomp, Catherine. "Unions, Civics, and National Identity: Organized Labor's Reaction to Immigration, 1881–1897." In *In the Shadow of the State of Liberty: Immigrants, Workers, and Citizens in the American Republic, 1880–1920*, edited by Marianne Debouzy. Urbana: University of Illinois Press, 1992.
Collomp, Catherine. "Immigrants, Labor Markets, and the State, a Comparative Approach: France and the United States, 1880–1930." *Journal of American History* (June 1999): 41–66.
Hahamovtich, Cindy. "'In America Life Is Given Away': Jamaican Farmworkers and the Making of Agricultural Immigration Policy." In *The Countryside in the Age of the Modern State: Political Histories of Rural America*, edited by Catherine McNicol Stock and Robert D. Johnston. Ithaca, NY: Cornell University Press.
Lee, Erika. *At America's Gates: Chinese Immigration during the Exclusion Era, 1882–1943*. Chapel Hill: University of North Carolina Press, 2003.
Mapes, Kathleen. "A 'Special Class of Labor': Mexican Migrants, Immigration Debate, and Industrial Agriculture in the 1920s." *Labor: Studies in Working Class History of the Americas* 1, 2 (June 2004): 65–88.
Mink, Gwendolyn. *Old Labor and New Immigrants in American Political Development: Union, Party, and State, 1875–1920*. Ithaca, NY: Cornell University Press, 1986.
Peck, Gunther. *Reinventing Free Labor: Padrones and Immigrant Workers in the North American West, 1880–1930*. Cambridge, UK: Cambridge University Press, 2000.
Reisler, Mark. *By the Sweat of Their Brow: Mexican Immigrant Labor in the United States, 1900–1940*. Westport, CT: Greenwood Press, 1976.

INDENTURED SERVITUDE

A shortage of labor plagued settlers in British Colonial America (1607–1775). Human brawn, aided only by animal and wind power, was required for most of the extremely labor-intensive tasks required in the American colonies. To meet this demand for labor, European settlers in British Colonial America relied on indentured servants. Though there were regional variations, this system of unfree labor thrived throughout British Colonial America.

Indentured servitude involved a written contract—an indenture—that a young person signed before coming to British Colonial America. This contract (indenture) specified that a laborer would work for a set number of years. The term ranged from 4–7 years, depending on specific circumstances. In return the indentured servant's passage to the colonies would be paid for and food and clothing would be provided for the duration of the contract. (The British American colonist who bought the indenture would pay these costs.) In some cases servants would also receive land or money (freedom dues) at the conclusion of their term. In the seventeenth and eighteenth centuries a lively trade in servants developed. Recruiters in England convinced young people to migrate to the colonies. In British Colonial America, colonists bought and sold indentures. Young men, often no more than teenagers, comprised the overwhelming majority of those who signed indentures. In many colonies, where men overwhelmingly outnumbered women, female indentured servants often faced the risk of sexual assault. Though servants usually signed the indenture voluntarily, they had no say over who bought the indenture or the type of labor they had to perform. Moreover indentured servants could neither marry nor take part in the political process. Servants legally belonged to the individual who purchased the indenture.

Indentured servitude flourished first in the English Chesapeake colonies of Virginia and Maryland during the seventeenth century. With the production and export of tobacco, beginning in the 1610s, planters turned to white indentured servants from England in order to meet the seemingly insatiable European craving for the American weed. The majority of these servants were young men. They cleared the land, planted, and tended the young plants before harvesting the mature leaves. The process involved intense labor. To encourage the emigration of servants as well as the growth and profitability of the Chesapeake colonies, planters received 50 acres of land under the headright system for every servant they paid to emigrate. For the young and destitute in England, the possibility of owning land in British Colonial America in return for serving as a servant proved to be a powerful inducement for making the voyage. Servant contracts sometimes even specified that a parcel of land would be granted on completion of the indentures. Yet most indentured servants in Virginia and Maryland did not survive their term of service. Disease, poor diet, and cruel treatment claimed thousands of servants' lives. While some successfully served the full term of their indentureship and managed to enter the ranks of the landowning planter class, others found it next to impossible to do so. Discontent among former servants found expression in 1675–1676 during Bacon's Rebellion in Virginia. This uprising, named after the insurgent leader Nathaniel Bacon, pitted land-hungry former servants against the royal governor who had tried to limit Anglo settlement on native American lands. After Bacon's Rebellion collapsed, planters gradually turned to African slave labor. For much of the seventeenth century, Africans in the Chesapeake colonies had served as indentured servants. Some Africans became landowners and had bought indentured servants as well. By the end of the seventeenth century however, especially after Bacon's Rebellion, racial antipathy toward those with black skins as well as the belief that black slaves would be more manageable than white servants led to the foundation of racially based slavery.

White indentured servants flocked to the English West Indies, especially the island of Barbados. From the 1620s to the 1640s, the English in the West Indies followed their counterparts in the Chesapeake colonies by growing tobacco. Just as in Virginia and Maryland, tobacco production spurred the emigration of a vast number of young English men and a few women who willingly sold themselves into servitude. Several factors worked against indentured servants in the West Indies however. First the islands proved to be a death trap for the English. The mortality rate from disease among the English servants in the West Indies surpassed that of the Chesapeake colonies. Second when the English West Indies turned from tobacco to sugar production in the 1640s, the labor system changed as well. As sugar supplanted tobacco, slavery surpassed indentured servitude as the primary labor system. By the 1640s, the English had fully colonized the small West Indian islands, making it highly improbable for white indentured servants to become planters. A rebellion by servants in the late

1640s on Barbados illustrates the level of frustration among those whose dreams of upward social mobility had been frustrated. Because of the transition to sugar and slavery, the English West Indies had ceased to be a major destination for white indentured servants by the early 1700s.

In the eighteenth century, planters in the Chesapeake colonies as well as those in the Carolinas and Georgia relied on both white indentured servants and African slaves. Colonial laws separated the two groups of laborers however. White servants were accorded the protection of colonial law while black slaves were defined as property. In some of the southern mainland colonies, most notably in South Carolina, African slavery was the major labor system.

Most indentured servants in the New England colonies (the Massachusetts Bay Colony, Plymouth Colony, New Haven Colony, Connecticut Colony, and Rhode Island) did not emigrate from England but rather were the children of the colonists themselves. Because colonial New England families tended to be very large, with six or more children being the norm, the region essentially produced its own labor force. The use of New England children as indentured servants served several purposes. First in colonial New England, where the Puritan faith predominated, indentured servants received religious instruction in the households where they worked. In this way the use of Puritan children as servants created communities bound together by shared religious belief. Second this system of indentureship allowed for extensive supervision over the large number of young people in New England. The placement of servants in the households of relatives increased the degree of oversight and control. Some of the strains experienced by New England's indentured servants found expression in cases of witchcraft. The historical record illustrates that on several occasions, young servants believed the Devil tempting them with promises of easing the burden of work if they would serve him. Other New England servants ran away. Many escaped the New England labor regime by going to sea. The most famous New England runaway, Benjamin Franklin, broke his indenture to his brother James by taking flight from his native Boston in 1723 and going to Philadelphia.

The middle colonies of New York, New Jersey, and Pennsylvania absorbed great number of servants from Europe. These colonies, especially Pennsylvania, received praise as the "best poor man's country." The French writer J. Hector St. John de Crevecouer, who never served as an indentured servant, applauded the region as a place where an indentured servant, through hard work and perseverance, could become a landowner. Others found the middle colonies disappointing. One servant, William Moraley, signed an indenture in 1729 and set sail with other servants to Philadelphia to seek his fortune. On his arrival Moraley was sold to a New Jersey Quaker. Unhappy with his dependent status, Moraley ran away only to be caught and returned to the Quaker's household. He completed his indenture in the early 1730s. Unable to find a place for himself in British Colonial America however, Moraley returned to his native England in 1734.

Indentured servitude in British Colonial America can be credited with laying part of the foundation for what would later be termed the American dream. During the Colonial Era, when a rigid European social hierarchy separated an elite leisure class from a mass of drones, coming to British Colonial America as an indentured servant appeared to be a way to escape dire poverty and substantially improve one's lot in life by potentially owning land. Many European promoters of colonization vigorously publicized the idea of upward social mobility during the seventeenth and eighteenth centuries. Indentured servitude did provide access to the status of an independent landowner for some migrants. For the majority of indentured servants however, life was filled with unending toil and hardship. For many indentured servitude led to an early death in British Colonial America. Other indentured servants, like Moraley and the more successful Benjamin Franklin, ran away. On several occasions discontent among indentured servants took the form of armed rebellion, most notably the 1675–1676 uprising in Virginia. However one chooses to interpret indentured servitude, this type of labor system helped to meet the urgent need for workers in British Colonial America.

JOHN M. LUND

References and Further Reading

Beckles, Hilary McD. *White Servitude and Black Slavery in Barbados, 1627–1715.* Knoxville: University of Tennessee Press, 1989.
Dunn, Richard. *Sugar and Slaves: The Rise of the Planter Class in the English West Indies, 1624–1713.* Chapel Hill: University of North Carolina Press, 1972.
Galenson, David W. *White Servitude in Colonial America: An Economic Analysis.* New York: Cambridge University Press, 1981.
Hotten, John Camden. *The Original Lists of Persons of Quality, Emigrants, Religious Exiles, Political Rebels, Serving Men Sold for a Term of Years, Apprentices, Children Stolen, Maidens Pressed, and Others Who Went from Great Britain to the American plantations, 1600–1700.* New York, 1874.
Klepp, Susan E., and Billy G. Smith. *The Infortunate: The Voyage and Adventures of William Moraley, an Indentured Servant.* University Park: Pennsylvania State University Press, 1992.
Morgan, Kenneth. *Slavery and Servitude in Colonial North America: A Short History.* New York: New York University Press, 2001.
Pagan, John Ruston. *Anne Orthwood's Bastard: Sex and Law in Early Virginia.* New York: Oxford University Press, 2003.
Salinger, Sharon V. *"To Serve Well and Faithfully": Labor and Indentured Servants in Pennsylvania, 1682–1800.* New York: Cambridge University Press, 1987.
Smith, Abbott Emerson. *Colonists in Bondage: White Servitude and Convict Labor in America, 1607–1776.* Chapel Hill: University of North Carolina Press, 1947.
St John de Crevecoeur, J Hector. *Letters from an American Farmer.* Gloucester, UK: P. Smith, 1968.
Towner, William. *"A Good Master Well Served": Masters and Servants in Colonial Massachusetts, 1620–1750.* New York: Garland Publishing, 1998.
Van der Zee, John. Diggins. *Bound Over: Indentured Servitude and American Conscience.* New York: Simon and Schuster, 1985.

INDEPENDENT UNION OF ALL WORKERS

In 1933, under the leadership of veteran Industrial Workers of the World (IWW) activist Frank Ellis, Hormel packinghouse workers in Austin, Minnesota, organized themselves and launched the Independent Union of All Workers (IUAW). The IUAW practiced many of the principles of the IWW—industrial as opposed to craft organization, a reliance on direct action, an emphasis on the values of solidarity, and a militant standing toward the employer—but it also went beyond its predecessor in its extension of wall-to-wall organizing to communities as well as workplaces. Over the next 4 years, it spread to at least 12 other midwestern communities, organizing not only packinghouse workers but also manufacturing, retail, transportation, and service workers. In 1937, amid a wave of turmoil in national labor politics, Minnesota Farmer Labor politics, and an economic collapse that shifted the labor climate, the IUAW voted to dismember itself, with groups of workers and networks of locals choosing to affiliate with existing American Federation of Labor (AFL) and Congress of Industrial Organizations (CIO) unions or organizing committees. Although the organization itself faded from existence, its dynamics, practices, and values left a living legacy for midwestern unions of packinghouse workers, warehouse workers and truckers, waitresses and department store clerks, and public employees.

641

Frank Ellis and a cadre of activists began the IUAW by building a strong shop-floor organization in the Hormel plant in the summer of 1933. They stopped production in the hog kill to force foremen to tear up Community Chest pledge cards as a way of protesting strong-arm management tactics as well as the low level of wages. A few months later, they walked off their jobs to join members of the Farm Holiday Association in picketing roads into Austin as part of their campaign for higher hog prices. Such actions inspired other Hormel workers to join the IUAW and to understand that collective direct action was the path to improved compensation and a recognition of workers' rights in the workplace.

In the country's first officially recorded sit-down strike, Hormel workers took over their plant on November 10, 1933, and held it—and millions of dollars' worth of equipment and semiprocessed meat—for the next three days. The IUAW leaders insisted that company management come into the occupied plant for negotiations, where according to local folklore, they felt a rise in temperature every time they turned down a union demand at the bargaining table. Farmer Labor party Governor Floyd B. Olson refused to dispatch the National Guard to retake Hormel's property from its workers. Instead he rushed to Austin to mediate a settlement. At the end of three days, the IUAW had its first contract, a substantial wage increase, and the momentum to spread beyond the Hormel plant itself.

Inside the plant and wherever they gained a foothold, the IUAW relied on direct action—slowdowns, stoppages, workplace protests, and—to expand workers' ability to control work rules, the pace of production, the systems of compensation, and the like. Their militant reputation—and their success—caught the imaginations of thousands of other workers, first in Austin and nearby communities like Albert Lea, and then across Minnesota and into North and South Dakota, Iowa, and Wisconsin. The IUAW sent teams of rank-and-file volunteer organizers into other communities, organized mass meetings featuring the kind of soapbox speaking that had been practiced by the IWW, and then offered practical support from picket lines to food pantries. In some communities they published newspapers, ran candidates for school board and city council, and promoted the vision of a society and culture in which workers were leaders.

In the late spring of 1937, a series of developments and events came together to create an organizational crisis for the IUAW. As the national economy plunged into the second trough of the Great Depression, unemployment leapt upward for the first time in 4 years, employers cut wages and dug in their heels against the further extension of union recognition and collective-bargaining agreements. Shifting political tides turned nationally against President Franklin Delano Roosevelt, while the Minnesota Farmer Labor party suffered the blow of the untimely death of Governor Olson, followed by increased infighting surrounding the new governor, Elmer Benson. Within the national labor movement, AFL leaders stepped up their efforts to undercut the new CIO unions, while CIO leaders and activists sought to consolidate their organizational breakthroughs.

The IUAW found itself in the midst of a hard-fought series of sit-down strikes in Albert Lea, 20 miles west of Austin, which included two substantial American Gas Machine manufacturing plants, three trucking warehouses, and the Woolworth's store. Coordinated sit-down strikes, linked by nightly marches led by the IUAW's Drum and Bugle Corps and bolstered by hundreds of militant rank-and-filers from the Austin Hormel plant, expressed workers' determination to win union recognition and improved conditions. When the Freeborn County sheriff launched a military attack, reminiscent of the Pacific Northwest violence against the IWW in the World War I era, on the "sitdowners" and the IUAW's hall, a showdown was precipitated, bringing Governor Benson himself to the scene. All of this happened while the IUAW founding spirit and chief strategist was locked away in state prison on questionable morals charges.

This crisis led to a complex negotiated settlement in which Albert Lea employers offered union recognition and contracts to local unions that would affiliate with specific AFL or CIO national unions. The IUAW leaders agreed to allow Albert Lea, and then Austin, and then other cities' members to vote on dissolving their "horizontal" organization in order to win security and apparent stability. In the next half dozen years, IUAW locals became part of the Packinghouse Workers' Organizing Committee-CIO (and then the United Packinghouse Workers of America), the Steel Workers' Organizing Committee-CIO (and then the United Steelworkers of America), District 50 of the United Mine Workers of America (and then the Oil, Chemical, and Atomic Workers' Union), the United Automobile Workers, and the Teamsters' Union. For many years, the particular locals they joined tended to manifest the dynamics, strategies, and values that had been inculcated by the IUAW. The vitality of this legacy was reflected in the Hormel strike of 1985–1986, when United Food and Commercial Workers' Union Local P-9, a descendant of the IUAW, waged a nationally significant struggle against the corporate demand for concessions.

PETER RACHLEFF

References and Further Reading

Halpern, Rick. *Down on the Killing Floor: Black and White Workers in Chicago's Packinghouses, 1904–1954.* Urbana: University of Illinois Press, 1997.

Horowitz, Roger. *"Negro and White, Unite and Fight!" A Social History of Industrial Unionism in Meatpacking, 1930–1990.* Urbana: University of Illinois Press, 1997.

Rachleff, Peter, "Organizing 'Wall-to-Wall': The Independent Union of All Workers." In *"We Are All Leaders": The Alternative Unionism of the Early 1930s*, edited by Staughton Lynd. Urbana: University of Illinois Press, 1996.

———. "The Failure of Minnesota Farmer Laborism." In *Organized Labor and American Politics, 1894–1994*, edited by Kevin Boyle. Albany: State University of New York Press, 1998.

See also **P-9 Strike**

INDUSTRIAL AREAS FOUNDATION
See **Alinsky, Saul David; Industrial Areas Foundation**

INDUSTRIAL DEMOCRACY

Industrial democracy was a protean concept used by a wide range of historical actors to frame debates about labor relations from the 1890s through the 1960s. Its origins can be traced to late nineteenth reformers, progressives, socialists, and Social Gospel advocates who worried that the rise of large-scale industrial capitalism was undermining the autonomy of workers and the quality of democracy in the United States.

Among the first to use the term industrial democracy was Lyman Abbott, an energetic Social Gospel reformer who succeeded Henry Ward Beecher as editor of the *Christian Union*. In Abbott's use, the term was meant as a critique of the "wages' system." Abbott advocated a host of reforms under the banner of industrial democracy, including profit sharing, cooperation, and incentive pay. Whether Abbott was the first American to use the term is not clear. What is clear is that by the 1890s, the term had gained wide currency among reformers. Henry Demarest Lloyd, Richard T. Ely, and many others began invoking notion of industrial democracy as a necessary antidote to growing corporate power during the depression of the 1890s and the merger wave that followed it. Work relations needed to become more democratic or else concentrated economic power would undermine American democracy, they warned.

The British reformers Sidney and Beatrice Webb provided an elaborate articulation of the notion in their 1897 book *Industrial Democracy*. To the Webbs, industrial democracy meant the organization of democratic trade unions, the recognition of those unions by employers, collective bargaining between employers and unions over the terms of labor, the development of a constitutional government of industry in which unions and employers developed policies jointly. Their ideas in turn influenced Americans like the economist John R. Commons, who advocated collectively bargained trade agreements in the United States as the proper way to advance industrial democracy in the early twentieth century.

A new phase in the dissemination of the industrial democracy ideal came when it was embraced by progressive reformer Louis D. Brandeis around 1910. Brandeis, who was also an advocate of "scientific management," came to believe that workplace efficiency could not be maximized without the active consent of workers. For him the idea of industrial democracy spoke to the necessity of finding ways through which employers and workers could cooperate in creating workplace rules. Influenced by Brandeis, reformer Robert G. Valentine won some converts to industrial democracy even among the followers of the guru of scientific management, Frederick Winslow Taylor. Brandeis also helped persuade some progressive businessmen, like the Boston retailers Edward and Lincoln Filene, to implement a form of industrial democracy through shop representation plans for their workers. Brandeis allies Felix Frankfurter, Walter Weyl, and Walter Lippmann were all writing about the need for the nation to democratize its workplaces in the years before World War I.

Still talk of industrial democracy remained largely confined to the world of middle-class progressive reformers until the 1913–1915 investigation of the U.S. Commission on Industrial Relations (USCIR) and the subsequent impact of the U.S. entry into World War I. In 1913, appointed President Woodrow Wilson appointed the USCIR to investigate the sources of labor violence in the nation and to recommend solutions. Labor lawyer Frank P. Walsh of Kansas City, Missouri, chaired the USCIR and through his committee's well-publicized hearings, Walsh became the most passionate and well-known advocate of industrial democracy in the nation. Walsh became a bitter opponent of company unionism practiced by employers like John D. Rockefeller, Jr. The only way for the nation to democratize its autocratic work relations, Walsh argued, was for the government to protect workers rights to organize unions. Walsh advocated national legislation that would allow workers to join unions without fear of intimidation or dismissal. Such legislation did not come to pass for nearly two decades, but on the eve of World War I, Walsh had succeeded in identifying industrial democracy with the cause of trade unionism. Thereafter labor activists increasingly adopted the term in their calls for union recognition. Even the radicals of the Industrial Workers of the World (IWW) began using the term to express their own vision.

The U.S. entry into World War I only widened the intense debate over industrial democracy. President Wilson unintentionally reinforced demands for industrial democracy by framing World War I as a war "to make the work safe for democracy." If Americans fought for democracy in Europe, they should also enjoy a measure of it in the places where they earned their livelihoods, argued labor activists. The extent to which industry might be democratized during the war was never clear. But the creation of the key war labor agency, the National War Labor Board (NWLB), in 1918 raised hopes that significant reforms could be won. Cochaired by Frank P. Walsh and former president William H. Taft, the NWLB actively promoted industrial democracy by calling on nonunion employers in war industries to bargain collectively with their workers through elected shop committees in cases where they refused to recognize unions. The NWLB's wartime stand helped legitimize workers' organizing efforts. The American Federation of Labor (AFL) grew by more than 1 million members during the war and broadly disseminated the idea that workers ought to have a say in shaping the terms of their work relations.

Following World War I, fierce conflicts took place between employers and unions over the survival of union organizations in mass-production industries where they had begun to take root during the war. Those conflicts led to the unprecedented strike wave of 1919. Employers emerged victorious during these strikes, uprooting recently formed unions in the steel, electrical-manufacturing, and meat-packing industries. But many large-scale employers were not able to roll back the clock to re-establish prewar patterns of labor relations. Rather employers had to recognize workers' demands for a voice in their workplace. Thus in the 1920s, large-scale employers in many basic industries created company unions and explicitly argued that such organizations would secure industrial democracy for their employees. By the end of the 1920s, it appeared that employers had largely succeeded in identifying company unionism with industrial democracy.

Yet the Great Depression undermined employers' efforts to claim that they were delivering on workers' demands for industrial democracy. As the welfare capitalism of 1920s' employers collapsed, workers once again called for independent union organization. Union organizing gathered momentum following the enactment in 1933 of Section 7(a) of the National Industrial Recovery Act, which provided for collective bargaining in industry. As in the World War I era, workers who sought to form unions did so under the banner of industrial democracy. Contesting the legitimacy of the employer-dominated employee representation plans (ERPs) that remained legal under the NRA, trade unionists argued that only independent union organizations could secure industrial democracy. When the 1935 Wagner Act triggered the formation of the Congress of Industrial Organizations (CIO), the demand for industrial democracy became central to CIO rhetoric. After the mid-1930s, industrial democracy had become fully identified with trade unionism's aspirations and had lost its previous connection to employers' welfare capitalism or the visions of Taylorite efficiency engineers.

What workers and labor activists meant when they used the term industrial democracy was still something of an open question however in the years before the United States entered World War II. For example left-leaning labor leaders like Walter Reuther of the United Automobile Workers (UAW) advanced plans for labor's comanagement of war industries under the banner of industrial democracy. But the war mobilization put on hold the most radical hopes for labor's comanagement of industry. Under the guidance of a second National War Labor Board (1942–1945), what instead emerged were union security arrangements that entrenched trade unionism in the nation's basic manufacturing industries and facilitated the expansion of collective bargaining between unions and employers, while demarcating the limits of union power. Nonwage benefits became a chief feature of wartime collective-bargaining agreements, but labor's efforts to achieve comanagement never came to pass.

When the war came to an end in 1945, labor movement waged an aggressive campaign to expand the limits of wartime industrial democracy. From 1945–1946, a huge strike wave swept the nation. This upheaval differed from the strike wave of 1919. After World War II employers did not attempt to crush unions. Rather employers simply resisted labor's efforts to take a hand in the management of industry. The UAW's strike against General Motors (GM) was indicative of how this postwar struggle played out. Autoworkers initially demanded that GM open its books to the union and allow the union a say in the pricing of its products. General Motors firmly resisted these demands and ultimately the UAW gave in on management issues in return for a considerable wage increase. In the postwar era most conflicts over the right to manage were settled in similar ways, with unions agreeing to better wages and benefits in lieu of greater say over how businesses were run. Unions simply lacked the political and economic power to force a different outcome in such struggles. Once the Taft-Hatley Act was passed in 1947, management's rights were further reinforced by that act's legal protections.

After 1947, the once contested meaning of postwar industrial democracy became clearer. Unions and collective bargaining had become firmly entrenched in basic manufacturing industry, but unions were unable to encroach on management rights. In this context the once insurgent possibilities of industrial democracy were tamed. Whereas the ideal of industrial democracy had once excited radicals and conveyed the possibility of worker-run industries, in the postwar era its meaning had been narrowed to what historian David Brody calls "workplace contractualism." Workplace contractualism amounted to trade union collective bargaining, the elaboration of jointly administered benefit programs, and the development of a workplace rule of law that circumscribed arbitrary and capricious treatment of workers by management. If this more modest form of industrial democracy fell short of the lofty hopes once entertained by radicals, it was nonetheless an enormous achievement. During the height of the uneasy postwar labor-capital accord (roughly 1947–1973) organized workers enjoyed a greater say over the terms and conditions under which they labored then they had ever enjoyed before or since that time. A semblance of democracy had indeed been brought to industry.

Yet no sooner had industrial democracy been entrenched in the form of the postwar collective-bargaining regime than the concept itself began to fall into disuse. By the 1970s, even trade unionists rarely spoke any longer about industrial democracy. At least four developments helped eclipse the industrial democracy ideal. First when the meaning of industrial democracy became clear in the postwar era, the concept suddenly proved less attractive to the wide range of groups who had once competed to define it. Neither employers nor radicals tended to invoke the concept of industrial democracy from the 1950s onward. No longer the protean ideal it had been early in the twentieth century, industrial democracy simply attracted fewer enthusiasts.

Second the very success of postwar workplace contractualism facilitated a subtle shift in workers' visions from industrial democracy to what Brody has called "industrial justice." Once unions' drive for access to decision-making in corporate boardrooms was blunted, workers turned to the task of creating what labor economist Sumner Slichter called "industrial jurisprudence," rules that would free them from arbitrary treatment. Defending and extending those shop-floor rules, not contesting the balance of power in industry, became the chief mission of the labor movement. Industrial democracy seemed an increasingly anachronistic term.

Third the civil rights revolution of the 1950s and 1960s fostered an alternative conception of worker empowerment. The rights consciousness spawned by the civil rights struggle did not usually channel workers' struggles into collective forms. Rather it helped to shift the locus of workers' struggles from picket lines to courtrooms. As this shift took place, the language of industrial democracy was increasingly supplanted by rights talk.

Finally the economic structures that had given rise to the idea of industrial democracy in the early twentieth century no longer existed in the post-1960s United States. The ideal of industrial democracy was the product of the distinctive historical era of "Fordist" mass production when employers sought to win the loyalty of workers whom they hoped to retain in life-time employment and when government was both deeply interested in, and broadly capable of, regulating workplace relations. In the years after the mid-1960s, the preconditions of industrial democracy evaporated as capital roamed the globe in search of cheaper labor, and government regulation of markets, including labor markets, rapidly receded.

If the idea of industrial democracy had emerged in the 1890s, by the 1990s it no longer resonated in debates about the workplace. When employers, labor leaders, or government officials debated labor questions in the 1990s, they no longer invoked the notion of industrial democracy. Instead they embraced vaguer terms like "labor-management cooperation" and "employee involvement." The distance between the early twentieth-century demand that industry be made democratic and the late twentieth-century plea for workplace cooperation between labor and management was considerable and called attention to how weak organized labor had become by the century's end.

JOSEPH A. MCCARTIN

References and Further Reading

Brody, David. "Workplace Contractualism in Comparative Perspective." In *Industrial Democracy in America: The Ambiguous Promise*, edited by Nelson Lichtenstein and Howell John Harris. New York: Cambridge University Press, 1992.

Derber, Milton. *The American Idea of Industrial Democracy, 1865–1965*. Urbana: University of Illinois Press, 1970.

Dickman, Howard. *Industrial Democracy in America: Ideological Origins of National Labor Relations Policy*. LaSalle, IL: Open Court, 1987.

Dubofsky, Melvyn. *The State and Labor in Modern America*. Chapel Hill: The University of North Carolina Press, 1994.

Gitelman, Howard M. *Legacy of the Ludlow Massacre: A Chapter in American Industrial Relations.* Philadelphia: University of Pennsylvania Press, 1988.

Golden, Clinton S., and Harold Ruttenberg. *The Dynamics of Industrial Democracy.* New York: Da Capa Press, 1973 (originally published, 1942).

Harris, Howell John. *The Right to Manage: The Industrial Relations Policies of American Business in the 1940s.* Madison: University of Wisconsin, 1982.

Lauck, W. Jett. *Political and Industrial Democracy, 1776–1926.* New York: Funk and Wagnalls, 1926.

Lichtenstein, Nelson, and Howell John Harris. *Industrial Democracy in America: The Ambiguous Legacy.* New York: Cambridge University Press, 1992.

McCartin, Joseph A. *Labor's Great War: The Struggle for Industrial Democracy and the Origins of Modern American Labor Relations, 1912–1921.* Chapel Hill: The University of North Carolina Press, 1997.

Montgomery, David. *The Fall of the House of Labor: The Workplace, the State, and American Labor Activism, 1865–1925.* New York: Cambridge University Press, 1987.

Plumb, Glenn E., and William G. Roylance. *Industrial Democracy: A Plan for Its Achievement.* New York: B. W. Heubsch, 1923.

Webb, Sidney J., and Beatrice Webb. *Industrial Democracy.* London: Longmans, Green & Co., 1897.

INDUSTRIAL UNION OF MARINE AND SHIPBUILDING WORKERS OF AMERICA (IUMSWA)

The Industrial Union of Marine and Shipbuilding Workers of America (IUMSWA) was founded on October 3, 1933, at New York Shipbuilding Corporation, Camden, New Jersey. Initially its only members were workers at the Camden yard. The union had an industrial rather than craft form of organization, which was inclusive of all production workers and was independent of the American Federation of Labor (AFL) and its craft unions that previously had members in numerous shipyards during World War I.

Capable leaders were crucial to the IUMSWA's early organizing success, with John Green the most important. He had worked in Scottish Clydeside shipyards since 1916, where he was active in the United Society of Boilermakers and Iron and Steel Shipbuilders. In 1923, he emigrated from Clydebank to Philadelphia, working in a number of manufacturing jobs before starting as a sheet metal worker at New York Ship in 1933.

Green also joined the Socialist party, where he met Moshe (M. H.) Goldstein, who served as the IUMSWA's chief legal counsel from the early 1930s through the 1960s, and Phil Van Gelder, who helped lead the New York Shipbuilding IUMSWA strike of 1934. Van Gelder had a degree from Brown University, but during the Depression, he became involved in union organizing, including with the Amalgamated Clothing Workers (ACW). Van Gelder never worked in a shipyard, but his organizing abilities and his connections to industrial unionists, such as Sidney Hillman and later, John L. Lewis, greatly advanced the IUMSWA in its early, tenuous years. Green and Van Gelder led the IUMSWA during its first decade as national president and national secretary-treasurer, respectively. Thomas Gallagher, who worked as a rigger in the New York Shipyard, was another central figure during the IUMSWA's first decade and served as the main leader of New York Shipbuilding's IUMSWA Local 1 after Green, later becoming the national union's first organizing director. In contrast to Green and Van Gelder, Gallagher identified with the Democratic party, which had a strong base in Camden.

In the early 1930s, the largest private shipyards in the Northeast were New York Shipbuilding; Fore River Shipyard (owned by Bethlehem Shipbuilding, in Quincy, Massachusetts); and Newport News Shipyard in Virginia. These major yards continued to receive minimal naval contracts as well as merchant, tanker, and passenger ship contracts during the 1920s and early 1930s when shipbuilding production reached a low point. When Franklin D. Roosevelt became president in early 1933, his administration substantially increased naval production and shipbuilding employment through National Industrial Recovery Act (NIRA) contracts to these big yards and also smaller but significant private builders, including Federal Shipbuilding (Kearny, New Jersey); Electric Boat (New London, Connecticut); Sun Shipbuilding (Chester, Pennsylvania); and Bath Iron Works (Bath, Maine).

The increase in production and jobs at New York Shipbuilding also was accompanied by restrictions on weekly working hours mandated under the new NIRA and a resultant pay cut that was deeply resented by the yard's workers. The company had installed a weak company union to prevent independent union organizing but failed to stop internal organizing. By fall 1933 workers voted 1,819 to 142 for the new IUMSWA and against the company union in a worker-sponsored poll.

The IUMSWA sought a charter from the AFL a few months later but was refused because it threatened existing jurisdiction claims by AFL metal trades unions. When John L. Lewis established the independence of the Committee of Industrial Organizations (CIO) in November 1936, he brought two independent unions into the new organization—the IUMSWA and the United Electrical Workers (UEW)—which effectively ensured the permanent split between the AFL and the CIO.

Initially New York Shipbuilding management refused to recognize the IUMSWA, precipitating a seven-week strike in 1934. New York Shipbuilding management's refusal to bargain in 1935 led to a second strike that lasted from March to August. The IUMSWA set up mass picket lines and gained extensive support from the community and such unions as the United Mine Workers (UMW), ACW, and locals of regional AFL unions. Congressional hearings were conducted to investigate the causes of the strike, and the U.S. Department of Labor, including Secretary of Labor Frances Perkins, intervened in efforts to mediate.

President Franklin D. Roosevelt finally broke the deadlock when he responded to Secretary Perkins's pleas and told the U.S. Navy and shipyard management that they had to negotiate with and recognize the IUMSWA, or else it would lose existing naval contracts. Management and the union then agreed to the establishment of a special arbitration board, ending the 11-week strike. The final settlement guaranteed full union recognition and a reasonable wage increase. Although IUMSWA Local 1 did not win the union shop, extensive internal organization enabled the IUMSWA to maintain relatively full membership throughout the yard. This stable membership base allowed the IUMSWA to begin organizing beyond Camden.

Organizing Expansion in the 1930s

Throughout its existence the IUMSWA was unable to organize in government yards due to AFL dominance. The AFL also dominated all West Coast yards except small repair yards in the Los Angeles region where the IUMSWA gained a small membership. As a result the IUMSWA was mainly concentrated in private Northeast port shipyards from the 1930s and later decades.

In the IUMSWA's early years, Van Gelder's efforts to direct organizing drives at Fore River, Newport News, Sun Ship, and Bath Iron Works failed in the 1930s largely because of these yards' well-organized company unions. The IUMSWA never won a union election at Newport News and lost elections at Bath Iron Works numerous times until 1955. The IUMSWA did win a victory at Fore River in mid-1945 (then the largest Congress of Industrial Organizations (CIO)

victory to date in New England) after a disastrous loss in 1941, and at Sun Ship in 1944, both led by organizer Lou Kaplan.

The IUMSWA made its first national breakthrough in the New York port region in 1936 at United's Staten Island Shipyard. Within a year the IUMSWA had locals chartered at a majority of the port region's repair yards, including those in New Jersey bordering New York City. However recognition came only after a bitter repair yard strike in mid-1937 that led to some gains but also losses of some yards.

Federal Shipyard (a subsidiary of U.S. Steel Corporation) was the most important early gain outside Camden. In spring 1937, inside IUMSWA organizers, directed by staff organizer Mike Smith (originally from New York Ship), won a majority on the company union, then voted it out of existence and replaced it with the IUMSWA. Following a massive strike of several days, management agreed to recognize the IUMSWA and signed a first contract. Full recognition and adherence to the grievance procedure by management did not occur until a March 1940 NLRB election that the IUMSWA won by a landslide.

World War II and Shipyard Organizing

By 1941, the Federal Shipbuilding gains and a series of NLRB election victories in other New York port region yards gave the New York port region a membership strength equal to that of the IUMSWA's original base in the Camden-Philadelphia-Delaware River region. This new membership concentration created factional rivalry within the union between the ports of Philadelphia and New York, but also between shipyard union locals, especially those in the largest yards, and the national officers directing union policy and organizing.

In the case of Federal Shipyard, the local had completely failed to sustain dues' collections of members from 1940–1942, leading to bitter fights within the local and suspension of the local's autonomy by the national office. In August 1941, Federal Shipyard workers briefly went on strike demanding enforcement of the National Defense Mediation Board (NDMB) decision calling for a maintenance-of-membership provision. The IUMSWA wanted a union shop with membership a condition of employment, but this NDMB alternative requiring continuous membership once signed up, for the life of the contract, gained the union's support. As a result of the strike and management's refusal to agree to the NDMB order, the U.S. Navy temporarily took over the yard, but the issue remained unresolved even after ownership returned to private management. Sustaining shipbuilding employment stability had become a major national defense production problem, especially after the attack on Pearl Harbor and the urgency of rapidly increasing the American naval fleet. The IUMSWA was one of the first CIO unions to agree to the no-strike pledge in support for war production, but workers—including those at Federal Shipyard—conducted numerous wildcat (unauthorized) strikes when their demands were not met.

President Roosevelt finally met with IUMSWA representatives, management, and government officials (including the Navy) in the White House in the spring of 1942, where he reiterated his unequivocal support for the NDMB, now the National War Labor Board (NWLB) decision endorsing the maintenance-of-membership provision on union security. The U.S. Steel's management capitulated, and the provision became standard throughout the defense industry, although failure to fully enforce the provision precipitated wildcat strikes at Federal until management agreed to government requirements.

Shipyard employment levels had a major influence on union-organizing success. Only 33,000 worked in private yards in 1933, but naval contracts boosted numbers to 48,700 in 1934 and by 1936 matched pre-Depression levels with over 60,000. As jobs became more secure, the demand for better wages increased. By 1941, private and government shipyards employed over half-a-million workers, with half of these in the North Atlantic region where the IUMSWA had its main membership. Peak World War II shipbuilding employment for all yards was 1,686,600 workers in 1943, with 1,400,000 in private yards. North Atlantic yards employed a majority of all shipyard workers, followed by the Pacific Coast region, and the remainder in Virginia, the Gulf Coast, and the Great Lakes. The IUMSWA membership reached 208,000 in 1943, the highest number attained over the union's 55-year history.

Almost one-fourth of this wartime membership was concentrated in a single yard, Camden's New York Ship, reaching some 50,000 at its peak. Management had difficulty running the yard with its own staff and turned to the union for assistance. Skilled shipyard workers who were IUMSWA members moved into foremen and subforemen positions, and organized a subforemen's division within Local 1. The union also assumed much of the responsibility for hiring and training new workers.

In New York Shipbuilding, Federal Shipbuilding, and the huge Bethlehem yards at Fore River and Sparrow's Point (Baltimore), these new workers included women and black workers, but these workers were generally concentrated in auxiliary yards that lasted only for the duration of the war. At Sun Ship, management created a separate yard with black employees only. This racial division among workers became an organizing target for the IUMSWA in two wartime election campaigns, the second led by organizer Lou Kaplan, which ended this employment segregation. In southern yards, particularly Mobile, Alabama, efforts to break down racial barriers were less successful, with IUMSWA organizers bowing to the tradition of segregation and discriminatory practices to secure union membership among white workers.

During World War II, the federal government regulated wages and hours through various agencies, including the tripartite Shipbuilding Stabilization Committee, but also through mediation efforts involving regional "zone conferences" of union and management representatives. The IUMSWA held sole representation only on the Atlantic conference, shared representation positions with the AFL metal trades unions on the Gulf and Great Lakes conferences, and had no position on the Pacific conference dominated by the AFL. Delays in implementing wage increases, which required approval from the NWLB, led to numerous wildcat strikes in most shipyards that were opposed by the IUMSWA national leadership.

Dissension also occurred at the local and national levels of IUMSWA over the presence of Communist party activists, particularly those elected to union office. At the 1941 IUMSWA convention, delegates approved an anti-Communist clause that later led to the expulsion of national General Executive Board (GEB) member, Irving Velson. Others who were not in the Communist party but who advocated a broad left coalition, including Secretary-Treasurer Van Gelder, later were targeted by IUMSWA President John Green. By the 1940s, Green served as a CIO vice-president and increasingly played a major role in attacking Communists within the CIO.

Postwar Dissension and the Collapse of American Shipbuilding

At the IUMSWA's January 1946 convention, an open split emerged between left and right factions in the national union. Van Gelder, recently returned from army service in Europe, challenged Ross Blood for his old position of secretary-treasurer and had substantial support from a Federal Shipbuilding delegation led by Lou Kaplan, but Green forces seated only a rightwing slate despite delegate election challenges. Other opposition came from New York Shipbuilding, led by Local 1 president Andy Reeder. After the defeat of the left at the January convention, Green called another convention in September to consolidate his forces. Van Gelder, Reeder, and others again tried to challenge the national leadership, but failed.

New York Shipbuilding Local 1 members remained alienated from the national leadership, but by the late 1940s, with Reeder's failure and departure, came under the rightwing opposition leadership of Tommy "Driftpin" Saul.

Shipyard employment collapsed at the end of the war, with all auxiliary yards closing and even Federal Shipbuilding shutting down by 1948. Strikes in shipbuilding in 1947 and 1948 gave workers some wage gains, but employment security remained precarious. Green decided to expand the IUMSWA's jurisdiction to regain membership. In 1947, the recently created CIO United Railroad Workers of America (URWA), made up of maintenance of way and shop crafts, merged with the IUMSWA. In early 1948, an anti-Communist group of Connecticut-based locals in the International Union of Mine Mill and Smelters, known as the Progressive Metalworkers' Council (PMC), seceded and joined the IUMSWA with Green's approval, over the strong objections of CIO heads Phil Murray and Alan Haywood. By January 1948, IUMSWA had 78,420 members, with 42,850 employed in shipbuilding, but by June 1950, IUMSWA membership had plummeted to 41,858, with only 25,000 in shipbuilding.

Following the membership gains from the URWA and the PMC, tensions arose between shipyard worker members and those in railroads and metal shops over national union positions and charges of national neglect by shipyard locals. As a result New York Ship's Local 1 led by Saul voted to disaffiliate with the IUMSWA in September 1948, and Sun Ship's IUMSWA local disaffiliated in April 1949. In 1950, the IUMSWA lost an NLRB election at New York Ship in a landslide to the AFL's Boilermakers' Union. This loss and the crisis over nonshipbuilding membership led Green to resign as IUMSWA national president in 1951, and national vice-president John Grogan, who came from the Hoboken repair yard in New Jersey, replaced him. Grogan reversed Green's earlier expansion plans and returned to organizing and consolidating the union's original base in shipbuilding. He also presided over the departure of the URWA and former PMC metal workers' locals into the United Steel Workers of America.

Final Decades to 1988 Merger

Grogan remained national president of the IUMSWA until his death in 1968, even though he was elected to the full-time position of mayor of Hoboken, New Jersey, in 1953. With the disaffiliation of the IUMSWA's largest local—in Camden—and the departure of half of the union's nonshipbuilding workers, membership in 1951 declined to 34,100 even though Bethlehem's eight Atlantic Coast shipyards alone still employed some 31,000 workers. World War II era national officer Andrew Pettis became national president after Grogan's death in 1968. In the 1970s, Eugene McCabe became national president, and in the early 1980s, Arthur Batson, Jr., became the last national IUMSWA president.

In the early 1950s, Japan overtook the United States in shipbuilding production, with American yards moving almost exclusively into naval contracts and abandoning virtually all merchant and tanker building. Production in the United States also shifted more to southern and Pacific Coast yards, devastating the IUMSWA. Its membership dropped to 25,600 in 1960, where it remained until the 1980s. By this time the combined employment at the nation's two biggest East Coast shipyards—the USWA's Newport News (specializing in aircraft carriers) and the AFL Metal Trades' Electric Boat (specializing in nuclear submarines)—exceeded the total national membership of the IUMSWA.

By 1988, New York Shipbuilding had closed, and Fore River management announced their yard's closure the following year, leaving only Maine's Bath Iron Works as the national union's single major yard. At only 13,000 members, the IUMSWA finally merged with the IAM, with 7,000 shipbuilding workers in a union mainly based in the aerospace industry, in 1989.

DAVID PALMER

References and Further Reading

Gifford, Courtney D., ed. *Directory of U.S. Labor Organizations: 1994–95 Edition.* Washington, DC: Bureau of National Affairs, 1995.
Mergen, Thomas. "History of the Industrial Union of Marine and Shipbuilding Workers." Ph.D. dissertation, University of Pennsylvania, 1968.
Palmer, David. "Organizing the Shipyards: Unionization at New York Ship, Federal Ship, and Fore River, 1898–1945." Ph.D. dissertation, Brandeis University, 1990.
———. *Organizing the Shipyards: Union Strategy in Three Northeast Ports.* Ithaca, NY: Cornell University Press, 1998.

INDUSTRIAL UNIONISM

Industrial unionism, which gathers all of the workers in an industry into a single labor organization, saw its heyday in the United States during the 1930s. Some workers and labor leaders challenged the more traditional craft or trade basis of organization quite a bit earlier however. In 1870, the Knights of St. Crispin (KOSC), a union of shoe workers, achieved almost total industrial organization and won a strike in Lynn, Massachusetts. One of the few successful factory workers' unions of its day, the KOSC was a contemporary of the national Knights of Labor (KOL), founded in Philadelphia in 1869 on principles of broad labor solidarity and dedicated to building a "cooperative commonwealth." The KOL admitted workers as individual members, and then placed them in trade assemblies when possible or in mixed assemblies when members of a single trade at a particular locality were insufficient in number. Because the mixed assemblies included unskilled workers and outnumbered the trade assemblies by the 1880s, the KOL took on a unique character that presaged the advent of industrial unionism. However the KOL's emphasis on the development of workers' cooperatives and its desire to organize all workers regardless of skill failed to produce an enduring organization at a time when the rapid concentration of industrial wealth; the abiding hostility of business corporations; and racial, linguistic, and religious barriers among workers made working-class cohesiveness very difficult.

By the late nineteenth century, the emergence of national business corporations and trusts, along with technological change, was weakening the power of trade unions through the geographic diffusion of production and the subdivision of labor into lower-skilled tasks. The first truly national businesses were the railroads, and it was there that one of the earliest efforts at modern industrial unionism took place. In 1893, Eugene Debs and 50 other railroaders founded the American Railway Union (ARU) in Chicago. Prior to this time most railroad workers had no union, and a minority belonged to five brotherhoods with no common alliance between them—the engineers, conductors, firemen, brakemen, and switchmen. The new organization was dedicated to bringing all categories of railway workers together, even car builders and coal miners in railroad employ. While the ARU was open to men and to women, its industrial unionism was still limited by race, since only white workers could join. The ARU led an 1894 strike by Pullman Palace Car employees and the ensuing nationwide Pullman car boycott. As a result of federal intervention and the union's violation of court injunctions, the ARU was virtually destroyed that same year.

Divisions in the Early AFL

By the time of the ARU's demise, the dominant national labor organization was the American Federation of Labor (AFL), born in 1886 and committed to trade unionism and trade autonomy. Although many of its founding members saw the AFL as a corrective to the KOL's mistakenly broad admission policies and consequently as a better guardian of the prerogatives of skilled workers, there were others who tackled the question of industrial unionism very early on. In 1901, the contest between advocates of craft and industrial organization was reflected in the AFL's Scranton Declaration, which on the one hand affirmed craft autonomy and on the other suggested that some rare industries might benefit from having all their workers organized in a single "paramount organization." On the basis of this second principle, the AFL gave one member union, the United Mine Workers (UMW), founded in 1890, jurisdiction over all workers in and around the mines, including those craftsmen that might normally have belonged to other organizations. The UMW was unusual, since the United Brewery Workers (UBW), which was already established on an industrial basis when it applied for AFL affiliation in 1887, was confronted with repeated demands to limit its organizational reach. Its membership in the federation led to years of bitter jurisdictional disputes and threats of expulsion that persisted through the 1930s. In yet another case, the craft-based International Ladies' Garment Workers' Union (ILGWU), founded by skilled male cloak makers in 1900, evolved into an industrial union after a 1909 strike by female shirtwaist makers in New York. The "uprising of the twenty thousand" brought these young Jewish and Italian immigrant women into the ILGWU, which achieved a female membership of 50% by 1916. In men's clothing, the AFL's United Garment Workers of America (UGW), which had been larger than the ILGWU prior to 1909, neglected the male counterparts of these same women. The immigrant men who labored in the ready-made suit sector abandoned the UGW and created their own industrial union outside of the AFL in 1915, the Amalgamated Clothing Workers of America (ACWA). The ILGWU and ACWA both proved the viability of industrial unionism and the potential for organizing women and immigrants, contrary to much of the rhetoric inside the AFL. Both of the garment unions were also overtly socialist.

The IWW

From 1905 through the First World War, the AFL was challenged by the radical Industrial Workers of the World (IWW), an openly anticapitalist labor organization that sought to organize workers on an industrial basis only. Critical of the "labor aristocracy" that had coalesced in the craft-based AFL, the IWW made a special effort to organize unskilled, foreign-born, and migratory workers that the AFL had ignored. Its principal founding union, the Western Federation of Miners (WFM), was itself an industrial union born in 1893 that had left the AFL in 1897 on account of the federation's neglect of workers in the Rocky Mountain States. Mirroring the WFM, the IWW devoted considerable attention to workers in the extractive industries of the West, including timber workers, miners, and agricultural workers. While the IWW was in theory composed of a large number of specific industrial departments, its practical organization was very loose, and its membership at any one time was small. The IWW organizers often gave form to workers' spontaneous struggles rather than building a permanent organizational edifice. The IWW's militancy and its opposition to the First World War invoked the wrath of employers and government, leading to its destruction by 1920.

The CIO

The heyday of industrial unionism in the United States came in the aftermath of the Wagner Act of 1935, a federal law that protected workers' right to join unions and unions' right to engage in collective bargaining. The opportunities presented by this New Deal era law re-opened old fissures within the AFL, causing the federation's advocates of industrial unionism to set up a Committee for Industrial Organizations (CIO) in November 1935. The committee, which sought to lead the AFL in organizing workers in mass-production industries, included the leaders of the UMW, ACWA (now in the AFL), and ILGWU, as well as leaders of the Typographical Union; United Textile Workers; Mine, Mill, and Smelter Workers; Oil Field, Gas Well, and Refining Workers; and the Cap and Millinery Department of the United Hatters. Rebuffed in its efforts to achieve industrial charters for workers in steel, automobiles, radio, and rubber, the CIO went ahead with its own organizing drives, broke with the AFL, and recast itself in 1938 as the Congress of Industrial Organizations under the direction of the UMW's John Lewis. The new unions it helped to create also subsumed the organizational efforts of the Trade Union Unity League, a collection of industrial unions under Communist leadership since 1929. The birth of the CIO corresponded to a shift in the Communist party line to a position of support for a unified democratic front against fascism, and Communists won some significant positions in the new unions, especially in the United Electrical, Radio, and Machine; Transport Workers; Maritime Workers; Fur and Leather Workers; Mine, Mill, and Smelter Workers; and International Woodworkers.

Because the CIO grew so rapidly—to 3.7 million members by the end of 1937—its success suggested that a tremendous latent demand for organization among ordinary production workers had gone unmet until the New Deal era. Workers certainly did exhibit substantial signs of militancy and determination, as most famously illustrated by a sit-down strike at General Motors in Flint, Michigan, from late December 1936 through mid-February 1937. The strike resulted in recognition of the United Automobile Workers and was the first time the CIO had obtained an agreement from an open-shop industry, no less one of the world's biggest corporations. The labor victory led to a wave of strikes and union organizing drives across the country, with sit-down strikes as the tactic of choice until mid-1937.

The advent of the Second World War allowed the industrial union movement to consolidate its membership gains if not its independence of action as the National War Labor Board adopted the principle of "maintenance of membership" in war industries. While not an endorsement of the closed shop, the rule required union members and new recruits to keep up their membership for the duration of a contract. In 1955, the CIO and the AFL merged, with the latter organization adding an Industrial Union Department in recognition of the permanent need for industrywide unionism. With few exceptions, such as the Union of Needletrades, Industrial, and Textile Employees (UNITE), which derives from a 1995 merger of the Amalgamated Clothing and Textile Workers' Union with the ILGWU, the major industrial unions in the United States as of 2005 have come down to us unchanged as a legacy of the CIO organizing drives of the 1930s.

PHILIP JACQUES DREYFUS

References and Further Reading

Babson, Steve. *The Unfinished Struggle: Turning Points in America Labor, 1877–Present*. Lanham, MD: Rowman and Littlefield, 1999.
Dubofsky, Melvyn. *Industrialism and the American Worker, 1865–1920*. Arlington Heights, IL: Harlan Davidson, 1985.

Dulles, Foster Rhea, and Melvyn Dubofsky. *Labor in America: A History*. Wheeling, IL: Harlan Davidson, 1993.

Foner, Philip S. *History of the Labor Movement in the United States*. New York: International Publishers, 1947.

Kessler-Harris, Alice. *Out to Work: A History of Wage-Earning Women in the United States*. New York: Oxford University Press, 1982.

Lynd, Staughton, ed. *"We Are All Leaders": The Alternative Unionism of the Early 1930s*. Urbana: University of Illinois Press, 1996.

Zieger, Robert H. *The CIO, 1935–1955*. Chapel Hill: University of North Carolina Press, 1995.

INDUSTRIAL WORKERS OF THE WORLD

Committed to organizing all workers regardless of race, skill, gender, or ethnicity into one large union dedicated to abolishing the wage system and overthrowing capitalism, the Industrial Workers of the World (IWW) embodied the revival of revolutionary fervor in the American labor movement in the first two decades of the twentieth century. From 1905–1924, the IWW inspired a spirit of radical working-class activism throughout the country that broke sharply from the business unionism advocated by the American Federation of Labor (AFL). Although its official membership was never very large, the IWW struck fear in employers who responded to the challenge of the Wobblies (a nickname for members of the IWW) with a concerted campaign of intimidation and repression that intensified during World War I. The IWW never regained its prewar militancy, but its legacy of direct action, industrial unionism influenced the American labor movement for decades to come.

Origins, Goals, and Membership

In June 1905, an assemblage of dissident radicals and labor activists gathered in Chicago to, in the words of keynote speaker and militant western mine unionist William D. "Big Bill" Haywood, create "a working-class movement that shall have for its purpose the emancipation of the working class from the slave bondage of capitalism" (P. Renshaw, *The Wobblies*, 1967). Delegates to the Chicago convention, what Haywood called the "Continental Congress of the working class," formed the Industrial Workers of the World. Those who attended—western miners, competing factions of socialists, industrial unionists, anarchists—agreed on little other than their hostility

toward the conservative craft unionism of the AFL. The Western Federation of Miners, the largest delegation in attendance for example had learned first hand the ineffectiveness of the AFL, which had proved an unreliable ally in the union's desperate struggles against mine operators in the Mountain West. Having experienced firsthand the multiple tactics that mine operators deployed to break their union—strikebreaking, martial law, private detectives—these veterans of the western mine wars came to Chicago with a sharpened class consciousness. They understood that industrial organization and securing allies across the labor movement rather than affiliation with the AFL was the only way to protect the interests of the working class. The preamble to the IWW's original constitution—"the working class and the employing class have nothing in common"—thus reflected the lived experiences of the workers gathered in Chicago. Declaring "an injury to one an injury to all," they advocated a cooperative, egalitarian spirit that they hoped would transform the American labor movement.

Although the delegates to the Chicago convention submerged philosophical differences in the interest of creating one big industrial union, factionalism quickly sapped the fledgling organization. In 1906, reformist socialists, after a conflict with revolutionary socialists, deserted the IWW. A year later moderates within the Western Federation of Miners persuaded its members to abandon the revolutionary industrial unionism of the IWW, diminishing the ranks of the Wobblies to perhaps less than 6,000. The internal debates within the Western Federation of Miners reflected a deeper debate within the IWW over the strategies and tactics the union ought to pursue to achieve the emancipation of the working class. Some saw industrial unionism as a means to more effectively organize the working-class vote, which would help to elect socialist political candidates. Others saw the exercise of the democratic ballot as flawed as the pure-and-simple unionism of the AFL. Political action, they argued, would lead only to the reform of capitalism, not its overthrow. Instead they favored an organization that would wage direct economic action, enabling workers to seize the means of production of entire industries. At the 1908 convention advocates or direct action gained the upper hand, ousted their opponents, and amended the constitution to eliminate political action as a viable tactic or strategy for achieving the abolition of the wage system. Among those expelled from the 1908 convention was the fractious Marxist ideologue Daniel DeLeon, who founded a faction of the IWW in Detroit. Although this splinter group, which later renamed itself the Workers' International Industrial Union, tried to rival the IWW, it never exerted much influence before it disbanded in 1924.

After the 1908 convention the IWW dedicated itself to the pursuit of two simultaneous goals. First it sought the practical task of organizing the masses of American industry into one big union. The IWW thus launched an aggressive organizing campaign that urged all workers regardless of skill level, race, ethnicity, nationality, or gender to join. This commitment to inclusiveness distinguished the IWW from exclusionary craft unionism of the AFL and its history of discouraging the participation of unskilled immigrant and African-American workers. The IWW's second and revolutionary goal was to "take possession of the earth and the machinery of production, and abolish the wage system," as it declared in its 1908 constitution. Direct action through industrial unionism would be the vehicle for achieving this utopian vision. By organizing all workers in all industries, the IWW would control the country's factories, mines, and railroads. Workers would then wage a general strike that would cripple capitalism and usher in a new day of a democratic, wageless, and classless society governed by workers themselves. Because of its revolutionary goals, the IWW pledged never to negotiate or seek peace with employers by signing binding contracts.

Direct-Action Campaigns before World War I

Achieving its utopian vision was a distant goal, so the IWW focused its energies on organizing unaffiliated workers. Despite the predominance of western radicals among the IWW's founders, the union gained national credibility from important victories in labor struggles in the industrial Northeast and Mid-Atlantic regions where immigrant factory workers and African-American longshoremen proved eager converts to the IWW's philosophy of direct action.

In 1912, the IWW supported the spontaneous strike of more than 20,000 textile workers who walked out in protest of wage cuts at the American Woolen Company in Lawrence, Massachusetts. Many of the strikers were young women aged 14–18 who had become malnourished and overworked as the company imposed wage reductions and forced them to endure the stress of a system designed to speed up the pace of work. "We want bread and roses, too" demanded the strikers in a phrase that became the signature slogan of the strike. Since most of the strikers were immigrants—Poles, Italians, Lithuanians, Russians, and members of several other nationalities—the IWW played a critical role in sustaining worker solidarity across difficult language barriers. The IWW distributed literature in dozens of languages and translated speeches, which sustained unity and solidarity as strikers maintained a massive picket line, held rallies, and organized stage parades through city streets. As the strike wore on, providing relief proved one of the greatest challenges to the strikers. The IWW's strike and relief committees served workers of different nationalities by providing supplies, maintaining soup kitchens, and distributing other critical aid. The strikers held their ground even as national guardsmen descended on Lawrence and the city imposed martial law and a ban on public meetings to disrupt their activities.

The IWW carefully cultivated public sympathy throughout the strike. Strike committees coordinated with labor sympathizers in nearby cities to aid the children of strikers by providing them care and temporary out-of-town safety during the duration of the conflict. The response was overwhelming; the image of underfed children in rags generated sympathetic publicity for the strikers and their cause. Distressed by the effectiveness of the strikers' ability to coordinate, Lawrence authorities moved to disrupt their strategy, declaring that children would not be allowed to leave the city. The tide of the strike turned when the police interfered by attacking a transport of 200 children destined for Philadelphia. A public outcry over the tactics of Lawrence authorities forced the mill owners' to settle, offering pay raises, overtime, and other improvements in working conditions.

In 1913, longshoremen in Philadelphia formed the interracial, multiethnic Local 8 of the IWW's Marine Transport Workers' Industrial Union. A long history of racial and ethnic conflict among Philadelphia's waterfront workers enabled employers to control the labor force of the city's docks. But longshoremen reversed that trend during a strike in 1913, when eastern European immigrants and African-Americans who worked the docks voted to affiliate with the IWW. Instrumental to the success of Local 8 was Ben Fletcher, who became one of the most prominent Wobblies in the United States. Fletcher, a Philadelphia native and young dockhand in his early twenties, ascended the leadership in the city's IWW. During the strike he emerged as a leader of Local 8. Fletcher was not the only black leader in Local 8: Several other key positions within the union, including those of business agents, meeting chairs, and secretaries, were held by African-Americans at one time or another. The union's careful efforts at political education and balancing the needs and interests of the union's different members made the union a powerful force on the Philadelphia waterfront for more than a decade.

The IWW's message of direct action appealed to the multitude of drifters—miners, loggers, farm hands—who toiled about the Trans-Mississippi West. The shift to an industrial form of agricultural—wheat on the Great Plains and fruits and vegetables in California and Washington—increased the demand for seasonal, migrant farm labor. Young, single, male, unskilled migrant farm hands endured an endless search for work, riding the rails from job to job, following the harvest season. At each work site, they settled into camps with poor lodging and inadequate bathing facilities and worked jobs that were strenuous, intensely supervised, and low-paying. During harvest season these hoboes became ripe recruits for the Wobblies. Thousands joined, forming in 1915 the Agricultural Workers' Organization (AWO), which later re-organized as the Agricultural Workers' Industrial Union. Until the late 1920s, these militant casual laborers built a union that was strongly centered at the level of the rank-and-file and for a while posed a formidable threat to employers. The IWW's organized farm hands in many ways pioneered the idea of industrial unionism in agriculture. The IWW also established a strong presence among the loggers of the timber camps of the Pacific Northwest. Here a mix of revolutionary appeals and the demands for immediate improvements in working and living conditions attracted thousands of loggers into locals that waged a series of strikes in the decade before World War I.

The Wobbly Counterculture

Beyond a commitment to waging direct-action campaigns against employers, the IWW spread a working-class culture that challenged the dominant values of competitive, acquisitive individualism. Through its newspapers the *Industrial Worker* and *Solidarity* and other publications, such as Covington's hall paper, the *Lumberjack* (later entitled *Voice of the People*), the IWW spread its political education of the working class, which drew on humor, song, and iconoclasm. Cartoons ridiculed Scissor Bill, the fictional American worker—and a ubiquitous presence at mines, mills, and lumber camps throughout the country—who resisted unionization and remained the dutiful servant of employers, earning nothing more than a life of sloth, gambling, drinking to excess, and residing in filth. Ernest Riehe's memorable Mr. Block cartoons, through mockery and humor, educated working-class readers on the values of class solidarity and industrial unionism. Mr. Block represented the naive American worker who faithfully believed that his material interests were served by obeying the law and remaining

faithful to the commands of his employers. As one IWW publication put it, "Mr. Block owns nothing, yet he speaks from the standpoint of the millionaire. . . . he licks the hand that smites him and kisses the boot that kicks him; he is the personification of all that a worker should not be." By following the adventures of Mr. Block, readers witnessed his discovery that the courts fail to protect him, that depositing wages in banks ensures him of no savings, that employer promises of plentiful jobs at high wages never materialize, and that the AFL only reinforces the power of capitalists. By raising the class consciousness of American workers through the humorous education of Mr. Block, Riehe and the IWW aimed to destroy the blocks on which capitalism was built.

The IWW spread is culture of class solidarity and industrial unionism through song as well as humor. The IWW music pledged to "fan the flames of discontent." In 1909, an IWW committee in Spokane, Washington, compiled the first of many editions of workers' songs, which became affectionately known among Wobblies as the "Little Red Song Book," after the color of its paperback cover. The songbook project reflected the talents of its compiler, J. H. Walsh, an energetic West Coast itinerant soapbox organizer who considered himself both an agitator and an entertainer. Wobbly music chronicled the travails of the male, migrant worker, who endured a life on the road with its endless search for work, crowding in unsanitary work camps, and exploitation at the hands of deceitful labor agents. Songs also urged direct action. They celebrated the uncompromising defiance of the IWW, mocked emasculated lackeys, such as Mr. Block and Scissor Bill; memorialized the heroics of legendary unionists, such as Joe Hill and rebel Elizabeth Gurley Flynn; mused at the destruction of property at the hands of Wobbly saboteurs; and promoted an ethic of cooperation and solidarity amid struggle.

But if songs registered workers' frustrations and lionized their militancy, nearly all of them struck a note that inspired dreams of the coming new day. Consider the chorus to Ralph Chaplin's "Commonwealth of Toil": "But we have a glowing dream / Of how fair the world will seem / When each man can live his life secure and free / When the earth is owned by Labor/And there's joy and peace for all/In the commonwealth of Toil that is to be" (*I. W. W. Songs*, 2003).

Although perhaps no more than 60,000 people ever belonged to the IWW at its zenith, many millions of American workers gained exposure to the IWW's revolutionary philosophy through the union's cultural propaganda of culture of humor, song, and militant class solidarity.

A masculine work life culture of the rails, mines, mills, and logging camps also spread the cultural values of the Wobblies. Hopping freights and living in tent colonies with other migrant workers, however unappealing, nurtured a masculine spirit of camaraderie, rebelliousness, and independence, values that the IWW taught in its newspapers, pamphlets, and stump speeches. Union delegates drifted through migrant camps, distributing IWW literature, buttons, and pasting stickers inside freight cars, rented rooms, and other places where migrants gathered. Organizers won many converts to the Wobbly cause when they displayed militant solidarity in action. Union men intimidated nonunionists, daring them to fistfights, shootouts, and other tests of masculinity. Wobblies enhanced their visibility and reputation among migrant workers when they stood together to resist eviction from freight cars. Engineers and conductors often harassed workers who rode the rails to work sites, trying to extort money from the migrants and forcing them off the train if they refused to pay. Wobblies defied these incursions on what they considered their right to ride the rails, resorting to coordinated acts of physical violence to repel railroad crews. The defiance of the Wobblies, not the deference of nonunionists, secured free passage to the next work site and taught the value of the militant, fighting spirit of the IWW to nonunion observers. Veterans of the rails and lumber camps thus served as emissaries of the IWW's counterculture of rebellious class solidarity.

Repression and Response

The IWW encountered coordinated repression, engineered by both the state and employers, to disrupt its organizing, its direct-action campaigns, and the spread of its cultural propaganda. To further its education of the working class, the IWW deployed a contingent of street-corner speakers and soapbox orators throughout western towns. They thundered before crowds of migrant, casual laborers and led public demonstrations against the abuses of private-employment agencies, or "employment sharks" in the vernacular speech of the IWW, who charged high job-placement and transportation fees to workers. Municipal officials drafted local ordinances that prohibited public-street speaking but exempted such religious organizations as the Salvation Army from the regulations. From 1909–1916, the IWW responded to these legal restrictions with its famous free-speech fights

in such places as Spokane, Washington, Fresno, California, and Minot, North Dakota. Wobblies defied local authorities with a coordinated plan by which one speaker would mount a soapbox and address the gathered crowd until the police intervened and arrested the offender for violating the ordinance. Immediately a second speaker would follow, leading to more arrests, until the IWW overwhelmed the jails and courts, forcing the police to release the prisoners. The demonstrators won public sympathy, not only from other radical groups, but also from civic groups and the mainstream press, which eventually led to the repeal of many of these ordinances. Despite victories in the free-speech fights, these battles divided Wobblies. Internal debates between advocates of soapbox organizing and those who feared that such tactics wasted critical union resources on courtroom costs raged, the latter insisting that time and money could be better spent organizing work sites and staging strikes.

Even as the Wobblies established a presence in mines, construction camps, logging fronts and sawmills, canneries, steel mills, and meatpacking plants, they confronted employers who had the authority to call on the coercive powers of the state to defend their interests over those of the IWW. Despite the IWW's victory at Lawrence for example, American Woolen slowly regained control over its mill. A recession in the textile industry in 1913 enabled mill operators to shift production to nonunion mills, fire unionists, and purchase the loyalty of workers who pledged to shun the Wobblies with promotions and other favors. Employer tactics undermined the IWW's persuasion with workers, who saw the union as powerless to protect the interest of its members. Membership dwindled, and a company-imposed stretch-out eroded pay gains won in the strike. Later that year the IWW endured another stinging defeat. The IWW supported a strike at the silk mills in Paterson, New Jersey, that quickly became one of the union's epic struggles. When silk operators rejected workers' demands, some 25,000 workers forced more than 300 silk mills to go idle. For more than 5 months, silk workers held together through a variety of tactics, including staging a celebrated pageant that dramatized the strikers' cause. Yet the employers' united front eroded worker unity as Paterson officials sanctioned police brutality against strikers, which employers succeeded in blaming on anarchists, a charge that stuck in this town with a reputation as a hotbed of anarchism. Violent repression of the strikers without fear of reprisal from local or state authorities emboldened the hand of company officials. The strike was defeated, and the IWW lost important credibility until the founding of the AWO in 1915 rejuvenated the union's mass appeal.

The onset of World War I posed even bigger challenges to the "one big union." When the war began in Europe in 1914, the union vowed to oppose it, arguing that it was a struggle between capitalist and imperialist powers in which the working class had no stake. When the United States entered the conflict in 1917, the IWW leadership never made an official antiwar declaration, although it refused to adopt a no-strike pledge and to suspend its commitment to class conflict for the duration of the war. Many Wobblies did resist the draft or went out on strike, but many others did not. Nevertheless Wobblies incurred the indiscriminate wrath of public officials and private citizens who condemned unionists as unpatriotic and pro-German, whose actions undermined American resolve and deprived the United States of mobilizing its vital war industries.

The passage of the Espionage Act (1917) empowered the federal government to intimidate and imprison such radicals as the Wobblies. At the pleading of the interests of the country's major industrial and agricultural interests, the federal government conducted a series of raids against the IWW. Federal agents stormed into union halls, libraries, and private homes, confiscating files, literature, supplies, office equipment, and even personal items. Thousands of organizers and rank-and-file Wobblies were arrested and indicted for violating the Espionage Act. In a series of mass trials, federal authorities prosecuted Wobblies for obstructing the war effort. In the largest of these trials, held in Chicago, William D. Haywood and scores of other Wobbly defendants were found guilty of sedition and sentenced to 20 years in prison.

Not only did the federal crackdown ensnare such IWW leaders as Haywood, but it took its toll on rank-and-file members as well. The federal investigations of the IWW were part of a larger federal campaign of fear waged against all kinds of alleged radicals. Vigilante groups, such as the American Protective League, worked in concert with state and local officials to expose and intimidate Wobblies who dodged the draft, failed to report for military training, or who were foreign-born and at risk for deportation as an enemy alien. Police arrested thousands of suspected Wobblies for vagrancy. Vigilantes in local loyalty leagues lynched, tar-and-feathered, and clubbed unionists. Even Wobblies who supported the war effort and served in the military were not immune from vigilante repression. For example war veteran and lumberjack Wesley Everest was lynched for resisting a mob of American Legionnaires who stormed the IWW union hall in Centralia, Washington, on Armistice Day in 1919. The war dealt a crippling blow to the IWW's offices, membership, and infrastructure.

Decline and Legacy

Although some pockets of Wobbly activism—such as the wheat fields of the Great Plains—saw a resurgence in the 1920s, the IWW never recovered from wartime repression. The union invested its limited resources and energies into the defense of wartime prisoners, which undermined any renewed efforts at organizing and direct action. Much of the leadership dispersed. After the war working-class radicals also began to gravitate toward the Communist Party of the United States of America (CPUSA), which was founded in 1919. Spearheaded by former Wobbly William Z. Foster, the CPUSA's Trade Union Educational League (TUEL) pushed to build industrial unionism within the trade union movement. Throughout the 1920s, the TUEL trained hundreds of field organizers who developed the skills, networks, and tactical experience to redirect working-class radicalism in the 1930s. Finally even the Wobbly revival on the plains was short-lived, since critical changes in agricultural technologies reduced agribusiness's dependence on migrant labor, the greatest source of new membership. The introduction of the automobile also undermined the work culture of the West, which weakened the Wobblies' ability to appeal to potential recruits. As workers traveled to work sites by car, they bypassed the sociability of riding the rails and the jungle camps, two places where activists had succeeded in wooing migrants to the Wobbly cause.

Despite its decline the IWW left important legacies. By taking seriously the importance of organizing unskilled workers, the IWW undermined the credibility of the AFL's craft unionism as a model for an effective labor movement. By organizing African-American longshoremen in Philadelphia, immigrant textile workers in Lawrence, and migrant harvest workers, and timber hands of various stripes, the IWW anticipated the industrial unionism of the Congress of Industrial Organizations, founded in the 1930s amid the Great Depression. The Wobblies direct-action tactics found renewed expression among activists in the United Mine Workers, the United Automobile Workers, and the Amalgamated Clothing Workers. Moreover the IWW's original idealism continues to inspire many on the left to this day. The union still maintains its own website (see References) where the project of working to build one big union remains alive. For many in the labor movement today, both activists and scholars, the IWW's expansive vision and idealism—that takes seriously the idea that "an injury to one is an injury to all"—is as relevant in today's world of global capitalism as it was in 1905 at the zenith of American industrial capitalism.

STEVEN A. REICH

References and Further Reading

Cameron, Ardis. *Radicals of the Worst Sort: Laboring Women in Lawrence, Massachusetts, 1860–1912*. Urbana: University of Illinois Press, 1994.

Cole, Peter. *Wobblies on the Waterfront: Interracial Unionism in Progressive Era Philadelphia*. Urbana: University of Illinois Press, 2006.

———. *Black Wobbly: The Life and Writings of Benjamin Harrison Fletcher*. Chicago, IL: Charles H. Kerr Press, 2006.

Crutchfield, J. D. "Jim Crutchfield's I.W.W. Page." www.workerseducation.org/crutch/

Dubofsky, Melvyn. *We Shall Be All: A History of the Industrial Workers of the World*. 2nd ed. Urbana: University of Illinois Press, 1988. (reprint).

———. *"Big Bill" Haywood. Lives of the Left*. New York: St. Martin's Press, 1987.

Hall, Greg. *Harvest Wobblies: The Industrial Workers of the World and Agricultural Laborers in the American West, 1905–1930*. Corvallis, OR: Oregon State University Press, 2001.

I. W. W. Songs. 19th ed. Chicago, IL: Charles H. Kerr, 2003. (reprint).

Industrial Workers of the World Songs, or Little Red Song Book. London, 1916. www.musicanet.org/robokopp/iww.html

Kimeldorf, Howard. *Battling for American Labor: Wobblies, Craft Workers, and the Making of the Union Movement*. Berkeley: University of California Press, 1999.

Kornbluh, Joyce L., ed. *Rebel Voices: An IWW Anthology*. Ann Arbor: University of Michigan Press, 1965.

Renshaw, Patrick. *The Wobblies: The Story of Syndicalism in the United States*. New York: Doubleday, 1967.

Salerno, Sal. *Red November, Black November: Culture and Community in the Industrial Workers of the World*. Albany, NY: State University of New York Press, 1989.

Sellers, Nigel Anthony. *Oil, Wheat, and Wobblies: The Industrial Workers of the World in Oklahoma, 1905–1930*. Norman, OK: Oklahoma University Press, 1998.

Tripp, Anne Huber. *The I. W. W. and the Paterson Silk Strike of 1913*. Urbana: University of Illinois Press, 1987.

Tyler, Robert. *Rebels of the Woods: The IWW in the Pacific Northwest*. Eugene: University of Oregon Press, 1967.

See also **Agricultural Workers Organization; Brotherhood of Timber Workers; Communist Party; DeLeon, Daniel; Fletcher, Benjamin Harrison; Flynn, Elizabeth Gurley; Foster, William Z.; Haywood, William D. "Big Bill"; Hill, Joe; Hoboes; Marine Transport Workers' Union; Western Federation of Miners/International Union of Mine, Mill, and Smelter Workers**

INJUNCTIONS

By definition an injunction is a court order directing a person, and if necessary his or her associates, to refrain from pursuing a course of action. For the labor movement, the injunction became a powerful legal weapon that was used to hamper its activities. From strikes to boycotts to peaceful picketing, U.S. courts would issue injunctions on the behest of employers to prevent workers from carrying out their forms of protest. Ever since the Pullman strike of 1894, curbing the use of the injunction became a serious quest on the behalf of labor.

Injunctions had their origin in the common law system of England. The king was given the power to prevent any sort of injury by banning someone from committing an act rather than taking action against such person after the injury was performed. Later on the English courts took on this responsibility with the idea of protecting property from any sort of threat and if the law provided for no other defense. In the United States however, the injunction was actually not used much, if at all, until 1877, when courts of equity issued injunctions to stop striking railroad workers. But the use of the injunction prior to Pullman had little if any far-reaching affects. For instance on March 26, 1886, Charles Bruschke, an Illinois furniture maker, obtained an injunction against his striking workers. On April 2, both sides appeared before the court to argue their case, with Bruschke winning a permanent injunction on May 20. Nevertheless the use of the injunction was not very widespread at this time.

In the United States if an immediate threat to property is seen, the courts will issue a temporary restraining order, a move that does not place blame on either side. If no further relief is seen, a temporary injunction will be issued to allow further investigation into the case. After viewing both sides, a judge may decide that more protection is needed and issue a permanent injunction.

However when it came to labor disputes, this path was rarely if ever taken. Courts tended to issue an injunction straight away. The problem concerning labor activities is that of time. When an injunction is issued, a hearing is scheduled for a later date. For a union, or a group of workers conducting a strike, this puts them in a precarious situation. Should they obey the injunction, they will lose the momentum of the strike. Should they disobey, they will be in contempt of court and face possible jail time.

Many labor groups and individuals protested the use of the injunction. They protested that this action was entirely judge-made law. There was no jury involved. Furthermore the side on whom the injunction was issued was not allowed to present its case until the hearing; only the petitioner had any access to state its position prior to that time. Also on many occasions, some judges issued blanket injunctions. When doing so many people would be placed under the requirements of the injunction but have no idea as to the situation and would therefore be liable for contempt of court.

The Pullman strike helped to promote the use of the injunction. In protesting wage cuts instituted by the Pullman Company against its workers, the American Railway Union (ARU), which was under the direction of Eugene V. Debs, called for a boycott of Pullman railroad cars to accompany the strike. The Pullman company turned to President Grover Cleveland for assistance. Under the guise of protecting the mails, Cleveland sent in federal troops both to maintain order and to protect the mails and interstate commerce. On the arrival of troops, violence broke out. A federal court issued an injunction against the ARU forbidding any interference with the mails or interstate commerce that the railroads provide, an action that Debs and the ARU ignored. Debs was jailed for contempt of court, and the strike eventually failed.

Once employers saw how the injunction could be used against the labor movement, its use picked up momentum. Ever since the celebrated 1842 Massachusetts case *Commonwealth v. Hunt*, unions had the legal right to exist as long as their purposes were legal. This was a matter of interpretation, especially when it came to the right to strike or conduct a boycott. In conducting strikes and boycotts, courts repeatedly defined and redefined what constituted a legal or illegal activity on the part of labor. The injunction was often used to create these new definitions.

On the other side were those who sought an injunction. A company owner rightfully considered his business his property. Should a labor dispute arise and he was faced with the possibility of a strike preventing him from conducting business, he would also face the loss of income and possibly find himself unable to open his company. An injunction would enable him to continue to use and enjoy his property.

Across the country the argument waged heavily on both sides. The injunction was denounced in the 1896 Democratic platform. Many of the injunction supporters were friends of big business and saw this court action as a way not only to ensure their profits, but also cut deep into labor activities, all while keeping the peace. Some took the middle road and examined injunction usage, distinguishing between proper and improper rulings. And as previously stated, the labor movement saw the injunction as a form of despotism, dictatorship, and harmful to society as a whole.

Writers and labor leaders weighed in heavily on the subject of injunctions. In 1930, Edwin Witt, a noted author and labor law specialist, called injunction judges kings. He argued that unions are painted as lawless when injunctions are ineffective. In 1919, Andrew Furuseth, a prominent national labor leader during the 1920s, argued that injunctions are "revolutionary and destructive of popular government." In 1923, Herbert Bigelow, another prominent labor leader, saw the issue as "a matter of life or death to organized labor." Others thought that injunctions prevented the vital dialog between labor and management that was so urgently needed.

Whenever possible labor organizations went out of their way to point out judges they believed to abuse the power of the injunction. Under the Chicago Federation of Labor (CFL), several judges met with labor's ire. Two particular judges were James Wilkerson and Jesse Baldwin, both of whom were accused of labor baiting. Judge Dennis Sullivan of the Superior Court of Cook County (the county in which the city of Chicago resides) was especially hated by the CFL, who even attempted to use the ballot box to oust him from his position. However Sullivan had the backing of the Chicago Bar Association and was apparently not repugnant to Chicago society and easily won re-election to the bench.

Many states saw the injunction abuses on the part of the courts and worked to pass legislation to curb its use. States like Illinois, Arizona, and New York worked to create legislation that would pass court approval. In many cases the American Federation of Labor (AFL) provided some guidelines and model language for these acts. By 1914, six states had laws that restricted the use of the injunction. Many felt that federal legislation would help in this quest. The first real piece of congressional law that originally seemed to favor labor was the Sherman Antitrust Act of 1890, which was meant to curb corrupt business activities. When the Sherman Act was actually later used against labor, it was strengthened with the Clayton Antitrust Act of 1914, which was dubbed the Magna Carta of labor. In Clayton labor was not deemed a "commodity or article of commerce" and forbade using the injunction unless there might be irreparable harm to property. Strikes, boycotts, and peaceful picketing were protected.

However three U.S. Supreme Court cases in 1921 put all back to square one: *Duplex Printing Press v. Deering, American Steel Foundaries v. Tri-City Trades*, and *Truax v. Corrigan*. *Duplex* involved the issue of secondary boycotts. In this decision the Court held that such boycotts were enjoinable under Clayton, which supposedly protected that very right. In *American Steel Foundaries*, Chief Justice, and former president, William Howard Taft applied the commerce clause of the U.S. constitution to uphold an injunction against striking workers, holding that the picketing presented an obstacle to interstate commerce. In *Truax*, an Arizona anti-injunction law, which used wording from the Clayton Act, was tossed out. The Court held that picketing deprived the owners of their property under the due process and equal protection clauses of the Fourteenth Amendment.

Using the Supreme Court decisions as a starting point, especially in light of the invalidation of the Arizona law, many states went back to work to draft new legislation that would apply the standards described in those decisions. Illinois was one such state. A new bill was drafted and submitted to the legislature in 1925. This bill provided sweeping rights for unions to exist, as well as greatly limited the use of the injunction unless there was irreparable harm to property. The bill was made into law. Its supporters knew one more hurdle was awaiting them: Court approval. Almost immediately after the passage of the law, one judge refused to issue an injunction under the language of the act. The law was not officially reviewed until the 1934 Illinois case of *Fenske Brothers v. Upholsterers International Union*. The Illinois Supreme Court found the law to be constitutional.

Opponents of the injunction knew that strong federal legislation was needed. On February 7, 1928, the U.S. Senate Judiciary Committee began to hold hearings concerning a federal bill. As with legislation on the state level, injunction opponents were looking for wording that would stand the test of constitutionality.

The dream of federal legislation became reality in 1932 with the Norris-LaGuardia Federal Anti-Injunction Act. This law spelled out "the public policy of the United States with respect to Employer-Employee relations." In this new law, federal courts were forbidden from using the injunction to sustain anti-union employment contracts or to prevent such activities as strikes, pickets, and boycotts. The act also addressed the "inequality of bargaining power between employers and employees" by limiting the court power to intervene in labor disputes. However while Norris-LaGuardia may have limited legal powers in some areas, in others labor organizations were still liable for civil suits and criminal activities.

Norris-LaGuardia was passed on the eve of the New Deal, a period that provided a great many legal benefits to organized labor. However in 1947, Congress passed the Taft-Hartley Act. At one point Congress considered repealing Norris-LaGuardia completely in order to allow courts to issue injunctions in case striking workers violated a no-strike clause. While repealing the law did not happen, Taft-Hartley did restrict many of the gains given to labor during the previous decade. The General Counsel of the National Labor Relations Board (NLRB) was required to seek an injunction against either unions or employers who violated the act, as well as obtaining an injunction against a secondary boycott.

In the early twenty-first century, the injunction issue is not a very prominent one. But for the period starting from the late nineteenth century through the post-World War II years, eradicating its use was indeed a major problem for the U.S. labor movement.

MITCHELL NEWTON-MATZA

References and Further Reading

Beckner, Earl. *A History of Labor Legislation in Illinois.* Chicago, IL: University of Chicago Press, 1929.

Brissenden, Paul. "The Campaign against the Labor Injunction." *American Economic Review* 23 (Mar. 1933): 42–54.

Donovan, Paul. "Legislation Affecting Labor Injunctions." *American Association Bar Journal* 16 (Sept. 1930): 561–563.

Forbath, William E. *Law and the Shaping of the American Labor Movement.* Cambridge, MA: Harvard University Press, 1991.

Frankfurter, Felix, and Greene, Nathan. *The Labor Injunction.* New York: Macmillan Company, 1930.

Friedman, Lawrence. *A History of American Law.* New York: Simon and Schuster, 1985.

Hall, Kermit. *The Magic Mirror.* New York: Oxford University Press, 1991.

Newton-Matza, Mitchell. "The Crack of the Whip: The Chicago Federation of Labor Battles against the Labor Injunction in the 1920s." *Journal of the Illinois State Historical Society* 93 (spring 2000): 82–107.

Taylor, Benjamin, and Witney, Fred. *U.S. Labor Relations Law.* Englewood Cliffs, NJ: Prentice Hall, 1992.

Tomlins, Christopher. *The State and the Unions.* Cambridge, UK: Cambridge University Press, 1985.

———. *Law, Labor, and Ideology in the Early American Republic.* New York: Cambridge University Press, 1993.

Tomlins, Christopher L., and King, Andrew J., eds. *Labor Law in America.* Baltimore, MD: Johns Hopkins, 1992.

Witte, Edwin E. "Social Consequences of Injunctions in Labor Disputes." *Illinois Law Review* 24 (Mar. 1930): 772–785.

Cases and Statutes Cited

American Steel Foundaries v. Tri-City Trades, 257 U.S. 184 (1921).

Duplex Printing Press Co. v. Deering, 254 U.S. 443 (1921).

Fenske Brothers v. Upholsterers' International Union of North America, 358 Ill. 239 (1934).

See also **Commonwealth v. Hunt; Norris-LaGuardia Federal Anti-Injunction Act; Pullman Strike and Boycott (1894)**

INTERNATIONAL ASSOCIATION OF MACHINISTS AND AEROSPACE WORKERS

From its underground beginnings in 1888, the International Association of Machinists and Aerospace Workers (IAMAW) has grown into a membership of over 730,000 in various North American industries. Along the way the union has won important rights for workers, including better pensions, stable health care through retirement, safe working conditions, and job security.

The Founding of a Union

On May 5, 1888, Thomas Wilson Talbot, a machinist in an Atlanta, Georgia, railway yard, gathered 18 of his fellow workers for a clandestine meeting in a railroad pit. Believing that railroad machinists needed a union to cope with problems particular to their craft, this small group formed the Order of United Machinists and Mechanical Engineers. The order, formed during a time when employers were often hostile to organized labor, remained underground for several years. Despite its secrecy the order spread beyond Georgia, thanks in part to the "boomers," men who traveled the railway lines for work. The boomers established local lodges in areas where they were not already present. Within 1 year there were 40 lodges; by 1891, there were 189.

With 34 locals represented, the first convention of the order was held on May 6, 1889, in the Georgia Senate chamber in Atlanta. Tom Talbot was elected grand master machinist (later known as the international president), and William L. Dawley was elected grand secretary (now known as the grand secretary-treasurer). The organization's name was changed to the National Association of Machinists, and a constitution was drawn up. It was also agreed that a journal, *Machinists Monthly Journal*, would be published monthly consisting of "no less than sixteen pages."

Also during the 1889 convention, the machinists sought a design for a union emblem. The winning entry was submitted by Frank French, representing Lodge 12 in Houston, Texas. The figures on the design were a flywheel, friction joint caliper, and the machinist's square with the initials of the organization in between the spokes of the flywheel. French's design featured symbols important to the members: "The flywheel is significant because it generates a lot of power once it gets started." French also explained that the calipers signified "that we extend an invitation to all persons of civilized countries who are practical machinists. The square signifies that we are square and honest."

Delegates of the second Grand Lodge Convention also adopted a secret code, known as the Russian Prison Knock Cipher, to be distributed to the membership. The code's purpose was to help machinists communicate with one another when organizing or on other union business. For many years officers and representatives of the IAMAW had no way of quickly communicating from one locality to another except by telegram. In many places the only telegraph office in town was in the railroad depot. This meant that the primary employers of IAM members, the railroads, could review union messages. At least to the eve of World War I, cards bearing new secret traveling passwords were reissued to officers and representatives every 6 months.

In 1890 and 1891, the machinists' union reached out to its first international members as a Canadian local was founded in Stratford, Ontario. Locals were also formed in Mexico. Consequently the name of the union was changed at the 1891 convention in Pittsburgh, Pennsylvania, to the International Association of Machinists. The international headquarters were moved to Richmond, Virginia, around this same time.

The IAMAW along with the boilermakers and blacksmiths signed a contract with the Atchison, Topeka & Santa Fe railroad in 1892. This was the first agreement entered into in the United States between a railroad company and an organized shop craft.

Acceptance of application into American Federation of Labor (AFL) affiliation would have been automatic were it not for the color bar, which went back to the IAMAW's southern beginnings. One of Thomas Talbot's primary objectives in working to establish this union had been to restore and enhance the image of machinists as aristocrats of labor. From the first membership was strictly limited to an exclusive fraternity of white male machinists. This meant no production workers, no specialists, no women, and no blacks. At the 1895 convention, the word black was removed from the constitution. That same year the IAMAW relocated its headquarters to Chicago, Illinois, and became affiliated with the AFL.

After a successful strike, Local Lodge 52 in Pittsburgh negotiated the IAMAW's first 9-hour day contract in 1898. In October 1899, many Canadian members won a 9-hour day after a 10-day strike against the Canadian Pacific Railroad. This also included a raise in minimum wage. By 1915, the IAMAW lobbied successfully for an 8-hour workday, increased wages, and improvement to work conditions in many shops and factories. They were especially successful in New England.

On the move again, the machinists established their headquarters in Washington, DC, in 1899. By the turn of the century, the young union had become an international organization that had grown to include 450 local lodges with a membership of 35,000.

Shortly thereafter IAMAW International President James O'Connell signed an agreement with the National Metal Trades' Association (NMTA), a group representing company owners' and employers' interests. Known as the Murray Hill Agreement, this contract provided there would be no discrimination against union labor, defined machinist in the terms of the IAMAW Constitution, stipulated extra pay for overtime, adopted an apprenticeship ratio, and most importantly, promised to put a 54-hour week into effect May 1, 1901, 1 year from the signing of the contract. One year after the agreement was signed however, the NMTA refused to pay workers the same pay for fewer hours per week, beginning 35 years of labor-management antagonism.

In 1911, the IAMAW began allowing some new types of workers into its ranks. Since its beginnings the IAMAW had been primarily composed of skilled, white, male railroad workers. In that year they changed their constitution to allow unskilled machinists as well as female workers. Women had been accepted into the IAMAW membership for some time despite language to the contrary in the constitution. James O'Connell pointed out, "We have female members . . . because of [union shop] agreements." By 1948, IAMAW membership was opened to all regardless of race or gender.

On June 28, 1915, the great strikes on the Illinois Central Railroad, the Harriman Lines, and the Pere Marquette Railroad were terminated. These strikes, in progress for more than 3 years, had been maintained at a tremendous cost to both organized labor and the railroad companies. This same year the union affiliated with the International Metalworkers' Federation. One year later automobile mechanics were admitted to the membership.

Changes in the Ranks: The War Years

During World War I, the Machinists' membership had reached 300,000, making it the largest union in the nation in 1918. However as the war ended and wartime production ceased, IAMAW membership sharply dropped off, plummeting to 80,000 by 1923. The situation worsened during the Great Depression: By 1933, membership was at only 50,000, and 23,000 of those workers were unemployed. The 1930s and 1940s did see new laws passed to help get the unemployed back to work under Franklin D. Roosevelt's New Deal and with industrial production for World War II. The jobs however decreased again with the end of the war and returning anti-union sentiment.

During the 1944 Grand Lodge Convention, delegates voted to establish an Education Department as well as a newspaper. President Harvey W. Brown persuaded the delegates to support publishing a supplement to the *Journal*. This would be a weekly IAMAW newspaper, the *Machinist*. Eventually the *Journal*'s production was cut back to twice a year, and then it was voted out of existence in 1956. The *Machinist* was closed down in 1994. It was replaced with a quarterly magazine, the *IAMAW Journal*, which is still in publication today.

The IAMAW disaffiliated with the AFL in 1945. This break was over the failure of the AFL to settle a jurisdictional dispute between the IAMAW and the United Brotherhood of Carpenters and Joiners of America, the Amalgamated Association of Street and Electric Railway Employees of America, and the International Union of Operating Engineers. The machinists argued that the AFL was assisting and encouraging these unions to trespass on the jurisdiction and raid the membership.

In 1947, Congress passed the Taft-Hartley Act (officially known as the Labor-Management Relations Act), which placed restrictions on union activities (specifically, it contained provisions that made closed shops illegal and outlawed secondary boycotts). Section 14(b), the most controversial, allowed states to pass right-to-work laws, which would enable them to regulate the number of union shops. The machinists worked with other AFL unions to repeal the act but to no avail. Because of the limitations imposed on union political activity by this act, the Machinists' Non-Partisan Political League was founded. Despite these reverses, the railroad machinists did manage to win a 40-hour workweek in 1949.

Postwar Years

Beginning in 1935 the machinists started organizing within the airline industry and won several victories. In 1936, the Boeing Company in Seattle, Washington, signed the industry's first labor agreement. By 1938, the IAMAW negotiated the first union agreement in air transportation with Eastern Air Lines.

In 1948, Lodge 751 went on strike in Seattle, Washington, against the Boeing Company. For the machinists the issues were preserving longstanding seniority rules that the company wanted to abolish and achieving a 10% per hour raise for all categories of labor. On strike for 4 months, the machinists went back to work under the terms set by the National Labor Relations Board. The IAMAW joined the International Transport Workers' Federation in 1950 and re-affiliated with the AFL in January 1951.

When the AFL merged with the Congress of Industrial Organizations (CIO) in 1955, Machinists International President Al Hayes was elected vice-president as well as chairman of the Ethical Practices Committee for the new organization. The shift of the IAMAW had changed the composition from skilled craftsmen into essentially an industrial union. The bulk of the membership had moved from the railroads to the metal-fabrication industry, with aircraft industry workers composing the largest component of the workers. From new worksites and plants in California down to Cape Canaveral (later Cape Kennedy) in Florida, aerospace workers began joining the IAMAW.

By 1964, the IAMAW changed its name yet again, this time to the International Association of Machinists and Aerospace Workers. The newly named union was able to shut down most of the airline industry 2 years later by striking against five major airlines in the business, including Eastern, National, Northwest, Trans World, and United Airlines. A united effort of 35,400 IAMAW members in 231 cities grounded the airlines for 43 days, finally winning 5% raises in three successive years as well as a cost-of-living escalator. The great airline strike of 1966 also led to President Lyndon B. Johnson eliminating the 3.2% limit on pay raises. This benefited both the public and private sectors by eliminating the cap on pay raises.

After 1970, several new departments were added to headquarters to meet members' needs as well as mirror the diversity of the members that formed the union. These included the Departments of Civil Rights (1976), Organizing (1976), Older Workers and Retired Members (1981), Women (1996), Automotive (2002), and Employment Services (2003).

At the 1984 convention in Seattle, Washington, delegates voted to fund the Placid Harbor Education Center in Maryland to train and educate members of the union as well as "to improve the level of understanding of workers in an ever-changing world." This center was later renamed the William W. Winpisinger Education and Technology Center in 1998 to honor the late international president.

The Late Twentieth Century and Beyond

In 1991, the Pattern Makers' League of North America merged with the machinists. The International Woodworkers of America would do the same in 1994. The IAMAW, the United Auto Workers (UAW), and the United Steelworkers of America in 1995 debated plans for unification by the year 2000. This unity plan would have created the largest, most diverse union in North America, with more than 2,000,000 active members and 1,400,000 retirees. However by 1999 the unification effort with the steelworkers and the UAW ended because of major philosophical differences. During the same year, the National Federation of Federal Employees affiliated with the IAMAW. In the twenty-first century, the union represents more than 200 industries and has become a large and diverse organization.

PAMELA HACKBART-DEAN

References and Further Reading

International Association of Machinists' Digital Publications." http://dlib.gsu.edu/spcoll/IAMAW/index.asp (2005).

Rodden, Robert G. *The Fighting Machinists: A Century of Struggle*. Washington, DC: Kelly Press, Inc., 1984.

See also **Taft-Hartley Act**

INTERNATIONAL BROTHERHOOD OF ELECTRICAL WORKERS

The International Brotherhood of Electrical Workers (IBEW) traces its roots to a convention of electrical workers held in a small room above Stolley's Dance Hall in St. Louis, Missouri. On November 21, 1891, 10 delegates representing 300 electrical workers in cities throughout the Midwest named their fledging organization the National Brotherhood of Electrical Workers (NBEW). Henry Miller was elected grand president at this first convention, and he immediately sought recognition by the American Federation of Labor (AFL). The federation acknowledged the need to organize the growing electrical industry and issued a national charter to the NBEW on December 7, 1891. In 1899, with the establishment of a local union in Ottawa, Canada, the organization formally became the IBEW.

The road to that historic meeting at Stolley's Dance Hall began in the 1840s when electricity left the experimental realm of the laboratory and was put to a practical commercial purpose in the form of the telegraph. Carried by wires strung on poles, the popularity of real-time communication over great distances spawned the new breed of construction workers referred to as linemen. These linemen led a nomadic life creating the spider web of telegraph lines across the continent. As more and more linemen were needed in the quest to connect coast to coast and city to city, there was no shortage of men attracted to this new and exciting opportunity for work and travel.

The second-half of the nineteenth century saw the emergence of many unions centered on individual crafts, and during the early years of the specialization of the electrical workers trade, there had been various attempts to organize linemen unions in particular cities and localities without much success. The fact that new telegraph lines were always emanating into new territories meant the workers were an itinerate and isolated workforce. However by 1880, there was enough support and communication among linemen to reach out for affiliation with the Knights of Labor, and while this relationship held for a while, an 1883 failed strike against the Western Union telegraph company subsequently broke up the first fledging union of electrical workers.

The failure of the strike did not dampen the urge to organize, and in 1884, a group of linemen, under the cloak of secrecy for fear of their loss of a job, formed a secret organization called the United Order of Linemen. Headquartered in Denver, this group did attain success organizing linemen in the midwestern and western states. However it was at the St. Louis Exposition of 1890 and the widely announced plan for the Expo to display to the world the wonders of electricity that provided, for the first time, a large project where electrical workers from across the country could work in one place for a prolonged period of time. Discussions among the electrical workers from different parts of the country highlighted the differences in pay and the general lack of safety measures, and these informal bull sessions became the spawning ground culminating in that first convention above Stolley's Dance Hall.

The 10 delegates at that first convention had set a far-reaching agenda, and during their convocation they composed a constitution, established a dues and per capita structure, planned for a death-and-strike benefit, and limited strike activity to only that sanctioned by national officers. Realizing that their dream of a better and safer life depended on increasing the membership, the delegates made organizing all workers in the electrical industry their primary goal. When the convention did adjourn, the delegates returned home flushed with vigor to carry the message to the unorganized in their respective cities. Some, like President Miller, went on the road traveling across the United States helping to set up locals and bring in new members wherever electrical work was being done.

The next convention in Chicago in 1892 saw the head count rise to over 43 local unions and an official membership of about 2,000. This convention also welcomed the first female telephone operators to become members and authorized the publication of a national magazine called the *Electrical Worker,* which has been published continuously under various names since the first issue in January of 1893.

While the majority of the early membership was concentrated in telegraph and telephone distribution, there was also another dynamic arising in the electrical industry. The growth of electrical power generators to provide electric street lighting and the much-desired electric lamps for use inside buildings produced electrical workers known as inside wiremen. With this new classification came new safety concerns and differing pay schedules, which needed to be addressed differently from linemen. A severe depression during the mid-1890s tested the bonds of brotherhood, but the union prevailed and entered the twentieth century claiming 24,000 members in 1905.

Several hardships that were holding back the IBEW from reaching its full potential were addressed early in the new century. The union had been struggling without a full-time, paid leadership that it needed to deal effectively with outbreaks of unauthorized strikes. The 1903 convention in Salt Lake City brought about the election and provision to pay a full-time salary to Frank J. McNulty as grand president. Given the opportunity to devote himself fulltime to the business of running an international organization, McNulty proved to be a strong leader effectively putting an end to wildcat strikes and restoring credibility with employers regarding contract obligations.

McNulty's 18 years as president were not without conflict. The long-simmering differences and dissensions between linemen and inside wiremen came to a head in 1908 with a large number of members rejecting the leadership of McNulty and holding their own convention, electing J. J. Reid as president. At one point the rebellious faction numbered almost three-fourths of the membership and rejected all initial efforts of the AFL to reconcile the opposing groups. It took a court decision in 1912 that declared the fractious convention of 1908 illegal and that all its actions were to be voided before the rebellious members would heed the AFL effort of reunification under President McNulty with no penalties to those who had seceded.

The Twentieth Century: Growth, Decline, Resurgence—Carrying the Union Torch

After full reunification membership rapidly began to increase. Most important to the growth of the union was the approach of World War I and the demand it put on the electrical industry. The effort to prepare the country possibly to be on the international war stage prompted the federal government to work with the IBEW and electrical contractors. The IBEW trained inside electricians, and linemen were hired through bona fide electrical contractors to build the military training camps, the arsenals, the navy yards, and even the Panama Canal. In 1917, the federal government took over the railroads, and 90% of the electrical workforce on the railroads joined the IBEW. In 1918, the National War Labor Board (NWLB) was established and endorsed the right to organize, leading many electricians employed in private-sector manufacturing to become IBEW members, and from 1913–1919, the membership exploded from 23,500 to 148,000 members.

The post-WWI United States brought hard times to all in the labor movement. Employers throughout the construction trades became enamored with the open-shop movement. An all out effort to break union influences over work rules was launched by anti-union forces, resulting in prohibitive legislation and antilabor court injunctions. Strike-breaking activities and terrorizing of members and potential members became common practice, and this combined with a depression in 1920–1921, led to IBEW membership dropping to 56,349 in 1925, a decrease of 70% in only 6 years.

Despite a decline in membership, the 1920s were still a time of great foresight for the IBEW. In 1920, the Council of Industrial Relations (CIR) came into existence as a compact between the IBEW and the National Electrical Contractors' Association (NECA). This agreement mandated representatives of employees and employers meet and discuss disputes arising in the industry and to abide by the mutually determined decisions and effectively eliminated strikes in the industry.

The 1920s also saw the formation of the Electrical Workers' Benefit Association in 1922 and the restructuring of the death benefit for union electricians. In 1928, the IBEW Pension Plan was instituted.

The IBEW suffered during the Great Depression, and financial difficulties resulted in canceling conventions from 1929–1941. Economic distress was felt throughout the industry and throughout the union. Officers' and representatives' salaries were cut, and some staff were laid off. However IBEW membership never dropped below 50,000 while other unions were forced out of existence.

New Deal legislation beneficial to workers affected the IBEW in a positive way by emphasizing the right of all workers to organize. However industrial semiskilled electricians did not have the training to stand side-by-side with IBEW trained construction electricians and linemen. This led to a protectionist attitude by long-time IBEW members, and this perceived arrogance was seen by industrial electricians as an indifference to their concerns. By the time the IBEW became ready to enjoin these workers, the United Electrical, Radio, and Machine Workers of America (UE) had filled the void. When John L. Lewis, leader of the newly established Committee for Industrial Organizations, endorsed the UE, the goal of the IBEW to enroll all electrical workers was thwarted.

As before the First World War, the buildup of the war effort saw great expansion in all phases of electrical work. Industrial production and electrical construction and distribution soared as the military relied on all things electrical and on the fledgling electronic infusion. Realizing the importance of labor in the war effort, Roosevelt appointed Daniel Tracy, IBEW international president (1933–1940, 1947–1954), to serve as assistant secretary of labor, thus guaranteeing organized labor would be a major player. Tracy worked hard to assure labor peace and harmony with the war effort and helped to craft a no-strike policy, wage-stabilization programs, and concessions on premium pay.

The economic stimulus leading up to WW II and continuing through the war years brought a large increase in IBEW membership. The IBEW membership grew from 50,000 in 1933 to 347,000 by the end of the war, picking up many utility, manufacturing, and government employees.

The Taft-Hartley Act of 1947 made organizing new members much more of a struggle for all of organized labor. However in 1947, training of electrical workers took on a new importance, and the IBEW-NECA National Joint Apprenticeship and Training Committee was established and became the major conduit of new workers coming into the industry.

During the postwar years the IBEW was forced to take a look at its policy concerning hiring of minorities. Historically the organization was overwhelmingly white. Through its history the union did have a legitimate contention that the transient nature of the work situation caused members to travel throughout the country and into racially segregated cities where work for blacks could not be guaranteed. However this statement could no longer hold as the civil rights movement drove down segregating laws.

The IBEW did not rush to hire minorities as either journeymen or as apprentices, but much of this resulted from a strong unwritten sentiment toward nepotism. The union did promote opening all aspects of membership to minorities during the early sixties in order to meet government standards for apprenticeships. However it took individual locals, such as New York City Local 3, to lead the way in demonstrating that minorities could become productive workers and good union members.

The second-half of the twentieth century saw a large decline of organized labor membership brought on by anti-union entities and right-to-work laws. The establishment of trade schools and nonunion electrical-training programs during the 1970s and 1980s specifically hurt IBEW recruitment efforts. In the early 1990s, the IBEW launched the Construction Organizing Membership Education Training (COMET) program. This aggressive organizing campaign became the model for organized labor and has been highly successful for all the skilled trades.

In 2005, IBEW membership stands at approximately 750,000. Union members are comprised predominantly of inside and outside electrical workers; utility workers; workers in cable broadcasting, radio and television, motion picture and telecommunications, railroad, manufacturing, and government.

The IBEW is headquartered in Washington, DC, and holds national conventions every 5 years. Principle officers are the international president, international secretary-treasurer, 11 international vice-presidents and a nine-member international executive committee.

MICHAEL V. DOYLE

References and Further Reading

Fink, Gary M., editor-in-chief. *Labor Unions*. Westport, CT: Greenwood Press, 1977.
IBEW staff. Who We Are: History. http://ibew.org/history/index.htm
Mulcaire, Michael A. "The International Brotherhood of Electrical Workers: A Study in Trade Union Structure and Functions." Ph.D. dissertation, Catholic University of America, 1923.
Palladino, Grace. *Dreams of Dignity, Workers of Vision*. Washington, DC: International Brotherhood of Electrical Workers, 1991.

INTERNATIONAL BROTHERHOOD OF RED CAPS/UNITED TRANSPORT SERVICE EMPLOYEES OF AMERICA

Founded in 1937, the International Brotherhood of Red Caps (IBRC), which changed its name to the United Transport Service Employees of America (UTSEA) in 1940, represented a largely unskilled occupational group dominated by African-Americans in an industry that was marked by pronounced racial divisions. Initially an interracial association affiliated with the American Federation of Labor (AFL) as a federal union (that is, affiliated directly to the AFL,

not to any of its constituent international unions), the IBRC became an all-black union shortly after its establishment; it soon disaffiliated in protest from the AFL and after 5 years as an independent body, joined the Congress of Industrial Organizations (CIO) in 1942. Possessing no critical skills enabling them to pressure their employers effectively in their workplaces, red caps relied almost exclusively on publicity and the federal government—in particular the courts and the administrative agencies overseeing labor relations in the railroad industry—to win contracts, wage increases, and improvements in working conditions.

The job category of red cap emerged only in the early 1890s. According to legend, a black teenager, James H. Williams, signaled his availability to carry passengers' bags at New York's Grand Central Station by affixing a piece of red flannel to his cap. Within several years, numerous stations were employing groups of station porters to deliver luggage to and from railroad passenger cars. While smaller stations employed only a few men, larger ones, such as Grand Central Station in New York City, placed as many as 500 men on their payroll by the mid-1930s. A U.S. Department of Labor study in 1942 estimated that 3,787 men worked as red caps throughout the country, while another 316 nonredcaps sometimes carried baggage. The employment status and job responsibilities of the red caps remained varied. In some stations, they performed janitorial services, while in others they focused exclusively on baggage carrying.

The men who secured jobs as red caps were a heterogeneous group by the early twentieth century. Although whites and a small number of Japanese worked as baggage carriers, African-Americans numerically dominated the job category. If the overall labor force was racially mixed, individual railroad stations tended to employ members of only one racial group. Requiring only a strong back and little formal skill, the job attracted men with little formal education, highly educated but unemployed black professionals, and black college students in search of money, especially during periods of high-seasonal travel or summer breaks.

Red cap wages and working conditions had been sources of complaint prior to their unionization in the 1930s. In rare instances red caps were salaried employees, but in many other cases they survived on gratuities alone. The Great Depression diminished the willingness or ability of rail passengers to tip generously. With no salaries, seniority rights, or grievance procedures, red caps experimented unsuccessfully with unionization during and after World War I. As one observer put it, red caps' bargaining position was extremely weak: If "every Red Cap in the Grand Central Station resigned," he noted, "they could be replaced by double the amount of men within 24 hours."

The upsurge in unionization during the 1930s in general, and the widely publicized efforts of the Brotherhood of Sleeping Car Porters in particular, provided the impetus for successful red cap unionization. In January 1937, an interracial group of Chicago red cap activists launched a unionizing campaign and founded the Brotherhood of Railroad Depot, Bus Terminal, Airport and Dock Red Caps, Attendants and Porters, which become AFL federal Local 20342. Blacks and whites divided leadership positions, with a white red cap serving as president and a black one, Willard S. Townsend, as vice-president. Seeking to build a larger organization, the local sponsored a multicity gathering in May 1937. The election of Townsend, an African-American, to the presidency of this larger body prompted the withdrawal of most white delegates, who eventually sought affiliation with the all-white Brotherhood of Railway Clerks. Second-class status within the AFL proved unacceptable to the black unionists, who withdrew their new organization from the federation to pursue an independent course of organizing red caps across the nation. At a conference held in January 1930, some 60 delegates representing as many as 4,000 workers officially founded the IBRC.

Over the next several years, the IBRC made civil rights and black equality a central tenet in its struggle for legitimacy. In fending off the jurisdictional claims of the white clerks' union, which insisted that all station workers—including freight handlers, janitors, and red caps—fell under its control, red caps charged their white challenger with outright discrimination and exclusion. A 1940 court decision awarding red caps in St. Paul, Minnesota, to the IBRC, according to one labor journalists, "struck the shackles of jim crow unionism from the legs of the Negro railroad worker and sounded the death knell for discriminatory practices which have enthroned prejudice in the railroad industry." That assessment, while incorrect, captured the spirit with which red cap activists framed their crusade. But when given a choice, station porters, objecting to the clerks' "color bar," overwhelmingly chose the IBRC in representation elections.

Their weak bargaining power in the labor market pushed red caps into a heavy dependence upon the federal government and the labor relations machinery enacted during the New Deal years. The first crucial step was to secure government recognition of its members' right to organize and bargain collectively. Managers of railroad stations claimed that red caps were not in fact railroad employees but technically were rather "privileged trespassers" or independent contractors working for tips. That definition of red caps' employment status if upheld would deprive them of access to the labor relations machinery—the National Adjustment Administration and the National Railroad Adjustment Boards—established under the terms of the Railway Labor Act of 1934. In late 1937 and 1938, the IBCR undertook a March Forward to Job Legality campaign, spearheaded by the union's white attorney, reformer Leon Despres, to convince the Interstate Commerce Commission (ICC) that red caps were bona fide railway employees. In September 1938, the ICC ruled in the red caps' favor, finding that the black workers' "'independent' status was wholly fictitious." Officially designated railroad employees, red caps now invoked the services of the governmental National Mediation Board to conduct union representation elections in numerous stations across the country, elections that the IBRC overwhelmingly won. In the contract negotiations that ensued in the late 1930s and early 1940s, the IBRC won grievance procedures and work rule improvements but few financial gains. Resorting to the newly passed Fair Labor Standards Act of 1938, red caps attempted to secure a minimum wage, which promised to be an economic boon for the majority of red caps working only for wages. Managers at over 200 railway stations responded by instituting a new "accounting and guarantee" system, which included gratuities as part of a red caps' salary as a means of evading the new law. The IBCR's court challenges to the system ultimately proved ineffective, as did its attempts to block a 10-cent-a-bag fee imposed by stations on passengers.

The IBRC's track record was a mixed one. The U.S. Department of Labor's Wage and Hour Division concluded in a 1941 study that unionization had brought observable improvements to red caps in the realm of seniority rights, a decrease in working hours, the elimination of the 7-day week, modest wage gains, and inclusion under unemployment compensation and retirement laws. The union had also successfully blocked the white clerks' union's effort to absorb and dominate black red caps in a racial, inequitable union structure. In 1942, the UTSEA's affiliation with the CIO provided it with an organizational platform from which to protest racial discrimination. On affiliation UTSEA President Willard S. Townsend was appointed to the CIO's executive board, the first black American to hold that position.

That limited success could not prevent the decline of red capping jobs. From the late 1940s through 1960s, railroad stations relied less and less on red caps' services. Rising baggage fees discouraged passengers from using station porters, while the long-term decline in railroad passenger traffic on account of competition from busses, cars, and planes decreased demand further. By 1955, one observer noted, rail passengers found "the search for the familiar red cap of a porter a desperate one." The advent of two-wheeled baggage carts and "Do-It-Yourself" plans in the mid 1950s displaced even more red caps. By 1972, the UTSEA, which then claimed only 1,700 members, merged with its former rival.

ERIC ARNESEN

References and Further Reading

Arnesen, Eric. *Brotherhoods of Color: Black Railroad Workers and the Struggle for Equality*. Cambridge, MA: Harvard University Press, 2001.
———. "Willard S. Townsend: Black Workers, Civil Rights, and the Labor Movement." In Nina Mjagkij, ed. *Portraits of African American Life Since 1865*. Scholarly Resources, 2003.

See also **Brotherhood of Sleeping Car Porters; Railway Labor Acts**

INTERNATIONAL BROTHERHOOD OF TEAMSTERS

Historically the International Brotherhood of Teamsters (IBT) has been one of the most powerful and most controversial of unions in the United States. Its power has stemmed from the union's strategic position in the transportation industry. The controversy has resulted from recurring charges of corruption against the union's leadership. Those charges reflect systemic factors in the union's jurisdiction and its governance that have encouraged corruption and undercut reform. But the corruption charges also often resulted from concerns by anti-union forces about this labor organization's strategic power. Some teamster officials have engaged in corrupt actions that betrayed the interests of the membership, but union opponents also used the label of corruption to tar aggressive union tactics that did not constitute a betrayal of union members.

Early Union History

The origins of the IBT lie in the growth of the teaming industry in the latter part of the nineteenth century.

Teamsters drove horse-pulled wagons, and in the growing cities of that era, they played a central role in the urban transportation network. The increasing scale of the teaming industry encouraged efforts at union organization, which took place at the local level in a number of cities in the late 1800s. The American Federation of Labor (AFL) worked to gather these local organizations into a new national union, and as a result, seven local leaders came together at the 1898 AFL convention to sign a national union charter creating the Team Drivers' International Union (TDIU), the organizational predecessor to the IBT. The union's first president was a Detroit teamster named George Innis.

The early years of this new national teamsters' union were marked by rapid growth and internal dissension. Partly by organizing new locals and partly by bringing existing local unions into the TDIU, the new union quickly grew to include 30,000 members by 1901. In many places, such as Chicago, team owners were encouraged to cooperate with the new union in return for its help in allowing them to control competition. Team owners would form an association that agreed to a closed contract with a local in exchange for the local policing the association's cartel arrangements. Intent on building a large union, TDIU leaders adopted an inclusive organizing strategy that welcomed African-Americans, recent immigrants, and even small-scale employers. The TDIU's constitution made team owners who employed less than five teams and who drove a wagon themselves eligible for membership. The inclusion of those employers generated dissension within TDIU, and in 1901 a secession movement resulted in the creation of a rival organization, the Teamsters' National Union (TNU). The AFL brokered a resolution of the conflict that allowed self-employed teamsters, but not employers, to remain members, and in 1903 TDIU and TNU merged to form the IBT.

The new organization's first president was Cornelius Shea, a Boston teamster, whose leadership generated much controversy. Shea led the union into a sympathetic strike against Montgomery Ward and Company in Chicago in the spring of 1905. The Chicago Employers' Association (CEA) joined this conflict on the side of Montgomery Ward and sought to use the strike to break the union's power in Chicago. Charges of corruption emerged as the CEA encouraged the state prosecutor's office to launch an investigation into the union's leadership. The investigation sought to link Shea to a local strike broker, John Driscoll, and also publicized salacious details regarding the teamster leader's private life. The strike ended in a draw, but Shea's reputation and that of the union's had been badly tarnished. Over the next

City employees picket City Hall/World Telegram photo by Dick DeMarsico. Library of Congress, Prints & Photographs Division, NYWT & S Collection [LC-USZ62-126870].

2 years, Shea stifled efforts within the union to unseat him, and as a result reformers turned to secession movements, most notably in 1906 with the formation of the United Teamsters of America (UTA). This internal dissension along with legal problems that stemmed from the 1905 Chicago strike brought the union to the brink of bankruptcy. In 1907, a reform candidate, Daniel Tobin, defeated Shea's effort for reelection. Tobin's victory marked a limited reform achievement. While Shea was ousted, Tobin found his ability to clean up particular problem locals in New York and Chicago limited. Faced with the threat of Tobin's intervention, local leaders simply pulled their organizations out of the national union, and in this way, the same tactic of secession proved equally useful to reformers and their opponents.

Transitional Era, 1910s to 1930s

A conservative union leader who described the IBT as "a business institution" that "must be run on business lines," Tobin led the union from 1907 to 1952. His leadership brought stability and financial health to the IBT. Tobin convinced the UTA to end its secession, and by 1915 the IBT had recovered from the membership losses of the previous decade. Over the next two decades, membership continued to grow at a steady pace reaching 90,000 by 1930. Carefully guarding the union's finances by discouraging local leaders from engaging in precipitous strikes, Tobin built the treasury up to $2.5 million by 1935. The union's constitution championed a democratic structure that sheltered local union autonomy, but Tobin circumvented those constraints. He built a strong hold over the organization through a network of loyal regional leaders who held the office of international representative. The international representatives owed their position to Tobin and dutifully represented him in their regions, intervening frequently in local union affairs and directing the union's frontlines during its conflicts with employers and other unions.

During these same years, the growth of the motor-trucking industry changed the nature of the union's core constituency. Firms hauling freight began to shift over to motor trucks in the first decade of the twentieth century, but the second decade marked a watershed in this transition. By 1930, according to

Tobin, 70% of the union's members drove motor vehicles, and horse-drawn wagons were becoming anachronisms. Trucking in this era was mostly short-haul, but to the extent that a long-haul interstate-trucking industry had emerged by the late 1920s and early 1930s, Tobin urged local union leaders to organize the drivers in this new industry.

Tobin's rhetoric, which celebrated a conservative craft-conscious ideal of unionism, conflicted with his aggressive policies in broadening the union's jurisdiction. Under Tobin's leadership, the IBT brought in categories of workers in various industries who did not drive but whose membership in the union would increase the organization's strategic position. The teamsters in this era laid claim to, among others, stable hands, employees in the ice and dairy industries, gas station attendants, and later warehouse workers. Like other AFL organizations, it became a kind of industrial union built around the organizational needs of its core membership, the drivers. This inclusive policy combined with the union's strategic role in the transportation industry allowed the IBT to take advantage of the more hospitable environment for organizing that emerged in the 1930s and early 1940s. In the same era, regional leaders, such as Dave Beck and Farrell Dobbs, pioneered new tactics that drew on the growing interstate-trucking industry. As a result, the membership ballooned to a half-million members by 1941, and the IBT became the largest union in the United States.

It also became known as one of the most corrupt. A study of union corruption published in 1938 labeled the teamsters "the most racketeer-ridden union in the United States." This notoriety stemmed from a number of factors. The IBT locals often sought to organize business sectors where entrepreneurs engaged in collusive arrangements to control competition. Local union leaders in those sectors convinced employers to accept collective bargaining by agreeing to participate in these collusive arrangements. By the late 1920s, those anticompetitive arrangements, many of which violated antitrust laws, were often described as racketeering. In addition Prohibition had transformed the nature of organized crime groups, which drew on the illegal liquor trade to become better organized and more aggressive over the course of the 1920s. In Chicago, New York, and elsewhere criminal gangs took on the role of regulating collusive arrangements in various industries, and in doing so, they sought to control the local unions involved. The teamsters' strategic role made their local unions frequent targets for criminal gangs. At the same time, opponents of organized labor, alarmed by its growing power, focused much of their attention on the IBT. Critics,

such as the conservative newspaper columnist Westbrook Pegler, used a broad definition of corruption to condemn the teamsters, whose ability to shut down road traffic during legitimate strikes was described as a kind of racketeering. The union's use of secondary boycotts and its participation in sympathy strikes brought similar condemnation.

Transformation of the Union Under Beck and Hoffa

Dave Beck served as president from 1952–1957, and James Hoffa held the office from 1957–1971. Like Tobin, both Beck and Hoffa described the IBT in business terms, and they sought to structure it accordingly. The union provided a service to its members, selling their labor at the highest price possible, and in order to achieve that end, both men saw a limited role for the rank-and-file membership. Instead they wanted union officials who acted as professionals, meaning well-compensated individuals who had accumulated a level of expertise and who would be required to achieve results or face dismissal. To promote this style of governance, the IBT developed layers of regional and industry-specific administration. On the West Coast, Beck had pioneered the creation of statewide joint councils and later a regional body, the Western Conference of Teamsters. In the 1940s and 1950s, at his urging, that same pattern of administration was extended across the rest of the country, which was divided into four large area conferences. At the same time, locals were also integrated into different regional trade divisions according to the kinds of industries in which their members worked. These trade divisions and conferences coordinated organizing campaigns and provided a new level of oversight on local leaders by keeping track of what proportion of their local's industry had been organized. Local leaders who failed to measure up faced the possibility that the national leadership might impose a trusteeship and oust them from office.

The size of the bargaining unit in the trucking industry also steadily grew. Beginning in the upper Midwest, Hoffa worked to bring all of the trucking locals into one national bargaining unit that would sign onto a national master freight agreement with the trucking industry. He achieved that goal in 1964, thus further integrating local unions into a national structure.

These changes created a more effective union administration, but at the cost of decreased local autonomy and by extension decreased union democracy.

The IBT could mount nationwide organizing campaigns that succeeded against stubborn corporate opponents like Montgomery Ward and Company. But areawide bargaining usurped the independent role traditionally played by local leaders in dealing with their local employers. It also left local leaders opposed to the national administration open to a new range of repercussions, including adverse grievance rulings against their membership at the conference level by grievance boards now dominated by the national leadership.

The relentless pressure to organize however also meant that the IBT was relatively open in this era to minorities and women as members. From its earliest years, the teamsters had welcomed African-American members. Historically the union had followed regional customs by having segregated locals in the South and mostly integrated locals in the North. Blacks served as local union officials and attended the union conventions as voting delegates. When racial tensions surfaced during the Chicago teamsters' strike of 1905, the union's leadership admonished white members to remember the valued role played by black teamsters in their union. By the 1930s, Tobin claimed that the IBT had more black members than any other union, and African-Americans probably made up about one-seventh of the membership. Without making a formal announcement, the union's southern locals were integrated in the late 1950s and early 1960s.

Similar to other biracial unions in this era however, the teamsters allowed a range of discriminatory practices to continue, especially at the local level. Many local unions, especially in local delivery and long-haul trucking jurisdictions, excluded African-American members or kept them out of the better jobs. Although about 200 thousand blacks belonged to the IBT by the 1950s, no blacks held office at the national level until the 1970s.

A similar pattern holds true regarding women's membership in the IBT. The union's broadened jurisdiction had resulted in female members as early as the 1930s, and they steadily grew in number in the 1940s and 1950s. By the 1960s, the union estimated that about 80,000 women belonged to the IBT out of a total union membership at the time of 1.7 million. The national leadership promised women equal treatment within the union. But while these women gained a range of benefits from their membership, it remained true that local leaders worked to keep them out of certain jobs and abetted employer practices that resulted in lower pay for women workers.

The IBT had become by the 1950s a diverse union whose 1.5 million members worked in a range of industries from various kinds of light manufacturing, food processing, and warehousing to the organization's more traditional jurisdiction in the trucking industry. Especially in trucking the union brought significant wage benefits to its membership. By 1956, 85% of all local truck drivers were part of a welfare plan through their job, and 50% of them had pension benefits. The IBT was known for its aggressive bargaining and tenacious organizing.

In the late 1950s, the IBT also once again became the center of controversy that stemmed from allegations of corruption. The McClellan Committee (1957–1959) held hearings that publicized charges of malfeasance against Dave Beck, and in the wake of the controversy that resulted, he chose not to run for re-election. The committee mounted a major effort to end Hoffa's career in a similar way but without success. Although it publicized his ties to organized crime figures and it highlighted his tolerance and even support for corrupt local leaders, Hoffa won election to the union presidency in 1957. The AFL-CIO cited the charges against him and the union's unwillingness to oust him as justification for expelling the IBT in 1957. Despite the outside pressures, Hoffa retained a firm grip on his office even after he was sent to jail on mail fraud and witness tampering charges in 1967. As with earlier waves of controversy, corruption charges in this era combined legitimate criticism with politically motivated hyperbole. Hoffa did have ties to organized crime; he did abet corruption at the local level; and he allowed the misuse of one of the union's largest benefit funds. But anti-union forces also depicted Hoffa and the teamsters' power as a threat to national security in an effort to justify new restrictions on union-organizing efforts.

Recent History

In an effort to gain parole, Hoffa resigned from the teamsters' presidency in 1971, and he was succeeded by Frank Fitzsimmons. Released from jail in 1971, Hoffa disappeared in 1975. He is generally believed to have been murdered in an effort by organized crime to block him from re-assuming the teamsters' presidency. This widely accepted explanation reflects the degree to which allegations of organized crime influence in the union continued after Hoffa's fall from power. Evidence indicates that his successors, Frank Fitzsimmons (president, 1971–1981), Roy Williams (president, 1981–1983), and Jackie Presser (president, 1983–1988), each had strong connections to organized crime figures. Efforts by reform groups, most notably Teamsters for a Democratic Union (TDU), to challenge these leaders proved unsuccessful. Insurgents enjoyed relatively few victories at the local level and thus had few delegates at the IBT conventions, where the national union leaders were elected. By the 1980s, the federal government had decided to intervene. The Justice Department cited organized crime's influence over the union to support a Civil RICO suit in 1988 calling for a court-imposed trusteeship over the union. A settlement reached on the eve of trial in 1989, led to a court-monitored consent decree that allowed a range of different types of government oversight.

This continuing oversight brought a measure of change to the IBT. Government-monitored direct elections held in 1991 led to the election of Ron Carey, a self-proclaimed reformer who received support from TDU. But Carey's effort to win re-election 5 years later was marred by a scandal involving the use of union funds to support his re-election campaign. The IBT's internal review board, created by the 1989 consent decree, removed Carey from office, and another election was held in 1998. This time James P. Hoffa, the son of James R. Hoffa, won in a victory that was widely seen as a defeat for the reformers. Supported by most of the union's long-time corps of officials, Hoffa has sought to end the government oversight on the grounds that it is no longer necessary.

These recent contests involving corruption and reform have taken place in the midst of dramatic shifts in the political and economic context facing the union. In 1979, Congress passed legislation deregulating the trucking industry, and the result was a 50% decline in the rate of union organization in the trucking industry. The union's membership fell from a peak of about two million in the mid-1970s to roughly 1.5 million by the year 2000. A political climate favorable to anti-union forces has undercut efforts to recoup membership losses with new organizing campaigns in the trucking industry. The existence of this large, unorganized segment in the trucking industry constrains the union's collective-bargaining position, but it remains true that teamster drivers enjoy better wages and working conditions than their nonunion counterparts. Those conditions in turn influence wages in the nonunion sector, where firms have to make their wages competitive in order to stave off organizing efforts. In this way the union continues to wield much influence in its key jurisdiction.

DAVID WITWER

References and Further Reading

Belzer, Michael H. *Sweatshops on Wheels: Winners and Losers in Trucking Deregulation.* New York: Oxford University Press, 2000.
Brill, Steven. *The Teamsters.* New York: Simon and Schuster, 1978.
Commons, John R. "The Teamsters of Chicago." In *Trade Unionism and Labor Problems,* edited by John R. Commons. New York: Ginn & Company, 1905.
Crowe, Kenneth. *Collision: How the Rank and File Took back the Teamster's Union.* New York: Charles Scribner's Sons, 1993.
Fraley, Oscar, and James Hoffa. *Hoffa: The Real Story by James R. Hoffa as Told by Oscar Fraley.* New York: Stein and Day Publishers, 1975.
Garnel, Donald. *The Rise of Teamster Power in the West.* Berkeley, CA: University of California Press, 1972.
James, Ralph, and Estelle Dinnerstein James. *Hoffa and the Teamsters: A Study of Union Power.* Princeton, NJ: D. Van Nostrand, 1965.
La Botz, Dan. *Rank and File Rebellion: Teamsters for a Democratic Union.* New York: Verso, 1990.
Leiter, Robert D. *The Teamsters Union: A Study of Its Economic Impact.* New York: Bookman Associates, 1957.
Neff, James. *Mobbed Up: Jackie Presser's High-Wire Life in the Teamsters, the Mafia, and the FBI.* New York: Dell Publishing, 1989.
Romer, Sam. *The International Brotherhood of Teamsters: Its Government and Structure.* New York: Wiley, 1962.
Russell, Thaddeus. *Out of the Jungle: Jimmy Hoffa and the Remaking of the American Working Class.* New York: A. A. Knopf, 2001.
Sloane, Arthur A. *Hoffa.* Cambridge, MA: The MIT Press, 1991.
Witwer, David. *Corruption and Reform in the Teamsters Union.* Chicago: University of Illinois Press, 2003.

See also **Beck, David; Chicago Teamsters Strike of 1905; Fitzsimmons, Frank E.; Hoffa, James P; Hoffa, James R; McClellan Committee Hearings; Organized Crime; Presser, Jackie; Racketeering and RICO**

INTERNATIONAL CONFEDERATION OF FREE TRADE UNIONS (ICFTU)

Origins and Early Years

The International Confederation of Free Trade Unions (ICFTU) was born in London, between November 29 and December 6, 1949. Founding American affiliates included the American Federation of Labor (AFL), the Congress of Industrial Organizations (CIO), and the United Mineworkers of America (UMW). Fifty-nine labor union centers from 53 countries representing more than 48 million members attended.

The ICFTU was a "dual union" center. It was a spin-off from the existing World Federation of Trade Unions (WFTU), founded in 1945 as the

671

labor counterpart to the United Nations' Organization and successor to the International Federation of Trade Unions (IFTU) founded in 1913. The CIO and most other major labor union centers had been enthusiastic early members of the WFTU. Its continuation of the broad alliance against Hitler and Japanese militarism during World War II meant that such Communist labor centers as the All-Union Central Council of Soviet Trade Unions were also members. The AFL steadfastly refused to work with Communists under any circumstances and thus never joined the WFTU, working instead to undermine the organization.

The WFTU became a major site of conflict in the emerging Cold War in the late 1940s. Outside the organization, the AFL's Free Trade Union Committee and U.S. government agencies fought to deny WFTU representation in major international bodies like the International Labor Organization and United Nations; the AFL and other agencies also sought to influence individual national labor centers in France and Italy and the re-emergent labor unions in Allied occupation areas of Germany and Austria. Inside the organization, sharpening international tensions led to growing opposition to WFTU Secretary-General Benoît Frachon who, although not formally a Communist, was considered to be acting as one through his opposition to the Marshall Plan, among other important international issues. After a shift in the internal balance of power during 1948 and 1949, the CIO was ready to join the British Trades' Union Congress (TUC) and other northwestern European labor centers in abandoning the WFTU to found a rival organization.

From the first, like other international organizations, the ICFTU, headquartered in Brussels, was an organization housing differing and often-competing constituents. The relationship between the ICFTU and European labor unions on the one side and the AFL (AFL-CIO after 1955) on the other was stormy. From the mid-1950s, relations between colonial and ex-colonial labor movements and the Europeans who led the ICFTU became increasingly tense. Much of the dissension was fueled by very close ties between national labor centers and their own governments, which pursued their foreign policies through international bodies.

The first secretary-general of the ICFTU was J. H. Oldenbroeck of the Netherlands, a veteran anti-Communist and leader of the powerful International Transport Workers' Federation. During World War II he had worked closely with the AFL and Office of Strategic Services (OSS), a forerunner of the CIA. Under Oldenbroeck, the organization of the ICFTU developed, as did its independence from AFL influence.

American Labor and the ICFTU during the 1950s and 1960s

Almost from the beginning, George Meany, president of the AFL (then AFL-CIO), regarded the ICFTU as insufficiently militant when it came to communism. For their part ICFTU leaders like Oldenbroeck lived in an environment where the strong presence of Communists was a reality. They disdained American missionary zeal on the issue. Friction quickly developed. The AFL refused to contribute funds to the organization. The Americans felt slighted by the ICFTU leadership. They slammed what they considered the ponderous approach of the European leaders in building a network of regional labor organizations to lead the fight against communism. Dominated by the AFL, in the Western Hemisphere the first regional section of the ICFTU was founded in 1951, the Organización Regional Interamericana del Trabajadores (ORIT). The AFL also refused to end its independent international activities, a move that led to more independent activities by the TUC. The resulting funding crisis meant the ICFTU was hamstrung. Strong U.S. anticolonial attitudes ran counter to the conservative colonial outlook of British, French, and Belgian unions. In 1951, existing difficulties were increased when Victor Tewson of the TUC was elected president of the ICFTU in contravention of an unwritten agreement that the organization should be led by representatives of the smaller affiliates to avoid struggles between the more powerful members. The personal rivalry of Meany and President Walter Reuther of the CIO was reflected in the support given by the CIO to Oldenbroeck and Tewson.

The merger of the AFL and CIO in 1955 meant a more united American approach to the ICFTU and to a temporary deal. The AFL-CIO agreed to renew its financial obligations to the ICFTU, channel its international work through the organization, and enlarge its secretariat. The 1955 Vienna Congress of the ICFTU accepted these proposals and in return promised that no affiliates would establish contacts with Communists. A new, powerful director of organization was to be appointed to provide a counterweight to Oldenbroeck. The job proved so politically sensitive it took a year to find a suitable candidate for the position. Charles Millard, Canadian director of the United Steelworkers of America was a compromise candidate. Millard was placed in an impossible position, caught between the efforts of the Americans and Europeans to dominate the ICFTU. With morale at ICFTU headquarters low due to Oldenbroeck's personal style of leadership (he did not like to share responsibility), the AFL-CIO once again withheld its financial commitments. Independent AFL-CIO activity in Africa after 1957 led to clashes with the British. By 1959, the ICFTU had upset the Americans, the British, and the Africans. It failed to develop a sound regional structure for the continent; omitted to consult Africans in instituting a training school; appointed the British union official Albert Hammerton as African regional director, a person previously criticized by Africans for his colonialist positions; and proved unable to respond to AFL-CIO pressure for a greater American presence to counter growing neutralist and Communist movements. The upshot was a vigorous American-led move to force the resignation of Oldenbroeck and the entire ICFTU leadership.

Despite the replacement of Oldenbroeck by the American-backed Omer Becu in 1960, relations between the AFL-CIO and the ICFTU improved little. The establishment of AFRO, the African Regional Organization of the ICFTU that same year was hardly a giant step forward. It was followed a year later by the establishment of the All-Africa Trade Union Federation and an intensified struggle within and among African labor unions over disaffiliation from any outside organizations. Eventually most left the ICFTU.

By 1965, George Meany had had enough. He demanded a full accounting of all monies donated to the ICFTU's solidarity fund and refused further funds until all unspent monies were returned and accounted for. Financial mismanagement of ICFTU monies in Africa was real. By 1968, when Reuther's United Automobile Workers (UAW) withdrew from the AFL-CIO, in part over foreign policy issues, the crunch arrived. Before withdrawing, Reuther and the ICFTU held talks concerning the application of the UAW for membership. The AFL-CIO was not informed, though Meany was subsequently told and asked not to oppose the application. Regarding this as interference in the internal affairs of a national affiliate, Meany requested the application be rejected, then took the AFL-CIO out of the ICFTU in 1969. Other reasons included condemnations of the United States over the war in Vietnam, supported by the AFL-CIO, and greater fraternization of the Europeans with Communist neighbors. The AFL-CIO remained affiliated with ORIT and increased its dominance. Throughout the 1960s, the AFL-CIO increased its activities independent of the ICFTU. In 1963, the American Institute for Free Labor Democracy (AIFLD) was founded as a partnership of the AFL-CIO, multinational U.S. corporations, and the U.S. government. In 1965, the African American Labor Center (AALC) was set up to oversee operations in Africa, and in 1968, as the Vietnam War entered its most severe phase, the Asian American Free Labor Institute (AIFLI) was established, both with heavy U.S. government financial support.

The End of the Cold War and the Evolution of the ICFTU

Only in 1982, after the death of Meany, did the AFL-CIO rejoin the ICFTU. The move was part of a major reconsideration of AFL-CIO foreign policy. By that time the ICFTU had sharpened its positions on human rights—for free labor, against slave labor, for women's rights, against child labor, for freedom of association, for workers' rights as a fundamental guarantee of human rights more generally. It was also focusing ever more tightly on the challenges posed by globalization. From the early 1980s, these were also issues of increasing concern for the AFL-CIO. Such concerns led to a much greater ICFTU effort in developing nations. In 1984, the final regional organization, the Asian and Pacific Regional Organization (APRO) was established. Working both through the major international organizations and on the ground, a remarkable transformation was enacted. Working together and separately, the AFL-CIO and ICFTU supported the independent Polish labor movement Solidarnosc in its efforts to represent the interests of working people outside government control and in campaigns for human rights in Chile, South Africa, and Turkey, among others.

As the Cold War ended in 1989 and 1990, the ICFTU was in a good position to consolidate its position as the most representative trade union organization in the world. By 1999, as the other world labor union federations—the WFTU and the formerly Christian World Confederation of Labor (WCL)—stagnated or declined in membership, the ICFTU grew to approximately 124 million members in 213 national trade union centers in 143 countries. Moreover by 1999, the ratio of members in developing countries to those in developed countries had risen dramatically to reach 48% of the total.

One of the central tensions in the ICFTU remained the North-South divide between industrialized and developing nations. The bureaucratic leadership of the ICFTU lagged behind the improving balance in membership and was challenged to integrate the concerns and struggles of workers from quite different environments. The ICFTU responses to issues of foreign debt, reform of multilateral institutions, international cooperation and free trade, and the liberalization of foreign investment were all challenged by leaders of workers of the South as bureaucratically rather than democratically determined and insufficiently sensitive to southern perspectives. Tensions led to the increased autonomy of the regional organizations after 1996. Reforms of ORIT in particular became models for calls to reform the ICFTU itself in a more decentralized direction.

By 2004, the ICFTU had grown to 234 affiliates in 152 countries with a combined membership of 148 million. It worked closely with the European Trade Union Confederation, the Trade Union Advisory Committee of the Organization for Economic Cooperation and Development (TUAC) and had deepened its historical working relationship with the International Trade Secretariats now renamed Global Union Federations (international groupings of national labor unions in a single trade). At its eighteenth world congress in December 2004 in Miyazaki, Japan, resolutions were passed for reforms that included a move toward unification with the WCL and tightening the relationship between the regional organizations and ICFTU headquarters to promote cohesive and concerted global action. Evidence of U.S. participation in the ICFTU can be seen in the fact that AFL-CIO President John Sweeney served that year as president of the TUAC and on the steering committee and executive board of the ICFTU, while AFL-CIO Executive Vice-President Linda Chavez-Thompson was president of ORIT.

STEPHEN BURWOOD

References and Further Reading

Carew, Anthony. "Charles Millard, a Canadian in the International Labour Movement: A Case Study of the ICFTU 1955-61." *Labour/Le Travail* 37, 1 (spring 1996): 121–148.
International Confederation of Free Trade Unions, www.icftu.org
International Confederation of Free Trade Unions. "Special 50th Anniversary Edition. How the ICFTU Has Influenced Global Developments Year after Year." *Trade Union World*, 3 (Mar. 1999), www.icftu.org
Jakobsen, Kjeld A. "Rethinking the International Confederation of Free Trade Unions and Its Inter-American Regional Organization." *Antipode* 33, 3 (2001): 363–388.
Morgan, Ted. *A Covert Life: Jay Lovestone Communist, Anti-Communist, and Spymaster*. New York: Random House, 1999.
Rathbun, Ben. *Point Man: Irving Brown and the Post-1945 Deadly Struggle for Europe and Africa*. Montreux, Switzerland, London, UK, and Washington, DC: Minerva, 1996.
Richards, Yevette. *Maida Springer: Pan-Africanist and International Labor Leader*. Pittsburgh, PA: University of Pittsburgh Press, 2000.
Weisband, Edward, and Christopher J. Colvin. "An Empirical Analysis of International Confederation of Free Trade Unions (ICFTU) Annual Surveys. *Human Rights Quarterly* 22, 1 (2000): 167–186.
Williamson, Hugh, "Globalizing Trade Unions." *Multinational Monitor* 16, 6 (June 1995): 26.

See also **American Federation of Labor; American Federation of Labor-Congress of Industrial Organizations; Meany, George; Reuther, Walter**

INTERNATIONAL FISHERMEN AND ALLIED WORKERS OF AMERICA

The International Fishermen and Allied Workers of America (IFAWA), a Congress of International Organizations (CIO) affiliate, represented fishing industry workers on the Pacific Coast of the United States in the years during and after World War II. The IFAWA focused on the protection of fishers' incomes and access to the fishery resource. While initially enjoying great organizational success, the union nevertheless became the target of successive attacks by the Federal Trade Commission (FTC) through the 1940s, which interpreted contractual demands for minimum fish prices as collusion to fix prices and restrain trade. These legal setbacks eventually forced IFAWA to reinvent itself as the Fisheries' and Allied Workers' Division of the International Longshoremen's and Warehousemen's Union (ILWU) in 1949. Along with the ILWU, the fishers were expelled from the CIO for alleged political affiliations later that year. The division was moribund by the mid-1950s.

The IFAWA emerged in 1937–1938, after a half-century of relatively isolated union action by Pacific fishers, with the affiliation of six smaller, regionally focused fishers' unions with the CIO. One year later these regional affiliates joined with several directly affiliated unions to create IFAWA, headquartered in Seattle. Nevertheless given its diverse parentage and the geographical specificity of each local's organizational and natural resource concerns, the union constitution allowed for considerable local autonomy, and the organization remained highly decentralized.

Like many other unions, IFAWA grew throughout World War II. At its peak in 1946, IFAWA membership exceeded 22,000, and the FTC declared that the "Pacific North West fishing industry is one of the most highly unionized industries of the country." Locals operated in every major fishing port on the coast, from Bristol Bay in western Alaska to San Diego, and members participated in virtually every commercially significant Pacific fishery—crab, salmon, sardine, tuna, herring, and halibut, for example—with the full range of commercial gear: Trawl, longline, purse-seine, and gill net, among others.

Three groups comprised the greater part of IFAWA's membership: Company fishers, fisher-boat owners, and shares' fishers. Company fishers fished with boats and gear owned by fish processors or "operators" and were paid a share of their catch. This arrangement was more common in more geographically isolated fisheries. Fisher-boat owners, or independents, owned or leased their boats and gear and sold their catch to operators by weight or piece. Shares' fishers crewed independent boats and were paid a share of the sale price of the catch, commonly after some agreed-on deduction for the cost of boat and gear maintenance. A proportionally less-significant fourth group, shore workers employed by the operators, performed a variety of jobs in the plants and on the docks.

Joe Jurich led IFAWA from its inception and remained president until the merger with the ILWU a decade later. Jurich's dynamism notwithstanding, the major organizing and strategic work was done at the local level in the face of challenges specific to fishery or locality. For example IFAWA's heated battles with the Seaman's International Union (SIU-AFL) in the early 1940s over participation in the Monterey sardine fishery was managed by Local 33, based in San Pedro, California, not by the international. Rather the international's principal organizational role was the representation of the union in three critical arenas: (1) To the membership, primarily through the publication of the union newspaper, the *International Fisherman and Allied Worker*, and the organization of fishery-specific coastwise conferences; (2) to state and federal fisheries managers through the conduct and publication of scientific research; and (3) before federal trade and labor regulators, the FTC in particular, in hearings and before the courts.

It is these latter two activities, and their institutional and ecological contexts, that make the history of IFAWA of particular interest. First the union's organizational form—a loosely coordinated set of virtually autonomous locals across thousands of miles of coast—reflected the ecological dimensions of the resource on which the membership depended. Not only would inconsistent pricing across regions undercut the power of all locals, but the mobility of the fish stocks, and the consequent risk of nonlocal risks to stock sustainability simultaneously encouraged vast geographical coverage and a commitment to local autonomy. The international's commitment to fisheries' science and population research was a logical result of these same pressures.

Second and most significantly in the union's history, the great majority of the international's attention—and that of powerful locals like San Pedro, San Francisco (Local 34), and Astoria, Oregon (Local 50), among others—was absorbed by the efforts of the FTC's antitrust division to indict the union under the Sherman Anti-Trust Act. The indictments, which began as soon as the union was organized in 1939, and continued unabated throughout the life of IFAWA and the ILWU fishers' division, were founded on the assertion that IFAWA's members were "independent contractors," engaged in the sale of commodities to processors. As such all efforts to set minimum fish prices constituted illegal price discrimination. Fishers' refusal to fish, a fishing strike, or "tie-up" was configured as restraint of trade.

The IFAWA, usually represented by Jurich and the union's California representative, Jeff Kibre, asserted that fishers were employees in everything but name. In the face of operator monopsony, the debt relations in which most fishers were involved with processors, and the perishability of fish that prevented the search for the highest price, even independent fishers were merely delivering fish to operators for what IFAWA called a "wage price." They argued that conflicts with processors were not the matter of the Sherman Act, but constituted labor disputes under the Norris-LaGuardia Act.

In the early 1940s, the legal interpretations of these conflicts varied: Despite the support, the FTC position from the Supreme Court in its decision in *Columbia River Packers Association v. Hinton*, the National War Labor Board generally recognized IFAWA's appeals for wage adjustments. By 1946, however, the courts had become far less sympathetic, and a series of defeats—especially in the Second Circuit's decision in *Local 36 of International Fishermen and Allied Workers of America v. United States*—created significant organizational instability, marked most notably by the secession of the membership-rich Alaska Fishermen's Union. The union never recovered; further indictments followed precedent, and locals collapsed or disaffiliated. The effort to save the union by joining the ILWU was further hampered by the disintegration of the CIO, and by 1957, even the Fisheries' and Allied Workers' Division was basically no more than a file folder.

GEOFF MANN

References and Further Reading

Crutchfield, James A. "Collective Bargaining in the Pacific Coast Fisheries: The Economic Issues." *Industrial and Labor Relations Review* 8, 4 (1955): 541–556.

Mann, Geoff. "Class Consciousness and Common Property: The International Fishermen and Allied Workers of America." *International Labor and Working Class History* 61 (2002): 141–160.

McEvoy, Arthur. *The Fisherman's Problem: Ecology and Law in the California Fisheries*. New York: Cambridge University Press, 1986.

Randall, Roger. "Labor Agreements in the West Coast Fishing Industry: Restraint of Trade or Basis of Industrial Stability." *Industrial and Labor Relations Review* 3, 4 (1950): 514–541.

Cases and Statutes Cited

Columbia River Packers Association v. Hinton, 315 U.S. 143 (1942).

Local 36 of International Fishermen and Allied Workers of America v. United States, 177 F.2d 320 (1949).

Norris-LaGuardia (Anti-Injunction) Act, Act of Mar. 23, 1932, c. 90, 47 Stat. 70.

Sherman (Anti-Trust) Act, Act of July 2, 1890, c. 647, 26 Stat. 209.

See also **Congress of Industrial Organizations; International Longshoremen's Association; Pacific Northwest; Sherman Anti-Trust Act**

INTERNATIONAL FUR AND LEATHER WORKERS' UNION

The International Fur and Leather Workers' Union (IFLWU) was the most left-wing of the Congress of International Organization's (CIO's) unions. The union was established in 1939, when the International Fur Workers' Union (IFWU), with its heavily Jewish—and smaller Greek—membership, merged with the recently created National Leather Workers' Association after a CIO-inspired industrial union campaign. The former organization itself was born of an earlier alliance, when eight American Federation of Labor (AFL) unions representing the various crafts of the fur trade joined together in 1913 to form the IFWU.

The 14,000-member IFWU was continually plagued by internal corruption, autocratic leaders, and constant factional battles. In the New York fur district, the industry's largest and most important center, organized crime soon managed to infiltrate the union, reaching accommodating arrangements with various employers. A radical group, led by Russian-born, New York Joint Board Chairman Ben Gold, an open Communist prominent within the national Communist party (CPUSA), began a concerted effort to regulate the industry and purge the union of all vestiges of criminal control. In a 4-month strike starting in February of 1926—waged mainly for a five-day, 40-hour week—Gold and his supporters challenged the district's employers and their organized crime supporters within the union. The strike ended in an unstable success and was followed the following year by yet another strike—mainly to enforce the settlement reached after the previous year's conflagration. Gold was not able to totally rid the union of corruption and was forced to wage a decade-long struggle against his right-wing enemies within the leadership of the international union—and the AFL. The Executive Council of the AFL and AFL President

William Green soon targeted Gold, appointing a special committee charged with ridding the New York City joint board of its Communist leadership. Faced with such concerted opposition, Gold lost his position as head of the joint board in 1928 but continued to lead the left-wing opposition group of the union, and then worked with the Trade Union Educational League and the Trade Union Unity League over the next few years to develop an industrial union, the Needle Trades Workers' Industrial Union, which would bring skilled and unskilled workers together in one expansive working-class organization. For the ensuing 7 years, unionization in the fur industry was sharply divided and chaotic. It was not until the spring of 1935, when the temper of trade unionism began to shift further to the left when the Communist party abandoned its "third-period" line and began once again to oppose dual unionism and emphasize unity and when rank-and-file workers had had enough of their organized-crime-tainted leadership that Gold returned and worked his way back into leadership of the IFWU. He was subsequently elected international president of the union in May of 1937. Soon afterward he took the IFWU out of the AFL and into the recently established CIO. In early 1938, Gold led the entire union in a successful strike that achieved wage increases and seasonal job security (the fur industry was a highly seasonal industry). Perhaps most important the strike finally unified the fur workers, forcing managers to sign an industrywide collective-bargaining agreement.

With the fur workers finally unified and the industry firmly organized, the new CIO-affiliated union shifted its focus to the leather trades and began cultivating an alliance with the National Leather Workers' Association, established by the CIO in 1937. In 1939, both the leather workers and the fur workers voted affirmatively for merging their two organizations and soon afterward established the IFLWU. The new industrial union immediately turned to organizing hitherto unorganized leather workers—in Pennsylvania, upstate New York, New England, and in the shops of the Midwest, close to the stockyards of Chicago.

During World War II, following the uncomfortable 1939–1941 alliance between Germany and the Soviet Union, codified in the Nazi-Soviet Pact, the union, like other left-led CIO unions, took on a hyperpatriotic stance and limited militant and radical action. It adopted a no-strike pledge for the duration of the war and accommodated to working out its demands through the War Labor Board. But the postwar era brought another turn. The IFLWU began to distance itself from the mainstream of the CIO. On foreign policy and domestic political issues, the union became an outspoken critic of the Truman administration. By 1948, Gold and his supporters turned away from the Democratic party and gave their support to Henry Wallace, former vice-president, who ran a full-employment, propeace, anti-Cold War campaign. The divergent path treaded by Gold and his union ultimately led to a fratricidal ideological battle within the CIO, finally culminating in the expulsion of the IFLWU in 1950, along with 10 other left-led unions.

Expulsion could be survived, but the Taft-Hartley Act of 1947 became Gold's and the union's Achilles' heel. In 1953, Gold was accused of perjury for signing a non-Communist Taft-Hartley Affidavit and was forced to resign as president of the union. He had publicly announced his withdrawal from the CPUSA in August of 1950 in order to sign the required non-Communist oath, required of all labor leaders under Section 9(h) of the act in order to gain for their unions the recognition and protections of the National Labor Relations Board (NLRB). A federal grand jury however determined that Gold had indeed perjured himself and was still involved in Communist party affairs and business; in April of 1954, he was sentenced to serve 1–3 years for violation of two counts of the Taft-Hartley Act. Though the Supreme Court would reverse Gold's conviction in January of 1958 because of FBI pressure on jury members and the government would ultimately drop its prosecution of the case, the immediate aftermath of the decision deeply harmed the union. As a result of Gold's 1954 conviction, in the summer of 1954, the IFLWU formally lost all NLRB protections.

In reality however many employers, like the Endicott Johnson Corporation—a large shoe and leather-manufacturing firm located in the southern tier of New York—and the various tannery mills in Fulton County, New York, had already taken advantage of the union's red reputation and vulnerability. They ceased negotiating with union representatives as early as 1947, even before the Taft-Hartley Bill had been signed, counting on favorable NLRB rulings against Communist-led locals.

Besides being targeted by employers and the government, from 1950–1955, the disaffiliated, independent union faced constant attempts throughout the country by CIO and AFL competitive unions to pick away at its membership. Finally in 1955, after much negotiation, a weakened IFLWU merged with the Amalgamated Butchers and Meat Cutters of North America. One of the conditions of that merger, set by George Meany, then president of the AFL (which was soon to merge with the CIO), and by Patrick E.

Gorman, secretary-treasurer of the Amalgamated, was the permanent removal of Gold from any leadership position in the union and the general "decommunization" of the union. Gold returned to the shops as a fur worker; his three decades of union leadership had ended.

In spite of the expulsion of Gold and many of his fellow Communist supporters in the IFLWU, the now-merged fur and leather division of the Amalgamated—the Joint Board Fur, Leather and Machine Workers' Union—persisted in following a progressive, left-wing track; it remained a radical voice and force within the AFL-CIO and the American labor movement. The union participated actively in the various civil rights and peace movements of the late 1950s–1970s, particularly under the leadership of Henry Foner, who had joined the IFLWU in 1948 as educational director. In 1961, following the death of Sam Burt, then president of the joint board, Foner was elevated to the presidency of the union and retained that position till his retirement in 1988—taking the union through yet another merger. Under the strain of a shrinking labor movement in the final decades of the twentieth century, the Amalgamated and its constituent unions began to explore mergers with other unions. In 1979, it joined with the Retail Clerks' International Union (RCIU), founded in 1888, to form the United Food and Commercial Workers' union (UFCW). The UFCW now has a membership of approximately 1.4 million workers.

GERALD ZAHAVI

References and Further Reading

Cammer, Harold. "Taft-Hartley and the International Fur and Leather Workers' Union." In *The Cold War against Labor*, edited by Ann Fagan Ginger and David Christiano. Berkeley, CA: Meiklejohn Civil Liberties Institute, 1987.

Foner, Philip S. *The Fur and Leather Workers Union: A Story of Dramatic Struggles and Achievements*. Newark, NJ: Nordan Press, 1950.

Gold, Ben. *Memoirs*. New York: William Howard, 1988.

Leiter, Robert D. "Fur Workers' Union." *Industrial and Labor Relations Review* 3, 2 (January 1950).

Spingham, Sandra Dawn. "Trade Unionism among the Jewish Workers in the Fur Manufacturing Industry in New York City, 1912–1929." Ph.D. dissertation, State University of New York at Binghamton, 1995.

Zahavi, Gerald. "Communism is No Bug-A-Boo: Communism and Left-Wing Unionism in Fulton County, New York, 1933–1950." *Labor History* 33:2 (spring 1992).

———. *Workers, Managers, and Welfare Capitalism: The Shoeworkers and Tanners of Endicott Johnson, 1890–1950*. Urbana: University of Illinois Press, 1988.

INTERNATIONAL LABOR DEFENSE

The International Labor Defense (ILD) was founded in Chicago on June 23, 1925. Closely associated with the Workers' party (which later became the American Communist Party) from its inception, the ILD satisfied V. I. Lenin's classic definition of a mass organization, one that was nominally non-Communist but firmly guided by the leadership of the party. In this way, Lenin theorized, non-Communists could gradually be drawn into the Communist orbit. The ILD was largely the brainchild of James P. Cannon, a leader of the Workers' party during the early 1920s when the American Communist movement was often split by bitter factional disputes. Cannon maintained that it had been inspired by a 1925 meeting in the Soviet Union with "Big Bill" Haywood, the leader of the Industrial Workers of the World (IWW) who had been indicted under the Sedition Act for his opposition to the involvement of the United States in World War I, jumped bail, and fled into exile in the Soviet Union. Convinced of the need for a legal defense organization that would defend activists in the labor movement and provide aid and assistance for their families, Cannon worked tirelessly to bring the organization into being. His efforts led to his election as national secretary at the 1925 meeting, a position he maintained until 1928, when he was expelled from the Communist party for his Trotskyite views.

For the ILD legal and political defenses were inextricably intertwined. It was firmly wed to the belief that legal strategies and tactics were in themselves inadequate to defend working-class people from a court system that was designed to represent the interests of the ruling classes. Although the ILD committed itself to securing the services of the most skilled, experienced, and politically adept lawyers it could find, it boldly linked its courtroom battles with sustained efforts at mass mobilization: Demonstrations, mass meetings, fund-raising events, petition drives, and telegrams and letters to established authorities. Moreover the ILD relied on its extensive network of international mass organizations, such as International Red Aid (known by its Russian initials MOPR) to mobilize international public opinion around its causes. These were the tactics the ILD pursued and fine tuned over the course of its existence.

Shortly after its emergence, the ILD plunged into the defense efforts mounted on behalf of Nicola Sacco and Bartolomeo Vanzetti, joining with liberals, radical anarchists, workers, immigrants, and people of conscience in an ultimately unsuccessful attempt to save their lives. By 1928, shortly before his expulsion, Cannon reported that the ILD had organized numerous new branches across the country; laid the basis for the defense campaigns of nationally known labor martyrs Tom Mooney and Warren Billings, as well as the Centralia, Washington, IWW workers; sponsored national tours on "revolution and counterrevolution in China" and "Polish fascism"; and dramatically increased the circulation of its magazine *Labor Defender*.

Cannon was replaced as national secretary by J. Louis Engdahl during a period that coincided with the 1928 Sixth Congress of the Communist International's (Comintern's) elevation of the Negro question as a central priority of the international Communist movement. The "black belt" of the South was named as the source of African-American oppression, the "black peasantry" as potential allies of the revolutionary working class. The Communist party shifted considerable effort and resources to organizing in the South; the ILD maintained a watchful eye for cases that captured these interests. One of the most important cases of this kind was the infamous Scottsboro case of 1931: Nine unemployed young black men were dragged off a freight train in Scottsboro, Alabama, and accused of raping two white women who, like them, were "hoboing" in search of jobs in Depression era America. Successfully wresting the defense of the Scottsboro boys from the hands of the National Association for the Advancement of Colored People (NAACP), the ILD aggressively waged a campaign throughout the 1930s that transformed it into a cause that generated international attention, led to two major Supreme Court decisions, and successfully derailed the sustained attempts of the State of Alabama to execute the Scottsboro defendants. The ILD also played a central role in bringing public attention to bear on the case of Angelo Herndon, an African-American Communist party organizer arrested in Atlanta, Georgia, in July 1932, for leading a biracial demonstration and indicted on a charge of incitement to insurrection—a law that carried a maximum penalty of death. Cases such as these, as well as the ascendancy of an African-American attorney to the position of national secretary after J. Louis Engdahl's death in late 1932, played a decisive role in bringing the ILD and the Communist party to the attention of the black community during the 1930s.

As a mass organization, the ILD from the beginning sought out reputable non-Communists to serve on its national executive board, but Communist party leadership ran the organization. In 1937, however, during the "popular-front" period, the ILD was re-organized; Vito Marcantonio, the radical congressman from East Harlem was named president; Anna Damon, a party member, became national secretary.

After the outbreak of World War II, the ILD's influence began to wane. By the end of the war, its status as a distinct organization had come to an end. It merged with the National Negro Congress and the National Federation for Constitutional Liberties to form the Civil Rights Congress, an organization that continued the struggle for civil rights and liberties into the mid-1950s.

JAMES A. MILLER

References and Further Reading

Foner, Philip S., and Herbert Shapiro. *American Communism and Black Americans: A Documentary History, 1930–1934*. Philadelphia, PA: Temple University Press, 1991.
James P. Cannon and the Early Years of American Communism: Selected Writings and Speeches, 1920–1928. New York: Sparticist Publishing Company, 1992.
Martin, Charles H. "The International Labor Defense and Black America." *Labor History* 26 (1985).

See also **Civil Rights Congress; Communist Party; Haywood, William D. "Big Bill"; Industrial Workers of the World; Mooney, Tom; National Association for the Advancement of Colored People; National Negro Congress; Sacco and Vanzetti; Scottsboro Case**

INTERNATIONAL LADIES' GARMENT WORKERS' UNION (ILGWU) (1900–1995)

The International Ladies' Garment Workers' Union (ILGWU) was founded as the principal representative of workers in the women's and children's sectors of the apparel industry in June 1900 at the Labor Lyceum, 64 East Fourth Street, New York, New York. Representatives of the Cloakmakers' Protective Union of Philadelphia, United Cloak Pressers of Philadelphia, Cloakmakers' Union of Baltimore, United Brotherhood of Cloakmakers of New York and Vicinity, Newark Cloakmakers' Union, and the Shirtmakers' Union of New York formed the ILGWU. Centered in New York, the union's mission was to improve wages and working conditions in women's and children's garment factories in the United States and Canada. At its founding the ILGWU affiliated with the American Federation of Labor (AFL).

As the end of the nineteenth-century drew near, the manufacture of clothing in the United States shifted from small artisan shops, individual homes, and immigrant-occupied tenements of urban industrial areas, such as New York's Lower East Side, to a growing number of factories. Though the roots of

factory-based apparel making can be traced to the 1840s, several factors spawned its expansion at century's end. The advent of the foot-powered sewing machine in 1846 and the mechanical cutting knife in 1876, along with the introduction of steam power by the 1880s, meant that large quantities of fabric could be made into finished clothing with greater efficiency. New technology transformed and enhanced production and resulted in more division of labor to meet growing consumer demand for ready-made clothing. Advances in transporting raw materials to manufacturers and finished goods to consumers opened new markets. Work-ready immigrants in urban areas contributed to the industry's growth as the nineteenth century drew to close.

In 1880, the typical New York garment-making establishment was owned by a German Jewish clothing retailer who employed small numbers of people. Most of the workers who made clothing for women and children—the focus of this study—were female. In the years to follow, tens of thousands of Jews emigrated from Russia and Eastern Europe in flight from pogroms, religious persecution, and political discrimination. Many possessed skills as tailors and seamstresses and entered the women's clothing industry *en masse* to be joined by Italian immigrants. By the dawn of the twentieth century, immigration significantly impacted U.S. apparel making.

Many workers were employed in so-called "inside shops" owned by a manufacturer who purchased raw materials, planned production, and hired immigrant labor to cut, sew, press, and finish fabric into consumer products. The manufacturer arranged for their sale in the marketplace. The main branches of the women's apparel industry included dresses, cloaks and suits, corsets and brassieres, undergarments, neckwear, rainwear, and infants' and children's wear. Although some large factories emerged in East Coast cities most garment-making establishments remained relatively small: The average factory employed about 30 people in 1899. Women's apparel making expanded to cities from coast to coast—including Cleveland, Chicago, St. Louis, Los Angeles, and San Francisco—but Manhattan remained a prime locale throughout the twentieth century.

Unionization began in the same city in 1879. The Knights of Labor established a short-lived workers' association that was superseded in 1883 by the Dress and Cloak Makers' Union and the Gotham Knife Cutters' Association of New York and Vicinity. Unions were also formed in Toledo, Baltimore, and Philadelphia. Worker-led protests of poor wages, long hours, and working conditions were common. The cloak trade workforce in New York struck in August 1885 demanding higher wages and shorter workdays.

Sweatshop of Mr. Goldstein 30 Suffolk St. Witness Mrs. L. Hosford. Location: New York, New York. Library of Congress, Prints & Photographs Division, National Child Labor Committee Collection [LC-DIG-nclc-04455].

In 1886, workers struck to protest contracting to small nonunion producers who paid pittance wages. The following year 30 walkouts were reported in the New York area over similar issues. Numerous garment strikes hit New York and Philadelphia in 1888 as workers demanded improved working conditions and higher wages. Disputes typically were settled with limited concessions to workers.

By the 1890s, the socialist United Hebrew Trades created the Operators' and Cloak Makers' Union No. 1 in Manhattan with affiliates in Chicago, Boston, Baltimore, and Philadelphia. After a major strike in New York in the spring of 1890, employers recognized the union. By the end of the year, the Operators' and Cloak Makers' Union No. 1 reported a membership of 7,000. However by 1892, the union was in disarray.

The tumultuous drive for unionization continued in 1892 with the formation of the International Cloak Makers' Union of America, headquartered in New York, where Barondess managed its metropolitan branch. The union had affiliates in Boston, Baltimore, Chicago, and Philadelphia and joined the AFL. The new union also set out to organize men's tailors and clothing makers, the traditional domain of the more conservative AFL-affiliated United Garment Workers' Union.

Over the next few years the pattern of union formation and dissolution in women's apparel continued, as did infighting between socialists, anarchists, and moderates. In June 1900, representatives from the several apparel unions met at Manhattan's Labor Lyceum to resolve cantankerous relations between workers and manufacturers. The conclave resulted in the formation of the ILGWU.

The union set out to organize workers, raise their wages, and win recognition. Garment manufacturers—in part to avoid the ILGWU and its demands for higher wages and better working conditions—expanded a practice that had its roots in the nineteenth century: Contracting to outside shops. Under this arrangement manufacturers and jobbers purchased fabrics, designed new styles, then contracted for the making of the garments. Small, highly competitive contractors bid on the orders, paying low wages and demanding long hours from employees. With its notoriously low wages and poor working conditions, contracting gave rise to the industrial sweatshop so often associated with garment making on Manhattan's Lower East Side. The system threatened unionization. Two significant strikes and a tragic fire brought public recognition to the struggles of garment workers and the ILGWU.

In 1909, 20,000 shirtwaist makers went on strike against New York employers. With support of the Women's Trade Union League, workers protested unsafe working conditions, low wages, long hours, and the imposition of employer-imposed taxes for electricity, sewing needles, and chairs. The ILGWU's shirtwaist makers affiliate, Local 25, spearheaded the strike, dubbed the "uprising of twenty thousand." Over 600 workers were affected. When the strike was settled, about half of the employers agreed to a 52-hour workweek, eliminated discrimination against hiring union members, ended all employer-charged taxes, and provided four annual paid holidays.

The uprising was followed in 1910 by the "great revolt" of 60,000 New York cloak makers. Worker grievances were similar to those prevalent in the uprising. Employers responded to the strike by forming the Cloak, Suit, and Skirt Manufacturers' Protective Association and issuing public statements claiming that workers were treated fairly. Louis Brandeis, Boston lawyer and later U.S. Supreme Court justice, mediated a settlement of the dispute by creating the historic protocol of peace.

While the protocol was in its infancy, tragedy struck at the Triangle Shirtwaist Company in March 1911. Located at New York's Washington Square, Triangle employed hundreds in a cramped, unsafe, multiple-story building where workers logged days of 12 hours or more. On March 25, 1911, during the daytime shift, a fire began on the middle floors of the building. Fueled by an abundance of cloth and other material, flames quickly spread. Frantic workers screamed for help and gasped for air from upper-story windows as flames billowed around. Rather than succumb to the inferno, some leapt from heights of eight stories. Sixty-two jumped to their end on the sidewalk below. Others died in the inferno bringing total fatalities to 146.

Strikes and the Triangle tragedy set the stage for Brandeis's labor-management relations experiment. The protocol of peace established several important precedents by creating a Committee of Grievances and a Board of Arbitration to mediate and arbitrate employer-union disputes and worker grievances, a Joint Board of Sanitary Control to oversee factory and employee health and safety, and a preferential union shop in which employer-hiring practices were limited to union members. The protocol was among early mediation attempts in U.S. labor-management relations. Within a few years its status was jeopardized by contracting.

The union expanded in other eastern cities, such as Philadelphia, Baltimore, and Boston, and by the end of World War I, had a membership of about 100 thousand. During the following decade, internal power struggles between Communists, socialists, and moderates nearly destroyed the ILGWU. In 1920, William Z. Foster formed the Trade Union Educational League (TUEL) to coordinate the work of leftist activists in the American labor movement. The TUEL policy advocated class struggle, international unification of industrial workers, mass organization

across industries, creation of a labor party, recognition of the Soviet state, and destruction of capitalism. Communists—led by Louis Hyman of the cloak makers and Charles (Sasha) Zimmerman of the dressmakers—expanded their influence in ILGWU affiliates and by 1924, elected a majority on the executive boards of key New York Locals 9 and 22. The ILGWU President Morris Sigman—a socialist who rejected Communist dogma—expelled TUEL supporters.

Conflict between radical and moderate forces peaked with a Communist-led strike in early 1926. Nearly 40,000 New York-based cloak makers walked off the job in protest over employer contracting to small nonunion factories outside of the New York area. The shutdown lasted 28 weeks at a total cost to the ILGWU treasury of $3 million. Sigman encouraged strike-weary, hungry, and penniless workers to affiliate with the union's more moderate influences. Most workers came back to the ILGWU, and Sigman successfully negotiated a contract with the employers that however lacked significant restrictions on contracting. Meanwhile Communists aligned themselves with the new Trade Union Unity League. In the needle trades disenchanted leftists joined the Needle Trades Workers' Industrial Union. Not all Communists followed this path. Hyman and Zimmerman rejected the move and remained with the ILGWU, becoming stalwart anti-Stalinists.

In 1928, Benjamin Schlesinger once again assumed the ILGWU's presidency (he had served in the post on two previous occasions: 1903–1904 and 1914–1923). David Dubinsky, the head of Local 10 representing garment cutters, assumed the post of secretary-treasurer. By the time of their ascendancy, the Communists had been expelled from ILGWU locals. Yet their actions and the impact of the 1926 strike endured. The union was bankrupt. Membership dwindled to 60,000, while New York members were threatened by unemployment and underemployment as the practice of contracting to nonunion factories expanded.

At its 1922 convention union delegates voted to levy a 4-dollar per-capita assessment to form the Eastern Out-of-Town Organizing Department to organize contractors that were sprouting in areas removed from the city. By the mid-1920s, the department enlisted 2,500 members organized in 29 locals in New Jersey, Connecticut, and on Long Island.

By the time Dubinsky assumed the presidency of the ILGWU in 1932, the union's future appeared grim. The Great Depression had caused a significant industrial slowdown; the union's membership dwindled to fewer than 25,000; and its financial situation remained precarious. Out-of-town shops had grown to a problem of major proportion. As the nation's economy stalled, competition among jobbers put tremendous pressure on contractors who were played against one another for even the smallest margins. Contractors responded by ignoring union agreements, paying below market wages, breaking the union altogether, and seeking the cheapest labor possible by fleeing to remote areas.

By the 1930s, the union expanded its definition of out-of-town to include a territory covering a one-hundred-plus mile radius from Manhattan, where it estimated that over 25,000 workers were employed in a virtual "sweatshop swamp." A 1933 general dress strike brought some organizing success, increased wages, and shortened hours, but problems remained as contractors continued to seek lower cost production. Pennsylvania's anthracite coal region and in particular its northernmost reaches around Wilkes-Barre and Scranton—which contained high-population concentrations and afforded relatively easy access to metropolitan markets—were prime locales for contractors who produced dresses and children's clothing for New York jobbers.

As the contracting system expanded during the 1920s and 1930s, out-of-town shops received nearly all of their work from New York jobbers. By 1937, nearly one-third of all cotton dresses sold in the eastern United States were manufactured in contract shops as was about 50% of all children's apparel.

The effect of low-cost competition from contractors impacted the New York dress industry as jobs were siphoned away. The ILGWU reported that, from 1946–1956, its membership declined by over 10,000 as a direct result of jobs going to lower-wage nonunion shops in Pennsylvania. The trend would continue well into the 1950s and 1960s as manufacturers moved production to the American South where the ILGWU would follow with organizing drives. By the late 1970s, and for the remainder of the twentieth century, apparel production shifted to Central and South America, Asia, and Pacific Rim nations. The ILGWU's membership dwindled to fewer than 200 thousand by the century's end.

Despite the union's peaks and valleys, throughout its history the ILGWU has been recognized as one of the foremost U.S. labor organizations, committed to social unionism, education of its members, and political activism. The ILGWU became the first American labor union to establish a health care center for its members in Manhattan in the early twentieth century. By the 1950s, union health care centers were established in nearly every major metropolitan area in the Northeast as well as in remote reaches where the apparel industry had spawned, such as Easton,

Pennsylvania, and locales in the American South. The ILGWU also established cultural and social institutions that served ILGWU members needs. These included a New York-based union leadership school; a "labor stage" for worker-based performing arts; a union-run vacation and education resort, Unity House, in the Pocono Mountains of Pennsylvania; and a union-owned radio station.

The ILGWU also constructed housing for member retirees in New York and was among the first unions successfully to negotiate health, welfare, and vacation funds in contracts with employers in the 1940s. The union nurtured its own chorus that conducted live musical performances in a variety of venues ranging from community fundraisers to political rallies and campaigns. And it implemented workers' education programs throughout its districts and locals to enlighten worker members on issues ranging from workplace health and safety to politics and political activism. The union was routinely active in voter registration drives and regularly endorsed and advocated for prolabor political candidates and incumbents, usually Democrats. Finally the ILGWU was at the forefront of an active national union label campaign from the 1960s to the mid-1980s to educate and encourage American consumers on the value of purchasing products made in the United States. Though it did not succeed in the long run, the union label campaign gained national acclaim as organized labor fought overseas imports of products ranging from apparel to electronics and children's toys.

In 1995, the ILGWU merged with the Amalgamated Clothing and Textile Workers' Union (ACTWU) to create UNITE! or Union of Needletrades, Industrial, and Textile Employees. The merger accompanied a 10 million-dollar campaign to organize domestic and overseas apparel workers in collaboration with the international labor movement. To assert such control, the new union turned to familiar practices reflective of its educational and political traditions.

The UNITE! members also took part in and supported massive protests targeted at the World Trade Organization's (WTO) third annual ministerial conference held in Seattle, Washington, in late 1999. In one of the largest (and most violent) protests of its kind, scores of protestors disrupted trade talks and demanded improved labor standards in developing economies and a greater voice for workers in trade agreements. Environmental, human, and labor rights' issues were the central focus of those concerned about negative repercussions of international free trade policy. Despite the perception of weakened clout and credibility, the WTO protests defined the labor movement's militancy in the arena of international trade, as did its spring 2000 opposition to the U.S. Government's move to normalize trade relations with the People's Republic of China in which UNITE! played an oppositionist role due in large part to workplace conditions in the Asian nation. In a related move UNITE! supported student-led antisweatshop campaigns to stop colleges and universities from selling apparel made with sweated labor. Student-inspired organizations, such as the United Students against Sweatshops, collaborated with the union and the Workers' Rights Organization.

On July 8, 2004, UNITE! merged with the Hotel Employees' and Restaurant Employees' International Union (HERE) to form UNITE HERE. The union represents more than 450,000 active members and more than 400,000 retirees throughout North America. The UNITE HERE is largely comprised of immigrants, including a high percentage of African-American, Latino, and Asian-American workers. The majority of UNITE HERE members are women.

In July 2005, UNITE HERE joined with three other labor unions—the Service Employees' International Union, International Brotherhood of Teamsters, and United Food and Commercial Workers—in boycotting the national AFL-CIO convention held in Chicago. The four unions comprise the Change to Win Coalition and have openly defied and challenged AFL-CIO policy and traditions and call for greater effort in grassroots organizing.

KENNETH C. WOLENSKY

References and Further Reading

Danish, Max. *The World of David Dubinsky*. Cleveland, OH: World Publishing, 1957.

Dubinsky, David. *A Life with Labor*. New York: Simon and Shuster, 1977.

Epstein, Melech. *Jewish Labor in the U.S.A.* Hoboken, NJ: KTAV, 1969.

Lorwin, Louis. *The Women's Garment Workers*. New York: Arno, 1969.

Stein, Leon. *Out of the Sweatshop*. New York: Quadrangle, 1977.

Tyler, Gus. *Look for the Union Label*. Armonk, New York: M. E. Sharpe, 1995.

Waldinger, Ruth. *Through the Eye of the Needle*. New York: New York University Press, 1986.

Wolensky, Kenneth C., Nicole H. Wolensky, and Robert P. Wolensky. *Fighting for the Union Label*. University Park: Pennsylvania State University Press, 2002.

See also **American Federation of Labor; Working-Class Feminism**

INTERNATIONAL LONGSHOREMEN'S ASSOCIATION

The International Longshoremen's Association (ILA) is one of the American Federation of Labor's (AFL's) oldest trade unions. Established in Chicago in 1892, the ILA would eventually expand its geographical base from the Midwest lake district to the Pacific Coast, the Gulf, and finally the Atlantic coastline. There had been numerous attempts to organize longshoremen beginning in the early nineteenth century. Most attempts were destroyed by economic conditions or employer intransigence. The economic and financial panics of the 1870s and 1880s did much to stall union organization. The Knights of Labor successfully organized New York's longshoremen, but a strike in 1889 witnessed a total destruction of the Knights' power. Contributing to this defeat was the use of Italian strikebreakers, and by the end of the nineteenth century, Italians dominated dock work in Brooklyn, Staten Island, and New Jersey.

In the Midwest and gulf ports, the story was different however. As early as 1877, tugboat worker Daniel Keefe had established a longshoremen's local in Chicago. He cautiously began to nurture locals in other midwestern ports. His perseverance paid off when longshoremen in Detroit and Cleveland and others agreed to use Keefe's Chicago local as a template. Because Keefe had also organized some Canadian locals, the title of the new organization would be the International Longshoremen's Association. By 1905, it appeared that the ILA's cautious approach was paying dividends. It had organized 100,000 longshoremen; 50,000 were from Great Lakes' ports, but New York remained as yet unorganized. Other ports of ILA strength were concentrated in the Gulf. Galveston, Mobile, and New Orleans were particular centers of union strength. Keefe's conservatism (he had close personal links with U.S. Senator Mark Hanna and the National Civic Federation) isolated him from many of the ILA locals. This was particularly the case with the Gulf longshoremen. These longshoremen fought bitter and violent battles against shippers and stevedores. Accustomed to fighting aggressively for advances, these longshoremen were wary of Keefe's cautious approach. In 1908, a stunned membership learned that Keefe had resigned. Taking his place was another Great Lakes ILA leader, T. V. O'Connor.

O'Connor appeared just as cautious as Keefe although relations with the AFL stood on happier ground. But O'Connor refused to support other maritime workers. In the Great Lakes region seamen had asked for support during a 1908 strike. O'Connor refused the plea leaving in his wake a hostile union

Longshoremen loading cargo onto a ship at Port Authority Piers, Furman St., Brooklyn, New York/World Journal Tribune photo by Matthew Black. Library of Congress, Prints & Photographs Division, NYWT & S Collection, [LC-USZ62-124237].

movement. Just as important the seamen lost the strike and personally blamed O'Connor and the ILA for their defeat. For all the lack of support for other maritime unions, the ILA's membership expansion continued apace. In 1911, there were over 307 locals. The majority were still in the Great Lakes region, but expansion had reached further into Canada, Puerto Rico, and the Atlantic ports of Baltimore, Philadelphia, Hampton Roads, and Norfolk, Virginia. The West remained a weak spot though. Although ILA locals were evident in San Diego, San Francisco, Oregon, and Washington, they held tenuous power and at times left the ILA fold accusing it of conservatism or acting like a company union.

Southern locals continued their strong showing. Just as dynamic these locals practiced a form of biracial unionism whereby black and white longshoremen were members together. Gulf longshoremen were unique in that they actively practiced a form of enlightened race relations. Although separated into white and black locals, white longshoremen recognized that accommodation to African-American dockworkers was a strategic necessity. Operating in a Jim Crow milieu, the New Orleans longshoremen paradoxically worked together to form a vibrant and successful alliance. Unlike longshoremen in the northern and midwestern ports, these longshoremen in New Orleans built a biracial labor movement that could actively resist employer power.

New York City, the largest port in the nation in terms of cargo handled and number of longshoremen, was still relatively unorganized. Stalling ILA efforts was the Longshoremen's Union Protective Association (LUPA). By 1912, the ILA had to share the spoils with the LUPA. Such dual unionism hampered a united front and left the majority of New York and New Jersey longshoremen unorganized. O'Connor dispatched organizers into the port and aggressively began organizing ILA locals. A district council was formed to represent the locals throughout the port. Such tactics bore fruit when the members of the LUPA either agreed to join the ILA or were simply absorbed. By 1914, the ILA had at last gained an impressive foothold. Such success was replicated in Boston and Baltimore. Philadelphia longshoremen however aligned themselves with the Industrial Workers of the World (IWW). Nonetheless the ILA was at last becoming a truly national organization. Encouraging such growth was a sympathetic federal government. President Woodrow Wilson's administration had done much to encourage trade union growth generally. The establishment of the Department of

Labor and the passage of the Clayton Anti-Trust Act made clear the shift toward more supportive government of trade union growth.

The organization of the New York longshoremen was beset with difficulties however. The giant port and its relatively large number of longshoremen, numbering approximately 30,000, were considered a very attractive prize by some union officials. The strong localism of the union made for unstable situations at times. The ethnic and racial character of the workforce added another layer to this traditional localism. Longshoremen locals tended to operate around specific piers. Such concentration was ethnically and race-based. On the west side of Manhattan, the Irish dominated the piers by the West Village, Chelsea, and Hells' Kitchen. In Brooklyn Italians controlled most of the locals, but in others there was a smattering of African-American and Scandinavian control. In New Jersey the mix was even more diverse with Italian, Czech, Polish, and Irish ethnics laboring. By the early 1920s, these same groups dominated the hiring process, thus preventing competition from so-called outsiders. In fact it merely confirmed a racial and ethnic hierarchy.

This hierarchy was no more evident than in Manhattan. Irish control of the more lucrative passenger terminals ensured a clear dominance in the port and in the union. Centered in this area was Local 791, known also as the "mother local." It was one of the largest and more militant of the union locals. It tended to lead the way in setting standards of work and wage demands. From Local 791 would come a future leader of the ILA, Joe Ryan. Ryan had moved through Local 791 to become the voice of the New York District Council.

But Ryan had to bide his time because once O'Connor stepped down from the presidency in 1921, he was replaced by another Great Lakes union official, Anthony Chlopek. Chlopek tried to continue the ILA goal of expansion but lacked the centralizing power to drive a nationwide campaign. Indeed the power had been transferred to the district and local levels, just as problematic employer offensives on the West Coast and at Gulf ports had rolled the union back. The ILA was now concentrated on the Great Lakes and the Atlantic Coast. The ILA barely hung on, and Chlopek retired a mere 6 years later in 1927.

For Joe Ryan his time had come to assume the presidency. He had made a name for himself by earlier supporting O'Connor and ridding New York of separatist tendencies. His presidency also represented a fundamental shift of power. The Great Lakes region, while obviously still important, could not compare in terms of numbers to the Atlantic Coast locals. As the major Atlantic ports were organized, a critical shift had taken place; consequently the center of power now resided in New York.

Joe Ryan would become a highly controversial figure. He became one of the longest ruling presidents, being in power from 1927 to 1954. His actions or nonaction with regard to criminal control of some New York locals would tarnish his image and that of the ILA. While at the helm, union locals in Brooklyn, Staten Island, Jersey City, and a smattering on the east and west sides of Manhattan became controlled by criminal elements. Notorious Italian and Irish gangsters used union locals as fiefdoms to control rackets, shake down employers and longshoremen, and organize theft on a large scale. To some extent the criminal infiltration on New York's waterfront coincided with Ryan's rule. When asked about the large number of ILA officials who had police records, Ryan merely responded that he was helping felons with an opportunity to go straight. Ryan also charged that Communist encroachment on the piers needed to be confronted with aggressive means. Indeed throughout his tenure as president, Ryan was always more concerned about Communist activity than that of criminal loading rackets.

The Port of New York's reputation for widespread criminal activity ensured that other regional districts were not pleased by the domination by New Yorkers of the ILA hierarchy. This resentment or alienation was no more apparent than with the West Coast longshoremen's revolt from the ILA. Since World War I, West Coast longshoremen had lacked a fighting organization and were forced to work with a company union. In 1934, these longshoremen rebelled against the arbitrary power of employers. A series of bloody street battles in San Francisco followed, resulting in deaths of two longshoremen. The ILA, and in particular, Joe Ryan, attempted to rein in the West Coast men urging that they remain patient and wait for the right moment to confront employers. The men rejected such overtures and instead formed a new union, the International Longshoremen's and Warehousemen's Union (ILWU). Led by Australian-born Harry Bridges, the ILWU was to become a permanent feature along the West Coast. The ILA had thus lost a significant membership section and would never regain its power on the West Coast.

Just as problematic, the ILA was facing a revolt within its ranks on the Atlantic Coast. Fed up with poor wages and working conditions, New York's rank-and-file were ripe for rebellion. Pete Panto, an Italian-American longshoreman from Brooklyn, helped create an organized opposition to the ILA hierarchy. In 1939, Panto was addressing meetings of thousands of Brooklyn's longshoremen. Panto was trusted by the men because he was one of them, a rank-and-file longshoreman. For the ILA leaders in Brooklyn, Panto's challenge was deemed a serious affront. Making the situation dangerous was that most of the Brooklyn union locals were controlled by mobsters linked to organized crime. Panto was warned to shut up and stop agitating against the established ILA leadership, but the momentum of the oppositional movement continued. In 1939, however, Panto went missing. Some union officials argued that his disappearance was a ruse to garner sympathy. His supporters believed that something more sinister was afoot. Chalk messages were written along the waterfront and in Brooklyn Heights asking, "Where is Pete Panto?" With Panto gone, the movement he had headed disintegrated. The message had clearly been sent; do not challenge the Brooklyn ILA leadership.

Not until after World War II was Panto's body discovered in a mob-run cemetery in New Jersey. He had been strangled and dumped in a lime pit. It was subsequently revealed that Panto had been murdered by members of Murder Inc. Murder Inc. was a notorious hit squad for the New York mob. The leading member was Albert Anastasia, whose brother, Tony Anastasia was the leader of the Brooklyn ILA. In response to Panto's disappearance, police officials did a short investigation, and the Brooklyn District Attorney asked Ryan to clear up the mob-dominated Brooklyn waterfront. Ryan agreed, but 20 years later in the 1950s, the same mob-related officials were still in power of most of the Brooklyn docks.

Panto's disappearance had a chilling effect on the insurgency. Lacking a respected leader, New York's longshoremen once again adopted a posture of grudgingly accepting their lot. Following Pearl Harbor and the entry of the United States into World War II, the ILA longshoremen were further defenseless in opposing the speed-up on the Atlantic Ocean docks. Sling loads increased, and the rhythm of work intensified. The only escape for many of the longshoremen was to leave the respective waterfronts for other jobs or enter the military. Indeed large numbers of Brooklyn and Manhattan longshoremen joined the armed forces. For those remaining, they experienced a dramatic deterioration of working conditions, including an almost absence of safety regulations on the job.

Once the war ended, the ILA confronted an angry and frustrated rank-and-file. Adding to the volatile mix were returning veterans who were no longer just going to accept the status quo. The spark for the revolt was a wage agreement negotiated by Ryan in 1945. Members of mother Local 791 walked off the job and were quickly joined by others throughout the port. Within days the port was shut down. For the first time, there appeared to be an organized opposition to the ILA leadership. Ryan responded by using redbaiting tactics when he blamed Communists for fomenting the trouble. True there was some Communist involvement, but it was peripheral at best. The charge was a potent one however. Those insurgent leaders who did emerge were quickly isolated and then violently attacked. William E. Warren and Sal Barone, for example, were viciously beaten, thrown out of the ILA, and told to stay away from the docks.

Such intimidation, although effective in the preceding case, could not forestall opposition to the ILA leadership. By 1948, returning veterans had transformed the political climate. These men had experienced death and destruction on a grand scale. Just as vital they had developed a distinct resentment of authority, whether military or union officialdom. Communist agitators were also active on the docks, particularly in Brooklyn. Trouble quickly followed another wage agreement that Ryan had negotiated. Again it was Local 791 that led the walkout. Local 791's leader, Gene Sampson, initially took charge of the revolt. Within days not only was the port of New York closed, but also ports in Boston, Philadelphia, and Baltimore. The rebellion had therefore spread to other ports. Ryan repeated his charge that Communists were spreading dissension and attempting to disrupt a "fine agreement." Such an accusation fell on deaf ears. Even the Federal Bureau of Investigation (FBI) was unimpressed with Ryan's accusation. In Brooklyn though, Communist influence was prevalent in the insurgency's leaders. Paul O'Dwyer, the brother of New York City Mayor William O'Dwyer, and Vincent Longhi, were both Communist sympathizers and helped create an oppositional organization. Such action was fraught with danger because gangsters were close by and could have easily attacked the organization.

The ILA was forced to renew negotiations. This time the ILA negotiated a larger wage increase and welfare fund. With such a turnaround, the opposition felt emboldened, and with the help of labor priests, they began organizing. In 1951, the situation was rife for change. Ryan had again negotiated a wage increase that was rejected by the rank-and-file. Correspondingly another wildcat strike broke out in New York and along the Atlantic coastline. Ryan's charge of Communist conspiracy rang hollow. The strike lasted for 11 days, resulting in a wage increase above that of Ryan's agreement. The strike also caught the attention of officials in New York. Governor Thomas Dewey unleashed an investigation of the ILA and its affiliated New York locals. What followed was a sensational series of hearings where a slew of ILA officials were cross-examined. Ultimately the hearings proved that the ILA was replete not only with criminal elements, but also members of organized crime.

The findings of widespread criminal infiltration forced the AFL to kick the ILA out of the established movement. The AFL created a rival union, the International Brotherhood of Longshoremen and a series of National Labor Relations Board (NLRB) elections were held. Each time however the New York men voted for the ILA. The ILA was eventually allowed back into the AFL after it promised to clean up the union. But the ILA has continued to be investigated for its criminal activities. Even as recently as the 1990s, a series of arrests of ILA officials highlighted the continuing involvement of criminal groups in the union.

COLIN DAVIS

References and Further Reading

Davis, Colin J. *Waterfront Revolts: New York and London Dockworkers, 1946–1961.* Urbana: University of Illinois Press, 2003.
Kimeldorf, Howard. *Reds or Rackets: The Making of Radical and Conservative Unions on the Waterfront.* Berkeley: University of California Press, 1988.
Russell, Maud. *Men along the Shore.* New York: Brussel and Brussel, 1966.

INTERNATIONAL TYPOGRAPHICAL UNION

One of the oldest and most successful trade unions in North America, the evolution and history of the International Typographical Union (ITU) reflected the strengths and weaknesses of American craft unionism.

Origins

Printers established some of the earliest trade unions in North America in response to trends that unfolded through the late eighteenth and early nineteenth centuries. During these years, even before mechanization, the division of labor eroded the importance of the long apprenticeships and training. This introduced "two-thirds" and "half-way" journeymen, as well as young boys into the shops and allowed employers radically to expand the size of the workplace. The process degraded the value of skilled labor, reduced wages, and simply throttled the kind of

mobility typified by the success of Benjamin Franklin in colonial days.

Journeymen in the craft began negotiating for better wages and working conditions as early as 1778, going on strike by 1786, and forming their own organizations in Philadelphia and New York by the 1790s, and in Boston, Albany, Baltimore, and Washington by 1815. That year also saw the first discussions begin about the need to establish a common wage scale for the northeastern seaboard.

Early efforts at national organization followed. In 1836, representatives from half-a-dozen locals formed a National Typographical Association, which reconvened in 1837. During these same years, there were also locals in at least 16 other communities as well as a Canadian society. In 1844, printers on the East Coast had a short-lived Order of Faust, apparently a fraternal organization named for the mythical, historical figure whose efforts created the craft.

The National Typographical Union

Near the middle of the nineteenth century, technological innovations converged to transform the craft. Early in the century, techniques of stereotyping allowed casts of forms for an entire page to be made and stored indefinitely. At about the same time, papermakers learned how to produce continuous rolls of paper, and steam-powered presses began to mechanize the process. In the 1840s, the Hoe rotary press combined these innovations in a way that made large-scale factory productions viable. The larger newspapers in New York and Philadelphia built massive new structures to house the gigantic new presses, the demands of which employed unprecedented numbers of workers, laboring by shift.

Journeymen working in these new concerns, together with others in less technologically developed smaller shops, held national conventions in 1850 and 1851 before organizing the National Typographical Union (NTU) on May 3, 1852. The NTU convened annually but had very little power over local organizations. It used its moral influence to attempt resolution of the varying standards among the locals for how to deal with wage scales, negotiations, and scabs. For example the NTU gradually drew New York's Co-operative Printer's Union representing job printers into its own No. 6, mostly newspaper printers.

The NTU could not overcome the different scale and orientation of the locals largely because local conditions were hardly similar in the craft as in the wider society. As this came to a head, the NTU postponed its 1861 convention, and the organization largely imploded under the impact of the Civil War. Still the wartime inflation and prosperity inspired new and larger reorganizations even as hard-pressed employers introduced women into the industry. By 1867, the NTU's own reconstruction involved renewed efforts to extend its power in relation to those of subordinate bodies and locals. In many respects the latter would long retain power.

Reconstruction of the union posed questions that came to a head at the 1869 convention. Although the NTU left whether or not to admit black members to the locals, many of which remained white-only, it decided 10 years later to require all locals to accept transfers of membership regardless of race. So, too, the NTU grappled with the question of the women who had entered the industry, opting for a distinct women's local in some cases. At the same time, the admission of Canadian locals transformed the NTU into the ITU.

Heyday: Shaping an American Craft Unionism

Locals organized within specific workplaces or chapels. In a craft where apprenticeship survived in such a state as not to provide many of the essential skills, the ITU became an arbiter of those skills. This suited the larger and more successful employers as well as the union, so the ITU gained much more control over the hiring and firing of workers than most American unions. This included control over the list of unemployed members who could substitute for the regularly employed, although a standardized ITU control over the sublist took until 1890. This went beyond the workplace as well because members "tramping" from job to job could replace their regular dues card with a traveling card that would be honored by all unions and therefore their employers.

Before the ITU assumed that authority, a series of secret societies within the union assumed that function. The Brotherhood of the Union, an antebellum forerunner of the Knights of Labor likely entered the union through the New York merger in the 1850s. Through the 1870s, it sought to secure the employment of the most committed unionists by taking control over hiring and firing in many chapels. This paradoxically established the foundations for cliquish privilege and corruption. After an ongoing battle at the conventions from 1880 to 1896, the ITU took on this authority and specifically placed the activities of the brotherhood beyond the bonds of acceptance.

Nevertheless as late as 1912, a secret society known as the Wahnetas had assumed the same functions as the brotherhood.

The only way the ITU could supersede what the Wahnetas or the brotherhood had done was to take control itself over the sublist and related issues. By the turn of the century, the progressives battled "administrationists" to do so, creating a unique two-party system within a North American union. (By the late 1920s, the independents would replace administrationists.)

Progressive Policy

From the 1880s into the 1920s, the ITU introduced a number of noteworthy innovations during this period. When the new Linotype machine finally allowed type to be set from a keyboard in the 1880s, union printers did not resist the machine but made it their own. Through rigorous training, they made sure that the overwhelming majority of Linotypes in use by 1915 were operated by unionists.

Insofar as the Linotype increased the exposure of printers to lead fumes, it afflicted many members with the printers' disease, tuberculosis. Given the ITU's long-standing interest in alimony and benefits, it opened a sanitarium in Colorado for treatment of the disease in 1892. Other reforms were even more directly associated with the wider ideology of progressive reform.

Printers had always preferred means other than strikes to impose their decisions. If a conflict became intense enough to inspire a work stoppage, other ITU locals might or might not respond with financial support. During the great strike wave of the 1880s though, the ITU began to put together a common defense fund to support the increasingly larger and more expensive local strikes. This forced the ITU to assume considerable control over job actions and encouraged collective bargaining and arbitration with employers. The approach reached its peak success during the First World War with the 1917–1922 arbitration agreement providing a legal alternative to litigation whereby both parties agree to submit their respective positions to a third party who would arbitrate or negotiate a resolution satisfactory to both sides.

In addition to arbitration, the ITU took up the idea of the referendum, which came to be used systematically to resolve questions in the union after 1889, and eventually used the referendum for its regular governance.

Organizing the Unorganized: The Congress of Industrial Organizations

From its inception the ITU functioned alongside other craft unions like that of the pressmen and lithographers. The Amalgamated Lithographers of America (1886) formed independently of the ITU, but the very success of the latter in elevating the wages and working conditions of compositors and typesetters inspired renewed efforts of these related crafts, creating the International Printing Pressmen's Union (1889), the International Brotherhood of Bookbinders (1892), the International Stereotypers' and Electrotypers' Union (1901), and the International Photoengravers' Union (1904). It was a founding participant in the American Federation of Labor (AFL).

The ITU extended its progressive unionism to industrial organization to break with the AFL in 1935, participating in the new Committee for Industrial Organization (CIO). Although this became a point of contention between the progressives and independents during the war, the ITU, like the other CIO unions, clashed with the government over National War Labor Board in 1943–1944, and after the war, Taft-Hartley Law 1947.

Postwar Demise

Despite the ITU's past adaptability, most locals and the international itself failed to adjust to the post-World War II technological and demographic changes in the industry. This proved fatal to the union's future.

After World War II, the officials who built the CIO and battled Taft-Hartley fared poorly in the climate of prosperity and anticommunism. Suburbanization and television drove a number of big-city dailies out of business. Eventually the Newspaper Preservation Act (1971) set aside earlier antitrust legislation by allowing rival publications to combine their production and delivery resources. This essentially authorized the extension of control by Gannett, Knight-Ridder, and Media General, Inc. over many urban newspapers.

The industry turned increasingly toward offset printing and photocomposition, and phototypesetting. These became commercially viable in the 1930s and became the dominant mode of printing in the 1950s. This technique conveys images to paper from rubber rollers, which pick up the ink from metal or paper plates. Dark parts of those plates repel water and absorb ink, while light parts repel ink and absorb water. These come from a photographic image of a sheet, the text for which was entered on a typewriter keyboard instead of a Linotype. This opened the craft to new workers, particularly women with good keyboarding skills.

Although the ITU and its locals fought the introduction of *ersatz* printing into the industry, it eventually established training programs for its members. However its main strategy was to negotiate guaranteed jobs for members already employed in the industry. Contrary to its own long traditions, the ITU never took stock of the state of the craft, much less opened itself to organization of the unorganized.

Unionism in the Computer Age

Computers transformed the craft entirely in the 1970s and 1980s. These made possible digital typesetting, while word-processing software and the quick-printing industry created an explosion in small-press publishing. Although at the center of this rapidly growing industry, ITU membership actually fell from over 106,634 in 1964 to only about 38,000 working members by the mid-1980s.

The cost of making printing profitable continued to encourage the concentration of media, which pit the ITU against more powerful employers. The deregulation of the 1980s brought ownership from outside of the industry to new levels. By then the large city newspapers moved digitized technology toward plateless printing, where images could be transferred by ink jet, photographic, or quick-copy techniques. While these remain ancillary to large-scale operations like a newspaper, they are frequently used for the production of printed matter in small quantity.

All these shifts further blurred the lines between the ITU and other unions like the Newspaper Guild, the Newspaper and Graphic Communications Workers' Union, and others. On the one hand employers ruthlessly exploited the persistence of these divisions. By 1975, the production of the *Washington Post* involved so many different unions that it successfully pit them against each other to win a pressman's strike. Similar scenarios had been played out earlier in many other cities.

On the other these developments made a new approach unavoidable. Through the 1970s into the 1980s, a series of mergers brought pressmen, bookbinders, stereotypers, electrotypers, photoengravers, and lithographers into the Graphic Communications International Union. By the mid-1980s, the ITU sought unions with which it might merge. In 1986, it folded its organization and resources into the Printing, Publishing, and Media Workers' division of the Communication Workers of America.

MARK LAUSE

References and Further Reading

A Study of the History of the International Typographical Union, 1852–1966. 2 vols. Colorado Springs, CO: International Typographical Union, 1967.

Lipset, Seymour Martin, Martin A. Trow, James S. Coleman. *Union Democracy: The Internal Politics of the International Typographical Union.* New York: Free Press, 1977. (reprint)

Stewart, Ethelbert. *A Documentary History of the Early Organizations of Printers.* Indianapolis, IN: International Typographical Union, 1907.

INTERNATIONAL UNION OF OPERATING ENGINEERS

Founded in 1896, the International Union of Operating Engineers (IUOE) has historically consisted of two branches of engineers: Stationary engineers and hoisting and portable engineers. In general stationary engineers operate, maintain, and repair equipment in buildings and industrial complexes, while hoisting and portable engineers operate heavy equipment used in the building and construction trades. Over the course of its history, the union has experienced its most impressive growth in the construction industry, and in the second-half of the twentieth century, the IUOE established itself as one of the strongest building trades unions in the United States.

Constituency

Five of the original six local craft unions that joined to form the IUOE in 1896 represented highly skilled stationary engineers who operated the steam engines that powered the heating and refrigeration systems in large commercial buildings (the word steam appeared in the union's title until 1927). Stationary engineers comprised a majority of the IUOE's membership until 1940, but their prestige was undermined by the decline of the steam engine. As central power plants replaced the single-building steam engine, the responsibilities of operating engineers gradually became the maintenance of central heating, air conditioning, refrigeration, and electrical systems. The stationary branch of the IUOE responded to these challenges in the post-World War II period by launching organizing drives in such other areas as nuclear power plants, oil and chemical refineries, hospitals, and public utilities.

In contrast to their stationary counterparts as well as to other building trades unions, hoisting and portable engineers generally benefited from technological change. In fact the job did not exist before the invention of the first practical hoisting engine in 1875. And as hoisting, pumping, cement mixing, and excavating machines improved, so did the job of the hoisting and portable engineer. In 1907, the American Federation of Labor (AFL) awarded the IUOE jurisdiction over all forms of construction equipment regardless of power source, thus ensuring that the union would survive the demise of the steam engine and would win a majority of its jurisdictional battles with other unions. After the IUOE amalgamated with the International Brotherhood of Steam Shovel and Dredgemen in 1927, they were poised to organize the operators of the heavy machines used in future highway and heavy construction projects, such as dams, airports, subways, pipelines, and bridges. In the post-World War II construction boom, these construction projects became the main source of employment for the IUOE and helped transform it from a financially weak organization of mostly stationary engineers into one of the most powerful unions in the building trades.

Leadership, Gains, and Conflict

Throughout its history the IUOE has remained committed to a course of business unionism, although since World War II, union leaders have exhibited flexibility in altering bargaining and organizational strategies to adjust to economic, technological, and political changes. Each general president and most international officers until 1921 were members of stationary locals, and every president since has come from the building trades division.

In the period that stationary engineers controlled the central organization, IUOE leaders focused on regulating entry to the craft and striking a workable balance between the international organization and local unions. In 1906, the IUOE began organizing lesser skilled workers into branch locals, each of which were subordinate to a parent local. In addition to serving as a substitute for a formal apprenticeship program, these branch locals also allowed the IUOE to neutralize the competition of nonunion workers for hoisting jobs, which would have undercut the union's wage rate. The most divisive internal conflicts that erupted during this period, particularly the problem of recalcitrant locals and internal jurisdictional disputes, were gradually resolved through amalgamation and the overall growth of the union's central organization during the 1920s and 1930s.

From 1940–1975, the IUOE enjoyed its greatest period of economic growth. Operating engineers had always enjoyed certain advantages when bargaining with employers. Contractors felt that they could depend on the IUOE to supply well-trained operators, which became increasingly important as contractors increased their investments in equipment and entered labor markets where they were unfamiliar with employers. In addition since operating engineers could halt an entire construction project simply by refusing to hoist materials, contractors were inclined to maintain good relations with the union. These factors combined with the expansion in the construction of highways, airports, pipelines, and other earth-moving projects to establish unprecedented wage settlements that significantly outpaced interest rates. With many of the union's internal disputes settled and the union experiencing healthy membership and financial growth, leaders in the post-World War II period were able to concentrate on reviving its stationary branch and moving into new fields, developing safety programs, pressing for workplace health and safety legislation, restructuring its job, and organizing training programs.

The IUOE leaders have also had to respond to external challenges. In the postwar period, building trades' unions were targeted by civil rights groups and protesters for excluding minorities and women. With passage of the Civil Rights Act of 1964, establishment of the Job Corps program, and implementation in 1969 of the Philadelphia Plan, the federal government also began to compel building trades unions to alter their membership and apprenticeship practices. The IUOE was resistant to any form of interference with its apprenticeship and membership policies, but in 1977 the union made inclusion of minorities a priority and created a department of civil rights.

More serious challenges to the IUOE's success however have been posed by the ascendance of political conservatism in the United States, economic recession and rising unemployment in the construction industry, and an aggressive open-shop drive led by large firms that purchase the services of contractors. Although by the 1960s, the National Labor Relations Board had begun applying Taft-Hartley regulations to building trades unions and anti-union state and national legislators launched attacks against prevailing wage legislation, contractors generally continued

to prefer IUOE labor. This soon changed however as the high-wage settlements of the 1960s had the unintended effect of making contractors responsive to anti-union campaigns launched by the large firms that blamed union wage rates for high construction costs. As a result the IUOE suffered substantial membership losses and watched as many of its collective-bargaining gains were rolled back. According to the union's historians, the IUOE regrouped after its nadir in the 1980s and began a period of new growth in the 1990s.

JOHN J. ROSEN

References and Further Reading

Mangum, Garth L. *The Operating Engineers: The Economic History of a Trade Union.* Cambridge, MA: Harvard University Press, 1964.
Mangum, Garth L., and John Walsh. *Union Resilience in Troubled Times: The Story of the Operating Engineers, AFL-CIO, 1960–1993.* New York and London, UK: M. E. Sharpe, 1994.

INTERNATIONAL WOODWORKERS OF AMERICA

The International Woodworkers of America (1937–1987) was unique among Congress of International Organizations (CIO) unions in two respects. First it was the most Canadian of international unions, with Canadians composing from 40%–60% of the union's membership throughout its history. Secondly it experienced an early internal political rift that would serve as a dress rehearsal for the conflict the labor movement experienced during the Cold War era. The history of the IWA demonstrates both the strength of the CIO's original industrial union strategy and that vision's limitations when confronted by the globalization of the economy at century's end. When the IWA finally divided into two national unions in 1987, one based in Canada and the other in the United States, the divorce demonstrated the limits of international union solidarity in this new world order.

Origins of Unionism in the Wood Products Industry

The lumber and sawmill industry had been the scene of turbulent labor unrest since the nineteenth century. This was especially the case in the Pacific Northwest, where the industry migrated as forests in the East and Midwest were cleared by the timber industrialists of the era. The wood products industry was an extremely dangerous place to work, especially for loggers. This group, dominated by unmarried men working in remote communities, provided a particularly fertile ground for labor radicalism. Early organizing success by the Industrial Workers of the World prompted fierce interunion rivalry between labor radicals, conservative craft unions, and a significant employer-dominated company union, the Loyal Legion of Loggers and Lumbermen. The vast majority of the industry's workers were unskilled, and the highly labor-intensive nature of production encouraged employers to squeeze workers with low pay and benefits. Seasonal fluctuations in product markets and chronic overcapacity led to frequent unemployment, further depressing the rural economies where logging and sawmills proliferated.

The IWA was founded in Tacoma, Washington, in July 1937, by woodworkers disaffected with the craft unionism policies of the United Brotherhood of Carpenters (UBC). The Timber and Sawmill Workers' union was given jurisdiction of the industry by the American Federation of labor (AFL) in the early 1930s but was never granted full membership status under the UBC constitution. Discontent exploded in the spring of 1935, when Oregon and Washington locals launched a regionwide strike. When insurgent unions (mostly in Washington State) opposed the UBC-led efforts to settle the dispute on less than acceptable terms, local leaders accused them of selling out and formed a rump Federation of Woodworkers' organization. They quickly sought affiliation with the national CIO and seceded from the UBC to form the new international union. Central to the IWA grievances were the second-rate status wood workers suffered within the UBC and the segregation of locals by craft, autocratically enforced by UBC officials. As delegates to the founding IWA convention sang, "We've gone CIO boys, we've gone CIO. The Carpenters and Joiners have always tried to corner our dough, but we'll stick together, for rank-and-file control." The IWA would be one of the most democratically structured of CIO international unions.

Canadian Influence and Disputes Over Communism

From the beginning the IWA was strongly influenced by its Canadian segment. The IWA's first president, Harold Pritchett, was a shingle weaver and member of the Canadian Communist party. He became only the second Canadian to head a U.S.-based international union. The Canadian region of the IWA was heavily influenced by left wingers, including leadership from the Communist party-affiliated Lumber Workers' Industrial Union, which fought a bitter, 5-month strike on Vancouver Island in 1934.

The IWA was split between a red bloc led by Pritchett and a white bloc of anti-Communists with strength in the Columbia River district of the union in Oregon and Washington. Observers have noted that the IWA "got redder as you went north," and this has been a source for debate about the politics of the union. One theory is that the northern mills encouraged a more radical rank-and-file because they were larger, more mechanized, and the workers more "proletarianized." Another relevant factor was the ethnic mix of workers within the IWA's two Pacific Northwest regions. The southern part of Region 3's membership (Oregon and Northern California) tended toward Germans of Midwest farming backgrounds, while Washington and Region 1 in British Columbia had more Scandinavians, and especially Finns, who are often associated with left-wing labor activism.

Rivalry with AFL Sawmill Workers

In addition to the battle over communism, the IWA faced significant resistance organizing from the rival AFL timber union (now known as the Lumber and Sawmill Workers [LSW]). Other AFL and CIO affiliates often joined the bitter disputes between the two, as the unions sought to enforce boycotts against their rival's products. An early partner of the IWA in these battles was the newly formed International Longshoremen's and Warehousemen's Union, another left-led union, whose successful 1934 coastal strike was a watershed historical moment for many Industrial Workers of the World (IWA) members. The recession of 1938, the red/white split, and fierce competition with the (LSW) exacted a serious toll on the new union. Membership fell from 40,000 at the first convention to 20,000 in 1938. The conflict prompted CIO President Phil Murray to install one of his staff, Adolph Germer, as organizing director, leading to a final showdown between the red and white blocs.

The white bloc deposed Pritchett in 1941 after his visa to enter the United States was denied when he attempted to attend the union's convention in Portland. The events surrounding Pritchett's defeat were notable because of the active involvement of the national CIO office, a precursor to the more open internecine warfare that the CIO would experience in 1947–1950. With white-bloc candidate Worth Lowery the new president, the left wing of the IWA retreated to British Columbia's District 3, where Harry Pritchett remained director.

Despite the ongoing political turmoil within the union, the IWA's first 15 years marked a remarkable organizing thrust that made the lumber and sawmill industry in the Pacific Northwest one of the most organized sectors in the entire North American manufacturing economy. Wartime labor policies boosted organizing, and by the late 1940s, 80% of the industry's workers were represented by a union.

Despite holding on to power in District 1, Pritchett's red bloc was seriously compromised by a fatal strategic decision made in 1948. Rather than submit to the Taft-Hartley Act's requirements to sign anti-Communist affidavits, British Columbia IWA leaders, on advice from the Canadian Communist party, took the region out of the IWA and formed an independent Woodworkers' Industrial Union of Canada. Shortly they faced raids from competing AFL and CIO unions, and the left-wing leadership was defeated. In 1950, the WIUC dissolved and went back into the IWA.

The IWA enjoyed great success in the 1960s and 1970s, with its membership peaking at 112,000 in 1977 as the housing boom drove a strong albeit cyclical industry. Significant strikes on both sides of the border strengthened pattern bargaining agreements in the United States and more centralized industrywide negotiations in British Columbia, where a corporate political environment encouraged government intervention in labor relations to stabilize crucial economic sectors.

Dissolution of the International Union

Despite success at the bargaining table, serious structural economic changes were at work that would undermine the strength of the IWA. Like other manufacturing industries, technological change was reducing employment drastically in wood products. Furthermore U.S.-based employers began increasingly to move operations to the South, where wages were considerably lower. Like other manufacturing unions of the era, the IWA found it difficult to organize in southern states or in the Canadian Maritimes, where a vicious anti-union campaign defeated IWA organizing efforts in Newfoundland in 1959. Finally in the late 1970s and 1980s, changing international markets for lumber would increasingly put Canadian and U.S. members at odds with each other as the United States imposed stiff tariffs on British Columbia lumber entering the country.

The organizational watershed for the IWA occurred in the early 1980s. Employers in the United States aggressively sought concessions from unions, often using permanent striker replacements, a tactic not possible under British Columbia's labor code. Louisiana Pacific was the first to challenge the wood products' unions, breaking the IWA and the LSW in a 1983 strike and instituting wage cuts of 10%. In British Columbia the IWA successfully fought back employer concessions after waging the longest strike in provincial history in 1986. But later that year, the U.S. woodworker bargaining system came apart when the Weyerhaeuser Corporation forced concessions of $4 per hour after threatening to replace IWA members who had been on strike for six weeks. The paths of the two regions had diverged significantly due to differences in the two national labor regimes and different strategies with regard to contract concessions.

The IWA was officially dissolved into two national unions in March 1987. Subsequent declines in membership led both unions to seek mergers with stronger organizations. The IWA-US became a division of the International Association of Machinists in 1994 and the Industrial, Wood, and Allied Workers of Canada (the renamed IWA) eventually returned to a U.S.-based union, merging with the United Steelworkers of America in 2004.

MARCUS WIDENOR

References and Further Reading

International Woodworkers of America Archives. Special Collections Department. Eugene: Knight Library, University of Oregon.

Jensen, Vernon H. *Lumber and Labor*. New York: Farrar & Rinehart, Inc., 1945.

Lembcke, Jerry, and William M. Tattam. *One Union in Wood: A Political History of the International Woodworks of America*. Vancouver, Canada: Harbour Publishing Company, 1984.

Neufeld, Andrew, and Andrew Parnaby. *The IWA in Canada: The Life and Times of an Industrial Union*. Vancouver, Canada: New Star Books, 2000.

"Diverging Patterns: Labor in the Pacific Northwest Wood Products Industry." *Industrial Relations* 34, 3 (July 1995).

"International Unionism in Retreat: The Dissolution of the International Woodworkers of America." In Gonick, Cy, Paul Phillips, and Jesse Vorst, eds., *Labour Gains, Labour Pains: 50 Years of PC 1003*. Halifax, Nova Scotia: Fernwood Publishing, 1995.

See also **Communist Party; Pacific Northwest; Taft-Hartley Act; United Brotherhood of Carpenters and Joiners of America**

INTERNATIONAL WORKERS' ORDER

The International Workers' Order (IWO) was founded on May 30, 1930, at Cooper Union in New York City by Yiddish-speaking left-wing Jews as a mutual-aid fraternal organization. William Weiner became the first president; Reuben Saltzman, the general secretary; and Kalman Marmor, the cultural director. The IWO provided low-cost life insurance for workers as well as credit, health care, and burial benefits. The IWO promoted a socialist pro-Bolshevik ideology, and its members actively supported progressive social causes, union struggles, and minority rights. The IWO federations provided a rich social and cultural life for their working-class members with summer colonies, choirs, theater groups, marching bands, sports leagues, and orchestras as well as language schools and summer camps for children.

The IWO emerged from divisions in the Workmen's Circle or *Arbeiter* Ring organized in New York in 1892 as a national labor fraternal order, an umbrella organization that encompassed labor Zionists, Bundists, and territorialists. All had a secular approach to Jewish identity, a concern with widespread anti-Semitism, and a desire to end class exploitation. An important undertaking of the *Arbeiter* Ring was the development of *shules* (schools) for children and summer camps where Yiddish language and literature were taught from a secular socialist point of view. They also incorporated drama, music, and dance into their programs, providing opportunities for impoverished immigrant children that would otherwise have been denied to them as well as an intellectual and social world for poor Jewish immigrants.

By the early 1920s, the *Arbeiter* Ring membership was split between the linke, those who supported the Bolshevik revolution, and those who remained Social Democrats. People took their politics seriously and were passionate about their views. The vituperation was bitter, the rhetoric vitriolic, and after a number of battles in the 1920s, the Left, or those who celebrated the Russian revolution and the emergence of the U.S.S.R. withdrew from the organization and called on others to follow and "help build a real proletarian Order."

At first the *international* in the name of the new organization was an aspiration that expressed a political outlook rather than a reality. The founders stressed the common class interests of workers avoiding what they viewed as the narrow chauvinism and nationalism of existing ethnic organizations. The approach was to first of all gather together existing fraternal organizations of varying nationalities, and then to organize language sections in other language communities. The strategy succeeded. From its beginnings as a Jewish workers' organization, it soon developed into a multi-ethnic and multiracial association. In addition to the large Jewish and English sections, there were 13 different language federations that were members by the mid-1930s, including the Hungarian Workmen's Sick, Benevolent, and Educational Federation; the Slovak Workers' Society; the Garibaldi American Fraternal Society (Italian speaking); the Polonia Society; the Ukrainian American Fraternal Union; the Rumanian American Fraternal Society; the Russian National Mutual Aid Society; the Croatian Benevolent Fraternity; the Cervantes Fraternal Society (Spanish-speaking); the Serbian-American Fraternal Society; the Carpathian-Russian Peoples' Society; the Hellenic American Brotherhood; the Czech Workers' Society; and the Finnish American Mutual Aid Society, a descendant of the Finnish Socialist Federation.

The IWO was unique in its attempt to attract blacks and ethnics into one organization and to offer insurance at the same rates to all working people regardless of race or occupation. At the time the IWO was the only organization where blacks could get insurance at the same rate as others and where people in high-risk occupations were welcome, which made the order attractive to coal miners in West Virginia and Pennsylvania. At its strongest in the 1940s, the order had a membership of 184,000. The largest ethnic group remained the Jewish section, which in 1944 became the Jewish People's Fraternal Order (JPFO). Jewish IWO members represented approximately one-third of the membership.

The leadership of the IWO were members of the Communist party, and this was reflected in IWO policy. However the majority of the rank-and-file, while favorably disposed toward the Soviet Union, were not party members, and not subject to party discipline. The structure of the organization allowed for considerable autonomy among the language groupings, which organized their own cultural and educational activities as they saw fit. The order flourished in the 1930s and 1940s, becoming the largest and most successful left-wing organization in U.S. history. A number of the language sections were part of a North American movement. For example the Jewish section had close ties with its Canadian counterpart, the Labour League, and the schools used both teachers and materials coming from New York. The Labour League in Canada became the United Jewish People's Order in 1945, which still exists.

Active in struggles to organize the CIO, IWO members engaged in campaigns for social security legislation and were very vocal in their opposition to anti-Semitism and the rise of fascism in the 1930s. Chartered as an insurance carrier by New York State, the IWO had certified insurance licenses in 17 other states and the District of Columbia. The left-wing politics of the international order, in particular the connection between IWO leaders and the Communist party ultimately destroyed the order during the height of the Cold War. In 1947, it was named a subversive organization and placed on the attorney general's list of subversive organizations. This list, supposedly to be used to ensure employee loyalty for federal government agencies, received national publicity and became the cornerstone of the Red Scare. In 1949, a time when the anti-Communist crusade had become a national obsession in the United States, the IWO was reviewed by the Mutual and Fraternal Bureau, a regulatory body that was part of the Insurance Department of New York State.

Although it was financially healthy, and its practices conformed to the insurance regulatory laws, James B. Haley, the insurance examiner for New York State found the order's fraternal activities unpatriotic and a "moral hazard," justifying withdrawing the license and liquidating the order. The case was heard in the Supreme Court in 1953, but the decision was upheld. The state took over the IWO and its assets, and the order was destroyed. It was the first and only time that an insurance company was disbanded for its unpopular politics. These included participation in the peace movement in the postwar years, in particular supporting the Stockholm Peace Petition, which proposed outlawing nuclear war. The IWO maintained that the Cold War was a threat to world peace. The organization was critical of American foreign policy—in particular the Marshall Plan, the Truman Doctrine, and U.S. engagement in Korea. By the 1950s, internal policy was no longer considered so radical: The battles for union recognition had largely been won, and Social Security, unemployment insurance, workers' compensation, public housing, and Fair Employment Practices were supported by most liberals.

After the IWO was eliminated, the Jewish section (Jewish People's Fraternal Order) reconstituted itself as the Jewish Cultural Clubs and societies. The camp, *Kinderland*, is thriving, and some of the Yiddish schools, now Sunday schools, still exist. The Canadian counterpart, the United Jewish People's Order still exists, as do the United Ukrainian Canadians. Although far smaller in numbers than previously, they represent an approach to ethnic identity that combines respect for one's heritage with the commitment to social justice.

ESTER REITER

References and Further Reading

Dinst fun Folk: Almanakh fun Yiddishn Folks Ordn. New York: Farlag fun Yidishn Folk Ordn, 1947.

Keeran, Roger. "National Groups and the Popular Front: The Case of the International Workers Order." *Journal of American Ethnic History* 4, 3 (Spring 1995): 23–29.

Liebman, Arthur. *Jews and the Left*. New York: Wiley, 1979.

Sabin, Arthur J. *Red Scare in Court*. Philadelphia, PA: University of Pennsylvania Press, 1993.

Tsen, Yoriker. *Yubilee fun Internatzionaler Arbeter Orden*. Cooperativa Folks Farlag fun Internatzationaler Arber Ordn, 1940.

Zaltzman, R. *Tsu der Geshikhte fun der fraternaler Bavegung*. New York: Farlag Internationatzaionale Arbeter Ordn, 1936.

INTERNATIONAL WORKINGMEN'S ASSOCIATION ("FIRST INTERNATIONAL")

Though short-lived and considered by most of its participants a failure, the International Workingmen's Association (IWA) is famous for being the only political organization founded and led by Karl Marx. Established in London in 1864 and officially pronounced dead by 1876, in its few short years the First International brought together a cadre of organizers who represented nearly all the existing variants of radical thought and ideology of its day. While its own initiatives and schemes all came to naught, its fame steadily grew along with the international renown of Marx, and subsequent international socialist congresses claimed themselves successors to its legacy.

Initially organized by an eclectic group of English and French artisans, expatriate revolutionists, trade unionists, and democratic reformers, the association was quickly pulled toward greater ideological discipline by Marx. While disagreeing with the party's majority of reformers, Marx believed that it could be a vehicle for spreading socialist principles at a crucial time in European and American history. Marx's tremendous energy, overawing intellectual leadership, and extensive contacts, helped the organization spread widely while his efforts at purifying the IWA's ranks by purging those elements that he deemed backward—a group that included not only anarchists, but leaders of the English trade union movement, Italian nationalists, Spanish syndicalists, and Yankee socialists (as Marx called native-born American radicals)—fractured it in many directions.

The IWA burst into international prominence with the French worker's revolt known as the Paris Commune of 1871. Though Marx and other IWA leaders had had little to do with the declaration of the commune that spring, or the events that led to its bloody suppression, a number of communard leaders declared themselves internationalists, and both governments and newspapers were quick to accuse the IWA of responsibility for it. Of course for revolutionaries and radical reformers from Moscow to Missouri, this only established the international's credentials and added to its prestige.

Founded first in the United States by German-American immigrants, many of them refugees from the European workers' rebellions of 1848, the IWA soon grew beyond the urban immigrant enclaves where it first took root. In the United States a uniquely American brand of social reform, a cross-class eclectic movement that encompassed abolition, feminism, temperance, spiritualism, communitarian socialism, and various health regimes, briefly joined forces with the competing socialist doctrines of Karl Marx. For a period of about 5 years, from 1867 to 1873, a significant number of native-born, English-speaking sections of the international had sprung up across the country, in both large cities, such as Baltimore and San Francisco, as well as in smaller places, such as Galveston, Texas; Terre Haute, Indiana; and Hammond, New York.

The U.S. IWA, for a fleeting moment in time in the early 1870s, was one big tent sheltering immigrant Marxists, communalists, anarchists, spiritualists, feminists, and land reformers, radical groups that had not been united in pursuit of a single cause since their members were joined in the abolitionist crusade against slavery. The IWA was an organization more characterized by its contradictions than its consistencies; it brought together those recognized as being the intellectual fathers of native anarchism with those credited with introducing Marxism to the United States. It enlisted both ideological atheists and the founders of American spiritualism. Among its members were trade unionists determined to preserve the privileges of the racially and gendered U.S. industrial caste system and the leading champions of the equal rights of women and minorities. Attracting both rich and poor, black and white, native and immigrant, men and women, the IWA stood at the crossroads of American society and American radicalism.

Of all the differences and potential divisions contained within the IWA, it was the deep ideological chasm between a hardening Marxist orthodoxy and the republican ideals of Yankee radicals that proved insurmountable. The diversity of individuals attracted to the IWA flew in the face of the strategy that Marx and his German American cohorts had hammered out for the United States. Marx had called for organizing a coalition of German and Irish workers who would together radicalize the American proletariat.

Such a vision of the IWA as a worker's vanguard capable of organizing and directing the fledgling U.S. industrial proletariat into a sharp tool of class struggle fared badly at recruiting American workers. Much to the chagrin of the IWA's class-conscious German American leaders, it instead found itself deluged with Yankee radicals who shared a distrust of coercive authority in any guise. By 1870, the American reform element outnumbered the socialist Germans and had a widely circulated newspaper of its own, *Woodhull & Claflin's Weekly*. By the fall of that year the block representing English language sections threatened to take control and democratize the IWA's American governing body, the central committee.

Yankee internationalists pursued their own broad egalitarian goals from under their new red umbrella. In New York native American reformers symbolically marched with African-American veterans in their foremost ranks. They organized black sections and railed against discrimination of all kinds in their newspapers. They nominated Victoria Woodhull and Frederick Douglass for the highest offices in the land. They worked with the National Woman Suffrage Association to secure women's franchise. From the viewpoint of the German Americans who maintained close ties to Marx in London, such actions were viewed as unscientific, idealistic, and simply wrong-headed. To them the Yankee radicals stood as the greatest obstacle to the success of their revolutionary strategy, and go they must.

In 1871, after but a year of coalition, the agents of Marxist orthodoxy in the United States became convinced that the reputation of their party among bona fide workingmen was in jeopardy because of their partner's pursuit of the moralistic and idealistic issues of women's rights, municipal ownership of utilities, and democratic reforms. In December of that year, a German American faction, led by Friedrich Sorge, expelled their fellow English-speaking radicals from the party, a move that spelled the end of the international in the United States and foreshadowed a similar schism and collapse of its parent organization in Europe. After the demise of the First International, the first U.S. Marxist movement, had destroyed itself, its so-called Yankee members continued their egalitarian and anticapitalistic crusade in a diverse array of causes, including providing leaders to such organizations as the Eight-Hour League, the Knights of Labor, and the Sovereigns of Industry.

TIMOTHY MESSER-KRUSE

References and Further Reading

Bernstein, Samuel. *The First International in America*. New York: A. M. Kelley, 1962.

Lause, Mark. "The American Radicals and Organized Marxism: The Initial Experience, 1869–1874." *Labor History* 33, 1 (spring 1992), 55–80.

Messer-Kruse, Timothy. *The Yankee International: Marxism and the American Reform Tradition, 1848–1876.* Chapel Hill: University of North Carolina Press, 1998.

See also **Marx, Karl**

IRISH

Irish people immigrated to the United States nearly continuously from the seventeenth century until the present day, making the Irish one of the largest, most sustained, and most influential of the population movements that shaped the American working class. Irish Catholics began moving to the United States in large numbers around 1830, and because they arrived early, spoke English, and settled primarily in large cities, they became powerful in institutions that would earn the loyalty of many subsequent members of the urban ethnic working class, including the Catholic church, the Democratic party, and organized labor. Their influence therefore was even greater than their numbers would suggest.

Before about 1830, most Irish emigrants were members of Ireland's minority Protestant community, many of them of Scottish descent and hailing from the Northern province of Ulster. A substantial minority were Catholic, but they settled in dispersed communities, and deprived of contact with other Irish Catholics, many did not retain ethnic or religious ties. Furthermore although discriminatory legislation significantly limited Irish Catholics' political rights and economic opportunities, most Irish Catholics were reluctant to leave Ireland. The early Irish-American community therefore comprised mostly Protestants, many of whom were hostile to their Catholic co-ethnics. After Catholics began immigrating in large numbers, the Protestant and Catholic Irish-American communities remained largely distinct, with different settlement and economic patterns and separate institutions. Protestant Irish-Americans are often referred to as the "Scots-Irish" and are discussed in a separate entry.

Irish Catholics began arriving in the United States in larger numbers in the early nineteenth century. Although very small numbers of Irish men and women fled to the United States in the late eighteenth, nineteenth, and twentieth centuries to escape being prosecuted by the British authorities for political offenses, the overwhelming majority of emigrants left Ireland for economic reasons. Starting in the early nineteenth century, changes in the agricultural economy made it more difficult for Irish people to support their families as farmers or farm laborers, and Ireland was actually losing rather than gaining industrial jobs that might have offered an alternative means of earning a living. Most Irish people were reluctant to emigrate and attempted to adapt to these economic challenges, most notably by subsisting on potatoes, a high-yield crop that could feed a family on relatively little land. However to improve their prospects or to avoid slipping into the ranks of the impoverished, some Irish Catholics, especially young men from relatively prosperous backgrounds, chose to come to America. This pattern was suddenly and tragically amplified when the potato crop failed repeatedly from 1845–1850. About a million people died in the Great Famine, and another 1.8 million desperate refugees made their way to North America, with the majority eventually settling in the United States. The famine refugees were, for the most part, not among the poorest Irish agricultural workers, most of whom could not afford passage to North America. However few brought savings or supplies with them, and most had only agricultural skills, which were not in demand in eastern and midwestern urban centers in which they settled. Moreover they faced significant prejudice, both because of their religion and ethnicity. Therefore they found jobs at the bottom of the economic ladder: In factories, as common laborers, and among women, in domestic service. After the famine ended, rates of emigration remained high, and although not nearly as desperate as famine-era refugees, later Irish immigrants continued to concentrate in cities and to find jobs as unskilled or semiskilled laborers. Two aspects of postfamine Irish immigration patterns are particularly notable. First an unusually high percentage of Irish immigrants were women. By the early twentieth century, more than half of all immigrants were female, most of them young, single women who hoped to find jobs and ultimately husbands in the United States. Second although many Irish immigrants dreamed of one day returning to Ireland, the overwhelming majority remained in the United States for the rest of their lives. In this they differed from most other immigrant groups, which had substantial rates of return to their home countries. Once they settled in the United States, Irish immigrants sent money back to Ireland, supporting remaining relatives and often paying for friends' or family members' passage to the United States. If Irish-Americans were unable to return to the land of their birth, they were considerably more successful at recreating their communities in the United States.

By the end of the nineteenth century, the Irish-American community was increasingly prosperous and stable. Although Irish immigrants were disproportionately likely to be unskilled laborers, many immigrants and most members of the second generation achieved a measure of economic mobility, gaining skills and sometimes entering the lower middle class. Young immigrant women were most likely to work in factories or domestic service, but their daughters and granddaughters often found jobs as teachers or clerical workers. There was also considerable geographic diversity in the Irish-American experience: Irish-Americans found fewer avenues to economic mobility in New England cities, such as Boston, than in midwestern and western cities, such as St. Louis or San Francisco, where anti-Catholic and anti-Irish prejudices were less entrenched.

If Irish-Americans were more prosperous by the end of the nineteenth century, they also benefited from no longer being the most recent or alien-seeming immigrant group. In the late nineteenth century, new immigrants from southern and Eastern Europe began arriving in the United States. Many of them, like Irish-Americans, were Catholics from agricultural backgrounds, and many settled in the same urban centers in which Irish-Americans had lived for decades. There was of course nothing new about Irish-Americans sharing urban space with members of other ethnic groups. Most notably in the nineteenth century, the Irish often lived in close proximity to African-Americans. Irish-Americans seldom felt solidarity with their African-American neighbors, and they seem to have been anxious to distance themselves from people who were even more despised and oppressed than themselves. Irish-Americans often refused to work with African-Americans, and their hostility sometimes spilled over into mass violence, as in the 1863 Draft Riots, which included appalling instances of racial violence. This attitude however stands in marked contrast to their approach to the new immigrants of the late nineteenth and early twentieth centuries. Irish-Americans may have felt superior to new immigrants, and new immigrants may have resented Irish-American power, but they nonetheless forged uneasy alliances. Irish-Americans came to act as "ethnic brokers," helping new immigrants negotiate their relations with the dominant society. In theory the relationship between the Irish and new immigrants was mutually beneficial: New immigrants could call on Irish-Americans' experience dealing with an often-hostile society, and Irish-American leaders gained a new constituency. In practice however, relations were sometimes much more unequal and strained. These alliances were often negotiated in institutions that the Irish did not found but in which by the late nineteenth century, they held considerable influence: The American Catholic church, labor unions, and urban political machines.

Irish Catholics began arriving in the United States during a period of profound religious change in Ireland. Although Irish Catholics had always identified strongly with the Catholic faith, it was only in the second-half of the nineteenth century that they became especially observant. Before the famine only about one-third of all Irish Catholics attended Mass each week; by the end of the nineteenth century, weekly Mass attendance was around 90%. The number of Irish priests and nuns also increased exponentially in the nineteenth century. The American Catholic church was transformed by the influx of Irish Catholics, who placed unprecedented demands on what had previously been a small, genteel institution dominated by Maryland planters. The newly observant Irish immigrants themselves helped achieve this transformation. Out of their meager paychecks, they donated money to build churches, schools, hospitals, and orphanages; Irish and Irish-American priests and nuns provided much of the staff for these institutions. By the time new immigrants from Eastern and southern Europe began arriving in the United States, the Irish dominated the American hierarchy, and they often clashed with immigrant Catholics who wished to retain their distinctive ethnic identities and traditions. Despite these tensions Catholicism could serve as a rallying point, uniting disparate people against a seemingly hostile, Protestant-dominant culture. Moreover although Irish Catholicism was usually conservative, stressing the individual's duty to submit to established authority, Catholic social thought also stressed that bonds of obligation were reciprocal and that employers had a duty to provide a decent standard of living for their workers. There was space in American Catholicism therefore for a labor movement, albeit usually a relatively conservative one.

Irish-Americans also became a significant force in politics, especially at the local level. Irish Catholic immigrants had considerable experience with mass politics before they ever arrived in the United States. From 1829–1847, the Irish Catholic leader Daniel O'Connell campaigned successfully to remove the last legal barriers to Catholics' full political participation and then unsuccessfully to gain a measure of independence for Ireland. O'Connell's strategy was to mobilize the entire Irish Catholic population, encouraging even the poorest people, who did not meet the property qualification for the vote, to donate a penny to the cause and organizing massive protests called "monster meetings" to put pressure on the British government. Before they set foot in the United States therefore, many Irish immigrants thought of themselves as political actors and of politics as a way of expressing group identity. Perhaps for this reason, Irish immigrants quickly adapted to American partisan politics, naturalizing and voting at higher rates than other nineteenth-century immigrants and for the most part, forming a strong attachment to the Democratic party. By the early twentieth century, they had come to dominate local politics in many American cities. Irish-Americans were particularly adept at managing political machines, institutions that won the support of voters by offering them tangible, individual benefits, such as jobs. In such cities as Chicago, machines ultimately became multi-ethnic institutions, but Irish-run machines were as likely to exclude new voters, who required jobs or other costly rewards to earn their loyalty, as to encourage them to participate in the political process. When machines did incorporate new ethnic or African-American voters, they often bought their loyalty with low-status and low-paying jobs or with federal benefits that were administered by local authorities. Machines may have helped incorporate new voters into the system therefore, but they also reinforced inequality within the system. By the mid-twentieth century, most urban machines were on the decline, but Irish-Americans continued to be disproportionately powerful in local politics and increasingly to make their mark on the national scene as well, culminating with the election of John F. Kennedy to the presidency in 1960.

If Irish-Americans were unusually active in American politics, they also retained an interest in the politics of their homeland. Many Irish-Americans hoped that Ireland would become independent of Britain, although they disagreed about whether this should be done through force or by peaceful means. During periods of heightened nationalist activity in Ireland, tens of thousands of Irish-Americans joined organizations and donated money to try to achieve that goal. Irish-American nationalism was often a conservative movement, led by members of the middle-class, eschewing economic goals, and stressing the need for Irish-Americans to adhere to middle-class standards of respectability in order to prove that Irish people were capable of self-government. Some historians have suggested that middle-class Irish-Americans used nationalism to obscure class divisions within the community and unite Irish-Americans behind middle-class leadership. Yet nationalism could also reinforce working-class consciousness and introduce Irish-Americans to radical politics. In 1879, nationalists in Ireland took up the cause of land reform, attacking the landlord system and adding an economic element to the movement for Irish independence. In the United States many nationalists believed that support for land reform was merely a tactic in the larger battle for Irish independence, but a faction of Irish-American nationalists, represented by Patrick Ford's newspaper the *Irish World and American Industrial Liberator*, fused nationalism, Catholicism, and demands for economic justice in both Ireland and the United States. Some

Irish-American nationalists supported Henry George's single-tax scheme, bringing them into contact with Protestant radicals whom they had previously viewed with hostility. Economic and social radicalism were always minority strains in Irish-American nationalism, but they continued to be present in the twentieth century. In the early 1920s, for instance, Chicago Federation of Labor President John Fitzpatrick founded the Labor Bureau for Irish Independence, which linked commitments to Irish nationalism, global anti-imperialism, and justice for workers.

This connection between nationalism and labor reflects the fact that the Irish were extremely well-represented in both the rank-and-file and leadership of American labor unions. Irish immigrants brought from Ireland traditions of labor protest, some of which were not suited to a modern capitalist economy. In the 1870s, the "Molly Maguires" attempted to bring premodern modes of protest to bear on the problem of industrial exploitation in Pennsylvania coalmines. Using ritualized forms of violence that were common in the Irish countryside, workers threatened and ultimately murdered mine officials in an attempt to force mine owners to fulfill what Irish peasants took to be employers' obligations to their workers. These efforts were futile, resulting only in the prosecutions of Irish-American workers, many of whom may have been innocent. Some immigrant contemporaries of the Molly Maguires had experience with British and Irish unions, and they may have been more likely than other first-generation Irish-Americans to participate in organized labor. However most Irish-American union leaders seem to have been American-born, such as Knights of Labor leader Terence Powderly, who was born in Pennsylvania in 1849, the son of Irish immigrants. Irish-Americans were so ubiquitous in the labor movement that it is hard to generalize about them: They were active in the most radical as well as the most conservative factions. It is probably safe to say however that they were more likely to be conservative than radical. Indeed some Irish-dominated unions, like some urban political machines, seemed more interested in securing benefits for their members by excluding outsiders than in forming coalitions with members of other ethnic groups or even more recent Irish immigrants. However Irish leaders could be found in the Congress of Industrial Organizations (CIO) and even the IWW, as well as the more-conservative American Federation of Labor (AFL).

In the 1920s, the flow of Irish immigration slowed because of laws restricting immigration and because the Great Depression eliminated the economic opportunities that drew Irish men and women to the United States. Young Irish people continued to emigrate in large numbers, but Britain, rather than the United States became their preferred destination. Perhaps because there were fewer recent immigrants to create a concrete bond to Ireland, the community seems to have lost some of its distinctiveness, and some scholars suggest that Irish-Americans' Catholic identity gradually supplanted their Irish affiliation. The Irish-American community was also increasingly middle-class, with rates of college graduation and white-collar employment higher than the overall population, and increasingly suburban. In the early twenty-first century, Irish-Americans no longer reliably support the Democratic party, and their voting habits look much like those of the population in general. Although the community has lost many of its distinctive characteristics, many Irish-Americans continue to be committed to their Irish identity.

In the 1980s, facing a recession in Ireland, Irish people again began to immigrate to the United States in larger numbers. They were aided in this by a visa program that favored the Irish, but many came as undocumented immigrants. Legal immigrants found jobs throughout the economy, including in professional occupations. Undocumented Irish immigrants were concentrated in such jobs as construction, restaurant work, and childcare. In recent years the Irish economy has experienced remarkable growth, and for the first time since the seventeenth century, Ireland has become an immigrant-receiving, rather than an emigrant-sending nation. Many Irish immigrants who arrived in the 1980s have decided to return to Ireland and pursue opportunities at home, something that was not possible for their earlier counterparts.

EMILY BRUNNER

References and Further Reading

Emmons, David M. *The Butte Irish: Class and Ethnicity in an American Mining Town.* Urbana: University of Illinois Press, 1989.

Kenny, Kevin. *The American Irish.* Harlow, Essex, UK, and New York: Longman, 2000.

———. *Making Sense of the Molly Maguires.* New York: Oxford University Press, 1998.

Meagher, Timothy. *Inventing Irish America: Generation, Class and Ethnic Identity in a New England City.* Notre Dame, IN: University of Notre Dame Press, 2001.

Miller, Kerby. *Emigrants and Exiles: Ireland and the Irish Exodus to North America.* New York: Oxford University Press, 1985.

IRON

See **Steel and Iron**

IRONS, MARTIN (OCTOBER 7, 1830–1900)
Knights of Labor

Martin Irons was a machinist and a Knights of Labor member who led the 1886 Southwest strike against railroad king Jay Gould's southwestern system of railways. The conflict was a pivotal event of the Great Upheaval of 1886, when Gilded Age working-class protest peaked. The walkout's defeat contributed to the decline of the knights. For Irons, who was haunted throughout his life by personal demons and tragedy, the strike brought first public recognition, and then controversy and hardship.

Irons was born on October 7, 1830, in Dundee, Scotland. His father was a sailor and sail maker, and his mother may have been a milliner. Irons was 14 when he arrived with a guardian in New York City. Six years later he began an itinerant life, moving about mostly in Kentucky, Ohio, and Missouri. In 1852, he married Mary Brown, also from Scotland. He often met with unemployment, drank heavily, and was a physically abusive husband, family sources reveal. Around 1876, Irons left Richmond, Missouri, where he had settled for 6 years and returned to an itinerant life without his family.

Around 1880, Irons arrived in Sedalia, Missouri. He married again, found a job as a machinist in a Gould system shop, and met with other workers to discuss labor issues. Once a member of the Grange, the Odd Fellows, and the Ancient Order of Workingmen, Irons joined the Knights of Labor, probably in 1884. By the fall of 1885, District Assembly (DA) 101, composed of about 5,000 knights across Gould's Southwest system, had elected him their master workman and chair of the executive board.

Like many railroad workers, Irons believed that Gould was conspiring to impose wage slavery on his employees and that only the enforcement of previous agreements and the recognition of DA 101 as the collective-bargaining agent on the Gould system could prevent this. The 1886 walkout began over precisely these issues. A massive, popularly supported strike in March 1885 and the knights' threat of a national railway strike later that year had resulted in much heralded contracts that railroad managers routinely ignored. Moreover railroad management widely discriminated against knights and consistently frustrated the efforts of Irons and other leaders to gain a hearing.

The general strike on the Gould system began on March 6, 1886. At a meeting in the midst of the conflict, Irons confided to Terence Powderly, the national knights' leader, that a mystery gunslinger had forced him at gunpoint to sign the strike order. Historian Ruth

Allen has accepted Irons's account although no independent evidence supports it. More likely Irons fabricated the story in order to distance himself from a failing walkout, one that DA 101 had undertaken without consulting the national knights. By the time Irons met with Powderly, railroad officials had obtained injunctions against strikers who interfered with freight traffic, and freight traffic was resuming with the aid of strikebreakers, returning strikers, and skilled trainmen. One week later and against Powderly's instructions, Irons pushed to expand the walkout to include knights throughout the country. A sympathy strike in East St. Louis that had paralyzed railway traffic in the region encouraged him, but a bloody clash there between prostrike crowds and railroad-employed deputies brought the state militia in to protect railroad property, effectively ending the 1886 walkout.

Much of the press and public associated Irons with the sabotage, riots, intimidation, and bloodshed that marked the strike in its final phase, although clearly many knights had engaged in these tactics. Irons insisted that he had consistently urged knights against violence, but the record suggests otherwise. Whatever the case the weight of the strike's failure fell disproportionately on him. His critics charged that he had aggressively pursued a clash with Gould in order to amass power. Embittered Sedalia knights forced him to resign and leave town. Blacklisted by the railways and alone (his second wife had died during the strike of pneumonia), Irons roamed in search of better circumstances in Missouri, Arkansas, and Texas, with little luck. He escaped various legal troubles, including a child molestation charge. Still despite his infamy, Irons never tired of discussing social and economic questions and was an active member of the People's party. During the 1890s, a doctor in Bruceville, Texas, took in and befriended an ailing and impoverished Irons, who died in 1900. In the decade after his death, Eugene Debs and Mother Jones praised him, and the Missouri State Federation of Labor voted to erect a monument in Bruceville to commemorate Irons's contributions to the labor movement.

THERESA CASE

References and Further Reading

Allen, Ruth. *The Great Southwest Strike*. Austin, TX: University of Texas Publications, 1942.
Case, Theresa A. "Free Labor on the Southwestern Railroads: The 1885–1886 Gould System Strikes." Ph.D. dissertation, University of Texas at Austin, 2002.
Dundee Old Parish Registers and Dundee Street Directories. Dundee, Scotland.
Labor Movement in Texas Collection. Austin, TX: Center for American History, University of Texas at Austin.

See also **Gilded Age; Knights of Labor**

ITALIANS

Italian migrant workers have been coming to North America since the earliest European settlements—a number of Venetian glass blowers had settled in Jamestown by 1622—and during the peak years of their migration, they constituted a critical, and heavily exploited, part of this country's working class. A handful of people from the peninsula that became Italy were enumerated in the 1820 U.S. census, and by 1850, a little more than a decade before Italy was united during the *Risorgimento*, the 3,645 Italians in the census were scattered across the country. Most of these early migrants, though certainly not all, were from provinces in northern Italy. There were population concentrations in New Orleans, San Francisco, and New York; over half the Italian migrants at that point lived in the South. There were agricultural settlements as well that extended the breadth of the country in places like Texas, New Jersey, and California.

The character of this immigration changed drastically during the peak years of Italian immigration. Over 300,000 arrived during the 1880s, and in the first decade of the twentieth century, over two million made the journey. From 1880–1920, over 4.1 million Italians entered the country. Most of these migrants came from southern provinces and the island of Sicily. Most were from rural areas, though some were artisans; few had solid industrial skills, and fewer could read. They were predominantly male—men outnumbered women by about 3 to 1. Their settlement patterns in the United States changed as well. Almost 97% arrived in New York, and many decided to settle there. By 1920, 400,000 Italian migrants made New York City their homes. There were sizeable Italian populations in Boston, Philadelphia, San Francisco, New Orleans, and growing populations in Chicago and in smaller and medium-sized cities, like Rochester, Utica, and Kansas City. But this wave of migrants concentrated mostly in the northeastern and mid-Atlantic states and mostly in large cities in those regions.

This summary though belies the complexity of Italian migration. Italians had a history of movement throughout Europe that preceded, and overlapped with, movement to the United States. Italian workers began seeking industrial employment to supplement sparse agricultural income in the earliest stages of industrialization on the European mainland. Seasonal journeys to industrial centers in Italy, France, Germany, and Switzerland extended across oceans when steerage rates on trans-Atlantic ocean liners began to drop in the late nineteenth century. Even then Italians did not necessarily head for the United States. By 1900, two of every three Italians

Family of Italians who came from nearby towns to pick beans as day laborers. Library of Congress, Prints & Photographs Division, FSA/OWI Collection [LC-USF34-057686-D].

who crossed the Atlantic sought other destinations, like Argentina, Brazil, or Montenegro.

Nor was there any guarantee they were going to stay. Most Italians were determined to return home once they made enough money to buy property in Italy. Not every Italian did so, but their return migration rates were as high as any other migrant group. Calculations of these rates are undependable at best, but historians estimate that from 30% to over 50% of Italian migrants left the United States. In 1908, the peak year of their migration, more Italians actually left the country than entered it. This was the second year of an economic depression in the United States. Nonetheless the statistic is telling.

Reception

The predominance of southern Italians in this massive wave of migrants, their penchant for return migration, their concentration in large cities, and their skill levels on arrival had enormous implications for working-class Italian migrants' reception in this country. At the end of the nineteenth and the beginning of the twentieth century, large-scale migration from across southern and Eastern Europe alarmed many native-born Americans. Politicians and labor leaders clamored for immigration restriction, and scholars in new social sciences like sociology began to characterize these new immigrants in racial terms. They considered them superior to Asians and Africans in the hierarchy of race but well below northern and western Europeans. Even in this scorned population, Italians, and especially southern Italians, were often singled out as the most contemptible. Scholarly works not only defined southern Italians as the lowest of European races, they often advised Anglo Saxons not to intermarry with them. They were considered, as one angry Italian migrant labor organizer put it, "the garbage of American social life."

Southern Italian immigrants at times experienced attitudes and treatment more similar to blacks than to other European immigrants. They were recruited to work on plantations to prod uncooperative ex-slaves. In the segregated South, they worked side-by-side with blacks, and their children often attended the same schools. Southern Italians suspected of crimes were occasionally lynched, a brutality almost exclusively endured by blacks. In the most infamous instance, 11 Italians in New Orleans were lynched in 1891. Three more were lynched in the city in 1896, and two in Tampa, Florida, in 1910.

As scorned as they were however, only the quality of their whiteness was challenged—rarely if ever the fact of it. Southern Italians may have been widely considered inferior to other European immigrants, but they still shared the privileges and advantages that whiteness conveyed in the United States. They did not face systematic, legalized segregation. They were not only legally allowed to naturalize (the naturalization law of 1790, not altered until 1952, reserved this opportunity solely for whites), they were encouraged to do so. Nor were they denied the right to vote—they were often criticized for not voting often enough.

Work

In many ways southern Italians were like the Irish immigrants who worked as manual laborers in the antebellum years—social commentators at the end of the nineteenth century commented explicitly that they were taking jobs that had previously belonged to the Irish and that Italian migrants were assuming their desultory social status as well. Certain Italian men actively sought outdoor manual labor, and Italian migrants moved in large numbers into the construction industry. They concentrated in other areas as well, especially in the garment and textile industries. Young, Italian immigrant women worked in the latter in large numbers. Many daughters in Italian families began work outside the home early to contribute to the family income. Most left this sort of work, if not when they married, then when their first babies were born. Married Italian women frequently sought work that enabled them to remain at home, taking in boarders, doing piece work for garment shops, or assembling artificial flowers or costume jewelry, often with the assistance of their small children.

Italian immigrant workers usually found employment through one of two means. The first was through *padrones*, or labor agents, who acted as intermediaries between them and potential employers. This system, more prevalent in the nineteenth than in the twentieth century, was often profoundly exploitive. *Padrones* often worked with employers to bilk immigrants out of their labor and their pay. *Padrones* were supplanted gradually by the links of chain migration—Italians migrating from the same region, village, or even street would seek each other out, and help each other find shelter and employment.

The work that these immigrants found was often extremely dangerous. In coalmines in Pennsylvania and Arizona, in Pennsylvania steel plants, and on building sites throughout the country, for example, Italian immigrant men faced potential injury or death daily. In textile and garment factories, Italian immigrant women risked disfigurement and mortal injury as well. In 1912, for example, a young girl testifying about unsafe conditions in textile mills showed U.S. senators how one of the machines had ripped off a piece of her scalp. The year before locked exit doors in the Triangle Shirtwaist factory in New York City had doomed 146 Italian and Jewish young women when lint from the machines caught fire. The image of these women leaping to their deaths to avoid the flames would haunt the city for decades.

Organizational Life

In the face of hardship and contempt and danger, Italian immigrants organized themselves, often drawing on institutions they had created in Italy. They formed mutual benefit societies, which provided a sense of community and often insurance in case of injury and funeral benefits in case of death. These associations' members usually organized themselves along regional lines or even by specific villages. Regionalism ran deep among Italian immigrants, in part because Italy itself had only existed as a nation since 1861, and in part because resentments between northern and southern Italians were so strong. Many also drew on the solace of religious faith. Despite the dominance of the Irish in the American Catholic hierarchy and their often open contempt for Italian Catholics, religious festivals were important events in Italian neighborhoods, and many—especially women—remained faithful church goers.

But the hesitance of many Italian immigrants about church services spoke to their wariness about certain organizations. There was a deep strain of distrust for the state and the church (often seen as one and the same in Italy) especially among southern Italian immigrants. Their anticlericalism kept many away from the church even if many still saw life through the lens of the religious imagery with which they had been raised. Their experience of the state as predominantly an oppressive institution contributed to very low rates of naturalization and use of the franchise among these immigrants.

Unions and Radical Organizations

It is small wonder then that the first migrant radicals to make their presence felt in Italian immigrant communities were anarchists. Like other Italian immigrant revolutionaries, these anarchists were small in number but deeply devoted and arduous activists.

As with so much of Italian immigrant life, much of this anarchist culture was rooted in Italy. The first anarchists to proselytize in Italian immigrant communities were sojourners from Italy who stayed in the country anywhere from a few weeks to a few years. They helped to develop anarchist circles, often named after Italian revolutionaries, in places like Tampa, Florida; Paterson, New Jersey; and Barre, Vermont. The most prominent of them, Luigi Galleani, also stayed the longest in the United States. Arriving in Paterson in 1902, he edited *la Questione Sociale* there before moving to Barre to join fellow immigrants from the Piedmont region in Italy who had settled there to work in the marble quarries and as sculptors. There he began the *Cronaca Sovversiva*, the most important voice of Italian immigrant anti-organizational anarchism in the United States, which reached anarchist men and women all over the country. He and his followers, Nicola Sacco and Bartolomeo Vanzetti among them, argued that a decent and dignified life for all could be achieved only by destroying existing institutions and starting over. Galleani encouraged his followers to act on their beliefs, publishing a bomb manual in about 1905, and certain of them responded—evidence points to their involvement in a number of bombings during and after World War I.

Italian immigrant syndicalists also considered the state an incurably corrupt institution but argued that unions should be the focal point of revolutionary activity. Though like the anarchists, relatively small in number, these syndicalists had an impact on the American labor movement that exceeded their numerical strength because of their willingness to risk prison time and even death in confronting factory owners and state officials. Led by people like labor activist and poet Arturo Giovannitti, they strived to use their *Federazione Socialista Italiana* (FSI) and its newspaper *il Proletario* to reach Italian immigrant workers. The apex of their efforts came in 1912, when they worked with the Industrial Workers of the World (IWW) to help over 20,000 striking textile workers in Lawrence, Massachusetts, achieve an unexpected victory. Soon after however disagreement about how to respond to World War I splintered the organization. Some of its members, among them former *il Proletario* editor Edmondo Rossoni, became staunch defenders of Italian nationalism and eventually joined Mussolini's Fascist party.

Although so few Italian immigrants voted in the early twentieth century, there was a small group who aligned themselves with the electoral strategies of the Socialist party. Their organization, the Federazione Socialista Italiana of the Socialist Party of America (FSI/SPA), was based in Chicago. Its members had some success organizing garment workers in the Midwest and on the East Coast.

World War I and Its Aftermath

While certain historians argue that their participation as soldiers in World War I gained Italian immigrants some level of respectability, wartime and postwar repression delivered a crushing blow to most Italian immigrant radicals. Italian anarchists, syndicalists, and even socialists were hounded, imprisoned, and deported. Though Italian immigrants took part in large numbers in the wave of postwar strikes that swept the nation, hostility to their perceived foreignness and fear even of moderate labor unions peaked in the late 1910s. The Red Scare, which stretched from the end of World War I into the early 1920s, had no clearer symbols among Italian immigrants than Sacco and Vanzetti, who were executed after a 7-year trial and series of appeals that revealed the potential injustice and danger Italian immigrants and radicals faced. As their appeals progressed, Congress passed two laws, one in 1921 and one in 1924, which slowed immigration from Italy (and elsewhere in southern and Eastern Europe and Japan) to a trickle.

The 1920s were marked by a decline in radical energies and by the rise of fascism in Italy—and increasing support for it among Italian Americans. Italian American radicals devoted much of their energy to combating Fascist supporters in Italian immigrant communities, often with considerable success. Carlo Tresca and his allies in New York for example made the streets unsafe for Fascists throughout the 1920s. But divisions among these radicals—particularly with the rising influence of the Communists in revolutionary circles—made successful opposition difficult. More importantly, opposition faced overwhelming enthusiasm for Mussolini and fascism among the Italian immigrant elite and in its press, as well as among many native-born Americans through the 1920s and early 1930s.

The 1920s also witnessed the emergence of corrupt labor organizers among Italian Americans. Unions in the clothing, garment, and construction industries and among dockworkers for example fell under the influence of organized criminal syndicates. These were not the first labor unions to fall prey to criminal elements; they would not be the last. And this corruption was neither specific to, nor confined to, Italian Americans. But here were roots of an association between Italian Americans and organized crime that continues to haunt them, especially through mass media and popular culture, to this day.

Italian Americans

By the 1930s and the 1940s, and especially by the end of World War II, Italian Americans were well on their way to entering the American mainstream. There was still of course support for fellow ethnics like Fiorello la Guardia, who became mayor of New York City. There were even remnants of past radical affiliations, most significantly in New York, where Italians in Harlem elected Communist sympathizer Vito Marcantonio to Congress repeatedly from 1936–1950. But most Italian American workers supported new Congress of Industrial Organization unions and Franklin Delano Roosevelt's New Deal. As sons and daughters—even grandsons and granddaughters—of Italian immigrants, most began to consider themselves part of the ethnic composition of a multiethnic United States.

MICHAEL M. TOPP

References and Further Reading

Cannistraro, Philip, and Gerald Meyer. *The Lost World of Italian-American Radicalism: Politics, Labor, and Culture*. Westport, CT: Prager, 2003.

Diggins, John P. *Mussolini and Fascism: The View from the United States*. Princeton, NJ: Princeton University Press, 1972.

Ewen, Elizabeth. *Immigrant Women in the Land of Dollars: Life and Culture on the Lower East Side, 1890–1925*. New York: Monthly Review Press, 1985.

Fenton, Edwin. *Immigrants and Unions, a Case Study: Italians and American Labor, 1870–1920*. New York: Arno Press, 1975.

Gabaccia, Donna R, and Franca Iacovetta. *Women, Gender, and Transnational Lives: Italian Workers of the World*. Toronto, Canada: University of Toronto Press, 2002.

Gabaccia, Donna R., and Fraser M. Ottanelli. *Italian Workers of the World: Labor Migration and the Formation of Multiethnic States*. Urbana: University of Illinois Press, 2001.

Guglielmo, Jennifer, and Salvatore Salerno. *Are Italians White? How Race Is Made in America*. Boston, MA: Routledge Press, 2003.

Guglielmo, Thomas H. *White on Arrival: Italians, Race, Color, and Power in Chicago, 1890–1945*. New York: Oxford University Press, 2004.

Mormino, Gary M., and George Pozzetta. *The Immigrant World of Ybor City: Italians and Their Latin Neighbors in Tampa, 1885–1985*. Urbana: University of Illinois Press, 1990.

See also **Anarchism; Catholic Church; Communist Party; Congress of Industrial Organizations; Immigration Restriction; Lawrence Strike (1912); Sacco and Vanzetti; Textiles; Triangle Shirtwaist Fire**

J

J. P. STEVENS CAMPAIGN (1963–1980)

In the spring of 1963, leaders of the Textile Workers Union of America (TWUA) selected J. P. Stevens as the target for a major organizing campaign. The second-largest textile firm in the nation, Stevens employed more than 36,000 people, the bulk of them in the South. For more than 30 years, textile unions had struggled to organize the growing southern textile industry, the region's largest employer. Across the South, employers fiercely opposed the union, often backed up by local politicians and community leaders. By the early 1960s, unions had only managed to sign up around 10% of the southern textile workforce, and most of these employees worked in small plants. Seeking to make more progress, TWUA leaders reasoned that if they could organize a large firm, other employers would look more favorably upon the union.

At Stevens, the battle between the two sides raged on until the fall of 1980, becoming a symbol of labor's determination to try and break through in the most nonunion area of the country. When an agreement was finally reached, the union called off a boycott of Stevens's products while the company agreed to recognize the union at the plants that it had managed to organize.

Labor Law Violations

TWUA leaders picked Stevens in the hope that the New York-based firm would look on it more favorably than southern-owned companies. This proved to be a miscalculation, as from the start Stevens repeatedly violated labor laws in order to thwart organizing. Like many other companies, Stevens had moved south after World War II, specifically because it wanted to pay lower wages and avoid unions. The Stevens CEO, Robert T. Stevens, a former secretary of the Army, disliked the way that his company had been picked out by TWUA and was determined to make a stand. For over 17 years, company officials argued that the union was an unwanted "third party" that would interfere with the direct relationship between management and its employees.

Stevens workers, however, received wages that were well below the manufacturing average, and they had few benefits. Many initially responded enthusiastically to TWUA, but company officials soon targeted activists. Between 1965 and 1976, Stevens was cited for violating the National Labor Relations Act (NLRA) in 15 different cases, paying out around $1.3 million in back pay to approximately three hundred workers. In a series of judgments by both the National Labor Relations Board (NLRB) and the courts, Stevens was accused of having open disregard for labor law.

At the heart of Stevens's strategy was the widespread dismissal of the union's most influential supporters. Supervisors used a wide range of pretexts in order to remove union advocates, even dismissing highly experienced workers as incompetent. Others were fired for practices that had long been tolerated, such as engaging in horseplay or buying soft drinks during company time. Such behavior led the national American Federation of Labor-Congress of Industrial Organizations (AFL-CIO) to brand the textile giant as the greatest labor law violator in the entire United States. Feeling that they could not allow such behavior to go unpunished, in the summer of 1976, the AFL-CIO threw itself behind a boycott. Earlier in the year, TWUA had merged with the Amalgamated Clothing Workers of America (ACWA) in order to form a bigger union that could bring Stevens to its knees. In the fall of 1976, the Amalgamated Clothing and Textile Workers Union (ACTWU) officially launched its boycott, the first time that this tactic had been attempted against an employer of Stevens's size. In doing so, activists particularly hoped to force the company to recognize the union at its plants in Roanoke Rapids, North Carolina, where the union had won an election in 1974 but had been unable to secure a contract.

The Campaign at Its Peak

The boycott brought the Stevens campaign to national attention, as thousands of protesters marched against the company in the nation's largest cities. "Don't Sleep with Stevens," they declared, a call for consumers to stop purchasing Stevens's sheets, a central part of its business. The union used issues of sexual and racial discrimination to mobilize the support of civil rights groups such as the National Association for the Advancement of Colored People (NAACP) and the Southern Christian Leadership Conference (SCLC), together with large parts of the women's movement and many church and student groups. In addition, the boycott was endorsed by 56 U.S. representatives and many high-profile figures, including the actress Jane Fonda, the sports commentator Myron Cope, and the economist John Kenneth Galbraith.

Alongside the boycott, the maverick activist Ray Rogers ran the first "corporate campaign" in U.S. history. As part of this, ACTWU's supporters disrupted Stevens's shareholders' meetings, securing publicity of the company's labor record. In addition, Rogers revealed that many of Stevens's directors were also CEOs of firms with union ties. Rogers successfully caused embarrassment and investor discontent, and two of the firm's directors were forced to resign.

At its peak, the Stevens campaign also inspired the film *Norma Rae* (1979). In the popular movie, Sally Field won an Oscar for her depiction of a character that was loosely based on Roanoke Rapids worker Crystal Lee Sutton. Following the movie's release, Sutton herself conducted a nationwide tour to promote the union's case, securing a great deal of positive press coverage in the process. As a public relations weapon, in fact, the boycott was clearly a success, although its economic impact on the firm was mild, especially as Stevens only sold around one third of its products directly to the consumer.

At its height, the campaign attracted a lot of attention from journalists. Detailed articles on the struggle appeared in national papers such as the *New York Times* and *Washington Post*, as well as in a range of journals that included *The Nation, Fortune, Business Week*, and *Time*. At the same time, journalist Mimi Conway produced a popular account of workers' struggle in Roanoke Rapids. Based largely on oral history interviews, Conway's work provided a vivid insight into workers' daily lives.

Since these contemporary accounts, historical scholarship has been limited. Some scholars have written articles exploring the making and impact of *Norma Rae*, while others have provided overviews of the campaign. Only recently has the entire campaign received its first book-length treatment. Making extensive use of recently released documents, Timothy J. Minchin's *"Don't Sleep with Stevens!": The J. P. Stevens Campaign and the Struggle to Organize the South, 1963–1980* provides an up-to-date account of the Stevens struggle.

Alongside the boycott and "corporate campaign," the union re-ignited its organizing efforts, yet it continued to struggle to make real gains. As Stevens had established such a harsh reputation, few workers were willing to risk discharge by signing union cards. Racial divisions also hurt organizing. ACTWU's leaders found that African-Americans, who were coming into the textile industry in increasing numbers, were more likely to join the union. They were still overwhelmingly concentrated in low-paid jobs, and many had been radicalized by the civil rights movement. Their activism, however, scared off whites, who saw the union as "black."

Following the 1980 settlement, the union continued small-scale organizing efforts until the fall of 1983, when the two sides settled all remaining NLRB charges. ACTWU abandoned its organizing efforts at Stevens's plants, while Stevens paid out $1.2 million and promised to obey the law in the future. Following this settlement, the two sides established a stable relationship at organized sites.

Significance of the Stevens Campaign

The Stevens campaign was not a complete victory for either side, and both were scarred by such a long fight.

For organized labor, the battle proved highly expensive, as it poured more than $30 million into the effort. At the time, this was the largest amount that a union had ever spent on a campaign against a single company. Despite all its efforts, the union never brought more than 7% of the company's workers under contract. While refusing to reveal how much it had spent, Stevens's corporate image was clearly harmed, and it had spent too much time fighting the union rather than modernizing its plants.

Overall, the Stevens campaign had a number of important consequences for U.S. labor relations. The company showed other firms that they could avoid unionization by deliberately violating labor laws. In subsequent years, many other executives copied these tactics, especially as the powers of the NLRB were further eroded during the 1980s. The willingness of some employers to openly disregard the NLRA prompted the AFL-CIO to fight for labor law reform, but labor-backed bills narrowly failed to become law in both 1978 and 1994.

Despite this, the campaign also highlighted to the labor movement that it could achieve the most if it worked with its allies in the broader community, a trend that has continued in subsequent years as striking has become less effective. The union's efforts, particularly its innovative "corporate campaign," brought Stevens to the bargaining table, no small achievement given the firm's virulent opposition to organized labor. Since the early 1980s, however, ACTWU's breakthrough has been undermined by the flight of the textile industry to the developing world, a trend that has undermined its ability to conduct further organizing. Ironically, in the years after the Stevens campaign, both managers and workers have come together to lobby for protection against cheap imports, yet this campaign has failed to convince Congress. In the 1980s and 1990s, the number of textile employees tumbled, and Stevens itself disappeared as a corporate entity in 1988, when it was bought out by a competitor and divided into three.

TIMOTHY MINCHIN

References and Further Reading

Conway, Mimi. *Rise Gonna Rise: A Portrait of Southern Textile Workers*. Garden City, NY: Anchor Press/Doubleday, 1979.
Daniel, Clete. *Culture of Misfortune: An Interpretative History of Textile Unionism in the United States*. Ithaca, NY: ILR Press, 2001.
Guzzardi, Walter Jr. "How the Union Got the Upper Hand on J. P. Stevens." *Fortune*, June 19, 1978, 86–89, 91, 94, 98.
Hodges, James A. "J. P. Stevens and the Union: Struggle for the South." In *Race, Class, and Community in Southern Labor History*, edited by Gary M. Fink and Merl E. Reed. Tuscaloosa: University of Alabama Press, 1994, pp. 53–64, 246–249.
———. "The Real Norma Rae." In *Southern Labor in Transition, 1940–1995*, edited by Robert H. Zieger. Knoxville: The University of Tennessee Press, 1997, pp. 251–272.
Kovler, Peter. "The South: Last Bastion of the Open Shop." *Politics Today* (March–April 1979): 26–31.
McConville, Ed. "The Southern Textile War." *The Nation*, October 2, 1976, 294–299.
Minchin, Timothy J. *"Don't Sleep with Stevens!": The J. P. Stevens Campaign and the Struggle to Organize the South, 1963–1980*. Gainesville: University Press of Florida, 2005.
Toplin, Robert Brent. "Norma Rae: Unionism in an Age of Feminism." *Labor History* 36 (Spring 1995): 282–298.
Truchil, Barry E. *Capital Labor Relations in the U.S. Textile Industry*. New York: Praeger Press, 1988.

JAMAICANS

More than any other modern international event, World War II motivated an unparalleled effort to recruit foreign labor for agricultural work in the United States. At the onset of WWII, farmers worried that they would face severe labor shortages because of the military draft and the high-paying defense industry jobs that had siphoned off many agricultural workers from farms, as well as the possibility of paying higher wages during the harvest season. In response, the U.S. government intervened on behalf of the growers and allowed them legally to import labor from Mexico and the British West Indies. On August 4, 1942, an executive order initiated the Mexican bracero program, which recruited Mexicans to work in the United States. Following the precedent of the bracero program, the U.S. government established a similar program to recruit workers from the British West Indies. The first agreements were reached with the colonial authorities in the Bahamas in March 1943 and with Jamaica in April 1943.

These two agreements established the British West Indies (BWI) Temporary Alien Labor Program and like the bracero program was formalized with the passage of Public Law 45, a series of farm labor appropriations acts authorizing the U.S. government to admit temporarily foreigners to perform agricultural labor in the United States. Other West Indians (from the Bahamas, British Honduras, St. Lucia, St. Vincent, Dominica, and Barbados) eventually joined the program; however, they never composed a significant portion of the farmworkers. Jamaicans always far outnumbered other Caribbean farmworkers, second only to the Mexican workers employed on the West Coast. Nearly 50,000 Jamaican men were recruited over the four years of the wartime program.

Several factors influenced the decision of the U.S. government to recruit large numbers of men from Jamaica. First, East Coast growers preferred Jamaicans to Mexicans because they spoke English. Jamaica was also considered an ideal source for foreign labor because of the island's geographical proximity to the eastern United States. Other factors included the island's high rates of unemployment, which meant there was significant support for any migration scheme that would alleviate the unemployment on the island. Additionally, the diplomatic relations between the crown colony governments of the islands, Great Britain, and the United States, allowed the intergovernmental agreement to be concluded easily.

In May 1943, the first Jamaican men recruited as farmworkers entered the United States. The average age of Jamaican men recruited as farmworkers was 25 years old; the oldest workers were 45 and the youngest not under 18. By the end of the first year, more than 11,000 Jamaican farmworkers were in the United States. They were dispersed throughout 14 states along the eastern seaboard from Florida to Maine. Workers harvested rhubarb, asparagus, peas, spinach, and beets in Pennsylvania; picked and harvested strawberries, spinach, onions, and potatoes in New York and New Jersey; worked on tobacco farms in Connecticut; and even helped bring in the sugar-beet crops in Idaho and Michigan. The harvesting of seasonal crops required significant stooping, squatting, and lifting, in the elements, from morning until late afternoon. During each contract period, Jamaican men moved from one locality to the next, with most ending the season cutting cane in Florida.

According to the intergovernmental agreement, the U.S. government, not individual farmers, employed Jamaicans, and they were guaranteed basic protections. The main provisions of the intergovernmental agreement guaranteed each man employment for at least 75% of the period for which he was contracted and that each man receive a minimum of 30 cents an hour and be required to work no more than six days a week. The agreement also stated that workers were not to "suffer discriminatory acts which would subject them to living conditions and sanitation and medical services . . . inferior to those afforded other agricultural workers" and would be housed in facilities maintained or approved by the U.S. government, and receive "all necessary food, health and medical care and other subsistence living facilities."

Despite the contract provisions, Jamaican farmworkers found that housing, food, and wage standards were frequently disregarded. Some Jamaicans, when housed by their employers, sometimes endured unsatisfactory housing in fairground cattle exhibition sheds and garages. Those not housed with their employers were placed in government camps called Farm Labor Supply Centers. These facilities were not permanent structures, usually army-issued tents, or prefabricated wooden huts, and included very basic accommodations. Provided with a cot and thin mattress, the typical quarters for the men were crude and furnished only to provide the men a place to sleep at the end of a long day of work. The quantity and quality of the food served in the camps was also a point of great frustration. Because of wartime rationing, certain food items, especially the products Jamaican men liked the most—meat, sugar, and rice—were in very short supply. The cold bologna and cheese sandwiches were the basis of many of the men's complaints. Yet, more than any other issue, dissatisfaction over wages was the most contentious. The Jamaican men's contract stated, "there shall be no strikes, lockouts, or stoppages of work during the period of employment," but they often organized work-slowdowns or stoppages and used other creative tactics to force farmers to improve their wages and comply with contract standards. Jamaican men were vulnerable to growers' threats of repatriation, and workers identified as "troublemakers" frequently found their contracts terminated, and they were sent home to Jamaica.

The BWI program was supposed to be a temporary expedient during a wartime emergency and concluded on December 31, 1947; however, the program lasted much longer. During the years 1947–1952, the BWI program converted into a temporary-worker program, as allowed under the provisions of the Immigration Act of 1917. Tripartite contracts were drawn up between the Jamaican workers, the Jamaican government, and U.S. employers. Employers wanting Jamaican farmworkers could, with authorization from the Immigration and Naturalization Service, recruit within Jamaica or other West Indian islands. In 1952, this temporary system received permanent sanction when the Department of Labor, under section H-2A of the new Immigration Nationality Act, authorized American employers to contract with West Indian men for farm work if they could prove that no domestic workers wanted the jobs. Under the program, U.S. agricultural employers, Jamaican workers, and the Jamaican government signed working contracts, thereby eliminating the U.S. government's involvement and liability. Farmworkers' wages and hours were set, and employers were required to provide suitable living and working conditions; however, with little official oversight, violations were rampant, and workers were reluctant to complain because of the threat of being sent home to Jamaica.

After 1952, American employers recruited in Jamaica, St. Lucia, St. Vincent, Dominica, and Barbados, although Jamaicans remained the largest group of West Indian farmworkers. Most Jamaicans worked as cane cutters under H-2A temporary contracts for Florida sugar plantations in the 1980s and early 1990s. They lived in atrociously inferior housing and were paid sub-minimum wages. However, by 1995, few Jamaicans were contracted to cut cane, and this change was in large part due to the mechanization of the Florida sugarcane harvest. Since 2002, the U.S. Department of Labor has reported that many apple growers have been hiring Jamaicans as H-2A workers in West Virginia, New York, and New England. Jamaicans work from tree to tree on 12-foot ladders hauling bags that they pack full of apples. The apple harvest season lasts no more than two months out of the year and is incredibly backbreaking. Under the H-2A provisions, problems of housing, food, wages, and general mistreatment of Jamaican farmworkers have continued to beleaguer the H-2A program, just as they did during World War II.

WENDI N. MANUEL-SCOTT

References and Further Reading

Hahamovitch, Cindy. "'In America Life Is Given Away': Jamaican Farmworkers and the Making of Agricultural Immigration Policy." In *The Countryside in the Age of the Modern State: Political Histories of Rural America*, edited by Catherine McNicol Stock and Robert D. Johnston. Ithaca, NY: Cornell University Press, 2001.

Manuel-Scott, Wendi. "Soldiers of the Field: Jamaican Farm Workers in the United States during World War II." Ph.D. diss., Howard University, Washington, DC, 2003.

Rasmussen, Wayne D. *A History of the Emergency Farm Labor Supply Program 1943–1947*. Agriculture Monograph No. 133. Washington, DC: U.S. Department of Agriculture, Bureau of Agricultural Economics, 1951.

Sokolowski, Jodi L. "Apple Season Draws Influx of Migrants to the Orchards." *The Winchester Star*, September 4, 2002.

Wood, Charles H., and Terry L. McCoy. "Caribbean Cane Cutters in Florida: Implication for the Study of the Internationalization of Labor." In *The Americas in the New International Division of Labor*, edited by Steven Sanderson. New York: Holmes and Meier, 1985.

JANITORIAL/CUSTODIAL

Janitors clean and maintain the buildings of urban America. Thus, their numbers have increased with the growth of cities and the industries that support them. In 1900, over 56,000 people worked in the occupation. In 2003, there were 2,064,350, making an average hourly wage of $9.77 or $20,320 annually. A manual occupation of low status, janitorial work has traditionally attracted a high proportion of immigrants and African-Americans. From the early twentieth century, janitors have been prominent trade unionists.

The Work

Janitorial work appears deceptively simple. Janitors clean floors, rugs, walls, and windows. They take out the garbage, empty wastebaskets, mow lawns, and shovel snow. They do numerous minor repairs to faucets and fixtures; they paint walls and fix damaged woodwork; and they make sure that heating and air-conditioning equipment works properly. In other words, they perform a set of low-skilled, manual, building service tasks. Nonetheless, this short summary leaves out the challenges of managing the numerous duties and dealing with the people who live or work in the buildings.

In contrast to factory workers, janitors do not typically work together in groups but rather service individual buildings by themselves or with a few co-workers. Also, unlike factory laborers, janitors do not usually work under the direct supervision of a superior. This quality of the job demands much of janitors, while constituting one of the occupation's main attractions. Since janitors are the responsible person on the spot, tenants or teachers go immediately to them to solve problems. This responsibility also means that they seldom work a normal day or week. At the same time, the janitor's responsibility for a building has meant that he could be "his own boss," an option that most manual laborers have not had.

The tasks that janitors perform are seldom physically strenuous in themselves but do require constant bending, stooping, and stretching, which can cause injuries like strained backs. Although rarely demanding individually, janitorial tasks can nonetheless be challenging in their multiplicity, timing, and required knowledge. The janitor has been the one managing the numerous duties, and the tasks themselves usually require more knowledge than is initially apparent. In the days of coal furnaces, maintaining a fire without burning too much fuel required skill and experience. Today, the furnace may be computer driven, but for that reason it requires sufficient experience with digital equipment to maintain basic operation. Many janitorial tasks in schools and offices impinge on health and safety codes. Unionized positions require knowledge of contractually defined work.

Thus, janitorial work has required more skills than is commonly assumed. Janitors need to read well enough to understand memos from supervisors and instructions on machines. They have to write sufficiently well to keep records. They need time management skills to orchestrate the complex menu of tasks. Yet, most important, they need social skills. The janitor is responsible to a building owner or manager but also—in many cases—to a union. Both can issue demands, which may conflict. Even more challenging are the frequent requests from teachers, tenants, and office workers. While not having direct authority over the janitor, these people commonly assume that they can make demands, too, in part because they feel socially superior. Learning to deal with, and manage, the building's users has typically been one of the janitor's greatest challenges. Thus, janitorial work can often demand levels of intelligence, self-discipline, and maturity that exceed considerably the occupation's menial status and low pay.

The Workers

Janitorial jobs have typically attracted recent immigrants and African-Americans. The ethnic and racial characteristics of male janitors in 1900 set a pattern that has largely remained: about 35% were immigrants, and another 15% were the children of immigrants. Thus, half were immigrants and their offspring. Just over 20% were African-Americans, leaving 30% American-born whites of native-born parents. This basic pattern of an occupation dominated by first- and second-generation immigrants and African-Americans has persisted. The origins of the foreign-born janitors have, of course, changed dramatically. While immigrant janitors formerly came from Europe, in the late twentieth century they typically came from Latin America.

African-Americans have been notable for their early and persistently strong representation in the occupation. African-Americans constituted over a fifth of janitors well before the Great Migration out of the South that began during World War I, and they still make up 20% of janitors and cleaners (see Figure 1).

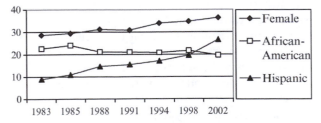

Figure 1.   Janitors and Cleaners by Sex, Race, and Hispanic Origin: 1983 to 2002.

A service occupation, janitorial work has fit with similar economic niches where, from an early date, African-Americans have earned a living in cities, such as waiting, barbering, and domestic service. Since janitorial work has grown rapidly, it became a substantial field of opportunity, especially for African-American males.

The representation of women in the janitorial workforce has changed significantly. In 1900, women made up about 14% of janitors. Today, they constitute over 35% of the workforce, and their proportion is expected to increase significantly in the future. The rise in the proportion of female janitors and cleaners is a reflection of the historic movement of women into the gainfully employed workforce during the last 40 years. Cleaning contractors have contributed to this larger trend by specializing in hiring women, particularly Hispanics. The rise of the cleaning contractors has reduced the number of traditional unionized janitorial jobs, where African-American males have been strongly represented. This development helps explain why the proportions of women and Hispanics have trended upward together in the janitorial workforce, while the percentage of African-Americans has decreased.

The age of janitors helps account for their historically prominent role in labor organizing. The occupation has traditionally attracted a substantial proportion of middle-aged men. A study of Missouri's school janitors in the 1930s found that their average age was 49. In 1998, 42% of janitors and cleaners were 45 years old or older. Since janitors perform light physical labor, the occupation has attracted manual workers who can no longer perform in more physically demanding jobs in fields such as construction or mining. The stability of the occupation has added to its attractions to older workers. In addition, traditional janitorial work has required maturity and social skills that come with age. At the same time, the low status and pay of janitors have meant that the occupation is not the first choice for workers. Thus, janitorial work has attracted older workers often with considerable background in other occupations, including experience with the trade unions. Even if such workers were only a minority among janitors, they have formed an experienced and reliable constituency for supporting unions.

The Industry

Since all buildings need to be cleaned and maintained, janitors and cleaners work across a range of industries. In 2003, local government, most notably school systems, hired over 20% of janitorial workers. Janitors employed by the federal government and by all colleges and universities together constituted another 5%. The remaining 75% worked primarily, though not exclusively, for private industry in residential buildings, offices, and hotels—that is, in the building services industry as traditionally understood.

Throughout its history, building services has been a metropolitan industry, which means first of all that its markets—including the one for labor—have been defined by cities and their economic hinterlands. Like other metropolitan industries, such as construction, building services has been characterized by numerous small- to medium-sized businesses, as well as, of course, some large ones. The apartment industry is the most obvious example, characterized by hundreds, if not thousands, of individual owners, even when national corporations may own the largest buildings in town.

The numerous businesses owning and operating buildings not only compete with each other but also try to manage their metropolitan markets. Historically, for example, they have tried to maintain a stable level of advantageous prices, which usually has required limiting access to their markets from outside competitors. Maintaining a price level also means disciplining local businesses that undercut it. Businesses' cooperative efforts to achieve these goals have typically been unstable, particularly because of the diverging interests between small and large firms. Unions have played a complicated role in the metropolitan building service industries, fighting for higher wages and better working conditions, while also sometimes cooperating to maintain agreed-upon price levels by, for example, disciplining businesses that pay below scale. When janitors' unions have gained control of the labor market in a metropolitan area, they have helped stabilize competition among building owners by putting a floor under wage reductions to gain cost advantages.

The substantial growth of contract cleaning firms in the last third of the twentieth century has brought a new level of competition to the building service industry and challenged the dominion of unions. The cleaning firms fit the mold of a metropolitan industry. In 2002, the nation had 51,345 firms providing janitorial services, and they hired more than 45% of the over 2 million janitors and cleaners. Although there were some large firms, these businesses employed an average of 18 workers. Also fitting the historical mold of the building service industry, the contract cleaners gained a competitive advantage by opposing unions and exploiting immigrants, in this case particularly, Hispanic women. Because the contract cleaners can provide cleaning services below the cost of unionized

janitors, they have started a trend toward outsourcing janitorial cleaning tasks.

Notably, however, because the buildings being serviced cannot be moved, these janitorial tasks cannot be outsourced overseas. Metropolitan markets are also subject to local political influence. These are two advantages to unions in an industry that is otherwise difficult and expensive to organize.

Unions and Politics

The dispersal of janitors across a metropolitan area has made organizing them complex and costly. The same dispersal has made their development of collective identities difficult. In addition, the numerous modest-sized employers in the industry require unions to confront and bargain with a host of businesses instead of a few. For much of the twentieth century, it was common for one janitor to service several residential buildings, often with different owners. Thus, the unions had to deal with more employers than they had members. The employment of a substantial minority of janitors by various governmental bodies has created further problems for unions, because government employees work under different laws and regulations.

These structural problems have helped push janitors' unions into politics from their earliest days. Most obviously, unions organizing publicly employed janitors have found political influence one of the few reliable means for aiding their members, since government workers have typically lacked legal collective bargaining rights, attaining them only since the 1960s. More generally, unions have used local politics to influence the real estate industry in which their members work. Historically, local governments have profoundly shaped the owners of real estate through court decisions, public works investment, zoning, building codes, and various health and safety regulations. Thus, gaining influence with these governments has been a means for shaping an often fragmented and complex industry. Ironically, the dispersal of the membership has aided the political influence of unions because they have members spread across political jurisdictions who know the local area intimately and engage in basic political work under the unions' central direction. In Chicago, the janitors' local was one of the most effective grassroots political organizations in the city.

Stable janitors' unions formed first in Chicago under the leadership of William F. Quesse, the native-born son of German immigrants. Quesse's local achieved a citywide contract in 1917 and went on to form the core of the new Building Service Employees International Union (BSEIU) in 1921. Other cities represented among the charter members were New York, Boston, St. Louis, and Seattle. Also from Chicago was a local of female school "janitresses." Quesse's Local 1 remained the center of power in the International for the next several decades. In the 1930s, Local 1 came under the influence of an alliance of Chicago and New York mobsters, who installed New Yorker George Scalise as head of the International. After Scalise was successfully prosecuted in the early 1940s, William McFetridge, Quesse's nephew, took over the leadership of both Local 1 and the International. Whereas Quesse supported a local Republican faction, Local 1 under McFetridge allied with Richard J. Daley's Democratic machine.

Both Local 1 and the International prospered after World War II. In 1968, the BSEIU changed its name to the Service Employees International Union (SEIU) to acknowledge its expanded organizing among health-care and government workers. In 2004, the SEIU had 1.7 million members across the United States, Canada, and Puerto Rico, making it the largest union in the AFL-CIO, as well as the source of some of its most energetic and innovative leadership. In 1995, John J. Sweeney moved from international president of the SEIU to president of the AFL-CIO. The SEIU has taken the lead in organizing the largely immigrant workers in the contract cleaning industry. Its Justice for Janitors campaign in the 1990s became a model for contemporary union organizing by mobilizing local communities to exert political pressure within metropolitan areas such as Washington, DC and Los Angeles.

JOHN B. JENTZ

References and Further Reading

Cranford, Cynthia. "Gender and Citizenship in the Restructuring of Janitorial Work in Los Angeles." In *Immigrant Women*, edited by Rita James Simon. New Brunswick, NJ: Transaction Publishers, 2001, pp. 21–47.
Dohm, Arlene. "Gauging the Labor Force Effects of Retiring Baby-Boomers." *Monthly Labor Review* 123, no. 7 (2000): 17–26.
Gordon, Colin. "The Lost City of Solidarity: Metropolitan Unionism in Historical Perspective." *Politics & Society* 27, no. 4 (1999): 561–585.
Jentz, John B. "Citizenship, Self-Respect, and Political Power: Chicago's Flat Janitors Trailblaze the Service Employees International Union." *Labor's Heritage* 9, no. 1 (1997): 4–23.
———. "Labor, the Law, and Economics: The Organization of the Chicago Flat Janitors' Union, 1902–1917." *Labor History* 38, no. 4 (1997): 413–431.
———. Unions, Cartels, and the Political Economy of American Cities: The Chicago Flat Janitors' Union in the Progressive Era and 1920s." *Studies in American Political Development* 14, no. 1 (2000): 51–71.
Mines, Richard, and Jeffrey Avina. "Immigrants and Labor Standards: The Case of California Janitors." In *U.S.-Mexico Relations: Labor Market Interdependence*, edited by Jorge A. Bustamante, Clark W. Reynolds, and Raúl A. Hinojosa Ojeda.Stanford, CA: Stanford University Press, 1992, pp. 429–448.
Slater, Joseph E. "Ground-Floor Politics and the BSEIU in the 1930s." In *Public Workers: Government Employee Unions, the Law, and the State, 1900–1962*, by Joseph E. Slater. Ithaca, NY: Cornell University Press, 2004, pp. 97–124.
United States Bureau of Labor Statistics. "Building Cleaning Workers." In *Occupational Outlook Handbook*, http://bls.gov/oco/ocos174.htm (accessed September 23, 2004).
———. "Occupational Employment and Wages, May 2003: 37-2011 Janitors and Cleaners, Except Maids and Housekeeping Cleaners." www.bls.gov/oes/2003/may/oes372011.htm (accessed October 13, 2004).
United States Census Bureau. *12th Census (1900), Occupations at the Twelfth Census.* Tables III and XXXVII, xxxiv–xxxv, cxiv. Washington, DC: Government Printing Office, 1904.
———. *Services to Buildings and Dwellings: 2002* (issued June 2004, as part of 2002 Economic Census, Administrative and Support and Waste Management and Remediation Services, Industry Series). www.census.gov/prod/ec02/ec0256i07.pdf (accessed September 23, 2004).
Witwer, David. "The Scandal of George Scalise: A Case Study in the Rise of Labor Racketeering in the 1930s." *Journal of Social History* 36, no. 4 (2003): 917–940.

See also **African-Americans; Justice for Janitors; Mexican and Mexican-American Workers; Service Employees' International Union; Southwest; Sweeney, John J.**

JAPANESE STRIKE IN HAWAI'I (1909)

Between May and November of 1909, nearly seven thousand Japanese workers struck sugar plantations on O'ahu in the territory of Hawai'i. The strike was instigated by a group that called itself "The Higher Wage Association." The Association was led by a small group of local intellectuals and writers, Motoyuki Negoro, Yasutaro Soga, and Kinzaburo Makino, who launched a campaign to increase the pay and improve working and living conditions of the largely Japanese workforce. The strike was a watershed in Hawai'i labor history because it was the first organized mass walkout of workers in the sugar industry. The strike united workers on many plantations and garnered the support of laborers on other islands and local business, trade, and union organizations. The strike also helped to consolidate the power of the Hawaii Sugar Planters' Association (HSPA), which represented all of the sugar plantation owners in the territory. Both sides used the power of the press to spread their messages, pitting Japanese- and English-language newspapers against one another in a war of words. Although the strike was eventually broken, the HSPA later conceded to many of the demands made by the striking workers, leading to higher pay and improved living conditions on the plantations.

The sugar industry in Hawai'i was established in the early 1840s. The industry enjoyed rapid growth after 1887 when the Kingdom of Hawai'i signed a reciprocity treaty with the United States guaranteeing Hawai'i's sugar duty-free entry into American ports. Because of years of depopulation due to introduced disease, the local Hawai'ian population was insufficient to provide enough labor for the industry. Sugar plantation owners, working in cooperation with the Hawai'ian government, began importing laborers from Asia, first China and, by the late nineteenth century, from Japan. During the first decade of the twentieth century, Japanese workers represented more than half the local workforce on sugar plantations.

Hawai'i plantation owners enjoyed a far-reaching control over their workers. According to Kingdom law, under the Masters and Servants Act, employees could be restricted to the plantation, could be jailed for failing to fulfill the terms of their contract, and enjoyed little to no legal recourse in the case of a dispute with an employer. After 1900, as a territory of the United States, the terms of labor contracting underwent liberalization, but Japanese immigrant workers were still subject to the dominion of plantation owners and managers. Workers were vulnerable to arrest, imprisonment, or deportation if they protested conditions on the plantations too strenuously.

Prior to 1909, labor strikes in Hawai'i were often spontaneous acts of resistance to the abuses of a *luna* (foreman) or a means to resolve a dispute over pay on a specific plantation. The 1909 strike was the first organized strike aimed at changing living and working conditions for all workers in the industry. Although it was confined to O'ahu, it was supported by plantation workers throughout the territory.

The 1909 strike was provoked by a call for higher wages. In July of 1908, Motoyuki Negoro published an editorial in *Nippu Jiji*, a Japanese-language newspaper in Honolulu. Negoro noted that the industry was enjoying an unprecedented level of profits and that workers had a right to share in those profits. The debate over higher wages continued throughout the year, eventually culminating in a meeting of the Japanese community leaders to discuss the issues. Those who wished to press ahead formed the Higher Wages Association and proceeded to formulate a set of demands to present to the Hawaii Sugar Planters' Association.

The petition presented to the HSPA documented the hardship of workers trying to survive on an average wage of 14 dollars a month. In addition to wage demands, the Higher Wage Association also stipulated that the HSPA address the substandard living conditions on the plantations. It called for an eight-hour workday, improved housing, sanitary and bathing facilities, and larger quarters to accommodate growing families. The petition also demanded an end to race-based wage scales that paid Japanese workers less than Portuguese and white workers.

The HSPA studiously ignored the demands of the workers as outlined in the petition. It refused to acknowledge or negotiate with the Higher Wage Association and instead began to plead its case before the public in the English-language press. It warned the white community of the potential for anarchy and unrest in the territory and suggested that the strike organizers were radicals, possibly Communists.

The strike began on May 5 when workers at Waipahu plantation presented their demands to local management. On May 9, 1,500 workers in Aiea walked off the job. By the end of the month, the Higher Wage Association estimated that 7,000 workers were striking all O'ahu plantations. The HSPA responded quickly; as an organization, it privately pledged to share the cost of the strike amongst its members so that no one plantation owner was vulnerable to excessive financial loss. Striking workers were kicked out of plantation-owned housing and charged with trespassing if they re-entered the premises. Plantation owners hired replacement workers from the Korean, Hawai'ian, and Portuguese communities, sometimes paying twice the going daily rate. The HSPA employed spies within the Higher Wage Association and used its influence in local government to harass the strike leaders. In June, the leadership of the Higher Wage Association and sympathetic writers and editors of the *Nippu Jiji* were arrested and charged with conspiracy. In August, they were convicted and sentenced to 10 months in prison and fined $300 each. Although they were eventually pardoned and released from jail, the HSPA demonstrated its potential power over union organizers because of the control it exercised over local government.

The arrest and imprisonment of the leaders crippled the strike. The strike fund was insufficient to take care of the thousands of workers and their families who, having been ousted from their plantation housing, were living in parks, beaches, and warehouses in Honolulu. On August 5, 1909, the Higher Wage Association voted to return to work.

In the months and years following the strike, the HSPA gradually conceded to many of the demands made by the strikers. It made incremental shifts in wage scales and instituted measures designed to make plantation camps more livable. The strike demonstrated the willingness and ability of workers to organize against the formidable power of the HSPA.

LORI PIERCE

References and Further Reading

Beechert, Edward D. *Working in Hawai'i: A Labor History.* Honolulu: University of Hawai'i Press, 1985.
Okihiro, Gary. *Cane Fires: The Anti-Japanese Movement in Hawai'i, 1865–1945.* Philadelphia: Temple University Press, 1991.

JEWISH LABOR COMMITTEE

The Jewish Labor Committee (JLC) formed in 1934 as a direct response to the Nazi seizure of power in Germany the preceding year. Its founders, composed of leaders from within the ranks of Jewish labor, sought to mobilize the general American labor movement to fight against fascism. In the years after the defeat of Nazi Germany, the JLC broadened its agenda on several fronts, including assisting survivors of the Holocaust, strengthening labor movements abroad, and fighting prejudice in the United States.

When the Nazis seized power in 1933, several American Jewish labor leaders convinced the American Federation of Labor (AFL) to call for a boycott of German products. Most American Jewish groups, such as the American Jewish Committee, believed a boycott would only lead to Nazi reprisals against German Jews or worse, an outbreak of anti-Semitism in the United States. Jewish labor leaders dismissed these concerns, and in 1933, convinced AFL leaders to call for the boycott. These Jewish labor leaders believed it necessary to create a permanent body to deal with this threat, and in February 1934, the JLC was created to develop more lines of attack against fascism and provide support for the victims of fascism.

The JLC formed with representation from the most powerful forces in the Jewish labor movement, most notably the International Ladies' Garment Workers' Union, the Amalgamated Clothing Workers of America, the United Hebrew Trades, the Workmen's Circle, and the Jewish Daily Forward Association. Its agenda consisted of four primary goals: raise awareness among the American public about the fascist threat, aid refugees of fascism, provide material and moral support for groups fighting fascism, and defend Jewish rights throughout the world.

At the AFL's 1934 convention, the JLC's president and founding member, Baruch Charney Vladeck, addressed the American Federation of Labor's annual convention and convinced AFL leaders of the need to create a special fund called the Labor Chest. The money from this fund was designated to assist refugees as well as promote various projects the JLC deemed necessary to educate the general public on the fascist threat.

In 1936, the JLC organized one of the largest of these projects. It sought to divert attention away from the Olympic Games in Berlin by organizing the World Labor Athletic Carnival at Randall's Island in New York, featuring athletes who did not wish to participate in the Berlin games. This "counter-Olympics" attracted prominent figures in labor and politics to serve as honorary chairpersons of the games, including the New York governor, Herbert Lehman, the New York City mayor, Fiorello LaGuardia, and the AFL president, William Green.

During World War II, the JLC succeeded in three major endeavors despite the immense obstacles created by the war. First, it made contact with underground forces in Nazi-occupied Europe and sent funds to assist them in fighting the Nazis. Second, it established a committee in New York composed of exiled European trade-union leaders, which maintained contact with partisans in Europe. Third, the JLC lobbied the U.S. government to provide visas for over a thousand European leaders in politics and culture, both Jewish and non-Jewish, and attained for them safe passage to the United States.

With the end of the war in 1945, JLC leadership believed the fate of Jewish children in postwar Europe needed to be addressed. Accordingly, it established the Child Adoption Program, which sought to provide these children with necessities such as clothes and food packages in addition to school supplies and toys. The program's leaders requested that union shops, locals, fraternal societies, or even individuals "adopt" a child for $300 each year.

Throughout the war years, the JLC supported Jewish immigration to Palestine as a practical solution to the refugee problem, especially since Congress refused to make exceptions to the immigration restriction laws of the 1920s. Yet, within the JLC, divisions among members over the issue of Zionism prevented the JLC from endorsing a Jewish state in Palestine until 1948. Most JLC members hailed from the Bund or General Jewish Workers' Union of Lithuania, Poland, and Russia. Bundists opposed nationalist movements such as Zionism as distractions from the socialist enterprise. Nonetheless, by the end of World War II, the realities of the Holocaust led most JLC members to view a Jewish state in Palestine as the only hope for Jewish survivors in Europe. By 1947, JLC leaders worked diligently to secure the votes within the United Nations supporting the partition of Palestine. With Israel's creation in 1948, the JLC spent the next few decades lending financial and moral succor to the Jewish labor movement in Israel and helping to develop Israel's infrastructure.

In addition to aiding Israel, the JLC implemented several plans to assist the survivors of the European war, including non-Jews. It sent clothing and food in mass quantities to European survivors, helped re-unite families separated during the war, built libraries, and provided shelter and food for children who lost their parents during the war. Domestically, the JLC developed educational programs to inform American workers on issues of prejudice. These programs, which received support from the general American labor movement, began a long-term commitment by the JLC to civil rights.

Initially, the JLC set up several committees at the local level in the United States and Canada designed to battle prejudice. Eventually, it assisted in the crea-tion of civil rights departments in several national unions in both countries, which led ultimately to the formation of the AFL Civil Rights Department. Dur-ing the 1960s, the JLC also played a role in the creation of the United Farm Workers.

Although founded as a reaction to the rise of Nazi fascism, the JLC became a pro-active organization dedicated to strengthening ties between labor and the Jewish community. Its actions before and during World War II demonstrate that Jewish and labor activists worked together in preventing, and later, alleviating the effects of Nazi persecution. Over time, the JLC expanded its agenda beyond the Jewish community to the national and international arena, leaving an indelible mark on the American labor movement and the Jewish community.

ADAM HOWARD

References and Further Reading

Epstein, Melech. *Jewish Labor Movement in the USA, Volumes I and II*. New York: Ktav Publishing House, Inc., 1969.
The Jewish Labor Committee Story. Publication of the Jew-ish Labor Committee, New York.
Kelman, Sidney. "Limits of Consensus: Unions and the Holocaust." *American Jewish History* 79 (Spring 1990): 336–357.
Lebowitz, Arieh. *Basic Bibliography: The Jewish Labor Movement in the United States*. New York, 1996.
Malmgreen, Gail. "Labor and the Holocaust: The Jewish Labor Committee and the Anti-Nazi Struggle." *Labor's Heritage* 3:4 (October 1991):

See also **Amalgamated Clothing Workers of America; International Ladies' Garment Workers' Union**

JEWS

During the twentieth century, the Jewish labor move-ment in the United States played a transformative role in the American labor movement. With the mass arrival of Eastern European Jews to the United States in the late nineteenth and early twentieth cen-turies, a new influx of Jewish workers entered the American labor force and brought a new sensibility to organized labor. After Jews were initially ostra-cized from the American labor movement by Gentile members resentful of the newcomers, Jews steadily worked their way to acceptance and helped imple-ment new approaches and innovations to trade union-ism and labor/management cooperation. Most of the Jewish influence within the American labor move-ment centered in the garment industry and in urban centers, especially New York, Chicago, Boston, and Philadelphia. By the mid-twentieth century, the num-ber of Jewish rank-and-file workers diminished, but Jewish leadership within the American labor move-ment remained influential for the rest of the century.

The first masses of immigrant Jewish laborers found themselves generally blocked from entry into unions belonging to the American Federation of Labor (AFL), the dominant labor federation at the turn of the twentieth century. Through a combination of obstacles, including high initiation fees, approval from union leaders for membership, or insistence on a foreign union card, Gentile union leadership generally blocked the entry of new Jewish arrivals. Through perseverance and the assistance of important allies such as the AFL president, Samuel Gompers, Jews began making headway into the American labor movement by the 1890s. Still, resistance to their pres-ence remained through the early twentieth century.

By the 1920s, Jewish labor suffered through a tu-multuous decade of strife caused by communist agita-tion within the garment industry and the increased influence of organized crime used by both manage-ment and union leadership to intimidate foes. These two elements would be subdued by union leaders during the 1930s, however, and the New Deal legis-lation of President Franklin Roosevelt's administra-tion opened up new opportunities for American labor to thrive. Jewish labor leaders recognized the opportunities offered first by the National Recovery Act (NRA) and then by the Wagner Act, and they introduced new innovations to American trade union-ism that would set a new standard for labor-manage-ment practices. Jewish-led garment unions, such as the Amalgamated Clothing Workers of America (ACWA) and International Ladies' Garment Work-ers' Union (ILGWU), created the first cooperative housing projects, pension and welfare funds, worker

Jewish family working on garters in kitchen for tenement home. Location: New York, New York. Library of Congress, Prints & Photographs Division, National Child Labor Committee Collection [LC-DIG-nclc-04274].

education institutes, and union health centers. Additionally, they provided funding for fellow labor movements outside the United States and became politically engaged in the civil rights movement of the 1950s and 1960s. In New York State, Jewish labor leaders formed two third parties, the American Labor Party (ALP) and the Liberal Party of New York, both of which shaped the state's political landscape for decades. Throughout the mid-twentieth century, Jewish labor leaders applied this expansive vision, inspired by the revolutionary movements of their youth in Eastern Europe, to the American labor movement. In the process, they played a major role in the evolution of the American labor movement from a "bread-and-butter" unionism to a movement encompassing a broader social vision for American society.

Origins of a Movement

Defining "Jewish unions" is problematic. Although many of the early garment unions based in New York City during the late nineteenth century consisted of Jewish majorities among workers, by the early twentieth century, union demographics had shifted. For example, the ACWA, one of the most powerful

garment unions during the twentieth century, originated under a predominantly Jewish membership. By the 1920s, however, this Jewish predominance diminished as Jews came to comprise just under half of the ACWA's membership. By the turn of the twentieth century, even the United Hebrew Trades (UHT), an organization founded in the 1880s explicitly to assist Jewish workers, accepted non-Jewish members and found that at various points during the 1930s, nearly half of its members were not Jewish.

Despite the demographic changes in union membership, however, Jewish leadership in these unions remained constant throughout the early and mid-twentieth century. Even with the large number of women comprising garment workers, the executive boards remained predominantly male and Jewish. By the mid-twentieth century, many Jewish garment workers had worked their way into the middle class, or at least their children breached it. Yet for decades, Jewish leadership remained entrenched, leaving a profound imprint on the American labor movement years after the number of rank-and-file Jewish unionists had dramatically diminished.

The dominance of Jewish leadership in the garment unions came only after a long struggle to create a labor movement among Jewish immigrants. During the 1880s, Jewish immigrants typically sought upward mobility as fast as possible, and therefore, never cultivated a strong trade-union movement. Many Jewish garment workers saw themselves as future employers and rarely engaged in the communal struggles necessary to form a vibrant and cohesive labor movement. In the early 1900s, the majority of the hundreds of thousands of garment workers in New York remained unorganized, and those unions that existed operated with minimal energy. Additionally, most of them had little connection with other American workers and little exposure to socialism. Thus, few immigrant Jews possessed a class-consciousness capable of sustaining a trade-union movement.

After 1905, this mentality changed rapidly. The second generation of Eastern European Jewish immigrants hit the shores of America with a bubbling romanticism for socialist ideals bred by revolutionary ferment in late nineteenth- and early twentieth-century Eastern Europe. Most arrived fresh from the abortive 1905 Russian Revolution, which despite its failure, left veterans of the revolt hopeful of applying their socialist vision in the United States.

This vision clashed, however, with the dominant attitude of the native, American labor movement, composed of non-Jewish workers. During the late nineteenth century, leaders of the emerging AFL embraced a labor philosophy known as "bread-and-butter" unionism. AFL leaders stressed wages, hours, and working conditions, shunning broader visions of social transformation. Many of the Jewish immigrants, imbued with socialist ideology, found this "bread-and-butter" unionism wanting. Their commitment to socialism encouraged workers to strive for a broad social vision that encompassed social insurance, government activism, and racial equality, all things anathema to AFL leaders of the early twentieth century. By the early 1900s, despite AFL resistance to such an expansive agenda, Jewish garment workers began to coalesce around the radical doctrine of their Eastern European homelands. They spent the first two decades of the twentieth century forming unions or strengthening previously existing ones.

The Jewish labor movement was not limited to the large memberships within the garment unions. Jewish workers also created labor organizations and associations to address their socialist vision such as the United Hebrew Trades. Founded in 1888, the UHT helped immigrants seeking food, shelter, and work, and provided financial support for sick workers, offered recreation opportunities, and educated workers in socialist principles. Additionally, by the early 1900s, Jewish workers formed fraternal organizations, most notably the Workmen's Circle (*Arbeiter Ring* in Yiddish), to promote social interaction and offer economic assistance and educational opportunities.

Jewish trade unionists also found assistance in many cases from Jewish community leaders. During the late nineteenth century, the mass arrival of Eastern European Jews to the United States raised concern among Jews already living in the country. Unlike Jewish immigrants of the mid-nineteenth century, many of whom came to the United States with some money and quickly assimilated, these new Jewish immigrants appeared quite foreign to most Americans and did not seem as readily assimilable as their predecessors. Despite these concerns among American Jews, some efforts were made to assist these new arrivals in their transition to life in the United States. Since many of these immigrants would be working in factories, notable American Jews sought to make their transition as smooth and quiet as possible. Some Jewish manufacturers tried to keep labor strife quiet by working with the newcomers in addressing labor issues. Additionally, Jewish community leaders sought to avoid trouble between manufacturers and workers by mediating disputes. In 1911, for example, Louis Brandeis arbitrated a cloakmakers' strike and drafted the protocol of peace, which helped establish a cooperative relationship between labor and management within the garment industry. Although many battles emerged between Jewish management and labor during the century, this attitude of quiet mediation and cooperation played a major role in allowing the Jewish labor movement to grow in an otherwise hostile environment.

The rising number of Jewish garment workers in the United States made it difficult for native garment union leaders to prevent them from joining their unions. Many native garment workers viewed these Jewish newcomers as aliens with radical beliefs, potentially undermining the garment unions. Even so, by World War I, Jewish-led labor battles had gained Jewish workers entry into established unions and had created new organizations such as the ACWA. The ILGWU emerged as a force in the garment industry after a 1909 strike among shirtwaist makers in New York known as the "Uprising of the 20,000." This strike marked the emergence of the ILGWU. Its gains continued in 1910 as a cloakmakers' strike, called the "Great Revolt," earned workers a 50-hour workweek, minimum wages for certain workers, and a Joint Board of Sanitary Control. Such hard-fought strikes won respect from AFL leaders. By the 1920s, as most Jewish labor leaders traded the radicalism of their youth for a more reform-minded approach to labor-management relations, they began to enjoy growing influence with the AFL. Yet, as the 1920s began, ideological conflicts within the Jewish labor movement and confrontations with organized crime nearly destroyed the Jewish labor movement in its nascent stages.

The 1920s: Struggles on Two Fronts

Despite Jewish labor's growing influence within the American labor movement, the 1920s proved a tumultuous decade for Jewish labor generally as communists engaged right-wing socialists in internecine conflicts that led in certain cases to destructive strikes, especially a 1926 strike that nearly destroyed the ILGWU. Additionally, organized crime entered the garment industry in growing numbers, with gangs working as strikebreakers for some manufacturers and strike enforcers for some labor unions.

Communism made major inroads within the Jewish labor movement during the decade, and many communists took an active role in union activities, including running for elected positions within the unions. Although the left wing of the Jewish labor movement also included anarchists and left-wing socialists, it was the communists whom union leaders such as Morris Sigman, David Dubinsky, and Alex Rose sought to purge from the garment industry. After anticommunist Jewish labor leaders actively sought the removal of communists from influential positions within the garment unions, the communists found themselves in retreat by the end of the decade. Still, the financial and psychological damage done to some garment unions, especially the ILGWU, lasted for years to come.

Organized crime also played a role in this weakening of the garment industry during this decade. Both manufacturers and unions hired gangsters from different gangs to work as "muscle" in either breaking strikes and protecting scabs or protecting picketers and attacking scabs. During a 1926 strike that paralyzed the garment industry, only the intervention of Arnold Rothstein, the influential gambler with mob connections, could successfully convince the gangs involved to cease their activities. This opened the way to a settlement but did not end mob influence within the Jewish labor movement. Mobsters infiltrated the trucking unions within the garment industry as well as some locals. By the early 1930s, Jewish labor leaders such as Sidney Hillman and David Dubinsky worked diligently to purge the mob from their unions. Their efforts met with generally good results, but some level of mob influence lingered for years to come.

A New Era

The 1930s proved both a successful and divisive era for Jewish labor. On the one hand, President Roosevelt's New Deal brought legal recognition to the labor movement through the Wagner Act as well as significant measures to protect union organizing. Concurrently, however, the labor movement fractured over the issue of organizing unskilled labor. Many Jewish labor leaders, including Sidney Hillman of the ACWA, David Dubinksy of the ILGWU, and Max Zaritsky of the United Hatters, Cap, and Millinery Workers' Union (UHCMWU), joined the Committee of Industrial Organizations (CIO) in an effort to organize the multitude of unskilled labor in the United States. Many AFL leaders feared losing bargaining leverage if they organized unskilled workers, whom management could easily replace with scabs. They preferred to focus their energies on skilled workers, much to the chagrin of Jewish labor leaders, who believed such a mentality to be parochial and out of touch with reality. For several American labor leaders, several of them Jewish, the future of the American labor movement lay with industrial unionism and the organizing of the unskilled laboring masses.

During the 1930s, Hillman, Dubinsky, and Zaritsky, along with John L. Lewis (the president of the United Mine Workers) and Charles P. Howard (the president of the International Typographical Union), pressed for the AFL to aggressively organize industrial workers, the labor movement's most energetic fighters during the 1930s, for major changes in worker-management relations. Prior to this period, industrial unionism remained stagnant on the AFL leadership's agenda, but by the 1930s, these labor leaders argued vehemently for the mass organization of industrial workers. In 1935, AFL apathy led Lewis, Howard, Hillman, Dubinsky, and Zaritsky to create the Committee for Industrial Organizations. They worked with AFL locals to convince the old craft unions that they could co-exist with industrial unions. By the late 1930s, fractures within the CIO over fears of dividing the labor movement led Dubinsky and Zaritsky to attempt peacemaking between CIO and AFL officials. They implored the AFL leadership to recognize the need for mass industrial organization while attempting to convince CIO leaders of the need for accommodation. Although Jewish labor leaders could not bridge this divide for nearly two decades, they served in the forefront of American labor's recognition of the need for mass industrial organization. While the ACWA remained in the CIO throughout the 1930s and 1940s, the ILGWU and UHCMWU rejoined the AFL by the 1940s.

With the onset of U.S. entry into World War II by 1941, the entire American labor movement experienced full employment. After the war, American labor enjoyed its greatest period of influence and prosperity. During this time, the Jewish labor movement played an important role in New York and national politics as well as supporting the international labor movement. The American Labor Party, founded in 1936 to support President Roosevelt's re-election, became a permanent New York state party dedicated to the ideals of the New Deal. After communists gained significant control within the party, right-wing socialists and liberals left the ALP to create the Liberal Party of New York. Both parties played influential roles in local New York politics and presidential elections during the mid-twentieth century.

Internationally, Jewish labor leaders worked through international labor organizations such as the International Confederation of Free Trade Unions (ICFTU) to strengthen free labor movements throughout the world. Additionally, garment unions provided direct assistance to several nations where labor movements sought aid, especially in Israel. Even before World War II, the Jewish labor movement assisted the Jewish labor movement in Palestine, known as the Histadrut. After the war, this assistance increased dramatically after the complete revelation of the Holocaust. Through generous donations, the Jewish labor movement helped the nascent state of Israel develop infrastructure and housing as well as lobby U.S. politicians to support Israel politically and financially.

The Decline of a Movement

By the 1960s, the Jewish labor movement moved into a steady decline as more and more children of union leaders and rank-and-file workers entered white-collar positions. David Dubinsky's retirement as the president of the ILGWU in 1966 signaled the end of an era. A continual increase in non-Jewish minorities ushered in a new era in the garment industry as Jewish labor leaders retired or died in office. Although some notable Jewish labor leaders continued to make an impact on the AFL-CIO's fortunes during the late twentieth century, an era of Jewish labor influence had passed. Yet, this influence, despite its eventual demise, left an immense impact on the American labor movement, both past and present.

ADAM HOWARD

References and Further Reading

Dubinsky, David, and A. H. Raskin. *David Dubinsky: A Life with Labor*. New York: Simon and Schuster, 1977.
Epstein, Melech. *Jewish Labor in the U.S.A., Volumes I and II*. New York: Ktav Publishing House, 1969.
Fraser, Stephen. *Labor Will Rule: Sidney Hillman and the Rise of American Labor*. New York: The Free Press, 1991.
Howe, Irving. *World of Our Fathers*. New York: Simon and Schuster, 1976.
Lebowitz, Arieh. *Basic Bibliography: The Jewish Labor Movement in the United States*. New York, 1996.
Parmet, Robert D. *The Master of Seventh Avenue: David Dubinsky and the American Labor Movement*. New York: New York University Press, 2005.
Shapiro, Judah J. *The Workmen's Circle: The First Seventy Years*. New York: Workmen's Circle, 1970.

See also **Amalgamated Clothing Workers of America; American Labor Party; Dubinsky, David; Hillman, Sidney; International Ladies' Garment Workers' Union; Liberal Party; Uprising of the 20,000 (1909)**

JOHNSON-REED (IMMIGRATION RESTRICTION) ACT (1924)

In enacting the Johnson Reed Immigration (Restriction) Act of 1924, Congress responded to a half century of concern about immigration. The legislators banned nearly all immigration from Asia and severely curtailed immigration from Southern and Eastern Europe through a system called "national origins." Newcomers from Africa were also limited to small quotas. The Western Hemisphere was left without numerical limits, but even that migration was brought to a near halt during the lean years of the Great Depression.

Asians

Prior to 1875, states managed immigration, but that practice ended when the United States Supreme Court held it to be a federal matter. Following that decision, federal lawmakers passed the Page Act in 1875, which barred prostitutes from coming to America. Seven years later, Congress went further and banned the entrance of Chinese laborers. The law responded to labor agitation against Chinese immigrants in California and growing racism in the United States overall. Racists argued that the Chinese were an inferior and unassimilable people who worked for virtual slave wages and depressed the American wage scale. Chinese merchants and their wives, students, and diplomats could still come to the United States, but the vast majority of potential migrants were barred.

When Japanese immigrants appeared in Hawaii and California, Californians created a diplomatic problem for President Theodore Roosevelt. The San Francisco school board announced that Japanese students were to be segregated. In 1907, President Roosevelt negotiated a diplomatic agreement with Japan (the Gentleman's Agreement) in which the federal government pressured the school board to reverse its decision and the government of Japan stopped allowing Japanese laborers to sail for America.

Other Asians faced similar hostility and racism. For example, Asian Indians were banned in 1917. Eventually, the Johnson-Reed Act barred virtually all Asians. Filipinos, who migrated to Hawaii and the mainland United States largely as agricultural workers, were not covered by the law. However, during the Great Depression, Congress gave them an annual quota of only 50. After 1945, when the Philippines became independent, they would no longer be eligible to migrate to the United States.

Europeans

Although the 1924 law banned nearly all Asians, the chief goal of the legislators was to curtail European immigrants, especially the largest source of immigrants after 1890: those from Southern and Eastern Europe. By 1910, nearly 15% of the American population was foreign-born. World War I did decrease immigration substantially, but after the war the large-scale movement of people to America renewed, and it increased the alarm of those who believed these newcomers were a danger to the United States.

By the 1920s, the calls for European immigration restriction could no longer be ignored. Business groups still wanted their labor for the growing industries of the United States, but labor leaders, such as Samuel Gompers, saw immigrants as competitors. Some Progressive reformers believed that the burgeoning immigrant communities supported corrupt urban bosses. A revived Ku Klux Klan saw many threats to American society, among them Roman Catholic immigrants and Jews, especially those from Russia and Poland, who, according to anti-Semites, could never successfully assimilate. After the Civil War, white southerners favored immigrants as workers, for many believed that blacks would not be reliable farmworkers. White southerners attempted to recruit Europeans and even Chinese, but these efforts proved to be unsuccessful. As a result, after 1900, southern white politicians turned against immigration, largely using racist arguments. Then World War I released a flood of anti-immigrant sentiment, as did the Russian Revolution of 1917. During World War I, German-Americans were persecuted, and immediately after, many "radical aliens" were rounded up and deported. This was not an unpopular move; many Americans feared that immigrants would import radical sentiments to America.

The rise of nineteenth-century racism crystallized in the "eugenics movement," which held that certain groups were inferior. This played a key role in the growing movement to restrict immigration from Europe as well as Asia. By 1900, a variety of academics, politicians, and popular writers were warning that the basic ethnic fabric of American society was in danger due to the "pollution" of America's demographic stock. The new racism acknowledged that Europeans were all white, but were whites of different abilities. Those who came before the late nineteenth century—the English, Scots-Irish, Scots, Germans, and Scandinavians—were deemed acceptable because of their alleged innate superiority. Even the Irish, who had been the victims of nativism in the nineteenth century because of their poverty and Catholicism, were becoming part of the desirable immigrant stream.

Among the popular eugenics writers was Madison Grant, the author of a popular 1916 book titled *The Passing of the Great Race*. Grant believed that the early Americans were from the Nordic race, but that that stock was now being diluted by mixing with those who came in later years.

Psychologists also took up the role of claiming that the Nordics were superior by nature. Carl Brigham of Princeton University, using the mental intelligence tests of the United States Army uncritically, said these tests proved that the Nordic or Old Stock Americans scored higher because they were naturally superior.

When barring Chinese beginning in 1882, Congress had also enacted a number of restrictions on other immigrants, such as persons "likely to be a public charge" (1891) or persons with certain diseases such as trachoma. Convicts were also added to the banned list, as were anarchists following the assassination of President William McKinley in 1901.

These growing restrictions kept few immigrants out; at Ellis Island 98% of Europeans managed to pass inspection and become legal immigrants. In the 1890s, a new anti-immigrant organization formed with a plan to cut the flow. The Immigration Restriction League, composed of elite Bostonians, suggested that a literacy test was needed for newcomers. The test would ban those over age 16 who could not read and write either English or their native tongue. In 1907, Congress created the Dillingham Commission, which echoed the recommendation. The literacy test passed in Congress, only to be vetoed by presidents Grover Cleveland, William Howard Taft, and Woodrow Wilson. Finally, in 1917, on the eve of the American entrance into World War I, Congress marshaled enough votes to override President Wilson's veto. Yet many Italian, Slovak, Greek, and Slavic immigrants, who would have had difficulty passing the exam in the 1890s, were more apt to be literate by the 1920s. In 1921, 805,000 immigrants passed through Ellis Island

and other ports of entry, with the prospect of millions of others wanting to come to America. If they were to radically reduce the flow, lawmakers had to find new ways, which they did in enacting the Johnson-Reed Act of 1924.

In 1921, Congress passed a one-year measure that limited immigration from the Eastern Hemisphere to approximately 350,000 annually, with each nation having a share based on its proportion of the foreign-born population of 1910. The act was extended the next year. Those who wanted more drastic cuts persuaded the legislators to cut the total and use 1890's foreign-born population as the base line. Because so few Southern and Eastern European immigrants had arrived before that date, the new law drastically reduced their immigration.

Although the restriction was extended several times, ultimately the national origins quotas used the 1920 census numbers, but the proportion was finally based on the entire white population and not simply the foreign-born. The change gave Southern and Eastern European nations more places than by using the 1890 figures. However, the quotas that went into effect in 1929 and that lasted until 1965 gave Great Britain, Germany, and Ireland over two thirds of the total of approximately 150,000 slots. Italy had fewer than 6,000 places, and Greece had only a few hundred, which was exactly what Congress and the administration intended. Using the population-derived formula, some nations had so few slots that the legislators gave them a minimum of 100.

The Western Hemisphere

The Johnson-Reed Act did not give the Western Hemisphere an overall limit or establish individual national quotas. Some in Congress insisted that Mexicans were just as inferior as Poles or Italians. Congress instead listened to the State Department, which said that quotas for the Western Hemisphere would hurt American foreign policy, and to agricultural interests, who claimed that Mexicans were needed to labor on American farms. Persons from the Western Hemisphere still had to pass a literacy test, pay a head tax, and satisfy other provisions of the immigration laws, but these were easily done. And if Mexicans and Canadians could not meet the requirements, many easily crossed the border, albeit illegally. There was no border patrol until 1924, and even after that date it was more interested in keeping liquor from flowing into the United States and catching Asians who were trying to evade immigration ports. However, during the Great Depression of the 1930s, federal, state, and local officials rounded up and deported several hundred Mexicans and their children, many of whom were American-born United States citizens, and shipped them back to Mexico. Many Europeans also faced difficulties in attempting to enter the United States during those years. Only 500,000 persons managed to gain entrance to America in the 1930s.

DAVID M. REIMERS

References and Further Reading

Daniels, Roger. *Guarding the Golden Door: American Immigration Policy and Immigrants since 1882*. New York: Hill and Wang, 2004.

Divine, Robert A. *American Immigration Policy, 1924–1952*. New Haven, CT: Yale University Press, 1957.

Gyory, Andrew. *Closing the Gate: Race, Politics, and the Chinese Exclusion Act*. Chapel Hill: University of North Carolina Press, 1998.

Higham, John. *Strangers in the Land: Patterns of American Nativism, 1860–1925*. New Brunswick, NJ: Rutgers University Press, 1955.

Hutchinson, E. P. *Legislative History of American Immigration Policy, 1790–1965*. Philadelphia: University of Pennsylvania Press, 1981.

Jacobson, Matthew Frye. *Whiteness of a Different Color: European Immigrants and the Alchemy of Race*. Cambridge, MA: Harvard University Press, 1998.

King, Desmond. *Making Americans: Immigration, Race, and the Origins of the Diverse Democracy*. Cambridge, MA: Harvard University Press, 2000.

Lee, Erika. *At America's Gates: Chinese Immigration during the Exclusion Era, 1882–1943*. Chapel Hill: North Carolina University Press, 2003.

Nagi, Mae M. *Impossible Subjects: Illegal Aliens and the Making of Modern America*. Princeton, NJ: Princeton University Press, 2004.

Roediger, David R. *Working toward Whiteness: How America's Immigrants Became White: The Strange Journey from Ellis Island to the Suburbs*. New York: Basic Books, 2005.

Solomon, Barbara Miller. *Ancestors and Immigrants*. Cambridge, MA: Harvard University Press, 1956.

Tichenor, Daniel J. *Dividing Lines: The Politics of Immigration Control in America*. Princeton, NJ: Princeton University Press, 2002.

Zeidel, Robert F. *Immigrants, Progressives, and Exclusion Politics: The Dillingham Commission, 1900–1927*. DeKalb, IL: Northern Illinois University Press, 2004.

See also **Immigration Restriction**

JOINT COUNCIL OF DINING CAR EMPLOYEES

During the 1930s, African-American railroad workers engaged in unprecedented union-organizing campaigns, the results of which were the formation of new, powerful labor associations. In this era, three substantial unions emerged: the Brotherhood of

Sleeping Car Porters (BSCP), which was affiliated with the American Federation of Labor (AFL); the United Transportation Workers (UTW), which was affiliated with the Congress of Industrial Organizations (CIO); and the Joint Council of Dining Car Employees (JCDCE), which was affiliated with the Federation but in practice worked with both the AFL and CIO. Like the BSCP and the UTW, the JCDCE was a "racial" union and was dedicated to advancing both labor and civil rights.

Black dining car workers formed the JCDCE to fight racial employment discrimination by employers and by other unions. Their battle was another chapter in a much larger struggle within the labor movement. From their inception in the nineteenth century, American labor unions had generally ignored the needs of African-Americans and frequently excluded them. This was particularly true of the national labor umbrella organizations: National Labor Union, the Knights of Labor, and the American Federation of Labor, the latter of which had the worst record on race relations. These labor organizations tended to bow to the racist attitudes and practices of their constituent unions, which were made up mostly of white workers. The major railroad unions were among the worst offenders. The Railway Mail Association only allowed as members workers "of the Caucasian race." The Brotherhood of Railway and Steamship Clerks, Freight Handlers, Express and Station Employees just admitted "white persons, male and female, of good moral character." Similar provisions were in most railroad labor organizations. By discriminating against minorities, whites in these unions secured higher wages, better benefits, and elevated their social standing. Similarly, railroad owners profited from the situation by exploiting their disadvantaged employees. Black railroad workers were paid less than their white counterparts, even when they did the same job. For example, occasionally a dining car ran without a white steward. In those instances, a black worker became a "waiter-in-charge," essentially a steward, but without the title, the higher wages, and the respect. Complaining to an all-white railroad union like the Brotherhood of Dining Car Conductors was fruitless. Black workers had to look elsewhere for redress of their many grievances.

By the early 1930s, there was an organizing model for black dining car workers to follow. In the 1920s, A. Philip Randolph had helped African-American sleeping car porters form a labor brotherhood. Although for years the Brotherhood of Sleeping Car Porters had floundered, in 1934, it received a new lease on life. The 1934 Railroad Labor Act, which was one of President Franklin D. Roosevelt's New Deal reforms, provided new bargaining rights to

unions. The BSCP used the law to wrestle a contract from the Pullman Palace Car Company. In 1937, the same year that the BSCP gained formal recognition from Pullman, Randolph helped to establish the Joint Council of Dining Car Employees.

The Joint Council grew out of the slow movement of dining car employees to form unions. In 1917, a group of black dining car workers created the Brotherhood of Dining Car Employees on the New York, New Haven and Hartford Railroad. The Brotherhood steadily gained members throughout the 1920s and early 1930s, and eventually it merged into the Hotel and Restaurant Employees' International (HRE), which was affiliated with the AFL. The formation of the Joint Council in 1937 represented the desire of many black dining car employees to unite the efforts of various union locals. Two dining car workers—Ishmael Flory of Oakland's HRE Local 456 and Solon Bell of Omaha's HRE Local 465—were instrumental in the formation of the JCDCE. Both Flory and Bell were exceptional organizers. By the end of the 1930s, the Council had 7,000 members in 15 locals. The Joint Council was also an integrated union that appealed to men and women. In 1939, there were 1,500 white cooks and waitresses who belonged to the JCDCE.

Like its close organizational cousins, the BSCP and the UTW, the leaders of the Joint Council pursued an agenda to improve the lives of dining car workers specifically and all African-Americans generally. All three unions were dedicated to eradicating discrimination in employment and inside the labor movement. The JCDCE and the BSCP faced an uphill battle to change the AFL. Despite Flory's and Bell's courageous efforts, very little progress was made. For example, for years, the AFL's Railroad Employee Department refused to integrate its annual convention. The leaders of the JCDCE as well as the BSCP protested, but they were simply not allowed to attend and represent their interests at the meeting.

Although the JCDCE and other black railroad unions worked harmoniously on occasion, the Joint Council's political outlook and its specific goals and methods often brought conflict with other unions and civil rights groups. The main problem related to Flory's and Bell's communist connections. Allegations that Flory was using his post to recruit for the Communist Party in an attempt to facilitate a takeover of the railroad industry resulted in punitive measures by the AFL on the Joint Council. Eventually, the HRE president, Edward Flore, fired Ishmael Flory and his comrade, Solon Bell, both of whom continued to labor on behalf of black dining car employees and established a rival union, the Dining Car and Railroad Food Workers Union. The challengers annoyed but did not defeat the JCDCE. The Joint Council also weathered the dramatic transformations in American transportation in the 1960s as railroad passenger travel was supplanted by air travel. Unlike the BSCP and the UTW unions, which faded and eventually merged into stronger unions, the JCDCE was one of the few original "racial" unions to survive.

ANDREW E. KERSTEN

References and Further Reading

Arnesen, Eric. *Brotherhood of Color: Black Railroad Workers and the Struggle for Equality.* Cambridge, MA: Harvard University Press, 2001.

Henderson, Alexa B. "FECP and the Southern Railway Case: An Investigation into the Discriminatory Practices of Railroad Unions during World War II." *Journal of Negro History* 61 (April 1976): 173–187.

Henderson, Elmer. "Political Changes among Negroes in Chicago during the Depression." *Social Forces* 19 (May 1941): 538–546.

Wesley, Charles H. "Organized Labor and the Negro." *Journal of Negro Education* 8 (July 1939): 449–461.

JONES, "MOTHER" MARY HARRIS (1837–1930)

Arrested once again in West Virginia in 1913, old Mother Jones used the labor and radical press to send out her missives to the world, and workers, organizers, and friends of labor responded with petitions, demonstrations, and letter-writing campaigns. Wrote T. J. Llewellen from Missouri to the Secretary of Labor, "I have carried a gun three times in the industrial wars in this country, and by the eternal, if any harm comes to the old Mother, I'm not too old nor by the same token too cowardly to carry it again." Margaret R. Duvall warned of an aroused working class "more dreadful than this country has ever seen" should any harm come to Mother Jones or her fellow prisoners. And A. Van Tassel of Ohio begged President Woodrow Wilson to free the Miners' Angel: "This beautiful hero of the labor movement has committed no crime, but is being slowly murdered because she insisted on agitating and educating the workers to realize their true status in society."

Who was Mother Jones? Aside from a progressive magazine named in her honor, and an occasional invocation of her famous line, "pray for the dead, and fight like hell for the living," she is a faded memory. Yet during the first quarter of the twentieth century, she was one of the most famous women in America.

Her friend Upton Sinclair, author of the great exposé of the Chicago stockyards, *The Jungle*, described her this way in his lightly fictionalized account of the Colorado Coal War of 1913–1914:

> There broke out a storm of applause which swelled into a tumult as a little woman came forward on the platform. She was wrinkled and old, dressed in black, looking like somebody's grandmother; she was, in truth, the grandmother of hundreds of thousands of miners....Hearing her speak, you discovered the secret of her influence over these polyglot hordes. She had force, she had wit, above all she had the fire of indignation—she was the walking wrath of God....She would tell endless stories about her adventures, about strikes she had led and speeches she had made; about interviews with presidents and governors and captains of industry; about jails and convict camps....All over the country she had roamed and wherever she went, the flame of protest had leaped up in the hearts of men; her story was a veritable Odyssey of revolt.

What Sinclair said was literally true; for 25 years this elderly woman did not have a permanent home, or as she explained to a congressional committee when asked where she lived, "my address is like my shoes, it follows me wherever I go." When she was in her 60s, her 70s, and her 80s, she renounced home, friends, and possessions to live on the road and be with her people, and out of that commitment grew working families' powerful sense of identity with her.

Her story is a difficult one to uncover because it is so shrouded in myth, much of it created by herself, especially in *The Autobiography of Mother Jones* (1925). For example, she says that she was born to Irish dissident parents on May Day, 1830. She followed her family to Canada, learned to be a school teacher and a dressmaker, and then found her true vocation in the 1870s, organizing the working class. In fact, she exaggerated her age to add to her venerability (she was born not on what became the International Workers' Holiday, but in August 1837), and her family came to America not because they were radicals fleeing the English, but because they were impoverished by the Great Hunger, or the Potato Famine, as Americans called it.

Mary Harris spent her early years in the city of Cork, where she witnessed the unspeakable horrors of the Famine—which she never discussed—then finished up her education in Toronto, including a semester at the normal school. As she became an adult, she left her family, first moving to Michigan to teach school, then briefly to Chicago, and then to Memphis, where she married an iron molder named George Jones, who was a member of William Sylvis's Molders' Union. Between 1861 and 1867, Mary and George Jones had four children. In the fall of that

President Calvin Coolidge and "Mother" Jones, half-length, standing outdoors. Library of Congress, Prints & Photographs Division [LC-USZ62-68543].

year, not long after she turned 30 years old, yellow fever struck her household. She was left to bury the dead, all of them, George and her four children. Mary Jones returned to Chicago and resumed dressmaking for the next three decades.

There is no reason to doubt that she became increasingly interested in the labor movement—after all, Chicago was the most radical city in America. But there is no evidence that she was an important player through the 1870s, 1880s, or 1890s, as she implies in her *Autobiography* when she discusses the 1877 Railroad Strike and the Haymarket Affair. Clearly, by the 1890s she had gotten to know some important men in the movement—Terence Powderly of the Knights of Labor, Eugene Debs of the American Railway Union (and soon to head the Socialist Party), and Julius Wayland, editor of the socialist newspaper *The Appeal to Reason*. We have evidence of her marching with a branch of Coxey's Army in 1894, and she was active organizing anthracite miners in Pennsylvania for the new United Mine Workers Union (UMW) in the 1890s.

But the important step for her was becoming "Mother Jones." Mary Harris was a poor Irish famine immigrant, a young school teacher and dressmaker, who drifted away from her working class Toronto family to pursue a life in the United States. Mary Jones was the wife of a working-class man and mother of a young family, until plague took them all and

left her a middle-aged widow, making ends meet sewing dresses in Chicago. It was in that shock city, which doubled in population every 10 years—a place where hundreds of thousands of people from overseas and from America's rural heartland came to start fresh—that she re-created herself and became somebody new. By the late 1890s, she was almost as dispossessed as an American could be—poor, of working class background, an Irish immigrant, widowed, elderly (she turned 60 years old in 1897). With precious little left to lose, in other words, she invented and inhabited the role of Mother Jones.

The new persona transformed Mary Jones. After about the turn of the century, she never called herself Mary; all of her letters were signed "Mother Jones," and union leaders, businessmen, even presidents of the United States all called her "Mother." She began to look the part, always wearing antique black dresses; she frequently referred to her advanced age, her impending mortality; and by her very looks she invoked a mother's claim to moral virtue. Yet Mother Jones skillfully combined her saintly image with hellfire oratory and raw physical courage. She stood up to police, private detectives, and national guardsmen; she flaunted judges' injunctions and defied governors; she was arrested several times, and spent months in prison. She organized the wives of workers for powerful demonstrations, and she cajoled, encouraged, and berated union workers to stay true to their organizations. As *Mother* Jones, she was able to make moral claims speaking for the family of labor. Her message rejected the untrammeled rule of the marketplace and substituted the necessity of creating humane communities for working families. She invoked wrenching images of blood stolen, bodies mangled, and youth exploited to dramatize the injustice of poverty in America. Above all, she gave working people hope and told them that their *collective* aspirations were in the best traditions of American freedom.

During the first decades of the twentieth century, the era of her greatest prominence, it is important to remember the conditions of laboring men and women. Roughly three quarters of a million men mined coal, were paid in company scrip, and made roughly $400 per year; their families often lived in company towns and had their lives policed by private armed guards who routinely abrogated their civil liberties. Half a million steelworkers labored on 12-hour shifts, six days a week. Not only men but millions of women and children worked in mills and sweatshops for pennies, sometimes with little option but to work or starve. Beyond simple working conditions, the transformation of America from the Gilded Age through the Progressive era—the re-organization of society, economy, law, politics, and culture that accompanied the growth of vast new concentrations of wealth and power in modern corporations—engendered an era of tremendous ideological ferment. It is best to think of Mother Jones as part of an age that produced the socialism of Eugene Debs, the anarchism of Emma Goldman, the struggle for black rights championed by W. E. B. Du Bois, the cracker-barrel radical journalism of Julius Wayland, and a host of others who responded to the crushing weight of corporate power with new and often radical ideas. All sought to mobilize Americans—through unions, through syndicalism, through politics—even to the point of open rebellion. Mother Jones, in other words, participated in contentious, even violent times.

She worked more for the United Mine Workers than for any other organization, especially in the early days of that organization when it was the largest industrial union in America, and she was instrumental in organizing anthracite miners in Pennsylvania and bituminous workers in the Middle West's Central Competitive Field. She broke with the UMW leadership as it turned more conservative early in the twentieth century. In 1903, she organized an early protest against child labor, the "March of the Mill Children," from Philadelphia to President Theodore Roosevelt's home on Long Island. Between roughly 1905 and 1912, she was on the road organizing for the Socialist Party, and for the radical Western Federation of Miners. She was a founding mother of the Industrial

Workers of the World, and a signer of that group's original charter. But she was willing to help out in any strike, so she worked for a while with copper miners in Calumet, brewery workers in Milwaukee, and garment workers in Chicago. She rejoined the Mine Workers as a paid organizer around 1912, just as it launched two massive efforts that ground on for months and turned quite violent in West Virginia and Colorado. "Medieval West Virginia," she said of the Mountain State, "with its tent colonies on the bleak hills! With its grim men and women! When I get to the other side, I shall tell God almighty about West Virginia." She certainly did not win all of the strikes she was involved with, but she was the most prominent and successful organizer of the Mine Workers, which was, in the early twentieth century, one of America's largest and most successful unions.

After the mine wars, she continued to travel about the country. She worked with Mexican revolutionaries based in the United States who sought their country's freedom from the tyranny of the Porfirio Díaz regime; she raised money for political prisoners like Tom Mooney in California; and she campaigned tirelessly from Chicago to Pittsburgh during the Great Steel Strike of 1919. Yet by the end of World War I, her health began to fail, as did her oratorical powers. She continued to make appearances, and she worked on her autobiography. She stayed embroiled in union politics, supporting various reformers in the United Mine Workers against the autocratic reign of John L. Lewis. On May Day, 1930, she and hundreds of well-wishers celebrated her hundredth birthday (she was really 93). Then, just six months later, she passed away.

She asked to be buried at the Union Miners' Cemetery in Mount Olive, Illinois, alongside the brave boys who fell in labor's cause. Thousands gathered to hear Father John Maguire's funeral oration, and tens of thousands more listened to the services over WCFL, Chicago's voice of labor:

> Today, in gorgeous mahogany furnished and carefully guarded offices in distant capitals wealthy mine owners and capitalists are breathing sighs of relief. Today, upon the plains of Illinois, the hillsides and valleys of Pennsylvania and West Virginia, in California, Colorado and British Columbia, strong men and toil worn women are weeping tears of bitter grief. The reasons are the same.... Mother Jones is dead.

Above all, working people thought of Mother Jones as one of their own. If her efforts led to a mixture of successes and failures, of some shops and even industries organized, others not, what is most striking is that she was heard at all. Mother Jones's greatest achievement was creating a loud and clear voice, for who could be more silenced in early twentieth-century America than an elderly widow, and a working-class immigrant at that. Yet she found a way to find and then raise her prophetic voice in the cause of America's workers. And she was heard.

ELLIOTT J. GORN

References and Further Reading

Featherling, Dale. *Mother Jones: The Miners' Angel*. Carbondale, Southern Illinois University Press, 1979.

Foner, Philip S. *Mother Jones Speaks*. New York: Monad Publishing, 1983.

Gorn, Elliott J. *Mother Jones: The Most Dangerous Woman in America*. New York: Hill and Wang, 2001.

Mother Jones. *The Autobiography of Mother Jones*. Chicago: Charles Kerr Publishing Company, 1990.

Steel, Edward M. *The Correspondence of Mother Jones*. Pittsburgh, PA: University of Pittsburgh Press, 1985.

———. *The Speeches and Writings of Mother Jones*. Pittsburgh, PA: University of Pittsburgh Press, 1988.

JOURNEYMEN CARPENTERS STRIKE IN NEW YORK (1833)

Strikes in the late eighteenth and early nineteenth centuries by journeymen cordwainers, house carpenters, and printers provide valuable lessons in American labor history. The strike of New York City's journeymen house carpenters of 1833 highlights the problematic situations many artisans faced when confronting their employer's whims, fancies, and heightened sense of power.

Artisans who engaged in combining faced conspiracy charges by the courts, which often led to heavy fines and imprisonment, as the example of the hatters of New York City in 1823 shows. However, such threats did not stop workers from going on strike. By the late 1820s, when labor's awakening first got under way, emboldened workers struck for the 10-hour day. As artisans in nearby Philadelphia in 1827 paved the way for America's nascent labor movement, in New York City that struggle took another step forward in 1833.

Facing greater vulnerability and insecurity, New York's journeymen carpenters felt compelled to demand higher wages and less hours of labor. As their own circular stated, they planned to "render justice where justice is due." Formerly they had been working for $1.37 a day, and now they wanted $1.50. The employers refused to grant the increase, and a strike ensued. At that point, the journeymen house carpenters issued an address "to the Citizens of New York" in mid-May, telling them that they were determined to adhere to their demands until they were met. Within days, they had deliberated and passed resolutions approving the conduct in general of the Journeymen House Carpenters as being the only means by which they could establish themselves as freemen and gain a compensation for their labors equivalent to the services rendered.

The New York *Evening Post* (June 10, 1833) counted between one to two thousand journeymen house carpenters on strike. Its editor claimed that rancorous feelings between the large body of useful mechanics and their recalcitrant bosses or master carpenters brought on the strike, commenting that not only had the artisans lost enormous wealth, but that wasted wealth had forever been "lost to the community," which resulted in a "total and irremediable loss." Responding to an editorial in the New York *Journal of Commerce* (May 22, 1833) urging every good citizen to "set his face like a flint against all combinations" that either raised or depressed the price, the Typographical Society quickly issued a circular "to the Journeymen Mechanics and Artisans of New York," calling upon all trades to appoint delegates to meet in "a general union." Declaring that "the time has now arrived for the mechanics of our city to arise to their strength," they determined not to ever again "submit to the thraldom which they had patiently borne for many years," nor "suffer employers" who took unfair advantage of their labor. As fellow mechanics engaged in the same cause, they promised to assist the striking journeymen carpenters by getting each member to donate 25 cents a week during the nearly month-long strike.

Before appealing for aid, 11 journeymen jewelers sent them $13. Afterward, the strikers appointed a committee to receive aid "from those who feel friendly towards us in the struggle for our right." Soon printers, tailors, masons, brush makers, tobacconists, and others helped them out. Next, some 15 trades met in separate meetings, passed resolutions of sympathy, made collections for the benefit of the strikers, and took new efforts to secure their self-protection; other enterprising men called a meeting to create "a general union of the Journeymen Mechanics and Artisans of every branch in this city." Thus aided by the contributions of nearly $1,200, the journeymen house carpenters, noted the *Morning Courier and New-York Enquirer* (June 3, 1833), could now afford to hold out.

The journeymen house carpenters won their battle and returned to work on their own terms on June 17: $1.50 for a day of 10 hours from March 10 to November 10, thereafter $1.37 for a day of nine hours for the reminder of the year.

On August 14, 1833, nine trades organized the General Trades Union (GTU); a year later, 20 more trades representing 11,500 men had joined somewhere between 20% and 30% of Manhattan's entire white male workforce—prompting the *Evening Post* to ponder such implications.

The birth of the city's trades union thus dates from the journeymen house carpenters strike of 1833. That strike not only became the nucleus around which the GTU was formed, but further, notes the historian Edward Pessen, the cornerstone upon which the early labor movement was based.

TIMOTHY C. COOGAN

References and Further Reading

Brown, James D. Jr. "A Curriculum of United States Labor History for Teachers." Sponsored by the Illinois Labor History Society.

Commons, John R., et al. *A Documentary History of American Industrial Society*. Vol. V. Cleveland, OH: Arthur H. Clark, 1910.

———. *History of Labour in the United States*. Vol. I. New York: Macmillan, 1918.

Constitution and Bye-Laws. New York Union Society of Journeymen House Carpenters. Manuscript, New York Public Library.

Finch, John R. *Rise and Progress of the General Trades' Union in the City of New York and Its Vicinity*. New York: James Ormond, 1833.

Hugins, Walter E. *Jacksonian Democracy and the Working Class: A Study of the New York Workingmen's Movement, 1829–1837*. Stanford, CA: Stanford University Press, 1960.

Morning Courier and New-York Enquirer, June 3, 10, 1833.

National Trades' Union, August 9, and December 12, 1834.

Pessen, Edward. *Most Uncommon Jacksonians: Radical Leaders of the Early Labor Movement*. Albany: State University of New York Press, 1967.

Wilentz, Sean. *Chants Democratic: New York City and the Rise of the American Working Class, 1788–1850*. New York: Oxford University Press, 1986.

JUSTICE FOR JANITORS

"*Si se puede!*" "Yes, we can!" janitors chanted on picket lines in cities across the United States, rattling noisemakers made from soda cans and stones. Justice for Janitors, a national campaign launched by the Service Employees International Union (SEIU) in 1987, combined street theater and civil disobedience with legal and corporate strategies to organize the janitorial industry. Justice for Janitor's astonishing success stood out in an era when American unions lost most organizing campaigns.

The SEIU started out as a Chicago janitors union in 1902, and the union built a strong core membership of janitors cleaning office buildings in urban markets, particularly New York City and Chicago. In the mid-1980s, a confluence of factors suddenly wiped out much of the union's strength. During the 1980s, commercial real estate ownership consolidated among a shrinking number of large developers and institutional investors. As real estate values tumbled in a cyclical crash, property owners began contracting out cleaning to independent janitorial companies that competed for business on price. Since labor constituted the single largest expense for a cleaning company, contractors constructed successful bids by trimming wages and benefits. In Los Angeles, for example, janitors' wages fell 36% from 1983 to 1989. Contractors hired newly arrived Central American immigrants, expecting quiescence from largely undocumented workers. In city after city, the union's predominantly African-American janitors swallowed contract concessions as they watched their membership evaporate.

A 1985 lockout in Pittsburgh roused the union to fight back. Members held the line against contract concessions in a yearlong struggle and galvanized the union to develop a plan to deal with the industry's transformation. The union's long-standing decentralization impeded a coordinated response. Powerful local presidents accustomed to autonomy and cordial contract bargaining sometimes refused to join multi-local campaigns, fearing erosion of their authority. Meanwhile, cleaning contractors had mushroomed into national and multinational firms with customer bases that far exceeded any local's ability to affect revenues enough to win with traditional union leverage like strikes.

The SEIU proceeded on two fronts: developing a centralized campaign apparatus, and deploying it in markets without resistant locals. The union created a new division to unite janitor locals under a coordinating umbrella. The division hired a crew of staffers, many from the United Farm Workers, with experience doing community organizing among Latino immigrants. A staffer, Stephen Lerner, helped craft the underlying theory: pressure building owners, not cleaning contractors, with demands for union recognition and fair contracts, since owners could oblige contractors to settle or lose the cleaning contract, and build the added cost of settlement into the contract terms.

They selected Denver in 1987 as the first market for new organizing and demonstrated the range of tactics that would characterize Justice for Janitors. The campaign attacked from above and below. Several contractors cleaned the Denver airport with union crews, while operating nonunion in the city. The union demanded that the political appointees on the airport governing board fire such "double-breasted" contractors unless they recognized the union in the city. Meanwhile, organizers laid out the plan to Latino janitors across the city and worked with community groups to build coalitions. A cadre of militant janitors marched on their bosses with demands for union recognition and marched in the streets to pressure politicians. Justice for Janitors caught Denver by surprise and won sizable gains within a year.

Buoyed by success, the union turned to Atlanta in 1988. A prominent Atlanta real estate developer with close ties to the Democratic Party looked like a promising target as Atlanta hosted the Democratic National Convention. African-American janitors cleaning his buildings demonstrated when he refused to recognize them, and the union picketed his convention events and dressed their delegates in Justice for Janitors T-shirts. But the mayor crossed the picket line, and the party brass sided with their fund-raiser over the janitors. Atlanta showed that political pressure and street militancy would not be enough in most cities.

Los Angeles and Washington, DC, were the laboratories for honing strategy. Beginning in late 1988, organizers in Los Angeles started talking to the overwhelmingly Latino janitors and building committees of workers willing to act as shock troops. Many workers had fled bloody civil war and insurgencies in El Salvador and Guatemala (and some had fought in those conflicts, as insurgents or soldiers) and found civil disobedience far less daunting than did native-born workers. Janitor committees heckled building owners at restaurants and country clubs by day and signed up members in house visits and on bus rides at night. Meanwhile, organizers tallied unpaid overtime hours and safety problems and used the union's lawyers to assemble legal complaints alleging employer violations of federal wage and hour and safety laws. And the campaign used leaflets and raucous demonstrations to compel office-building tenants to force building owners to settle with the union. Tenants resented the publicity but invariably complained to owners, thus accomplishing the union's goals. After registering modest successes, the union came up against an intransigent employer in Century City, a large office complex. Janitors and organizers agitated for a strike. The workers struck in May 1990 and ran a noisy picket line filled with community allies. Tensions rose among building owners and police. On June 15, as janitors and their allies marched toward Century City, the police attacked, clubbing marchers in full view of television cameras. Public support for the janitors boiled over, obliging the mayor to speak out for the janitors and driving the union's powerful New York local president to finally threaten the cleaning contractor to settle in Los Angeles or risk unrest in New York. The contractor settled, and with a major contractor defeated, janitors rapidly seized the rest of the market, winning a master agreement by 1991.

Building owners proved more intractable in Washington DC, where they had a strong industry association to coordinate their opposition and the union had scant membership. The union dug in and experimented with tactics like protesting zoning changes desired by developers and challenging favorable real estate tax assessments. Civil disobedience escalated from marches and building-lobby demonstrations to highly coordinated mass actions like blocking major traffic arteries during rush hour. The local's African-American leadership, unprepared for an infusion of Latino workers, bucked the International and resisted the campaign. After seven years of pitched battle, the International called a public truce to ratchet down the hostilities and trusteed the local. In 1997, the union finally began picking up settlements.

Several key organizing and bargaining concepts shaped Justice for Janitors. First, the union abjured National Labor Relations Board (NLRB)-supervised elections to demonstrate a majority and compel employer bargaining. With extremely high turnover among janitors and many undocumented workers, an election would represent only a snapshot in time of a fluctuating membership. Moreover, the NLRB procedures treated the cleaning contractor as the employer rather than the building owner, who actually controlled the bargaining relationship. Instead, organizers built a militant minority among janitors and pressed for recognition via a majority of signed union cards or a community election. This spared the union the endless litigation and arcane bureaucratic maneuvering that the NLRB election procedure had become. Second, the union negotiated "trigger" agreements with cleaning contractors that initially granted recognition and union rights but modest wage and benefit improvements. Once the union signed up a majority of contractors in a market, the agreements "triggered" negotiations among all the contractors to set a market rate. This strategy forestalled the problem of making a union contractor uncompetitive in a market shaped by labor costs. With a majority of contractors organized, no contractor was disadvantaged by the extra costs for higher wages and benefits. Trigger agreements functioned as a mechanism for pattern bargaining in the service sector, and the SEIU exported the practice to its other service-sector campaigns. The SEIU also laid the groundwork to link markets in national campaigns by lining up contracts in multiple cities to terminate on the same dates. And in 1995, the SEIU required all janitor contracts to include a provision stipulating the right to honor picket lines

Critics generally assailed Justice for Janitors from two directions: union democracy and the trigger agreements. Where recalcitrant local officials refused to participate, the SEIU simply removed them, installing trustees to run the locals and then running the trustees for the presidency. In some cases, these trustees came from the rank and file, like Rocio Saenz, a Mexican-born janitor who took over the Boston local; others came from the ranks of union staff organizers, like Mike Garcia in Los Angeles or Michael Fishman in New York. At the same time, the SEIU merged small city locals, many of which represented workers in multiple industries, into regional or state-wide janitorial locals; it was hard for rank-and-file workers to campaign or win office in these staff-run organizations.

As for the trigger agreements, which some derided as settlements for a "nickel and dues checkoff," criticism subsided abruptly after the SEIU ran a national rolling strike to win health-care benefits in 2000. In April, janitors walked out in Los Angeles, San Diego, and Chicago; as contracts expired in 30 markets, including New York, Cleveland, Chicago, and Seattle, contractors settled quickly, some before expiration. That October, janitors in Stamford and Hartford, Connecticut, struck for union recognition. Janitors routed contractors across the country, winning sizable wage increases and health-care benefits. The union turned to organizing the suburban markets around its strongholds and picked up Orange County, Long Island, suburban Chicago, and northern New Jersey. In 2000, Ken Loach, a leftist British filmmaker, produced "Bread and Roses," a Hollywood movie based on the Los Angeles campaign. Justice for Janitors had arrived.

In 2005, 20 years after launching Justice for Janitors, over 70% of janitors in 23 of the top 50 U.S. cities were organized. Despite its great successes, however, the union had lost ground. The South remained overwhelmingly nonunion, and burgeoning suburban office markets added janitors much faster than the union could organize them. The SEIU estimated that its density in the industry had slipped from 40% in the 1950s to 10% in 1980 to 6% by 2000. But a victory in 2005 offered hope. Janitors in New York, Chicago, and dozens of other cities honored picket lines thrown up by Houston janitors working for the same building contractor. The contractor folded quickly, and the union won a master agreement in Houston, marking the first real beachhead in the South.

JENNIFER LUFF

References and Further Reading:

Bread and Roses. Directed by Ken Loach. 2000.
Waldinger, Roger, et al. "Helots No More: A Case Study of the Justice for Janitors Campaign in Los Angeles." In *Organizing to Win: New Research on Union Strategies*, edited by Kate Bronfenbrenner et al. Ithaca, NY: Cornell University Press, 1998.

See also **Service Employees' International Union**

K

KANSAS COURT OF INDUSTRIAL RELATIONS

The Kansas Court of Industrial Relations was an experiment in state-mediated labor relations that grew out of the Kansas coal strike of 1919. The court was actually a three-man board appointed by the governor that could make rules concerning labor relations, settle disputes, and take over and run businesses. It allowed for collective bargaining but declared strikes illegal. The Kansas Court of Industrial Relations was abolished in 1925 by the Kansas Legislature after the Supreme Court of the United States overturned a number of its decisions and curtailed its power.

In November of 1919, the United Mine Workers (UMW) declared a national strike and thousands of Kansas miners heeded the call. The strike was declared illegal by President Wilson, and the UMW called it off, but 12,000 Kansas miners led by Alexander Howat, president of UMW District 14, stayed out and threatened the state with a coal shortage heading into winter. In response the Kansas Supreme Court allowed the state government to take over the mines. Republican Governor Henry Allen still could not induce the miners to return to work, so he called for volunteers and got about 10,000 mostly college student volunteers to work as scabs, many of them recruited during halftime of the Kansas–Missouri football game. These volunteers were reinforced by the Kansas National Guard and about 600 regular army troops.

This strike was soon defeated, and state control of the mines lasted only three weeks, but Governor Allen wanted to avoid any future strikes in vital services. The month following the coal strike, Allen called a special session of the state legislature of Kansas in January of 1920 to establish a labor arbitration board that would have authority over any labor disputes in an industry that affected the public welfare. This new Kansas Court of Industrial Relations was given the power to regulate working hours, fix a minimum wage, prohibit strikes, run certain industries if necessary, and levy severe penalties for noncompliance.

The court attracted considerable national attention as an experiment, but because it severely curtailed the rights of workers to strike and gave the government almost unlimited power to arbitrate labor disputes, it was vehemently opposed by organized labor. In 1922, Allen used the court to outlaw picketing during a railroad strike and even arrested his friend William White, editor of the Emporia Gazette, for putting a placard in favor of the strike in his window. White subsequently became the first Kansan to win the Pulitzer for his attack on this arbitrary arrest and his defense of free speech.

Some employers also objected to the activities of the court, as in the case of the Wolff Packing Company, which was ordered to increase wages to its workers in January of 1921. Wolff Packing Company appealed this decision to the Supreme Court of the United States, arguing that the decision violated the company's Fourteenth Amendment right to have no property taken without due process. In the case *Chas. Wolff Packing Co. v. Court of Industrial Relations of State of Kansas*, 262 U.S. 522 (1923), the Supreme

Court unanimously overturned this decision of the Kansas Court of Industrial Relations on the grounds that the declaration of a legislature that a business is concerned with the public interest is insufficient grounds for regulating that business. This severely curtailed the Kansas Court of Industrial Relation's power.

The court heard 166 cases over its 5-year existence and was lauded by many politicians as a novel experiment, but it was generally regarded as a failure.

SAMUEL MITRANI

References and Further Reading

Bowers, John H. *The Kansas Court of Industrial Relations: The Philosophy and History of the Court.* Chicago, IL: McClurg, 1922.

See also **United Mine Workers of America**

KEARNEY, DENIS (1847–1907)
Workingmen's Party of California

Denis Kearney was a leader of the Workingmen's Party of California (WPC) in the late 1870s and a vehement advocate of Chinese exclusion. A polarizing figure with scant labor background, Kearney was an electrifying speaker whose racist oratory helped nationalize the issue of Chinese immigration.

Kearney was born on February 1, 1847, in Oakmount, County Cork, Ireland. The second of seven sons from a poor family, he went to sea as a cabin boy at age eleven and over the next decade worked his way up to first mate and captain. He married Mary Anne Leary in 1870 and 2 years later settled in San Francisco, where he purchased a draying, or trucking, business. He became an American citizen in 1876. Although he had little formal schooling, he attended a club known as the Lyceum of Self-Culture, at which he participated in weekly debates and developed his speaking skills.

Kearney burst onto the public scene in 1877 in the wake of the national railroad strike after members of an "anticoolie" club barged into a workers' meeting in San Francisco in July and commandeered the audience. With shouts of "on to Chinatown," gangs of white men and boys roamed the city, attacking Chinese homes and property. Kearney joined a vigilante group to suppress the rioters, or "hoodlums," as the press labeled them. In August many of these hoodlums, along with workers and sympathizers, began gathering at a large, vacant space near City Hall, called the sandlots. Amid the glow of bonfires and torches, sandlot speakers—led by Kearney, who had switched sides—denounced corporations, monopolists, and Chinese immigration. On August 22, Kearney helped organize the Workingmen's Trade and Labor Union of San Francisco and was named secretary.

The momentum of these nightly meetings led to formation of the WPC, and on October 5, Kearney was made president. The party's most fiery orator, Kearney laced his speeches with incendiary comments. "There isn't an honest man in office today," he told one crowd. "The only way to get laws passed in our favor is to surround the Capitol with bayonets and shoot those who vote against us." Kearney was arrested in November for incitement to riot—the first of many such arrests—but acquitted in January 1878. Under Kearney's direction, the party grew, and although his defiant rhetoric and uncompromising personality caused dissension, he remained its leader, chief organizer, and spokesman. Kearney attracted followers by uttering class-based appeals, but he directed his most vicious attacks at Chinese immigrants. The "moon-eyed lepers," with their "putrid carcasses," could live on "rice and rats," he declared. The Pacific Coast was "cursed with parasites from China.... My chief mission here is to secure the expulsion of Chinese labor from California." Sandlot meetings began and ended with Kearney's trademark cry, "the Chinese must go." As he later wrote the English historian Lord Bryce, "Every speech and every document written by me ended with the words, 'And whatever happens the Chinese must go.'" (D. Nunis, *Pacific Historical Review* 36, 1967)

In early 1878, WPC candidates scored victories in San Francisco, Santa Clara, Oakland, and Sacramento. The party's swift ascent alarmed Republicans and Democrats, and in the election for delegates to the state constitutional convention in June, the two major parties nominated a joint nonpartisan slate. Still the WPC captured one-third of the delegates. Flushed with success, Kearney embarked on a tour of the East in the summer of 1878. He spoke in more than a dozen cities, from Boston and Washington to New York and Chicago. Newspapers everywhere reported his denunciations of "capitalistic vagabonds," "lecherous bondholders," and "Asiatic lepers"; the enormous press coverage turned the "howling hoodlum" into a national figure and working-class spokesman. Kearney voiced little interest in unions, however, urging workers instead to abandon the two major parties. "The Workingmen's party must win," he said in Cincinnati, "if it has to wade knee deep in blood and perish in battle." Hoping to cement an alliance with the fledgling Greenback-Labor party,

Kearney also campaigned in Massachusetts for Ben Butler, then running for governor as a Greenbacker. Although showering him with attention, the press excoriated Kearney as a Communist and demagogue, and most workers, union leaders, and labor advocates—who initially welcomed him—soon spurned him for his lack of substantive ideas and his race baiting of Chinese immigrants.

Largely discredited in the East, Kearney returned in November to California where he still retained a sizable following. He campaigned heavily in support of the new state constitution, which Californians approved in May 1879, and steered the WPC toward nominating a large slate of candidates for the upcoming statewide elections. In August, two weeks before the voting, a would-be assassin shot the WPC candidate for mayor of San Francisco, putting the city on edge. Kearney counseled peace, and the party swept to victory, electing the chief justice of the Supreme Court, five associate justices, 11 senators, 17 assemblymen, and the mayor of San Francisco, who recovered. Both the WPC's and Kearney's influence reached their zenith. Leaders of the National Greenback-Labor party, then mounting a serious challenge for the White House in 1880, took notice of these victories and sought to capitalize on them. By winning over Kearney, they hoped to win over the WPC, gain workingmen's votes, and thereby capture California. The Greenbackers invited Kearney to become a leader of the party, and he readily accepted. Emboldened by his newfound respectability, he ratcheted up the intensity of his sandlot speeches. Proposing to build a gallows on the sandlots, he declared, "If I hear any man plotting to kill me, I will kill him so help me God." For uttering these words, Kearney was arrested.

While Kearney was in prison, the WPC split over whether to support the Greenbackers or the Democrats for president. The state Greenback party meanwhile repudiated Kearney. Undeterred, Kearney, released from prison in May 1880, immediately headed to the Greenbackers' national convention in Chicago. In what would be the final major speech of his life, Kearney attacked his enemies as "beggars... robbers...pimp[s] and nincompoops" and declared, "The Chinese must go, even if we are to deluge the state of California in blood." His speech polarized the convention, and he returned home to find the WPC collapsing and the Greenback party imploding. Most WPC members returned to the Democratic fold, and the Greenbackers quickly faded. A year later Kearney himself provided an epitaph: "There is no Workingmen's Party now, and it would take a telescope larger than Lick's to find a vestige of the giant that shook not only the state but the nation." Kearney all

but disappeared from politics. He later inherited a fortune, invested in wheat, sugar, and oil, and died in obscurity on April 24, 1907, in Alameda, California.

Kearney leaves a legacy both familiar and unique. He fits into a long line of charismatic figures who combined rabid populism with vicious racism. Like Mike Walsh in the 1840s, Tom Watson at the turn of the century, and George Wallace in the 1960s, he gained notoriety by spouting class-conscious, racist epithets. A magnetic orator who both attracted and repelled, Kearney rallied supporters to form a vibrant third party, yet his querulous, mercurial personality played a central role in its demise. He became synonymous with the anti-Chinese crusade, which led to passage of the Chinese Exclusion Act in 1882.

ANDREW GYORY

References and Further Reading

George, Henry. "The Kearney Agitation in California." *Popular Science Monthly* 17 (Aug. 1880): 433–453.

Gyory, Andrew. *Closing the Gate: Race, Politics, and the Chinese Exclusion Act.* Chapel Hill: University of North Carolina Press, 1998.

Kauer, Ralph. "The Workingmen's Party of California." *Pacific Historical Review* 13 (Sept. 1944): 278–291.

Nunis, Doyce B., Jr., ed. "The Demagogue and the Demographer: Correspondence of Denis Kearney and Lord Bryce." *Pacific Historical Review* 36 (Aug. 1967): 269–288.

Posner, Russell M. "The Lord and the Drayman: James Bryce vs. Denis Kearney." *California Historical Quarterly* 50 (Sept. 1971): 277–284.

Shumsky, Neil Larry. *The Evolution of Political Protest and the Workingmen's Party of California.* Columbus: Ohio State University Press, 1991.

See also **Chinese Exclusion Acts**

KEATING-OWEN CHILD LABOR ACT (1916)

The Keating-Owen Child Labor Act of 1916 banned goods produced by child workers from interstate and foreign commerce and was the first statute that prescribed federal regulation of child labor. The act set a minimum age of 14 for factory work, an 8-hour day for workers between the ages of 14–16, a 6-day week, and prohibited work between the hours of 7:00 P.M–6:00 A.M. With bipartisan support in Congress, President Woodrow Wilson signed it into law on September 1, 1916, to take effect exactly 1 year later. Its passage culminated decades of activism by social justice reformers and labor advocates, investigations compiled by the U.S. Children's Bureau, and public educational campaigns waged by the National Child Labor Committee (NALC) to combat the evils of child labor. After being in effect for only 9 months, the Supreme Court overturned the Keating-Owen Child Labor Act with its *Dagenhart* decision on June 3, 1918.

Child labor reform was a complex proposition involving the minimum age and maximum hours for children across diverse industries and regions in the country. Labor and social reformers began investigating the exploitation of child workers in the late nineteenth century and campaigned for the enactment of state regulation. By 1900, 26 states had passed laws for compulsory school attendance, minimum employment age, or laws that prohibited children from night work or work in dangerous industries. However the patchwork of state laws lacked enforcement, were ignored by employers, and circumvented by needy working-class families. A national movement to end child labor began in the twentieth century and was organized by the NALC.

A federal solution to child labor faced strong resistance from manufacturers' associations and fractiousness among political moderates and progressives. When in 1906, Senator Albert Beveridge suggested that goods produced by children be banned from interstate commerce, objections arose questioning federal interference in parental and states' rights; NALC added its support and lost members, and American Federation of Labor (AFL) President Samuel Gompers argued federal intervention undercut labor's autonomy. Federal attention was sustained during the administrations of Roosevelt and Taft that supported a study of children's and women's working conditions by the Bureau of Labor, banned child labor in the District of Columbia, and created the U.S. Children's Bureau. In 1914, NALC drafted what became the Palmer-Owen bill (Rep. A. Mitchell Palmer [D-PA] and Sen. Robert L. Owen [D-OK]), which, like the Beveridge bill, banned from interstate commerce goods produced by children under the age of 14 and set an 8-hour day for workers aged 14–16. Although President Wilson doubted its constitutionality, he gave his support, and on February 13, 1915, it passed the House, with sectional opposition from representatives of southern manufacturing states—North Carolina, South Carolina, Mississippi and Georgia—where more than one-quarter of cotton and textile mill workers were children. The bill did not make it to the Senate before adjournment and was reintroduced to Congress the following year. Sponsored by Representative Edward Keating (D-CO) and Senator Owen, it passed the House, 343 to 46, and the Senate with 52 votes for the bill, 12 against, and 32 abstentions.

Anticipating the passage of the Keating-Owen bill, the executive committee of Southern Cotton Manufacturers raised a suit to challenge it before the U.S. Federal Court in North Carolina, which resulted in an injunction of the act's provisions in the state on August 31, 1917. The Supreme Court received *Hammer v. Dagenhart* quickly and in a 5-4 decision ruled that the act had transcended congressional power of the Commerce Clause (Article I, Section 8, Clause 3) and that authority rested in the states. Since its passage many workplaces had conformed to the Keating-Owen Child Labor Act, yet the lifting of federal regulation reversed child labor's decline. Reformers continued their campaigns, gaining support for a tax on profits produced with child labor (Pomerene Amendment to the Revenue Act of 1919) and a constitutional amendment in 1924. However not until the New Deal's provisions during the 1930s would the standards set by the Keating-Owen Child Labor Act be realized.

RACHEL A. BATCH

References and Further Reading

Hindman, Hugh D. *Child Labor: An American History*. Armonk, NY: M. E. Sharpe, 2002.

Lindenmeyer, Kriste. *A Right to Childhood: The U.S. Children's Bureau and Child Welfare, 1912–1946*. Chicago: University of Illinois Press, 1997.

Sallee, Shelley. *The Whiteness of Child Labor Reform in the New South*. Athens: University of Georgia Press, 2003.

Trattner, Walter I. *Crusade for the Children: A History of the National Child Labor Committee and Child Labor Reform in America*. Chicago, IL: Quadrangle Books, 1970.

Cases and Statutes Cited

Hammer v. Dagenhart, 247 U.S. 251 (1918).

See also **Child Labor; Children's Bureau Fair Labor Standards Act; Family Wage; Hull-House Settlement (1889–1963); Jones, 'Mother' Mary Harris; National Child Labor Committee**

KEEFE, DANIEL (SEPTEMBER 27, 1852–JANUARY 2, 1929)
Seamen and Longshoremen Union Leader

An example of the union bureaucrat of the late nineteenth century, Keefe comfortably traversed the world of union hall and corporate office. Concerned primarily with upholding the terms of the labor contract, Keefe was the quintessential union leader in the mold of Samuel Gompers and the American Federation of Labor (AFL).

Keefe began his career as a union functionary by organizing seamen who worked along the Great Lakes ports of the Midwest. Prior to that he had worked as a tugboat hand along the Great Lakes, which had given him an invaluable insight into the working conditions of seamen throughout the region. What he saw appalled him. Long hours and low wages were the norm. On board the ships the seamen confronted unsanitary conditions, poor food, and tyrannical skippers. Therefore in 1878, Keefe began to organize these men, quickly gaining results. The seamen joined the new organization, the Lake Seamen's Benevolent Association (LSBA), in great numbers. The LSBA established wage rates for all members, which were generally pasted or pinned to a wall near the docks. The union also encouraged collective action in defending their rights. Seamen for example refused to work with nonunion labor. Union members also boycotted merchants or landlords who serviced nonunion seamen.

Such tactics bore fruit as the LSBA took firm control over hiring and wages. Ship owners counterattacked in 1880–1881 by bringing in replacement labor and discharging union members. The situation was made more difficult due to internal strife within the LSBA. Sailors had been fighting a running battle to exclude from their ranks seamen who worked on steam-driven vessels. The sailors were losing the battle however, as steam ships were rapidly displacing sailing ships. The bickering weakened the union just as the employers embarked on their anti-union campaign. By 1881, the LSBA had been effectively destroyed on the Great Lakes.

Keefe then turned his attention to the Great Lakes' longshoremen. As with his organizational strategy with the seamen, Keefe traveled from port to port signing up new members. By 1892, Keefe had successfully organized 11 locals from Chicago to Buffalo. Keefe called an organizational meeting in Detroit, and there the assembled delegates agreed on the name of the International Longshoremen's Association (ILA). The ILA adopted an aggressive policy of expansion. Not content to just organize longshoremen, the ILA reached out to other workers along the Great Lakes coastline. Correspondingly Keefe helped bring into the ILA fold marine engineers and oilers, tugboat workers, marine pilots, fishermen, grain elevator workers, steam shovel engineers, and marine pile drivers. To a large extent Keefe had succeeded in creating an industrial union. By the end of this initial round of organizing, the ILA had organized 40 marine occupations.

Such territorial advancement encountered resistance. Other unions, most notably the Seamen's Unions, cried foul. For the next few decades, a jurisdictional war broke out as a series of unions charged that Keefe had trampled on their areas of operation. Keefe's political posturing reflected the labor movement's conservative tilt. Once signed, Keefe insisted that ILA locals abide by the contract. When union locals refused and embarked on strike action during the life of the contract, Keefe was merciless in his response. Keefe supplied strikebreakers to break industrial action by his local unions. For Keefe, the contract was sacrosanct; any action that threatened the terms of the contract, whether strikes or boycotts, were perceived as being unwarranted, and at worst, ungrateful.

Keefe's comfortable relationship with employers was epitomized by his relationship with U.S. Senator Mark Hanna and the National Civic Federation (NCF). The group was created ostensibly to steer a middle course between employers who espoused a rabid anti-unionism and radical trade union leaders. Keefe's reputation as a no-strike labor leader was considered particularly attractive. Keefe's elevation as supposed responsible labor leader and member of the NCF had a remarkable effect on him. By the turn of the century, he carried himself more as a successful businessman as he dressed in elegant clothes and smoked expensive cigars.

But for all his conservative leanings, Keefe remained a union leader. Under his tenure the ILA grew into a fighting organization. By 1905, the ILA had 100,000 members. The ports of the Great Lakes had been organized, as had those in Galveston and New Orleans. But in 1908, Keefe abruptly resigned from the ILA. The episode remains clouded in mystery. The most likely reason is that the AFL leadership (who resented Keefe's expansionist aims) had pressured ILA officials to force him out. Whatever the reason, Keefe was a union leader who oversaw the rapid expansion and consolidation of the ILA. Unfortunately such a strategy resulted in a union that refused to support other maritime unions in recognition battles, and in some extreme cases, the same union disciplined its own members for violating signed contracts by striking.

COLIN DAVIS

References and Further Reading

Larrowe, Charles P. *Maritime Labor Relations on the Great Lakes.* East Lansing: Michigan State University, 1959.
Russell, Maud. *Men along the Shore.* New York: Brussel and Brussel, 1966.

KELLEY, FLORENCE (SEPTEMBER 12, 1859–FEBRUARY 17, 1932)
Antisweatshop Activist

Florence Kelley dedicated her life to industrial reform, serving as a prominent leader in the antisweatshop movement. As the daughter of William "Pig Iron" Kelley, a radical Republican congressman and Caroline Bartram Kelley, a Quaker and abolitionist, she made an early commitment to social reform that persisted throughout her life. Kelley earned her bachelor's degree in 1882 as a member of the first generation of college-educated women. She trained in the social sciences both at Cornell University and at the University of Zurich after the University of Pennsylvania refused her admission on account of her sex. During her studies abroad, Kelley became a socialist and translated into English Friedrich Engels's *The Condition of the Working Class in England in 1844* and a Karl Marx speech on free trade. When Kelley returned to New York in 1886 with her Russian husband and three children, she continued her socialist activities and began to focus her energies on reforming the circumstances of wage-earning women and children.

Kelley became a leader in the antisweating movement when she moved to Illinois with her children in 1891. Divorced, Kelley became a resident at the Hull-House settlement in Chicago where she immersed herself in industrial reform activities. In 1892, she joined with the Illinois Woman's Alliance in reporting on the neglect of school children in the city's poorest wards. That year she also conducted an investigation of the labor conditions in the Chicago garment industry for the Illinois Bureau of Labor Statistics, participated in a survey of the city's tenements for the federal commissioner of labor, and was one of the key speakers at a mass meeting denouncing the sweatshop. Kelley and other Hull-House residents enlarged this study and produced the *Hull-House Maps and Papers* (1895), depicting the occupation, nationality, and living conditions of the residents of Chicago's nineteenth ward. With this evidence Kelley drafted and secured a state law that set maximum hours for women, prohibited child labor, set factory safety standards, and provided for state inspections. Governor John Altgeld appointed Kelley the chief factory inspector, and with a staff of 11, she immediately began to document violations for the state's attorney. Frustrated that most of the violations were not prosecuted, Kelley secured her law license and prosecuted some of the cases herself.

In the mid-1890s, Kelley and the antisweating campaign endured setbacks, leading Kelley to engage in a new consumer-based strategy. In 1895, in *Ritchie v. Illinois* the Illinois Supreme Court held that the 8-hour provision in Kelley's factory law was unconstitutional because it inhibited female workers and their employers' freedom to contract. The following year John Tanner won the governor's election and fired Kelley as chief factory inspector. In response in 1897, she joined with wealthy clubwoman Ellen Henrotin to create an Illinois Consumers' League, modeled after the New York league that worked to use the purchasing power of middle-class women to improve the treatment of factory workers. In 1898, she represented the Illinois League at a multibranch convention and suggested that they create a white label that they would award to goods produced under fair conditions. The branch leagues created the National Consumers' League (NCL) to coordinate this effort and chose Kelley to run its operations. Kelley moved with her children to the Henry Street settlement house in New York in 1899 to serve as the NCL secretary.

Kelley led the NCL for three decades. She expanded the organization, developing additional local leagues throughout the North and West and led the national and local leagues in their white-label and protective-labor legislation campaigns. Initially Kelley supervised inspections of working conditions in factories throughout the country, assessing which companies should receive an NCL white label. The league conferred the distinction to those who followed state labor laws, did not use home manufacturing or child labor, and did not require overtime. It then urged middle-class female consumers, through ethical and economic appeals, to purchase only goods with a white label. Kelley enhanced the campaign by reviving her state and federal legislation efforts to establish factory safety standards, maximum hours and minimum pay for female workers, and efforts to defend existing laws against constitutional challenges. Most significantly the NCL submitted a brief through then-Attorney Louis Brandeis in the defense of Oregon's maximum hour law for women. The brief included sociological evidence collected by the NCL that illustrated the hazards of working long hours in factories. The U.S. Supreme Court upheld the Oregon 10-hour law in *Muller v. Oregon* (1908).

Kelley took the NCL agenda beyond its membership and broadened her social reform work. She sought assistance for the antisweating campaigns from numerous organizations, including the Women's Trade Union League, the General Federation of Women's Clubs, the National Congress of Mothers, and the National American Woman Suffrage Association (NAWSA), educating them on the hazards of sweating and the importance of protective labor legislation. She assisted in the creation of the National Association for the Advancement of Colored People (1909) and the Women's International League for Peace and Freedom (1919). She fought for woman suffrage, serving for a time as vice-president of the NAWSA. She worked with Lillian Wald and other Henry Street settlement residents in the establishment of the U.S. Children's Bureau in 1911 and in conjunction with the NCL, provided key support for the Sheppard-Towner Maternity and Infancy Protection (1921) that provided federal funds for health care to working mothers and their children.

Kelley persevered in her social and labor reform work in the 1920s as the political climate became more conservative and opposition to labor reform from the courts, the legislature, and some other women's organizations intensified. During the Red Scare and its aftermath surrounding World War I, Kelley had to defend herself against right-wing, anti-Communists attacks. Kelley and the NCL also fought against the 1921 Equal Rights Amendment (ERA) proposed by the National Woman's party, which she and the NCL perceived as an indirect attack on protective labor reforms for women. In 1923, in *Adkins v. Children's Hospital* the U.S. Supreme Court found that a state minimum-wage law for women was unconstitutional, and in 1926 Congress stopped funding the health care programs created under the Sheppard-Towner Act. When the Great Depression began, Kelley and the entire labor movement endured even more opposition to labor reform.

Kelley died in 1932, but her work survived her. During the New Deal years in the 1930s, the U.S. government adopted many of her labor reform efforts, most significantly the 1938 Fair Labor Standards Act that included minimum wage and maximum hours for men and women.

GWEN HOERR JORDAN

References and Further Reading

Sklar, Kathryn Kish. *Florence Kelley and the Nation's Work: The Rise of Women's Political Culture, 1830–1900.* New Haven, CT: Yale University Press, 1995.
———. "Kelley, Florence." In *Women Building Chicago 1790–1990: A Biographical Dictionary,* edited by Rima Lunin Schultz and Adele Hast. Bloomington: Indiana University Press, 2001.
Wade, Louise. "Kelley, Florence." In *Notable American Women, 1607–1950. A Biographical Dictionary,* edited by Edward T. James, Janet Wilson, and Paul S. Boyer. Cambridge, MA: Belknap Press of Harvard University Press, 1971.

Cases and Statutes Cited

Adkins v. Children's Hospital 261 U.S. 525 (1923)
Muller v. Oregon 208 U.S. 412 (1908)
Richie v. People 155 Illinois 98 (1895)

See also **Hull-House; Illinois Woman's Alliance; National Consumers' League; Women's Trade Union League**

KENNEY O'SULLIVAN, MARY (JANUARY 8, 1864–JANUARY 18, 1943) Cofounder, American Women's Trade Union League

Mary Kenney O'Sullivan was a labor activist and a reformer. The daughter of immigrant railroad workers, she became the first woman organizer for the American Federation of Labor (AFL) and was one of the founders of the American Women's Trade Union League. She especially fostered cross-class alliances among women and used them to advance the interests of laboring women.

Kenney's labor activism was infused with demands for gender equality. Kenney's first job in Chicago was for a bindery company. The bindery trade was one of many that divided tasks by gender and paid a lower wage for women's jobs. Kenney organized her sister workers in the trade to both overcome its gender division and to secure better working conditions.

Kenney sought assistance for organizing her first union from the Ladies Federal Labor Union 2703 (LFLU), a new organization founded to organize female workers. Kenney went from shop to shop persuading female bookbinders to come to an organizational meeting where the LFLU, in its first undertaking, helped the workers form the Women's Bookbinding Union No.1 (WBU). Kenney was elected the WBU delegate to the Chicago Trades and Labor Assembly.

Kenney next accepted help in her organizing efforts from Hull-House settlement founder Jane Addams. Hull-House became the meeting place for the WBU and many of the settlement's residents and middle-class affiliates assisted Kenney in organizing unions, managing strikes, and providing direct assistance to female workers. Kenney also persuaded Addams to found Jane Club, a housing cooperative for working women situated near Hull-House. Kenney served as president of the cooperative.

In 1891, AFL President Samuel Gompers appointed Kenney the federation's first national female organizer. The AFL authorized the position for only a 5-month trial period. Kenney began her service on the East Coast, traveling from New York to Massachusetts attempting to organize women working in the trades. Most notably Kenney worked with Leonora O'Reilly in organizing the Local 16 of the United Garment Workers in New York. Against Gompers's recommendation however, the AFL terminated Kenney's appointment after 5 months, explaining that her low success rate did not justify the financial costs. Its decision demonstrated the AFL's tenuous relationship with female workers. Gompers nonetheless encouraged Kenney and other female labor leaders to continue to organize female workers.

Kenney returned to Chicago and Hull-House in 1892, where she resumed her organization efforts and developed a friendship with labor activist Florence Kelley. Kenney assisted Kelley in her campaign against child labor and the sweating system. Kelley's tactics included both investigations of industries that employed women and children, paying under factory wages to complete work at home, and drafting legislation to abolish such work and regulate the hours of work for women and children. Kenney assisted Kelley in the investigations and chaired a mass meeting in support of a bill Kelley drafted to end sweating and improve working conditions for women and children. The bill included a provision for the creation of a state inspector's office with deputies to enforce the prohibitions in the legislation. When the bill was enacted in 1893, Kenney was appointed a deputy inspector to serve under chief inspector Florence Kelley.

In the fall of 1893, Kenney moved to Boston to work with social reformer Hannah Parker Kimball and labor activist Jack O'Sullivan. The following year Kenney and O'Sullivan married. The pair continued their labor activities throughout their marriage. Kenney became a member of the board of directors of the Boston Women's Educational and Industrial Union (BWEIU), which lobbied for protective labor legislation, provided services to female workers, studied industrial conditions in the city, and assisted in organizing unions. She was also a member of a women's federal labor union organized primarily by her husband for the AFL that comprised laborers and professionals who worked for labor interests. When O'Sullivan died in a train accident in 1902, Kenney secured employment as a property manager for a real estate association to support herself and her children and continued her labor activism.

In 1903, wealthy reformer and socialist William English Walling solicited Kenney to assist him in establishing an American Women's Trade Union League (WTUL). Modeled after the British WTUL, the American league joined workers, social reformers, and settlement workers with an aim to organize women into trade unions. Kenney was elected the WTUL's national secretary.

Kenney remained active in the WTUL over the next decade but broadened her activist work in a myriad of directions. Kenney joined with wealthy female reformers to found a summer camp for the children at the Boston Dennison House settlement. She also worked as a trade union reporter for the *Boston Globe* and became a peace activist and woman's suffrage proponent. She supported suffrage because she believed it would help laborers improve their working conditions. She spoke out in anger at antisuffragists, accusing them of not caring about workers.

In 1912, Kenney stopped organizing and ended her relationship with the AFL. She had long urged the AFL to hire more female organizers and pay more attention to the conditions of working women, but her disappointment in the organization climaxed over the AFL's failure to aid striking mill workers in Lawrence, Massachusetts. Though the AFL did not typically lend its support to unskilled workers, Kenney publicly criticized the federation and lent her support to the Industrial Workers of the World (IWW), an organization whose mission focused on organizing unskilled workers. When the strike settled, Kenney became an inspector for the Massachusetts Board of Labor and Industries, a position she held for the next 20 years. Kenney retired in 1934 at 70 years of age. She died 9 years later.

Kenney devoted her entire life to the labor movement. Most prominently, she joined her efforts to organize women with the work of middle-class female reformers, significantly facilitating cross-class alliances among women to advance the labor movement.

GWEN HOERR JORDAN

References and Further Reading

Carson, Mina. *Settlement Folk Social Thought and the American Settlement Movement, 1885–1930.* Chicago, IL: The University of Chicago Press, 1990.

Kenneally, James J. *Women and American Trade.* Montreal, Canada: Eden Press Women's Publications, 1981.

Kenney, Mary E. "Organization of Women." *Age of Labor* 2 (1893): 2.

Nutter, Kathleen Banks. "O'Sullivan, Mary Kenney." In *Women Building Chicago 1790–1990: A Biographical Dictionary*, edited by Rima Lunin Schultz and Adele Hast. Bloomington: Indiana University Press, 2001.

O'Sullivan, Mary K. "The Labor War at Lawrence." *Survey* (Apr. 16, 1912): 72.

———. "O'Sullivan Autobiography." *Papers of the Women's Trade Union League and Its Principal Leaders.* Microfilm Collection 7. Woodbridge, CT: Research Public.

Payne, Elizabeth Anne. *Reform, Labor, and Feminism: Margaret Dreier Robins and the Women's Trade Union League.* Urbana: University of Illinois Press, 1988.

Tax, Meredith. *The Rising of the Women Feminist Solidarity and Class Conflict, 1880–1917.* New York: Monthly Review Press, 1980.

See also **Hull-House**

KIRKLAND, LANE (1922–1999)

Lane Kirkland was the American Federation of Labor-Congress of Industrial Organization's (AFL-CIO's) second president. The federation's Kirkland Years, 1979–1995, were contentious, controversial, and ultimately damaging to the labor movement as a whole. The question that historians grapple with is: How much was Kirkland responsible for the AFL-CIO's untimely downturn during the 1980s and early 1990s? Kirkland's detractors point out his administration's many failings. The AFL-CIO seemed powerless to stop the antilabor actions of President Ronald Reagan. Even President George H. W. Bush's "kinder, gentler" conservatism went virtually unchallenged. Under Kirkland's watch, the labor movement seemed to grow frail, unresponsive, and sluggish, unable to provide answers to the difficulties presented by an unfriendly federal government, rising costs of living, and the dramatic changes in the economy. Kirkland's patriots point out that organized labor and the AFL-CIO's chief did the best that they could do in the face of Reaganomics, de-industrialization, and the triumph of political conservatives. They agree that the state of the labor movement has seemingly returned to the 1920s nadir. But they assert that Kirkland's leadership brought unity back to organized labor. Moreover as President Bill Clinton once said, Kirkland was a "five-star general in the global fight for human liberty," supporting democratic movements in Europe, Central America, and the Middle East. Finally Kirkland was the self-proclaimed standard bearer for New Deal Democrats, stumping for the working class's bread-and-butter interests and holding the line against unchecked identity politics.

Joseph Lane Kirkland was the second of Randolph and Louise Kirkland's five children. Born on March 12, 1922, Lane grew up in Camden, South Carolina. He was the product of a fine southern aristocratic family. His male ancestors were men of distinction: planters, judges, politicians, industrialists, entrepreneurs, and even adventurers. Although his parents were not wealthy, Lane had a happy childhood. His father was a cotton buyer and later a cotton broker. In good economic times, the family got by with little to spare. In bad times, like most of the late 1920s and through the 1930s when the bottom dropped out of the cotton market, life was rough. It was during the lean years of the Great Depression that Lane developed many of his life-long personal characteristics, such as his optimism and equanimity and his politics, which were decided, unabashedly "Rooseveltian." In addition to an adherence to liberal politics, the family as a whole seemed to have liberal views on race. Lane grew up in an integrated neighborhood, and relations between the family and African-Americans appeared to be quite respectful and cordial.

Kirkland's experiences with unions happened outside his middle-class family. In his teenage years, Lane developed a serious case of wanderlust. In 1939, following in the footsteps of his ancestor who had joined the American expedition to circumnavigate the globe, Lane went off to sea, joining the crew of the *S.S. Liberator*, a merchant ship. He remained with the merchant marine after the United States formally entered the Second World War in 1941. During the war he joined Local 88 of the Masters, Mates, and Pilots' Associations, thus beginning a five-decade association with organized labor. Still the draw to devote his life to the labor movement was not an obvious one to Kirkland, and after the war, he toyed with various career moves. But in 1947, Lane went to hear the AFL President William Green speak about unions and the vicious assault on them, specifically the passage of the Taft-Hartley Act. Green, who had all the rhetorical tools of a Baptist minister, moved Kirkland, spurring him to ask Green for a job with the federation. Green gave him a post as a researcher and speechwriter.

Through the late 1940s to the early 1960s, Kirkland's *ad hoc* assignments grew in importance. From writing speeches for the Democratic vice-presidential candidate in 1948, Alben Barkley, to penning those of presidential candidate Adlai Stevenson in 1952, Lane became a top spokesperson for the AFL. His work brought him within the closeted circles of political power in the United States. Perhaps nothing illustrates this more than the passage of the 1964 Civil Rights Bill. In 1963, the AFL-CIO finally stepped up its somnambulant campaign for civil rights. President John F. Kennedy (JFK) had on his desk an omnibus civil rights reform bill, which included a provision for a new federal fair employment practices commission (FEPC). The inclusion of an FEPC into the legislation made it quite controversial, causing JFK to shy away from it. It was at this moment that AFL-CIO President George Meany sent his top legislative aide, Andrew Biemiller, as well as Lane Kirkland, to speak with Kennedy. Biemiller and Kirkland convinced the president not to drop his support for fair employment. In the end President Kennedy listened to Meany, Biemiller, and Kirkland, as well as several influential civil rights leaders, such as A. Philip Randolph and

Roy Wilkins, and the bill that passed after his assassination contained the FEPC, which was rechristened the Equal Employment Opportunity Commission.

Despite the legislative advances during the Lyndon Johnson years and Kirkland's appointment in 1969 to be the AFL-CIO's secretary-treasurer, the 1960s were a troubled time for him. His first marriage fell apart in 1969. He witnessed with great apprehension the disintegration and transformation of the Democratic party. In Kirkland's view, the singular goal of liberal politics was to advance the standard of living for the working class. He had very little use for antiwar protestors, feminists, environmentalists, and gay rights activists. Kirkland frequently lamented the introduction of so-called identity politics into his Democratic party. To the end Kirkland remained an anti-Communist, bread-and-butter unionist. He was thus devoted to Great Society politics: the War in Vietnam and the War on Poverty. Unfortunately for him this political outlook was best suited for the Cold War of the 1950s and early 1960s, and not the decades that followed the Vietnam War and Watergate.

By the time Kirkland was elevated to the AFL-CIO presidency in 1979, he was already something of an anachronism. Throughout the 1970s, large segments of the labor movement, including coal miners and truck drivers, were seeking more democratic, less bureaucratic solutions to their problems. Despite his great sympathies with workers everywhere, Kirkland was a product of the federation's bureaucracy. Moreover he was not always comfortable in the national spotlight as George Meany had been, particularly with reporters and the New Left's social activists. Rather than adapt his style to new political realities, Kirkland instead charged ahead, leading with what he knew and understood: Fighting for a better deal for workers and fighting against communism across the globe.

Initially Kirkland's political goals found fertile ground. He and President Jimmy Carter got along well. Together they had worked on a labor-management-government arrangement, the so-called National Accord, which ideally would have ushered in a new era of cooperation and give labor unions unprecedented influence in the formation of national economic policy. Kirkland fashioned the outline of the National Accord in preparation for the 1980 presidential election. The AFL-CIO and its member unions went all out for their candidate, Jimmy Carter. Unfortunately for Kirkland, drumming up political support within the labor movement proved much harder than originally thought. Although union leaders backed Carter, many rank-and-file members voted for Ronald Reagan and conservative contenders for the U.S. Congress. Reagan's ascendancy was a disaster for the AFL-CIO on the domestic level. And yet Kirkland was able to use Reagan's hard Cold War stance in the world to propel the federation's desire to create more democratic unions around the world.

Reagan's "morning in America" policies were tremendously damaging to the labor movement and workers generally. Under Reagan's leadership, conservatives in the federal government launched long-planned attacks on unions and living standards. They wanted to enact all sorts of reforms from lowering the minimum wage to reducing federal support for collective bargaining and workers' rights. President Reagan first showed the nature of his administration in 1981. Instead of bargaining with striking air traffic controllers, who belonged to the Professional Air Traffic Controller Organization (PATCO), Reagan fired all 10,000 workers. They were subsequently blacklisted as well. While supportive of the workers, the AFL-CIO seemed powerless to rein Reagan in. Kirkland was left with the job of rallying laborers and drumming up support for Walter Mondale's lackluster 1984 presidential campaign.

After the stunning and stinging defeat of organized labor's candidate, Kirkland began to focus more on international issues. He had always been interested in foreign affairs and diplomacy. As a died-in-the-wool cold warrior, Kirkland became the AFL-CIO's point man on the U.S. attempt to challenge the Soviet Union in Europe and Central America. He had been involved in carrying out some of the logistics for the operations surrounding the Bay of Pigs fiasco. In the late 1980s, Kirkland became an important voice in the national debates about Cold War foreign policy. Politically he was to the left of Reagan but to the right of those on the Left. He derided any actions to support the oppressive and murderous right-wing dictatorships and was equally critical of the left-wing Central American revolutionaries and governments. He supported middle-of-the-road democratic forces, especially trade unions set up on the federation's model. At the time Kirkland's moderate view seemed to win few converts. However his position became vindicated with the political transformations in Poland and Nicaragua. Kirkland's support for Lech Walesa's Solidarity Movement was decisive and instrumental in the creation of a prodemocracy, non-Communist Poland. (It also made Kirkland a Polish national hero.)

Kirkland's emphasis on foreign policy as well as his particular political outlook in the Cold War was controversial within the AFL-CIO. Not everyone wanted the federation to adopt a moderate tone in the U.S. approach to the global fight with the Communists. Moreover some felt that the concern with international issues was taking the focus away from the eroding position of organized labor within the United States. Beginning with the failed PATCO strike, unions suffered a series of setbacks. Encouraged by their victories in the early 1980s, anti-union employers and their associations mounted a frontal assault on organized labor. These right-wing forces found sympathy, support, and assistance from the federal government. President Reagan's appointees on the National Labor Relations Board turned that agency into a decidedly pro-employer body. During the 1980s, workers lost about half of their petitions for certification for collective bargaining. Making matters much worse were dramatic and expansive changes to the American economy. Technological innovation, federally sanctioned use of permanent replacement workers, and de-industrialization worked together to deskill and downsize the labor force. All workers suffered as high-paying manufacturing jobs were replaced by low-paying service jobs, but unions and unionists bore the heavy burdens. By the end of the 1980s, union density was at historic lows.

Kirkland tried the best he could to stem the rising conservative tide against organized labor. In the 1980s, he worked tirelessly to bring unity back to the fractured labor movement. His efforts culminated in the re-entry of three major unions—the United Automobile Workers (1981), the Teamsters (1987), and the United Mine Workers (1989)—into the AFL-CIO. Kirkland also led the charge against such potentially antilabor initiatives as North American Free Trade Agreement (NAFTA). Finally he worked to diversify and harmonize the labor movement by encouraging women and minorities to take more leadership positions within the AFL-CIO and by adopting neutral stands on such critical social issues as abortion. Despite these accomplishments, many in the labor movement in general, and the AFL-CIO in particular, felt as though the emperor was fiddling while Rome was burning.

Following the election of President Bill Clinton in 1992, forces within the AFL-CIO began to organize a challenge to Kirkland's presidency. In October 1994, at the federation's annual convention, a group of unionists collectively known as the New Voice, engaged in surprise attacks on Kirkland. Taken completely off guard, he became very defensive and resistant to the calls for reform. In particular the New Voice unionists, who were led by John Sweeney, Linda Chavez-Thompson, and Rich Trumka, wanted a renewed focus on organizing new union members; a new approach to the national media; and new support for women, minorities, and low-income wage earners. Rather than fight his vocal opponents, Kirkland decided to retire in the spring of 1995. He was

devastated by the rebuke, which he saw as a condemnation of all that he had accomplished over the last five decades. Moreover at 72, he had been eyeing retirement for some time. In his place the AFL-CIO chose Tom Donahue, who served as president until October 1995, when the federation elected Sweeney. After his ouster Kirkland faded from public view while traveling, enjoying his family, and working on a memoir that was never published. He died in 1999.

To this day Kirkland's critics have not mollified their views of him. Perhaps we are all still too close to the events to make a decisive judgment. It remains difficult to answer the question whether Kirkland could have done more to reverse organized labor's decline since the 1980s. In the midst of a hostile political environment and during one of the most transformative periods in American economic history, he was able at least to keep the AFL-CIO together, challenge some of the more pernicious politicians and public policies, and score some victories, especially on the international stage. But Kirkland's inability or unwillingness to engage in new organizing campaigns, his disregard of the media, and old-style political style did hamper the growth of the federation. Weighing these historical factors will be the work of future labor historians.

ANDREW E. KERSTEN

References and Further Reading

Buhle, Paul. *Taking Care of Business: Samuel Gompers, George Meany, Lane Kirkland, and the Tragedy of American Labor.* New York: Monthly Review Press, 1999.
Kirkland, Lane. *Labor and the Liberal Tradition.* New York: League for Industrial Democracy, 1971.
Puddington, Arch. *Lane Kirkland: Champion of American Labor.* Hoboken, NJ: Wiley, 2005.

See also **American Federation of Labor-Congress of Industrial Organizations**

KNIGHTS OF LABOR

On May 4, 1884, the Union Pacific Railroad Company slashed pay rates for all of its workers. Over 12,000 machinists, yardmen, freight handlers, firemen, and engineers from Nebraska to Oregon struck in protest. In Denver, Colorado, a committee of railroad laborers came to editor and Knights of Labor (KOL) organizer Joseph Buchanan's office for help. The men convinced Buchanan to address a group of local picketers. When he arrived the KOL leader heard militant rhetoric that revealed both workers' anger and their spirit of collectivism. He helped provide expression for the raw passions of these men and their fellow operatives in other cities by creating KOL District Assembly (DA) 82, which represented all Union Pacific employees from Omaha to Portland. Over the next decade DA 82 proved one of the KOL's strongest affiliates, and its workers earned the highest pay on any railroad line.

During the next year, 1885, tensions between Denver's railroad laborers and their employer arose again, this time spilling over into a citywide display of working-class militancy. Picketers, rioters, paraders, and boycotters blended as a series of actions supported the KOL insistence that all workers receive the remuneration their work had earned them. The housewives and female laborers belonging to Denver's two women's local assemblies of the KOL, for example, appeared on Monday May 18, the first day of the strike, to halt scabs by pushing them into irrigation ditches. Buchanan quipped that a "scab tried to get through the line" and "half a dozen women gave him the 'ditch degree.'" "Those house wives of labor" he wrote, "were fervent believers in the virtues of water." Later that evening protestors marched two miles "loudly singing the battle hymn of organized labor in the West, 'Hold the Fort, ye Knights of Labor!'" Buchanan remembered that the singing stopped twice. First the crowd held "a little bonfire" outside the office of the *Rocky Mountain News*, burning recent issues that had condemned the strike. Second the "nearly two thousand voices" stopped singing to issue "cat-calls, groans, and hisses" at Shed's Cheap Store. The KOL organized a boycott of the store because it refused to recognize the local clerks' union.

To understand Buchanan's activism is to understand the KOL. Born in Missouri in 1851, he eventually chose journalism and union organizing as his trades and went to Colorado in 1878. Between his arrival and his decision to move to Chicago in 1887 in order to aid KOLs falsely accused and erroneously convicted of a bombing at the city's Haymarket Square, he created a number of local assemblies and two district assemblies and led two major railroad strikes, coal miners' strikes, parades, and boycotts. He was a craft union printer who helped organize the Denver Trades Assembly, and he was the KOL's leading organizer in the country. As editor of the Rocky Mountain West's largest labor newspaper, the *Labor Enquirer*, he encouraged workers to find a vision of political economy that resonated most with them, all the while insisting that they privilege pragmatism over dogma. The pages of the *Enquirer* proved eclectic as readers found the writings and speeches of theorists who ranged from doctrinaire Marxists to anarchists to utopian co-operativists to land reformers. No matter their ideological bent, he consistently reminded his readers that organizing, striking, and boycotting achieved the desired short-term ends of all proponents of the labor movement. His commitment to possessing multiple views led him to join two different socialist societies and endorse Greenback, Union Labor, and Republican candidates for office.

The range of Buchanan's antimonopolistic thought as well as the various actions that resulted from it reflected the changing industrial order. Knights of Labor across the country shared the sense that their rights as citizens were being usurped by corporations. The long hours for low pay, not to mention the dangerous conditions found in factories, mines, and on railroad lines, challenged workers' conception of work and reward. Most KOLs accepted the labor theory of value or the idea that labor created all wealth and therefore workers deserved the lion's share of what they produced. Deciding exactly what the fair share of the fruits of their labor provided often proved difficult. Instead of seeking a wage formula, workers by the 1870s were willing to accept the wage bargain as a transitory phase that allowed them to save enough money eventually to purchase their land or buy a workshop. In the Jeffersonian tradition that many postbellum Americans still held dear, owning land or a small shop signified the promise of American freedom. From this perspective the creation of a permanent wage workforce existing on subsistence pay threatened to prevent generations of laborers from ascending to the promised status of independence. Thus many workers joined the KOL in order to prevent their bosses from keeping them in a dependent state or turning them into wage slaves.

During the 1870s, chronic unemployment and constant wage cuts heightened workers' fears that they now lived in a world where social mobility was dead. When railroad owners cut their laborers' pay yet again, workers' responded by participating in the Great Strike of 1877. With evidence of a collective opposition to wage slavery, KOL leaders outlined the organizations' beliefs and aims in its Preamble and Declaration of Principles. The 1878 document argued that the unchecked "aggressiveness of great capitalists and corporations" would result in the "hopeless degradation of the toiling masses." To ensure that workers received "the wealth they create," KOL favored abolishing the wage system and replacing it with cooperatives. Recognizing the complete restructuring of the nation's economic order would take time, the KOL's declaration also called for more immediate changes to limit the inequalities workers faced. Protecting public lands for "actual settlers" instead of granting acreage to railroad companies, promoting workplace safety, ending child labor, and making 8 hours the standard workday were among the reforms KOL demanded. Buchanan emerged as the KOL's best organizer because like the order's manifesto, he successfully mixed practical objectives and actions with idealistic goals and rhetoric.

The KOL rank-and-file members accepted this blend of pragmatism and radicalism because they realized that it allowed the ideological and strategic flexibility necessary to construct a national labor movement. Most also realized that much of the KOL's emerging strength resulted from the fact that power within the order flowed from the bottom up. Local, district, state, and national trade assemblies existed under the umbrella of national bodies, which included the general assembly, the general executive board, and the grand master workman. Some local and district assemblies consisted of a single trade, while others were mixed or accepted all those regardless of occupation who wanted to join the order in a given area. The KOL barred lawyers, bankers, speculators, gamblers, and drunkards, since they understood them to be nonproductive workers and immoral human beings. Leaders and members proudly spoke of their acceptance of immigrants, African-Americans, and women. Organizers and elected leaders however also took equal satisfaction in their support of Chinese exclusion and their insistence to ban Asian immigrants from their locals. Many KOL publications, influenced by the racist pseudoscientific writings of the day, considered Chinese workers inassimilable and therefore a permanent pool of cheap labor. Thus in order to understand the KOL and their many contradictions, we must look at some of the battles the workers who belonged to the over 12,000 local assemblies organized in roughly 3,000 communities, fought with their employers, and each other. Only then we can grasp how an organization with 110,000 workers in 1885 could grow to 729,000 members in the next year, and then fall to roughly 250,000 members by the end of the 1880s.

Philadelphia tailors created the Nobel and Holy Order of the Knights of Labor in 1869, and chose Uriah Stephens their leader. Influenced by the Masons, these garment cutters founded a fraternal order committed to ritual and secrecy and as a result remained rooted mostly in the Philadelphia area until the 1870s. By 1876, the unskilled laborers in Pittsburgh's emerging industries and a number of Pennsylvania's coal miners joined the order and changed the face of the organization. Crucial to the transformation of the KOL from a fraternal organization into a federation of industrial workers was a change in leadership. Terence Powderly, an Irish Catholic former railroad worker turned machinist,

won the order's top post of grand master workman in 1878. In 1881, Powderly convinced members to abandon secrecy. He also pushed organizers to bring laborers in the emerging factory towns of Buffalo, Chicago, Cleveland, Detroit, and Milwaukee into the KOL and demonstrated his commitment to building an organization for industrial workers by moving the KOL's headquarters from Philadelphia to Pittsburgh. As more and more workers joined the order, Powderly and other leaders pushed new members to focus on their similarities, such as their opposition to wage labor, rather than their differences, namely, political beliefs that ranged from socialism to anarchism to general reform. Indeed this commitment to unity can be found in the KOL's motto, adopted in 1882, that "an injury to one is the concern of all."

National leaders' commitment to fostering a working-class culture of unity certainly contributed to the order's growth, but victories on the industrial battlefield proved the real engines of expansion. Workers throughout the nation were becoming more militant as indicated by the increasing number of strikes. In 1881, for instance, there were roughly 101,000 workers involved in 474 strikes compared to 407,000 workers participating in 1,432 strikes in 1886. In fact from 1881 to 1900, at least 22,739 strikes occurred. From 1880 to 1884, most of these protests were spontaneous, but after 1884, they were increasingly called by unions. Officially the KOL opposed strikes except in extreme circumstances, but the reality of power flowing from the bottom up meant that local leaders followed the wishes of their constituents rather than national officers. For example when a manager on railroad magnate Jay Gould's Wabash line fired a KOL-affiliated shop man in 1885, his fellow workers refused to handle any more cars. The walkout spread, and Gould eventually backed down. The Wabash strike stirred workers' faith in the power of organized collective action. From July 1885 to June 1886, 6,200 new district assemblies formed. In fact the executive board suspended the granting of new charters for 40 days in early 1886 to try and catch up on the flurry of requests for membership. For a brief period then workers won strikes, membership rolls swelled, and militant actions, not Powderly's rhetoric of cooperation with capital, determined the order's course.

Suggesting the promise of a truly inclusive grassroots working-class movement was the fact that 60,000, or ten percent, of the order's new cardholders were African-Americans. Also, female operatives claimed nearly a ten percent share of the KOL total membership as well. As the women belonging to Denver's local assemblies illustrated, they could be as militant as the white male majority. This democratic spirit did have its limits.

The Rock Springs Massacre in September 1885 provided an example of white workers' willingness to subscribe to social Darwinism and use brutality in attempting to control the labor supply. Union Pacific coal miners, belonging to DA 82, marched from their union hall to the outskirts of the small Wyoming town. Earlier in the day a fistfight between white and Chinese miners saw the whites call a strike. Although the Chinese outnumbered white coal diggers 331 to 150, whites still surrounded Chinese homes with rifles and revolvers. Many of the Asian immigrants fled by train, as did two white foremen who received death threats, but some remained. As evening settled on Rock Springs, the white KOL members set fire to the local Chinatown, and then shot at those exiting their burning homes. In the end 28 Chinese died, 15 were wounded, and the 14 white miners arrested were acquitted.

Divisions over political beliefs and organizational structure also led to violence and revealed the weakness that existed within the order. Attempting to build on the momentum of the southwestern victory and promote unity through a common reform agenda, both national and regional leaders advocated an 8-hour day movement. The shorter hours movement garnered support from both craft unionists who, led by New York cigar maker Samuel Gompers, belonged to the Federation of Organized Trades and Labor Unions (FOTLU), and Chicago's Anarchist International. Members of both organizations belonged to the KOL. The FOTLU's leaders proposed that workers across the country strike on May 1, 1886 for 8 hours. By early spring 8-hour rallies were held around the country. But all was not well within the KOL. On March 13, Powderly informed local and district assemblies that he opposed the strike plan, arguing that the order did not have the necessary funds for strike relief that this massive action would require. By that point however, Chicago workers proved too excited to wait for May 1 and struck early. Powderly and his supporters found themselves in an increasingly difficult position by the end of April as nearly 50,000 Chicago unionists had made 8 hours the standard workday. As May 1 approached, those who insisted on caution appeared to lack nerve. Despite the grand master workman's objections, KOL members struck.

On May 1, 1886, about 200,000 workers went on strike across the nation; 40,000 lived in Chicago. On May 3, antilabor police captain John Bonfiled ordered some of his men to attack picketers outside the McCormick reaper plant. At least two unionists were fatally shot, and a number of other demonstrators were wounded. In opposition to this extreme act of police brutality, labor activists organized a protest rally at Haymarket Square on May 4. As speakers condemned city leaders for their indifference to the murdered strikers, a bomb exploded killing four policemen. Policemen who had marched to the middle of the square just before the blast opened fire on the crowd. Employer and police hyperbole aided by the *Chicago Tribune*'s anti-union flair stirred public fears that they sat on the brink of revolution. Over the next three weeks, Chicago's district attorney incited 31 people for the murder of Mathias Degan, a police officer killed by the bomb. Eventually eight men stood trial for conspiracy to commit murder, and the judge found all of them guilty. After the appeals process, the State of Illinois sanctioned the hanging of four of the conspirators.

Workers across the nation protested the convictions and voiced their opposition to state-sponsored repression. Worried about the image of the KOL, Powderly however refused to authorize an official protest. Already angered by his lack of support for the 8-hour strikes, opposition to Powderly within the order grew. The divisions that workers had put aside during their efforts to acquire pragmatic reforms ended with Haymarket. More specifically the leaders of DA 49 in New York had long pushed their fellow KOLs to follow a more radical path that included organizing laborers into only mixed locals and forbidding organization along craft lines. They had fought with Gompers and the cigar makers over this issue in 1875. By 1886, they held a majority of spots on the KOL's general assembly, and during the KOL's annual meeting, they passed a motion removing the cigar makers from the order. Gompers and other purged workers responded by forming the American Federation of Labor (AFL).

Buchanan found himself at the center of this affair. The order's best organizer argued that by expelling the cigar makers the executive board was dividing the labor movement and destroying the KOL. Instead of siding with Buchanan, the thin-skinned Powderly rebuked the Denver printer. Buchanan had critiqued Powderly based on the master workmen's failure to support the accused Haymarket bombers. Powderly countered by claiming that Buchanan had injured the order's image both because of his support for the conspirators and his membership in socialist organizations. In early 1887, Buchanan decided to leave Denver and move to Chicago to defend the convicted Haymarket bombers and try to build an anti-Powderly base. He soon found himself expelled from the KOL.

Buchanan failed largely because the order was hemorrhaging members. In February 1887, Powderly realized the error of his ways regarding the cigar makers, but by that point Gompers rejected any type of peace. By July 1888, the once powerful KOL stood at 220,000 members. By 1890, that number would fall to 100,000. Although the national office would not disband until 1917, the KOL had become ineffective as a national movement by the early 1890s. Yet the number of members should not be the only test of strength.

In some places, such as the Rocky Mountain West, workers maintained the tradition Buchanan started and continued to work with each other across union and skill lines by engaging in collective actions on both the industrial and political fronts. In Butte, Montana, for example, virtually every male wage by 1890 received $3 per day. This rate, originally set by the Butte Miners' Union, became the standard. When some laborers excavating a cellar discovered, on May 3, that contractors planned on paying them a daily rate of only $2.50, they stopped working. Unionists across the city met and threatened a general strike. By May 6, 500 Butte unionists walked picket lines in support of the common laborers' demand for a 3-dollar day. By early June the strike was successful, and the KOL-affiliated Butte Workingmen's Union emerged to represent all unskilled labor in the city.

The unity of Butte workers by the 1890s was also displayed in the political arena. Nationally KOL locals across the country attempted grassroots political efforts from 1885–1888 and then worked with farmers and eventually became tied to the Populist movement in the early 1890s. Following this trend Butte workers created a Workingmen's party in 1888, but only two of the candidates the unionists supported proved victorious. Divisions over tactics, ideology, and religion blunted the promise of this movement. Leaders of the District Assembly 98 (headquartered in Butte) tried again by joining forces with the Helena Trades and Labor Assembly and the Farmers' Alliance to organize the Independent Labor in 1890. The party's platform calling for the 8-hour day, a more stringent mine inspection law, equal wages for men and women, and stronger enforcement of the Chinese Exclusion Act. Like its predecessor the Independent Labor party failed. Eventually Montana's KOL succeeded in the mid-1890s as members of the Populist party when they elected local officials and a governor who ran on a fusion Populist-Democratic ticket. Although the KOL's political efforts proved limited nationally, they functioned as a building bloc for Socialist party victories in the Progressive Era.

In the end the KOL strength also proved its weakness. Power did flow from the bottom up, and that meant that skilled organizers could mould workers' passions into a culture of unity that translated into victories on the industrial battlefield. It also meant that national leaders had troubles controlling factional crises, setting strike policy, healing ideological divisions, and articulating a clear political agenda. The order demonstrated that the class struggle had to start on the local level and that workers could have some success nationally when they maintained their culture of unity.

JOHN ENYEART

References and Further Reading

Enyeart, John P. "'The Exercise of the Intelligent Ballot': Rocky Mountain Workers, Urban Politics, and Shorter Hours, 1886–1911." *Labor: Working-Class History of the Americas* 1 (fall 2004): 45–69.
Fink, Leon. *Workingmen's Democracy: The Knights of Labor and American Politics.* 1983.
Laurie, Bruce. *Artisans into Workers: Labor in Nineteenth-Century America.* 1989.
Oestreicher, Richard. Jules. *Solidarity and Fragmentation: Working People and Class Consciousness in Detroit 1875–1900.* 1986.
Schneirov, Richard. *Labor and Urban Politics: Class Conflict and the Origins of Modern Liberalism in Chicago, 1864–1897.* 1998.
Weir, Robert E. *Beyond Labor's Veil: The Culture of the Knights of Labor.* 1996
———. *Knights Unhorsed: Internal Conflict in a Gilded Age Social Movement.* 2000.

KNIGHTS OF ST. CRISPIN AND THE DAUGHTERS OF ST. CRISPIN

Massachusetts shoemakers organized the International Knights of St. Crispin (KOSC), founded in 1867, to oppose the impact of industrialization on shoemaking. The post-Civil War introduction of steam-powered machinery increasingly divided work by job and specialization. Resistance to the power of industrial capitalism required factory workers to organize and confront their employers over wage cuts and control of work processes. In 1868, Lynn shoe workers organized the first KOSC craft lodge in Massachusetts. The transnational activities of the KOSC, led by the craft lodges in Massachusetts, expanded into shoe centers in the American Northeast and Canada. The mechanization of sewing light leather already employed many female shoe workers. Seeking to protect women who migrated to northeastern shoe centers in search of higher wages, the national Daughters of St. Crispin (DOSC), founded in 1869, sought to represent the economic interests of female shoe workers, both migratory and resident in shoe towns. Led by female workers, the DOSC organized separately from the KOSC but cooperated in strikes and in pressuring employers to arbitrate wages and grievances.

Borrowing the patron saint from English cordwainers, the KOSC transferred artisan values into the emerging post-Civil War shoe factory. These men organized the most successful union of industrial workers in the early 1870s, representing various jobs from skilled lasters to teams of bottomers. Native-born Massachusetts residents, migratory Yankee workers from Maine and New Hampshire, and Irish immigrants joined the Crispin movement, which in 1870 reflected the interests of about half of all American shoe workers. At the same time, the activism of artisan-trained shoe workers in Canadian factories in southern Ontario and Quebec provinces made the KOSC organization international.

Efforts by large New England manufacturers to dominate the American shoe market through higher productivity and lower costs confronted shoe workers with intensifying mechanization, wage cuts, and concentrated, exhausting seasons of production. Crispinism represented both a critique of industrial capitalism and a labor organization. Employers defined labor costs as just another commodity in their calculations and blamed supply-and-demand forces for wage cuts. Crispins feared that wealth and power were concentrating to undermine their fair share of the value created by factory labor. They denied that their labor was a commodity to be buffeted by market forces.

By 1869, the Crispin organization in Massachusetts, spearheaded by activists in Lynn, Worcester, and Brockton, claimed 30,000 members/sympathizers. Two thousand Lynn lasters in Unity Lodge backed by Mutual Lodge with 500 members organized in 1870 to seek a citywide wage scale protected by arbitration. They timed a strike over wages to interrupt the fall busy season. Many small manufacturers, wishing to stabilize wage levels, agreed to arbitration. While unfilled orders piled up, a citywide wage scale was negotiated for 1 year with five Crispins and five manufacturers as a joint board of arbitration in Lynn. This agreement was renewed in 1871. As the leading center of shoe production in New England, Lynn factories joined by others throughout Essex County in Massachusetts set the scale of wages for the Crispin organization expanding in such shoe centers as Utica, New York, and Philadelphia. Similar agreements stabilized wages in Toronto and Hamilton, Ontario.

The KOSC in Lynn became politically active to protest the state legislature's refusal to grant a charter for the KOSC in 1869 and successfully offered Labor Reform party candidates for state offices, winning local elections. In 1878, the offshoot Workingmen's party candidate and long-time Crispin activist beat the incumbent mayor, a large manufacturer and key opponent of the KOSC. The KOSC in Massachusetts joined the statewide push for the 10-hour day and advocated cooperative shoe factories as an alternative to industrial capitalism. The KOSC opposed Chinese immigration based on the destruction in 1870 of the KOSC in North Adams, Massachusetts, by Asian strikebreakers.

In late 1868, female workers in Lynn shoe factories organized Central Lodge No. 1 of the DOSC to prevent wage cuts. Thirty-one female delegates from DOSC lodges in the Northeast met in Lynn in 1869 to form the national association. The sexual division of labor, which assigned women to machine-stitching uppers, created no serious competition with male workers. The KOSC and the DOSC cooperated but met separately as organizations and in negotiations on wages.

Twenty-four DOSC lodges formed in late 1869, the largest in Rochester, New York, while together the KOSC and DOSC won strikes in Syracuse and Baltimore in 1871. The DOSC represented the self-supporting boarding stitcher and the female-head of family to a greater extent than residents living in male-headed families.

To protect working women's mobility, the KOSC and the DOSC joined forces in 1871 when Lynn shop owners who subcontracted stitching for large manufacturers attempted to stop the turnover of skilled working women during the busy season who left to seek higher wages elsewhere. Infuriated stitchers struck, rejecting the requirement of a week's notice backed by a wage deposit or the disgrace of a dishonorable discharge. The DOSC and the KOSC in Lynn quickly backed the strikers, forcing the employers to agree that stitchers could leave any shop without penalty.

As Lynn manufacturers sought to dominate the national market in high-buttoned ladies shoes, the KOSC and the DOSC faced downward pressure on wages. The depression years, 1873–1878, which reduced demand for fancy styles and crowded labor markets, cut earnings. The national DOSC collapsed in 1874 and the Lynn lodges in 1879. From 1875–1878, arbitration of wages and grievances in Lynn settled strikes, protected profits, and maintained wages for union men. In 1878, Lynn manufacturers, eager to sustain their dominant position in the reviving shoe market, undermined Crispin arbitration. Local lodges struck, while the manufacturers fired Crispins and recruited strikebreakers in the depression-era labor market. After five weeks the Lynn Crispins lost the right to arbitration, but not the right to organize in lodges. Without a negotiated citywide wage scale, their fight to sustain wages failed. Still the KOSC and the DOSC had developed effective organizations to oppose the power of industrial capitalism.

MARY H. BLEWETT

References and Further Reading

Blewett, Mary H. *Men, Women, and Work: Gender, Class, and Protest in the New England Shoe Industry, 1780–1910.* Urbana: University of Illinois Press, 1988.
———. *We Will Rise in Our Might: Workingwomen's Voices from Nineteenth-Century New England.* Ithaca, NY: Cornell University Press, 1990.
Commons, John R. "American Shoemakers, 1648–1895: A Sketch of Industrial Evolution." *Quarterly Journal of Economics* 24 (Nov. 1909): 39–83.
Dawley, Alan. *Class and Community: The Industrial Revolution in Lynn.* Cambridge, MA: Harvard University Press, 1983.
Hall, John Philip. "The Knights of St. Crispin in Massachusetts, 1869–1879." *Journal of Economic History* 18 (June 1958): 161–75.
Kealey, Gregory. "Artisans Respond to Industrialism: Shoemakers, Shoe Factories, and the Knights of St. Crispin." *Historical Papers* (June 1973): 137–57.
Lescohier, Don D. "The Knights of St. Crispin, 1867–1874: A Study of the Industrial Causes of Trade Unionism." *Bulletin of the University of Wisconsin* 355 (Madison, WI, 1910)
Palmer, Bryan. *A Culture in Conflict: Skilled Workers and Industrial Capitalism in Hamilton, Ontario, 1860–1914.* Montreal, Canada: McGill-Queen's University Press, 1979.

KNOW-NOTHING PARTY

In the mid-1850s, the Know-Nothing party, the nickname of what was officially termed the American party, rose to national prominence by vowing to curb the influence of foreigners and Catholics in public life and pledging to safeguard the federal union from corrupt politicians and sectional extremists. Native-born skilled workers comprised an important Know-Nothing constituency, especially in industrializing cities. Know-Nothings supported American workers' requests that government counteract economic slumps and combat immigrant job competition. The ascendancy of Know Nothings worsened ethnic divisions among workers, but by the late 1850s, those conflicts receded in the face of renewed struggle over slavery's status in the West. Almost as fast as it rose, the Know-Nothing party declined as voters' allegiance shifted to the free-soil Republicans in the North and proslavery Democrats in the South.

The Know-Nothing party traced its origins to the American Republican party, a short-lived, anti-immigrant and anti-Catholic party that fielded candidates in 1844 and 1845. Shortly after those elections, New York City's American Republican mayor James Harper and Thomas R. Whitney, an engraver and Whig party activist, helped found the Order of United Americans (OUA), a semisecret nativist society. The OUA remained small and confined to the urban Northeast. In 1853, it merged with another secret society, the Order of the Star Spangled Banner, which restricted membership to native-born Protestants who swore to vote only for men of the same status. The device of an oath-bound secret society prevented opponents from gauging Know-Nothing strength until election day and enforced loyalty that would override voters' attachments to the established Whig and Democratic parties.

In 1853, the name Know-Nothing first appeared in print in the New York *Tribune*. It is unclear if the term referred to members' directive to tell outsiders that they "knew nothing" about the order or if observers who were unable to learn anything about the secretive group coined the phrase.

Anti-immigrant nativism, which was often intertwined with Protestant hatred for Catholics, had a history dating back to the colonial rivalry between Protestant England and its Catholic rivals, France and Spain. Nativism as a force in elections and government has tended to be most intense when spikes in immigration coincide with turmoil in national politics, as occurred in the mid-1850s.

Pre-Civil War immigration peaked from 1845–1854. During those years almost three million immigrants arrived in the United States, more than four times the number that had come during the previous 10-year span. Hard hit by the potato famine and declining opportunities for tenant farmers, Ireland supplied the largest number of newcomers. The states of western Germany, which were affected by crop failure and pressure on handcraft industries, came in a close second.

Immigrants provided a convenient target for voters anxious about disruptive social change. Native-born Americans complained that European newcomers lacked knowledge of republican political institutions and were therefore easily manipulated by scheming office seekers. Protestant bigots claimed that Catholic immigrants owed a primary allegiance to the Pope and acted as Vatican foot soldiers in a plot to subvert American liberty. Xenophobes also believed that immigrants drank to excess, committed crime, and generally disrespected American cultural values. Know-Nothings addressed these concerns with proposals to extend naturalization to 21 years, restrict immigrant voting and office holding, teach Protestant values in public schools, disband immigrant militia units, and investigate allegations of sexual abuse by Catholic priests and nuns.

Earlier campaigns on these nativist issues had failed, but the Know-Nothings benefited from voter anger at established parties that made any alternative, even one as ethnically divisive as the American party, seem attractive. Simultaneous with increased immigration, conflict over the spread of slavery to lands recently conquered from Mexico had severely weakened voter allegiance to the Whigs and Democrats. Not only were parties unable to resolve the sectional conflict, but their lingering obsession with Jacksonian era economic fights about credit and currency failed to address new cultural concerns related to schools and alcohol as well as immigration. Voter dissatisfaction with the major parties also embraced a more general critique of party politics as inherently corrupt. Know-Nothings responded to this discontent by promising to safeguard the federal Union from extremists in either section, combat cultural anxiety by attacking immigrants, and replace venal office seekers with virtuous public servants.

For wage earners, political and cultural corruption mattered less than did immigrant competition for jobs and the impact that an influx of unskilled labor had on the trend toward division of labor and the replacement of the artisan shop with the factory assembly line. A drop in the roller-coaster business cycle exacerbated long-term economic forces that contributed to nativism. The 1850s witnessed the end of a long boom spurred by westward expansion, housing construction, and railroad building. Three times during the decade (in 1851, 1854, and 1857) economic panics closed banks, cut off employment, and ate up working families' meager savings. Amid these downturns employers continued to experiment with mass-production techniques in such industries as textiles, iron-making, and food processing, which lowered wages and lessened the need for skilled craftsmen. In this environment fear of foreign competition encompassed several issues: Head-to-head competition for jobs in an oversupplied labor market; competition with the foreign products imported from abroad; and the more abstract problem of the transition toward mass production and an increasing reliance on unskilled labor. In the early 1850s, the Order of United American Mechanics, a nativist trade union, supported strikes in industries pressed by hard times. Spurred by this activity, American-born skilled workers responded to Know-Nothing promises to reduce job competition by curbing immigration; protect American industry by raising the tariff; offset unemployment with public works; and at the local level,

bolster employee-negotiating power by supporting trade unions.

In 1854, the formal American party emerged from secrecy to campaign for offices across the country. From 1854–1856, the American party elected seven governors, eight U.S. senators, 104 members of the federal House of Representatives, and took majority control of eight state legislatures. Although they had supporters in the countryside and small towns, Know-Nothings were particularly influential in cities. They won control of municipal governments in most of the country's largest metropolitan centers, including Baltimore, Boston, Cincinnati, Louisville, New Orleans, Pittsburgh, Philadelphia, St. Louis, and San Francisco.

The exceptions to Know-Nothing victory proved the rule of nativism's ethnic polarization of the electorate. Ironically it was the home of the OUA, New York City, where Know-Nothings failed to win a majority. That result reflected the greater share of foreign-born voters in New York's electorate, where they made up half of those eligible to vote and could easily defeat a nativist candidate. Immigrant voters in the other major cities quickly banded together with Democrats and wealthy professionals alarmed at the labor militancy of some Know-Nothing partisans. Know-Nothings lost power the fastest in cities that resembled New York's demography; that is, places where the foreign-born comprised a majority or near majority of the electorate.

Political violence, a not uncommon feature of nineteenth-century urban politics, accompanied the rise of the Know-Nothings. The widespread nativist conviction that existing laws failed to stop foreign-born vote fraud encouraged some Know-Nothings to use force against immigrants who tried to cast ballots, lawfully or not. Street gangs affiliated with the rival political factions as well as partisan police joined in these election riots. Among the worst was Louisville's Bloody Monday riot in 1855, during which 22 people died, and the combined tally of 17 deaths and more than 250 injuries at Baltimore's municipal and federal elections in 1856. Violence distorted vote totals and further undermined public confidence in the political process.

In office the American party had difficulty enacting its agenda. In a few states, bans on immigrant militias and restriction of public-works employment to the native-born were put into effect. The Know-Nothing stronghold of Massachusetts enacted a 2-year delay on voting rights for naturalized citizens, but the law was quickly repealed by the next Republican party administration. More extreme proposals to outlaw Catholic convents and lengthen naturalization failed.

At the municipal level, Know-Nothings managed to deliver on many of their promises to native-born workers. American party administrations in cities across the country increased municipal spending on public works, created more working-class jobs in government by professionalizing police and fire departments, extended city services to newer, cheaper neighborhoods on the edges of growing cities, and permitted unions to wage strikes without police interference. In a few places, such as New Orleans where a stevedore won the mayoralty, Know-Nothings placed wage earners in positions of power, but most leaders belonged to the class of lawyers and business professionals who traditionally predominated in the high offices of all parties.

Know-Nothing success was cut short by controversy over slavery's status in the West. The 1854, Kansas-Nebraska Act spurred this conflict by lifting a 33-year-old ban on slavery in those territories and permitting voters in the new states to adopt slavery should they so choose. Like the Whig party, which provided the American party with many of its leaders, the slavery question bedeviled Know-Nothings, who would have rather talked about other issues. In the South nativists were staunchly proslavery, while in the North most Know-Nothings opposed the Kansas-Nebraska Act, and many had joined the party in 1854 and 1855 because at that point the Know-Nothings represented the most credible opponent to the spread of slavery. The fledging Republican party, created in the western states in 1854 and competitive across the North by 1856, made free soil its primary objective. The option to vote for a forthright antislavery extension party in the 1856 presidential election coincided with violence in Kansas and the caning of Republican Senator Charles Sumner by a South Carolina congressman outraged by Sumner's inflammatory free-soil speech, "The Crime Against Kansas."

Poised to expand on their victories of 1854 and 1855, the American party instead collapsed. At the party's presidential nominating convention in February 1856, northern and southern delegates argued over endorsing proslavery laws like the Kansas-Nebraska Act. A united southern delegation aided by a few northern conservatives resolved "to abide by and maintain the existing laws on the subject of slavery, as a final and conclusive settlement of that subject." Afterward 63 of 75 northern delegates repudiated the platform and began the American party's disintegration as a national force. The convention nominated former Whig President Millard Fillmore, a northerner who supported the Fugitive Slave Law and other pro-Southern elements of the Compromise of 1850. Fillmore ran on a platform that emphasized nativism, sectional comity, and support for popular sovereignty in Kansas. Northern Know-Nothings tried to field an independent ticket but watched helplessly as most of their supporters transferred allegiance to the Republicans. Fillmore, who carried only one state (Maryland), finished a distant third behind victorious Democrat James Buchanan and Republican challenger John C. Frémont. Because Republicans had little support in the South and the increasingly proslavery Democrats were in decline in the North, the fall of the Know-Nothings alarmed Americans committed to preserving the Union.

The American party survived until 1860 and beyond in three of the slave South's three largest cities–Baltimore, Louisville, and New Orleans. In the urban South, the American party stood for a more conservative version of the free-labor politics that drew workers to the Republican banner in the North. Southern big-city Know-Nothings expanded their local support by playing on urban resentment against proslavery rural Democrats who dominated state legislatures. Although southern Know-Nothings did not explicitly attack slavery, they supported the concerns of free-wage labor and thereby posed a threat to the unity of southern whites in support of slavery. During the secession crisis many of these former Know Nothings backed the Union and volunteered for service in federal regiments.

The meteoric rise and fall of the Know-Nothings destabilized the established system of party competition and voiced skilled workers' concerns about immigrant competition and economic change.

FRANK TOWERS

References and Further Reading

Anbinder, Tyler. *Nativism and Slavery: The Northern Know Nothings and the Politics of the 1850s.* New York: Oxford University Press, 1992.

Gienapp, William E. *The Origins of the Republican Party, 1852–1856.* New York: Oxford University Press, 1986.

Holt, Michael F. *The Rise and Fall of the American Whig Party: Jacksonian Politics and the Onset of the Civil War.* New York: Oxford University Press, 2001.

Mulkern, John R. *The Know Nothing Party in Massachusetts: The Rise and Fall of a People's Movement.* Boston, MA: Northeastern University Press, 1990.

Overdyke, W. Darrell. *The Know Nothing Party in the South.* Gloucester, MA: Peter Smith, 1968 (reprint, 1950).

Towers, Frank. *The Coming of the Civil War in the Urban South.* Charlottesville, VA: University of Virginia Press, 2004.

Voss-Hubbard, Mark. *Beyond Party: Cultures of Anti-artisanship in Northern Politics before the Civil War.* Baltimore, MD: The Johns Hopkins University Press, 2002.

See also **Antebellum Era; Artisans; Fugitive Slave Acts; Order of United American Mechanics**

KOHLER STRIKE (1954)

Lasting from 1954 to 1965, the strike of United Auto Workers (UAW) Local 833 against the Kohler Co. of Kohler, Wisconsin, stood out as the longest industrial dispute in U.S. history throughout the second-half of the twentieth century. The 1954 Kohler strike was notable for more than its extraordinary longevity, however. Undertaken against an adamantly anti-union employer, embroiled in congressional-level efforts to demonize UAW leaders, and marked by violence and profound community division, this strike expressed the confrontation between early twentieth-century welfare-capitalist strategies and the competing culture of union solidarity that had emerged within the unions of the Congress of International Organizations (CIO) in the 1930s as they clashed anew in the context of Cold War politics. The rhetoric of the strike also highlighted the significance to labor-management battles of competing labor geographies.

Kohler of Kohler is a family owned company, in business since 1873, most famous for its manufacture of plumbing fixtures. It was located in Sheboygan, Wisconsin, 50 miles north of Milwaukee on the shore of Lake Michigan until its founder, Austrian-born John-Michael Kohler, moved it four miles west to the relatively undeveloped community of Riverside in 1898. The firm passed to the founder's sons in 1900 and ultimately to Walter Jodok Kohler, the only remaining adult son by 1905 (his younger half-brother Herbert, who would be in charge of the plant in the 1950s, was still in school). Walter Kohler oversaw the new plant's expansion throughout the first decades of the twentieth century. He retained a series of planners and landscape architects to develop a residential community adjacent to the plant, featuring company-built homes available for purchase, the American Club dormitory for immigrant workers, and an increasingly elaborate array of clubs, sports, and uplifting recreation designed to enhance the daily lives of worker-residents. Incorporated as Kohler Village in the 1910s, the town had some 400 homes and duplexes in addition to the dormitory by the 1920s.

Though the Kohler Company had weathered strikes by skilled molders at its Sheboygan, Wisconsin, factory, there had been no signs of labor agitation in the Kohler Village plant prior to the 1930s. The first twentieth-century union at the Kohler Company was Federal Union Number 18545, chartered by the American Federation of Labor (AFL) in August 1933. Declining piece-work rates and hours, disputes over "cull" rates charged for defective products, favoritism to Kohler Village homeowners in the case of layoffs coupled with mandatory contracts pledging to use scarce wages to make mortgage payments to the Kohler Village, and an accumulation of complaints about harsh working conditions were among the issues that motivated Local 18545. The recent passage of the National Industrial Recovery Act and its Section 7(a) providing federal endorsement, if not enforcement, for workers' unionization rights also inspired the new union's members: Indeed, as would be the case in the 1950s, workers' desire for the dignity of an independent voice in determinations of conditions became one of the strongest motivations for unionization at Kohler. Almost immediately the firm countered with the formation of the Kohler Workers' Association (KWA), a company union meant to give organized expression to Kohler officials' assertions of the company's willingness "to confer at anytime with any employee, group of employees, or their representatives..." (W. Uphoff, *Kohler on Strike*, 1966). When Local 18545's requests to discuss grievances with company officials met with repeated rebuffs, the union called a strike effective July 16, 1934. Eleven days later the tensions surrounding the strike led to a violent clash in which two workers were killed by "special deputies" protecting the plant and village. A (pre-Wagner Act) National Labor Relations Board (NLRB) hearing held in September considered complaints by the union regarding discharges for union activity, refusal to bargain collectively, and interference with the company's self-organization through the promotion of a company union. Though the NLRB found such interference, it decided that the wrong could be remedied by an election between Local 18545 and the KWA, which the KWA won with 62% of counted votes. Local 18545's strike dragged on until a quiet settlement was reached to permit wartime expansion of the company in 1941. The KWA remained the main organization handling Kohler employee grievances.

The 1954 Kohler strike developed out of growing dissatisfactions and aggressiveness on the part of KWA members in the 1950s. Both the UAW-AFL and the UAW-CIO had responded to continued interest among Kohler employees for an independent union, but the KWA continued to win NLRB elections through 1951. By then KWA officials had themselves become interested in possible UAW-CIO representation as they sought more substantial gains with regard to wages and work conditions and met with resistance from the Kohler Company. In 1952, the KWA membership voted to affiliate with the UAW-CIO, and won an election certifying itself to bargain as Local 833-UAW. The new union signed a first contract with the company in February 1953, bringing, among other things, a dues check-off, arbitration, and a wage gain. However soon after bargaining began in 1954 for a new contract, the company proved unyielding on major issues, including arbitration, union security, seniority, pensions, insurance, lunch breaks for workers in units with continuous shifts, and wages. Bargaining broke down in April, and Local 833 struck the Kohler plant on April 5.

Union and company tactics early in the strike demonstrated the outrage and acrimony the company had inspired as well as the ferocity of its anti-union sentiment. Convinced that the company was determined to break the strike and destroy the union, and outraged at Kohler officials' allegations that the strike was engineered by militant outsiders, Local 833 rallied masses of 2,000 or more pickets to demonstrate support for the union and prevent the company from operating. The company stockpiled weapons and tear gas while its representatives grimly refused to negotiate on any of the union's demands on the grounds that the union's mass picketing and other strike strategies were illegal.

The company's complaints against the union reflected in part the opposing perceptions and uses of industrial, community, and private space invoked in the course of the conflict. For decades company publicity had touted the factory's idyllic village of proud home-owning employees as proof that the quality of Kohler products derived from a well-ordered balance of industrial and domestic life. Strikers upset this balance by blocking other workers' movements from home to factory, "disturbing the peace" with bullhorns and sound systems used for outdoor meetings, and intimidating those who crossed picket lines to work at the plant by taking industrial issues to their front lawns (thereby also disturbing prevailing gendered divisions of space between home and work promoted by the company). These actions formed the core of the complaints lodged by the company with the Wisconsin Employment Relations Board (WERB) charging the union with unlawful picketing and intimidation under Wisconsin law. The union's own publicity and legal maneuvers signaled the alternative geography in which members charted their affiliations. While the company labeled picketers as outsiders upsetting the friendly labor relations and locally oriented lives in Kohler, union publicity claimed that unionized workers nationwide, with the higher wages and benefits they had won through union contracts, represented the appropriate range of affiliation for Kohler workers. Union lawyers followed suit by filing a complaint against the company for failure to negotiate with NLRB and arguing that due to Kohler's considerable interstate commerce,

it was the NLRB and not WERB that held final jurisdiction. The union's tactics themselves acquired broader geographical reach after the strike had dragged on for a year with no signs of resolution. It pursued a nationwide boycott of Kohler products that often involved strikers following Kohler delivery trucks to distant destinations to picket their recipients. The boycott also relied on the expanded labor support available through the recent AFL-CIO merger.

Before the NLRB case could be heard, the Kohler strike came before another federal body—the U.S. Senate's Select Committee on Improper Activities in the Labor and Management Field, known as the McClellan Committee. Beginning in early 1957, McClellan committee hearings had exposed the corruption and intimidation rampant especially in the Teamsters' Union. Republican members of the committee, especially Senator Barry Goldwater, were determined to direct its investigations at the UAW as well, particularly its president, Walter Reuther, and saw the Kohler strike as the ideal vehicle. Along with right-wing, anti-Communist, and anti-union groups like Dean Manion's For America and *Manion Forum*, which Herbert Kohler, Jr., also supported, they were eager to undermine the higher expectations for wages and benefits that large industrial union contracts inspired among workers nationwide, boost the popularity of state-level right-to-work laws, and curb what they perceived as the growing political influence of big labor, all of which they associated with "Reutherism." The McClellan Committee's Special Counsel, Robert Kennedy, doubted that it could effectively uncover information on the strike that voluminous testimony already taken by the NLRB had not. But repeated news stories claiming that he and his brother, committee member Senator John F. Kennedy, were deliberately shielding Reuther by ignoring the situation in Kohler forced him to ask Committee Chair Senator John L. McClellan to approve an investigation and hearings. Months of mismanaged inquiry undertaken by Republican appointees and followed up by Special Counsel Kennedy himself managed to reconfirm before a national audience the profound local hatreds bred by the strike but no flagrant union corruption. Contrary to their instigators' intent, the McClellan Committee's Kohler hearings gave local union officials and UAW President Reuther a national platform to admit their mistakes and air their convictions, which proved more compelling than the company's intransigent anti-union stance and the accompanying tactics of spying and stockpiling weapons that the hearings exposed.

The NLRB's extensive hearings on the union's charges of unfair labor practices had meanwhile stretched from 1955 to 1959. The board handed down its first ruling on the case on August 26, 1960. It found that though the Kohler strike began as an economic strike, which would not have entitled strikers to re-instatement under the Taft-Hartley Act of 1947, it became an unfair labor practices strike as of June 1, 1954, when the company gave a wage increase to nonstriking employees though it had refused demands for wage increases during negotiations. The company was therefore ordered to dismiss any workers hired on or after June 1, 1954, if necessary to re-instate strikers in their old positions. The board upheld the company's discharge of 77 employees for misconduct. Both union and company filed appeals to aspects of the ruling that favored the opposite side.

Negotiations between the company and the union finally resumed in June 1962, after the Supreme Court refused the company's appeal of a Circuit Court's decision upholding the August 1960 NLRB decision. A new contract, the first in 9 years, was reached on October 7, with modest but meaningful gains in the areas of dues check-off, arbitration, seniority, layoffs, insurance, and pensions, among others, though no general wage increase. But court appeals dragged on until, in October 1965, the Supreme Court turned back a second appeal from the company, this time regarding a Circuit Court ruling that effectively expanded the number of former strikers eligible for re-instatement under the August 1960 NLRB order. With the company and union engaged in negotiating a new contract that involved changes in the pension program, the issue of the former strikers' eligibility status became inescapable. A series of high-level negotiations between company and union officials ensued, culminating in the company's agreement to pay strikers $4.5 million in back wages and pension credits and the union's agreement in return to press no further charges related to the strike.

The longest strike to that date in U.S. history was over. According to the strike's most assiduous scholar, Walter Uphoff, relations between the company and union improved from the early 1960s as they settled into a working routine of regular grievance adjustments and contract negotiations. This was itself an extraordinary achievement considering that only court orders had persuaded the company to comply with laws mandating good-faith bargaining. A two-week strike ensued in the 1980s when the company—like many others with UAW contracts—proposed a two-tier wage system in order to decrease its contractual commitments to employees. However unlike so many unionized U.S. workers of the late-twentieth century, those at the Kohler Village plant have yet to see their unionized jobs disappear overseas. The company has established plants in an ever-wider global circle of less union-friendly locations—beginning with Spartanburg, South Carolina, during the strike and proceeding to Texas, Mexico, and China, among others. But it has also maintained employment levels at its plant in Kohler, and recently even announced plans to expand its Wisconsin plant. Ironically as jobs protected by the historic contracts pioneered by the CIO in the 1930s and 1940s have become ever scarcer, the Wisconsin plumbing factory once known for its steely determination to repel such contracts has become a most remarkable destination among union-recommended vacation spots—the location of a factory tour where union labor can be seen at work.

KATHRYN J. OBERDECK

References and Further Reading

Lichtenstein, Nelson. *The Most Dangerous Man in Detroit: Walter Reuther and the Fate of American Labor*. New York: Basic Books, 1995.

Kennedy, Robert F. *The Enemy Within*. New York: Harper and Brothers, 1960.

Oberdeck, Kathryn J., "Class, Place, and Gender: Contested Industrial and Domestic Space in Kohler, Wisconsin, 1920–1960," *Gender and History* 13,1 (Apr. 2001): 97–137.

Perlstein, Rick. *Before the Storm: Barry Goldwater and the Unmaking of the American Consensus*. New York: Hill and Wang, 2001.

Uphoff, Walter. *Kohler on Strike: Thirty Years of Conflict*. Boston, MA: Beacon Press, 1966.

U.S. Senate, 85th Congress, 2nd Session. *Hearings before the Select Committee on Improper Activities in the Labor or Management Field, February 16–March 4, 1958*. Washington, DC.

KU KLUX KLAN (RECONSTRUCTION AND WWI ERA)

In its successive incarnations since the 1860s, the Ku Klux Klan (KKK) has proven the most powerful reactionary movement in American history. Yet in each of the three eras in which its organizers worked, they recruited different social groups, identified different challenges, targeted different enemies, and had a different relationship to working-class Americans and the labor movement. The two constants over more than a century have been a commitment to white supremacy and an embrace of terrorism as a political tool.

The Reconstruction-Era KKK

The first Ku Klux Klan aimed to restore planter power and white supremacy in the South in the wake of emancipation and the awarding of citizenship rights to former slaves. The organization began in 1866, at a time when fraternal orders with elaborate secret rituals were a popular form of association for American men. It was established on this model in Pulaski, Tennessee, its name taken from a Greek word signifying a circle (*kuklos*). But the new order soon turned to vigilante activity as former Confederate leaders and such Democratic party stalwarts as Nathan Bedford Forest realized the value its hooded costumes and strict secrecy could have for paramilitary activity. As congressional Reconstruction opened the way to new republican state governments, including African-Americans and those committed to democratizing the region's political economy, the KKK movement spread across the former Confederacy in 1867–1868.

In this era the movement was exclusively southern, largely rural, and its leaders came from the ranks of planters, merchants, and professionals, although the rank-and-file crossed classes. The KKK's primary objective was to reverse the revolutionary change wrought by the Civil War and radical Reconstruction: To restore as much of the prewar social order as it could manage to. Above all KKK leaders aimed to keep agriculture labor servile, if technically free, and to maintain white elites' control of government. For its part as a coalition between freedmen, free blacks, white small-holding farmers, and former Whigs devoted to a free-labor vision of the South's future, the Republican party threatened both agricultural employers' power and white supremacy. This dual challenge made it anathema to Klansmen and their allies in the Democratic party. The violence they inflicted on freedmen had no counterpart in the Western Hemisphere: One in ten of the black participants in the constitutional conventions of 1867–1868 suffered violent reprisals, in which seven were killed outright.

The KKK's signature practice was masked terrorism under cover of darkness. In a typical raid, a band of hooded KKK night riders abducted a local black Republican activist from his home at night, flogged, beat, or otherwise tortured him, sometimes killed him, perhaps also raping women in the family or burning it out of its home or destroying churches or schools. Sometimes Klansmen assaulted whites for Republican party activism or for affronting local moral codes in some way, but their main focus was the defense of racial hierarchy. The movement was usually most active in communities where blacks and whites lived in relatively equal numbers and Republicans and Democrats were in sharp competition, such as the Upcountry. There vigilantism swung otherwise tight elections, decimated Republican party organizations, and weakened community institutions.

Because so many white southerners agreed with the KKK, its terrorism was nearly impossible to prosecute locally. At worst local law enforcement officials participated in the night riding; at best, they like other critics were intimidated by the KKK and unable to secure indictments and convictions from white jurors. This stalemate made federal intervention essential to suppress the widespread violence and lawlessness that threatened to undermine democracy. Congress carried out major investigations (also unintentionally creating rich documentation for later generations of historians) that led to legislation such as the Ku Klux Klan Act of April 1871, which enabled military arrests and federal trials. Thanks to them the KKK conspiracy was nearly overcome in the early 1870s, although freelance intimidation and violence resumed after federal troops were withdrawn.

The Second KKK

After the defeat of Reconstruction, leading white southerners promoted a mythology of the lost cause that lionized the KKK. In mass membership organizations, such as the United Sons of the Confederacy and the United Daughters of the Confederacy, they glorified the old South and secession and credited the KKK with saving southern civilization from the supposed peril of black rule. As elites reconciled across the Mason-Dixon line in the Gilded Age, the South's mythology became the nation's. Leading historians at premier U.S. universities pilloried Reconstruction such that the KKK appeared a salutary force. The most influential version of this revisionist narrative was the blockbuster film by D. W. Griffith, *Birth of a Nation*, released in 1915. After a private showing for Washington leaders in the White House, President Woodrow Wilson, whose historical writing was quoted in the film, described the racist epic as "history written with lightning."

In the same year the film was released, an Atlanta huckster and avid fraternalist named William Joseph Simmons revived the KKK and used showings of *Birth of a Nation* to recruit. The order's message of "100 percent Americanism" enjoyed wide approval thanks to the hyperpatriotic climate cultivated by the federal government to wage World War I.

But it was not until after the armistice that the second KKK really took off. In the nationwide unrest that followed in the war's wake, the KKK's message attracted a wide swath of native-born, Protestant, white Americans faced with bolder challenges from African-Americans; unprecedented labor struggle and radical mobilization following the Bolshevik revolution; feminist challenges to male power; and a younger generation disdainful of Victorian moral codes and determined to see salacious movies, patronize dance halls, and engage in other modern practices that shocked adults. The new KKK proved most popular in Indiana, where one in four eligible men joined, but it enjoyed great electoral success in places as far-flung as Oregon and Arkansas. Unlike the old KKK, this one did better in urban than in rural areas. The city of Chicago alone hosted 20 different klaverns (chapters) and claimed 50,000 members; in one 1921 march, 10,000 Chicagoans took part. Nationally the KKK is reliably estimated to have enrolled about two million dues-paying members in some four thousand local chapters over the decade.

The KKK of the 1920s had a more wide-ranging agenda than those of other eras. It joined the earlier movement's commitment to white supremacy with modern anti-Semitism; anti-Catholicism; anticommunism; hostility to immigrants; antipathy to liberals; support for old-time religion; and a defense of Victorian gender roles and sexual values. The KKK leaders denounced enlightenment thinking and the Protestant social gospel then popular for encouraging "alien ideas." Local purity campaigns joined all these causes together, often in extralegal Prohibition enforcement. Staking out a place as the most devoted defender of what today would be called family values in the face of what it called moral breakdown, the KKK became so popular that it was able to practice vigilantism with relative impunity in many small-town communities in the South and Southwest. Historians have estimated in fact that approximately half of the victims of KKK terrorism in the 1920s were whites accused of violating local moral codes.

Yet whereas in the Reconstruction era, extralegal violence was the KKK's sole activity of note, in the 1920s, members typically engaged in nonviolent practices common to many social movements, albeit with KKK content. They attended business meetings to discuss ideas and plan activities, campaigned for sympathetic political candidates or against offending businesses, worked for laws against interracial marriage and against U.S. participation in the World Court, came together for picnics and religious revivals, and mobilized for shows of strength in rallies lit by burning crosses. Through such practices, the KKK became a formidable force in American politics.

At least 75 members of Congress in the early 1920s were said to owe their seats to the KKK. In 1924, the national conventions of both major parties voted down resolutions condemning the KKK. By then the KKK also claimed to have recruited 30,000 Protestant ministers and three-quarters of the delegates to the Southeastern Baptist Convention.

Historians have divided over how to interpret this incarnation of the KKK. Riding the crest of the wave of social history in the 1970s that stressed demographic research, downplayed ideas, and sought to identify the real problems behind social movements and their rational answers, some scholars became self-conscious revisionists. Pointing to the KKK's broadly middle-class ranks and many of its leading activists' long records of civic involvement, they depicted members as populists concerned about elite domination of politics and threats to established community standards. Some other historians saw prejudices of various kinds as the core of the KKK's appeal but assumed local conditions determined activists' thinking: That, for example, blacks were the focus in Alabama and Catholics in Pennsylvania. Actually regardless of where they appeared, KKK publications and speeches usually discussed numerous targets and sought to connect issues by, for example, blaming Jews for hard times or Catholics for the failures of Prohibition.

Admittedly a movement this diverse in its antipathies and broad in its catchment poses interpretative challenges that defy conventional class analysis. But if we understand class as socially constructed and class identity as shaped historically by race and gender affiliations and understand middle-class people as having a kind of class consciousness of their own, then the catchment becomes more explicable. It embodied an American variant of reactionary populist politics akin to those developing at the same time in Europe; KKK leaders if not rank-and-file members sensed the family resemblance and expressed feelings of kinship with the Italian Fascist leader Mussolini in particular. No longer forcing the KKK movement into a Procrustean bed as either populist or racist, an approach employing this kind of class analysis can reveal how the two characteristics worked together to give the movement its powerful appeal.

The KKK spokesmen framed their cause in the kind of Janus-faced republican idiom popular in nineteenth-century America. Imperial Wizard Hiram Evans, for example, portrayed the KKK as "once more the embattled farmer and artisan"—now mobilized to fight off "radicalism, cosmopolitanism," and "the alien-minded 'Liberal'" along with other enemies. The republican tradition had long excluded most Americans from citizenship—whether slaves, property-less labor, or women and children—so its assumptions proved congenial to KKK leaders, who ignored all that did not suit their purposes.

The KKK's class politics built on republicanism's basic distinction between property owners with a stake in society and others seen as objects of control. The movement attracted many skilled workers and seemed untroubled by the kind of racially exclusive business unionism practiced by most affiliates of the American Federation of Labor (AFL). Yet KKK leaders excoriated the majority of the contemporary working class, African-Americans, and the new immigrants. The KKK spokesmen construed these groups in biological terms as a threat to the nation, building on the antidemocratic theory of such racist writers then in vogue as Lothrop Stoddard and Madison Grant. Denouncing the militant labor organizations of the unskilled as the work of racial aliens—whether the Industrial Workers of the World or industrial unions more generally—KKK leaders also sometimes helped employers suppress labor struggle with vigilantism.

As powerful as it was at its peak in 1924, the second KKK faltered thereafter and was nearly moribund by the end of the decade everywhere but in the South, where it would continue for decades in numerous derivatives as a force for white supremacy. Historians have offered various explanations of the movement's demise. Some have pointed to the scandals that plagued its leaders, most dramatically in Indiana where the powerful DC Stephenson was found guilty of second-degree murder for the rape of a girlfriend that resulted in her suicide attempt and death. The widely publicized murder trial and ensuing revelations of Stephenson's empire of political corruption tarnished the movement irrevocably. Others have suggested that the rank-and-file recoiled once they realized the extent of the movement's authoritarianism. Still others have argued that the KKK

subsided when the threats its members perceived passed: as the labor movement ebbed, Congress enacted draconian immigration restriction in 1924, the NAACP lost its postwar *élan*, and so forth. With progressive activism on the defensive and conservatism triumphant in Washington, few felt the urgency they had in the early 1920s to pay dues and participate.

Whatever the precise causes of the movement's decline, the stunning power amassed by the KKK in its prime offers a chilling reminder of the indigenous American cultural traditions that have enabled terrorism when carried out by native-born white men styling themselves as victims and standing up for goals and values widely shared among their peers.

NANCY MACLEAN

References and Further Reading

Chalmers, David. *Hooded Americanism: The History of the Ku Klux Klan*. 3rd ed. Durham, NC: Duke University Press, 1987.
Evans, Hiram Wesley. "The Klan's Fight for Americanism." *North American Review* 223 (1926): 33–63.
Jackson, Kenneth T. *The Ku Klux Klan in the City, 1915–1930*. New York: Oxford University Press, 1970.
Lay, Shawn, ed. *The Invisible Empire in the West: Toward a New Historical Appraisal of the Ku Klux Klan of the 1920s*. Urbana: University of Illinois Press, 1992.
MacLean, Nancy. *Behind the Mask of Chivalry: The Making of the Second Ku Klux Klan*. New York: Oxford University Press, 1994.
Moore, Leonard J. *Citizen Klansmen: The Ku Klux Klan in Indiana, 1921–1928*. Chapel Hill: University of North Carolina Press, 1991.
Trelease, Allen W. *White Terror: The Ku Klux Klan Conspiracy and Southern Reconstruction*. New York: Harper & Row, 1971.

See also **African-Americans; Civil War and Reconstruction; Gilded Age; World War I**

L

LABADIE, JOSEPH A. (1850–1933)
Knights of Labor

The Detroit organizer of the Knights of Labor, the first president of the Michigan Federation of Labor, and ultimately a major influence on individualist American anarchism, Joseph A. Labadie contributed to numerous organizations and publications in one of the most turbulent and formative periods of American labor history.

Born in Paw Paw, Michigan, Joseph A. Labadie (commonly known as "Jo" Labadie) moved to Detroit in 1872, where he started working as a printer at the *Detroit Post and Tribune*. Joining the International Typographical Union proved to be the start of a long career in labor activism and organization. Six years later, in 1878, Labadie was among the founders of the first chapter of the Knights of Labor in Detroit, sanctioned by the Philadelphia-based organization. Although Labadie quickly became a key figure in the Knights' Detroit organization, controversy existed from the very beginning. While wholeheartedly agreeing with the emphasis on education and the solidarity of the working class, Labadie criticized the Knights' elaborate rituals involving secret handshakes, initiation ceremonies, and magnanimous titles, as noted in Carlotta R. Anderson's *All American Anarchist*, calling them "excessive rigamarole" and "the habits and the fears and the ignorance of our barbaric ancestors."

Labadie's involvement in the Knights of Labor coincided with his interest in socialism. During the 1870s and early 1880s, socialism in Detroit attracted a majority of foreign-born immigrants, most notably from Germany. When Labadie decided to join the Socialist Labor Party (SLP) in 1877, he was one of the few native-born members of the organization in Detroit. One of the consequences of Labadie's interest in socialism and the SLP was the publication of *The Detroit Socialist*, an English-language newspaper with Labadie as a major contributor. In addition to his activities with the SLP and the Knights of Labor, Labadie also served as the first president of the Detroit Trades Council, which was founded in 1880.

The break from socialism as well as the Knights of Labor for Labadie came in the 1880s. Labadie's interest in anarchism, along with his long-lasting association with Benjamin Tucker, began in the early 1880s. The same period saw Labadie's involvement in a variety of publications (including the *Advance and Labor Leaf* and the *Three Stars*) and movements, including his interest in Greenbackism and Henry George's single tax movement. A frequent contributor to Tucker's *Liberty*, Labadie's decision to leave the Knights of Labor came after the Haymarket bombing of 1886 in Chicago. While the Knights of Labor became the target of accusations for having connections with anarchists and labor upheaval in general, its leader, Terence Powderly, determinedly denounced anarchism and refused supporting the Haymarket anarchists. Labadie challenged the Knights' leadership for corruption and authoritarianism, visited the Haymarket anarchists in Chicago where they were imprisoned, and following a particularly vehement and sharp clash in a Knights of Labor convention, decided to part ways with Powderly.

In 1888, Labadie appeared at the forefront of labor organization in Detroit once again, as he became one of the founders of the Michigan Federation of Labor, functioning as its first president. Labadie's involvement with anarchism intensified during the 1890s, as a wave of violent acts, including the attempted assassination of the Carnegie Steel Company's chairman Henry Clay Frick by Alexander Berkman in 1892 for his brutal tactics during the Homestead strike, and the assassination of President McKinley by Leon Czolgosz in 1901, brought anarchism and anarchists to the center of public attention and reaction. Labadie, while condemning the assassination of McKinley, diverged from many individualist anarchists of the time as he avoided the attempt to categorically distance anarchism from these acts, and explained them as natural consequences of the existing political system and the oppression of labor.

Despite his prolific output as an anarchist columnist and lecturer paralleling his vigorous involvement in labor and anarchist organization, which included arranging speeches by Emma Goldman in Detroit, Labadie's reputation in his home city never suffered. In fact, when his dedication and degree of radicalism were questioned by some anarchists as well as mainstream journalists, Labadie was dismayed. As much as Labadie might have resented such implications, his reputation as the popular "gentle anarchist" of Detroit proved to be helpful on several occasions: in 1908, when the city postal inspector banned Labadie's mail for featuring anarchist material and quotations, an immediate public outcry ensued. Following this incident, a few months later the water board commissioner attempted to fire Labadie for being an anarchist and faced a scathing response from the Detroit press.

Joseph A. Labadie's historical significance for the history of labor and anarchism has often been overlooked, despite his influence and achievements. A considerable part of his lasting legacy can be found in the Joseph A. Labadie Collection, donated to the University of Michigan in 1911. The Labadie Collection is still one of the richest resources for manuscripts and other primary sources on the history of labor and anarchism in the United States.

AXEL B. CORLU

References and Further Reading

Anderson, Carlotta R. *All-American Anarchist: Joseph A. Labadie and the Labor Movement*. Detroit: Wayne State University Press, 1998.
The Labadie Collection. Special Collections Library, University of Michigan. www.lib.umich.edu/spec-coll/labadie/.
Martin, James J. *Men against the State: The Expositors of Individualist Anarchism in America, 1827–1908*. Colorado Springs, CO: Ralph Myles Publisher, 1970.

See also **Berkman, Alexander; Goldman, Emma; Haymarket Affair (1886); Homestead Strike (1892); Knights of Labor; Socialist Labor Party**

LABOR DAY

Labor Day was founded in New York City in 1882 and has been celebrated by workers in the United States on the first Monday in September ever since. Labor Day was born from the labor movement of the Gilded Age, which was diverse, national, and on the upswing. The first Labor Day celebration was called by the Central Labor Union of New York, a recently formed umbrella organization that included workers from different nations and with different political affiliations. Labor Day eventually became the first national holiday dedicated to a specific class or ethnic group, and its celebration and meaning have changed with the times.

Labor Day was initiated with two goals in mind. First, its proponents wanted to project an image of a united group of producers organized together against monopoly to the general public. Second, Labor Day was intended to be a festival that could bring together the various strands of the working-class movement, socialists, Knights of Labor, anarchists, craft unionists, Single Taxers, and Labor Party activists. The first Labor Day parade was organized to coincide with a Knights of Labor meeting, and it was followed by a picnic. Its organizers sought to create a festival that would have a very general political content that could appeal to as wide a range of workers as possible and that would send a message to the politicians without prompting repression or scaring off the middle class. These conflicting goals of uniting the working class while addressing the general public have been present in Labor Day festivities ever since.

The first Labor Day was a resounding success. As many as 250,000 New Yorkers turned out to watch from 10,000 to 20,000 disciplined paraders (mostly men and a few women) march in formation with floats, banners, and uniforms from Lower Broadway to Union Square. Typical banners read: "Labor Creates All Wealth," "Labor Built This Republic, Labor Shall Rule It," "The Government Must Own the Railroads and Telegraphs," and "Labor Will Be United." Members of each union carried the tools of their trade, a tradition that dated back to guild processions in the European Middle Ages. The parade was also full of patriotic imagery, including American flags and a drum-and-fife corps; at least one speaker quoted Thomas Jefferson.

Labor Day quickly became part of the nation's working-class traditions. The following year, the Central Labor Union decided to repeat the affair. In 1884, the national Federation of Organized Trades and Labor Unions (the precursor to the American Federation of Labor, AFL) called on workers to participate, and by 1886, workers were celebrating Labor Day throughout the country.

Workers also pushed to have Labor Day recognized by state and local governments and by their employers. A number of cities passed municipal ordinances recognizing the holiday in 1886, Oregon became the first state to enshrine it in 1887, and by 1894, Labor Day was recognized by 24 states, most of which had strong Populist or labor movements. In general, these state and local laws recognized the holiday but did not enforce it as a day off for all workers. Employers were much harder to convince, and for two decades after the first Labor Day parade, the holiday was essentially a one-day general strike in many cities.

By the late 1880s, AFL unions had taken over the job of organizing Labor Day parades in most cities. In the aftermath of Haymarket and the ensuing repression and propaganda campaign against unions as a foreign ideology threatening American values, the AFL moved to strip Labor Day of any radical implications. Red flags and radical speakers were banned, and all marchers were given little American flags. While Labor Day had patriotic symbolism from the beginning, this symbolism was made more prominent at the expense of radical critiques of capitalism. In the 1890s, this pushed many radicals and immigrants to avoid Labor Day and to celebrate May Day instead, which had been born out of the struggles over the eight-hour day centered in Chicago in 1886 and had been celebrated as an international day for workers since 1890.

By the early 1900s, Labor Day had become a permanent part of the American calendar. While the AFL continued to organize Labor Day parades and picnics around the country, and while Samuel Gompers continued to stress the importance of Labor Day parades for demonstrating the strength and patriotism of the labor movement, many workers wanted to use their hard-won three-day weekend for a holiday with friends or family. This was the period when the tradition of the Labor Day barbecue was born.

In the ensuing decades, the AFL made great attempts to make Labor Day fit the mood of the day. In 1918, during World War I, with the labor movement under attack for being less than 100% American, Gompers even renamed Labor Day "Win the War for Freedom Day." During the 1920s, Labor Day celebrations across the country adapted to the conservative mood of the times. In New York, Labor Day marches were abandoned in favor of celebrations at the Army's Fort Hamilton, where participants watched infantry drills and mock air battles. Labor Day celebrations were open to speeches by politicians, and their class character was diluted by the participation of many nonworkers.

In the 1930s, Labor Day celebrations were reinvigorated by the upsurge in the labor movement and attracted hundreds of thousands of participants in many cities. Labor Day marches once again took on a class character and incorporated images from the current popular culture. In Los Angeles in 1937, for instance, Popeye and the Keystone Cops chased away scabs, while an actor dressed as Abraham Lincoln declared all racial groups equal. Also in the 1930s, women were included in Labor Day celebrations on a more equal footing with men, especially in those celebrations organized by the Congress of Industrial Organizations (CIO) instead of the AFL. From 1942 to 1944, unionists stayed on the job during Labor Day and dedicated the holiday to winning World War II.

Since the end of that war, Labor Day has become a fixture of the American scene that is often celebrated like any other anesthetized American three-day weekend, with traffic jams and barbecues. At certain moments, however, union leaders will still call large marches or demonstrations of labor's power and organization on their traditional holiday. In 1959, for instance, over 115,000 New Yorkers marched down Fifth Avenue to protest the Eisenhower recession and the attacks on the labor movement. In 1982, 150,000 people protested Ronald Reagan's domestic policies in New York, and there were smaller marches in Chicago, Indianapolis, and Denver, among other cities. While Labor Day has lost much of its original vigor, it remains the only national holiday dedicated to the working class.

SAMUEL MITRANI

References and Further Reading

Baker, B. Kimball. "The First Labor Day Parade." *Worklife* (September 1976): 24–26.

Hunt, Richard P. "The First Labor Day." *American Heritage* 33 (August/September 1982).

Kazin, Michael, and Steven J. Ross. "America's Labor Day: The Dilemma of a Workers' Celebration." *The Journal of American History* 78, no. 4 (March 1992): 1294–1323.

Stewart, Estelle M. "Origin and Significance of Labor Day." *Monthly Labor Review* 43 (August 1936): 279–284.

See also **American Federation of Labor; Gompers, Samuel; May Day**

LABOR REPUBLICANISM

Labor republicanism developed from ideas about government and society that gained currency in the transatlantic world in the eighteenth century. In England, criticism grew within radical circles about the corrupting influence of self-seeking placemen and their supporters in parliament. In France, the monarchy became the target of opponents to an entrenched and unaccountable political and social hierarchy.

Republicans held that government rested on the consent of the governed, who through regular elections authorized their representatives to govern for the common good. The polity consisted of "free men" whose social and economic independence as property owners entitled them to the franchise. Citizens replaced subjects in republican discourse; rule by law instead of by men served as a republican benchmark; and civic-mindedness and not the pursuit of personal gain pervaded republican society.

Between 1763 and 1776, when American colonists grieved that British imperial policies infringed on their "rights as free-born Englishmen," republican ideas were central to an incisive critique of British rule itself. In the Atlantic seaports, artisans joined tradesmen and merchants in defying colonial authority, and especially in Philadelphia from 1774 to 1776, tavern and coffeehouse customers debated the arguments for national independence.

Thomas Paine, a former corset maker and excise man who migrated from England to Philadelphia, popularized much of the emerging republican case for independence in a widely distributed and read pamphlet, *Common Sense*. Paine vehemently denounced monarchic rule as inimical to peace and prosperity and vigorously contended that Americans had an opportunity to erect a government on sound principles. Artisan readers of *Common Sense* and other tracts by Paine during the Revolutionary War imbibed an ethos of uncompromising egalitarianism and nationalism that helped to define their identity as Americans in the young republic.

Independence resonated with special meaning to master and journeymen craftsmen in the pre-industrial era. Just as the newly formed United States of America was free of foreign domination, artisans practiced their trades and earned their livelihoods, free of control by others. Their independence emanated from finely honed skills, breadth of knowledge, well-grounded experience, and personal initiative. Carpenters, cordwainers, and printers, among others, expressed pride in their labor, which they considered vital to the nation's economic and social welfare. Indeed, artisans viewed themselves as the heart and soul of a republic of "small producers," essential to wise government and political stability.

Accordingly, they participated in debates over the ratification of the U.S. Constitution and generally endorsed the federalist case for a stronger central government. Enticed by Thomas Jefferson's vision of a nation propelled by yeoman farmers and urban mechanics, artisans supported the Virginian planter's successful candidacy for the presidency in 1800 and helped form the base of the Democratic-Republican Party for the next two decades.

Artisan Republicanism

Artisans not only marked their republicanism by exercising their citizenship rights in elections. Between 1788 and 1825, artisans in New York City used such occasions as Independence Day (4th of July), Evacuation Day (November 25, 1783, when British troops left New York), and the opening of the Erie Canal in 1825 to demonstrate their patriotism and celebrate their status as free men and independent producers. In orderly processions they carried banners and transparencies that displayed symbols of their trades and craft societies. These festivals featured an iconography that powerfully expressed values embedded in the artisans' political and work cultures.

To artisans, the small independent workshop was the microcosm of a republican society. Masters, journeymen, and apprentices worked alongside each other in self-directed but interdependent activity. Mutuality, co-operation, and convivial relations bonded producers within a tightly knit community free of hierarchy and exploitation. Any suggestion that the calculus of economic efficiency should govern the organization of production met with hostility. Typical was the response of a journeyman drug maker in 1830, who dismissed the observation of an English immigrant that a more detailed division of labor would increase productivity: "This is a free country; we want no one person over another which would be the case if you divided the labor."

That the process of industrialization by the 1820s and 1830s had manifestly rendered the republican imagery of the workshop as increasingly idyllic did not reduce the steadfastness or intensity by which artisans upheld republican values. Disputes between masters and journeymen, which prompted restrictive judicial interpretations of the common law and definitions of property rights at the expense of journeymen, compelled artisans to recognize the reality of social and economic divisions. Yet in doing so, they re-affirmed the vitality of the founding principles of the American republic as expressed in the Declaration of Independence. Journeymen defended their militancy in the face of "haughty and overbearing" masters who in the pursuit of private gain sought to deny journeymen of their natural, inalienable rights as "free men" and thereby defy the republic itself.

Artisans' republicanism was most manifest as they assumed leadership in the labor movement in the 1820s and 1830s. The growth of craft-based journeymen societies to achieve "just compensation" in the 1820s; the intervention of Workingmen's Parties in Boston, New York, and Philadelphia (1828–1830) to contest the state's promotion of "monopolistic privilege"; and the emergence of citywide general trade unions, which brought together craftsmen, outworkers, and factory operatives between 1833 and 1836 to halt the imposition of economic "vassalage" by employers keen to reduce labor costs signaled a shift in consciousness in recognition of the widening chasm between masters and journeymen and employers and wage workers.

Labor republicanism, as defined and understood by artisans in this sense, constituted both a language of class with its distinctive terminology, structure, and tonality as well as the rudiments of an ideological critique of the social relations of production that capitalist accumulation of wealth engendered. In this context, Ely Moore, the leader of the New York Workingmen's Party, defended journeymen's concerted activity at the workplace and in the political arena as an antidote to the corrupting influence of a "new aristocracy" of manufacturers and bankers. Addressing the New York General Trades Union in 1834, he warned delegates of the dangers posed by a "widening distinction between employer and the employed," including the perpetuation of a "system that fostered dependency," subverted "the natural rights of man," and was "hostile to the spirit and genius" of republican government.

Labor republicanism as a body of thought was not without its anomalies and tensions. Despite offering an imprimatur to artisans to organize trade unions and political parties with aspirations to represent all producers, at times it existed more as a radical subculture in competition with evangelical Protestantism, which many Anglo-American workers in the 1830s and 1840s embraced. Consequently, its claim to encapsulate a vision of labor in a republican society rested on an appeal to a rationalist sensibility. Although republicanism possessed elements of a code of ethics in its critique of aggrandizing capitalists, it lacked the moral fervor of religious revivalism that spoke to the emotional needs of artisans and other workers confronted with the insecurities and anxieties of a market-driven economy.

Moreover, republicanism's emphasis on the rights and liberties of individuals was predicated on the existence of a durable political and cultural consensus. Yet economic changes attendant to industrialization bore witness, and the property rights of individuals became subject to redefinition. In part, republicanism did display an elasticity in this regard, as artisans asserted that their labor constituted a form of property that they "owned" just as much as a merchant owned his business or a yeoman farmer owned his land. However, master craftsmen increasingly were acting as incipient entrepreneurs who regarded the journeymen's skills as a commodity to be purchased at the right price.

Labor Republicanism and Wage Labor

Concomitant to these different readings of property rights were conflicting interpretations of what wage labor signified. Informed by abolitionists' critique of slavery in the South, wage labor was a form of "free" labor since wage workers were not bound to their employers in that they were free to seek other employment opportunities and could advance economically and socially. A more pessimistic interpretation stressed that wage labor constituted another and more insidious form of dependency that entailed a deterioration in workers' position. Labor spokespersons sometimes referred to wage workers as "hirelings" who were shown scant respect by those who retained their services. In the 1830s, "wage slavery" entered republican discourse as an emotive term, indicating that manual workers were entrapped within an "iron chain of bondage."

This metaphor was not coincidental, since "freedom," "slavery," independence, and servility were charged with racial meanings. For many antebellum white Americans, chattel slavery was the lot of African-Americans, who purportedly were "unfit" to act as autonomous agents. Any suggestion that white wage workers were being made slaves of any sort raised the fear that they were falling from republican grace and succumbing to a degradation associated with an inferior race.

Likewise, republicanism's ethos was coded in terms of gender. Republican independence signified "manliness," a set of traits that entitled some men to enjoy the rights and fulfill the responsibilities of citizenship. Personal integrity, honesty, native intelligence, and self-respect were manly characteristics, cultivated in a republican society that did not tolerate social hierarchies based on inherited titles, imposed ranks, or permanent classes. That some seemingly acquiesced to if not accepted a status less than that of "free men" convinced many white workers that a "republican" labor movement justifiably had no room for "unmanly" African-Americans and Chinese immigrant "coolies."

Notions of manliness, nevertheless, revealed ambiguities in labor republicanism. Republican thought traditionally deemed women as lacking the prerequisites for citizenship, although women served the patriot cause during the War for Independence and subsequently were expected to uphold the ideal of "republican motherhood." In part, republicanism's ambiguity paralleled the tensions in the legal code between women as "femme covert" and as "femme sole" whereby women's status before the law oscillated between one absorbed with that of their fathers or husbands and one that deemed women as autonomous individuals capable of thinking and acting for themselves.

Women drew greater attention from the labor movement as their position in a market economy grew in the 1830s and 1840s. In some respects, the employment of women in mechanized factories and labor-intensive urban sweatshops epitomized the degradation of wage labor and the erosion of the artisans' world, and as such became a target of approbation.

Yet, as women workers, especially in New England's cotton textile industry, began to organize against wage reductions and long hours, they asserted their claim to a place within a republican society. Their language of protest—be it to justify their strikes to the general public or explain their petition for a 10-hour day—evoked images familiar with male artisans. Standing firm against the "oppressing hand of avarice," female operatives in Lowell, Massachusetts, declared they remained "daughters of freemen" and possessed "unquestionable rights" as an inheritance of their "patriotic ancestors." In short, by dint of their concerted activity and the meaning they attached to it, women workers helped to make labor republicanism less gender specific by the mid-nineteenth century.

Labor Republicanism in the Gilded Age

Labor republicanism's "golden age" occurred during a period of accelerated industrialization, marked by sweeping technological innovation, the development of national capital, labor and consumer markets, and the emergence of powerful corporations. This fundamental transformation of the American economy represented a challenge to the labor movement over the last quarter of the nineteenth century. Members from the National Labor Union, Knights of Labor, and individual unions upheld time-honored principles in their advocacy of workers' individual rights and collective interests. Expressed in declarations, speeches, songs, and poems through such publications as the *National Labor Tribune*, the *Journal of United Labor*, and *John Swinton's Paper*, an alternative value system and vision of American society were cultivated.

The attempts of industrialists to reduce labor costs and wrest control over the labor process from craft workers spurred trade unionists and labor reformers to re-affirm bedrock republican values. Puddlers in Pittsburgh's steel mills referred to an "intrinsic customary value" of labor, independent of the interplay of supply and demand. Ideas about natural justice were prominent in a critique of industrial capitalism and underpinned arguments for workers' claims to the product of their labor as a "competence" and "fair" or "living" wage. Labor, therefore, was construed in terms of equity as a means of securing a "dignified" life that allowed workers to own a house and sustain a family without wives/mothers and children having to work.

An emphasis on the distribution of wealth revealed a growing sensitivity to social and economic relations in a capitalist society. To advocates of the eight-hour day, such as Ira Steward, freedom from excessive toil and just compensation were two sides of the same coin, emblematic of full emancipation. Whereas Steward believed that wage labor did not prevent workers from "moving out of the slavery of poverty" into "the freedom of wealth," spokespersons from the Knights of Labor, such as George McNeil and Uriah Stephens, regarded wage labor as part and parcel of inequality and the lack of freedom. McNeil categorically declared that "there is an inevitable and irresistible conflict between the wage system and the republican form of government." Stephens called on Knights to fulfill their noble duty and oppose the usurpations of "an accursed slavery, a heaven denounced tyranny and a degrading atheistic idolatry."

These different representations of wage labor suggest that labor republicanism was multivalent. For some, it provided the logical foundation for a program—setting out practical aims and objectives. For others, it supplied the labor movement with the moral energy and fortitude necessary to persevere in the face of intense opposition. In any event, republicanism permeated a movement culture that simultaneously defended American values and dynamically recast them to contest the perceived threat industrial capitalism posed to American democracy. At a time when "self-made" captains of industry such as Andrew Carnegie lauded the pursuit of private interest and the acquisition of wealth as fundamental to a democratic society, Gilded Age labor activists spoke of promoting the "commonweal" whereby workers could "develop their intellectual, moral, and social faculties" and "share in the gains and honors of an advancing civilization."

The Knights of Labor, in particular, envisioned a society in which cooperation, equality, and community defined social, economic, and cultural life in contrast to the egotistical individualism, the concentration of wealth and power, and the ethos of unbridled competition that industrial capitalism both fed on and encouraged. In a language that combined the temperament of a devout Christian and the clearheaded logic of a political economist, the Knights unreservedly launched a crusade to redeem the republic by nurturing the values and mobilizing for a program that would make "industrial and moral worth and not wealth the true standard of individual and natural greatness."

The Knights' appeal rested also on its inclusiveness. Membership in its assemblies and lodges was open to wage earners, farmers, merchants, doctors, and educators. The Knights drew from "producerist" precepts at the heart of artisan republicanism that validated the contributions of the producers of wealth at the exclusion of those who expropriated wealth, such as bankers and land speculators. Likewise, its program was comprehensive—aimed at redressing economic grievances, codifying the rights of labor, altering institutional arrangements, or otherwise checking unequal power relations.

The Knights rapidly declined in the 1890s, and concurrently much of labor's crusading spirit ebbed. Concomitantly, republicanism's compelling vigor began to wane within movement discourse. Its guiding principles and core values no longer were salient in labor's program and strategic orientation. By the turn of the century, greater stress was placed on the nuts and bolts of organization at the workplace and political arena to wrest concessions from employers and the state and to establish the legal legitimacy of trade unions.

Even when there was no change in labor's objectives, a shift in emphasis emerged. For example, advocates of the eight-hour day turned to arguments focusing on workers as consumers rather than on workers as producers. Workers were entitled to "an American standard of living" and not just the fruits of their labor. Proto-Keynesian assertions that a shorter workday and higher wages would stimulate demand and thereby promote economic prosperity became more common.

In a sense, republicanism's decline coincided with workers' accommodation to the growth of industrial capitalism. Nevertheless, even as labor leaders assumed a business- and statesmanlike posture, the raison d'être of trade unionism in the twentieth century remained its pursuit of justice and equality, once at the heart of labor republicanism.

RONALD MENDEL

References and Further Reading

Fink, Leon. *In Search of the Working Class: Essays in American Labor History and Political Culture.* Urbana: University of Illinois Press, 1998.
Glickman, Lawrence. *A Living Wage: American Workers and the Making of a Consumer Society.* Ithaca, NY: Cornell University Press, 1997.
Krause, Paul. *The Battle for Homestead 1880–1892: Politics, Culture, and Steel.* Pittsburgh, PA: University of Pittsburgh Press, 1992.
Rodgers, Daniel. "Republicanism: The Career of a Concept." *Journal of American History* 79 (June 1992): 11–38.
Schneirov, Richard. *Labor and Urban Politics: Class Conflict and the Origins of Modern Liberalism in Chicago, 1864–1897.* Urbana: University of Illinois Press, 1998.
Schultz, Ronald. *The Republic of Labor: Philadelphia Artisans and the Politics of Class, 1720–1830.* New York: Oxford University Press, 1993.
Wilentz, Sean. *Chants Democratic: New York City and the Rise of the American Working Class, 1788–1850.* New York: Oxford University Press, 1984.

See also **Artisans; Gilded Age; Knights of Labor**

LABOR RESEARCH ASSOCIATION

The Labor Research Association (LRA) was founded in 1927 by Robert Dunn (1895–1977). It continues to this day as a New York-based nonprofit organization that provides research and educational services for unions. Today, the LRA is known for hosting an annual dinner that honors labor leaders. The LRA also assists unions in bargaining preparations and strategic planning. It is managed by a board of directors composed of union and other labor leaders.

Robert Dunn was born in Huntington, Pennsylvania, on June 1, 1895, and eventually graduated from Yale University. He began his career in 1918 as an organizer and economic researcher for the Amalgamated Textile Workers Union. He was also secretary of the New England Civil Liberties Committee, a division of the American Civil Liberties Union (ACLU) from the beginning of that organization in

1920. He served on the board of directors of the ACLU from 1933 to 1941. After founding the LRA in 1927, he served as its executive secretary until 1975. Dunn was interested in the Soviet Union and visited that country as the research director of the Quaker Relief Committee in 1922–1923 and as the secretary of the American Trade Union Delegation to Russia in 1927.

He founded the LRA in order to collect data on labor and the economy for unions. This data included statistics, general information, and analysis by the LRA. To this end, the LRA published the *Labor Fact Book* biennially. The *Labor Fact Book* contained a systematic analysis of the facts and statistics it compiled, including in its first decade such questions as the nature of the Great Depression, the relations of white and black workers, and the meaning of Fascism. The LRA was influenced by the Communist Party and took many of its definitions and questions from that organization's viewpoint. The LRA also put out a series of monographs, mostly written by Dunn, called the "Labor and Industry Series." These include *Labor and Automobiles* (1929), *Labor and Textiles* (1931), and *Labor and Steel* (1934).

The LRA continued to espouse a Marxian viewpoint and to publish books through International Publishers, the Communist Party's publishing house, into the 1950s. The book *Monopoly Today*, put out by the LRA in 1950, for instance, asserted that four hundred men ruled the American economy and analyzed the different groups of monopolies that dominated the nation. The LRA also published books on American imperialism and on theoretical questions such as wage determination (see *New Concepts in Wage Determination*, edited by George Taylor and Frank Pierson, 1957).

The LRA has continued to mount an intellectual critique of academic economics from the viewpoint of labor and the working class until the present day. While the openly Marxian perspective was less evident in LRA publications in the late twentieth and early twenty-first centuries, the organization still put out articles with titles like "'Invisible Hand' Not a Solution: Laid-off Workers Need More Protection" (November 15, 2001). The LRA's analysis of the Enron scandal, for instance, asserts that Enron illustrates the "inherent corruption in the system of capital accumulation itself" (Greg Tarpinian, "The Enron Collapse: Symptom of a Corrupt Economic System," Jan 21, 2002). In the early twenty-first century, the LRA began a new project, LRA Photography, dedicated to photographing working people. The LRA has continued the tradition of intellectual work in the service of the labor movement.

SAMUEL MITRANI

References and Further Reading

Labor Fact Books. 1928 to the present.
Labor Research Association. "Labor and Industry Series."
Labor Research Association. *Monopoly Today*. New York: International Publishers, 1950.
LRA Web Site. www.laborresearch.org. Contains an index of articles cited.
Taylor, George, and Frank Pierson, eds. *New Concepts in Wage Determination*. New York: McGraw-Hill, 1957.

LABOR THEORY OF VALUE

The "labor theory of value," the doctrine that "labor creates all wealth" and that workers should therefore receive the "full fruits of their labor," had broad support in nineteenth-century America. Rooted in ancient notions of justice, the labor theory of value was given modern legitimacy in the philosophy of John Locke, who held that one's labor was a form of personal property, as inviolable as one's home, crops, or tools. Artisans, farmers, and politicians agreed, at least rhetorically, that the people who did useful labor were both morally superior to and more worthy of political power than the idle rich, the shiftless, and, in general, those who consumed wealth rather than produced it. Enslaved people also invoked the labor theory of value as a justification for the common practice of appropriating food and other items that, they believed, properly belonged to them by virtue of their productive labor.

The labor theory of value was the bulwark of "producerism," the notion that those who grew the nation's crops and produced its goods were the moral, economic, and political heart of the American republic. What made the labor theory of value so popular in the nineteenth century was that the concept of "labor" was very broad, and might include, depending on who was defining it—in addition to manual laborers, skilled workers, and farmers—merchants, entrepreneurs, and professionals. The first working-class organizations in the Jacksonian era endlessly repeated the claim that "labor creates all wealth" and, accordingly, demanded that workers both receive their fair share of that wealth and that they play a central role in the governance of the republic. In the 1870s and 1880s, America's first great national labor union, the Knights of Labor, embodied this broad definition of what it called the "producing masses" by welcoming—in addition to artisans and other manual workers—merchants and small businessmen, and explicitly excluding only those who "lived by the sweat of other men's brows."

The labor theory of value was central to labor and farmer discourse well into the late nineteenth century. The Knights of Labor used the phrase "full fruits of his toil" in the preamble to their platform. Workers, it claimed, should be able "to secure to the workers the full enjoyment of the wealth they create." Both the St. Louis and Omaha platforms of the People's Party, the political offshoot of the Populist movement, declared: "Wealth belongs to him who creates it. Every dollar taken from industry without an equivalent is robbery" (Knights of Labor, pp. 22, 30; Destler, pp. 25–27). Many farmers and workers clung to the belief that they were entitled to nothing less than the "full fruits of their labor."

Although they continued to embrace the labor theory of value, beginning in the late nineteenth century, American workers began to redefine its meaning, from an individual to a collective concept. Samuel Gompers, the leader of the American Federation of Labor, for example, insisted that living wages represented workers' fair share of productive value. But Gompers and other advocates of high wages invoked "fair share" in a new way. Whereas earlier in the nineteenth century, proponents of "fair" or "honest" or "just" wages described them as a return for individual labor yields, in the late nineteenth century, advocates for workers described the fair share, often also called a "living wage," in collective terms, as the worker's rightful "share in the products of common toil" (Lloyd, 51). This redefinition was necessary as increasingly industrial workers labored alongside large numbers of other people, making it difficult to measure the value of individual labor. Instead, wages resulted from the aggregate claims of a group of workers to their rightful share of the social product that they collectively created.

These revisers of the labor theory of value refused to separate remuneration and production. Their claims for fair wages or living wages, however expansively construed, were a demand for wealth earned by the sweat of workers' brows. This is why Samuel Gompers insisted that the living wage should be understood as an "entitlement" rather than "charity" ("Minimum Living Wage," and *Lowell Mail*, pp. 432–435). These claims to economic justice depended on the labor theory of value; living wages came out of the reserves of wealth that workers themselves created. As the radical Bob Ingersoll framed it, the demand for a high standard of living was not a claim for unearned wealth but a way to establish economic justice in the classic producerist sense. "Why should labor fill the world with wealth and live in want?" he asked in 1882 (Ingersoll). Through the twentieth century, organized labor continued to make this argument about the collective value of labor as a justification for wage demands. For example, the socialist newspaper, the *New York Call*, described

a "Fundamental Principle that each worker has an undeniable right to enjoy the full benefit of all that he or she produces" (June 29, 1908).

Although workers continue to invoke the labor theory of value, since the late nineteenth century competing theories of value have emerged. Beginning in the late nineteenth century, the major challenge to the producerist moorings of the labor theory of value has been marginalism, the insight first promoted by economists in the 1870s that what is most important for decision making is the marginal or last unit of consumption or production. The marginalist revolution in economics suggested that value was best thought of as what consumers were willing to pay for a good or service. This meant that measuring the value of work could not occur outside of the marketplace; according to this theory, it was ultimately consumers who determined the value of labor. Marginalism challenged the notion that the absolute value of labor could be determined, even if one defined production in collective terms; they understood the determination of labor value as a relative process, shifting the meaning of value from the production to the consumption side, or in the language of economists, from the supply to the demand side.

As the marginalist revolution gained prominence, workers often phrased their wage demands in consumerist rather than producerist terms, weakening the hold of the labor theory of value. "The living wage is based, not on the value of a man's work, but on his requirements as a man in civilized society," one advocate declared (Crowther, p. 26). Rejecting the dogma that "wages must be proportionate to the value of services rendered," another advocate of living wages argued that it was impossible to separate value from questions of power: "every one knows that there is little connection between value of services and wages paid; the employer pays no more than he must" (Sullivan, 284–289). "Under the present social system," wrote the progressive reformer Scott Nearing in 1915, "there is no relation between the social needs of a man and the wage which he receives." In a frontal assault on the labor theory of value, Nearing argued that the "the term worth should be abandoned." For Nearing, a living wage should be "a return in proportion to social needs." In 1915, Nearing denounced the "American Wage" as "anti-social" because it was "fixed wholly independent of social relations" (Lehrer, p. 91). In 1916, he condemned the view that the worker receives wages "in proportion to his product." In truth, he wrote, wages "are never fixed on that basis" (Sherman, pp. 66–67; Nearing, 872–873).

Notwithstanding the acceptance of marginal thinking by many working-class organizations, organized labor and many ordinary workers continued to posit a chastened version of the labor theory of value throughout the twentieth century, a belief that seems likely to continue to motivate manual laborers well into the future. Labor demands for good wages continue to be grounded in the idea that, even in a modern economy, the value of goods and services should be reflective of the labor that helped create the product. When Walter Reuther, the head of the United Auto Workers' Union in the post-World War II years, asked the big automobile companies to "open the books," he was making the case that workers, responsible for the profits of these corporations, deserved a share of the wealth they created. But even here, labor's claims rested less on the labor theory of value than on the claim that justice demanded that workers earn decent wages that would allow them to live with dignity. Many late twentieth-century and early twenty-first century "living wage" campaigns, for example, while stressing the productive value contributed by the labor force, have emphasized far more American affluence, social justice, and the benefits of extending mass consumption as justifications for paying workers livable wages.

LAWRENCE B. GLICKMAN

References and Further Reading

Crowther, December 30, 1922, p. 26.
Destler, Chester McArthur. *American Radicalism, 1865–1901: Essays and Documents.* New York: Octagon Books, 1963.
Ingersoll, Robert. "The Infidel." *San Francisco Truth,* September 20, 1882.
Knights of Labor. *Labor: Its Rights and Wrongs.* Washington, DC: Labor Publishing Company, 1886.
Laurie, Bruce. *Artisan into Worker: Labor in Nineteenth-Century America.* New York: Hill and Wang, 1989.
Lehrer, Susan. *Origins of Protective Labor Legislation for Women, 1905–1925.* Albany: State University of New York Press, 1987.
Livingston, James. *Pragmatism and the Political Economy of Cultural Revolution, 1850–1940.* Chapel Hill: University of North Carolina Press, 1994.
Lloyd, Henry Demarest. "A Living Wage by Law." *The Independent,* September 27, 1900, pp. 2330–2332.
Lloyd, Henry Demarest. "The Safety of the Future Lies in Organized Labor." 13th Convention, AFL, December 1893. *AFL and CIO Pamphlets. 1889–1955.* Westport, 1977 (microfilm).
Meek, Ronald L. *Studies in the Labour Theory of Value.* 2nd ed. London: Lawrence and Wishart, 1973.
Nearing, Scott. "What Are Men Worth?" *Railroad Trainmen* (October 1916): 872–873.
Sherman, Steve, ed. *A Scott Nearing Reader: The Good Life in Bad Times.* Metuchen, NJ: The Scarecrow Press, 1989.
Sullivan, J. W. "Business Methods in Marketing One's Labor." *AF* (April 1911): 284–289.
Wilentz, Sean. *Chants Democratic: New York City and the Rise of the American Working Class, 1788–1850.* New York: Oxford University Press, 1984.

LABOR'S NON-PARTISAN LEAGUE (1936–1944)

Leaders from the Congress of Industrial Organizations (CIO) created Labor's Non-Partisan League (LNPL) in April 1936 to increase organized labor's influence in American politics. The United Mine Workers of America (UMWA) president, John L. Lewis, and the Amalgamated Clothing Workers of America (ACWA) president, Sidney Hillman, played leading roles in the formation of LNPL. In an attempt to emphasize its independence from the CIO and its multi-union composition, the League's first president, George Berry, came from the International Printing Pressmen and Assistant's Union, an American Federation of Labor (AFL)-affiliated union. Eli P. Oliver, an organizer for the ACWA, became the vice president. In reality, LNPL possessed only nominal independence from the CIO, whose leaders, particularly Hillman and Lewis, created and controlled the organization.

Just a few months prior to forming LNPL, Hillman and Lewis had created the CIO to challenge the craft-oriented AFL. Upset with the AFL's refusal to alter its organization to accommodate the structural changes that had occurred in the workplace, they formed the CIO to organize these workers into industrial, rather than craft, unions. The CIO experienced substantial early gains, particularly in the fledgling United Auto Workers Union in the wake of the successful Flint sit-down strike. Legislation supported by President Franklin D. Roosevelt, such as the National Industrial Recovery Act (NIRA, 1933) and, after the Supreme Court ruled the NIRA unconstitutional, the National Labor Relations Act (1935), greatly improved the union-organizing environment. Encouraged by the support of Roosevelt and other labor-friendly Democrats, CIO leaders formed LNPL to increase labor's power and effectiveness in politics.

The formation of LNPL represented an important shift in organized labor's previous stance toward politics. It also demonstrated further differences between the AFL and the CIO. The AFL only occasionally became involved in electoral politics, proudly maintaining that it remained independent of either party by rewarding its political friends and punishing its enemies. LNPL activities represented a more expansive, organized, and partisan foray into electoral politics than AFL leaders had ever envisioned. Although its name suggested that LNPL would be independent of either political party, the League almost immediately became closely aligned with the Democratic Party and rarely supported Republican Party candidates. The long political alliance between organized labor and the Democratic Party began in 1936 with the creation of LNPL and its support of Roosevelt.

The League provided Roosevelt's 1936 re-election campaign with substantial financial and institutional backing. LNPL spent around $1,000,000 in its efforts to re-elect FDR, much of it going to the Democratic Party. Lewis's own UMWA contributed a large portion of the money. LNPL also provided important organizational assistance to Roosevelt and the Democratic Party. LNPL election activities included publishing and distributing pamphlets, organizing rallies, radio addresses, press releases, and public statements. In addition to its primary focus on the presidential election, state and local CIO unions that had political activists and increasing CIO union memberships organized support at both the state and local levels for other Democratic Party candidates. Roosevelt's landslide victory (532 electoral votes to the Republican challenger Alf Landon's 8) in 1936 and the election of a number of LNPL-supported governors, such as Frank Murphy in Michigan and George Earle Jr. in Pennsylvania, demonstrated to many CIO leaders that LNPL was a critical component of the new industrial labor movement and that organized labor should have a permanent presence in American politics.

Success in the 1936 elections encouraged LNPL's continued political activities. In early 1937, the national LNPL offices moved to become an integral part of the Democratic Party, the Roosevelt presidency, and the New Deal coalition. Its initial activities focused on supporting Roosevelt's political agenda. For example, LNPL supported the President's ill-fated Supreme Court packing plan. Although formed as a top-down organization interested primarily in national politics, local LNPL organizations in a number of cities, like Detroit, Pittsburgh, and Akron, ran and supported candidates for local offices, such as city council and mayoral races, in 1937.

The emerging alliance between LNPL and the Democratic Party also encountered difficulties. Some LNPL leaders, like the outspoken Lewis, rebuked Roosevelt for his lack of support of union efforts, particularly after the Little Steel Strike Massacre on Memorial Day in 1937, which left 10 strikers shot dead after confrontations with law enforcement. By 1939, Lewis, who now chaired and dominated the LNPL national offices after the ouster of George Berry in 1938, grew increasingly disenchanted with Roosevelt. Lewis supported Republican Wendell Willkie in the 1940 presidential campaign, while most CIO leaders, including Sidney Hillman, supported Roosevelt's bid for an unprecedented third

term. Lewis's support of Wilkie created chaos in LNPL, particularly when Lewis ordered LNPL to stay out of the campaign. Some local and state LNPL offices disregarded Lewis's directive and supported Roosevelt. Lewis resigned as president of the CIO after Roosevelt's victory but maintained control of the national LNPL offices.

LNPL went in two directions after the 1940 election. The Lewis-controlled national LNPL offices struggled between 1941 until 1944. Its activities slowed considerably and focused primarily on lobbying Congress on labor-related legislation, such as antistrike bills and wage and price control legislation. In a few strong CIO cities, local LNPL offices developed into independent political arms of the local labor movement that no longer had a direct connection to the national LNPL. These local efforts remained close to the Democratic Party. The creation of the Congress of Industrial Organizations-Political Action Committee (CIO-PAC) in 1943 spelled the end of LNPL. The locally active LNPLs merged into the larger, more coordinated and directly CIO-affiliated CIO-PAC structure. The increasingly inactive Lewis-led national LNPL quietly shut its offices in 1944. The CIO-PAC built on the earlier success of LNPL and further tied organized labor to the Democratic Party as an integral part of the New Deal coalition, a process that LNPL had started when it supported FDR's re-election campaign in 1936.

JOSEPH M. TURRINI

References and Further Reading

Dubofsky, Melvyn, and Warren Van Tine. *John L. Lewis: A Biography*. New York: Quadrangle, 1977.

Fraser, Steven. *Labor Will Rule: Sidney Hillman and the Rise of American Labor*. New York: The Free Press, 1991.

Nelson, Daniel. "The CIO at Bay: Labor Militancy and Politics and Akron, 1936–1938. *The Journal of American History* 71 (December 1984): 565–586.

Spencer, Thomas T. "Labor's Non-Partisan League, 1936–1944." *Labor's Heritage* (Spring/Summer 2004): 35–47.

See also **Congress of Industrial Organizations**

LABORERS' INTERNATIONAL UNION OF NORTH AMERICA

In April 1903, Samuel Gompers, the president of the American Federation of Labor (AFL), called a meeting of all independent laborers' unions in Washington, DC. Gompers argued that the other construction trades often treated laborers—who performed unskilled, low-status work on construction sites (hod carriers, for example, carried mortar to bricklayers)—as second-class members of the house of labor. Laborers, therefore, would be better able to protect their interests by consolidating all the independents into one international union. On April 13, 25 delegates representing over 8,000 workers formed the International Hod Carriers' and Building Laborers' Union of America (IHCBLUA). During its first decade, the AFL laborers' union survived challenges from two independent unions—the Building Laborers' International Protective Union of America and the Laborers' Protective Union of America. Thereafter, the leadership of presidents Domenico D'Alessandro (1908–1926) and Joseph V. Moreschi (1926–1968) created a relatively stable early history.

The AFL's Laborers' union grew unevenly but persisted through numerous jurisdictional and name changes. In 1912 alone, the Laborers' union changed labels twice, first to the International Hod Carriers' and Common Laborers' Union of America (IHC-CLUA) and then to the International Hod Carriers', Building and Common Laborers' Union of America (IHCB & CLUA). The membership grew gradually until 1913, when the union appropriated its first funds for organizers, added road construction workers, and raised membership to nearly 25,000. During the building boom of the 1920s, the Laborers' grew to approximately 96,000. However, the Depression hit the IHCB & CLUA hard, and its numbers dropped to 27,000 by 1933. Although private construction did not recover until after World War II, the Laborers' prospects gradually improved over the 1930s. In 1931, Congress passed the Davis-Bacon Act, which protected wage rates for construction workers on government-financed projects. In addition, public works projects during the second half of the New Deal years were good for the union, bringing the rank and file to over 101,000 in 1937 and 200,000 in 1942. Post-World War II organizing campaigns, combined with the addition of trades such as the National Association of Post Office Mail Handlers in 1958, added strength. In the 1950s and 1960s, the Laborers' International Union of North America (LIUNA) signed a number of agreements with national employers' associations, such as the National Pipeline Association, Association of Railway Track Contractors of America, Inc., Associated General Contractors of America, National Contractors' Association, Building Trades Employers' Association, and General Contractors' Association. In 1965, the union changed its name one final time to the Laborers' International Union of North America (LIUNA), reflecting the union's increased scope.

The Laborers' history is tied to the history of public works and government contract law. Laborers and other construction trades, of course, are essential to public works projects. Consequently, they have been beneficiaries of the expansion of the nation's infrastructure. In addition to the Davis-Bacon Act, the Federal Highway Act (1944) was a great boon to the Laborers' union. Since the late 1940s, the Laborers have been at the center of lobbying efforts for occupational safety. The 1949 National Pipeline Agreement, for example, included groundbreaking safety regulations for thousands of workers. In addition, in 1962, the Laborers formed the AFL-CIO Building and Construction Trades Department Safety Committee, and a massive lobbying effort succeeded in prompting the creation of the Occupational Safety and Health Administration (OSHA). Laborers have also played key roles in safe removal of asbestos and in 1988 established a pioneering Health and Safety Fund.

As a union encompassing many low-skilled workers, the Laborers have had a problematic relationship to the history of trade unionism more generally. The conventional view of the AFL is that it was a bastion of "pure and simple unionism," providing a protective house of labor for skilled workers. The Laborers, however, represent Gompers's and the AFL's efforts to expand its jurisdiction to include lower-skilled workers in order to oppose competing unions. The Laborers' history with regard to racial discrimination fits squarely into the broader narrative of trade unionism. Despite the AFL's claims that it disavowed racist practices, contemporaries and historians have noted that African-Americans and Mexicans did not hold an equal place in the Laborers' ranks during the first half of the twentieth century. Well into the century, black laborers in the IHCB & CLUA were forced to reside in segregated locals.

Throughout much of its history, the Laborers' union has had notorious ties to organized crime. The construction industry's large and relatively constant revenue streams have made it an attractive target for organized crime. Additionally, once organized crime members infiltrated the construction trades, the unions' exclusivity facilitated their control over material flows and job distribution. The federal government began investigating these connections in the early twentieth century, culminating in the 1980s and 1990s when LIUNA was at the center of a national controversy over organized crime and unions, with significant implications for national politics. In 1986, the President's Commission on Organized Crime named LIUNA one of the "bad four" unions for its ties to racketeering, along with the International Brotherhood of Teamsters (IBT), Hotel and Restaurant Workers (HRW), and the International Longshoremen's Association. In 1994, after many successful efforts to clean other unions of organized crime elements, the U.S. Department of Justice (DOJ) presented LIUNA with a 212-page complaint against the Laborers' president, Arthur A. Coia. In an unusual settlement, the DOJ agreed to leave Coia in office and put LIUNA in charge of cleaning its own ranks of organized crime. Republican members of Congress charged that LIUNA received a "sweetheart deal" because Coia had strong connections to the Democratic Party and President Bill Clinton and Hillary Clinton. In 1996, the House Committee on the Judiciary's Subcommittee on Crime heard two days of testimony on the Justice Department's handling of allegations that labor was connected to organized crime. In turn, labor leaders such as Coia and the AFL-CIO head John Sweeney rejected the 1996 hearings, arguing that they were merely partisan efforts to undercut organized labor's newly energized organizing campaigns. In 1999, Coia stepped down from the union's presidency, and a year later the federal government gave up its option to take charge of LIUNA. By 2000, LIUNA's self-policing ousted at least 220 corrupt officials, 127 of whom had proven connections to organized crime.

While LIUNA dealt with allegations of corruption, the Laborers saw two distinct movements to increase the numbers and power of rank-and-file members. In 1994, Coia established a new organizing department, which included the Volunteer Organizer in Community Empowerment (VOICE) program. New organizers increased the Laborers' numbers to over 800,000 by focusing on low-skilled workers in new sectors. In 2003, LIUNA also joined the Immigrant Workers Freedom Ride Coalition. In addition, Laborers members led an unofficial grassroots movement to democratize the union. The Laborers' history reveals the ambiguities of the American union movement. Throughout its history, the Laborers' union's various incarnations have represented sectors of the working class that other trade and industrial unions often overlooked. Yet, the Laborers' history also highlights American unions' struggles with corruption and imperfect union democracy.

JEFFREY HELGESON

References and Further Reading

Greenhouse, Steven. "Embattled Head of Laborers Union Announces His Retirement." *The New York Times*, December 7, 1999, section A, p. 19, column 2, National Desk.
———. "Republicans Questioning Federal Deal with Union." *The New York Times*, July 14, 1996, section 1, p. 14, column 1, National Desk.
———. "Union Cleanup Praised: U.S. Oversight Is Eased." *The New York Times*, July 21, 2000, section A, p. 20, column 5, National Desk.
Laborers' International Union of North America's monthly journal, *The Laborer*.
Mercey, Arch A. *The Laborers' Story, 1903–1953: The First Fifty Years of the International Hod Carriers', Building and Common Laborers' Union of America*. Washington, DC: Ransdell, 1954.
Randolph, Philip A. "The Trade Union Movement and the Negro." *The Journal of Negro Education* 5, no. 1 (January 1936): pp. 54–58.
Tomlins, Christopher L. "AFL Unions in the 1930s: Their Performance in Historical Perspective." *The Journal of American History* 65:4 (March 1979): 1021–1042.
United States Congress. House Committee on the Judiciary Subcommittee on Crime. Administration's Efforts against the Influence of Organized Crime in the Laborers' International Union of North America: Hearings before the Subcommittee on Crime of the Committee on the Judiciary, House of Representatives, One Hundred Fourth Congress, Second Session, July 24 and 25, 1996.

See also **American Federation of Labor; Brotherhood of Sleeping Car Porters; Construction Trades; Davis-Bacon Act; Gompers, Samuel; Occupational Safety and Health Administration**

LABOR-MANAGEMENT COOPERATION

"Labor-management cooperation" (LMC) is a rather complex concept in the labor relations lexicon, as its meaning changes depending on who is using it and for what purpose. In the early twentieth century, it denoted key ideological splits within both management and labor. By mid-century, that version of the issue had been settled in favor of a specific form of cooperation. Subsequently, either unions or managements periodically employed the concept, or invoked the sentiment, whenever they were feeling particularly weak—or particularly strong. In the last quarter of the century, when unions still had substantial, if eroding, strength in many important sectors, labor-management cooperation enjoyed something of a fad among management for motives that were decidedly mixed. By the beginning of the twenty-first century, however, with unions representing less than 10% of private-sector workers, the concept faded, as did the entire field of "labor relations" in favor of "human resources" in nonunion workplaces.

In the early years of the last century, key proponents of labor-management cooperation formed the National Civic Federation (NCF) with hopes of preventing class divisions from "dissolving society" by addressing "industrial problems through evolutionary rather than revolutionary processes." Samuel Gompers, the president of the American Federation of Labor (AFL), and John Mitchell, the head of the United Mine Workers (UMWA), were key labor spokespersons for this view, while corporate and political leaders associated with the NCF included Andrew Carnegie, William H. Taft, Alton Parker, George Perkins, and August Belmont.

The issue for the labor movement then was whether to use trade unions to negotiate a better deal with capitalist employers or as but part of a larger effort to replace the capitalist system with a "cooperative commonwealth"—that is, one form or another of socialism. Eugene Debs, a railroad unionist who ran for U.S. president as a Socialist from 1900 through 1920, and William ("Big Bill") Haywood of the Industrial Workers of the World (IWW) condemned Gompers's and Mitchell's participation in the Civic Federation. Haywood claimed unions that took this approach were "poisoned and polluted with the virus of the pure and simple trade union that . . . proclaim [ed] the identity of interests of capital and labor." In 1911, a dissident group within the AFL and the UMWA scored labor leaders' membership in the NCF as "class collaboration" designed "to chloroform the labor movement into a more submissive mood."

On the business side, the primary focus was on whether to accept labor unions as institutional representatives of workers. Business advocates of labor-management cooperation argued that negotiating some terms and conditions of employment with AFL-style unions was preferable to the potential social and political upheavals that would result if there were no mechanism for workers to articulate their grievances and improve their conditions. This view was anathema to most employers at the time, even those who were forced by strikes and boycotts to bargain with unions occasionally. Many corporations, as Debs and Haywood were quick to point out, wanted to have it both ways. U.S. Steel, for example, was a prominent member of the Civic Federation, extolling the virtues of "cooperation" in speeches and documents but going to great lengths to systematically suppress any and all union activity in its mills and mines.

Cooperation Wins as Collective Bargaining

With the National Labor Relations Act (NLRA) and other labor legislation in the 1930s, the federal government weighed in strongly in favor of a specific form of labor-management cooperation—government-regulated collective bargaining. By legislating certain rights and protections for workers, the government required private employers to recognize and bargain in good faith with duly elected unions. Responding to the social and economic upheavals of the Great Depression, the NLRA channeled worker activity into a very specific form of labor union defined nearly exclusively as an institution for collective bargaining. Though communists, socialists, and other revolutionary unionists were prominent in organizing millions of workers into unions within this government-regulated system, the system decisively ended the internal labor movement debate over whether to negotiate with capitalists or to replace them with an altogether different, socialist system. Legally sanctioned strikes forced powerful corporations, one by one from 1937 to 1941, to recognize and bargain with unions.

In the new system, labor-management cooperation was conceived of as necessarily adversarial. That is, though areas of common interest between workers and management were recognized, it was assumed that there would always be deep and abiding differences in real material interests. The way to reconcile these differences was through negotiations, enforced by (peaceful and legally regulated) economic strikes and lockouts or the threat thereof, and by what became elaborate systems of mediation and arbitration by third-party, often government, agencies. Labor-management cooperation, in other words, was seen as enemies negotiating with each other rather than going to war to eliminate each other. Employers, when they had to, recognized and negotiated with unions. Unions abandoned the revolutionary socialist option in favor of negotiating better and better terms and conditions of employment with capitalist employers.

Legally inscribed as an adversarial system, in the immediate post-World War II period it was open as to what all would be covered by the legal requirement to negotiate "terms and conditions." The principal AFL unions that had formed the Congress of Industrial Organizations (CIO)—the miners and the clothing unions—had long traditions of offering highly competitive employers what amounted to business plans for limiting competition to protect prices and profits. This was also part of the traditional "sales pitch" of the AFL building trades unions: that by cooperating with workers through their unions, employers could stabilize (and thereby increase) the quality and quantity of their production and, thus, their profits. Postwar CIO unions employed similar appeals to "labor-management cooperation" in a different form, proposing tripartite Industry Councils where government, employers, and unions would cooperate to ensure profitability, increased wages, and better conditions within a regime of stable prices that would stimulate economic growth. Employers almost uniformly saw this form of labor-management cooperation as an illegitimate challenge to their "right to manage." Both through negotiations and legislative restrictions, this wider participation of unions in "managing" entire industries was rejected by business and government. Though there were occasionally echoes of this broader approach, for the most part unions subsequently narrowed their focus to wages, benefits, and shop-floor power through what became highly elaborate grievance-ending-in-arbitration systems.

Cooperation as Unions Decline

Faced with declining productivity growth and economic stagflation in the 1970s, many unionized employers turned to a shop-floor form of labor-management cooperation for a variety of reasons. Likewise, as plant closings began to proliferate in the late 1970s and early 1980s, some unions broached the idea of "industrial policy" modeled on the CIO's Industry Councils, while others traded contract concessions for investment guarantees and seats on companies' board of directors. In general, management was most interested in greater "cooperation" at the shop-floor level, while unions often emphasized "cooperation" at higher levels where companywide decisions were being made.

Labor-management cooperation in the workplace itself came in a variety of forms with an even greater variety of names and emphases. "Quality of Work Life" (QWL), for example, emphasized a joint process of improving workplace amenities, morale, and productivity. "Employee involvement" focused more on gaining worker input and insight into how to improve specific work processes in order to improve product quality and/or productivity. These programs were usually initiated by management in union workplaces, and unions had a variety of responses to them. Most unions were suspicious of them, fearing they would undermine the steward and grievance systems that enforced contract provisions concerning job classifications and work rules. Some, most importantly the United Auto Workers (UAW), embraced the concept at the leadership level and experimented with various forms of cooperative shop-floor improvement processes, but not without both explicit and tacit resistance on the part of local UAW leaders and workers. Even well-defined programs, like those at General Motors at various times, played out very differently division by division and plant by plant. Local management, particularly at the departmental and front-line supervisor levels, were generally unenthusiastic, and even where elaborate programs had seemed to foster a more co-operative environment with tangible improvements in product quality or productivity, they could be rapidly eroded by labor-management disputes at higher levels.

As union-heavy industries restructured—not only manufacturing with its plant closings and severe downsizing, but telecommunications, airlines, trucking and others—these programs were sometimes forced upon and other times advocated by union workers as efforts that could improve the prospects of their company or industry. Though the overall record of these "labor-management cooperation" programs is mixed at best, there were some dramatic success stories of plants or companies being turned around. These successes, however, typically involved crisis situations, and while some analysts credited labor-management cooperation for these turnarounds, others saw "worker participation in management" as the moving force.

As union power has eroded in industry after industry and as nonunion employers in growing economic sectors have greatly improved their ability to resist union organization, some form of LMC program has become a standard, but unimportant, element in most union workplaces. In nonunion workplaces, an entirely different terminology is used because workers have no collective power to cooperate or not. Though many large employers devote substantial resources to "human capital development" and other efforts to maintain "employee morale and commitment," others deliberately churn their workforces, accepting high levels of worker absenteeism and turnover in return for a complete absence of any threat of worker organization. From the beginning, the concept of labor-management cooperation assumed a certain level of collective worker power that made cooperation a necessary or appealing option for management. In the private sector in the United States, worker power has decreased to well below that level.

JACK METZGAR

References and Further Reading

Bluestone, Barry, and Irving Bluestone. *Negotiating the Future: A Labor Perspective on American Business*. New York: Basic Books, 1992.
Commission on the Future of Worker-Management Relations. *Report and Recommendations*. Washington, DC: U.S. Departments of Labor and Commerce, December 1994.
Kochan, Thomas A., Harry C. Katz, and Robert B. McKersie. *The Transformation of American Industrial Relations*. New York: Basic Books, 1986.
Parker, Mike, and Jane Slaughter. *Working Smart: A Union Guide to Participation Programs and Reengineering*. Detroit: Labor Notes, 1994.
Weinstein, James. *The Decline of Socialism in America: 1912–1925*. New York: Random House, 1967.

LABOR-MANAGEMENT RELATIONS ACT

See **Taft-Hartley Act**

LAFOLLETTE CIVIL LIBERTIES COMMITTEE

Strikebreakers and labor spies harassed American workers and subverted labor organizations from the earliest days of industrialization. The LaFollette Civil Liberties Committee paraded these shadowy figures before the nation in dramatic hearings from 1936 through 1939, exposing employers' anti-union tactics and affirming the need for federally protected labor rights. The Committee's hearings built public support for the National Labor Relations Act and hamstrung employers from openly attacking workers organizing unions. Reactionary labor leaders opposed to state oversight of labor allied with congressional conservatives in 1938 to undermine the Committee.

American workers won sweeping new federal rights to organize and bargain collectively with the 1935 passage of the National Labor Relations Act. However, employers ignored the law, expecting the Supreme Court to invalidate it along with other New Deal legislation. As the National Labor Relations Board (NLRB) prepared its test cases for the Supreme Court, Heber Blankenhorn, an NLRB staffer and former aide to Senator Robert F. Wagner, argued that the NLRB needed a public relations strategy as well. Blankenhorn had organized the Army's first military propaganda unit during World War I and also investigated the steel industry's use of spies and strikebreakers during the 1919 steel strike. Blankenhorn outlined his strategy in a 1935 letter: "Tear open the whole infamous system which rules labor relations in steel, auto manufacture, rubber, much of textiles, much of mining and general manufacture. Let the country, through public hearings, judge what these great industrialists really want when they declare the Labor Relations Act 'unconstitutional.'" After Blankenhorn lobbied leaders of the AFL and CIO along with members of Congress, Senator Robert M. LaFollette Jr. agreed to chair the hearings.

The Committee on Education and Labor opened hearings in April 1936 to investigate "violations of free speech and the rights of labor" and received an appropriation for a full investigation that fall by a subcommittee including LaFollette and Senators Elbert D. Thomas of Utah and Louis Murphy of Iowa. Subpoenas summoned the heads of major detective firms, including the Pinkertons and Burns, to testify about their business and clients. Company presidents, spies, and strikebreakers were also called. Committee staffers seized the trash cans of recalcitrant detective agencies and laboriously pieced together shredded documents to produce client lists, revealing that storied firms like Studebaker, Endicott-Johnson, and Pennsylvania Greyhound all used undercover operatives. The CIO, just beginning its massive drives in auto and steel, invited Committee staffers to witness strikebreaking on its picket lines, and the Committee held hearings on the strikes at Republic Steel and the Harlan County coal mines as they happened. The Michigan governor, Frank Murphy, said the hearings greatly assisted negotiations during the General Motors sit-down strikes. Lengthy investigations of employers' associations like the National Metal Trades Association and the National Association of Manufacturers exposed their reliance on blacklists and professional armed strikebreakers. The Committee was far from impartial and functioned more as a propaganda agency than as a disinterested enquiry.

A congressional hearing on employer violations of labor rights was not a new idea; the LaFollette Committee mirrored earlier congressional investigations, such as the Homestead hearings of 1893 and the Commission on Industrial Relations in 1913. The Committee's findings were not new either—progressives and trade unionists had complained of spies and blacklists for 50 years, and a synthesis of those earlier accounts formed the initial basis for the Committee's work. The Committee's findings resounded less because they were revelatory, but rather because they were suddenly relevant. Unionists who suspected spies in their ranks or endured strikebreakers' attacks could call in Senate investigators to subpoena their enemies before Congress.

Blankenhorn, hoping to eradicate labor espionage and strikebreaking, tried to require agencies to turn over lists of all their undercover operatives. When the agencies refused, the Senate declined to prosecute them for failing to comply with subpoenas, permitting spies the protection of secrecy. But employers feared bad publicity and rapidly stopped using detective agencies and strikebreaking firms. Both industries began to wither. LaFollette drafted a bill titled the Oppressive Labor Practices Act that would have prohibited employers from using strikebreakers and labor spies and from stockpiling weapons. (The NLRA did not specifically prohibit these acts.)

However, a backlash had begun. Leaders of the AFL resented the Committee's close alliance with CIO unions that had bolted the federation. Moreover, the AFL saw the NLRB's endorsement of industrial organizing as a fulfillment of their worries about state involvement in labor relations. In the summer of

1938, the NLRB ruled against the AFL and for the CIO in a case involving West Coast longshoremen. Outraged AFL leaders began a concerted attack on the NLRA, allying with employers to roll back key provisions of the law, and they began working with Representative Martin Dies, the chair of the newly created House Un-American Affairs Committee (HUAC) investigating Communism. Among HUAC's first targets was the LaFollette Committee. An AFL official, John Frey, testified in August 1938 that Communists were working closely with LaFollette investigators. (Indeed, several LaFollette staffers turned out to be avowed Communists.) A strange and bitter conflict developed between the two committees, with the HUAC threatening to hold hearings on the La Follette Committee. President Roosevelt publicly supported the LaFollette Committee, and it received enough funding to conduct a major investigation into California agricultural labor. But its bill died in committee, and the LaFollette Committee folded in 1941.

The battle over the LaFollette Committee shows the schism within the labor movement over its relation to the state in the 1930s. The CIO embraced an expansive state regulatory regime, and its collaboration with the LaFollette Committee revealed the potential for a state alliance to discipline employers and shift power to workers. The AFL feared state control and CIO ascendance enough to sabotage this alliance, despite the benefits all workers enjoyed from impairing employers' anti-unionism. Meanwhile, as strikebreaking and labor espionage waned, employers developed new tactics to defeat unions. A labor spy told Congress in 1938 that lawyers were taking all the union-busting business, since attorney-client privilege shielded them from Congressional subpoena.

JENNIFER LUFF

References and Further Reading

Auerbach, Jerold S. *Labor and Liberty: The LaFollette Committee and the New Deal.* Indianapolis, IN and New York: Bobbs-Merrill, 1964.
Gall, Gilbert J. "Heber Blankenhorn: The Publicist as Reformer." *The Historian* (August 1983).
Gross, James A. *The Reshaping of the National Labor Relations Board.* Albany: State University of New York Press, 1981.

See also **Blacklists; National Labor Relations Board; Strikebreaking**

LAFOLLETTE SEAMEN'S ACT (1915)

On March 4, 1915, President Woodrow Wilson signed the Seamen's (aka LaFollette) Act, best known for having secured the "sailor's freedom," that is, the right to quit a ship at port without incurring criminal charges of desertion. Within a comprehensive and complex piece of legislation (requiring 21 pages of dense, single-space type to enumerate its 20 sections), legislators attempted, among other ends, "to promote the welfare of American seamen...abolish arrest and imprisonment as a penalty for desertion...and to promote safety at sea." What might be considered the "free labor" provisions of the act centered on the decriminalization of desertion (now reduced to a forfeiture of wages earned), formal abolition of flogging and other forms of corporal punishment (replaced by a graduated code of punishment of disorderly conduct), an anticrimping ban on advance wages or the allotment of wages to any but the sailor's immediate family, and a "half-wage clause" allowing the sailor to depart at any port during a voyage with half his earnings to date. Second, the act set firm controls on the hours and conditions of labor. In particular, these work-related measures divided sailors into two and firemen into three watches at sea and limited all seamen to nine-hour days in port; in addition, they specified minimal requirements for shipboard diet, sleeping space, and adequate toilet facilities. Third, explicit concern for passenger as well as crew safety mandated lifeboat design, access, and certified emergency training by the crew. Fourth, the act ventured into the arena of hiring and skill restriction: within five years of the passage of the act, 65% of the deck crew were to be rated as "able seaman," defined by three years' service at sea or on the Great Lakes; in addition, English-language requirements—justified by concern for communicative safety—also clearly intended to shift crews toward higher native-American quotients. Finally, in perhaps its boldest move, the authors of the act specified its application not only to "all vessels of the United States but also, and within a year, to "foreign vessels."

The political history of the Seamen's Act is reasonably well documented. Behind the eponymous author of the legislative act, Senator Robert LaFollette, the real father of the maritime labor reforms was the Seamen's Union leader, Andrew Furuseth. An Oslo-born sailor and fisherman, who jumped ship in 1880 to make his home in San Francisco, Furuseth was a self-taught exponent of sailor union federation, craft unionism, and ultimately, political regulation of the waterfront. In the wake of the *Titanic* disaster of April 1912, the force behind maritime labor and safety reform gained inexorable logic. A less-trumpeted source of support for the bill was anti-Asian racism; both the language and skill requirements in the bill aimed to reduce international maritime traffic in "cheap labor" and thus promote the return of "Caucasians" to the industry. By 1912, both major party conventions had adopted resolutions sympathetic to the sailors' cause. When the Democrats not only retook the White House and control of both houses of Congress in November 1912, but also the bill's former cosponsor, William B. Wilson, was named Secretary of Labor, labor reform forces gained the edge they needed.

LEON FINK

References and Further Reading

Auerbach, Jerold S. "Progressives at Sea: The La Follette Act of 1915." *Labor History* 2 (Fall 1961): 344–360.
Weintraub, Andrew. *Andrew Furuseth: Emancipator of the Seamen.* Berkeley: University of California Press, 1959.

Statute Cited

U.S. Statutes at Large, 63rd Cong., 3d sess., 1915, 38, pt. 1, 1164–1185.

LANDRUM-GRIFFIN ACT (1959)

Officially titled the Labor-Management Reporting and Disclosure Act, this law resulted from the McClellan Committee hearings (1957–1959) on union corruption. Those hearings offered opponents of organized labor an opportunity to pass new restrictions on unions' ability to organize new members. But the legislation also represented efforts to empower the rank-and-file union membership in hopes that they could police their own unions.

This legislation emerged at a time of strength for organized labor. Unions had grown during the early 1950s, reaching a peak of membership in 1956 that included roughly one third of the nonagricultural workforce. The merger of the AFL and CIO in 1955 allowed organized labor to present a united front that should have strengthened their political hand in Congress. The off-year elections in 1958 demonstrated organized labor's apparent strength as efforts to pass right-to-work legislation in several states, including California, went down to defeat. However, the revelations of union corruption presented by the McClellan Committee undercut public sympathy for labor unions. Even those congressmen who had been elected with the support of organized labor in 1958 felt pressure to support anti-union corruption legislation, regardless of whether or not a bill was harmful to unions.

Meanwhile, business interest groups had been rallying support for amendments to the Wagner Act that would strengthen employers' ability to resist union-organizing efforts. An employer counteroffensive to union growth had been gaining strength in the 1950s. The economic downturn in 1957 combined with the growing presence of foreign competition bolstered employer efforts to resist further union gains. The U.S. Chamber of Commerce and the National Association of Manufacturers both sought legislation that would curb unions by restricting organizational picketing and banning secondary boycotts. Their efforts received support from the White House, where the Eisenhower Administration led a Republican Party committed to supporting business interests and hostile to organized labor.

For these groups, the McClellan Committee hearings represented an opportunity to achieve their legislative goals. As one member of the Chamber of Commerce observed, "The McClellan hearings gave us the train to ride on; they were the bulldozer clearing the path." In particular, the McClellan Committee hearings provided the public with a powerful new symbol of the danger presented by union power, in the form of James R. Hoffa and his apparently corrupt administration of the nation's largest union, the Teamsters. Congressmen invoked Hoffa's name in their legislative proposals. For example, Senator John F. Kennedy, who had served on the McClellan Committee, told Congress that his proposed bill would "stop those practices [upon] which, based upon the testimony before our committee, it would appear Mr. Hoffa's career and power are based— and will in short, virtually put Mr. Hoffa and his associates out of business."

Key provisions of the Landrum-Griffin Act reflected the ways in which anti-union forces seized the opportunity provided by the McClellan Committee hearings by placing new legal barriers in the path of union-organizing efforts. In particular, it imposed restrictions on using pickets in organizing efforts, and it closed a loophole that had allowed the continued use of secondary boycotts, a practice that the Taft-Hartley Act (1947) had attempted to end.

But many other aspects of the bill had little to do with the priorities of business groups; instead, these provisions regulated union governance in the interest of protecting the democratic process within labor organizations. Business groups had feared that such proposals might justify similar new regulations on corporate governance; moreover, an empowered rank and file could encourage union militancy. But Senator John L. McClellan, whose committee had helped create the opportunity for this legislation, championed these union governance proposals. He depicted the effort to empower union members as a kind of voluntarist solution both to the problem of union corruption and to the growing power of organized labor.

Members would police their own organizations by booting corrupt officials out of power. And an empowered membership would restrict the authority available to union leaders, thus offering a natural break in the aggregation of power by individuals such as Hoffa.

To achieve this goal, Landrum-Griffin sought to protect union democracy by setting up new standards for union governance. It drew on the revelations of the McClellan Committee to impose new regulations on union officeholders. The law specified that union officers held a position of fiduciary trust with regard to their members. Legally, this meant that actions in violation of that trust, for instance, misappropriation of union funds or engaging in conflicts of interest, were now violations of federal law. Certain persons were now barred from holding union office. Individuals convicted of certain crimes, including murder, assault, and extortion, were banned from holding union office for a period of 13 years. The law also barred anyone "who is or has been a member of the Communist Party." It was decreed that unions must make their finances transparent. Officers were required to file annual public reports on the internal finances of their organizations, including information on the officers' salaries. Finally, a number of provisions sought to guarantee democratic union elections. New guidelines regulated election procedures and provided avenues for appeal in cases of intimidation or fraud. The law created a "Bill of Rights of Members of Labor Organizations" that protected members' ability to speak out on union affairs and guarded them against unfair disciplinary action.

Union leaders at the time argued strongly against these union governance proposals, claiming that they would hamstring effective union government. But the initial predictions that the law would foster instability by encouraging frequent turnover in union officeholders have not been borne out over time. Instead, critics have frequently argued that the law has not offered enough help to insurgent movements within unions. Thus, although the law proved helpful to reform efforts in the United Mine Workers Union in the early 1970s, insurgents in the Teamsters Union had less success in using the law to unseat their leadership. Ironically, the law designed to put Hoffa out of business had little impact on him or his union in subsequent years.

DAVID WITWER

References and Further Reading

Bellace, James R., and Alan D. Berkowitz. *The Landrum-Griffin Act: Twenty Years of Federal Protection of Union Members' Rights.* Philadelphia: Industrial Research Unit, The Wharton School, University of Pennsylvania, 1979.
Lee, R. Alton. *Eisenhower and Landrum-Griffin: A Study in Labor-Management Politics.* Lexington: University Press of Kentucky, 1990.
McAdams, Alan K. *Power and Politics in Labor Legislation.* New York: Columbia University Press, 1964.
Witwer, David. *Corruption and Reform in the Teamsters Union.* Urbana: University of Illinois Press, 2003.

See also **Hoffa, James R.; McClellan Committee Hearings; Organized Crime**

LAUNDRY

Laundry workers have always done some of the hardest and most necessary work in society. Nevertheless, laundry work has almost always been considered a low-skilled, menial job ideally suited to women, often women of color. The term "laundry worker" hides a multitude of tasks and identities. "Laundry worker" has been used to refer to laundresses or washerwomen who washed clothes and flatwork (sheets, tablecloths, and other flat pieces) by hand in private homes; steam or power laundry workers who labored in highly mechanized industrial settings; Chinese hand laundry workers who operated small neighborhood laundries; and industrial or linen supply laundry workers who cleaned linens, uniforms, and newly manufactured garments. The post-World War II popularity of dry cleaning and coin-operated laundries expanded the category to include new groups of workers. Although working conditions have varied considerably across time and place, laundry workers have almost always earned abysmally low wages, and at no time in history have a majority of the workers labored under the protection of union contracts.

Pre-Industrial Laundry Work

The occupation of laundress has deep roots in European culture. In pre-industrial Europe, laundresses washed garments by trampling them underfoot in a tub or shallow stream or by pounding them with a wooden bat or against rocks at the edge of a stream or well. While neither method required soap, some laundresses added a cleaning agent to the water, usually made of urine, dung, or lye. Like their European counterparts, colonial and nineteenth-century Americans with the economic means employed laundresses or domestic servants to do all or part of the family wash. In the pre-Civil War South, slaveholders often removed their female slaves from the fields to do the household laundry on the weekend. In 1870, there were close to 60,000 laundry workers in the United States. Gender ideologies associating laundry work with domesticity meant that almost all of these workers were women, significant numbers of whom were African-American.

Pre-industrial laundry required significant physical strength and endurance. Before the advent of private plumbing and urban water systems, laundresses had to collect water from springs, wells, creeks, or pumps and transport it home over what were often considerable distances. Using a stove, open hearth, or boiler, the water was boiled and transferred into wooden or galvanized washtubs, where the laundress scrubbed the pieces on a washboard or by hand. In the nineteenth century, most laundresses made their own soap and starch from lye, animal fat, and wheat bran. After rinsing the soapy garments in boiling or bluing water, the laundress rubbed boiling starch into the shirts, linens, and other pieces that had to be ironed. Excess water was squeezed out with a small hand-cranked wringing machine that pressed the articles between two parallel rubber rolls or by hand. Using heavy flatirons that weighed as much as 12 pounds, ironing, the final part of the job, brought no reprieve from the arduous labor involved in washing. Although by the 1850s laundresses could purchase small household tools such as wringers, the work remained hard. While many laundresses took in the washing of two or three families a week, in the nineteenth century, most laundresses earned no more than $4 to $8 a month, out of which they were expected to provide their own soap, starch, and wood.

While laundry work paid relatively little, it offered some advantages over household service work, one of the major occupational fields for women in nineteenth- century America. Unlike domestic servants who worked in their employers' homes, most laundresses worked in the privacy of their own homes, where they could set the pace of work and rely upon family members for help. Tera Hunter's study of African-American laundresses in the urban South (census data reveals that in the nineteenth century, laundresses were more numerous in the South than the North) reveals that laundresses often allocated space within their communities to do the work collectively, taking care of one another's children, pooling their resources, and engaging in community-building activities. Hunter's analysis also reveals that black laundresses engaged in acts of resistance ranging from "borrowing" their employers' garments to creating trade union-like organizations.

Industrialization and Laundry Work

By the 1860s, industrialization had created a wide divergence in how, where, and why people washed clothes for money. While the overwhelming majority of laundry workers continued to wash garments by hand at home, by the 1860s a growing number of women and men were seeking employment in one of the nation's new steam laundries (by 1920 the U.S. Census had replaced the title steam laundry with power laundry; steam and power laundries have also been called commercial laundries).

In her comparative analysis of steam laundries in the United States and Britain, Arwen Palmer Mohun argues that technological and cultural factors facilitated the growth of the laundry industry. By the late 1800s, mechanized washing machines, flatwork ironers (large ironing machines that pressed flatwork between padded rollers and steam-heated chests or cylinders), extractors (centrifugal drying machines that expelled water from clothes by spinning them at high speeds), and steam presses could wash, dry, and iron clothing and flatwork in a portion of the time it took the laundress or housewife. The earliest machines were operated by hand cranks, foot treadles, or hand levers; by the 1920s, many of the machines were operated by pushing a button. The introduction of laundry machinery facilitated the move of the work from the home to the factory, where the labor process was broken down into increasingly smaller parts, and where the site of skill was transferred from the worker to the machine.

The proliferation of washable fabrics also played an important role in the emergence of the laundry industry. The development of manufactured cloth and the growth of the ready-made clothing industry in the nineteenth century meant that for the first time, most Americans could afford to own many articles of clothing, most of which were made of cotton, a fabric that was easily washed. Growing fears about the spread of germs and new middle-class social mores that condemned the wearing of smelly or dirty clothing contributed to the demand for laundry workers, and for new methods of laundering. Between 1860 and 1890, the number of laundry workers (both hand and steam) in the United States jumped from 38,633 to 246,739, a more than 600% increase.

Carole Turbin's examination of Troy, New York, the capital of the nation's shirt, collar, and cuff industry, and home to some of the nation's first steam laundries, reveals the impact that mechanization would have on the American laundry worker. In the mid-1800s, collar laundries in Troy typically employed 20 to 30 women who washed, starched, and ironed collars and cuffs by hand. Because the work required familiarity with different ironing techniques and starching, as well as manual dexterity, Troy's laundry workers were considered highly skilled. As skilled workers, the women, the vast majority of whom were Irish, were among the first women laundry workers in the United States to establish formal trade unions. Under the able leadership of Kate Mullaney, in 1864, the women organized the Troy Collar Laundry Union and within a year had increased wages from $2 to $3 a week to $8 to $12. The activities of Troy's laundry workers challenged widely held beliefs that women made poor trade unionists.

In an attempt to increase productivity and reduce their reliance on women's traditional skills, as the nineteenth century progressed, Troy's collar laundry owners implemented ironing and starching machines and cut wages. Mechanization was accompanied by an increased division of labor, and the women found themselves confined to one part of the laundering process. Once considered skilled workers, mechanization transformed the women into machine tenders who could be easily replaced.

Laundry Workers at the Turn of the Twentieth Century

Although until 1909, the U.S. Census aggregated hand and steam laundry workers, evidence suggests that in 1900, the vast majority of the nation's 385,000 laundry workers were still employed in private homes. As before, the majority of the workers were women. Between 1870 and 1910, women composed between 87% and 99% of the nation's laundry workforce. Census data reveal that laundry workers were on average older than women employed in most other occupations and were more likely to be married. As work that could be done at home using home-based skills, laundry work attracted women with families, who were able to combine paid work with domestic responsibilities such as child care.

Laundry work was not only gendered, it was also racialized. Between 1890 and 1910, approximately two thirds of the nation's laundry workers were African-American; in the southern United States, close to 90% of the region's laundry workers were black. Laundry work ranked third in importance in the employment of black women, preceded only by agricultural laborers and servants and waitresses. Conversely, relatively few native white women of native parentage were employed as laundry workers. In 1900, 2.4% of these women were employed as laundry workers, compared to 19.2% of all wage-earning African-American women. Of the approximately 75,000 women laundry workers of foreign parentage (many of whom were also of foreign birth), the predominant groups were Irish and German. Evidence suggests that at the turn of the twentieth century,

steam laundry jobs were open only to white women of native or foreign birth.

Alongside the more than 300,000 women employed as laundry workers in 1900, 50,000 men worked as launderers, half of whom were Chinese. Racially discriminatory hiring practices and exclusionary trade union tactics confined Chinese men to low-paying service work traditionally performed by women. Many of the laundries run by Chinese men were referred to as hand laundries, small, neighborhood businesses where clothes were washed and ironed by hand. By the 1910s, hand laundries (which by this time could be found in most large cities except those in the South) used either a combination of hand methods and electric appliances to wash the clothes on site, or sent them out to be washed in a steam laundry, after which they were returned to the hand laundry for ironing. Throughout the twentieth century, hand laundries remained small-scale establishments, often consisting of little more than two or three rooms where the owner and a few paid employees lived and worked. Although most hand laundry workers labored between 10 and 16 hours a day in hot, wet, and steamy conditions, wages were typically low.

The Ascendancy of Power Laundries, 1900–1950

While a relatively small number of cities had steam laundries as early as the 1850s, it was not until the early 1900s that the power laundry industry really took off. The dirt and grime that accompanied urban industrial living, the increased number of people living in apartments (many of which provided no washing facilities), the rising numbers of women working outside the home, and the decreased availability of household servants fueled the expansion of the industry at the turn of the century. In 1909, the first year in which steam laundries appeared in the census, 5,186 establishments employed close to 125,000 workers (called laundry operatives), over two thirds of whom were women. The steam laundry was one of the few industries in which the number of female employees exceeded that of males. The growth in the power laundry industry did not lead to the immediate elimination of hand laundering. In 1910, half a million laundry workers continued to work in private homes, using hand methods or an electrically operated washing machine. Thirty years later, the ratio between steam and hand laundry workers had reversed. By 1939, approximately 7,000 power laundries employed 249,000 workers, close to two thirds of whom were women. Conversely, by the 1950s, only

75,512 laundry workers labored outside of commercial laundries.

In the early 1900s, power laundries could be found in every state of the union. They were, however, most numerous in large cities such as New York and San Francisco, and were less common in the South where technological developments lagged and where the abundance of poorly paid black washerwomen acted as a disincentive to industrialization. As an industrial job, increasing numbers of both native white women and men entered into the laundry trades. By 1930, 30% of the nation's power laundry workers were men, and over one half of the women were native white. Power laundries were also one of the first industries to employ significant numbers of African-American women. By 1930, close to 50,000, or one-third, of the nation's female power laundry workers were black, and an additional 10,000 African-American men were employed in power laundries. A U.S. Department of Labor Women's Bureau survey found that four in five power laundry workers in the South were African-American. In cities such as New York and Chicago, most power laundries had ethnically and racially diverse workforces. As in the nineteenth century, laundry work continued to be done by women who were on average older than women employed in other industries and who were more likely to be married.

Most power laundries were relatively small operations employing between 20 and 50 workers. In their early years, power laundries received the bulk of their business from commercial establishments such as hotels, and from the laundering of men's shirts. To increase sales from families, in the 1910s power laundry owners implemented cheaper semifinished services such as wet wash, in which garments were washed, but not dried or ironed. The wet-wash family bundle was a huge hit. By the 1940s, approximately half of the commercial laundry business came in the form of family service work.

In addition to power laundries that catered primarily to families and individuals, institutions such as hospitals and hotels sometimes built their own laundries. Linen supply and industrial laundries provided and laundered (usually on a rental basis) linens such as work uniforms, towels, bed linens and protective apparel to service, industrial, and government users. Alongside power laundries, in the early 1900s, in New York, Baltimore, and a number of other cities, social reformers and public health officials constructed public laundries where the poor could wash their clothing at a fraction of the cost of a commercial laundry.

In commercial laundries, approximately three quarters of the employees were productive workers, defined as workers engaged in the actual laundering process. Under this broad heading fell the markers, washers, dryers, flatwork ironers, press operators, starchers, sorters, and checkers. Men were employed as washers and dryers, while women performed all the other jobs, usually composing over two thirds of all productive workers. Markers undid the soiled articles, marked them, and sent them to the washroom, where washers placed the articles into large cylinder washing machines. Next, garments were sent to the extractors or dryers, while sheets, pillow cases, and other flat pieces went to the flatwork department, where workers fed the pieces into moving rollers. At the other side of the machine, a group of workers caught and folded the hot, freshly ironed pieces. Flatwork ironing, which usually employed the largest group of women workers, was described as one of the hottest and hardest jobs in the industry. Articles that could not be handled by the flatwork machines, such as shirts or suits, went to the pressers or shirt finishers, who ironed the pieces on pressing machines. A small laundry would likely have a few general, multipurpose presses, while large laundries would have dozens of specialized pressing machines. In the early 1900s, starchers starched by hand or machine collars or other such pieces. Many laundries also employed hand washers or ironers to handle delicate pieces that could not be put through the machines. Finally, sorters or checkers collected all the articles and packaged them for return to the customer. Not all laundry workers were productive workers. Nonproductive workers included routemen or drivers (who delivered laundry and engaged in sales work), repair maintenance or mechanical workers, office workers, and foremen. With the exception of office workers and sometimes foremen, most of these workers were male.

While the use of power-operated machinery increased daily output, it did not significantly lessen the workload, as power laundry workers spent long hours operating heavy presses and carrying bundles of heavy clothing in a hot, wet, and noisy working environment. As many of the machines lacked proper safety guards, mechanized laundry work was also extremely dangerous; workers regularly burned their fingers on the machines or chemicals, or worse, got a finger, hand, or arm caught in one of the revolving rollers or extractors. Unlike laundresses, who were usually self-regulated, in an industrial setting, laundry workers had to contend with the direct supervision of the owner or foreman, frequent speedups, and excessively long working hours. In 1909, 75% of the nation's power laundry operatives worked 54 hours or more a week. Despite laws prohibiting women from working more than 10 hours a day (the constitutionality of which was upheld by the Supreme Court in 1908 in the famous *Muller v. Oregon* decision involving an Oregon laundry owner), 12- and 13-hour days were common.

Tainted by its association with women's domestic labor, power laundry work quickly became one of the lowest-paying industrial jobs. In the early 1900s, many workers earned as little as $3 or $4 a week. Labor investigations reveal that there were significant wage differentials between workers. Like most industries of this period, the laundry was organized along racial and patriarchal lines, with black women confined to the lowest-paying jobs of flatwork ironing and pressing, while men were employed as washers, drivers, and mechanical workers, the highest-paying jobs. A 1930 Women's Bureau survey found that median earnings for white women laundry workers were $16.10 a week, and for black women workers $8.85 a week.

Laundry Unions and Legislation, 1900–1960s

In 1900, in Troy, New York, the American Federation of Labor (AFL) chartered the first international union of laundry workers, the Shirt, Waist and Laundry Workers' International Union. With jurisdiction over all the workers involved in the making and laundering of shirts and collars (the union never tried to organize home laundry workers), the new union quickly spread to San Francisco, where in 1901 a group of workers organized a local of 1,000 laundry workers. Although the majority of laundry workers were women, most of the union's leaders were men, and union contracts tended to institutionalize existing sex-based wage differentials. In 1909, the AFL limited membership in the union to those engaged in laundry work and changed the union's name to the Laundry Workers' International Union (LWIU). Drivers were to be organized separately by the AFL-affiliated International Brotherhood of Teamsters. By 1930, the LWIU had only 6,000 members, and most of its locals were disorganized and poorly funded. Wages in the industry remained low and working conditions bad.

The New Deal ushered in the first national effort to regulate laundry workers' hours and wages. Under the National Industrial Recovery Act (NIRA), in 1934, a nationwide laundry code established a maximum 40-hour workweek (with an allowance of overtime) and minimum hourly rates of pay that varied according to three population groups and five geographic regions. Rates were set lowest in the South, where in many places a 14-cent hourly wage was established, and highest in Boston, New York, Los Angeles, and San Francisco, where a 30-cent rate was established. As most of the workers in the South were African-American, the code formalized existing wage differentials across racial lines. In 1938, like other service workers, laundry workers were exempted from the Fair Labor Standards Act (FLSA), which established minimum working conditions for workers in interstate production. It was not until 1967 that amendments to the FLSA finally brought laundry and dry-cleaning workers under its umbrella, establishing a minimum wage of $1 per hour, in many places well below a living wage.

The New Deal labor legislation with the most impact on laundry workers was the 1935 National Labor Relations Act (Wagner Act), which granted workers the right to organize and bargain collectively. The mid-1930s witnessed a wave of strikes and organizational activities among laundry workers across the country. By 1950, the LWIU had over 50,000 members and was no longer the only major union organizing laundry workers in the country. In 1937, laundry workers in New York City withdrew from the AFL-affiliated LWIU and affiliated with the Amalgamated Clothing Workers of America (ACWA), one of the founding Congress of Industrial Organizations' (CIO) unions. By 1941, almost all of NYC's approximately 30,000 laundry workers, significant numbers of whom were African-American, were organized under the ACWA. The new union secured major wage increases and established a health center and benefit fund for its members. Outside of New York City, Washington, and Detroit, most of the workers continued to organize under the AFL-affiliated Laundry and Dry Cleaning Workers' International Union (LDCIU), and in 1947, an estimated 30% to 40% of laundry workers labored under collective bargaining agreements. Unionized workers were concentrated in large cities in the Pacific region, Northeast, and Middle Atlantic. In the South, most laundry workers remained outside the trade union fold.

In 1957, the AFL-CIO expelled the LDCIU and its approximately 75,000 members on corruption charges and a year later chartered the Laundry, Dry Cleaning and Dye House Workers International Union (LDDIU). In 1961, 128,000 or 23%, of the workers in the laundry and dry-cleaning industry were covered by contract under the LDCIU, the LDDIU, or the ACWA. Most of the organized workers continued to be located in large cities in the Middle Atlantic, East North Central, and Pacific regions of the country.

The Laundry Industry and Laundry Unions, 1960–2004

By the 1960s, the laundry and dry-cleaning industry had become one of the major service industries in the United States. Well over half a million workers, two thirds of whom were women, were employed in power laundries (catering to families), linen supply and industrial laundries, hand laundries, diaper service laundries, dry-cleaning businesses, rug cleaning plants, cleaning and pressing establishments, laundry and garment service plants, and coin-operated laundries. In the 1960s, the rapid proliferation of coin-operated laundries, new fabrics which required little or no ironing, and improved and affordable home washing and drying machines forced power laundries to diversify and offer new services such as dry cleaning, carpet cleaning, and alterations. Many power laundries also implemented labor-saving technologies such as automated wash systems and automatic flatwork processing machines. While power laundries struggled to maintain sales, in the 1960s and 1970s, industrial and linen supply laundries capitalized on the increased construction of hospitals and nursing homes, institutions that produced large amounts of laundry. In the 1960s, laundry workers continued to be among the lowest-paid workers in the country. In 1961, gross average hourly earnings of workers in laundry and dry-cleaning plants were $1.27, compared with $1.70 for workers in the retail trade and $1.49 for workers in general merchandise stores.

By 1987, of the approximately 400,000 workers employed in the laundry, dry-cleaning, and garment service industry, close to two thirds of whom were women, only 33,180 were employed in power laundries, compared with 45,416 workers in coin-operated laundries and a little over 100,000 in linen supply or industrial laundries. The largest group of workers in the industry now worked in dry-cleaning establishments, establishments that employed more men than women. In the 1960s, 1970s, and 1980s, most power laundry workers continued to labor in relatively small plants that employed around 20 employees, while linen supply and industrial laundry workers were employed in larger plants that were often part of multi-unit chains. In the 1990s, the largest private industrial laundering companies in the United States were California's Aratex, the National Linen of Atlanta, and Cintas, a uniform supply outfit headquartered in Cincinnati, Ohio. At the turn of the twenty-first century, many laundry workers employed in the public sector saw their jobs outsourced to private companies such as Cintas.

At the end of the twentieth century, laundry workers across the nation complained of poverty wages, dangerous and oppressive working conditions, and inadequate benefits. Workers described being forced to work in sweltering plants, denied water or bathroom breaks, and being forced to handle bloody sheets with little to no sanitary protection. Women earned less than men, who continued to work as washers and drivers. In cities such as New York and Washington, Hispanic workers, some of whom were undocumented, joined the already large numbers of black workers in the laundry industry. At the turn of the twenty-first century, undocumented Mexican immigrants were found working 72 hours a week in NYC laundries for as little as $3.00 or $4.00 an hour (in violation of minimum wage laws).

By the end of the 1990s, laundry and dry-cleaning workers in the United States were represented by the Union of Needletrades, Industrial and Textile Employees union (UNITE), an AFL-CIO-affiliated international union representing workers in apparel, textile, and industrial laundries, and by the LDCIU (then affiliated with the Service Employees International Union). With only 8,000 members across the country, in 1998, UNITE began a massive campaign to organize the nation's industrial laundry workers. In November 1998, nearly 3,000 National Linen laundry workers in the South voted to join UNITE. Sparked by low wages, unaffordable health insurance, and unfair treatment, in the late 1990s, laundry workers in NYC, Baltimore, Washington, Chicago, and a host of other cities went on strike and secured what were in many instances groundbreaking contracts (including features such as immigrant rights protection and protection against sexual harassment). In April 2001, the nearly 9,000 members of the LDCIU voted to affiliate with UNITE, bringing the total number of laundry workers in UNITE up to almost 40,000, representing 90% of the unionized laundry workers in the United States.

In 2004, UNITE-HERE (UNITE merged with the Hotel Employees and Restaurant Employees International Union in 2004) began a major organizing effort among the mostly unorganized workers in the uniform laundry industry. With over 27,000 employees, in 2005, Cintas was the largest uniform rental provider and industrial launderer in North America, and, according to UNITE-HERE, was responsible for keeping wages low and working conditions bad in the industry. In 2003, current and former Cintas employees filed class-action charges with the Equal Employment Opportunity Commission, alleging widespread discrimination against people of color and women in hiring and promotion policies, job assignments, and work environment. Despite the efforts of

UNITE-HERE and the nation's laundry workers, in the early twenty-first century, many laundry workers continued to labor under highly exploitative conditions without union protection.

JENNY CARSON

References and Further Reading

Best, Ethel L., and Ethel Erickson. *A Survey of Laundries and Their Women Workers in 23 Cities.* United States Department of Labor, Women's Bureau. Bulletin no.78. Washington, DC: Government Printing Office, 1930.

Cowan, Ruth Schwartz. *More Work for Mother: The Ironies of Household Technology from the Open Hearth to the Microwave.* New York: Basic Books, 1983.

Hunter, Tera. *To 'Joy My Freedom: Southern Black Women's Lives and Labors after the Civil War.* Cambridge, MA: Harvard University Press, 1997.

Jones, Jacqueline. *Labor of Love, Labor of Sorrow: Black Women, Work, and the Family, from Slavery to the Present.* New York: Vintage Books, 1995.

Malcolmson, Patricia E. *English Laundresses: A Social History, 1850–1930.* Urbana: University of Illinois Press, 1986.

Mohun, Arwen P. *Steam Laundries: Gender, Technology, and Work in the United States and Great Britain, 1880–1940.* Baltimore: Johns Hopkins University Press, 1999.

Siu, Paul C. P. *The Chinese Laundryman: A Study of Social Isolation.* New York: New York University Press, 1987.

Turbin, Carole. *Working Women of Collar City: Gender, Class, and Community in Troy, New York, 1864–86.* Urbana: University of Illinois Press, 1992.

See also **African-Americans; Amalgamated Clothing Workers of America; Atlanta Washerwomen's Strike (1881); Domestic Service; Fair Labor Standards Act; Gender; Housework; Minimum-Wage Laws; National Industrial Recovery Act; National Labor Relations Board; Springer, Maida**

LAW AND LABOR

Law has profoundly shaped the experience of American workers both individually and collectively. Since the first European settlement of North America, an array of rules has governed the employer's authority, the labor market, workplace conditions, social insurance, equal employment, and perhaps most significantly, the legitimacy of protest. Given coherence by the status of its subjects rather than by a specific form or jurisdiction, the set of regulations we call "labor law" crosses traditional legal boundaries, touching on contracts, torts, association, antitrust, criminal law, regulation, and civil rights. Throughout this history, the state confronted workers most spectacularly during strikes, boycotts, and other disputes. Yet, in some periods, the law governing employment focused less on class conflict than on the free movement of labor, the health and welfare of workers, and the rights of employees.

During the last four centuries, this mix of traditions, judicial precedents, statutes, and administrative interpretations traced an arc from the oppressively paternalistic laws governing colonial servitude to the free-labor precedents of the antebellum era, from the reactionary rulings of late nineteenth-century judges to the relatively proworker regulatory legislation of the twentieth century. Rather than evolving steadily, law changed dialectically, first strengthening employer authority, and then eroding traditional bonds; constructing new worker rights, and then weakening those protections.

Law profoundly influenced the trajectory of the American labor movement. The state's harshness alienated workers, severing organized labor's roots in antebellum reform and making its leaders skeptical toward the government. Only during the Great Depression, when lawmakers appealed to labor by guaranteeing the right to organize, did union workers fully embrace the law as a vehicle for improving their condition. Though labor's marriage to the state forced workers to suppress their most radical tendencies, the relationship proved fruitful into the 1970s, when an increasingly hostile government sped a decline in union fortunes.

Though the law gradually ceased supporting collective action, the government continued to shape the workplace in powerful ways into the twenty-first century. In particular, the civil rights legislation enacted between the 1965 and 2000 promised workers fair treatment regardless of race, creed, sex, or physical impediment. Such laws offered employees significant benefits, but required them to petition the government as individuals, not as members of a broader class.

Colonial governments of the seventeenth and eighteenth centuries regulated work by applying European (primarily British) precedents to the novel circumstances they found in North America. The colonies inherited long-standing doctrines giving masters authority over their employees. Moreover, while the shortage of labor in the colonies could have empowered workers, it instead led employers to use the law to secure their control over human capital. Thus, a large percentage of American settlers worked under some form of legal coercion, either as indented servants, as sailors, or as slaves.

At first, the hazards of settlement prompted harsh laws compelling workers to labor. In 1612, the Virginia governor, Sir Thomas Dale, implemented "Laws Divine, Morall and Martial," which punished idle colonists by forcing them to lie all night with neck and heels together. Repeat offenders could be whipped and eventually sent to a year's service in English galleys. As the colonies grew more secure, they adopted the more moderate British common law, but the courts still reserved harsh sentences for recalcitrant servants and slaves.

For the most part, colonial laws neither stipulated, nor enforced, specific codes regulating the workplace, but rather guaranteed the authority of the master and defined his responsibilities to his servants. The loose principle underlying such rules was paternalism. The law used the family as a metaphor for the workplace, identifying the employer as father and the employees as his offspring. By this logic, the law obliged servants to obey their master's will as the Bible commanded children to honor their parents. The government granted masters the right to physically punish refractory servants, and constables assisted employers seeking to recover runaway apprentices. In return, the law required the employer to provide room and adequate food for the worker. Economic realities seemed to affirm the familial analogy, as many employees were young, worked for blood relatives, and lived and labored in their master's home. Yet, the law of master and servant offered workers little protection, obliging the employer to provide only minimal provision for his employees. Without the emotional bonds that stilled the parent's switch and filled the child's bowl, many servants found paternalism miserable rather than comfortable.

For white workers, this wretched dependency was both temporary and contractual. Servants (or their parents acting on their behalf) consented to their condition by signing indenture papers and offering bonds against their disobedience. In return for years of toil, apprentices received training and access to a trade. Some indentured servants labored to repay the cost of their passage from Europe. Others were teenage girls, who worked for their keep while awaiting marriage. Sailors submitted to more extreme discipline than ordinary servants, but received wages and served only for a much shorter time.

By contrast, colonial law denied slaves brought from Africa the protections afforded by time-limited contracts. Because slaves did not negotiate legal agreements with their masters, their rights were subject to the continual depredation of legislatures. Beginning in 1661, colonies like Virginia expanded the master's authority, making enslavement a permanent inheritable condition and slaves a form of salable property. Laws gave the master the almost absolute right to punish his slaves as he saw fit, reserving only the power of execution to the state.

The law further bolstered slavery by enforcing severe punishments for resistance. When New York City slaves rebelled in 1712, killing nine whites, courts ordered the execution of 21 insurrectionists by burning and the wheel. Moreover, such protests often encouraged newly repressive laws. After the 1739 Stono rebellion, South Carolina enacted the severe "Negro Act," which barred slaves from growing their own food, assembling in groups, earning their own money, or learning to read.

Though the War of Independence promised law more favorable to the laborer, the new republic quickly disappointed workers. Thousands of journeymen, sailors, apprentices, and slaves had fought on the colonial side, inspired by the rhetoric of social upheaval and democracy. Yet, the new government denied the franchise to men without property, while expecting these workers to pay for the war through excise taxes. The Constitution of 1787 not only greatly strengthened the position of creditors, but also guaranteed the slaveholder's right to human property.

Most significantly, early American courts reimplemented the common law, defying those workers who hoped the revolution might sweep away the oppressive vestiges of British rule. Early national magistrates not only guaranteed masters their traditional legal authority over servants, but also enforced employer control. Sheriffs routinely jailed irresponsible sailors, runaway apprentices, and fugitive slaves pending the return of their masters.

Courts also used common law to suppress the earliest American labor unions. In England, the doctrine of conspiracy had long prohibited journeymen from organizing. Though guilds and corporations could obtain charters from the crown granting specific rights and duties, independent journeymen's associations were seen as threats to the authority of the sovereign. Over the angry denunciations of workers, who felt the First Amendment to the Constitution guaranteed freedom of association, early American courts applied this principle to unions. The first such trial, *Commonwealth v. Pullis*, occurred in 1806, when the Philadelphia court convicted journeymen cordwainers (that is, shoemakers) on charges of conspiracy for seeking higher wages. Referencing British common law, the presiding judge, Recorder Moses Levy, condemned the defendants as dangerous outlaws. Later verdicts in cities like New York, Boston, and Pittsburgh affirmed this notion.

In the 1830s, three main factors—the market revolution, the establishment of universal white male suffrage, and the construction of a transformative liberal ideology— combined to shatter the common-law rules governing work in the North. Improvements in transportation, the specialization of labor, and the introduction of machinery eroded the economic basis for paternalism. Manufactories employing bands of independent operatives replaced master craftsmen with dependent apprentices and journeymen boarding in their households. As white workers won the vote, they demanded the courts cease harassing their unions. And finally, with the rise of the antislavery movement, many Americans questioned the contradictions between Enlightenment individualism and traditional forms of authority.

Influenced by these forces, northern judges began undermining paternalism and offering workers an ambiguous new freedom. The foremost figure in this transformation was Lemuel Shaw, the chief justice of the Massachusetts Supreme Court. A Whig dedicated to market liberalism, Shaw made the worker's consent the basis for the labor agreement. Moreover, Shaw's rulings replaced asymmetrical relationships based on status, such as master and servant, with legally enforceable contracts between officially equal parties. Such decisions denied not only the master's special authority over his servant, but also the employer's responsibility to care for his employees. Finally, Shaw proposed abstract rules to govern these contracts and the rights of the individuals who made them.

In the year 1842, Shaw rendered two judgments that redefined antebellum labor law: *Farwell v. Boston & Worcester Railroad Co.* and *Commonwealth v. Hunt*. The *Farwell* decision is best known for limiting the employer's responsibility for workplace accidents, but it also enunciated Shaw's notion of the wage bargain as a contract between equal partners. The plaintiff, a railroad engineer, sued his employer after a switchman's negligence resulted in an accident that left Farwell's hand crushed. Shaw ruled in favor of the defendant, holding that the employer's liability for accidents was not implicit in the labor contract. Farwell might win damages from his "fellow servant," but not from the railroad, which was responsible only for mishaps caused by its overt neglect. Shaw further ruled that workers assumed the risks of employment upon accepting work. Employees who deemed a job dangerous might either demand higher wages, seek a contract explicitly indemnifying the employer, or quit. The Farwell decision thus also enunciated the principle of employment at will, which gave workers and businesses the equal right to make and terminate labor contracts.

Shaw's second key ruling, *Commonwealth v. Hunt*, also affirmed employment at will, this time giving workers the right to strike to protest labor conditions. The case arose when members of the Boston Society of Journeymen Bootmakers left their jobs, refusing to work alongside Jeremiah Horne, a former associate suspended for violating union rules. A jury convicted the society's members, including John Hunt, of criminal conspiracy. But what the trial judge saw as an unlawful boycott, threatening to the peace and welfare of the community, Shaw interpreted as men exercising their constitutionally protected freedom of association. Denying the master's right to compel labor and affirming the worker's right to quit, Shaw could only view strikes as mere agglomerations of lawful individual decisions. By this logic, the bootmakers' union was no different from the fire companies, temperance societies, and party organizations that constituted the primary mode of self-improvement and political participation for millions in the Jacksonian Era.

While Shaw overturned Hunt's conviction, he did not give unions free rein. Rather, he subjected associations to a rigorous "means-ends" test. Workers could coordinate walkouts as long as their practices and goals were legal. Strikers could exercise their freedoms of contract and association by withholding their labor until they received a specific wage. But unionists could neither use threats, force, or violence (unlawful means), nor seek to injure an employer or nonunion worker (an unlawful end) through otherwise legitimate economic pressure. In essence, Shaw sought to make the conspiracy doctrine consistent with the Bill of Rights, while channeling collective protest into what he saw as socially productive forms.

These two decisions had a profound, if mixed, effect on workers. Shaw liberated Massachusetts laborers from the burdens of obedience imposed by master and servant law. Under employment at will, the state could no longer imprison employees who declined to fulfill their labor agreements. Shaw legalized the strike, offering labor unions a legitimate means of raising their members' wages. Yet, Shaw also eradicated the protections that paternalism had offered servants and greatly reduced the employer's implied responsibilities to his employees. Shaw left laborers liable for the exploding number of workplace accidents. Workers were free to quit but still financially responsible for the damages they caused by breaking contracts. And while the means-ends test legalized the wage strike, it barred a range of other union tactics, such as picketing and boycotts.

During and after the Civil War, lawmakers applied the principles of market liberalism to new regions and expanded their meaning for the American worker. But doctrines that had freed antebellum laborers increasingly confined the workers of the late-nineteenth century. The employee's formal equality in court merely accommodated the employer's superior power to set the terms of labor contracts. Moreover, the war initiated an economic transformation that only increased the scale, scope, and technological sophistication of American enterprise. Laborers quickly found themselves free either to accept corporate terms, or to starve.

Workers in the former Confederacy found the end of paternalism liberating but not entirely emancipatory. With the end of slavery, the authors of Reconstruction sought to replace the old regime with a contractual scheme of northern origin. But the balance of power that emerged during Reconstruction greatly favored employers, for the new system offered freedpeople few special protections in acknowledgment of their poverty. Moreover, the white "redeemer" governments of the 1870s and 1880s further skewed the scales by passing laws restricting the southern worker's ability to exploit his market value. Legislatures enacted statutes barring vagrancy, seeking to tie workers to their old masters. They made laws prohibiting northern agents from recruiting workers, protecting southern employers from the pressures of the national labor market. Southern states used the criminal law to maintain a pool of coerced labor, sending poor whites and blacks to chain gangs and prison farms for petty offenses including debt and breach of contract. And looming over all was the threat of white violence, which discouraged not only African-American protest, but also dissent, and even hard negotiation.

During the late-nineteenth century, labor law became increasingly pre-occupied with unions and worker protest. The law itself had provided a major impetus for the development of the labor movement. Beginning in the 1870s, workers bitterly dissented not against the degradation of their skill wrought by the second industrial revolution, but also the eclipse of antebellum republicanism, which had promised white male producers control over American government. As railroads, refiners, and manufacturers came to dominate the Gilded Age political system, unions like the Knights of Labor grew rapidly, promising to build a "cooperative commonwealth" that recognized workers' rights.

Rather than accommodating this political dissent, the post-Reconstruction state acted to suppress the emerging movement. Faced with unprecedented worker activism, public officials concluded that normal legal institutions were insufficient to maintain the social order, and they asked the army to crush strikes. In 1877, for instance, President Rutherford Hayes called on troops to suppress "The Great Upheaval," a nationwide railroad walkout. Firing indiscriminately into crowds of protesters, soldiers killed over 30 workers. Though politicians were generally reluctant to deploy the military in this fashion, federal troops or state militias crushed a number of major uprisings, including the Homestead Steel strike of 1892 and the Pullman boycott of 1894.

As workers adopted more aggressive methods and radical goals, they ran headlong into the conspiracy doctrine enunciated in *Commonwealth v. Hunt* (1842), which still barred boycotts or strikes designed to punish an employer. Moreover, many state legislatures superseded common law by passing criminal conspiracy statutes not only defining many forms of collective protest as unlawful, but also making union officials criminally liable for the actions of their constituents. Labor leaders found themselves subject to regular criminal conspiracy indictments, trials, fines, and imprisonment.

Most significant, Gilded Age unions had to overcome court orders restraining picketing, some strikes, and even speech itself. Before the Civil War, injunctions were uncommon; courts expected businesses injured by workers to either sue for damages or file a criminal complaint. Judges reserved their equity jurisdiction—the term for their authority to issue writs—for cases involving imminent and irreparable harm, such as the felling of an ancient tree.

Yet, late-nineteenth-century employers increasingly viewed traditional criminal and civil remedies as insufficient. Criminal trials were slow, and juries were sympathetic to labor. Suing a union for damages proved nearly impossible, for unincorporated unions had no legal standing in a court of law. They could neither sue, nor be sued, except in the name of their individual members, most of whom had few financial resources. Charging that labor's legal incapacity made it impossible to seek redress through normal means, employers asked the court issue injunctions barring strikers from committing any act that might damage their trade or property.

Courts eagerly embraced these arguments, enjoining innumerable strikers over the course of the following decades. Painting themselves as defending civilization against barbarism, judges wrote expansive orders, barring even speech encouraging protest or educating the public about labor disputes. Additionally, judges often considered employers' complaints ex parte, that is, without evaluating the union's side of the story. Finally, judges often fined and jailed violators for contempt upon the mere allegations of the plaintiff. Thus, unions found themselves subject to serious punishments without any of the normal protections constitutionally guaranteed to criminal defendants, such as trial by jury.

The combination of indictment and injunction seriously hampered labor activism. The constant threat of prosecution restrained union ambitions, and the costs of defending members drained union treasuries. Courts played an active role in suppressing the most dramatic protests of the era, especially the Pullman boycott of 1894. When members of Eugene Debs's

American Railway Union decided to honor striking workers at the Pullman Palace Car Company by demanding their employers uncouple Pullman sleepers from trains, federal courts sprung into action. Claiming authority under the Interstate Commerce Act of 1887—a recent law intended to regulate the power of railroad corporations—judges issued injunctions prohibiting continued protest and then jailed violators for contempt of court. Debs himself received a six-month sentence for violating a federal injunction.

Meanwhile, Gilded Age judges used their authority as interpreters of the Constitution to thwart the popular demand for legislation shielding workers from the market. Courts rejected statutes barring child labor, setting wages and hours, and ordering factory inspection, charging that these regulations interfered with a worker's right to make his or her own bargains. Such rulings radically expanded Lemuel Shaw's market liberalism, for these judges used the doctrine of "freedom of contract" not to alter common-law precedent, but to void acts of the legislature. Judges also developed new interpretations of the Fourteenth Amendment (1868), charging that regulatory legislation denied citizens their "life, liberty, and property without due process of law" while statutes giving workers special rights deprived employers of "equal protection." In the landmark case *In re Jacobs* (1885), the New York Court of Appeals used these arguments to invalidate a law barring the manufacturing of cigars in tenements, a provision meant to discourage sweatshops. Harkening back to Lincoln's free labor ideology and the powerful image of the independent artisan living in his shop, Judge Robert Earl construed the reform as an unconstitutional infringement upon the right to property.

Frustrated with such decisions, many workers abandoned their faith in government. While the Knights of Labor had lobbied for new law protecting the rights of producers, its rival, the Federation of Organized Trade and Labor Unions (later renamed the American Federation of Labor), aggressively enlisted craftsmen in trades like construction, obtained exclusive "closed shop" agreements with employers, and directly imposed their terms through strikes, boycotts, and fines. Contrary to common belief, AFL unions rejected legally enforceable contracts, asserting their own jurisdiction over the labor market, making their own private laws, and enforcing them through internal disciplinary procedures. Craft unions rooted their power in the skill and loyalty of their members, competing with, rather than capitulating to, the state. In doing so, they solved a problem long plaguing unions, namely, how to maintain a labor agreement without relying upon hostile courts.

Though private governance—often misleadingly termed "voluntarism" or "business unionism"—allowed unions to survive, it encouraged craft labor's ugliest tendencies. The emphasis on internal discipline and market control prompted unions to exclude perceived outsiders, not only African-Americans, women, and some immigrants, but also members of competing trades. For almost a decade, beginning in 1903, the United Association of Plumbers and the International Association of Steamfitters fought a pitched jurisdictional battle over who might install steam heat in the nation's buildings. The closed shop alienated middle-class observers, who saw the private enforcement of agreements, especially when violent, as a serious threat to the social order and rule of law. Union delegates often succumbed to the immense temptation to accept bribes offered by employers seeking to circumvent work rules.

Finally, the repudiation of the state made the AFL an inconsistent partner in reformers' efforts at gaining legislation sheltering all workers. Craft unions spent much of their considerable political energy seeking either license laws for specific trades like barbering, or statutes exempting unions from antitrust prosecutions and prohibiting judges from enjoining peaceful picketing. Seeing the courts as irretrievably biased, workers used their political influence to shelter themselves from judicial power.

Nevertheless, a coalition of professionals and some unions renewed the push for protective legislation during the Progressive Era (1900–1919). Reformers carefully constructed new statutes restricting child labor, setting maximum hours, and implementing minimum wages to survive judicial scrutiny. Lawmakers addressed the problem of workplace accidents through social insurance programs, such as workers' compensation, and by expanding the employer's legal responsibility for safety. By 1906, 25 states had modified or abolished Shaw's fellow-servant rule, while almost as many had revised the doctrine of assumption of risk.

Progressive Era judges slowly and intermittently warmed to such legislation, rejecting some statutes, but allowing those protecting populations deemed deserving public support. Most infamously, the U.S. Supreme Court's *Lochner v. New York* (1905) decision invalidated a New York state law limiting the baker's workday. But just three years later, in *Muller v. Oregon* (1908), the same court upheld the state's authority to set maximum hours for women, a group of workers judges deemed worthy of public protection. The high court invalidated the federal child labor law, but affirmed similar state legislation. Though laws faced rigorous scrutiny, trends seemed to favor the reformers. For instance, in 1911, the New York Court of

Appeals voided that state's workers' compensation law. But in 1917, the U.S. Supreme Court issued decisions validating three different mandatory accident insurance schemes.

By contrast, the law continued to deny labor organizations legitimacy deep into the so-called Progressive Era. Judges still enjoined picketing and jail violators for contempt of court without jury trial. Grand juries still indicted union officials for conspiracy to boycott, restrain trade, and injure employers and nonunion workers. Meanwhile, criminal courts found ways to prosecute labor leaders engaged in graft, extortion, and embezzlement, responding to urban reformers who demanded that the state begin policing the internal administration of unions.

Similarly, Progressive Era appellate courts constructed new doctrines that affirmed employer prerogatives at the expense of unions. Adopting contemporary antimonopoly rhetoric to their own uses, "open shop" employers asked the courts to protect their authority to employ whomever they choose and to affirm the nonunion worker's right to choose his associations. Impressed by the arguments of new advocacy groups like the American Anti-Boycott Association, reputed reformers like the federal judge William Howard Taft turned restraint-of-trade laws against union pickets, boycotts, and exclusive agreements. Moreover, appellate courts affirmed open-shop premises, ratifying the worker's right to join an association and quit work, but severely limiting the union's ability to govern the economy. Most significant, in the series of decisions titled *Loewe v. Lawlor* (1903–1917), the United States Supreme Court ruled that the Sherman Anti-Trust Act of 1890 applied to labor unions, upholding a Danbury, Connecticut, milliner's lawsuit against the United Hatters Union.

These victories oddly disappointed many businessmen. Though injunctions forestalled the unionization of manufacturing, they failed to break labor's hold on trades like construction. Moreover, employers struggled to collect the judgments that courts awarded. Indeed, victorious hat manufacturer Dietrich Loewe went bankrupt waiting for unionists to obey the court, forcing him to accept charity from a collection of wealthy businessmen. Here open-shop employers found themselves hoist on their own rhetoric. Seeing unions as unlawful conspiracies, businessmen refused to offer labor any form of legal recognition. But without "standing" or state-sponsored corporate form, unions could only be sued as mere associations of individuals. Under these conditions, even a successful claim like Loewe's proved impossible to collect, requiring as it did thousands of lawsuits for nonpayment.

Modern collective bargaining emerged from this paradox, as many Americans began seeing legally enforceable labor contracts as a middle ground between individualism and the closed shop. Reformers, stability-minded businessmen, and some unions began working to construct frameworks under which workers exchanged strikes, boycotts, and violence for arbitration, higher wages, shorter hours, and employer recognition. Such contracts had appeared in construction as early as the 1880s, but seldom in manufacturing until New York's clothing producers signed the famed "Protocol of Peace" of 1910.

New laws such as the Clayton Act of 1914, which exempted unions from federal antitrust law, validated such agreements. Called "Labor's Magna Carta" by Samuel Gompers, the Clayton Act expanded labor's legitimate space for the first time since *Commonwealth v. Hunt* in 1843. Almost immediately upon its passage, however, courts began limiting the range of acceptable strikes under the exemption. For instance, in *U.S. v. Norris* (1918), the federal judge Arthur Loomis upheld the conspiracy conviction of Chicago teamsters officials for boycotting a building material dealer. The Clayton Act thus did not legitimize unions as such, but instead offered a contractual ideal to which they could aspire.

During World War I, the federal government further enshrined what was called "responsible unionism," aiding unions that engaged in lawful collective bargaining. Seeking worker support for the war and an end to costly strikes, Congress enacted statutes creating extraordinary new agencies like the National War Labor Board, which arbitrated over 1,200 industrial disputes, often siding with workers. Trumpeted as "industrial democracy," these laws appeared to apply the war's principal ideological justification to economic life, formally ending the state's traditional hostility to labor. Indeed, under the new regime, both craft and industrial workers gained significant improvements in their condition, including the eight-hour day.

Yet, the wartime institutionalization of labor also resulted in the demonization of unions that opposed American entry into the conflict. Federal officials imprisoned Eugene Debs, accusing the Socialist Party presidential candidate of violating the Espionage Act of 1917 by giving speeches encouraging workers to resist conscription. Federal courts suppressed radical labor unions like the Industrial Workers of the World (IWW), arresting their leaders for espionage and sedition, crushing their strikes, and permitting vigilante violence against rank-and-file Wobblies. Moreover, when governments removed and even reversed their support for labor after the 1918 armistice, unionization drives collapsed. Most famously, in 1919, steel manufacturers suppressed a national strike by marshaling local police and state troopers against workers energized by labor's recent successes in other industries.

During the 1920s, Progressive law grew still more stifling. The courts demanded that labor act "responsibly," but declined to reward obedient workers by legitimizing unions or validating protective legislation. On the ground, indictments and injunctions bolstered open-shop drives in construction, teaming, metalworking, and printing. The federal judge James Wilkerson's expansive court order severely impeded the enormous railroad shopmen's strike of 1922. Higher courts blessed such judicial interference in labor disputes. In *American Steel Foundries v. Tri-City Central Trades Council* (1921) and *Duplex Printing Press v. Deering* (1921), the U.S. Supreme Court narrowed the scope of the Clayton Act's labor exemption, ruling that federal judges could still enjoin unions engaged in coercive picketing, sympathy strikes, and secondary boycotts. As justices expanded equity jurisdiction in labor cases, they also made unions more vulnerable to lawsuit. In *United Mine Workers v. Coronado Coal* (1922), the U.S. Supreme Court ruled that employers could sue unincorporated labor unions under the Sherman Act by name in court. This ruling effectively barred unions from presenting themselves as loose associations to avoid compensating individuals and firms injured by strikes. Finally, in *Adkins v. Children's Hospital* (1923), the Supreme Court revived the *Lochner* precedent, voiding a Washington, DC law creating a board setting minimum wages for women and children as an unconstitutional offense against freedom of contract. Under these conditions, union ranks shrank to prewar levels.

The stock market crash of 1929 and the ensuing Great Depression transformed American law, unleashing an unprecedented wave of labor activism and broad improvements in the working lives of ordinary workers. Depression-era labor law continued long-term trends begun in the 1890s, but radically departed from the past in its overt sympathy for unions and its willingness to employ federal power. While prior reformers had urged that the state permit workers to strike, the law of the 1930s actively encouraged workers to organize and forced employers to collectively bargain. While Progressive lawmakers had offered support to unions that abided middle-class norms, the New Deal initially endorsed labor in almost all its forms. Finally, the Depression saw Congress establish a federal program of social insurance, not to mention national standards for minimum wages, maximum hours, and child labor.

As the Depression worsened, Americans demanded that government promote economic stability by fostering cooperation. The federal government responded first by removing barriers to union activism. In 1932, Congress enacted the Norris-LaGuardia Act, which elaborated the worker's right to union membership. The law barred employers from forcing workers to sign yellow-dog contracts promising not to join a union. More significant, the law denied U.S. district and appellate court judges the authority to issue injunctions in nonviolent labor disputes. After years of fruitless lobbying, workers were finally free from constant federal judicial interference.

After winning election in 1932, President Franklin Roosevelt proposed New Deal legislation actually mandating various forms of economic organization, including labor unions. The centerpiece of Roosevelt's program was the National Industrial Recovery Act of 1933 (NIRA), which required businesses to organize "code authorities" and design industrial rules governing conditions in each field. Section 7A of the statute re-affirmed the worker's right to join a labor organization and required that industries permit unions to participate in the code-writing process. In theory, the federal government backed these provisions, giving union wage scales the force of law.

Many unions prospered under the recovery act. Even before the legislation became law, the United Mine Workers of America (UMWA) union appealed to prospective members by claiming, "the president wants you to join a union." Quickly organizing the bituminous coal miners, the UMWA gained employer recognition and a seat at the National Recovery Administration (NRA) code authority. Other unions found NIRA disappointing, and the experiment in cartelization was short-lived. In the *Schechter Poultry* decision of 1935, the U.S. Supreme Court ruled the recovery act an unconstitutional delegation of executive power. But the NIRA nonetheless represented an unprecedented peacetime intervention on behalf of unions that began a two-decade-long expansion of the size and power of the labor movement.

The void left by the death of the NIRA was filled by a still more radical piece of legislation: the National Labor Relations Act of 1935 (NLRA). Often called the Wagner Act, after its progenitor, New York Senator Robert F. Wagner Sr., the NLRA not only re-iterated the worker's right to join a union, but built a legal framework for collective bargaining that remains in place today. The law required employers to recognize unions winning certification elections as legitimate representatives of the workers. It created the National Labor Relations Board (NLRB) to oversee certifications and arbitrate labor disputes. Even more than the NIRA, the Wagner Act electrified the labor movement, enabling the long-awaited organization of basic industries like steel and auto.

The legitimacy offered unions by the New Deal was far less restrictive than any proposed before. Though the National Labor Relations Board used its power to favor certain unions over others, diverse organizations received state support. The federal government did take steps to ensure that labor's new power was not misused. Passing the Anti-racketeering Act of 1934 (ARA), lawmakers tried to protect workers from criminals like Murray "The Camel" Humphreys, who coveted unions for their treasuries and their power. Written in consultation with AFL leaders, the ARA reconfigured the relationship between labor and the criminal justice system. Rather than limiting worker protest, racketeering law aimed to limit the exploitation of labor by undefined outsiders. While this vagueness made unions susceptible to arbitrary prosecution in future decades, it represented a triumph for unions once buffeted by the simultaneous harassment of courts and gangsters.

Other New Deal programs and regulations similarly transformed the worker's experience. The Social Security Act of 1935 created a national, nearly universal, system of old age insurance, financed through a payroll tax. Retirement, once a luxury reserved for the wealthy, was now available to manual laborers. The Fair Labor Standards Act of 1938 abolished child labor and established the 40-hour workweek for many job classifications, overtime pay, and minimum wages. Moreover, the law replaced the patchwork of competing state provisions with a national standard, ending the statutory race to the bottom that had long stymied protective legislation in poorer regions of the nation.

Finally, the Great Depression saw the U.S. Supreme Court purge its lingering hostility to government regulation of the labor contract. In *West Coast Hotel v. Parrish* (1937), the court upheld a Washington law setting minimum wages for women. In *NLRB v. Jones and Laughlin* (1937), the court disappointed corporations by affirming the constitutionality of the Wagner Act. Taken together, the 1937 decisions overturned two generations of precedent invalidating protective legislation. The individual's right to "freedom of contract" would no longer trump the public will.

During World War II, the state revived the principle of "responsible unionism," helping unions that endorsed government policy, but repudiating those deemed too radical or independent, such as the West Coast longshoremen and even the United Mine Workers. Offering significant aid to workers who agreed to forgo strikes and raise productivity, the federal government helped many internationals grow rapidly during this period. But it also foreshadowed the use of ideological and tactical litmus tests to suppress labor's most aggressive tendencies.

By the end of the war, labor's growing power inspired politicians of both parties to favor new laws containing unions. The 1947 Taft-Hartley Amendment to the NLRA ended 15 years of comparatively unfettered union activism. Though the law continued to support collective bargaining, it made organizing far more difficult. Under Taft-Hartley, federal judges regained the authority to interfere in peaceful labor disputes suspended by the Norris-LaGuardia Act of 1932. Taft-Hartley required union officers to file affidavits swearing they were not Communists. The law barred unions from engaging in "unfair labor practices," including jurisdictional strikes and secondary boycotts. The amendment allowed states to pass "right to work" laws, enabling employees in unionized workplaces to decline union membership. These provisions had a profound impact on labor organizing, especially in the South, where CIO attempts to unionize the textile industry stalled.

In the 1950s and 1960s, lawmakers also placed new restrictions on the administration of labor unions. In 1957, the Senate held hearings to investigate charges of corruption and gangster domination in unions like the International Brotherhood of Teamsters, leading to the Labor-Management Reporting and Disclosure Act of 1959 (aka, Landrum-Griffin), which proposed to guarantee democracy, freedom of speech, and official probity in unions. Seeking to promote politically conservative and personally honest leadership, the law forbade former Communists and ex-convicts from holding a union office for five years. Moreover, federal prosecutors began aggressively pursuing union officials under the 1934 Anti-racketeering Act and its successor, the Hobbs Act of 1946. Though these prosecutions undoubtedly stemmed the movement's most violent, collusive, and corrupt elements, they nonetheless put labor on the defensive, undermining the movement's reputation without offering well-administered unions any additional support.

The civil rights revolution of the 1960s radically altered the trajectory of American labor law. Once focused on the legitimacy of unions and their tactics, the law grew increasingly concerned with the rights of individuals to employment, fair treatment, and a safe workplace. The Civil Rights Act of 1965 and its subsequent amendments prohibited employers from discriminating against prospective and current employees on the basis of race, creed, or gender. To help victims of workplace bias seek redress through the federal courts, the law created the Equal Opportunity Employment Commission. In 1970, Congress passed the Occupational Safety and Health Act, which set standards for safe work environments, protecting employees from hazardous materials, noise, machinery, temperature, or unsanitary conditions.

Though its support is often forgotten, the AFL-CIO lobbied hard for all these laws, occasionally over the objections of more conservative affiliates and their members.

By the end of the twentieth century, workers found their once-strong legal position under political assault. By filling the federal courts and administrative agencies with officials hostile to unions, Republican presidents like Ronald Reagan successfully vitiated the Wagner Act without amending it legislatively. Refusing to defend the right to join a union, the courts contributed to the decline of organized labor's share of the workforce. By contrast, employees actually gained new civil rights during this period. Despite business opposition, laws such as the Americans with Disabilities Act of 1990 and the Family and Medical Leave Act of 1993 retained the overwhelming support of both legislators and the public. It remains unclear, however, whether workers can retain these rights without a strong labor movement to lobby for their continuation.

ANDREW WENDER COHEN

References and Further Reading

Cohen, Andrew Wender. *The Racketeer's Progress: Chicago and the Struggle for the Modern American Economy.* New York: Cambridge University Press, 2004.
Dubofsky, Melvyn. *The State and Labor in Modern America.* Chapel Hill: University of North Carolina Press, 1994.
Ernst, Daniel. *Lawyers against Labor: From Individual Rights to Corporate Liberalism.* Urbana and Chicago: University of Illinois Press, 1995.
Fink, Leon. "Labor, Liberty, and the Law: Trade Unionism and the Problem of the American Constitutional Order." *Journal of American History* 74 (1987): 904–925.
Forbath, William. *Law and the Shaping of the American Labor Movement.* Cambridge, MA: Harvard University Press, 1991.
Geoghegan, Thomas. *Which Side Are You On?: Trying to Be for Labor When It's Flat on Its Back.* 1991.
Hattam, Victoria. *Labor Visions and State Power.* New Haven, CT: Yale University Press, 1993.
Lichtenstein, Nelson. *State of the Union: A Century of American Labor.* Princeton, NJ: Princeton University Press, 2002.
McCartin, Joseph. *Labor's Great War: The Struggle for Industrial Democracy and the Transformation of the American Workplace, 1912–1921.* Chapel Hill: University of North Carolina Press, 1998.
Morgan, Edmund. *American Slavery, American Freedom.* New York: W. W. Norton and Co., 1975.
O'Brien, Ruth. *Workers' Paradox: The Republican Origins of New Deal Labor Policy, 1886–1935.* Chapel Hill: University of North Carolina Press, 1998.
Orren, Karen. *Belated Feudalism: Labor, the Law, and Liberal Development in the United States.* New York: Cambridge University Press, 1991.
Tomlins, Christopher. *Law, Labor, and Ideology in the Early American Republic.* Cambridge: Cambridge University Press, 1993.
———. *The State and the Unions: Labor Relations, Law, and the Organized Labor Movement in America, 1880–1960.* New York: Cambridge University Press, 1985.
Wilentz, Sean. *Chants Democratic: New York City and the Rise of the American Working Class, 1788–1850.* New York: Oxford University Press, 1986.
Witte, Edwin. *The Government in Labor Disputes.* New York: McGraw-Hill, 1932.

LAWRENCE STRIKE (1912)

For nine weeks during the winter of 1912, more than 15,000 Lawrence, Massachusetts, textile workers, most of them Southern and Eastern European immigrants, waged a spirited strike marked by creative mass tactics, cooperation among a dozen or more ethnic groups, determined activism by women militants, and assistance from the Industrial Workers of the World (IWW). Several thousand more stayed off the job but avoided strike activities. Often called the "Bread and Roses" strike, the walkout was the high point of the IWW's efforts among eastern factory workers and led to pay increases for workers throughout the New England textile industry.

Dominated by the worsted and cotton goods industries, Lawrence was a city of crowded tenement districts and huge factories. Southern and Eastern Europeans, who were an important part of New England's mill labor force, were especially numerous in Lawrence, where the textile industry had added 10,000 jobs since 1905. The strike highlighted Lawrence's ethnic fault line. Most strikers were Southern and Eastern European immigrants and Franco-Belgians, with important support among the Germans. The largest groups were Italians, Poles, Lithuanians, and Syrians (Lebanese). There were smaller groups of Jewish, Armenian, Russian, Lettish, and Portuguese strikers, along with a scattering from other ethnicities. Despite the strikers' overtures, relatively few Irish, French-Canadian, English, or Yankee workers backed the strike committee.

The strike was sparked by a state law cutting the workweek for women and minors from 56 to 54 hours effective January 1. Because of the integration of men's and women's jobs, nearly every worker was placed on the 54-hour schedule. The owners' refusal to adjust pay rates to maintain take-home pay triggered the walkout, which was fueled by underlying discontent over working conditions. IWW Local 20, a tiny 300-member organization, was the key reason Lawrence was the only Massachusetts mill town where a major strike erupted over this statewide issue. By pressing mill officials about their plans and agitating on the job and in the neighborhoods, Local 20 activists built a loose strike movement. On January 10,

Strike in Lawrence, Massachusetts, with many children posed on sidewalk. Library of Congress, Prints & Photographs Division [LC-USZ62-98168].

they convened a meeting of 1,000 Italians, who voted to strike unless they received their full wages. The next day, 300 weavers, mostly Polish women, struck the Everett Mill because their pay envelopes were short two hours' wages. On January 12, after paymasters distributed wages at the big mills along the Merrimack River, strikers ran down the aisles pressuring others to join them and spread the walkout by marching from mill to mill.

The national IWW had no role in the prestrike agitation; but once workers had walked off the job, the strikers sent for an IWW organizer, Joe Ettor, who helped them co-ordinate their efforts. An engaging speaker, Ettor encouraged the strikers by connecting local events to a broader social analysis and insisting that they would win because the owners could not "weave cloth with bayonets." With his assistance, the strikers refined their structure, which already included a multi-ethnic strike committee, set up relief and publicity subcommittees, and mobilized mass demonstrations. The strikers adopted demands that included a 15% pay hike, double time for overtime, elimination of the premium system under which some workers had to meet monthlong production or attendance standards to receive their full pay, and no discrimination against strikers.

After Ettor's arrest in late January, William D. ("Big Bill") Haywood became the IWW's lead organizer. Elizabeth Gurley Flynn also played an active role in the strike, working closely with women strikers, helping evacuate strikers' children, and assisting with outreach. The IWW did not control the strike, but the strikers listened carefully to the organizers' advice. As many as 10,000 joined Local 20 before the strike's end.

The strikers promoted participation through mass meetings, parades, and open strike committee meetings. Carrying American flags and singing the "Internationale" and the "Marseillaise," thousands followed local Italian, Syrian, and Franco-Belgian bands in huge parades that wound through the tenement districts and the main business district. Hundreds packed daily strike committee meetings where delegates reported on developments in their communities and debated tactics and strategy. The strike's institutional core, however, was the committee's ethnic branches, which drew on individual groups' personal networks and institutional resources. Through these branches, strikers mobilized street actions, promoted solidarity, punished scabs, administered relief, reached out to fellow ethnics in other cities, and voted on policies proposed by the strike committee.

The strikers faced stiff opposition from civic leaders, the militia, and the American Federation of Labor (AFL), as well the mill owners. Despite their ambivalence toward the mills, municipal leaders like Mayor Michael Scanlon worried about the social order. In particular, they distrusted new-immigrant-led mass protests. In mid-January, a prominent local undertaker, John Breen, planted dynamite at a Syrian strike supporter's laundry and at a cobbler's shop next to the print shop where Ettor received his mail.

Only Breen's transparent bungling betrayed this scheme to smear the strikers and jail Ettor. Most local AFL leaders also opposed the strike. Although the AFL's United Textile Workers of America (UTWA) had few members in Lawrence, its hostility to the walkout re-inforced this opposition. Motivated by organizational jealousy and antiradicalism, the UTWA's national president, John Golden, denounced the strike, tried to undermine relief efforts, and supported a back-to-work drive.

Local officers and out-of-town police challenged the strikers, and the militia sealed off the main mill district. After two weeks, the authorities stepped up the pressure. On January 29, marchers attacked trolleys carrying strikebreakers. The police and militia monitored the confrontations but did not interfere. In response, Governor Eugene Foss sent more troops. That evening, a striker, Annie LoPizzo was shot to death when police broke up a street demonstration. Police quickly arrested Ettor and the Italian Socialist Federation leader Arturo Giovannitti, who they feared would replace Ettor. Although the two were speaking elsewhere in town when LoPizzo was shot, the authorities charged them with creating a violent climate that caused her death. Several weeks later, the police arrested the striker Joe Caruso as a third accessory. All three faced possible death sentences. Besides the arrests, Colonel Leroy Sweetser, who directed the militia's efforts, banned strike meetings on the Lawrence Common and ordered mounted troops and infantry to patrol city streets, including the tenement districts. On January 30, John Ramey, a teenage Syrian mill worker, died from a bayonet wound in the back.

Women's Strike Activism

To avoid more bloodshed, the strike committee suspended mass demonstrations for two weeks. When large protests resumed, women took the lead. Although underrepresented on the strike committee and bargaining team, they played a central role in the strike. Nearly every Southern and Eastern European woman had a direct stake in the strike, either working in the mills or running her household with mill earnings from boarders and family members. Strikers' wives, mothers, sisters, and daughters joined together with women operatives, who composed roughly 40% of the strikers. Women's militancy was hardly unique to Lawrence, but their high-profile involvement both as strikers and strike supporters and their sustained, large-scale participation set Lawrence apart. Like men, they drew on gendered social networks of daily life to mobilize demonstrations, administer relief, and promote the strike in their neighborhoods.

Effective relief work was crucial to maintaining the strike. The IWW and strikers raised over $72,000 through labor, radical, and ethnic networks across the Northeast and Midwest. Working through ethnic subcommittees, strikers and their families investigated needs, distributed relief goods, and ran soup kitchens. The strike committee evacuated more than 250 children to other cities. The IWW and out-of-town supporters made careful preparations, investigating prospective foster homes, giving physical examinations to the children, and requiring signed permission from the children's parents. On February 11, 119 children left for New York. In the following weeks, others left for New York; Hoboken; Philadelphia; Barre, Vermont; and Manchester, New Hampshire. The evacuations, which eased parents' concerns and provided valuable publicity for the strikers, outraged municipal leaders. Besides strengthening the strike, the departures portrayed Lawrence as a grim city with ill-clothed, malnourished children. On February 24, police clubbed and arrested women trying to put their children on a train. The authorities then charged several mothers with child neglect. The depot incident backfired, prompting a U.S. House Rules Committee hearing in Washington, DC, where young strikers presented dramatic testimony about their jobs and living conditions.

Continued mass picketing, publicity from the Washington hearing, and congressional threats to investigate the woolen tariff cracked the owners' determination. With American Woolen, the largest employer, wavering, the owners tried to establish the framework for a citywide settlement with minimal concessions at the Arlington Mill, a corporation that employed relatively large numbers of English and Irish workers. When the strikers defeated this back-to-work maneuver, American Woolen offered to negotiate. Convinced that an agreement with the largest employer would set the terms for every mill, the strike committee dropped its insistence on citywide negotiations and sent a nine-member committee to bargain with American Woolen officials. These were the first negotiations between the mills and the strike committee. On March 13, the strikers ratified the American Woolen agreement that included a 5% raise for pieceworkers; a 5% to 22% increase for those paid by the hour, with the highest raise for the lowest-paid workers; a two-week premium period; time and one quarter for overtime; and a no-discrimination pledge. The other mills granted similar terms, although several refused a formal agreement with the strikers. On Monday, March 18, the strikers resumed work.

After the settlement, unrest swept New England's textile industry. Workers in Barre, Vermont, and in Lowell and other Massachusetts mill towns transformed Lawrence strike support work into agitation for their own raises. Once they struck, operatives called in the IWW. In April, the Lowell showdown prompted New England mill owners to declare a regionwide 10% raise that benefited over 125,000 textile workers.

Lawrence workers and managers continued to struggle over poststrike power relations. Walkouts erupted over discrimination and working conditions. Despite some gains, workers often found themselves outmatched as the owners resisted demands from one department or ethnic group. Local 20 members were unable to wage constant strikes or to focus their full strength on narrow demands involving limited numbers of workers.

During the summer and early fall, the movement to free Ettor, Giovannitti, and Caruso grew into an energetic campaign with huge demonstrations, ambitious speaking tours, extensive publicity, and threats of a general strike. This activism mobilized support across the United States and sparked large European protests. In November, jurors acquitted the three prisoners. By then, the defense campaign had become entangled with Local 20's fate and Lawrence civic leaders' battle against the IWW.

Frustrated by shop-floor conditions and swayed by calls for a general strike to save the prisoners, Italians as well as some Poles struck several mills on September 26–28. To gain control over the agitation, Local 20 called a one-day citywide mill strike for September 30, the first day of the trial. The divisive strike left Local 20 ill-prepared for the mills' counteroffensive, which included an aggressive blacklist.

The September turmoil also provided an opening for municipal leaders. Seizing on the "No God, No Master" slogan on a sign carried by out-of-towners at an Ettor-Giovannitti-Caruso demonstration, Mayor Scanlon and Father James O'Reilly, the dean of Lawrence's Catholic clergy, launched an anti-IWW "God and Country" campaign. With a Columbus Day parade by over 25,000 as its high point, the campaign combined boosterism, nationalism, inflammatory anti-IWW rhetoric, and intimidation. In this volatile atmosphere, Jonas Smolskas, a Lithuanian mill worker, was killed in a fight provoked by his IWW button. Although the God and Country campaign had limited appeal to former strikers, it became the template for municipal leaders' future efforts to quell labor militancy and their struggle to stigmatize the 1912 strike as an affront to Lawrence and to the nation.

Unable to counter the owners' power on the job, Local 20 unraveled. Lawrence workers abandoned the IWW, but the 1912 strike left its mark on local labor activism. During the next decade, Lawrence workers drew on their 1912 experiences as they mobilized strikes that eliminated the premium system (1918), won the 48-hour week for 54 hours' pay (1919), and blocked a 20% pay cut (1922).

DEXTER ARNOLD

References and Further Reading

Arnold, Dexter. "'A Larger Battle': Lawrence and the 1912 New England Mill Strikes." In *Work Recreation and Culture: Essays in American Labor History*, edited by Martin Henry Blatt and Martha K. Norkunas. New York: Garland Publishing, Inc., 1996, pp. 183–199.

Cahn, William. *Lawrence 1912: The Bread and Roses Strike.* Intro by Paul Cowan. New York: The Pilgrim Press, 1980.

Cameron, Ardis. *Radicals of the Worst Sort: Laboring Women in Lawrence, Massachusetts, 1860–1912*. Urbana: University of Illinois Press, 1993.

Dubofsky, Melvyn. *We Shall Be All: A History of the Industrial Workers of the World*. Chicago: Quadrangle Books, 1969.

Foner, Philip S. *History of the American Labor Movement*. Volume IV: *The Industrial Workers of the World, 1905–1917*. New York: International Publishers, 1965.

Watson, Bruce. *Bread and Roses: Mills, Migrants, and the Struggle for the American Dream*. New York: Viking, 2005.

See also **Flynn, Elizabeth Gurley; Haywood, William D. "Big Bill"; Industrial Workers of the World**

LEAGUE FOR INDUSTRIAL DEMOCRACY (LID)

The League for Industrial Democracy (LID), an educational group devoted to the ideals of social democracy and trade unionism, began its existence as the Intercollegiate Socialist Society (ISS), founded in New York City on September 12, 1905. The socialist novelist Upton Sinclair had drafted a call for a meeting to found a group for the "purpose of promoting an intelligent interest in Socialism among college men and women." At the founding meeting of the ISS, Sinclair complained that in his own years as a college student, none of his professors had ever discussed "proposals to eliminate poverty and social injustices." Accordingly, he decided that "since the professors would not educate the students, it was up to the students to educate the professors." Sinclair was just a few days short of his twenty-seventh birthday when he chaired the meeting, and he was by no means the oldest person present. The group was not intended to be restricted to currently enrolled college students; any college graduate who supported its aims could join.

Only a tiny percentage of Americans enjoyed the privilege of higher education in the early twentieth century, and college and university students had traditionally been as conservative as their professors. The creation of the ISS, which would grow within little over a decade to include roughly a thousand members at 70-odd campus chapters, thus represented an important turning point in the history of campus politics and the American Left as the first national organization of radically inclined students.

The years leading up to the First World War were heady times for American radicals, on and off campus. The Socialist Party grew to over a 100,000 members, and its presidential candidate, Eugene Debs, attracted a million votes in the 1912 election. The ISS recruits included many students who would later make their mark on American politics. Walter Lippmann, perhaps the most influential political journalist of the mid-twentieth century, founded the Harvard University chapter in 1910. The ISS began publishing a quarterly journal, Intercollegiate Socialist, in 1913, and sponsored speaking tours and conferences that were attended by many students. John Reed, a member of the ISS Harvard chapter, who would later gain fame as author of *Ten Days That Shook the World*, an account of the 1917 Bolshevik Revolution in Russia, would write that the ISS's impact upon prewar campuses "was potent":

All over the place radicals sprang up.... The more serious college papers took a socialistic, or at least a progressive tinge.... It made me, and many others, realize that there was something going on in the dull outside world more thrilling than college activities.

Harry W. Laidler, a junior at Wesleyan University when he attended the founding meeting of the ISS in 1905, became the group's executive director in 1910; he would define the organization's purpose as "primarily a study, not a political propagandist organization." (Laidler remained in the leadership of the ISS, and its successor organization, for an astonishing five decades.) But it was not going to prove easy to separate the intellectual fortunes of the ISS from the political fortunes of the broader radical movement.

American entry into the First World War in 1917 took the bloom of the socialist rose. The Socialist Party and other radical groups like the Industrial Workers of the World (IWW) came under official attack for opposing the war; radical leaders were imprisoned, and radical publications banned from the mails. College and university campuses were as intolerant as the larger society; antiwar professors

lost their jobs, and the ISS shriveled. By 1920, few ISS chapters survived outside of New York City.

In 1921, the Intercollegiate Socialist Society changed its name to the League for Industrial Democracy (LID). By dropping the reference to socialism, the new name was intended to be more inclusive and less inflammatory. The change also reflected a shift in organizational perspective. The LID would increasingly function as a kind of think tank for trade unions under socialist or social democratic leadership.

Although Harry Laidler had defined the ISS and the LID's mission as primarily educational, the organization and its supporters played an increasingly activist role in the 1920s. In the early years of the decade, the LID encouraged the creation of the nationally organized Farmer Labor Party, and in 1924, it endorsed the independent presidential campaign of Robert M. La Follette. Despite the LID's efforts, the 1920s would not prove a propitious decade for any group that challenged the status quo from the left. Corporate-sponsored "welfare capitalism" schemes attracted far more attention from the general public than the League's advocacy of a worker-controlled "industrial democracy."

However, the onset of the Great Depression in the 1930s seemed to vindicate the LID's criticisms of capitalism, and the group's influence spread. In 1932, it organized a formal student affiliate, the Intercollegiate League for Industrial Democracy, in part to compete with the Communist-led National Student League (NSL). Chapters of the group were founded on over a hundred campuses, enrolling several thousand members who were active in backing Norman Thomas's presidential campaign on the Socialist ticket in 1932. In 1934, the LID's student affiliate adopted a new name, the Student League for Industrial Democracy (SLID). Meanwhile, the parent organization was also growing. LID's speakers were in demand in union halls as well as on college campuses, and the group's pamphlets circulated widely. Adopting a new form of communication, the LID sponsored a series of talks on current affairs on the NBC radio network.

In addition to its educational work, the LID plunged into social and political activism. The group published a magazine titled *The Unemployed* to spur the demand for unemployment insurance. LID members played a significant role in the revival of the labor movement in the 1930s; a Detroit LID member named Walter Reuther, for example, would make a name for himself in his efforts to organize an industrial union in the traditionally open-shop auto industry. The LID was also active in defending the civil liberties of workers and radicals, founding a legal defense group called the Workers Defense League (WDL).

But in the second half of the 1930s, the LID, like the Socialist Party, faltered. To the dismay of LID elders, its student affiliate SLID and the Communist-led NSL merged in 1935 to form the American Student Union (ASU). The Communists exercised effective control over the ASU until the group collapsed in disarray after the signing of the Nazi-Soviet Pact. Factional battles within the Socialist Party spilled over into and damaged the LID. And many LIDers disagreed with Norman Thomas's opposition to U.S. entry into World War II, leading Thomas to resign as LID's codirector.

In the aftermath of World War II, the LID shed much of its residual anticapitalist sentiments, supporting policies of liberal reformism at home, and anti-Communism abroad. Apart from reviving SLID in 1945 as a campus affiliate, the group undertook few new initiatives in the 1940s and 1950s. The LID was on its way to becoming an ideological retirement home for lapsed radicals, kept alive by the charity of a few leaders of the garment workers unions who retained a sentimental attachment to the socialist ideals of their youth.

Two political developments led to a brief revival in the LID's fortunes in the 1960s. One was the merger of a left-wing splinter group led by the former Trotskyist Max Shachtman with Thomas's Socialist Party at the end of the 1950s. The "Shachtmanites" included a number of talented and energetic young activists like Michael Harrington (soon to gain fame as the author of *The Other America*, the book that helped spark the "War on Poverty"). The Shachtmanites concentrated their political efforts within the LID, and in 1964, Harrington was elected the chair of the group. Writing in the *New York Post*, the journalist James Wechsler celebrated Harrington's new appointment and predicted that as a leader of the LID, he would emerge as a unifier of "the scattered legions among the liberal intellectual community, the civil rights activists and the more enlightened sectors of organized labor."

The other important development was the transformation of the largely moribund SLID into a new group called the Students for a Democratic Society (SDS) between 1960 and 1962. The SDS would soon emerge as the center of the New Left, a radical movement destined to have an enormous impact on American campuses in the 1960s.

But for a third time in the twentieth century, the LID's seemingly bright prospects proved chimerical. The "scattered legions" of American liberalism would end the 1960s even more scattered as a result of conflicts over the Vietnam War and American race relations. The SDS split with the LID in 1965, after a series of bruising generational confrontations, most famously the battle at the SDS's founding convention between Tom Hayden and Michael Harrington over the issue of anti-Communism. Harrington found himself in the unenviable position of being attacked from his left by youthful radicals like Hayden, and from his right by his former comrades among the Shachtmanites, who were increasingly adopting a neoconservative worldview. By the end of the 1960s, he had been marginalized within the LID leadership, and resigned soon afterward. Although showing few signs of life after Harrington's resignation, the LID survived for the remainder of the twentieth century and into the start of the next century, as a front organization for the Shachtmanite-controlled Social Democrats, USA.

MAURICE ISSERMAN

References and Further Reading

Isserman, Maurice. *The Other American: The Life of Michael Harrington*. New York: Public Affairs Press, 2000.
Johnpoll, Bernard K., and Mark R. Yerburgh, eds. *The League for Industrial Democracy: A Documentary History*, 3 vols. Westport, CT: Greenwood Press, 1980.
Sale, Kirkpatrick. *SDS*. New York: Random House, 1973.

LEAGUE OF REVOLUTIONARY BLACK WORKERS

The League of Revolutionary Black Workers was founded in Detroit by a coalition of radical black autoworkers, students, and intellectuals in the early months of 1969. It was designed to serve as a coordinating body for numerous black revolutionary union movements that black workers had developed in the auto plants of Detroit in 1968. The League openly expressed a Marxist-Leninist orientation and focused its organizational efforts solely on black workers. The League contended that black autoworkers occupied a strategic position within the capitalist economy and should therefore be the primary focus of revolutionary struggle.

Detroit's black revolutionary union movement developed in the wake of the July 1967 uprising and was nurtured by a radical community that included prominent black Marxist writers C. L. R. James, James and Grace Lee Boggs, Uhruhu (a militant group of nationalist and socialist black students associated with Wayne State University), the Socialist Workers Party, and the Communist Party. In September 1967, caucuses of black autoworkers began meeting at Dodge Main (Hamtramck assembly plant) for discussions. Also that fall, *The Inner City Voice*, a radical black newspaper, began publication in Detroit. Its editors, John Watson, Ken Cockrel, and Mike Hamlin, would later join with nine production workers from the Dodge Main plant in May 1968 to establish DRUM (Dodge Revolutionary Union Movement), the first of Detroit's black revolutionary unions. Founding members of the League included production workers Luke Tripp, General Baker, Chuck Wooten, Ernest Allen, and James Forman. The initial stimulus for the formation of DRUM was a spontaneous, interracial wildcat strike by 4,000 workers at Dodge Main on May 2, 1968. Chrysler responded by firing seven workers (five black, two white). Eventually, all but two (both black) were rehired. In the aftermath of the wildcat strike, DRUM began publishing a weekly newsletter and devoted its first issue to an assessment of the recent strike, which it argued was caused by a production speedup. In addition, the newsletter decried the unfair punishment administered to the striking black workers and accused Chrysler of racist labor policies.

After a series of more DRUM-inspired wildcat strikes, fund-raising, and a public attack on the Detroit chapter of the Urban League, the revolutionary union movement spread to other Chrysler plants, resulting in the creation of FRUM (Ford Revolutionary Union Movement) and ELRUM (Eldon Avenue Revolutionary Union Movement). As the black revolutionary union model spread throughout Detroit and the nation, the League of Revolutionary Black Workers was created in an effort to provide direction and coordination for the individual affiliates. The League briefly published its own circular titled *Spear*, but *The Inner City Voice* soon became the League's official newspaper. The League consistently demanded an increase in the number of black people employed at all levels of the auto industry, lobbied to get black workers' union dues channeled into the local black community for self-determination, and called for equal pay for black workers at Chrysler plants in South Africa.

Throughout its five-year existence, the League of Revolutionary Black Workers had a contentious relationship with the United Auto Workers International and Local 3. The League accused the UAW leadership of assisting Chrysler management in the maintenance of a racist system by failing to respond to black workers' complaints. The UAW and Local 3 considered DRUM a threat from its beginning. The UAW argued that DRUM would split the Dodge workers, rendering their union ineffective, and criticized the DRUM newsletter as extremist and hateful. Moreover, the League assailed the UAW for endorsing an annual Detroit police field day. Since the Detroit Police Department was widely criticized by the local black community for racist and brutal policing, the UAW's support for the Detroit police seemed

especially galling. The UAW's endorsement of the police field day was seen by many in the League as proof of an alliance between the UAW and the police department. The League intensified its confrontation with the UAW by calling for a demonstration and march on a UAW convention being held at Cobo Hall in Detroit on November 8 and 9, 1969. The League demanded that the purpose of the convention be changed to consider a complete restructuring of the UAW to a model that better reflected the needs of black autoworkers. The UAW chose to end the convention early to avoid an embarrassing racial confrontation.

The League made several attempts to gain control of local unions by running League candidates in official union elections. League members hoped that taking part in union electoral politics would lend them legitimacy in the eyes of nonaligned black workers, demonstrate black solidarity, raise worker consciousness, and ultimately increase League membership. Amid a massive turnout by retired white UAW members and accusations that local police assisted the UAW by suppressing the League's election-day carpooling efforts, the League of Revolutionary Black Workers failed to get any League members elected to a union office.

The pressures of national growth and intense internal dissension resulted in an organizational split in June 1971. The disagreements that contributed to the division included ideological differences concerning nationalist or class-based consciousness, cooperation with white radicals, whether the League's struggle should be national in scope or more local, and whether its focus should expand to include sexism and imperialism. Three of the League's seven executive board members left the League to work for the Black Workers' Congress, a national black Marxist-Leninist group. The various factions eventually decided that the League would be an affiliate of the Black Workers' Congress along with other worker organizations and student and community groups. But the intense debate exposed irresolvable tensions. Both organizations continued to exist in Detroit for a brief time. However, ideological tensions gave way to personal hostility and a battle over the League's Black Star Publishing company, Black Star Productions, and Black Star bookstore brought organizational activities to a minimum as the League gradually faded away. Many League members went on to join various other labor and political organizations.

Despite its ultimate demise, many Detroit observers credit the League of Revolutionary Black Workers for a significant increase in the amount of black foremen and union stewards in Detroit. The League's activities are often recognized as having resulted in relatively safer and cleaner work environments. The League was also successful in establishing its own printing and film production facilities, which resulted in the production of numerous newsletters, a book on political theory, and a documentary film of the League's history titled *Finally Got the News*. In addition, several League members were actively involved in the Detroit chapter of the Black Panther Party.

JOSEPH LIPARI

References and Further Reading

Georgakas, Dan, and Marvin Surkin. *Detroit, I Do Mind Dying: A Study in Urban Revolution*. New York: St. Martin's Press, 1975.

Geschwender, James. *Class, Race, and Worker Insurgency: The League of Revolutionary Black Workers*. Cambridge: Cambridge University Press, 1977.

Thompson, Heather Ann. *Whose Detroit? Politics, Labor, and Race in a Modern American City*. Ithaca, NY: Cornell University Press, 2001.

See also **DRUM, FRUM, ELRUM**

LEGGETT, WILLIAM (1801–1839)
Labor Activist and Abolitionist

Born in 1801, William Leggett was a writer, journalist, and Democratic Party activist who advocated prolabor and antislavery positions through his editorials and the "Locofoco" wing of the New York Jacksonian Democracy. Born in Savannah, Georgia, Leggett grew up in New York City. After a truncated course of study at Georgetown College and an 1819 stay with his parents on the Illinois frontier, in 1822, Leggett entered the Navy as a midshipman, but was court-martialed for insubordination after four years at sea under the brutal and often arbitrary disciplinary regime typical of the British and American navies. He soon published two volumes of maritime poetry as well as quite a few short stories regarding the sea and the frontier life he had seen in Illinois, all of which earned him some renown. Foreshadowing his future political views, his fiction often condemned abusive ship captains, and one story set forth a sympathetic portrayal of a free black on the frontier. In 1829, after 10 months of editing his own literary journal, the *Critic*, he joined William Cullen Bryant's *New York Evening Post* as a part-owner and literary critic, eventually editing the paper himself for 16 months in 1834 and 1835. Leggett left the *Post* in late 1836 and edited two journals, the *Plaindealer* and the *Examiner*, until both failed toward the end of 1837. Leggett's main contributions to the history of American labor lie in his intellectual leadership of the Locofoco wing of the New York Democracy, his opposition to government preferences and monopoly, his support of labor organizing and the right to strike, and his advocacy of abolition and universal manhood suffrage for blacks. In 1839, soon after being appointed by President Van Buren as diplomatic agent to Guatemala, Leggett died before his voyage to Central America.

Although he proclaimed a lack of interest in politics when he began at the *Post*, Leggett proved a quick student of Bryant's Jacksonian Democratic views. From June 1834 to October 1835, while Bryant was traveling in Europe, Leggett assumed the editorship of the *Evening Post* and wrote many of the fiery editorials upon which his reputation is based. Those editorials, however, so antagonized key advertisers and Democratic Party officials that the *Post* approached financial ruin, hastening Bryant's return to America and Leggett's eventual departure.

Leggett argued that the principle of "equal rights," derived from Thomas Jefferson, and the principle of "free trade," derived from classical political economy, should be the guiding precepts of the Jacksonian Democracy. Leggett was an ardent opponent of the "Money Power," that interlocking constellation of banks, merchants, and capitalists that derived their wealth from the labor of the farmer and urban worker, because it violated both equal rights and free trade. Leggett was particularly suspicious of government action that violated these principles by distributing benefits to some and not to others, and sounded this theme of "antimonopoly" throughout his career. In Leggett's able hands, these ideas became potent weapons against wealth and privilege, and he wrote blistering editorials on numerous subjects, including banking, the rights of labor, and abolition of slavery.

The bank issue was a prime exemplar of Leggett's equal rights and free trade philosophy. Supportive of Andrew Jackson's veto of the Bank Bill, Leggett opposed state-chartered banks as well, while most Jacksonian Democrats supported the so-called pet banks where the Jackson administration deposited federal funds. On this question, Leggett applied the same critique of federal monopoly charters to state monopoly charters. Leggett argued that legislatively granted bank charters were available only to the wealthy and politically influential, and hence violated the principles of equal rights and free trade just as the Bank of the United States had done. Rarely one to criticize without offering an alternative, Leggett became a prime exponent of general incorporation laws to make the process of incorporating a matter of complying with statutorily prescribed conditions open to all. Such statutes were passed throughout the Union in the decades after Leggett's death.

Of course, the bank issue was not simply or solely of interest to antimonopoly ideologists. Small-scale artisans and others in the "laboring classes" had long argued that the banking system was rigged to hold down the honest mechanic by limiting access to capital to those with wealth or political connections. Further, employers paid wage laborers not in hard specie, but in bank notes that often proved to be fraudulent or worthless. Thus, the bank issue was a labor issue. On other labor issues as well, Leggett was very supportive of the nascent American labor movement. Leggett condemned the doctrine of labor conspiracy, which held the organization of labor unions to be a criminal act, and he supported the right of workers not only to organize but to engage in strikes as well, though he believed strikes to be, for the most part, an ill-advised attempt to get around the laws of free trade.

Indeed, when labor activists seemed to violate the principle of free trade directly, Leggett parted company with them. Leggett had only harsh words regarding the flour riot of 1837, when a large crowd, believing that several flour merchants were holding large stores of flour from the market during that hungry winter of high bread prices, stormed their warehouses and made off with the flour. To Leggett, the flour riot was an inexcusable violation of the principle of free trade. Carrying these principles to their logical conclusion as usual, Leggett subsequently opposed legislation to compensate the flour merchants for their losses, because that would improperly involve the government in insuring the property of merchants but not of others.

It was on the issue of slavery that Leggett most raised the ire of mainstream Jacksonian Democrats. By the mid-1830s, several slave states had passed legislation banning abolitionist literature from their mails, and antiabolition riots occurred in various cities, including New York. Though critical of these attempts to restrict the flow of ideas and use violence against abolitionists, Leggett initially opposed abolition on the ground that it would create ruinous competition for white wage workers. Over time, however, Leggett found it impossible to reconcile his beliefs in equal rights and free trade with the forcible compulsion of labor inherent to the peculiar institution, and he joined the abolitionist cause. Unlike some abolitionists, moreover, Leggett favored not only the end of slavery, but equal political rights for blacks (and women) as well. For these apostasies, he was denied a Democratic nomination to Congress in 1838.

Leggett's intellectual leadership of the Locofoco wing of the New York Democratic Party represented a chance to put his equal rights and free trade principles into action. Originating during the state banking fights of 1835, the Locofocos advocated measures to ease the burdens of debt on the laboring classes and found their ideological leader and guiding light in Leggett, whose principles of equal rights and free trade became their own. In the Locofocos, the emerging labor movement found, for the first time, a sympathetic ear within the political party system, though a minority one at that.

Though his equation of equal rights and free trade would become increasingly difficult to sustain in the decades after his death, William Leggett's contribution to the labor movement was substantial. Along with George Henry Evans and a few others, he was among the first to present a critique of slavery rooted, at least in part, in labor ideas, and his advocacy of equal rights for blacks and women was certainly quite progressive for his day. His use of the antimonopoly tradition to serve labor's cause continued to resonate throughout the nineteenth century. Perhaps most important, Leggett saw that the labor movement, even in its earliest days, was a political force to be reckoned with by the major parties.

MATTHEW S. R. BEWIG

References and Further Reading

Earle, Jonathan H. *Jacksonian Antislavery and the Politics of Free Soil, 1824–1854.* Chapel Hill: University of North Carolina Press, 2004.
Headley, Joel Tyler. *The Great Riots of New York: 1712–1873.* Reprint. Indianapolis, IN: Bobbs-Merrill, 1970.
Hofstadter, Richard. "William Leggett, Spokesman of Jacksonian Democracy." *Political Science Quarterly* 58, no. 4 (December 1943): 581–594.
Hugins, Walter. *Jacksonian Democracy and the Working Class.* Stanford, CA: Stanford University Press, 1960.
Leggett, William. *A Collection of the Political Writings of William Leggett, Selected and Arranged, with a Preface, by Theodore Sedgwick, Jr.* Reprint. New York: Arno and the New York Times, 1970.
———. *Democratick Editorials: Essays in Jacksonian Political Economy.* Indianapolis, IN: Liberty Press, 1984.
Procter, Page S. "A Source for the Flogging Incident in White-Jacket." *American Literature* 22, no. 2 (May 1950): 176–177.
Seelye, John. "Buckskin and Ballistics: William Leggett and the American Detective Story." *Journal of Popular Culture* 1, no. 1 (1967):

See also **Abolitionism; Antebellum Era; Evans, George Henry; Locofoco Democrats**

LEMLICH, CLARA SHAVELSON (1886–1982)

Clara Lemlich Shavelson (1886–1982) is best known as a leader of the *fabrente Yidishe meydlekh*, the fiery Jewish immigrant girls, whose militancy and dedication to the ideal of bread and roses helped to galvanize the early twentieth-century U.S. labor movement. In 1909, the young shirtwaist maker delivered an impassioned speech in Yiddish at New York's Cooper Union that sparked an "uprising" of 30,000 garment workers—most of whom were East European Jewish immigrant girls between the ages of 15 and 25. The strike, which was the largest strike by women in the United States to that time, paralyzed New York's garment industry and set off a decade of labor militancy by garment workers across the country. Lemlich's role as the catalyst for the 1909 strike ensured her place as a bit player in histories of the early twentieth-century labor movement, East European Jewish immigration, and women's militancy before the 1960s. Lemlich even had a walk-on in the 1986 Broadway hit *I'm Not Rappaport* as the symbol of an idealistic generation of immigrants whose values had been abandoned in the materialistic frenzy of the 1980s.

While these mentions of Lemlich made her into an icon for her generation of immigrant women, telescoping her long activist career into one cameo appearance oversimplifies her complex legacy. Suffragist, communist, community organizer, and peace activist, Clara Lemlich Shavelson was active in revolutionary and left-wing politics from her teen years in the Ukraine until her last years in a California nursing home, where she helped organize the orderlies into a union and convinced the home administrators to honor the United Farm Workers' grape and lettuce boycott. She was also a dedicated promoter of Yiddish culture, cofounder and longtime member of the Emma Lazarus Federation of Jewish Women's Clubs, birth mother to three children who carried on her tradition of radical activism, and political mother to a generation of Jewish radical activists who came of age in the 1930s and modeled themselves on her example.

Lemlich was born in 1886 in Gorodok, Ukraine, to deeply religious Jewish parents. Like most girls in late nineteenth-century East European Jewish villages, she was taught to read and write Yiddish but was offered no further Jewish schooling. Breaking from the tradition of many of their Jewish neighbors—who distrusted everything associated with the Russian authorities—Lemlich's parents allowed her to attend the local Russian-language public school. When Clara was denied admission to Gorodok's only public school because she was a Jew, her parents reacted angrily, banning Russian language, books, and music from their home. Already a rebel, the young Lemlich refused to abide by her parents' prohibition. She had amassed quite a collection by the time her father found and burned her secret library of Russian classics. Undaunted, Lemlich began collecting again

and, now in her teens, she read and collected revolutionary texts by Lenin, Trotsky, and Marx, among others. By the age of 17, Lemlich was a committed socialist. She would remain so for the rest of her life. The violent Kishinev pogrom of 1903 convinced Lemlich's parents that the time had come to leave the Ukraine. The family moved to New York in 1905.

A highly skilled dressmaker, young Clara quickly found work in a Lower East Side garment shop. It took her little time to begin organizing her fellow workers to protest conditions that, she said, reduced human beings to the status of machines. Clara accepted the tutelage of older workers in the fundamentals of trade unionism, but she firmly rejected their insistence that women and unskilled workers could not be organized. Lemlich organized a series of strikes in garment shops around New York between 1907 and 1909, laying the groundwork for a general strike to improve wages, hours, and conditions in the shirt and dress trades. Despite the warnings of Samuel Gompers (the first president of the American Federation of Labor—AFL) and middle-class reformers in the Women's Trade Union League that young women workers could not sustain a general strike, Lemlich called on her fellow shirtwaist makers and dressmakers to attend a meeting in the Great Hall of the People at New York's Cooper Union in November 1909. After a series of labor leaders urged caution, Lemlich jumped on the stage and began exhorting the crowd of young women workers in Yiddish. "I am one of those who suffers from the abuses described here, and I move that we go on a general strike," she shouted. The New York garment uprising that followed sparked similar strikes in Philadelphia, Cleveland, Chicago, Iowa, and Kalamazoo, Michigan, resulting in an unprecedented 40% of women garment workers organized into unions by 1919.

After the 1909 strike, Lemlich was blacklisted from the garment trades. For a few years she channeled her considerable energies into suffrage activism, helping to found and sustain the Wage Earner's League for Woman Suffrage. Here again, Lemlich's uncompromising and fiery nature got her in trouble, this time with the historian Mary Beard, who controlled funds earmarked by more affluent suffragists to pay a working-class suffrage organizer. Beard fired Lemlich in 1912 for refusing to moderate her radical politics to suit the vision of cross-class sisterhood espoused by middle-class women reformers.

Retiring briefly into the role of wife and mother, Lemlich married the printer's union activist Joe Shavelson in 1913 and moved to the Brooklyn immigrant neighborhood of Brownsville, where she gave birth to three children: Irving, Martha, and Rita. Almost immediately, Clara Shavelson began organizing wives and mothers around the primary issues affecting their workplace—the cost of food and housing. She organized kosher meat boycotts in 1917 to protest price increases in staple foods. After World War I, she led a rent strike movement that swept New York's immigrant neighborhoods, when a postwar housing shortage dramatically raised the cost of housing and inflation threatened the hard-won working-class standard of living.

In 1926, Shavelson joined the Communist Party USA and immediately began pushing its leaders to organize not only on the shop floor but in the sphere of working-class housewives—neighborhood markets, parks, and kitchens. That same year, Lemlich founded the United Council of Working Class Housewives (UCWCH). Like a women's union auxiliary, the UCWCH provided aid to striking workers by raising funds, opening community kitchens, and establishing collective child-care arrangements so that women workers could walk the picket lines.

The limits of such work quickly became clear, and in 1929, Shavelson and her neighbor Rose Nelson organized the United Council of Working-Class Women (UCWW) to organize around women's unpaid labor in the home. Shavelson and Nelson insisted that consumption was inextricably linked to production, making the working-class housewife as important a part of the class struggle as were her wage-earning husband, sons, and daughters. Through the UCWW, Shavelson led rent strikes; anti-eviction demonstrations; meat, bread, and milk boycotts; sit-ins and marches on Washington calling for controls on the costs of housing and staple foods, and the construction of more public housing and of more public schools. Over the next few years, she built a national working-class housewives movement. The UCWW changed its name to the Progressive Women's Councils and forged coalitions with a wide range of progressive women's groups, mothers' leagues, neighborhood groups, and union auxiliaries to protest "the high cost of living." In 1935, Shavelson and Nelson led a nationwide meat boycott that shut down 4,500 butcher shops in New York City alone. Though the strike began in Jewish and African-American neighborhoods in New York, it spread to Chicago, Detroit, Los Angeles, Minneapolis, Cleveland, St. Louis, and Seattle, soon involving women of many racial, religious, and ethnic backgrounds. The 1930s housewives' coalition alleviated the worst effects of the Depression in many working-class communities by bringing down food prices and rent and utility costs; preventing evictions; and spurring the construction of more public schools, housing, and parks.

After World War II, housewife organizers conducted two more nationwide meat boycotts, and led annual marches on Washington to lobby elected officials on matters of concern to working-class housewives. Through her decades of community organizing, Shavelson and the housewives' organizations she organized and spurred to action convinced many municipalities to pass rent-control laws. The housewives' movement increased support in Congress for federally funded public housing. It also paved the way for the modern tenants' and consumer movements. Finally, Shavelson and the housewife activists she inspired brought gender politics into union and working-class homes, illuminating previously hidden power relations between husbands and wives, parents and children. Long before the 1960s women's movement, Shavelson knew and made sure that other working-class activists understood that the personal was deeply political.

Shavelson returned to the garment shop floor in 1944, when her husband Joe became too ill to continue working. She quickly became active in a range of union causes, serving on the American Committee to Survey Trade Union Conditions in Europe. As an organizer for the American League Against War and Fascism, she spoke regularly against nuclear weapons and the intensifying arms race. Her passport was revoked after a visit to the Soviet Union in 1949. In 1951, the year her husband, Joe, died, Shavelson was subpoenaed to testify before the House Committee on Un-American Activities. Her husband had been under investigation before his death. Her son remained the subject of FBI surveillance for the next two decades. Government harassment did not silence Shavelson, however. Shavelson maintained a vigil in front of the Foley Square Courthouse and later in Washington, DC to protest the arrest, trial, and execution of famed "atom spies" Julius and Ethel Rosenberg. She also actively protested the U.S. role in the 1954 coup in Guatemala that overthrew democratically elected President Jacobo Arbenz Guzman. Her daughter Martha recalls Shavelson's courage in the face of government harassment during the 1950s. "Others burned books from their own shelves," Martha remembers. "Not Clara." She grew more stubborn and more certain. In 1954, when Shavelson retired from the International Ladies' Garment Workers' Union (ILGWU), the unrepentant radical was denied a pension on a technicality. After a long battle, she was awarded two honorary stipends by the ILGWU president, David Dubinsky, but she never did receive the pension she had earned from the union she helped to found—and which hailed her as a pioneer on every major anniversary.

Nine years after the death of her husband, Shavelson fell in love again and married an old labor movement acquaintance named Abraham Goldman.

She lived with him until his death in 1967. At age 81, beginning to suffer from Alzheimer's, Shavelson moved into the Jewish Home for the Aged in Los Angeles. While the home was located in Boyle Heights, Shavelson enjoyed a wide circle of friends among the area's Jewish radical community. When the home moved into the San Fernando Valley, she was cut off from her accustomed political and ethnic atmosphere and began to withdraw into herself. Still, Shavelson remained feisty into her 90s, advising and helping to organize the home's orderlies into a union. She also shamed the home's administrators into honoring the United Farm Workers' boycott of nonunion grapes and lettuce by reminding them how many of the home's residents were former union activists themselves. Even if they no longer understood, she insisted, they would be very upset to know they were eating "scab" grapes and lettuce. Shavelson died on July 12, 1982, at the age of 96.

Clara Shavelson was once described by her friend and political collaborator Rose Nelson as a "spark plug" who set off conflagrations wherever she was. Sparks and spark plugs are fitting metaphors for the life of this explosive woman revolutionary.

ANNELISE ORLECK

References and Further Reading

Buhle, Mari Jo. *Women and American Socialism, 1870–1920.* Urbana: University of Illinois Press, 1981.
Orleck, Annelise. *Common Sense and a Little Fire: Women and Working-Class Politics in the United States, 1900–1965.* Chapel Hill: University of North Carolina Press, 1995.
Scheier, Paula. "Clara Lemlich: 50 Years in Labor's Front Line." *Jewish Life* (November 1954).
Tax, Meredith. *The Rising of the Women: Feminist Solidarity and Class Conflict, 1880–1917.* New York: Monthly Review Press, 1980.

See also **International Ladies' Garment Workers' Union (ILGWU) (1900–1995); Jews; Women's Trade Union League**

LEWIS, JOHN L. (1880–1969)
Founder, Congress of Industrial Organizations

John Llewelyn Lewis served as the president of the United Mine Workers of America (UMWA) for four decades and was a founder and first president of the Congress of Industrial Organizations (CIO), from its origins in 1935 until 1940. During his tenure as a labor leader, he earned a contradictory reputation, both as an autocrat who repressed those who challenged his authority in the UMWA and, later, as the militant voice for America's industrial working class during the massive CIO organizing drives of the New Deal era. Always controversial, Lewis later broke ranks with the CIO, became a strong opponent of President Franklin Roosevelt, and led coal miners during a series of national walkouts during World War II. Following the war, Lewis negotiated a groundbreaking pension and heath-care system for union coal miners, but faded into obscurity as the coal industry and his union went into steep decline.

Early Career

Lewis, the son of Welsh immigrants, was born in 1880 in Iowa. While much of Lewis's early life remains sketchy, his family moved frequently, leaving the coalfields on at least one occasion. By the late 1890s, Lewis had followed his father underground, and he became the secretary of his local union in 1901. Lewis, however, had other ambitions. He managed the local opera house and performed in several productions. He ventured west from 1901 to 1905, where exactly and what he did remain a mystery. Lewis returned to Iowa and resumed work in the mines. He also ran unsuccessfully for local political office and failed in his efforts to establish a grain and feed business. Lewis married Myrta Edith Bell in 1907 and relocated with his extended family to the coal-mining town of Panama, Illinois.

Lewis soon rose to prominence in the UMWA in Illinois, where he caught the eye of the American Federation of Labor (AFL) president Samuel Gompers, who appointed him to various organizing posts and helped launch his career as a labor leader. Lewis continued his involvement in internal UMWA politics, however, and he remained a close ally of the then-president John P. White, who appointed him "international statistician" in 1917. Lewis soon became business manager of the *United Mine Workers Journal* and then vice president of the union after White resigned to take a post in the Wilson administration. Lewis quickly edged out the president, Frank Hayes, and became temporary head of the UMWA in 1919. The following year, Lewis won a bitter election to become the international president of the miners' union, a position he would hold until 1960.

Lewis spent his first decade as the president of the UMWA, consolidating his control over the union by eliminating his political rivals. Building on his victory in the UMWA, Lewis challenged Gompers for president of the AFL in 1921, presenting himself as a radical and more militant alternative. But Lewis was soundly defeated at the AFL's national convention when opponents from within the UMWA openly opposed him. Lewis later had one of his UMWA lieutenants, William Green, named the AFL president after Gompers died in 1924. Lewis spent the rest of the decade running those who had opposed him in the 1921 election out of the miners' union, shrewdly pitting his more opportunistic opponents, like the Kansas militant Alex Howat and the Illinois leader Frank Farrington, against each other, isolating them, and using their own mistakes to eliminate them as political threats. Most of them were eventually expelled from the UMWA.

With his more principled opponents, like the Pennsylvania socialist John Brophy, Lewis often resorted to red-baiting to marginalize them within the UMWA. When that failed, he employed repressive tactics against his opponents. While Lewis became the best-known labor Republican in the 1920s, many of his specific political beliefs remained vague and ill-defined, perhaps because he had to contend with a substantial leftist challenge within his own union during his first decade as president. Brophy and many other UMWA activists supported mild efforts to nationalize the nation's coal industry, and the union had endorsed such proposals at some of its conventions. Lewis, a shrewd political operative, used their politics against them. He appointed Brophy and other leftists to a Nationalization Research Committee to study the issue. He then worked to undermine and demonize the committee, portraying the committee as the tool of outside liberal and socialistic interests bent on controlling the UMWA. When Brophy ran against Lewis for UMWA president in 1926, he faced the full wrath of the UMWA president's well-oiled political machine. Lewis closed the pages of the union's journal to Brophy, and then portrayed the District 2 president as a communist and socialist stooge. Lewis, in full control of the UMWA's electoral system, soundly defeated Brophy in the election. Like Lewis's less principled opponents, Brophy also found himself expelled from the UMWA.

Though Lewis emerged from the 1920s in full control of the UMWA, the union was just a shell of its former self. Throughout the 1920s, the coal operators mounted a concerted campaign to roll back union gains while nonunion companies continued to expand. The operators succeeded in banishing the UMWA from most of the southern and outlying districts in the years after World War I. The union's "Jacksonville Agreement," negotiated with federal help in 1924, sought to preserve wages and working conditions with large operators in the northern coalfields. The agreement proved unenforceable, and the companies that had signed it openly violated it. Without federal support, UMWA membership declined from 400,000 to under 80,000 at the end of the 1920s, as the onset of the Great Depression ravaged the nation's coalfields. The economic crisis produced a final round of dissent, centered in Illinois, the only viable region left in the UMWA by the late 1920s. Heavily divided, the dissidents, who called themselves the "True" UMWA, met the same fate as those who had earlier tried to oust Lewis. They were red-baited and denounced as "dual unionists," and their attempt to wrest control of the UMWA from Lewis failed miserably. Lewis remained atop the union in the early 1930s, but the UMWA lay in tatters.

The CIO Era

At this low point, the miners and their president stirred to action, and they transformed the labor movement in the United States in the process. Though Lewis, a Republican, had endorsed Herbert Hoover for president in 1932, Franklin D. Roosevelt and his New Deal helped bring the UMWA back. Encouraged by Roosevelt's programs, particularly section 7a of the National Industrial Recovery Act, miners flocked to the UMWA in 1933 and 1934, and the union and its president returned to national prominence. The UMWA controlled nearly 90% of the country's production in 1934, once again emerging as a powerful force in the nation. Lewis, meanwhile, reached out to his former opponents on the left, including the talented Brophy. He restored their union membership and drew on their organizing skill to expand UMWA influence. The UMWA president became increasingly disillusioned by the lackluster efforts on the part of the AFL, then headed by his old ally William Green, to organize workers in the automobile, rubber, and steel industries. Poor tactics by the craft union-dominated AFL had left these workers unorganized and disillusioned during the early years of the New Deal. The UMWA, which functioned on an industrial basis, had thrived with its aggressive organizing programs.

Events transformed Lewis into the most important voice for the millions of unorganized workers in the United States, and he embarked upon the most dramatic and successful phase of his long career in the labor movement. In his criticisms of the AFL, Lewis found important allies in Sidney Hillman, the president of the Amalgamated Clothing Workers of America (ACWA), and David Dubinsky, the head of the International Ladies' Garment Workers' Union (ILGWU). Together with other industrial union advocates, they began to push for reform within the AFL, urging the organization to embrace the opportunities the activist federal government presented. Their efforts to encourage more aggressive organizing in heavy industries failed, and by the mid-1930s they were ready to branch off from the AFL. After a dramatic confrontation between Lewis and the carpenters' union president, William Hutcheson, during the AFL convention in 1935—Lewis punched him in the face after the two men quarreled—Lewis, Hillman, Dubinsky, and other industrial union supporters created the Committee for Industrial Organization. Though the industrial unions essentially functioned independently of the AFL, they would remain within the umbrella organization until 1938, when the Congress of Industrial Organizations officially separated itself from its old parent. Dubinsky and the ILGWU, however, would remain in the AFL.

Lewis dominated the CIO in its early years, drawing on the UMWA's treasury to finance the organization's activities and staffing it with his miners' union allies. Brophy became the CIO's director, and Adolph Germer, a former miner who also had opposed Lewis, was named field representative. Even Powers Hapgood, a UMWA militant who had opposed Lewis and suffered beatings at the hands of his thugs, was brought into the CIO fold. Along with Lewis, these organizers demonstrated a stunning amount of skill that led to early organizing victories. In the winter of 1936, Lewis and the CIO staff encouraged the militance demonstrated by rubber workers at Goodyear's operations in Akron, Ohio. Thousands of workers idled the company's operations through March, when the CIO reached a settlement with management that resulted in modest changes. Most important, however, the workers and their union, the United Rubber Workers (URW), had survived.

Later, in December, workers at Fisher Body plants in Flint, Michigan, owned by auto giant General Motors (GM), shut off their machinery, forced company guards and foremen out of the shops, and took control of the plant, initiating a major sit-down strike. They refused to leave until the company agreed to recognize their union, the United Automobile Workers (UAW). Lewis initiated a complex series of negotiations that involved the company, the federal government, and state officials. The workers, boldly defying the company's efforts to evict them, remained inside the plant for six weeks, providing Lewis and the CIO with the support they needed to force an agreement with GM. Lewis, with the workers flocking to the CIO banner, refused to back down from his demand for union recognition through the winter months of 1937. Finally, under pressure from Lewis

and federal officials, General Motors agreed to recognize the UAW in February. It was perhaps Lewis's greatest moment as a labor leader, and he watched as other major automakers began to sign agreements with the union in the months that followed. CIO membership swelled.

Lewis and the CIO enjoyed less success in their attempts to organize the steel industry, a key sector of the economy, with close ties to the coal industry. The Steel Workers Organizing Committee (SWOC) was formed in June 1936, after the AFL's attempts to organize the steel industry faltered. The CIO put 200 organizers into the campaign, and Lewis installed his trusted UMWA ally Philip Murray as the president of SWOC, but the efforts made only limited headway. The CIO's victory at General Motors, however, convinced management at United States Steel, the industry's leader, to compromise. Lewis and the U.S. Steel head, Myron Taylor, began a series of negotiations in January 1937, after they famously met at the Mayflower Hotel in Washington, DC. Near the end of February, the two leaders reached a deal that granted a 5% wage increase, a 40-hour week, overtime, a grievance procedure, and, most important, recognition of the United Steelworkers of America (USWA). Lewis and the CIO ran into stronger opposition with the smaller "Little Steel" companies that made up the rest of the industry, however. The organizing drive in the spring of 1937 was met with violence, most prominently in Chicago, where 10 strikers were killed and dozens wounded in a brutal attack on Memorial Day. The drive to organize these companies had faltered by the middle of July.

The industrial organizing tactics pushed by Lewis and the CIO signaled a major shift in the manner in which labor unions sought to bring workers into the movement. This was particularly true with regard to African-American workers, who had largely been ignored by AFL unions, many of which practiced segregation or refused to allow black workers to belong to their organizations at all. By contrast, Lewis and his supporters in the CIO proved among the strongest advocates for the rights of African-Americans in the mainstream labor movement. When the UMWA moved into the southern coalfields in the 1930s, it reached out to black coal miners, welcoming them into the same local unions as white miners without hesitation. The UMWA did conform to many of the requirements of Jim Crow—in particular, African-Americans were relegated to secondary status in terms of leadership positions in the union, and many locals initially adhered to segregated seating arrangements—but in other ways, Lewis and the miners issued strong challenges to southern norms.

Lewis sought to equalize wage rates among black and white miners, and African-Americans participated in union grievance committees and were brought on as paid staff members.

The efforts at reform reached outside the workplace as well. Lewis and other UMWA officials denounced the disfranchisement of African-Americans in the South. Lewis addressed both the National Association for the Advancement of Colored People (NAACP) and the National Negro Congress conventions in 1940, where he spoke strongly in favor of black rights. Brophy, in a 1938 address to the National Negro Conference, denounced lynching and stressed the interracial organizing efforts of the CIO. The UMWA secretary-treasurer, Thomas Kennedy, a close Lewis ally, sharply criticized racial discrimination in the labor movement at the same convention. These strong words resonated with African-Americans, who embraced the cause of industrial unionism and provided the foundation on which the movement rested in most parts of the South.

Going It Alone

At the height of the CIO's influence, however, Lewis did an about-face, and he began to clash openly with many of his former allies. His actions grew increasingly secretive and arbitrary in the late 1930s. He removed CIO staffers like Brophy and replaced them with family members or allies he could control. Tensions within the CIO grew between Lewis and Hillman, particularly after the ACWA president took a job in the Roosevelt administration. Hillman agreed with Roosevelt's foreign policy direction, which increasingly moved the United States toward intervention in World War II. Lewis, an isolationist, was staunchly opposed to the administration on this issue. Hillman also believed that co-operation between labor and government was positive, while Lewis worried that the increasing federal presence, and the defense industry buildup in particular, was a threat to the labor movement. Increasingly, Lewis began to issue a series of sharp attacks against Hillman for his support of administration policies.

Tensions came to a head in the fall of 1940. Lewis reverted to his Republican sentiments and endorsed Wendell Willkie for president, sharply denouncing Roosevelt and vowing to resign as CIO president if workers did not follow him into the GOP. While the CIO made no formal endorsement, most officials in the organization and its membership supported Roosevelt in the election. Lewis resigned soon after,

handing over the CIO presidency to his former UMWA lieutenant, SWOC head Philip Murray.

As the CIO president, Murray attempted to move the organization away from UMWA domination. Lewis responded with a series of harsh attacks on Murray, and he attempted to put the CIO president through a series of humiliating punishments for his independence. Lewis publicly advanced the idea that the CIO and AFL should re-unite, with both Murray and the AFL president Green retiring. He then billed the CIO for $1.6 million that the UMWA had loaned the organization during its early days. When Murray suggested that Lewis was spreading chaos in the CIO, the UMWA president threatened to charge him with slander and had Murray's membership in the miners' union revoked. The UMWA formally left the CIO in 1942, closing the door on the most remarkable phase of Lewis's career.

The UMWA would mostly pursue an independent path in the years that followed. It briefly re-united with the AFL after World War II, but left again in 1947, after Lewis refused to comply with provisions of the Taft-Hartley Act. Increasingly, the UMWA and its president became isolated from the currents of the mainstream labor movement. Lewis, in fact, would finish his career in relative obscurity.

Lewis first led the miners in a series of walkouts during World War II, defying both the federal government and public opinion. The war caused demand for coal to grow, and it took a toll on the miners as they struggled to meet production demands. Deaths in the mines increased, outpacing combat casualties during the first year of the war. As inflation surged, meanwhile, pay remained stagnant, due in part to the federal government's "Little Steel Formula," which attempted to control wartime inflation by limiting increases in wages and benefits. Lewis alternately led the miners and followed their lead in a series of walkouts during 1943 that idled the nation's coalfields. Eventually, the federal government intervened, seizing the coal mines and raising wages under a plan to pay workers for the time they traveled to and from the coal face (called "portal to portal" pay). When the government returned the mines to private hands, however, the strikes resumed. Eventually, the miners won a wage increase with the help of the Roosevelt administration, though not as much as they had initially hoped for. Meanwhile, the UMWA and Lewis became national pariahs. Congress passed the Smith-Connally Act in the midst of the UMWA's strikes. This measure made it a crime to encourage workers to go on strike during the war and required notices of the intent to strike, secret ballots on the issue, and a 30-day "cooling off" period.

The Final Battle

Beginning in 1945, Lewis began the last major initiative in his career as a labor leader when he pushed for the creation of a health and pension system for UMWA members that would be financed by a royalty on every ton of coal produced by union miners. In the spring of 1946, after another round of walkouts, the federal government imposed a settlement on the operators that included a jointly administered Welfare and Retirement Fund for injured, sick, and retired miners and their families. But it would take years of fighting and negotiations before the coal operators would actually agree to the proposal. In the meantime, they fought Lewis and the UMWA every step of the way. The opposition of the operators provoked a series of strikes throughout the remainder of the 1940s, culminating with the 1949–1950 national walkout, which saw the permanent establishment of the system.

After the 1949–1950 strike, Lewis established dominance over the board that oversaw the Fund when he engineered the nomination of his close ally, Josephine Roche, as a "neutral trustee" in 1950. Though Lewis realized his dream of a health and pension system for coal-mining families, the industry's persistent economic problems led to rounds of cutbacks in the 1950s and 1960s. A series of hospitals constructed by the Fund that served isolated communities in Appalachia had to be sold or closed to keep the system solvent. Since the Fund was bankrolled by production, the UMWA encouraged mechanization, which cost miners jobs, and discouraged walkouts, including those over safety issues. Meanwhile, nonunion production began to rise in the 1950s and 1960s, at the same time that the coal industry entered a deep recession. Miners responded with a series of violent organizing drives, particularly in parts of Tennessee and Kentucky, where the coal-purchasing policies of the Tennessee Valley Authority had encouraged the creation of small, nonunion operations. Despite these occasional violent episodes, Lewis became known more for his co-operation with the industry than for his confrontation with it during the 1950s. He grew increasingly close to Cyrus Eaton, a financier based in Cleveland, Ohio, and George Love of Consolidation Coal Company, the industry leader.

When Lewis finally retired in January 1960, both the Fund and his union were on shaky ground. The UMWA president spent his last years continuing to oversee the Fund, but overall, he faded into obscurity. The union, meanwhile, suffered under the leaders that followed Lewis. Thomas Kennedy succeeded him as president, but died three years later. W. A. "Tony" Boyle became the UMWA president in 1963, but he lacked Lewis's charisma and his talent for managing the union. Though Lewis had brought Boyle out of the union's obscure Montana district, the new UMWA president had learned little from his mentor, and Lewis eventually repudiated him in private. When Joseph A. "Jock" Yablonski, a former Lewis loyalist, challenged Boyle for the UMWA presidency in 1969, many hoped the former president would endorse the insurgency. Though Lewis indicated his support, he died on June 11, 1969, before a formal meeting with Yablonski could take place. Yablonski lost the flawed election to Boyle—the UMWA president's political machine made sure the results were favorable—and assassins later murdered the insurgent, his wife, and daughter. Boyle and several other UMWA officials eventually were convicted of arranging the killings. Many speculated whether the system within the UMWA that Lewis had built over the preceding decades had created the atmosphere that allowed such brutality and corruption to flourish.

Ultimately, John L. Lewis left a mixed legacy. In his early career as a labor leader, Lewis suppressed rank-and-file activism in the UMWA and solidified dictatorial control over the organization. Then, in the wake of the economic collapse of the Great Depression, Lewis emerged as a militant unionist and eloquent spokesman for the unorganized, creating the CIO and transforming the American labor movement in the process. In the midst of this effort, he suddenly reversed course, turning on his union and political allies and taking the miners down an independent path that ultimately left them on the margins of the American labor movement. In his final years, Lewis forced the coal operators to agree to a groundbreaking health and pension system for miners. But this, too, proved an elusive dream, as cutbacks and financial problems, the product of the problematic economics of the coal industry, continually plagued the program.

ROBERT H. WOODRUM

References and Further Reading

Dubofsky, Melvyn, and Warren Van Tine. *John L. Lewis: A Biography.* New York: Quadrangle/The New York Times Book Co., 1977.

Finley, Joseph F. *The Corrupt Kingdom: The Rise and Fall of the United Mine Workers.* New York: Simon and Schuster, 1972.

Fox, Maier. *United We Stand: The United Mine Workers of America, 1890–1990.* Washington, DC: United Mine Workers of America, 1990.

Lewis, Ronald. *Black Coal Miners in America: Race, Class, and Community Conflict, 1780–1980.* Lexington: University of Kentucky Press, 1987.

Mulcahy, Richard. *A Social Contract for the Coalfields: The Rise and Fall of the United Mine Workers of America Welfare and Retirement Fund.* Knoxville: University of Tennessee Press, 2000.

Zieger, Robert H. *The CIO: 1935–1955.* Chapel Hill: University of North Carolina Press, 1995.

———. *John L. Lewis: Labor Leader.* Boston: Twayne Publishers, 1988.

See also **Amalgamated Clothing Workers of America; American Federation of Labor; Boyle, W. A. (Tony); Brophy, John; Congress of Industrial Organizations; Dubinsky, David; Gompers Samuel; Hapgood, Powers; Hillman, Sidney; United Mine Workers of America; United Rubber Workers of America; United Steelworkers of America**

LIBERAL PARTY

Formed in 1944 after a clash with American Labor Party (ALP) leadership, the Liberal Party of New York State sought to continue the ALP formula of supporting President Roosevelt's re-election while endorsing liberal Democrats or Republicans (typically the Liberal Party endorsed Democrats) and occasionally fielding its own candidates. Although the Liberal Party consisted of a small membership compared with the major parties, Democrats and Republicans recognized the Liberal's Party's significance in deciding close elections. Although the ALP counted more registered voters than the burgeoning Liberal Party, the ALP grew steadily isolated during the late 1940s and early 1950s from the mainstream labor movement as communist influence within it increased. When the ALP ceased to exist by 1956, the Liberal Party became the sole labor party in the state and grew to increase its influence over the next three decades.

The International Ladies' Garment Workers' Union president, David Dubinsky, and the United Hatters, Cap, and Millinery Workers' International Union vice president, Alex Rose, led many labor leaders and rank-and-file members out of the ALP due to the increasing communist influence within the party. In many respects, the Liberal Party was a non-communist replica of the ALP, led by trade unionists but also including liberal thinkers and activists such as the theologian Reinhold Niebuhr. Therefore, it competed for many of the same voters as the ALP during its early years, typically trailing behind in members. The Liberal Party's first attempt to make a splash in New York politics occurred in its incipient year when Dubinsky and Rose wanted the party to endorse the former Republican presidential candidate Wendell Willkie for mayor of New York City. They presumed that Willkie would be endorsed by the New York Republican Party, making him a fusion candidate with support from the Republican and Liberal Parties. However, Willkie died of a heart attack shortly before the campaign commenced. Nonetheless, the Liberal Party persevered, supporting a number of liberal Democrats as well as liberal Republicans such as Jacob Javits, beginning with his first election to Congress in 1946. Over the next few years, however, the party worked diligently to develop a base and came to play a major role in the 1948 presidential election.

In early 1948, Liberal Party leaders recognized Truman's need to win New York, and they believed he would consider changes in his policies if those alterations would win him the state. New York State's 47 electoral votes offered a potentially decisive number of votes in a close election, and Truman appeared to be heading into a tight finish with the Republican nominee, Thomas Dewey. In 1948, an extraordinary division within the Democratic Party occurred, threatening to cost Truman crucial votes and tip the election to Dewey. To the political left, Henry Wallace of the Progressive Party threatened to carry off liberal votes. On the political right, Strom Thurmond endangered Truman's ability to win traditionally Democratic votes in the South. Winning New York offered a way to compensate for these likely lost votes.

Ostensibly, this led Truman to seek backing from Liberal Party voters. New York offered any presidential candidate the greatest number of electoral votes in the country. During the 1944 and 1948 presidential campaigns, the Republicans nominated Dewey, the governor of New York, specifically to win his own state. In the previous 70 years, only Woodrow Wilson had won the presidency without winning New York. With this in mind, Truman recognized the importance of securing as many New Yorkers' votes as possible.

Truman needed the votes of New York trade unionists and liberals to carry the state. He wanted the help of a political apparatus capable of publicizing his message among these union members and liberals. New York Democratic leaders did not have the same level of influence with this crucial voting bloc and more important, they believed Truman had no chance to win New York. The Liberal Party offered an organization with prominent labor leadership and an ability to galvanize labor and liberal voters through a party structure. It maintained a prominent position within the state electorate, its leadership enjoyed wide access to the local media, and its organizational and financial resources promised a candidate mass exposure to New York voters.

By September 1948, the Liberal Party, satisfied with Truman's stances on issues important to it, including labor, housing, foreign policy, and civil rights, put its weight behind his candidacy. While the New York Democratic Party leadership distanced itself from Truman and focused on assisting local candidates, the Liberal Party provided Truman his most organized support system in the state. This was most evident when the Liberal Party sponsored a rally for Truman at Madison Square Garden. Typically, a presidential candidate's own party sponsored such an event, but only the Liberal Party offered Truman this promotional event in New York.

Ultimately, Truman lost New York in a close finish, but the Liberal Party had established itself as a player in national and state politics. With the ALP's demise and eventual extinction in 1956, the Liberal Party became the most important third party in New York State politics. In 1960, the party once again played a crucial role in a presidential campaign. The Democratic candidate, John F. Kennedy, sought support from the Liberal Party, and he gained crucial votes he needed to secure New York with much assistance from Liberal Party supporters. In 1965, the Liberal Party endorsed liberal Republican John Lindsay for New York City mayor. Again, the party put a candidate over the top, and Lindsay won the mayoralty. By 1969, New York City appeared on a downturn, and Lindsay lost the Republican primary for mayor. The Liberal Party offered Lindsay the opportunity to run as the Liberal Party candidate, and he won re-election with the backing of his new party.

With Dubinsky and Rose's deaths during the 1970s, the Liberal Party lost momentum. It drifted through much of the 1980s and 1990s. The party's support of Rudolph Giuliani in his three elections for mayor angered many of its constituents, leading to the formation of a rival party, the Working Families Party. By 2002, the Liberal Party failed to get the required 50,000 votes to qualify for the New York State ballot. This marked the first time that the Liberal Party failed to make the state's ballot since the party's inception in 1944. Accordingly, the party shut down its headquarters in late 2002 and ceased its existence in January 2003.

ADAM HOWARD

References and Further Reading

Dubinsky, David, and A. H. Raskin. *David Dubinsky: A Life with Labor*. New York: Simon and Schuster, 1977.

Epstein, Melech. *Jewish Labor Movement in the USA, Volumes I and II*. New York: Ktav Publishing House, Inc., 1969.

Parmet, Robert D. *The Master of Seventh Avenue: David Dubinsky and the American Labor Movement*. New York: New York University Press, 2005.

See also **American Labor Party; Dubinsky, David**

LIPPARD, GEORGE (1822–1854)
Writer

George Lippard contributed to the imagination of the nineteenth-century American labor movement, through his journalism, his fiction, and his invention of rich and ritualistic culture of the American labor secret society, the Brotherhood of the Union. A romantic and eccentric figure, so self-denying that he could be seen walking around Philadelphia in clothes tied together with twine, he balanced dark thoughts about machinery enslaving the working man against his optimism that "The Continent of America is the Palestine of Redeemed Labor."

Early on, George Lippard had social and educational advantages over his eventual working-class audience. Born into a prosperous German farming family near Yellow Springs, Pennsylvania, in 1822, he was the son of a schoolteacher, Daniel Lippard, and his wife, Jemima. Due to a series of deaths in the family, George was raised by maternal aunts and educated with an eye toward first the ministry, and then the law. By 1840, he was beginning to write his first novel and, bored with the law, joined the Philadelphia newspaper *The Spirit of the Times*, covering the police beat.

Over the next decade, Lippard worked as both a fiction writer and a journalist, serving as chief editor of the *Citizen Soldier* and eventually founding his own newspaper, *The Quaker City*, in 1848. As a journalist, George Lippard covered labor issues, writing floridly about the dehumanizing power of machinery. As an author of sensationalist novels that first appeared in serialized form in "story papers," Lippard specialized in a form of the Gothic that drew on his experiences as a crime reporter, mixing pornographic levels of violence with patriotic narratives. His work reveals a strong sense of place, evoking the sights of Pennsylvania—from the woods of his boyhood to the teeming streets of Philadelphia—in his narratives. Unlike his contemporary and friend Edgar Allan Poe, Lippard created fictional worlds predicated on the idea that cities had secret lives and that working people were dogged by great, corrupt conspiracies. Although panned by contemporary critics, his novels hit a nerve and were best sellers with an avid working-class readership.

Lippard's concern for the "lower ten thousand" had appeared before his official involvement with the labor movement. In 1848, he found an outlet for his social reformism when he attended one of the annual Industrial Congresses then being held in cities up and down the East Coast. Like many labor reformers of his day, Lippard both feared and thought it possible to avoid the importation of European class differences. In a milieu in which Fourierism, land reform, the ten-hour day, and various other prescriptions swirled, Lippard proposed a harmony of interests between employer and employee. This would be achieved through the fraternity of a secret society, the Brotherhood of the Union. Founded September 1, 1849, the Brotherhood of the Union eventually had "circles" or locals in 20 states. According to Lippard's own statement of purpose for the organization, it took for its basis "the principle of Brotherly Love in the Gospel of Nazareth, and the affirmation of the Right of Man to life, liberty, land and home in the Declaration of Independence." This combination of patriotism and Christianity was intended to have the widest possible appeal to native-born artisans. Lippard also endorsed the popular movement, led by the National Reform Association, to secure a homestead for every working man—but by 1852, he had become convinced that the Industrial Congresses were nothing but a sham and that his Brotherhood was the only route to the regeneration of mankind.

Given the high profile of the secretive Masons in antebellum politics, Lippard emulated that group by using ritual and theatrics to bind the members of his union together. Initiates in the Brotherhood of the Union could buy, or have their wives sew, regalia for their meetings according to patterns that Lippard created. The speeches and initiation ceremonies that characterized the order were all written by Lippard himself. Dressed in their robes, members of the Brotherhood could eventually aspire to be leaders, the leadership positions having been named after great American patriots: not only the expected George Washington, but also Robert Fulton, who inaugurated the age of steam travel on the waterways, and Stephen Girard, the Philadelphia philanthropist who endowed a secondary school for the orphaned sons of industrious mechanics. Lippard himself was repeatedly elected to three-year terms as Supreme Washington of the Brotherhood of the Union—the highest possible leadership position—until his death.

The success that Lippard enjoyed as a journalist, popular author, and labor reformer was not mirrored in his home life. He had married Rose Newman in 1847 and fathered a son and a daughter, but between 1849 and 1851 both children died in infancy, and his adored young wife succumbed to tuberculosis. The

Brotherhood of the Union was the only bright star in his firmament, and he continued to promote it, traveling around the country giving speeches, and keeping in contact with local leaders by letter. Lippard died—reportedly of "a heavy cold"—at the age of 32, on February 9, 1854. He left behind not only his corpus of writings, but also an enduring legacy of labor activism in Philadelphia. The Brotherhood of the Union helped to unify labor reformers through some lean years of unionism and to provide a model for the ritual, the reformism, and some of the rhetoric of interclass harmony of the Knights of Labor. In a testament to the popularity of Lippard's blending of working-class patriotism and religiosity, the Brotherhood of the Union persisted as an organization into the twentieth century, describing itself as a friendly society based on the teachings of the Gospel of Nazareth and the Declaration of Independence.

JAMIE L. BRONSTEIN

References and Further Reading

Butterfield, Roger. "George Lippard and His Secret Brotherhood." *Pennsylvania Magazine of History and Biography* 74 (July 1955): 291–309.

Denning, Michael. *Mechanic Accents: Dime Novels and Working-Class Culture in America*. London: Verso, 1987.

Reynolds, David S. *George Lippard*. Boston: Twayne, 1982.

———. *George Lippard, Prophet of Protest: Writings of an American Radical, 1822–1854*. New York: Peter Lang, 1986.

Streeby, Shelley. *American Sensations: Class, Empire, and the Production of Popular Culture*. Berkeley: University of California Press, 2002.

LIVING WAGE

The concept of the "living wage" has been central in the ideology of organized (and unorganized) labor since the 1870s. Generally defined by its working-class promoters as a wage sufficient to allow workers and their families to live in comfort, the living wage linked earning levels with contemporary standards of appropriate consumption. The British labor radical Hugh Lloyd Jones popularized the term in 1874, which was first used in the late 1860s, in a series of articles in *The Beehive*. Across the Atlantic, at roughly the same time, the Boston labor leader Ira Steward used the phrase "living wage" several times in his unpublished manuscript, "The Political Economy of Eight Hours," which was written between 1872 and his death in 1883. After the 1877 national railroad strike, "living wage" became a key word in American labor rhetoric. It remains so today. The key reason for the popularity of the phrase "living wage" is that it provided a means for American workers to make the system of wage labor, which was becoming dominant in late nineteenth-century America, consistent with republic ideals of free labor. According to labor advocates, living wages could provide workers with the ability to maintain their position as key citizens of the American republic, a position previously ensured only by independent proprietorship.

For most of the nineteenth century, American workers decried wage labor. They claimed that wage labor denied workers the "full fruits" of their labor and reduced the proud American citizen-worker to a "wage slave," a term of derision popularized in the Jacksonian era as the incipient crisis of wage labor led to the rise of the organized labor movement. Free workers did not want to be identified with lifelong "hirelings," whom they condemned as emblematic of slavery. The very word "wages," one worker in the 1850s declared, was "odious." Wage work was a form of compulsion, the opposite of the free labor system that they valued. In a society that, until 1865, countenanced chattel slavery, these were serious charges.

In the decades after the Civil War, however, a striking transformation began, as many workers for the first time pondered the possibilities of wage labor. In coming to accept the necessity of wages, workers also redefined wage earning to make it consistent with their vision of a just world. They began to interpret wages not as slavery but as a potential means of escape from slavery. George Gunton, a pamphleteer for the American Federation of Labor (AFL), declared, "Wages are not a badge of slavery but a necessary and continual part of social progress." While not all labor leaders shared Gunton's optimism, almost a vast number of them participated in the redefinition of wage labor from slavish to liberating.

The linchpin of this transformation was the demand for a "living wage," usually defined as remuneration commensurate with a worker's needs as citizen, breadwinner, and consumer. Most workers closely paired the living wage with the idea of an "American Standard of Living," a related idea that developed at approximately the same time. Indeed, proponents often defined one in terms of the other, as in John Mitchell's comment that, "The living wage means the American Standard of Living." The AFL president, Samuel Gompers, declared in a well-publicized 1898 debate that a living wage should be "sufficient to maintain an average-sized family in a manner consistent with whatever the contemporary local civilization recognizes as indispensable to physical and mental health, or as required by the rational self-respect of human beings." Although others put forth very different definitions, most proponents of the living wage shared a new, positive vision of wage labor, one that linked it to an expansive and expanding standard of living.

Living wages, proponents held, should offer to wage earners in the post-Civil War years what independent proprietorship had promised in the antebellum era: the ability to support families, to maintain self-respect, and to have both the means and the leisure to participate in the civic life of the nation. In this worldview, the level of wages became what Gompers called "the barometer which indicates the social, political and industrial status" of a society. Advocates of the living wage described it in explicitly political terms as a "right"—often they used the phrase "inalienable right"—the violation of which made republican citizenship impossible. Living wage advocates merged wage labor with citizenship rather than defining the two as incompatible. Workers "have burned the new words of the living wage into the bill of rights," Henry Demarest Lloyd announced in a pamphlet published by the American Federation of Labor in 1893, connecting the economic realm of wages to the political realm of citizenship.

Labor was not alone in constructing the living wage discourse. Not all business leaders and politicians accepted the idea of the living wage. Many of its enemies associated the living wage with the rejection of the "natural" economic laws of supply and demand, freedom of contract. But from the start, a large number of reformers, politicians, and business as well as religious leaders joined labor in debating the meaning of the living wage. Pope Leo XII's 1891 encyclical *Rerum Novarum* advocated that "remuneration must be enough to support the wage earners in reasonable and frugal comfort." An American priest, John A. Ryan, published *A Living Wage* in 1906, a book that helped shift the living wage discourse away from its working-class roots and toward a broader, societywide issue. Protestant ministers, influenced by the Social Gospel, also described living wages as a social obligation of employers. The idea was closely tied to Progressive Era minimum wage legislation and New Deal economic policy. Many of these middle-class promoters of the living wage endorsed it as a way to minimize working-class protest and to incorporate organized labor into the political system. In 1921, the Anthracite Coal Commission endorsed the living wage as a bulwark against revolution: "all American wage earners have a fundamental economic right to at least a living wage, or an American Standard of Living....Failure to realize this right breeds revolutionary agitation, and prevents our self-governing Republic from being what it should be."

Yet in the process of the broad diffusion and acceptance of the living wage, the working-class notion of a consumerist living wage was redefined downward. Many Progressive supporters of the living wage did not have in mind what Ira Steward and Samuel Gompers did when they endorsed a living wage, but rather what they called a "minimum wage," a bare subsistence amount that fell far short of the consumerist ideals posited by workers. State minimum wage laws, first passed in Massachusetts in 1912, reflected the ideal of subsistence rather than abundance. Many politicians and commentators conflated this minimum wage with the much more robust living wage.

While use of the term in the expansive working-class sense had diminished, a consumerist complex of ideas flourished and became central to New Deal political economy, and indeed through the post–World War II years. The working-class and middle-class visions of the living wage occasionally found common ground in the 1920s, when prominent business leaders and politicians supported the living wage and policy makers began to promote the benefits of working-class consumption. In the next decade, a marriage was sealed; in the consolidation of the New Deal Order, the rival versions of the living wage ideology converged in public policy and political economy to become accepted as economic common sense. In language recalling labor's consumerist turn, Franklin Roosevelt declared in a Fireside Chat of 1938, "We suffer primarily from a failure of consumer demand because of a lack of buying power." By the post–World War II years, the living wage had become so integral to the American social contract that some commentators viewed the payment of living wages as a problem solved by the post–New Deal political economy. In these years, labor's demands for high wages, purchasing power, and an American Standard of Living gained a receptive public reaction. The living wage was a central part of the "social bargain" of the post–World War II decades, in which business leaders and politicians accepted the existence and claims of organized labor in exchange for a reduction in shop-floor militancy.

With the economic turmoil of the 1970s, however, and the rise of global competition in many industries, many businesses once again rejected the ideal of the living wage. The weakening of organized labor in this period meant that the main champion of living wages had lost its bully pulpit. Discarding their faith in the broadening of mass consumption as the key to a modern economy, business leaders and their trade organizations argued that the only way for companies to compete was to keep labor costs to a minimum. Throughout the 1970s and 1980s, the federal minimum wage, first set at 25 cents an hour with the Fair Labor Standards Act of 1938 and subsequently increased to account for inflation, stagnated in real dollars. In this period, as the "New Deal bargain" crumbled in the midst of neoliberal market forces, the living wage lost its hold on the popular imagination as an essential element of labor relations.

In the 1990s, the living wage idea was reborn, as an alternative to the legal minimum wage, which had dramatically declined in real dollars in the last third of the twentieth century. Advocates of the revived living wage brought back two related arguments of the idea's originators. They claimed that the payment of living wages would improve, not weaken, local economies, and they argued that living wages were a political and moral necessity. As the Association of Community Organizations for Reform Now (ACORN), an activist group that has promoted living wage campaigns, notes on its Web site (*www.livingwagecampaign.org/*): "The concept behind any living wage campaign is simple: Our limited public dollars should not be subsidizing poverty-wage work. When subsidized employers are allowed to pay their workers less than a living wage, tax payers end up footing a double bill: the initial subsidy and then the food stamps, emergency medical, housing and other social services low wage workers may require to support themselves and their families even minimally. Public dollars should be leveraged for the public good—reserved for those private sector employers who demonstrate a commitment to providing decent, family-supporting jobs in our local communities."

The living wage campaigns of the 1990s and early 2000s generally sought to pass local ordinances requiring private businesses that benefit from public money to pay their workers a living wage, generally defined as the equivalent to the poverty line for a family of four (currently $9.06 an hour), though ordinances that have passed range from $6.25 to $13.00 an hour, with some newer campaigns pushing for even higher wages. In 1994, Baltimore became the first city to pass a so-called living wage ordinance, raising the minimum wage for city workers and those businesses that did business with the city to several dollars above the legal minimum. By the end of 2004, more than 100 living wage ordinances were on the books in cities and counties across the country. In addition, students at many American universities have demanded living wages for university employees and for those who make the goods that bear their school logos. Furthermore, the living wage idea has been exported to other countries. Campaigns for living wages have been waged in countries ranging from South Africa to Canada. In an era of capital mobility and plentiful cheap labor, advocates have even promoted a "global living wage," as an attempt to ensure that global capital pays livable wages wherever it employs workers.

LAWRENCE B. GLICKMAN

References and Further Reading

Glickman, Lawrence. *A Living Wage: American Workers and the Making of Consumer Society*. Ithaca, NY: Cornell University Press, 1997.

Kessler-Harris, Alice. *A Woman's Wage: Historical Meanings and Social Consequences*. Lexington: University of Kentucky Press, 1990.

Luce, Stephanie. *Fighting for a Living Wage*. Ithaca, NY: ILR Press, 2004.

———. "'The Full Fruits of Our Labor': The Rebirth of the Living Wage Movement." *Labor History* 43 (Nov. 2002), 401–409.

Pollin, Robert, and Stephanie Luce. *The Living Wage: Building a Fair Economy*. New York: The New Press, 1998.

LIVING WAGE CAMPAIGNS

In 1994, faith-based, labor, and community activists in Baltimore, Maryland, pressured their city council to adopt a living wage ordinance, a law that required any firm holding a service contract with the city to pay its workers a wage high enough to allow a full-time worker with a family of four to meet the federal poverty line. The campaign was launched for several reasons. First, the federal government had been slow to raise the national minimum wage for the previous two decades, so in real terms its current value had fallen well below its historic peak. In 1994, the federal minimum wage was $4.25 per hour: 38% below where it should have been if it had kept pace with inflation since 1968. The living wage ordinance was designed to begin raising the minimum wage for at least some workers.

Second, living wage campaigns built on the concept of prevailing wage laws, which set wage standards for government construction contracts. The Davis-Bacon Act, passed in 1932, was created in part to establish government as a model employer. Third, local efforts to revitalize urban centers had not resulted in living wage employment for the bulk of urban residents. In the late 1970s and 1980s, cities like Baltimore pumped millions of public dollars into economic redevelopment projects. Even when these efforts resulted in increased employment, residents found that the jobs tended to be low-wage, service-sector positions without benefits. Concerns shifted from simple job creation to the need for a living wage.

Finally, the living wage campaign built on a historical use of the term. In the late nineteenth century,

most workers in industrializing countries realized that they would not be able to stop the growth of wage labor. They then demanded that they be paid a living wage that would guarantee their subsistence and reduce their exploitation. Early advocates of a living wage for industrial laborers included Catholic priests, trade unionists, and women's movement activists.

Since the Baltimore victory, other coalitions formed around the United States to campaign for living wage ordinances in their cities and counties. As more and more campaigns were successful, the scope of the ordinances expanded. Soon, cities were passing living wage ordinances that applied to not only service contractors, but recipients of economic development assistance, firms operating food and beverage concessions on city-owned property, and direct employees of the city or county. The ordinances were also expanded in terms of content. In addition to mandating a higher hourly wage, new ordinances tended to include automatic indexing (so that the wage would increase each year with the rate of inflation) and a requirement that employers either provide health insurance or pay a higher wage to cover the cost of health insurance. Some ordinances also mandated paid days off and required local hiring from community hiring halls, and included language that assisted unions (such as giving employers with a history of labor law violations lower priority for receiving contracts or subsidies).

Living wage supporters then broadened their efforts in an attempt to cover more workers by launching campaigns to establish citywide minimum wage laws under the living wage banner. For example, in 2002, voters in New Orleans, Louisiana, passed a ballot initiative that would require all employers operating within city limits to pay their employees $1 more than the federal minimum wage of $5.15. This measure was eventually overturned by the State Supreme Court, but subsequent efforts are still on the books in several cities. Santa Fe, New Mexico, and San Francisco, California, set citywide minimum wage rates of $8.50 per hour in 2003, indexed to rise with inflation. The Madison, Wisconsin, City Council also established a citywide minimum wage, starting at $5.70 per hour in 2005, increasing to $7.75 plus indexing in 2008.

In the late 1990s, the living wage concept also spread to college campuses. In the most publicized effort, students at Harvard engaged in a three-week sit-in during 2001, occupying an administration building. They had been calling on Harvard University to pay its direct and contracted employees a living wage for several years but met with no success. After their sit-in, the university agreed to convene a task force to develop solutions. In the end, they agreed to several of the students' demands, including raising contracted workers' wages to the level of unionized direct employee wages.

Opposition and Support

By 1998, based on the popularity of the living wage concept and the rapid spread of campaigns, journalists and academics began to refer to a living wage *movement*. The concept of a living wage has generally received significant public support: for example, polls over the last several decades show that a majority of Americans favor an increase in the minimum wage. Nonetheless, the movement has, at times, faced strong opposition. This has included local and national business associations, most notably the Employment Policies Institute; many city administrators, particularly from economic development departments; and some academics. In the late 1990s, when it became clear that most living wage ordinances were passing at the local level, employer associations worked to pass state-level laws that would pre-empt local living wage ordinances. As of 2004, 12 states have laws that pre-empt various forms of living wage ordinances.

In addition to general public support, the list of living wage advocates includes a variety of community, faith-based, and labor organizations. Most prominent is the community-based ACORN (Association of Community Organizations for Reform Now), which runs a national Living Wage Resource Center. Also very active is the Brennan Center for Justice, at the New York University School of Law, which provides legal and technical support for campaigns around the country. Other groups that have been involved in a number of campaigns include Jobs with Justice, the Industrial Areas Foundation, and local legal services offices. Unions have also been involved in the movement, particularly locals of the Service Employees International Union (SEIU) and the Hotel Employees and Restaurant Employees Union (HERE). These unions already represent some of the low-wage workers covered by the ordinances, and have been active in organizing new members through the living wage campaigns. The AFL-CIO endorsed the living wage movement at the national level, and local labor councils have provided support in many cities. Academics such as Robert Pollin from the Political Economy Research Institute at the University of Massachusetts-Amherst have been very involved in the movement as well.

Relevance of the Movement

Judged as a social movement, the campaigns for a living wage have enjoyed much success. Ten years after the initial ordinance was passed in Baltimore, more than 120 local governments have passed a living wage law. Few campaigns have been defeated. In numerous cities, unions and community organizations have achieved a variety of goals through the living wage movement, such as building new labor-community coalitions and organizing workers into unions.

Judged as policy, the outcomes are less clear. First, critics have noted that ordinances cover only a small proportion of low-wage workers. The Economic Policy Institute estimates that in 2000, approximately 38 million workers were earning wages below the living wage level. Even a generous estimate of the number of workers receiving a raise through a living wage ordinance would suggest the campaigns are only providing living wages for fewer than 5% of these workers.

Second, some living wage advocates have discovered that getting the ordinances implemented can be more difficult than getting the law passed in the first place. Research by Stephanie Luce shows that cities are unlikely to rigorously enforce the laws on their own. However, she finds that living wage advocates who have become involved in implementation have had success in significantly improving monitoring and enforcement. Still, implementation remains an issue in many cities.

Third, debate is ongoing about whether living wage ordinances lead to lower employment. Research by the economists Scott Adams and David Neumark concludes that living wage ordinances do result in a modest reduction of employment, and these authors and others conclude that other policy tools such as the Earned Income Tax Credit are more effective methods to reducing poverty. However, these claims are disputed by economists such as Mark Brenner, Peter Hall, Ken Jacobs, and Michael Reich, who find in their empirical work little evidence of negative outcomes. Rather, they find that employers are able to absorb the costs of the living wage through other means. This includes savings achieved through lower turnover and absenteeism as well as reduced profits. It also includes "cost pass-throughs": in some cases, cities are paying a higher amount for their contracted services in order to ensure that workers are getting a living wage. In other cases, employers are able to raise prices for their goods or services.

STEPHANIE LUCE

References and Further Reading

Adams, Scott, and David Neumark. "When Do Living Wages Bite?" *Industrial Relations* 44, no. 1 (2005): 164–192.

Brenner, Mark D. "The Economic Impact of the Boston Living Wage Ordinance." *Industrial Relations* 44, no. 1 (2005): 59–83.

Fairris, Dave. "The Impact of Living Wages on Employers: A Control Group Analysis of the Los Angeles Ordinance." *Industrial Relations* 44, no. 1 (2005): 59–83.

Glickman, Lawrence. *A Living Wage: American Workers and the Making of Consumer Society.* Ithaca, NY: Cornell University Press, 1997.

Luce, Stephanie. *Fighting for a Living Wage.* Ithaca, NY: Cornell University Press, 2004.

Pollin, Robert, and Stephanie Luce. *The Living Wage: Building a Fair Economy.* New York: The New Press, 2000, 1998.

Reich, Michael, Peter Hall, and Ken Jacobs. "Living Wage Policies at San Francisco Airport: Impacts on Workers and Businesses." *Industrial Relations* 44, no. 1 (2005): 106–138.

Reynolds, David. *Living Wage Campaigns: An Activist's Guide to Building the Movement for Economic Justice.* Washington, DC: ACORN, 2003.

See also **Davis-Bacon Act; Minimum-Wage Laws**

LLOYD, HENRY DEMAREST (1847–1903)
Social Reformer

Henry Demarest Lloyd is not well known today, but during the nineteenth century, he was one of the most influential of American social reformers. His voluminous writings earned him the label of "the first muckraker," and his screed against Standard Oil, *Wealth against Commonwealth*, has arguably become one of the masterpieces of the American reform tradition. Lloyd also played an important role in most of the critical events of labor turmoil in the United States from the late 1880s until his death in 1903.

Lloyd's relatively genteel background made it difficult to predict his eventual turn to radicalism. Yet, as was so common in the annals of nineteenth-century reform, Lloyd's strenuously Protestant background helped nurture a desire to improve the world. His father, Aaron, was originally a Dutch Reformed pastor, although when Henry was young, Aaron gave up the ministry to work in a customs house and operate a small bookshop. Henry got through Columbia College on a scholarship, and he also graduated from that institution's law school. Soon afterward, he became the public relations agent for the American Free-Trade League.

Decisive to Lloyd's political blossoming was his move to Chicago in 1872 to become the *Chicago Tribune*'s literary editor. Marriage to the wealthy daughter of one of the paper's owners, William Bross, followed the next year. He and Jessie went on to have four children. Lloyd worked his way up the ranks to chief editorial writer for the *Tribune* before resigning in 1885, the result of political conflicts with the newspaper's chief owner, Joseph Medill.

Lloyd had already turned his attention to pressing Gilded Age political matters while at the *Tribune*, but he gained national attention with the 1881 publication of "The Story of a Great Monopoly" in *Atlantic Monthly*. Here Lloyd explored the corrupt connection between railroads and corporations, particularly the ties between the Pennsylvania Railroad and Standard Oil.

The next 20 years of Lloyd's life would witness an astounding literary output as well as the cementing of his position as one of the age's most important allies of the labor movement. Always prone toward mental fragility, Lloyd suffered a nervous breakdown while traveling in Europe after leaving the *Tribune*. Lloyd's studies during his recovery pushed him far enough to the left that, upon his recuperation, he became one of the primary advocates for clemency for the Haymarket anarchists. This in turn led to his disinheritance from his father-in-law, but Lloyd's many real estate investments allowed him to continue his career as an agitator based out of two elegant homes in Winnekta, Illinois (his main residence), and Sakonnet Point, Rhode Island (his summer abode).

Lloyd's pre-eminent standing in the labor movement came with the publication in 1888 of his "The New Conscience; or, The Religion of Labor" in the *North American Review*. Standing firm against social Darwinism, Lloyd instead foresaw the coming of the co-operative commonwealth. Lloyd, however, never ascended to a purely philosophical plane. The following year, for example, Lloyd learned of the very concrete situation of coal miners in Spring Valley, Illinois, who had been locked out by a company with connections to the rapacious financier Jay Gould. Using to great advantage his background in public relations, Lloyd brilliantly exposed the plight of the miners in his 1890 *A Strike of Millionaires*.

The exploitation of labor was always one of Lloyd's main reasons to indict the large corporations inhabiting the new economic landscape of the Gilded Age. Yet one of Lloyd's strengths was his ability to also consistently keep his feet in the world of middle-class reform. Few works were more important to developing a joint labor/middle-class indictment of big business than Lloyd's magnum opus, *Wealth against Commonwealth* (1894). Here Lloyd accused John D. Rockefeller's Standard Oil of being an enemy of consumers as well as a menace to representative government.

The same year as the publication of *Wealth against Commonwealth*, Lloyd threw himself insistently into the nitty-gritty of radical political affairs. Never comfortable with the stringent emphasis on class in both Gompersite and Socialist rhetoric, Lloyd believed it necessary to bring both farmers and the urban working class together before the age of the cooperative commonwealth could be declared. And this alliance did make it further in Chicago, and in Illinois, than anywhere else in the country. Yet soon the Populists embraced the cause of free silver, which alienated most urban workers, who then turned even more emphatically to the building of defensive craft unions—of which most farmers were suspicious. Lloyd's own overwhelming defeat for Congress on a Labor-Populist ticket portended the split in an alliance that, arguably, never had more than a small chance of success.

After the 1896 Populist debacle, Lloyd gave up his hopes of transforming the national political scene. In his final years, Lloyd grasped after a number of nonconventional reforms that might empower labor and bring about true social democracy. He first turned to producer and consumer co-operatives, writing *Labour Copartnership* in 1898. Two years later, he penned *Country without Strikes* to celebrate New Zealand's effective and just application of compulsory arbitration. Lloyd also threw himself into campaigns for municipal ownership of utilities—particularly, public transportation in Chicago.

A good part of the reason for Lloyd's eclectic reforms, and, in the end, for his ineffectiveness, was his attraction to but ultimate discomfort with much of the militancy and uncompromising nature of the socialist spirit. Lloyd hoped ultimately for a more broad-based political philosophy that could bring together citizens and create social harmony (and he did to some extent find this in the Christian and Fabian branches of socialism). While scholars have often viewed such dismissal of social conflict as a bourgeois fantasy, the overall historical failure of socialism might help us to rethink the value of Lloyd's often radical and staunchly democratic middle-class reformism.

Lloyd died young, broken in spirit and in health. The previous year had, ironically, seen his greatest conventional acceptance into the mainstream when he joined Clarence Darrow and the United Mine Workers president John Mitchell to successfully argue labor's cause before the commission set up by President Theodore Roosevelt to arbitrate the great 1902 Pennsylvania coal strike. Lloyd's memorial service brought 5,000 labor and civic reformers to Chicago to celebrate the life of this unconventional but most steadfast ally of workers.

ROBERT D. JOHNSTON

References and Further Reading

Destler, Chester McArthur. *Henry Demarest Lloyd and the Empire of Reform*. Philadelphia: University of Pennsylvania Press, 1963.
Digby-Junger, Richard. *The Journalist as Reformer: Henry Demarest Lloyd and* Wealth against Commonwealth. Westport, CT: Greenwood, 1996.
Jernigan, E. Jay. *Henry Demarest Lloyd*. Boston: Twayne, 1976.
Thomas, John L. *Alternative America: Henry George, Edward Bellamy, Henry Demarest Lloyd, and the Adversary Tradition*. Cambridge, MA: Belknap Press of Harvard University Press, 1983.

See also **Haymarket Affair (1886); Mitchell, John; Populism/People's Party**

LOCHNER v. NEW YORK (1905)

One of the most infamous cases in the history of the Supreme Court, *Lochner v. New York*, has, in many circles, a reputation close to that of *Dred Scott* or *Plessy v. Ferguson*. In striking down almost all forms of protective labor legislation in *Lochner*, the court majority seemed to go out of its way to sanction the most extreme form of laissez-faire capitalism. The case, however, had surprising complexities, and *Lochner*'s legacy cast an incomplete shadow for American workers.

Although Supreme Court justices receive most of the attention of historians who study *Lochner*, the origins of the case lie in the agitation of workers seeking to create better work conditions. Concerned about low wages and long work hours, bakers in postbellum New York state formulated a two-prong response. One was unionization, which proceeded steadily but in an incomplete fashion through to the end of the century. The other was agitation for shorter hours, which began in earnest during the 1880s. By the end of that decade, employees of union bakeries were working 10 hours a day, but Italian and Jewish immigrants often labored up to 14 hours a day in nonunion shops.

In 1890, Henry Weissman, a German immigrant, took over editorship of the *Baker's Journal*, the voice of the Journeymen Bakers Union. Weissman turned the organ into an effective mouthpiece for protective labor legislation. By 1893, the New York legislature limited bakery work to 10 hours a day and 60 hours per week—although the law offered no sanction to employers who violated the limit. Such penalties came in 1895, and the legislature ratified the law in 1897.

For its first few years, the law was largely ignored, with employers little concerned about enforcement and employees themselves either intimidated or themselves ambivalent about a law that prohibited overtime. Around 1900, at least one third of bakeries were apparently still working their employees longer than 60 hours per week. And while bakers were launching a major unionizing offensive, their employers were also organizing—to fight the rise of organized labor.

In the midst of these hostilities, conditions for bakers in New York City were generally improving, but employers held the upper hand upstate. There, in 1901, Joseph Lochner, a bakery owner in Utica, committed the offense that led the way to the Supreme Court. Lochner "permitted and required" Aman Schmitter to work more than 60 hours in a week. Moreover, Lochner had already been convicted of the same offense in 1899. He refused to offer any defense before the Oneida County Court, and upon his conviction, the Master Bakers Association announced a constitutional appeal.

The bakeshop employers argued along several main lines. First, they denied that the statute was a health measure, a purpose that courts seemed to be requiring of protective labor legislation before declaring such laws a legitimate exercise of the government's police powers. Bread made by overworked employees did not represent a menace to the public health, and there seemed to be no convincing reasoning that overwork affected the health of the employees themselves. Second, the law was illegal "class legislation" because there was no compelling reason to single out bakers over other kinds of employees. Third, the statute restricted the liberty of employees to make their own full and free contractual arrangements, a right supposedly guaranteed under the Fourteenth Amendment.

Lochner lost his case in close split decisions through the New York state court system, with the majority of justices arguing that the legislature, and not the courts, was the proper body to decide such matters. The case then ascended to the Supreme Court, where the employers picked up a key ally: none other than Harry Weissman, the former editor of the *Baker's Journal* as well as the secretary of their union, and arguably the key figure behind the passing of the New York law in the first place. Weissman had left the union in 1897 and, in a move common at the time, set up his own bakeshop. After that enterprise failed, he earned his law degree and entered politics. Weissman's motivations for his ideological turnaround remain unclear. Indeed, after the Supreme Court made its decision in the case, he announced his actual support for the law—stating curiously that his only concern had been the statute's outlawing of overtime pay.

The Supreme Court heard arguments in the case in February 1905. Initially, a majority of justices were set to uphold the law, but a mystery justice (likely Joseph McKenna or Henry Billings Brown) switched and created a new 5-4 majority to strike down the statute. Accepting all of the key arguments of the bakeshop owners, Rufus W. Peckham composed the majority opinion. In turn, two separate dissents offered stinging rebukes to the majority. John Marshall Harlan argued that workers could not "voluntarily" agree to labor for long hours because they had so little power in relation to employers. Harlan also cited medical evidence to argue that the health hazards of long bakeshop work were indeed substantial enough to sanction legislative regulation.

The opinion of Oliver Wendell Holmes was even more emphatic, and it has become a classic in its own right. Holmes accused the majority of allowing reactionary economic perspectives to override the clear legitimacy of such legislation. The Court had no right to override the wishes of the majority of citizens as expressed through the legislature, and he decried the interpretation of the Fourteenth Amendment as supposedly enacting "Mr. Herbert Spencer's Social Statics"—a key text of the era's social Darwinism.

Public outcry against the Court's decision came fast and furious, and scholars have largely agreed with Holmes and the other dissenters. Indeed, much of the period from Reconstruction to the New Deal is known as the Supreme Court's Lochner Era—an age that supposedly witnessed the Court mandating an unrelenting conservatism. Yet while there is much truth to this portrait of the case and the era, other historians have noted that *Lochner* was a strange precedent, applied in a quite haphazard manner as the Supreme Court took up other related cases. Indeed, as early as 1908, the Court seemed to retreat significantly from *Lochner* when it upheld female protective labor legislation in *Muller v. Oregon*, and Holmes and others believed that the Court had effectively overturned *Lochner* in the 1917 case of *Bunting v. Oregon*. Yet, the Court re-affirmed *Lochner* in 1923's *Adkins v. Children's Hospital*, and it was not until the New Deal that the New York bakeshop case finally became a dead letter.

ROBERT D. JOHNSTON

References and Further Reading

Bernstein, David E. "The Story of *Lochner v. New York*: Barrier to the Growth of the Regulatory State." In *Constitutional Law Stories*, edited by Michael Dorf. Westbury, NY: Foundation Press, 2004, pp. 325–358.

Gillman, Howard. *The Constitution Besieged: The Rise and Demise of Lochner Era Police Powers Jurisprudence.* Durham, NC: Duke University Press, 1993.

Kens, Paul. *Lochner v. New York: Economic Regulation on Trial.* Lawrence: University of Kansas Press, 1998.

Ragan, Fred D. "'Mere Meddlesome Interferences': The Apogee of Substantive Due Process." In *Historic U.S. Court Cases, 1690–1990: An Encyclopedia*, edited by John W. Johnson. New York: Garland, 1992, pp. 269–277.

Sunstein, Cass R. "Lochner's Legacy." *Columbia Law Review* 87 (893): 873–919.

Urofsky, Melvin I. "State Courts and Protective Legislation during the Progressive Era: A Reevaluation." *Journal of American History* 72 (June 1985): 63–91.

Cases and Statutes Cited

Adkins v. Children's Hospital 261 U.S. 525 (1923)
Bunting v. Oregon 243 U.S. 426 (1917)
Lochner v. New York 198 U.S. 45 (1905)
Muller v. Oregon 208 U.S. 412 (1908)

See also **Bunting v. Oregon** (1917)

LOCOFOCO DEMOCRATS

The term "Locofoco" was used first to designate the radical wing of the New York Democracy, then to refer to radical Jacksonians in other states, and finally as a synonym for the entire Democratic Party. The Locofoco Democrats flourished between 1835 and the early 1840s. Labor unions and labor activists provided much of the leadership, and working-class districts regularly voted more heavily for Locofoco candidates than more affluent areas. The rise of the Locofocos in New York was a direct result of Andrew Jackson's Bank War, which the future Locofocos had strongly supported. Jackson's 1833 decision to move federal funds from the Bank of the United States to state banks made banking a more attractive investment opportunity nationwide. In early 1835, the newly elected Democratic majority in Albany, despite heated opposition from Democrats like the newspaper editor William Leggett and various labor leaders, wasted no time in rewarding their friends and supporters with new state bank charters. To their critics, the same political, social, and economic problems would arise from New York's grant of state banking charters as resulted from the Bank of the United States, namely, the corruption of the political process by cronyism and monopoly power, the raising up of a social elite composed of those able to secure charters, and the inflation and outright fraud suffered by wage laborers owing to the effects of the note-issuing powers of the banks.

At the October 1835 Democratic nominating meeting, the regular Democrats of Tammany Hall forced through their pro-Bank slate of candidates despite the opposition of many at the meeting, whose attempt to offer an alternative ticket was ignored and then cut short when the gas was turned off and the room plunged into darkness. Ready for this tactic, the insurgents proceeded to light candles with new friction matches, known as locofocos. The Locofoco Democrats then nominated candidates opposed to the rash of state-chartered banks and supportive of hard money, antimonopoly, and labor union rights in general. Though these candidates lost to their regular Democratic opponents, the Locofoco wing of the party had been born.

William Leggett, the editor of the *New York Post* during William Cullen Bryant's absence, became the tribune of Locofocoism by means of his vitriolic and cogent editorials during the spring and summer of 1835 attacking the charters and other policies of the legislature. Though he was an important intellectual inspiration of the Locofocos, a severe illness in late 1835 sharply curtailed his direct participation in the movement. Instead, the actual leadership was provided by the politician Alexander Ming Jr.; labor union leaders John Commerford, Levi Slamm, and Robert Townsend Jr.; former Workingmen's Party activists George H. Evans, John Windt, Gilbert Vale, Isaac Smith, and Joel Curtis; and the political economist Clinton Roosevelt.

In January 1836, the Locofocos organized a separate party, the Equal Rights Party, which ran its own candidates as well as fusion nominees with the Whigs. In local elections in April 1836, the Locofocos defeated Tammany nominees for city office and in November elected two candidates to the state assembly. They also elected at least one congressman. However, the Locofocos never intended to build a new party, but to bring the rest of the Democracy around to their way of thinking. After Martin Van Buren's administration adopted a large part of the Locofoco program, especially its hard-money financial policies, Tammany went along, and after 1838 the Equal Rights Party ran no further separate tickets.

Outside of New York, the term "Locofoco" was used to describe the left-wing tendency within the Jacksonian Democratic Party, particularly in the states of the Northeast, where the labor movement was strongest and bank issues most salient. Throughout the region, attempts at the state level to issue new state bank charters were met with criticism and hostility from those radicalized by the Bank War. In Pennsylvania, for example, Locofocos favored hard-money state-banking reform. Leadership of the Pennsylvania Locofocos was provided by the union leaders John Ferral, William English, and Thomas Hogan; the radical editor Thomas Brothers; and Congressman Henry Muhlenberg, who ran for United States Senate as a Locofoco.

The Locofocos were supporters not only of hard money, but also of antimonopoly generally, and of the rights of labor in particular. The bank issue itself was a labor issue. Small-scale artisans and others in the "laboring classes" had long criticized the banking system, which they said unduly restricted their opportunities by limiting access to capital to those with wealth or political connections. Further, employers paid wage laborers not in hard specie, but in bank notes that often proved to be fraudulent or worthless. Locofocos believed that a hard-money policy that curtailed the issuance of bank notes, especially in small denominations, would cure these ills. The Locofocos also supported labor's efforts to attain the 10-hour workday and the right to organize labor unions and strike.

By late 1837, the Locofocos had largely won over the Van Buren administration to their way of thinking, as demonstrated by Van Buren's presidential message advocating the independent treasury plan, under which the federal government would no longer deposit its funds in private banks, but in its own treasury. Locofoco sentiment was at its high point through 1840, when the independent treasury plan was finally approved by Congress and Van Buren issued an executive order mandating the 10-hour day on federal public works. After the Whig victory in the 1840 elections, however, the radicals gradually lost power in the Democratic Party, owing in part to the issue of slavery, on which the Locofocos split, some calling for abolition while others rejected it.

The Locofoco Democrats are important to labor history because they represent the first instance of a major political party taking the labor movement and its ideas and interests seriously. The Locofocos advanced a broad agenda that was generally very sympathetic to the labor movement, and spoke a language of equal rights and popular democracy that struck a responsive chord in the working class. Their hard-money, prolabor, and antimonopoly policies continued to provide a wellspring of ideas and policies for left-leaning Democrats through the remainder of the nineteenth century.

MATTHEW S. R. BEWIG

References and Further Reading

Byrdsall, Fitzwilliam. *History of the Loco-Foco or Equal Rights Party*. New York: 1842.

Degler, Carl N. "The Locofocos: Urban 'Agrarians.'" *Journal of Economic History* 16 (September 1956): 322–333.

Earle, Jonathan H. *Jacksonian Antislavery and the Politics of Free Soil, 1824–1854*. Chapel Hill: University of North Carolina Press, 2004.

Hofstadter, Richard. "William Leggett, Spokesman of Jacksonian Democracy." *Political Science Quarterly* 58 (December 1943): 581–594.

Hugins, Walter. *Jacksonian Democracy and the Working Class*. Stanford, CA: Stanford University Press, 1960.

Leggett, William. *A Collection of the Political Writings of William Leggett, Selected and Arranged, with a Preface, by Theodore Sedgwick, Jr.* Reprint. New York: Arno and the New York Times, 1970.

Schlesinger, Arthur M. Jr. *The Age of Jackson*. Boston: Little, Brown and Company, 1945.

Trimble, William. "Diverging Tendencies in New York Democracy in the Period of the Locofocos." *American Historical Review* 24 (April 1919): 396–421.

———. "The Social Philosophy of the Loco-Foco Democracy." *American Journal of Sociology* 26 (May 1921): 705–715.

LONGSHORING

For the most part, longshoring work has been site- and job-specific. At first glance, it appears that longshoring is merely the loading and unloading of ships, whether sail, steam, or diesel. But at each port in the United States and throughout the world, the work has unique qualities and a distinct tempo. Some of this uniqueness is determined by the cargo that is being discharged. Whether it is cotton in New Orleans, iron ore in Detroit, or lumber in Portland, each in its own way prescribes a certain form of labor. Longshoring in various locales has also been affected by the ethnic and racial profile of the men engaged in the work. For every port along the incredible length of the U.S. coastline, there emerged a distinct but fluid racial and ethnic patterning. As the process of longshoring was changed by technological development, new groups undertook the work. In many cases the changing composition of the workforce was a bilateral process, whereby the men decided for themselves who should do what in and around the ship; at other sites it was employers who determined who should work and where.

Just as vital in this evolving story has been a collective sense of community. Unlike many other occupations, longshoring necessarily encompassed gang labor. Such labor created and re-inforced a group ideal, a sense of collective not always experienced by other workers. As will be seen, working in gangs encouraged a form of trust and dependency that could overcome ethnic, and at times, racial differences.

When examining longshoremen chronologically, one is struck immediately by the nearly total absence of colonial or early nineteenth-century studies. Historians have tended to focus their attention on the twentieth century, and such emphasis has left the earlier period relatively unstudied. What is certain is that longshoremen played an invaluable role in the emerging colonial economy and culture. Trade was the lifeblood of the British imperial system. The ports of Boston, New York, Philadelphia, Baltimore, and Charleston were dynamic lynchpins in the economic and financial success of colonial development. What is evident is that longshoremen held a tenuous social status. Surrounding communities long regarded longshoremen as brutes with no regard for long-term welfare for themselves and their families. They were stereotyped as short-tempered, quick to use their fists, and constantly in a state of near or total drunkenness. Such a perception would continue up to and throughout the twentieth century.

These colonial longshoremen generally lived close to their work, which necessitated obtaining cheaper lodgings along the waterfront. Such living arrangements forced longshoremen to work close in to the bustling environment of a port. Thus, incorporated into the longshoremen's world were heavy and exhausting work, and physical surroundings marked by taverns, brothels, gambling, and opium dens. Many of the longshoremen moved easily to and from laboring jobs along the waterfront. They also moved back and forth over the water's edge. Many were former seamen who wanted to enjoy a spell onshore or because of family circumstances needed to be close to home. Indeed, the job of longshoring has always constituted an entry point for seamen. Crispus Attucks, the first casualty of the American Revolution, was both a seaman and a longshoreman. Killed by British troops during the Boston Massacre of 1770, Attucks had been protesting British soldiers doing jobs normally done by dockside laborers.

Longshoring throughout the United States was structured as casual employment. That is, the men lined up for work every day and were then allocated jobs. Such a casual hiring system was rife with exploitation and danger. It was common to pay a kickback to obtain a job. Other than insecurity of employment, longshoring was an occupation that encompassed diverse job categorization. A myriad of jobs came under the rubric of longshoring. In New Orleans, for example, the job was broken down by skill and race. The highest skilled job was that of cotton screwman. These men packed the cotton bales into the ships' holds using specialized machinery that literally screwed the bales into place. The cotton screwmen's skilled status was predicated on judgment and strength. Each ship had a different size hold, and in some cases, a different shape. The ability of the screwmen to adjust to the differing hold designs ensured their skilled status. Elsewhere in the hierarchy labored longshoremen who loaded agricultural goods. Many of the latter jobs were held by slave and freed blacks.

Each group suffered from the same structural constraints, however. Although pay could vary widely, it was the unpredictability of work that was feared the most. Unlike factory work, the availability of work varied from day to day. The arrival of ships has always been dependent upon the weather and the tides, and more crushing was the loss of a ship at sea, which reflected back at the dock with a loss of work. It was also a seasonal trade, as in the case of cotton in New Orleans.

Irregular work was a constant theme for longshoremen throughout the United States and the world—they were victims of the vagaries of the sea and weather, and trading patterns. International shippers were always looking for ways to cheapen the costs of transporting their goods. For longshoremen then, work was conditioned by insecurity.

Another common trait of longshoring was that it was an entry job for first-generation immigrants. In San Francisco, for example, Irish immigrants made up the majority of longshoremen at the end of the nineteenth century. Although the dominant group, the Irish composed just 25% of the total workforce. Other principal groups were Scandinavians (17%), Germans (14%), British (6%), and Italians (6%). African-Americans were not a presence at this time, but during World War I and II, their numbers exponentially increased. On the Great Lakes, a similar immigrant profile was clear: Irish immigrants predominated, joined by Swedes, Germans, and French-Canadians.

In New York, African-Americans constituted the largest group of longshoremen up until the 1840s. Once the Irish diaspora grew as a result of the Great Famine, African-Americans were displaced in Manhattan. The Irish then came to dominate the piers along the west side of Manhattan. In Brooklyn, large numbers of Norwegians and Swedes controlled the docks, although there was an Irish presence there also. Immigrant entry to the work was influenced by employer strategy. Beginning in the 1870s, a fledgling union was formed in the Port of New York. To counter this development, shippers and stevedores imported large numbers of Italian-Americans and African-Americans as strikebreakers. Such a tactic dramatically transformed the ethnic and racial profile of New York's longshoremen. By the beginning of the twentieth century, Italians had an entrenched hold on the docks in Brooklyn, Staten Island, and in Jersey City and Hoboken, New Jersey. African-Americans were not so fortunate in establishing control over certain docks. Unable to control a pier or piers, they were left to function as a floating pool of labor. Not for the first time, employers played a significant role in influencing the racial and ethnic makeup of its workforce. A similar racial and ethnic makeup was present in Boston, where Irish dominated, followed by Italians, and a small percentage of African-Americans.

African-Americans were a much larger presence in Philadelphia: by 1910, they composed nearly 50% of the workforce. Many of these black longshoremen had migrated from North Carolina, Virginia, and Maryland. Following World War I, blacks increased their numbers to over 60%. Some of this increase can be attributed to the Great Migration, during which southern longshoremen migrated to Philadelphia from New Orleans and Mobile, Alabama. The Philadelphia port became a magnet for first-generation immigrants also. The largest ethnic group was the Poles, followed by Lithuanians, Italians, Irish, and Jews.

In the South, however, an ethnically diverse labor force was generally absent. Reflecting a distinct absence of mass migration into the region, the work was dominated by native-born whites and blacks—although in Galveston, Texas, workers of Hispanic origin were present.

In the early twentieth century, most longshoremen worked with little or no union protection. This lack of institutional protection ensured that erratic employment became the norm. Symptomatic of this insecurity was the method of getting work—the "shape-up." The shape-up was a simple method whereby hiring foremen would pick the men who would work that day from the crowd. Such a system made for rank favoritism and discrimination. It was common on most of the nation's waterfronts to pay a bribe or kickback to obtain a job. Such a system bred insecurity but also had another effect: it helped maintain a union-free environment. Anyone judged to be a union agitator or sympathizer could easily be ignored at the shape-up, effectively removing them from work and ultimately the docks.

At the beginning of the twentieth century, only a small number of longshoremen had won union recognition. They included Gulf Coast men in New Orleans and Galveston, Great Lakes longshoremen, and a few locals on the eastern seaboard and the West Coast. The principal union at this time was the International Longshoremen's Association (ILA). Its power base was the Great Lakes, and its first leader was Daniel Keefe. Keefe was instrumental in capturing most of the longshoremen working the ships along the Great Lakes, including Chicago, Cleveland, Detroit, and smaller ports like Marquette and Escanaba. Keefe and his successors were conservative in their dealings with employers and shippers. Reflecting the dominant ideological stream of the American Federation of Labor (AFL), the ILA leaders rarely challenged the status quo. Indeed, Keefe's comfortable posture when dealing with employers was reflected in his membership in the National Civic Federation. By World War I, the ILA's center of strength began to shift toward the eastern seaboard as union locals were established in Boston, New York, Philadelphia, and Baltimore.

During this period, the ILA was directly challenged by the Industrial Workers of the World (IWW). Philadelphia longshoremen overwhelmingly supported the IWW. Not until the 1920s was the ILA able to break the IWW's hold, after importing ILA strikebreakers from New York. On the West Coast, the situation was just as volatile but did not have such a sanguine result for the ILA. The West Coast men vacillated between creating their own organization or a tenuous alliance with the ILA. After a failed strike, a company union was installed. A similar defeat occurred on the Gulf Coast. For decades, longshoremen in New Orleans, for example, had practiced a successful form of biracialism. But a strike defeat in 1923 ended years of union strength and racial compromise. Union strength of the longshoremen fluctuated between union stability on the Great Lakes and expanding representation on the Atlantic seaboard to outright defeat on the West and Gulf coasts.

The 1929 stock market crash and accompanying Great Depression would help transform the situation. The turning point for the nation's longshoremen came as events unfolded on the West Coast. Longshoremen in San Francisco had long bridled at their lack of trade union protection and being forced to join a company union, the Longshoremen's Association of San Francisco. A combination of forces transformed the situation in the early 1930s. The passage of the National Industrial Recovery Act (NIRA) gave the longshoremen at least a semblance of maneuverability. The ILA began to challenge the company union, and finally, communists, supported by seamen in the Marine Workers Industrial Union (MWIU), began to actively organize. The key to success, however, was the men themselves and their rank-and-file leaders. Most notably, Australian-born Harry Bridges took the helm. With the issue of union recognition uppermost, San Francisco longshoremen went out on strike in 1934. The strike was a bloody affair resulting in the violent deaths of two strikers. Other San Francisco unions pledged their support for the longshoremen, and threats of a general strike were made. With such an outpouring of support, the strikers won union recognition, but the victory also unleashed a battle within the ILA. The established leadership, dominated by the New York office, preached caution and patience. Led by Harry Bridges, West Coast longshoremen viewed such directives as superfluous. Suspicious of ILA intentions, the men decided to form their own union, the International Longshoremen's and Warehousemen's Union (ILWU). This break from the ILA was to become permanent; in the twenty-first century, the ILWU continues to represent West Coast longshoremen.

The example set by the likes of Harry Bridges encouraged others to challenge the conservatism of ILA officials. In New York, for example, members of the rank and file emerged calling for greater democracy within the ILA. Led by Brooklyn longshoreman Pete Panto, the men challenged the ILA leadership of Joe Ryan. Mysteriously, Pete Panto disappeared in 1939, and not until after World War II would the true story of Panto's disappearance become public knowledge. He had been kidnapped by members of Murder Inc., strangled, and dumped into a lime pit in New Jersey. The removal of Panto effectively ended the rank and file's challenge. Unlike their cousins on the West Coast, New York longshoremen would continue to labor without effective union protection. By World War II, the ILA had been captured by rogue criminal elements resulting in poor wages and working conditions.

World War II transformed the work relations on the New York waterfront and elsewhere. Young longshoremen left the docks in droves to join the armed forces. But as the U.S. Army and Navy took ever-increasing control of loading and unloading in the port of New York, a more steady form of employment became the norm. Regular gangs were recognized as being far more efficient than individuals occasionally hired from a shape-up. By the end of the war, over 60% of longshoremen were laboring in regular gangs. Regular employment took away from the ILA and the shippers the power to hire and fire. Gaining expertise on certain cargo lines, the longshoremen in turn could now demand and receive on-the-spot wage awards.

The speed and rhythm of work had, however, increased. Sling loads became heavier, and thus the job was more hazardous. In terms of hours lost due to disabling injury, longshoremen outranked coal miners and were only slightly behind loggers. The most dangerous jobs involved working in the hold: falling objects were one of the major killers of longshoremen. Working on the deck or the dock was also dangerous, where common injuries included crushed hands, feet, and ankles.

Longshoremen throughout the United States adopted a fatalistic attitude toward the hazards of their job. While on the West Coast the ILWU worked hard to improve safety on the job, such activity was noticeably absent on the East Coast and Gulf.

Pilfering cargo was just as common. On ships and docks throughout the United States and the world, longshoremen routinely took possession of such things as candy, liquor, tools, and even food from the ships' galleys. The longshoremen had a sense of entitlement when justifying such action. Contraband was either consumed on board ship or taken off the waterfront to either be sold or consumed at home. Nicknames tended to be correlated to place of origin, or related to form of dress or food eaten. So, for example, nicknames such as Staten Island Joe and Hoboken Harry were used to identify someone by their place of origin. Others pertained to the food eaten by longshoremen such as "Chicken" and "Cheese," or by their dress; for example, the man who always wore a red shirt to work was labeled as the "bullfighter." The common form of dress, uses of nicknames, and pilferage activities became identifying markers. Such clear markers ensured that longshoremen could recognize one another, both on the job and off.

The longshoring workforce was traditionally an older one. In most of the ports, older men dominated the work. By the late 1940s and early 1950s, the nation's longshoremen still labored with their hands. Winches on board the ships still carried the cargo to and from the hold, but the men continued to use the hook to fill or empty the sling. Younger men did play a large role in changing the trade union culture. This was especially true in New York. Longshoremen returning from the war challenged the established ILA hierarchy and unleashed a series of wildcat strikes that resulted in the end of the shape-up and the establishment of medical centers in Manhattan and Brooklyn. For the ILWU men, their focus was on the deportation hearings of their leader, Harry Bridges.

By 1960, the ILA and ILWU had become established entities in the lives of their members throughout the United States. The year 1960 also represented a turning point for longshoremen. Containerization had become a new phenomenon in their lives. The hand labor of the previous centuries had been replaced by the mechanized loading of vast tonnage. Both the ILA and ILWU negotiated deals with their respective employers guaranteeing protecting jobs while accepting the new technology. The introduction of containerization immediately transformed longshoremen's work. Smaller gangs were needed, and new skills were developed. The crane operator now became the lynchpin in the process. The longshoremen were able to barter certain arrangements where half the gang would work while the other half rested. Also, if the set work was completed before time, the gang was able to leave work but get fully paid. While able to negotiate a semblance of protection, the longshoremen witnessed women entering the job. In 1982, the first woman hired on the West Coast was the daughter of a longshoreman.

Containerization, then, dramatically transformed the longshoring process. Most dramatic of all was its effect on the numbers employed. The number of East

Coast longshoremen dropped from 51,000 in 1952 to 15,000 in 1972. Generous retirement payments and incentives convinced many on the West and East Coast to accept redundancy. The job, however, would never take on the earlier qualities of gang solidarity, and traditional longshoring communities faded away.

COLIN DAVIS

References and Further Reading

Arnesen, Eric. *Waterfront Workers of New Orleans: Race, Class, and Politics, 1863–1923*. Urbana: University of Illinois, 1994.

Beck, John P. "They Fought for Their Work: Upper Peninsula Iron Ore Trimmer Wars." *Michigan History* 1989 73(1): 24–31.

Broeze, Frank. *The Globalisation of the Oceans: Containerisation from the 1950s to the Present*. St. Johns, Newfoundland: International Maritime Economic History Association, 2002.

Davis, Colin J. *Waterfront Revolts: New York and London Dockworkers, 1946–1961*. (Urbana: University of Illinois Press, 2003.

Finlay, William. *Work on the Waterfront: Worker Power and Technological Change in a West Coast Port*. Philadelphia: Temple University Press, 1988.

Nelson, Bruce. *Workers on the Waterfront: Seamen, Longshoremen, and Unionism in the 1930s*. Urbana: University of Illinois, 1990.

Wellman, David. *The Union Makes Us Strong: Radical Unionism on the San Francisco Waterfront*. Cambridge, MA: Cambridge University Press, 1995.

See also **Bridges, Harry Renton; International Longshoremen's Association; Keefe, Daniel; National Industrial Recovery Act**

LORD DUNMORE'S PROCLAMATION

On November 15, 1775, John Murray, the fourth Earl of Dunmore and royal governor of the colony of Virginia, issued a proclamation concerning the ongoing military actions taking place in eastern Virginia. He demanded that all able-bodied white men in the colony rally to his banner immediately on pain of being declared a traitor. Further, Dunmore proclaimed that any able-bodied male indentured servant or slave who was owned by a rebel would be granted his freedom if he ran away to Dunmore and enlisted as a soldier in the loyalist cause.

Context

Colonial Virginia was a slave society, its economy dependent upon the racial and class-based exploitation of African slaves for its continued existence. By the 1770s, there were close to 190,000 slaves in the colony, composing 42% of the overall population. These slaves primarily worked in the fields growing the staple crop of the Chesapeake region, tobacco. Though tobacco cultivation was becoming less lucrative in the long-settled Tidewater regions, white settlers from these areas were rapidly moving into the Piedmont and the backcountry. These settlers took slaves with them and began replicating the staple-crop, slave society of the Tidewater.

Earlier in 1775, during a period of heightened tension, Dunmore had threatened to grant freedom to the slaves. Slaveholding colonists were worried that slaves might be inspired to revolt anyway. Indeed, slave resistance and running away seem to have increased over the spring of 1775—one group even appeared on Dunmore's doorstep at the Governor's Palace in Williamsburg to offer its services. It was not, however, until fighting had broken out between royal troops and patriot militias that Dunmore seriously considered the idea. He signed the proclamation on November 7 but did not issue it until a week later, after his troops had defeated the Princess Anne County militia at the Battle of Kemp's Landing in southeastern Virginia.

Slaves

Roughly 1,000 slaves escaped bondage by joining Dunmore. About half were women and children—expressly not covered by the terms of the proclamation. The freedmen and freedwomen served Dunmore's army as sailors, foragers, and most notably as soldiers. A special "Ethiopian Regiment" was formed. The freedmen wore badges with the legend "Liberty to Slaves"—a direct response to their former masters, whose uniforms bore the slogan "Liberty or Death."

The vast majority of slaves did not run away to Dunmore's army. Many seem to have chosen instead to stay together with families and communities. Dunmore's decision to offer freedom only to able-bodied men certainly caused fewer to join him than might have if emancipation had been offered to all slaves. Some, likely, were suspicious of such a limited declaration and chose the devil they knew over the one they did not. Dunmore's influence was also largely limited to the Chesapeake Bay region—it would have been difficult for slaves from the Piedmont to have both heard about the proclamation and to have made their way across hostile territory to reach Dunmore's camp.

Nevertheless, there is no doubt that Dunmore's proclamation influenced slaves both in Virginia and through the southern colonies to resist their patriot masters, lending outside support to an internal rebellion that the slaves had already begun.

Masters

On the other hand, the white population of Virginia found itself polarized by Dunmore's proclamation. The threat of a full-scale slave rebellion, while always in the background, now seemed closer than ever. Neutral and loyalist white Virginians quickly joined the patriot cause.

Whites in Virginia and beyond feared that slaves across the South would hear of Dunmore's proclamation and be inspired to revolt. Maryland cut off all communication with Virginia to prevent this event, while in North Carolina militias mustered with the dual objects of opposing a British incursion from the north and of apprehending Dunmore agents rumored to be working to incite slaves in that colony. In South Carolina, whites attributed the growth of a runaway population on Sullivan's Island to the effects of Dunmore's proclamation.

Significance

Across the colonies, whites assumed that Dunmore's radical proclamation would be rescinded by the Crown. When George III refused to recall the proclamation and remove Dunmore as governor, it became one of the final pushes toward independence. Indeed, the general complaint that the king had inspired "domestic insurrections"—a direct reference to the slave revolts of 1775—became the crowning grievance of the Declaration of Independence.

A historiographical shift in our understanding of Lord Dunmore's proclamation has taken place over the past several decades. The central point of this shift is the question of slave agency and slave resistance. Earlier authors (Selby, Quarles) have seen the proclamation as providing an inspiration for slaves to escape. More recent works (those by Frey and Holton) argue the reverse: slaves were resisting their masters before and during the events leading up to Dunmore's proclamation. It was this insurgency that persuaded Dunmore to issue his proclamation—he knew that slaves would respond to his call. Thus, slave resistance led to Dunmore's proclamation, not the other way around.

Further, this recent re-interpretation of Dunmore's proclamation supports a progressive reading of the Revolution. In Virginia, Holton and Frey argue, the Revolution was a class war: not between great planters and yeomen farmers but between slaveowners and slaves.

JOSHUA BEATY

References and Further Reading

Berlin, Ira. *Many Thousands Gone: The First Two Centuries of Slavery in North America.* Cambridge, MA: Belknap Press of Harvard University Press, 1998.
Frey, Sylvia. *Water from the Rock: Black Resistance in a Revolutionary Age.* Princeton, NJ: Princeton University Press, 1991.
Holton, Woody. *Forced Founders: Indians, Debtors, Slaves, and the Making of the American Revolution in Virginia.* Chapel Hill: University of North Carolina Press for the Omohundro Institute of Early American History and Culture, Williamsburg, VA, 1999.
———. "Rebel against Rebel: Enslaved Virginians and the Coming of the American Revolution." *Virginia Magazine of History and Biography* 105 (1997): 157–192.
Quarles, Benjamin. "Lord Dunmore as Liberator." *William and Mary Quarterly*, 3rd series, 15 (1958): 494–507.
———. *The Negro in the American Revolution.* Chapel Hill: University of North Carolina Press for the Institute of Early American History and Culture, Williamsburg, VA, 1961.
Selby, John E. *The Revolution in Virginia, 1775–1783.* Williamsburg, VA: Colonial Williamsburg Foundation, 1988.

LOUISIANA FARMERS' UNION

The Louisiana Farmers' Union was an organization of small farmers, tenants, and wage laborers that sought to improve conditions for rural workers in the state's sugar and cotton plantation regions in the second half of the 1930s. Although the union achieved some gains, its interracial makeup, communist affiliations, and the threat that it posed to the plantation system provoked violent responses from landowners and local officials. This repression, along with changing economic conditions during World War II, contributed to the union's demise in the early 1940s.

In the early twentieth century, rural workers in Louisiana were among the most poorly treated laborers in the nation. Sharecroppers and tenants in the cotton-producing parishes worked land owned by their employers in return for a portion of the income from the crops they produced. They received payment only once per year, after the crops had been harvested and sold. Lacking cash, they relied on landlords or local merchants to provide them with seeds, fertilizer, food, and other necessities throughout the crop season. The costs of these supplies (plus interest) were deducted from their payments at settlement time. In the sugar parishes, tenant farming was less common, and planters relied on wage laborers, who were paid more regularly throughout the year. However, payment was often in scrip redeemable only at the plantation store. Both systems were vulnerable to abuse by employers, and many planters used their control over prices, credit, and accounts to cheat workers out of their earnings. The housing provided for workers on most plantations was also substandard, often consisting of leaky shacks with no electricity or indoor plumbing. White supremacist ideologies and the South's Jim Crow system of racial oppression helped to justify and maintain the conditions endured by the predominantly black workforce. If plantation laborers complained, they risked economic or physical reprisals from landlords or police.

In 1931, the Communist Party began organizing black sharecroppers in the South in an attempt to transform them into a revolutionary vanguard. Party activists soon learned that the region's rural workers were more interested in gaining concrete improvements in their living and working conditions than in overthrowing the government. Organizers in Alabama encouraged local people to form the Share Croppers' Union (SCU) and use collective action to put pressure on plantation owners. Planters retaliated by evicting, beating, and lynching union members. Seeking a more hospitable environment, the union moved its headquarters to New Orleans in 1936. The New Orleans office was run by a small group of communist and left-wing activists that included Clyde Johnson, a Communist Party member from Minnesota; Gordon McIntire, a Texan who had attended the left-leaning Commonwealth College in Arkansas; Clinton Clark, a native of Louisiana and former sharecropper; and Peggy Dallet, another Louisianan who had helped to organize local chapters of other liberal and leftist organizations. Most of the group were in their early 20s, and Clinton Clark was the only African-American among them.

After the move, union leaders sought to further strengthen the organization by forming alliances with other farmers and workers unions. Johnson believed that joining forces with the larger National Farmers' Union (NFU) might provide some protection for union members, and in 1937, SCU locals began transferring into the NFU. The Louisiana locals became the Louisiana Farmers' Union (LFU), a state division of the NFU. Although the union welcomed white people as well as African-Americans, most of its members were black.

Local leaders and activists played important roles in the LFU. Organizers encouraged them to write to the central office about their problems and published members' letters in the union newspaper. The union's rank and file frequently made suggestions for action and debated new policies at the local level before decisions were made at state conventions. Union activities addressed long-standing grievances of rural black people, such as low pay, unfair crop settlements, inadequate school facilities, and exclusion from political participation.

To combat planter abuses of the tenancy system, the LFU offered literacy and math classes for members and lobbied federal officials to require written contracts between landowners and their employees when they participated in the new farm subsidy programs established during the New Deal. Union representatives attended hearings held by the Department of Agriculture to determine wages and conditions in the sugar industry and persuaded government officials to require modest increases in pay for plantation workers each year. The union also helped members obtain loans and other assistance for low-income farmers offered by the Farm Security Agency (FSA), providing a chance for them to achieve farm ownership and economic independence. Many locals attempted to improve educational facilities in their communities by raising money for buildings and equipment and pressuring school boards to provide more funding. The LFU also joined with other rural unions in the 1930s to advocate greater participation by poor farmers in setting policy and administering government farm programs.

Like their counterparts in Alabama, plantation owners in Louisiana responded to union organizing efforts with intimidation and violence. Local newspapers accused the union of fomenting class warfare and highlighted the participation of black people and communists in an attempt to discredit it. Employers threatened to evict workers or physically harm them if they joined the union. Police and local officials arrested and harassed union members, and in June 1937, local leaders Willie and Irene Scott had to temporarily flee their home in West Feliciana Parish to avoid being lynched. Activists organized to protect themselves and fight back against the violence, forming armed guards to protect their homes and families. Nonetheless, repression took its toll, and fear of reprisals prevented many people from becoming involved in union activities.

After growing to about three thousand members by 1940, the LFU began to lose support and resources as the nation prepared for and then entered World War II. The poverty of its members and their irregular dues-paying habits meant that the union relied heavily on outside contributors to fund its activities. Most donations came from liberals and other sympathizers with left-wing causes, many of whom were angered by the union's stance on the war in the late 1930s and early 1940s. In keeping with the Communist Party line, LFU leaders advocated neutrality in the European conflict until Germany invaded the Soviet Union in June 1941. Party activists then switched to all-out support for the fight against fascism, refocusing their attention away from the rural South and further undermining the LFU.

Economic changes wrought by the war also contributed to the union's decline. New jobs in construction and defense industries drew many of the LFU's rural poor constituents away from the plantations. Landowners responded to the loss of their cheap labor supply by mechanizing as many operations as possible or by switching to livestock farming and other activities that required fewer workers. In the next few decades, the old plantation system gradually disintegrated, displacing thousands of rural workers and leading to increasing out-migration from the rural parishes. The political and economic shifts of the 1940s left few active LFU members by the end of the war. Although some locals may have continued to hold meetings, official union activity ceased after the mid-1940s.

For a brief period, the LFU provided a vehicle through which black plantation workers in Louisiana challenged the power of their employers and struggled against the system of white supremacy that kept them poor and oppressed. It brought improvements in the lives of many of its members in the form of higher pay, increased access to educational opportunities, and political empowerment. Perhaps more important, union activity was part of an ongoing fight for freedom and justice by African-Americans that continued beyond the 1940s. In the 1950s and 1960s, former LFU members were among the black farmers, workers, homemakers, and students who participated in the civil rights movement in Louisiana and helped to bring an end to the Jim Crow system.

GRETA DE JONG

References and Further Reading

Becnel, Thomas. *Labor, Church, and the Sugar Establishment: Louisiana, 1887–1976*. Baton Rouge: Louisiana State University Press, 1980.
Conrad, David Eugene. *The Forgotten Farmers: The Story of Sharecroppers in the New Deal*. Urbana: University of Illinois Press, 1965.
Daniel, Pete. *The Shadow of Slavery: Peonage in the South, 1901–1969*. Illini Books ed. Urbana: University of Illinois Press, 1990.
de Jong, Greta. *A Different Day: African American Struggles for Justice in Rural Louisiana, 1900–1970*. Chapel Hill: University of North Carolina Press, 2002.
Fairclough, Adam. *Race and Democracy: The Civil Rights Struggle in Louisiana, 1915–1972*. Athens: University of Georgia Press, 1995.
Kelley, Robin D. G. *Hammer and Hoe: Alabama Communists during the Great Depression*. Chapel Hill: University of North Carolina Press, 1990.

See also **Agriculture Adjustment Administration; Civil Rights; Communist Party; Share Croppers Union (1930s); Southern Tenant Farmers' Union**

LOUISIANA SUGAR STRIKE (1887)

The Louisiana Sugar Strike was carried out by overwhelmingly African-American wage workers on sugar plantations in southern Louisiana, organized by the Knights of Labor, in November 1887. It resulted in the infamous "Thibodaux Massacre," in which a large number of strikers and organizers were slain. Among the most violent labor episodes nationally during the Gilded Age, the massacre culminated labor conflict on sugar plantations since the abolition of slavery and precluded further efforts to organize sugar workers until the mid-twentieth century.

The strike's origins can be traced to the slave era. During the nineteenth century, sugar plantations dominated the alluvial lands along the Mississippi River and numerous bayous. Sugar production required large concentrations of land, labor, and capital, and sugar planters ranked among the South's wealthiest slaveholders. Sugar making also gave rise to large, complex slave communities and a well-defined division of labor. The fall harvest necessitated a disciplined labor force to toil intensively yet with clocklike precision. The uncompromising nature of sugar production, which was a semi-industrial endeavor, and the delicate equilibrium of plantation routine caused contemporaries to liken sugar plantations to "factories in the field" and gave them their well-deserved reputation as death traps for slaves.

The federal capture of New Orleans during the Civil War led to the implementation of monthly wage labor. Responding to the breakdown of plantation discipline following their arrival, federal officers improvised a system in which workers received monthly wages and basic necessities. By war's end, wage labor was firmly entrenched on sugar plantations, and former slaves continued to work in gangs under white supervision. During the war, half of workers' wages had been withheld until completion of the crop, in order to secure planters sufficient labor, and this practice continued into the 1870s, despite workers' objections. Conflict also arose over wage rates, working conditions, provisioning, and other matters. In constructing the new labor system, workers benefited from the exigencies of sugar production, the emergence of a functioning labor market, and their own political empowerment during Radical Reconstruction, but conflict and occasional violence characterized relations between planters and workers.

Although workers by the latter 1870s had secured full monthly wage payment and other favorable terms, the end of Reconstruction in 1877 strengthened planters by placing the state's coercive power at their disposal. Responding to dramatic changes in the world sugar market and to their own economic woes, planters lowered wages during the early 1880s and replaced cash payments with nontransferable plantation scrip. By the mid-1880s, the Knights of Labor—which first began unionizing railroad workers in Morgan City, a transportation hub west of New Orleans—was tapping into sugar worker discontent and organizing locals along Bayou Teche in St. Mary Parish and along Bayou Lafourche in Assumption, Lafourche, and Terrebonne parishes. In fall 1887, predominantly white labor leaders called for wage increases and abolition of scrip payment, and they set a strike deadline for November 1, around the traditional start of the harvest. As former slaveholders and as men of property, planters adopted a hard line—refusing to negotiate, vowing to evict strikers from their estates, and calling upon local and state authorities for assistance.

On November 1, some 10,000 workers along Bayous Teche and Lafourche went on strike. Most plantations remained idle, although some operated with white labor from New Orleans. A state militia detachment and several paramilitary groups arrived in the Lafourche Parish town of Thibodaux. Sheriffs' posses were organized, and local white men deputized. Planters evicted strikers and their families, many of whom congregated in Thibodaux and other towns. During the next three weeks, as attempted negotiations failed, tensions increased and the situation became more volatile. Sporadic violence also occurred. Strikers in several instances allegedly shot into operating sugar mills. During a "riot" in one St. Mary Parish town, whites killed several strikers. Newspapers fanned the flames of racial and labor conflict. Since the state militia could not remain on duty indefinitely, it eventually withdrew and was replaced by posses and paramilitary groups from as far away as Shreveport. On November 21, in response to continuing "lawlessness" and to rumors of strikers' plans to attack Thibodaux, the parish judge, Taylor Beattie, a former Republican, declared martial law in the town. Pickets were established, but tensions further heightened.

In the early morning of November 23, shots were fired at a picket guard. This so-called attack precipitated a frenzy of violence, which lasted for the next three days, by various white forces against black strikers and Knights organizers. "Instigators" were identified and singled out for especially brutal treatment. State militia units returned to Thibodaux but did little to stop the slaughter. By November 25, the worst was over, although whites continued to comb the woods and swamps for strikers and labor leaders. Shots rang out for several more days, and bodies turned up weeks later. There was no official estimate of the number of casualties. Press reports, which downplayed violence against blacks, conceded at least 30 black fatalities, although some local white residents privately admitted that more than 50 strikers died. It became part of the oral tradition of the black community along Bayou Lafourche that the total number of casualties—killed, wounded, and missing—numbered in the hundreds.

The massacre ended both the strike and the Knights of Labor's organizing efforts in the sugar region, as the defeated sugar workers returned to the plantations on their employers' terms. Although planters would continue in the years ahead to bemoan their inability to control labor, and although employers could not exercise the same authority over free workers as masters had over slaves, black people in southern Louisiana were left with few alternatives to the plantation economy. In a few short years, moreover, a white supremacist social order characterized by legal segregation, disfranchisement, and racial violence would emerge. The 1887 sugar strike was but one among a number of setbacks suffered by the Knights of Labor that contributed to its ultimate demise, and not until the 1940s did a national labor organization again attempt to unionize black workers on southern Louisiana sugar plantations.

JOHN C. RODRIGUE

References and Further Reading

Foner, Philip S., and Ronald L. Lewis, eds. *The Black Worker: A Documentary History from Colonial Times to the Present*. Vol. 3. *The Black Worker during the Era of the Knights of Labor*. Philadelphia: Temple University Press, 1978.

Gould, Jeffrey. "Louisiana Sugar War: The Strike of 1887." *Southern Exposure* 12 (November–December 1984): 45–55.

Hair, William Ivy. *Bourbonism and Agrarian Protest: Louisiana Politics, 1877–1900*. Baton Rouge: Louisiana State University Press, 1969.

Rodrigue, John C. *Reconstruction in the Cane Fields: From Slavery to Free Labor in Louisiana's Sugar Parishes, 1862–1880*. Baton Rouge: Louisiana State University Press, 2001.

Scott, Rebecca. *Degrees of Freedom: Louisiana and Cuba after Slavery, 1862–1914*. Cambridge, MA: Harvard University Press, 2005.

LOVESTONE, JAY (1897–1990)
Communist Party of America

Jay Lovestone, a leading Communist and then Communist oppositionist for nearly two decades before World War II, emerged in the postwar era as the major architect of the AFL-CIO's anti-Communist foreign policy through his leading of the federation's International Department until his retirement in 1974. Born Jacob Liebstein in czarist Russia in 1897, his family immigrated to New York 10 years later, settling on New York's Lower East Side before moving to the Bronx. Graduating from City College after only three years in June 1918, Liebstein had been radicalized in college, becoming the president of the Intercollegiate Socialist Society. Formally changing his name to Jay Lovestone upon becoming a naturalized citizen in February 1919, Lovestone, who had been an antiwar Marxist and identified with the Socialist Party of America's (SPA) left wing, expressed political sympathy with the Bolshevik Revolution. When the SPA split in late summer 1919, he joined the Communist Party of America (CPA) at its founding convention and was elected to membership on the party's Central Executive Committee.

Becoming a protégé of the CPA leader, Charles E. Ruthenberg, with the formation of the legal Workers Party, at the end of December 1921, Lovestone edited the party newspaper, *The Worker*, and quickly rose through the ranks, putting in countless hours under Ruthenbergs' tutelage. As one of the leaders of the American Communists and of the Ruthenberg Caucus, Lovestone traveled in January 1925 with his mentor and factional rivals, William Z. Foster and James P. Cannon, to Moscow so that the Communist International's American Commission could attempt to resolve the two groups' differences, which was not achieved. However, at the Workers Party convention in August 1925, the Ruthenberg Caucus, of which Lovestone was a main organizer, gained control of the party with the help of Moscow.

Throughout 1926, Lovestone worked diligently to bolshevize the American party. When Ruthenberg died in early March 1927, Lovestone was elected acting secretary, although the Foster-Cannon faction was not willing to concede the party's leadership to the young leader without a fight. After defeating his rivals at the convention in late summer 1927, Lovestone obtained strong control of the organization. Lovestone's leadership tenure would last less than two years. After the October 1928 expulsion of the Trotskyists from the party, Lovestone was expelled eight months later, with Moscow's blessing, at the end of June 1929 for supporting Bukharin and the policy of "American exceptionalism." Fellow Lovestoneites were purged by the end of August 1929.

Upon his expulsion, the inveterate Communist immediately organized a rival political organization in 1929, first named the Communist Party (Majority Group) and later the Communist Party (Opposition). In the organization's newspaper, the *Revolutionary Age*, later renamed the *Workers Age*, the Lovestoneites supported the Soviet Union while calling for more freedom for foreign Communist parties. Through Lovestoneite activity in the International Ladies' Garment Workers' Union (ILGWU) in the early 1930s, Lovestone developed close relations with and became an advisor of David Dubinsky, the union's president. Lovestone and his followers also became influential in the United Auto Workers, with more than a dozen serving in President Homer Martin's administration in the late 1930s.

Disheartened by Bukharin's execution in 1938 and disillusioned by Moscow's treatment of the Workers' Party of Marxist Unification (*Partido Obrero de Unificación Marxista*—POUM) during the Spanish Civil War, Lovestone formally broke with Communism and the Soviet Union in 1939. In response, he transformed his party into a democratic socialist organization, the Independent Labor League (ILL). However, the ILL survived for less than two years before being dissolved by Lovestone at the end of December 1940.

In 1941, without an organizational home or job, Lovestone was chosen by Dubinsky to run the labor division of the New York chapter of the Committee to Defend America by Aiding the Allies (which later changed its name to Citizens for Victory). This position, which he held through 1943, required Lovestone to get the U.S. trade union movement to support FDR's efforts in aiding the British; after Germany's invasion of the Soviet Union in June 1941, Lovestone was responsible for delivering labor support to Russia.

Introduced by Dubinsky to George Meany in 1941, the American Federation of Labor (AFL) secretary-treasurer at the time, later to become the AFL president and the first AFL-CIO president, Meany selected Lovestone to run the federation's foreign affairs. Beginning in 1944 until his forced retirement in 1974, Lovestone led the AFL's, and then after the AFL-CIO merger in 1955, the combined federation's foreign affairs activities. As executive secretary of the Free Trade Union Committee (FTUC), formed at the 1944 AFL convention "with the mandate of assisting free unions abroad," Lovestone operated this group out of the ILGWU's headquarters in New York with only two assistants, working quietly behind the scenes becoming "one of the masterminds of the Cold War" (Morgan, p. 144).

In the immediate postwar period, Lovestone toiled diligently to prevent the European trade unions from becoming Communist-dominated. For example, in France, Lovestone attempted to split the Communist-led *Confederation Generale du Travail* (CGT) by financially supporting the anti-Communist *Force Ouvriere* and sabotaging CGT-directed strikes in 1947 and 1948. In Italy, Lovestone successfully adopted a similar strategy of dividing the major trade union federation, the CGIL, controlled by the Communists and Socialists, in the late 1940s. In addition, under Lovestone's tutelage, the FTUC promoted its anti-Communist agenda in the 1950s and 1960s in unions of African and Asian nations, such as Tunisia, Morocco, Algeria, and India, many of which were beginning to emerge from colonialism.

Not surprisingly, Lovestone strongly backed U.S. involvement in Vietnam throughout the 1960s and 1970s, working with and financially supporting the anti-Communist Confederation of Vietnamese Labor (Confederation Vietnamienne du Travail—CVT). He even helped to organize the prowar demonstration among 100,000 construction workers in New York in late May 1970. Although Lovestone supported Nixon's foreign policy, he would renounce him for his opening to Communist China later in the 1970s.

There is no doubt that Jay Lovestone was a controversial figure in the U.S. trade union movement. To those anti-Communist Cold Warriors found in the upper echelons of the AFL-CIO, Lovestone was undoubtedly viewed as an unsung hero for the role he played in combating Soviet influence in the world's trade unions. However, for others, his legacy is viewed considerably more negatively. By turning the U.S. trade union movement into an instrument of government policy and for sabotaging other nations' unions that derived legitimate support from workers, Lovestone's actions demonstrate how the Cold War divided the working class to capitalists' benefit.

VICTOR G. DEVINATZ

References and Further Reading

Alexander, Robert. *The Right Opposition: The Lovestoneites and the International Communist Opposition of the 1930s.* Westport, CT: Greenwood Press, 1981.

Buhle, Paul. "Spies Everywhere." *Radical History Review* 67 (Winter 1997): 187–198.

Carew, Anthony. "The American Labor Movement in Fizzland: The Free Trade Union Committee and the CIA." *Labor History* 39, no. 1 (February 1998): 25–42.

Klehr, Harvey, John Earl Haynes, and Fridrikh Igorevich Firsov. *The Secret World of American Communism.* New Haven, CT: Yale University Press, 1995.

Morgan, Ted. *A Covert Life: Jay Lovestone: Communist, Anti-Communist, and Spymaster.* New York: Random House, 1999.

LOWELL FEMALE LABOR REFORM ASSOCIATION (LFLRA)

The Lowell Female Labor Reform Association (LFLRA) formed in the winter of 1845 with 13 officers and two additional members drawn from the thousands of young women who then filled the textile mills of antebellum America's most famous industrial city. By spring, the association's ranks swelled into the hundreds, under the dual mottos of "Try Again" and "Union, for Power." Sarah Bagley, the association's president, stated that the organization's purpose was to give workingwomen a sense of both personal autonomy and collective responsibility to defend themselves from the increasingly exploitative conditions of factory labor. Workers needed not only to speak out against the injustices of the factory system, but also organize to fight those inequities and take back control of their labor. The association, clearly seeing links between gender and class on shop floors where male overseers always supervised female workers, insisted that female factory operatives had to challenge male corporate power, which had expanded virtually unchecked since the city began to produce cloth in the early 1820s. Yet, despite sometimes fiery rhetoric and bold assertions of women's rights to organize and agitate in public, this organization rarely made a sustained effort to confront directly the terms of industrial capitalism.

The LFLRA was one of the first stable organizations of female operatives in the nation. These women, who had often been excluded from workingmen's groups, helped publish the *Voice of Industry* and a widely circulated series of "Factory Tracts." The association also sponsored an industrial reform lyceum and various fairs and rallies to publicize its messages and raise money. Perhaps most important, this organization became an influential force in the campaign for a 10-hour workday through its publications, petition drives, and even testimony before the

Massachusetts legislature. In fact, the association's peak years of activism—1845 to 1847—parallel the high point of 10-hour agitation in that decade. The fortunes of both these crusades were intimately linked, and they rose and fell together.

The LFLRA, with Bagley at the helm, tried to steer a middle course between agitation and restraint in the campaign for labor reform. Unlike many antebellum craft unions, this association was filled with semi-skilled operatives who had little or no organizational experience or individual bargaining power, and hence received no meaningful recognition from management. Thus, the group did not propose any work rules to control production processes, or hiring procedures to regulate labor recruitment, or standard lists of piece rates to maintain wages. Moreover, the association's constitution called for strikes only as a last resort. The organization did not want to renounce this weapon, but there seemed to be a general agreement among most Lowell workers in the 1840s that strikes were not the most effective means to change the workplace. Therefore, the LFLRA, despite its frequent scorching public pronouncements against corporate abuses such as long hours, wage cuts, and increased workloads, did not direct any major walkouts. Many women came to see the organization as a mechanism for airing their grievances forcefully and publicly and securing their rights through popular pressure and political activism, while at the same time avoiding direct conflict with overseers and mill owners.

Interest in labor reform associations spread to female operatives in other industrial cities. Larger factory communities may have been particularly conducive to organizing such groups because the sheer number of young female workers in these mills made collective protest a more realistic option for aggrieved employees. Workers in Manchester, New Hampshire, organized their own Female Labor Reform Association, as did operatives in nearby Dover and Nashua, and in the Massachusetts seacoast city of Fall River. The LFLRA's secretary, Huldah Stone, corresponded with these other groups and offered a vision of solidarity among women workers that transcended any one location, occupation, or industry.

Yet ironically, as the LFLRA and its sister organizations became better coordinated and perhaps better able to protest more forcefully at the point of production, they also remained cautious and continued to channel their efforts into petitions and publications. They still avoided strikes, perhaps because they now worried about compromising the very organizational structure they had built up. So, the LFLRA remained more outspoken than many workingmen's groups in its written demands for significant reforms in the factory system, but these women rarely engaged in direct confrontation with corporate power to press those demands.

As female operatives became more involved in these local labor reform associations, and eventually in regional organizations such as the New England Workingmen's Association (NEWA), they faced new challenges to their arguments for women's activism. Sarah Bagley, when she addressed the NEWA in May 1845, defended the right of women to speak publicly for themselves, even as she re-assured her mostly male audience that female activists would not threaten the men's sphere of power and politics. Bagley wedded her crusade for workingwomen to more traditional concepts of female nurturing and morality so as not to jeopardize the support of workingmen by making her demands seem too strident. She made the fight for labor reform, whether women acted on their own or in support of men, a key to protecting women's health and dignity. Those who protested did not violate ideals of female modesty; they defended women's true virtue from the encroachments of greedy factory owners.

By January 1847, just two years after its founding, the LFLRA transformed itself into the Lowell Female Industrial Reform and Mutual Aid Society. The association's name change was more than cosmetic; it reflected a deeper shift from a group centered on workingwomen's own agenda for labor reform, to an organization devoted to bringing middle-class notions of moral uplift to female operatives. The new society was not necessarily a wholesale capitulation to pressure from management, or to possible divisions within the women's own ranks. But the new group did prove to be even more cautious in its public actions and often quite limited in its critiques. The emphasis was now, more than ever, on ideals of female friendship and nurturing. Labor reform was now to be found in "the elevation and cultivation of mind and morals" and in this society's relief programs for destitute and lonely workers. The goal was to connect middle-class ideals of respectable womanhood with a working-class ideology of collective action and the dignity of labor. Yet this society never clearly explained how it would reconcile those divergent ideas into one unifying organizational philosophy. By the end of the decade, perhaps burdened by these internal contradictions, the society had disbanded.

DAVID A. ZONDERMAN

References and Further Reading

Dublin, Thomas. *Women at Work: The Transformation of Work and Community in Lowell, Massachusetts, 1826–1860.* New York: Columbia University Press, 1979.

Early, Frances H. "A Reappraisal of the New England Labor Reform Movement of the 1840s: The Lowell Female Labor Reform Association and the New England Workingmen's Association." *Social History* 13 (1980): 49.

Foner, Philip S., ed. *The Factory Girls.* Urbana: University of Illinois Press, 1977.

Zonderman, David A. *Aspirations and Anxieties: New England Workers and the Mechanized Factory System, 1815–1850.* New York: Oxford University Press, 1992.

See also **Bagley, Sarah George; New England Workingmen's Association**

LOWELL TURNOUTS (1834, 1836)

In the winter of 1834, and again in the fall of 1836, thousands of young women workers walked off their jobs to protest wage cuts in the textile mills of Lowell, Massachusetts. The sight of female factory operatives taking to the streets in protest over their working conditions, in the midst of antebellum America's "model" industrial city, sent shock waves through counting rooms and drawing rooms across the nation. Managers may have aimed deliberately at the reduction of women's wages because they assumed these women would accept such cuts meekly; these men were gravely mistaken. The walkouts, some of the largest yet organized by American workers, served notice that the Lowell "mill girls" were also the "daughters of freemen"—willing to stand up for what they saw as the very rights their fathers and grandfathers had fought for not so long ago. Without a personal artisanal background to draw on, these women tapped into the inheritance of their forefathers' republican status—they organized themselves as workers to protect the legacies of their middle-class family roots.

The 1834 turnout began on a Friday evening, February 14, with the dismissal of one worker. But she was no ordinary factory hand, and the strike was not an entirely spontaneous action. This woman had already spoken up at several meetings where workers complained about a 15% pay cut scheduled to take effect on March 1 and signed pledges to quit work when wages were cut, or pay a $5 fine for going back on their word. She urged her fellow operatives to give their notice to quit, withdraw their savings from local banks, and return to their country homes (if they could). After she learned of her discharge (which she may have been expecting) and received her pay, she waved her bonnet in the air to signal other workers looking into the office windows. Her compatriots immediately left their looms and spindles, gathered round their fired comrade, formed a procession of nearly eight hundred workers, and marched through the city drawing out other employees from all the mills.

By the following day (Saturday), the protesters' ranks were reported to be over two thousand strong. Strike leaders issued a proclamation rooting their actions in the traditions of the American Revolution and pledging themselves to the ideals of solidarity and mutual assistance. The issue at hand was more than a matter of wages and money to these women. Yes, they had to preserve their economic rights as free labor; they deserved to be treated with respect and paid a just wage for their daily toil. But they also believed that it was imperative for all of them to band together to guard their political rights as citizens of a free republic (though they could not vote); they deserved to be recognized as the moral equal of any male overseer or owner. Furthermore, a worker's fundamental equality and independence was a right due all honest American workers, not a favor to be bestowed or removed at management's discretion. And these women saw a clear connection between asserting their status as American citizens and preserving their respectability as women. For only a free female operative paid a just wage could hold herself above any potentially contaminating influences in the factory.

Although the strike began with bold assertions of workers' unity and appeals for respect, the protesters' fervor subsided quickly. Advanced planning and enthusiastic rallies were no match for corporate wealth and power. The overall economic climate was sluggish, and the corporations seemed in no hurry to make concessions to resolve this disruption in production. The operatives discovered, by Monday, that they were the ones who would have to move rapidly if they wanted to protect their jobs. New recruits already streamed into the city inquiring about the jobs left open by strikers, several leaders were summarily fired, and others returned to work at the reduced wages.

But life in Lowell did not return immediately to the status quo. Some strikers left the company boardinghouses and rented their own quarters; others demanded that the banks pay out their accounts in cash and made good on their plans to hire wagons that took them back to their rural homes. One former overseer recalled that in some mills there were looms that lay idle until September 1835.

In October 1836, operatives in Lowell again turned out over the issue of declining wages. Actually, in this instance, the workers' boarding charges went up without any corresponding raise in pay, and the net effect was a decrease in earnings. Harriet Hanson Robinson, who wrote a book about her childhood in Lowell (*Loom and Spindle*), reported that the strike spread from room to room, and mill to mill. Protesters again tried to do some advanced planning and targeted vulnerable areas in the production process, knowing if they shut down particular rooms, then the whole factory would have to stop running. For example, weavers—though they were relatively well paid and felt the increase in boarding costs less—were also well organized and led many facets of the walkout. They urged other workers to leave their departments; if enough workers joined in, even if they did not compose a majority of the workforce, they could still shut down the mills. Eventually, 1,500 women walked out and formed a procession through the city streets. The marchers did not have banners or music, but they sang their own songs.

This walkout proved to be a harder-fought battle than the 1834 protest. Once again, thousands of women assembled to hear speeches about their rights as the daughters (or more likely, granddaughters) of revolutionary patriots. Many operatives held out for more than two weeks. There were reports that a "Factory Girls' Association" had formed and quickly enrolled 2,500 members. The organization demanded that manufacturers communicate with its officers and that no sanctions be taken against any members. Yet some strikers did face corporate reprisals. And after a month of agitation, the strike concluded much as the one in 1834 had. Some workers left the mills altogether and returned to their families; other straggled back to their jobs under the new rates. But one observer did report a crucial difference: this time, the corporations rescinded the board increase for workers paid by the day. Thus, about 40% of the women employees (those paid a daily wage) did win their basic demand. In this instance, the mills were faced with thousands of strikers and a shutdown dragging on for weeks in the midst of a sales boom. So, the owners may have been more anxious to settle this dispute than they had been two years earlier, and more willing to show some flexibility in making modest concessions.

The mill operatives of Lowell, in the turnouts of 1834 and 1836, protested as workers, as women, and as the "daughters of freemen." The strikers, usually living on their own away from their families, still invoked strong images of their personal heritage in defense of their bold actions. Their rhetoric and conduct displayed a radical new vision of women's power through public protest, embedded in a language of traditional rights inherited through their patriarchal lineage. Patriotism meant fighting for fairness, not blind obedience to those in authority. Militancy was a necessary tool to secure liberty and protect status. The strikers demanded that the historical ideals of respect, justice, and equity be honored within the new factory system. And they insisted that they would not play the role of dutiful daughters for any

substitute father-manager in the scheme of corporate paternalism. Rather, they would take the lessons of discipline and interdependence learned in the mills and use those principles to build networks for collective protest. Thus, these strikers drew on the ideology of republicanism, citizenship, and self-determination—all patriotic, mainstream democratic themes—blended with the language of class- and gender-consciousness and solidarity to support their struggles as workers and as women.

DAVID A. ZONDERMAN

References and Further Reading

Dublin, Thomas. *Women at Work: The Transformation of Work and Community in Lowell, Massachusetts, 1826–1860.* New York: Columbia University Press, 1979.
Robinson, Harriet H. *Loom and Spindle; or, Life among the Early Mill Girls.* New York: Thomas Y. Crowell, 1898.
Zonderman, David A. *Aspirations and Anxieties: New England Workers and the Mechanized Factory System, 1815–1850.* New York: Oxford University Press, 1992.

See also **Textiles**

LOYAL LEGION OF LOGGERS AND LUMBERMEN

The origin of the Loyal Legion of Loggers and Lumbermen began with the 1917 Pacific Northwest lumber strike. By August of that year, 50,000 lumber workers shut down approximately 75% of the industry regionwide. The primary issues for the workers involved their demands for an eight-hour day, wage increases, and improvement in living conditions in logging camps. Employers were most intransigent over the eighthour day. Even though striking workers were forced to return to the logging camps and lumber mills, the Industrial Workers of the World (IWW) and American Federation of Labor (AFL)—both of which had competed for leadership of the strike—urged workers to "strike on the job." This tactic of working only eight hours a day and intentionally slowing down on the job severely reduced production.

The federal government grew concerned over the low production of lumber and decided to act. Lumber, especially spruce, was a primary manufacturing material for building military aircraft. In early October, the War Department dispatched Colonel Bryce P. Disque to investigate the production problem and to find a solution that would meet the military's needs. After consulting with members of the academic community, labor leaders, and lumber company owners in the region, Disque came to the conclusion that the continuing problems of labor unrest were caused by difficult working conditions, low pay, and the lack of an eight-hour day among the lumber industry's workforce. Disque's plan was to use federal troops to begin logging operations in the spruce timber region of the Pacific Northwest and to create an organization to deal with the industry's labor-management problems. It was necessary for Disque to get as many lumber company owners to agree to this scheme as possible. With a sufficient number of them giving their approval, the War Department allotted him 100 officers and 25,000 troops to staff his Spruce Production Division (SPD). In order to solve the long-term problems of the industry as a whole, however, Disque established the Legion. This organization was designed to provide a forum for workers and employers to resolve disputes in the industry. The federal government and lumber company owners considered the SPD to be a temporary wartime measure. They considered the Legion as a possible permanent solution to industrial unrest. By December, the Legion grew in membership as loggers, mill and kiln hands, and employers joined. Its membership peaked by the war's end with more than 100,000 members and over 1,000 locals. The membership was primarily native-born men, though a small number of immigrants and women were also members.

Soon after the creation of the Legion, the issues that caused the strike and that continued to plague the industry were brought up at local meetings. In early 1918—at Disque's urging—employers began to implement the eight-hour day in an effort to bring their operations to normal production levels. On March 1, 1918, Disque, after receiving agreement from two hundred representatives of the Pacific Northwest lumber industry, declared the eight-hour day, the 48-hour workweek, and time and a half for overtime in effect throughout the Pacific Northwest. Living conditions and wages also improved over the course of 1918. These improvements in working and living conditions severely weakened the organizing efforts of the IWW and AFL.

At the end of the war, Legion locals overwhelmingly voted to continue the organization. Members elected delegates from each local to represent them at the district boards. Both worker and employer delegates were chosen by the boards to serve at the Headquarters Council, headed by Colonel Disque. Funding for the Legion came from member dues and contributions from employers. For several years, the organization remained a strong force in the region's timber industry. Locals could be found throughout the Pacific Northwest, including northern California. The Legion's constitution stipulated that locals elect a special committee for negotiations and grievance issues with employers. The organization established a wage scale and continued to support the eight-hour day. It also published a bulletin and other periodicals.

Nevertheless, membership began to dwindle as employers grew less supportive of employee participation. The experiment in employer and employee collaboration in such an organization revealed its limits with workers' concerns over wages and working conditions in conflict with employers' concerns over profits and production levels.

By 1921, the Legion had a membership of just 10,000, never rising above that number throughout the decade. In 1935, a major strike again gripped the region. At first, the Legion opposed the strike but later demanded a wage increase, thus further alienating employer support. The final end came with the Supreme Court decision upholding the Wagner Act (1935). The act re-invigorated AFL organizing in the timber industry. The new Congress of Industrial Organizations (CIO) also proved too competitive for the Legion. Even the last-ditch effort to remove employer members, accept the right to strike, and change the organization's name in order to meet the recognition requirements of the National Labor Relations Board (NLRB) could not save the Legion from extinction.

GREG HALL

References and Further Reading

Ficken, Robert E. *The Forested Land: A History of Lumbering in Western Washington.* Seattle: University of Washington Press, 1987.

Hyman, Harold M. *Soldiers and Spruce: Origins of the Loyal Legion of Loggers and Lumbermen.* Los Angeles: Institute of Industrial Relations, University of California, 1963.

Jensen, Vernon H. *Lumber and Labor.* New York: Farrar & Rinehart, Inc., 1945.

Mittelman, Edward B. "The Loyal Legion of Loggers and Lumbermen: An Experiment in Industrial Relations." *The Journal of Political Economy* 31, no. 3 (June 1923): 313–341.

Tyler, Robert. *Rebels of the Woods: The I.W.W. in the Pacific Northwest.* Eugene: University of Oregon, 1967.

———. "The United States Government as Union Organizer: The Loyal Legion of Loggers and Lumbermen." *The Mississippi Valley Historical Review* 47, no. 3 (November 1960): 434–451.

LUCIA, CARMEN (APRIL 3, 1902– FEBRUARY 1985)
Union Organizer

Carmen Lucia was a lifelong unionist who organized workers across the United States. Joining the Amalgamated Clothing Workers of America (ACWA) at age 14, Lucia became a tenacious organizer for the United Hatters, Cap and Millinery Workers International Union (UHCMW), affiliated with the American Federation of Labor (AFL). While working for the UHCMW, Lucia led numerous organizing drives, became one of the union's first female vice presidents in 1946, was appointed a labor delegate to France in 1950, and participated in education, health care, women's rights, and other humanitarian causes.

Two years after her birth in Calabia, Italy, in 1902, Lucia's family immigrated to Rochester, New York, where several relatives had already settled to work in the city's thriving garment industry. Raised in Rochester, Lucia's worldview was shaped by her father's periodic layoffs at Stein-Bloch garment factory and, later, by his membership in the ACWA. Additionally, she was influenced by her older brother's experiences as an organizer for the Industrial Workers of the World (IWW) and, perhaps most poignantly, the death of a 17-year-old girl shot during a garment strike in 1913 while standing near Lucia, who had sneaked out of her house to picket with her father. Consequently, over the course of her upbringing, Lucia developed a hatred of poverty and a belief that unions could improve the lives of working people.

At age 12, Lucia dropped out of school to help raise her siblings, 13 in all, and two years later began working at Stein-Bloch as a machine operator. At Stein-Bloch she became chairperson of the ACWA local, in charge of roughly two hundred laborers. When tensions developed between the union and Stein-Bloch in 1924, Lucia was appointed spokesperson and in this capacity led her first strike. While the stoppage accomplished few gains, Stein-Bloch refused to rehire Lucia. However, Abraham Chapman, the vice president of Rochester's ACWA, was impressed by Lucia's charisma and at the time desired someone with Italian-language skills and hired her as his secretary. Between 1924 and 1930, Lucia worked for Chapman, became a valuable asset to the ACWA, and rose to the position of interpreter and director of complaints.

Although Lucia dropped out of school at a young age, her mother had taught her the value of a bilingual education by teaching Carmen to read through English and Italian-language newspapers. Thus, at age 25, upon learning that evening courses were being offered to female workers by the Industrial Department of Rochester's Young Women's Christian Association (YWCA), Lucia embraced the opportunity to participate. There, Lucia was mentored by Elizabeth Hiss, the department's director, who had Lucia take courses in labor history, debate middle-class university students on various topics, and attend community functions at local churches and synagogues, where Lucia spoke out on behalf of Rochester's labor force. Through her friendship with Hiss, in 1927 and 1930, Lucia enrolled in the Summer School for Women Workers in Industry at Bryn Mawr College in Philadelphia, where she met Hilda (Jane) Worthington Smith (director of Bryn Mawr, 1920–1933), who further mentored Lucia. Soon, Lucia began writing labor and inspirational poetry that was published in *Shop and School* by Bryn Mawr; *Spring Magazine*, published by the Affiliated Schools; and the *Hat Worker*, the official newspaper of the UHCMW. In this context, Lucia befriended multiethnic Euro-American female workers, some of whom were Marxists. Later on she was appointed student representative for the Affiliated Summer Schools for Workers in Industry, Inc., a program affiliated with the Brookwood Labor School, the Barnard School of Columbia University, and the University of Wisconsin, where she would serve as secretary of the joint committee from 1934 to 1936. Lucia was also elected class president in 1930. Through these programs, Lucia developed a middle-class female support network and became a lifelong advocate of educational programs for workers and women in particular. In fact, Lucia would become the vice president of the National YWCA, a member of the League of Women Voters, and a board member of the Affiliated Schools for Workers.

In 1930, Lucia broke with the ACWA over a dispute concerning the treatment of Italian workers. However, through her studies at Bryn Mawr, Lucia met Louis Fuchs, of the Independent Neckwear Workers Union (NWU), who hired her as a full-time organizer, sending her to New Haven, Philadelphia, and then Chicago. In 1931, in New Haven, Lucia called a strike at the Seigman and Son Hat Company, during which she drew on her experiences at Bryn Mawr and obtained middle-class support from the broader community through connections to women activists and students attending the Divinity School of Yale. While the strike (which lasted from February to November) was ultimately lost, Lucia gained much respect from her union, given that during the ordeal she was beaten by three assailants, arrested, and boldly returned to the picket line.

During the Great Depression, Lucia married Leo Kowski, the financial secretary of the ACWA. She retained her maiden name as a marker of independence and delivered their first and only child, Marguarita, in 1932. Due to illness, Kowski did not work, and when in 1934 the NWU asked Lucia to help organize workers in Philadelphia, she accepted. During a strike in Philadelphia, Lucia drew community support by highlighting the female members of the labor force. Lucia asked women workers to picket while wearing white dresses with bright red sashes. After the strike was won, the NWU sent Lucia to Chicago, where another garment strike was in progress. While attempting to speak to a replacement worker, Lucia placed her hand on the female worker's shoulder and immediately after was dragged into an alley by a Chicago police officer, who beat her, pulled her arm out of its socket, and then arrested her. After she was bailed out of jail by the NWU, Lucia fearlessly rejoined the picket line. Embroiled in an internal altercation within the NWU, Lucia quit the union. In 1935, she met Max Zaritsky, of the Cloth Hat and Cap Makers of North America, who shared many of Lucia's ideals and hired her to organize West Coast garment workers.

Between 1935 and 1950, Lucia organized garment workers on behalf of the UHCMW in Los Angeles and San Francisco. She later went to Texas and worked in operations in Dallas, Garland, Longview, and Corsica. Upon briefly returning to Illinois (DeKalb), Lucia established herself at the union's central office in Atlanta (1944–1960), from which she led campaigns as far north as Norwalk, Connecticut, and Holyoke, Massachusetts. Lucia then chaired the union's southern organizing drive in Greenville, Alabama; Winchester, Tennessee; and Richmond, Virginia. In 1950, she was elected a labor delegate to France, under the State Department's Economic Cooperation Administration, in affiliation with the Marshall Plan. Upon returning to the United States, she continued to work for the UHCMW throughout the 1960s, by which time she was championing the Equal Rights Amendment. In 1974, at the age of 72, and after 39 years of union service, Lucia retired from the UHCMW. In 1980, she returned to Rochester, where several of her brothers and sisters still resided, and in February 1985, Lucia passed away.

JOHN H. FLORES

Selected Works

The Carmen Lucia Papers can be located at the Southern Labor Archives, Georgia State University.

"First a Troublemaker, Then a Troubleshooter: Carmen Lucia, United Hatters, Cap and Millinery Workers International Union (1902–1985)." In *Rocking the Boat: Union Women's Voices, 1915–1975*, edited by Brigid O'Farrell and Joyce L. Kornbluh. New Brunswick, NJ: Rutgers University Press, 1996.

Gamel, Faye Phillips. "The Hat Lady: A Career Biography of Carmen Lucia." Master's thesis, Georgia State University, 1979.

Martin, Christopher T. "New Unionism at the Grassroots: The Amalgamated Clothing Workers of America in Rochester, New York, 1914–29." *Labor History* 42, no. 3 (2001): 237–253.

See also **Amalgamated Clothing Workers of America; American Federation of Labor; Brookwood Labor College; Industrial Workers of the World; United Hatters', Cap and Millinery Workers' International Union**

LUDLOW MASSACRE (1914)

The 1913–1914 southern Colorado coal strike was one of the most violent labor conflicts in American history. The strike's denouement came on April 20, 1914, when 12 children, six miners and union officials, and one National Guardsman were killed in a day-long battle between the Colorado National Guard, which had been called to break the strike, and residents of a tent colony near the Ludlow, Colorado, railroad station. Ludlow was the largest of seven tent colonies that the United Mine Workers (UMW) had built to house the more than 9,000 mostly Southern and Eastern European and Mexican immigrant miners who were thrown out of company housing when they went on strike. The massacre set off a 10-day-long war between National Guardsmen and incensed miners, who were intent on exacting revenge for the Ludlow killings. Twenty-nine more people were killed during those 10 days, before President Woodrow Wilson sent the Army to restore order.

Like many well-known historical events, the Ludlow Massacre has been distorted by misstatement and exaggeration. Though some histories of the massacre contend that the Colorado National Guard planned an attack on the Ludlow tent colony, the truth was more complicated. Relations between Guardsmen and the striking miners were far from harmonious during the six months the Guard was on strike duty. The poisoned atmosphere that developed between the Guard and the miners created the preconditions for the Ludlow Massacre.

By the spring of 1914, the coal-mine operators, led by the Rockefeller family-owned Colorado Fuel and Iron Company (CF&I), had all but defeated the miners' strike. The National Guard had helped the operators import thousands of nonunion workers into their mines, leaving the UMW with little leverage to negotiate a settlement. The miners, however, refused to surrender. On Sunday, April 19, 1914, the day before the Ludlow Massacre, the Greeks in the Ludlow tent colony treated their neighbors to a celebration of the Greek Orthodox Easter. After roasting lamb, the tent colonists played baseball. In what was perhaps an apocryphal story, several women participating in the game said later that a few National Guardsmen showed up at the ball field. The Guardsmen and colonists exchanged insults, and as the soldiers left, they hinted that they would soon attack the colony. It was this story that has probably left the impression that the Guard had planned an invasion.

Next morning, a detail of National Guardsmen came to Ludlow looking for an Italian miner. Louis Tikas, a Greek immigrant who had become a union organizer and then the popular leader of the Ludlow colony, said the man in question was not there and refused to allow a search. Tikas thought he had good reason to keep the soldiers out. Guardsmen had frequently used intimidation and violence against the miners and their families as they attempted to force the strikers back to work. The Guard had also torn down the nearby Forbes tent colony several weeks earlier. Most miners and their families already loathed the Guard, and after Forbes's destruction, they vowed that they would not allow soldiers into their camps again.

What followed was a series of misunderstandings and mistaken perceptions. It remains impossible to determine who fired the first shot, but by 10 a.m., the Guard and the miners were exchanging a torrent of rifle fire. Charlie Costa, an Italian immigrant and striking miner who would die that day along with his wife and children, led the miners out of the tent colony in an effort to draw the National Guard's fire away from the women and children still in the tents. Costa's plan failed. In addition to keeping the miners pinned down just outside the colony, the Guard poured rifle and machine gun fire into the tents. The women and children inside rightfully believed that fleeing would get them shot, but the canvas tents provided scant protection from the gunfire. With little choice, some women and children climbed into the pits that many colonists had dug in the earth beneath their tents early in the strike after the Baldwin-Felts detectives hired by the coal operators fired on the tent colonies. These pits served as hiding places.

By early evening, the Guard had succeeded in fighting its way into the tent colony. They set the tents ablaze, but also found women and children still hiding in the tents. Guardsmen had a very difficult time getting these colonists to come out because they believed that the soldiers were going to kill them. The soldiers eventually pulled more than a few women and children out of the fire that quickly engulfed the entire tent colony, but failed to find all who were still alive and hiding underground. It was not until the following afternoon that the bodies of two women and eleven children were found in the pit beneath a tent. The Guard had also taken Louis Tikas and two other miners prisoner. All three men were killed while in the Guard's custody.

The miners who escaped Ludlow could think of nothing but revenge. For the next 10 days, they destroyed the mine companies' property while fighting the Guard. The army's arrival in southern Colorado ended the violence, but the strike eventually ended in defeat for the miners. This outcome was not unique for workers who faced hostile military intervention during a strike. The National Guard's court-martial acquitted all the men charged with crimes stemming from Ludlow, but the Ludlow Massacre did have some lasting impact. John D. Rockefeller Jr. introduced his Industrial Representation Plan at the CF&I's mines shortly after the strike ended. The plan instituted a system of company-sanctioned representation for the miners and became a model for company unions. Nevertheless, Colorado's coal miners struck eight more times during the following two decades, and the UMW won a contract with the CF&I in 1933. For students of labor history, the Ludlow Massacre vividly illustrates the volatile conditions that military intervention in labor conflicts often created and reveals the class, racial, and ethnic tensions that drove military strikebreaking.

ANTHONY DeSTEFANIS

References and Further Reading

Beshoar, Barron B. *Out of the Depths: The Story of John R. Lawson, a Labor Leader*. Denver, CO: Golden Bell Press, 1958.

Gitelman, Howard M. *Legacy of the Ludlow Massacre: A Chapter in American Industrial Relations*. Philadelphia: University of Pennsylvania Press, 1988.

Gorn, Elliot J. *Mother Jones: The Most Dangerous Woman in America*. New York: Hill and Wang, 2001.

Long, Priscilla. *Where the Sun Never Shines: A History of America's Bloody Coal Industry*. Chapters 12–14. New York: Paragon House 1989.

———. "The Women of the Colorado Fuel and Iron Strike, 1913–14." In *Women, Work, and Protest: A Century of U.S. Women's Labor History*, edited by Ruth Milkman. Boston: Routledge & Kegan Paul, 1985, pp. 62–85.

McGovern, George S., and Leonard F. Guttridge. *The Great Coalfield War*. Boston: Houghton Mifflin Company, 1972.

Papanikolas, Zeese. *Buried Unsung: Louis Tikas and the Ludlow Massacre*. Salt Lake City: University of Utah Press, 1982.

LUTHER, SETH (1795–1863)
Writer and Labor Activist

Seth Luther was born in Providence, Rhode Island. His father was a veteran of the Revolutionary War. His mother was active religiously. Trained as a carpenter, Luther practiced a strain of Baptist egalitarianism that he preached in the streets of Providence and laced into the philosophy of the emerging national workers' movement in essays in the 1830s. These militant pamphlets in the Jacksonian Era extolled labor rights, like the 10-hour day, as well as the necessity for suffrage rights without property qualifications. Luther matched the ardor of his literary output with concrete union organizing on a local and national level. In Rhode Island, he was a key figure in a civil uprising in 1842—the Dorr War. He followed his own dictates and took up arms for the right of an unfettered franchise and landed in prison. Like many social pioneers he eventually suffered a nervous breakdown and was institutionalized until his death in an asylum.

His political career had its genesis in Providence's First Baptist Church, where Luther apparently offered his own take on Scripture not long after the War of 1812. At the same time he worked his trade as a carpenter, he also moonlighted as a bookseller and vendor of religious portraits. Despite his literary skills, Luther seemed to have little business sense and a host of medical problems that curtailed his activities. He went to debtor's prison in 1823, saddled with almost $1,000 of liability. He successfully petitioned the General Assembly to release him later in the year. In 1824, the church expelled him for "disorderly walking," a catchall phrase that could include drinking, unsanctioned religious activity, or other problems.

Luther traveled frequently, allegedly walking hundreds of miles during various trips. He appeared in Rhode Island again in 1831 when he had an indirect experience in a racial riot in Providence. The state mobilized the militia, including Luther, who later complained that many male citizens had to serve as troops involuntarily without the right to vote due to a property qualification of $134 of taxable realty. That seemingly small figure still disenfranchised about 60% of all white males in the state by 1840. Rhode Island, the most urban industrial state in the nation, soon had more propertyless factory workers than land-rich farmers.

The 1830s was an active decade in Luther's life and rise to labor prominence. He wrote his first pamphlet in 1833 about the voting situation in Rhode Island, *Address on the Right of Free Suffrage*. He agitated the question of the 10-hour workday—perhaps the linchpin of the era's workingmen's parties. He crisscrossed New England, hawking copies of a regional labor newspaper. He helped found the Trades Union of Boston and Vicinity and participated in the pioneering National Trades Union that flourished until the Panic of 1837.

Despite his broad, geographical labor career, Luther flexed his muscular efforts primarily in his home state. In the 1830s, he joined a band of skilled workers who challenged the role and rights of laborers throughout society and, in particular, agitated fiercely for local manhood suffrage. Employing the rhetoric of the American Revolution, these tradesmen joined forces with liberal-minded professionals in Rhode Island to boil the arguments into a material force in the upcoming Dorr War in 1842. In his quest for political freedom, Luther, who became a brilliant orator as well, often declared "Peaceably if we can, forcibly if we must!

He was in a group of armed demonstrators who tried to capture the state arsenal in Providence in the year of the uprising, after his rebel cohorts used an extralegal election to bifurcate the state between reformers and the forces of the status quo. The ensuing insurrection, more smoke than fusillade, ended quickly when the ruling law and order group activated the militia and pursued the mutineers relentlessly but with only incidental violence.

Charged with treason under martial law, Luther spent a year in prison and published a rare poem of gratitude to the women who supported the campaign. After his release, he embarked on a tour to champion the uprising, which eventually became part of the 1844 Democratic presidential campaign. He spent time in Illinois recuperating mentally before rejoining his colleagues in Rhode Island and re-igniting the old labor quest of a 10-hour workday.

In 1846, he abandoned his usual tunnel vision for unions and suffrage by writing to President Polk, offering his patriotic services in the Mexican War. Apparently, on his way to the conflict, Luther entered a bank in Boston, brandishing a sword, and demanded a $1,000 in Polk's name. He became a patient at two asylums in Providence before being transferred in 1858 to a facility in Brattleboro, Vermont, that charged less than its Rhode Island counterparts. The city fathers in Providence hoped to save scarce municipal funds in that depression year.

Luther died in 1863, unnoticed for the most part, in the midst of a much crueler civil war than the one he helped instigate. A local paper wrote that he led a useless life. He was buried in an unmarked grave at the Vermont asylum. He wielded the precepts of the American Revolution and natural equality more vehemently than his sword in the Boston bank. Louis Hartz wrote that Luther possessed a unique global consciousness in that era about the drive for class equality. The Rhode Island Heritage Hall of Fame inducted Seth Luther, the deranged bank robber, into its ranks in 2001.

SCOTT MOLLOY

References and Further Reading

Gersuny, Carl. "Young Luther in Debt." *Rhode Island History* 56 (June 1999): 52–60.
Hartz, Louis. "Seth Luther: The Story of a Working-Class Rebel." *New England Quarterly* 13 (September 1940): 401–418.
Molloy, Scott, Carl Gersuny, and Robert Macieski, eds. *Peaceably If We Can, Forcibly If We Must!: Writings by and about Seth Luther*. Kingston: Rhode Island Labor History Society, 1998.

See also **Dorr War**

LYNN SHOE STRIKE (1860)

The great New England shoe strike of February and March, 1860, led by shoe workers in Lynn, Massachusetts, involved town-centered artisan men, women stitchers working by hand in their homes or by machine in small factories, and rural outworkers in Massachusetts, Maine, and New Hampshire. The strike represented the most widely supported and powerful demonstration of American labor protest prior to the Civil War.

The 1860 strike was a response on many levels to the slow industrialization of New England shoemaking during the early nineteenth century. In the pre-industrial phase, artisan shoemakers produced the entire boot or shoe in small shops called "10-footers." As the market for their shoes expanded, daughters and wives in artisan families began to assist the shoemakers but did not enter the shops. In their kitchens, women hand-sewed the uppers for the shoes in a process called "binding." The female binders then passed that part to the artisans, who completed the shoe. A distinct gender division of labor became established. As demand for boots and shoes rose, shoemakers or the merchants, who handled the sale of the shoes and often supplied leather to the artisans, began to hire women as shoe binders. Their wages remained low. If possible, young women left their families to earn higher wages in New England textile factories.

The artisan system of shoemaking in New England became altered by centralization and mechanization. The shoemakers, now called "bottomers," began in the 1830s and 1840s to protest low wages and a lost independence. Merchants responded by hiring shoe bottomers in rural New England, linked by wagon. By the 1850s, the sewing machine was adapted to stitch leather. The merchants or shoe bosses brought sewing machines into their central shops, where they distributed leather and assembled the completed shoes for sale. Highly skilled leather cutters also worked in the central shops. At first, female stitchers operated the sewing machines by foot power, but shoe bosses quickly attached the machines to steam engines. Meanwhile, shoe binders working at home in Lynn, Salem, and Marblehead had the chance to rent sewing machines. Their work remained in their homes, but the machines had to be laboriously hand-cranked, sometimes by children as their mothers or sisters stitched.

Machines run by steam power stitched uppers much faster, while the uniformity of machine stitching represented an improvement over hand work. Wages for stitchers in factories outpaced both machine work and handwork at home. Factory stitchers, usually young, unmarried women, worked for 10 hours a day, six days a week, under the constant discipline of centralized management. They earned high wages and did not, like shoe binders, have to provide or furnish their own thread, needles, and wax. All of these groups—shoe bottomers, shoe binders, home machine workers, and factory stitchers—participated in the shoe strike of 1860. The issues that arose during the strike revealed the opportunities and challenges of industrialization as it reshaped the work of men and women. The strike also featured the persisting values of artisan work culture and gender relations within the family.

Artisan shoemakers in Lynn launched the strike on February 22, 1860, the birthday of George Washington, to commemorate the link between their struggle for independence against the shoe bosses with the political rights of artisan men achieved in the War of the Revolution. Artisans in Lynn and Natick, Massachusetts, led the action. Male shoemakers sought the support both of other shoemakers throughout New England and of women workers in the shoe trade. Female moral support would blunt criticism of violence against teamsters taking materials to rural shoemakers and organize the support of families for the strike. But as the strike spread, conflicts began to emerge between men and women strikers and between factory stitchers and shoe binders.

Many shoe binders and factory stitchers saw the strike as an opportunity to advance their interests as workingwomen. A coalition forged between factory workers and lower-paid home workers held out the hope for higher wages for all women engaged in shoe work, whether married or single, family resident or boarder, and wherever they stitched. Higher wages for women's work in the home and in the factory meant that single women could anticipate—once they married—reasonable wages for homework. The factory girls occupying a strategic place in centralized operations could deny the shoe bosses sewn uppers to deliver to rural bottomers. Workingwomen organized in early 1860 to demand higher wages for female factory workers and homeworkers.

Artisan shoemakers who had initiated and organized the strike objected, regarding men's rights and wages as primary. During the debates over the purpose of the strike, women homeworkers had to choose between supporting the strike as women workers with their own interests or as female members of artisan families. Many remained loyal to their husbands, fathers, and brothers, abandoning the coalition with factory stitchers and their wage demands. Women who supported the male strikers thus reflected gender relations within the artisan family, values that defined women as secondary earners in a family wage system within which they were socially and economically subordinate. The alliance of male bottomers and female homeworkers prevailed, and the factory girls deserted the strike.

Street processions and marches to other shoemaking towns featured the men and women strikers carrying banners proclaiming support for increases in male wages and female moral support for the strike. On March 7, one banner carried by women supporters summed up their position: "Weak in physical strength but strong in moral courage, we dare battle for the right, shoulder to shoulder with our fathers, husbands and brothers." The values of artisan culture shaped and dominated the 1860 strike, which represented the last stand of pre-industrial work against the emerging factory system. After the regional strike failed in March, the impetus of mechanization and centralization brought more male workers into the factory, eliminating both the work of artisan bottomers and shoe binders, the key supporters of the strike.

MARY H. BLEWETT

M

MAJOR LEAGUE BASEBALL PLAYERS ASSOCIATION

The most powerful labor organization in the United States at the turn of the twenty-first century was the Major League Baseball Players Union, an association of millionaire athletes who had turned the tables on management and seemingly had the upper hand in the sport, winning all eight negotiations since 1968. This was a dramatic reversal from the early days of baseball when players were described as chattel by shortstop John M. Ward of the New York Giants, organizer of the Brotherhood, the first baseball union in 1885. The Brotherhood fought against maximum salaries and the reserve clause (which restricted players to their teams in perpetuity), and established the short-lived Players' League in 1890. The next brief efforts at unionization were the Protective Association of Professional Baseball Players, formed in 1900, and the Base Ball Players' Fraternity in 1912.

In 1946, Robert Murphy, a Congress of International Organizations (CIO) lawyer, formed the American Baseball Guild to equalize the playing field between management and labor. He sought a $7,500 minimum salary, an arbitration system for resolving contract disputes, replacing the reverse clause with long-term contracts, and insurance and pension benefits. He convinced the Pittsburgh Pirates, a team located in a strong prolabor city, to strike, but they backed down at the last minute under pressure from management. The owners did make concessions, including $25 a week for spring training meals ("Murphy money"), a $5,000 minimum salary, a small pension plan, and representation on the owners' and league presidents' council.

In 1953, after Commissioner Ford Frick refused to give the players a full accounting of the pension fund and the owners refused to raise the minimum salary to $8,000, team representatives, led by Ralph Kiner and Allie Reynolds, hired J. Norman Lewis as legal counsel. The owners excluded him from their meetings with player reps, and then the ballplayers founded the Major League Baseball Players Association (MLBPA). In response, owners agreed to fund the pension with revenue from the All Star game and World Series.

In 1959, the weak MLBPA replaced Lewis with Judge Robert Cannon, whose goal was to become baseball commissioner. Seven years later the MLBPA offered Cannon $50,000 to become their full-time administrator, but he declined. The members, led by Robin Roberts and Jim Bunning, chose a new tactic, influenced by rising NFL salaries, fears about their pensions, the dual Koufax-Drysdale holdout, and the social activism of the 1960s. They hired Marvin J. Miller, chief labor economist with the United Steelworkers, as executive director.

Miller sought to destroy the paternalistic character of player-management relations by introducing an adversarial model, learning the players' main grievances, and shaping their collective consciousness to see themselves as professionals meriting proper compensation. Miller scared the owners, who established the Player Relations Committee (PRC) to deal with him through professional negotiator John J. Gaherin. In 1968, after Miller threatened to seek federal mediation, the owners signed the first Basic Agreement of any sport. The path-breaking 2-year contract raised the minimum pay from $7,000 to $10,000, granted players the right to be represented by agents, and established grievance procedures adjudicated by the commissioner. Then in 1969, veteran players sat out spring training to secure higher pension funding.

A bitter fight emerged between the union and PRC in 1972. Owners were upset at rising payrolls and their declining power, while the players were still concerned about pension funding. The union voted 663-10 to authorize a strike in spring training that lasted until April 13 and got their pension contributions raised to $5.9 million. The press attacked the players as spoiled, pampered, and irresponsible.

In 1973, the MLBPA focused on securing independent grievance arbitration and a breakthrough occurred when the owners agreed that players with 2 years' experience could request "final offer salary arbitration" after the expiration of their contract. The player and owner would each submit a salary to a board comprised of a representative from labor and management plus an independent arbitrator, and they would pick between the two proposals. This opportunity helped many players get big raises as teams became more responsive to their demands in hopes of avoiding final arbitration.

The MLBPA and Free Agency

The union supported players' rights to control their own destiny. In 1969, the MLBPA financed Curt Flood's suit to block his trade from the Cardinals to the Philadelphia Phillies. The case went to the Supreme Court in 1972, which rejected his complaint because baseball was exempt from antitrust law. Two years later, Catfish Hunter was declared a free agent by arbitrator Peter Seitz because annuity installments stipulated in his contract were not paid. Hunter then signed a 5-year, $3.75-million contract with the Yankees, which opened the eyes of star players.

Miller believed a player who completed a season without a signed contract, would become a free agent. In 1975, two players completed the season unsigned—pitchers Andy Messersmith of the Dodgers and the injured Dave McNally of the Expos. After the season Seitz ruled they were now free agents. McNally retired, but Messersmith signed a multiyear contract with the Braves for $1.75 million. The owners responded by locking out the players from spring training, but Commissioner Kuhn ordered the camps open under pressure from television and certain key owners. That summer negotiators agreed to grant

free agency after 6 years, but teams signing these players had to give the old team a selection in the amateur draft. Players also won many perks, including firstclass airfare, severance pay, and input on working conditions Average salaries shot up to $76,000 in 1977, the first year of widespread free agency, and $143,000 by 1980.

In the early 1980s, when there was widespread union busting and forced givebacks throughout the United States, the baseball owners also fought back. They wanted better compensation in the form of a comparable player. That would discourage teams from hiring free agents, which resulted in higher salaries, lack of control over their players, uncompetitive play, and economic uncertainty. The union responded with a strike on April 1 that lasted 8 days. Shortly thereafter, a 4-year Basic Agreement was signed that did not alter free agency, while raising the minimum salary to $35,000 in 1984.

The growing hatred and distrust of players and management propelled a major strike in 1981 that began on June 12 and lasted 7 weeks. The public was irate and blamed the players. By then the players' strike fund was nearly spent, while the owners' insurance was about to expire, and they would lose their television revenue. The settlement gave owners who lost a free agent protection of 26 of their 40 man rosters, leaving only journeymen and minor leaguers as compensation. A split season was declared, and the winners of the prestrike season and the poststrike season advanced to the playoffs.

Miller retired in 1982 and was replaced by Ken Moffett, a former mediator, who lasted less than 2 years. Miller temporarily "unretired," and gave way to his assistant, Don Fehr, a brilliant attorney, who led the MLBPA to great successes, protecting players' jobs and rights.

In the 1986 round of negotiations, the owners cried poverty, claiming a total loss of $166 million although attendance was high and television revenue was up to $200 million. The union authorized a strike date on August 6 after they had made most of their salaries but before the owner would get 80% of the national TV revenue. Two days later an agreement was reached that established eligibility for arbitration after 3 years, the salary minimum was boosted to $60,000, and compensation for free agents through the amateur draft was restored. Thereafter owners then stopped bidding for free agents. The union sued, and arbitrators twice found the owners and the commissioner guilty of collusion to fix the player marketplace. The teams were fined $280 million.

The 4-year basic agreement signed in 1990 called for two new teams, boosted salary minimums to $100,000, raised the pension contribution to $55 million, and granted salary arbitration to the most experienced second-year men. Two years later the owners hired a new negotiator, Richard Ravitch, with the hopes of busting the union.

In 1994, with players getting 60.5% of total revenues, the owners proposed sharing revenue with the players, with salaries capped at 50% of revenues, ending salary arbitration, and granting free agency in 4 years. The MLBPA was prepared to go to the barricades to maintain the status quo, and with a strike fund of $165,000 per man, called a strike for August 12. The owners responded provocatively, refusing to make a scheduled $7.8 million pension contribution. The bitter and suspicious negotiations fell apart, and the strike followed. The players returned to work after 232 days following a court injunction that restored the old terms of the expired Basic Agreement. In 1996, a new agreement was reached. The players accepted interleague play, which began in 1997, two more teams in 1998, a minimum salary of $200,000 in 1999, and a 35% luxury tax on at least five teams. The current Basic Agreement, signed in 2002, established revenue sharing among teams and raised the minimum pay to $300,000. Since then the union's main concern seems to have become protecting players accused of drug usage. Random testing for steroids was agreed to in 2003, and in 2005, year-round testing for steroid use was introduced, with a 10-day suspension for the first offense.

The MLBPA's successes set a standard for labor relations in professional sports. Miller remolded a company union into a powerful collective that won major gains at the bargaining table, which the players, through a united front, have since maintained and expanded. The achievement of a grievance procedure in 1968 was the foundation for all future gains. Thereafter the union used the strike as a tactic to demonstrate the solidarity of the membership to secure even more gains.

STEVEN A. RIESS

References and Further Reading

Burk, Robert F. *Much More Than Just a Game: Players, Owners & American Baseball since 1921*. Chapel Hill, University of North Carolina Press, 2001.

Korr, Charles P. *The End of Baseball as We Knew It: The Players Union, 1960-81*. Urbana: University of Illinois Press, 2002.

Miller, Marvin. *A Whole Different Ball Game: The Sport and Business of Baseball*. New York: Birch Lane Press, 1991.

Rader, Benjamin G. *Baseball: History of America's Game*. 2nd ed. Urbana: University of Illinois Press, 2002.

Staudohar, Paul D. "Baseball Negotiations: A New Agreement." *Monthly Labor Review* 125 (Dec.2002): 15–21.

Staudohar, Paul D., ed. *Diamond Mines: Baseball & Labor*. Syracuse, NY: Syracuse University Press, 2000.

MAQUILADORAS

Maquiladora is the name for a sector of the Mexican economy in which foreign-owned firms assemble products from parts and other inputs that come largely from outside of Mexico. Most of the assembled products are then exported from Mexico. The *maquilidora* sector's development has served as a model for similar activities in developing countries throughout the world. This type of development is an example of "flexible production" that has typified economic globalization. New technologies make it possible for the production of goods to be broken up into smaller parts so that the manufacturing of a product can occur in different locations.

The *maquiladora* sector has its origins before the birth of today's form of globalization. From 1942-1964 the United States and Mexico engaged in a cooperative venture known as the *Bracero Program* that enabled Mexican agricultural workers to enter the United States and help harvest particular crops during specified time periods. Once the crops were harvested, these workers were transported back to Mexico. The Mexican workers were needed in the United States initially because of labor shortages caused by World War II. Mexico for its part had a surplus of agricultural workers. But in 1964 the United States unilaterally canceled the *Bracero Program*, which caused a social and political crisis in the Mexican border towns. In response the United States and Mexico entered into a new agreement known as the Border Industrialization Program (BIP). It was designed to ease Mexican unemployment in the border towns. The United States and Mexico amended tariff codes to allow U.S. firms to export intermediate products to Mexico for assembly into finished products without paying Mexican tariffs. These products would then be exported from Mexico back to the United States with tariffs limited to the value added by Mexican assembly. Mexico at the time had a development strategy called "import substitution," which was geared toward promoting economic self-sufficiency. The BIP ran counter to this strategy because it relied on foreign investors. Nevertheless Mexico attempted to maintain its broader economic policy by placing restrictions on the BIP: Requiring dual U.S.-Mexican ownership of BIP plants, restricting their location to U.S.-Mexican border areas, and requiring that all BIP products be exported immediately from the country.

The initial size of the program was quite modest. By 1971, there were only two hundred *maquiladoras* employing about 30,000 workers. Working conditions in these plants were very bad and wages low. The government-controlled union, the Confederation of Mexican Workers (CTM), deliberately took a hands-off policy in the *maquiladoras* in order to attract foreign investors. But they soon lost control, and militant independent union organizing ensued. As wages increased many owners threatened to pull out. When a major recession hit in 1975, employment actually declined in the *maquiladora* sector. In 1976, the CTM regained control over organizing in the *maquiladora* zones and allowed the Mexican government to take repressive measures against dissident worker organizations. Nevertheless from 1977–1981 continued militant worker activity enabled real wages to grow rapidly. But in 1981–1982, a severe recession and a drastic peso devaluation caused wages and employment to decline once again, and independent union activity ceased.

In 1982, there was a debt repayment crisis in much of the developing world, and Mexico was one of the first to declare its inability to pay off massive foreign loans. In response the International Monetary Fund (IMF) agreed to provide a bridge loan to Mexico so it could continue making payments on its debts. By 1985, IMF pressure resulted in the adoption of a structural-adjustment program that constituted a new economic development strategy. At this point Mexico officially abandoned its import-substitution strategy. The new development model aimed to achieve economic growth through exports, wage, and inflation reduction, privatization of state enterprises, lowering tariffs on foreign goods, and easing barriers to foreign capital. The old BIP was transformed into the *maquiladora* sector and became the centerpiece of this new strategy. During the next decade, restrictions on *maquiladora* development were greatly reduced, including ownership provisions, location, and even the requirement that the goods be exported. *Maquiladora* products could now compete directly with Mexican manufactured goods.

The Mexican government with U.S. approval also initiated an aggressive program to recruit U.S. firms to move production to Mexico. As a result of these efforts the growth of employment in the *maquiladora* sector took off, growing 17.5% from 1982 to 1990 to nearly 500,000 workers. Most of these workers were employed in electric and electronic equipment and products and transportation equipment, particularly automobiles.

In 1994, Mexico, Canada, and the United States entered into an agreement known as the North American Free Trade Agreement (NAFTA). The NAFTA greatly accelerated the developmental approach initiated in 1985. This included removing any further restrictions on *maquiladora* activity. Militant labor activity had largely been eliminated at this point as well so that *maquiladora* wages and working conditions were generally poor. This resulted in a large jump in employment in the *maquiladora* sector so that by 1998, there were over 3,000 *maquiladora* plants employing over one million workers. Their location was concentrated in border areas, but there were now *maquiladora* operations throughout the nation.

Part of the significance of the evolution of the *maquiladora* sector is that it became a model for other parts of the world. Beginning in 1971, there began a period of rapid growth of similar assembly operations known as export-processing zones (EPZs), largely in Asia and the Caribbean. There are now more than 200 EPZs in such nations as India, China, Taiwan, Malaysia, South Korea, the Philippines, Honduras, and Columbia. Total employment in developing-nation EPZs is now more than four million.

The growth of EPZs generally has led to the displacement of many workers, contributing to the decline of union membership in the United States. It is part of the process of globalization in which capital has become highly mobile, which creates new challenges for organized labor. The EPZs have been controversial within the nations where they are located as well. This is due in part to the fact that wages, working conditions, and environmental impacts have been poor, and union activity has been suppressed by EPZ governments. But in addition there is considerable question of how great a positive impact they really have. In the Mexican case, *maquiladora* activity has ended up displacing more manufacturing jobs than it created. During the past decade, manufacturing employment has declined by nearly 10% even though output has increased by 38%. In part this is due to the fact that *maquiladoras*, like all EPZs, do not use goods produced nationally in the production process. The Mexican content of *maquiladora* products over the past decade is less than 3%. And the *maquiladora* operations have put some Mexican firms that had over 90% Mexican content out of business. Furthermore with the rapid growth of EPZs throughout the world, rising wages in one nation can result in firms leaving for lower wage locations. This is beginning to happen in Mexico as a number of *maquiladora* firms move to China's EPZs.

DAVID C. RANNEY

References and Further Reading

Arroyo, Alberto et al. *Lessons of NAFTA: The High Cost of "Free" Trade.* Toronto: Canadian Centre for Policy Alternatives, 2003.

Dicken, Peter. *Global Shift: Transforming the World Economy.* 3rd ed. New York: Guilford Press, 1998.

Kamel, Rachae, and Anya Hoffman. *The Maquiladora Reader: Cross Border Organizing since NAFTA.* Philadelphia, PA: American Friends Service Committee, 1999.

See also **Globalization**

MARCH ON WASHINGTON MOVEMENT

The Negro March on Washington and its successor the March on Washington Movement were both efforts by African-Americans in the 1940s to mobilize around the related issues of racial and economic discrimination faced by African-American workers. Behind both efforts was A. Philip Randolph, a labor and civil rights activist, who by 1941 was a national African-American leader, who had led the Brotherhood of Sleeping Car Porters and the National Negro Congress. Randolph's lifelong political commitment was to convince Americans of all races of the interrelationship between economic inequalities and racial discrimination. Such a commitment inspired his efforts in the 1940s.

The Negro March on Washington for Jobs and Equal Participation in National Defense, 1941

The origin of the Negro March was in the preparedness efforts in the United States in the late 1930s. As European countries increased their demand for certain American products, many American workers began to feel as if the Great Depression was relenting. African-Americans were less likely to notice, because the companies supplying weapons, engine parts, and other products to the Allies were often the same companies who were least likely to employ many African-Americans in well-paying jobs. Likewise African-Americans also found less opportunity if they answered the call of recruiters from the armed services. All branches discriminated against blacks, and all segregated them from white members. African-American organizations, such as the National Association for the Advancement of Colored People (NAACP), the Urban League, and Randolph's National Negro Congress, took notice of this dual inequality and began to demand that the federal government intervene. But their testimony at congressional hearings, their leaders' meeting with President Franklin Roosevelt, and their reports had caused little change by the end of 1940.

Randolph resolved that different tactics were necessary. Inspired by his own involvement in mass marches and labor strikes, he called for other African-Americans to join him in a mass march on Washington to demand an end to segregation in the armed forces and equal access to defense jobs. He recruited the leaders of most major African-American organizations to lend their names to his efforts and began

recruiting marchers from cities with large African-American populations. Starting with a goal of 10,000 marchers, by late June he believed that 100,000 black men and women might attend the July 1 march. The march was to take place at the Lincoln Memorial and include addresses by all the major African-American leaders. In addition Randolph invited President Roosevelt and First Lady Eleanor Roosevelt to attend.

President Roosevelt, the first lady, and his aides did not believe the march was a good idea. They feared the march would be used by German officials to highlight the contradictions in U.S. racial policies. They also feared that a large mass of African-Americans in the nation's capital might result in rioting—of white people or black people. As a result they put pressure on Randolph and the other organizers of the march to cancel in June 1941. But these leaders refused to change their plans unless they received some significant action on the part of the president. The negotiations were tense and hurried, since the march was just weeks away. Finally on June 25, the president signed Executive Order 8802. This order did not address all the problems that had inspired the march; most noticeably, it did not directly address the segregation and unequal treatment of African-Americans in the military. Yet it did create a commission on Fair Employment Practices that had the power to investigate companies with defense contracts and punish those that discriminated on the basis of race, religion, or national origin. This commission had the most far-reaching federal powers to fight racial discrimination at the time. Its issuance was seen as a major victory of the Negro March leaders. And the march was canceled in response.

The March on Washington Movement's Successes and Failures

The problem of being a successful threat of a march but not an actual march struck the march organizers as soon as they had canceled. And this problem inspired the creation of the March on Washington Movement (MOWM)—a group that never marched on Washington but did train activists and keep African-Americans mobilized during the 1940s. In July 1941, Randolph and other leaders urged their supporters to stay mobilized to make sure that the president's executive order met their expectations. The American declaration of war in December 1941, however, made marching on Washington an even more radical act, since both Japanese and German officials might use such acts to publicize the pervasive

Civil rights march on Washington, D.C. Library of Congress, Prints & Photographs Division, U.S. News & World Report Magazine Collection [LC-DIG-ppmsca-03128 8].

discrimination African-Americans still experienced. Accordingly as Randolph organized the MOWM, he had to balance his desire to mobilize as many African-Americans as possible to work on both economic and civil rights issues with the need to remain patriotic. The need for the group became more obvious as it became clear that the Fair Employment Practices Commission held hearings but rarely invoked its powers to halt contracts with companies that continued to discriminate. The group sponsored a series of mass meetings in Detroit, New York, and St. Louis. Still Randolph found that leaders of other African-American organizations, such as the NAACP and the Urban League, were less inclined to support his efforts when they were associated with a permanent group rather than a single group. And without their support and funds, Randolph and his supporters began to foster protests focused on civil disobedience. Younger activists joined the organization because of this tactic of nonviolent direct action. For example Bayard Rustin, a former Communist, youth activist, and draft resister, became very influential in the group. The MOWM local groups and national conferences influenced such groups as Congress of Racial Equality (CORE), which soon used direct action to challenge segregated buses and services for interstate travelers. Though the March on Washington Movement did not last past the 1940s and never held a march in the nation's capital, its influence was profound. People involved with the MOWM in the 1940s went on to play crucial roles in organizing

subsequent efforts to win better treatment of black workers in both the North and the South.

LUCY G. BARBER

References and Further Reading

Barber, Lucy G. *Marching on Washington: The Forging of American Political Tradition.* Berkeley: University of California Press, 2002.

Bracey, John H., Jr., and August Meier "Allies or Adversaries? The NAACP, A. Philip Randolph, and the 1941 March on Washington." *Georgia Historical Quarterly* 75 (spring 1991): 1–17.

Garfinkel, Herbert. *When Negroes March: The March on Washington Movement in the Organizational Politics for FEPC.* Glencoe, IL: The Free Press, 1959.

Pfeffer, Paula F. *A. Philip Randolph, Pioneer of the Civil Rights Movement.* Baton Rouge: Louisiana State University Press, 1990.

See also **A. Philip Randolph Institute; Don't Buy Where You Can't Work Campaigns; Fair Employment Practice Committee; National Association for the Advancement of Colored People; Randolph, A. Philip; Rustin, Bayard**

MARINE TRANSPORT WORKERS' INDUSTRIAL UNION

The Marine Transport Workers' Industrial Union (MTW) was one of the largest, most important, and durable segments of the Industrial Workers of the

Marine truck transport units. Marine Corps transport workers study the assembly of one of the many weapons the leathernecks use in war exercises at New River, North Carolina. Library of Congress, Prints & Photographs Division, FSA/OWI Collection [LC-USE6-D-005785].

World (IWW), commonly referred to as the Wobblies. The MTW organized sailors, longshoremen, and other workers in the marine transport industry—shipping—on an industrial basis. The MTW was the most international component of an organization ideologically committed to fighting global capitalism yet it was primarily a North American outfit. The MTW simultaneously engendered tremendous respect among many thousands of sailors and animosity from rival unions, employers, and governments.

Shipping, domestic and international, was—and is—essential to the global economy. There are few industries that better embody the market adage "time is money" than shipping. The knowledge that the ship must sail on time provided an opening for longshoremen and sailors to exert pressure "at the point of production" by declaring quickie strikes just before a ship set sail.

Shortly after its founding in 1905, the fledgling revolutionary union started organizing in marine transport. Wobblies first targeted the longshoremen of Hoboken, New Jersey, across the Hudson River from Manhattan. As the largest port in America by a large margin, organizing New York was essential to any maritime union. Interestingly the Irish immigrant James Connally spearheaded the effort. Connally

later took IWW ideals and tactics back to Ireland, where he organized simultaneously for the class struggle and Irish independence, ultimately martyred in the 1916 Easter Rebellion. The MTW remained active on the piers and aboard the ships that docked in Manhattan, Brooklyn, and Hoboken into the 1940s.

However as in most other U.S. ports, the MTW never supplanted its rivals, the International Longshoremen's Association (ILA) and International Seamen's Union (ISU), both of which belonged to the more mainstream and conservative American Federation of Labor (AFL). The AFL operated on a craft model, spawning more than a dozen maritime unions divided by region and type of work; by contrast the MTW was an industrial union, meaning that regardless of craft, all workers belonged to the same organization. Also the MTW never signed contracts, so that its members always could deploy workers' ultimate weapon, their ability to strike. This tactic raised the ire of employers but won respect from many sailors in an often-brutal industry.

In 1912, the IWW created the National Industrial Union of Marine Transport Workers (NIUMTW) as part of its efforts to establish nationwide unions in important industrial fields. The NIUMTW was founded in part to convince certain AFL sailors to re-affiliate. Engine room workers, who performed some of the dirtiest and hardest work on coal-fired steamships, were overwhelmingly dark-skinned, a huge percentage on Atlantic vessels being Spanish and Portuguese. These men were alienated from the AFL because of its racist tendencies and more conservative policies. Efforts to get the thousands of AFL firemen to join the IWW failed, though the MTW continued to command loyalty from these radical sailors, who often were dual unionists (paying dues into an AFL union and the MTW). Around 1917, the IWW created different MTW sections for the Atlantic, Pacific, Great Lakes, and Gulf of Mexico. Curiously its largest branch remained a separate entity.

In a real sense the history of the MTW is that of Local 8, though technically it did not originally belong to the MTW. In May 1913, several thousand Philadelphia longshoremen struck for higher wages and union recognition. The union that this diverse dock workforce chose to represent them was the IWW, chartered as Local 8. Local 8 did what no other MTW or IWW branch did: Line up thousands of workers and keep them for years. Simply put Local 8 was the most durable branch in the entire IWW, representing Delaware River longshoremen for almost a decade, dramatically improving their wage rates, work conditions, power, and prestige. Perhaps most noteworthy about Local 8 was that approximately half of its members, and its most important leader, Ben Fletcher, were African-American. Though ideologically committed to equality, in practice there were few nonwhite Wobblies. Thus the IWW celebrated Local 8 for proving that IWW vision and tactics could overcome the traditional bogeyman of (working-class) America: Race.

For decades the MTW proved itself to be thoroughly international, apropos of the industry. A quick perusal of its newspaper, the *Marine Worker*, indicates in how many different ports of call throughout the world the MTW organized. True the parent union's name suggested a global strategy, but in practice the IWW was mostly U.S. and Canadian. By contrast the MTW had branches across the seven seas. The MTW organized in numerous Latin American ports, for instance, in Valparaiso, Chile, that nation's largest port, and Tampico, Mexico, using its control of area sailors to create a wedge into that city's important oil industry. The IWW gained the loyalty of sailors based in Hamburg and other German ports, as in Sweden and Britain. Similar to other movements, Wobbly sailors proved instrumental in the distribution of IWW literature and ideas. Moreover it was in this industry that a transnational working-class identity fully revealed itself; during Local 8's 1920 strike, for example, British sailors and Spanish firemen refused to scab on Philadelphia longshoremen. Wobbly sailors later castigated AFL sailors for working ships that supplied the Fascists in the Spanish Civil War.

In 1917, when the IWW suffered from massive federal persecution, the MTW was well-represented. Five Philadelphia residents associated with the MTW were arrested (Walter Nef, Jack Walsh, E. F. Doree, and Fletcher of Local 8; Manuel Rey, a Spanish-born sailor, led the MTW on the Atlantic Coast; he was replaced by Genaro Pazos, another Spanish sailor based in Philadelphia). In the aftermath of this repression, the MTW, now numbered 510, struggled to survive. The MTW maintained an active presence along both coasts (Boston to Norfolk, Seattle to San Pedro) as well as in the Gulf (especially New Orleans, later Galveston and Houston). Local 8, still the largest and most important branch, maintained its impressive strength notwithstanding the loss of its entire leadership.

Despite repression the MTW joined the postwar wave of labor militancy that swept the nation and world, in part inspired by the nascent Soviet Union. In 1920, Local 8 called out its four thousand members and thousands of other workers in a failed 6-week strike for the 8-hour day. In 1922, sensing the weakness of the IWW and a turning tide away from labor, employers locked out Local 8 members and exploited growing racial tensions to tear the most important MTW outpost asunder. The IWW maintained its presence in Philadelphia for the rest of the decade but never asserted the authority that it commanded in the 1910s. The MTW also undertook major strikes in Portland, Oregon, in 1922 and San Pedro (an L.A. port) in 1923. This last strike agitated for the release of the remaining Wobblies languishing in state and federal prisons due to the Red Scare. This persecution continued unabated well into the 1920s, notably when the San Pedro hall was raided and members brutally beaten in 1924.

While most IWW unions emerged from World War I far weaker, such was not the case for 510. In fact amid a crushing depression across the Atlantic maritime world in the early 1920s, the MTW challenged the ISU for dominance. Each union claimed more than 5,000 members, and the MTW flourished as a massive ISU strike failed in 1921-1922 despite strong MTW support. Throughout the 1920s, even though Lenin ordered American Communists to "bore from within" the AFL, the MTW remained strong enough that Communists considered whether it should be the target for infiltration. Though the IWW repeatedly rejected such overtures, many in the MTW still flirted with communism.

The MTW maintained significant influence among sailors in the Atlantic, Pacific, and Gulf into the 1940s. It is clear that the insurgent sailor and longshore unions of the Congress of Industrial Organizations (CIO) drew much of their inspiration and ideology, as well as some members, from the MTW. By the same token, the Communist Marine Workers' Industrial Union (a clear rip-off of MTWIU) also were inspired by, and competed with, Wobblies. The MTW maintained halls in numerous ports on all four coasts into the late 1940s, so younger sailors in a second postwar world still encountered old-time Wobblies, but it faded by the end of that decade.

The legacy of the MTW is quite strong. Influential among sailors for more than 30 years, the MTW was a force to be reckoned with across the United States and the globe. Although rarely did the MTW command a majority of any ship's crew, it often was instrumental in securing gains for sailors—thanks to a militant and committed membership. And the story of Local 8 is among the most impressive in the entire IWW. The MTW also deserves notice for working tirelessly to challenge nationalist identities and create an international union.

PETER COLE

References and Further Reading

Bekken, Jon. "Marine Transport Workers IU 510 (IWW): Direct Action Unionism." *Libertarian Labor Review* 18 (1995): 12–25.

Cole, Peter. *Black Wobbly: The Life and Writings of Ben Fletcher*. Chicago, IL: Charles H. Kerr, forthcoming/ 2005.

———. "Shaping Up and Shipping Out: The Philadelphia Waterfront during and after the IWW Years, 1913– 1940." Ph.D. dissertation, Georgetown University, 1997.

Dubofsky, Melvyn. *We Shall Be All: A History of the Industrial Workers of the World*. 2nd ed. Urbana: University of Illinois Press, 1988.

Kimeldorf, Howard. *Battling for American Labor: Wobblies, Craft Workers, and the Making of the Union Movement*. Berkeley: University of California Press, 1999.

Nelson, Bruce. *Workers on the Waterfront: Seamen, Longshoremen, and Unionism in the 1930s*. Urbana: University of Illinois Press, 1990.

Marine Worker. Detroit, MI: IWW Collection, Walter Reuther Archives, Wayne State University.

See also **Fletcher, Benjamin Harrison; Industrial Workers of the World; International Longshoremen's Association**

MARITIME LABOR

Maritime labor gave birth to the American colonies. In 1773, Newburyport, Massachusetts, was home to 700 adult males, of whom the jobs of nearly 600 have been determined. Among the business and professional men were 140 who described themselves as merchants, shipbuilders, distillers, or shipmasters linked to the sea. The town's 21 shopkeepers depended on water imports. Maritime artisans included shipwrights, boat builders, sail makers, coopers, mast makers, and caulkers. Over 50 were mariners, truck men, or laborers working on the waterfront. Nearly 60% worked with some link to the sea.

Privateering, in contrast to piracy, was a legal trade in which warring states granted permits to loot enemy shipping. These permits were called Letters of Marque, and although the state often took a share, it was more profitable than service in the regular navy and attracted the best seamen. American fortunes were thus made during both the Revolution and the War of 1812. Privateering was the merchant sailor's main opportunity for earning income until it was ended by the Declaration of Paris in 1856. In New York City the roster of privateers was known as "the social register" by their wealthy heirs. Robert Randall, the conscientious son of a privateer captain, established Sailor's Snug Harbor "to support aged, decrepit and worn out seamen." Snug Harbor still serves Randall's intent, and over 14,000 older seafarers have passed through its eighteenth-century halls. Many of these were foreign-born, as were many American merchant sailors.

Most seamen were tied to ships like medieval serfs were tied to the land. The independent-minded United States ironically made this servitude into law in its first statutes in 1797 by outlawing resignation from merchant ships for the duration of the voyage. This law was in effect until phased out in the late nineteenth century. If a sailor left a ship, he could be apprehended by shore-side authorities and returned— or his pay could be forfeited and his belongings confiscated and sold in the captain's "slop chest." The nineteenth century saw the evolution of the "land sharks," the combination of boarding house owners, "runners," and saloon owners, who could bind a man in cycles of debt.

Brave sailors went on strikes even before they had unions. Indeed many mutinies might be considered strikes. Mutinies on merchant ships were single-ship actions and might be short and unrecorded, and unless they became violent, they were often successful. The first recorded strike was in 1803 in the port of New York City, as a result of which the men won an increase from $10 a month to $17 a month. The next portwide strike was in Boston in 1837, when pay was only slightly higher than 34 years previously.

The search for speed under sail created beautiful tall ships, but it also created more hazardous working conditions aloft, and perhaps it made the seafarers more assertive. Strikes appeared early in the nineteenth century, and wages rose as did the length of the topmasts, although the unhealthy conditions remained stubborn. The glory days ended in the Civil War, as British steamers took over, and American crews were left on the beach. Further the Confederate raiding ships burned many of the beautiful clipper ships of that era of wood and sail.

The Search for Speed under Steam

In 1850, the Collins Line pioneered government subsidies to steam shipping—these totaled $385,000 per year without any stipulations for labor conditions—although there was a safety clause that all Collins ships must be built to pass naval standards.

Labor unionism proceeded fitfully and by discreet maritime regions. One early organization of maritime labor was the Stewards' and Cooks' Marine Benevolent Society formed in New York in 1837. The first sailors' union was organized in New York by black Americans in 1863 as the American Seamen's Protective Union Association. In this same year Great Lakes' sailors came together in Chicago as the Seamen's Benevolent Union, which in 1892 became part of the International Seamen's Union (ISU) of the East Coast and the Gulf ports. The Great Lakes' men also established the Lakes Seamen's Union in 1878.

The first sailors' union on the West Coast was organized in San Francisco in 1866 as the Seamen's Friendly Union and Protective Society, but it did not collect dues and was replaced by the Seaman's Protective Association in 1880. This combination was founded to block the hiring of Chinese sailors, but it collapsed when its treasurer absconded with the union funds. Steamship sailors started their own union and opposed the radical Coast Seamen's Union until the two united under the conservative leadership of Andrew Furuseth in 1891 as the Sailors' Union of the Pacific. "Andy" Furuseth was so conservative that he quizzed prospective members on the elements of sailing ship rigging. Radicals at the turn of the last century were good organizers, but their appeal for violence may have cost public support. The modern Marine Transport Workers' Industrial Union still has a logo of a fist holding up a cargo hook.

The Anglo-American–owned *RMS Titanic* went down in 1912 in an accident that seems to grow ever more complex in its causes because modern divers are still making discoveries. The contemporary British and American court proceedings found no liability, and so the owners went unpenalized for the problematic design of the ship, marred by a slow rudder and short water-tight bulkheads. Captain Smith was drowned and could not testify about his errors of speed and observation. However just 3 years later, the capsize of the Great Lakes' excursion ship *Eastland* started a 20-year court battle over corporate responsibility.

The U-Boat Menace and Nationalized Shipbuilding

World War I brought on government shipbuilding by the Emergency Fleet Corporation, which built 2,382 ships in 18 months. These were the well-riveted "Hog Islanders," which gave good but slow service in both world wars. Seamen on these chartered ships were able to earn $90 a month plus a dollar an hour overtime—the best wages in merchant history. Certainly there were hazards, like U-boats and the fatal influenza and the delayed enforcement of the LaFollette Seaman's Act. At the end of the war, the Merchant Marine (aka Jones) Act of 1920 added workmen's compensation to sailor welfarism. After the war the shippers, and Admiral W. S. Benson of the U.S. Shipping Board, beat down wages, and the International Seamen's Union membership dropped from 115,000 to 16,000.

Diversity afloat was partially and temporarily realized in the 1921 achievement of the Black Star Line, created by black Americans to promote trade with Africa. Black nationalist Marcus Garvey in 1921 raised money from black Americans to buy the ships, but Garvey was not a businessman, and the line was finally bankrupted by his incompetence and fraud—or perhaps by sabotage. Still the short career of the Black Star Line drew worldwide attention.

Radicals in Power

The 1930s saw competition between conservative and radical union factions, but there was still an advance in unionization. The radicals were often the most active in recruiting and particularly contributed to sympathy strikes. On the West Coast the venerable conservative Furuseth held on to power, along with his associate Victor Olander, national secretary of the ISU, through a combination of deference-from-below and highhandedness-from-above. They opposed radical leader Harry Bridges who wanted a federation of sailors with longshoremen. Olander asserted that this was a tactic to destroy the International Seamen's Union, and the conservatives prevailed.

In 1933, the crew of the *Diamond Cement* participated in the first U.S. sit-down strike. It succeeded with support by East Coast waterfront workers. On the West Coast, the *S. S. California* crew struck for parity of pay with East Coast scales. By striking in place in a sit-down strike, they kept nonstrikers from moving the cargo ship. The owners threatened to bring charges of mutiny until President Franklin D. Roosevelt's Secretary of Labor Frances Perkins intervened on behalf of the men, but Secretary of Commerce Daniel C. Roper supported the firing of strike leaders. Failure of the ISU to support the men weakened that union, while another sit-down strike on the *S.S. American Trader* divided the ISU and led to the rise of Joe Curran, a leftist disciple of Harry Bridges.

In 1937, Joe Curran and Jack Laurenson left the International Seamen's Union (ISU) to form the National Maritime Union. An election led to the fall of the ISU and its absorption into the American Federation of Labor (AFL). Harry Lundeberg, head of the Sailors' Union of the Pacific helped reorganize this into the AFL Seafarers' International Union (SIU), which rapidly assumed a more activist stance with its drive for hazardous—duty pay in war zones—achieving a 33.3% bonus for African runs. The SIU's bold actions before the war gained both bonuses and a mediation procedure that helped smooth the path to victory at sea.

During World War II, the American Merchant Marine went from 55,000 men to 215,000. Of these 6,830 were killed, about 11,000 were wounded, and 604 became prisoners, of whom 10% died in prison. The percentage of Merchant Marine deaths during the war was greater than the percentage for any other service, yet they were denied the benefits granted to other services. They did not get draft deferments until mid-1942. Their Liberty ships were often ill-equipped, lightly armed, and slow targets for the numerous U-boats—if they did not first burst their welded seams.

Hollywood gave the unsung merchant mariners public recognition in 1943 when it made the film *Action in the North Atlantic*, but otherwise the merchant mariners suffered from the stigma of radicalism. This film began in a union hiring hall and followed the all-star crew along their hellacious passage to Murmansk, where they met a beautiful woman line handler as the other dockworkers shouted "*tovarich!*"

The New Internationalism

In 1961, American freighters usually had a young crew of 45 men, with an average age of 30 plus. By 1991, a similar ship carried 22. Maritime unions had their largest memberships in the 1970s. But now a union member's working time may be limited to a half a year to give more members a chance at the better jobs. After the voyage the seaman goes to a union hall and gets a dated National Shipping card, whose date determines the priority of that man—or since 1964—that woman. The person between ships then must drive from one port to another in search of a berth. The average age of persons in this system is now over 55.

Containerized cargo, which started replacing break-and-bulk cargo in the 1950s, dealt a heavy blow to the longshoremen's union, which had often supported seamen's unions in the past. Seamen themselves also suffered work loss from new labor-saving technology: Better metal finishes reduced the need for the constant chipping and painting of iron ship technology, frozen meals and microwaves needed only one cook, and the simple installation of a toilet near the bridge saved one person per watch. Electronics saved the time of the navigation officers, and the worried radioman was replaced by a few small boxes. The need for human observation with binoculars has been reduced by position-plotting radar.

The post-World War II emergence of Flags of Convenience (FOC) has dealt a further blow to the leverage of maritime labor. This practice of hiding ownership under weak-state flags has led to human rights' abuses, ecological abuses, and contractual abuses that are difficult to prosecute. Ship maintenance, crew training, paperwork, and crew communication can easily be skipped over and concealed. Mariners may be stranded in foreign ports, and marginal owners may simply cut all resources from a worn-out ship and let it drift, as in the case of *Mercedes I*, which went ashore at the Florida estate of Mollie Wilmot in 1984 and drew brief public attention. The best real hope for FOC seamen lies in the coordinated, global campaigns of the International Federation of Transport Workers.

Although the U.S. Merchant Marine has withered under international competition, there are still good careers available. The Merchant Marine Academy at Piney Point, Maryland, now accepts international students and places its graduates internationally. A union-run school is the Seafarers Harry Lundberg School of Seamanship of the SIU that trains beginning and advanced students in U.S. standards, also at Piney Point, Maryland. There are many regional and state schools in shipping, fishery, oceanography, and related seamanship studies, such as Maine Maritime Academy at Castine, Maine. Sailing-ship experience is still widely respected for its instinctive feeling for wind and wave and its bravery. The American Sail Training Association can still teach tall-ship skills to students who dare.

JOHN HEINZ

References and Further Reading

Bolster, W. Jeffrey. *Black Jacks: African-American Seamen in the Age of Sail.* Cambridge, MA: Harvard University Press, 1997.

Bunker, John. "A History of the Seafarer's International Union." *Seafarer's Log,* www.seafarers.org/about history.xml

Butler, John A. *Sailing on Friday: The Perilous Voyage of America's Merchant Marine.* Dulles, VA: Brassey's, 1997.

Cogill, Burgess. *When God Was an Atheist Sailor: Memories of a Childhood at Sea, 1902–1910.* New York: W. W. Norton & Co., 1990, 1985.

Encyclopedia of the American Left. 2nd ed. New York: Oxford University Press, 1998.

Heitzmann, William Ray. *Opportunities in Marine and Maritime Careers.* Lincolnwood, IL: VGM, 1999.

Heyden, Sterling. *Wanderer.* New York: Knopf, 1963.

Hilton, George Woodman. *Eastland: Legacy of the Titanic.* Stanford, CA: Stanford University Press, 1995.

Rediker, Marcus Buford. *Between the Devil and the Deep Blue Sea: Merchant Seamen, Pirates, and the Anglo-American Maritime World, 1700–1750.* New York: Cambridge University Press, 1987.

Runyan, Timothy J. *Ships, Seafaring, and Society: Essays in Maritime History.* Detroit, MI: Wayne State University Press, 1987.

The Women's Great Lakes Reader, edited by Victoria Brehm. Tustin, MI: Ladyslipper Press, 2000.

Weintraub, Hyman. *Andrew Furuseth, Emancipator of the Seamen.* Berkeley: University of California Press, 1959.

See also **Bridges, Harry Renton; Furuseth, Andrew; LaFollette Seaman's Act; Longshoring; Marine Transport Workers' Industrial Union; National Union of Marine Cooks and Stewards; Perkins, Frances; Rosie the Riveter**

MARX, KARL (1818–1883)

Few have left so massive and complicated a legacy as Karl Marx. He wrote voluminously, politicked incessantly, and long after his death, his name and his thought—and all manner of variations on them, to various and hotly contested degrees of fidelity—continue to exercise an enormous influence on intellectual and political life across the planet. He vigorously denounced any "great man" theory of history, but for present purposes, it is difficult to avoid if for no other reason than his significance for labor history and labor historians is virtually unparalleled. Marx never visited North America, but he wrote a great deal about the New World and the United States, and in addition to the global influence of his thought, there are two other main ways in which this significance relates to the American context. First his occasional reflections on the United States throughout his theoretical works and his many journalistic contributions analyzing the Civil War, indicate that the United States played an important role in the formulation of Marx's critical theory. Most notably it frequently serves as a counter-example to Europe in his analysis of capitalist development. Second his thought is enormously important to the practice of labor history in the United States and to American labor radicalism.

Life and Work

Marx was the great historicizer, and it is a crucial lesson of Marx's work that it is only comprehensible in light of the specific histories that produced it, especially the larger context of nineteenth-century European radicalism. He was born in Trier, Prussia, in 1818, the *petit bourgeois* son of a lawyer. The family was of Jewish heritage but converted to Protestantism when Marx was a young boy. He attended the gymnasium in Trier and studied philosophy at universities in Bonn and Berlin. While in Berlin he became associated with the so-called Youngor Left Hegelians, a group of thinkers interested in the revolutionary and atheistic possibilities they read in Hegel's idealist philosophy. He would later break with them, but he never let go of Hegel, whose *Logic* (1830) would prove essential to his critical dialectical method.

In 1841, Marx left Berlin for Bonn, but the political climate prevented him from finding the university post he sought, and he accepted an offer to help run the *Rheinische Zeitung,* a radical newspaper published in Köln. Not long after he was appointed editor-in-chief. The radical-democratic turn the newspaper took under Marx's leadership led to its official suppression in early 1843, and Marx moved to Paris to publish a similar journal, the *Deutsche-Französische Jahrbücher.* Only one issue of the *Jahrbücher* was printed, but in Paris Marx met Friedrich Engels (1820-1895), his life-long collaborator, friend, and financial supporter. With Engels he developed the materialist political philosophy they outlined in *The German Ideology* (1845), which denounced the Young Hegelians' idealism as blind to the true forces of history: the "mode of production," the historically specific manner in which real individuals produce and reproduce their material life. He extended the materialist argument in his 1847 excoriation of Pierre-Joseph Proudhon's utopian socialism, *The Poverty of Philosophy*.

At the request of the Prussian government, Marx was expelled from France for his revolutionary writing and political activity, and in 1847, he and Engels moved to Brussels. There they joined the Communist League, at whose request they cowrote the *Communist Manifesto*, which appeared in February 1848. The Manifesto develops a materialist theory of revolutionary social change from the contradictions and antagonisms immanent to the productive structure of bourgeois-capitalist society. Even if it is necessarily among his more programmatic, less subtle works, the *Manifesto* presents some of Marx's best-known ideas and commitments in their early stages of development. These themes include a materialist political economy, the movement of class and class-consciousness, a progressive-revolutionary theory of history and the proletariat, and internationalism (that is, "Workers of all countries, unite").

With the failure of the German revolution of 1848, for which he and Engels had returned to Prussia, he fled again to Paris but almost immediately went in exile to London, where he remained until his death. In England Marx and his family lived in poverty, often supported entirely by Engels, and for a time his political activity slowed. Eventually however London proved the stage of his most lasting political and intellectual contributions. On the one hand, in 1864 he helped found and lead the International Workingmen's Association (IWA)—the so-called First International, a worker's movement that helped plant the seeds of Communist internationalism. On the other hand, it was during this period of more than 30 years of relative sedentariness that Marx produced, with the exception of the *Manifesto*, his most influential works, among them the unpublished notebooks published as the Grundrisse (1939), written between 1857–1858, the *Contribution to a Critique of Political Economy* (1859), and his *magnum opus, Capital: A Critique of Political Economy*.

Capital is Marx's greatest intellectual and political legacy. He only succeeded in completing and publishing the first of four projected volumes in 1867. Nonetheless since the end of the nineteenth century, *Capital* has been published as a three-volume critique of the capitalist mode of production. Volume 1 is primarily an analysis of the social relations of production under capitalism, Volume 2 (1885) discusses the process of circulation, and Volume 3 (1894) is presented as a consideration of capitalism in general. It is important to note however, that what stand today as Volumes 2 and 3—and as *Theories of Surplus Value* (1861–1863), sometimes described as Volume 4-were compiled by Engels and others from notes left by Marx after his death. Indeed the chronology implied by the volumes' ordering obscures the fact that despite much of interest therein, most of the material was written before Volume 1 appeared in print and represents in many cases early, and often presumably incomplete, formulations of the arguments in Volume 1.

Volume 1 develops in detail the critical theory of capitalism and its constituent concepts and methods. These provide the foundation for all subsequent Marxisms, of which there have been many (a short list might include Kautskian, Leninist, Trotskyist, Maoist, Gramscian, and Althusserian, among others). Common to virtually all of them however is Marx's fundamental historicization of capitalism. In contrast to those he called *bourgeois* political economists, who naturalize capitalism and its attendant individualism and competition as either a state of nature or as the realization of historical progress—thus the subtitle *A Critique of Political Economy*—Marx argues that capitalism is one historically contingent "mode of production" (and thus mode of social organization) in the trajectory of human development. Basing his analysis on the experience of industrial revolution in Europe, England in particular, he considers the evolution of capitalism from previous modes, particularly feudalism, and thus demonstrates that capitalism is neither natural nor an historical end point but a mode from which others will inevitably emerge.

His method of analysis was dialectical, derived from Hegel's theory of historical movement stripped of its idealism; as Engels later wrote, the materialist dialectic showed that Hegel had the form of movement right but that the relation between ideas and material life was "placed upon its head"—what was needed was to turn Hegel on to his feet. It suggested that the contradictions implicit in the struggle between the various classes capitalism produced, and in the inevitable conflict between humans' emancipatory desires and the increasing material and political burdens of life under capitalism, would lead to the supercession of capitalism by revolutionary forces with great liberatory potential. Although Marx does not suggest in his later work the precise forms the future will take, his critique is nonetheless based on the fact that if workers were to act, to determine the shape that revolutionary potential, then subsequent modes of production would increasingly provide for greater freedom, greater security, greater wisdom for all.

Volume 1 also contains many of Marx's most influential theoretical contributions. For example the book begins with a discussion of the commodity, which Marx argues is the fundamental unit of capitalist production. In the often-cited passages on the "fetish of the commodity," he argues that the relations of production under capitalism hide its fundamentally social basis, leading both capitalists (those owning and controlling access to the means of production) and workers (those without means of production, thus forced to sell their labor power to gain access) to imagine life under capitalism as constituted by the relations between things (inanimate objects are thus fetishized or accorded the qualities of living things), as opposed to the relation between people. It also presents, among other ideas, his theory of money as the standard equivalent (one commodity that over time emerges as the standard of measure), his explanation of the complex relation between use-value (qualitative value-in-use) and exchange-value (quantitative value-in-exchange), the distinction between labor and labor-power, and his outline of the labor theory of value (the hotly contested notion that all value is produced by labor, an idea he adopted from political economists David Ricardo and Adam Smith).

The importance of these ideas notwithstanding, Marx frequently described his discovery of the "law of surplus value" as his most important contribution. With the benefit of hindsight, it is hard to disagree. The concept is straightforward: Capitalist production is predicated on growth, but that expansion is impossible unless among the commodities mobilized by capitalism, there is one that is not only of value but produces value in excess of itself. The only such commodity is labor power, which produces surplus value, value that exceeds what is necessary for its reproduction. The ideological power of capitalist relations of production resides in the secret expropriation of surplus value in the "hidden abode of production." There the wage-form, which represents the return to the worker for a specific amount of time and effort, conceals from the worker the fact that only part of the day is spent working to earn the means of his or her own reproduction, and the rest of the day's value is appropriated directly by the capitalist. There is therefore no such thing as a just wage rate, for the wage form itself mystifies exploitation; capitalism is by definition exploitative. Even when the wage is high, constant agitation for better working conditions, better wages, and less work are always just and in workers' interests. Wherever Marx's legacy is heralded by wage earners, it is almost always with some reference to the idea of surplus value, and the critique of exploitation, politics, and theory of justice it generates. It is among his most direct influences on the politics and lives of working people, who even when

they have explicitly rejected Marx and Marxism, they have nonetheless often leaned hard on his concept of surplus value.

Marx and the United States

The meaning of the United States in the development of Marx's critique of capitalism is underappreciated. For him and for other Europeans before and after, the United States was a crucial historical anomaly. Hegel called the United States "the land of the future": "It is for America to abandon the ground on which hitherto the History of the World has developed itself" (*The Philosophy of History*, 1956). For Marx this land of the future was key to the process and analysis of capitalist development.

The United States thus stood as an instructive counterexample to the legacy of feudalism in Europe. It was a place "where bourgeois relations of production imported together with their representatives sprouted rapidly in a soil in which the superabundance of humus made up for the lack of historical tradition" (1970: 55). It was consequently a fascinating test case of the cultural and political-economic implications of unfettered capitalism: "The abstract category 'labour,' 'labour as such,' labour *sans phrase*, the point of departure of modern economics, thus becomes a practical fact only there . . . in the most modern society" (1970: 210). The transparency of the commodification of labor was part and parcel of American social relations' bourgeois modernity: "Nowhere are people so indifferent to the type of work they do as in the United States, nowhere are people so aware that their labour always produces the same product, money, and nowhere do they pass through the most divergent kinds of work with the same nonchalance" (1977: 1014, note 23). Moreover in its struggle over the question of slavery, the United States suggested an analysis of the complex articulation of modes of production that characterized the capitalist world system. "The fact that we now not only call the plantation owners in America capitalists, but that they *are* capitalists, is based on their existence as anomalies within a world market based on free labour" (1973).

He followed the U.S. Civil War—"a world upheaval" (Marx and Engels, 1961)—with intense interest and wrote about it for the New York Tribune and the Vienna *Presse* (1861–1862). To Marx the war pivoted primarily on the increasing significance of the West in American national development (Marx and Engels 1961). He thus framed it as an historically determined destruction of slavery—and thus of its expansionary pretensions—by a bourgeois revolution, which despite its contradictory possibilities, all workers had cause to celebrate. In the United States, as he writes in *Capital* (Volume 1) "Every independent workers' movement was paralysed as long as slavery disfigured a part of the republic. Labour in white skin cannot emancipate itself where it is branded in a black skin. However, a new life immediately arose from the death of slavery. The first fruit of the American Civil War was the eight hours' agitation, which ran from the Atlantic to the Pacific, from New England to California, with the seven-league boots of the locomotive" (1977).

Marx's conclusions from his analysis of the United States were nevertheless far from salutary for American labor. He believed the political and demographic significance of the West was diminishing, stranding immigrants in the tenements of eastern cities. "The great republic has therefore ceased to be the promised land for emigrating workers. Capitalist production advances there with gigantic strides, even though the lowering of wages and dependence of the wage-labourer has by no means yet proceeded so far as to reach the normal European level" (1977). This only reinforced the fact that despite its relative lack of history, the United States was "economically speaking, still a colony of Europe" (1977). Indeed in many ways the postbellum era boded no better for American than for European workers, since it brought with it rapid concentration of capital in the hands of "speculative companies" and "a finance aristocracy of the vilest type" (1977).

The significance of Marx and his thought in American labor history is much more complex and diffuse. Marxism first came to North America with the political activities of German immigrants like Joseph Weydemeyer, with whom Marx corresponded frequently after 1848. Many of them joined the IWA, whose international headquarters were based in New York between 1872 and the organization's collapse four years later. Marxism soon gained currency with many American radicals—prominent Socialists like Daniel De Leon, journalist, activist, and member of the Socialist Labor party; and Eugene V. Debs, trade union leader and member of the Socialist party, for example, both claimed a life-long reading of Marx had greatly influenced their work and ideas. De Leon, who emigrated from Germany, wrote an English translation of Marx's best-known work of history, *The Eighteenth Brumaire of Louis Bonaparte* (1852). Activist-intellectuals like W. E. B. Du Bois (1935) and Oliver Cox (1959) developed brilliant Marx-inspired analyses of the nexus of race and class oppression in the United States. Many others, like William Z. Foster, labor and Communist party leader before World War II, or Elizabeth Gurley Flynn, activist and founder of the American Civil Liberties Union, populate American labor history. Inevitably the extent to which any of these was Marxist (not to be conflated with Communist) is contestable, and a laundry list of great men and women who considered themselves Marxists obscures the profoundly subtle ways in which Marx's thought articulates with, or informs much of, the activity and intellectual vigor of the American Left. Even in the case of anti-Marxists like Samuel Gompers, Marx's shadow is cast over the working-class politics of the United States.

Perhaps the most obvious way in which Marx continues to play a crucial part in American labor however is in its historiography. Marx's thought has significantly shaped the work of some of the most prominent U.S. labor historians, many of whom make it clear that their historical work is itself an explicit and radical political statement. The work of such seminal contributors as Philip S. Foner, Herbert Gutman, Ruth Milkman, David Montgomery, David Roediger, and Alexander Saxton is situated in this tradition. In addition much nonhistorical scholarship that is of continued significance to labor historians in the United States, like Harry Braverman's labor process analysis (1974) or the segmented labor market literature, are more or less orthodox extensions of Marxist political economy. Indeed any understanding of American labor historiography demands an engagement with Marx's thought in a manner he would probably never have anticipated. And his American legacy as such is perhaps less constituted by his role in U.S. labor history than by the force of his ideas and their persistent capacity to illuminate and historicize the American working-class experience.

GEOFF MANN

References and Further Reading

Althusser, Louis, and Étienne Balibar. *Reading Capital*, trans. B. Brewster. New York: New Left Books, 1970.

Aronowitz, Stanley. *The Shaping of American Working-Class Consciousness*. Durham, NC: Duke University Press, 1988.

Braverman, Harry. "Labor and Monopoly Capital: The Degradation of Work in the Twentieth Century." *Monthly Review* (1974).

Cox, Oliver C. "Caste, Class, and Race." New York: *Monthly Review* (1959).

Davis, Mike. *Prisoners of the American Dream: Politics and Economy in the US Working Class*. New York: Verso, 1986.

Du Bois, W. E. B. *Black Reconstruction in America, 1860–1880*. New York: Atheneum, 1969. (reprint, 1935)

Edwards, Richard, Michael Reich, and David Gordon. *Segmented Work, Divided Workers: The Historical Transformation of the United States*. Cambridge, UK: Cambridge University Press, 1982.

Foner, Philip S. *History of the Labor Movement in the United States.* Vols. 1–10. New York: International Publishers, 1947–1994.

Gramsci, Antonio. *Selections from the Prison Notebooks,* trans. Q. Hoare and G. N. Smith. New York: International Publishers, 1971.

Gutman, Herbert. *Work, Culture, and Society in Industrializing America.* New York: Vintage, 1977.

Hegel, Georg W. F. *The Philosophy of History,* trans. J. Sibree. New York: Dover, 1956. (reprint, 1843)

———. *Logic, The Encyclopædia of the Philosophical Sciences,* Part I, trans. W. Wallace. Oxford, UK: Oxford University Press, 1975. (reprint, 1830)

Marx, Karl. *The Poverty of Philosophy,* trans. H. Quelch. Chicago, IL: Charles H. Kerr, 1910. (reprint, 1847)

———. *The Eighteenth Brumaire of Louis Bonaparte,* trans. D. De Leon. Chicago, IL: Charles H. Kerr, 1914. (reprint, 1852)

———. *A Contribution to the Critique of Political Economy,* trans. S. W. Ryazanskaya. Moscow, Russia: Progress Publishers, 1970. (reprint, 1859)

———. *Grundrisse,* trans. M. Nicolaus. New York: Vintage, 1973. (reprint, 1939)

———. *Capital.* Vol. 1, trans. B. Fowkes. London, UK: Penguin, 1977. (reprint, 1867)

———. *Capital.* Vol. 2, trans. D. Fernbach. London, UK: Penguin, 1977. (reprint, 1885)

———. *Capital.* Vol. 3, trans. D. Fernbach. London: Penguin, 1977. (reprint, 1893)

———. *Theories of Surplus Value,* Books. 1-3, trans. E. Burns. Amherst NY: Prometheus Books, 2000. (reprint, 1905–1910)

Marx, Karl, and Friedrich Engels. *Letters to Americans, 1848–1895: A Selection.* New York: International Publishers, 1953.

———. *The Civil War in the United States.* New York: Citadel Press, 1961.

———. *Manifesto of the Communist Party.* New York: International Publishers, 1983. (reprint, 1848)

———. *The German Ideology.* Amherst NY: Prometheus Books, 1998. (reprint, 1845)

Milkman, Ruth. *Gender at Work: The Dynamics of Job Segregation by Sex during World War II.* Urbana: University of Illinois Press, 1987.

Nimtz, August H. *Marx, Tocqueville, and Race in America: The "Absolute Democracy" or "Defiled Republic."* Lanham MD: Lexington Books, 2003.

Obermann, Karl. *Joseph Weydemeyer: Pioneer of American Socialism.* New York: International Publishers, 1947.

Roediger, David R. *The Wages of Whiteness: Race and the Making of the American Working Class.* New York: Verso, 1991.

Runkle, Gerald. "Karl Marx and the American Civil War." *Comparative Studies in Society and History* 6, 2 (1964): 117–141.

Saxton, Alexander. *The Indispensable Enemy: Labor and the Anti-Chinese Movement in California.* Berkeley: University of California Press, 1971.

See also **Civil War and Reconstruction; Communist Party; DeLeon, Daniel; International Workingmen's Association; Labor Theory of Value; New Left; Politics and Labor, Nineteenth Century; Popular Front; Socialist Labor Party; Socialist Trade and Labor Alliance; Socialist Workers' Party**

MASON, LUCY RANDOLPH (JULY 26, 1882–1959)
Southern Labor Organizer

The daughter of an Episcopal minister, Lucy Randolph Mason was born in Virginia. To be born a Mason in the Commonwealth of Virginia was no minor matter; one forebear wrote the Virginia Bill of Rights, and another cousin was Robert E. Lee. Despite her lineage, Mason's family relied on her father's small church salary. But they bestowed on Mason a commitment to community service. In 1903, in an early example of her interest in the rights of labor, she refused to ride Richmond's trolley cars, in support of a strike by streetcar operators.

At 22 Mason taught herself stenography and found a job with a Richmond law firm that often handled large insurance casualty cases stemming from industrial injuries. Mason witnessed how little protection employers afforded workers injured on the job. She toured factories and saw first-hand poor working conditions. She was particularly struck by the effects of these conditions on female workers. In one instance a 17-year-old woman lost part of her hand on the job. A lawyer who employed Mason convinced the woman to accept a 75-dollar settlement. Mason's outrage directed the rest of her life.

Mason became convinced of the need for labor unions to assist working people. She noticed that union workers were the best paid, 8-hour days, and time off. Two years into her employment at the law firm, she became a member of the Union Labor League of Richmond and began lobbying for an 8-hour working day for women. Mason gravitated toward protective legislation for women, a position that would later divide suffragists but that reflected Mason's belief at the time that white, middle-class women must protect women less fortunate than themselves.

In 1914, Mason resigned to care for her ailing father. She remained there until 1923, when her father's death allowed her to accept a full-time position as general secretary of the Richmond Young Women's Christian Association (YWCA). Mason's work with the association cemented her concern for the working class and her belief that labor unions were a way of alleviating some of the problems among working people. In addition a growing interest in securing aid for all of Richmond's citizens, both black and white, led to Mason's public disavowal of segregation. While religion certainly played a major role in Mason's thinking, it seems likely that her experience with the YWCA contributed much to her radical thinking on race. Mason almost single-handedly defeated the Richmond city council's segregation ordinance in 1929.

Mason's work in Richmond drew the attention of national women's groups. In 1932, she went to work full time for the National Consumers' League (NCL), devoted primarily to labor rights for women. The NCL produced several well-trained women, including Francis Perkins. Prior to Mason's appointment, the league advocated primarily for white, immigrant, working-class women, creating a pattern of interclass cooperation with middle-class activists acting as liaisons between the working class and the government. In part Florence Kelley, her predecessor, designated Mason her replacement to redirect the league's focus to the newly industrializing South.

As part of her southern strategy, Mason traveled throughout the region in the 1930s, establishing local branches of middle-class women and female workers. Mason worked especially to develop either inter-racial branches or white and black branches that would work together. Such a task was not surprisingly very difficult in the South. Inter-racial branches working for fair employment practices not only challenged industrialists' ability to gain access to cheap, unorganized labor, but also assailed the notion of white supremacy that undergirded that system. Southern manufacturers typically opposed the league's efforts, and such controversy made the organization of local branches almost impossible for Mason. Thus while she could win converts on issues like protective legislation, she was not able to change many minds on the issue of race. Despite her energetic direction of the league and a growing friendship with Eleanor Roosevelt, Mason seemed unable to build a viable southern initiative. The tension within the league finally came to a head in 1937 and Mason resigned.

Mason's desire to work in her home region in support of organized labor directed her next profession. In 1937, when the Congress of Industrial Organizations' (CIO's) John Lewis tapped Sidney Hillman to direct the energies of the newly formed Textile Workers' Organizing Committee (TWOC) to create a southern campaign, he sent Mason to Hillman to assist in the work. As the head of an organization with purported ties to communism, Lewis immediately saw the advantages of having a public relations representative with "blood in her veins bluer than indigo." Hillman assigned her to his Atlanta office where she remained the rest of her life.

Union activists knew that a southern strategy was necessary for the strength of unions as a whole. The growing textile industry in the South represented over 200,000 virtually unorganized workers alone, the largest industrial group in the region in 1934. The lack of organization in the South forced down wages, with repercussions in the North. But the South presented its own organizing challenges. Race was the fulcrum on which the southern labor drama turned. Southern capital was notoriously anti-union and a confederation of politicians, ministers, and newspaper editors reinforced that fervor. Mason's appointment as a southern ambassador for the CIO was meant to mitigate the ire of factory owners, ministers, and editors, who used race baiting, charges of communism, and the specter of outside agitators to control cheap labor. Mason's job was to organize among elite white people like herself to accept labor unionism and inter-racialism in order to smooth the CIO's way in the South.

Mason was almost alone as a female organizer in a male arena. Yet she was highly effective. As with her work for the NCL, Mason used her identity, her status as a southern lady, to camouflage her radical actions; in short she used her image self-consciously to accomplish her goals. In many instances of potential violence, the presence of a soft-spoken, white-haired, elderly lady from Virginia calmed tensions. Certainly the fact that a person like Mason would attach herself to such a suspect cause diffused its threat for many southern officials. More importantly Mason's status paved the way for many southern editors to listen to labor's demands and to consider union organizing because it seemed less dangerous when supported by Mason. Thus Mason lent legitimacy to the labor movement.

In time civil rights cases constituted the bulk of Mason's work for the CIO. While her focus was on persuading elite whites either to aid labor or at least to step aside, she also responded to the concerns of workers whose rights had been violated as they tried to organize. She visited their homes and helped with leaflet distribution to protest their cases. As war loomed, factory owners manipulated the issue of patriotism to elicit any anti-union sentiment. Sixteen states in the South and Southwest passed sabotage and sedition laws to prevent union organizing, and this restrictive atmosphere circumscribed union activity until the country entered the war in 1941. Mason's work garnered much suspicion. She wrote Eleanor Roosevelt that "a friend heard I am a dangerous person, that I am down here to incite the Negroes to an uprising as part of the CIO program." And she was.

The CIO sought to organize the textile industry, which presented unique challenges. There were over 6,000 textile plants in 29 states, employing over one million workers. Each plant represented an array of economic situations and organizing challenges. Although the South represented one of TWOC's greatest challenges, Hillman allocated only 30% of the textile campaign organizers to the South, including Mason, in what would prove later to be a serious underestimation of the need there as well as a harbinger of the CIO's postwar defeat. She set off on a letter-writing effort to win support for TWOC's efforts. Hillman appeared to heed Mason and "preached the virtues of moderation" to his southern TWOC representatives.

Mason informed President Roosevelt of her plans. She would call for his intervention in the years to come when resistance to a particular strike became violent or a union organizer disappeared; more importantly in some instances, she would receive his help. At other times Mason wrote Roosevelt regarding a particular situation but received no detectable reply from the president. She did however use that relationship to pressure local authorities. She also used the contacts she had made through the NCL to aid in the labor struggle in the South, writing to Molly Dewson, among others.

Letter campaigns helped Mason to develop working relationships with an important contingent of liberal newspaper editors. She corresponded regularly with Ralph McGill, Hodding Carter, and Virginius Dabney. She grew especially close to Jonathan Daniels; Daniels would write Mason often for clarification of labor issues, and he attempted to introduce her to other editors. Mason also maintained a close friendship with the journalist and essayist Lillian Smith.

Mason was careful to investigate the conditions of workers and the responses to their attempts to organize, so that accurate information appeared in the press. A favorite forum for Mason was the college campus. She believed that labor and the higher education community must collaborate to support the union cause. Mason also increasingly involved herself in national events and became tied to a variety of progressive efforts in addition to her work with labor. In June 1938, President Franklin Roosevelt convened the Committee on Economic Conditions in the South, and in the summer of that year, the president issued a 15-chapter report it had drafted. Its most well-known assertion was that "the South was the nation's number one economic problem." Lucy Mason compiled much of the information in the report and was the committee's only female member.

In 1942, Mason turned 60 and years of traveling and intervening in stressful civil liberties cases began to take its toll. Illness limited the last 10 years of her work for the CIO. She focused on encouraging inter-racialism. Mason could not have predicted the impact the Cold War would have on the American labor movement. However tentative the CIO's commitment to inter-racialism may have been, the CIO's small steps across the racial divide made it vulnerable to charges of radicalism, where in the context of the Jim Crow South, it surely was. In mobilizing against union organizing in the postwar period therefore, employers were able to marry inter-racialism and anticommunism by literally conflating unionism and miscegenation.

Given the even greater obstacles to unionization in the postwar period, Mason's ability to appeal to owners, government officials, police, ministers, editors, and other opinion-makers was especially important and offered the greatest potential to southern labor organizing in the postwar period. Ultimately however few resources, pervasive racism, and anti-union fervor overwhelmed her contributions, and the CIO's Operation Dixie. Labor unions backed away from civil rights activity and inter-racial work as their southern members increasingly joined newly forming White Citizens' Councils. However as the CIO relaxed its commitment to racial equality, Mason redoubled hers. Race relations captured her attention most fully at the end of her life. She participated in a variety of initiatives dedicated to eradicating racism and increasing inter-racial cooperation. She seemed to understand that education and intervention by whites were crucial to improved racial interactions.

Mason spent the last active years of her life writing a book that documented her experiences with the CIO. The process of writing the book was valuable but ultimately debilitating. With the book published in 1952, Mason was too tired to continue working. She retired from the CIO in 1953 and died in 1959.

Through moral suasion and an active campaign of publicity that used her access to an elite white base of power, Mason was able for a time to help aid the cause of labor and racial justice in the South. But it would fall to a new generation to enforce the truth of Mason's prediction that whites and blacks could work together.

SUSAN M. GLISSON

References and Further Reading

Draper, Alan. *Conflict of Interests: Organized Labor and the Civil Rights Movement, 1954–1968.* Ithaca, NY: ILR Press, 1994.

Egerton, John. *Speak Now against the Day: The Generation before the Civil Rights Movement in the South.* New York: Knopf, 1994.

Honey, Michael. *Southern Labor and Black Civil Rights: Organizing Memphis Workers.* Urbana: University of Illinois Press, 1993.

Mason, Lucy Randolph. *To Win These Rights: A Personal Story of the CIO in the South.* New York: Harper, 1952.

Salmond, John A. *Miss Lucy of the CIO: The Life and Times of Lucy Randolph Mason, 1882–1959.* Athens: The University of Georgia Press, 1988.

MAY DAY

May Day is the international workers' holiday. It was celebrated in the Soviet Union and then in the Communist countries of Eastern Europe as a major national holiday, and it is still celebrated by unions and workers' parties throughout Europe, but it actually originated in the United States.

The Origins of May Day

May Day emerged in the late nineteenth century out of the struggle by American workers for the 8-hour day. Throughout the nineteenth century, workers fought to shorten the workday, first to 10 hours, then to 8. By the 1880s, these fights had generally been unsuccessful. A work week of 10 hours, 6 days a week was the norm, with many workers putting in 12-15 hours, sometimes 7 days a week. The Knights of Labor (KOL), which was the largest and most important workers' organization for most of the 1880s, called for the 8-hour day but did little on a national level to organize fights for it. The KOL pushed Congress to pass a law limiting the workday to 8 hours, but this never happened. The American Federation of Labor (AFL), founded as the Federation of Organized Trades and Labor Unions of the United States and Canada in 1881, also declared for the 8-hour day and at first also proposed legislation as the means to procure it.

The various attempts to get laws passed to limit the workday, going back to the original 10-hour movement in the first part of the century, had all been resounding failures. Even when specific localities did pass laws limiting hours, they invariably included the caveat that if workers contracted for a longer day, they could work it. A fight over just such a law in Chicago was actually the first May Day fight for shorter hours, though it was not yet called May Day. On May 1, 1867, workers paraded and struck throughout Chicago to try and enforce an Illinois law calling for the 8-hour day, but they were defeated. In the mid-1880s, a group of people within the AFL began pushing for militant action instead of legislation as the surest path to win the 8-hour day. To this end George Edmonston, founder and first president of the Brotherhood of Carpenters and Joiners, introduced a resolution in 1884 that from May 1, 1886, 8 hours would constitute a full workday. This resolution passed 23-2, and May Day was born, at least as an idea. This date was probably selected for two reasons. First it was traditional for carpenters to rally together and get employers to sign contracts on May 1. It is also possible that Edmonston chose May 1 to commemorate the Chicago strikes of 1867.

There was a long distance between declaring that from May 1, 1886, on 8 hours would constitute a workday and actually putting that demand into effect. The first problem was to enlist the aid of the KOL, much larger than the AFL at that time. While the national leadership of the KOL refused to support any kind of national strike wave for the 8-hour day, many local assemblies of the KOL supported the plan. Throughout late 1885 and early 1886, both local KOL assemblies and unions affiliated with the AFL held mass meetings, put out circulars, and prepared themselves for a fight. Workers rushed into the movement as it picked up steam and put more militant leaders at its head. Anarchosyndicalists organized in the International Working People's Association gained mass support, especially in Chicago, by advocating militant action to win workers' demands. In Chicago alone these anarchists put out five papers in three different languages, had perhaps 5,000 members, and were in the leadership of the biggest unions in the city. This mass movement was not centrally coordinated; in New York, craft unions did most of the work, in Chicago it was the anarchists and the KOL; in Cincinnati a Trades' Assembly and the local KOL predominated. Despite this lack of central coordination, by late April 1886, about 250,000 industrial workers were involved, and many employers granted the 8- or 9-hour day before May 1 to avoid strikes.

On May 1, 1886, perhaps 400,000 workers struck and demonstrated across the country. This strike wave was centered in Chicago, though it included smaller cities and towns like Mobile, Alabama; Galveston, Texas; Argentine, Maine; Duluth, Minnesota; and many others. In Chicago about 30–40,000 workers struck, with 45,000 having already won the 8-hour day. In the first May Day parade in the world, about 80,000 workers marched up Michigan Avenue. Railroads, stockyards, and many other industries were closed. From May 1 to May 3, the movement grew. A 7,000 additional strikers went out in Milwaukee on May 2; about 20,000 workers paraded in Baltimore on May 3. Then, on May 4, tragedy struck.

Haymarket

The seeds of Haymarket were planted at the McCormick Reaper Works, where a lockout and strike that had started in February continued into May of 1886. On May 3, the Lumber Shovers' Union held an 8-hour rally near the plant where August Spies, one of Chicago's main anarchist leaders, was to speak. When the shift change bell rang at the McCormick plant, about 500 people left the crowd to demonstrate

May Day Parade, women marchers, New York. Library of Congress, Prints & Photographs Division [LC-DIG-ggbain-03326].

against the scabs still working at the factory. In the ensuing scuffle, police fired into the crowd, immediately killing one demonstrator. Three more died later of their wounds, and many more were injured.

Spies called for a meeting in Haymarket Square the next day to protest police brutality. With rain threatening and competing demonstrations taking place throughout the city, only about 3,000 people arrived at the demonstration. During the speeches, it began to thunder, and by the time 180 police arrived to disperse the crowd, only perhaps 200 demonstrators were left. As the police encircled this small crowd, a bomb exploded in front of the police killing one instantly and wounding over 70. The remaining police fired indiscriminately into the crowd and at each other, killing at least one demonstrator and wounding many others. Six more police later died from the wounds, at least some of which were sustained from their fellow officers.

In the aftermath of this bombing, the city elites cracked down on the leaders of the working class movement. On May 5, the mayor of Chicago declared martial law. The main newspapers and business leaders of the city called for blood. The police arrested hundreds of people and finally prosecuted eight men: August Spies, Albert Parsons, Samuel J. Fielden, Michael Schwab, Adolph Fisher, George Engel, Louis Lingg, and Oscar Neebe. These were eight of the main leaders of the workers' movement, and none of them

could have thrown the bomb. Spies, Parson, and Fielden actually spoke at the rally. Fielden was the speaker when the bomb exploded. The others did not even attend the rally. At the same time, the elites of the other cities affected by the movement launched their own repression. Cincinnati deputized 1,000 special police. In Milwaukee militia fired on a crowd and killed at least nine workers. In the face of this repression, it was impossible to maintain the 8-hour day movement, and by mid-May the strikes were over. Some had been defeated, but almost 200,000 workers did gain the 8-hour day.

The eight Chicagoans were tried in June of 1886. The prosecution charged that they were guilty, not because they threw the bomb, but because the unknown bomb thrower was influenced by their ideas. Their trial was presided over by Judge Joseph Gary, future president of U. S. Steel and namesake of Gary, Indiana, who appointed a bailiff to select jurors who were evidently biased against the defendants. None were workers, and one was even a relative of one of the murdered police officers. After a farcical trial, all eight were convicted. Judge Gary condemned seven of the eight to be hanged, and gave Neebe 15 years of hard labor. Before sentencing, Spies and Parsons gave rousing speeches invoking the power of the workers' movement. After the verdict an international movement was launched to save the condemned men. Two of the condemned, Fielden and Schwab, had their sentences commuted to life imprisonment. Lingg committed suicide, and Spies, Parsons, Engel, and Fisher were hanged on November 11, 1887. In 1888, Illinois Governor John Altgeld pardoned the Haymarket martyrs, one day after the Haymarket Martyrs' Monument was dedicated in Waldheim cemetery.

International May Day

The first international May Day was celebrated on May 1, 1890, in cities throughout Europe and the United States after a call from the AFL and the Paris Socialist Congress that also founded the Second International. May 1 was chosen for an international 1-day strike for the 8-hour day and to commemorate the Haymarket martyrs. In many countries workers demonstrated rather than striking, but across Europe and the United States, this first international May Day was greeted with such enthusiasm that May Day was celebrated again in 1891 and became an annual international day to demonstrate for the 8-hour day. In the United States, the peaceful enactment of Labor Day as a national holiday in 1894 took some of the steam out of May Day. The AFL decided to support Labor Day, and by 1901, it abandoned any mention of May Day.

In Europe workers organized massive demonstrations and strikes on May Day during the whole period leading up to World War I. In the United States, May Day became the holiday of the Left. The Socialist party and the Industrial Workers of the World organized the main May Day rallies, while the main unions did not participate. After the Russian revolution, when May Day became an official holiday in the Soviet Union, its celebration in the United States was repressed in the first Red Scare. During the Great Depression, the Communist party of the United States, sometimes in alliance with the Socialist party, organized large May Day rallies, but during the Cold War after World War II, May Day almost passed out of existence as an American holiday. In Europe and in much of Latin America however, May Day remains a major holiday of workers and the Left.

SAMUEL MITRANI

References and Further Reading

Avrich, Paul. *The Haymarket Tragedy*. Princeton, NJ: Princeton University Press, 1984.
Foner, Philip. *May Day: A Short History of the International Workers' Holiday, 1886–1986*. New York: International Publishers, 1986.

See also **Haymarket Affair (1886)**

McBRIDE, JOHN (1854–1917)
President of Both the United Mine Workers and the American Federation of Labor

John McBride led the last and most substantial challenge to business unionism's domination of the American Federation of Labor (AFL), mobilizing forces that wanted to transform the federation into a partisan organization.

McBride was born in 1854 near Massillon, Ohio, to immigrants Thomas and Bridget McBride. Thomas McBride, a coal miner and part owner of a mine, served as an American Miners' Association official in the 1860s. McBride followed his father into the mines at the age of eight, working as a helper before becoming a full-fledged miner. He joined the local union and in the 1870s, became an officer in local and regional unions. By 1880, McBride had become the most important miners' union official in Ohio, leading the formation of the Ohio Miners' Union in 1882 and serving as president until 1889. McBride mixed trade unionism with politics, winning terms in the Ohio House of Representatives (1883–1887), receiving the Democratic nomination for secretary of state (1886), and losing an Ohio Senate bid (1890). He headed Ohio's Bureau of Labor Statistics from 1890–1892, when he became United Mine Workers (UMW) president.

In the 1880s, McBride insisted that market forces posed the greatest threat to the welfare of miners and that the fortunes of miners and operators were linked. With "too many mines and too many miners," the coal industry was suffering. McBride worked to eliminate this competition through the creation of a national miners' union and the negotiation of a nationwide agreement between miners and operators to set wages, divide markets, and establish price differentials based on costs. Without competition, coal prices would rise allowing operators to increase wages.

McBride's strategy was partly successful. He guided regional miners' unions through a series of mergers that resulted in the 1890 formation of the UMW and helped miners and operators forge an agreement on markets, wages, and prices covering much of the bituminous field stretching from western Pennsylvania to Illinois. Although the agreement probably improved conditions for miners and operators, too few operators respected the agreement.

The Panic of 1893 destroyed the union's agreement with operators. As demand for coal dropped, operators scrambled to find markets, cutting prices and wages. McBride (and many operators) thought that only the UMW could improve market conditions.

A strike would cut supply, increasing coal prices to enable operators to pay the negotiated scale. McBride convinced the UMW's annual convention to launch a nationwide strike on April 21, 1894.

The strike began well. By mid-May, about 180,000 of the nation's 193,000 miners were out. Initially there was cooperation between operators and miners, with some operators providing strikers with above-ground work. By late May McBride believed that market conditions would allow operators to pay the negotiated scale and met with operators in Cleveland in hopes of ending the strike. In Cleveland operators disagreed among themselves. Some were willing to pay the scale; others refused. McBride felt betrayed, charging reluctant operators with continuing the strike in order to unload stockpiles at inflated prices. Failure in Cleveland transformed the strike. Miners began disrupting shipments from nonstriking mines and stockpiles, and authorities in several states mobilized troops. The strike petered out.

The strike's failure and other events that year—Pullman boycott, Coxey's march, conviction of Eugene Debs—convinced McBride that cooperation between capital and labor was impractical, that state and federal governments had become tools of capital, and that only political action could help workers. In fall 1894, McBride, with support from Ohio's leading trade unionists and urban federations, engineered a state labor-Populist alliance. Ohio's Populist platform, written by McBride, demanded the "collective ownership . . . of all such means of production and distribution as the people may elect to operate."

McBride's support of Populism helped him defeat Samuel Gompers for the AFL's presidency that December. President McBride worked to expand the labor-Populist alliance, but his efforts were hindered by allegations of bribery, illness, the AFL's constitution, and business unionists on the federation's executive board. McBride's supporters and opponents saw the AFL's 1895 presidential election as determining the federation's political stance in 1896 and beyond. By a very small margin, Gompers defeated McBride.

The Populist nomination of William Jennings Bryan fragmented the coalition that had supported McBride's efforts to transform the federation, ushering in an era in which business unionism dominated the AFL. McBride campaigned for Bryan in 1896, and then disappeared from federation affairs. Returning to Ohio, he ran a labor newspaper and a saloon until his death.

MICHAEL PIERCE

References and Further Reading

McBride, John, and T. T. O'Malley. "Coal Miners." In *The Labor Movement; The Problem of Today*, edited by George McNeill., Boston,MA: Bridgeman and Co., 1886.
Pierce, Michael. "The Populist President of the American Federation of Labor: The Career of John McBride." *Labor History* 41, 1 (2000): 5–24.

See also **American Federation of Labor; Coxey's Army; Gompers, Samuel; Populism/People's Party; Pullman Strike and Boycott; United Mine Workers of America**

McCARRAN-WALTER ACT (1952)

The Immigration and Nationality Act of 1952, or the McCarran-Walter Act, served to reaffirm the principles of immigration restriction and the national-origins quota system first set in place in 1924. In part a reaction to the Cold War concerns about subversion and in part an effort to codify and restructure the many existing statutes on immigration, work on the act began in 1947 and ended 5 years later with the passage of the bill over President Truman's veto.

Although the 1952 act was largely an affirmation of the status quo, it did depart from the previous acts in several ways. First although it continued the national-origins quota system that allotted 85% of the 154,277 visas available each year to residents of northwestern Europe, it did end Asian exclusion and racial restrictions against naturalization, allotting a minimum of 100 visas to each Asian nation each year. At the same time, not only were quota numbers for Asian countries kept very low, they were also allotted on the basis of race, not country of birth as in Europe.

Second the act instituted a system of preferences to help determine which applicants of countries with oversubscribed quotas would be given the right to immigrate. The first preference was reserved for workers with special training or job skills of use to the United States; the second through fourth levels were allotted to various relatives of American citizens and residents. For countries with surplus quotas, like Great Britain, such preferences would not be used, but for other countries with considerable waiting lists, like Italy or Greece, the preferences were intended to help consular officers sort through the applicants to find the most desirable.

Other innovations in the act included providing nonquota status to alien husbands of American citizens and residents and the introduction of a system-of-labor certification to prevent new immigration from having an adverse affect on the work and wages available to American citizens, though this particular provision was rarely put into practice.

Although the act passed by an overwhelming majority and even over the president's veto, the debate over the act was quite heated, and several of its provisions fraught with controversy. The most fundamental debate was between those advocating continued restrictionism and those arguing for a more liberal policy. While those advocating continued restriction, led by Senator Pat McCarran (R-NV) and Congressman Francis Walter (D-PA), highlighted the importance of safeguarding national security and maintained that the national-origins system was vital to these efforts, those favoring liberalization, like Congressman Emanuel Cellar (D-NY), linked American immigration policy to foreign policy, and declared that an equitable system free from the charges of racism and nativism to be needed to garner international support for American leadership of the free world. One proposal for making the act fairer and less overtly racist was to pool unused quotas for the use of countries with many would-be immigrants and small quotas, like those in southeastern Europe.

An important issue receiving much attention in the hearings over the proposed bills was the issue of Asian exclusion. Cracks had already emerged in the system with the repeal of the Chinese Exclusion Acts as a war measure in 1943 and the repeal of exclusion against Asian Indians and Filipinos in 1946. Although the McCarran proposal provided for the repeal of Asian exclusion, it did not mean equitable treatment of Asian and European immigrants, since it kept Asian quotas on a basis of race rather than one of nationality. Many witnesses, including a representative from the American Federation of Labor (AFL), advocated placing Asians on the same country-of-birth formula as Europeans, arguing that it would bolster American efforts to fight communism in Asia.

Another source of controversy in the debate over the bill was its provisions for restricting the immigration of subversives. The McCarran bill actually liberalized existing policies to allow former members of subversive parties to enter provided they had renounced their prior activities. Still some liberal reformers felt that these provisions were not open enough and moreover extended far too much discretionary power to the attorney general to make exclusion decisions without any provision for judicial review.

In spite of the controversy and extended debate, restrictionists won the day on all of these points. In the end the argument for protection of borders and the importance of considering national security when determining immigration policy was paramount. Interestingly enough the economic argument was seldom raised by restrictionists although concern over immigrant competition with the American worker had been vital in past debates over immigration policy. A combination of the postwar boom, cold war security concerns, and a difference in opinion within organized labor over the act (the AFL was in favor of restriction, whereas the Congress of Industrial Organizations [CIO] was against it) lessened the impact of the economic factor in these proceedings.

Racial or ethnic considerations by contrast were vital, as can been seen by the final version of the act, which maintained the system of open doors for immigrants from northwestern Europe (and for non-Asian migrants from the Western Hemisphere, since the quota system was not applied in the Americas) and restriction against everyone else. Additionally in the final vote, the minority of senators and representatives against the bill were predominantly representing communities in the northeastern United States that had strong ethnic blocs opposing the bill. These concerns, when combined with the national mood of suspicion early in the Cold War, ensured that the Immigration and Nationality Act of 1952 did little more than maintain the status quo.

MEREDITH OYEN

References and Further Reading

Briggs, Vernon M., Jr. *Immigration Policy and the American Labor Force.* Baltimore, MD: Johns Hopkins University Press, 1984.

Divine, Robert A. *American Immigration Policy, 1924–52.* New Haven, CT: Yale University Press, 1957.

Graham, Otis L., Jr. *Unguarded Gates: A History of America's Immigration Crisis.* Lanham, MD: Rowman and Littlefield Publishers, 2004.

Ueda, Reed. *Postwar Immigrant America: A Social History.* Boston, MD: Bedford Books of St. Martin's Press, 1994.

McCLELLAN COMMITTEE HEARINGS

Formally the U.S. Senate Select Committee on Improper Practices in the Labor or Management Field, this body commonly was referred to by the name of its chairman, Senator John L. McClellan, a conservative Democrat from Arkansas. The McClellan Committee's hearings helped to make labor corruption a national concern at the same time as the committee's conservative majority promoted a broad interpretation of the term corruption, one that justified efforts to curb organized labor. The result was the passage of legislation, the Landrum-Griffin Act (1959), which imposed new restrictions on union-organizing tactics.

The committee's formation grew out of hearings on corruption in the Western Conference of the Teamsters' Union held in late 1956 by the Permanent Subcommittee on Investigation of the Senate's Government Operations Committee. McClellan, who chaired that committee, asked Congress to authorize and fund a more in-depth investigation in labor racketeering, and the result was the formation of this new select committee with an initial 2-year mandate and preliminary budget of $350,000. McClellan and the committee's chief counsel, Robert Kennedy, brought together the largest investigative staff of any congressional committee up to that time. Over the next 2.5 years, the committee questioned 1,525 witnesses in testimony that eventually filled over 50 bound volumes. These hearings and the committee's findings were widely publicized, and they drew public attention to the problem of labor corruption. In 1959, opinion polls revealed that Americans now listed labor union problems as one of the nation's most significant problems, equal in importance to concerns about education, the space race, and national defense.

But at the same time as the committee drew public attention to the phenomenon of union corruption, it also promoted a particular political agenda. Conservative senators hostile to organized labor dominated the eight-member committee. McClellan was joined by another southern Democrat, Sam Ervin, while the Republican members of the committee included longtime anti-unionists: Carl Curtis, Karl Mundt, and Barry Goldwater. The moderate committee members with more sympathy for labor included John F. Kennedy and Irving Ives. The only prominent prolabor Senator, Pat McNamara, a Michigan Democrat, resigned after the first year to be replaced by Frank Church, a junior Senator from Idaho. The conservatives who made up the committee's majority asserted that organized labor had gained too much power and they hoped that the committee's revelations regarding union corruption would build support for new restrictive legislation. Thus although the original mandate for the committee involved looking at the activities of employers and their representatives, in fact the committee focused almost exclusively on unions. Blame for improper activities was assigned to union leaders. When employers paid money to union officials, the committee almost always depicted those payments as examples of union extortion even if the employers had initiated the arrangement in hopes of

achieving a more lenient contract. Moreover the hearings promoted a definition of corruption that included organizing tactics by unions, such as secondary boycotts, that were aggressive but technically legal.

In its efforts to focus public attention on the problem of union corruption, the McClellan Committee investigated a number of different unions, including the United Auto Workers' Union, the Carpenters' Union, and the Operating Engineers, among others. But by far the committee spent the most amount of time investigating the Teamsters' Union, making this organization and its leader, James R. Hoffa, into prominent symbols of the problem of labor corruption. Ironically the early McClellan Committee hearings, which had brought down Hoffa's predecessor as Teamster president, Dave Beck, made Hoffa's rise to the union's leadership possible. The committee demonstrated Hoffa's connections to organized crime figures and raised questions about his administration of the union. The hearings made Hoffa notorious, but they failed to shake his political strength within the Teamsters.

The committee's investigation was also shaped by the advent of a gathering of organized crime figures in Apalachin, New York, that the New York State Police stumbled on in November 1957. Apalachin appeared to confirm the existence of the Mafia as a nationwide organization, and the McClellan Committee held a series of hearings on the threat posed to the country by this criminal conspiracy. Criminal figures testifying at these hearings regularly invoked their Fifth Amendment privilege against self-incrimination, and their refusal to answer questions was depicted as confirmation of the existence of a tightly organized conspiracy. The committee argued that the existence of the Mafia combined with its ties to such labor leaders as Hoffa made the need to pass new restrictive legislation all the more urgent.

DAVID WITWER

References and Further Reading

Hutchinson, John. *The Imperfect Union: A History of Corruption in American Trade Unions*. New York: E. P. Dutton, 1970.

Kennedy, Robert F. *The Enemy Within*. New York: Harper & Brothers, 1960.

Mollenhoff, Clark. *Tentacles of Power: The Story of Jimmy Hoffa*. Cleveland, OH: The World Publishing Company, 1965.

Witwer, David. *Corruption and Reform in the Teamsters Union*. Urbana: University of Illinois Press, 2003.

See also **Beck, David; Hoffa, James R.; International Brotherhood of Teamsters, Landrum-Griffin Act, Organized Crime**

McENTEE, GERALD W. (JANUARY 11, 1935–)
American Federation of State, County and Municipal Employees (AFSCME)

Gerald W. McEntee was born in Philadelphia, and educated at parochial schools before attending LaSalle College, where he graduated with a degree in political science in 1956. The son of William J. McEntee, the original organizer and leader of Philadelphia's Municipal Workers' Union, McEntee's early years were immersed in the world of labor politics. Following the completion of his college education, McEntee took a position as an organizer with the American Federation of State, County, and Municipal Employees (AFSCME) and was placed on staff with his father at Philadelphia's AFSCME District Council 33. From 1957 to 1969, he worked as one of the council's lead political strategists and as a negotiator in bargaining contracts with the City of Philadelphia.

Gerald McEntee's place within the labor movement centers primarily on his successes as an organizer. In the late 1960s, he helped boost District Council 33's membership in a series of aggressive campaigns that brought in new locals representing cafeteria and library workers at the University of Pennsylvania, employees at the Philadelphia Zoo, and over 1,000 women who served as school crossing guards. In the summer of 1969, with approval from AFSCME International President Jerry Wurf, McEntee shifted his organizing activities beyond Philadelphia toward an ambitious attempt to organize the over 75,000 state employees of the Commonwealth of Pennsylvania. Appointed director of the AFSCME's Pennsylvania Organizing Committee (POC), McEntee had just one other organizer assigned to work with him, Buck Martin, an AFSCME representative from Johnstown Municipal Employees' Local 630. Believing that a drive to organize all of Pennsylvania's state workers would take about 5 years, McEntee divided Pennsylvania's 67 counties between him and Martin and began making contacts with workers in union halls, private homes, and political gatherings in the last months of 1969. The success of the POC campaign would be based on two objectives: A political campaign to restructure Pennsylvania's existing public-sector labor laws and a simultaneous effort to secure support for AFSCME representation among the thousands of unorganized state employees.

The political climate for an overhaul of Pennsylvania's labor laws seemed promising in the late 1960s. Although Pennsylvania's laws officially recognized the right of state workers to join associations that advanced their position as government employees, these laws stopped short of granting the right to bargain collectively. In the mid-1960s, however, challenges to state laws were initiated by Pennsylvania police and firefighter associations. With bipartisan support, Raymond P. Shafer, Pennsylvania's moderate Republican governor, approved of measures to grant collective-bargaining rights to uniformed personnel. Pennsylvania citizens voted in favor of the legal changes in a 1968 referendum, giving hope to nonuniformed state employees that they could gain similar rights. Soon after Governor Shafer formed a commission to review existing state labor laws, which ultimately recommended a complete overhaul of the Commonwealth's guidelines regarding public employees.

The AFSCME championed the committee recommendations and lobbied for the adaptation of a new law protecting the organizing rights of state workers. McEntee coordinated an extensive lobbying campaign in support of the newly proposed Public Employees Bargaining Law, also known as State Bill 1113, while also organizing activities among state workers to put public pressure on state legislators. A master of media relations, McEntee orchestrated a picket of 5,000 government employees at the state capital building in Harrisburg in April 1970, receiving much publicity across the state. In July 1970, such political pressures paid off with the passing of Act 195, providing Pennsylvania's government workers the legal right to organize and collectively bargain for the first time.

In the days immediately following the passing of Act 195, hundreds of state workers signed cards authorizing AFSCME to represent them in collective-bargaining sessions. Through early 1971, AFSCME continued to expand its membership among Pennsylvania's employees despite a crowded organizing field of competing unions. A key AFSCME victory came in March 1971, when the union gained exclusive bargaining representation for the Commonwealth's maintenance and trade employees, signing the first statewide unit contract covering approximately 17,500 members 8 months later. By July 1973, a master contract for 75,000 workers across the Commonwealth was signed, providing a 6.5% wage increase over 2 years. Soon after a new statewide organization Council 13, with eight regional district councils was established, with Gerald McEntee elected president. The success of McEntee's campaign became AFSCME's national model for similar organizing efforts, helping to expand its membership to the one million mark in 1978.

McEntee's success in organizing Pennsylvania—the largest and most successful organizing campaign in U.S. labor history—launched him into national prominence. McEntee gained attention again in July 1975 when he led Council 13 in the nation's first strike against a state government, an action that resulted in substantial pay increases for Pennsylvania AFSCME members and underscored the union's militant stance. Following the death of AFSCME International President Wurf in December 1981, McEntee ran for the union's top position, challenging William Lucy, AFSCME's secretary-treasurer who many considered Wurf's handpicked successor. In a hard-fought campaign, McEntee won a narrow victory and has consecutively won re-election as AFSCME president since then. Among his innovations as national AFSCME leader was the establishment of labor's first in-house broadcasting studio, the Labor Network News, in 1982. Located in AFSCME's Washington, DC, offices, the network was equipped with television cameras, tape decks, and editing equipment for use in press conferences and panel discussions, with the capacity to broadcast to four million viewers.

McEntee has been an important voice in shaping debates over the goals and direction of organized labor in the twenty-first century. Most significant was his early involvement in the formation of the New Voice for American Workers' coalition in 1995. Formed in response to the failure of the American Federation of Labor-Congress of Industrial Organizations (AFL-CIO) leadership to reverse downward trends in union membership, and in the face of such serious defeats of labor causes as the failure to stop enactment of the North Atlantic Free Trade Agreement (NAFTA), the inability to secure health care reforms with the Clinton administration, and most importantly the 1994 loss of Congress to the Gingrich Republicans, the New Voice coalition sought to recharge organized labor as a potent force in U.S. politics and culture. In October 1995, John Sweeney, the international president of the Service Employees' International Union (SEIU), was elected as a reform candidate to the presidency of the AFL-CIO. With McEntee's support, Sweeney encouraged new organizing campaigns in the American workplace, including service and retail sectors, to bolster labor power in the United States. Despite the initiatives of the New Voice platform, organized labor continued to decline through the first years of the twenty-first century, leading some prominent leaders of the AFL-CIO, especially SEIU president Andy Stern, to question the federation's commitment to organizing and its ability to represent the concerns of working Americans. Through these debates, McEntee was a staunch critic of Stern's efforts to restructure the AFL-CIO and supported Sweeney's re-election as federation president in 2005. In the summer of 2005, the SEIU along with seven other national unions broke with the AFL-CIO to form a new national labor federation, Change To Win, a move that McEntee strongly opposed.

A proponent of socially engaged unionism that addresses social issues beyond the formal workplace, Gerald McEntee has been at the head of numerous progressive causes since the 1960s. In 1999, he was among the national labor leaders who urged the formation of a new progressive political coalition at the Seattle protests against the World Trade Organization. McEntee has played a powerful role as the primary spokesperson of the progressive wing of the Democratic party. In 1999, he cast AFSCME's support behind Al Gore, leading to labor's early endorsement, helping him to secure the Democratic nomination. McEntee has been an outspoken critic of the policies of the George W. Bush administration and an active antiwar voice in Washington. In 2003, McEntee was an early backer of antiwar candidate Howard Dean but broke with him following Dean's disappointing performance in the Iowa Caucus, eventually shifting AFSCME's support to John Kerry. At the dawn of the twenty-first century, McEntee remains the most vocal spokesperson for organized labor in the United States.

FRANCIS RYAN

References and Further Reading

Billings, Richard N., and John Greenya. *Power to the Public Worker*. Washington, DC: R. B. Luce, 1974.
Brutto, Carmen. *The History of AFSCME Council 13*. Harrisburg, PA: AFSCME District Council 13, 1998.
Dark, Taylor E. "Debating Decline: The 1995 Race for the AFL-CIO Presidency." *Labor History* 40, 3 (Aug. 1999): 323–343.

See also **American Federation of State, County, and Municipal Employees (AFSCME); Donahue, Thomas; Kirkland, Lane; McEntee, William J.; Sweeny, John J.; Wurf, Jerry**

McENTEE, WILLIAM J. (JUNE 8, 1903–MAY 22, 1983)
President of Philadelphia's AFSCME District Council 33

A native of Philadelphia, William J. "Bill" McEntee was one of the early pioneers of municipal unionism in the United States. In an era when public workers enjoyed no legal rights to organize, McEntee forged ahead in establishing a tradition of labor activism among this neglected segment of the U.S. labor force. His bold actions in organizing municipal workers, especially in blue-collar divisions, and his success in gaining advancements in wages and job protection, set a precedent for big-city labor-management relations that would later emerge across the United States by the 1970s. As the original organizer of Philadelphia's Street Cleaning Bureau, which was one of the most ethnically and racially diverse workplaces in the city, McEntee helped forge a new tradition of interracial unionism in Philadelphia.

A sanitation truck driver who started with the City of Philadelphia's Street Cleaning Bureau in 1924, McEntee's union involvement began in the early 1930s when he initiated an organizing campaign among the city's sanitation workers, eventually securing affiliation with a chapter of Philadelphia's Teamsters' Union. In October 1938, McEntee led a week-long strike that stopped the city's trash services, securing an agreement with Philadelphia's Republican leadership guaranteeing wage increases and increased job security for 2,500 workers in the city's street-cleaning, highway maintenance, and water bureaus. During this strike McEntee allied the municipal workers with the new American Federation of Labor (AFL) union with jurisdiction over local government workers, the American Federation of State, County, and Municipal Employees (AFSCME). In July 1939, the City of Philadelphia signed a contract with AFSCME, accepting the union as the exclusive collective-bargaining agent for all of its blue-collar employees, the first major city in the United States to accord AFSCME such recognition.

In 1944, McEntee was elected the first president of Philadelphia's AFSCME District Council 33, a position he held for 24 years. Under McEntee's leadership, AFSCME expanded its membership there, with new locals established across city departments, reaching a membership of 12,000 by 1960. Philadelphia achieved important settlements with the city through these years, including wage increases, establishment of a civil service system, and the securing of a 40-hour workweek. In 1947, pay demands by District Council 33 led to the forming of a financial review committee that uncovered corruption and graft in key municipal offices, giving rise to a powerful political reform movement that McEntee placed AFSCME behind. Through the 1950s, McEntee secured a political alliance with the reform administrations of Democratic Mayors Joseph Clark and Richardson Dilworth and with their support, secured the nation's first municipal employees' health and welfare fund supported completely through city funding, which became the model for all public-employee health programs across the United States.

Besides his position as head of AFSCME DC 33, McEntee also played an important role as a leader of both regional and national labor movements, serving as a vice-president of the city's AFL Central Labor Union and as a regional vice-president to the AFSCME international board, positions he maintained for almost 25 years. Through his years as a national AFSCME leader, McEntee was a supporter of the union's founder and president, Arnold Zander, and remained a staunch ally through Jerry Wurf's insurgency for the union presidency in the early 1960s. In 1964, McEntee was Zander's running mate at the international convention in Denver, losing in a close election to Wurf's reform coalition. Following this defeat, McEntee continued to serve as a national AFSCME leader, working with Wurf on the union's Constitution Revision Commission that implemented changes in union procedure and regional planning that heralded the most successful membership drives in AFSCME's history. In 1968, McEntee stepped down as president of Philadelphia's District Council 33. In 1981, McEntee's son, Gerald W. McEntee, who successfully organized 75,000 Pennsylvania Commonwealth employees in the 1970s, succeeded Wurf as international AFSCME president.

FRANCIS RYAN

References and Further Reading

Billings, Richard N., and John Greenya. *Power to the Public Worker*. Washington, DC: R. B. Luce, 1974.
Slater, Joseph. *Public Workers: Government Employee Unions, the Law and the State, 1900–1962*. Ithaca, NY: ILR Press, 2004.

See also **American Federation of State, County and Municipal Employees (AFSCME); McEntee, Gerald W.; Quill, Michael J.; Wurf, Jerry**

McGLYNN, FATHER EDWARD (SEPTEMBER 27, 1837–JULY 1, 1910)

Father McGlynn was pastor of St. Stephen's Church on East Twenty-Eighth Street in New York City from 1866–1887. His advocacy of social justice and defiance of ecclesiastical authority resulted in his excommunication in 1887.

McGlynn spent most of his formative years in New York's Lower East Side. His first assignment as a priest was as an assistant to Father Thomas Farrell, who was a vehement opponent of slavery and a staunch supporter of Abraham Lincoln. During the Civil War, he served as acting pastor in three churches in lower Manhattan.

McGlynn earned praise for his efforts in securing an orphan asylum within Stephen's parish shortly after he became pastor. Yet in 1870, his refusal to establish a parochial school for Catholic children drew the ire of his superiors. Here he demonstrated a characteristic outspokenness that would lead to controversy. In an interview with the *New York Sun*, he recalled his own experience in local schools as he defended public education, rejecting the position of the church.

McGlynn became a centre of attention again when he enthusiastically embraced the views of Henry George, who proposed a single tax on land not used productively and advocated the cause of the Irish Land League in the early 1880s. In describing *Progress and Poverty* as "a poem of philosophy, prophecy and prayer" whose conclusion is "more like an utterance of an inspired seer of Israel," he testified to the impact of George's major work. Like many Irish Catholic Americans, he saw an intimate connection between the "struggle against landlordism" in Ireland and the antimonopoly movement in the United States inspired by Henry George.

Consequently Archbishop of New York Michael Corrigan demanded that McGlynn cease to espouse views that contravened church doctrine. Matters came to a head when McGlynn spoke at Chickering Hall in October 1886 on behalf of George's independent candidacy for mayor, supported by a coalition of the city's major unions through the United Labor party (ULP). Corrigan suspended McGlynn from fulfilling priestly functions for 2 weeks and extended the suspension when McGlynn in two interviews with the *New York Tribune* reiterated his support for the single tax. Then in January 1887, Corrigan named Arthur Donnelly as the new pastor of St. Stephen's Church.

Neither Corrigan's punitive measures nor the close defeat of George, who finished second to the Democratic party candidate, Abram Hewitt, dimmed McGlynn's belief that the remedy to poverty remained "the abolition of private ownership of land and the restitution to all men of their rights in the soil." He continued to insist that social and economic relations were accountable to a higher law than the rules of a free market. He quoted from the scriptures, especially Leviticus and Jesus's Sermon on the Mount, to underscore his conviction that Christians had an obligation to seek justice for the less fortunate, which during an era of accelerating inequality meant opposition to the "monopolisation of land for profit."

Encouraged by the support of parishioners who pledged not to contribute to the maintenance of St. Stephen's Church until McGlynn was re-instated as its pastor and editorials in New York's Irish press, including the *Irish World* and *Catholic Herald*, he remained unbowed. He was elected president of the Anti-Poverty Society, formed in March 1887 to campaign for the single tax, and embarked on a hectic speaking tour that included Boston, Philadelphia, Washington, DC, and Cincinnati, among other cities. In June when Pope Leo III summoned McGlynn to appear at a tribunal to answer for his disobedience, the Anti-Poverty Society organised a march in his support estimated at 30-40,000 strong. In July the Vatican excommunicated McGlynn after he defiantly failed to appear at the tribunal.

Over the next 3 years, McGlynn dedicated himself to promoting the program of the Anti-Poverty Society, although his influence—as did the vitality of social reform—began to wane. During the 1887 statewide elections, George ran for secretary of state as a candidate for the ULP, but a split between Socialists and the single-tax camp and the failure of the city's unions to mobilise for the campaign resulted in a poor showing. Conspicuously such erstwhile supporters like the *Irish World* withheld its support from McGlynn and the ULP. Then in 1888 the alliance between McGlynn and George ruptured when the latter endorsed Grover Cleveland's Democratic candidacy for president, an act that McGlynn felt sabotaged the integrity of the singe-tax movement.

Meanwhile behind the scenes, McGlynn's restoration within the church began. Mgr. Francisco Satolli on behalf of Pope Leo XII, conducted an investigation of McGlynn's standing among Catholic parishioners and discovered the excommunicated priest had broad support among other clergymen and that the Vatican's decision in 1887 continued to divide the Church. McGlynn helped his cause when he provided a lengthy statement explaining his views on the private property and the land question that appeared not incompatible with the sentiments expressed in Pope Leo's Encyclical "*Rerum Novarum*" in 1891 that "workingmen have been surrended...to the hardheartedness of employers and the greed of unchecked competition."

Accordingly in 1892, McGlynn was re-instated into the church as a priest, and in 1894, McGlynn was appointed pastor of St. Mary's Church in Newburgh, New York. Although he lectured around the country on the theme of social and economic justice, a chronic heart condition restricted his activities after 1899.

RONALD MENDEL

References and Further Reading

Bell, Stephen. *Rebel, Priest, and Prophet: A Biography of Dr. Edward McGlynn*. New York: The Devin-Adair Company, 1932.

Foner, Eric. "Class, Ethnicity, and Radicalism in the Gilded Age: The Land League and Irish America." *Politics and Ideology in the Age of the Civil War*, edited by Eric Foner. New York: Oxford University Press, 1980.

Miller, Kerby. *Emigrants and Exiles: Ireland and the Irish Exodus to North America*. New York: Oxford University Press, 1985.

Post, Louis, and Charles Leubuscher. *An Account of the George-Hewitt Campaign in the New York Municipal Election of 1886*. New York, 1887.

McGUIRE, PETER J. (JULY 6, 1852– FEBRUARY 18, 1906)
Cofounder, American Federation of Labor

Peter McGuire was a central figure in the labor movement during the Gilded Age. He served as the general secretary of the United Brotherhood of Carpenters and Joiners from its founding in 1881 until 1902. Along with Samuel Gompers, he helped launch the American Federation of Labor (AFL) in 1886.

McGuire cut his teeth as a labor activist at the onset of a protracted economic depression in 1873. He was elected as a member of the Committee of Public Safety, formed to press the authorities to provide public relief for the city's unemployed workers. He spoke, both in English and German, at impromptu street corner meetings and more formal rallies, culminating in the mass public meeting at Tompkins Square on January 13, 1874, which the police violently broke up, resulting in scores of injuries and the arrest of 35 demonstrators.

As unemployment and economic hardship mounted, McGuire increasingly became more involved in the nation's burgeoning socialist movement. In 1874, he helped to establish the Social Democratic party of North America (SDP), which was inspired by the writings of the German Socialist Ferdinand Lassalle. He contributed to the SDP's newspaper, the *Toiler*, which advocated independent working-class political action in pursuit of collectively owned and managed "productive associations in industry," and over the next 2 years tirelessly toured the country on behalf of the party. With the formation of the Workingmen's party, which encompassed the SDP, in 1877, McGuire's reputation as a rousing speaker and energetic organiser grew. He ran the party's election campaigns for local and state offices in Connecticut and garnered over 9,000 votes in Cincinnati's council elections that year.

Later in 1877, McGuire relocated to St. Louis, where he rose to prominence in the city's Trades' and Labor Assembly. He lobbied state legislators to enact bills that would require adequate ventilation in mines, regulate child labor, and establish a State Bureau of Labor Statistics. For his efforts he was appointed deputy commissioner in 1879, but he quit after 6 months in post.

His remaining 3 years in St. Louis saw McGuire renew his commitment to independent political action. On his election as president of the Trades' and Labor Assembly, he was chosen as a delegate to the national convention of the Greenback-Labor party in 1880, and despite his vocal support of the party's election efforts, he refused the nomination to run for the office of secretary of state in Missouri.

By 1881, however, McGuire turned his attention to the nuts-and-bolts of trade unionism. The disappointing performance of the Greenback-Labor party led to a sober reassessment of the potential of independent political action. McGuire's intermittent stints as a carpenter gave him first-hand experience with the deteriorating employment conditions in the trade. Lastly his involvement in a wave of strikes by carpenters and railway workers in St. Louis convinced him that to sustain the momentum of labor militancy, effective trade union organisation was necessary.

Accordingly McGuire directed his energies to building a national carpenters' union. In 1881, he was elected the general secretary of the United Brotherhood of Carpenters at its inaugural convention with a salary of $15 per annum. He also became editor of the union's monthly journal, the *Carpenter*, where he gave practical council to newly formed locals as well as developed his vision of a transformative trade unionism that would uplift workers individually and collectively.

The union's formative years tested McGuire's organizing skills. Membership only incrementally rose in the first 3 years, since competition from three other unions, the United Order of Carpenters, the Amalgamated Society of Carpenters (ACS), and the Knights of Labor (KOL) forestalled the Brotherhood's progress. However McGuire's and the union's leadership in the 8-hour movement in 1886 became a turning point, as membership increased more than threefold to over 21,000. The Brotherhood's growth spurred McGuire's efforts to seek agreements with competing unions. The Brotherhood overcame threats posed by the KOL assemblies in Washington, DC, and Chicago by 1887, and in 1888 at a special conference in Philadelphia, the United Order of Carpenters and the Brotherhood agreed to merge and form the United Brotherhood of Carpenters and Joiners (UBCJ).

The UBCJ's continued growth and organizational stability represented a model for the AFL's leadership, which since 1886 had sought to promote national unions representing distinct crafts or trades. In recognition of the UBCJ's achievements, the union agreed to spearhead a renewed drive for the 8-hour day at the urging of Gompers, the AFL's president, in 1890. The union's involvement in 141 strikes in 36 cities involving over 54,000 workers triggered another surge in membership, which more than doubled to 53,000 by the end of the year.

Nevertheless most of the 1890s presented serious challenges to the UBCJ. Firstly jurisdictional conflicts with the International Woodworkers' Union (IWU), which along with the UBCJ, claimed members in shops that made doors, blinds, sashes, and stairs, and with the ASC festered. Secondly McGuire and the union's General Executive Board discovered that their authority was contested by some districts dissatisfied with official union policies. Thirdly in 1893, and during the ensuing years of economic depression, pressure mounted at union conventions to join forces with the Socialist Labor party (SLP) in the political arena. Lastly McGuire, beginning in 1894, faced calls to loosen his grip on the union's operational affairs.

McGuire steadfastly faced these challenges. He was instrumental in negotiating an agreement with the ASC in 1895 that called for the mutual recognition of the membership cards of each union and used his diplomatic skills to prevent a breakdown in relations between the Brotherhood and the IWU. Likewise he steered the General Executive Board away from any direct confrontation with districts that did not consistently respect jurisdictional agreements. Although he remained a Socialist, McGuire's intervention in convention debates stressed that members' interests were not served by a political alliance with the SLP.

Ironically though in large measure because of the UBCJ's expansion in the 1890s, the General Executive Board sought to redistribute some of the general secretary's powers to other full-time, salaried officials. When attempts to modify the union's constitution failed, McGuire's opponents charged him with financial malfeasance, which initially resulted in his suspension in 1901 and his resignation in 1902.

Notwithstanding his anticlimactic forfeiture of leadership, McGuire could take a lion's share of the credit for the gains made by carpenters in the previous 20 years. Union membership rocketed to 122,000, the 8-hour day had been introduced in over 500 cities, and carpenters were among the highest paid manual workers in the nation. Whereas McGuire could envision only a national union capable of advancing carpenters' collective interests, by 1902 the UBCJ had become a flagship affiliate of the AFL at a time when

employers and the general public contested the very legitimacy of trade unionism.

RONALD MENDEL

References and Further Reading

Christie, Robert. *Empire in Wood: A History of the Carpenters' Union*. Ithaca, NY: Cornell University Press, 1956.

Ehrlich, Mark. "Peter J. Mc Guire's Trade Unionism: Socialism of a Trade Union Kind?" *Labor History* 24 (Spring 1983): 165–197.

Galenson, Walter. *The United Brotherhood of Carpenters and Joiners: The First Hundred Years*. Cambridge, MA: Harvard University Press, 1983.

See also **American Federation of Labor; United Brotherhood of Carpenters and Joiners of America**

McNAMARA BROTHERS

John J. McNamara and his younger brother James B. McNamara were union activists associated with the International Association of Bridge and Structural Iron Workers (BSIW) who were tried for murder after a dynamite bomb destroyed the *Los Angeles Times* building on October 1, 1910. The explosion caused the deaths of around 20 people and destroyed over half-a-million dollars in property. While many at the time considered the brothers' arrest to be a frame-up, and despite the retention of Clarence Darrow to head up the defense, both men pleaded guilty and served prison terms.

Los Angeles employers had long been hostile to unions, and Harrison Gray Otis, the owner and publisher of the *Times*, had helped organize the virulently anti-union Merchants' and Manufacturers' Association. When San Fransisco unionists began a concerted organizing campaign in the Los Angeles building trades in the summer of 1910, Otis's *Times* served as a mouthpiece for the employers and goaded the metal trades workers who walked off their jobs on June 1. The metal trades' unions decided to engage in industrial terrorism in an attempt to better their bargaining position, a practice that had been effective in their struggle against the National Erectors' Association (NEA), an anti-union group fighting for the open-shop in the construction industry. In the period from 1908–1911, the BSIW had detonated 87 bombs in an attempt to gain union recognition from the NEA and its members. Most of these bombs were relatively harmless however, with no loss of life associated with any attack other than the October bombing of the *Times* plant.

When the metal trades strike began in June, the Los Angeles unions contacted John J. McNamara, who was the secretary-treasurer of the BSIW, and requested the assistance of Herbert Hockin, who had been one of the leading dynamiters for the union. When Hockin was unavailable, John sent his brother James instead. James McNamara had been Hockin's apprentice since 1909 and was a skilled dynamiter in his own right. James set the bomb behind the *Times* printing plant, but he had only intended to cause minor damage to the building. Unfortunately he failed to notice the barrels of flammable ink that were stored in the alley where he had placed the bomb. After the building was destroyed, James was distraught and fled first to Salt Lake City and then to Chicago. Nevertheless by December, he appeared to have recovered, and he helped Ortie McManigal plant another bomb at the Llewellyn iron works on the West Coast. When that bomb injured a night watchman, plans for two more bombs, including one at the *Times* auxiliary plant, were scrapped. After a short break however, James and McManigal began bombing again, planting at least five bombs in March of 1911.

John J. McNamara was arrested on April 22, 1911 by agents working for William J. Burns, a private detective who had been retained by the mayor of Los Angeles to investigate the *Times* bombing. James and his partner McManigal had been arrested 10 days earlier carrying a suitcase full of explosives. McManigal agreed to cooperate in exchange for a lighter sentence, and the McNamara brothers were quickly extradited to California. The extradition was carried out with great secrecy and with minimal respect for due process, giving rise to the claim that the McNamaras had been kidnapped by the detectives, as had happened during the Haywood-Moyer-Pettibone murder case of 1906, when three leaders of the Western Federation of Miners were abducted by Pinkerton detectives so that they could be smuggled into Idaho to stand trial for the murder of governor Frank Steunenberg.

Samuel Gompers and the American Federation of labor (AFL) immediately began a campaign to free the two brothers. The labor movement maintained that the McNamaras were innocent and that the *Times* explosion was a result of Otis's negligence rather than a dynamite bomb at all. Labor Day 1911 was renamed McNamara Day, and massive crowds attended demonstrations across the United States demanding that the brothers be set free. Hundreds of thousands of dollars were raised for the defense fund, and the AFL retained Clarence Darrow to serve as the chief defense attorney.

Unfortunately the brothers were guilty, and Darrow knew it. He did everything in his power to ensure that the McNamaras would be acquitted, going so far, it was alleged, as to bribe witnesses and jurors. The case against the brothers was too strong, and in order to prevent James from getting the death penalty, Darrow convinced the two unionists to plead guilty. James B. McNamara pleaded guilty to murder and was given a life sentence, while his brother John J. McNamara plead guilty to participating in the bombing of the Llewellyn iron works and was given 15 years. While the decision to pleaded guilty probably saved James's life, it had some harsh repercussions for the labor movement both in California and nationally.

Socialist labor lawyer Job Harriman was running for mayor during the McNamara trial, and when the brothers plead guilty, his campaign collapsed. Many on the Left criticized Darrow for his timing, since the lawyer chose December 1, four days before the mayoral election, for his clients to change their pleas. Before the McNamaras' confession of guilt, Harriman was the frontrunner for the upcoming runoff election. Moreover the guilty plea struck a blow at the reputation of Gompers and the AFL, which had protested so vigorously regarding the brothers' innocence. In the aftermath of the trial, Darrow was himself put on trial for the bribing of one of the jurors in the McNamara case, although he was eventually acquitted.

After his incarceration, James McNamara moved increasingly to the Left, eventually joining the Communist Party USA. He died in prison on March 8, 1941. His brother John was released from prison in 1921 but was shunned by the labor community. He died two months after his younger brother in May of 1941.

AARON MAX BERKOWITZ

References and Further Reading

Cowan, Geoffrey. *The People v. Clarence Darrow: The Bribery Trial of America's Greatest Lawyer*. New York: Times Books, 1993.

Kazin, Michael. *Barons of Labor: The San Fransisco Building Trades and Union Power in the Progressive Era*. Urbana: University of Illinois Press, 1987.

McNEILL, GEORGE EDWIN (1837–1906)
Eight-Hour Day Activist

George Edwin McNeill was born in Amesbury, Massachusetts, in 1837. His father was a Scotch-Irish immigrant who sent him to work in a local woolen mill after he turned 15. There McNeill later remembered, he had his "baptism in the labor cause" when the factory's workers unsuccessfully struck to retain the customary quarter-hour forenoon break.

After 4 years in the factory, McNeill moved to nearby Boston and soon became active in that city's flourishing labor movement. There in a city known for its great orators and its radicalism, McNeill honed his elocutionary skills in both the temperance and abolitionist movements but gravitated to the 8-hour movement then being placed on a new intellectual footing by the self-taught labor economist, Ira Steward. Steward came to rely on McNeill's organizing skills, later describing him as a "walking convention." When Steward organized the Grand Eight-Hour League in 1863, an attempt to forge a union between elite reformers and trade unionists in the state, he tapped McNeill as its first secretary.

After the war McNeill's scope of activities widened considerably. In 1867, he helped found and served as the first president of the self-improvement-oriented Workingmen's Institute. Two years later he was nominated as the deputy director of the newly formed Massachusetts Bureau of Labor Statistics, a post that he made into a bully pulpit for his 8-hour, labor reform, and anti-Chinese ideas. In 1874, he wrote the charter for the Rochester Labor Congress that would later be adopted as the statement of principles of the Knights of Labor (KOL). When Boston's 8-hour men and New York's German Marxists combined in 1878 to form a short-lived Marxist-inspired labor union, the International Labor Union (ILU), McNeill was tapped as its first president.

After the demise of the ILU, McNeill continued his labor reform efforts through the KOL, quickly rising to become an officer of Boston's district. McNeill aligned himself with the KOL faction that advocated the organization of national trade unions within the order. Later when this idea was more effectively carried forward by the American Federation of Labor (AFL), McNeill became an advocate of some sort of functional alliance between the two organizations; and when that idea proved unpopular, McNeill jumped ship and became an ally of Samuel Gompers.

Through these years he supplemented his small official salary by selling insurance and by taking on the editorship of the Boston Labor Leader, a labor weekly. In 1886, he agreed to place his name in candidacy for the office of mayor of Boston on a labor ticket but with little hope of success. The last decades of his life were spent primarily as a writer, authoring a number of pamphlets that were widely circulated by the AFL, including "The Philosophy of the Labor

Movement" (1893) and the "Eight Hour Primer" (1889). His best-known work was as the editor of the historically important volume, *The Labor Movement: The Problem of To-Day* (1887) to which many of the key figures of the labor movement of that time contributed, including both Gompers, and Terence Powderly, leader of the KOL.

TIMOTHY MESSER-KRUSE

References and Further Reading

Messer-Kruse, Timothy. "Eight Hours, Greenbacks, and 'Chinamen': Wendell Phillips, Ira Steward, and the Fate of Labor Reform in Massachusetts." *Labor History* 42: 2 (2001): 133–158.

Montgomery, Robert R. "'To Fight This Thing Till I Die': The Career of George Edwin McNeill." In Ronald C. Kent, et al., eds., *Culture, Gender, Race, and U.S. Labor History*. Westport, CT: Greenwood Press, 1993.

MEANY, GEORGE (1894–1980)
American Federation of Labor, American Federation of Labor-Congress of Industrial Organization.

George Meany today remains among the most controversial figures in American labor history. Arguably the debates about his legacy are a function of the tremendous power he wielded. In fact in many ways, he was the American Federation of Labor's (AFL's) (and later the American Federation of Labor-Congress of Industrial Organizations' [AFL-CIO's]) strongest, most influential boss, rivaling only John L. Lewis for his ability to project his will over others and over the American economic and political systems. As the leader of the largest labor organization in the United States, Meany used his office to transform and modernize the AFL so that it became more than just a bread-and-butter organization. Under President Meany's administration, the AFL focused its political energies on improving the lives of workers and decreasing the pernicious influences of corruption and discrimination. Also under Meany the AFL (and AFL-CIO) increased its presence on the world stage, becoming a force fostering the growth of anti-Communist, pro-Western labor unions. What makes Meany's career in labor politics all the more amazing is his circuitous and improbable rise to power.

Just weeks after the collapse of the Pullman Strike of 1894, a son was born to Michael J. Meany and Anne Cullen Meany. They named him William George Meany. The boy was known universally as George, and in fact he only learned about his first name in his teen years. George grew up in a household that was infused with politics and religion. His parents were the American-born children of Irish immigrants who had strong feelings about Irish nationalism and Roman Catholicism as well as unions. As Meany later put it, workers in his neighborhood put labor "Organ-I-zation" on "par with their religion."

Michael Meany was the president of a sizeable plumbers' union in Bronx, New York, and a cog in the local Democratic political machine. George grew up aspiring to be just like this father. Specifically he wanted to be a plumber. But the craft that seemingly came naturally to his father did not for the son. In fact Michael did not want his son to follow in his footsteps. Perhaps he knew that George's gifts did not relate to bending, fitting, and fixing pipes. Moreover the life of a construction worker was a precarious one, since lay-offs and slack times were unpredictable and potentially devastating. Against his father's wishes, in 1910, George became a plumber's apprentice working on various projects in the city. After 5 years of training, in 1915, he decided to take the test to become a journeyman plumber. Michael aided him as much as possible, handpicking the examining board. The help did not matter, since the 21-year-old apprentice failed his test. He did however pass the next year, sadly shortly after his father had died of pneumonia.

Despite how much Michael Meany was loved, George received a rude initiation into Plumbers' Local 463 (later Local 2). The local of 3,600 plumbers was a closed local, meaning that it rarely accepted new workers in order to control the supply of labor and the availability of work. The introduction of new members always sparked fears in older unionists that there might be a glut of plumbers scrapping for a small number of jobs. At Meany's initiation on January 17, 1917, five hundred angry plumbers showed up at the union hall to boo and harass their new brothers in a vain attempt to get them to quit before they went through the ritual. The rough treatment did not scare Meany away. In fact, 5 years later, he was elected to be the business agent of the union, checking wages and working conditions and ensuring that the plumbers honored their contractual obligations. Moreover Meany enforced the closed-shop arrangements on construction jobs, rooting out the nonunion laborers on job sites and sending them packing. The full-time post was a big step up for Meany, who now had more money to support his growing family.

Meany used his position as the plumbers' business agent as a springboard to larger, more powerful bureaucratic positions. The 1920s and 1930s thus constituted the formative years in the development of not only Meany's power within the labor movement but also his political philosophy. With each step up the ladder in the labor movement's hierarchy, Meany's became more committed to certain ideological positions. For example in 1921, a major scandal was exposed in New York City. The city's dock builders' business agent, Robert P. Brindell, was sentenced to 10 years for taking a bribe during a strike. Needless to say Brindell lost his post on the citywide building trades council, a position that Meany filled in 1922. Meany's hard-nosed political abilities along with his dedication to craft unionism and his unstinting probity caught the eye of his union brothers around the state, and in 1934, they made him the president of the New York State Federation of Labor. As NYSF president, Meany began to demonstrate the other major tenet of his labor philosophy. During the early 1930s, he became a strong proponent for governmental action to relieve the horrible effects of the Great Depression and to reform the economy in order to build more stability into the lives of workers. Specifically he backed state laws for unemployment insurance and for expanding prevailing wage protections. Meany's lobbying also brought him in association with other labor leaders, most importantly the Teamsters' Dan Tobin, who helped him get the post with the AFL that he held for 13 years: The AFL's secretary-treasurer.

When he entered the office for the first time, Meany was quite disappointed. The secretary-treasurer had no power or duties. It was, as a Meany biographer once put it, like the U.S. vice-presidency, without the glory. William Green, the 72-year-old AFL president, liked it that way. Green had no compulsion to encourage the younger, more energetic upstart. Nevertheless within just a few years, Meany had transformed the post into a position of considerable power. His moment of opportunity came in heady months following the Japanese attack on the naval installation at Pearl Harbor. The AFL had been integrally involved in President Franklin D. Roosevelt's defense efforts, and once the war formally started, the AFL role expanded greatly. Meany served as Green's lieutenant on several wartime assignments, none more important than the National War Labor Board, a body that set wage, hour, and working conditions rules for the arsenal of democracy. Meany was also instrumental in President FDR's attempt to bring the AFL and CIO together if only for the duration. Although this failed, Meany's status as a powerful labor broker was nonetheless heightened.

After the war Meany's power and influence within the labor movement continued to grow, especially during the disastrous fight over the Taft-Hartley Act. In early 1947, Senator Robert A. Taft (R, OH) and

Representative Fred Hartley (R, NJ) proposed a series of amendments to the Wagner Act designed to constrict the power of unions. Labor leaders and the rank-and-file unionists fought against the "slave labor act" tooth-and-nail but to no avail. To fight the law's implementation and to ensure that organized labor developed a more potent political voice, Meany helped to form Labor's League for Political Education (LLPE). The LLPE not only lobbied Congress for more favorable labor legislation but also got out the vote for labor-friendly politicians. The LLPE represented well Meany's outlook on politics. More than other AFL leaders, he wanted to engage and influence politicians, elections, and public policy.

Meany had free reign to develop his political outlook when in 1952, he succeeded Green as the third AFL president. In his later years Green had become feeble and ineffective, but the new AFL president soon proved that he was a dynamo. Practically speaking Meany's presidency had four central tenets. First Meany wanted the labor movement to become much more active in American and international politics. Second this new political influence was to be used to advance what one scholar has termed laborite Keyneseanism, which called for government spending for jobs and economic security, not only in the United States but also elsewhere in the free world. Third Meany used his office to push out of the labor movement those he deemed as corrupt, particularly the racketeers and Communists. Fourth Meany sought to unite all workers under a single banner. Arguably this was Meany's greatest achievement.

Partially the merger between the AFL and the CIO in 1955 was about timing. In 1952, both Green and Philip Murray died, and thus both the AFL and CIO gained new leadership. The CIO's new chief, Walther Reuther, the former head of the United Automobile Workers, was no stranger to the labor schism that had divided the house of labor. And, yet like Meany, Reuther firmly believed that in the conservative 1950s the labor movement was stronger unified rather than divided. Almost immediately after entering their offices, Meany and Reuther started negotiating. In fact they restarted conversations begun during the Second World War when President Franklin D. Roosevelt had urged the labor federations to rejoin. This time however the old obstructions did not resurface. Within 3 years Meany along with Reuther had hammered out an agreement. Meany played a crucial role in getting his AFL colleagues to allow the new AFL-CIO to organize along industrial lines. As Meany explained later, he put down the "craft revolt" within the AFL that sought to prevent the new Industrial Union Department from operating.

The new AFL-CIO, whose formal marriage was consummated on December 5, 1955, indeed created a larger if not more powerful and more unified labor movement. As its spokesman Meany quickly used his new position to propel his agenda and philosophy on both a national and international stage. Among his first actions was to crack down on corrupt unions. As noted earlier Meany had long battled against corruption within the labor movement. As AFL-CIO president, he launched investigations into the worst offenders, namely, the International Longshoremen's Association (ILA) and the International Brotherhood of Teamsters. Both unions were eventually expelled from the AFL-CIO. The battle against the grafters however exposed a weakness within the labor federation and with Meany's leadership. In 1959, 2 years after the Teamsters were kicked out of the AFL-CIO, A. Philip Randolph, the Brotherhood of Sleeping Car Porters' president and still the leading civil rights figure in the United States, demanded that the AFL-CIO's leadership take the same pro-active stance on civil rights and expel the unions who had broken code of the AFL-CIO by segregating and discriminating against minority workers. In Randolph's view employment discrimination was akin to the kind of insidious corruption practiced by the Teamsters and ILA. Such a proposal drew the ire of Meany who at the 1959 AFL-CIO convention denounced Randolph, belittling him viciously saying, "Who the hell appointed you as the guardian of all the Negroes in America?" The convention's fiery exchange became legendary and a touchstone moment in the history of the labor and civil rights movements. Although Meany had helped to draft and pass the initial AFL-CIO resolution on civil rights, he did not pursue the issue so vigorously as he did the other initiatives, such as the anticorruption campaign.

Rather for nearly three decades, the Meany presidency was synonymous with bread-and-butter unionism, the global anti-Communist crusade, and the growth of the AFL-CIO's influence in American electoral politics. In a way Meany's business agent mentality never left him. He constantly looking to defend his organization and expand benefits for its members. By the middle-1950s, this meant that Meany became a regular in the hall of Congress and the Oval Office. Moreover Meany's impact on politics expanded after he set up the Committee on Political Education (COPE), the get-out-the-vote arm of the AFL-CIO. With his political connections and with his ability to deliver votes, Meany became an important ally of presidents. It was often Meany's endorsement that either cleared or blocked a candidate's path to the White House. Ignoring decades of AFL tradition, Meany took very public stands in every presidential contest from 1952 to 1976 (with the exception of 1972). He was perhaps closest to President John F. Kennedy. The AFL's chief looked on the young president as his adopted Irish nephew. However Meany's relationship with President Lyndon B. Johnson may have been the most productive. In addition to lending support for Johnson's war in Vietnam and his War on Poverty, Meany helped LBJ with the passage of the 1964 Civil Rights Act and the 1965 Voting Rights Act. To this day, historians argue how much Meany influenced the Civil Rights Act, particularly its fair employment provision. It is clear that Meany's support and suggestions did have some salutary impact on the landmark law.

President Meany's political efforts were not always successful, and his record as labor's power broker is decidedly mixed. He was not always very adept at stopping the advances of conservative political forces. For example he proved powerless to stop the passage of the Landrum-Griffith Act in 1959, which further curtailed the power of unions. He also failed to exert any influence over Presidents Nixon, Ford, and Carter. Nixon refused to listen to Meany's objections to the creation of the Philadelphia Plan, the first attempt at affirmative action. Ford ignored Meany's ideas on curbing inflation. However Carter's relationship with Meany was the most contentious. Carter had earned the backing of Meany and the AFL-CIO by promising a more labor-friendly administration and offering the opportunity for the passage of progressive labor legislation long blocked by Republicans. But once in office President Carter turned his back on Meany and reneged on pledges concerning wages, taxes, and inflation.

Although one can blame labor's troubles on the ascendancy of modern political conservatism, Meany's frustrations were partly his own fault. He rarely allowed anyone to join him in the public limelight. In essence he was the sole public face for the AFL-CIO. It was Meany who met with congressmen, various presidents, and the press. It was Meany who made the appearances on television, especially the important and popular Dick Cavett Show. Not allowing subordinates or even others in the labor movement to share this national stage created two problems. First since Meany did not in fact represent all opinions in the labor movement, his inflated public presence generated considerable tension among unionists. In order to get their messages heard, labor leaders like Randolph and Reuther had to establish their own organizations outside the AFL-CIO. Although consequential, necessary, and useful in their own right, at times these groups like Randolph's Negro American Labor Council and Reuther's UAW-Teamster Alliance contributed to the divisions within the labor movement at a

time when conservative forces were on the attack. Second the appearance of Meany as the AFL-CIO's sole leader made the issue of succession problematic. Like Green, Meany did not give many public duties to his lieutenants. As such when Lane Kirkland, Meany's alter ego, assumed the AFL reins in 1980, few unionists, politicians, or citizens knew him well. And, at the dawning of Reagan's years, the lack of a strong, popularly backed chief of the AFL-CIO did not make it easy for organized labor to survive the onslaught of modern conservatism in the 1980s and early 1990s. Thus labor's modern troubles as well as its organizational strengths are both legacies of Meany.

ANDREW E. KERSTEN

References and Further Reading

Goulden, Joseph C. *Meany: The Unchallenged Strong Man of American Labor*. New York: Antheneum, 1972.

Robinson, Archie. *George Meany and His Times: A Biography*. New York: Simon and Schuster, 1981.

Zieger, Robert H. "George Meany: Labor's Organization Man." In *Labor Leaders in America*. Melvyn Dubofsky and Warren Van Tine, eds. Urbana: University of Illinois Press, 1987.

MECHANICS' LIEN LAW

Advocacy of stronger and more widely applicable mechanics' lien laws was a salient demand of the antebellum labor movement, starting with the Working Men's parties of the late 1820s and the Locofoco Democrats of the 1830s. The term mechanic meant a skilled artisan or craftsman, such as a carpenter, while a lien is a right or claim against property created by law as an incident of contract. Thus a mechanics' lien is a right or claim that secures to a craftsman a priority of payment for work performed or materials provided in the improvement of real property, for example, the construction or repair of a building. If the property owner fails to pay for work or materials used in improving his/her property, a mechanics' lien holder can file a lien against the property for the money owed. English common law did not provide for such a lien. Instead the mechanics' lien is a creation of statute whose origins are found in Roman law, which had a similar privilege.

The first mechanics' lien law in the United States was enacted in 1791 by Maryland. The statute applied only to master builders who provided labor or materials in the construction of buildings in the new capital in Washington, DC. Thomas Jefferson and James Madison were key members of the special commission that recommended adoption of the mechanics' lien law to speed construction of the capital by ensuring builders that they would be paid. Neighboring Pennsylvania followed in 1803, and by 1855 at least 19 of the 31 states had passed mechanics' lien laws, but these often applied only to specified urban areas and only to the master builder who contracted with the property owner, not to subcontractors or employees, who were called journeymen in that period.

The mechanics' lien laws became a labor issue because journeymen artisans argued that they too should receive the protections of these laws. To them the main purpose of the lien law was to protect honest mechanics from insolvent or fraudulent master builders who refused to pay their workmen after construction was complete. The journeymen mechanics urged that in those circumstances, they should be able to file a lien against a property owner even if the owner had paid the contractor, concluding that this policy would not only serve the economic development goals touted by the master builders but also would ensure compensation to those whose labor actually created the wealth represented by the finished project. These nineteenth-century construction workers transformed a bourgeois legal innovation intended to encourage economic development into an engine of economic fairness and wealth redistribution. Indeed understood in the context of political economy, the mechanics' lien challenged the usual assumption underlying wage labor that the worker retains no interest in the product of his/her labor, which belongs entirely to the employer. Instead the mechanics' lien protects the wageworker by giving him/her a security interest in the product of his/her labor, even after it has become the property of the consumer.

Politically the Working Men's parties took up the cause of expanding the mechanics' lien and enjoyed considerable support from journeymen who worked construction like carpenters, masons, and laborers. The Jacksonian Democrats however were eager to lure journeymen away from the Working Men's parties and successfully made the issue their own by sponsoring laws to extend the lien to employees. Nevertheless the radical implications of the mechanics' lien law continued to rankle those who exalted contract and property rights over all else; they could not abide extensions of these statutes to cover entire states, to bind not only fee-simple owners of property, but also to those with any legal or equitable interest, including as early as 1836, a lessee. In 1848, Maine even extended the lien's protections to lumber workers who cut and floated logs down rivers to mills only to be refused payment by their employers.

The mechanics' lien law reforms of the 1830s were some of the first labor laws passed in the United States. The evolution of the nineteenth-century mechanics' lien into the present-day contractors' lien, which is beyond the scope of this entry, would reveal much about the parallel development of the construction industry and the building trades, especially the struggle between employers and workers for control over wages and wealth. Despite the fact that contemporary contractors most often limit the property owner's liability to the contract price, the mechanics' lien laws constituted an important point of origin for the history of American labor legislation.

MATTHEW S. R. BEWIG

References and Further Reading

Browne, Peter A. A Summary of the Law of Pennsylvania Securing to Mechanics and Others Payment for Their Labour and Materials in Erecting any House or Other Building. Philadelphia, PA: J. Maxwell, 1814.

Farnam, Henry W., and Clive Day, eds. Chapters in the History of Social Legislation in the United States to 1860. Washington, DC: Carnegie Institution, 1938.

Hartz, Louis. Economic Policy and Democratic Thought: Pennsylvania, 1776–1860. Chicago, IL: Quadrangle Books, 1948.

Hilliard, Francis. An Abridgment of the American Law of Real Property. 2 vols. Boston, MA: Charles C. Little and James Brown, 1838.

———. The American Law of Real Property. 2 vols. New York: Banks, Gould, 1855.

———. Ibid. Albany, NY: Weare C. Little, 1869.

Hugins, Walter. Jacksonian Democracy and the Working Class. Stanford, CA: Stanford University Press, 1960.

Manson, N. C. "Mechanics' Liens," The Virginia Law Register 2 (Nov. 1896): 489–514.

Marks, Edward. Jensen on the Mechanics' Lien Law (and Related Procedures) of the State of New York. 4th ed. New York: Clark Boardman Co., 1963.

Phillips, Samuel L. A Treatise on the Law of Mechanics' Liens on Real and Personal Property. Boston, MA: Little, Brown, and Co., 1874.

Scott, Samuel Parsons. The Civil Law. 17 vols. New York: AMS Press, 1973.

Sergeant, Henry J., and E. Spencer Miller. A Treatise on the Lien of Mechanics and Material Men, in Pennsylvania, with the Acts of Assembly Relating thereto, and Various Forms. 2nd ed. Philadelphia, PA: Kay & Brother, 1856.

Sumner, Helen. "Citizenship (1827–1833)." In History of Labour in the United States, Volume I, by John R. Commons, et al. New York: MacMillan, 1918.

Wilentz, Sean. Chants Democratic. New York: Oxford University Press, 1984.

MECHANICS' UNION OF TRADE ASSOCIATIONS OF PHILADELPHIA

This association of trade unions emerged in winter 1827–1828 following a series of meetings held by Philadelphia tradesmen in spring and fall and led by William Heighton, the English-born shoemaker and radical labor activist. Heighton had called for such a union in two speeches in April and November 1827, and in January 1828, a meeting of his fellow unionists formally endorsed the constitution and bylaws of the Mechanics' Union of Trade Associations (MUTA), launching what historians consider the first labor movement in the United States (and arguably in the world).

The MUTA was structured along the lines outlined by Heighton in his addresses. It was administered by executive officers and financed by dues of 10 cents per member per month levied by a finance committee composed of one representative from each affiliated union (nine at first, and then 15 at the height). The MUTA had a strike fund that was made available to unions on strike to raise wages or improve conditions. It also resolved disputes between unions and organized unions of skilled workers, bringing at least five trade societies and a benevolent society into the fold. Unskilled workers, female workers, and African-American workers did not belong to the MUTA as individuals or as groups even though Heighton sympathized with unskilled labor and personally supported the struggles of textile operatives in and around the city.

The vision of the MUTA reflected Heighton's ambitious vision of transcending the narrow concerns of trade unionists and the immediate interests of labor as a whole. It pursued the related objectives of raising the social awareness of workingmen and putting forth a program of economic reconstruction. The first of these gained expression in the *Mechanics' Free Press (MFP)*, the nation's first labor newspaper published and edited by workers for workers. The labor sheet, edited by a committee that included Heighton, covered the local and national economy, carried news of union and labor affairs, and offered editorial opinion on a wide variety of topics. It also founded the Mechanics' Library Company with reading and debating rooms that offered books and journals to subscribers and sponsored public debates on such propositions as "Should Money Be Eliminated from the Economy and Barter Stores Substituted Instead?" In a similar spirit, the paper reprinted texts otherwise inaccessible to struggling workers, most notably perhaps John Gray's, *Lecture on Human Happiness* (1825), the primitive socialist pamphlet that had strongly influenced Heighton's thinking. The MUTA members who took this doctrine more seriously could patronize one of several barter stores or a producers' cooperative-styled, "labor for labor," which used labor time as the medium of exchange.

The MUTA is perhaps best known for its precedent-setting foray into third-party politics under the banner of the Working Men's party. Such a step was inevitable given the union's reconstructionist vision but still came as something of a surprise because of its timing. Heighton had hoped that the union's didactic organizations would prepare the membership for independent politics down the road, which is why the original constitution made no mention of political action. Nonetheless the MUTA was barely a month old when in January 1828, the membership passed a bylaw, clearly with Heighton's approval, stating that 4 months before the fall elections, the MUTA would nominate candidates for public office who reflected "interests and enlightenment of the working classes." The bylaw added that "party politics shall be entirely out of the question," indicating that the "workies" did not think of themselves as a party in the formal sense so much as an independent force out to run its own candidates and influence the regulars (L. Arky, "Mechanics' Union," 1952). Thus it reflected the aversion to "tyrant party" that would characterize third parties for the rest of the century. Indeed it was the mainstream press and the political regulars that called the MUTA's political association the Working Men's party, and it stuck.

Labels aside, the Working Men had no choice but to mimic the regulars of the new second-party system. They developed an ambitious reform platform headed by demands for tax-supported public schools (in favor of the state's spotty "pauper schools" for the poor), an end to chartered monopolies and paper money in small denominations, fairer taxation, and other planks reflecting popular needs and interests. They also nominated candidates every year from 1828 to 1831, concentrating on city races, and then including local races for the state senate and assembly as well as Congress, typically backing a minority of unaffiliated office seekers along with a majority of candidates on the slates of the regulars—usually more Democrats than federalists. The Working Men's amateurism proved harmful throughout but especially so in the initial campaign, as regulars disrupted nominating meetings and harassed their voters at the polls. Candidates endorsed by the Working Men mainly drew a disappointing 240 to 540 voters out of 9,000 cast. The party then ebbed and flowed over the next 3 years, in 1829 tripling its vote, helping elect over a dozen candidates, and boasting the balance of power; in 1830, the Working Men lost the balance of power despite increasing their tally by an average of 300 votes and electing about the same number of candidates as a year earlier. It then faired badly in 1831 and simply collapsed.

As for the MUTA, it faded and then disbanded in fall 1829. For his part Heighton went through a roller-coaster of feeling and emotion. Within days of the 1828 election, he called for disbanding the original nominating machinery because it was too closely tied to the narrow base of the unions. Looking to expand the party's following, he restructured the political organization along geographic lines, starting with ward committees and building upward to district groups, mimicking the regulars. Though this reform increased turnout, the election of 1830 left Heighton bitterly disappointed. So much so that he turned on his own people, denouncing the "blindness" and "sappiness" of the workers and then leaving the city for good. (*MFP*, Oct. 29 1830 and Mar. 2, 1831.)

The MUTA was not simply the first of a long line of failed insurgencies that would litter the political terrain for the rest of the century. It essentially infused Jacksonian democracy with its popular agenda of educational reform and economic populism. Though President Andrew Jackson was no friend of the big banks, it is likely that when he declared war on the U.S. Bank in 1831, he was following the lead of the newly awakened workies of the city. The MUTA also established the organizational template and intellectual framework of reform unionism for the rest of the century. Its successors in Philadelphia and other cities after 1830 would establish their own presses, reading rooms, and other organizational forms of a "movement culture," inspired by the powerful idea that labor is the source of all wealth. It was those threads that bound the MUTA to the Knights of Labor in the last third of the century.

BRUCE LAURIE

References and Further Reading

Arky, Lewis H. "The Mechanics' Union of Trade Associations and the Formation of the Philadelphia Working Men's Movement. Ph.D. dissertations, Univ. of Pennsylvania. 1952.
———. "The Mechanics' Union of Trade Associations and the Formation of the Philadelphia Working Men's Movement." *Pennsylvania Magazine of History and Biography*. 76 (Apr. 1952): 146–176.
Commons, John R., et al. *History of Labor in the United States*. Vol. 1. New York. The Macmillan Company, 1918.
———. *Documentary History of American Industrial Society. 1910–11*. Vols. 5–6. New York: Russell & Russell, 1958.
Foner, Philip S. *William Heighton: Pioneer Labor Leader of Jacksonian America*. New York: International Publishers, 1991.
Foster. A. Kristin. *Moral Visions and Material Ambitions: Philadelphia Struggles to Define 1776–1836*. Lanham, MD: Lexington Books, 2004.
Laurie, Bruce. *Working People of Philadelphia, 1800–1850*. Philadelphia, PA: Temple Univ. Press, 1980.
Mechanics' Free Press. Philadelphia, PA: 1828–1831.
Pessen, Edward. *Most Uncommon Jacksonians: The Radical Leaders of the Early Labor Movement*. Albany, NY: State Univ. of New York Press, 1967.
Schultz, Ronald. *The Republic of Labor: Philadelphia Artisans and the Politics of Class, 1780–1830*. New York: Oxford Univ. Press, 1993.
Shelton, Cynthia J. *The Mills of Manayunk: Industrialization and Social Conflict in the Philadelphia Region, 1787–1837*. Baltimore, MD: Johns Hopkins Univ. Press, 1986.
Sullivan, William A. "Did Labor Support Andrew Jackson?" *Political Science Quarterly* 62 (Dec. 1947): 569–580.
Wallace, Anthony F .C. *Rockdale: The Growth of an American Village in the Early Industrial Revolution*. New York: Alfred A. Knopf, 1980.

See also **Heighton, William**

MEMORIAL DAY MASSACRE (1937)

On May 30, Memorial Day, 1937, outside the Republic Steel works in Chicago, a large crowd of workers and their supporters rallied to protest the decision by the Chicago police to ban picketing at the steel mill. The city's mayor had affirmed the right of the striking workers to picket, and legal precedent seemed to uphold the right to picket peacefully as well. The rally began as a picnic held nearby the Republic Steel works, but after a series of speakers, a large contingent of the crowd decided to approach the factory and try to picket. In their way stood over 200 police officers, who refused to allow the marchers to picket the steel works. As a group of marchers approached the police line, the Chicago police opened fire, killing 10 demonstrators. Most of the strikers were shot in the back as they tried to flee. The police also launched tear gas canisters into the crowd. After the barrage of gunfire and gas, the police moved through the crowd swinging clubs, beating several people senseless. The police also allegedly refused medical aid to the injured and flung demonstrators into overcrowded paddy wagons. In addition to the dead, nearly 60 lay wounded, from both gunfire and the beatings that followed. It was later discovered that Republic Steel had helped to arm the police for their confrontation with the strikers and their sympathizers.

The crowd almost certainly held no real armaments, though some observers would later claim that a few marchers were carrying sticks and rocks. The police may have begun their rampage after a demonstrator threw either a rock or a tree branch at them. Nevertheless there can be no doubt that even if the police were provoked by a few rowdies in the crowd, they reacted with indiscriminate and massive violence. The police were never held accountable for their actions either. The coroner who investigated the bodies of the demonstrators—shot in the back—ruled their deaths justifiable homicide.

The U.S. Senate's LaFollette Civil Liberties' Committee held hearings on the Memorial Day Massacre in June and July of 1937. The Chicago police maintained that they had intervened to prevent the striking workers from invading the plant. Police claimed that agitators and radicals headed the crowd, that the crowd was heavily armed, and that the police acted only in self-defense. One crucial piece of evidence negated all of the police claims. A filmmaker from Paramount Pictures had captured the massacre on a newsreel. The motion picture industry had not shown the film publicly, fearing that it would incite riots. Yet the LaFollette Committee obtained the footage and held a private screening.

The committee allowed one reporter, Paul Anderson, to view the newsreel. Anderson wrote a vivid account in the *St. Louis Post Dispatch* of July 17, 1937, recounting the violence in great detail. Anderson described the ordeal of a man who was paralyzed after being shot through the spine. The man struggled to rise as police dragged him toward a paddy wagon, then crumpled to the ground helplessly clawing at the grass. Anderson reported the beating of a young girl, shoved into a paddy wagon with blood streaming down her face. Perhaps most dramatically, Anderson revealed the singular shout that rose above the din on the sound track of the film, "God Almighty!" (R. Hostader and M. Wallace, *American Violence*, 1970). Anderson's article revealed to the public the injustice of the massacre. Until the Post-Dispatch printed his piece, most news organizations had either ignored the incident or congratulated the police for their heroism in defeating a revolutionary mob.

The LaFollette Committee concluded that the police had reacted with undue force. The committee held that the intent of the marchers had been to picket the plant, not to invade it nor engage in any sort of violence. The committee also found no evidence that revolutionaries had provoked the crown into a violent confrontation with the police.

The Memorial Day Massacre took place as the Steel Workers' Organizing Committee (SWOC) of the Congress of Industrial Organizations (CIO) undertook an organizing campaign in the "little-steel" sector. The SWOC had already organized the giant of American steel, U.S. Steel. Yet smaller steel companies remained unorganized. The name little steel was something of a misnomer; over 200,000 employees worked for the firms that made up little steel. The CIO leadership mistakenly thought that organizing these smaller companies would be easy. But little steel remained staunchly anti-union, using police and private detective forces to beat back picketing strikers. The Memorial Day Massacre was just the most severe incident in a long summer of violence at steel mills nationwide.

Ultimately the brutal methods used by little steel prevailed. Almost every company in little steel remained nonunion as workers returned to the mills in the face of employer intransigence.

The defeat of the little-steel campaign struck a heavy blow to the CIO's organizing hopes, although the CIO still grew dramatically for several years. The defeat of the little-steel campaign stood as one of the CIO's first major defeats after a series of decisive victories in organizing the core industries of the economy. The extraordinary violence that accompanied the organizing drive also alienated President Franklin D. Roosevelt, usually a strong supporter of labor. At a press conference during the little-steel campaign, Roosevelt famously told the labor movement and the steel industry, "a plague on both your houses."

STEVEN DIKE-WILHELM

References and Further Reading

Auerbach, Jerold. *Labor and Liberty: The LaFolette Committee and the New Deal.* Indianapolis, IN: Bobbs-Merrill, 1966.

Bernstein, Irving. *Turbulent Years: A History of the American Worker 1933–1941.* Boston, MA: Houghton Mifflin, 1969.

Hostader, Richard, and Michael Wallace. *American Violence: A Documentary History.* New York: Alfred A. Knopf, 1970.

Sofchalk, Donald G. "The Chicago Memorial Day Incident: An Episode of Mass Action," in *Labor History* 6, 1 (winter 1965).

Zeiger, Robert. *The CIO: 1935–1955.* Chapel Hill: University of North Carolina Press, 1995.

MEMPHIS SANITATION STRIKE (1968)

The 1968 Memphis sanitation strike is most often remembered as the backdrop to the assassination of Martin Luther King, Jr. Yet the strike was much more than just a tragic setting. It represented a shift in the focus of the civil rights movement from a struggle for social and political change to a campaign for economic justice. The Memphis strike also embodied the promise and problems of coalition building between labor and civil rights activists who had long sought a more permanent alliance.

Historical Background

In the late 1960s, Memphis, Tennessee, was the perfect crucible for a labor-civil rights alliance. Mechanization of agriculture in the surrounding rural areas, especially the fabled Mississippi Delta, had pushed thousands of black migrants off plantations and into the city over the preceding two decades. These migrants created a strong and vibrant community held together by the spiritual power of Christian faith and the cultural power of blues music. Economically however black workers in Memphis struggled for meager wages in a segregated job market. Though there was a relatively strong trade union movement in Memphis, it was dominated by white union leaders for whom civil rights were not a top priority.

The black employees in the Memphis Public Works' Department who handled the city's garbage collection were near the bottom of the labor ladder. The city openly discriminated against these men in hiring, promotion, and daily task assignments, sending them home without pay on rainy days, while their white coworkers remained on the clock. Until the mid-1960s, when the city grudgingly purchased pushcarts and mechanized trucks, Memphis sanitation workers had to carry leaky 50-gallon drums of garbage on their backs, suffering both humiliation and workplace injuries. In addition to discrimination and poor working conditions, the wages paid to black sanitation workers were so low that 40% of them still qualified for welfare even though most had a second job.

Workers had tried to organize a union in 1964 and 1966, only to see their efforts crushed by the city. Then in 1967 and 1968, a number of events galvanized black workers and the black community. First Henry Loeb, a conservative businessman and staunch segregationist, rode a white backlash against civil rights activism into the mayor's office. Then when a garbage truck malfunctioned, crushing two black workers to death, the city gave their families a month's salary and $500 for expenses but sent no representatives to the funerals and offered no further compensation. Around the same time, white supervisors once again sent black workers home without pay on a rainy day. More than 1,300 black sanitation workers responded to these incidents with a strike on February 12, 1968. They demanded higher wages, an end to discrimination, recognition of their union, and dues check-off.

The Strike

Initially the American Federation of State, County, and Municipal Employees (AFSCME) provided most of the support for the striking sanitation workers. But on February 23, police attacked black ministers and community supporters as well as strikers during a march that followed failed negotiations with the city council. Within days black ministers led by James Lawson organized a support group called Community on the Move for Equality (COME). This was now both a strike and a civil rights campaign. When a court injunction prohibited AFSCME members from leading marches and economic boycotts, leadership of the movement shifted increasingly to ministers and civil rights activists.

The AFSCME President Jerry Wurf came to Memphis within a week of the strike, but organized labor alone could not get the national publicity needed to win the strike. Roy Wilkins, the president of the National Association for the Advancement of Colored People (NAACP), and Bayard Rustin, the organizer of the 1963 March on Washington, both appeared in Memphis. On March 18, Martin Luther King, Jr., came to the city and spoke to an overflowing crowd of over 10,000 people. At the mass meeting he promised to return and lead a march to pressure the city to negotiate with the union in good faith. He called for a general strike of black workers, joined by black students in a school walkout that could shut much of the city down.

On March 28, King returned to Memphis and marched at the front of a throng of strikers and their supporters. Many of the strikers carried or wore placards bearing the slogan that had become the strike's rallying cry: "I AM a Man." Workers and most of the marchers faithfully followed King's call for a nonviolent demonstration, but by 1968, many black youth had grown tired of such pacifist tactics. A group known as the Invaders popularized the arguments of Stokely Carmichael and other Black Power leaders that power would never be given by white authorities; it had to be taken. With King at the front of the march, nonmarchers and unidentified youth in the rear ranks turned to violence, smashing storefronts and breaking windows. Lawson and other ministers, fearing for King's life, removed him from the march. Police attacked marchers and looters indiscriminately, wounding many and later killing a 16-year-old youth named Larry Payne. The black community angrily responded with more arson and looting, and Mayor Loeb and the state's governor brought in the National Guard to occupy the town.

King's visit to Memphis was part of a movement against poverty, racism, and war, called the Poor People's Campaign, aimed at creating an encampment in Washington, DC, similar to the Bonus Marchers protest of 1932. Segregationists, conservatives, and some liberals now attacked King, claiming he could not lead such a demonstration in the nation's predominantly black capital without setting off massive riots. King promised that he would return to Memphis, this time to lead a truly nonviolent protest in hopes of maintaining his campaign and his credibility as a leader. The Memphis sanitation strike had now become a microcosm of the movement. Devotees of nonviolence like King vied with advocates of armed self-defense like the Invaders. Economic justice and cultural nationalism were becoming as important to civil rights and black union activists as social equality and political rights. Civil rights activists were moving northward and into urban areas to tackle housing, job and school segregation, institutional racism as insidious as and perhaps more resilient than that of the rural South.

The strike along with other events made 1968 a turning point for both the labor and the civil rights movements. Some union leaders hoped that the racial divisions and political conservatism that had kept southern states solidly anti-union for decades might be overcome with an organizing drive among the region's newly mobilized black working class. The fate of AFSCME, through no choice of its national leaders, was also on the line. Wurf and his regional director P. J. Ciampa had not done anything to instigate the Memphis strike and did not welcome it. They considered a garbage strike in the middle of the winter bad timing, and they did not want to take on an anti-union southern administration. Black workers themselves, led by former sanitation worker T. O. Jones, had decided to strike back at a city that had exploited and disrespected them. With King's entry into the Memphis strike and with the March 28 riot however, the issues became larger, and the outcome more charged with meaning. Wurf believed the fate of southern labor organizing and AFSCME's future among public employees hung in the balance. At the local level, there was a practical question of how long the strikers could afford to rely on their families and the union for sustenance and support. The sanitation strike had become a campaign that King, the workers, and AFSCME could not afford to lose.

The Mountaintop

King returned to Memphis on April 3 and gave one of the most powerful speeches of his career, hoping to fire up the crowd for the upcoming nonviolent march. Tired, but unbowed, King expressed a guarded optimism for the movement, even though he knew that he might never live to see its triumph. He began his speech by chronicling the black freedom movement's victories up through 1968. He thanked God for the opportunity to be present for such historical struggles. As he reached the climax of the oration, he imagined the movement as having reached a metaphorical mountaintop, a great vista from which he and his followers could see the land of freedom. "I may not get there with you," he concluded prophetically, "but...we as a people will get to the Promised Land."

The next day, April 4, 1968, James Earl Ray shot and killed Martin Luther King, Jr., at the Lorraine Motel. Riots erupted across the country as black communities expressed rage and frustration at King's cold-blooded murder, creating the most widespread urban upheaval of the 1960s. The nation mourned, as did the sanitation workers, but in Memphis the movement redoubled its efforts. The 1,300 striking men refused to stop marching and meeting even though the National Guard once again occupied their town. Though the federal government had been unwilling to intervene earlier, President Lyndon Johnson finally sent Undersecretary of Labor James Reynolds to mediate the labor dispute, and he sent Attorney General Ramsey Clark to find King's killer and prevent more violence.

The movement continued, and the specter of King's death haunted the negotiations between city and AFSCME leaders until April 16. That day the mayor finally agreed to a 15% pay raise for the workers, a ban on racial discrimination in hiring and promotions, a step-by-step grievance procedure, a guarantee that union members and strikers would not be fired or discriminated against, within a memorandum of understanding that informally acknowledged the union. The AFSCME did not get a union shop, but the agreement allowed union members to deduct dues through their credit union. All of these measures stabilized the union's existence and at last guaranteed city workers the freedom to organize. It was a victory not just for the sanitation workers, but for police, firemen, parks, hospital, and other city workers who had been denied union rights in the past.

The AFSCME Local 1733 grew to become the largest single union in the city, as employees in various city departments, both blacks and whites, organized. The victory of the strike also spurred public-employee organizing throughout the South and the country, as AFSCME became the fastest growing and one of the largest unions in the nation. Wurf said it represented the triumph of the principle of labor, civil rights and community alliances, and he hoped it would lead to unionization of the South. Out of this struggle also came a heightened visibility for black workers. William Lucy, one of the organizers in the strike, became secretary-treasurer of AFSCME, and head of the Coalition of Black Trade Unionists. Others involved in the strike went on to play major organizing roles. Lawson became a staunch ally of Justice for Janitors and other immigrant-organizing drives after he became pastor of a church in Los Angeles. King's organization, the Southern Christian Leadership Conference, joined with Hospital Workers' Local 1199 to organize black hospital workers in Charleston, South Carolina, in 1969, and for a time it appeared that a labor–civil rights alliance might indeed open the way to southern unionization.

Though the Memphis sanitation strike provided an inspiring victory, it came at a serious cost. King's death was only part of the tragedy. The promise of a lasting alliance between the labor and civil rights movements floundered, as growing militancy and separatism in the movement coincided with a backlash among working-class whites cultivated by conservative political leaders. Plant closings and attacks by conservative national administrations after 1968 decimated both workers and industrial unions. The labor and civil rights movements retreated from the mountaintop that King had envisioned, and the promised land of freedom, equality, and economic justice seemed ever more distant as anti-union governments and corporate power overwhelmed local movements. Still the Memphis strike exemplified the potential power of the labor, civil rights, and community alliance even if such a national coalition has not yet materialized.

STEVE ESTES and MICHAEL HONEY

References and Further Reading

Beifuss, Joan Turner. *At the River I Stand: Memphis, the 1968 Strike, and Martin Luther King*. Memphis, TN: B & W Books, 1985.

Estes, Steve. *I Am a Man: Race, Manhood, and the Civil Rights Movement*. Chapel Hill: University of North Carolina Press, 2005.

Green, Laurie B. "Race, Gender, and Labor in 1960s Memphis: 'I Am a Man' and the Meaning of Freedom." *Journal of Urban History*, 30, 3 (2004): 465–489.

Honey, Michael. *Southern Labor and Black Civil Rights: Organizing Memphis Workers*. Urbana and Chicago: University of Illinois Press, 1993.

———. *Black Workers Remember: An Oral History of Segregation, Unionism, and the Freedom Struggle*. Berkeley: University of California Press, 1999.

———. *The Last Crusade: Martin Luther King, the Poor People's Campaign, and the Sanitation Workers' Strike in Memphis*. New York: W. W. Norton, forthcoming 2006.

Posner, Gerald. *Killing the Dream: James Earl Ray and the Assassination of Martin Luther King, Jr.* New York: Random House, 1998.

Sokol, Jason. "Dynamics of Leadership and the Memphis Sanitation Strike of 1968." *Tennessee Historical Quarterly* 60 (winter 2001): 258–283.

See also **African Americans; American Federation of State, County, and Municipal Employees; Civil Rights; Poor People's Campaign; Rustin, Bayard; Wurf, Jerry**

MEXICAN AND MEXICAN-AMERICAN WORKERS

Mexican and Mexican-American labor history has its roots in the eighteenth century when the southwestern states were under the control of Spain and Mexico. In northern Mexico, many colonial settlers engaged in ranching and subsistence farming, while some managed large landed estates. This frontier period ended in the decades after the Texas Revolution (1836) and the conquest and annexation of northern Mexico following the U.S.-Mexican War (1848). By the late nineteenth and early twentieth century, this population became more diverse as Mexican immigrants entered the United States dwarfing the small colonial population of Californios, Tejanos, and the Hispanos of New Mexico and southern Colorado. Mexican-ancestry residents of the U.S. Southwest came from a variety of southwestern cultural groups, including mestizos (mixed Spanish, Mexican, and indigenous ancestry), former colonial settlers, U.S. citizens, immigrants, and aliens, with each of these mingling as they migrated across the North American continent beyond the confines of the U.S.-Mexico border or the American Southwest.

From Colonial Settlers to a Laboring Class: 1748–1890

In late colonial New Spain and Mexico, an estimated 100,000 colonials lived in northern communities stretching across the present day states of California, Arizona, New Mexico, Texas, Colorado, and other U.S. states. Although there were many large landholding families in California settled on relatively new grants carved from the large, indigenous mission-trust lands, the majority of settlers in the former Spanish colony of *Nuevo Santander* in present day Tamaulipas, Mexico, and Texas, for example, were small-to-medium-sized family ranchers who settled in 1748, living on both sides of the Rio Grande River. Like earlier settlements in New Mexico, community life was local and family-based. This was a military frontier defined by warfare with *indios bárbaros* (Spanish for indigenous peoples) where settler soldiers engaged primarily in ranching and livestock husbandry. These frontier folk engaged in seasonal labor

Mexican workers recruited and brought to the Arkansas valley, Colorado, Nebraska and Minnesota by the FSA (Farm Security Administration), to harvest and process sugar beets under contract with the Inter-mountain Agricultural Improvement Association. Library of Congress, Prints & Photographs Division, FSA/OWI Collection [LC-USW33-031869-C].

patterns as groups of Hispanicized indigenous people, many of whom did much of the killing and stripping of the cowhides and sheering of sheep each year, came together in communal work crews that involved adjacent landowners and hired hands in the annual round up and processing of hides and wool.

This colonial-ranching frontier ended in the decades after the U.S. annexation of Texas and northern Mexico. In the years after the annexation, colonials tried to maintain their property and customs in opposition to the waves of Anglo-American migrants who entered the Southwest intent on building their own ranches, often by accumulating Spanish and Mexican deeds across the region. Throughout the nineteenth century, downward mobility and land loss defined the era for these newly incorporated Mexican-Americans as much as agricultural, economic, and transportation development defined this period for Anglo-American settlers and U.S. capitalists who developed and incorporated the region. Many former landowners and skilled workers in Texas and California were proletarianized in this period of rapid change and economic and cultural transformation just as the ethnic make-up of Mexicans and Mexican-Americans was changing itself.

Mexican and Mexican-American Migrants and Workers: 1890–1945

The postannexation period was one of rapid regional development of the agricultural, transport, and extractive industries across the Southwest, each of which relied on Mexican immigrant workers. This dependence became more acute in the period of European and Asian immigration restriction after 1917 and 1924 as western and midwestern employers sought out an ever-larger reserve of Mexican immigrant workers. Beginning in the 1890s, the annual immigration of Mexicans into the United States increased yearly, reaching a high point in the period from 1920–1930 and bringing the total Mexican ancestry population to just under 1,500,000, with the largest number, nearly 700,000, living in Texas, although many scholars agree that the number may have been higher. As of 1930, some estimate that nearly 10% of Mexico's population resided in the United States. The majority of those who would come to call themselves Mexican-Americans in the twentieth century entered the United States at this time in search of work and stability.

Many Mexican migrants entered the United States as they fled from rural poverty, exploitation, and the violence and chaos of the Mexican revolution after 1910. Although many professionals and artisans retained some of their status in the United States, most workers from Mexico entered the United States as common laborers and unskilled workers in a time of economic development and expansion. Migration was often a multistaged process. Many migrated first within Mexico, often working in U.S.-owned extractive and rail industries in their home country before entering the United States to work in these same industries. Others escaped the vast *haciendas* (ranches) of northern Mexico in the revolutionary period for border cities before moving on to permanent settlement in the newly established agricultural boomtowns and modernizing cities of the Southwest. These migrants built communities of workers as they settled near their workplaces in the agricultural regions of Texas, California, and other southwestern states. Mexican migrants lived in communities rooted in Mexican politics and folkways even as life in the United States and the establishment of community institutions increasingly tied them and their children to their new homes.

Once in the United States newly arrived Mexicans established or expanded communal and ethnic institutions, much like other immigrants, which allowed for the maintenance of community through such entities as mutual-aid societies, Catholic churches and other religious organizations, and informal networks of kith and kin. In the western states, community and ethnically based institutions provided a foundation for community mobilization that the region's weak labor unions, then often restricted to Anglo-Americans and perpetually under attack by state and employer coalitions, failed to provide. In some circumstances these mutual-benefit societies and religious community organizations established their own independent labor unions, sometimes confined to a single labor action. In other cases these efforts led to the formation of more lasting organizations, such as the *Confederación de Campesinos y Obreros Mexicanos* (CCOM) in 1928, which at its height organized over 3,000 workers into 50 locals. In the mining towns of Arizona, *mutualistas* provided key support to Mexican workers and the mining unionization efforts of the late nineteenth and early twentieth centuries.

Organized labor in the United States was not welcoming when it came to Mexican and Mexican-American workers. Throughout the 1920s and 1930s, despite several American Federation of Labor (AFL) organizing efforts in the Southwest led by Clarence Idar, high-level labor relationships with the Regional Confederation of Mexican Workers (CROM), Mexico's powerful labor organization, focused on convincing these Mexican unionists to support voluntary immigration restriction after the AFL had failed to restrict Mexican workers in the U.S. immigration acts passed following World War I. Prior to World War II, the AFL would not focus on organizing Mexican and Mexican-American workers in the United States as equals but rather on lobbying in the United States and Mexico to restrict Mexican immigration.

Although Mexican and Mexican-Americans labored in a variety of fields, many of these migratory workers began work in the United States in the years before the Great Depression as highly mobile railroad workers. Tens of thousands of Mexican immigrants worked for the railroads, often living in rail-car camps or in the urban neighborhoods of Kansas City, Milwaukee Chicago, Detroit, Minneapolis-St. Paul, or Pittsburgh, as well as Los Angeles, and the border city of El Paso and numerous other railroad towns across the Southwest. In some cases these camps became the nucleus for the establishment of Mexican *colonias* (colonies or neighborhoods), which led to the establishment of Mexican religious, cultural, and social institutions. These institutional developments were often supported by Mexican consular officials who sought to maintain an affinity for Mexico and Mexican citizenship on the part of these laborers. Railroad work often led these workers into other industries in the places they settled, including meatpacking and the expanding steel industry in cities like Chicago, East Chicago, and Gary, Indiana.

For the large number of Mexican immigrants who settled in agricultural areas across the Southwest and Texas in particular, where nearly 400,000 Mexican-ancestry residents lived, these agricultural communities often became a home base for what increasingly became a migratory labor work world. Like those who established the *colonias* of the urban centers, immigrants to the Southwest established new social and religious organizations as they also often encountered established Mexican-American residents. In the rapidly developing agricultural industries of the Southwest and West, many of these settlers established homes in the cities of major harvesting regions, where their work often focused on a single citrus, vegetable, nut, or fruit crop in southern California and south Texas. From the start however, many

Mexican workers supplemented these local wages by migrating to harvest other nearby local crops or were recruited to work at the state or regional level with many traveling across the United States by the 1930s. Migration grew increasingly sophisticated as organized groups first traveled by horse-drawn cart at the local level and later moved across the nation in a migrant stream powered by railcars, large trucks, and eventually personal automobiles. The work these migrants (increasingly whole families) did was specific to the crops they traveled to harvest, yet relied on the specific skills one gained with experience tending and harvesting crops for processing and family consumption.

In the early twentieth century, Texas migrants harvested cotton, moving with the crop as it ripened in an annual migration pattern known as the "big swing," with similar migration patterns developing with the maturation of cotton production in other southwestern states. In California migration brought workers north from southern California each season as they harvested trees and vines in one of the largest annual human migrations in North America.

For many of the migrants who began their journey in Texas, migration became an annual and circular labor migration. This migrant stream brought them from the U.S.-Mexico border region to the West, Northwest, and Midwest each year. From Texas migrants traveled to the central valley of California, the Pacific Northwest, Great Plains, and Midwest, often moving in extended-family- and neighborhood-based work crews. Although often considered an uprooted population, migrant workers often hailed from relatively stable local communities where they returned home each season. At these home bases in Texas, migrants often owned small homes, businesses, and increasingly sent their children to school.

Although there were many attempts to organize harvest workers in winter harvest areas of California, Texas, and Arizona after 1900, most of these efforts succeeded in organizing workers yet failed when it came to establishing a permanent union. Agricultural unionism often failed due often to the seasonal nature of the workforce, the perishability of the crops, as well as sustained employer and police harassment of radical organizers and workers. From the Imperial Valley of California to the urban processing facilities of San Antonio, Mexican, Latino, and Mexican-American activists successfully organized these workers even if the unions failed to survive. Militant unionists in the West almost perennially sought to organize harvest workers on the large industrial farms in California and other states, and each year faced grower opposition backed by the state police power. In 1933, several California-based unions merged to form the Confederation of Mexican Farm Workers' and Laborers' Unions (CUCUM), combining 5,000 members into a single agricultural labor organization yet failed to establish a permanent trade union movement.

In southern California, Mexican immigrants settled near the expanding city of Los Angeles and in smaller agricultural towns in a region where Mexican colonials had long been a settled population in colonial cities. In Los Angeles Mexican immigrants joined the settled community near the *placita* (center of original Spanish city) and entered into the heterogeneous, east LA immigrant neighborhood, joining Jews, Asians, and other immigrants in Boyle Heights and surrounding areas. By 1930, Los Angeles had a Mexican-ancestry population of nearly 100,000 of a total county population of over 2 million people. Working in Los Angeles factories, construction trades, and the service industry, these immigrants became the nucleus for the nation's largest urban concentration of Mexicans and Mexican-Americans. Like other southwestern agricultural centers, greater Los Angeles and southern California generally witnessed the development of agricultural boomtowns and large-scale farming operations that resembled those in south Texas and Arizona. Growers recruited Mexicans as a labor and harvest workforce, segregating them from the Anglo ranchers and small businesspeople in small Mexican districts that often stood in stark contrast to Anglo-American neighborhoods.

In the midwestern United States, Mexicans often found better working conditions and higher pay in that region's booming industries. Although most of these workers journeyed north as male contract workers, families soon took root in the developing ethnic enclaves of large midwestern cities. Like other ethnics and immigrants in the Midwest, Mexican-ancestry workers lived in work-based, ethnic communities, founding and attending ethnic churches and sending their children to public and parochial schools near their places of employment, thereby establishing a community life that would continue for much of the twentieth century.

With the onset of the Great Depression, the United States, with the support of nativist groups and the Mexican government, repatriated several hundred thousand Mexicans from 1929–1932. After 1932, with the continued support of the Mexican government, the number of annual repatriations dropped to the tens of thousands. Despite this troubling policy, Mexican immigrant labor was soon in demand as employers recruited workers from Texas and Mexico once again.

With the passage of the National Labor Relations Act (NLRA) in 1932 and the formation of the Steel Workers' Organizing Committee (SWOC) by the

Congress of Industrial Organizations (CIO), Mexican-American workers joined the growing ranks of industrial unionists. The SWOC organized at U.S. Steel's Chicago South Works, where Mexican workers comprised 11% of SWOC membership. Mexican workers were also involved in the organization of "little-steel" plants on both sides of the Illinois-Indiana state line on Chicago's South Side. At a rally on May 30, 1937, commonly known as the Memorial Day Massacre, the Chicago police fired into a crowd of these Mexican and other ethnic union members killing and injuring several. When SWOC finally organized the mills of Chicago, Mexican immigrants across the region joined the ranks of the settled working class raising children who lived Mexican and American lives in the multiracial and multi-ethnic cities of these northern states.

Mexican-Americans in the midwestern and southwestern states were a largely working-class population engaged in migrant agricultural labor and settled industrial work, and in some cases both. The ties of ethnicity however allowed for the development of a small and often-unstable ethnic middle class that provided workers with Mexican foods, entertainment, as well as familiar social and cultural activities. The 1920s witnessed the birth of the League of United Latin American Citizens (LULAC), founded in 1929 as a departure from the often Mexico-oriented mutualist organizations of the late nineteenth and early twentieth centuries. Although considered middle class in orientation, LULAC pressed for naturalization and an embrace of U.S. citizenship as well as the maintenance of ethnic and cultural folkways, as they made social and civil rights claims as citizens and Caucasians within the United States. Granted the status of white ethnics by the naturalization provisions of the Treaty of Guadalupe Hidalgo (1848), LULAC used this legal status to press for an end to the segregation, discrimination, and other disabilities faced by Mexican-Americans in the Jim Crow era.

Mexicans and Mexican-Americans after 1945

From midcentury to the end of the twentieth century, Mexican and Mexican-American labor history witnessed the continued influx of documented and undocumented Mexican immigrants, leading to greater heterogeneity in the Mexican-American population. While some came first as guest workers and others came illegally, many became residents and later citizens. Moreover, Mexican-American workers and returning veterans grew more aggressive about

their rights as American citizens to claim a place in civil society.

As Mexican-American citizens were making increasing demands for civil rights, the United States established and then extended a wartime bilateral program to recruit temporary workers from Mexico. The *Bracero* guest worker program began as an emergency labor program during World War II. The United States had operated a similar program without much input from the Mexican government during World War I. In theory, *braceros* were guaranteed basic wage rates and healthy living and working conditions and were not to compete with domestic workers.

The *Bracero* Program had mixed results. What began as a wartime program to remedy a labor shortage created opportunities for Mexican workers and some Mexican-American entrepreneurs. Yet when this program continued in peacetime, it pitted *braceros* and Mexican-American workers against one another, since the program subsidized and helped to maintain a low-wage labor market in agriculture and related industries through 1964, when organized labor and Mexican-American activists brought the program to an end. Even with this bilateral agreement between the United States and Mexico, the *Bracero* Program itself accepted illegal entry and allowed for the conversion of undocumented entrants to *braceros* and the "paroling" of captured undocumented workers to employers. From 1947–1949, for example, more than 140,000 illegal Mexican workers were legalized through these procedures. Likewise the Immigration and Naturalization Service and the Border Patrol in some cases had a policy of lax enforcement during harvest seasons, and Mexico did little to stop or regulate the outflow. *Braceros* and undocumented workers displaced *Tejano* and other workers, since labor once done locally was now contracted to *braceros*. This competition, many Mexican-American activists feared, may have led domestic harvest workers to migrate to the midwestern and northwestern states in increasing numbers after 1940 in search of seasonal agricultural, food-processing, and cannery work, and higher wages.

The 1950s and 1960s witnessed increasing militancy and organization among Mexican-American workers. Union membership became a fact of life in the midwestern steel industry and the urban-industrial areas of the Southwest as Mexican-Americans continued to press for citizenship and civil rights in the United States. The perennial issue of agricultural unionism again gained prominence in the late 1950s as community and labor organizers sought to build harvest worker unions in California. In 1959, a coalition of Filipino, Mexican-American, and Anglo-American workers in California succeeded in organizing the

Agricultural Workers' Organizing Committee (AWOC) with support from the AFL-CIO. The organizing success of AWOC provided community activist Cesar Chavez with an opportunity to build his small United Farm Workers' Union in the mid-1960s as he joined the AWOC and eventually the two merged and formed the United Farm Workers' Organizing Committee (UFWOC). Chavez's leadership of this labor movement inspired the creation of similar agricultural unions in Wisconsin, led by Jesus Salas, and in Texas, led by Antonio Orendain, as well as a large number of community organizations and civil rights groups that also drew inspiration from Chavez. Until his death in 1993, Chavez's union was central to the Mexican-American community's effort to claim labor and civil rights in the United States. Together with Chavez's union, the only other union to maintain itself as a viable labor union into the twenty-first century was the Farm Labor Organizing Committee (FLOC) founded in Ohio by former Texas farm worker, Baldemar Velasquez, which by the end of the twentieth century was organizing immigrant workers in North Carolina and the American South and operating a joint FLOC/UFW union office in Mexican cities.

Conclusion

The history of Mexican and Mexican-American workers has been defined by the constant overlap of Mexican-American workers, Mexican immigrant workers, and undocumented workers, a process that has created a heterogeneous and often-splintered Mexican-American or Latino population in the United States increasingly diverse and separated by layers of acculturation, English language proficiency, nativity, citizenship, and immigration status. By 2000, the total Hispanic population of the United States had grown to over 35 million, with nearly 60% of this total being of Mexican ancestry.

At the close of the twentieth century, Mexican and Mexican-American workers continue to include millions of undocumented workers who increasingly labor in the nonunionized service, domestic, agricultural, meatpacking, and light industrial sectors, providing a reserve of cheap labor for the U.S. economy as the North American Free Trade Agreement (NAFTA) weakens the position of labor unions and the working class on both sides of the U.S.-Mexico border.

There are some late twentieth-century cross-border success stories, such as the Service Employees International Union (SEIU), which incorporated such organizers as Eliseo Medina, formerly of the UFW,

and immigrants to organize these often-transnational workers through the successful national Justice for Janitors campaign. For middle-class and mixed-ancestry Mexican-American workers, acculturation and prosperity have most prominently expanded in California and Texas, leading to rising income and education levels even as the majority of Mexican immigrants and Mexican-Americans remain an overwhelmingly low-income and working-class community today.

MARC S. RODRIGUEZ

References and Further Reading

Calavita, Kitty. Inside the State: The Bracero Program, Immigration and the INS. New York: Routledge, 1992.
Ferriss, Susan, and Ricardo Sandoval. The Fight in the Fields: Cesar Chavez and the Farmworkers Movement. New York: Harvest Books, 1998.
Gomez-Quinones, Juan. Mexican American Labor, 1790–1990. Albuquerque: University of New Mexico Press, 1994.
Montejano, David. Anglos and Mexicans in the Making of Texas, 1836–1986. Austin: University of Texas Press, 1987.
Ochoa, Gilda, and Enrique Ochoa. Latino Los Angeles: Global Transformations, Settlement, and Political Activism. Tucson: University of Arizona Press, 2005.
Ruiz, Vicki. From Out of the Shadows: Mexican Women in the Twentieth-Century America. New York: Oxford University Press, 1999.
Sanchez, George J. Becoming Mexican-American: Ethnicity, Culture, and Identity in Chicano Los Angeles, 1900–1945. New York: Oxford University Press, 1995.
Valdes, Dennis. Al Norte: Agricultural Workers in the Great Lakes Region, 1917–1970. Austin: University of Texas Press, 1991.
Valdes, Dionicio Nodin. Barrios Norteños: St. Paul and Midwestern Mexican Communities in the Twentieth Century. Austin: University of Texas Press, 2000.
Vargas, Zaragosa. Labor Rights are Civil Rights: Mexican American Workers in Twentieth-Century America. Princeton, NJ: Princeton University Press, 2004.
Weber, Devra. Dark Sweat, White Gold: California Farm Workers, Cotton, and the New Deal. Berkeley: University of California Press, 1996.

MIDWEST

The Midwest holds an enigmatic place in U.S. labor and working-class history. It is popularly regarded as the conservative heartland of the United States, a racially homogenous and culturally traditional region dominated by employers and middle-class ideology. In contrast labor historians know the region for its militancy and organizational innovation. Indiana was home to railway union leader and Socialist Eugene Debs; Mineworkers' Union leader John L. Lewis was an Iowan. Chicago was the birthplace of the Industrial Workers of the World (IWW) and the American Communist party. The Congress of Industrial Organizations (CIO) emerged from the massive auto, steel, and meatpacking plants of Flint, Detroit, and Chicago, as well as from smaller industrial centers like Akron, Ohio; Anderson, Indiana; and Austin, Minnesota. Racially and ethnically diverse since the mid-nineteenth century, the midwestern working class has been created by waves of migration from Europe, Latin America, and the rural and southern United States.

The story of midwestern labor and working-class history follows closely the rise and fall of a regional, industrial network based in its earliest days on proximity to natural resources and transportation routes and in the twentieth century, on supplying national and global markets for manufactured goods and agricultural commodities. Spread out across hundreds of small industrial towns, as well as concentrated in metropolises like Chicago, Detroit, and Kansas City, midwestern industry sustained a working class that significantly shaped the political trajectory of the United States, especially in the mid-twentieth century. A period of decline and reconfiguration from the 1970s to the 1990s decimated many of these working-class communities as employers and the federal government shifted investment to the American South and West.

The region we now know as the Midwest was once part of a global trading network linked to the French, Spanish, and English empires. In the seventeenth century, the interior of North America was too remote for much direct European colonization, but the French in particular succeeded in building a profitable trade in animal furs. This trade was based on the personal and economic alliances between French men, Indian women, and their mixed race (métis) descendants. Working as indentured or contract laborers, and less frequently as independent contractors, French coureur de bois (runners of the woods) packed out from Montreal for years at a time, trading and living with American Indians and in some cases becoming permanent settlers. The Indian women who married these traders and laborers played a central role in the fur trade as the cultural bridge between French and Indians, as the embodiment of family-structured trading networks, and as agriculturalists whose produce was crucial to provisioning fur trade workers.

With the independence of the United States from Britain, the region began to take on its modern political form, splitting the trajectories of U.S. and Canadian workers, although migration across the border has been a constant. American leaders like Thomas Jefferson looked to the territory north and west of the Ohio River to fulfill dreams of a democratic society built on the foundation of yeoman farmers. The Northwest Ordinance of 1787 stipulated that the region would be free of slavery and promised to treat Indian communities fairly. Most Euro-American settlers disregarded the latter promise, in large part because their ideas of private property and resource exploitation were at odds with those of Indians. After nearly a century of intermittent warfare, Euro-American settlers had succeeded in moving most American Indians out of the lower Midwest; however, a significant Indian and métis presence remains in the upper Midwest.

By the Civil War the region had a widely dispersed industrial network and working class. The first industrial centers of the region were Ohio and Mississippi River towns, and only later ports on the Great Lakes. Pittsburgh, Cincinnati, and St. Louis provisioned their agricultural hinterlands, processing raw materials into preserved meats, timber, and pig iron. But they were primarily trading entrepots rather than industrial cities at this point. A network of canals and railroads began to take shape after the 1830s, opening the region's interior and linking it closer to national and global markets. Canals and railroads created a broad network of small industrial towns, each with manufacturers who took advantage of some local advantage, such as access to resources or skilled workers.

With the canals came the first large wave of immigrant wageworkers. Canal labor was primarily drawn from Irish and German immigrants, and especially in the early years, they faced horrendous conditions. During the building of the Illinois and Michigan Canal (completed in 1848), contractors routinely held back pay for their laborers, often because they had not been paid themselves by the canal corporation. Malaria, cholera, and other communicable diseases swept through the shantytowns that shadowed the path of the canal, their victims buried in anonymous mass graves. Although the first railroads started fast on the heels of canals, both forms of transportation co-existed for several decades, with canals offering a lower priced alternative to the railroad for crops, coal, and timber. By the 1850s, railroad building far outstripped the canals, and railroads would remain a major regional employer for the next century.

The quickly expanding regional economy nurtured a vision of shared interests among workers, farmers, and small business owners—what historians call "producerism." Although this notion benefited those who were able to settle down in one place, the dynamic regional economy also encouraged the "boomers"—highly mobile workers and speculators who followed each new economic boom—to see themselves as always on the verge of breaking through. It would take the economic crisis of 1873, and the long deflationary period that followed, to shake the labor movement of this producerism. But along the way, the philosophy shifted from one that supported the emerging market economy to an oppositional, even millennial critique of capitalism as a betrayal of the American democratic project. Although the Midwest was certainly not alone in this producerist outlook, the region produced some of the most vocal exponents of oppositional producerism through the populist and socialist movements of the late nineteenth century.

The great rail strike of 1877 announced a generation of militant strikes and equally militant employer and government opposition to unionization. Originating in the East, the strike spread through midwestern rail centers rapidly. In Chicago the rail strike spread to other industries, especially among immigrant workers, and led to the infamous Battle of the Viaduct, in which an armed militia fired on a crowd of workers and their families gathered near a busy rail crossing on the city's Southside, killing 14 people. St. Louis workers declared a general strike paralyzing the city for nearly a week.

These first mass strikes were followed a decade later by the growth of the Knights of Labor (KOL) and the Eight-Hour movement. As in other regions, the KOL assemblies in the Midwest were spread evenly between small and large industrial towns and included all kinds of workers: Men and women, black and white, wage laborers and farmers. Chicago and Detroit witnessed mass demonstrations on May 1, 1886, in support of the 8-hour day. Shortly afterward Chicago anarchist labor leaders were caught up in a dubious prosecution, and eight were found guilty of conspiring to bomb police officers. The wave of anti-radical suppression that accompanied the prosecution of the Haymarket defendants weakened both labor and radicalism in the Midwest. In the years after, radicals celebrated the Haymarket martyrs as working-class heroes, while mainline trade unionists learned to shun radicalism.

Whatever their political orientation, workers in the Midwest would play a central role in the long struggle for industrial unionism and government social provision that culminated in the formation of the CIO and the New Deal, respectively. The employers they faced were among the nation's richest and staunchly anti-union, the same corporations that were transforming the United States into a leader of the industrial world, including the Pullman Palace Car Company, U.S. Steel, International Harvester, Ford, and the meatpacking giants Swift and Armour. These heavy industries relied on a new wave of southern and eastern European migrants who took semi-skilled jobs that had been routinized following the thinking of Frederick Winslow Taylor. In a series of major confrontations from the 1890s to World War I, these employers were able to defeat unionization and maintain the open shop. The shifting position of the federal government in this struggle would prove decisive.

Railroad industry workers first sought to bridge their many craft union rivalries in the American Railway Union (ARU) of the 1890s, led by the charismatic Hoosier Debs. In 1894, the ARU took up the cause of the workers who built and repaired Pullman sleeping cars, declaring a boycott on the handling of Pullman cars. Employers and their supporters in the press labeled the boycott an insurrection. The federal government sent troops to Chicago over the objections of Illinois governor John Altgeld. Debs and other ARU leaders were jailed, and within a decade, most of the major trade unions had been crushed in massive strikes, including the meatpackers and teamsters in Chicago.

The intensity of employer and government anti-unionism pushed some homegrown labor leaders toward radicalism, most notably Debs, who became a Socialist while in prison. Responding to labor's crisis, a group of radicals and industrial unionists founded the IWW in Chicago in 1905. At its outset the IWW included the well-established Western Federation of Miners, and was supported by Debs and other well-known Socialists, suggesting the seriousness of the effort. By 1912, the miners' union and the Socialist Party (SP) had officially parted with the IWW. But left-wing Socialists like those associated with the Charles H. Kerr Publishing Company of Chicago remained supporters of the IWW. From 1915 to 1924, the IWW had notable success in organizing agricultural workers in the Great Plains and far West despite intense local and federal repression.

The advent of war in Europe during 1914 began a fundamental re-orientation of midwestern working-class communities and industrial structure. First and foremost the war cut off the flow of new workers from Europe, prompting employers to scramble for new sources of labor. The wartime labor shortage created an opportunity for African-Americans, Mexican immigrants, Mexican-American migrants, and working-class women to enter industrial employment in large numbers. The war also created opportunities for unions: As inflation undermined workers' standard of living, unionization and radicalism gained a new hearing. The frequency of strikes in the United States reached an all-time high during this decade, as workers, unions, and working-class activists put into practice a form of unionism that was appropriate for the new scale of work. The American Federation of labor (AFL) experimented with forms of industrial unionism, especially in Chicago's Stockyards' Labor Council and in the effort to organize the steel industry. In both cases former IWW and future Communist leader William Z. Foster played a prominent role. Success in meatpacking proved short-lived, with employer hostility on the rise with the end of wartime regulations. Whether the union's collapse was due to hostility among European ethnic groups, between Europeans and African-Americans, or because of the union's complex organizational structure is a subject of debate among historians.

Midwestern workers and farmers were also active in politics, forming important factions within the Republican and Democratic parties as well as in various third-party efforts. In North Dakota for instance, former leaders of the state Socialist party repackaged themselves as the Non Partisan League and in 1916 won a statewide election. They were able to pass profarmer and proworker legislation and in the war years prevented the passage of a criminal syndicalism law, the likes of which was used in other states to cripple the IWW. Socialist and prolabor mayors were elected in Milwaukee, Wisconsin, St. Paul, Minnesota, and Sioux City, Iowa. With the collapse of the union and left movements after the war, the Progressive party emerged as the last gasp of midwestern opposition. With Wisconsin's Robert LaFollette as its presidential candidate, the party advocated nationalization of railroads and a variety of proworker and profarmer reforms. LaFollette won more than 16% of the national vote in 1924, including a majority in Wisconsin and as much as 40% in several upper midwestern and western states.

The mid-1920s were a time of reckoning for the region. The expansive post-Civil War economy that incorporated the vast lands of midcontinent North America in the national and international economy had spawned a widely flung society of small towns with a mixed industrial and commercial base servicing the agricultural and extractive hinterlands. World War I had masked the extent to which this process had reached its end even before the war, as railroad construction ground to a halt and capital investment began a re-orientation toward urban-centered mass production, construction, and cultural industries. The extractive and transportation industries continued to be important economic power centers and large employers in the region, but after the mid-1920s, farming, timber, mining, and railroads were all in decline. The small industrial towns that relied on them would languish first in the hidden depression of the 1920s and then openly in the Great Depression of the 1930s. The recovery of the World War II years for the most part simply siphoned off population and business away from these smaller towns. Only in the 1950s, as industries began the decentralization of production away the metropolitan areas with their militant unionized workforces, would the population and economies of the towns grow again.

The 1920s also marked a shift away from the highly fluid labor markets of Gilded Age capitalism. The high turnover rates typical of modern factories were sapping profits, and many large employers sought to stabilize their workforces through welfare and training programs. Although the employee welfare programs pioneered by midwestern employers like Ford, Pullman, and International Harvester were generally sacrificed during the lean years of the 1930s, employers' hostility to high-turnover rates remained constant. The increasing stability of working-class communities, especially immigrant communities, translated into political power in the 1930s as the Democratic party solidified its New Deal coalition with programs like Social Security and the codification of collective bargaining in the National Labor Relations Act (1935). Nevertheless unionization remained elusive in many industries until World War II.

Contrary to notions of a Golden Age of employer-union harmony, the region experienced major strikes throughout the 1940s and 1950s. Moreover despite their alliance within the Democratic party, white and African-American communities continued to struggle over urban neighborhoods, a conflict that would create opportunities for employers and conservative politicians. Already in the early 1950s, large manufacturers moved production out of metropolitan areas to newer rural and small-town factories where the workforce was overwhelmingly white. The jobs that were left in the big cities usually went to the workers with the most seniority. In many cases these were white workers who had been in the factories since the 1930s, and black workers who had landed jobs during the war were thrown into unemployment with devastating effects on their communities.

Beginning with the oil crisis of the early 1970s, midwestern industry went into a long decline, with the automobile and steel sectors leading the way. Turning their early twentieth-century strategy of consolidation on its head, employers now sought industrial decentralization in order to escape the high land, transportation, and labor costs associated with their metropolitan operations. Rather than upgrading their urban midwestern plants, employers built new factories in rural areas and in the South. In this way they hoped to escape the power of militant and well-organized union locals.

Although unions sometimes fought these relocations directly, the more common strategy was to work with employers to increase the productivity of the older plants. The result was an intensifying split between rank-and-file workers bearing the brunt of the speed up and their union officials who seemed sometimes to side with employers. In Detroit and other auto industry towns, this brewing dispute over productivity combined with racial and generational divisions resulted in some cases in open rank-and-file revolt, as in the case of the Dodge Revolutionary Union Movement. Workers at newer auto plants, like the Lordstown, Ohio, General Motors assembly plant opened in 1966, faced intense demands for increased productivity. With an assembly line timed to produce a record 100 cars an hour, workers at Lordstown launched a strike in 1972 that became a national symbol of the rebelliousness of young workers.

The conflict over productivity became more intense as a number of large employers threatened bankruptcy, and others, like Wisconsin Steel, simply closed shop. Federal loan guarantees designed to save the Chrysler Corporation, for instance, required massive layoffs, wage and benefit cuts, and work-rule concessions by the United Auto Workers (UAW). By the mid-1980s concessionary bargaining held sway, and unions generally fought to limit the erosion of wages and benefits. Labor's defensive position was manifested in a series of strikes and lockouts that seemed to foster as much conflict within the labor movement as between unions and employers. The strike of Austin, Minnesota, Packinghouse Workers' Local P-9 against Hormel ended in failure and trusteeship for the local after the Minnesota National Guard was called out to protect replacement workers. The boom economy of the mid-1990s did little for midwestern industrial workers. A long-running battle between the UAW and Caterpillar ended with a clear management victory. A 3-year lockout of workers at the A. E. Staley corn products plant in Decatur came shortly after the firm was purchased by a British-based multinational. The unions' feeling of embattlement was best illustrated by their billboard advertisements outside of Decatur and Peoria, Illinois, that announced to drivers "You Are Now Entering a War Zone." Facing de-industrialization and intense employer anti-unionism, once powerful industrial unions like the Packinghouse Workers, and the Rubber Workers were forced to merge with larger unions.

The declining power of unions undermined the power of prolabor Democrats, and the party increasingly sided with probusiness positions aligned with the emerging global economy. The 1994 North American Free Trade Agreement (NAFTA), served another blow to the industrial base of the Midwest as employers transferred labor-intensive work to Mexico and capital-intensive work to Canada. The increasingly global outlook of midwestern industrial employers was illustrated best by a series of foreign buy-outs, most prominently the 1998 purchase of Chrysler by German automaker Daimler-Benz. In contrast to the manufacturing sector, public-sector and service-sector unions in the region experienced strong growth in the 1990s and 2000s, even expanding into previously nonunion workforces, such as home healthcare workers. However the vulnerability of public-sector unions was underscored in 2005 when Indiana's recently elected Republican governor revoked the collective-bargaining rights of state employees and canceled existing contracts.

FRANK TOBIAS HIGBIE

References and Further Reading

Barrett, James R. *Work and Community in the Jungle: Chicago's Packinghouse Workers, 1894–1922*. Urbana: University of Illinois Press, 1987.

Fink, Deborah. *Cutting into the Meatpacking Line: Workers and Change in the Rural Midwest*. Chapel Hill: University of North Carolina Press, 1998.

Franklin, Stephen. *Three Strikes: Labor's Heartland Losses and What They Mean for Working Americans*. New York: Guilford Press, 2001.

Ginger, Ray. *The Bending Cross: a Biography of Eugene Victor Debs*. New Brunswick, NJ: Rutgers University Press, 1949.

Grossman, James. *Land of Hope: Chicago, Black Southerners, and the Great Migration*. Chicago, IL: University of Chicago Press, 1998.

Hamper, Ben. *Rivethead: Tales from the Assembly Line*. New York: Warner Books, 1991.

Higbie, Frank Tobias. *Indispensable Outcasts: Hobo Workers and Community in the American Midwest*. Urbana: University of Illinois Press, 2003.

Laslett, John H. M. *Colliers across the Sea: A Comparative Study of Coal Miners in Scotland and the American Midwest*. Urbana: University of Illinois Press, 2000.

Lichtenstein, Nelson. *Walter Reuther: The Most Dangerous Man in Detroit*. Urbana: University of Illinois Press, 1995.

Meyer, Stephen. *The Five-Dollar Day: Labor, Management, and Social Control in the Ford Motor Company, 1908–1921*. Albany: State University of New York Press, 1981.

Register, Cheri. *Packinghouse Daughter: A Memoir*. St. Paul: Minnesota Historical Society Press, 2000.

Sleeper–Smith, Susan. *Indian Women and French Men: Rethinking Cultural Encounter in the Western Great Lakes*. Amherst: University of Massachusetts Press, 2001.

Valdés, Dennis Nodin. *Al Norte: Agricultural Workers in the Great Lakes Region, 1917–1970*. Austin: University of Texas Press, 1991.

Cases and Statutes Cited

See also **Debs, Eugene V.; Foster, William Z.; Industrial Workers of the World; Knights of Labor**

MIGRANT FARMWORKERS

Workers who labor for wages on farms in the United States can be broken down into several groups: Year-round hired hands, local seasonal laborers, and migrant farmworkers—those who must leave their home for an extended period of time to work for wages on a farm. The first and second subsets of agricultural laborers were part of the American labor experience beginning in the colonial era. Migrant farmworkers however emerged later in time. The study of these workers poses unique problems for labor historians. Migrant farmworkers are ethnically and racial diverse, native-born and immigrant, men, women, and children, geographically mobile, lack long-term labor union affiliations and local community ties, and work in other nonagricultural jobs. These are only a few of the distinctive features of the migrant farm-worker

population that has evolved since the middle of the nineteenth century, making them a group of workers who do not fit neatly into any one, two, or even three areas of study.

Farmworker Origins

In the decades leading up to the Civil War, farmers began to specialize in commercial agricultural products, taking advantage of an advancing market economy and a revolution in transportation. In the old Northwest and prairie states, the first uses of migrant farmworkers took place, though on a scale much smaller than what would appear later in the century. With the introduction of the reaper and mechanical thresher in the 1840s and 1850s, western farmers could plant wheat and other grain crops on a much larger scale. Although farmers could plant and tend their crops with their own labor, that of their families, and perhaps with the help of a hired hand or two, the harvest of these crops required extra temporary labor. The sparsely populated countryside did

Dispossessed Arkansas farmers. Bakersfield, California. Library of Congress, Prints & Photographs Division, FSA/OWI Collection [LC-USF34-002327-C].

not have sufficient labor sources. Therefore, native-born men—white and black—and European immigrants from urban areas provided a migrant farm-worker supply for the crucial harvest period. These workers would migrate with the ripening grain from South to North in Ohio, Indiana, and Illinois. Out in California Gold Rush miners stimulated an expansion of the existing agricultural economy. Native Americans became a major source of seasonal and migrant farm labor.

After the Civil War, the need for migrant farm-workers accelerated, especially in areas of the West: the Great Plains, California, and the Pacific Northwest. The Great Plains are a more arid region than the Midwest prairies in that annual rainfall is on average 20 inches or less a year. Despite modest precipitation, grain crops, especially wheat, thrived. By 1900, the creation of five transcontinental railroad lines with their connecting lines helped farmers reach growing urban consumer markets. Just as with the Midwest farmers, Great Plains farmers could plant hundreds and even thousands of acres of wheat. Still the limits of technology required that they employ seasonal labor for the harvest. Again sufficient harvest labor could not be supplied by area workers. Therefore migrant labor was necessary. California agriculture experienced a similar phenomenon. Wheat and other grain crops predominated in the state and required extensive use of seasonal and migrant farm labor. Even when the state's farmers moved to truck farm-ing, that is vegetable and fruit production for sale in urban areas, limits of agricultural technology compelled both large and small farmers to use temporary harvest labor. At the end of the nineteenth century, the Pacific Northwest developed both grain- and fruit-growing agricultural industries that could not rely only on local seasonal labor. Whether picking apples or harvesting wheat, migrant farm laborers were essential to the region's farmers.

Work-Life Culture

Migrant laborers at this point in their history tended to be young, native-born, white men, though African-Americans and European immigrants could be found in the harvest sites on the Great Plains and in the West generally. California was unique in that wave after wave of Asian and later Latino immigrants made their way into the few employment avenues open to them, namely, farm labor. Nevertheless until the advent of World War I, young, white, native-born men dominated the migrant farm labor workforce. Migrant workers as a group made up a substantial portion of the 150 thousand agricultural laborers employed annually in California. On the Great Plains, the migrant portion of 200 thousand or so agricultural laborers could be broken down into three major groups. One cohort migrated to work sites through-out the West and lived on their earnings during the winter months in towns and cities in the region. The second were farmers who supplemented their annual income by working harvests. Out-of-work tradesmen, students, and young men out to experience the West made up the final group. Migrant farmworkers though also labored in nonagricultural jobs on a seasonal basis as well.

Migrant farmworkers developed distinctive cul-tures of work and life on the road in search of employment. Before the advent of the automobile, migrant workers had to travel by freight train. They would stop in area farm towns to find employ-ment where they were usually tolerated only during the harvest period. It was customary for workers to go to the center of town and wait for farmers from the countryside to arrive and to offer employment. Work-ers would have to determine whether to accept the wages, room, board, and hours offered. Once workers completed the harvesting job, they had to move on to find other employment. Though some purchased tick-ets on passenger trains, others stole rides on freight trains. Between jobs workers stayed in "jungles." Jungles were temporary communities situated well outside of towns but near a railroad line and a stream or some other water source. In these camps, a worker could make a meal, sleep, socialize, and become in-formed about other employment. As these workers traveled from workplace to workplace, they carried their bedding and other belongings on their backs in the form of a bundle. Migrant farmworkers were commonly referred to as bindle stiffs.

The East Coast was another region of significant migrant farm-worker formation. As early as 1870, the Northeast, specifically southern New Jersey, devel-oped a truck-farming industry that could supply the major cities of New York, Philadelphia, and Newark with fresh fruits and vegetables. Unlike California, which had much larger farming operations and a larger workforce that tended to be isolated from the local workforce, the East Coast had smaller truck-farming operations, and farms had to tap into existing urban labor sources. Therefore Italian tradesmen and their families supplemented their income by turning to summer harvests. These Northeast farmers also relied on African-American men from the upper South to migrate seasonally to perform a variety of farm labor tasks. With refrigerated railroad car con-nections established between the Southeast and Northeast, truck farming expanded in the South, with farmers turning to sharecroppers and their families to harvest crops seasonally.

Radicalism and Reform

The first successful effort at organizing migrant farm labor in the early twentieth century was by the Industrial Workers of the World (IWW). The IWW organized thousands of agricultural laborers with the Agricultural Workers' Organization (AWO), later renamed the Agricultural Workers' Industrial Union (AWIU). The strategy of the AWO and AWIU was to embrace the work life culture of migrant farmworkers. As long as these workers were predominately white and male, the IWW proved successfully. The AWO and AWIU job delegates rode the rails, lived in jungles, and worked the harvest job sites with the workers they sought to organize. From 1910 to 1925, the IWW had its greatest triumph in organizing workers on the Great Plains. As migrant farm laborers though turned to second-hand automobiles to search for work, the IWW lost its ability to bring new workers into the union. The AWIU job delegates failed to adapt an organizing strategy that could accommodate workers making their way through the harvest in small groups, living out of their cars and trucks, and soliciting farmers for work directly at the job site. Also changes in harvest technology of wheat and other grains crops, especially after 1930, eliminated the need for large numbers of migrant farmworkers on the Great Plains. In the second-half of the 1920s, farmers began to use the combine, which put into one mechanized operation harvesting and threshing wheat.

The federal government's interest in migrant farmworkers and agricultural labor generally began with the U. S. Industrial Commission (USIC). It met from 1898 to 1902 and determined that immigrant workers would benefit in the long run by taking up agricultural labor. The USIC believed that the agricultural ladder could provide agricultural workers with avenues to farm ownership and independence. First they would have to work as hired hands and seasonal workers, but eventually, the commissioners believed, they would be able to establish their own farms. Nevertheless the Division of Information, which was overseen by the Department of Commerce and Labor, was unable to arrive at an efficient distribution program. With the advent of the Wheatland Strike of 1913 and concerns about child labor, progressives sought to address the problems of migrant farm labor with reform of labor camps and improvement in working conditions. Another federal inquiry, the Commission on Industrial Relations

(CIR), investigated agricultural labor in the context of other industrial relations. The CIR focused on labor militancy, such as the success of the IWW, and the fact that armies of migrant laborers stole rides on freight trains to traverse major portions of the country searching for work. The CIR understood that the agricultural ladder had broken down in an era of industrial agriculture. Only with a national distribution system of labor could workers and employers have their needs met. During World War I, the Department of Labor created the U.S. Employment Service to deal with rationalizing farm labor needs. With several hundred free employment bureaus, the service placed tens of thousands of farmworkers. But with the end of war, Congress cut the service's funding.

Federal Intervention

The Dust Bowl and the Great Depression of the 1930s accelerated trends in migrant farm labor that had been developing for several decades. Even though single men, whether native-born or immigrant, dominated migrant farm labor through the 1920s, more and more families of harvesters made their way into the army of workers with the availability of cheap, second-hand cars and trucks. The Great Depression pushed farmers and their families into the ranks of migrant farmworkers due to the Dust Bowl and to other economic catastrophes. Urban families and single men were forced into farm labor as well. Streams of migrant farm laborers fed farmers' demand for workers. The most notable migrant stream was from the Great Plains to California. Workers from the plains though also trekked to the Pacific Northwest. Still other workers made their way from Texas to the berry harvests in Arkansas and Michigan. Other workers journeyed from the South to the Midwest and Northeast to find labor on truck farms and in sugar beet fields. These migrant streams were ethnically and racially diverse. Native-born blacks and whites, and immigrant workers, especially Asians and Latinos, could be found integrated into the same migrant labor streams and work places, but they could also be segregated in both labor streams and work sites.

At the end of the 1920s and through the 1930s, agricultural labor strikes erupted in California and in other farming areas of the country. Despite the effort of migrant and seasonal farmworkers to join unions— some of the most militant efforts led by Communists— their right to organize into labor unions was exempt in the Wagner Act (1935). Therefore subsequent efforts by the Congress of Industrial Organizations (CIO) and the American Federation of Labor (AFL) were seriously hampered during the rest of the 1930s and into the 1940s. Still workers were able to improve wages and working conditions due to some strike actions despite the brutal reaction by farmers' associations. The poor working and living conditions that led to strikes attracted public sympathy for migrant farmworkers, especially when coupled with the writings of John Steinbeck and Carey McWilliams and by government hearings, such as those led by Senator Robert La Follette.

Unlike progressives, New Deal officials tried to make migrant farmworkers the responsibility of the state. New Deal officials in the Departments of Labor and Agriculture tried to find ways that the federal government could act to help but not empower farmworkers. Their efforts resulted in attempts to settle strikes and to create migrant labor camps in order to alleviate difficult living conditions. Within the Department of Agriculture, officials in the Resettlement Administration (RA) at the end of the decade were able to create labor camps on both coasts. Their efforts to alleviate the problems that migrant farmworkers experienced whether on the East Coast, West Coast, or anywhere in between, were thwarted by officials in the Agricultural Adjustment Administration, who were preoccupied with the interests of farm owners as opposed to migrant farmworkers, seasonal agricultural laborers, sharecroppers, or tenant farmers. Where farmers would not or could not provide farm labor housing, the RA's Migratory Camp Program did provide migrant workers a safe, clean place to live while working on truck farms. Employers though continued to complain about labor shortages and the fact that migrants organized successful strikes out of the camps. With the outbreak of World War II, the federal government transformed the camps into centers of labor distribution. A new agency, the Emergency Farm Labor Supply Program, brought agricultural laborers from Mexico and the Caribbean, along with over 100 thousand prisoners of war to meet the needs of farmers.

With war production moving into full swing in 1941, white, native-born agricultural laborers found more employment options. African-Americans, Latinos, and other minority groups found agricultural labor one of only several limited employment opportunities. The war though motivated government officials to focus their efforts on attaining sufficient farm labor for farm owners as opposed to assisting farm laborers in securing better working and living conditions. The Farm Security Administration, which succeeded the RA, created fixed and mobile farm labor camps to facilitate the placement of farmworkers for employers. Eventually this commitment on the part of the federal government led to the Labor Importation Program, also known as the Bracero Program in the Southwest. Federal officials negotiated agreements with Mexico to bring thousands of Mexican nationals into the United States. to work as agricultural laborers. The program was extended to the East Coast, using workers from Puerto Rico and other Caribbean islands. Despite the introduction of foreign workers, domestic migrant workers continued to be employed as agricultural laborers. After 1948, the Bracero Program continued but by state government arrangements rather than strictly through the federal government and Mexico. Several hundred thousand workers were imported during the 1950s on an annual basis. This practice ended in 1964 due to a series of legal challenges.

Postwar Unionization and Advocacy

Efforts by native-born and immigrant agricultural laborers to organize into effective labor unions continued after the war. There are three phases of postwar farmworker organizing. The first phase, 1947–1955, was led by the National Farm Labor Union (NFLU). The AFL chartered the NFLU with an industrial model for its structure. The union focused on large-scale farming operations in California, initiated several strikes, and lobbied against the Bracero program. Nonetheless the leadership failed to understand the cultural attributes of the significant migrant, ethnic minority, and immigrant portion of the workforce. The second phase, 1956–1964, was led by the Agricultural Workers' Organizing Committee (AWOC). The AFL-CIO created AWOC, but again the organizational model was not well-suited to the migrant nature of the workforce. Moreover the leadership sought to organize white elements of the workforce and overlooked the strong presence of immigrant, Latino, and Asian farmworkers.

The third phase—beginning in the mid-1960s and continuing to the present—had its origins with the Cesar Chavez and other union and social reform advocates. A series of successful strikes in 1965 led to a grape boycott that galvanized critical nationwide support for migrant and seasonal farm laborers. The culmination of these efforts led to the formation of a union that both spoke to the economic needs and cultural attributes of a farmworker population that was primarily made up of ethnic minorities and immigrants. That union, the United Farm Workers (UFW), officially affiliated with the AFL-CIO in

1972. With the passage of California's 1975 Agricultural Labor Relations Act (ALRA), the UFW had the right to organize farmworkers and collectively bargain with employers. The ALRA however could be compromised by powerful associations of farmers and by employer strategies to undermine the effectiveness of the law. Other states with an agricultural economy that required migrant farmworkers did not follow California's lead with such protective legislation for agricultural laborers. Moreover government officials have tended to view migrant farmworkers as a social problem and a labor-distribution issue. Such media exposes as *Harvest of Shame* at the beginning of the 1960s and decade after decade of state and federal governmental investigations have led to school programs for migrant children and some improvements in housing and working conditions. However such legislation has not led to political or economic empowerment for migrant farmworkers.

At the beginning of the twenty-first century, migrant farmworkers in the United. States can be found in all 50 states, though most are concentrated in California, Texas, and Florida. A contemporary guest worker program, H-2A, allows employers to import immigrant workers when they can successfully argue that they are experiencing a lack of sufficient availability of laborers for their crops. Lack of available workers includes laborers unwilling to accept certain wages and working conditions. The result is to pit domestic workers against immigrant workers. Despite the current guest worker program and the lack of legal protection for organizing efforts among migrant farmworkers, agricultural laborers are still an active part of the labor union movement. The UFW in the West and the Farm Labor Organizing Committee in the East and such advocacy groups as Student Action with Farmworkers seek to empower agricultural laborers, placing them at the center of the struggle for economic and social justice.

GREG HALL

References and Further Reading

Edid, Maralyn. *Farm Labor Organizing: Trends and Prospects.* Ithaca, NY: ILR Press, 1994.
Griffith, David Craig. *Working Poor: Farmworkers in the United States.* Philadelphia, PA: Temple University Press, 1995.
Griswold del Castillo, Richard, and Richard A. Garcia. *Cesar Chavez: Triumph of Spirit.* Norman: University of Oklahoma Press, 1995.
Hahamovitch, Cindy. *The Fruits of Their Labor: Atlantic Coast Farmworkers and the Making of Migrant Poverty, 1870–1945.* Chapel Hill: The University of North Carolina Press, 1997.
Higbie, Frank Tobias. *Indispensable Outcasts: Hobo Workers and Community in the American Midwest, 1880–1930.* Urbana: University of Illinois, 2003.
Jamieson, Stuart. *Labor Unionism in American Agriculture.* Washington, DC: United States Government Printing Office, 1945.
Martin, Philip L. *Harvest of Confusion: Migrant Workers in U. S. Agriculture.* San Francisco, CA: Westview Press, 1988.
McWilliams, Carey. *Factories in the Field: The Story of Migratory Farm Labor in California.* Boston, MA: Little, Brown, and Company, 1939.
———. *Ill Fares the Land: Migrant and Migratory Labor in the United States.* Boston, MA: Little, Brown, and Company, 1942.
Street, Richard Steven. *Beasts of the Fields: A Narrative History of California Farmworkers, 1769–1913.* Stanford, CA: Stanford University Press, 2004.
Thompson, Charles D., Jr., and Melina F. Wiggins, eds. *The Human Cost of Food: Farmworkers' Lives, Labor, and Advocacy.* Austin: University of Texas Press, 2002.
Valdes, Dennis Nodin. *Al Norte: Agricultural Workers in the Great Lakes Region, 1917–1970.* Austin: University of Texas, 1991.

MILLER, ARNOLD (1922–1985)
President, United Mine Workers of America

Arnold Miller was president of the United Mine Workers of America (UMWA) from 1972 to 1979. He won his first term under the insurgent banner of Miners for Democracy (MFD) against Tony Boyle after a federal court overturned Boyle's fraud-ridden 1969 electoral victory over Jock Yablonski. Assassinated in December 1969, Yablonski had begun to unite the decentralized 1960s rank-and-file coal miners' movement around his candidacy. The MFD carried his fight to fruition with the election of Miller, who received 55% of the votes in December 1972.

A 1972 MFD convention had nominated Miller for president, Pennsylvania-based Mike Trbovich for vice-president, and Harry Patrick of northern West Virginia for secretary-treasurer. A southern West Virginia coal miner beginning at age 16, Miller was badly wounded in World War II, after which he returned to the mines as a repairman and electrician. He had served as president of his local for 1 year before black lung disease and arthritis ended his mining career at age 48 in 1970.

Miller had no connection to the old order (indeed he had never attended a national UMWA convention). However he was closely associated with the militant movement that won the landmark Federal Coal Mine Health and Safety Act (1969), establishing black lung benefits and federal responsibility for mine health and safety. Miller had been president of the West Virginia Black Lung Association (BLA) and had supervised the association's widely circulated *Black Lung Bulletin*. Soft-spoken and modest in demeanor, he had a strong knack for the public relations side of organizing, which made him well-known among the networks of activist miners and organizers, and the media. He was also a newcomer to formal organizational leadership in a union that had long concentrated administrative power and responsibility at the top. Miller was about to take on the challenging task of restructuring and leading a union with some 140,000 members (down from over 400,000 a generation earlier) facing complex contractual and pension-related issues and difficult organizing tasks in a time of ongoing rank-and-file unrest.

The new leadership promptly carried out fundamental changes in the UMWA. Miller dismantled the corrupt Boyle apparatus. He removed both hired administrators and the 20 appointed International Executive Board (IEB) members and replaced them with people from the MFD's network of activists. Elections were held for the IEB positions within several months. The UMW Journal was transformed from a self-serving mouthpiece of the national leadership into a serious source of information for miners. The Miller administration cut salaries for top leaders and prioritized mine health and safety, securing the endangered Health and Retirement Funds, and organizing new members. It carried out the 1973 UMWA convention with unprecedented rank-and-file involvement and participation, and it implemented membership ratification of the 1974 collective-bargaining contract.

The new president, apparently fearful of organized factionalism and even "dual unionism," also hastened to abandon MFD as a rank-and-file vehicle. Furthermore Miller at times undercut the BLAs, which had spread from West Virginia to other states. However undermining the organized channels for the grassroots movement did not make his tenure any easier. A strong core of former Boyle supporters won IEB seats in Boyle's old strongholds and came to constitute a persistent base of hostile opposition to Miller. At the same time, rank-and-file protest continued in the mid-1970s. This included frequent wildcat strikes. With no unifying leadership or clear program, the unpredictable wildcats created legal problems and dilemmas for the reform administration. The wildcats also added pressure on the production-linked Health and Retirement Funds, which began making cuts in medical services. Increasingly isolated from the wave that had catapulted him to the presidency, Miller gradually became estranged from the network of activists, many of whom exited from his staff. The top three leaders split into hostile factions, and

Patrick opposed Miller for the presidency in a three-way race (1977). Miller won a second term, but his governance of the UMWA was becoming less effective.

The problems were most exemplified by the 1978 contract, signed after a 110-day strike, with few gains. The final agreement included replacement of the long-cherished across-the-board free medical care with company-by-company private plans, and the defeat of a hoped-for local right to strike between contracts. Many miners were disappointed. Fending off attempts to recall him and prematurely aging from the toll of work and war-related injuries, Miller suffered a stroke and resigned in 1979. Sam Church, a former Boyle supporter who had joined forces with Miller as the MFD leaders split apart, became president. Miller died in 1985.

Criticisms of Miller's shortcomings must be tempered by the fact that the weakening of the UMWA's bargaining power had deep historical roots that would have proved daunting for any leader. No one before or since has solved the problem of unionization in either the western states, where strip mines have continued to increase their proportion of production, or in the historically nonunion, small mines in Appalachia. But the UMWA's stubborn and often creative survival, furthered by the accession of a new generation of progressive leadership beginning with Richard Trumka and continuing with Cecil Roberts, certainly owes much to the election of Miller, to the reforms he implemented, and to the movement of which he was part.

PAUL SIEGEL

References and Further Reading

Brody, David. In *Labor's Cause: Main Themes in the History of the American Worker*. New York: Oxford University Press, 1993.
Clark, Paul F. *The Miners' Fight for Democracy: Arnold Miller and the Reform of the United Mine Workers*. Ithica, NY: New York State School of Industrial and Labor Relations, Cornell University, 1981.
———. "Legacy of Democratic Reform: The Trumka Administration and the Challenge of the Eighties." In *The United Mine Workers of America: A Model of Industrial Solidarity?* edited by John H. M. Laslett. University Park: University of Pennsylvania Press, 1996.
Goldstein, George S. "The Rise and Decline of the UMWA Health and Retirement Funds Program, 1946–1995."
Green, James R. "'Tying the Knot of Solidarity': The Pittston Strike of 1989–1990." In *The United Mine Workers of America: A Model of Industrial Solidarity?* edited by John H. M. Laslett. University Park: University of Pennsylvania Press, 1996.
Hume, Brit. *Death and the Mines: Rebellion and Murder in the United Mine Workers*. New York: Grossman Publishers, 1971.

See also **Black Lung Associations; Boyle, (W. A.) Tony; Federal Coal Mine Health and Safety Act; Miners For Democracy; United Mine Workers of America**

MILLS, C. WRIGHT (1916–1962)
Sociologist

As a sociologist and radical social critic, C. Wright Mills was one of the most significant intellectuals in the mid-twentieth-century United States. He was also one of the many American thinkers of his era to be profoundly shaped by an engagement with the labor movement. Born in Waco, Texas, Mills studied at the University of Texas before receiving his Ph.D. from the University of Wisconsin in 1942. Beginning in the early 1940s, Mills associated himself with a group of left-wing anti-Stalinist intellectuals centered in New York City and began to develop a radical critique of American society.

During World War II, Mills was pessimistic regarding the potential of organized labor to transform American society. However following the war, Mills was drawn to the upsurge of union activity and became hopeful that labor could serve as a radical agency of social change. In 1946, Mills joined the Inter-Union Institute for Labor and Democracy, a consortium of labor-oriented intellectuals headed by the venerable union journalist, J. B. S. Hardman. Mills also became a frequent contributor to the institute's magazine, *Labor and Nation.* Also in 1946, in his capacity as research associate at Columbia University's cutting-edge research bureau, the Bureau of Applied Social Research, Mills established a Labor Research Division of the bureau and began to conduct an extensive survey of American labor leaders. In 1947, Mills wrote an enthusiastic report on the United Automobile Workers convention for *Commentary* magazine.

Mills presented the results of this survey in his first book, *The New Men of Power: America's Labor Leaders*, published in 1948. The book alternated unevenly between the empirical results of Mills's study and his speculative analysis of the radical political potential of the labor movement.

DANIEL GEARY

References and Further Reading

Geary, Daniel. "The 'Union of the Power and the Intellect': C. Wright Mills and the Labor Movement." *Labor History* 42, 4 (2001): 327–345.
Mills, C. Wright. *The New Men of Power.* New York: Harcourt, Brace, 1948

MINERS FOR DEMOCRACY

From 1970 through 1973, Miners for Democracy (MFD) led a coalition of insurgent coal miners in electing new leadership for the United Mine Workers of America (UMWA), who then democratically restructured the union. The MFD was born literally at the funeral of Joseph A. (Jock) Yablonski, his wife, and his daughter, who were brutally murdered on December 31, 1969. A coterie of his followers and family agreed to carry on. Yablonski had mounted a strong though unsuccessful challenge to incumbent W. A. (Tony) Boyle for the presidency of the UMWA in an election tainted by massive fraud. Boyle's 1969 election was ultimately overturned by federal intervention, and he was later convicted of ordering the murder of Yablonski.

Origins: Militancy, Despotism, Crisis

The roots of the MFD, and the insurgency from which it grew, lie in the legendary yet contradictory career of John L. Lewis, who headed the UMWA for four decades, ending in 1960. Alongside his legacy as standard-bearer of the early CIO, for which the actions of militant UMWA miners prepared the path, stands a more complex and conservative Lewis. He supported, even demanded, modernization and corporate consolidation of the historically fragmented and competitive coal industry, with collective bargaining as the price. The mixed results included the unionization of large mines under even larger corporations, with historic gains for coal miners. Among those gains were, post-World War II, the pioneering UMWA Health and Retirement Funds, won by militant strikes, with a network of clinics and hospitals in the underserved Appalachian coalfields.

Modernization, along with competition from other fuels, also resulted in massive job loss from 1950 to 1970, leaving Appalachia's coal-dependent economy in a devastating crisis, and the UMWA weakened. Lewis's project was incomplete, since a cost-cutting sector of mostly nonunion, small mines remained, especially in eastern Kentucky and Tennessee. Lewis ran the UMWA itself as both a dictatorship, gradually removing district autonomy, and in some respects, as a business enterprise, with growing cronyism in the 1950s.

Boyle, a UMWA functionary, soon stepped into the magisterial Lewis's ill-fitting shoes. He took to greater lengths the suppression of internal democracy and the corruption, which extended to the cherished Health and Retirement Funds. Sweetheart deals with operators signaled Boyle's retreat from the redeeming elements of militant struggle.

Challenge from Below

As the 1960s began union miners faced economic insecurity and life-threatening health and safety problems. They were further stymied by near absence of district autonomy, by "bogus" locals of retirees under the national leadership's thumb, and then by violence and intimidation at the 1964 UMWA convention. Without access to leaders or voting rights on contracts, insurgent miners tapped into both their militant traditions of direct workplace action and the democratic spirit of rebellion in the 1960s.

Wildcat strikes grew throughout the eastern coalfields. Miners from eastern Kentucky creatively deployed roving pickets. Local and district electoral challenges were mounted in Pennsylvania's District 5 and Ohio's District 6. The Disabled Miners and Widows of Southern West Virginia challenged inequities of the Health and Retirement Funds, with both direct and legal actions, and the Black Lung Associations (BLAs), won unprecedented federal legislation in 1969, aimed at workplace health and safety.

Forging Unity

The diverse rank-and-file movement began to coalesce around Yablonski's 1969 campaign. Yablonski was a veteran UMWA leader from Pennsylvania's District 5, among the few areas where district autonomy had survived. Although he had long ceased to be an active miner and had in fact been part of Boyle's machine, Yablonski had an easy rapport with miners. Moreover during his brief time as a reform leader, he seemed to grasp the historical moment that had arrived. He understood the issues facing miners and connected the demands for union democracy with substantive issues from black lung and mine safety to problems of poor services in coal field communities and in a visceral way, to national political issues.

Perhaps not surprisingly, the MFD, in carrying the fight to victory, tended to see unity overwhelmingly in terms of wresting power from the Boyle clique. However the potential of the coalition to connect the many demands of the rank-and-file movement, which involved sharp conflict with the coal operators as well as with Boyle, was partly lost.

MFD's Base

By the early 1970s, the contours of the rank-and-file coal miners' upsurge had formed around a cross-generational alliance. Many young miners were entering the industry as it began to recover from its long slump. Impatient with conditions, without ties to the old guard's patronage and intimidation, they formed a receptive base for the MFD, especially in larger unionized mines. Older, often disabled miners had taken initiative in forming the militant Disabled Miners and Widows group, and the BLAs. African-Americans, such as Robert Payne, Charles Brooks, and Bill Worthington, and women, such as Helen Powell, Anise Floyd, and Sara Kaznoski (widow of a miner killed in the infamous Mannington disaster) played important roles, though they were little known to the media.

Such organizations and leaders sparked wildcat strikes on broad health, safety, and pension issues that gave the movement much of its momentum, and they often made connections to community-based and poor peoples' struggles. Most of these "movement soldiers," notably the African-Americans, were not brought into the leading core of the MFD, which points to the nature and limitations of MFD unity. Boyle's strongest base was among another set of older and retired miners who were susceptible to his influence and control, especially at smaller mines and in areas where the union was relatively weak.

Legal and Electoral Victories; the End of MFD

The MFD's legal arm, led by Yablonski's sons, Ken and "Chip" Yablonski, and other attorneys, secured the intervention of the Justice Department and the judiciary, which previously had ignored the Yablonski campaign's complaints. They won court-ordered restoration of district autonomy (which signaled the end of dictatorial control), the overturning of the 1969 election, and federal oversight of the resulting 1972 election. Three miners headed the MFD ticket, chosen at a 1972 convention that was attended by over 400 activist delegates. Arnold Miller, West Virginia BLA president, ran for UMWA president. Mike Trbovich, MFD vice-presidential candidate from Pennsylvania, had chaired Yablonski's campaign. Harry Patrick, from northern West Virginia, had become the self-styled spokesman for younger miners and ran for secretary-treasurer.

The campaign tapped into networks built by the grassroots movement, for example, through rank-and-file publications, such as the Black Lung Bulletin that Miller had started. It was estimated that the three candidates visited 400 bathhouses and talked to 60,000 miners. The MFD ticket won, capturing 55% of the 127,000 votes cast. That margin, while impressive, revealed also a significant residual base of support for the old guard and perhaps a mistrust of the MFD attorneys and other outsiders against whom Boyle endlessly railed.

Following victory the MFD withered. Apparently swayed by old fears regarding dual unionism, the top MFD leaders made no secret before the election of their belief that once Miller was elected, the MFD would be redundant, since "we will have democracy." Miller would have even preferred the abandonment of the BLA, which survived thanks to the determination of Worthington. Among the MFD's leading core, only Patrick mourned its passing, but rank-and-file objections were heard. In District 5 and West Virginia's District 17, candidates kept the MFD apparatus and name alive in the 1973 elections, brought about by democratization, for district officers and the International Executive Board (IEB). The planned demise of MFD may have contributed to the winning of several IEB seats by Boyle supporters, which was to be one source of the Miller administration's many problems. The profound structural reform of the UMWA is a post-MFD story.

Politically the last direct traces of the MFD disappeared (late 1970s) when the Miller-Trbovich-Patrick troika split into hostile factions, none of which retained power. Although Miller was a sincere reforming champion of coal miners, his gradual isolation from the continuing 1970s rank-and-file ferment helped to limit the movement's accomplishments in that era. Whether preserving the MFD would have by itself made a difference is uncertain given the organization's own limitations.

Nonetheless MFD's accomplishments in its short history were considerable. The MFD's stirring grassroots victory over Boyle rescued the nation's longest surviving industrial union, and UMWA militancy lived to fight again. The celebrated 1989 Pittston strike, under the presidency of the young and dynamic Richard Trumka, with its direct action and appeal to communities and progressive networks, is in part a tribute to the legacy of the MFD and the movement from which it grew. The MFD can also be credited with helping to inspire rank-and-file activism elsewhere, for example among Teamsters and Steel Workers. Thus the MFD is linked to successful reform of the UMWA and to a post-1960s history of workers fighting uphill battles to revitalize the labor movement from below as the economic retrenchment that first struck the coal industry spread throughout the economy.

PAUL SIEGEL

References and Further Reading

Brody, David. In *Labor's Cause: Main Themes in the History of the American Worker*. New York: Oxford University Press, 1993.

Clark, Paul F. *The Miners' Fight for Democracy: Arnold Miller and the Reform of the United Mine Workers*. Ithaca, NY: New York State School of Industrial and Labor Relations, Cornell University, 1981.

Dubofsky, Melvyn, and Warren Van Tine. *John L. Lewis: A Biography*. New York: Quadrangle, 1977.

Finley, Joseph, E. *The Corrupt Kingdom: The Rise and Fall of the United Mine Workers*. New York: Simon and Schuster, 1972.

Green, James R. "'Tying the Knot of Solidarity': The Pittston Strike of 1989–1990." In *The United Mine Workers of America: A Model of Industrial Solidarity?* edited by John H. M. Laslett. University Park: University of Pennsylvania Press, 1996.

Hume, Brit. *Death and the Mines: Rebellion and Murder in the United Mine Workers*. New York: Grossman Publishers, 1971.

Lewis, Ronald L. *Black Coal Miners in America: Race, Class, and Community Conflict, 1780–1980*. Lexington: University Press of Kentucky, 1987.

Nyden, Paul. "Miners for Democracy: Struggle in the Coal Fields." Ph.D. dissertation, University of Michigan: University Microfilms International, 1974.

See also **Black Lung Associations; Boyle, W. A. (Tony); Coal Mining; Federal Coal Mine Health and Safety Act; Miller, Arnold; United Mine Workers of America**

MINIMUM-WAGE LAWS

Labor reformers began to call for a legal minimum wage in United States in the late nineteenth century, arguing that those persons forced to sell their labor for a wage should be paid fairly for their work. Workers called for a "living wage," which was understood at that time to mean a familywage—an amount necessary for a male worker to support a wife and children at home. These demands grew into an effort to institute minimum-wage laws. As these were passed, the courts limited their coverage to women and children, framing them as protective legislation for the most vulnerable workers. Despite the gendered connotations of the term and legislations, many women were among the leaders of the early fight for wage standards. The first state minimum wages were passed from 1912–1923, but by the 1930s, due to new court rulings and shifts in the strategy of female reformers and the labor movement, states and eventually the federal government passed minimum wages for most workers, male and female.

In 1938, the federal government ratified the first national minimum-wage law, called the Fair Labor Standards Act (FLSA). In addition to setting a minimum hourly wage, it also required employers to pay workers working more than 40 hours per week overtime pay of time-and-a-half (this provision was amended significantly in 2004). The FLSA obviously had broader coverage than the patchwork of state minimum-wage laws, but it still included major coverage exemptions, such as domestic and agricultural workers. These exemptions particularly affected African-American workers, who were disproportionately represented in the exempted industries. The FLSA established a federal minimum wage of 25 cents an hour, to be raised to 40 cents by 1945. The law did not establish a formula for determining the wage level, and the wage was not indexed to inflation. This meant that future revisions were left up to congressional action. Over the years Congress revised the FLSA several times to raise the wage. Revisions also broadened coverage to retail establishments in 1961; to hospitals, nursing homes, schools and colleges, and laundries in 1966; and to domestic, and state and local government workers in 1974.

In the early twenty-first century, the minimum wage covers four specific categories. These include firms that have at least two employees and that do at least $500,000 per year in business; government agencies, schools and preschools, and hospitals and businesses providing medical or nursing care for residents; individuals not covered in the first two categories but whose work regularly involves them in interstate commerce (for example, producing goods that will cross state lines); and domestic workers.

Several states have set state minimum-wage rates higher than the federal level at different times since the passage of the FLSA. As of 2004, 12 states had rates higher than the federal, ranging from $5.50 in Illinois to $7.16 in Washington. Only Washington state has a minimum wage that is indexed to inflation (Alaska passed but later repealed a law requiring indexing). Seven states, all in the south, have no state minimum wage. Two states—Ohio and Kansas—have state rates lower than the federal, although this affects only those workers not covered by the federal minimum wage.

The real value of the minimum wage (the value adjusted for inflation) rose relatively consistently from its enactment in 1938 to 1968, but it has fallen on average since then. By the end of the 1980s, the real value of the minimum wage was $4.50 per hour (in 1999 dollars), the lowest it had been since 1955. By 2000, the real value had climbed slightly but was still far below its 1968 peak value.

As part of the national living-wage movement, local coalitions began efforts to pass citywide minimum wage laws in the late 1990s, searching for other ways to raise minimum wages besides waiting for a federal increase. (Before then only the District of Columbia had a citywide minimum wage, set at $1 above the federal minimum.) As of 2004, Santa Fe, New Mexico; San Francisco, California; and Madison, Wisconsin had established citywide minimum wages ranging from $5.70 in Madison (set to increase to $7.75 plus indexing in 2008), to $8.50 per hour plus indexing in Santa Fe and San Francisco.

The value of the minimum wage and the types of workers covered have always been hotly contested. Despite steady public support for regular increases to the federal minimum wage, employer lobbyists, particularly from such low-wage industries as restaurants and hotels, have been vociferous opponents. The issue has also been regularly debated among academics. While mainstream neoclassical economic theory predicts that an increase in the minimum wage leads to reduced employment, economists David Card and Alan Krueger gained attention in the 1990s with their research examining the real impact of minimum-wage increases in several cases. For example they compared fast-food restaurants on the New Jersey–Pennsylvania border after New Jersey raised its state minimum wage from $4.25 to $5.05 in 1992. Contrary to the conventional wisdom among neoclassical economists, Card and Krueger found that employers did not automatically reduce employment. Rather their findings suggest that several factors came together to pay the higher wage. First the fast-food restaurants were able to raise prices by a small amount. Second employers found that with the higher wage, they had higher productivity—perhaps due to lower turnover and absenteeism. These factors can allow employers to cover a higher minimum wage without reducing employment. However other economists, such as David Neumark and William Wascher, continue to challenge Card's and Krueger's findings, and there is no consensus within the field as to the merits of a minimum-wage increase. Even if political forces align to pass another increase to the federal minimum wage soon, the lack of indexing assures the issue will remain on the agenda in years to come.

STEPHANIE LUCE

References and Further Reading

Card, David, and Alan B. Krueger. *Myth and Measurement: The New Economics of the Minimum Wage.* Princeton, NJ: Princeton University Press, 1995.

———. "Minimum Wages and Employment: A Case Study of the Fast-Food Industry in New Jersey and Pennsylvania: Reply." *American Economic Review* 90, 5 (2000): 1397–1420.

Economic Policy Institute. "Minimum Wage Issue Guide." www.epinet.org/content.cfm/issueguides_minwage_minwage

Figart, Deborah M., Ellen Mutari, and Marilyn Powers. *Living Wages, Equal Wages: Gender and Labor Market Policies in the United States.* London, UK: Routledge, 2002.

Glickman, Lawrence B. *A Living Wage: American Workers and the Making of Consumer Society.* Ithaca, NY: Cornell University Press, 1999.

Neumark, David, and William Wascher, "Minimum Wages and Employment: A Case Study of the Fast-Food Industry in New Jersey and Pennsylvania: Comment." *American Economic Review* 90, 5 (2000): 1362–1396.

Nordlund, Willis J. *The Quest for a Living Wage: The History of the Federal Minimum-Wage Program.* Wesport, CT: Greenwood Press, 1997.

Sklar, Holly, Laryssa Mykyta, and Susan Wefald. *Raise the Floor: Wages and Policies That Work for All of Us.* New York: MS Foundation for Women, 2001.

U.S. Department of Labor, "Minimum Wage." www.dol.gov/dol/topic/wages/minimumwage.htm.

Waltman, Jerold. *The Politics of the Minimum Wage.* Urbana: University of Illinois Press, 2000.

See also **Living Wage Campaigns**

MINING, COAL

Coal is a fossil fuel that has been mined by working people, slave and free, in the United States since the colonial period. The labor of coal miners initially centered in the Appalachians and the Midwest provided the raw materials for heating homes, running the railroads, making steel, and keeping factories humming. Severe threats to miners' lives and limbs, as well as economic hardships, were a regular feature of life for coal miners and their families. In response to these shared conditions, coal miners pioneered socially conscious industrial unionism. Coal mining became increasingly mechanized through the twentieth century. As a result employment of coal miners has dropped dramatically since its historic peak during the World War I era of more than 700,000 to some 74,000 today, though production of coal has doubled to over one billion tons annually.

Early Coal Mining Industry

The first recorded observation of coal by a European in what became the United States appears in the 1679 journal of Belgian-born missionary Louis Hennepin, who traveled with La Salle and noted deposits of coal on the Illinois River near modern-day Ottawa, Illinois. But long before Illinois coal miners were to begin digging in the early 1800s, colonists had discovered coal far to the east, and the coalfields of Richmond, Virginia, formed the first U.S. coal-mining region in the early 1700s. Early miners included European immigrant farmers who mined coal to use or sell to blacksmiths, as well as enslaved Africans, who were leased to owners of coal lands. Coal was discovered in western Virginia in 1742. By the early 1800s, mining in the Kanawha valley employed large numbers of enslaved workers, who mined coal for the booming salt industry of that region. Some slave owners who contracted out to the salt industry requested their slaves not be placed in the mines, so as to protect their investment in human chattel. In the United States as a whole in 1840, there were some 6,800 mine workers who produced less than 2 million tons of coal.

High-carbon, nearly smokeless, extremely hard anthracite coal was available in a six-county area of eastern Pennsylvania—Carbon, Columbia, Lackawanna, Luzerne, Northumberland, and Schuylkill—but iron makers preferred charcoal, since anthracite was difficult to burn. In 1840, however, the development of the hot-blast method for smelting iron, which successfully burned anthracite, boosted the value of hard coal. By 1853, anthracite miners brought up some 11 million tons, and until the 1860s, their region produced more coal than all other regions combined, which included bituminous or soft coal fields in Ohio, Indiana, Illinois, western Pennsylvania, Maryland, and Virginia. The baking of coal into coke as a fuel for the steel industry also expanded, with an annual production of three million tons by 1880, centered in the Connellsville region of southwestern Pennsylvania.

The spread of industry and railroads westward opened up new fields for soft-coal mining. In Illinois the completion of the Illinois Central in 1855 spurred coal development, and by 1879, the state's miners had dug over 2.6 million tons. By 1907, the state was second only to Pennsylvania in coal production. Similarly in southern West Virginia, where Kanawha County operators had sent coal to their commercial customers down the Ohio River on flatboat, the arrival of the railroads in the 1800s transformed the industry. West Virginia coal production increased from a mere 489,000 tons in 1867 to over 89 million tons by 1917.

West of the Mississippi, in the Colorado and Wyoming coalfields, the Union Pacific, the Atchison, Topeka, and Santa Fe, and other companies wrangled over coal lands and employed miners in towns like Crested Butte, Colorado, and Rock Springs, Wyoming.

Mining Work: The Hand-Loading Era

Underground coalmines came in three basic varieties: Drifts, slopes, and shafts. Drifts were dug straight into a coal vein that was visible in the side of a hill or bluff. Slopes were dug on a gradual downward slant from ground level. Shafts were dug straight down, hundreds of feet in depth. Regardless of how miners entered the mine, the most common approach to getting coal out was the room-and-pillar method, still widely in use today. The mine was organized around a central transport tunnel called the main entry. Branching off from the main entry at right angles was a series of side entries. As one proceeded down a side entry along which coal was hauled, smaller tunnels branched off at right angles, like side streets, at regular intervals. Walking down one of these side streets, some 15–35 feet wide, depending on the quality of the coal, one sooner or later would confront a solid wall of coal, the "working face." The side street, up to 400 feet long when the coal is fully mined or worked out was the room in which the miner worked. Along the side walls or ribs of the room, at periodic intervals, were cross-cuts. These were relatively narrow openings, equivalent to alleys between the side streets, which led to the adjoining room. The cross-cuts allowed the air to circulate up through each working room to the face and enabled miners to pass easily between rooms. Between two cross-cuts, stood a four-sided block of coal, the pillar, which served to hold up the roof of the mine. Coal veins varied in thickness from 2–25 feet. Lying both above and below the vein were layers of dirt, soapstone, and slate, which formed the bottom and roof of the mine.

The distinguishing characteristic of the early slope and drift mines was the multiplicity of roles taken on by the pick miner. On a typical workday, mine cap on and carbide lamp lit, he walked into the mine on his own power and headed toward his entry. As he arrived at his room, he surveyed the scene. There stood wooden mine props he had capped and pushed into place to support the roof. Next to the right rib sat his hand-cranked augur drill alongside a keg of black blasting powder, which he used to "shoot" the coal. Shooting involved drilling holes into the face of the coal, filling them with explosive, setting the fuses correctly, and then lighting the charges. Next to the left rib, he spied his pick, which he had used for 3 hours the previous afternoon undercutting the coal-face. At times lying on his side, he had carved out a 6-inch-high and six-foot-deep empty shelf, so that the coal had room to fall. A length of wooden coal car tracks ran up the center of the room toward the face; he had just added the last section after undercutting the previous day. Sprawling across the front of his room were 5 tons of freshly cut coal he had blasted before leaving work the evening before. All he needed now was an empty coal car, which if the mine were small enough, he would fetch himself, fill with chunks of coal, and push to the mine bottom, perhaps towed by his trusty mine dog.

Until the mid-twentieth century, coal miners were paid by the ton. This meant that when a miner had dug enough coal for his own tastes, he put down his tools, walked out of his room and went home for the day. This miner's freedom was the envy of many workers who labored under factory discipline and the bane of many a mine manager's existence. The character of the pick miner as an independent contractor selling his services and product to the mine owner could also encourage divisions with other mine workers who were not, properly speaking, miners. In the anthracite fields in particular, it was common for pick miners to hire laborers as subcontractors. The nineteenth-century conception of the miner as an independent skilled artisan helps explain why early mining union leaders, such as Illinois's Daniel Weaver, became small mine owners and did not see a conflict between their status as workers and businessmen.

As the nineteenth century progressed, the pick miner was joined by a growing army of mine workers, called company men, who were paid by the day. Trappers—often young boys—secured the doors. In anthracite boys also worked picking slate out of the coal in the aboveground breaker. Timbermen, mule drivers, and later locomotive motormen also took their place in the mines. With the introduction of shaft mining, a "cager" took charge of loading and unloading coal and miners between the bottom and the surface. A variety of general bottom laborers cleared coal and slate from the tracks, brought supplies to miners, built wooden "brattices" that kept the air course running correctly, and performed other needed tasks. With the proliferation of deeper and larger shaft mines in the late nineteenth century, the hoisting engineer became a regular addition to the mine along with the pumpman, who managed the process of forcing water hundreds of feet upward to the surface. Mine workers with a specialty in laying iron and then steel track were hired as tracklayers. They not only laid track on the entries, but gradually took over from the pick miner the laying of track in individual rooms.

While the pick miner held a special place in the more primitive mines, the development of new undercutting technology in the 1870s and 1880s began to eat away at the centrality of the miner's craft skills by providing a mechanical substitute for the miner's pick. Initial designs included a rotating cutter bar armed with steel teeth as well as a long cylindrical punch machine that repeatedly struck the coal like a jackhammer; both models were powered by compressed air. The preferred technology became the electric-powered chain undercutter, first sold in 1893, which worked like a wide chainsaw ripping into the bottom of the coalface. No longer did a miner need to be skilled with the pick—the machine did it for him. The widespread adoption of the undercutting machine heralded the entrance of a new brand of worker into the coalmines: The loader. Depending on the degree of mechanization and specialization in the mine, many loaders continued to timber their working places, lay rail, and set shots. Increasingly though loaders, who were often new immigrants from southern and eastern Europe and in the western mines, from China and Japan, spent their time on one task—shoveling coal.

In addition to facing the challenges of mechanization, coal miners, coal loaders, and mine laborers all had to contend with chronic underemployment. From 1913 to 1918 (a span that includes 2 years of economic depression as well as the war boom), the national average of coal-mining days worked was 206.5, or two-thirds of a possible 312. But this average conceals wide swings in employment over time. In Illinois for instance, in the year ending February 1919, mines worked an average of 256 days. But for the year ending June 30, 1924, the average dropped to 140. In local mines that produced fuel for home heating, miners were often were laid off starting April 1. In shipping mines that sold to manufacturing companies and railroads, a number of factors limited regular work. The chaotic railroad system often left mines without cars to pick up coal, and the intense competition between mining companies operating at low margins meant that mines often shut down for lack of customers. At the same time, mines had to retain a skeleton workforce to maintain the mine physically and keep it safe, which encouraged overproduction, lowered coal prices, and created pressure to lower tonnage and day rates.

Coal Mining Hazards

From 1839 to 2006, there were 614 coalmine disasters killing five or more workers, totaling 13,805 deaths.

But the number of injuries was always far higher. During the 1930s, for instance, coal miners averaged annually 1,500 deaths and about 81,000 injuries. The dangers of coal mining stemmed from four main sources, described by miners as bad air, bad top, bad roads, bad shots. In the period following the Civil War, many relatively shallow mines were still ventilated by the natural method—that is, particularly in colder weather, the warmer air underground rose, pulling the colder air down the shaft and through the workings. Mine operators also commonly installed a furnace at the foot of the shaft, which had a similar drawing effect (and also tended to start mine fires, such as the landmark Avondale disaster that killed 110 miners in Plymouth, Pennsylvania, in 1869). Increasingly though as mines got deeper and miners demanded higher standards, coal companies installed large electrically powered drawing fans, which pulled the air through an intricate maze of entries, crosscuts, and doorways to provide air for every working area of the mine. Miners were particularly wary of methane gas, or "fire damp," which is naturally emitted by coal, is colorless and odorless, hangs near the roof of the mine, and is highly explosive. Methane buildup caused many explosions, such as the Wadge mining disaster of 1942 in Mount Harris, Colorado, that killed 34.

Less dramatic but possibly even more deadly were a variety of gases that conspired to rob miners of their health over time. The primary two were black damp or choke damp (carbon dioxide), produced by burning black powder and given off by all organic matter, living and dead, underground; and white damp (carbon monoxide), produced mainly by powder explosions and fires. Odorless, colorless, and normally mixed in with healthy air, these two invisible poisons were slow and insidious underground killers. Coal dust as well posed a danger to the lives of mineworkers. Nearly every activity in the mine stirred up dust, from moving along the haulage ways by foot, car, or mule to undercutting, blasting, and loading coal. Not only did coal dust magnify the destructive effect of a gas explosion, but it killed miners "by the inches." As late as the 1930s, while medical authorities had realized the dangers of silica dust, they failed to recognize the negative effects of plain coal dust on miners' health. Miner's asthma was not recognized by the federal government as pneumoconiosis, or black lung disease, until the 1960s, although doctors in the United States and England had identified the disease in the nineteenth century.

Roof falls, or bad top, killed more miners than any other mining hazard. A study of Illinois miners found that in 1916, for example, 63% of the mine deaths and 38% of the injuries in one region resulted from some type of roof fall. Most of these incidents occurred in the miner's or loader's room. When coal companies were sued in court for injuries or death caused by bad top, they often claimed that the miner's inattention and irresponsibility had resulted in his death. In some cases miners had not taken full precaution in setting roof props, but one main reason for this was the piece-rate system of payment and miners' intermittent employment—if miners took more time to set props, they might miss the chance to load enough coal for the few days they were working.

Work on the haulage roads could also be a source of considerable anxiety. Rotten railroad ties, sagging rails, falling coal, failing entry props, lingering smoke from shooting coal, and above all, piled up coal-dust on the roads could make for treacherous conditions. The coal debris—known as "gob"—beside the tracks made walking hazardous. Mine managers did routinely order dusty entries sprinkled and cleaned, but state laws generally gave them wide legal latitude in deciding on the frequency of sprinkling.

Finally especially in mines where miners shot their coal "off the solid"—meaning it was not undercut, and they used extra powder to get the coal down—there was always the chance of a blown-out or "windy" shot, in which the deadly force of the explosion was directed outward into the room rather than into the block of coal. Such a mishap, perhaps combined with coal dust, is believed to be the cause of the worst mining disaster in U.S. history, the Monongah, West Virginia, explosion of 1907 that took the lives of 362 miners.

The Evolution of Coal-Mining Unionism

Anthracite miners pioneered the first short-lived union in the Schuylkill region in 1848–1849, when miner John Bates mobilized some 5,000 miners to fight for pay increases. Within another decade the first attempts at a national union of coal miners took root in the Midwest. Founded by British-born miners and former Chartists, Daniel Weaver and Thomas Lloyd, the American Miners' Association (AMA) emerged in the course of a successful 1861 strike in St. Clair County, Illinois. Strikers targeted mine operators who shortchanged miners on the true weight of coal they dug by claiming it was intermixed with too much slate. In response the AMA, and later unions, demanded that operators allow for a union check-weigh man, who would ensure that miners' daily tonnage was accurately weighed. Miners from Ohio, Pennsylvania, Maryland, and West Virginia joined Weaver and Lloyd in establishing the AMA,

which lasted until the economic depression of 1867 depleted its membership. As midwestern coal miners began to recover from the initial blows of the postwar economic depression, they formed in 1872 the Miners' Benevolent and Protective Association, which encompassed coal diggers from Illinois, Indiana, and Missouri. With a proven record of leadership ability and 23 years in the mines, Walton Rutledge was chosen first secretary, serving for 2 years until the organization became part of the Miners' National Association (MNA), established in 1874.

Meanwhile in 1868, led by Irish-born John Siney from St. Clair, Pennsylvania, in Schuylkill County, the anthracite miners struck to enforce a new 8-hour law. They then formed the Workingmen's Benevolent Association (WBA), which promoted cooperatives, sick and death benefits, trade agreements with employers, and arbitration of disputes. In 1870, its members signed the first written contract with coal operators. The price was the sliding scale of wages pegged to the price of coal. Strikes, in the WBA's view, were primarily for restricting the supply of coal to raise its price on the market, hence allowing employers to raise wages. This conception of the harmony of interest between coal miners and their employers, based on the model provided by famed unionist Alexander McDonald of the Scottish miners, would die hard, although the WBA lasted only until 1875. It was a casualty of the Panic of 1873 but also of an anti-union campaign unleashed by Franklin B. Gowen of the Reading Railroad, who bought up Schuylkill coal lands, lowered wages, and offered a benefit plan for miners to undercut the WBA. Gowen then collaborated with Allan Pinkerton to combat the Molly Maguires, whose brand of retributive justice Gowen linked in the minds of many with the cause of coal unionism.

For the next 15 years, a succession of national unions, none lasting more than a few years, followed the WBA. The MNA had limited participation from anthracite miners, though Siney served as its president and the group had 35,000 members spread across 12 states by 1875. But legal attacks on Siney and other leaders, as well as conflicts within the MNA over the utility of arbitration, severely weakened the group by 1876. Coal miners were also a large part of the Knights of Labor (KOL), often in mixed assemblies that contained a variety of types of workers, and sometimes in local trade assemblies of miners only. Complaints from coal miners about this situation led the KOL to establish National Trade Assembly (NTA) No. 135 in 1886. But just before the KOL acted, in 1885 prominent mining unionists John McBride, Chris Evans, and Daniel McLaughlin led the formation of the National Federation of Miners and Mine Laborers. The federation called for the 8-hour day, state laws for miners' health and safety, an end to convict mining, mine run of coal (which meant miners were paid for the full weight of coal mined before it was run over screens), and an end to company stores. That year the federation's representatives from Illinois, Indiana, Ohio, and Pennsylvania—the Central Competitive Field (CCF)—met in Columbus, Ohio, with a group of coal operators and for the first time agreed on an interstate scale of wages. In 1888, some elements of NTA No. 135 left the KOL and merged with the federation to create the National Progressive Union of Miners and Mine Laborers (NPU). Formal rivalry with the KOL finally ended on January 22, 1890, in Columbus, Ohio, when 198 delegates of the NPU and NTA No. 135 joined together to form the United Mine Workers of America (UMWA).

The constitution of the new union set forth the UMWA's objectives: To secure decent earnings, to do away with payment in scrip to company stores, to advance mine safety, to win the 8-hour day, to obtain education for miners' children, to enact laws protecting miners' health and safety, and to adjust differences with employers peacefully, so that strikes would become unnecessary. A national coal strike in 1897 finally brought CCF operators and the UMWA agreement in 1898 on a union scale, the 8-hour day, and mine run of coal. While the agreement left out West Virginia, the anthracite miners, and miners in the South and West, it was a milestone for the new miners' union.

Mechanization of Mining

As the fledgling union began to flex its muscles and organize miners into a solid mass, coal operators were steadily mechanizing the mines. Undercutting machines were just the first step, as companies such as the Jeffrey Manufacturing Company and later, Joseph Joy and his Joy Machine Company, began to build and sell mechanical loaders. Joy's 4BU loader debuted in 1922 and was used mainly in non-union mines at first, given well-grounded expectation of opposition from UMWA members. The loader operated by means of rotating scooping arms that gathered the blasted coal onto a conveyer that carried the coal onto a shuttle.

As coal production plunged after World War I, UMWA President John L. Lewis championed the idea that there were too many mines and too many miners. A consolidation of the industry, with a higher degree of mechanization, would create long-term stable employment for the nation's miners. Indeed by 1948,

nearly two-thirds of all coal in the United States was mechanically loaded and 90% was mechanically undercut. All that remained to mechanize was the removal of coal still done by blasting. Jeffrey already had developed an entry driver, a machine that would cut through coal to create tunnels in the mine. The next step was the continuous miner, introduced in the late 1940s, which used a rotating drum equipped with steel teeth for cutting bits. By the early twenty-first century, the latest versions could mine coal at the rate of 38 tons a minute. Setting props was also mechanized by the introduction of machines that drill steel bolts into the mine roof. Not only were roof bolts safer, but they allowed mechanical loaders and continuous miners to move more freely through the mine.

Despite the overall decline in death and injury in the mines during the twentieth century, machinery introduced new dangers. From 1929 to 1944, for instance, explosions caused by electricity were responsible for the majority of mining deaths. Loading and mining machines kicked up a great amount of dust. And the huge capital outlay for loading machines put pressure to speed up production, to use more blasting powder to create more loadable coal, and to shoot coal with men in the mines. All of these combined to create the Centralia, Illinois, mine disaster of 1947 that killed 111 men.

The UMWA and the Changing Demographics of Coal Mining

Coal miners in the pre-Civil War era were overwhelmingly drawn from England, Wales, and Scotland. After the Civil War, they were joined by those of Irish and German extraction. As mechanical undercutters entered the mines, miners from southern and eastern Europe joined the mine workforce. In the West Union Pacific Railroad hired Chinese- and then Japanese-born coal miners in Wyoming. The early generations of miners often resented the new immigrant coal loaders, whom they viewed as interlopers, and in Rock Springs, Wyoming, in 1885 KOL miners rioted against Chinese miners, killing 28 and wounding 15. On the other hand, by 1907 in Rock Springs, Japanese miners became part of the UMWA local. Similarly starting in 1918, District 12 of the UMWA, covering the state of Illinois, printed its union constitution in English, Serbo-Croatian, Polish, Lithuanian, Italian, and French. And not surprisingly, in newly unionizing sections of the Pennyslvania coalfields, such as Windber in the 1920s, Slovak and Hungarian miners flocked into the leadership of the union. Unionized Mexican-born miners worked in the mines of the Rocky Mountains and the southwest. A central leader of the Colorado miners was Louis Tikas, a Greek immigrant who was martyred in the Ludlow Massacre of 1914.

Negotiating the terrain of Jim Crow segregation was perhaps more difficult, and the extent to which the UMWA succeeded has been vigorously debated by historians. African-Americans were among the nation's first coal miners in the Chesapeake. After the Civil War, they continued to work privately owned mines in Tennessee and Alabama, hired out by prison officials to mine owners as convict laborers. A rebellion by black and white free miners in Tennessee helped put an end to private convict mine labor by 1896. At the same time, African-American miners also labored as free workers in the Alabama mines, where they formed over half of unionized miners by 1902, though they met in segregated locals. Similarly in West Virginia, black miners were roughly one-quarter of the coal-mining workforce in southern West Virginia in 1910, and by 1931 in some counties they made up one-third of the total.

While the image of coal mining as an exclusively male occupation persists today, female coal miners had toiled in British mines for centuries until forced out by an act of Parliament in 1842. Though they were kept out of American mines by custom, law, and union opposition, women did work sporadically in U.S. mines as part of a family labor system, primarily in small mines leased by coal miners in the Appalachian region. During World War II, the employment of women increased, as they took aboveground jobs working in mine shops and tipples. In the early 1970s, under the impact of the women's movement, affirmative action in the steel industry, which owned captive mines, and a spurt of new hiring due to the oil crisis, women were hired to work underground. They formed the Coal Employment Project in 1977 to advocate for women facing discrimination and sexual harassment from mine managers and male coal miners. By 1979, nearly 3,000 women had been hired as underground miners, mainly in West Virginia, Pennsylvania, Illinois, and Alabama. The UMWA women were coldly received by the international union leadership, but with the election of Richard Trumka as international UMWA president in 1982, they began to receive more official support.

Coal Mining and the Government

As early as 1870, reacting to the horrors of the Avondale disaster, Ohio miners proposed legislation regulating the mines. An act passed in 1874 provided for two separate openings in mines employing over 10 miners, specified the volume of air to circulate in the mines, required daily inspection before work by a fire boss or fire viewer, gave miners the right to appoint a check-weigh man at the mine, and mandated the appointment of mine inspectors to enforce the law. With the help of Illinois miners' leader Daniel McLaughlin, later elected to the state general assembly on the Greenback-Labor ticket, Illinois passed a similar mining law in 1872. Other coal-mining states followed in rapid succession, though coal operators strenuously opposed legal regulation. Passage of laws did not guarantee enforcement however, and mine inspector services were generally underfunded and understaffed, with West Virginia the worst and Ohio the best.

Federal regulation began with an 1891 act of the U.S. Congress that regulated coalmines only in federal territories. Revisions in the early 1900s provided for specialized shot firers to shoot coal when miners were out of the mine and for watering down or removal of coal dust. As of 1902, the law applied only to mines in Indian Territory (Oklahoma) and New Mexico Territory employing 20 or more miners. Popular outrage over the Monongah disaster and the Cherry, Illinois, mine fire of 1909 that killed 259 miners helped propel Congress to create the U.S. Bureau of Mines in the Department of the Interior in 1910. Even though the bureau established mine-safety stations in the coalfields, conducted research on coal dust, and promoted rock dusting, now standard practice in underground mines, its dual commitment to boosting the mining industry and protecting miners limited its effectiveness.

Federal government involvement in the coal-mining industry expanded in 1902 when President Theodore Roosevelt personally intervened to mediate a strike by coal miners against the Pennylvania anthracite operators. While only a third of the 150,000 anthracite miners belonged to the UMWA, nearly all the miners walked out over a range of issues including tonnage and daily pay rates and disputes over weighing of coal. The UMWA International President John Mitchell publicly faced off against Reading Railroad President and coal operator George Baer, whose J. P. Morgan-controlled company owned many mines in the anthracite region. After 6 months on strike, as operators refused to budge, miners refused to return to work, and cold weather was approaching, Roosevelt called representatives of the miners and operators to the White House for a historic meeting. While the deadlock remained, pressure from Roosevelt on J. P. Morgan, along with the continuing intransigence of the miners, resulted eventually in an agreement from miners and operators to submit their claims to an arbitration board. Once the miners returned to work in October 1902, the Anthracite Coal Strike Commission, led by Roosevelt's Commissioner of Labor Carroll Wright, conducted 3 months of hearings involving over 500 witnesses. The outcome was a compromise on wages and hours and the establishment of an ongoing arbitration board to hear anthracite cases. While the UMWA was not recognized as a bargaining agent for the miners, Mitchell claimed victory, and some have viewed the settlement as a de facto recognition of the union. Though the anthracite miners were not solidly unionized by the UMWA for decades, the intervention of President Roosevelt is often seen to mark a progressive break in a long pattern of open federal strike breaking. The government was now in the mediation business, and a long series of federal coal commissions would follow.

It was not until 1941 that Congress empowered federal mine inspectors to enter mines in the states. In 1947, shortly after the Centralia, Illinois, disaster, Congress provided for the promulgation of a federal code of regulations on mine safety, Title 30 of the Code of Federal Regulations (30 CFR). Five years later, after the West Frankfort, Illinois, disaster that killed 119, Congress passed the Federal Coal Mine Safety Act. It provided for annual inspections of larger mines and gave the bureau the power to issue violation notices and imminent danger withdrawal orders. Civil penalties could be assessed against mine owners for violating such orders but none for violating safety provisions in the first place.

In 1966, the law was extended to cover all coalmines. Under the impact of the Farmington, West Virginia, disaster in 1968, which killed 78, as well as grassroots pressure in West Virginia, powered by a broader Miners for Democracy movement against the Tony Boyle leadership of the union, Congress passed the Federal Coal Mine Health and Safety Act of 1969 (Coal Act). This law extended coverage to surface mines, required four inspections per year of every underground mine, initiated fines for company safety violations and criminal penalties for willful violations. It also for the first time provided compensation for miners with black lung. In 1973, the secretary of the interior created the Mining Enforcement and Safety Administration as a separate agency from the Bureau of Mines. Finally in 1977, Congress enacted the Federal Mine Safety and Health Act, establishing the Mine Safety and Health Administration (MSHA), which moved to the Department of Labor, enhancing miners' legal rights to report safety violations and consolidating all federal mining-safety regulations. In that year Congress also passed the Surface Mining Control and Reclamation Act. It resulted mainly from concerns about the environmental impact of strip mining but also provided for federal regulation of coal-mining safety on federal land as well as on Indian reservations, where Navajo and Hopi people mine coal for Peabody Energy.

Coal Mining Today

Coal miners work today in 25 different states. The majority, some 41,000, still work underground and one-third of them are unionized. Workers in surface or strip mines are a growing minority of the mining workforce and only 22% belong to a union. They mine the majority of coal, which is mainly used to fuel electrical power plants. Though most coal is still mined east of the Mississippi, the top coal producing state today is Wyoming, including its Powder River Basin, where miners extract over one-third of all coal mined in the United States. Death and injury rates have fallen substantially. But the Sago Mine disaster in Tallmansville, West Virginia, in January 2006, killing 12 miners at a nonunion mine that had been cited for numerous serious safety violations by the MSHA, points to the challenges facing coal miners today.

CARL R. WEINBERG

References and Further Reading

Adams, Sean Patrick. *Old Dominion, Industrial Commonwealth: Coal, Politics, and Economy in Antebellum America*. Baltimore, MD: Johns Hopkins University Press, 2004.

Beik, Mildred Allen. *The Miners of Windber: The Struggles of New Immigrants for Unionization, 1890s–1930s*. University Park: The Pennsylvania State University Press, 1996.

Blatz, Perry K. *Democratic Miners: Work and Labor Relations in the Anthracite Coal Industry*. Albany: State University of New York Press, 1994.

Calderon, Roberto. *Mexican Coal-Mining Labor in Texas and Coahuila, 1880–1930*. College Station: Texas A & M University Press, 2000.

Corbin, David Alan. *Life, Work, and Rebellion in the Coal Fields: The Southern West Virginia Miners, 1880–1922*. Urbana and Chicago: University of Illinois Press, 1981.

Derickson, Alan. *Black Lung: Anatomy of a Public Health Disaster*. Ithaca, NY: Cornell University Press, 1998.

Dix, Keith. *What's a Coal Miner to Do? The Mechanization of Coal Mining*. Pittsburgh, PA: University of Pittsburgh Press, 1988.

Fishback, Price. *Soft Coal, Hard Choices: The Economic Welfare of Bituminous Miners*. New York: Oxford University Press, 1992.

Fox, Maier B. *United We Stand: The United Mine Workers of America, 1890–1990*. Washington, DC: International Union, United Mine Workers of America, 1990.

Goodrich, Carter. *The Miner's Freedom: A Study of the Working Life in a Changing Industry.* Boston, MA: Marshall Jones Co., 1925.

Graebner, William. *Coal Mining Safety in the Progressive Period. Lexington:* University Press of Kentucky, 1976.

Ichioka, Yuji. "Asian Immigrant Coal Miners and the United Mine Workers of America: Race and Class in Rock Springs, Wyoming, 1907." *Amerasia* 6, 2 (June 1979): 1–24.

Laslett, John H. M. *Colliers across the Sea: A Comparative Study of Class Formation in Scotland and the American Midwest, 1830–1924.* Urbana and Chicago: University of Illinois Press, 2000.

Laslett, John H. M., ed. *The United Mine Workers of America: A Model of Industrial Solidarity?* University Park: The Pennsylvania State University Press, 1996.

Letwin, Daniel. *The Challenge of Interracial Unionism: Alabama Coal Miners, 1878–1921.* Chapel Hill and London: University of North Carolina Press, 1998.

Lewis, Ronald. *Black Coal Miners in America: Race, Class, and Community Conflict, 1780–1980.* Lexington: University Press of Kentucky, 1987.

Long, Priscilla. *Where the Sun Never Shines: A History of America's Bloody Coal Industry.* New York: Paragon House, 1989.

Moore, Marat. *Women in the Mines: Stories of Life and Work, 1920–1994.* New York: Macmillan/Twayne, 1996.

Shapiro, Karin. *A New South Rebellion: The Battle against Convict Labor in the Tennessee Coalfields, 1871–1896.* Chapel Hill and London: University of North Carolina Press, 1998.

Smith, Barbara Ellen. *Digging Our Own Graves: Coal Miners and the Struggle over Black Lung Disease.* Philadelphia, PA: Temple University Press, 1987.

Tintori, Karen. *Trapped: The 1909 Cherry Mine Disaster.* New York: Atria Books, 2002.

Trotter, Joe William. *Coal, Class, and Color: Blacks in Southern West Virginia, 1915–32.* Urbana and Chicago: University of Illinois Press, 1990.

Wallace, Anthony F. *St. Clair: A Nineteenth-Century Coal Town's Experience with a Disaster-Prone Industry.* New York: Alfred A. Knopf, 1987.

Whiteside, James. *Regulating Danger: The Struggle for Mine Safety in the Rocky Mountain Coal Industry.* Lincoln and London: University of Nebraska Press, 1990.

Wieck, Edward A. *The American Miners' Association: A Record of the Origin of Coal Miners' Unions in the United States.* New York: Russell Sage Foundation, 1940.

See also **Anthracite Coal Strike (1902); Boyle, W. A. (Tony); Knights of Labor; Lewis, John L.; Ludlow Massacre (1914); Miners for Democracy; Molly Maguires; Trumka, Richard L.; United Mine Workers of America**

MINING, HARDROCK

Hardrock mining—mining metals from ore-bearing rock—was practiced for centuries to glean copper, tin, and precious metals. The work processes and labor relationships of U.S. hardrock mining varied over time and region and with the kind of ore being mined. Hardrock miners have been prominent in U.S. labor history for their militant industrial unions, for brutal confrontations with employers and the state, and for their leadership in founding the Western Federation of Miners (WFM), Western Labor Union (WLU), Industrial Workers of the World (IWW), and Congress of Industrial Organizations (CIO). This entry covers the California Gold Rush through the post-World War II period, concentrating primarily on the earlier decades.

Industrialization

From the 1848 discovery of gold at Sutter's Fort, a series of gold and silver rushes drew prospectors to the North American West. Small groups of placer miners panned or sluiced ore from California's streams and gravel beds and developed a system of law and custom that required work and occupation in good faith to own a claim. Placers were rapidly depleted, to be replaced by lode, or quartz, mining: Deep-shaft operations that removed the rock from which placer metals had eroded, in which the ore was not naturally separated but must later be milled or refined. Mining rapidly became an industrial enterprise requiring massive capital investment to sink shafts, purchase machinery, build railroads, and refine ore. Work and ownership became separate: Miners worked for wages; mines belonged to stockholders who neither worked nor occupied them.

Industrialization brought new demands for metals. Wisconsin's lead mines attracted an international workforce by the mid-nineteenth century, and steel production drove the development of the Minnesota iron range. By the late nineteenth century, a burgeoning electronics industry spurred copper mining in Arizona, Utah, Montana, and Michigan. Silver camps closed throughout the Rockies after the 1893 repeal of the Sherman Silver Purchase Act, but gold-based currency and new cyanide and chlorination processes for separating base from precious metals made it profitable to refine low-grade gold ores. The U.S. government closed silver and gold mines during World War II to divert labor to base metals. Then new atomic industries led to a postwar boom in uranium mining. By the late twentieth century, rising gold prices and new refining methods, like heap leach cyanide production, made it profitable to work low-grade ores and prompted an extension of open-pit mining from base metals to gold. Leadville, Colorado, represented in microcosm the trajectories of hardrock development: A brief gold boom after 1858 was followed by extensive underground silver mining after 1876, and then in the twentieth century, by molybdenum for steel production.

Mining industrialization eroded some skills but demanded new ones to run hoists, set dynamite charges to break out the most ore and least waste rock, run tramming systems, and refine complex ores. Underground miners risked cave-ins and explosions. The dangers increased with dynamite, cyanide, power drills that spewed rock dust, inadequate timbering, improperly grounded electric hoists, and other technologies that increased both the profits and the hazards of hardrock mining. Mining communities have born the environmental costs of heavy metals and dangerous chemicals in their soil and water tables.

Mining Workforces

The instabilities of an extractive industry—limited ore supplies, high recovery costs, and unstable markets— created boom-and-bust hardrock communities whose mobile workforces followed the changing fortunes of the industry. Hopes for wealth or decent wages drew diverse workers. The California gold rush attracted hopeful prospectors, particularly from the U.S. North and Midwest, Mexico, Chile, China, Ireland, Cornwall (UK), France, and Germany. Some doubtless dreamed of riches; they were pushed as well by drought, famine, revolution, factories that eroded artisans' skills and independence, and by worked-out mines where they had honed their skills. Subsequent booms and the pits and shafts of industrial mining attracted selectively diverse workforces. International migrations fed the processes of workforce and class formation that determined who worked underground for wages and who mined the short-lived placers; who sojourned in the diggings, and who stayed to labor.

After the gold rush, native-born Americans tended to move quickly and disproportionately out of mining, as industrial operations attracted more immigrants and skilled miners from eastern coal and lead mines. By 1870, in the industrial mining town of Grass Valley, California, only one workingman in four was a native-born American. While French gold seekers and New England craftsmen might sojourn briefly in the goldfields, the Irish potato famine, diminished Cornish tin reserves, famine and warfare in China's Guandong Province, and other dislocations propelled more permanent migrants, followed in the early twentieth century by more Slavs, Swedes, Finns, Italians, Japanese,

and Greeks. British miners came from Wales, from the Yorkshire coalfields, and especially from generations of Cornish miners who had dug tin, copper, and china clay. By the end of the nineteenth century, Cornwall lost at least a third of its population. Many migrated multiple times: To dig lead in Wisconsin, copper in Australia and Michigan, silver in Nevada or Idaho, gold in Colorado. Some Irish miners dug coal in Pennsylvania; their sons sought the relative safety and higher wages of hardrock.

The ethnic compositions of local workforces varied. Chain migrations might draw Cornish to Michigan's Upper Peninsula, Irish to Butte, Finns to Michigan and Minnesota. On Nevada's Comstock Lode, the Cornish and Irish each comprised a third of all miners. A majority of Idaho miners in 1870 were Chinese; almost half of the rest were immigrants. In 1900, Butte was 26% first- or second-generation Irish; in the Cripple Creek gold district, 70% of miners were native-born, but three in ten adults were second-generation immigrants.

Racial hierarchies and barriers divided the hardrock social landscapes. Ethnicity could operate positively for the Irish who worked in Marcus Daly's Butte mines, or for the Cornish, hired by foremen and shift bosses for whom Cornishness connoted skill regardless of actual experience. In contrast Mexicans, Chileans, and Chinese were run out of many hardrock centers and restricted to the placers. Subjected to a selectively enforced California Foreign Miners' Tax from 1852–1870, the Chinese were allowed underground only in deadly quicksilver mines. Comstock miners organized a Workingmen's Protective Union "to protect the interests of the white workingman against the encroachments of capital and Coolie labor." Miners supported enactment of the Chinese Exclusion Act of 1882 and led anti-Chinese riots throughout the West in 1885 and 1886.

A "white man's camp" was idealized throughout the hardrock West, but the meanings of whiteness varied. In Rossland, B.C., most gold miners came from Britain, the United States, or Canada and traced their ethnic origins to England, Scotland, Ireland, or Wales, but significant minorities of Swedes, Italians, and Germans also labored there. More Italians and Chinese lived in Rossland than in Colorado gold camps, but they faced heavy discrimination. In Utah native-born miners and immigrants from northern and western Europe tried to exclude Greeks, Japanese, and Mexican Americans from their WFM local. Italians and Finns mined in 1910. Ethnic tensions divided the Butte Irish and Cornish, and these old-timers from the newcomers. In 1912, 500 Finnish miners complained that the Butte Miners' Union refused to support Finnish members. In Arizona and New Mexico, a dual labor system separated white workers from Mexicans and Mexican-Americans. In Colorado Mexicans, Italians, and Greeks worked in coal but not hardrock. The white man's camp of Cripple Creek excluded Mexicans, Asians, southern and eastern Europeans, but not African-Americans.

White men's camps enforced the local practices of racial exclusion and the assumptions of a mining industry that employed only men. Women were vastly outnumbered; California mining populations were 97% male in 1850. In Colorado a year after the Pike's Peak boom, women were outnumbered 17 to 1. But as the placers dwindled and quartz mining stabilized, the ratios became somewhat more balanced—in 1870, almost 4 Californians in 10 were female. By 1900, there were three men to each two women in the industrial mining centers of Cripple Creek and Butte. Placers and boomtowns attracted more young single men, while stable deep-shaft mining attracted older, experienced miners who married, bought homes, built schools, and organized.

Hardrock communities offered narrow options for women. As wives, mothers, and wageworkers they supplied men's domestic needs, their social and sexual desires, cooking, cleaning, sewing, washing, and providing companionship for the male majority. Not until the 1970s did women join men underground, when enforcement of Title VII of the Civil Rights Act opened mining to a few women who often faced considerable male resistance.

Hardrock Unions

Hardrock miners organized to protect their health, their families, their wages, and their control of the workplace. The international migrations that brought experienced miners to North America brought with them histories of ethnic and racist antagonism but also the class analyses and organizing experience gained in the mines of Cornwall and Durham and all the underground workings where experienced miners taught younger men their mining skills and lore.

Miners' agendas and their calculus of success developed from what they had left and what they experienced in the rapidly industrializing U.S. mines. Keeping women out of the mines was an achievement for Cornishmen; keeping children in school was a huge gain for the sons of eastern coal miners. Women and boys worked underground in England until 1842, when the Mines and Collieries Act forbade the employment of boys under 10 and of all females in British mines, although "bal maidens" continued the arduous labor of breaking ore for little pay on the surface.

Hardrock miners organized their first U.S. union as Nevada's Comstock Lode industrialized, founding the Virginia City Miners' Protective Association on May 30, 1863. By the end of the decade, there were miners' locals in most of the major lode-mining centers, many formed by mobile Comstock miners who patterned their constitutions on the Comstock unions. The Working Men's Association of Butte was formed in 1878; it became the Gibraltar of unionism as Local No. 1 of the WFM. Leadville miners founded a Miners' Cooperative Union as a Knights of Labor Assembly in 1879, lost it in a bitter strike the following year, and then reorganized in 1885. By the early 1890s, miners had organized in most Colorado hardrock camps, many in Knights of Labor Assemblies that offered mutual aid and sometimes more militant resistance. Four Idaho locals formed the first association of hardrock unions in 1889, the Coeur d'Alenes Executive Miners' Union.

Confronting new technologies that eroded experienced miners' skills and the shared dangers of underground work, miners sought uniform minimum wages for all mine workers and organized industrial unions to match the growing power of an increasingly integrated mining industry. They based their organizing strategy on the mutual cooperation necessary for workers whose safety underground was interdependent and on a labor theory of value reinforced by the placer camp ethos that based ownership of wealth on the labor that produced it. The WFM's slogan was "Labor Produces All Wealth; Wealth Belongs to the Producer Thereof."

Hardrock unions fought often-defensive battles to resist wage cuts or stripping orders and to protect jobs and the right to organize. The first locals on the Comstock established a $4 minimum daily wage for all mining labor. In 1883, southwestern Colorado mine owners formed the San Juan Miners' Association and broke the $4 day in Telluride and Silverton. Coeur d'Alenes miners struck in 1892 to resist a wage cut from a uniform $3.50 day to $3 for miners and $2.50 for surface workers. In 1894, Cripple Creek gold miners struck to maintain a $3 day for 8 hours.

As mine owners organized to oppose their workers' demands, the miners' locals recognized the need for a central organization of their own. The Coeur d'Alenes Executive Miners' Union corresponded with unions in Montana, Colorado, and Idaho, and representatives of 15 local unions met in Butte on May 15, 1893, to form the Western Federation of Miners.

Known for its commitment to industrial unionism, its endorsements of the Socialist party, its role in founding the Western Labor Union in 1898 (which became the American Labor Union in 1902), and the

IWW in 1905 as alternatives to the conservative craft unionism of the American Federation of Labor (AFL), the WFM has engaged labor historians who debated the roots of its militancy and the violence of many hardrock strikes. The WFM won its first victory in the 1894 Cripple Creek strike, atypical because the state intervened to protect miners' rights and civil peace rather than mine owners' property. The WFM waged strikes in Leadville in 1896, the Coeur d'Alenes again in 1899, Telluride in 1901, throughout Colorado (including Telluride and Cripple Creek) in 1903–1904; in Goldfield, Nevada, in 1906–1907; Lead, South Dakota, in 1909; Calumet, Michigan, in 1913–1914; and Bisbee, Arizona, in 1917. Aptly called labor wars, the strikes often pitted unions, infiltrated by mine owners' detectives, against state force and organized mine owners. Yet the strikes were but one aspect of a union that provided health care, insurance, fellowship, and education for its members; that worked to extend union benefits to other workers; and that generated considerable internal debate about political and industrial strategies. It won a notable legal victory with a Supreme Court decision that legalized limiting hours of work underground.

The disastrous strike defeats in Colorado in 1903–1904 prompted the WFM to become the largest founding member of the IWW. In the 1904 strike aftermath, the Colorado legislature overturned the defeat of Governor James Peabody, who had sent troops to strike areas and used them to deport union leaders from the state, declaring him elected on condition that he relinquish the office to his lieutenant governor. This political manipulation led some miners to abandon politics in favor of industrial organization that might someday lead to workers' control of production. It convinced others to pursue political reform, and still others to continue to work for socialism.

The IWW seemed initially to offer an industrial alternative to the AFL; the WFM hoped that the United Mine Workers, who organized coal miners, might withdraw from the AFL and join the IWW, where the two miners' unions might merge. That did not happen, and political divisions within both the IWW and the WFM led the WFM to leave the IWW in 1908. Vainly pursuing a merger with the UMW, the WFM joined the AFL in 1912. In 1916, the union changed its name to reflect its industrywide jurisdiction and became the International Union of Mine, Mill, and Smelter Workers (Mine-Mill).

Like many unions, Mine-Mill lost members during the 1920s, and then regrouped as one of the nation's most militant industrial unions to help found the CIO in 1936. Struggling with racist divisions, the WFM began organizing Mexicans, Japanese, Italians, and Greeks before World War I and continued after World War II to organize Mexican miners in New Mexico and Arizona, and African-American miners in the U.S. South. But in the Cold War backlash, Mine-Mill leaders and organizers were prosecuted for allegedly falsely signing the anti-Communist affidavits required under the Taft-Hartley Act. Mine-Mill was one of the unions expelled from the CIO for alleged Communist domination. Some union leaders had been Communist party members, a not-uncommon commitment during the 1930s and World War II. Some resigned their party memberships in order to be able to sign the Taft-Hartley affidavits. But the threat of the union in the 1940s and 1950s, as in the preceding decades, lay in the power to organize hardrock miners regardless of race or skill, not in an international Communist conspiracy.

One moving legacy of the postwar period was a film, *Salt of the Earth*, a cooperative production of blacklisted Hollywood filmmakers and Mine-Mill, based on the strike of Mine-Mill Local 890 against New Jersey Zinc in Bayard, New Mexico. Most of the actors were Mexican-American miners and their families whose stories powerfully linked the inseparable inequalities of race, class, and gender in hardrock mining.

Mine-Mill persisted throughout the 1950s and 1960s but lost ground to raids by other unions, particularly the United Steelworkers of America. Its support dwindled in the face of racist attacks, anticommunism, and new challenges from an internationally organized mining industry. Mine-Mill merged with the Steelworkers in 1967.

Labor historians have long debated the heritage of conflict in hardrock mining, locating its origins in frontier violence, the lack of a middle class, or the recklessness of an unstable and mobile workforce. Yet hardrock miners' strategies are more accurately located in the industrial conditions they faced and in histories of class-based cooperation. For most radicalism and reform were not opposed strategies. The most militant union leaders were married men who protected homes, families, and communities. Hardrock miners confronted conflict but wrote a heritage of industrial organizing and mutual protection and of an industrial landscape wrought from the metals they dug and refined. This heritage continues to be written from sources as complex and as rich as the changing workforces, work processes, and the ore-bearing rock itself.

ELIZABETH JAMESON

References and Further Reading

Brown, Ronald C. *Hard-Rock Miners: The Intermountain West, 1860–1920*. College Station, Texas: Texas A & M University Press, 1979.

Dubofsky, Melvyn. *We Shall Be All*. New York: Quadrangle/The New York Times Book Co., 1969.

Emmons, David M. *The Butte Irish: Class and Ethnicity in an American Mining Town, 1875–1925*. Urbana: University of Illinois Press, 1989.

Jameson, Elizabeth. *All That Glitters: Class, Conflict, and Community in Cripple Creek*. Urbana and Chicago, Ill.: University of Illinois Press, 1998.

Jenson, Vernon H. *Heritage of Conflict: Labor Relations in the Nonferrous Metals Industry Up to 1930*. Ithaca, NY: Cornell University Press, 1950.

Johnson, Susan Lee. *Roaring Camp: The Social World of the California Gold Rush*. New York: W. W. Norton & Company, 2000.

Lingenfelter, Richard E. *The Hardrock Miners: A History of the Mining Labor Movement in the American West, 1863–1893*. Berkeley: University of California Press, 1974.

Lorence, James J. *The Suppression of Salt of the Earth: How Hollywood, Big Labor, and Politicians Blacklisted a Movie in Cold War America*. Albuquerque: University of New Mexico Press, 1999.

Mann, Ralph Emerson. *After the Gold Rush: Society in Grass Valley and Nevada City, California, 1849–1870*. Stanford, CA: Stanford University Press, 1982.

Mellinger, Philip J. *Race and Labor in Western Copper: The Fight for Equality, 1896–1918*. Tucson: University of Arizona Press, 1995.

Mercier, Laurie. *Anaconda: Labor, Community, and Culture in Montana's Smelter City*. Urbana and Chicago: University of Illinois Press, 2001.

Mouat, Jeremy. *Roaring Days: Rossland's Mines and the History of British Columbia*. Vancouver: University of British Columbia Press, 1995.

Owens, Kenneth N. *Riches for All: The California Gold Rush and the World*. Lincoln: University of Nebraska Press, 2002.

Peck, Gunther. *Reinventing Free Labor: Padrones and Immigrant Workers in the North American West, 1880–1930*. New York: Cambridge University Press, 2000.

Wyman, Mark. *Hard Rock Epic: Western Miners and the Industrial Revolution, 1860–1910*. Berkeley: University of California Press, 1979.

See also **Congress of Industrial Organizations; Cripple Creek Strikes; Industrial Workers of the World**

MITCH, WILLIAM A. (1881–1974)
President, United Mine Workers of America

William A. Mitch served as president of the United Mine Workers of America (UMWA) in Alabama for more than three decades, leading the organization back from a crushing defeat in the years after World War I and building District 20, as the southernmost branch of the union is known, into one of its most solid strongholds. In the process he helped transform Birmingham into a center for industrial unionism, fighting to establish the United Steelworkers of America in the city's iron and steel mills and speaking out forcefully for the rights of African-American workers. Though he is best remembered for his efforts in the South, Mitch's union career actually began in Indiana, where he rose to prominence as an activist in the miners' union, supporting nationalization of the nation's coal industry and eventually becoming a close ally of legendary UMWA president John L. Lewis.

The Indiana Years

Mitch was born in Nelsonville, Ohio, in 1881, and he accompanied his father into the coalmines as a boy. He eventually settled in Indiana, where miners elected him secretary-treasurer of District 11 in 1915. Like many miners Mitch held socialist sympathies, and he unsuccessfully ran for Congress from the fifth district in 1920 as a member of the Labor party of Indiana. During the campaign Mitch garnered national attention for his denunciation of American Federation of Labor (AFL) President Samuel Gompers and his policy of supporting the friends of organized labor and opposing its enemies. Instead of supporting either Democratic or Republican candidates, as Gompers advocated, Mitch believed that workers should form their own party and use it to advance their interests. That same year Mitch helped deliver Indiana to John L. Lewis in the UMWA presidential election, cementing a political relationship between the two men that would last the rest of their lives.

In 1921, Lewis appointed Mitch to the union's Nationalization Research Committee, where he served with John Brophy, president of UMWA District 2, and Christ Golden, leader of District 9. Lewis, a conservative on economic matters, never fully supported nationalizing the coal industry, and though the concept had much support within the UMWA ranks, the union president merely used the issue to strengthen his control over the union. He and his supporters criticized the committee as a tool of union outsiders—"a bunch of Greenwich Village reds" in the words of Lewis's handpicked editor of the union's newspaper—and the other members soon resigned. Mitch managed to survive the crisis, distancing himself from Brophy, who emerged as Lewis's main rival in the UMWA. The nationalization effort faded away.

By the middle of the 1920s, Mitch was firmly in Lewis's political camp in the UMWA, but the Indiana branch of the union began to suffer. An employer offensive and the chaotic economics of the coal industry in the 1920s caused political turmoil within the national UMWA, and in the Indiana district as well. Though Mitch enjoyed enough support to remain secretary-treasurer throughout the decade, miners in District 11 regularly turned other state leaders out of office. Indiana remained one of the few regions with a viable union presence during the Great Depression, but the number of employed miners dwindled from 18,000 to just 7,500 in 1931. Mitch's support for Lewis eventually became a liability. He worked tirelessly to limit the spread of a rebellion against Lewis that swept through the neighboring Illinois district in the late 1920s. In response the rebels worked hard to unseat Mitch as an Indiana UMWA official. Their efforts bore fruit in 1931, when Mitch was defeated for re-election as secretary treasurer of District 11. Adolph Germer, a leader among the dissidents, proclaimed Mitch's defeat a successfor Lewis's opponents in the UMWA. If so it proved one of the few victories ever recorded by the anti-Lewis bloc within the union.

The defeat caused something of a crisis for Mitch, who, after 16 years as a union officer had only limited options for employment in an industry ravaged by the Depression and declining union membership. He briefly considered practicing law, having been admitted to the Indiana bar after completing college extension courses. Lewis however rarely forgot his allies, and Mitch eventually landed a post as a "special representative" with the UMWA.

Out of this defeat however, Mitch was reborn. In the summer of 1933, Lewis sent Mitch to Alabama to head up the efforts to re-establish District 20, which had been destroyed in the wake of a disastrous strike in 1920–1921. The ravages of the Great Depression— Birmingham once was described as the worst hit city in the country—and the programs of President Franklin Roosevelt had dramatically altered the balance of power in Alabama. The coal miners of the Birmingham district meanwhile were ready to bring their old union back, and they enlisted in the ranks of the miners' union by the thousands. In Alabama Mitch joined his old friend William Dalrymple, a UMWA organizer and later, William Raney, a former Indiana associate. By 1934, the miners' union represented 90% of the miners in the state, and Mitch found himself president of one of the strongest districts in the UMWA.

Organizing one of the most important industries in an anti-union state however was not without challenges. Mitch and the UMWA had a difficult time dealing with the local affiliate of United States Steel Corporation, called the Tennessee, Coal, Iron, and Railroad Company (TCI). Though the union signed its first contract with TCI in 1934, it would not enjoy exclusive bargaining rights with the company until 1941. The UMWA's battles with the notorious Alabama Fuel and Iron Company (AFI), headed by the reactionary Charles DeBardeleben, often resulted in violence and on at least one occasion, the outright murder of a union activist. The AFI remained unorganized until it closed in the early 1950s.

Mitch has been described as very conservative in his methods of organization. While there is a degree of legitimacy to this argument, on the issue of race, the District 20 president often defied southern customs. In particular the UMWA organized both black and white miners into the same locals in Alabama and often flaunted segregation ordinances during local meetings as miners of both races participated. Though the union remained in the control of whites like Mitch at a time when most observers believed it had a black majority, the UMWA provided a forum from which African-Americans could improve their standard of living and even stake a claim to limited leadership positions in the union. Mitch undoubtedly exercised caution when he confronted the color line in Alabama, but even his critics on the left recognized his ability to rally support among African-Americans. He fought against the poll tax and spoke out often for the rights of black workers outside the workplace.

As president of the state AFL, called the Alabama State Federation of Labor (ASFL), Mitch attempted to encourage craft unions to organize African-Americans, with mixed results. A former ASFL lawyer accused him of practicing "what the Communists preach on Negro equality in the ranks of the United Mine Workers of America and in Organized Labor." Later as president of the state Congress of Industrial Organizations (CIO), called the Alabama State Industrial Union Council (ASIUC), he supported the efforts of the Southern Conference for Human Welfare, a popular front group that sought to bring liberals and leftists together to campaign against the poll tax and other instruments of oppression against African-Americans. Mitch's views on race were complex, and he admitted to another union official "that I have always handled it with gloves on . . . and the Negroes have cooperated splendidly."

Mitch resigned as president of the ASFL after the AFL expelled industrial unionists from its ranks and became the first president of the ASIUC. Lewis also tapped the District 20 president to head up the southern efforts of the Steel Workers' Organizing Committee (SWOC). Under his leadership the ranks of union members in the state swelled, and Alabama became a center of union activity in the South with large numbers of miners and factory workers opting for representation. Almost a quarter of the state's workers were unionized by the mid-1950s, a testament to his legacy.

When the UMWA and CIO split in 1942, Mitch resigned as head of the ASIUC. Mitch, who had often found himself the target of red-baiting attacks by industrialists and craft unionists, engaged in his own round at his final ASIUC convention. He denounced critics of Lewis at the event and branded the UMWA president's opponents as Communists. The miners' union left the state CIO a short time later. During World War II, Mitch led the UMWA in Alabama during bitter national walkouts in 1943 and 1945. He also helped establish the landmark health care and pension system the union negotiated with both the federal government and coal operators in the years after the war.

Later Career

But the decades after the war were exceedingly difficult for the aging District 20 president and the union in Alabama. The coal industry in Alabama suffered from declining markets, and the number of miners dropped dramatically from 21,975 miners in 1945 to 7,400 in 1960. Production plummeted from 18 million tons of coal to 12–13 million tons a year in the 1950s. The UMWA's influence in Alabama waned along with the declining fortunes of the industry.

Lewis retired as president of the national union in 1960, but Mitch, by this time an elderly man, continued as head of the Alabama branch for several years. New UMWA President W. A. "Tony" Boyle began to tighten his grip on District 20, appointing one of his supporters as secretary-treasurer of the Alabama organization. Mitch resigned as president in 1963 but continued to represent District 20 on the international executive board (IEB) until 1967, when he retired from that position. Tellingly Boyle replaced Mitch on the IEB with Albert Pass, one of his loyalists who was then also the secretary-treasurer from the union's District 19 in Tennessee. Pass would later be convicted along with Boyle and other UMWA officials of arranging the murder of union insurgent Joseph A. "Jock" Yablonski, his wife, and daughter in 1969.

Mitch died in a nursing home in Birmingham on July 12, 1974. He was remembered for his efforts to bring the UMWA back in Alabama as well as for his work with the steelworkers and the CIO. "His weight and influence were felt throughout the labor movement in Alabama," proclaimed Howard Strevel of the steelworkers. Indeed Mitch had played a role in most of the major developments of the UMWA and the southern labor movement in the middle of the twentieth century, a time that saw workers in the South and the rest of the nation realize a standard of living they could not have imagined during the depths of the Great Depression. Near the end of his career, Mitch had been hailed as a "dyed in the wood Alabamian" and "a man of integrity and a born leader of men" by the state's largest newspaper. Sadly few outside of Alabama recognized Mitch's contributions to the labor movement in the region, including the UMWA, which devoted just four sentences to his passing.

ROBERT H. WOODRUM

References and Further Reading:

Alexander, Peter. "Rising from the Ashes: Alabama Coal Miners, 1921–1941." In *It Is Union and Liberty: Alabama Coal Miners and the UMW*, edited by Edwin L. Brown and Colin J. Davis. Tuscaloosa: University of Alabama Press, 1999.

Dubofsky, Melvyn, and Warren Van Tine. *John L. Lewis: A Biography*. New York: Quadrangle/The New York Times Book Co., 1977.

Fox, Maier. *United We Stand: The United Mine Workers of America, 1890–1990*. Washington, DC: United Mine Workers of America, 1990.

Kelley, Robin D.G. *Hammer and Hoe: Alabama Communists during the Great Depression*. Chapel Hill: University of North Carolina Press, 1990.

Mitch, William A. Papers. State College: Historical Collections and Labor Archives, Paterno Library, Pennsylvania State University.

Norrell, Robert J. "Caste in Steel: Jim Crow Careers in Birmingham, Alabama." *Journal of American History* 73, 3 (1986): 669–694.

———. "Labor at the Ballot Box: Alabama Politics from the New Deal to the Dixiecrat Movement." *Journal of Southern History* 57, 2 (1991): 201–234.

Stein, Judith. "Southern Workers in National Unions: Birmingham Steelworkers, 1936–1951." In *Organized Labor in the Twentieth-Century South*, edited by Robert H. Zieger. Knoxville: University of Tennessee Press.

Taft, Philip. *Organizing Dixie: Alabama Workers in the Industrial Era*, edited by Gary M. Fink. Connecticut: Greenwood Press, 1981.

United Mine Workers of America Archive. State College: Historical Collections and Labor Archives, Paterno Library, Pennsylvania State University.

Woodrum, Robert H. "The Rebirth of the UMWA and Racial Anxiety in Alabama, 1933–1942." *Alabama Review* (forthcoming).

———. "Race and Industrial Transformation in the Alabama Coalfields, 1933–2001." Ph.D. dissertation, Georgia State University, 2003.

———. "Reforming Dixie: Alabama Coal Miners and Rank-and-File Rebellion in the United Mine Workers of America, 1963 to 1978," M.A. thesis, Georgia State University, 1997.

See also **Lewis, John L; United Mine Workers of America**

MITCHELL, H. L. ("MITCH") (1906–1989)
Socialist Labor Activist

Harry Leland Mitchell devoted his life to organizing southern agricultural workers, a group often ignored by the mainstream labor movement and denied the protections of national labor law. Cofounder of the interracial Southern Tenant Farmers' Union (STFU) in the 1930s, Mitchell can be considered a product of what historian James Green has called grass-roots socialism. The pre-World War I Socialist party had an especially strong presence in Oklahoma, Texas, Louisiana, and Arkansas, a tradition of agrarian radicalism rekindled by Mitchell and his fellow STFU organizers during the years of the Great Depression.

Born in Halls, Tennessee, in 1906, Mitchell spent his formative years in the small-town South during the first two decades of the twentieth century. Even then west Tennessee, the hinterland of Memphis, remained an area rooted in the plantation economy, cotton production, and the racial legacy of slavery. As a boy of 11, Mitchell witnessed a frenzied mob of 500 whites applaud the lynching of a black man in front of the courthouse in nearby Dyersburg, Tennessee. As a young man, Mitchell worked as a newspaper boy, a sharecropper, a deliveryman, and even a bootlegger.

His early experiences with hard work and witnessing racial injustice proved fertile ground for the ideas of the American Socialist party, which Mitchell first encountered in Eugene V. Debs's 1920 presidential campaign. Largely denied the opportunity of formal schooling, Mitchell educated himself with the *Little Blue Books* published by E. Haldeman-Julius, editor of the Girard, Kansas, socialist mass-circulation newspaper, *Appeal to Reason.*

In 1927, Mitchell moved across the Mississippi River to Tyronza, a small town in the Arkansas delta, to join his father, Jim, who worked there as a barber. At first Mitchell tried his hand at growing cotton but soon realizing that "the landlord got one bale, and the boll weevil the other," he established a dry cleaning business and talked socialism to anyone who would listen.

By 1932, he and one of his local converts, gas station owner Clay East (their adjacent businesses in the center of town were known by community wits as Red Square), had chartered a Tyronza local of the Socialist party and invited Norman Thomas to the delta to address the area's impoverished tenants and sharecroppers. While there Thomas conducted research for the Socialists' pamphlet on cotton tenancy, *The Plight of the Sharecropper* (1934), which helped expose the planters' misappropriation of Agricultural Administration Act (AAA) payments owed to sharecroppers under the New Deal.

Socialism was not entirely out of place in rural Arkansas in the 1930s. Mitchell, East, and Christian Socialist Howard Kester, who joined them in 1935, easily tapped into the dormant sentiments of southwestern agrarian radicalism, dating back to the Populists of the 1890s. From 1900–1920, the socialism of Debs had fired the imagination and expressed the aspirations of workers and farmers in Arkansas, Louisiana, Oklahoma, and Texas. Radical interracial unions, including the Industrial Workers of the World—affiliated Brotherhood of Timber Workers, had a presence in the region. By the 1930s, small farmers and migratory workers who had sought economic opportunity in this region had sunk into the status of dependent proletarians and peasants. In response to this transformation, Socialists like Mitchell revived the radical tradition as rural working people cast around for a political response to the depression. The STFU became their vehicle.

Mitchell is best known for his work with the STFU, first organized in Tyronza in 1934. Founded by a handful of black and white sharecroppers, the STFU initially sought to secure a fair share of government AAA payments for those who worked the land and to protect them from unjust evictions. Part agricultural labor union able to conduct strikes, part advocacy and lobbying organization, this interracial movement of the poor pioneered many of the tactics that would come to characterize civil rights and labor movements in the rural South in future generations. Despite his own devout atheism, Mitchell joined forces with Christian Socialists like Kester and Ward Rogers, and local African-American preachers like E. B. McKinney. The union also embraced the principle of nonviolence but more out of tactical necessity than fundamental principle. Finally Mitchell recognized that the powerless and isolated sharecroppers of the delta would have to call on more established and well-connected organizations in order to succeed. Thus he readily forged alliances with friends in New Deal agencies, the National Association for the Advancement of Colored People (NAACP), liberal churches, backers of farm co-operatives, and by 1937, the industrial labor movement in the nascent Congress of Industrial Organizations (CIO).

The STFU's brief alliance with the CIO proved ill-fated however, in part because of the enmity between Mitchell and the Communist party leadership of the CIO agricultural workers union, UCAPAWA. During World War II many sharecroppers left the land to work in industry, further weakening the STFU. In the aftermath of the war, Mitchell took the STFU, now renamed the National Farm Labor Union (NFLU), into the Amalgamated Meat Cutters and Butcher Workmen of the American Federation of Labor (AFL). The NFLU retained its interracial leadership structure at a time when many AFL unions remained segregated or excluded blacks altogether.

As president of the NFLU from 1948–1960, Mitchell worked in Washington D.C., where he and his second wife, Dorothy Dowe, lobbied on behalf of farm workers' national interests and remained part of an active network of southerners attempting to liberalize their home region. Although unable to secure extension of NLRB coverage to agricultural laborers, Mitchell did help them win rights to social security benefits. Under Mitchell's guidance, the NFLU also spearheaded organizing drives in the late 1940s and early 1950s among fruit pickers in California's central valley and strawberry and sugar-cane workers in Louisiana. Mitchell always claimed that the persistent efforts of the NFLU to turn organized labor's attention to the plight of agricultural workers helped pave the way for Cesar Chavez and the United Farm Workers in the 1960s.

During the late 1960s, Mitchell himself made efforts to bring student activists from the Southern Students' Organizing Committee together with trade union organizers in the sugarcane fields of Louisiana. In the last decades of his life, retired from organizing campaigns, Mitch continued to reach out to the younger generation. Traveling around the country to college campuses, he regaled students with the colorful history of union organizing among the dispossessed and made sure numerous libraries acquired the micro-filmed collection of the STFU's records. Through these activities Mitchell kept alive the memories of social activism that would help inspire a new cohort of students, scholars, trade unionists, and civil rights workers intent on bringing interracial social justice to the South.

ALEX LICHTENSTEIN

References and Further Reading

Dunbar, Anthony P. *Against the Grain: Southern Radicals and Prophet, 1929–1959*. Charlottesville: 1981.
Kester, Howard. *Revolt among the Sharecroppers*. Knoxville: 1997. (reprint, 1936)
Mitchell, H. L. *Mean Things Happening in This Land: The Life and Times of H. L. Mitchell, Co-Founder of the Southern Tenant Farmers'Union*. Montclair: 1979.

See also **Amalgamated Meat Cutters and Butcher Workmen; Chávez, César Estrada; Congress of Industrial Organizations (CIO); Industrial Workers of the World; Southern Tenant Farmers' Union; United Farm Workers of America**

MITCHELL, JOHN (1870–1919)
President, United Mine Workers of America

Along with Samuel Gompers and Eugene Debs, John Mitchell ranks as one of the most influential figures in the U.S. labor movement during the period from the late 1890s to World War 1. It was during the early years of his tenure as president of the United Mine Workers of America (UMWA), a position he held from 1898 to 1908, that the industrial union of coal miners, founded in 1890, emerged from years of depression and defeat to become the largest union in the American Federation of Labor (AFL) and a source of organized labor's new power during the Progressive Era.

After labor's debacles during the crisis-ridden 1890s, economic recovery and the political climate of the late 1890s brought about favorable times for the resurgence of the labor movement. The successful national strike that the UMWA launched in 1897, when it had less than 10,000 members, proved to be a turning point in its fortunes. Before the strike Mitchell had been relatively unknown, but his success in organizing southern Illinois miners during the conflict brought him attention and led to his election to the union's vice-presidency. The watershed strike resulted in the re-establishment of the joint-conference system, a system involving formal meetings and direct negotiations between the miners and the operators for the purpose of securing industrial peace. The unprecedented interstate agreement that followed in 1898 brought bituminous miners higher wages and the 8-hour day and stabilized the soft coal industry in the four key states that comprised the important central competitive field of production. Mitchell was a beneficiary of these events, and his meteoric rise to a position of power coincided with the UMWA's growth, newfound stability, and expanding influence.

Under his leadership the UMWA then went on to win prestigious victories in the hard-coal region during the strikes of 1900 and 1902, when the anthracite miners, mine workers, and breaker boys secured higher wages, shorter hours, and better working conditions. The victories won him the fierce loyalty of hard-coal miners, established the union in the district, and earned him widespread acclaim throughout the nation. Mitchell was lauded for his conservative rhetoric, his ability to unify the disparate nationalities and avoid serious violence, his ambitious efforts to garner broad public support, and his skill in mustering assistance from the nation's power brokers, including Senator Mark Hanna, President Theodore Roosevelt, and the financier J. P. Morgan, to win settlements from the virulently anti-union monopolistic coal-carrying railroads. Although the 1902 strikers did not achieve their most important demand—union recognition—they established a lasting tradition and proclaimed October 29, 1902, as the first Mitchell Day to honor the man and the union's achievements. The strikes had catapulted Mitchell into national prominence and increased middle-class support for the notion that conservative trade unions might be legitimate. By the end of 1902, the UMWA had over 300,000 members, the trade union movement was resurgent, and Mitchell was at the peak of his influence.

The UMWA president's greatest successes occurred during the general prosperity from 1898 to1904, a time when he was as responsible as AFL President Gompers for eschewing radicalism and actively advocating a nonradical, pure-and-simple unionism course for the labor movement, a policy that many, then and since, have contested. Like Gompers, Mitchell accepted many of the basic tenets of capitalism and saw no irreconcilable conflict between capital and labor. In his view many employers were progressive, and contracts were sacred. He became an ardent champion of conservative trade unions and trade agreements with limited purposes. It was one thing for workers to seek to raise wages, end child labor, or eliminate the most exploitative working conditions, but it was something else for them to seek workers' control or challenge existing business prerogatives. In his speeches and writings, he ridiculed socialism and the radical political and economic alternatives of his day as unachievable dreams. Ultimately the complex and contradictory labor leader placed his faith for a solution to the labor problem more in the hands of prominent capitalists and powerful politicians than he did in the working classes. For such reasons he, like Gompers, readily joined the nation's power brokers and became a member (from 1899 to 1911) of the National Civic Federation (NCF), a controversial organization of capitalists, labor leaders, and the general public that sought to avert socialism in the United States by promoting moderate reforms, business recognition of conservative trade unions, and acceptance of collective bargaining. The NCF and its goals were never accepted by the major coal corporations, the National Association of Manufacturers, or many other businesses.

Meanwhile the economic downturn that occurred in 1904 set the stage for Mitchell's undoing and revealed the shortcomings of his policies. The sentiment for radical political and economic alternatives was growing throughout the country. Union miners reluctantly accepted his decision to approve the operators' demands for a wage cut in 1904, but the failure of his 1906 strike policy to offset union defeat or even retain the much-valued interstate joint-conference system was decisive. Radicals and rivals combined forces against him, and he resigned the union's presidency in 1908. His questionable dealings with powerful class enemies, his ongoing participation in the business-dominated NCF, plus various shady business transactions had aroused serious conflict-of-interest issues and opposition. In 1911, a disgruntled UMWA convention forced the ousted leader to choose between membership in the UMWA or the NCF; he kept his union membership but retained his faith in the NCF and in conservative unionism. In the context of the changed times and the growth of radical movements, he became increasingly irrelevant to the labor movement.

Mitchell has been described as a complex man whose loyalties were divided, a miners' Moses, a failed labor bureaucrat, and the personification of all that is good and bad in the American labor movement. Perhaps the roots of his contradictory impulses lay in his early years. The son of an Irish immigrant coal miner, born in Braidwood, Illinois, in 1870, he had experienced a childhood fraught with family tragedy and extreme poverty. The difficult struggle for survival that he and working-class families endured in the coalfields left a deep and lasting imprint on him. That struggle prompted him to join the Knights of Labor in 1885, and then the United Mine Workers in 1890, and to become a fervent lifelong advocate of trade unions and trade agreements; but it also fostered his personal desire to escape the status of a permanent wage earner. When he died, largely unheralded, in 1919, he left a personal fortune worth nearly $350,000. That money did not come from his employment on the New York Workers' Compensation Commission or the Industrial Commission of New York but from the dubious investments he had made in notoriously anti-union corporations.

In many ways Mitchell was a tragic figure who embodied the greater tragedy of an American labor movement that once militantly challenged the capitalist system but eventually succumbed to the temptations of "business unionism." Nonetheless to this day, union miners celebrate Mitchell Day to commemorate the historic contributions he made to the labor movement in 1900 and 1902 and to inspire contemporary generations to continue the broader struggle for workers' rights.

MILDRED ALLEN BEIK

Selected Works

Mitchell, John. *Organized Labor: Its Problems, Purposes, and Ideals and the Present and Future of American Wage Earners*. Philadelphia, PA: American Book and Bible House, 1903.
———. Foreword by Samuel Gompers. *The Wage Earner and His Problems*. Washington, DC: P. S. Ridsdale, 1913.

References and Further Reading

Glück, Elsie. *John Mitchell, Miner: Labor's Bargain with the Gilded Age*. New York: The John Day Company, 1929.
Gowaskie, Joseph M. "John Mitchell and the Anthracite Mine Workers: Leadership Conservatism and Rank-and-File Militancy." *Labor History* 27, 1 (winter 1985–1986): 54–83.
Laslett, John H. M. *Labor and the Left: A Study of Socialist and Radical Influences in the American Labor Movement, 1881–1924*. New York: Basic Books, 1970.
Madison, Charles A. *American Labor Leaders: Personalities and Forces in the Labor Movement*. New York: Frederick Ungar, 1950.
Phelan, Craig. *Divided Loyalties: The Public and Private Life of Labor Leader John Mitchell*. Albany: State University of New York Press, 1994.
———. "The Making of a Labor Leader: John Mitchell and the Anthracite Strike of 1900." *Pennsylvania History* 63 (winter 1996): 53–77.
Warne, Frank Julian. "John Mitchell: The Labor Leader and the Man." http://history.osu.edu/projects/coal/1902 AnthraciteStrike/MitchellLaborLeader/MitchellLabor Leader.htm (2004–).
Wiebe, Robert H. "The Anthracite Strike of 1902: A Record of Confusion." *The Mississippi Valley Historical Review* 48, 2 (Sept. 1961): 229–251.

See also **American Federation of Labor; Anthracite Coal Strike (1902); Arbitration; Collective Bargaining; Debs, Eugene V.;** *Gompers v. Buck's Stove and Range Co.;* **Gompers, Samuel;** *Hitchman Coal & Coke v. Mitchell* **(1916); Mining, Coal; National Civic Federation; Socialist Party of America; United Mine Workers of America**

MOLLY MAGUIRES

Twenty young Irishmen were hanged in the anthracite region of northeastern Pennsylvania in the late 1870s, and 20 more were sent to prison, convicted of a series of killings stretching back to the Civil War. They belonged to an ethnic fraternal society called the Ancient Order of Hibernians (AOH) and were convicted on the evidence of a Pinkerton detective and labor spy, James McParlan, who had infiltrated their organization. Because they left us virtually no evidence of their own, almost everything we know about the Molly Maguires was recorded by their enemies. At the showcase trials of the 1870s, the prosecution offered no plausible explanation of motive and nor it seems was one expected—for the explanation of Irish depravity was simply that the Irish were depraved by nature.

This argument, while perfectly circular, was surprisingly powerful in the nineteenth-century United States, and it laid the groundwork for a powerful and enduring myth. Nobody did more to articulate that myth than Allan Pinkerton, founder of the famous detective agency, whose ghost-written history *The Molly Maguires and the Detectives*, published in 1877 as the trials and executions were proceeding, celebrated McParlan's triumph over Irish barbarity. Pinkerton's highly pejorative account laid down a narrative line that would remain dominant for at least the next two generations, providing a staple plot for American dime-novel fiction and even for a Sherlock Holmes novel, *The Valley of Fear* (1914).

In certain Irish-American and labor circles meanwhile, a counternarrative flourished based on a notion of the Molly Maguires as innocent victims of oppression, whether economic, religious, or ethnic. This position however too often turned the dominant mythology on its head, retaining the central explanatory category of evil but transferring it from Irish workers to their nativist or capitalist enemies. Evil as a timeless attribute of individual or group character is not a useful category of historical analysis. The popular countermyth, while it was undoubtedly consoling and empowering, was ultimately as implausible as the pernicious narrative it arose to encounter. To state the matter bluntly, there were Molly Maguires in Pennsylvania, and they killed people.

The historian's task is to explain why they did so. Clearly what is needed is an explanation that breaks free of the two extremes of interpretation—the Irish simply as savages or the Irish simply as scapegoats. Only in the 1930s did the task of historical analysis get underway when Anthony Bimba (rather dogmatically) and J. Walter Coleman (with greater subtlety) pointed out what a handful of radical dissenting

Pneumatic steam hammer and forges, blacksmith shop at mines, Scranton, Pa. Library of Congress, Prints & Photographs Division [LC-USZ62-72474].

voices in the 1870s had tried in vain to explain: The Molly Maguires were one element in a concerted struggle between labor and capital for control of the lower anthracite region of Pennsylvania, and their story made no sense outside that context. If labor history provides one essential context for understanding the Molly Maguires, immigration history provides the other. Any account of the subject today must take as its starting point a precept widely accepted by American historians but difficult to put into practice, that is, we cannot make proper sense of the lives of immigrant workers in the United States without a detailed knowledge of the lands from which they came.

Irish Origins

To make sense of the Molly Maguires then we must begin with Irish history. In Ireland secret societies, generically known as Whiteboys and Ribbonmen had been waging a losing struggle against land enclosures, tithes, and rack renting since the 1760s, a struggle that featured threatening letters (or "coffin notices"), beatings, burnings, and assassinations. The Irish Molly Maguires, who emerged toward the end of the Great Famine (1845–1851), were so-named because their members (invariably young men) disguised themselves in women's clothing, used powder or burnt cork on their faces, and pledged their allegiance to a mythical woman who symbolized their struggle against injustice. Ireland in the first-half of the nineteenth century was notorious for its tradition of clandestine rural violence, of which the Molly Maguires were one of the last manifestations. In north-central Ireland, where many of the men involved in the Pennsylvania episode originated, the terms Molly Maguires, Ribbonmen, and Ancient Order of Hibernians were sometimes used interchangeably. Immigrant workers carried some of their traditions with them to the United States, and from the 1830s onward, faction fighters and Ribbonmen made their presence known on the public works, canals, and railroads of the United States, where Irish manual labor was in heavy demand. The Molly Maguires of Pennsylvania represented the most concerted, dramatic, and tragic transatlantic outgrowth of this rural Irish tradition in the industrial United States.

According to the interpretation laid down in the 1870s, the Molly Maguires were a conspiratorial organization imported direct from the Irish countryside. There is however no evidence at all that anyone in Ireland conspired to export any such organization nor that any of the individuals convicted in Pennsylvania were involved in violent activities before they left Ireland. But they did arrive in the United States with particular forms of cultural memory and distinctive traditions of social protest; faced with appalling conditions in the mines of Pennsylvania, they responded by deploying a specific form of collective violence, rooted in Irish rural history, that featured the familiar tactics of coffin notices, beatings, sabotage, and assassinations. The Pennsylvania Molly Maguires do not appear to have worn women's clothing, but some of them reportedly "blacked up" for disguise. Like their Irish counterparts, they were led by tavern keepers, and they called on strangers from neighboring lodges to carry out beatings and killings, pledging to return the favor at a later date. There is no doubt then that the American Molly Maguires existed even if they never assumed the diabolical form depicted by contemporaries. They were not a figment of the conspiratorial imagination, whether nativist or capitalist; indeed if Irish immigrant workers had not been engaged in collective violence of some sort, the mythology created about them could never have carried the persuasive power it so evidently did.

But what was the institutional reality behind the exaggerated descriptions of contemporary observers? According to the prosecuting attorneys, the term Molly Maguires was just another name for the AOH, an assertion that made the Mollies appear like part of a vast national and international conspiratorial network. An otherwise peaceful Catholic fraternal society, the AOH had branches in Irish settlements across the United States as well as in Ireland, England, and Scotland. The local lodges in the hard-coal region of Pennsylvania, according to the prosecuting attorneys, acted as a cover for a group of depraved Irish killers. Some AOH lodges in Pennsylvania were undoubtedly used for violent purposes; yet that still begs the question of why the Molly Maguires operating within those lodges acted as they did and why contemporaries were so concerned about the threat they posed.

Labor Struggles

If the inherent depravity of Irish workers can no longer serve as an answer to this question, where do the real answers lie? They are to be found neither in national character nor in individual pathology, but instead in the detailed history of labor and capital in Pennsylvania's lower anthracite region during the era of Civil War and Reconstruction.

There were two quite distinct, and only tenuously connected, waves of Molly Maguire activity in Pennsylvania, the first in the 1860s and the second in the 1870s. The first wave, which included six of the 16 assassinations, occurred during and directly after the Civil War. At the heart of this violence was a combination of resistance to the military draft with some form of rudimentary labor organizing by a mysterious group of mine workers, known variously as the Buckshots, the Committee, and the Molly Maguires. Nobody was convicted of any crimes in the 1860s; only during the trials of the following decade was the first wave of violence retrospectively traced to individual members of the AOH and hence to an organized conspiracy by the Molly Maguires. The violence abated after 1868, mainly because of the formation of a powerful new trade union, the Workingmen's Benevolent Association (WBA), which united Irish, British, and American workers across lines of ethnicity and skill. At its height in the early 1870s, the WBA enlisted some 30,000 members. Its rise and fall neatly divides the first wave of Molly Maguire violence from the second and much better known outbreak that followed the destruction of the union in the summer of 1875.

In the late 1860s and 1870s, the labor movement of the anthracite region took two distinct but overlapping forms: A powerful and inclusive trade union movement open to all mine workers regardless of ethnicity or skill; and a shadowy, sporadic, and exclusively Irish group, manned by unskilled laborers, led by tavern keepers, practicing violence, and known as the Molly Maguires. Favoring collective-bargaining, strikes, moral force, and third-party politics, the leaders of the WBA publicly condemned violence by labor as both inherently wrong and tactically counterproductive, singling out the Molly Maguires for repeated criticism. Yet Franklin B. Gowen, the president of the Reading Railroad, determined to secure his monopolistic goals, repeatedly insisted that the Molly Maguires were merely the terrorist arm of the union movement, whose claims to nonviolence were but a smoke screen. By collapsing the distinction between the two forms of labor organization, Gowen eventually succeeded in destroying the power of both.

Matters moved to their tragic climax after October 1873, when Gowen hired Pinkerton to gather information against both arms of the labor movement, and Pinkerton dispatched James McParlan to the anthracite region. After infiltrating the inner circle of the local AOH with remarkable ease, McParlan spent 2.5 years working undercover among the mineworkers before fleeing for Philadelphia in March 1876 when his cover was blown. Several other Pinkerton agents infiltrated the WBA. In June 1875, after a desperate 6-month struggle against Gowen and his railroad (the legendary Long Strike), the WBA went down to its final defeat. In the disarray that followed, the Molly Maguires stepped up their activities, with the last six assassinations attributed to them taking place during that summer alone. In January 1876, the arrests began, and in the spring and summer, the famous trials got underway. With the labor movement in its various forms now utterly defeated, Gowen completed his conquest of the local economy.

The Trials and Executions

It was during the trials and executions that the myth of the Molly Maguires was perfected. The trials, conducted in the midst of enormously hostile national publicity, were in several respects a travesty of justice. The defendants had been arrested by the private police force of Gowen's private Coal & Iron police, acting in close cooperation with the Pinkertons. They were convicted on the evidence of an undercover detective whom the defense attorneys accused (albeit somewhat half-heartedly) of being an agent provocateur, supplemented by the confessions of a series of informers who turned state's evidence to save their necks. Irish Catholics were excluded from the juries. Most of the prosecuting attorneys worked for railroads and mining companies. Remarkably Gowen himself appeared as the star prosecutor at several trials, and his florid courtroom speeches were rushed into print as popular pamphlets. Mere membership in the AOH was presented as de facto membership in the Molly Maguires, which in turn was presented as evidence of guilt. Even by nineteenth-century standards, the arrests and trials were flagrant in their abuse of judicial procedure and their flaunting of corporate power.

The first 10 Molly Maguires were hanged on a single day, June 21, 1877, known to the people of the anthracite region ever since as Black Thursday or the Day of the Rope. Six men were hanged in Pottsville that day and four in the neighboring town of Mauch Chunk (now called Jim Thorpe), in a spectacle carefully choreographed to assert the outraged majesty of the law and the awesome might of

corporate capital. The Reading Railroad's Coal & Iron police patrolled the streets and guarded the jails; special trains were added to transport the coffins. Ten more men would die before the hanging was done. Some of those executed were no doubt guilty as charged; most of them were involved in some sort of Molly Maguire violence even if they had not committed the actual crimes of which they were convicted; all had fought for justice in their own way. Ultimately the Molly Maguires had no place in the industrial United States, and their rural-based tradition of direct, retributive justice died with them on the scaffold. Although the coalmines of Pennsylvania would see plenty of violence in years to come, the Molly Maguires were the last of their line.

KEVIN KENNY

References and Further Reading

Bimba, Anthony. *The Molly Maguires*. New York: International Publisher, 1932.
Broehl, Wayne G., Jr. *The Molly Maguires*. Cambridge, MA: Harvard University Press, 1964.
Coleman, J. Walter. *The Molly Maguire Riots: Industrial Conflict in the Pennsylvania Coal Region*. Richmond, VA: Garret and Massie, 1936.
Dewees, Francis P. *The Molly Maguires*. Philadelphia, PA: J. B. Lippincott & Co., 1877.
Doyle, Sir Arthur Conan. *The Valley of Fear*. New York: Collier, 1914.
Kenny, Kevin. *Making Sense of the Molly Maguires*. New York: Oxford University Press, 1998.
Pinkerton, Allen. *The Molly Maguires and the Detectives*. New York: G. W. Carleton, 1877.

See also **Irish**

MOONEY, TOM (1892–1942)
Socialist Party Activist

Thomas Mooney was born in 1892 to Bernard and Mary Mooney, Irish immigrants in Holyoke, Massachusetts. Mooney's father was a miner and an organizer for the Knights of Labor, and Tom grew up in an atmosphere pervaded with labor violence. Tom became an apprentice foundryman at the Dean Steam Pump Company when he was 14, and when he was 20, he joined the International Molders' Union. In 1907, Tom went on a trip to Europe that he won by selling subscriptions to a socialist magazine; there he was converted to socialism. When he returned to the United States, he moved west to Stockton, California, where he joined the Socialist party. Along with his wife Rena, Tom began to sell socialist literature and in the process, came to the attention of Eugene Debs, who enlisted Mooney in his campaign. As Mooney's commitment to socialism deepened, he also became an advocate of industrial sabotage and direct action.

After 1912, Tom and Rena moved to San Francisco where they became involved in organizing the workers at the Pacific Gas & Electric Company. Along with his partner, Warren Billings, Mooney began to steal explosives from rock quarries and work sites and use them to bring down electrical transmission towers in an attempt to force the utility's management to deal with the union. Mooney managed to win acquittal when accused by company detectives of involvement in the dynamiting. Billings however served time for transporting dynamite on a passenger train.

On 22 July 1916, a bomb exploded during the San Francisco Preparedness Day Parade, killing 10 and injuring 40 others. The bomb went off during a bitter organizing drive at the Market Street Railway, part of the San Francisco streetcar system. Less than a month before, three transmission towers providing power to the streetcars were dynamited, and Mooney and Billings were the prime suspects. When the Preparedness Day bomb went off, Mooney and Billings were quickly apprehended along with a number of their associates.

Mooney's wife and associates were eventually acquitted, but Tom and Billings were found guilty of setting the bomb. It quickly became apparent however that most if not all of the testimony used against Mooney and Billings in the trial had been perjured. Moreover it appeared that the District Attorney Charles Fickert and Mooney's prosecutor, Eddie Cunha, had bribed and coached witnesses to place Mooney and Billings at the scene of the crime. Evidence that would have provided an alibi for Mooney, including a photograph placing Mooney blocks away from the blast at the time of the explosion, mysteriously disappeared. All in all the district attorney's office had engaged in a massive frame-up against Mooney and Billings.

While the initial trial did not spark much interest or concern in the American labor movement, once it was revealed that Mooney and Billings were the victims of a frame-up, the case became an international cause. With World War I still in full swing, the Germans used pro-Mooney propaganda in an attempt to influence European and American workingmen against the U.S. war effort. President Woodrow Wilson became involved in the case, intervening on behalf of Mooney after a group of anarchists protested in front of an American embassy in Russia. None of this was terribly successful however. Governor William Stephens of California refused to pardon Mooney,

and the California Supreme Court remained staunchly hostile to appeals by the two prisoners. When the Wickersham Commission, a federal commission set up by President Wilson to investigate Mooney's guilt, concluded that the case against Mooney and Billings was a politically motivated frame-up, the state government took up the mantle of State's Rights and resisted calls for new trials or pardons.

Meanwhile the Mooney-Billings defense committees were hampered by political sectarianism and personal conflicts. The original head of the defense committees, Bob Minor, was forced out as a result of factional conflicts within the International Workers' Defense League. Ed Nolan, who succeeded Minor, left after strategic disagreements with Mooney. Tom's wife, Rena, then succeeded as the head of the defense committees. Unfortunately Rena began an affair with another Mooney defense worker, which ruined her relationship with her husband. While Mooney was unable to publicly break with his wife for fear that it would hurt his image, the betrayal was a severe blow to the defense committees. Eventually Rena's sister, Belle Hammerberg, took over as head of the defense. Together Mooney and Hammerberg managed to convince the judge at his original trial and all nine of the jurors still alive to publicly state that they believed Tom Mooney to be innocent. Once again however in 1930, the California Supreme Court refused to grant Mooney or Billings a pardon.

Mooney's defense was dealt another major blow when Billings, in an attempt to win parole from prison, revealed the truth about his and Mooney's involvement with industrial sabotage. Billings admitted that at the time when the Preparedness Day bomb went off, he was squirting varnish remover on high-priced automobiles in an attempt to coerce local repair shops (who were bound by a 1-year guarantee to fix paint jobs on certain brands of cars) to deal with the Machinists' Union. Even worse for Mooney, Billings admitted to working as a spy and saboteur for a number of different unions. Billings even named Mooney and other high-ranking figures in the labor movement as being involved in these plots. Once again however Billings was denied a pardon or parole.

Mooney and Billings were eventually released from prison but not until 1939. Mooney was pardoned at the time of his release, but Billings was not pardoned until 1961. The Depression, along with such activists as Upton Sinclair, had done much to change the tone of California politics. When State Senator and Socialist Culbert Olson was elected governor, it was clear that both men would soon be pardoned. Billings emerged from prison repentant. One of the top chess players in the country, Billings eventually became a watchmaker and served as vice-president of the Watchmakers' Union. Mooney however was rendered bedridden soon after his release and died on 6 March 1942.

AARON MAX BERKOWITZ

References and Further Reading

Hunt, Henry Thomas. *The Case of Thomas J. Mooney and Warren K. Billings*. New York: Da Capo Press, 1971.
Frost, Richard H. *The Mooney Case*. Stanford, CA: Stanford University Press, 1968.
Ward, Esolv Ethan. *The Gentle Dynamiter: A Biography of Tom Mooney*. Palo Alto, California: Ramparts, 1983.

See also **Socialist Party of America**

MORGAN, ELIZABETH CHAMBERS (JUNE 16, 1850–FEBRUARY 11, 1944)
Women's Labor Organizer

Elizabeth Morgan was a pioneering women's labor organizer, radical reformer, and advocate for working children. She was among the first women who publicly illuminated the serious hardship working women and children suffered in manufacturing industries, and she was one of the leading female activists to use political action in efforts to better the situation of working women and children. An avowed Socialist, through legislation and organization, Morgan attempted to protect and promote wage earners who suffered from what she believed were the evils of capitalism.

Morgan's experiences as a laborer drove her work as an organizer. She began working in a factory in Birmingham, England, when she was 11 years old. When she was 17, she married machinist Thomas Morgan; together they were able only barely to get by economically. In 1869, the couple immigrated to Chicago, where they had two children. Although they hoped to find a better life in Chicago, they were instead confronted with similarly harsh working conditions. The Morgans became staunch Socialists and both began careers as labor activists.

Morgan's first organizing efforts produced fleeting results. During the 1873 depression, she helped establish a cooperative society, the Sovereigns of Industry, which lasted only a short while. In 1881, Morgan was one of the founders of a women's labor union, Local Assembly 1789, which affiliated with the Knights of Labor. The union advocated for wages for women that were equal to men's, restrictions on child labor, and suffrage for women and African-Americans. By the

end of the decade however, it fell apart over political and ideological differences among its members.

In 1888, Morgan helped found a much stronger organization, the Illinois Ladies' Federal Labor Union No. 2703 (LFLU). The LFLU affiliated with the American Federation of Labor (AFL) and the Chicago Trade and Labor Assembly (CTLA) as one of the few female labor unions in either organization. Morgan served as the LFLU delegate to the CTLA. Its membership included wage-working women from several different trades and middle-class reformers. Its mission was to protect laboring women and children from abusive employers through investigation, legislation, enforcement of laws, and organization. Toward this aim the LFLU organized 23 local craft unions for women, all affiliated with the AFL.

The work of the LFLU illuminated the need for an additional organization that would focus on reforming the social conditions that negatively affected most laboring women and children. Within months of its founding, Morgan and several other LFLU members, together with other female Socialists, union agitators, and settlement workers in Chicago, formed the Illinois Woman's Alliance (IWA). During its 6-year existence, the IWA fought for the elimination of sweatshops, compulsory education for children, and anti-child labor laws and worked to provide immediate relief for the poor through clothing drives and campaigns for public baths.

In the early 1890s, Morgan was a force in the antisweatshop campaigns in Chicago. In 1891, she investigated the working conditions in the city's garment industry for the CTLA and reported on the existence of sweating practices. She explained that women and children were hired to sew pieces of clothing for substandard pay and were required to complete the work either in their tenement or in overcrowded shops without ventilation for 10–14 hours a day, 6 days a week. Morgan's report demanded enforcement of the child labor laws and sanitation inspections of the shops.

In 1892, Morgan participated in additional local and national investigations of the sweating system. As a member of the IWA Committee on Child Labor, Morgan reported on the harsh labor conditions in a number of new sweatshops in Chicago. This and other reports prompted Congress to conduct its own investigation. Morgan was among those who testified and assisted in an investigation led by Florence Kelley and sponsored by the Illinois Bureau of Labor Statistics. Their report citing gross abuses prompted the state legislature to conduct its own investigation.

The Illinois legislature finally took action in 1893. Based on its own investigation of factory work conditions, conducted by a committee that included Morgan and Kelley, the general assembly passed the Factory and Workshop Inspection Act. It established health standards for shops, set the minimum mandatory age to work in manufactories at 14, and limited the amount women could work to 8 hours a day, six days a week. Businessmen who opposed the act formed the Illinois Manufacturers' Association to challenge it. In 1895, the Illinois Supreme Court overturned the 8-hour day provision of the act.

In 1894, debates among IAW members over strategy caused divisions within the organization to intensify. Morgan and other socialist members of the alliance called for strikes and political agitations to secure their aims. Many of the IWA's middle-class members advocated less confrontational and more conventional means to effect labor reforms. Morgan left the organization when the IWA adopted the more conservative approach. Months later the differences resulted in the demise of the alliance.

Morgan's call for strikes and political action to support laboring women received a slightly better reception at the AFL. At its 1894 convention, the AFL approved Morgan's resolutions demanding the passage and enforcement of compulsory education laws, an 8-hour day for women and children, and abolition of the sweating system. The AFL's ambivalence toward women laborers however was reflected in its treatment of Morgan. Morgan's few supporters within the AFL nominated her for the office of first vice-president, the highest office a woman had sought within the federation. Despite her record of service, she resoundingly lost the election.

Morgan finished her career by assisting her husband in his new law practice, defending wage earners. When her final attempt to establish an organization of wage-earning women failed in 1894, she began to study law with her husband. Though she never sought her law license, Morgan spent 17 years providing legal assistance to workingmen and women.

Morgan retired in 1912 after almost 40 years of advocacy for laboring women and children. She was a leader who used radical strategies to expose publicly and alter politically the abuses laborers suffered in the industrial capitalist system. She was also one of the critical actors who attempted to build cross-class alliances among women to further the cause.

GWEN HOERR JORDAN

References and Further Reading

DeVault, Ileen A. "'To Sit among Men': Skill, Gender, and Craft Unionism in the Early American Federation of Labor." In *Labor Histories: Class, Politics, and the Working-Class Experience*, edited by Eric Arnesen, Julie Greene, and Bruce Laurie. Urbana: University of Illinois Press, 1998.

Scharnau, Ralph "Morgan, Elizabeth Chambers." In *Women Building Chicago 1790–1990: A Biographical Dictionary*, edited by Rima Lunin Schultz and Adele Hast. Bloomington: Indiana University Press, 2001.

———. "Elizabeth Morgan, Crusader for Public Reform." *Labor History* 14, 3 (1973): 340–351.

Sklar, Kathryn Kish. *Florence Kelley and the Nations' Work: The Rise of Women's Political Culture, 1830–1900*. New Haven, CT: Yale University Press, 1995.

Tax, Meredith *The Rising of Women: Feminist Solidarity and Class Conflict, 1880–1917*. New York: Monthly Review Press, 1980.

Cases and Statutes Cited

Richie v. People, 155 Ill. 98 (1895).

See also **Knights of Labor; Morgan, Thomas J.; Sovereigns of Industry**

MORGAN, THOMAS J. (OCTOBER 27, 1847–DECEMBER 10, 1912)
Socialist Trade Unionist

During the last quarter of the nineteenth century, the name Thomas J. Morgan became synonymous with the socialist movement in Chicago. Egotistical and combative, Morgan had a genius for organizing. He voiced the sentiments of the working class with personal knowledge, deep feeling, and stinging sarcasm. Morgan held a number of leadership posts and exuded enormous energy in his committee work, his editorial writing, and his fiery speeches. He possessed an uncanny gift for drafting resolutions. While holding fast to socialist principles, Morgan embraced immediate social reforms and sought short-term political alliances with progressive labor and farmer elements.

From Birmingham to Chicago

Born on October 27, 1847, in Birmingham, England, of English and Welsh parentage, Morgan was one of nine children. He began work alongside his poverty-stricken, nail-making parents at age nine. He obtained a rudimentary formal education in parochial and Sunday schools and later studied mechanical drawing in night school.

Morgan's father joined the Chartists, a political movement of reformers who would make Parliament more democratic and responsive to the needs of workers. Young Morgan began reading Jeremy Bentham and John Stuart Mill and attending political mass meetings of workers. He joined the Brass Workers' Society in 1864 and 3 years later helped to organize a small cooperative grocery store.

He married Elizabeth Chambers Morgan on January 26, 1868. Born in 1850, Elizabeth came from a poor factory-operatives family of 10 children. Feeling trapped by the injustices of a society based on privilege and profits, the newlyweds decided to emigrate, seeking freedom and opportunity in the United States. Thomas Morgan arrived in Chicago on May 12, 1869, with 12 dollars in his pocket. He found work as a machinist and brass finisher, employed for most of his wage-earning career at the Illinois Central Railroad's Car Works.

Radical Political Activist

Morgan's political activities took him from a brief flirtation with the Republican party to independent labor and socialist political action. The turning point came with the onset of the national depression of 1873, when he endured 15 bitter weeks of unemployment. Disgusted by the major political parties' inaction and galvanized by the hard times, he marched with other jobless workers demanding the city provide direct relief and work projects. His experiences with labor activism brought him into contact with socialist ideas. Morgan's full commitment to socialism came after a Chicago address by P. J. McGuire in 1876.

During the nationwide railway strikes of 1877, he walked off his job at the Illinois Central railroad. Before the imposition of overwhelming force broke the Chicago general strike, he urged strikers to remain nonviolent as they pressed their wage and hour demands. He soon became a prominent figure in the Workingmen's party and its successor, the Socialist Labor party (SLP). In 1878, thanks in part to Morgan's leadership, the SLP elected Chicago's first socialist alderman as well as four members of the Illinois legislature and added three aldermanic posts in 1879. Despite Morgan's call for unity, friction between the SLP's political and trade union factions sapped the party's strength.

Following two local incidents that had a national impact, Morgan played the leading role in founding a new labor party. On May 3, 1886, strikers at the McCormick Harvester Works clashed with scabs and police, and the next day a bomb broke up a peaceful protest meeting at Haymarket Square. Working with other labor leaders, Morgan channeled worker discontent into the United Labor party (ULP). Operating as a coalition of trade unions, the ULP became Chicago's most successful workers' party, winning eight seats in the state legislature and one aldermanic post. After 2 years however the labor party disappeared, a victim of factionalism, red-baiting, and the lure of the major parties.

Morgan also made common cause with money and agrarian reformers. In 1880, he supported the Greenback-Labor party and in 1894 joined Henry Demarest Lloyd in backing a labor-Populist alliance. His political action brought some notable legislative victories. Morgan authored Chicago's first factory inspection statute and assisted his wife in securing passage of similar legislation at the state level. He successfully spearheaded the long-standing labor demand for the establishment of an Illinois Bureau of Labor Statistics.

Trade Unionist and Labor Lawyer

As a militant trade unionist, Morgan left his imprint on several labor bodies. His affiliations included the Machinists' and Blacksmiths' Union, the Knights of Labor, the Chicago Metal Workers' Union, and the Socialist Trade and Labor Alliance. He helped organize the Chicago Trade and Labor Assembly and the International Machinists' Union.

At the 1890 convention of the American Federation of Labor (AFL), Morgan won approval of the first women's suffrage resolution in the federation's history, but the delegates refused to accept direct representation of the SLP. After contentious debate the 1892–1894 conventions turned down Morgan's socialist initiatives to endorse independent political action and collective ownership of all means of production and distribution. Morgan received only scant support in his quest for two AFL offices, president and second vice-president.

With the outbreak of the 1893 depression, Morgan quit his job at the Illinois Central, enrolled in the Chicago College of Law and was admitted to the bar in 1895. He saw the law profession as an opportunity to contend for both workers' rights and public ownership. He condemned the rise of Chicago's anarchist movement and led the political wing of the SLP into the new Socialist party (SP).

No longer a wage earner, alienated from the new, young party professionals, and outraged by stock-jobbing schemes and what he considered leadership misconduct, Morgan's influence waned as he became half muckraker and half traducer. He stayed active by attending national conventions of the SP in 1901, 1904, 1908, and 1910, by editing a caustic little paper called the *Provoker* (1909–1911), and by organizing the Socialist Education League (1912). Headed for retirement in California, he was killed on December 10, 1912, in a train wreck in Williams, Arizona.

Often partnering with his wife, Morgan's activism spanned an era in Chicago of economic and political reform and radicalism. Morgan achieved national recognition as a militant trade unionist and a socialist firebrand.

Throughout his life Morgan retained his faith in political action as a remedy for labor's ills. He believed that immediate social reform could be achieved through legislative action. He ran unsuccessfully on socialist tickets for a variety of public offices, including alderman, mayor, and U.S. senator. He used independent labor parties as a vehicle for educating workers about socialism. An agitator rather than a theoretician, Morgan maintained a steadfast belief in independent politics and socialist principles.

RALPH SCHARNAU

References and Further Reading

Dell, Floyd. "Socialism and Anarchism in Chicago." In *Chicago: Its History and Its Builders, a Century of Marvelous Growth*, edited by J. Seymour Curry. Vol. 2. Chicago: S. J. Clarke Publishing Company, 1912.

Fine, Nathan. *Labor and Farmer Parties in the United States, 1828–1928*. New York: Rand School of Social Science, 1928.

Kipnis, Ira. *The American Socialist Movement, 1897–1912*. New York: Columbia University Press, 1952.

Mittelman, Edward B. "Chicago Labor in Politics, 1877–96." *Journal of Political Economy* 28, 5 (May 1920): 407–427.

Scharnau, Ralph W. "Thomas J. Morgan and the Chicago Socialist Movement, 1876–1901." Ph.D. dissertation, Northern Illinois University, 1970.

———. "Thomas J. Morgan and the United Labor Party of Chicago." *Journal of the Illinois State Historical Society* 66 (spring 1973): 41–61.

Schilling, George A. "History of the Labor Movement in Chicago." In *Life of Albert R. Parsons with Brief History of the Labor Movement in America*, edited by Lucy E. Parsons. Chicago: Mrs. Lucy Parsons, publisher and proprietor, 1889.

See also **American Federation of Labor; Great Upheaval (1886); Greenback-Labor Party; Knights of Labor; McGuire, Peter J.; Morgan, Elizabeth; Populism/People's Party; Railroad Strikes (1877); Socialist Labor Party; Socialist Trade and Labor Alliance**

MORRISON, FRANK (1859–1949)
American Federation of Labor

Frank Morrison served as the secretary of the American Federation of Labor (AFL) from 1897 to 1935 and was its secretary-treasurer from 1936 to 1939. He was born in Frankton, Ontario. In 1865, his family moved to Walkerton, Ontario, where he became a printer. In 1886, he moved to Chicago, where he joined the International Typographical Union, Local 16. He studied law at Lake Forest University from 1893 to 1894, and became a member of the Illinois bar in 1895. From the inception of the AFL to his death, Morrison was a major political ally of Samuel Gompers. Among other posts, he chaired the wages and hours subcommittee of the Committee on Labor of the Advisory Commission of the Council of National Defense during World War I and attended the International Labor Conference of 1919 organized by conservative unionists at the same time as the Peace Conference that produced the Treaty of Versailles.

For his entire political life, Morrison stood for moderation and cooperation with the government as well as pure-and-simple unionism. Morrison was consistently opposed to socialism as well as to most strikes. Along with Gompers Morrison consistently argued that labor should win a place for itself as a conservative, responsible partner with business owners and the government. As a result Morrison often testified in Congress and played a role in much of the labor legislation passed during the early twentieth century. For instance he advocated in Congress for the creation of a separate Department of Labor, distinct from the Department of Commerce, in the hopes that such a department might regulate wages, hours, and working conditions from a friendlier standpoint than the Department of Commerce. In 1934, he testified before the National Advisory Council in favor of the creation of the Social Security System.

Morrison consistently defended the AFL's stance against organizing unskilled immigrants or black workers. During the McKees Rocks, Pennsylvania, steel strike of 1909, for instance, Morrison was reported to say of the strikers, "They are only hunkies." While the AFL did not officially exclude black workers, it did in practice, and Morrison was complicit in this position. In 1934, under pressure from the Brotherhood of Sleeping Car Porters, the AFL conducted an internal investigation of race discrimination in the federation, but it declined to present the results at the 1935 convention, though it did bring the Brotherhood of Sleeping Car Porters into the AFL.

Morrison was also opposed to the drive to organize the mass-production workers during the early 1930s. When John L. Lewis and other American Federation of Labor (AFL) leaders split from the AFL to form the Congress of Industrial Organizations (CIO), Morrison remained a staunch defender of the old union federation.

At times however Morrison's activity on behalf of the AFL got him into trouble with the system he tried so hard to win a place in, especially since before the New Deal, the government at all levels was generally opposed to any kind of union activity, no matter how moderate. In 1908, Morrison was sentenced to 6 months in prison along with Gompers and John Mitchell, another AFL leader, for violating a court injunction against boycotting Buck's Stove and Range Company, though he did not actually serve any time. He also presented Robert M. La Follette with the endorsement of the AFL as candidate of the Progressive party in 1924, an exception to the usual AFL policy of opposing working-class political action outside the two-party system.

SAMUEL MITRANI

References and Further Reading

Greene, Julie. *Pure and Simple Politics, the American Federation of Labor and Political Activism, 1881–1917*. Cambridge, UK: Cambridge University Press, 1998.

See also **American Federation of Labor; Gompers, Samuel**

MUSIC

Music has always been an integral part of work and the labor movement. Work songs are those sung during the process of work, and they refer to the job itself or attitudes toward work. Labor songs by contrast are used to exhort workers to join unions, to explain their circumstances, and offer a collective solution. Work songs can be traced back to pre-industrial society, while the tradition of labor songs developed along with the large-scale industrialization that took place after the Civil War.

Work Songs

The richest tradition of work songs in the United States comes from African-Americans. Slaves used music both to coordinate their work and to reflect on their fate. In use and style the songs they sang reflected the African cultures they had been forced to leave: Music was a central element in daily life, involving verbal improvisation and participation. Songs had a variety of uses, among which was setting the tempo for work. Yet even in work situations, songs might comment on all sorts of issues ranging from gossip to protest against slavery itself.

Hymns and spirituals expressed the slaves' most profound hopes and concerns and like secular songs were subject to the folk process whereby old songs were constantly revised to fit new situations. These were not sung only in church but were used as rowing, field, and work songs, and their call-and-response patterns meant the individual participated in an ongoing dialogue with his or her community. Often the songs spoke of ultimate justice and freedom.

In the years following emancipation, black laborers continued to work to the accompaniment of song, increasingly secular rather than religious. Song leaders played an important role in setting the pace of work, communicating instructions, and providing diversion. Work songs described and commented on shared problems, including the foibles of white bosses. While such songs declined in the latter part of the twentieth century, from the 1930s to the 1960s, work songs could still be found in southern prisons, where working conditions most resembled those of slavery times.

Other categories of songs related to work include agricultural and pastoral, domestic, street cries, and chants. There is also a large volume of songs related to specific occupations. Sea shanties are the best example in the Anglo-American folk tradition, but such songs also encompass farmers, cowboys, lumberjacks, and prison work gangs. These songs also have historically served a variety of functions, from directing particular tasks to providing diversion from work itself.

Nineteenth-Century Labor Songs

Social movements have always used music to unite, encourage, and inspire participants. The labor movement is no exception. Music is less easily suppressed than political tracts; it appeals to emotion as well as intellect and does not require a high level of education for the listener to understand and be moved by it. In pre-industrial times work songs, spirituals, and ethnic music served important community-building functions. But the formative years of the U.S. labor movement in the late nineteenth century brought with it a tradition of songs and song-poems that directly addressed the dramatic changes in working conditions that accompanied industrialization and offered a simple solution: Join the union.

This tradition began with the struggle for the 8-hour day, but the songs associated with it also commented on working conditions, the experience of immigrants, and a common dislike for the boss. The rousing chorus of "8 Hours"—"8 hours for work, 8 hours for rest, 8 hours for what we will!"—one of the most popular song-poems in U.S. history, could be heard at rallies, demonstrations, and parades.

The most popular song-poem of the nineteenth century came from the Knights of Labor. Typical of the songs of this period, "Storm the Fort, Ye Knights," based on the tune "Hold the Fort") exhorted workers to participate in a moral crusade and projected a vision of an alternative republic based more on cooperation than competition. It offered an optimistic, determined working-class message, which was pegged to a melody borrowed from an evangelical hymn. From this came a long heritage of labor songs based on familiar melodies. Other songs from this period portrayed the United States as a land controlled by an aristocracy of wealth in which workers had lost the rights their forefathers had fought to achieve. These songs often offered alternative visions, especially a republic of and for workers. Poets used the terminology of the Revolutionary Era and the shared heritage of the idea of freedom as tools to criticize social injustice and keep up the spirits of struggling workers. In a later period recorded songs of work and the labor movement reflected a wide variety of musical styles and perspectives.

Songs by and about immigrants also emphasized issues of social justice, pointing out discrimination and calling for genuine equality of opportunity. For instance, "No Irish Need Apply" suggested that Irish immigrants sometimes had a difficult time finding employment because of the stereotypes about them. The Protestant majority questioned their loyalty and their work ethic, criticizing them for celebrating different holidays and drinking too much. The song asserts the pride of the Irish and their determination to make a place for themselves.

Labor Songs and the Left in the Twentieth Century

Some of the most well-known and long-lasting labor songs came from the Industrial Workers of the World (IWW), whose vision of "One Big Union" was relatively popular among workers in the early years of the twentieth century. The IWW (or Wobblies, as they were known) printed and distributed a *Little Red Songbook* that was used as an organizing tool.

"Songs to fan the flame of discontent" reached workers in mines and mills, lumber camps, and hobo jungles across the United States. Most often the songs were based on new lyrics written to a familiar tune, often a hymn. One of the most well-known Wobbly songwriters was Joe Hill, who was executed in Utah in 1915. His words, "Don't mourn, organize," and his songs left a significant and lasting legacy to those who continued to fight for workers' rights. A song later written about Hill by Earl Robinson, set to a poem by Alfred Hayes, was sung and recorded many times.

Another Wobbly songwriter, Ralph Chaplin, penned the words to "Solidarity Forever," generally considered to be the anthem of the labor movement. The melody came from "The Battle Hymn of the Republic," which had already been transformed into "John Brown's Body." Instead of "Glory, glory hallelujah, his soul is marching on," the chorus says "solidarity forever, for the union makes us strong." The song was used not only by the IWW, but again in the organizing drives of the Congress of Industrial Organizations (CIO) in the 1930s.

Some immigrants to the United States brought with them a musical heritage that was qualitatively different than either the African-American or the Anglo-American folk and religious traditions. Urban European workers were used to singing in choruses, and those who wrote songs about their work and their labor-organizing efforts in the United States at first attempted to use this choral tradition. Thus such composers as Charles Seeger and Elie Seigmeister wrote art songs aimed at secular European immigrant workers. One problem with such songs was that they were difficult to use at a march or a rally because they were technically difficult. Thus writers concerned about workers' fate turned to using a more indigenous, rural folk style in their compositions. The songs may not have been authentic folk songs, but they were more accessible; both words and melody were easily remembered, and a group could sing them on the move if necessary, without musical accompaniment. These labor songs, written and sung in a style loosely based on Appalachian folk music, served an important purpose in the 1930s when labor organizing was at its height.

The Great Depression brought enormous problems for working people around the world who struggled to make ends meet. In the United States, songs played an important part in calling attention to these struggles and encouraging workers to fight for their rights. Yip Harburg's "Brother, Can You Spare a Dime" evoked images of people who had worked and fought for their country but were now going hungry. More commonly popular music denied that problems existed—"Life is Just a Bowl of Cherries"—or at best offered escape—"No Depression in Heaven." The tradition of labor songs thus developed outside the bounds of popular music, particularly in the hands of Communists and other left-wing writers who were critical of Tin Pan Alley for its avoidance of the most pressing issues of the day. The Communist movement drew on earlier traditions and materials to write and adapt songs addressing such working-class issues as unemployment and labor unions. In their preference for folk-style music, they intended to create an alternative musical tradition as well as an alternative vision.

Many of the songs written and sung during the Depression Era suggest that if workers joined unions, many of their problems would be ameliorated. In 1932, Florence Reece, the wife of a miner, wrote a song called "Which Side Are You On?" in the midst of an intense strike by the National Miners' Union in Harlan County, Kentucky. Many prominent outsiders—artists, writers, and journalists among them—came to observe for themselves the events in "bloody Harlan," and it was these observers who helped spread the song along with the issues raised in the strike.

The first distribution of such songs by a union was the 1935 recording of the International Ladies' Garment Workers' Union (ILGWU) chorus. The 12 songs on the two 78-RPM records included "Hold the Fort" and "Solidarity Forever." The ILGWU also produced the popular labor musical *Pins and Needles*. Another musical that addressed workers issues in a more esoteric form, *The Cradle Will Rock*, based on Marc Blitzstein's original music, had a big impact on labor theater if not on song.

Woody Guthrie, Pete Seeger, and People's Songs

One of the most well-known singers and song writers from the Depression era is Woody Guthrie, whose many original compositions about labor and other issues left a lasting legacy. Guthrie was an authentic folk singer whose compositions came from personal experience—he hailed from Oklahoma and had seen the Dust Bowl firsthand—but he was also a member of a broad Communist movement that intended to use song as a weapon to help workers overthrow the capitalist system. Guthrie's theory of songwriting was less crude than the phrase "song as a weapon" might suggest, and many of his songs continue to be recorded and sung, from "Pastures of Plenty" to "So Long, It's

Been Good to Know You." Guthrie's "This Land Is Your Land" still is sung by school children all over the United States, but few people know the origins of the song as a critique of an economic system that, in Guthrie's view, bred vast inequalities.

Songs were disseminated by performers such as Guthrie and Pete Seeger. They were also created, revised, and spread through the interactions of writers, singers, and labor organizers at such institutions as Commonwealth College in Arkansas and Highlander Folk School in Tennessee. "Roll the Union on" came from Commonwelth and "We Shall Overcome" from Highlander. The first album of general union songs was recorded in 1941 by the Almanac Singers. *Talking Union* consisted of class-conscious lyrics set to traditional folk tunes, many of which became classics.

After World War II Seeger began an organization called People's Songs, Inc., with a vision of a singing labor movement. In its short-lived existence (1946–1949), People's Songs disseminated songs on a variety of issues, including labor, racial equality, and peace. The work of People's Songs carried on the links between labor and other movements for social change. Such connections are exemplified in the song that became the anthem of the civil rights movement, "We Shall Overcome." Originally a hymn, "I'll Overcome Someday," the song was adapted by black textile workers and brought to Highlander Folk School. Zilphia Horton adapted it and taught it to others, including Seeger, who added more verses to it. When Guy Carawan sang it in the North Carolina sit-ins in 1960 to protest segregation, the word overcome took on new meaning.

Popular Music

By this period some labor songs had carried over into popular music. Merle Travis had already composed and recorded two of the most famous mining songs, "Dark as a Dungeon" and "Sixteen Tons," but by the 1960s, country music regularly included commentary on work. In the late 1970s, "Take This Job and Shove It" was number one on the country music charts. In the 1960s and 1970s, songs also documented contemporary labor struggles, such as that of migrant farm laborers.

As the conditions of labor changed however, and sessions at the bargaining table became more common than picket lines, songs became less useful as tools for labor organizing and expressions of solidarity. As the context and the nature of work changed, so did the songs, with less emphasis on accessibility and participation. The 1960s brought more attention to individual singer-songwriters who performed and recorded for a mass audience in contrast to the group singing and songwriting activities of an earlier era. Yet writers and performers, such as Bob Dylan, drew on the legacy of Woody Guthrie and the issues of the People's Songs era. Rock musician Bruce Springsteen carried on this tradition in subsequent years, writing and singing about the conditions of workers and promoting a vision of a more cooperative society. Harkening back to Guthrie as well, Springsteen argued that the point was not to write propaganda but to tell stories in order to enable a mass audience to walk in the shoes of the oppressed. While he did write and sing about his own experience, Springsteen was still an interpreter whose recordings differed, particularly in style, from those of workers who performed their own songs.

Singers and songwriters addressed new themes from the 1970s on, including the environment, women's liberation, consumerism, and jobs moving overseas. Their songs did not always comment directly on issues of work and labor organizing, but many writers continued to make these links. Dave Rovics for instance called one of his songs criticizing U.S. imperialism "Pray for the Dead and Fight Like Hell for the Living," evoking memories of the feisty Mother Jones, one of the most important and successful labor organizers in the early twentieth century. New occupational songs appeared as well, such as those about truck driving. Old and new songs commemorated heroes and heroines of the labor movement, such as Mother Jones and those who wrote and sang about them, including Joe Hill and Woody Guthrie.

ROBBIE LIEBERMAN

References and Further Reading

Cohen, Ronald D. *Rainbow Quest: The Folk Music Revival and American Society, 1940–1970.* Amherst: University of Massachusetts Press, 2002.
Dunaway, David King. *How Can I Keep from Singing: Pete Seeger.* New York: McGraw-Hill, 1981.
Foner, Philip S. *American Labor Songs of the Nineteenth Century.* Urbana and Chicago: University of Illinois Press, 1975.
Green, Archie. *Only a Miner: Studies in Recorded Coal-Mining Songs.* Urbana and Chicago: University of Illinois Press, 1975.
Green, Archie, ed. *Songs about Work: Essays in Occupational Culture for Richard A. Reuss.* Bloomington: Special Publications of the Folklore Institute No. 3, Indiana University, 1993.
Glazer, Joe, and Edith Fowke. *Songs of Work and Freedom.* Garden City, NY: Dolphin Books, 1961.
Greenway, John. *American Folksongs of Protest.* Philadelphia: University of Pennsylvania Press, 1953.
Halker, Clark. *For Democracy, Workers, and God: Labor Song-Poems and Labor Protest, 1865–1895.* Urbana and Chicago: University of Illinois Press, 1991.
IWW. *Songs of the Workers, to Fan the Flames of Discontent (Little Red Songbook).* Chicago, IL: Industrial Workers of the World, 1964.
Klein, Joe. *Woody Guthrie: A Life.* New York: Alfred A. Knopf, 1980.
Kornbluh, Joyce. *Rebel Voices: An IWW Anthology.* Chicago: Charles Kerr Press, 1998.
Korson, George. *Minstrels of the Mine Patch.* Philadelphia: University of Pennsylvania Press, 1938.
Levine, Lawrence. *Black Culture and Black Consciousness.* New York: Oxford University Press., 1977.
Lomax, Alan. Woody Guthrie, Pete Seeger, *Hard-Hitting Songs for Hard-Hit People.* New York: Oak Publications, 1967.
Lieberman, Robbie. *"My Song Is My Weapon": People's Songs, American Communism, and the Politics of Culture 1930–1950.* Urbana and Chicago: University of Illinois Press, 1989.
Reuss, Richard. *Songs of American Labor, Industrialization, and the Urban Work Experience: A Discography.* Ann Arbor: Program on Workers' Culture, Labor Studies Center, University of Michigan, 1982.

MUSTE, A. J. (1885–1967)
Pacifist and Labor Activist

Abraham Johannes (A. J.) Muste gained his greatest renown as a respected leader and public spokesperson for the radical wing of the post-World War II American peace movement, where he promoted militant pacifism's vision of a nonviolent world through the pursuit of social justice and peace. For almost two solid decades, from 1919 through the late 1930s, Muste worked to create opportunities for working-class empowerment. His grassroots organizing efforts, his work as director of an innovative program in worker education, and his promotion of a revolutionary model of labor action and politics emphasized the potential of militant protest and foreshadowed the radical democratic thrust of Depression Era industrial unionism. In the process Muste helped sustain a tradition of independent radicalism and militant democracy among the American working-class.

Accidental Beginnings: The Lawrence Strike of 1919

Muste began his career in the early 1910s as a sheltered and inexperienced Dutch Reformed Minister.

Born in the Netherlands and brought to the United States as a child, Muste initially adopted the orthodox Calvinist inclinations of his family and the west Michigan Dutch immigrant community in which they lived. He attended seminary in New Jersey and New York, where he gained basic theological training, and then accepted his first ministerial job in upper Manhattan. Life in New York City changed Muste's life. The activist members of Muste's congregation and the tumult of the city brought this novice minister into contact with the precepts of the social Gospel, the reform agendas of leading social welfare advocates, and the public struggles of local workers fighting to improve the conditions of their lives. By the time of U.S. entry into the First World War, Muste, who had moved to a new congregation in the Boston area, had thoroughly imbibed of these progressive impulses, and by the end of the war, he had learned both the perils and promises of taking a principled and nonconformist stance. His outspoken advocacy of Christian pacifism during wartime cost him his job, forcing him to seek work and build community with nearby Quakers and other Christian opponents to war. At the same time, Muste's growing commitment to socialist ideals and working-class struggles began to alienate him from the same liberal antimilitarists who had come to his aid. He emerged from the experience a committed radical and respected organizer of the unorganized working class.

A 1919 strike in the textile mills of Lawrence, Massachusetts, the site of an earlier general strike of 1912, became Muste's crucible. In February of that year, a renegade group of workers revolted against a pay cut instituted by Lawrence employers and agreed to by their union representatives and walked out on strike, bringing 15,000–30,000 workers onto the streets with them. As part of a small fellowship of faith-based activists then living in Boston, Muste and two friends traveled to Lawrence to observe the events and quickly found themselves swept into the center of events. The members of the strike committee, acting in opposition to the American Federation of Labor (AFL), were essentially on their own, with little experience, minimal command of the English language, an immigrant constituent base divided by ethnicity and language, and almost no contacts outside their limited circle. Aware of the obstacles they faced and their desperate need for help, they asked the visiting Muste to become their committee's executive secretary. Although he had no formal union training or working-class credentials, Muste accepted the invitation, stepped into the political vacuum, and helped lead these workers through 16 weeks of difficult protest to victory.

Brookwood Labor College: An Experiment in Worker Education

The lessons Muste learned from the Lawrence experience—the importance of having strong and capable leadership at the grass roots, the need to forge unity among disparate groups, and the ways in which principled risk-taking could foster solidarity and political power—shaped his activism and defined his work on behalf of the organized and unorganized working class. Muste immediately moved into the newly formed Amalgamated Textile Workers of America, where he worked for 2 years as the unions' general secretary. His more lasting influence came through his work with Brookwood Labor College in Katonah, New York, which he directed from its inception in 1921 until his departure 1933. At Brookwood Muste advanced a unique vision of worker education that helped shape a generation of militant labor organizers and union advocates.

Brookwood Labor College began, as did Muste's labor career, as an outgrowth of the progressive strain of politically engaged pacifism that ultimately moved in a more revolutionary direction. Its founders, William and Helen Fincke, were members of the pacifist Fellowship of Reconciliation who, like Muste, sought to link the quest for peace with the fight for social justice, a difficult quest during a time in which labor and progressive activists faced full-scale repression and attack. With Muste at the helm, Brookwood forged ahead, making strong connections to leading progressives and militant trade unionists and developing an innovative curriculum that linked intellectual development to organizing experience. The school's goal was simple: To create effective labor leaders at the local level. To achieve this goal, Brookwood recruited students from a variety of regions and occupations; taught classes that ranged from sophisticated studies of psychology and sociology to basic public speaking, writing, and organizing skills; and sent its students out to apply what they learned to real-world situations. It was a stimulating environment that built community and confidence and gave Brookwood and Muste strong reputations within the progressive wing of the American labor movement. Brookwood's pedagogical emphasis on worker democracy and militant action, which strongly encouraged its students to think outside of established bureaucratic and political frameworks, ultimately brought the college into conflict with the more conservative elements of organized labor. In 1928, the leaders of the AFL publicly condemned the college as antagonistic and subversive and instructed member unions to no longer supply Brookwood with students or funds. Ironically the school's nondoctrinaire approach to labor activism also earned it the ire of the Communist party, which also denounced the school that very same year. Charting an independent radical course was no easy task during the tumultuous years of the 1920s.

The Era of the Musteites

Neither Muste nor Brookwood folded in the face of these attacks. According to Muste, the school maintained its vitality for several more years but ultimately closed as a result of Depression Era financial constraints and factional infighting. Muste in the meantime had begun to develop what he hoped would become a politically powerful revolutionary workers' movement. In May 1929, he founded the Conference for Progressive Labor Action (CPLA). Through the CPLA Muste and his cohorts, many of them graduates of Brookwood, advanced an explicitly Marxist but non-Communist agenda that presaged much of the later work of the not-yet-formed Congress of Industrial Organizations (CIO). Their efforts reflected the growing dissatisfaction felt by progressive and radical unionists with both the rightward-leaning AFL and the Soviet-dominated Communist party. The CPLA believed that it could encourage alternative forms of labor activism that better served the needs of the American working class.

The Musteites, as CPLA's followers were called, called for organizing the unorganized into broad-based industrial unions (a direct challenge to the bureaucratic trade unionism of the AFL); advocated wide-ranging nondiscrimination clauses; and worked on behalf of the unemployed. During their heyday the Musteites lent skilled and militant leadership to a number of important strikes, including a series of violent labor conflicts in southern textile mills in 1929 and a mass protest and picketing campaign among autoworkers at Toledo Auto-Lite in April 1934. The CPLA also made a strong impact by organizing jobless Americans into Unemployed Leagues in Ohio, West Virginia, Pennsylvania, and North Carolina. Seeking direct political power, the CPLA merged in December 1933 with the Trotskyite Communist League of America to form the short-lived American Workers' party. In all of these efforts, the Musteites displayed their commitment to increasing the power of American workers at the grass roots.

The Return to His Pacifist Roots

In the summer of 1936, Muste experienced a religious reconversion that brought him back to his Christian pacifist roots. He reconnected with the pacifist Fellowship of Reconciliation (FOR) where he won election to the organization's National Council and found employment as chair of the FOR's Committee on Industrial Relations. There he continued his pursuit of social justice for working-class Americans and participated on the periphery of vanguard labor protests, including a 1936 nonviolent "lie down" strike at a textile mill near Reading, Pennsylvania. In May 1937, Muste took on the directorship of New York City's Labor Temple, where he preached a doctrine of Christian social responsibility that linked religious practice to the defense of working-class struggle. In April 1940, he returned to the FOR as executive secretary, beginning the next and final phase of an activist career that would not end until his death in 1967. Even with peace and nonviolence at the center of his political agenda, Muste retained his militancy, his belief in the importance of skilled and visionary leadership, and his dedication to economic justice as a fundamental part of his work for social change.

MARIAN MOLLIN

Selected Works

Muste, A. J. *The Essays of A. J. Muste*, edited by Nat Hentoff. New York: The Bobbs-Merrill Company, 1967.

References and Further Reading

Hentoff, Nat. *Peace Agitator: The Story of A. J. Muste*. New York: Macmillan, 1963.
Robinson, Jo Ann Oiman. *Abraham Went Out: A Biography of A. J. Muste*. Philadelphia, PA: Temple Univ. Press, 1981.

See also **Brookwood Labor College**

MYERS, ISAAC (JANUARY 13, 1835– JANUARY 26, 1891)
African-American Labor Organizer and Activist

From the Civil War years until his death in 1891, Issac Myers was one of Baltimore's most prominent African-American citizens. Over the course of three decades in public life, Myers wore multiple hats, including those of labor organizer, community activist and spokesperson, postal detective, businessman, newspaper editor, and church leader. During the

Reconstruction years, Myers emerged as perhaps the nation's most staunch and well-known advocate of trade unionism for black workers. By the 1880s, however, his commitment to labor organization had waned as he became embittered by white workers' reluctance to abandon their hostility toward their black counterparts. Business, Republican party politics, and the African Methodist Episcopal Church occupied his organization and emotional energies in the last decade of his life. Myers's transformation from a preacher of the gospel of trade unionism to full-throated opponent of organized white labor illustrates the contradictory impulses toward black advancement in the late nineteenth century and the persistence of racial barriers to labor unity.

Myers was born free in Maryland, a slave state with the country's largest free black population, in 1835. Little is known of his parents, who were reported to be poor, not unlike many other free blacks in the border states. Late nineteenth-century accounts of his life state that he attended a private religious day school—no public schools were open to free-black children at the time—where he received the equivalent of a common school education. At the age of 16, he apparently left school and apprenticed to a prominent local black caulker, James Jackson, and within 4 years Myers was reported to have been superintending the caulking of some of Baltimore's largest clipper ships under construction. In 1860, he left the ship yards to assume the position of chief porter and shipping clerk in the wholesale grocery of Woods, Bridges, and Company, where he would learn crucial business skills that he would shortly put to good use on behalf of the city's black community.

The outbreak of racial conflict in Baltimore's shipyards immediately following the Civil War pushed Myers into a public leadership role as a community activist. In September 1865, white caulkers engaged in a successful month-long strike against Baltimore's shipyards, resulting in an all-white employment policy requiring the eventual dismissal of black shipyard workers. Displaced black caulkers quickly mobilized community support on their behalf, winning local support for the creation of a Mutual Joint Stock Company that soon became the Chesapeake Marine Railway and Dry Dock Company. Myers, who local accounts named as one of the black caulkers' leaders, was the likely source of the proposal to form the all-black company; joining with other community leaders drawn from the ranks of the African Methodist Episcopal Church and the Methodist Episcopal Church. Myers became a founder and director of the new enterprise, which leased facilities and gave employment to as many as 300 black dockworkers before it closed its doors in 1883.

Active on behalf of the Republican party in Maryland in the years immediately following the Civil War, Myers also organized black workers in cities across the South, earning a reputation as a strong supporter of black labor activism. In 1869, he accepted the invitation of the National Labor Union (NLU), an assemblage of white craft unions, to address its delegates. Speaking on behalf of the small black delegation at the convention, Myers sought to transform the white labor federation's unprecedented invitation into a permanent interracial relationship. On a practical level Myers assured his white listeners that they now had "nothing to fear from the colored laboring man," who desired only to see "labor elevated and made respectable," just as whites did. But he did express concern with the racial division of labor that relegated blacks to unskilled work. "American citizenship with the black man is a complete failure," he concluded, "if he is proscribed from the workshops of the country," as had long been the case. Myers called on white workers of the newly reunited nation to follow the NLU's example by finishing "the good work of uniting the colored and white workingmen of the country." Notwithstanding Myers's endorsement of Republican President Ulysses S. Grant and his opposition to the repudiation of the national debt (positions white workers objected to), his address was apparently greeted with respect, punctuated by enthusiastic applause.

Although the NLU was not interested in pressing its constituent white unions to drop their policies of racial exclusion, black workers in the upper South pressed forward with plans to organize. In July 1869, Myers presided over a gathering of 30 black delegates at the Douglass Institute in Baltimore to establish a statewide black labor association. In December of that year, Myers, representing the Baltimore Colored Caulkers' Trade Union Society, joined with over two hundred black delegates in Washington, DC to spearhead an effort to establish a Colored National Labor Union (CNLU) aimed at fostering black trade unionism. In its brief existence, the CNLU served as a clearinghouse for black trade unionists and politicians. Preaching the fundamental unity between labor and capital, it opposed employment discrimination; endorsed cooperatives, vocational training, and public education for blacks; supported the Republican party; and memorialized Congress on behalf of black southerners seeking public land, low interest loans, and civil rights. As the CNLU's first president, Myers traveled widely to encourage black workers to organize in self-defense and avoid becoming "the servants of servants." The "watchword of the colored men must be organize!" he told a group of African-Americans in Norfolk,

Virginia. In 1871, the former slave and noted abolitionist Frederick Douglass succeeded Myers as CNLU president, a testament to the growing influence of black Republican politicians in the organization. The CNLU quickly faded from the scene.

Over the course of the 1870s and 1880s, Myers was active in his support for the Republican party. For his efforts he was rewarded with a patronage position in the U.S. Post Office as a postal detective. By 1879, he was operating a coal yard in Baltimore; in 1882, he became owner and editor of a political newspaper, the *Colored Proprietor*, and held another patronage job as a U.S. gauger, a post he held until early 1887, when a Democratic assumed the position as collector for the port of Baltimore. Myers remained active on behalf of the Republicans, organized a Colored State Industrial Fair Association in Maryland, and founded and led a Colored Business Men's Association.

By the 1880s, if not earlier, Myers's stance toward organized labor had turned decidedly negative. "All branches of the trades are governed by rules and regulations which are so framed as to exclude the colored man," he explained to the readers of the *Christian Recorder* in 1881. Myers attributed the greatest antiblack animus to working- and middle-class whites, particularly immigrants. "Everywhere, the white trades unions prohibits the admission of colored men as members, and white contractors, no matter how favorable, are prohibited from employing colored mechanics," he complained. With white oppression and black workers' own failure aggressively to embrace what few opportunities there were, he predicted that black "mechanics will gradually drop into obscurity and the grave." The evolution of Myers's perspective from pro- to anti-union reflected less an objective shift in the relationship between black and white workers—the white hostility he objected to had not changed considerably over time—than it did Myers's growing pessimism about the realistic prospects of interracial labor collaboration. When the rise of the Knights of Labor in Baltimore in the mid-1880s temporarily united black and white workers, Myers was nowhere to be seen. This new opportunity to create an interracial alliance, which many Baltimore blacks embraced, failed to win back the man who had once been the country's most prominent black labor leader.

Myers's final years were devoted to politics, business, and the church. For 15 years he served as the Bethel A. M. E. School of Baltimore as superintendent, transforming it, one contemporary claimed, into "the banner Sunday-school of the world." In his final years, he had been elected president of a project to build a home for elderly A. M. E. Church ministers. He died of a stroke after a brief illness in 1891.

ERIC ARNESEN

References and Further Reading

Foner, Philip S., and Lewis, Ronald L. *The Black Worker: A Documentary History from Colonial Times to the Present.* Vol. 2: *The Black Worker during the Era of the National Labor Union.* Philadelphia, PA: Temple University Press, 1978.

Hill, John Louis. *When Black Meets White.* Cleveland, OH: Argyle Publishing Co., 1924.

"The Late Isaac Myers, of Baltimore, MD." *A. M. E. Church Review* 7 (Apr. 1891): 351–356.

Matison, Sumner Eliot. "The Labor Movement and the Negro during Reconstruction." *Journal of Negro History* 33, 4 (Oct. 1948): 426–468.

Paul, William George. "The Shadow of Equality: The Negro in Baltimore, 1964–1911." Ph.D. dissertation, University of Wisconsin, 1972.

Thomas, Bettye C. "A Nineteenth-Century Black-Operated Shipyard, 1866–1884: Reflections Upon Its Inception and Ownership." *Journal of Negro History* 59, 1 (Jan. 1974): 1–12

See also **African-Americans; Emancipation and Reconstruction; National Labor Union; South**

N

NATIONAL AD HOC COMMITTEE OF BLACK STEELWORKERS

The National Ad Hoc Committee of Black Steelworkers was founded in 1964 by African-American members of the United Steelworkers of America (USWA). The first nationwide African-American protest organization in the USWA, it waged major struggles against racial discrimination in USWA policies and practices. Although it did not achieve all of its goals, it succeeded in improving African-Americans' prospects within the union and the steel industry. Its struggles led to changes within the USWA that paved the way for its agreement to sign the Consent Decree in 1974. The Committee disbanded in the early 1970s.

At the dawn of the 1960s, African-American steelworkers faced significant barriers to advancement due to discriminatory policies and practices within major steel companies. Although African-Americans formed a significant percentage of the USWA's membership, they felt that their issues were not adequately addressed by the union. Departments were highly segregated by race, which affected the type of work performed as well as black workers' mobility within a company. In general, African-American steelworkers were confined to unskilled, dirty, dangerous, lower-paying jobs such as in blast furnaces and open hearths, and were denied access to cleaner, safer, and more highly compensated positions dominated by whites. They were able to rise to skilled positions only in so-called black departments and advanced into skilled positions in "white departments" only after years of hard work and persistence. Blacks' mobility was further constrained by the fact that seniority was accrued within departments—that is, blacks who transferred to other departments risked losing their hard-earned seniority. The situation was worse at the executive level, as an exceedingly small percentage of leadership positions in both the steel companies and the USWA were filled by African-Americans. African-Americans were discriminated against in promotions, and their positions were the most vulnerable to automation and layoffs.

These disadvantages remained despite the existence of a top-level USWA Civil Rights Committee, union contracts that contained nondiscrimination clauses, fair employment committees at the local level, and public pronouncements by union leaders. The USWA president, David McDonald, promised to fight racial discrimination, and the union vowed to work with the federal Committee on Equal Employment Opportunity (EEO), but significant racial disparities persisted.

In the 1950s, organized labor and unions responded to McCarthyism by taking more conservative stances, as organizations that called for social justice and racial equality were increasingly branded as Communist and anti-American. By the early 1960s, African-American unionists in many industries, frustrated by barriers to progress and inspired by the growing civil rights movement, began to organize protest groups. Among these were the Negro American Labor Council (NALC), which brought together over one thousand union members from the steel, rubber, and auto industries, and the United Negro Protest Committee. However, organized labor was not receptive—even unions considered to be progressive, such as the United Auto Workers (UAW) and the USWA, denounced the African-American activism as anti-union and counterproductive. This is the context in which the National Ad Hoc Committee of Black Steelworkers was founded.

The Ad Hoc Committee formed in the summer of 1964, when a group of African-American activists within the USWA called a meeting at the union's International Convention in Atlantic City. Important members of this committee included Curtis Strong, Rayfield Mooty, Aaron Jackson, and Hugh Henderson. Elections for key USWA offices, including the position of president, were scheduled for 1965, and the Committee members recognized this as an opportune time to organize and use the African-American vote as leverage to force changes in the union's racial practices. They agreed to present a three-point agenda to both presidential candidates: 1) the re-organization of the union's Civil Rights Committee into a full-blown department led by an African-American; 2) greater African-American representation on district and national staffs; and 3) the inclusion of an African-American on the union's international executive board.

In December 1964, the incumbent president, David McDonald, dismissed the demands of Committee representatives in a meeting that lasted less than 15 minutes. The Committee fared better with the challenger I. W. Abel, who recognized that African-Americans, then composing 20% to 30% of the union's membership, could swing the vote in his favor. Abel agreed to the first two of the Committee's three demands, contending that the third would require a change in the union's constitution, and thus won the support of the group. Abel defeated the incumbent McDonald in a very close election in which the northern black vote sealed Abel's victory.

As promised, Abel re-organized the union's Civil Rights Committee into a new department, led by an African-American. He appointed other African-Americans, including Curtis Strong, to the staff and addressed the 1966 conference of the NALC. However, Abel failed to fully integrate the union's decision-making bodies, and the union's system of delegating blacks to low-paid, unskilled "black jobs" persisted. In 1966, the group picketed U.S. Steel's Pittsburgh headquarters and openly criticized Abel at the USWA convention later that year.

The Ad Hoc Committee continued to fight for change, holding two national meetings in 1967. The meetings spawned demonstrations against major steel companies, letters of protest, and discrimination lawsuits against both the USWA and the larger steel industry. The Committee tried repeatedly to meet with Abel to discuss the union's racial problems but was continually ignored. It decided to up the pressure by organizing a picket line protest at the USWA's International Convention in August 1968; this would be the group's first action that directly targeted its union. The Committee also agreed on three new demands: 1) elimination of all discrimination in the USWA; 2) full integration in policy-making positions within all levels of district and national offices (including the earlier demand of an African-American on the Executive Board); and 3) revision of the union's civil rights program. Abel and other USWA leaders tried to preempt the strike through various political means, but their attempts were ineffective—the picket line garnered national media attention. The Committee's resolutions were voted down, but after the convention, Abel responded by hiring more African-Americans in staff positions.

The Committee continued its organizing and recruiting efforts and began to include more women in its efforts. Responding to Abel's efforts to hire black staff after the 1968 protests and by his promise to fight for an African-American on the Executive Board, the Committee endorsed his re-election in 1969 and helped him win a second term. In 1972, the USWA agreed to appoint an African-American to the Executive Board. Committee members viewed it as a hollow victory, however, criticizing the appointment—in a new position of vice president for human affairs—as tokenism and yet another instance of institutional segregation.

By this time, black steelworkers were increasingly turning to the courts for help, as well as forming new organizations outside of the USWA. Committee members, recognizing the limitations of a black reform movement within a predominantly white institution and acknowledging the frustrations of its constituency, voted to disband. Some local chapters continued on but lacked the power of a national movement. African-American steelworkers never again achieved the level of power they held during the high points of the Committee's fight for equality. In 1974, the USWA signed the Consent Decree, agreeing to pay $31 million in damages to minority steelworkers and promising more progressive hiring practices.

DAVID PURCELL

References and Further Reading

Foner, Philip Sheldon. *Organized Labor and the Black Worker, 1619–1981*. New York: International Publishers, 1982.

Hill, Herbert. *Black Labor and the American Legal System: Race, Work, and the Law*. Madison: University of Wisconsin Press, 1986.

———. "The Problem of Race in American Labor History." *Reviews in American History* 24, no. 2 (1996): 189–208.

Hinshaw, John H. *Steel and Steelworkers: Race and Class Struggle in Twentieth-Century Pittsburgh*. Albany: State University of New York Press, 2002.

Needleman, Ruth. *Black Freedom Fighters in Steel: The Struggle for Democratic Unionism*. Ithaca, NY: ILR Press, 2003.

Stein, Judith. *Running Steel, Running America: Race, Economic Policy, and the Decline of Liberalism*. Chapel Hill: University of North Carolina Press, 1998.

See also **African-Americans; National Negro Labor Council; Steel and Iron; United Steelworkers of America**

NATIONAL AGRICULTURAL WORKERS UNION

See **Southern Tenant Farmers' Union**

NATIONAL ALLIANCE OF POSTAL AND FEDERAL EMPLOYEES

The National Alliance of Postal and Federal Employees (NAPE) evolved over the course of the twentieth century, from an all-black industrial union to an interracial trade organization. Founded in Chattanooga, Tennessee, on October 6, 1913, by African-American railway mail clerks, the National Alliance of Postal Employees came into existence only after the American Federation of Labor (AFL)-affiliated Railway Mail Association adopted a Caucasian-only clause in its national constitution. At the time, the Railway Mail Service formed one of the central departments of the postal service, operating wooden cars that created hazardous work conditions, and subsequently large casualty numbers, for the black mail clerks who worked on them. Given the risks, whites were reluctant to work in these positions. However, when the major railroads replaced the cars with steel containers in 1913, the Railway Mail Association launched an effort to systematically remove black clerks from its memberships. Along with a racially discriminatory program implemented by President Woodrow Wilson's newly appointed postmaster general, Albert Burleson, to make the railroads' postal operations "lily white," the black clerks faced dismal job prospects.

Led by Robert L. Bailey of Indianapolis, Indiana, Louis J. Harper of Atlanta, Georgia, and Henry Mims of Houston, Texas, representatives from railway centers in 13 states held a national convention to draft a constitution that advocated protective measures for their families (such as the creation of a beneficiary and insurance department), established a national journal that advanced their common cause, and created an organization to represent black workers who wished to file grievances and petitions with the Post Office Department. Throughout its early history, the Alliance grew rapidly from its southern base, establishing branches in New York City, Detroit, Chicago, Cleveland, Pittsburgh, and Cincinnati. Between 1920 and 1939, 11 districts were formed and the number of Alliance memberships grew slowly.

District and local Alliance members engaged in a wide variety of civil rights issues affecting the employment of African-American postal workers throughout the 1920s and 1930s, such as: demanding equal promotion and pay raises for postal employees; calling for an end to the Wilson Administration's use of photographs to accompany civil service applications; and waging an extensive publicity campaign against the segregation of mail crews and sorting rooms in southern areas. Branches of the National Alliance also co-operated with other organizations working for the political and economic advancement of African-Americans, such as the antilynching campaigns waged by the National Association for the Advancement of Colored People (NAACP), the employment initiatives of the National Urban League, and the "Back to Africa" movement of Marcus Garvey and the Universal Negro Improvement Association.

In the Great Depression years of the 1930s, NAPE membership faced new challenges when the Postmaster General instituted pay cuts and furloughs without monetary compensation for mail employees. World War II witnessed the involvement of organization leaders in Fair Employment Practice Committee (FEPC) hearings throughout the country in response to complaints of job discrimination in post office hiring and the promotion of Africans as timekeepers, window clerks, and scheme examiners. The Alliance campaigned for the hiring of black women to permanent positions in federal service. In 1945, Alliance activism reached a high-water mark when NAPE leaders pushed for permanent FEPC legislation. Branch applications for memberships declined sharply after 1948, however, when black postal employees faced wholesale suspensions under President Harry S. Truman's Federal Employees Loyalty Program, most notably in Cleveland, Chicago, Los Angeles, New York, and Philadelphia. Postal Loyalty boards directed their investigation against black and Jewish employees, inquiring about the employees' attitudes toward topics ranging from interracial marriage and community activism to items relating to national security such as the Truman Doctrine and the Marshall Plan.

In addition, NAPE members faced increased scrutiny as a result of a measure stipulated in the Taft-Hartley Act of 1947. While much of the legislation focused on industrial-labor management relations in the private sector, a section of the measure barred Alliance employees and other postal union members who wished to exercise their right to bargain collectively in the workplace from doing so. By the close of the 1950s, however, the Alliance had succeeded in pressuring the U.S. Post Office Department to create a Board of Appeals and Review as an impartial body to adjudicate the grievances of postal employees. Throughout the nation, Alliance local representatives worked diligently to promote grassroots voter registration drives and civil rights issues affecting its membership.

In 1962, the Alliance was dealt an administrative blow when the union's industrial status prevented its rank-and-file membership from being included in Executive Order 10988 as a "national exclusive" craft entity and entitled to collective bargaining rights. However, the Alliance managed to reach new heights despite these administrative setbacks. In 1965, the Alliance opened its memberships to include all federal employees. Changing its name to the National Alliance of Postal and Federal Employees (NAPFE), the Alliance worked in collaboration with the leadership of the Manhattan-Bronx Post Union (MBPU) and the National Association of Letter Carriers (NALC) when New York's clerks, mail handlers, maintenance workers, and letter carriers walked off the job for higher wages in 1970. By the late 1970s, the Alliance had created a definitive public image, with its representatives making numerous visits to Capitol Hill to appear before committees of the House and Senate to discuss legislation affecting the Union's interests.

In the early twenty-first century, with over 70,000 members organized into more than 141 local chapters in 37 states, the Alliance was at the forefront of employee-management relations, addressing issues such as mail security, federal job privatization, and health care, not to mention the challenges of globalization. It held biennial conventions throughout its 10 districts and published the *National Alliance* and the legislative newsletter for all federal employees in every branch of government. Furthermore, it offered the Ashby B. Carter Memorial Scholarship Program and a host of grants to the dependents of its rank-and-file membership and hosted a number of fundraising activities for community organizations and auxiliary affiliates. It also forged alliances with the World Confederation of Labor and the Leadership Conference on Civil Rights.

ROBERT F. JEFFERSON

References and Further Reading

Glenn, Alonzo L. *History of the National Alliance of Postal Employees, 1913–1955*. Cleveland: s.n., 1955.

The Kaiser Index of Black Resources, 1948–1986. Brooklyn, NY: Carlson, 1992.

Leadership Conference on Civil Rights. "Our Coalition." www.civilrights.org/about/lccr/coalition%5Fmembers/.

Moore, Jacquelyne C., ed. *Public Information Kit*. Washington, DC: National Alliance of Postal and Federal Employees, 1996.

National Alliance of Postal and Federal Employees. "History of NAPFE." www.napfe.com/NAPFEabouthistory.asp.

NATIONAL ASSOCIATION FOR THE ADVANCEMENT OF COLORED PEOPLE (NAACP)

One of the nation's most prominent civil rights organizations, the National Association for the Advancement of Colored People (NAACP) is most famous for its Supreme Court victories in the 1950s and 1960s. In cases like *Brown v. Board of Education*, the NAACP remade constitutional law. In particular, the NAACP successfully attacked racially segregated education, transportation, and housing, as well as racially discriminatory voting procedures. For much of its history, labor issues were peripheral to the NAACP's wide-ranging agenda. Nonetheless, the NAACP consistently struggled with whether, and how, it would represent poor and working-class African-Americans.

The Early NAACP

Founded in New York City on the hundredth anniversary of Abraham Lincoln's birthday, the NAACP emerged in 1909 in direct response to riots in Lincoln's birthplace of Springfield, Illinois. The increase in white-on-black violence after the turn of the twentieth century might have been the immediate catalyst, but the problems the new organization sought to challenge extended far beyond such incidents. As laws and customs pervasively established racial segregation and discrimination in the late nineteenth and early twentieth centuries, the Supreme Court largely eviscerated post-Civil War constitutional protections for the formerly enslaved. The founders of the interracial NAACP sought to reverse this negative trend by expanding legal protections for African-Americans.

Throughout its history, the NAACP struggled to develop a strategy for addressing the problems of African-American workers. One of the Association's

People marching with signs to protest segregation in education at the college and secondary levels. Library of Congress, Prints & Photographs Division, Visual Materials from the NAACP Records [LC-USZ62-116817].

original goals was to help African-Americans find employment. Early in the NAACP's history, however, it informally arranged with the National Urban League to divide the pursuit of African-American advancement into legal equality and economic advancement. The NAACP focused on the former through litigation efforts and lobbying, while the Urban League concentrated on the latter through social work and community organization.

The Association's peripheral treatment of economic issues reflected the elite status of its founders. Although they were well equipped to handle their mission, the founders were unrepresentative of the vast majority of African-Americans who sought to fulfill basic economic needs. As a result, the Association thought that attacking the segregation and discrimination that affected the race as a whole was the best way to represent working-class as well as higher-status African-Americans.

Despite its focus on racial discrimination in education and housing, the early NAACP did not entirely eschew economic matters. Legal and economic inequalities were often inextricably linked in a Jim Crow system that completely subordinated African-Americans. In the first two decades of its existence, the NAACP frequently struggled with how best to incorporate workers' interests into its program. Theoretically, union organizing might have been the most effective way, but it presented major obstacles for African-Americans. Most unions in the early twentieth century were defined by the race of their membership—white—as well as by their class composition. Unions' exclusionary and discriminatory practices led many African-Americans to view employers as friendlier than fellow white workers. The twin problems of hostile unions and African-American views contributed to the NAACP's reluctance to embrace union organizing as an answer to black workers' difficulties.

Instead, as reflected by articles in *Crisis*, the official organ of the NAACP, the Association considered numerous, sometimes inconsistent ways to assist working African-Americans: promoting socialism, cooperatives, northern migration, and black-owned businesses. The NAACP advocated on behalf of southern agricultural workers by publicizing egregious incidents of racial violence and horrifying working conditions. The NAACP, usually represented by fieldworker Walter White, investigated and publicized lynchings, massacres, and widespread practices of peonage and involuntary servitude. In particular, it publicized the Elaine, Arkansas, massacre in 1919 and the peonage that followed the Mississippi River flood in 1927.

The NAACP in the Great Depression

During the Great Depression, the NAACP's labor-related activities greatly expanded as a result of several factors: the Depression's devastating economic impact on African-Americans, widespread criticism of the NAACP for its labor policies, discriminatory federal responses to the economic crisis, and competition for loyalty from other organizations.

In a nation pre-occupied with poverty and saturated with class politics, the NAACP realized that it could avoid economic issues only at its own peril. Stinging critiques came from a group of young Howard University intellectuals dubbed the "Young Turks." They criticized the NAACP for placing too much emphasis on racial discrimination and not enough on economic inequality and working-class solidarity. For them, the upper-class status of the NAACP prevented it from representing workers and seeking equality beyond that needed for elites.

With a myriad of left-leaning organizations embracing the more class-based strategies the Young Turks favored, the NAACP's claims to race leadership faltered. As the Communist Party, the International Labor Defense (ILD), the National Negro Congress (NNC), and other Popular Front organizations attempted to gain African-American members, the NAACP competed for loyalty and membership. The ILD notably challenged the NAACP when it battled to represent nine young African-American men "legally lynched" for rape in Scottsboro, Alabama.

As a result of these pressures to address labor issues, the NAACP took on a variety of projects targeted to help poor and working-class African-Americans. One of its main tasks was to address race discrimination in federal programs. It called on the Roosevelt administration to implement New Deal programs in a nondiscriminatory fashion. It also lobbied (albeit unsuccessfully) to require the withholding of federal certification under the National Labor Relations Act (NLRA) to any union that discriminated on the basis of race. Beyond these federal targets, the NAACP also adopted a grassroots approach to economic issues by supporting local boycotts of retail businesses that refused to hire African-Americans.

The creation of the Congress of Industrial Organizations (CIO) in 1935 offered the NAACP a more politically mainstream way of helping African-American workers—by allying with organized labor. Unlike the American Federation of Labor (AFL), the CIO officially opposed racial discrimination from its inception. Although in practice CIO member unions at the local level continued to exclude African-Americans, the NAACP saw the CIO as a friend and began a long and ambivalent alliance with organized labor.

Overall, during the 1930s, the NAACP expressed a greater commitment to economic issues than it had in the past, and some branches and youth councils even more actively pursued economic goals. Nonetheless, the NAACP never adopted labor issues as part of its core litigation agenda. The NAACP's notable litigation successes were reserved for areas like equal pay for teachers and access to graduate education, which garnered more support from middle-class than working-class African-Americans.

The NAACP in World War II

During World War II, the NAACP broke with previous practice by including labor issues in its core litigation agenda. This decision stemmed from the growing political and economic power of African-American workers during the war. Economically, after the high unemployment rates of the Depression years, war production needs created an economic boom, a far tighter labor market, and greater market power for African-Americans. On the political side, African-Americans in the North became swing voters valued by the Democratic Party. They became increasingly vocal about their demand for victory over fascism not only abroad, but at home where discrimination still hampered African-American progress. In this context, African-American workers began demanding the same rights that white employees had insisted on during the Depression.

As employment discrimination became the most nationally prominent civil rights issue of the day, the NAACP saw political, economic, and institutional opportunities to attack the problems African-American workers faced. Although the NAACP occasionally intervened to assist agricultural workers suffering peonage and other egregious labor practices in the South, it usually limited such intervention to passing on the complaints of agricultural workers to the United States Departments of Justice and Agriculture.

In the main, the NAACP addressed black industrial workers' concerns in the North, Midwest, and West. Industries frequently excluded African-Americans from jobs altogether, segregated them into the lowest-paying jobs, and denied them promotions. Unions also discriminated against African-Americans by excluding them altogether or segregating them into largely powerless auxiliary locals.

Under Walter White's leadership, the NAACP made significant headway in the 1940s tackling labor problems with political and legal tools. In the political arena, the NAACP joined A. Philip Randolph and his all-black Brotherhood of Sleeping Car Porters to compel the Roosevelt administration to end employment and union discrimination in war industries. They successfully pressured Roosevelt to create the Fair Employment Practice Committee (FEPC) in exchange for halting a massive protest march during the war. Following this success, the NAACP persisted in its efforts, lobbying to transform the FEPC into a more powerful and permanent administrative forum to redress race discrimination in employment. It joined lobbying groups such as the National Council for a Permanent FEPC to help in these efforts.

In the legal arena, the NAACP pursued litigation in three main areas during the 1940s. The lawyers Thurgood Marshall, Prentice Thomas, and Marion Wynn Perry brought lawsuits across the country against boilermakers' unions that excluded African-American shipyard workers and segregated them into auxiliary locals. It challenged union and employer discrimination in New York under a pioneering fair employment practice law. And it supported the lawyer Charles Hamilton Houston's efforts to end employer and union discrimination on the railroads.

These lawsuits frequently pitted the NAACP against discriminatory labor unions, but the NAACP managed simultaneously to strengthen its alliance with organized labor. Following a 1941 strike at Ford Motor Company's River Rouge plant in Michigan, unity grew between the NAACP and the CIO. Labor leaders increasingly spoke at NAACP annual conventions, and the NAACP represented itself at activities sponsored by organized labor.

The NAACP's World War II emphasis on industrial concerns reflected the Association's recognition that African-American workers might bolster the Association's membership. Previously, the NAACP sought support from middle-class blacks and wealthy, philanthropic whites. The NAACP had therefore focused on issues of middle-class concern like education, as well as on issues like lynching, whose shock value garnered support from whites. As black industrial workers earned wages in the 1940s that enabled them to afford NAACP membership dues, the Association began to consider working-class African-Americans fruitful targets for membership. In an attempt to attract such workers, the NAACP created a new staff position in its Washington office devoted entirely to labor issues. Clarence Mitchell, a political activist who had worked for the federal Fair Employment Practice Committee, was hired for the job.

The new attention to workers appeared to pay off in membership terms, as the size of the NAACP expanded considerably during the 1940s. The NAACP grew from 355 branches and a membership of 50,556 in 1940 to 1,073 branches and a membership of around 450,000 in 1946. The Association's budget grew from $54,300 in 1930, composed of a combination of contributions and membership dues, to more than $319,000 in 1947, entirely from membership dues. This tremendous growth was due at least in part to the new membership of working-class African-Americans.

The NAACP in the Postwar Era

The NAACP continued to pursue labor activities in the decade after World War II ended, although its school desegregation cases overshadowed its other work. The NAACP continued its two-pronged attack on labor problems. First, the NAACP cooperated with other civil rights, labor, and religious groups in lobbying for civil rights and labor legislation. In 1950, the NAACP formed the Leadership Conference on Civil Rights (LCCR), which included over 30 organizations and a wide array of labor leaders, including the liberal Democrat Walter Reuther and the more conservative AFL leader George Meany. The NAACP-labor alliance lobbied for a permanent FEPC, the repeal of antilabor laws such as the Taft-Hartley Act, and an end to union and employment discrimination.

That alliance stood in tension with the NAACP's second labor program: challenging race discrimination in unions. Unions at local levels often remained uncooperative with their national leaders' efforts to end discrimination and ally with the NAACP. Some black unionists nonetheless cautioned the NAACP against prioritizing its civil rights agenda over labor policies. When the Association conditioned its support for a pro-union railroad law on a nondiscrimination requirement, one African-American union member warned the NAACP not to defeat the bill entirely.

The conflict between supporting and condemning unions took an institutional form. Clarence Mitchell, who graduated from labor secretary to director of the NAACP's Washington Bureau in 1952, not surprisingly emphasized co-operation with unions on a national level. His replacement as NAACP labor secretary was his institutional rival, Herbert Hill, who primarily attacked discrimination within unions. Roy Wilkins, who became executive secretary in 1955, frequently attempted to mediate between the two.

To challenge discrimination in labor unions, Hill used grassroots economic political pressure as well as state and federal administrative tools. In 1953, he began conducting workshops to teach black union members how to wield power in discriminatory unions. After the AFL-CIO merger in 1955, the NAACP educated the labor federation's staff about race discrimination. Also among the NAACP's main goals during this period was targeting large corporations that adopted discriminatory labor practices when moving to the South to capitalize on cheap labor.

Hill also launched direct attacks on particular unions. In New York, he was instrumental in the desegregation of New York City's Sheet Metal Workers Local 28. In Atlanta, he targeted discrimination in the International Ladies' Garment Workers' Union, a longtime ally of the NAACP that did not receive the criticism well. Nationally, the NAACP challenged widespread race discrimination in the steel, oil, automobile, and airline manufacturing unions. Building trades unions were especially recalcitrant and opposed NAACP challenges to their racial practices. In 1969, Hill facilitated the creation of the National Afro-American Builders, Inc. to help African-American builders gain skills necessary to bid for larger construction jobs.

Under Hill's direction, the NAACP also addressed agricultural labor practices in the 1950s. Hill investigated the conditions of migratory farmworkers and wrote a compelling booklet on the subject titled *No Harvest for the Reaper: The Story of the Migratory Agricultural Worker in the United States*. In New York, the NAACP called for government reform of agricultural labor camps. Hill had exposed several upstate New York camps where African-American farmworkers recruited from the South labored in oppressive conditions. On the federal level, when the NAACP supported raising the federal minimum wage in 1955, it lobbied for inclusion of both domestic and agricultural workers.

Throughout the 1950s, the NAACP used federal and state administrative agencies to redress labor problems. Lacking a federal law to attack discrimination, the NAACP turned to state fair employment agencies as well as less effective federal agencies. It filed complaints of employment discrimination with the Office of Government Contract Compliance, an agency President Eisenhower created by executive order in 1954 to supervise businesses with federal contracts. It also filed complaints against segregated and discriminatory unions with the National Labor Relations Board (NLRB).

In the early 1960s, direct action protests by groups such as Martin Luther King's Southern Christian Leadership Conference and the Student Nonviolent Coordinating Committee spotlighted the concerns of African-Americans. In December 1962, two civil rights leaders sought to capitalize on momentum from these protests. Known for their long-standing advocacy of African-American workers, Bayard Rustin and A. Philip Randolph planned the event with economic issues in mind. They decided to call the protest a "March for Jobs and Freedom." The NAACP was one of the many organizations that took part in the historic march, which is now remembered for Martin Luther King's antidiscrimination focus in his "I Have a Dream" speech. Other speakers, including Walter Reuther of the United Automobile Workers, focused on economic issues.

The NAACP Legal Defense and Educational Fund after 1956

After 1956, the NAACP and the NAACP Legal Defense and Educational Fund (LDF) became distinctly separate organizations with different agendas. The two groups had essentially served as a single organization since 1939, when the NAACP created the LDF largely for tax reasons. The 1956 split was apparent in the types of activities undertaken by the two groups. While the NAACP continued to pursue lobbying for prolabor legislation, the LDF focused on school desegregation litigation.

The LDF turned its litigation focus toward labor issues after passage of the 1964 Civil Rights Act. Under the direction of Jack Greenberg, the LDF launched a plan to file 1,000 complaints after the law's equal employment section (Title VII) went into effect in 1965. The LDF targeted large corporations such as General Motors and U.S. Steel, which offered well-paying blue-collar jobs in areas with high black unemployment. Rather than seeking employment per se, the LDF aimed to perfect the law itself.

One of the LDF's first successful cases authorized the use of class-action suits. The case targeted discrimination in Tennessee's Werthan Bag Company, later mentioned in the 1989 movie *Driving Miss Daisy*. In another notable LDF victory, the Supreme Court established that job qualification tests must relate to abilities needed to perform a job. It accepted LDF arguments that a test by the Duke Power Company unfairly discriminated against blacks who were equally capable to perform a desired job.

The LDF successfully targeted discrimination in the federal government after 1972, when Congress amended Title VII to allow such suits. The LDF notably won discrimination cases against NASA, the Postal Service, the army, the navy, the air force, and the Immigration and Naturalization Service.

It also proved successful in discrimination suits against city and state governments involving teachers, police officers, and firefighters.

Since the 1990s, the Legal Defense Fund has won court cases against Shoney's Restaurant, the Nashville Banner, and Shell Oil Company. It has also pursued employment discrimination cases against Abercrombie & Fitch clothing retailers, AVX (a South Carolina-based high-tech components manufacturer), the City of Chicago's fire department, and the New York City Parks Department and Board of Education.

The NAACP after 1964

Like the LDF, the NAACP's labor activities changed with the passage of the 1964 Civil Rights Act. The law, a result of public pressure following violent demonstrations in the South, appeared to spell victory for the NAACP's years of efforts lobbying for such legislation. The NAACP leader, Herbert Hill, organized local committees to educate African-American workers about their rights under the statute. He helped numerous African-American workers file complaints against governmental and private employers as well as unions. Between 1965 and 1977, the NAACP filed several thousand complaints on behalf of African-American workers with federal agencies like the Equal Employment Opportunity Commission (EEOC) and the National Labor Relations Board. The same year the Civil Rights Act became law, the NAACP legal counsel, Robert Carter, finally convinced the NLRB to deny certification to segregating and discriminating unions.

Throughout the 1970s, the NAACP looked beyond workers to the poor more generally, lobbying for expanded assistance to the poor and pressing for higher minimum wages, welfare reform, and full employment.

Under Benjamin L. Hooks, who headed the NAACP from 1977 to 1993, Benjamin Chavis, who took over until 1995, and Kweisi Mfume, who led the organization from 1995 to 2005, the NAACP has continued to pursue litigation against companies when complaints are insufficient to redress employment discrimination. In 1996, the NAACP launched its Economic Reciprocity Initiative to publicize the practices of major American industries in areas such as hiring, job promotions, advertising, and charity work. The goal was to promote those companies with favorable practices toward African-Americans while economically harming ones with poor results. The NAACP successfully sued Cracker Barrel in 2001 for employment discrimination and intervened in a lawsuit against Coca-Cola filed by current and former employees.

RISA L. GOLUBOFF

References and Further Reading

Anderson, Carol. *Eyes off the Prize: The United Nations and the African American Struggle for Human Rights, 1944–1955.* New York: Cambridge University Press, 2003.

Bates, Beth Tompkins. "A New Crowd Challenges the Agenda of the Old Guard in the NAACP, 1933–1941." *American Historical Review* 102 (April 1997): 340–377.

Eisenberg, Bernard. "Only for the Bourgeois? James Weldon Johnson and the NAACP, 1916–1930." *Phylon* 43 (1982): 110–124.

Goluboff, Risa L. "Let Economic Equality Take Care of Itself": The NAACP, Labor Litigation, and the Making of Civil Rights in the 1940s. *UCLA Law Review* 52 (2005): 1393–1486.

Hamilton, Dona Cooper, and Charles V. Hamilton. *The Dual Agenda: Race and Social Welfare Policies of Civil Rights Organizations.* New York: Columbia University Press, 1997.

Jonas, Gilbert. *Freedom's Sword: The NAACP and the Struggle against Racism in America, 1909–1969.* New York: Routledge, 2005.

Kellogg, Charles Flint. *NAACP: A History of the National Association for the Advancement of Colored People, Volume I, 1909–1920.* Baltimore: 1967.

Meier, August, and John H. Bracey Jr. "The NAACP as a Reform Movement, 1909–1965: 'To Reach the Conscience of America.'" *Journal of Southern History* 59 (February 1993): 3–30.

NAACP Detroit Branch. "Economic Reciprocity Report Cards." www.detroitnaacp.org/economics/cards.asp (accessed May 26, 2005).

Nelson, H. Viscount. "The Philadelphia NAACP: Race versus Class Consciousness during the Thirties." *Journal of Black Studies* 5 (March 1975): 255–276.

Record, Wilson. *Race and Radicalism: The NAACP and the Communist Party in Conflict.* Ithaca, NY: Cornell University Press, 1964.

Tushnet, Mark V. *Making Civil Rights Law: Thurgood Marshall and the Supreme Court, 1936–1961.* New York: Oxford University Press, 1994.

Watson, Denton L. *Lion in the Lobby.* New York: William Morrow Publishers, 1990.

Wynn, Daniel W. *The NAACP versus Negro Revolutionary Protest.* New York: Exposition Press, 1955.

Zangrando, Robert L. *The NAACP Crusade against Lynching, 1909–1950.* Philadelphia: Temple University Press, 1980.

Cases and Statutes Cited

Brown v. Board of Education, 347 U.S. 483 (1954)
Bull v. AVX, 112 F.3d 508, 4th Cir. (S.C.), May 02, 1997
Griggs v. Duke Power Co., 401 U.S. 424 (1971)
Hall v. Werthan Bag Co., 251 F.Supp 184 (M.D. Tenn. 1966)
Hughes Tool Co., 147 NLRB 1573 (1964)
Civil Rights Act of 1964, Pub. L. 88–352, July 2, 1964, 78 Stat. 241

See also **African-Americans; Civil Rights Act of 1964/ Title VII; Elaine, Arkansas Massacre (1919); Fair Employment Practice Committee; March on Washington Movement; National Negro Congress; Peonage**

NATIONAL ASSOCIATION OF COLORED GRADUATE NURSES

There is no record of what prompted Martha Franklin, in the fall of 1906, to write about five hundred letters to other black nurses to find out about their work. She wrote to individual nurses, to directors of training schools for black nurses, and to members of black alumnae and other nursing organizations. Franklin must have known that their situations were difficult at best. Soon after formal nursing education appeared in the United States in the mid-1870s, scores of hospital nurse training schools sprang up all over the country. Students spent two or three years working in the wards until they graduated, when a new group of students were enrolled. Most hospital nurse training schools were segregated, and black graduates found particular difficulty finding employment where race, as well as gender and occupation, factored against them.

Franklin was a Connecticut native who graduated in 1897 as the only African-American in her class at the Women's Hospital Training School for Nurses in Philadelphia. Franklin was a private-duty nurse in Connecticut when she started her marathon correspondence. In August 1908, Franklin's letters resulted in 52 black nurses meeting at St. Mark's Methodist Episcopal Church in New York City. They gathered at the invitation of Adah Thoms, the president of the Lincoln School for Nurses Alumnae Association. During this three-day meeting, goals were developed to advance the standards and best interests of trained nurses, break down discrimination in the nursing profession, and develop leadership within the ranks of black nurses.

The black physicians' organization, the National Medical Association, was also meeting nearby, and various members lent their support to their nursing colleagues. At the close of the three-day meeting, Franklin was offered the position of president and Thoms was elected treasurer. Three days later, the National Association of Colored Graduate Nurses (NACGN) was formed with 26 charter members.

This first meeting of black nurses reflected the activism of the new profession of nursing as a whole. The Nurses' Associated Alumnae of the United States and Canada, known after 1911 as the American Nurses Association (ANA), was organized in 1897.

In 1909, 52 black nurses gathered in Boston for the first annual NACGN meeting. One member was Mary Eliza Mahoney, who had graduated in 1879 and was acclaimed as the first African-American graduate nurse in the United States. The early years of the NACGN continued with annual meetings in different cities at the invitation of local groups or alumnae associations. These early meetings were a testament to the dedication and strength of the membership. These women overcame the expense and physical and mental hardships inherent in forming and sustaining an organization of working black women at this time of Jim Crow laws and widespread racial discrimination. In turn, the organization gave black nurses a stronger professional identity and groomed them in organizational leadership while shielding them from "the excessive racism, hostility, and denigration of their white colleagues."

The meetings involved presentations on such topics as the high incidence of tuberculosis and the high infant mortality among blacks as well as the conditions that spawned them—poor housing and lack of health facilities and employment opportunities. The nurses also discussed the unfair practice of some southern states that barred black nurses from taking the national nursing examination.

The role of the NACGN assumed a new urgency when the ANA restructured in 1916. Membership in the ANA, previously through alumnae associations, now was available only with membership in state nurses' associations. Since 16 southern state associations and the District of Columbia denied membership to black nurses, they were now effectively denied membership in the ANA. The ANA allowed the Alumnae Association of Freedmen's Hospital in Washington DC to retain membership, but future black graduates from these southern states were effectively barred from joining.

The NACGN formed a national nurses' registry in 1918, much the same as the ANA operated, to help its members find work. Membership steadily increased. In 1920, when the NACGN became incorporated in the state of New York, there were about 500 members. In 1926, the NACGN borrowed space for a headquarters office within the offices of the National Health Circle for Colored People, in New York City, and in 1928, the first issue of the NACGN's organ, the *National News Bulletin*, appeared. Yet, as the Great Depression took its toll and strategies to achieve integration with white nurses floundered, membership in the NACGN dropped to just 175 in 1933.

From this low point, the NACGN somehow managed to regroup itself, as the historian Darlene Clark Hines has described, through a combination of factors. In 1934, the first of a series of regional conferences, supported by the Rockefeller Foundation, was held. Attended by black and white nurse leaders, as well as representatives from other disciplines, the discussions included the relationship between the NACGN and the ANA, the NACGN structure, and the status of black nurses. The black nurse leaders Estelle Massey Riddle and Mabel Keaton Staupers became involved with the organization, along with Congresswoman Frances Payne Bolton and the Julius Rosenwald fund administration, while some key white nurse leaders expressed concern with the black nurses' *de facto* exclusion from the ANA.

Estelle Massey Riddle, the first African-American nurse to hold a master's degree, was the NACGN president from 1934 to 1939. Mabel Keaton Staupers was hired as the first executive secretary, a post she held for the next 12 years. Staupers proved a staunch and energetic supporter of the NACGN for many years, eventually serving as the NACGN's last president. Also in 1936, the NACGN moved into its own office, strategically located in the same New York building as the three main white nursing organizations. Over the years, Congresswoman Bolton and the Julius Rosenwald fund continued their support.

The NACGN consistently stood for improved education for blacks, along with improved, nonsegregated educational and work opportunities for black nurses. The thrust for better care for black patients was continued during these years, as the NACGN worked with the National Urban League and the National Association for the Advancement of Colored People to improve conditions in black hospitals. Additionally, the NACGN co-operated with other nursing organizations on a variety of fronts, including the national Fair Employment Practices Act and the Bolton Bill amendment, which created the Cadet Nurse Corps.

ANA membership for black nurses remained a thorny issue; in 1939, 16 southern state associations still denied membership to black nurses. The two other major nursing organizations, the National League of Nursing Education and the National Organization of Public Health Nurses, both granted individual membership to black nurses when necessary.

Following the war, the ANA's position changed, although this was not immediately reflected by the state associations. The ANA membership voted in 1948 to allow individual membership to black nurses who were barred from their state associations. By 1953, all the states, except Georgia, admitted black nurses. Mabel Staupers wrote in 1984: "The war did a lot towards bringing it about. When people are sick they know no prejudice . . . I also feel that the ANA grew up."

In 1950, with all black nurses now eligible to join the ANA, the NACGN leaders considered that the major charge of its later years was fulfilled—black nurses from every state could now join the ANA. Mabel Staupers was elected president of the NACGN and oversaw its dissolution. The final membership meeting was held in January 1951 at St. Mark's Methodist Church, the site of the NACGN founding over 40 years earlier.

Thus, years before the start of the civil rights movement, a group of black nurses joined together to work for improved health care for black Americans as well as racial equality within nursing. Disturbingly, in 1971, the National Black Nurses' Association was formed following concerns about a lack of black representation in the ANA leadership.

BRIGID LUSK

References and Further Reading

Campinha-Bacote, Josepha. "The Black Nurses' Struggle toward Equality: An Historical Account of the National Association of Colored Graduate Nurses." *Journal of the National Black Nurses' Association* 2, no. 2 (1987): 15–25.

Carnegie, M. Elizabeth. *Path We Tread: Blacks in Nursing, 1854–1990.* 2nd ed. New York: National League for Nursing Press, 1991.

Davis, Althea T. *Early Black American Leaders in Nursing: Architects for Integration and Equality.* Boston: Jones and Bartlett, 1999.

Hine, Darlene Clark. *Black Women in White: Racial Conflict and Cooperation in the Nursing Profession, 1890–1950.* Bloomington: Indiana University Press, 1989.

Kalisch, Philip A., and Beatrice J. Kalisch. *Advance of American Nursing.* 3rd ed. Philadelphia: Lippincott, 1995.

Mosley, Marie Oleatha Pitts. "A New Beginning: The Story of the National Association of Colored Graduate Nurses, 1908–1951." *Journal of National Black Nurses' Association* 8, no. 1 (1996): 20–32.

Smith, Gloria R. "From Invisibility to Blackness: The Story of the National Black Nurses' Association." *Nursing Outlook* 23 (April 1975): 225–229.

Staupers, Mabel Keaton. *No Time for Prejudice.* New York: Macmillan, 1961.

Thoms, Adah B. *Pathfinders: A History of the Progress of Colored Graduate Nurses* New York: Kay Printing, 1929.

NATIONAL CHILD LABOR COMMITTEE

The National Child Labor Committee (NCLC) was formed on April 15, 1904, as an organization dedicated to the abolition of child labor and to promoting the well-being and education of children in the United States. The organization focused on raising public awareness about the employment of children in the industrial, service, and agricultural sectors and on securing the passage of child labor regulations and compulsory education laws.

During the late nineteenth and early twentieth centuries, the United States witnessed an unprecedented period of industrial and urban expansion. With this growth came what many Americans saw as intolerable social problems. From the 1890s through World War I, years commonly known as the Progressive Era, large numbers of middle-class men and women established reform organizations meant to combat the nation's ills. They focused on myriad issues ranging from urban poverty, political corruption, and temperance to woman suffrage, immigration restriction, and industrial regulation. During this time, growing numbers of children in the United States worked in textile factories, coal mines, glasshouses, and food canneries, as well as in fields picking produce, in city tenements manufacturing piece goods, and on the streets as peddlers, newsboys, and messengers. These working children drew the attention of many middle-class social reformers. Shaped by a mix of humanitarian objectives and fears of social degeneracy and decay, a strong child labor reform movement emerged in the United States by the turn of the twentieth century.

In line with other progressives, child labor reformers looked to use the state to bring about change. As early as the 1820s, labor organizations pressed for state laws restricting the employment of children in mills and factories. In 1836, Massachusetts was the first state in the United States to enact such legislation, outlawing the employment of children in manufacturing establishments who were under 15 years old and did not attend school at least three months a year. Massachusetts passed another act in 1842 limiting the workday of children in mills and factories to 10 hours. In the decades that followed, other industrialized states passed similar statutes. By the turn of the century, numerous states in the North and Midwest had child labor laws applicable to a variety of occupations that set minimum ages of hire, established educational requirements, and prohibited night work by children.

Organized labor, as well as groups established by middle-class social reformers, including religious organizations, consumer leagues, and women's clubs, was integral in the passage of these child labor statutes. Yet, the laws and their enforcement were uneven, and as late as 1902, no southern state had a child labor law. Owners of industrial enterprises in the North, especially cotton textile manufacturers, argued that the absence of child labor legislation in the southern states gave unfair advantage to manufacturing enterprises located there. This led some northern manufacturers to open and operate factories in the South to circumvent regulations in their home states.

This lack of uniformity among state laws highlighted the fact that child labor was not only a pressing social and economic problem, but that it also was national in scope and called for a concerted, coordinated nationwide effort to eradicate it. Leaders of child labor reform groups who worked at the local and state levels, therefore, created the National Child Labor Committee. Edgar Gardner Murphy, chairman of the Alabama Child Labor Committee, and members of the New York Child Labor Committee, especially Felix Adler, who was one of the New York group's founding members, spearheaded the 1904 formation of the NCLC. Edgar Gardner Murphy, a minister from Montgomery, organized the Alabama Child Labor Committee in 1901, and two years later, he and his organization helped secure the passage of a child labor law in Alabama, the first twentieth-century child labor law enacted in the South. Murphy sat on the NCLC's first board of trustees, as did Felix Adler, a Columbia University professor and the committee's first chairperson. The NCLC selected the University of Pennsylvania sociologist Samuel McCune Lindsay as its first general secretary and the southerner Alexander McKelway and the northerner Owen Lovejoy, both ministers and longtime child labor reform advocates, as assistant secretaries. Headquartered in New York City, about one third of the NCLC's first members were from the South, with the remaining two thirds hailing from northern states. The organization counted among its founding members some of the foremost social reformers in the United States, including the settlement house pioneers Jane Addams and Lillian Wald, and the general secretary of the National Consumers' League, Florence Kelley, as well as academicians, journalists, labor and religious leaders, and progressive politicians and businessmen.

The NCLC focused much of its early twentieth-century activities on collecting information about the employment of children and disseminating it to the public, with the intention of arousing widespread sentiment against child labor and support for legislative restrictions of it. The organization first sent investigators into textile mills, factories, and coal mines, where some of the most flagrant abuses of child labor occurred, and then focused on children who did industrial homework, worked in the street trades, and labored as itinerant farmworkers. The reports of these investigations often included graphic accounts of the realities, effects, and hazards of child labor and statistics documenting appallingly low education rates and literacy standards among the nation's child workers. The NCLC published these findings in its quarterly publication, *The Child Labor Bulletin*, in the weekly social reform magazine, *The Survey*, as well as in book and pamphlet form, and in academic journals. It used the editorial pages of newspapers, leaflets, and mass mailings to reach an even wider audience.

It was the photographs of children working in a variety of industrial and agricultural settings, especially those taken by the NCLC investigator Lewis Hine, that had the most profound and lasting impact on public opinion. In 1909, Hine published the first of his photographic exposés documenting children at work, "Day Laborers before Their Time" and "Child Labor in the Carolinas." Two years later, he began an extensive investigation and compiled a far-reaching photographic record of children at work, traveling throughout the eastern United States, from cranberry bogs in New England to oyster canneries along the Gulf Coast. The photojournalism of Lewis Hine, as did the written reports of NCLC investigations, thrust the issue of child labor into the national spotlight and political discourse.

In spite of advances made by state child labor committees and the NCLC in the passage of child labor laws at the state level, disparities continued to exist, and the NCLC increasingly focused on the enactment of federal child labor legislation that would apply to all states evenly. In 1906, Senator Alfred Beveridge of Indiana introduced into Congress a bill that would make illegal the interstate transportation and sale of goods produced by companies employing children under the age of 14 years. A heated debate ensued among the members of the NCLC's board over whether the organization should endorse the Beveridge bill, and divided the NCLC between a faction preferring to continue lobbying for regulatory laws at the state level and another seeing federal intervention as the most expeditious, albeit constitutionally controversial, route to the eradication of child labor. The NCLC ultimately voted to endorse the Beveridge bill, a decision that led to the resignation of Edgar Gardner Murphy and other leading southern members from the organization.

The movement for federal child labor legislation faced staunch opposition from a number of fronts, including not only employers but also parents of working children who needed their income to keep the family economy afloat. Despite support from the NCLC and other social reform groups, the Beveridge bill failed to pass. It did, however, garner enough attention and interest to facilitate the creation of the U.S. Children's Bureau in 1912. The Beveridge bill was also the basis of the Keating-Owen Child Labor bill, which NCLC endorsed and for which it actively lobbied. The Keating-Owen Act became law on September 1, 1916.

Although the U.S. Supreme Court declared the Keating-Owen Act unconstitutional in 1918, the NCLC continued to push for federal child labor regulations. In 1919, the NCLC supported the enactment of the Child Labor Tax Act, which levied a 10% excise tax on goods produced by children, and, after the Supreme Court deemed it unconstitutional in 1922, worked aggressively to secure a constitutional amendment that would give Congress explicit constitutional authority to regulate child labor. Though approved by Congress in 1924, the states failed to ratify the amendment. In 1938, the NCLC finally saw its goal of the enactment of a permanent federal child labor law realized with the inclusion of minimum age provisions within the Fair Labor Standards Act.

The National Child Labor Committee continued to work for improvements in federal child labor legislation, especially to extend the protections afforded by the Fair Labor Standards Act to children working as agricultural laborers, and in education requirements and standards. The NCLC continues to be a leading advocacy group for youth in the United States and is a clearinghouse for information relating to child labor law compliance and enforcement, education, and youth employment. The NCLC celebrated the centennial anniversary of the organization in 2004.

BETH ENGLISH

References and Further Reading

Davidson, Elizabeth. *Child Labor in the Southern Textile States*. Chapel Hill: University of North Carolina Press, 1939.
Goldberg, Vicki. *Lewis W. Hine: Children at Work*. New York: Prestel, 1999.
Hindman, Hugh. *Child Labor: An American History*. Armonk, NY: M. E. Sharpe, 2002.
Kheel Center for Labor-Management Documentation and Archives, Cornell University Library. "Guide to the National Child Labor Committee Publications." http://rmc.library.cornell.edu/EAD/htmldocs/KCL05242.html.
Levine, Marvin. *Children for Hire: The Perils of Child Labor in the United States*. Westport, CT: Praeger, 2003.
Sallee, Shelley. *The Whiteness of Child Labor Reform in the New South*. Athens: University of Georgia Press, 2004.
Trattner, Walter. *Crusade for the Children: A History of the National Child Labor Committee and Child Labor Reform in America*. Chicago: Quadrangle Books, 1970.
Zelizer, Viviana. *Pricing the Priceless Child: The Changing Social Value of Children*. New York: Basic Books, Inc., 1985.

See also **Child Labor; Fair Labor Standards Act; Family Wage; Keating-Owen Child Labor Act (1916); Law and Labor; National Consumers League; rogressive Era**

NATIONAL CIVIC FEDERATION

The National Civic Federation (NCF) emerged out of the era of "Great Upheaval" in labor relations between the mid-1870s and mid-1890s. It reflected the heightened anxiety of businessmen and the middle-class public over the growing polarization between labor and capital and the increasing power of unprecedentedly large corporations in manufacturing, transportation, and finance. Through a novel tripartite structure, some of the largest corporations crafted what they hoped would be an institutional forum for cultivating "responsible" labor and some measure of business accommodation to legitimate grievances of labor, while policing the competitive marketplace to reduce excessive and destructive competition. They recruited allies among civic leaders and the national officers of the American Federation of Labor (AFL). In so doing, they also incurred the wrath of left-wing labor leaders and what they termed "anarchists" among businessmen, their archrivals in the National Association of Manufacturers and its avowedly "open shop" movement.

The origins of the NCF lay in the depression of 1893 and the Pullman strike and boycott. Shortly after the closing of the Columbian World's Exposition in Chicago, a coalition of civic and business leaders prompted by Rev. William T. Stead, the author of *If Christ Came to Chicago*, called a public meeting at which the assembled reformers, including Jane Addams, Henry Demarest Lloyd, the banker Lyman Gage, and others called for the formation of a "civic federation" to pursue the goals of social amelioration and class reconciliation. Months later, early in the strike of Pullman car shop employees, a delegation from the Chicago Civic Federation (CCF) tried unsuccessfully to persuade George M. Pullman to meet with his striking employees. In November 1894, following the collapse of the massive Pullman boycott itself, the CCF convened a Congress on Industrial Conciliation and Arbitration to re-affirm the goals of industrial mediation. Through the appointment of a National Commission, the CCF hoped to influence states and the federal government to pass new legislation establishing boards of arbitration and support a new national legislative initiative to resolve future railroad labor disputes. That initiative eventually took the form of the Erdman Act of 1898. In the context of the return of prosperity in 1897 and an accelerating pace of corporate consolidation in what came to be called the "great merger movement," the CCF sponsored high-profile national conferences on foreign policy (1898) and the "trust problem" (1899).

During the CCF's early years, a one-time Kansas City journalist and conservative civic promoter, Ralph Easley, served as its secretary and chief organizer. Indeed, it was Easley's vision of an influential national organization committed to industrial conciliation that precipitated the formation of an organizing committee for such a body at the National Conference on Trusts. Despite some opposition from within the CCF, Easley managed to call another National Conference on Trade Agreements in 1900, out of which a tripartite board was appointed for a National Civic Federation that, in its early years, would be committed to industrial conciliation. Included as members were Samuel Gompers, the president of the American Federation of Labor, and John Mitchell, the president of the United Mine Workers of America, whose organizations both experienced considerable growth and national prominence in that period.

Also recruited to the NCF in its first year were the Republican boss and former industrialist Mark Hanna and the corporate titans Charles Francis Adams, Andrew Carnegie, and key figures in the J. P. Morgan investment firm, including George W. Perkins. As the NCF's organizational structure expanded into a series of functioning departments—Trade Agreements, Welfare, Immigration, Commission on Public Ownership of Utilities—its membership also reached deeper into the corporate and labor worlds. Other key members included, for business, Elbert Gary, Samuel Insull, Cyrus McCormick, and August Belmont and for labor, besides Gompers and Mitchell, William Mahon (Streetcar Employees) and Frank Sargent (Locomotive Firemen), along with public representatives, Easley, Seth Low, and John R. Commons. As the focus of the NCF shifted, so too did its membership, though Easley provided continuity as the perpetual hub of the organization.

In its earliest years, the NCF's chief pre-occupation lay in labor conciliation. Although frequently operating behind the scenes, the NCF helped diffuse conflict or produce trade agreements that brought potentially disabling strikes to a conclusion. Most notable among these were the Steel Strike of 1901, the Anthracite Coal Strike of 1902, and the Machinists' Strikes of 1901 and 1904. Emblematic of these efforts was the behind-the-scenes work of the NCF (notably Easley, Mitchell, and Morgan) to craft first a temporary agreement in the 1901 Anthracite coal dispute and then a resolution of the bitter five-month strike in 1902, through a presidentially appointed commission that left the miners without formal recognition but in possession of a trade agreement granting wage concessions and creating a board of arbitration that would hear future grievances. The NCF hailed the agreement as a model for future labor-management conciliation.

Officially committed to fostering labor-management peace through negotiation, the NCF approach did not in fact reflect the day-to-day practice of many of its most influential corporate members. This is perhaps most notably true in the case of the U.S. Steel Corporation and its president, Judge Elbert Gary, who like many of his colleagues, maintained a determined anti-union posture throughout the period of the NCF's greatest influence.

Almost from the outset, the NCF positioned itself as an alternative to the more aggressively anti-union National Association of Manufacturers (NAM), which after 1902 spearheaded an "open shop" campaign that sought to roll back trade union gains in cities across the country through locally organized Citizens' Industrial Associations (CIA). Its leaders, David Parry and James Van Cleave, also supported high-profile prosecutions in the famous Danbury Hatters' and Buck's Stove and Range cases of union officials, including NCF member Samuel Gompers, for backing trade union boycott activity. Quietly, some key corporate members of the NCF assisted in Gompers's legal defense.

Socialists and industrial union opponents of the AFL leadership consistently attacked Gompers, John Mitchell, and William D. Mahon for their participation in the NCF. Gompers saw such participation as the logical outgrowth of the stature the AFL had acquired in the buoyant years 1897 to 1904, and he regarded this position as a crowning personal and organizational achievement. His opponents viewed such participation as nothing short of class collaboration with fundamentally anti-union corporate elites.

After 1905, the NCF's focus shifted somewhat from direct mediation of labor-management disputes to promotion of corporatist measures that might ameliorate class friction in a number of areas: employee welfare, regulation of trusts (through amendment of the Sherman Anti-Trust Act), public utilities regulation, workers' compensation, child labor, and immigration. The NCF, and especially its secretary Ralph Easley and president Seth Low, played major roles in the efforts of corporate reformers allied with both Theodore Roosevelt and Woodrow Wilson to craft new regulatory legislation that would both limit the effects of unpredictable court decisions under the Sherman Anti-trust Act and move the federal government toward a greater administrative role in the trust-dominated marketplace. These goals came to be embodied to some degree in the Clayton Antitrust and Federal Trade Commission Acts of 1914.

Although its labor members did not always join wholeheartedly in its initiatives, the NCF pioneered some new legislation (such as state-level workers' compensation laws) and promoted new arenas of corporate innovation (welfare capitalism of the 1920s). Some of these efforts bore fruit well after the NCF itself ceased to be an influential force in public life. During and after World War I, a cadre of "enlightened" businessmen continued to seek ways to secure the position of America's largest corporations against unnecessary competition, while at the same time limiting the growth of more aggressive forms of unionism and independent labor and socialist politics.

Easley and the NCF steadily lost influence in the postwar era. But the seeds of its corporatist vision had been planted and eventually bore fruit in the New Era and New Deal.

SHELTON STROMQUIST

References and Further Reading

Glück, Elsie. *John Mitchell, Miner: Labor's Bargain with the Gilded Age*. New York: Greenwood Press, 1969; originally published 1929.

Green, Marguerite. *The National Civic Federation and the American Labor Movement, 1900–1925*. Washington, DC: Catholic University Press, 1956.

Montgomery, David. *The Fall of the House of Labor: The Workplace, the State, and American Labor Activism, 1865–1925*. New York: Cambridge University Press, 1987.

Sklar, Martin. *The Corporate Reconstruction of American Capitalism, 1890–1916*. New York: Cambridge University Press, 1988.

Stromquist, Shelton. *Reinventing "The People": The Progressive Movement, the Class Problem, and the Origins of Modern Liberalism*. Urbana: University of Illinois Press, 2006.

Weinstein, James. *The Corporate Ideal of the Liberal State, 1900–1918*. Boston: Beacon Press, 1968.

NATIONAL CONSUMERS LEAGUE

For over a century, the National Consumers League (NCL) has been a leader in the movement to improve the pay and working conditions of factory laborers. Throughout the twentieth century, it consistently believed that these reforms would ameliorate some of the negative effects of capitalism and lead to an increase in the working classes' economic and political power. Its operations employed a dual strategy, coupling its campaign to use consumers' economic power to persuade factory owners to improve working conditions for laborers with efforts to enact and enforce legislation that established safety standards, minimum wages, and maximum hours. Founded in 1899, the League began by uniting white, middle-class, women reformers with trade unionists to end the sweating system for women and children in cities throughout the United States. By the end of the twentieth century, the NCL employed a similar strategy in its efforts to improve the working conditions for all laborers in factories throughout the world.

The NCL originated from the Working Women's Society (WWS), established in New York in 1886, and its successor, the Consumers League of New York (CLNY), created in 1890. The WWS was composed of both working-class and middle-class women who sought to improve the working conditions of laboring women. The working-class women attempted to organize workers into unions and advocated for protective legislation while the middle-class members worked to educate female consumers and use their purchasing power to end the sweating system for women laborers. After four years, the Society divided along class lines and dissolved. The middle-class members, led by Josephine Shaw Lowell and Maud Nathan, established the CLNY to enlarge their campaign.

The CLNY inspired the creation of other state consumer leagues and ultimately the formation of a national league. It borrowed the strategy of a similar organization operating in London that created a "white list" of businesses that maintained acceptable working conditions for their employees and did not use home manufacturing or child labor. Local leagues established throughout the North and Midwest each employed this strategy. By 1898, the local leagues sought to co-ordinate their efforts and founded the NCL to create a consumers' "white label," modeled after the union label, that it awarded to manufacturers who met its labor standards. The following year, the socialist and settlement worker Florence Kelley, who had been active in forming a league in Illinois and had proposed the label strategy, became the first secretary of the NCL.

Kelley served the NCL until her death in 1932. Throughout her tenure she attempted to arouse and exploit the moral conscience of women consumers through both economic and ethical arguments. She explained that when employers maintained unsanitary factories and used tenement manufacturing, they were both inhibiting the use and development of technological advances that could lower the cost of goods and were endangering public health through the sale of dirty products. Kelley also emphasized the human costs of hazardous work for long hours and low pay to the workers, their children, and their homes and asked middle-class women, as good citizens, to use their consumer power to help. Kelley used these arguments as the basis for the white label campaign.

The white label campaign required extensive fieldwork and a publicity operation. The NCL began by investigating and documenting working conditions for urban laborers throughout much of the country. Within five years, it awarded the white label to more than 60 factories. It publicized its work, in part, through the manufacturers and retailers that complied with its standards. Most prominently, it forged an agreement with the garment manufacturer and department store tycoon John Wanamaker to create window displays that illustrated the contrast in working conditions between sweatshops and model factories and featured Wanamaker's clothes with a white label. For those companies that persisted in using the sweated labor, Kelley led the League in a legislative campaign.

The NCL worked with state leagues and numerous other organizations including trade unions, the National Women's Trade Union League, settlement house workers, and state and federal agencies to pass protective labor laws, establish agencies to oversee their enforcement, and defend them against legal challenges. In the first two decades of the twentieth century, the League assisted in the enactment of a number of state laws that limited child labor, established safety standards for factories, and set maximum hours for women workers. It played a critical role in defending the constitutionality of Oregon's labor law in a case that went to the United States Supreme Court. Kelley and her colleague Josephine Goldmark, through Goldmark's brother-in-law Louis Brandeis, submitted a brief to the Court that outlined the League's extensive evidence of the injurious results of sweated labor. When the Court upheld the maximum hours law for women in 1908 in *Muller v. Oregon*, more than 15 states enacted similar laws. In 1909, the NCL drafted a minimum wage law for women modeled after a British law. It was enacted first in 1912 in Massachusetts and subsequently in 14 additional states.

By the 1920s the NCL made its legislative work primary. In 1918, it ended its white label campaign without abandoning its belief in what it called "ethical consumerism." Florence Kelley explained that workers through their unions and collective bargaining were able to secure better working conditions than the standards set by the League at the turn of the century in its label campaign. Focusing on Congress and state legislatures, the NCL expanded its efforts to secure protective labor laws into the southern states, broadened its efforts beyond white women and children to include white men and black men and women, and sought health care for women and children outside of the factory. One of Kelley's greatest legislative efforts was the NCL's advocacy of the Sheppard-Towner Maternity and Infancy Act. Passed in 1921, it provided federal funds to states for maternity and child health programs.

The NCL's legislative campaigns suffered setbacks in the mid-1920s. In 1923, the Supreme Court struck down the District of Columbia's minimum wage law. In 1926, Congress refused to continue to fund the Sheppard-Towner Act. The NCL also fought against the National Woman's Party's Equal Rights Amendment, believing that the amendment would undermine the protective labor legislation that remained. The NCL persevered and intensified its legislative efforts during the Great Depression, securing some of its most significant reforms during the New Deal era.

During the 1930s, the NCL assisted in the enactment of state and federal labor legislation and in operating the agencies created to oversee regulation enforcement. The NCL led efforts to allow state involvement in labor contract negotiations, worked with the National Recovery Administration during its existence (1933–1935) in setting and enforcing minimum wage and maximum hours codes, and was instrumental in securing wage and hours laws in several southern states. In 1933, President Roosevelt appointed the NCL member Frances Perkins as secretary of labor, and the NCL member Clara Beyer was a regional director for the National Labor Relations Board (NLRB). Most prominently, the NCL lobbied extensively for the Fair Labor Standards Act, which passed in 1938, codifying into federal law its labor reform efforts.

Beginning in the 1940s, the NCL once again faced external opposition. Professional male experts replaced NCL members in governmental positions who oversaw the new labor laws. NCL members were frustrated both because they were marginalized and because the labor legislation and its implementation left the wages and working conditions for countless laborers unreformed. The League struggled to maintain its mission, even temporarily changing its name during World War II to the National Consumers League for Fair Labor Standards, to distinguish itself from emerging groups that championed consumers' rights. During the 1950s, Cold War politics and antilabor forces required some NCL members to defend their activism. For the following 30 years, the NCL's influence significantly diminished.

In the 1980s, the NCL began to regain some public stature when it expanded its original program of using consumer power to improve working conditions for wage laborers beyond United States borders. The NCL was responding to the public exposition of deplorable working conditions in many of the factories in the global apparel industry. After World War II, a number of factors caused a rise in violations of the hard-fought protective labor laws, including a shift of production outside of the United States, a decrease in inspections of factories, rescission of some

labor restrictions in the United States and an absence of regulation in manufacturing sites outside the United States, an increase of poor immigrants in the United States, and a decrease in the power of labor unions. The NCL joined the antisweatshop campaigns led first by the National Labor Committee and then the Department of Labor, in a fight it had championed a century earlier.

At the turn of the twenty-first century, the NCL worked with the federal government, trade unionists, and other nongovernmental organizations to set labor standards for the global apparel industry and ensure their enforcement through public and private power. Once again, one of its primary tools to set and enforce a minimum wage, maximum hours, prohibitions on child labor, and health and safety standards was to appeal to consumers and use their economic power to persuade companies to improve their treatment of their workers. In 1995, it worked with Secretary of Labor Robert Reich as he set forth a "white list" of manufacturers that followed the government's labor standards. In 1997, it joined the Apparel Industry Partnership, creating labor codes and awarding "No Sweat" labels to companies that complied. Time will reveal the effect of these efforts, but at the turn of the twenty-first century, the spirit of the NCL persisted.

GWEN HOERR JORDAN

References and Further Reading

Boris, Eileen. "'Social Responsibility on a Global Level': The National Consumers League, Fair Labor, and Worker Rights at Century's End." In *A Coat of Many Colors: Immigration, Globalization, and Reform in New York City's Garment Industry*, edited by Daniel Soyer. New York: Fordham University Press, 2005, pp. 211–233.

Sklar, Kathryn Kish. "The Consumer's White Label Campaign of the National Consumers' League, 1898–1918." In *Getting and Spending: European and American Consumer Societies in the Twentieth Century*, edited by Susan Strasser, Charles McGovern, and Matthias Judt. Washington DC: Cambridge University Press for the German Historical Institute, 1998, pp. 17–35.

———. "Kelley, Florence." In *Women Building Chicago 1790–1990: A Biographical Dictionary*, edited by Rima Lunin Schultz and Adele Hast. Bloomington: Indiana University Press, 2001, pp. 650–653.

Storrs, Landon R. Y. *Civilizing Capitalism: The National Consumers' League, Women's Activism, and Labor Standards in the New Deal Era*. Chapel Hill: The University of North Carolina Press, 2000.

Cases and Statutes Cited

Adkins v. Children's Hospital 261 U.S. 525 (1923)
Muller v. Oregon 208 U.S. 412 (1908)

NATIONAL EDUCATION ASSOCIATION

The National Education Association (NEA) is a teachers' union that evolved from a professional association. Numbering 2.7 million members in 2005, the present organization developed from an 1857 meeting called by Thomas W. Valentine and Daniel B. Hagar, presidents of the New York and Massachusetts State Teachers' Associations, to form a National Teachers' Association (NTA). The meeting attracted about 100 educators who regarded themselves as "practical teachers," in distinction from the state officials, college presidents, and reformers who composed other educational associations. Working together, these founding members hoped to professionalize their occupation. They resented existing lay governance of education and sought to become a self-regulating profession with control over preparation, qualifications, and practices in the field.

Women soon outnumbered men in teaching, but only "gentlemen" qualified as full members according to the NTA Constitution. At the 1857 meeting, two women signed the Constitution; however, women were not accepted as full members until 1866, when the Association replaced the word "gentlemen" with "persons." Several women served as officers of the Association and addressed annual meetings in subsequent years. Nevertheless, women's participation in the Association did not nearly match their proportions in teaching in the late nineteenth century.

The founders identified themselves as "practical teachers," but their annual meetings reflected their swift ascent to administration as men profited from the nineteenth-century bureaucratization of schools and moved into these newly created, better-paying positions. In 1870, the NTA changed its name to the National Education Association, after merging with the American Normal School Association, the National Association of School Superintendents, and the Central College Association, all organizations that brought more administrators into the membership. To re-inforce the national scope of their ambitions, leaders selected a different city to host the annual meeting each year. Addresses typically concerned developments in educational theory and federal aid to education. Annual meetings were also the venue for elections and important committee appointments, such as those to recommend curricular reform for secondary and elementary education.

Membership grew, but it did not keep pace with the soaring numbers employed in U.S. schools. Between the Civil War and 1900, the number of teachers tripled, but less than 1% joined the NEA. Focused on influencing educational policy and raising professional

Secretary, National Education Association (NEA), displays emblem to John W. Studebaker, U.S. Commissioner of Education. Library of Congress, Prints & Photographs Division, FSA/OWI Collection [LC-USE6-D-005523-a].

prestige, the leadership showed little interest in the problems facing ordinary classroom teachers, whose meager salaries did not permit regular annual meeting attendance. The NEA passed occasional resolutions in favor of better pay, but for the most part, leaders expressed faith that professionalism would secure better salaries.

Seeking an infusion of members and activity, the NEA recruited as president Thomas W. Bicknell, editor of the *Journal of Education* and the former president of the American Institute of Instruction. A tireless promoter, Bicknell billed the 1884 meeting as "the greatest educational show on earth," drawing attendance of nearly 5,000. Not only the NEA's most successful, the program was also the NEA's most inclusive to date, with two African-American men and five white women addressing the general assembly. The organization's effort to appeal to women teachers and reformers succeeded; 54% of those attending were women.

Bicknell popularized attendance at the annual meeting, but he was also instrumental in creating an elite circle within the NEA, the National Council of Education. Formed in 1881, the Council consisted of 51 members appointed by NEA leaders to deliberate and hand down important decisions on educational questions. It soon became a lightning rod for concerns about centralized authority in education. Responding to members' demands for more open discussion, the Council more than tripled in size during its 60-year history, while its mandate grew outmoded. The Council was created to deliver expert opinions; but the NEA Research Division, created in 1922, provided the data and expert analysis on which the Association came to rely.

Criticism of the NEA and the Council's elitist orientation mounted as women classroom teachers struggled for representation. Women's attendance at annual meetings grew in the 1890s, but their numbers did not translate to influence. Women teachers controlled their own urban associations, like the Chicago Teachers' Federation, and local successes raised their expectations for a national organization that would pursue their priorities. Facing new demands from classroom teachers, established NEA leaders guarded their power. At the 1903 annual meeting, the NEA president, Nicholas Murray Butler, proposed narrowing the electoral process. Instead of the affiliated state associations selecting the members of the nominating committee, Butler suggested the president should appoint them. Infuriated by Butler's grab for power, the Chicago Teachers' Federation activist Margaret Haley turned the vote against him. She argued that his proposal would create an

undemocratic "self-perpetuating machine," designed to block women from positions of authority.

Demanding that teachers share in the wealth they helped to create, Haley explicitly connected classroom teachers' and workers' rights. She galvanized a following at the 1904 annual meeting with her speech, "Why Teachers Should Organize," in which she contended that schools were becoming too much like factories and urged the importance of teacher welfare and independence to the protection of the nation's democratic ideals. The NEA leadership charged Aaron Gove, the Denver superintendent of schools, with responding to Haley's address. Gove agreed that teachers deserved better terms and conditions of work, but he warned that organizing would lead to class division within the profession and harm the schools. Gove argued the efficiency of centralized authority, insisting that "despotism can be wielded with a gloved hand." These and similar expressions of patronizing paternalism motivated classroom teachers to embrace Haley's call to organize for better conditions of employment. The first known strike by NEA-affiliated teachers took place that same year in Saline County, Illinois, where teachers refused to sign contracts until the school board met their salary demands. Though strikes remained rare, issues such as salaries, pensions, and tenure began to show up on the NEA agenda.

Conflicts of Gender and Rank

When administrators dominated the NEA in the nineteenth century, organizational priorities emphasized educational policy and building a profession. As classroom teachers made their opinions known at annual meetings, teachers' rights and welfare attracted new attention. They exposed how the NEA, boasting about 2,300 members in 1900, did not represent the tens of thousands of teachers in the nation. NEA leaders continued to consider professionalization their primary objective, but they no longer dismissed classroom teachers' concerns.

Pressure from teachers produced significant changes in NEA activities and personnel. In 1903, the NEA undertook its first investigation of salaries, tenure, and pensions, steered by a committee which included Catharine Goggin, a Chicago Teachers' Federation activist. The women teachers of Chicago and New York proved their growing power when they joined forces in 1910 to elect Ella Flagg Young, the superintendent of Chicago public schools, as the NEA's first female president. Young instigated the creation of the Department of Classroom Teachers, establishing a place in the administrator-dominated organizational structure for teachers, and she secured funding for further study of teachers' salaries. As a consequence of her leadership, the NEA endorsed women's suffrage, teachers' councils, and equal pay for equal work. It also adopted the practice of alternating the presidency between the sexes.

Attempting to blend administrators' priority on improving education with teachers' priority on improving the terms and conditions of employment, the NEA embarked on a massive re-organization in 1917. Leaders recognized that organizational growth depended on women teachers, but power in the organization remained concentrated among two groups of male administrators, superintendents and normal school principals. As the historian Wayne J. Urban has observed, neither group sought to make the NEA a teacher-driven organization, but normal school principals advocated greater consideration of classroom teachers' concerns. One of the most contentious aspects of the re-organization was the replacement of open-floor voting, by all members attending the annual meeting, with a new Representative Assembly, the representatives chosen by the state associations. As membership approached 10,000, leaders insisted that a Representative Assembly would make the organization more democratic. Teachers objected, having learned to mobilize their local associations for important votes at annual meetings. They anticipated correctly that the Representative Assembly would privilege administrator-dominated state associations and reduce the power of their own local associations.

Several other factors diminished teachers' influence within the NEA in the 1920s. The creation of the labor-affiliated American Federation of Teachers (AFT) in 1916, with its strong base of local associations, siphoned away some militant teachers' dissent. Electing women as NEA presidents in alternate years gave teachers representation at higher levels, but some of the power that had been vested in the presidency shifted to the new full-time executive secretary, J. W. Crabtree, hired to direct the re-organization in 1917. Most significant, however, was the impact of World War I. The war effort attached a sense of urgency to improving public schools, most evidently in the NEA's successful Commission on the Emergency in Education. After the war, the NEA capitalized on anti-union sentiment by advocating teacher councils as an alternative to teacher unions like the AFT. Teacher councils were simply advisory groups with no power to act, but with the postwar red scare and backlash against organized labor, the NEA's approach won widespread support. The administrator-dominated

NEA leadership overcame the AFT's challenge and formed an alliance with the veterans of the American Legion, cosponsoring patriotic publications and school events. Friend to the NEA, the Legion became a vocal critic of the AFT. In the 1920s, membership in the AFT declined while the NEA surged to over 220,000 by 1932.

Revenue from membership enabled the NEA to expand its Washington, DC, headquarters with the Research and Legislative Services divisions, bolstering the organization's ambitions for building the profession. In 1917, the entire staff consisted of the executive secretary and a few clerks; by the early 1930s, operations grew to occupy a staff of 140. The Research Division gathered information on education, mostly concerning salaries and school finances. Its publications supplemented the information collected by the small federal Bureau of Education. The Legislative Services Division lobbied Congress; its main focus was the creation of a federal Department of Education, an effort that continued until 1979, when President Jimmy Carter made Education a cabinet position. In the intervening years, Legislative Services built broad-based support for NEA initiatives, especially among state governors, women's clubs, and organized labor.

The Depression quelled lingering conflicts between administrators and teachers. Faced with salary cuts and job losses, both groups put a priority on preserving school funding. Nearly 25% of NEA members lost their jobs by early 1933, and the organization lost a similar percentage of members by 1936. NEA leaders staved off the decline in membership with attention to teacher welfare issues, advocating for gender equity through a single salary scale and better salaries for rural teachers. It also made new efforts to protect the rights of married women teachers. Conscious of Depression-era rises in AFT membership, the much larger NEA still maintained its commitment to educator professionalism, promoting its initiatives to benefit teachers as initiatives that in turn benefited children, schools, and American society.

With the coming of World War II, the NEA pushed toward becoming a significant voice in Washington. It created the Commission on the Defense of Democracy in Education, seeking to launch an offensive against ideological and financial attacks on public education and replicate its WWI public relations success linking organizational and military objectives. The NEA also strengthened its relationship to government by lending educational assistance to the reconstruction of Germany and Japan. After the Soviet Union launched the Sputnik satellite, Congress passed the 1958 National Defense Education

Act, providing federal funding to education. Though it might have represented a victory, the legislation disappointed NEA leaders because it did not give education professionals discretion in the way the funds were used. Decades of NEA lobbying finally paid off when President Lyndon Johnson, a former schoolteacher, signed the Elementary and Secondary Education Act of 1965, providing $1 billion in federal subsidies annually.

On issues of teacher welfare and rights, however, the NEA took a conservative turn. A series of strikes erupted immediately after the war, but the NEA essentially ignored teachers' complaints about rising inflation and stagnant pay. NEA calls for gender equity also faded away. By the 1950s, most large school districts had adopted a single salary scale for men and women teachers, but NEA leaders did not promote this accomplishment. Instead, they celebrated the abolition of "the celibacy rule," noting that married women now outnumbered single women in teaching. Yet the message was not about winning greater freedoms; rather it re-assured members that work in schools did not make them less feminine.

In retreat on gender equity, the NEA also proved reluctant to confront racial discrimination. Segregated state and local associations existed across the South and in many border states. Despite having all-black affiliates, the NEA made little effort to serve those members, aside from cooperating with the all-black American Teachers' Association (ATA) to obtain the same accreditation for black high schools that white schools had. When the Supreme Court issued its 1954 decision in *Brown v. Board of Education*, the NEA responded cautiously. Southern politicians threatened to close the public schools, intimidating supporters of desegregation with a movement of "massive resistance," which put children out of classrooms and teachers out of work in several southern counties. While northern, western, and urban contingents of the NEA supported *Brown*, southern state associations opposed it, worried about alienating whites. Unlike AFT leaders, who were quick to advocate compliance with *Brown*, NEA leaders preferred the risks of stalling to those of acting.

Becoming a Teacher-Driven Organization

Conservative professionalism helped make the NEA the largest educator association in the nation, but competition with the labor-affiliated AFT was a persisting threat. Membership reached nearly 700,000 during the 1957 centennial year, though the goal had been one million. The NEA developed a strong base among women and rural teachers, but leaders recognized their weakness lay among teachers in large cities, especially a new cohort of high school teachers whose numbers nearly doubled between 1954 and 1964. An NEA study titled "Angry Young Men in Teaching" identified these teachers as the primary source of growing militancy. Several teacher strikes in New York City culminated in a resounding AFT victory in 1962, prompting the NEA to reconsider its relations with city teachers and local organizations.

The NEA began to re-invent itself as a union in the 1960s, though its history as a professional association shaped the kind of representation it offered teachers. The NEA advocated "professional negotiations" as an alternative to collective bargaining, and in place of strikes, the organization placed "sanctions" on school districts, warning members not to accept positions in them. Though the national leadership was uneasy with language of unionism, the contracts that NEA locals negotiated did not differ substantially from AFT agreements. Yet NEA discomfort with unionism produced serious repercussions when the state association in Florida called a statewide walkout, following the lead of several city locals. Committed to its no-strike policy, the NEA encouraged Florida teachers to resign rather than strike. This strategy, as the historian Marjorie Murphy noted, asked teachers to break their legal contract of employment rather than the Association's policy of professionalism. The mass resignation prompted legislators to pass the desired education funding, but the problem of negotiating thousands of teachers' return to work, after they resigned, compelled the NEA to rethink the practical wisdom of its no-strike policy. The NEA soon joined the Coalition of American Public Employees, operating outside the umbrella of organized labor, but as a union nonetheless.

As the NEA blended its move to unionism with its long commitment to professionalism, the organization reached a more progressive position on race in public education. In 1964, the Representative Assembly voted to mandate desegregation within its affiliates and merge with the ATA. Concerns that black teachers would have little influence in the NEA stalled the merger temporarily, while efforts to desegregate state associations in Mississippi and Louisiana continued until the 1970s. In the meantime, however, the NEA went on record in support of desegregation, mandatory busing, and protecting black teachers' rights. Having taken strong positions in favor of racial justice, the NEA was able to rise above the highly publicized Ocean Hill-Brownsville conflict in 1968 between AFT locals and urban black communities regarding the community's prerogative to force teacher transfers. While the AFT defended predominately white teachers' seniority rights, Elizabeth Koontz, the NEA's first African-American female president, invoked the NEA's ethos of professionalism, affirming the organization's commitment to building partnerships between teachers and communities of color.

Unionization and desegregation altered the distribution of power within the NEA structure. Administrator-dominated state associations, once the seat of organizational power, took a back seat to the more progressive locals and the national. As teacher support and services emerged as new priorities, locals assumed responsibility for negotiating contracts while the national organization concentrated on building political influence for teachers in Washington and creating the NEA's first Political Action Committee. Recognizing that women remain its largest constituency, the national resumed its advocacy of gender equity in the 1970s, endorsing the Equal Rights Amendment. With the organization focused on serving teachers, the organization revised its Constitution in 1973, substantively reducing the authority of the executive secretary and state associations and placing more power in the hands of teachers.

Immersed in collective bargaining and considerably more teacher-driven, the NEA at the turn of the twenty-first century shared much in common with the AFT. Both groups considered several proposals to merge the two organizations, none of them successful. In 2000, they entered into the NEA FT partnership, which facilitates collaboration between them. Though no longer dominated by administrators, NEA members, still largely women, continue to show some discomfort with the adversarial aspects of unionism. Today, the NEA prides itself on responding to teacher's concerns and makes the case that improved terms and conditions of work for teachers will reap broader social and educational benefits. This "New Unionism" represents a partial return to the NEA of the early and mid-twentieth century, when co-operation characterized the main thrust of organizational activities, while continuing to pursue goals adopted in the 1960s and 1970s to work toward improving teachers' welfare and securing their rights.

KAREN LEROUX

References and Further Reading

Lowell, Susan Butler. *Pressing Onward: The Women's Historical Biography of the National Education Association.* Washington, DC: The Association, 1996.

Murphy, Marjorie. *Blackboard Unions: The AFT and the NEA, 1900–1980.* Ithaca, NY: Cornell University Press, 1990.

Tyack, David B. *The One Best System: A History of American Urban Education.* Cambridge, MA: Harvard University Press, 1974.

Urban, Wayne J. *Gender, Race, and the 1National Education Association: Professionalism and Its Limitations.* New York: Routledge Falmer, 2000.

———. *Why Teachers Organized.* Detroit: Wayne State University, 1982.

Wesley, Edgar B. *NEA: The First Hundred Years: The Building of the Teaching Profession.* New York: Harper & Brothers, 1957.

West, Allan M. *The National Education Association: The Power Base for Education.* New York: Free Press, 1980.

See also **American Federation of Teachers; Teaching**

NATIONAL FARM LABOR UNION
See **Southern Tenant Farmers' Union**

NATIONAL FEDERATION OF FEDERAL EMPLOYEES

When the American Federation of Labor (AFL) chartered the National Federation of Federal Employees (NFFE) in 1917, it took the unusual step of creating an early version of industrial unionization. Open to federal government workers in all agencies and in all occupations, it became the first general federal service union that was not organized around craft or government department. Prior to its creation, the most active unions with exclusively federal employees had been postal workers, and in 1904, the International Association of Machinists had established District 44 exclusively for civilian workers employed by the military.

NFFE emerged at a time when groups of government employees, including postal workers, were fighting for the right to lobby Congress on issues such as pay. The Lloyd-La Follette Act of 1912 recognized the right of postal employees to join unions without penalty and for all federal employees to petition on their own behalf, thus setting the stage for union organization outside the postal service. Several years later, the Borland Rider to an appropriation bill attempted to lengthen the workday for federal employees, encouraging the establishment of a number of small unions, including one in 1916 representing mostly women in the Treasury Department's Bureau of Engraving and Printing. A group of these government unions then organized into the Federal Employees Union. When the Borland Rider appeared, the Stenographers and Typists Union asked Samuel Gompers and the AFL to join them in opposing the law. AFL leaders did so, successfully defeating the

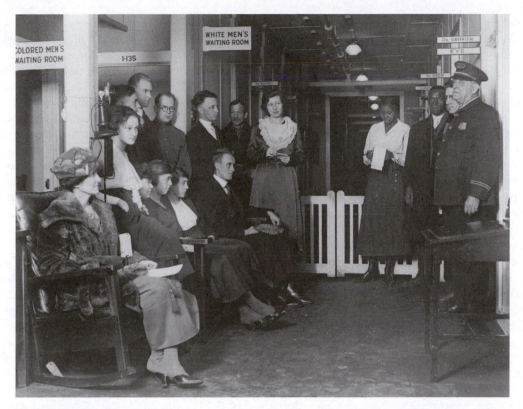

Group of federal employees waiting for treatment at the Public Health Service Dispensary #32, which has recently been opened for the exclusive benefit of government workers. Library of Congress, Prints & Photographs Division [LC-USZ62-108282].

measure while also seizing the opportunity to organize further federal workers. Using the Federal Employees Union as a core, the AFL formally chartered a new union, NFFE, at their September 1917 convention. Immediately flexing its muscle, NFFE helped defeat Democratic Representative William P. Borland in Missouri's 1918 primary race.

Open to all civilian employees of the United States government or the District of Columbia, NFFE started with over 60 locals and 10,000 members. Local 2 represented most Washington, DC, agencies with some exceptions. The Bureau of Engraving and Printing union, for instance, formed Local 105, and its president, Gertrude McNally, went on to become the secretary-treasurer of NFFE in 1925. She served in this post until 1953. Luther Steward became president in 1917, and remained in this office for 37 years. Together, they therefore had significant influence on the union's tone and direction.

Objectives and Tactics

Adamantly opposed to use of the strike, NFFE instead saw itself as a lobbying organization or pressure group. Consequently, its strategies included petitioning Congress, generating positive publicity for its aims, and using union members to work with agency administrators to further a mutually beneficial agenda. Hence, it eschewed militant tactics in favor of parades and mass meetings to promote its cause. Its mission was "to advance the social and economic welfare and education of employees of the United States and to aid in the perfection of systems that will make for greater efficiency in the various services of the United States." Committed to raising salaries, it sought to eliminate inconsistencies in pay; support the reclassification of occupations, in order to provide uniformity within and across agencies; extend the merit system, thus eliminating patronage positions; and establish annual and sick leave, a Saturday half holiday, and retirement plans.

NFFE's efforts to extend the classification system to the field service (a reference to the federal workforce outside of Washington, DC) set the stage for its break with the AFL. From its inception, NFFE put much of its energy behind classification of government jobs, believing that greater uniformity in describing and classifying occupations would standardize pay across the federal service. Congress passed the Classification Act in 1923, but it excluded field service and craft workers. The Welsh Act of 1928 called for a reconsideration of classification of these two groups of workers, an effort that NFFE leadership vigorously supported. A legislative measure considered in 1931 would have established a Personnel Classification Board to determine classifications and wage rates for all government positions, including crafts. The AFL's executive council, however, objected to this plan, perceiving it as an effort to undermine existing craft control over occupations and pay standards. Most craft workers had their pay set by wage boards, which used prevailing private-sector wages to set pay rates. Although the legislation would not have abolished wage boards, it would have made them subservient to the proposed Personnel Classification Board. AFL leaders sided with craft workers in rejecting the legislation. The NFFE president, Luther Steward, angered by the AFL's opposition to this classification measure, called for a vote on whether NFFE should disengage from the AFL and become an independent union. When the vote was held in December 1931, NFFE members narrowly voted to leave the AFL. Once NFFE became independent, the AFL took the unusual step of immediately establishing a competing federal government union, the American Federation of Government Employees, which siphoned off approximately one third of NFFE's members. In June 1932, NFFE was left with some 64,000 members. By 1937, the union had recovered some of its losses, with over 600 locals and 75,000 members in more than 35 federal agencies. NFFE remained independent until 1999. Faced with stiff competition from other unions in the 1980s and 1990s, it began to look for a partner that would help strengthen its finances and membership. A search committee recommended a partnership with the AFL-CIO's International Association of Machinists and Aerospace workers, which went into effect in 1999. Consequently, after a 67-year absence, NFFE returned to the AFL.

NFFE devoted most of its resources to bread-and-butter issues, including lobbying for overtime pay, revisions to the efficiency rating system, and of course, extension of the merit system. In 1937, NFFE formally affiliated with the primary pressure group for merit reform, the National Civil Service Reform League, with President Steward and Secretary-Treasurer McNally sitting on the League's council. Union leaders also continued to support vigorously the creation of a civil service court of appeals.

They remained adamantly opposed to striking and to any hint of collective bargaining, frequently criticizing the more left-leaning United Federal Workers of America, affiliated with the Congress of Industrial Organizations (CIO), for supporting collective bargaining rights and for their more aggressive tactics in pursuing goals. Steward, for instance, played a key role in President Franklin D. Roosevelt's decision to issue a statement defining public employee union rights. NFFE's president had asked Roosevelt to speak at the union's Twentieth Jubilee Convention in 1937, but the President declined. Instead, Roosevelt drafted a letter to be read at the convention in which he clarified the differences between private- and public-sector unionization. Arguing that "collective bargaining, as usually understood, cannot be transplanted into the public service," Roosevelt noted that in the case of public employees, "the employer is the whole people, who speak by means of laws enacted by their representatives in Congress." He went on to emphasize that "militant tactics have no place in the functions of any organization of Government employees." Steward strongly supported Roosevelt's statement. In keeping with its desire to use collective weight to influence Congress, NFFE became a charter member of the National Legislative Council of Federal Employee Organizations, designed to coordinate lobbying activities of the general government unions.

NFFE's identity as a lobbying organization devoted to upholding the merit system was much in evidence when President John F. Kennedy issued Executive Order 10988 in 1962 granting limited bargaining rights to federal employees. His order established informal, formal, and exclusive bargaining rights for employees based upon the percentage of union employees in any given unit. NFFE's president, Vaux Owen, vigorously objected to the order's private-sector terminology, stipulating that collective bargaining did not belong in the public sector. He also opposed establishment of exclusive recognition for unions representing a majority of employees in a unit, arguing that it would curtail an employee's right to choose any union. Finally, he voiced opposition to the order's "conflict-of-interest" clause, which held that managers or supervisors could not hold office in a union. Owen complained that this provision created class distinctions and adversarial relationships in an environment otherwise free of these conflicts. Further, he noted that a number of NFFE members, who were supervisors, would be in violation of the order. To combat the order, NFFE initiated an unsuccessful lawsuit claiming that the executive order was unconstitutional because federal employees had been exempted explicitly from the National Labor Relations Act (NLRA), and yet Executive Order 10988 applied NLRA models to these employees. In 1965, the Washington, DC, District Court ruled that the dispute over the order should be settled within the executive branch. After the ruling, NFFE's executive council, led by a new president, Nathan T. Wolkomir, voted to drop the suit. Eventually, the union came to embrace collective bargaining and saw its membership rise as a consequence of employees' expanded rights.

Yet even in the 1970s, NFFE hesitated to support reforms it perceived as threatening to the merit system. President Jimmy Carter's Civil Service Reform Act of 1978 abolished the Civil Service Commission, replacing it with the Office of Personnel Management (OPM) to handle personnel programs; the Merit Systems Protection Board (MSPB) to manage the merit system and protect federal whistleblowers from retribution; and the Federal Labor Relations Authority to oversee labor-management relations. The law also created a Senior Executive Service (SES), which enabled high-ranking supervisors to transfer from agency to agency without losing their rank. Finally, to make the bureaucracy more flexible, the measure loosened personnel rules, making it easier for agencies to hire, fire, promote, and discipline employees, and weakened veterans' preference. NFFE perceived the law as a presidential attempt to politicize the bureaucracy, calling the SES a haven for political appointees, the MSPB a tool of agency management, and the OPM an agency controlled by the White House. This concern with patronage and political influence was also clear in NFFE's opposition to efforts in the early 1970s to liberalize the Hatch Act of 1939, which had severely limited the political activities of federal employees. Not until 1977 did NFFE leadership, under pressure from members, favor some revisions to the law, including the ability of employees to run for local political offices. Nevertheless, the organization remained staunchly in favor of the Hatch Act's prohibition against partisan activity in federal offices and pushed for stronger penalties for those violating the law. While it favored further revisions to the law in the late 1980s, it continued to advocate for a civil service free of partisanship.

Membership

NFFE's conservatism may partially have been a reflection of its diverse membership, which included blue- and white-collar workers in occupations ranging from janitor to chemist. Among white-collar employees, the union had large numbers of clerical workers as well as mid-level administrators, and it tended to be stronger in old-line agencies, probably in part because

it was the first general public service union. For instance, among its members was Dr. Howard Edson, the president of Local 2 in 1937, and a scientist in the Department of Agriculture who had taken an active role in classification during the 1920s. Harrison E. Meyer served as the president of the Civil Service Commission branch of Local 2. He began his government career as a page, working his way into clerical positions, and eventually into mid-level administration. Meyer's upward movement reflected the experience of many NFFE members, and the union therefore remained a strong proponent of promotion from within. In its early years, members did not tend to be strong supporters of the private-sector organized labor movement, and into the 1970s, the union's constitution continued to bar communists from joining. Like many federal worker unions, NFFE had many female members and a strong advocate in longtime Secretary-Treasurer McNally. It did not, however, encourage black membership until after the civil rights movement.

As the first general union for federal government workers, NFFE broke new ground in organizing across occupations, pay grades, and gender. It represented an early version of industry-based organizing, and as such, its membership focused on improving pay and working conditions in federal agencies, largely through collective pressure on Congress and agency administrators.

MARGARET C. RUNG

References and Further Reading

Johnson, Eldon. "General Unions in the Federal Civil Service." *Journal of Politics* 1 (February 1940): 23–56.
Levine, Marvin, and Eugene G. Hagburg. *Public Sector Labor Relations.* St. Paul, MN: West Publishing Co., 1979.
Mosher, Frederick C. *Democracy and the Public Service.* New York: Oxford University Press, 1968.
Nesbitt, Murray. *Labor Relations in the Federal Government Service.* Washington, DC: Bureau of National Affairs, 1976.
"NFFE History." www.nffe.org/nffe-1917.html (2005).
Rung, Margaret. *Servants of the State: Managing Diversity and Democracy in the Federal Workforce, 1933–1953.* Athens: University of Georgia Press, 2002.
Spero, Sterling D. *Government as Employer.* New York: Remsen Press, 1948.
Van Riper, Paul P. *History of the United States Civil Service.* Evanston, IL: Row, Peterson & Co., 1958.

See also **American Federation of Government Employees; American Federation of Labor; United Government Employees; United Public Workers of America/ United Federal Workers of America**

NATIONAL FOOTBALL LEAGUE PLAYERS ASSOCIATION

The National Football League Players Association (NFLPA) was formed in 1956 during a meeting at the Waldorf Astoria hotel in New York City. Such notables as Don Shula and Frank Gifford were in attendance. The demands of the players upon the National Football League (NFL) owners were initially very basic: a minimum salary of $5,000 per year, equipment and uniform allowances, and injury pay. The owners, however, rejected these demands. This early defeat of the NFLPA would illustrate the conflict between the owners of NFL franchises and the players. Over the next 50 years, issues such as free agency, salary caps, the college draft, and two major players' strikes would grab headlines and lead to the cancellation of both games and television contracts.

The players were resolute in their demands, despite their early snubbing by the NFL owners. The next step for the NFLPA was litigation. In the first of a series of court cases related to playing conditions and pay in the NFL, the Supreme Court ruled in 1957 (*Radovich vs. NFL*) that the NFL was subject to antitrust laws. Shortly after this decision, the owners gave in to the demands that the NFLPA had articulated in 1956. Once these demands were met, the NFLPA demanded even more from the owners. These new demands were related to pay for preseason games and medical and retirement benefits. The owners met some of the players' demands, but only modestly (the mandatory retirement age remained 65).

The players, looking to capitalize on their court victory, tried to join the AFL-CIO, but they were refused admission. After this, the players briefly considered joining the Teamsters, but the NFLPA did not join the union and thus remained an association and not a union. The next challenge to the NFLPA was competition from the American Football League (AFL). The players in the newer and smaller AFL had their own association. The NFL owners therefore could play one association off the other. This in effect was the case, even after the two leagues merged. These same dynamics would be repeated in the 1980s with the short-lived United States Football League (USFL). In 1968, the NFLPA threatened a strike, but the owners locked them out. A landmark collective bargaining agreement followed, with the players getting a lot less than what they originally demanded. Finally, the two players' associations merged, with John Mackey to head the new group. Shortly after this, the NFLPA was certified by the National Labor Relations Board (NLRB).

Recognition by the NLRB meant that the NFLPA was now a union, although an extremely weak one with respect to the NFL team owners. In July 1970, there was another strike during training camp by the players. The agreement that ended the strike gave certain concessions to the NFLPA, including an increase in minimum salaries, pension and dental benefits, as well as agents being allowed for players. Despite these gains, many union reps were cut by teams. Another tactic used by owners was the "Rozelle rule," which prevented players from moving to other teams once their contracts were up. So, despite modest gains, the NFLPA realized it needed more clout and savvy if it was to beat the owners in the complex field of labor relations.

Toward these goals, the NFLPA moved its headquarters to Washington, DC, and began a program to educate players as to their rights with respect to the owners. The players' union then voted to file suit against the NFL again over the Rozelle rule in a case that came to be known as *Mackey vs. NFL*. In 1974, the NFLPA declared "No Freedom, No Football," and the players went on strike again. This time around, the demands on the owners were more ambitious: arbitration over contracts and an end to the college draft. Despite the fact that this new round of demands was unmet, the players ended the strike and played for the next several seasons with their disputes still unresolved. In 1976, the owners were found guilty of violating antitrust laws, and a new round of collective bargaining ensued between them and the NFLPA. Emboldened by its victory in court, the NFLPA made even more demands, which concerned free agency and a share of the revenues from TV rights and ticket sales. The irony in all of this was that union membership went down for the players' union despite league expansion during this time.

In 1982, the players struck again over the issues of modified free agency and the issue of revenue sharing with the owners. The NFL owners had a unique advantage in professional sports in that they shared the TV revenues and gate receipts among themselves. Therefore, they usually presented a united front with respect to the players. The NFLPA made a modest proposal that would allow the more talented players to get paid more, but the owners rejected this for two reasons. First, they did not want to give up their lucrative TV and attendance money. Second, because a new league was forming (that is, the USFL), the owners realized that the NFLPA would now be in an inferior bargaining position. Finally, a compromise was reached, and the regular season was resumed, with a modified nine-game season and a larger playoff format. The owners did agree to a percentage of their gross team revenues going to the players as a good faith gesture. As in the 1974 strike, the players were still at a disadvantage, though. The NFLPA realized that it represented people in a very dangerous game that had short careers, so any future decision to strike would have to be weighed carefully. The owners, for their part, stuck together and rode out the competition from the rival USFL for the next few years. They could always raise the price of tickets or add more amenities to their stadiums such as skyboxes.

The leader of the 1982 players strike now became the executive president of the NFLPA. Gene Upshaw wanted to pride himself on truly representing the interests of the players and not the lawyers. The collective bargaining agreement after the 1982 season expired before the 1987 season and left many issues unresolved. The players voted to strike, and this time the owners meant business. They hired replacement players for three games. This promptly ended the strike, as the NFLPA "punted" because it realized that its bargaining position had deteriorated. Despite this, the owners refused to allow the players to return immediately, and the NLRB would later cite them for this. In the meantime, the NFLPA returned to court to fight on a more level playing field. In a case in Minnesota federal court, the NFL owners' "Plan B" free agency was determined to be unfair. The owners appealed this decision and won. Despite this, the NFLPA did win back pay for the players who were not allowed to return immediately at the end of the 1987 strike. In 1989, the players met and agreed to end their status as a union.

A series of court cases, the first involving Freeman McNeil of the Jets, ended in a defeat for the owners—and again stated that "Plan B" free agency was struck down. Other settlements in the *Brown vs. NFL* and *White vs. NFL* cases resulted in clear victories for the players involved. These new court victories resulted in the players voting to make the NFLPA a union again in 1993. A new agreement after this with the NFL owners allowed a share of the teams' revenues to go to the players. After many court battles, strikes, reversals, and broken promises by the owners, the NFLPA had finally won respectability for its players and had solid material results to prove it. Like the game of football itself, with its seesaw battles for mere yards, the struggle between the NFLPA and the NFL owners had been a hard-fought fight. In the end, the NFLPA definitely finished in the win column for the interests of the players.

TIMOTHY A. BERG

References and Further Reading

MacCambridge, Michael. *America's Game: The Epic Story of How Pro Football Captured a Nation.* New York: Random House, 2004.

Moraniss, David. *When Pride Still Mattered: A Life of Vincent Lombardi.* New York: Simon & Schuster, 1999.

NATIONAL HOCKEY PLAYERS ASSOCIATION

For nearly 40 years, the National Hockey League Players Association (NHLPA) has been the sole employee bargaining unit with the National Hockey League (NHL). Its creation came at a time of increasing awareness of the unequal power distribution between employers and employees in the professional sports industry. According to many critics, however, the NHLPA, until the 1990s, was no more than a company union that protected the interests of the employers rather than those of the union membership.

Early in the history of professional hockey, skilled players had many options that enhanced their bargaining power. Multiple professional leagues appeared in the early 1910s. Of importance were the National Hockey Association (NHA), created in 1909, and the Pacific Coast Hockey Association (PCHA), founded in 1911. Contracts were negotiated between individual players and management, often the owner of the club. Although professional in name, professional hockey seasons rarely lasted more than four months of the year. Thus, all players had other careers beyond and, sometimes, during the season. Unlike professional baseball, which had established a national commission by 1903 to oversee the industry, the NHA and PCHA in particular raided each other's players for much of the 1910s. Highly skilled players also could choose to remain in the amateur leagues, where some top-level clubs provided players with jobs and/or under-the-table payment. These options gave highly skilled players leverage when professional clubs came calling and partly explained why players did not see the need to organize themselves.

Organizing a player union also had to overcome the culture of professional team sports. Ideas of team unity and loyalty were drummed into the players' consciousness early on. For a team sport that had a great potential for violence amongst the participants, team members learned quickly to stick up for one another, especially during fights. Often a siege mentality existed within a team and, in turn, re-inforced and magnified the us-against-them mentality. It was not unusual for players to carry their animosities toward other teams' players beyond the games. Management also cultivated a form of loyalty based on paternalism. Players were trained to follow orders of the coach and, by implication, management. The idea of loyalty, team unity, and submission to authority made organizing on a leaguewide basis difficult. Indeed, the first organized effort to challenge management's prerogative did not come until after the NHL replaced the NHA as the major league in eastern Canada. Disputing the length of the season in their contracts, Hamilton Tigers players refused to participate in the 1925 playoffs unless they were paid an extra $200 per person. In turn, the NHL president, Frank Calder, suspended the players and fined each $200. The Hamilton owners then sold the entire roster to the new entry into the NHL, the New York Americans, for the following season.

The Hamilton players challenge, however, came at a period of major NHL expansion after its creation in 1917. Between 1924 and 1926, the league membership increased from four to 10 teams. Despite increased job opportunities with the expansion, the only other major league, the Western Hockey League, which had six franchises, went out of business in 1926, giving the NHL a monopoly in the industry. Furthermore, the Great Depression soon made jobs scarce when some NHL franchises faltered. By the end of the Second World War, the league had only six franchises left.

The first leaguewide effort to organize players did not result in a union. In 1946, a Detroit insurance agent, C. Jean Casper, convinced a group of players to form a pension society. The players then approached the owners for an additional contribution. Although the Detroit club had contributed into the plan, other owners, led by Toronto's Conn Smythe, disliked this act of independence and headed off the players' effort by establishing a pension society administered by the league, the National Hockey League Pension Society. Owners began contributing to the plan using portions of the revenues from the all-star and playoff games in 1957. Revenues from international exhibition games involving the NHL were added to the fund when the league began organizing these tournaments in the 1970s.

Whereas the NHL began to enjoy a period of stability and prosperity after the Second World War, player discontent surfaced. With the assistance of a New York attorney, Milton Mound, Ted Lindsey, a Detroit player, began secretly signing up players in the league and on February 12, 1957, announced the formation of the NHLPA. If the owners could not stomach a player-controlled pension society, the league had no wish to recognize this first player union. Owners and managers intimidated players by ridding those involved in the union. Under tremendous pressure, players from the Detroit Red Wings decided to leave the NHLPA on November 13, 1957, thus squashing the union.

The next effort to form a union came in 1967. On June 6, a group of players announced the new NHLPA, under the leadership of the Toronto attorney and player agent R. Alan Eagleson. Unlike the 1957 version, it was accepted by the owners, in part because of the league's concern that the Teamsters Union was considering organizing professional sports. Despite management's recognition of the NHLPA as a bargaining unit, the NHLPA did not initiate negotiation for a collective bargaining agreement (CBA) until 1975. Between 1967 and 1991, when Eagleson was the executive director, the NHL and the NHLPA concluded only four (1976, 1981, 1984, and 1988).

For a large part of the NHLPA history, Alan Eagleson was the lightning rod around whom praises and criticisms revolved. Despite improvements to the players' salaries and benefits and the elimination of the reserve clause, some players and player agents soon doubted Eagleson's effectiveness as a union executive director. They complained about conflicts of interests in Eagleson's multiple roles as union executive director, player agent, practicing lawyer, and, later, a director of Hockey Canada. They argued that Eagleson was often unresponsive to their queries on union business and that he seemed to favor those represented by his own player agency. Some retired players, led by Carl Brewer, also charged that Eagleson often sided with management in issues such as pension funds and disability insurance. Observers noted that the NHL players' gains lagged far behind those in the other professional sports, despite favorable bargaining positions—an investigation was conducted by the U. S. Justice Department on possible violation of antitrust laws in 1971 and the appearance of a rival league, the World Hockey Association (WHA), in 1972. Interestingly, Eagleson brokered the merger between the WHA and the NHL in 1979, eliminating jobs and the bidding war for players. A movement to oust Eagleson emerged around the 1980s and led to his resignation in 1991 when the FBI began investigating his affairs. In 1998, Eagleson pled guilty to charges brought by both the Canadian and American governments.

Between 1992 and 2005, Robert W. Goodenow, a Detroit lawyer and player agent, succeeded Eagleson as the executive director of the NHLPA. Goodenow's terms of employment demanded that he relinquish his other careers. Unlike Eagleson, Goodenow was much more militant. Indeed, the first player strike occurred a mere four months after Goodenow took office. Both sides reached a new CBA 10 days after the strike began. Negotiations for a new CBA broke down again before the start of the 1994–1995 season, and this time, the owners locked out the players.

On January 20, 1995, a new agreement was signed by both sides, and the league operated a shortened schedule. The 1995 agreement was extended to 2004, when the NHL owners insisted on and the union strenuously objected to a salary cap. United by a resolve to control salaries, the NHL owners locked out the players for the entire 2004–2005 season. In July 2005, a new CBA with a salary cap was agreed upon by both sides. Amid criticisms by a few players on how he handled the negotiations, Goodenow resigned as executive director on July 28 and was replaced by the NHLPA senior director of business affairs and licensing, Ted Saskin. The latest CBA was scheduled to expire after the 2010–2011 season, with an option for the NHLPA to re-open negotiation for a new agreement after the 2008–2009 season. Saskin is only the third executive director of the NHLPA. Whereas Eagleson was deemed too friendly to management and Goodenow the opposite, it will be interesting to see how Saskin guides the union after a substantial defeat in the last agreement.

JOHN CHI–KIT WONG

References and Further Reading

Beamish, Rob B. "The Impact of Corporate Ownership on Labor-Management Relations in Hockey." In *The Business of Professional Sports*, edited by Paul D. Staudohar and James A. Mangan. Urbana and Chicago: University of Illinois Press, 1991, pp. 202–221.

Conway, Russ. *Game Misconduct: Alan Eagleson and the Corruption of Hockey*. Toronto: Macfarlane Walter & Ross, 1995.

Cruise, David, and Alison Griffiths. *Net Worth: Exploding the Myths of Pro Hockey*. Toronto: Penguin Books, 1992.

Dowbiggin, Bruce. *The Defence Never Rests*. Toronto: HarperCollins Publishers Ltd., 1993.

Eagleson, R. Alan, with Scott Young. *Power Play: The Memoirs of Hockey Czar Alan Eagleson*. Toronto: McClelland & Stewart, 1991.

Gruneau, Richard, and David Whitson. "The Work World of Pro Hockey." In *Hockey Night in Canada: Sport, Identities, and Cultural Politics*. Toronto: Garamond Press, 1993.

Holzman, Morey, and Joseph Nieforth. *Deceptions and Doublecross: How the NHL Conquered Hockey*. Toronto: The Dundurn Group, 2002.

Kidd, Bruce. "Brand Name Hockey." In *The Struggle for Canadian Sport*. Toronto: University of Toronto Press, 1996.

Meagher, Gary. "Inside the NHL—the Business Side of Hockey." In *Total Hockey*, edited by Dan Diamond. New York: Total Sports, 1998, pp. 129–142.

Morrison, Scott. "The Rise and Fall of R. Alan Eagleson." In *Total Hockey*, edited by Dan Diamond. New York: Total Sports, 1998, pp. 118–120.

Wong, John Chi-Kit. *Lords of the Rinks: The Emergence of the National Hockey League, 1875–1936*. Toronto: University of Toronto Press, 2005.

NATIONAL INDUSTRIAL RECOVERY ACT

The National Industrial Recovery Act (NIRA) was the Roosevelt administration's signature economic revitalization act of the First New Deal. The bill passed during the first "Hundred Days" as a part of the crash legislation session passing laws designed to stem the tide of the Great Depression and restore prosperity and employment to the nation. The Act set up a complicated new bureaucracy, the National Recovery Administration (NRA), headed by the retired general Hugh Johnson. Most significant for labor organizations in the country, Section 7a of the Act provided the first federal recognition of the rights of employees to form unions.

The National Recovery Administration was charged with setting codes for major industries throughout the nation. The codes were to be agreed upon in council between government, industry, and to a lesser extent, labor representation. Economic advisers in the Roosevelt administration saw excessive competition as destructive to the economy and as one of the prime causes of the Great Depression. The administration hoped to use the NRA as a means of managing and reducing competition. In practice, however, the NRA was less than successful. Many businesses resented government interference of any sort in their affairs and refused to cooperate. Henry Ford, for instance, tried to steer the Ford Motor Company clear of any involvement whatsoever in the NRA. The NRA tended to benefit big business at the expense of small businesses; many small businesspersons and progressive-minded legislators saw the NRA as furthering monopolistic behavior on the part of big firms at the expense of consumers and small producers. The NRA did, in fact, encourage oligopolies in industry, as the committees writing codes were able to set quotas for production, prices, and wages.

The codes written by the NIRA brought stability to a few industries that had been decimated by cutthroat competition, but many of the codes proved unworkable. The NIRA did score one major achievement, writing a code for the textile industry that virtually eliminated child labor. Some of the codes established minimum wages in industries, and many unskilled workers saw real wage increases after their industries adopted NRA codes. Skilled workers, however, frequently saw their wages decrease. Overall, the NRA failed in its goals of increasing employment and purchasing power. After a temporary increase, real wages overall actually began to decline under the NRA.

The NRA also had a difficult time selling its plans to the public and to local businesses. To counter this, the NRA devised a Blue Eagle emblem, with the slogan, "We do our part!" The NRA used the emblem along with several publicity stunts to try to build public support for the program. The Blue Eagle also served as one of the few real enforcement mechanisms of the program—businesses that refused to abide by their industry codes would have the Blue Eagle logo denied to them. Thousands of posters with the NRA eagle were distributed around the country to be hung in shop windows. After an initial period of public support, enthusiasm faded, and for most of its brief existence, American support for the program was tepid at best. When the U.S. Supreme Court declared the NIRA unconstitutional in 1935, most Americans were indifferent.

Business had always been lukewarm toward the NIRA. Some business leaders had seen government intervention in the economy as inevitable and urged the business community to act decisively in shaping that intervention, but many were unconvinced. Yet in the context of the Great Depression, the NRA seemed to be a reasonable compromise. In exchange for the ability to act collusively to fix prices and production schedules, businesses had to accept some sort of government oversight and involvement in the marketplace. The single provision of the Act that most angered business was Section 7A, which provided for collective bargaining for employees in industries covered by the Act.

Section 7a of the NIRA read, in part, "employees shall have the right to organize and bargain collectively through representatives of their own choosing." Section 7a also prevented yellow-dog contracts and gave the executive branch authority through the NRA's system of codes to set minimum wages and maximum hours by industry. The passage of the NIRA set off a furious organizing spree amongst the nation's workers. Much of the organizing occurred at the grassroots level, as workers, frustrated by the grim economic conditions of the Depression, the legacy of 1920s union busting, and union ineffectiveness, began demanding organization into unions. Section 7a of the NIRA seemed to give not only government sanction for unionism, but for many workers, implied Roosevelt administration approval of their unionization efforts as a tool for economic recovery.

Yet the organizing efforts of 1933–1935 were only of limited effectiveness. The American Federation of Labor (AFL) proved largely incapable of accommodating the influx of workers, many of whom were unskilled or semiskilled. William Green, the president of the AFL, responded by trying to organize workers into a new system of federal unions, to keep the traditional affiliates of the AFL skilled and free of unskilled immigrant labor. Industry signed on to the NIRA politically but balked at giving in to the new wave of organization. Employers held that the NIRA did not provide any structure for dealing with employee organizations. Specifically, they would claim that the law did not require an employer to recognize a union as the sole bargaining agent for all employees merely because a majority of workers supported it. This contention led to a resurgence of company unionism as employers attempted to thwart the wave of organization by bargaining with company-organized and financed unions that clearly represented a minority of employees. Many of the codes that the NIRA established in industries allowed employees to be arbitrarily dismissed; many union activists felt that this provided a method for employers to dismiss union sympathizers. Employers also resorted to cruder methods, employing labor spies, guards, and other methods of dubious legality to thwart the employee offensive. This led to a rash of strikes in 1934. Thousands of strikes brought out over 1.5 million workers in the year. Whereas workers had struck in past years over issues such as hours, wages, and working conditions, union recognition drove the strike wave of 1934.

The NIRA lacked any effective enforcement mechanisms to deal with the labor unrest of 1934. The Act provided for a National Labor Board (later the National Labor Relations Board, NLRB) to oversee the implementation of Section 7a. Robert Wagner, a senator from New York, chaired the board. From the outset, Wagner saw both the National Labor Board and Section 7a as insufficient to protect the interests of American workers. His experiences on the National Labor Board led him to begin considering new legislation to guarantee the right of American workers to organize. This legislation would emerge later as the National Labor Relations Act (or Wagner Act).

The experiences of the AFL during the regime of the NIRA brought major changes. The inadequacy of the AFL's federal union strategy in organizing unskilled and semiskilled workers was apparent to insurgents like John L. Lewis within the union movement. Lewis led the UMW to massive organizing gains during the NIRA. Lewis used the increased pull that his successes granted him to force the creation within the AFL of the Committee for Industrial Organizing, which would later splinter into the independent Congress of Industrial Organizations. The AFL, too, would eventually be forced to back away from its strictly craft method of organization and adapt to the new regime of mass organization in large industry. Finally, the creation of the National Labor Board and the federal guarantee of the right to organize unions convinced many in the labor movement of the need to turn to the federal state for progress in labor relations.

The U.S. Supreme Court declared the NIRA unconstitutional in 1935. In *Schechter v. United States* (or as it came to be known, the sick chickens case), a unanimous Court ruled that the Act had overstepped the bounds of the commerce clause of the Constitution. The Court also ruled that the NRA's system of codes was unconstitutional in that it usurped the legislature's power to create law. The Schechter Poultry Corporation had been convicted for violating the poultry codes of the NIRA, specifically for violating wage and hour provisions of the code and for selling diseased chickens. The invalidation of the law brought to an end the Roosevelt administration's most ambitious plans to reform the American economy. The ruling, coupled with the Supreme Court's invalidation of the Agricultural Adjustment Act (AAA), also seemed to threaten much of the New Deal.

The National Industrial Recovery Act left a mixed legacy. While the NRA largely failed to raise wages and therefore purchasing power of the working class in the United States, it did help to set in motion the 1930s union movement that would achieve a vastly increased standard of living for many American workers. As the centerpiece program of the Roosevelt administration's effort to end the Great Depression, it surely was a disappointment. But as with much of the New Deal, it did achieve some small successes in economic reform, even as it failed to fix the American economy overall.

STEVEN DIKE-WILHELM

References and Further Reading

Bernstein, Irving. *Turbulent Years: A History of the American Worker, 1933–1941*. Boston: Houghton Mifflin, 1969.
Leuchtenburg, William E. *Franklin D. Roosevelt and the New Deal, 1932–1940*. New York: Harper and Row, 1963.
Rauch, Basil. *The History of the New Deal, 1933–1938*. New York: Creative Age Press, Inc., 1944.
Watkins, T. H. *The Great Depression: America in the 1930s*. Boston: Little, Brown, and Company, 1993.

NATIONAL LABOR REFORM PARTY

The National Labor Reform Party (NLRP) was the political organization of the National Labor Union (NLU). Officially established in 1870, the NLRP entered candidates in the 1872 elections.

The NLU represented a coalition of local trade unions, trade assemblies or citywide federations, and a handful of national trade unions and Eight-Hour Leagues that emerged in the New England and mid-Atlantic states. Between 1866, when it was founded, through 1872, the NLU advanced a program that stressed the eight-hour day, producer co-operatives, the abolition of contract and convict labor, and currency reform. From its very conception, the NLU was politically orientated. At its founding congress, following a long and heated debate, the NLU endorsed the formation of an independent labor party "as soon as possible."

The NLU began to make headway following the election of William Sylvis from the Iron Molders Union as its president. He and Richard Trevellick, the president of the International Union of Ship Carpenters and Caulkers, devoted their energies to propagate the NLU's program at local meetings in 1868. By the end of the decade, there were more than 120 new affiliates, including 14 national unions.

Effectively, the NLU was a forum for the labor movement through which strategic objectives were identified, priorities established, and specific measures for action developed. For example, a centerpiece of the NLU's program was currency reform. Inspired by the theories of Edward Kellogg, who in *Labor and Other Capital* proposed that the government issue greenbacks (paper currency) at 1% interest, the NLU adopted the "interconvertibility plan."

This plan called for the abolition of the national banking system, the recognition of the federal government's exclusive authority to fix interest rates, and the reduction of interest on government bonds to 3% and their convertibility into greenbacks. In the eyes of William Sylvis and Andrew Cameron, the editor of the Chicago-based labor newspaper the *Workingmen's Advocate* and a founder of the NLU, implementation of this plan would foster the growth of producer co-operatives since they would have access to low-cost credit and enable small business to expand and thereby provide more employment.

Rarely did the NLU directly sponsor a campaign or provide leadership in implementing its program. In the movement for the eight-hour day, spokesmen such as William Sylvis exhorted local unions and state Eight-Hour Leagues to wage campaigns, but without any guidance, let alone co-ordination, from the NLU itself. Nevertheless, the CLU showed a capacity to engage in practical activity. In 1867, it successfully lobbied Congress to repeal the contract labor law, enacted during the Civil War, and matched this success in 1868 when Congress passed legislation introducing an eight-hour day for manual workers employed by the federal government.

The endorsement of currency reform and the eight-hour day led the NLU to place greater emphasis on political action. At the 1870 congress, the NLU, in the face of opposition from most national unions, split into two branches—one "political" and the other "industrial," and established an executive committee of the National Labor Reform Party. In 1872, the NLU's political branch officially changed its name and modified its program to include exclusion of Chinese immigrant laborers and reduction of the tariff.

Preparation for independent political action received a boost from the experience of labor politics in Massachusetts. Here the Knights of St. Crispin spearheaded the formation of the Independent Party in 1869, which gained more than 13,000 votes and elected one state senator and 22 assemblymen under its banner. Although the following year the newly named Labor Reform Party lost most of its seats in the state legislature, a vigorous campaign led by Wendell Phillips, who ran for governor, helped to secure the establishment of a state Bureau of Labor Statistics, one the party's key proposals.

The NLRP's campaign in the 1872 elections was ill fated from the start. Among much disquiet from labor leaders, Judge David Davis from Illinois, with no ties to the labor movement, became the party's presidential candidate. Then within weeks, he withdrew his candidacy after dissidents within the Republican Party launched the Liberal Republican Party and made Horace Greeley its standard-bearer. The NLRP lost all creditability following the last-minute selection of Charles O'Connor, a former Tammany Hall Democrat from New York, to run for president. Consequently, the NLU collapsed, as only seven delegates turned up to its "industrial convention" that year.

Historians' judgment of the NLRP and concomitantly the NLU has been mixed. At one extreme, the NLU and NLRP were deemed as misguided and ineffective, "led by labor leaders without organizations and politicians without parties" (Ware). Less severe was the verdict that the NLU and NLRP were inevitably enfeebled by an inability to reconcile two conflicting "philosophies"—one based on political and social reform and the other predicated on "pure and simple" trade unionism (Rayback). Another assessment stressed the bona fide commitment to equal pay for women workers and its fraternity with African-American trade unionists as well as its promotion of independent labor politics, although it criticized its muddled programmatic orientation (Foner).

Notwithstanding these different interpretations, the NLU and NLRP were significant in the development of the labor movement during the Gilded Age. Their leaders underscored the importance of establishing a national body by which organized labor could articulate objectives and formulate strategies. At a time when wage labor became more embedded and economic inequality more manifest, they recognized that workers would need to organize politically *and* industrially. These lessons drawn from the short-lived existence of the NLU and NLRP would guide the next generation of labor activists.

RONALD MENDEL

References and Further Reading

Foner, Philip. *A History of the Labor Movement in the United States*. Volume I. New York: International Publishers, 1947.

Montgomery, David. *Beyond Equality: Labor and the Radical Republicans*. New York: Knopf, 1967.

Rayback, Joseph. *A History of American Labor*. New York: Free Press, 1966.

Ware, Norman. *The Labor Movement in the United States, 1860–1895: A Study in Democracy*. New York: D. Appleton and Company, 1929.

NATIONAL LABOR RELATIONS ACT

See **Dunlop Commission;** *National Labor Relations Board v. Jones-Laughlin Steel Corporation* **(1937)**

NATIONAL LABOR RELATIONS BOARD

On July 5, 1935, President Franklin Delano Roosevelt signed the National Labor Relations Act (NLRA), or Wagner Act, which created the National Labor Relations Board (NLRB), an independent federal agency charged with protecting workers' rights to organize and bargain collectively with their employers through representatives of their own choosing, or to refrain from such activities. The Wagner Act replaced the National Labor Board (NLB) (August 1933 to June 1934) and the original National Labor Relations Board (June 1934 to July 1935), which consisted of representatives from organized labor, industry, and the federal government and sought to mediate labor disputes to voluntary resolutions. Senator Robert Wagner of New York worked closely with the ineffective NLB and "old" NLRB, and in the 1935, legislation crafted a new NLRB to enforce rights rather than mediate disputes. The new NLRB's responsibilities were to hold union elections and to prevent or remedy unfair labor practices (ULPs). Legal challenges to the NLRB began immediately after its creation and consumed most of the board's energy until the Supreme Court affirmed its constitutionality in 1937. In the decades after that ruling, legal struggles persisted, the NLRB grew increasingly unpopular, and Congress made the board friendlier to business interests through amendments to the NLRA in the 1947 Taft-Hartley Act and the 1959 Landrum-Griffin Act.

The NLRB consists of a central board in Washington, DC, and field offices (51 as of 2006) that handle approximately 90% of the election petitions and ULP complaints. The president appoints, with the consent of the Senate, five board members for five-year terms and one general counsel for a four-year term. The NLRB's field offices investigate and seek voluntary resolutions to ULP complaints. If the parties are unwilling to settle at that point, the case goes before an NLRB administrative law judge, who decides whether the case will go to the five-member board. The parties may appeal the board's decision to the U.S. Court of Appeals, and then to the Supreme Court. In order to separate the board's prosecutorial and judicial functions, Taft-Hartley made the general counsel independent from the five-member board. Subsequently, the general counsel investigated and prosecuted ULP complaints and oversaw the field offices, while the five-member board acted as an appellate court for cases decided by administrative law judges. In order to hold an election for union representation, or for decertification of an existing union, a union, individual, or employer must file a petition with the NLRB. The petition must have the support of at least 30% of the employees. If all criteria are met, the government-sponsored election is held within 50 days of filing the petition. The NLRB's jurisdiction extends to employers involved in interstate commerce, with the exception of airlines, railroads, agriculture, and public employees.

The board's structure insulates the vast majority of NLRB cases from direct influences in Washington, DC, while subjecting the highest levels of the board to partisan politics. The president holds the power of appointment and Congress influences the NLRB through Senate confirmation of appointees, appropriations, and oversight and investigation. Between 1935 and 1937, partisan disputes focused on constitutional challenges to the NLRB. Once the Supreme Court sanctioned the board in 1937, the NLRB's zealous legal staffers tackled a flood of new election petitions and ULP complaints. This period of aggressive enforcement ended in late 1939, when the House of Representatives' "Smith Committee," named for the committee chair, Harold Smith (R-VA), held special hearings on the NLRB. The Smith Committee focused on alleged communist influence on the board and the board's ostensible bias toward bargaining units defined by industry rather than craft, a charge that grew out of the rivalry between the American Federation of Labor (AFL) and the Congress of Industrial Organizations (CIO). The hearings turned popular opinion against the NLRB and began a movement for amendments to the Wagner Act that ultimately led to Taft-Hartley and Landrum-Griffin. From the early 1960s to the late 1970s, the board enjoyed relatively high esteem for its role in maintaining "industrial peace," but beginning in the early 1980s, persistent conservative attacks cut the board's budget and made Senate confirmation proceedings highly contentious. Partisan wrangling has often left the board without its full complement of five members. Labor relations policy changed most dramatically when parties brought NLRB cases to the Supreme Court or when Congress amended the NLRB's powers.

Through the NLRB, the federal government shaped four main areas of employer-employee relations. First, the Court has reshaped employers' traditional rights to hire and fire workers. In *NLRB v. Mackay Radio* (1938), for example, the Court decided that strikers maintained their status as employees, but employers were allowed to hire permanent replacements during a strike. In addition, in *Phelps Dodge v. NLRB* (1941), the Court found that workers could not be dismissed for union affiliation and that they had the right to be re-instated and to collect back pay. Second, in *Textile Workers v. Darlington Co.* (1965), the Court significantly limited an employer's right to close one operation of a multipart business if the closure meant to discourage unionization. Third, from 1935 to 1947, the NLRB considered virtually any employer's speech against labor unions or unionization campaigns to constitute a ULP. In reaction against this "totality of conduct doctrine," Taft-Hartley included a free speech amendment, Section 8 (c), which states that no written or oral statement regarding a union or unionization campaign "shall constitute or be evidence of an unfair labor practice . . . if such expression contains no threat of reprisal or force or promise of benefit." Finally, Congress has passed multiple measures limiting union activities. Picketing per se was never a central issue for the NLRB because the 1932 Norris-LaGuardia Act legalized peaceful picketing in labor disputes. However, Taft-Hartley charged the NLRB with enforcing its prohibitions against the closed shop, wildcat strikes, jurisdictional strikes (picketing against a rival union), and secondary boycotts (boycotting a company doing business with a struck company). Landrum-Griffin re-inforced these proscriptions on union practices and extended the NLRB's control over union financial practices.

Over time, employers and unions grew more sophisticated in their approach to the NRLB process. Employers have successfully used the NLRB to delay organizing campaigns until worker fatigue set in and the campaign folded. Unions increasingly avoided the long NLRB election process, turning instead to "card check" agreements with employers, meaning that an employer recognizes and bargains with a union when a majority of employees have signed union cards. Unions have also taken advantage of the Supreme Court's decision in *NLRB v. Town & Country Electric* (1995), which upheld the constitutionality of "salting." Especially popular in the building trades, "salts" are union workers who covertly or overtly apply for jobs at nonunion worksites in order to pressure nonunion employees to accept union workers or to drive nonunion contractors out of business.

Even as unions avoided the NLRB and the unionization of the private workforce has declined, the NLRB has maintained its relevance by ruling that workers employed by temporary agencies can join unions and that nonunion employees have a right to representation during disciplinary hearings.

JEFFREY HELGESON

References and Further Reading

Bennett, James T. "The National Labor Relations Board: Some Preliminary Perspectives." *Journal of Labor Research* 22, no. 4 (Fall 2001): 695–698.

Bodah, Matthew M. "Congress and the National Labor Relations Board: A Review of the Recent Past." *Journal of Labor Research* 22, no. 4 (Fall 2001): 699–722.

Brooks, Robert R. R. *Unions of Their Own Choosing: An Account of the National Labor Relations Board and Its Work.* New Haven, CT: Yale University Press, 1939.

Gross, James A. *Broken Promise: The Subversion of U.S. Labor Relations Policy, 1947–1994.* Philadelphia: Temple University Press, 1995.

———. *The Making of the National Labor Relations Board.* Albany: State University of New York Press, 1974.

———. *The Reshaping of the National Labor Relations Board.* Albany: State University of New York Press, 1981.

Leroy, Michael H. "The Formation and Administration of Labor Policy by the NLRB: Evidence from Economic and ULP Strike Rulings." *Journal of Labor Research* 22, no. 4 (Fall 2001): 723–760.

Leslie, Douglas L. *Labor Law in a Nutshell.* St. Paul, MN: West Publishing Co., 1979.

Miller, Edward B. "NLRB Decisions on Economic Strikes and Unfair Labor Practice Strikes: A Response to LeRoy." *Journal of Labor Research* 22, no. 4 (Fall 2001): 739.

O'Connell, John F. "The NLRB at the Grassroots." *Journal of Labor Research* 22, no. 4 (Fall 2001): 761–776.

Williamson, Charles M. "Labor Policy and the Immediate Future of the National Labor Relations Board: Comment on LeRoy." *Journal of Labor Research* 22, no. 4 (Fall 2001): 777–780.

Witney, Fred. *Wartime Experiences of the National Labor Relations Board, 1941–1945.* Urbana: University of Illinois Press, 1949.

Cases and Statutes Cited

Fansteel Metallurgical Corp. and Amalgamated Association of Iron, Steel and Tin Workers of North America, Local 66, 5 NLRB 930, 949 (1938) enf. denied 98 F2d 375 (C A 7 1938), enf. as mod. 306 U.S. 240 (1939)

NLRB v. Jones & Laughlin Steel Corp., 301 U.S. 1 (1937)

NLRB v. Mackay Radio & Telegraph, 304 U.S. 333 (1938)

NLRB v. Town & Country Elec., Inc., 516 U.S. 85 (1995)

Phelps Dodge Corp. v. NLRB, 313 U.S. 177 (1941)

Textile Workers v. Darlington Co., 380 U.S. 263 (1965)

Anti-Injunction Bill/Norris-LaGuardia Act (29 U.S.C.A. § 101 et seq., 1932)

Labor Management Relations Act (Taft-Hartley Labor Act), (29 U.S.C.A. § 151 et seq., 1947)

Labor-Management Reporting and Disclosure Act/Landrum-Griffin Act, (29 U.S.C.A. § 401 et seq., 1959)

National Labor Relations Act/Wagner Act (29 U.S.C.A. § 151 et seq., 1935)

See also **Landrum-Griffin Act (1959); Law and Labor; Norris-LaGuardia Federal Anti Injunction Act; Taft-Hartley Act**

NATIONAL LABOR RELATIONS BOARD v. FANSTEEL METALLURGICAL CORP.
See **Fansteel v. United States**

NATIONAL LABOR RELATIONS BOARD v. JONES-LAUGHLIN STEEL CORPORATION (1937)

In April 1937, the U.S. Supreme Court found in the *Jones-Laughlin* decision that the Wagner Act (or the National Labor Relations Act) of 1935 was constitutional. At issue was the reach of the commerce clause of the United States Constitution. The first attempt of the federal government to guarantee the right of workers to engage in collective bargaining, Section 7a of the National Industrial Recovery Act (NIRA) of 1933, had been invalidated by the Supreme Court in 1935. In *Schechter Poultry Corporation v. United States* (or the "sick chicken" case), the Supreme Court invalidated the NIRA, finding that Congress had overstepped its powers granted to it by the commerce clause. *Jones-Laughlin* established that the federal government could legitimately act to protect the rights of workers to unionize through the National Labor Relations Board (NLRB).

Opponents of the Wagner Act argued that the United States government and the National Labor

Relations Board had no power to regulate collective bargaining in industries that were not directly engaged in interstate commerce. Specifically, they argued that manufacturing was an industry of production, and not of commerce, so that the law should not apply to manufacturing industries. Further, they argued that the Wagner Act violated the due process clause of the Fifth Amendment to the U.S. Constitution by giving a regulatory agency arbitrary power over a private corporation. Finally, opponents of the Wagner Act complained that the bill delineated unfair bargaining practices for employers, and not for unions. Proponents of the Act argued that the government was acting within its legitimate constitutional authority to regulate and promote interstate commerce by ensuring stable labor relations. Proponents also argued that because corporations could redress their grievances to a court, the Wagner Act did not violate the due process rights of businesses. In a 5–4 decision, the court held that the Wagner Act was constitutional and could be broadly applied to private workplaces, manufacturing included, around the country. The Court also found that the Act did not violate the due process clause of the Fifth Amendment. The Court left the issue of unfair bargaining practices open, seeing it as a question of policy, not constitutionality. The Taft-Hartley Act of 1947 delineated unfair bargaining practices for unions as well.

In the short time between the passage of the Wagner Act and the *Jones-Laughlin* decision, many employers had chosen to defy the NLRB. The decision freed the NLRB from dealing with voluminous legal challenges to its authority and allowed the Board to effectively oversee union certification and collective bargaining disputes. The decision also impacted trade unions. In the wake of *Jones-Laughlin*, legal disputes over union recognition declined. Unions increasingly turned their attention to issues of working conditions, wages, and hours.

STEVEN DIKE-WILHELM

References and Further Reading

Koretz, Robert, ed. *Statutory History of the United States: Labor Organization*. New York: Chelsea House, 1970.
Taylor, Benjamin J., and Fred Witney. *U.S. Labor Relations Law: Historical Development*. Englewood Cliffs, NJ: Prentice Hall, 1992.

Cases and Statutes Cited

National Labor Relations Board v. Jones & Laughlin Steel Corporation, 301 U.S. 1 (1937)

NATIONAL LABOR UNION

The Civil War, with its labor shortages, price inflation, and productivity increases, revived a trade union movement that had languished since the industrial depression of the 1850s. At the very peak of the war, new labor organizations formed at all levels, from new locals, citywide trades assemblies, and abortive national organizations such as the International Industrial Assembly of North America to international bodies such as the International Workingmen's Association, founded in 1864. However, it was not until after the war that a serious attempt at national organization, bringing representatives of the leading trade unions together, was successful.

The need for nationwide labor organization was the outcome of the increasing interconnectedness of markets both for goods and labor. Many trade union leaders realized that they could no longer rely on strong local organizations to protect their working conditions, and their dreams of winning greater victories, such as the eight-hour day, rested on the marshaling of labor's forces throughout the country. As early as 1860, the National Union of Machinists and Blacksmiths proposed establishing a national federation of all trades, though no action was taken as the war crisis engulfed the country. The Molders union revived the idea in early 1864, and the Bricklayers along with the Coachmakers endorsed it in 1866.

Originally, the concrete plan for a conference to organize a national union federation centered on the trades unions that had first proposed it. But after the call for both local and national trades unions to convene in Baltimore was published, objections by labor associations that were not organized on a trade basis, led by the New York City Workingmen's Union, pushed the Baltimore conference organizers to broaden their invitation to include all labor organizations, including those, such as the Eight-Hour Leagues, that did not specifically represent groups of workers.

In August 1866, 77 delegates met in Baltimore and founded the National Labor Union (NLU). It was, like the Industrial Congresses of the 1850s and the National Trades Unions of the 1830s, a cross-class organization with good representation of both social theorists and reformers and trade unionists, but unlike the older attempts at national union, it actually developed the beginnings of a permanent institutional structure of local corresponding secretaries, annual meetings, and a standing executive committee. Largely the doing of the Molders union president, William Sylvis, the NLU convened without him when he fell ill just days before the opening session.

Delegates readily agreed upon their goals of winning the eight-hour day, abolishing the wage system through producer cooperatives and land reform, and increasing the power of trade unions, but they divided on the means of achieving their aims. Some conceived of the NLU as becoming a centralized union, others as a loose federation, and still others as a political party. In the end, those who believed the best way to achieve the eight-hour day was through legislative action carried the day, and the NLU resolved to take the form of a political reform organization rather than a strictly trade union federation.

Steady promotion of the NLU by the labor publisher Jonathon Fincher and the cajoling of William Sylvis succeeded in attracting delegates from a majority of existing national trade unions to a second convention of the NLU held in Chicago in 1867. This time, the able and popular Sylvis chaired the proceedings, but the convention was marked by the increasing strength of a vocal group of greenbackers who were determined to steer the NLU into the swamp of partisan politics. A few spokespersons, such as the German socialists, continued to champion the idea of making the NLU into a centralized national union, but they were thwarted by trade union leaders jealous of their own power and independence.

The majority, led by the greenback pamphleteer Alexander Campbell, and including two of the most influential delegates, the founder William Sylvis and the labor editor Andrew Cameron, supported currency reform because they were attracted to its promise of empowering workers, unifying workers and farmers (the conference began in this year to refer more to "industrial classes" than "workingmen"), and creating the basis for market prosperity for all Americans, all without substantially re-ordering or centralizing the American state. Following the teachings of Edward Kellogg first published two decades before, these delegates held that the "money power" used the gold standard and high interest rates to rob workers of the fruits of their labor. The remedy was to adopt paper or "greenback" currency and for the government to keep interest rates low through a complicated "interconvertible bond" scheme that would also finance the independent enterprises, farms, and cooperative ventures of "producers" throughout the nation.

Given the racially charged context of the times in which it operated, it was inevitable that the NLU would be forced to address the question of inclusion or exclusion of racial minorities in the ranks of organized labor. Like most trade unionists of his day, the NLU committee charged with drafting a statement of principles stressed the importance of facing the fact that slavery had ended, "unpalatable as the truth may be to many, it is needless to disguise the fact that they [African-Americans] are destined to occupy a different position in the future, to what they have in the past," and that interracial cooperation was a policy about which they had little choice. The question, the committee concluded, was "shall we make them our friends, or shall capital be allowed to turn them as an engine against us?" Or as William Sylvis put it at the 1867 convention, "The negro will take possession of the shops, if we do not take possession of the negro."

However, when the principle of interracial organizing and cooperation was put to the next annual conference in 1867, the question exposed a deep split between the labor reformers, who largely came out of an abolitionist tradition, and the trade union leadership, whose organizations practiced racial exclusion. In the end, the question was deemed too problematic and was deferred as too difficult to resolve by two consecutive conferences. It was, finally, the standing executive committee that forced the NLU to confront the issue by inviting African-American delegates to its 1869 conference. Nine attended, including the eloquent Isaac Myers of the Colored Caulkers' Trade Union Society, who was made chair of the committee on cooperation. Under pressure from the labor reformers, the NLU then resolved that it knew "neither color nor sex, on the question of the rights of labor" and urged "colored fellow members to form organizations in all legitimate ways." Thus, the NLU endorsed the principle of racial equality without challenging the exclusionary practices of trade unions but rather urged that black workers be aided in forming their own unions that would be "invited to cooperate with us in the general labor undertaking."

Race was an issue underlying many of the NLU's concerns and one that further divided trade unionists and broad-minded labor reformers. In an early compromise that would come to characterize the general attitude of the American trade union movement, the convention denounced the American Emigrant Aid Society and the federal law of 1864 that established an enforcement mechanism for immigrant labor contracts, but studiously avoided condemning immigration itself. Such a posture of condemning "importation" but welcoming immigration conformed to prevalent economic thinking about wages and distanced the labor movement from the vicious nativism of an earlier day. A year later, after Congress repealed the 1864 contract labor law, the NLU turned its attention to what it perceived as a new and greater threat looming over the American worker—the importation of Chinese "coolies." This carefully drawn distinction between "importation" and immigration, meant to paper over the differences between labor reformers and union regulars, broke down by 1870, when the NLU declared that "the presence in our country of

Chinese laborers" was an "evil" and demanded its prevention by legislation.

The tensions between trade union interests and labor reformers took a more public form at the next NLU convention held in New York in 1868 with the appearance of Elizabeth Cady Stanton, who claimed admittance on the basis of her membership in the Woman Suffrage Association. Trade union delegates threatened to walk out until Sylvis, a strong advocate of women's rights, worked out a compromise whereby Stanton took her seat, with the body voting to neither endorse nor condemn women's suffrage. However, the following year, a similar attempt on the part of Susan B. Anthony for credentials was denied after the vigorous protest of New York's Mike Walsh, who accused her of representing a scab union. However, none of this altered the NLU's statement of principles, which included a demand for equal pay for equal work for women, a measure trade unionists endorsed both as a matter of justice and out of the hope that this would retard the expansion of female labor.

In spite of its impoverished finances and still shakily organized state, the NLU claimed some significant successes in 1868 and 1869. In June, after lobbying by NLU representatives, Congress voted to establish the eight-hour day for federal employees. One year after the NLU demanded the establishment of a federal Department of Labor, Massachusetts became the first state to establish a Labor Bureau. And in 1869, Andrew C. Cameron, the editor of the *Workingmen's Advocate*, was sent as the official delegate of the NLU to the International Workingmen's Association conference at Basle, Switzerland—the first time an American labor federation attempted to affiliate with an international body.

The NLU continued even after the death of its founder, William Sylvis, in 1869 under a new president, Richard Trevellick, to whom credit was given for winning passage of the federal eight-hour law and who was most closely allied with the labor reform rather than the trade union wings of the NLU. However, by this time, the decline of the organization was evident, as only half as many delegates attended the 1870 convention in Cincinnati as had met in Philadelphia the year before. Interest in the NLU flagged most among the leaders of national trade unions, who looked skeptically upon the political drift of the organization and desired to create a federation of trade unions separate from the labor reform elements that played such a prominent part in the NLU. As a means of addressing these concerns while at the same time moving forward with its political strategy, the NLU resolved to split itself into two organizations, one a political party to nominate candidates for office

and the other a conference to deal strictly with "industrial" issues.

As promising as this strategy sounded in theory, its realization was thwarted by the deep political intrigues it invited. The political wing of the NLU met in convention in Columbus, Ohio, in February 1872 (ironically where the strictly industrial American Federation of Labor would be founded in 1886), calling itself the National Labor and Reform Party, and nominated Judge David Davis, Abraham Lincoln's former campaign manager and Supreme Court justice, for president. Judge Davis thanked the party for the honor but did not clearly indicate if he accepted or declined until months later after the Democratic and Republican conventions, when it was too late for the labor reformers to select someone else, thus derailing the labor party movement before it even began. The partisan taint of this affair further tarred the reputation of the NLU as an impractical debating society, and the "industrial" congress of the NLU that met in Cleveland that year attracted only seven delegates, and all recognized the need to make a fresh start under a new name and organizational scheme. The following year, the same national union leaders who had once been a part of the NLU began meeting under the new banner of the Industrial Congress.

TIMOTHY MESSER-KRUSE

References and Further Reading

Bloch, Herman, and Carol Banks. "The National Labor Union and Black Workers." *Journal of Ethnic Studies* 1, no. 1 (1973): 13–21.

Grossman, Jonathan. *William Sylvis, Pioneer of American Labor: A Study of the Labor Movement during the Era of the Civil War*. New York: Columbia University Press, 1945.

Montgomery, David. *Beyond Equality: Labor and the Radical Republicans, 1862–1872*. 1967. Reprint, Urbana: University of Illinois Press, 1981.

See also **Civil War and Reconstruction**

NATIONAL MINERS UNION

The National Miners Union (NMU) had its origins in domestic and international developments of the 1920s, including a disastrous 1927 coal strike and the expulsion of virtually all radicals from the United Mine Workers of America (UMWA). The desire of radical miners to form a union outside the UMWA co-incided with the Comintern's declaration of the Third Period in the summer of 1928, which called for the organization of independent communist unions within the United States. Organized in Pittsburgh in early September 1928 from the remnants of

Striking miners drawing rations, West Virginia. Library of Congress, Prints & Photographs Division, Theodor Horydczak Collection [LC-H823-1308-004-x].

the UMWA's "Save the Union Movement," the NMU affiliated itself with William Z. Foster's Trade Union Educational League (TUEL), which was re-organized into the Trade Union Unity League (TUUL) in late summer 1929. The program of the NMU advocated the six-hour day and five-day week (designed to distribute work among more miners), organization of the unorganized, the creation of a national labor party, nationalization of the mines, support of the Soviet Union, the release of all workers arrested for strike-related activities, the organization of women and children, and racial and gender equality.

National and regional NMU leaders were members of the Communist Party (CP). John Watt, William Boyce (an African-American), Patrick Toohey, Freeman Thompson, Thomas Meyerscough, and Frank Borich occupied the top national offices within the NMU; a number of important CP officials, including William Z. Foster, Jack Johnstone, and William Dunne, were closely involved in NMU actions. Although the union was officially charged with the building of the Party, rank-and-file miners viewed the CP as separate from the NMU and were far more likely to join the NMU than the CP, despite the fact that the NMU required its members to attend Party meetings.

Between 1929 and 1933, the NMU led strikes in Illinois, Pennsylvania, Ohio, West Virginia, Kentucky, Utah, and New Mexico. In the fall of 1929, the NMU conducted a strike in the central and southern coalfields of Illinois. Although approximately 10,000 miners responded to the union's strike call, the UMWA issued a barrage of red-baiting propaganda, while the state police cordoned the area and arrested the strike's leaders, ending the strike after a week and establishing a pattern of opposition from the UMWA and state officials that plagued NMU organizing efforts.

In May 1931, the NMU launched a strike against wage reductions that spread rapidly through western Pennsylvania, eastern Ohio, and West Virginia, eventually involving 40,000 miners. Lasting 12 weeks, the ill-fated strike was marked by red baiting from the UMWA, police violence, a shortage of union organizers, and internal conflict over strike goals. In January 1932, the NMU entered the strike-ridden Harlan County, Kentucky, taking up a strike abandoned by the UMWA. The NMU was quickly met with extraordinary violence from armed vigilantes, who killed several miners and a young communist organizer. As relief workers were blocked from entering the county and miners were discharged and blacklisted, the strike collapsed. Although the strike failed to win union recognition, it brought national attention to the plight of the region's coal miners and produced a wealth of music, including Florence Reece's frequently adapted labor anthem, "Which Side Are You On?"

Following the defeats in Illinois, Pennsylvania, Ohio, West Virginia, and Kentucky, the NMU turned west, first waging an unsuccessful strike in Carbon

County, Utah, and finally turning to Gallup, New Mexico, in August 1933. In New Mexico, the governor declared martial law. The National Guard arrested NMU leaders and held them in a military stockade. Despite UMWA propaganda that divided white and Spanish-speaking miners, the NMU was able to thwart company attempts to force all miners into the UMWA by arguing that NRA Section 7a provided workers with the right to choose their union. Although technically a success, as the strike ended, the NMU was unable to prevent massive blacklisting and eviction of Spanish-speaking strike leaders. The NMU abandoned organizing after the Gallup strike and was officially decertified by the CP in early 1935, as the Comintern moved away from dual unionism toward a united front against fascism.

During its brief existence, the NMU was thwarted by a number of persistent problems. First, there were struggles over goals and tactics. The disparity in numbers recruited for the NMU as opposed to those joining the CP makes it clear that miners were vastly more interested in solving wage and workplace grievances than in building a revolutionary movement. The NMU also suffered from a persistent shortage of trained organizers and a lack of funding for relief and legal expenses, especially after 1931. Although most of the miners recruited by the NMU had been previously abandoned by the UMWA, the strikes led by the NMU raised fears of communist infiltration into the coalfields and had the ironic result of breathing new life into the UMWA. As Irving Bernstein wrote in *The Lean Years*, companies preferred UMW chickenpox to NMU smallpox.

Despite its organizing failures, the NMU did spotlight the plight of the nation's coal miners. In both Pennsylvania (1931) and Kentucky (1932), William Z. Foster called on Theodore Dreiser to generate positive publicity outside the coal region and provide relief through the National Committee for the Defense of Political Prisoners. The "Dreiser Committee," which included Malcolm Cowley, Edmund Wilson, John Dos Passos, Anna Rochester, and other left-wing writers, investigated conditions and held open hearings in both regions. Their interviews with miners in Kentucky were published as *Harlan Miners Speak*. The publicity generated relief donations and prompted a congressional investigation but did little to alter conditions or influence the outcome of the strikes.

The NMU also advanced the cause of racial and gender equality within the labor movement. Unlike the UMWA, the NMU insisted on equality for African-Americans, Spanish-speaking Americans, and resident aliens. The NMU also stressed the importance of women, employing them as organizers and looking to local women for strike leadership. NMU strikes produced a number of remarkable women, including Florence Reece, Aunt Molly Jackson and her half-sister Sarah Ogan Gunning from West Virginia, and Dominica Hernandez from New Mexico.

ELIZABETH RICKETTS

References and Further Reading

Barrett, James R. *William Z. Foster and the Tragedy of American Radicalism*. Urbana: University of Illinois Press, 1999.
Dreiser, Theodore, ed. *Harlan Miners Speak: Report on Terrorism in the Eastern Kentucky Coalfields*. New York: Harcourt, Brace and Company, 1932.
Gaventa, John. *Power and Powerlessness: Quiescence and Rebellion in an Appalachian Valley*. Chicago: University of Chicago Press, 1980.
Hevener, John W. *Which Side Are You On? The Harlan County Coal Miners, 1931–39*. Urbana: University of Illinois Press, 1978.
Powell, Kent Allan. *The Next Time We Strike: Labor in Utah's Coal Fields, 1900–1933*. Logan: Utah State University Press, 1985.
Vargas, Zaragosa. *Labor Rights Are Civil Rights: Mexican American Workers in Twentieth-Century America*. Princeton, NJ: Princeton University Press, 2005.

See also **Foster, William Z.; Lewis, John L.; Trade Union Unity League; United Mine Workers of America**

NATIONAL NEGRO CONGRESS

In February 1936, over 750 delegates from 28 states registered their names at the Eighth Regiment Armory in South Chicago for the first conclave of the National Negro Congress (NNC). During the conference sessions, black intellectuals, labor leaders, artists, and clerics debated issues relating to trade unions, youth, women, churches, businesses, fascism, and interracial relations. The NNC hoped this cross-section of African-Americans would ignite a nationwide movement of New Deal activism that would expand democracy to include African-American workers. Over the next five years, the NNC became one of the most prominent black organizations to fight for racial equality. Its members organized thousands into unions, opened new sectors of employment to black workers, demonstrated against extralegal violence, and resurrected a proud African-American culture based upon the history of the Reconstruction Era.

A younger group of black leaders laid the groundwork for the NNC during the previous decade. In the early Depression years, economic hardship leveled race-based institutions in northern city neighborhoods, leaving a void in professional leadership. Black nationalists (splinter groups from Marcus Garvey's 1920s movement), Communists, Socialists, and others filled some of this space by orating on street corners, forming unemployment councils, and marching against the immediate crises of hunger and homelessness. Before the first NNC conference, John P. Davis, a Bates College and Harvard-trained intellectual, formed the Joint Committee on National Recovery (JCNR) to testify in Washington on behalf of black labor at the National Recovery Act wage hearings. Davis pointed out that New Deal legislation omitted the largest sections of black labor and allowed for race-based differences in wages, giving African-Americans a "raw deal" rather than a New Deal. At a spring 1935 Howard University conference of black leaders, Davis, the socialist and union leader A. Philip Randolph, the liberal sociologist Ralph Bunche, and the Communist leader James W. Ford charted new ways to address racial discrimination. This meeting corresponded with the Communist Party's shift away from a revolutionary strategy to one of a Popular Front alliance with liberals to fight fascism. In addition, a few maverick unions within the American Federation of Labor (AFL) had stormed out of the Federation's 1935 annual meeting when the Federation voted against organizing industrial workers. These larger circumstances weighed heavily on the minds of the black leaders gathered at Howard; they concurred that black America needed to focus more on its working class through a united coalition that they bequeathed the National Negro Congress.

In its nascence, the NNC formed local councils in northern and western cities and fostered a vital partnership with the Committee for Industrial Organization (CIO). John P. Davis convinced national CIO leaders to hire several NNC organizers, who worked to persuade black workers to join these new unions. In the Great Lakes region, NNC leaders helped organize thousands of black steel workers, while NNC mass meetings and publicity on the West Coast brought co-operation between white and black workers during the 1936 maritime strike. In the South, black tobacco workers organized in advance of a CIO campaign. Over five hundred delegates traveled to Richmond in February 1937 to inaugurate the Southern Negro Youth Conference (SNYC), an offshoot of the NNC's youth council. Three months later, black tobacco stemmers, soon to be joined by the SNYC organizers James Jackson and Chris Alston, went on strike there. Between 1937 and 1940, young SNYC activists in the South and NNC organizers in the North formed alliances with African-American industrial workers, organized them into unions, waged several successful strikes, and reoriented many black middle-class community leaders to endorse these actions as respectable means of protest. Moreover, the NNC surmised that the organization of millions of black industrial workers would leave the conservative American Federation of Labor no choice but to reverse its discriminatory practices. The NNC's local councils threw their support behind the Randolph Resolution, named after its president, to provide equal access in all AFL locals or risk expulsion. While the AFL nonetheless evaded the resolution, Randolph's own union, the Brotherhood of Sleeping Car Porters, secured a charter from the AFL and company recognition by 1937.

Meanwhile, the NNC combined this momentum in unions with local antiracist actions. The council in Washington, DC, for example, fought against police brutality, while the NNC's national leaders agitated for federal antilynching legislation. In Detroit, the local council rallied against white supremacists to minimize racial tensions between the city's automobile workers. Other actions taken by the Congress included campaigning for jobs on public utilities, creating tenant councils to improve housing conditions and eliminate restrictive covenants, organizing domestic workers, and supporting international antifascist campaigns in Ethiopia and Spain. Seeking to elect sympathetic government representatives, NNC leaders allied with Labor's Non-Partisan League in 1938 to promote progressive candidates. While the NNC aided certain local candidates to win elections, they encountered a tougher road within the Democratic Party. White supremacist representatives blocked antiracist legislation, revealing the Janus-faced nature of the Democratic Party's "New Deal."

During the late 1930s, the NNC proved very effective in allying liberal and left organizations (both in black communities and interracial Popular Front networks) in pursuit of progressive goals, but by 1940, international political developments split this unity. The NNC increasingly cast its lot with two larger forces: the CIO and the Communist Party. The CIO (with NNC assistance) ushered hundreds of thousands of African-Americans into unions for the first time in American history. As members of these unions, NNC activists hope to push them to endorse antidiscrimination within their own ranks, with their employers, and in local and national political matters. The Communist Party (CP) also became an important source of militancy for the NNC. Some key Negro Congress members had ties to the CP, but as the NAACP and other liberal groups affirmed, the CP did not control the NNC. During this first Popular Front period (1936–1939), mid-level Communists in the NNC ranks had a remarkable degree of freedom to act without national CP leaders interfering, and dedication to the black freedom struggle made them vital members of local NNC councils. In the summer of 1939, however, after Josef Stalin signed a nonaggression pact with Adolph Hitler, tensions that had been manageable exploded into controversy. Top Communists now made demands upon local NNC leaders to switch from antifascism to an antiwar stance (calling it imperialism) in foreign policy. This switch meant that Communists in the NNC suddenly took a defiant stance against President Roosevelt and others who increasingly supported armed intervention against the Nazis. Conservative forces within government and labor circles, especially the congressional committee chaired by Martin Dies of Texas, attempted to use this political turmoil to derail the CIO by exposing Communists and fellow travelers within its ranks. Meanwhile, John L. Lewis, though not a Communist, also opposed intervention in the Second World War because he believed it would sacrifice working-class men at the behest of elites. Thus, the two most effective NNC allies demanded a drastic shift in foreign policy matters that affected domestic ones. The conflict enervated local NNC councils, and by its 1940 convention in Washington, the organization suffered a national split when A. Philip Randolph resigned his post as president.

This break hampered the NNC's membership as a mass-based organization, but it did not destroy it. After leaving the NNC, Randolph and his allies began the March on Washington Movement that resulted in President Roosevelt issuing Executive Order 8802 in June 1941 that established the first federal Fair Employment Practice Committee (FEPC). That same month, the unpalatable alliance between Hitler and Stalin ended abruptly when the Nazi army invaded the Soviet Union. Now, the NNC became the leading critic of antiwar leaders like John L. Lewis, who had already been discredited by supporting the Republican candidate, Wendell Willkie, in the presidential election of 1940 and had resigned his post as leader of the CIO.

During the Second World War, a remarkable group of young women assumed leadership roles at the NNC's new headquarters in New York and SNYC's in Birmingham. With most men in the armed services, Thelma Dale Perkins, a Howard graduate student and Washington Youth Federation and SNYC leader, became acting executive secretary of the NNC. Alongside Max Yergan, the NNC's new president, Dale and other female leaders pressured the FEPC to act against discriminatory employers and secured jobs for blacks in war industries jobs (like the Glen L. Martin aircraft plants) as well as in public utilities employment. While the NNC and SNYC honored the no-strike pledge of the CIO and prioritized winning the war (echoing the Communist Party's policy), they also embraced the "Double V" campaign to eliminate fascism abroad alongside racism at home. SNYC

leaders like Augusta Jackson (Strong) and Esther Cooper (Jackson) put women at the center of an Abolish the Poll Tax week (in May 1941) as well as protests against military inequality and police brutality. Both the NNC and SNYC began to publish monthly magazines (the NNC's *Congress View* and the SNYC's *Cavalcade*) that featured a creative mix of politics, poetry, and black history. Through these publications, their editors evoked a black oppositional culture that highlighted slave rebels of the past, compared the Second World War to the Civil War as a new emancipation, and deemed the postwar reconversion as a second Black Reconstruction for American democracy.

At the end of the war, the NNC and SNYC took on new life. Re-organized local councils thrived in states like New York, Michigan, California, and South Carolina. The NNC, now led by Revels Cayton, a black Communist who had ties to the maritime unions on the West Coast, re-oriented the NNC's leadership by forming a black labor council to recruit thousands of black CIO members and returning veterans as their troops to fight Jim Crow. As its Detroit Council pronounced in 1946, the NNC would seek to remove the barriers of second-class citizenship in America by enforcing Roosevelt's "Four Freedoms." Freedom from fear meant freedom from lynching; freedom from want meant freedom to work and join unions at all skill levels. To enact this vision, NNC members helped organize veterans into the United Negro and Allied Veterans of America, while the SNYC established special veterans councils and became less youth-oriented. In the fall of 1946, they helped bring two thousand delegates to Washington for the American Crusade to End Lynching. This coalition sought to shame leaders in the nation's capital into punishing those responsible for lynching blacks (often returning veterans), enacting a federal law against lynching, and ending the disfranchisement that allowed southern white supremacists to remain in office and filibuster such legislation. Thereafter, the NNC sponsored a tour of Paul Robeson, while the SNYC invited the historian Herbert Aptheker to speak to local councils, black colleges, and labor unions about their agenda for postwar reconversion. Through these tours, they hoped to inspire local councils by promoting militant versions of black history and culture that they compared to their contemporary local struggles.

The postwar NNC and SNYC refused to believe the United States had to return to its laissez-faire approach to white supremacy or that the United States and Soviet Union had to devolve into Cold War hostility. Due to what the NNC considered U.S. government hypocrisy in speaking of freedom without supporting civil rights, it petitioned the United Nations in June 1946 on "behalf of the 13 million oppressed Negro citizens of the United States" to expose the housing, health, education, civil liberties, and violence that violated the U.N.'s charter. By 1947, these African-American activists threw their support and energies behind former Vice President Henry Wallace, whose Progressive Party featured a strong antiracist platform and neutrality with the Soviet Union. Antagonism by both the United States and the Soviet Union, however, offered little room for middle ground. Wallace's integrated tour of the South turned violent and Wallace garnered fewer votes in the 1948 presidential election than NNC and SNYC leaders expected.

More than any other measure, the passage of the 1947 Taft-Hartley Act (over Truman's veto) destroyed any hope the NNC and SNYC had in generating an immediate and militant working-class movement among African-Americans. The Act forced national CIO leaders to choose between government protection and keeping Communist and other left forces within their ranks. Much to the dismay of NNC leaders, the CIO chose the latter option. Beginning in late 1946, the CIO harassed and eventually purged NNC and SNYC allies from their positions, and the attorney general listed both organizations as "subversive." In this new Cold War atmosphere, the NNC merged into the newfound Civil Rights Congress in 1947, and the SNYC regrettably folded two years later.

While their members did not succeed in enacting their postwar motto, "Death Blow to Jim Crow," the NNC and SNYC generated much more than a seedbed for the civil rights movement that followed it in the 1950s and 1960s. The NNC and SNYC cultivated black working-class leadership and focused upon economic issues as the principal means for racial advancement. As the organizations struggled against Jim Crow policies, their alliance with leftist CIO unions and the Communist Party became their most important sources of power but also increasingly compromised their ability to lead a mass movement. The NNC cultivated an oppositional black culture and fostered militant antiracist campaigns that forced American institutions to enact racial and labor reforms for the first time since Reconstruction. During the Cold War, however, these leaders would be relegated to the background of mass movements of southern students and church members. The demise of the NNC and SNYC decoupled collaboration between labor and antiracist activists that had flourished during the late 1930s and 1940s. The legacy of this uncoupling became visible again in the late 1960s, when, after black activism dismantled Jim Crow

barriers in the South, black workers still lacked access to unions and skilled employment.

ERIK S. GELLMAN

References and Further Reading

Bates, Beth Tompkins. "A New Crowd Challenges the Agenda of the Old Guard in the NAACP, 1933–1941." *American Historical Review* 102, no .2 (April 1997).

Gellman, Erik S. "'Carthage Must Be Destroyed': Race, City Politics, and the Campaign to Integrate Chicago Transportation Work, 1929–1943." *Labor: Studies in Working-Class History of the Americas* 2, no. 2 (Summer 2005).

———. "'Death Blow to Jim Crow': The National Negro Congress." Ph.D. Dissertation, Northwestern University, 2006.

Naison, Mark. *Communists in Harlem during the Depression*. Urbana: University of Illinois Press, 1983.

Papers of the National Negro Congress, Schomburg Center for Research in Black Culture, The New York Public Library.

NATIONAL NEGRO LABOR COUNCIL

In 1950, African-American workers, determined to resist discrimination in the workplace and defend their civil rights within the larger community, prepared the way for the formation of the National Negro Labor Council (NNLC). More than 900 delegates met in Chicago in June not only to discuss the status of black workers since World War II but to create an entity to fill a void. At the time, there was no national organization dedicated to securing rights for African-American laborers. The Chicago gathering established a permanent organization, and on October 27, 1951, more than one thousand black workers, representing tens of thousands more, met at the first convention of the NNLC in Cincinnati, Ohio. Although the delegates were largely black, whites were welcomed and present at the founding convention. One third of the delegates were women. The NNLC was primarily concerned with realizing full citizenship rights within the workplace. To that end, the NNLC pledged to fight for full economic opportunity and to end discrimination in the workplace and in the unions. The centerpiece of the NNLC's political platform was its resolve to incorporate a Fair Employment Practice Committee (FEPC) clause in every union contract. Within a year, 23 Negro Labor Councils had been established in major industrial areas. The NNLC, branded by mainstream labor organizations as a tool of the Soviet Union and a creation of the Communist Party, was a victim of the anti-Communist crusades of the early 1950s and dissolved in 1956. Nevertheless, the organization presented a significant challenge to the institutional racism embedded within organized labor and provided a model for labor activists who carried the legacy of the NNLC forward into the 1960s.

The predominately black labor activists who attended the National Labor Conference for Negro Rights in June 1950 in Chicago mobilized around the issue of the backsliding that had occurred since the end of World War II in terms of equal economic opportunity for black workers. Black workers who had made substantial gains within industry during World War II blamed both management and union officials for lack of progress in terms of job opportunities for African-Americans less than a decade after the end of the war. Nevertheless, delegates to the Cincinnati convention pledged to remain within their respective unions even as they built local councils of the NNLC, which functioned as independent black caucuses within established unions. Mainstream labor officials tried to dismiss NNLC councils by charging the organizers with fostering dual unionism. The NNLC challenged dependence on white control both within the workplace as well as the community; indeed, black autonomy was a hallmark of the organization.

The most active local—the Detroit Negro Labor Council—included several key black activists from United Auto Workers (UAW) Local 600, the largest local in the world, with the largest black membership in the union, representing thousands of black workers at the River Rouge Plant of Ford Motor Company. Two leaders from Local 600, who had locked horns with Walter Reuther, the president of the UAW, on several occasions, helped lead and shape the NNLC. William R. Hood, the president of the NNLC, was the recording secretary of Local 600, and Coleman A. Young, a militant UAW organizer and the former director of the Wayne County (Detroit) CIO Council, was elected executive secretary. Hood etched the theme of autonomy on the NNLC convention by drawing from a speech written by Vicki Garvin, the executive secretary of the NNLC in New York City, which sent a message to white America—white trade union leaders and other white leaders—declaring they should no longer assume that they can tell African-Americans what they should do to attain their rights and how they should do it. White leaders were on notice that henceforth, while black Americans would like the cooperation of whites, they no longer felt the need to ask for permission from liberal whites before proceeding in their struggle.

With that as a preface, the UAW officials clashed with the Detroit chapter of the NNLC over several issues. The NNLC structure was criticized for weakening the union and its leaders were portrayed as Communists. Reuther directed autoworkers who had signed a petition brought forth by the Detroit NNLC for a local FEPC ordinance to withdraw their names. Although the petition campaign was not successful, the 40,000 signatures showed there was a reason for union officials to take the NNLC seriously.

The NNLC's agenda included a fight for 100,000 new jobs for African-Americans, a focus on securing the right of black women to equal job opportunities, a commitment to securing an FEPC clause in every union contract, and a pledge to work for civil and human rights of African-Americans. The NNLC lobbied for and secured positions that had been denied black workers. One campaign targeted clerical and administrative positions in the Sears-Roebuck chain, another concentrated on discrimination in hiring and promotion within the hotel industry, and yet another focused on breaking down exclusion of black pilots and stewardesses from the airline industry. The NNLC also had a southern strategy, designed to open up factory production jobs to African-American men and women throughout the South even as it challenged the AFL and the CIO to unionize unorganized southern black and white workers. Initiating its southern campaign in Louisville under the banner, "Let Freedom Crash the Gateway to the South," the NNLC made a few inroads at the General Electric, Westinghouse, and Ford Motor Company plants. The NNLC never was able to replicate its limited success in Louisville in other areas of the South for lack of resources.

The NNLC's struggle was against union politics as much as it was against industrial management. The strength of its largest chapter in Detroit depended on the members from Local 600. Tensions between the militant activists and Reuther, which predated the formation of the NNLC, continued to plague the young organization. Reuther played the red card with abandon. His charges were re-inforced when the House Un-American Activities Committee (HUAC) accused the NNLC of Communist domination. The NNLC won a few battles against the HUAC, but the politics of the McCarthy era won the day by putting the NNLC on the defensive. The organization finally disbanded when faced with the enormous costs connected with its defense in 1956.

BETH THOMPKINS BATES

References and Further Reading

Foner, Philip S. *Organized Labor and the Black Worker, 1619–1981*. New York: International Publishers, 1981.
The Freedom Train. New York: Filmmakers Library, 1995.

Thompson, Mindy. *National Negro Labor Council: A History*. Rutgers University Library, Special Collections and University Archives. New Brunswick, NJ.

See also **League of Revolutionary Black Workers**

NATIONAL RIGHT TO WORK COMMITTEE

Dedicated to weakening federal and state labor law, the National Right to Work Committee (NRWC) co-ordinated legislative campaigns and court challenges to dismantle the legal protections unions won in the New Deal. Initially formed to lobby for state "right-to-work" laws, in the 1980s the Committee expanded its purview to include attacks on public-sector unionism, union political activity, and "card check" agreements. The Committee achieved only moderate success in winning state right-to-work laws but established itself as a brain trust and institutional center for conservative antiunion strategy.

Fred A. Hartley, a retired New Jersey congressman and cosponsor of the Taft-Hartley Act, founded the NRWC in 1955 with financial backing from business interests. Eighteen states already had right-to-work laws, and the NRWC aimed to increase that number by helping co-ordinate state-level campaigns. In its first big push, the NRWC got right-to-work measures on the ballot in six states; labor's superior political power prevailed in five states. Backed by business groups like the U.S. Chamber of Commerce and the National Association of Manufacturers as well as dues paid primarily by small businesses, the NRWC shrugged off the defeats with new referenda in 1961 and 1966. The NRWC ran sophisticated and well-financed campaigns, many featuring disgruntled current or former union members decrying corruption in their own unions. *And Women Must Weep*, a 1963 NRWC film depicting picket-line violence, became a staple of employer antiunion campaigns. Nevertheless, 50 years of concerted effort resulted in victories in only four states. By 2005, 22 states had right-to-work laws. The NRWC's signal victory in this era was defensive: in 1966, the NRWC helped beat back a federal amendment to Taft-Hartley that would have outlawed state right-to-work laws.

This victory exposed the NRWC to attack, however; unions and congressional allies demanded an IRS review of the NRWC's tax-exempt status, arguing that its lobbying activities should invalidate the privilege. In 1968, the NRWC was obliged to create a separate advocacy foundation and restyle itself as a lobbying organization. While the NRWC continued to push for state right-to-work laws (winning in Oklahoma as late as 2001), the NRWC and its foundation devoted increasing resources to related but distinct campaigns. The NRWC took up legislation and court cases focused on the boundary between the rights of individual union members and the autonomy and authority of their unions. In this realm, the NRWC registered real gains.

A signal victory concerned unions' use of dues revenues for political lobbying. Beginning in the 1950s, the NRWC brought lawsuits on behalf of union members who argued that their First Amendment rights to free speech were violated when their unions lobbied for political causes to which they were opposed, using dues collected under closed-shop contracts. These arguments made little headway until the 1970s. In a series of cases culminating in the 1988 ruling *Communications Workers v. Beck*, the Supreme Court prohibited both public- and private-sector unions from using dues for purposes other than union representation and collective bargaining without the permission of each union member. The NRWC vigorously enforced the new rule by soliciting and representing plaintiffs alleging union breaches of the law. The ruling burdened unions with added reporting requirements but did not seriously hamper lobbying, as most members neither knew about nor exercised their right to retrospective dues rebates. Still, the NWRC and its allies used the principle for new state referenda in California, in 1988 and 2005, requiring unions to obtain prospective permission from members before spending dues on lobbying. Labor defeated both, at great expense.

In the late 1990s, the NRWC began challenging neutrality and card check agreements. Unions frustrated with the byzantine bureaucracy of the National Labor Relations Board turned to negotiating private agreements that obliged employers not to fight workers' organizing attempts and to recognize the union based on a majority of signed union cards. (Employers agreed to these terms only under duress, usually from pressure at the bargaining table or from a sustained pressure campaign by the union.) Workers represented by the NRWC argued that these agreements constituted an improper collaboration between employer and union, and only a secret ballot election supervised by the NLRB could ensure workers' freedom to choose or reject unionization. As of late 2005, the Supreme Court had not ruled on these cases.

JENNIFER LUFF

References and Further Reading

Gall, Gilbert J. *The Politics of Right to Work: The Labor Federations as Special Interests, 1943–1979*. Westport, CT: Greenwood Press, 1988.

See also **Taft-Hartley Act**

NATIONAL UNION OF MARINE COOKS AND STEWARDS

An excellent historical example of the melding of workers into a functional union is the National Union of Marine Cooks and Stewards (NUMCS). At first glance, it seems logical that cooks and stewards would be in the same union. After all, cooks make the meals and stewards serve them. Since the word "marine" is in the title, this implies the workers are on ships. But the formation of this particular union was both long and arduous. It is also a symbol of how far unionization has come, and changed, since the 1930s.

Historically, some of the strongest American unions have been located on the waterfront. This is partially because the area where the work is to be performed is so confined. Longshoremen, teamsters, and stevedores work on the waterfront, a strip of land dockside where everyone knows which ships are coming in, how much cargo they are carrying, what outbound containers have to be loaded, and when the ship is leaving.

Because of the tight fabric of union cooperation on the waterfront, management forces have found it very difficult to break the hold of the unions on the docks. One of the largest strikes that affected the waterfront came in 1934, when the Teamsters precipitated a nationwide strike that drew more than 100,000 workers off their jobs nationwide. It was in this melee that the National Union of Marine Cooks and Stewards—originally the Marine Cooks' and Stewards' Association of the Pacific—was formed.

What made the NUMCS different was that its members were primarily black. Prior to 1934, blacks were considered second-class citizens, particularly on the docks. This was partially because in the early days of unionization there were so few of them that could work on the docks. The NUMCS had a number of other distinctions that set it apart from other unions. Because the socialist movement had made inroads into the black community, many assumed that the union was "red" as well as black. Additionally, since the NUMCS readily admitted gays, it was referred to as the "Red, Black, and Gay" union.

The General Strike of 1934 was a turning point in American union labor race relations. The West Coast ILA (International Longshoremen's Association) president was Harry Bridges, an Australian-born activist. Bridges understood that the ILA needed black workers for both solidarity and membership. So he opened the doors of the ILA on the West Coast to black members. It was a risky move, as many union members did not trust the blacks because they had not participated in previous strikes—and many blacks did not trust that their union brothers and sisters not to be racist.

What tipped the balance was the ILA demand of what is now known as the "hiring hall" system. Before 1934, almost all union labor on the waterfront was done on the basis of who the employer wanted to hire. The unions were looked upon as providers of labor in the generic. Then the employers would hire the specific laborers they wanted. This, naturally, led to a situation where certain union members got the lion's share of the work and the others got what was left. Being black had meant that you were not hired at all, the reason there were few blacks in the unions at that time.

The "hiring hall" system was a significant change in the way members were hired. Instead of having the employer choose which specific person it wanted—and to keep the union hierarchy from doing the choosing—union members were hired on the basis of which member had the most seniority who was in the union hall at the moment the job was available. Blacks viewed this as the best possible mechanism to parcel out work, as it had nothing to do with race.

When the strike was over, the hiring hall system was implemented. Overnight, blacks flooded into the union. The system was color blind, so blacks believed they had an equal chance of getting jobs and moving up in seniority. Another result was the formation of the National Union of Marine Cooks and Stewards. With the implementation of the hiring hall system, there was finally a mechanism to ensure fairness in hiring.

Created at the dawn of the hiring hall system, the National Union of Marine Cooks and Stewards was instrumental in spreading the concept to other coastal communities. This is significant because the ILA strike that had created the new system only affected West Coast cities. But the establishment of the National Union of Marine Cooks and Stewards necessarily meant that the hiring hall system had to be implemented nationwide for that union. It did not take long for other coastal cities to see the merit of the new system. The result is a national union database that uses the hiring hall system.

But the history of the NUMCS has not been without controversy. It was a very vocal, Communist-led union until the 1950s, when it came under scrutiny during the witch hunts of the McCarthy era. The subsequent investigations almost destroyed the union. By 1952, many of its leaders were imprisoned or blacklisted. The CIO, seeking to put as much distance as possible between itself and the radicals of any union, purged itself of the NUMCS and eight other unions. It was not until the death of Joseph McCarthy in 1957 and the end of the Red Scare that the NUMCS was welcomed back into the CIO, which by then had merged with the American Federation of Labor (1955) to create the AFL-CIO.

In the final analysis, the national significance of the National Union of Marine Cooks and Stewards is not so much what the members do as what the union did. By recognizing the importance of the hiring hall system, it formed and was one of the first—if not the first—union to use the concept nationwide. Its pioneering effort has proved a benefit to all unions. Very few unions can make that claim.

STEVEN C. LEVI

References and Further Reading

Giacomo, Paul. *National Union of Marine Cooks and Stewards*. NUMCS, 1944.
www.hartford-hwp.com/archives/45a/336.html.

NATIONAL UNION OF TEXTILE WORKERS

The National Union of Textile Workers (NUTW) was formed in 1890 as the American Federation of Labor's (AFL) primary vehicle for organizing textile workers. Initially, membership in the NUTW was limited mainly to skilled workers in northern textile mills. But the NUTW ran into immediate difficulties because there were already separate unions for most of the textile industry's skilled positions, including loom fixers and weavers. The NUTW also contended with the ongoing migration of textile production from the North to the South. Therefore, the union's long-term prospects depended on making inroads among southern textile workers.

The AFL had shown no previous interest in organizing southern mill hands. The Knights of Labor had paid some attention to the growing number of cotton-mill workers, but the Knights had a much broader focus and did not target any specific industry. The Farmers' Alliance and the People's Party (Populists) of the late nineteenth century both recognized the necessity of forging connections with industrial workers, but these organizations were concerned mainly with the issues bedeviling agriculture. Ironically, many Alliance members and Populists saw cotton mills as examples of society's decline, even as many farmers fled their fields for work in the fast-growing industry.

The NUTW's attempt to organize textile workers, particularly in the South, was motivated in part by a struggle between the AFL and Socialists for leadership of the American labor movement. The AFL emphasized its relatively moderate agenda of organizing skilled workers to improve their wages and working conditions, contrasting these goals with the inflammatory anticapitalist rhetoric of the Socialists. Socialists, however, had gained notoriety and no small measure of support through their high-profile leadership in particular labor conflicts, particularly that of Eugene Debs in the Pullman Strike of 1894. Daniel De Leon's Socialist Trade and Labor Alliance (STLA) challenged the AFL in key northern industries, including textiles, and the deep depression of the mid-1890s enhanced the appeal of more radical unionism. Since textiles continued to be a major industry in the Northeast, the NUTW and the STLA locked horns in that region. Both organizations, however, also had an eye on the South.

Moving South

In 1895, the AFL head, Samuel Gompers, toured the South and reported on the rapid growth of cotton mills, which seemed immune to the national depression. Despite the southern textile industry's relative good fortune, there was evidence as well of widespread discontent among its workers, who disliked their long hours and low pay but had few options given the state of agriculture. From the perspective of northern labor leaders, whether moderate or radical, the race was on to see which union would reap the harvest of discontented southern mill hands. Ironically, southern unionizing efforts gained some vocal support as well from northern textile industrialists, who hoped that the organization of southern workers would diminish the regional wage differential that gave the South a competitive advantage.

The realities of southern organizing, however, quickly complicated these northern dreams. The NUTW's first campaign started in 1896 at the Eagle and Phoenix Manufacturing Company in Columbus, Georgia, a booming textile town. The union gained popularity when Eagle and Phoenix management ordered a 10% wage reduction. In response, over 1,700 workers, skilled and unskilled alike, went on strike and formed the NUTW's first southern local. While a boon for the fledgling union, this influx of new members also revealed what would be one of the organization's persistent weaknesses. The NUTW had meager financial resources and could offer little assistance to striking workers. When the company held out and refused to bargain, workers had no way to replace their paychecks. Eventually, many striking employees along with a number of outside strikebreakers returned to work, production resumed, and the strike crumbled. Eagle and Phoenix magnanimously offered to rescind the wage cut when, in management's opinion, conditions allowed.

Failure in Columbus sparked further conflict in the South between the NUTW and the Socialists, complicated by a temporary fusion of the unions when the NUTW's general secretary, a Socialist, created a new labor organization. Gompers, however, cracked down and purged the NUTW of any outward Socialist influences. In the North, this resulted in the defection of many locals from the NUTW to the STLA. The South still seemed, at least on the surface, to be up for grabs. But no matter what the outcome of the inter-union squabbling in the South, the Eagle and Phoenix strike suggested that southern mill owners wanted no meaningful unionization, whether conservative or radical.

Focusing on urban areas, the NUTW found ambiguously advantageous circumstances in Atlanta in 1897. Black men had been allowed to work in southern cotton mills only as menial laborers, and few black women had ever been hired, despite large numbers of white women mill hands. But the huge Fulton Bag and Cotton Mills broke the color line by hiring 20 black women. White workers protested by walking off the job and joining the NUTW. Once again, however, lack of money undercut the local union. The strike fizzled as workers struggled without their paycheck and union leaders were fired. Without power or influence and committed to a segregated workforce, the NUTW local clung to existence.

Persistence and Futility

Despite these setbacks, the NUTW persevered. Between 1898 and 1900, organizers claimed to have chartered 54 locals in Virginia, North and South Carolina, Alabama, and Georgia. Yet it was unclear how a "local" was defined. It could be a few sympathetic workers in a Piedmont mill, or a few hundred in Atlanta. In any event, it seemed clear that these new locals were not generating much in the way of dues, which limited the power of each of them. Although in 1900 the NUTW claimed 5,000 dues-paying members, mostly in the South, the union never generated a significant strike fund, yet found it impossible to function without one.

Management bodies responded to NUTW campaigns by claiming that organizers were foreign-influenced "outsiders" who favored race mixing and that disgruntled employees showed ingratitude. The union's national leaders lent credence to the race-mixing charge, offending many white members, by opposing grandfather clauses that prevented blacks from voting. Top NUTW leadership also supported child labor legislation, which management saw as an infringement on its rights and which many workers, who appreciated their children working beside them, also viewed with skepticism.

Lack of finances, however, continued to be the NUTW's main liability. In an effort to conserve money, the union offered strike relief only to locals that had been chartered for six months. However, most workers appealed to the NUTW for recognition and support only in the midst of strikes. Rejection of requests for strike assistance discouraged union membership, but so did unfulfilled promises of relief. Mill owners tightened the screws with selective firings, lockouts, evictions from company housing, and blacklisting. The NUTW did win some specific demands, usually small wage increases for specific workers in various mills. But most of the union's efforts in dozens of textile communities ended in disaster, fueling cynicism among mill hands about the value of organization.

In 1900, the NUTW appealed to southern mill workers by promoting the 10-hour day. This campaign was hotly contested by mill managements, in part because the market for southern textiles had been undercut by the Boxer Rebellion in China, the destination for much southern production. In the summer of 1900, there were nearly 30 strikes and lockouts in North Carolina alone. The biggest, involving over 1,000 workers, arose from the arbitrary dismissal of an employee at the Haw River Mills in Alamance County. Management responded by firing anyone who admitted membership in the NUTW, hiring strikebreakers, and holding out against initially unsympathetic local public opinion. Once again, however, strikers had minimal resources, could not hold out, and were blacklisted when seeking employment elsewhere. The NUTW offered little financial relief, and the workers ultimately conceded. Some version of this story was repeated in nearly every case. For example, for a major strike in Danville, Virginia, the NUTW had a strike fund of $2,700 to support some 2,000 workers. The AFL eventually sent another $4,000, but this still could not offset even a week's worth of pay.

At its peak in 1900, the NUTW might have claimed 6% of the southern textile labor force as members. A year later, the remaining southern NUTW locals merged with a number of northern locals, ones that had left in the mid-1890s, to form the United Textile Workers of America. The NUTW had few tangible successes, but in its brief existence it did manage to bring into focus many grievances held by southern mill workers. There was certainly widespread discontent, and mill hands were not reluctant, at least initially, to strike in pursuit of their goals. The lessons learned during those conflicts, however, heightened skepticism about the usefulness of unions and reinforced the high stakes of labor activism. These themes would recur in later textile conflicts. Mill owners, especially those in hundreds of tiny Piedmont communities, ultimately held much more power than did the NUTW.

DANIEL CLARK

References and Further Reading

Carlton, David. *Mill and Town in South Carolina, 1880–1920.* Baton Rouge: Louisiana State University Press, 1982.

Fink, Gary. *The Fulton Bag and Cotton Mills Strike of 1914–1915: Espionage, Labor Conflict, and New South Industrial Relations.* Ithaca, NY: ILR Press, 1993.

Flamming, Douglas. *Creating the Modern South: Millhands and Managers in Dalton, Georgia, 1884–1984.* Chapel Hill: University of North Carolina Press, 1992.

Hall, Jacquelyn Dowd, James Leloudis, Robert Korstad, Mary Murphy, Lu Ann Jones, and Christopher Daly. *Like a Family: The Making of a Southern Cotton Mill World.* Chapel Hill: University of North Carolina Press, 1987.

McLaurin, Melton Alonza. *Paternalism and Protest: Southern Cotton Mill Workers and Organized Labor, 1875–1905.* Westport, CT: Greenwood Publishing Corporation, 1971.

Mitchell, George Sinclair. *Textile Unionism in the South.* Chapel Hill: University of North Carolina Press, 1931.

Newby, I. A. *Plain Folk in the New South: Social Change and Cultural Persistence, 1880–1915.* Baton Rouge: Louisiana State University Press, 1989.

See also **American Federation of Labor; Debs, Eugene V.; DeLeon, Daniel; Gompers, Samuel; Knights of Labor; Populism/People's Party; Socialist Trade and Labor Alliance; Textiles; United Textile Workers**

NATIONAL URBAN LEAGUE

The National Urban League (NUL) was founded in 1911 in New York City. The League was the product of the merger of three social work agencies: the National League for the Protection of Colored Women (founded by Frances Kellor in 1905), the Committee for the Improvement of Industrial Conditions Among Negroes (1906), and the Committee on Urban Conditions Among Negroes (1910). Originally the National League on Urban Conditions Among Negroes (NLUCAN), in 1920, the name was shortened to the National Urban League (NUL). From the outset, the NUL focused on black migrants' acculturation, jobs, and housing. The League taught lessons in everything

from choosing a vocation and job-search strategies to cooking, cleaning, and personal hygiene. The League also sought to shape policy with empirical research and provided social services such as job placement, education, and health care. Finally, the NUL built training centers and provided fellowships to encourage young African-Americans to enter professional social work.

The League's programs of "interracial co-operation" originated in the Progressive Era's emphasis on rational solutions to social problems and top-down reform. The League's founders included white philanthropists and reformers such as Ruth Standish Baldwin, the wife of railroad magnate William H. Baldwin; L. Hollingsworth Wood, a Quaker involved in the New York Colored Mission; and the Columbia University professor E. R. A. Seligman. The NUL's African-American founders were members of what W. E. B. DuBois called the "talented tenth." The Howard University dean Kelly Miller and the physician and civic leader George Cleveland Hall exemplify the League's roots in higher education and social reform. The League's first two executive directors, George Edmund Haynes and Eugene Kinckle Jones, were both college-educated black professionals. These leaders built NLUCAN on the model of prominent agencies that worked to assist transnational immigrants to New York City.

The NUL added affiliates in cities across the country. For most of the century, local chapters were relatively autonomous compared, for example, to NAACP chapters and achieved uneven success. Although some white officials in southern cities did attempt to set up NUL chapters, creating organizations based on the principle of interracial co-operation was especially difficult where "social equality" was anathema. The most notable southern affiliate was in Nashville, Tennessee, and was led by the sociologist George Haynes. Haynes met the challenge of interracial work in the South by concentrating on professional social work training at Fisk University. Although Haynes sought to connect the university to the broader community, it was in New York City that the League's attention to urgent social problems took shape. In the national office, Eugene Kinckle Jones worked with relative autonomy and with the greater resources available in the city to shift the center of the League's activities away from Haynes's educational approach.

In addition to the affiliates work, the NUL's influence spread through its journal *Opportunity*. In 1923, the Fisk University sociologist Charles S. Johnson founded the League's alternative to *The Crisis*, the organ of the National Association for the Advancement of Colored People (NAACP). Together, they provided widely read platforms for black poets, novelists, and intellectuals. The League's magazine did not match the distribution of *The Crisis*, but *Opportunity* provided an outlet for the League's substantial research and drew a larger white audience.

The NUL included an executive director, a board of directors, field organizers, and professional staff. A president, largely a figurehead, ran the interracial board, which was generally the most conservative element of the organization. For the most part, the League's executive directors shaped the organization's programs. George Haynes led the League from Nashville during its first eight years. His partner in New York City, Eugene Kinckle Jones, was the NUL's executive secretary from 1919 to 1941. Jones's tenure coincided with the Great Migration, Harlem Renaissance, Great Depression, and the onset of World War II. It was an achievement just to keep the League alive, especially when donations virtually dried up in the 1930s. The longtime League organizer Lester B. Granger led the League from 1941 until his retirement in 1961. Granger struggled to raise money for the League, but under his leadership, the NUL did expand its Vocational Opportunity Campaigns. Whitney Young replaced Granger and served until he drowned while on a trip to Lagos, Nigeria, in 1971. In an era of increasing conservatism, Vernon E. Jordan (1972–1981), John Jacob (1982–1994), Hugh Price (1994–2003), and Marc Morial (2003–) have attempted to sustain the League's dramatic revitalization under Young.

Controversial History

The NUL sits at the center of controversies over the character and effectiveness of liberal reform in African-American history. Some students of the Progressive Era's legacy for African-American reform movements argue that the NUL was a regressive institution of social control. Others insist that the League has been a necessary supplement to organizations with different approaches. Finally, historians point out the mediating role the NUL has played between revolutionaries, liberals, and conservatives.

The NUL and the NAACP provide a convenient point of comparison for this debate. The NAACP, founded by W. E. B. DuBois and others in the Niagara Movement just two years before NLUCAN, also developed programs based on Progressive Era liberalism. For many years, historians argued that the NUL and NAACP exemplified a split between Booker T. Washington and W. E. B. DuBois. Those who equated Washington's industrial education and the League's vocational guidance argued that the NUL represented an urban version of Washington's accommodationist self-help ideology. The NAACP, on the other hand, was said to reflect DuBois's more confrontational politics. This comparison ignores a number of key points. Washington played little role in the League's founding and later was only peripherally connected to the NUL's work. In addition, the NUL's vocational guidance programs trained African-Americans for industrial and white-collar work. DuBois did have a central part in the NAACP's origins and probably did more to shape the NAACP's public image than any other individual through his *Crisis* articles. However, DuBois never held unchallenged control over the NAACP's programs. Most important, historians have pointed to the overlaps and ambiguities in the two organizations' ideologies and programs, concluding that the NUL and the NAACP often enjoyed a complementary and supplementary relationship. Leaders in both organizations believed in the power of public education, but neither was originally a mass-based civil rights organization. During their first two decades, the major difference between the NUL and the NAACP was that while the NUL focused on social work and vocational guidance, the NAACP concentrated on reform via pressure on government institutions and legal strategies to fight discrimination.

Still, the NUL's history raises debates over the strengths and weaknesses of the NUL's cooperation with the white power structure. Numerous scholars argue that the NUL's reliance on funding from white philanthropists such as Ruth S. Baldwin, John D. Rockefeller, and Julius Rosenwald of Sears, Roebuck, and Co. prevented the League from pursuing fundamental social or economic change. From this point of view, the NUL has been at best a paternalistic, reformist organization.

The historiographical debate over the League's effectiveness has been most pointed in biographies of Whitney M. Young, the NUL executive director from 1961 to 1971. In 1970, the *New York Times* columnist Tom Buckley voiced the popular critique of the NUL as an organization of lackeys to the white power structure in his article "Whitney Young: Black Leader or 'Oreo Cookie'?" Nancy Weiss's 1989 biography rehabilitated Young's image by highlighting achievements. Young turned the League into a premier civil rights organization and secured funds from corporations, foundations, and the federal government. In 1998, Dennis C. Dickerson revised Weiss's portrayal, adding that Young's work with white business and political leaders was grounded in activism in working- and middle-class black circles. In these biographies, Young's attempts to mediate between civil rights activists and elite whites represent the NUL's dilemma more generally, especially the difficult middle ground the agency attempts to hold between antagonistic groups of different races and classes.

Another controversial aspect of the League's history is its relationship to trade unions and strikebreaking during its first two decades. During the Great Migration, the NUL's job placement services engendered criticism from both white employers and trade unions. The NUL responded to African-Americans' employment demands and during World War I assisted the United States Employment Service (USES) in recruiting African-American workers. Many employers (some of whom relied on black labor when it was convenient) saw the NUL-backed USES as an incursion into their right to choose workers based on race. For their part, white trade unions perceived NUL job placement, and black workers in general, as real threats to their jobs and unions. Worst of all, black workers carried the stigma of strikebreakers. During the massive 1919 steel and packinghouse strikes, the League jumped into the middle of this controversy. At a Detroit conference that year, the NUL declared its position on unionization: black workers should join unions and bargain collectively when unions did not discriminate. However, if excluded, black workers should form their own collective and negotiate with white employers and unions. At the same time, the NUL actively pursued job placements throughout the 1919 strikes. According to the historian James Grossman, in 1919, in Chicago alone, 14,000 blacks found jobs through the League. By straddling the middle of the strikes and continuing to place thousands of black workers in jobs, the NUL exacerbated tension with trade unions. However, historians point out that for African-American laborers, who were last hired and first fired, accepting a strikebreaking job was a pragmatic choice in a hostile economic environment.

A New Context

In 1961, the League's new executive director, Whitney M. Young, reshuffled the League's national office and began a fund-raising campaign that ultimately created the League's most dynamic period. As the historian Nancy Weiss points out, between 1961 and 1970, the League's budget increased significantly, from $340,000 to $14,279,000; the number of affiliates increased from 63 to 98, and its professional staff expanded from 300 to more than 1,200. Although some League affiliates had already taken on projects for civil and legal rights, the NUL remained committed to social service, education, and research

activities. This began to change during Young's tenure. Young reformed the League's popular image by working closely with groups such as the Southern Christian Leadership Conference, the Congress of Racial Equality, and the Student Non-Violent Coordinating Committee. Young used his charisma to forge lucrative connections with corporations, gain access to the highest levels of the federal government, and make the Urban League one of the primary civil rights organizations. According to his biographers, Young played important intermediary roles throughout the decade—between leaders of the 1963 March on Washington, between corporate and government officials and the other major civil right leaders, and between black and white liberals and the increasingly radical youth-based movements of the late 1960s.

Young was not alone in his desire to revise the League's programs. The general political climate of the 1960s included greater federal and private resources for fighting racial discrimination. In addition, after 1966, the Black Power Movement brought a newly energized commitment to black nationalism, self-determination, and in some cases, racial separatism. This rapidly changing political context caused many inside the League to move away from its traditional emphasis on interracial co-operation and appeasement of the white power structure.

For Young and the NUL, the resurgent popular emphasis on self-determination and racial pride did not translate into racial separatism. Instead, Young and his allies in the NUL moved toward racial pluralism while constructing innovative programs targeting social problems in the ghettos. The NUL created a National Skills Bank that connected black workers with jobs that fit their skill levels; on-the-job training programs in concert with the Department of Labor; a Broadcast Skills Bank to direct African-Americans into radio and television; and a Secretarial Training Project. These new programs dramatically increased the number of people who received job training and placement from the NUL. No longer was progress measured in terms of "pilot placements," jobs secured by an individual black candidate for the first time, which had been the Industrial Department's standard for so many years. In addition, as part of the "New Thrust" mass organizing in ghettos that began in 1968, many League affiliates moved their offices from central business sections of their cities to the center of black majority neighborhoods. The League created voter education and registration, labor education, and youth development programs. Clearly, though the NUL now focused its attention on centers of black life rather than interracial co-operation, the organization remained committed to the transformative power of jobs, education, and the democratic process. The League's persistent faith in reform paid off in grants from philanthropic groups such as the Ford Foundation and the federal government.

After Young's death, League leaders remained committed to providing social services and funding research projects in majority black communities. The NUL has maintained its nonpartisan, interracial social work. In addition to its traditional employment and education services, the League assists black veterans, fights for open housing and consumers' rights, and helps find adoptive houses and tutors for inner-city children. Since the mid-1970s the League has also produced an annual report, *The State of Black America*, carrying on its tradition of using scientific social research to influence public policy.

JEFFREY HELGESON

References and Further Reading

Dickerson, Dennis C. *Militant Mediator: Whitney M. Young, Jr.* Lexington: University Press of Kentucky, 1998.

Ferguson, Karen. *Black Politics in New Deal Atlanta.* Chapel Hill: University of North Carolina Press, 2002.

Grossman, James R. *Land of Hope: Chicago, Black Southerners, and the Great Migration.* Chicago: University of Chicago Press, 1989.

Moore, Jesse Thomas Jr. *A Search for Equality: The National Urban League, 1910–1961.* University Park: Pennsylvania State University Press, 1981.

Parris, Guichard, and Lester Brooks. *Blacks in the City: A History of the National Urban League.* Boston: Little, Brown and Company, 1971.

Strickland, Arvarh E. *History of the Chicago Urban League.* Urbana: University of Illinois, 1966.

Weiss, Nancy J. *The National Urban League, 1910–1940.* New York: Oxford University Press, 1974.

———. *Whitney M. Young, Jr., and the Struggle for Civil Rights.* Princeton: Princeton University Press, 1989.

Wilson, Sondra Kathryn, ed. *The Opportunity Reader: Stories, Poetry, and Essays from the Urban League's Opportunity Magazine.* New York: The Modern Library, 1999.

See also **Civil Rights; Du Bois, W. E. B.; Great Migration; National Association for the Advancement of Colored People (NAACP); Progressive Era; Strike Wave (1919); Strikebreaking**

NATIONAL WAR LABOR BOARD (WWI)

Created by presidential proclamation in 1918, the National War Labor Board (NWLB) served as the primary U.S. government agency for resolving labor disputes during World War I. The 12-member body was cochaired by Frank Walsh, a prolabor Kansas City attorney who had gained fame as chair of the U.S. Commission on Industrial Relations, and William Howard Taft, a former Republican president of the United States. By the time it ceased operations in August 1919, the Board had handed down nearly 500 rulings in disputes over pay, hours, and employee representation.

The origins of the NWLB are rooted in the strike wave that swept the country once the United States declared war on Germany in April 1917. In the first six months of the war, more than 280,000 workers engaged in over 1,100 strikes, substantially impairing the U.S. war effort. Initial government efforts to achieve labor peace relied on a patchwork of industry-specific boards in army barracks construction, shipbuilding, coal, and railroads. In January 1918, President Wilson assigned Secretary of Labor William B. Wilson to establish a unified labor policy. The resulting War Labor Conference Board (WLCB), with five members for labor, five for management, and Walsh and Taft representing the public, reported to the president in late March 1918. On April 8, Wilson created the NWLB, with a nearly identical membership.

Representing labor on the new Board were Frank Hayes (the president of the United Mine Workers of America), William L. Hutcheson (the president of the United Carpenters), Thomas Savage (a member of the Executive Council of the International Association of Machinists), Victor Olander (the secretary-treasurer of the Illinois Federation of Labor and the top official of the International Seamen's Union), and Thomas A. Rickert (the president of the United Garment Workers). The employer representatives were L. F. Loree (the president of the Delaware and Hudson Railroad), C. Edwin Michael (the former vice president of the National Association of Manufacturers and an iron manufacturer), Loyall A. Osborne (the vice president of Westinghouse), W. H. Van Dervoort, (an East Moline, IL manufacturer), and B. L. Worden (the head of the Submarine Boat Corporation and the Lackawanna Bridge Co). Members also had seconds, who served in their absence.

The mission of the Board was to keep war industry workers on the job. Its guiding principles aimed at balancing the needs of business and the demands of workers. Workers had the right to organize unions without management interference as long as they did not use "coercive" tactics. "Existing conditions," whether union or open shop, were to be maintained. Women and men were to receive equal pay for equal work, though women were not to be assigned work "disproportionate" to their strength. The right to the eight-hour day would be upheld where it was legally required by state law. Workers and managers would co-operate to avoid production delays and to provide information about available skilled workers to the government. Wage levels should be based on prevailing local standards. And finally, for their part in the Great War, workers were entitled to a living wage.

Each case that came before the NWLB was assigned to a "section" of the Board consisting of one management and one labor member. The pair relied on information provided by impartial staff investigators sent into the field. The section could also choose to dispatch a pair of partisan investigators. If the section could not agree on the case, the full Board would decide it. In the event that the full Board could not reach unanimity, the case went to one of 10 presidentially appointed umpires who alone issued a decision. Umpires included prominent politicians and business leaders, such as Henry Ford, Walter Clark, the chief justice of the North Carolina Supreme Court, and the U.S. Housing Corporation president, Otto Eidlitz.

Since the Board did not result from an act of Congress, its rulings did not have legal sanction, unless both employer and employees had jointly submitted the case. In its very first case, members of the Commercial Telegraphers Union of America (CTUA) working at Western Union asked the NWLB to intervene when the company president, Newcomb Carlton, fired workers for joining the union. When Carlton refused to comply with a Board compromise proposal, thus exposing the Board's weakness, President Wilson convinced Congress to nationalize the telegraph and telephone lines and appointed Albert Burleson as administrator. The strongly antilabor Burleson stalled on implementing the NWLB's subsequent award of a wage increase to Western Union workers, but Wilson's action gave the NWLB some teeth.

Though the Board was split evenly between labor and employer representatives, the pressures of labor unrest, the need for uninterrupted production, Wilson's strong stand in the Western Union case, plus the moderating influence of Taft on the employer side resulted in a series of prolabor rulings. In a case brought by striking foundry workers in Waynesboro, Pennsylvania, the Board raised the minimum laborers' hourly wage from 22 cents to 40 cents, which became a precedent for further rulings. After labor and employer members of the Board deadlocked on eight-hour cases from Wheeling, West Virginia, and Bridgeport, Connecticut, a major munitions production center, umpires Ford, Clark, and Eidlitz awarded the eight-hour day to workers. Women employees, including Schenectady electrical workers, were also awarded wage increases, though the Board accepted lower minimums for women than for men. Low-paid black laborers in New Orleans and elsewhere made wage gains; similarly, though, when black Birmingham steelworkers encountered vigilante racist violence in the course of an organizing campaign, the Board failed to intervene.

In its attempt to maintain "existing standards," the Board dealt with the sticky issue of employee representation by recommending, in a majority of collective bargaining cases, that shop committees be established in plants throughout the country. While the committees were meant to postpone the issue of unionism, in Bridgeport, radical leaders of District 55 of the International Association of Machinists led a strike against an inadequate Board ruling and then swept the shop committee elections. Union activists at General Electric employed NWLB hearings to win new members and then used shop committees to organize the Electrical Manufacturing Industry Labor Federation, uniting electrical workers from Pennsylvania to New York to Massachusetts. After the Armistice, however, as the leverage of Board labor representatives evaporated, employers such as Eugene Grace of Bethlehem Steel successfully flouted Board authority and used NWLB-recommended shop committees as a barrier to unionization. Considering that these committees became a primary vehicle for companies to avoid unions in the subsequent decade, historians have differed on whether Board policy should be seen positively as providing the basis for later prolabor New Deal reforms or viewed as a kind of Trojan horse for the open shop.

CARL R. WEINBERG

References and Further Reading

Bing, Alexander. *Wartime Strikes and Their Adjustment.* New York: E. P. Dutton, 1921.

Conner, Valerie Jean. *The National War Labor Board: Stability, Social Justice, and the Voluntary State in World War I.* Chapel Hill: University of North Carolina Press, 1983.

Dubofsky, Melvyn. "Abortive Reform: The Wilson Administration and Organized Labor, 1913–1920." In *Work, Community, and Power: The Experience of Labor in Europe and America, 1900–1925,* edited by James E. Cronin and Carmen Sirianni. Philadelphia: Temple University Press, 1983.

Haydu, Jeffrey. *Making American Industry Safe for Democracy.* Urbana: University of Illinois Press, 1997.

McCartin, Joseph. *Labor's Great War: The Struggle for Industrial Democracy and the Origins of Modern American Labor Relations, 1912–1921.* Chapel Hill: University of North Carolina Press, 1997.

Montgomery, David. *The Fall of the House of Labor: The Workplace, the State, and American Labor Activism, 1865–1925.* Cambridge: Cambridge University Press, 1987.

NATIONAL WAR LABOR BOARD (WWII)

As the United States edged closer to involvement in and then entered World War II in December 1941, organized labor, management, and the government each maneuvered to protect their interests. Labor hoped to consolidate the membership gains and legal legitimacy secured by the New Deal and to extend its collective bargaining victories into nonunion shops and industries, particularly those that benefited from defense production. For its part, big business wanted to hold the line against further union advances. Government, interested foremost in uninterrupted defense production, sought to create mediation mechanisms that would settle any labor disputes to both parties' satisfaction with a minimum of disruption. All looked to the state-mandated industrial relations pioneered during the First World War, characterized by a tripartite mediation War Labor Board, for guidance.

When defense production for the Allies increased in 1940 and 1941, Congress of Industrial Organizations (CIO) unions tried to win concessions from recalcitrant employers with large government contracts, most notably Ford Motor Company, Bethlehem Steel, and Allis-Chalmers. Organized labor's representatives on the National Defense Advisory Commission failed to get the government to deny defense contracts to corporations that violated the National Labor Relations Act (NLRA), and the resulting strikes began to retard defense production by the spring of 1941. That March, President Roosevelt established the National Defense Mediation Board (NDMB) to help resolve these defense industry labor disputes. The 11-member NDMB had a mandate to "exert every possible effort to assure that all work necessary for national defense shall proceed without interruption and with all possible speed" but was handicapped by its inability to compel arbitration that would be binding on both labor and management.

The NDMB collapsed in November 1941, when its two CIO members resigned over the Board's refusal to grant a closed shop to the United Mine Workers in its ongoing dispute with U.S. Steel. Only a month later, however, with U.S. entry into the war, President Roosevelt issued an executive order reconstituting the Board as the National War Labor Board (NWLB).

Like the NDMB before it, the NWLB's 12 members were drawn evenly from representatives of labor, business, and the "public"(in reality, seen as representing the interests of government). Labor members included Philip Murray, the president of the CIO, Thomas Kennedy of the United Mine Workers, and two representatives from the rival American Federation of Labor (AFL). Business sent representatives of large corporations accustomed to negotiating with unions, such as U.S. Rubber's Cyrus Ching, who had long advocated co-operation with organized labor. William H. Davis, the one-time head of the New York state mediation service, chaired both the NWLB and its predecessor. Davis was joined by men with extensive experience in mediating labor disputes and balancing competing interests in public life, including Wayne Morse, who had arbitrated the fierce West Coast longshore strikes during the 1930s, and Frank Porter Graham, the liberal president of the University of North Carolina. No women sat on the Board, though the NWLB did issue rulings that enforced equal pay for equal work done by men and women in war production. Graham, in particular, also helped the Board lend a sympathetic ear to black workers who demanded equal treatment in the wartime workplace, and sought to abolish racial inequities in wage structures.

Unlike the National Defense Mediation Board or its World War I predecessor, the NWLB had the power to decide disputes in a legally binding manner and to bring sanctions to bear against both unions and businesses that refused to abide by its decisions, including plant seizures. The major tasks of the NWLB, in the words of its final report, consisted of "the settlement of labor disputes which endangered the war effort and the stabilization of wages as an integral part of the over-all program to prevent inflation." Between 1942 and 1945, the NWLB decided over 17,000 disputes involving over 12 million employees, which impacted a majority of unionized workers in the United States. In only 40 cases did the NWLB call on the government to seize defense plants to compel adherence to its rulings. The NWLB's strongest sanctions against organized labor came in its power to revoke union security provisions, fringe benefits, or collective bargaining contracts that it had helped unions secure. Thus, more often than not, the Board proved able to enlist union leaders in heading off unauthorized disputes or quelling wildcat strikes.

If the NWLB carried out its mediation function effectively and protected workers' right to organize and bargain collectively, its efforts to stabilize wages proved far less satisfactory to labor. In an effort to restrain rapidly advancing wartime inflation, the NWLB laid down a policy in July 1942 that capped wage increases at about 3%, a figure the Board claimed matched the gap between the increase in cost of living and wage gains over the past 18 months. This so-called Little Steel Formula of wage stabilization placed the burden of inflationary restraint on wage earners and proved immensely unpopular with rank-and-file workers, who regarded it as a wage freeze. Nevertheless, increased overtime and more elaborate fringe benefits compensated in part for the artificial ceiling on the pay packet.

The mandated wage restraint notwithstanding, of the many wartime administrative agencies designed to oversee war production, the NWLB was the only one in which organized labor proved able to wield some influence. Despite grumbling by workers about limited wage increases, restrictions on labor mobility, and the no-strike pledge, the NWLB placated labor leaders by granting "maintenance of membership" to the unions. Under these agreements, all newly hired workers in a union shop would be automatically enrolled in the union after a 15-day waiting period. The union security thus gained proved instrumental in encouraging the growth of organized labor during the war. For unions, this proved an essential component of the wartime industrial relations regime because of the enormous influx of unorganized workers into the defense industries; for big business, "maintenance of membership" represented a major capitulation to labor's historic quest for the universal closed shop. As the NWLB noted in its final report, "no issue presented to the War Labor Board precipitated more furious debate than union security."

Some scholars argue that the NWLB, despite its brief existence, had a long-lasting effect on the shape of American labor law. The basic structure of collective bargaining agreements as overseen by the state, the means of arbitration and mediation of disputes, and a sharply delineated arena of managerial prerogatives, as well as the requirement that trade unions police the behavior of their members, can all be seen as significant legacies of the Board's decisions.

ALEX LICHTENSTEIN

References and Further Reading

Atleson, James B. *Labor and the Wartime State.* Urbana: University of Illinois Press, 1998.

Dubofsky, Melvyn. *The State and Labor in Modern America.* Chapel Hill and London: University of North Carolina Press, 1994.

Lichtenstein, Nelson. *Labor's War at Home: The CIO in World War II.* Philadelphia: Temple University Press, 2003.

U.S. Department of Labor. *Termination Report of the War Labor Board.* Washington, DC: 1947.

See also **American Federation of Labor; United Mine Workers of America; World War II**

NATIVE AMERICANS

American Indians worked for wages since their earliest encounters with the developing capitalist economy. They cleaned homes and minded children for colonial officials, picked crops and herded cattle for frontier farmers and ranchers, and scouted out their enemies for the U.S. military during the nineteenth-century Indian wars. When the transcontinental railroad brought industrial development to the western landscape, American Indians found work in industries that drew other migrants to the region from across the globe: in mining, lumber, railroads and large-scale commercial agriculture.

While they labored alongside Asian, Latino, and Euro-American migrants, their specific experience under U.S. control set American Indians apart from other workers. U.S. policy and treaties dictated the terms of American Indian existence to the most intimate detail. Federal bureaucrats in what would become the Bureau of Indian Affairs (BIA) would attempt to control every aspect of their daily lives, including where Indians would live, how they would make a living, what they learned in school, and how they would engage their spiritual worlds. Non-Indian workers faced similar types of federal intervention and assimilationist programs, including initiatives that transformed the slave labor system in the South and legislation that regulated working conditions and restricted immigration. But the history of treaty making between American Indians and the U.S. government established the precedent of indigenous people asserting their rights to sovereignty, not simply the civil rights of fully enfranchised citizens demanded by other racialized minority groups.

During the course of the nineteenth century, when other American workers faced problems of mechanization and industrialization, and fought for control over the workplace and the eight-hour day, American Indians were engaged in a life-or-death struggle to hold on to their homelands. This history of armed conflict, colonial control, and dispossession would profoundly determine how American Indians would be incorporated into the capitalist market as well as what types of individual and collective strategies they would develop to survive and persevere.

Indian land was pivotal to American expansion and the pursuit of "Manifest Destiny" in the nineteenth century and made possible the development of intercontinental railroads and extractive industries that formed the backbone of the U.S. West's economy until World War II. By the beginning of the twentieth century, American Indians lost most of their land in a series of wars, treaties, and congressional actions. By 1887, American Indians held approximately 136 million acres of land, 6.8% of what they occupied prior to European contact. The 1887 General Allotment Act (the Dawes Act) further reduced their holdings by two thirds, carving up tribally held territory into individual homesteads and opening up the remaining land to white settlement.

Reformers saw the Dawes Act as the best solution for the "Indian Problem." By "killing the Indian to save the man," it was supposed to transform Indians into yeoman farmers and help them achieve a level of civilization (as defined by federal lawmakers) necessary for incorporation into American society. Some took advantage of this mandate and became successful farmers and ranchers. But for the most part, the Dawes Act dealt a decisive blow to their subsistence cultures, rendering many American Indians landless and homeless.

Boarding Schools and the "Making" of Indian Workers

For reformers, civilizing the Indians required more than assigning them allotments of land. Assimilation required American Indians to abandon their cultures, languages, and tribal affiliations. With these goals in mind, Richard Henry Pratt founded the Carlisle Indian School in 1879, a boarding school for Indians that emphasized a vocational rather than an academic curriculum. Far from home and forbidden to speak their native languages, American Indian students learned the social expectations of industrial society. They marched in military formation, donned Victorian-era clothing, and marked their time according to the bells of a clock. Mostly, they learned about wage work from the "outing system," an apprenticeship program at the heart of assimilationist curriculum. Students performed a variety of jobs in this program, but they primarily found themselves doing unskilled, agricultural labor or domestic work for western employers. According to Lewis Meriam, the author of a major exposé on Indian Policy in 1928, these schools were not preparing students to land lucrative, skilled jobs. They were simply supplying the schools and surrounding employers with a source of cheap labor. As a result, according to the anthropologist Alice Littlefield in *Native Americans and Wage Labor*, such an education "was not so much assimilation as proletarianization." Even with useful vocational training, Indians would find little access to well-paying jobs once they left the boarding school environment. Racism that barred other workers of color from access to the skilled trades applied to Indians as well.

The Indian New Deal

During the New Deal era, American Indians experienced a brief reprieve from the draconian assimilationist programs of the previous 50 years. Under John Collier, the commissioner of Indian affairs, American Indians saw an end to allotment, the development of day schools, and increasing support for tribal identity. For Collier, Indian culture was something to be preserved, not extinguished. The 1934 Wheeler-Howard Act, the hallmark of his administration, authorized tribes to set up their own governments and created programs that encouraged craft production and other forms of cultural expression.

Commonly known as the "Indian New Deal," the legislation also extended Depression-era work and relief programs to American Indian communities. Ironically, while many American workers were losing their jobs as the economy crumbled in the 1930s, many American Indians were experiencing wage work for the first time. They found jobs in the growing BIA bureaucracies and in the Indian Civilian Conservation Corps clearing trails, building campgrounds, and working on reservation land conservation projects. And in one short-lived experiment, Indian women were put to work in small, reservation-based mattress factories.

But for the Navajos, meager wages did not make up for the New Deal's unwitting assault on their cultural economy. According to conservation specialists, Navajos' sheep, goats, and cattle were overgrazing their rangelands, and the resulting erosion threatened the economic viability of their livestock industry. The BIA's answer for repairing and preserving those rangelands included reducing Navajo livestock holdings by more than 50%. It was a harsh measure—a long-term solution that threatened the short-term survival of their pastoral culture. It firmly embittered a generation of Navajos, many of whom would subsequently vote against the ratification of the Indian Reorganization Act. After livestock reduction, many had to abandon their families and herds to look for other ways to earn a living, including railroad maintenance, agricultural labor, and assorted domestic jobs in reservation boarding towns. As the Navajo example suggests, Collier's policies, while anti-assimilationist, may have done as much to pull American Indians into the capitalist marketplace as boarding schools and allotment had accomplished in the generation before.

World War II halted the New Dealer's efforts, redirecting people and resources away from Indian conservation and labor programs. Like other Americans, native people joined the war effort, enlisting in the military and finding work in defense-related industries. According to the historian Allison Bernstein, 44,000 American Indians served in the armed forces, and many more worked in weapons depots, mining, and other heavy industries. American Indian women joined up as nurses and members of the Women's Army Corps. Soldiers and workers sent a substantial percentage of their paychecks home to their loved ones on the reservation, supplying those communities with a new and significant source of income. When the war ended, these veterans would return to their homes with cash in their pockets and heightened expectations about their rights and responsibilities as citizens. They would be part of a new generation of American Indian leaders who would begin to establish new tribal governments and test the boundaries of sovereignty promised by New Deal-era reforms.

Termination and Relocation

After the war, the mood in Congress shifted once again toward a more assimilationist Indian policy. In 1953, legislators were determined to "get out of the Indian business" once and for all, and passed a series of laws, including Concurrent Resolution 108 and Public Law 208, that enabled states to extend their jurisdictions over Indian land, thus terminating their federal reservation status. Not all states exercised this option, nor did all tribes find their reservation status terminated. This was a devastating blow to nascent tribal governments, such as the Menominee in Wisconsin, who had been somewhat successful in developing a relatively small, yet viable, lumber industry. Still, without federal support they could not compete with large-scale corporate operations. For many tribes, termination meant further loss of their land base as well as a direct attack on their political and economic sovereignty.

Like other federal policies, termination did not turn out as legislators expected. Coupled with this legislation was a voluntary federal program that offered to relocate reservation residents to urban areas such as Denver, Albuquerque, San Francisco, and Phoenix as well as Midwestern cities such as Minneapolis and Chicago. Many American Indians took advantage of this project, hoping to find a way out of the poverty they faced at home on the reservations. But migration did not mean that American Indians would completely abandon their reservation communities, as policy makers had hoped. Since at least the late nineteenth century, native people ventured beyond their reservation's boundaries to find work; but they would also come back, contributing their earnings and labor to the survival of their families. Picking carrots for commercial growers in Phoenix, repairing railroad tracks near Kansas City, or packing produce

in Oakland did not necessarily mean that American Indian workers would completely assimilate the values and culture of the dominant society. Nor did it mean that they would lose their connections with their kin at home. The result was not necessarily assimilation, but what the historian Eric Meeks terms "resistant adaptation." American Indians did not choose between their cultures and their jobs. Instead, they developed strategies that enabled them to make a living in ways that resonated with their own cultural practices and responsibilities.

In the 1950s and 1960s, sizable urban Indian communities emerged in Los Angeles, San Francisco, Phoenix, and other western cities. But many native people returned to the reservation or created broader urban/reservation migration streams of relatives and friends who might come and go as needed. New social movements grew from these urban enclaves that would demand significant reform in U.S. Indian policy, including the repeal of termination and legislation that afforded greater respect for cultural, political, and economic sovereignty.

Native Americans and Labor Unions

The history of Native Americans and organized labor in the United States reflects considerable tension and ambiguities, mirroring the experience of other workers of color. Like Mexican-Americans and African-Americans, they confronted racial discrimination at work and in the union hall, where white union members denied them access to the building trades and other highly skilled jobs. In fact, labor unions that traditionally organized workers in Arizona and New Mexico mining districts, in towns that bordered reservations, have been at best ambivalent toward American Indians. At worst, unions were outright hostile, viewing Native American workers as potential strikebreakers who depressed wages and working conditions for the rest of the membership. In mining towns such as Ajo and Bisbee, Arizona, or even Gallup, New Mexico, American Indians were not even afforded conventional company housing. Instead, they lived in segregated areas on the margins of those communities called "Indian villages" and performed jobs that were designated "Indian work." Union members would do little to challenge such discrimination until the 1970s, when they found themselves competing with Indians for jobs in large-scale, extractive industries and other corporate operations on reservation land. After that, Indian workers would demand access to those jobs, not as a civil right, but as a right to tribal sovereignty.

Since 1958, when workers at the Texas Zinc uranium processing mill tried to organize a union on the Navajo Reservation, the status of unions on reservation land has been in question. With the development of Indian gaming, this issue remains a difficult problem between trade union activists who assert their rights under federal labor law and tribal authorities who insist on their sovereign jurisdiction. In some cases, native labor activists have successfully bridged this divide by demanding that their tribal governments enact guidelines to promote safer working conditions and cooperate with unions to develop apprenticeship programs for young American Indian workers. In 1977, Native Americans throughout the United States developed the Tribal Employment Rights Ordinance, an initiative independent of other federal programs that gives hiring preference to Native American workers in non-tribally operated companies on reservation lands.

Other workers of color, Mexican-Americans and African-Americans in particular, transformed their unions into social movements that advocated broad, civil rights agendas. Many American Indians eventually joined unions such as the United Farm Workers, United Mine Workers, and Laborers' International and significantly improved their wages and working conditions as a result. But unions themselves did not serve as vehicles for social justice, as they had under César Chávez and A. Philip Randolph. American Indian working-class history is complicated by a long-fought struggle over land and sovereignty, treaties, and armed resistance. A civil rights agenda, one that ensured equal rights for all American citizens, did not adequately address the demands of indigenous communities that also wanted power over their own lands, cultures, and economies. Labor demands might translate well into civil rights, but not into treaty obligations.

COLLEEN O'NEILL

References and Further Reading

Adams, David. *Education for Extinction: American Indians and the Boarding School Experience, 1875–1928.* Lawrence: University Press of Kansas, 1995.
Bernstein, Alison. *American Indians and World War II: Toward a New Era in Indian Affairs.* Norman: University of Oklahoma Press 1991.
Fixico, Donald Lee. *Termination and Relocation: Federal Indian Policy, 1945–1960.* Albuquerque: University of New Mexico Press, 1986.
Harmon, Alexandra. *Indians in the Making: Ethnic Relations and Indian Identities around Puget Sound.* Berkeley: University of California Press, 1998.
Hosmer, Brian C. *American Indians in the Marketplace: Persistence and Innovation among the Menominees and Metlakatlans, 1870–1920.* Lawrence: University Press of Kansas, 1999.
Hosmer, Brian C., and Colleen O'Neill, eds. *Native Pathways: American Indian Culture and Economic Development in the Twentieth Century.* Boulder: University Press of Colorado, 2004.
Hoxie, Frederick E. *Parading through History: The Making of the Crow Nation, 1805–1935.* New York: Cambridge University Press, 1995.
Knack, Martha, and Alice Littlefield, eds. *Native Americans and Wage Labor: Ethnohistorical Perspectives.* Norman: University of Oklahoma Press, 1996.
Knight, Rolf. *Indians at Work: An Informal History of Native American Labour in British Columbia, 1858–1930.* Vancouver: New Star Books, 1978.
Meeks, Eric V. "The Tohono O'odham, Wage Labor, and Resistant Adaptation, 1900–1930." *The Western Historical Quarterly* 34, no. 4 (Winter 2003): 469–490.
Myer, Melissa. *The White Earth Tragedy: Ethnicity and Dispossession at a Minnesota Anishinaabe Reservation.* Lincoln: University of Nebraska Press, 1994.
O'Neill, Colleen. *Working the Navajo Way: Labor and Culture in the Twentieth Century.* Lawrence: University Press of Kansas, 2005.
Pickering, Kathleen Ann. *Lakota Culture, World Economy.* Lincoln: University of Nebraska Press, 2000.
Rosier, Paul C. *Rebirth of the Blackfeet Nation, 1912–1954.* Lincoln: University of Nebraska Press, 2001.
Stuart, Paul. *Nations within a Nation: Historical Statistics of American Indians.* New York: Greenwood Press, 1987.

NESTOR, AGNES (JUNE 24, 1880–1948)
Progressive Era Trade Unionist

Agnes Nestor, a self-described pioneer woman trade unionist, was a groundbreaking labor leader and political activist during the Progressive Era. Nestor dedicated her life to the promotion of workingwomen's needs. To this end, she advocated for women's unionization, protective legislation, and woman suffrage. Her successes make Nestor one of the most influential and significant female labor leaders of the early twentieth century.

Agnes Nestor was born in Grand Rapids, Michigan, on June 24, 1880. Her mother, Anna McEwan, suffered a lifetime of health problems after working in the cotton mills of upstate New York as a child. Agnes's father, Thomas Nestor, was a machinist by trade and active in machinists' unions and the Knights of Labor. In Grand Rapids, he managed a grocery store and served several terms in the city government. In 1896, an economic depression drove Thomas to seek work in Chicago. His family followed several months later in 1897.

Agnes began working for wages when she moved to Chicago with her family. She found a job as a glove maker at Eisendrath's Glove Factory, where she stayed for the next nine years. Almost immediately,

Nestor realized the disadvantages of the piecework system. She shared grievances with the women in her department, such as having to purchase their own needles and oil for the sewing machines, having their pay docked for the cost of power to run their machines, and dealing with disrespectful foremen. When the male glove cutters at Eisendrath's went on strike in the spring of 1898, Nestor and the glove makers followed suit in order to make their own demands on management. Nestor quickly assumed a leadership role amongst the women workers, and with the support of the Chicago Federation of Labor (CFL), the strikers won. As a result of her experiences organizing on the picket line, Nestor became convinced that women required separate all-women's locals in order to see their interests properly served. She went on to organize the Glove Makers' Local 2 at Eisendrath's in 1902 (Local 1 was all men). During this time, Nestor also published the first of her many written pieces, "A Day's Work Making Gloves." Nestor's early commitment to workingwomen's self-organization shaped her political approach and activity in the labor movement.

As Nestor agitated for workingwomen's needs, she encountered an extremely supportive environment, both from her family and the labor movement. The experiences and pro-union stance of her parents supported Nestor's ideology from the days of her first strike. Her father, in particular, applauded his daughter's unionism, and he instructed her from his own experiences in the labor movement. The strike at Eisendrath's allowed Nestor to work with the Chicago Federation of Labor Organization Committee. Sophie Becker, the only woman on the CFL Organization Committee, particularly inspired Nestor. In addition, Nestor regarded John Fitzpatrick, the head of the CFL Organization Committee at this time, as a great mentor and friend. Over the next few years, she often sought his advice and received his support. This network shaped Nestor as she rose to become a great labor leader.

As the first president of her Glove Makers' local, Nestor served as a delegate to a 1902 American Federation of Labor conference in Washington, DC, to organize the International Glove Workers Union of America (IGWUA). Nestor acted as an officer of the IGWUA from 1903 until her death in 1948. At the second IGWUA convention, held in Gloversville, New York, in 1903, Nestor made her first public speech and was elected vice president on the executive board of the union.

The summer of 1904 brought a great strike in the Chicago Stockyards, including some three thousand women workers. The Chicago branch of the National Women's Trade Union League (WTUL), formed in 1903, actively supported the strikers. The WTUL interested Nestor because it was the only organization of its time that sought to unionize women as a mechanism for social reform. As president of her local, Nestor attended a meeting of the Chicago WTUL at Hull-House, where she met Mary McDowell, Jane Addams, and Ellen Gates Starr. Nestor joined forces with the Chicago branch of the WTUL in 1904. She served on the national executive board in 1906 and also held the office of president of the Chicago branch from 1913 until her death in 1948.

In 1906, Nestor became the secretary-treasurer of the IGWUA, a full-time, paid position. This appointment marked Nestor's transition to full-time labor organizing. She continued to lead and organize women workers in various industries, including involvement in Chicago's first large strike for garment workers in 1911.

In addition to promoting women's self-organization, Nestor sought to support women workers through legislation. Beginning in 1909, Nestor and the WTUL lobbied every session of the state legislature for an eight-hour day for women until the bill finally passed in 1937. Nestor believed that protective laws would ensure greater security for workers than unions alone could provide. She stood against the National Woman's Party (NWP), which argued that protection for women would jeopardize the passage of the Equal Rights Amendment. In opposition, Nestor wrote a scathing critique of the NWP platform in her 1926 report of the Women's Industrial Conference.

Throughout her career, Nestor supported women's suffrage. Her experiences as a worker and organizer led Nestor to see suffrage as a key to better working conditions for women and children. She pointed out that the ballot ensured women's vote for worker safety and the appointment of female inspectors in the factories. In addition, women voters would have a voice in the appointment of police and court positions, two institutions that often turned against strikers. In 1910, Nestor outlined her position in her published piece "The Working Girl's Need for Suffrage."

Nestor's influence reached both the local and national levels. In 1914, President Wilson appointed Nestor to the Vocational Educational Commission, out of which came the 1917 Smith-Hughes Act, which offered federal aid to vocational education. Nestor ensured that women would properly benefit from this act, advocating that women needed support for technical training in addition to domestic science. Additionally, Nestor served on several wartime labor commissions and played a crucial role in the 1920 creation of the Department of Labor's Women's Bureau.

Nestor died on December 28, 1948. Eulogized as the workingwoman's best friend, Agnes Nestor helped to shape the role of women in the labor movement. Her commitment to workingwomen's needs informed her political approach and strategy for reform. As an early twentieth-century woman's trade unionist, Agnes Nestor stands out as a pioneering and prominent labor leader.

CATHERINE O. JACQUET

References and Further Reading

Hirsch, Susan E. "Agnes Nestor." In *Women Building Chicago, 1790–1990: A Biographical Dictionary*, edited by Rima Lunin Schultz and Adele Hast. Bloomington: Indiana University Press, 2001, 623–626.
Mason, Karen M. "Testing the Boundaries: Women, Politics, and Gender Roles in Chicago, 1890–1923." Ph.D. diss., University of Michigan, 1991.
Nestor, Agnes. "A Day's Work Making Gloves." 1898?
———. "The Eight-Hours Day." *The Survey* (December 30, 1916).
———. "The Experiences of a Pioneer Woman Trade Unionist." *American Federationist* 36 (August 1929).
———. "The Trend of Legislation Affecting Women's Hours of Labor." *Life and Labor* 7 (May 1917).
———. "Ushering in a New Day." *Life and Labor* 11 (June 1921).
———. "The Women's Industrial Conference." *American Federationist* 33 (March 1926).
———. *Woman's Labor Leader: An Autobiography of Agnes Nestor*. Rockwell, IL: Bellevue Books, 1954.

See also **Chicago Federation of Labor; Women's Trade Union League**

NEW ENGLAND ASSOCIATION OF FARMERS, MECHANICS, AND OTHER WORKING MEN

On February 16, 1832, more than 80 men gathered at the Marlborough Hotel on Washington Street in Boston's central commercial district to form the New England Association of Farmers, Mechanics, and Other Working Men (NEA). The NEA did indeed encompass farmers, mechanics, and other workingmen from the across the region, but the Association's leaders also included men who earned their living from "mental labor." Charles Douglas, the first president and editor of the organization's newspaper (*New England Artisan*), was a physician, and Jacob Frieze, the founding secretary, was a Universalist minister.

The NEA was distinct from—though certainly cognizant of—the trade unions and workingmen's political parties also active in the early 1830s. The Association addressed issues of immediate import to workers such as the demand for a 10-hour workday and broader topics such as the morality of child labor and the need for wider access to public education. The organization reached deliberately across occupational categories and class lines to build a coalition to improve working conditions and elevate workers' status. The NEA saw political action as an essential component of this struggle for labor rights but tried to avoid plunging into the hurly-burly of parties, campaigns, and electioneering.

The NEA's constitution, ratified at its first convention, included a public pledge that all its members work a 10-hour day—or risk expulsion from the organization. Moreover, the assembly set March 20 as the date to put the 10-hour workday into effect. No one mentioned the word "strike"; nevertheless, on March 20, 1832, ship caulkers, carpenters, painters, masons, and other tradesmen in Boston walked off their jobs and demanded the 10-hour day. Employer associations quickly countered with denunciations and lockouts; soon each strike collapsed. Though the NEA did not play a prominent role in leading these protests, the organization never denied that its call to action helped to inspire the work stoppages.

The Association also issued a report on education that focused on children in textile mills, their long hours of labor, and their lost opportunities for schooling. The report offered a disturbing account of young workers being exploited and kept in ignorance; of children growing up with stunted bodies and minds unprepared to assume the duties incumbent upon citizens in a republic. The authors recommended that "a committee of vigilance be appointed in each State" to publicize abuses at the workplace and petition legislatures for the 10-hour day and mandatory education for all children employed in factories. Thus, the NEA was one of the first labor reform organizations to insist that government had the right and the duty to regulate the conditions of labor, especially by legally limiting the length of the workday for those who could not secure such protections for themselves through negotiations or contracts. Here again, the Association never pursued this political petition drive with much consistency or vigor, but labor reform groups in the 1840s picked up on this campaign and often made legislation for the 10-hour day a centerpiece of their public pronouncements.

The NEA continued to press for a 10-hour workday and the education of factory children at its next convention in the Representatives' Chamber of the Massachusetts State House on September 6, 1832. Those assembled re-elected Charles Douglas as president; and taking note of the recent wave of failed strikes in Boston, the delegates retracted any plans to expel members or local affiliates who were compelled to work more than 10 hours a day. The Association learned quickly that public declarations had limited effect on recalcitrant employers and that workers should not be punished further for losing a courageous battle to limit working hours.

The Association returned to the Marlborough Hotel for its annual meeting on October 2, 1833. The organization's new president—William Thompson, a farmer from the western Massachusetts town of Northampton—was urged to appoint traveling lecturers who could help distribute copies of newspapers and convention proceedings across the region. At this same meeting, delegates from New Haven, Connecticut, noted the absence of representatives from factory towns and villages—despite the Association's sympathetic reports on the plight of industrial operatives. Thus, the NEA's ranks were missing an essential component of the emerging antebellum working class: textile operatives and urban women workers such as seamstresses and domestics.

This failure to bring women into the fold may have been a key reason why the Association disintegrated after one final lackluster meeting in the fall of 1834 in Northampton. By this time, the NEA was pursuing a strategy to recruit more members from rural areas. The organization published an address that never mentioned the 10-hour workday but focused instead on financial problems plaguing farmers. The Association demanded the repeal of what it proclaimed were unjust laws regulating mortgages, debt, banks, public education, and criminal courts and urged all its members to go to the ballot box to gain redress. The new emphasis on agrarian politics, despite the organization's insistence that it was still distinct from any political party, further marginalized factory operatives and other wage-earning women and made the NEA a close adjunct of the Massachusetts Workingmen's Party. The descent into the electoral maelstrom of Jacksonian Era politics may well have sealed the Association's fate—after the 1834 campaign season concluded, the NEA was never heard from again.

DAVID A. ZONDERMAN

References and Further Reading

Commons, John R., et al. *History of Labor in the United States.* Vol. 1, Ch. 5. New York: Macmillan, 1918.
Darling, Arthur B. "The Workingmen's Party in Massachusetts, 1833–1834." *American Historical Review* 29 (October 1923): 81–86.
Murphy, Teresa. *Ten Hours' Labor: Religion, Reform, and Gender in Early New England.* Ithaca, NY: Cornell University Press, 1992.

NEW ENGLAND LABOR REFORM LEAGUE

The New England Labor Reform League (NELRL) held its first convention on January 27–29, 1869, in the Melodeon Theatre on Washington Street in Boston's central commercial district. The league was essentially the brainchild of Ezra Heywood, a 40-year-old Congregational minister turned Garrisonian abolitionist, pacifist, philosophical anarchist, and advocate of both "free love" and his own version of labor reform. Heywood's abiding commitment to the NELRL—calling meetings, renting halls, writing resolutions, and publishing pronouncements—kept the organization going for nearly two decades. However, his idiosyncratic definition of labor reform also triggered irrevocable splits with other activists and advocates and relegated this organization to the sidelines in the broader movement for justice at the workplace.

When Heywood wrote his call for the League's founding convention, he had the support of local Boston labor newspapers, such as the *American Workman* and the *Daily Evening Voice*; unions, such as the Knights of St. Crispin (shoe workers); and activists, such as Ira Steward and George McNeill. He believed that this new organization would embody his vision of a truly classless movement, dissolving differences between working-class activists and middle-class reformers and restructuring relations between labor and capital. To realize this bold ideal, Heywood insisted on opening the speaker's rostrum to a range of nostrums on taxes, tariffs, and currency, as well as discussions of working hours and wages. He placed great emphasis on debate and public edification, and not on specific plans for collective action. If Heywood showed any preferences among the cacophony of competing schemes, he opted for a broad individualistic, antimonopolistic, philosophically anarchistic critique rooted in currency reform.

Once Heywood let his preferences be known, activists such as Steward and McNeill—outspoken proponents of the emerging postwar eight-hour movement—quickly sought to extricate themselves from any alliances with the mercurial ex-minister. By the end of the League's second convention, in May 1869, hopes for a stable coalition between eight-hour advocates and Heywood's supporters were dashed in a series of bitter floor debates. Steward's camp insisted that labor reform had to be both pragmatic and programmatic—workers could not waste their time debating monopoly power in the abstract; they had to restrain corporate power at the point of production by first limiting the hours of labor. Heywood clung to his definition of the League as a forum where many visions of labor reform could be discussed (including his own preference for currency reform). Yet, even as he insisted that the meeting was open to all opinions, Heywood tried to control the agenda through prewritten resolutions. Many workers left the conclave bitterly resentful of what they saw as Heywood's high-handed and hypocritical tactics.

Steward and McNeill's departure meant that Heywood no longer had to deal with organized opposition to his leadership of the League or to his policy of free-ranging (some would say unfocused) debate. The few workers who turned out for the League's fall 1869 meeting left before adjournment, grumbling about the gathering's antilabor tone and the constant chatter concerning party politics. Thus, within less than a year of its inception, the League lost most of its initial support from working-class men and women in Boston. Despite its name, many workers concluded that this organization simply had no idea what labor reform meant to people on the shop floor. The League's resolutions continually subordinated basic workplace demands to vague schemes for financial transformations that were supposed to cure all social ills. In reality, however, such ideas often benefited only those with far more money than the workers whom the League professed so much sympathy for. Workers insisted that labor reform was not an abstract set of propositions to be bandied about; social change had to be rooted in a clearly defined course of collective action to secure specific improvements in working conditions. The growing rift between Heywood's remaining supporters in the League and the broader labor reform community in Boston revolved around two competing maps of social change—one started with theories about financial reform and their dissemination through public debate; the other began with improving conditions on the job as a way of liberating workers to become agents for broader economic and political transformations. The fight in this League was seen by many participants as a contest for the ideological soul of labor reform itself.

Whatever the NELRL's faults and fault lines, the treasurer's report at the January 1870 convention revealed that this league was financially robust compared with most other reform groups of the early postwar period. The organization collected nearly five thousand dollars in its first year from book sales, membership dues, and donations. Most of the funds were expended to distribute 30,000 books and pamphlets, sponsor lectures, and rent halls for meetings. Clearly, the League was spending a substantial amount of time and money to promote its brand of labor reform, but the group's strategy remained rooted in conventions, resolutions, and publications. The organization continued to frown on actively organizing workers or working to rebuild its tattered alliances with other labor reform groups. In fact, the more that eight-hour associations and trade unions dismissed the league as irrelevant to their campaigns for workers' rights, the more the NELRL rejected these groups as narrow-minded special interests that underestimated their own constituents' intelligence.

To their credit, Heywood and his wife, Angela, frequently criticized the exploitation of women in the urban economy, especially those working in the garment trade and in domestic service. The Heywoods shared a conviction that equitable pay for workingwomen was part of a much larger crusade to gain full economic, social, political, and sexual equality for all women. They also believed that equal rights should be extended to all people regardless of race, nationality, or religion and that universal equity lay at the heart of a truly reformed society. Yet, here again, the Heywoods stopped at grand pronouncements and rarely offered any concrete strategies for achieving social equality.

By the mid-1870s, Heywood's antimonopoly rhetoric became so pronounced that his convention resolutions lacked even a veneer of sympathy for basic workplace reforms. He publicly condemned the entire movement for a shorter workday because he saw it as inextricably linked with party politics and a corrupt state. Furthermore, he proclaimed that employers deserved the League's "full sympathy in resisting legislative or trade-union interference." Heywood's aggressively individualistic, antistatist, and now avowedly anti-union pronouncements signaled his and the League's nearly complete break with every other labor reform organization. The League became a hollow shell with few if any working-class members, content to preach its own negative version of labor reform to a rapidly diminishing circle of adherents. Yet the group continued to meet, at least on an annual basis, well into the 1880s. It even pointed to its own longevity as proof that its antagonistic definition of labor reform was actually the most accurate assessment of social conditions in Gilded Age America, though few others cared to listen to such claims.

For most of its nearly two-decade existence, the New England Labor Reform League sought to liberate all individuals from what the organization defined as unnatural legal, political, economic, and social constraints. Many workers embraced antimonopoly arguments—especially those criticisms directed at manufacturing corporations and financial institutions. But Heywood insisted that his philosophy of individual freedom also compelled him to condemn trade unions, producer co-operatives, and legislative limits on the workday—the very institutions and ideas that many other labor reformers considered essential building blocks for workers' emancipation. Heywood often spoke with conviction and sympathy about the injustices heaped on American workers and the need for equity and fairness in American society. But the organization he led became a labor reform group opposed to virtually all popular ideas for labor reform. Thus, the NELRL doomed itself to irrelevance within the campaign it claimed to be championing.

DAVID A. ZONDERMAN

References and Further Reading

Blatt, Martin Henry. *Free Love and Anarchism: The Biography of Ezra Heywood*. Urbana: University of Illinois Press, 1989.

Montgomery, David. *Beyond Equality: Labor and the Radical Republicans, 1862–1872*. Urbana: University of Illinois Press, 1981.

See also **Knights of St. Crispin and the Daughters of St. Crispin; McNeil, George Edwin; Steward, Ira**

NEW ENGLAND WORKINGMEN'S ASSOCIATION

Organized labor in New England all but disappeared following the Panic of 1837, but as the economy began to revive in the early 1840s, so too did labor agitation. New England workers experienced industrial life in ways that varied by industry, sex, and skill. But widespread complaints of low wages, long hours, weak control over apprenticeship, and intensified labor conditions brought on by the speedup, stretchout, and premium system reflected rising discontent. In Fall River, Lowell, Manchester, Dover, Milford, Woonsocket, and throughout New England during the early 1840s, workers responded by waging petition campaigns and organizing community-based associations to improve labor conditions. In June 1844, one such organization, the newly organized Fall River Mechanics' Association, issued a call to New England workers to assemble in convention. The "prevailing system of labor," they charged, was "at war with the . . . physical, intellectual, social, moral and religious" well-being of labor. A convention, they suggested, would bring together "the united wisdom and judgment of various Mechanics' Associations," creating a force of "incalculable benefit." On October 16, 1844, delegates convened at Boston's Fanueil Hall to create the New England Workingmen's Association (NEWA).

Hoping to maximize participation by the region's workers and their supporters, NEWA delegates set an inclusive course for the organization. After a heated debate about participation, delegates ruled to open their doors to "all those interested in the elevation of the Producing Classes, and Industrial Reform, and the extinction of Slavery and Servitude in all their forms." Thomas Almy, the editor of *The Mechanic*, the Fall River newspaper that issued the call, observed that perspectives on reform were "as dissimilar as are the conditions of society." Women did not attend the founding convention, though a "ladies association" from Fall River provided a banner proclaiming "Union is Strength." Despite their initial absence, women played a vital role in NEWA, marking a radical departure from previous labor organizations.

Opening itself to widespread participation also meant dealing with competing visions of labor's interests. Mechanics made up the majority of the 207 delegates present, but the large numbers of reformers in attendance aggressively pushed their own reform agendas. Representatives from Brook Farm, such as George Ripley, Parke Goodwin, and L. W. Rychman, used the convention to convince delegates of the virtues of Fourierism, while George Henry Evans, Thomas Devyr, and Alvan E. Bovay tried to win converts to their ideas on land reform. Working-class delegates objected to both of these grand utopian undertakings, though not vigorously enough to derail them. Many workers were interested in the idea of establishing producers' cooperatives, in which labor, not capital, would be rewarded with the fruits of its own labor. Working-class delegates expressed universal support for the 10-hour workday.

Advocacy for a 10-hour workday had deep roots in the region, though the movement in the 1840s took a new and decidedly political direction. In the 1830s, the New England Association of Farmers, Mechanics, and Other Workingmen had tried unsuccessfully to secure such ends by organizing regional strikes. But NEWA eschewed strikes in favor of petitioning. The political emphasis of NEWA was no doubt influenced by President Martin Van Buren's executive order of March 31, 1840, establishing a 10-hour workday for all federal employees. Unable to secure protection under this federal legislation, New England workers stressed the need for state legislatures to take up the 10-hour challenge. The political emphasis of the movement for the 10-hour workday limited female participation in some respects, most notably at the ballot box, but the commitment to petitioning state legislatures centered on tactics and skills familiar to female members, particularly those engaged in raising abolitionist petitions. Women in Lowell, Manchester, Dover, and elsewhere organized Female Labor Reform Associations (FLRA) that operated under the umbrella of NEWA, providing energy, organization, and moral authority to the movement.

One of the most effective organizing tools for NEWA was the newspaper *The Voice of Industry*, initially published in Fitchburg by William F. Young. In April 1845, *The Mechanic* ceased publication, but by October, NEWA made *The Voice* its official organ, moved the paper to Lowell, and appointed Sarah Bagley, the president of the Lowell FLRA, to its three-person publishing committee. Huldah J. Stone, the secretary of the Lowell FLRA, served as a correspondent to the paper. In early 1846, the Lowell FLRA purchased the paper's press and type and, over the next couple of years, held numerous fundraising activities to pay for it.

Throughout its brief existence, groups vied for influence over NEWA. NEWA held its second convention in Lowell in March 1845. Horace Greeley, Robert Owen, Albert Brisbane, and other Associationists spoke, dominating the meeting, leading the president, W. H. Channing, to note: "Much complaint was made by the members about the want of interest felt by the workingmen for the cause of reform." At the third convention in Boston, May 1845, Associationists again dominated the convention with extended discussion of Fourierism. Associationists and land reformers were largely absent from the fourth convention in Fall River, September 1846, leaving working-class members to re-assert more immediate and practical labor reforms, such as the 10-hour day. Members of NEWA assembled in convention in Lynn in January 1846, Manchester in March 1846, and in Nashua September 1846. At the Nashua convention, the New England Workingmen's Association renamed itself the Labor Reform League of New England.

The League met in Boston in January 1847 and remained under the influence of the Associationists until the organization's disappearance. In July, however, 10-hour advocates scored a victory when the New Hampshire legislature, under the weight of a statewide petition drive, passed the first state law limiting the workday to 10 hours. It was a hollow victory. The law contained a clause limiting the workday to 10 hours, "unless otherwise agreed by the parties." Many manufacturers merely issued their employees new contracts containing the clause, with a simple command: sign or be blacklisted. Workingmen and workingwomen gradually lost interest in NEWA. Members who had earlier advocated cooperative stores became involved in the New England Protective Union movement, while other elements became involved in the Industrial Congresses of the 1850s. By 1849, the entire Association disappeared.

ROBERT MACIESKI

References and Further Reading

Blewett, Mary H. *Constant Turmoil: The Politics of Industrial Life in Nineteenth-Century New England*. Amherst: University of Massachusetts Press, 2000.
Commons, John R., et al. *A Documentary History of American Industrial Society*. Vol. VIII Cleveland, OH: Arthur H. Clark Company, 1910.
Dublin, Thomas. *Women at Work: The Transformation of Work and Community in Lowell, Massachusetts, 1826–1860*. New York: Columbia University Press, 1979.
Foner, Philip S. *History of the Labor Movement*. Vol. 1, *From Colonial Times to the Founding of the American Federation of Labor*. New York: International Publishers, 1975.
Lazerow, Jama. *Religion and the Working Class in Antebellum America*. Washington, DC: Smithsonian Institution Press, 1995.
Murphy, Teresa. "The Petitioning of Artisans and Operatives: Means and Ends in the Struggle for a Ten-Hour Day." In *American Artisans: Crafting Social Identity, 1750–1850*, edited by Howard B. Rock, Paul A. Gilje, and Robert Asher. Baltimore: Johns Hopkins University Press, 1995, pp. 77–97.
Ware, Norman. *The Industrial Worker, 1840–1860*. Chicago: Ivan R. Dee Publishers, 1990.

See also **Brisbane, Albert; Evans, George Henry; Fourierism; Luther, Seth; New England Association of Farmers, Mechanics, and Other Workingmen; New England Labor Reform League**

NEW LEFT

The New Left was a movement of white, college-educated youth that stood for radical democracy in the United States and around the world. The American New Left existed from around 1960 into the early 1970s. The idea of a "New Left" originated in Great Britain in the 1950s. This term was associated there with young Marxists unhappy with existing left-wing politics. The radical American sociologist C. Wright Mills, author of *The Power Elite* (1956), brought the term "New Left" to the U.S. scene, penning a "Letter to the New Left" in 1960, published in *New Left Review*, the journal of the British New Left, and then republished in the United States. Besides straddling the Atlantic, Mills offered a connection to an earlier era in American radicalism, having published political writings since the 1940s, a time when the labor movement stood at the center of the American left.

The relationship between labor and the New Left was far weaker, although not nonexistent. The young American radicals' thinking echoed the argument Mills had made in his first book, *The New Men of Power* (1948), that union leaders had become absorbed into the "power elite." The young leftists, like many liberals, were persuaded that the United

States in the 1950s had become, as John Kenneth Galbraith put it in the title of his 1958 book, *The Affluent Society*. Economic inequality persisted, as the continued presence of the poor attested. But the industrial working class, most young radicals feared, had become comfortable enough that they were "part of the system," no longer natural rebels. Members of the New Left saw a need for a challenge to this system if its flaws were to be rectified, but they expected that, with perhaps a small number of exceptions, that challenge would not come from labor. Instead, they looked to African-Americans, who were rising up against the Jim Crow system of white supremacy in the South, to youth in general, and to the poor. From the beginning, the New Left's strategic thinking about change in America was tied to a hope for insurgencies and a determination to support, and perhaps to help guide, such insurgencies.

Post-Scarcity Radicalism

The New Left had several sources and inspirations, in addition to Mills's writings. These included the civil rights movement, especially its youth wing, as embodied in the Student Nonviolent Coordinating Committee (established in 1960); the pacifist radicalism of the 1950s, as encountered in the pages of *Liberation* magazine (founded in 1956); the journal *Studies on the Left*, published in Madison, Wisconsin, starting in 1959 under the influence of the historian William Appleman Williams, which indicted American liberals for their collusion with capitalism and imperialism; and even critical religious thought such as that encountered in university YMCAs and YWCAs (Young Men's/Women's Christian Associations) across the country. Marxism and other traditional economically oriented leftist perspectives were present in this mix of influences, but other moral and analytical perspectives predominated.

The young radicals began by thinking that university-educated people like them would pioneer new ideas that would make life worth living in the America of the future, even as they would fight rearguard battles against the remaining vestiges of unfairness and authoritarianism, which they saw epitomized in southern segregationism and the power that its representatives wielded in the U.S. Congress. All of this they promoted under the slogan "participatory democracy." They pictured organized labor as a potential partner in pursuing this agenda, but not as moral leaders of a New Left alliance. New Left activists formed their main organization in 1960 when they changed the name of the Student League for Industrial Democracy

(SLID), a small union-funded group, to Students for a Democratic Society (SDS). The name change indicated a shift away from economic issues to a less class-oriented focus on issues of power. Yet the young activists hoped to retain their ties to sympathetic labor unions. Their 1962 manifesto, the "Port Huron Statement," in which they advanced an agenda focused on the imbalances of power that they discerned in the U.S. political system—imbalances that, at that date, they connected only obliquely to economic power relations and inequalities—was adopted at a Michigan retreat owned by the United Auto Workers (UAW). SDS sought to point the way toward a newly meaningful life in a society whose material wealth held the capacity to provide the essentials of physical existence to all. New Left thought reflected a belief that the United States had entered a "post-scarcity" age, when the basic struggle for survival need not dominate people's lives. Ever fewer person-hours were required to produce the economic value needed to sustain the country's population. While labor leaders in the 1960s tended to worry over the prospects of increased unemployment that this trend augured, New Left radicals, as well as many liberals, thought that the coming challenge was to find ways of making increasing amounts of leisure time meaningful, to enhance one's "quality of life" rather than merely piling up ever greater quantities of goods. The New Left did not grapple seriously with the question of how to ensure a sufficiently broad dispersal of the country's growing wealth so as to make this "leisure problem" the salient one for all Americans.

In keeping with its theme of honoring and promoting democracy, the New Left took a "plague on both your houses" attitude toward the Cold War between the United States and the Soviet Union. The young radicals saw neither superpower promoting democracy around the world; instead, both sides simply pursued power and sought to make pawns of peoples in the Third World. Moreover, members of SDS felt that the intellectual and political battles over communism had wasted the energies of the previous generation in America and that the harsh anticommunism that had dominated political life in the 1950s had done much damage to the cause of democratic progress by stifling dissent and promoting conservatism. The New Left's announcement that it intended to stay on the sidelines of the Cold War was controversial and earned them accusations of naïveté about communism, or worse, from the start. The young radicals, while they had no use for the Soviets, sympathized with Third World revolutionaries, thinking that such forces might represent a middle way between the dogmas and corruptions of the United States and the USSR. They took an admiring view of the Cuban revolution in particular, even viewing the youthful cadres of nationalist movements of Africa and Latin America as models they might emulate in the United States. Still, early SDS activists sometimes indicated they wished to moot international issues, to place them on the back burner so that they could focus on the issues of power and authenticity within the United States. The escalation of the Vietnam War in the 1960s would make that impossible.

A Host of Challenges

The environment in which the New Left operated changed drastically in the second half of the 1960s, and the movement was transformed in turn. Soon the slogans changed from "protest" to "resistance" and on to "revolution." Several factors converged to create a maelstrom of political change.

First, the New Left could not help but oppose the U.S. effort to vanquish the Vietnamese revolution. In the early 1960s, the young radicals already had developed a critical view of U.S. actions in the Cold War. Their anti-imperialism made the war, after it was expanded dramatically in 1965, come to seem like their most urgent business. It also fed the New Left's galloping estrangement from the U.S. social and political system, in its mind's eye changing the insurgencies it always had wished to sponsor from levers for social reform into battering rams that might bring down a violent system. The structures of that system closest at hand for the young radicals were the universities themselves. The radicals became increasingly knowledgeable about the involvement of U.S. universities in doing war-related research, and this prodded the New Left to view universities in a new light: as agents of social repression, hostile to social change, and logical targets of leftist agitation. The New Left's absorption in the war issue spurred the development of a set of critical perspectives on the U.S. role in the world that had a strong and unprecedented influence upon U.S. intellectual life.

Second, the African-American movement turned away from the doctrines of nonviolence and interracialism that had characterized its early years, and its increased militancy affected the New Left, just as the black movement had inspired the New Left in earlier years. White leftists no longer could entertain notions of enlisting the black or the poor as the shock troops, figuratively speaking, in New Left scenarios of social change. Some white radicals envisioned the relationship working the other way around, with them in a supporting role. In part, the message of the new "black power" movement among African-Americans was that white radicals should organize among whites to advance the cause of social transformation and should cease involving themselves in the affairs of people of color.

Third, the counterculture of white middle-class youth, associated with the use of hallucinogenic drugs, the loosening of customary sexual mores, communal living, and a rejection of acquisitive consumerism, gained a legion of followers across the country in the late 1960s and early 1970s. The New Left felt it had to respond to this movement, for it was a momentous development among the only constituency the New Left had—white college-educated youth. Many young leftists became deeply involved in the counterculture, both out of such strategic considerations and because they were moved by the same yearning for a more authentic life that moved their nonpolitical peers. Leftists involved in the "hippie" counterculture hoped that such an alternative culture could have a profound political impact. By winning ever more members of the educated young away from loyalty to the dominant social system, a politically conscious counterculture might provide the key to a bloodless revolution.

A fourth development of the post-1965 years was the rise of a new feminist movement, which spread from its initial reform constituency to young firebrands, most of them in the New Left or the black movement, who promoted more total change in social practices. This emergence of "radical feminism" had a profound impact on the New Left. Many of the men in the left derided it as unimportant, but resisted it fiercely, thus betraying the centrality of its concerns to the youth culture in which the New Left was deeply implicated. But feminism's disintegrative impact on the New Left arrived only after the radicalizing effect of the three developments mentioned above had taken hold. The trajectory of the New Left in its second phase—changing from a reform movement with some daring ideas to a revolutionary movement experimenting with different strategies for promoting a political upheaval—resulted from these other developments, not from the rise of feminism. The rift between men and women in the movement over gender issues shaped the final years of the New Left, after 1968.

The New Working Class

The post-1965 phase of the New Left's existence featured one important intellectual development that bears special relevance to the question of the New Left's relations with the labor movement. That is the development of what was dubbed "new working-class theory." Since the New Left's membership was college-educated and largely "raised in at least modest comfort," as the "Port Huron Statement" put it, it is widely and correctly viewed as a middle-class movement. Yet education and standard of living are not the only ways to define one's class location. Some New Left radicals, starting in 1966, asserted that college-educated young people formed a new working class, one whose future occupations might be salaried and would require bachelor's degrees, but an exploited set of employees nonetheless. This emphasis on one's relation to the means of production basically expressed an updated Marxist analysis.

The appeal of this analysis to New Left radicals stemmed from the dawning realization within the movement that its only base of support lay in the college-educated white youth that populated this new working class, a realization that the black movement drove home with its assertion that radicals within each major social group in U.S. society should organize among their peers alone. New working-class theory was a way of understanding and justifying the simple fact that white middle-class youth were basically on their own in the New Left. This theory said that this relatively privileged youth was not a parasitic social class, living off the surplus created by truly exploited people and out of touch with the experience of oppression. It said that New Left radicals and their peers were, instead, central to the unfolding drama of social as well as cultural change in the United States and morally justified in trying to bring down a system that oppressed not only others but them, too. Morally it did not matter that the New Left had weak and conflicted relations with the labor movement, if the New Left actually spoke on behalf of a new segment of labor, one unrepresented by the trade-union movement.

The vogue of new working-class theory passed by the end of the 1960s, as the war and the worsening racial conflict in the United States commanded immediate attention from the New Left. It became harder to assert that the New Left should content itself with tending its own fields. Many New Left radicals after 1968 departed into desperate, if usually feckless, efforts to support the struggles of African-American militants and Vietnamese revolutionaries. Yet, at the same time, many others in the New Left immersed themselves further in counterculture and feminist activities, announcing in deeds if not in words that they would continue to work for the development of a dissident consciousness within the white middle class/ new working class of which they were members. These two different emphases, which sometimes overlapped in the lives of individual activists who maintained multiple commitments, were the lasting legacies of the New Left. New Left radicals sided with domestic and foreign insurgencies by palpably subordinate peoples against the U.S. power structure, and they sided with themselves, nurturing seeds of dissidence among the white college-educated population. Because the New Left in general did not view organized labor as representatives of an oppressed minority poised for insurgency, because the early leaders of SDS, who had at least hoped to maintain an alliance with liberal union leaders, had been eclipsed by younger radicals with less interest in labor, and because initially sympathetic labor officials had been estranged by the New Left's increasing radicalism, the traditional labor movement never attained a central role in New Left thought.

DOUG ROSSINOW

References and Further Reading

Chun, Lin. *The British New Left*. Edinburgh: Edinburgh University Press, 1993.

Evans, Sara. *Personal Politics: The Roots of Women's Liberation in the Civil Rights Movement and the New Left*. New York: Alfred A. Knopf, 1979.

Gosse, Van. *Where the Boys Are: Cuba, Cold War America, and the Making of a New Left*. London: Verso Books, 1993.

Isserman, Maurice. *If I Had a Hammer...: The Death of the Old Left and the Birth of the New Left*. New York: Basic Books, 1987.

Levy, Peter B. *The New Left and Labor in the 1960s*. Urbana: University of Illinois Press, 1993.

Mattson, Kevin. *Intellectuals in Action: The Origins of the New Left and Radical Liberalism, 1945–1970*. University Park, PA: Penn State University Press, 2002.

McMillian, John, and Paul Buhle, eds. *The New Left Revisited*. Philadelphia: Temple University Press, 2003.

Miller, James. *"Democracy Is in the Streets": From Port Huron to the Siege of Chicago*. New York: Simon & Schuster, 1987.

Rossinow, Doug. *The Politics of Authenticity: Liberalism, Christianity, and the New Left in America*. New York: Columbia University Press, 1998.

Vickers, George R. *The Formation of the New Left: The Early Years*. Lexington, MA: Lexington Books, 1975.

NEW ORLEANS GENERAL STRIKE (1892)

This strike came two months after the Homestead Strike in Pennsylvania and two years before the great Pullman Strike of 1894. As Roger Shugg wrote in a 1938 article in *The Louisiana Historical Quarterly*, it was "the first general strike in American history to enlist both skilled and unskilled labor, black and white, and to paralyze the life of a great city." The strike involved at least 20,000 workers in 49 AFL unions. Two delegates from each union orchestrated the strike in a Workingman's Amalgamated Council that represented black and white alike. Their demands included union recognition, the 10-hour day, and a preferential closed shop. Workers from every trade and skill level participated in the strike, including the organized hatters, shoe clerks, and musicians, but the powerful waterfront unions did not play an active role.

The strike began because the employers refused to grant union recognition. On November 5, 1892, all of the Council's member unions—including the streetcar drivers, the electric, light, and gas workers, and the marine and stationary firemen—responded to the general strike call. The mass walkouts happened at a peak time in seasonal business and shut down the city for three days. No violence was associated with the strike, even though the pickets left the city in darkness for three nights. Mayor John Fitzpatrick, a former longshoreman, supported the workers and resisted sending out the police against them, but Governor Murphy J. Foster backed the business interests. His threat to call out the state militia and impose martial law broke the strike. In poststrike arbitration, the workers won the 10-hour day and overtime pay, but the united employers refused to grant union recognition. After the strike, a lawsuit filed in Federal District Court charged 44 union leaders with conspiracy to restrain trade, but the Federal Circuit Court postponed indefinitely this first effort to invoke the Sherman Anti-Trust Act against labor.

In *Origins of the New South*, C. Vann Woodward argued that the New Orleans general strike of 1892 challenged the "Old South labor philosophy of the New South doctrinaires." Two years after a state law pioneered Jim Crow on Louisiana railcars, the Workingman's Amalgamated Council certainly demonstrated that the many races of workers could join to resist the exploitation of organized labor. Both the Council and the strike represented the peak of a remarkable era. Since at least the 1870s, strong black unions and the structure of segregation had forced the organized workers to find terms to accommodate all. The results were profound. Eric Arnesen noted that by 1886, most New Orleanians in the trades commanded the same wage scale for the same work, regardless of race. In the next four years, the craft unions outpaced the Knights of Labor throughout the state. Between 1891 and 1892, more new AFL unions were chartered in Louisiana than elsewhere in the South, a handful fewer than Ohio, Indiana, and Illinois. The general strike was a product of that momentum, but it also marked the end of the era.

Scholars estimate that half the population of the city supported the Council, but the allied business interests presented an even more formidable front.

The united employers were represented by the Board of Trade and commanded support from most newspapers in the city, the commodity exchanges, the railway lines, and the governor of the State of Louisiana. When state power decided the strike, the employers learned an important lesson. Partly as a result, they determined they must develop an alliance with the leaders of the Choctaw Club, a new political machine on the rise in the late 1890s. Meanwhile, labor's biracial alliance collapsed. After a devastating 1894 strike, competition for work and white-on-black violence destroyed the structure of co-operation, and organized labor did not recover for almost a decade.

EDIE AMBROSE

References and Further Reading

Arnesen, Eric. *Waterfront Workers of New Orleans: Race, Class, and Politics, 1882–1923*. Oxford: Oxford University Press, 1991.

Fairclough, Adam. "The Public Utilities Industry in New Orleans: A Study in Capital, Labor, and Government, 1894–1929." *Journal of Louisiana History* 22 (Winter 1981).

Marshall, F. Ray. *Labor in the South*. Cambridge, MA: Harvard University Press, 1967.

Northrup, Herbert R. "The New Orleans Longshoremen." *Political Science Quarterly* 57 (1942).

Rosenberg, Daniel. *New Orleans Dockworkers: Race, Labor, and Unionism, 1892–1923*. New York: State University of New York Press, 1988.

Shugg, Robert W. "The New Orleans General Strike of 1892." *The Louisiana Historical Quarterly* 21 (1938).

Wells, Dave, and Jim Stodder. "A Short History of New Orleans Dockworkers." *Radical America* (1976).

See also **American Federation of Labor; Gilded Age; Industrial Workers of the World; Injunctions**

NEW SOUTH

In the wake of the Civil War, an emerging cohort of business entrepreneurs and newspaper editors advocated the building of a "New South" based on the growth of southern industry, the diversification of agriculture, and the attraction of northern investment. It was time to "put business before politics," proclaimed the editor of the *Atlanta Constitution* and New South booster Henry Grady, in a famous 1886 speech urging sectional reconciliation and southern economic development. "The Old South rested everything on slavery and agriculture," he continued. "The New South presents a perfect democracy...and a diversified industry that meets the complex needs of this complex age."

The "New South" did experience economic growth and attract outside capital. Between 1869 and 1899, the region's manufacturing output and value of products multiplied six times, and capital investment increased 10-fold. Nevertheless, the South continued to lag behind the rapidly expanding manufacturing base of the northern states; with nearly a third of the nation's population in 1900, the region was responsible for only 10% of national nonagricultural income. Much of the South's economic development rested on extractive industries like timber, naval stores, and mining or low-wage manufacturing based on agricultural products, like tobacco and cotton textiles. Indeed, in the latter case, low wages and a manufacturing environment with little threat of labor organization or state regulation represented the region's primary competitive advantage over the North, establishing a pattern that would attract capital and bedevil labor reformers and organizers for decades to come.

Meanwhile, despite the calls for diversification, the agricultural sector stagnated. The price of cotton, the South's main commodity crop, failed to increase sufficiently in this period to permit investment and modernization of southern agriculture. Low prices and steep mortgages drove many small landholders into the ranks of tenants and sharecroppers; by 1900, two thirds of all southern cotton producers worked land owned by someone else. With limited urbanization, a weak home market for foodstuffs made agricultural diversification difficult. In the words of the historian James C. Cobb, in the last three decades of the nineteenth century, "southern agriculture and southern industry remained locked in a mutually dependent relationship in which the weaknesses of one reinforced the weaknesses of the other."

The persistent gap between optimistic rhetoric and economic reality that characterized the New South proved perilous to the region's working class. For rural workers, African-Americans in particular, the system of sharecropping meant dependence on landlords, little income, and no possibility of upward mobility. Others fell into debt peonage and found they had to work out a debt to a landlord or turpentine camp operator in perpetuity or be sent to a chain gang or convict camp. Coal miners competed against the forced labor of convicts, leased by southern states to mine owners for a pittance. The South's most impressive industrial success, the rapid expansion across the Piedmont of textile manufacturing from 10,000 employees in 1870 to 100,000 30 years later, drew on the cheap and unskilled labor of displaced white tenant farmer families and almost entirely excluded blacks. Nearly a quarter of southern textile workers in the 1880s and 1890s were children, and over 40% were women. Textile workers, scorned as lazy and uncouth, lived and labored in mill towns completely dominated by the textile owners.

Both black and white southern workers attempted to better their condition during this period, sometimes in concert with one another. The interracial United Mine Workers successfully organized the coalfields of Alabama and Tennessee, the Knights of Labor made inroads in Richmond and other cities, and dockworkers in New Orleans built a successful union, to name but three examples. However, the New South's largest industry, textiles, remained impervious to organization. Despite these occasional successes, however, most southerners continued to labor long hours, under difficult conditions, for low wages or, in the case of sharecroppers, peons, and convicts, no wages at all. If some blacks joined unions to improve their conditions, other African-American leaders, most notably Booker T. Washington, urged black workers to accept their degraded place in the labor market and make their peace with the economy of the New South in lieu of pursuing political or civil rights.

Historians continue to debate the nature of the New South's political economy, a discussion that mirrors ongoing debates about globalization and the developing world in the twenty-first century. Some argue that the South followed the best path of economic modernization possible under the circumstances, making the most of limited resources and an economy devastated by the Civil War. Others maintain that deeply engrained patterns of economic dependency, labor exploitation, employer control, and racial domination set the New South on a peculiar path of growth that continued to deny the fruits of the region's wealth to its working people well into the twentieth century.

ALEX LICHTENSTEIN

References and Further Reading

Arnesen, Eric. *Waterfront Workers of New Orleans: Race, Class, and Politics, 1863–1923*. Urbana: University of Illinois Press, 1994.

Cobb, James C. *Industrialization and Southern Society, 1877–1984*. Lexington: University Press of Kentucky, 1984.

Grady, Henry W. "The New South." Speech of December 22, 1886. http://douglassarchives.org/grad_a12.htm. (1996–).

Letwin, Daniel. *The Challenge of Interracial Unionism: Alabama Coal Miners, 1878–1921*. Chapel Hill: University of North Carolina Press, 1998.

Wiener, Jonathan M. "Class Structure and Economic Development in the American South, 1865–1955." *American Historical Review* 84 (May 1979): 970–1006.

Woodward, C. Vann. *Origins of the New South: 1877–1913*. Baton Rouge: Louisiana State University Press, 1951.

Wright, Gavin. *Old South, New South: Revolutions in the Southern Economy since the Civil War*. New York: Basic Books, 1986.

See also **Convict Labor in the New South; Peonage; Sharecropping and Tenancy; Tennessee Convict Uprising (1891–1892); Textiles; United Mine Workers of America; Washington, Booker T.**

NEW YORK CITY FISCAL CRISIS (1970s)

The 1970s New York City fiscal crisis began in the spring of 1975, when the city lost its ability to borrow money in the private market and teetered on the edge of bankruptcy. It was a key turning point in the city's history. The fiscal crisis led to a rapid dismantling of the city's liberal political and social order, which had originated during the New Deal period of the 1930s and 1940s, and had developed even further during Mayor John Lindsay's two terms (1966–1972), and its replacement with a new political order based on fiscal austerity. New York's 1970s fiscal crisis had national significance given the importance of the city, how its fiscal crisis was seen as an example of the failures of liberal social and economic policies, and how the solution to the crisis (the imposition of fiscal austerity and demands for givebacks from its unions) would soon be replicated in other U.S. cities and in the nation's private sector.

The fiscal crisis was a particularly significant moment for New York's working class because of the central role played by the city's municipal unions during the crisis and the impact of the fiscal crisis on all working-class New Yorkers. The municipal unions were a central political actor during the fiscal crisis and played a central role in keeping the city out of bankruptcy by investing close to $3 billion of their members' pension fund assets in city securities. At the same time, they were forced to accept wage freezes and the firing of thousands of their members. Also, it was the city's working class and middle class that bore the brunt of the cuts in social services and layoffs that the city imposed during the fiscal crisis.

The city's fiscal crisis had several causes. One was the loss of tens of thousands of city jobs (particularly in the manufacturing sector) during the 1960s and early 1970s. During the same period, the city went through a significant demographic shift, as over 300,000 New Yorkers, many of whom were middle class, left the city to move to the suburbs or other areas of the country and were replaced with a massive influx of poor African-Americans and Puerto Ricans. The onset of the worldwide recession of 1973 further weakened the city's economy.

While New York City was hemorrhaging jobs and its tax base was declining, the city's municipal expenditures increased significantly. During Mayor John Lindsay's two terms (1966–1972), spending on welfare, higher education (particularly after the creation of an open admissions policy at the City University of New York), and health care skyrocketed. One cause for the increase in city expenditures was rapidly growing labor costs as the city's municipal workforce grew in large numbers and these workers won significant wage increases and better pensions. Between 1961 and 1975, the city's labor costs quadrupled. These increases in labor costs were not out of line with increases in most of the nation's other major cities. These gains were won by militant municipal unions. Led by such men as Victor Gotbaum of District Council 37 of the American Federation of State, County, and Municipal Employees (AFSCME) and Al Shanker of the United Federation of Teachers (UFT), the city's municipal unions went on a series of strikes during the second half of the 1960s that gained national attention.

In order to pay for these increased expenditures, the city needed more revenue, but only rarely did the city raise taxes to pay for these increases (one of the few exceptions was a commuter tax enacted in 1966) because of growing opposition to any tax increases by the state legislature and the city's City Council and its Board of Estimate, which were increasingly influenced by middle-class homeowners in Brooklyn, Queens, and Staten Island, who opposed any tax increases. Instead, the city chose to issue increasingly large amounts of short-term debt to raise needed revenue. By 1974, the city, under Mayor Abe Beame (1973–1977), was issuing over $7 billion in short-term debt a year. Considering that the city's operating expenses in 1974 were only a little over $10 billion, the city had reached a point at which it was covering over 70% of its operating expenses with short-term debt.

During the 1960s and early 1970s, the nation's large investment banks, which functioned as both underwriters and major purchasers of this city debt, were quite happy to go along with this policy, since they made significant profits from it. However, by late 1974, banks such as Chase Manhattan and Citibank began to reconsider their role in the city's financing. Many were reeling from significant losses from domestic and international investments and were increasingly worried about the city's ability to honor its debt and the Beame administration's willingness to rein in city spending. Therefore, they quietly began to sell their own city notes and bonds, and in March 1975, they informed the city that they would no longer underwrite the sale of New York City securities. This decision by the banks cut the city off from private capital; without this money, the city moved quickly in the direction of defaulting on its loans and having to declare bankruptcy.

The city managed to avoid bankruptcy, but only after a series of actions were taken that significantly limited the elected city officials' control over the city's finances and budget, and the city was forced to make large cuts in its budget and lay off tens of thousands of municipal workers. Perhaps the most significant step was taken by Governor Hugh Carey and the state legislature during the summer and fall of 1975, when they created the Municipal Assistance Corporation (MAC) and the Emergency Financial Control Board (EFCB), which were given enormous power over the city's finances, budget, and collective bargaining power.

Blamed for being one of the main causes of the fiscal crisis by the banks, the Ford administration, and the city's newspapers, New York's municipal unions faced their worst crisis since the Great Depression. Despite their insistence that their members' wages and benefits were not out of line with municipal workers in other cities (which was accurate), the city fired approximately 25,000 municipal employees and reduced its municipal workforce by an additional 40,000 through attrition by 1980. Also, the municipal unions were forced to make a series of major concessions, such as agreeing to the deferment of an already-negotiated wage increase won in 1974, a wage freeze for the duration of the fiscal crisis, and less generous pension benefits for new members.

Faced with this crisis, as well as wildcat strikes by members of several unions in protests over the layoffs, Gotbaum of District Council 37 and the majority of other municipal union leaders developed an overall strategy in the summer of 1975 that would determine, to a great extent, what they would do for the duration of the crisis. Having concluded that striking was futile and determined to maintain their institutional power, they chose a strategy based on not directly opposing fiscal austerity, but on using their political power and their control of their members' pension fund assets to maintain some degree of institutional power and to protect their members as best as they could within the context of fiscal austerity.

To a certain extent, this strategy was successful. Using their control over the assets of their members' pension funds, which the city desperately needed access to in order to stave off bankruptcy, and the threat that they would go on strike if too many givebacks were demanded, the municipal unions remained an important player within the new political environment created by the fiscal crisis. Also, there were no more significant layoffs after 1975. Moreover, in

1977, in what was most likely a reward for their agreement to accept significant concessions, to keep strikes to a minimum, and to not directly oppose policies of fiscal austerity, the state legislature granted the city's municipal unions the right to an agency shop. Agency shop, which had been one of the municipal unions' main legislative goals since the mid-1960s, allowed the unions to automatically collect union dues or an amount equivalent to union dues directly from the paychecks of all workers covered by the union contract regardless of whether the worker was a union member. It is important to note that the state legislature chose not to make agency shop permanent. Instead, it granted the unions agency shop only for two years and made it clear that it might not be renewed for unions that went out on strike.

However, their membership did suffer significant layoffs, wage freezes in a period of galloping inflation, and significant givebacks concerning pension plans and work rules. Also, the municipal unions' acceptance of fiscal austerity put considerable limits on their power and their actions during the fiscal crisis and made them less inclined to work with, in any significant way, other groups in the city that were attempting to contest the imposition of a new political regime based on fiscal austerity. For example, despite their intense dislike of Mayor Edward Koch because of his actions during the 1980 transit strike and at the bargaining table, the municipal unions chose not to oppose his re-election by joining a broad coalition made up of most of the city's labor movement, liberal Democrats, and activists within the city's African-American community that supported State Assemblyman Frank Barbaro during the 1981 mayoral campaign.

However, it is not clear that the municipal union leadership had other viable alternatives under the circumstances. The 1970s were a remarkably difficult time for municipal unions in most of the nation's cities. A combination of fiscal crises at all levels of government, a conservative taxpayer revolt, and high inflation led elected city officials to turn against municipal unions that had emerged in the 1960s as a major political force. In cities across the country, elected city officials began to lay off municipal workers and demand significant wages cuts. Municipal unions found that striking, which many had used to great success in the 1960s, was no longer an option as much of the public had now turned against them and city officials proved willing to take strikes and, in some cases, permanently replace striking workers.

The city's working and middle classes bore the brunt of cuts in spending and government programs that were imposed during the 1970s fiscal crisis, given that it was these groups that most relied upon city services. From the layoff of municipal workers to the imposition of tuition at the previously free City University, to a subway fare increase and increases in class sizes in the already troubled public school system, the city's working and middle class made tremendous sacrifices and confronted deteriorating city services.

While New York's 1970s fiscal crisis ended in the early 1980s, its legacy continues to this day. Wages, work conditions, and fringe benefits for the city's municipal employees have never totally recovered from the hit they took during the 1970s fiscal crisis. New York City's municipal unions have continued to pursue a relatively conservative and narrow interest-group strategy into the post-fiscal crisis period, as their endorsement of Mayor Rudolph Giuliani in his 1997 re-election campaign demonstrated. New York's once robust liberal political culture, which rested on a strong labor movement, has never totally recovered from the blow it suffered during the 1970s fiscal crisis.

MICHAEL SPEAR

References and Further Reading

Bailey, Robert. *The Crisis Regime: The MAC, the EFCB, and the Political Impact of the New York City Fiscal Crisis.* Albany: SUNY Press, 1984.

Freeman, Joshua. *Working-Class New York: Life and Labor since World War II.* New York: The New Press, 2000.

Shefter, Martin. *Political Crisis/Fiscal Crisis: The Collapse and Revival of New York City.* New York: Columbia University Press, 1992.

Spear, Michael. "A Crisis in Urban Liberalism: The New York City Municipal Unions and the 1970s Fiscal Crisis." Ph.D. diss., Graduate Center of the City University of New York, 2005.

Tabb, William. *The Long Default: New York City and the Urban Fiscal Crisis.* New York: Monthly Review Press, 1982.

Wallace, Mike. *A New Deal for New York.* New York: Bell & Weiland Publishers, 2002.

NEW YORK CITY HOSPITAL STRIKE (1959)

The seven-week strike by maintenance and service workers at six New York City nonprofit hospitals, which began on May 8, 1959, proved a signal breakthrough for hospital worker unionism in the United States. Organized by Retail Drug Employees and Hospital Workers Union Local 1199—a maverick outfit with roots in the Communist-led fringe of 1930s-era CIO industrial unionism—the "battle of '59," as it would later be known by insiders, was one of the first northern conflicts effectively to draw on the emergent energy of the civil rights movement,

even as it also relied on the peculiar labor politics of New York City for victory.

On the heels of a collective bargaining settlement at Montefiore Hospital the previous year, Local 1199 demanded union recognition from 40 voluntary, nonprofit institutions represented by the staunchly anti-union Greater New York Hospital Association. Strategically selecting six Jewish-endowed hospitals where the union, itself led by the Jewish pharmacists Leon Davis and Elliott Godoff, had amassed its strongest cadre, the union struck in defiance of both the law (nonprofit-sector workers were not included in national or state labor laws) and the convention of selfless service on the part of health-care employees. President Davis himself was forced to hide out from process servers during much of the strike.

The prolonged conflict challenged the political values and loyalties of a city and public accustomed to think of itself as a relatively "liberal" oasis. In the workplace, the union tapped pent-up demands for dignity and self-respect within a low-wage, largely black and Latino labor force that had shared neither in the postwar boom nor in the city's otherwise powerful labor movement. By organizing themselves, the nearly 3,000 workers who walked picket lines in 1959 added a new and increasingly powerful voice to the city's public face. In particular, two African-American strike activists—Lenox Hill diet clerk Doris Turner and Mt. Sinai orderly Henry Nicholas—would attain future prominence (and some notoriety) within the union.

Outside the workplace, Local 1199's public relations director, Moe Foner, assembled an impressive political coalition behind the strikers. In addition to donations from 175 local unions and critical support from the city Central Labor Council chieftain Harry Van Arsdale, Foner enlisted the black socialist and civil rights activist Bayard Rustin to coordinate community support for the strikers. Soon, Eleanor Roosevelt, Congressmen Adam Clayton Powell and Emanual Cellar, and other liberals had joined forces on a Committee for a Just Settlement cochaired by A. Philip Randolph and the theologian Reinhold Niebuhr.

With union pressure unavailing on hospital trustees, the strike ended in a compromise settlement arranged by Mayor Wagner and the veteran mediator William H. Davis. Instead of direct union recognition and an official presence in the hospitals, the workers formally gained only a Permanent Administrative Committee (PAC) of hospital and "public" representatives who would themselves try to resolve future labor grievances. Formally, neither the union nor the strikers had achieved their goals; on the ground, however, the militant self-organization of hospital workers had forever changed social relations in the affected institutions. Within a year of the creation of the PAC, some 3,000 workers were enrolled in collective bargaining agreements at seven New York City hospitals, and in 1963—thanks to another massive political campaign and a sympathetic response by Governor Nelson Rockefeller—city hospital workers were officially given the right to organize. Henry Nicholas could thus justifiably look back on the 1959 strike as "a defeat, but the greatest defeat the union ever encountered."

Despite several years of internal turmoil, by the late 1980s, Local 1199 had grown into a national presence of some 200,000 workers; in 1989, it formally joined the Service Employees International Union, where it continued to function as an aggressive, grassroots-oriented force within the labor movement.

LEON FINK

References and Further Reading

Fink, Leon, and Greenberg Brian. *Upheaval in the Quiet Zone: A History of Hospital Workers' Union, Local 1199.* Urbana: University of Illinois Press, 1989.

See also **Foner, Moe; Randolph, A. Philip; Rustin, Bayard; Service Employees' International Union**

NEWMAN, PAULINE M. (1890–1986)

Pauline M. Newman (1890–1986) was a labor pioneer and a die-hard union loyalist. In 1909, when she was not yet out of her teens, she became the first woman appointed general organizer by the International Ladies' Garment Workers' Union (ILGWU). That labor union was so heavily influenced by Jewish immigrant socialists that Newman referred to it as "the Jewish movement"—and saw it as both a cultural and political foundation for Jewish progressivism in the United States during the first half of the twentieth century. Despite ongoing battles with the men who ran the ILGWU, Newman worked for that union for more than 70 years—as an organizer, labor journalist, health educator, and liaison between the labor movement and elected officials in Albany, New York, and in Washington, DC. A leader and inspirational figure in the early twentieth-century tenant, labor, socialist, and suffrage movements, Newman's influence on labor politics and the emerging welfare state was deep and lasting.

A tough Lithuanian Jewish immigrant with an acerbic tongue and a penchant for tweeds and slicked-back hair, Newman was described by male colleagues in the labor movement as "capable of smoking a cigar with the best of them." In an era when the idea of unionism was synonymous with notions of brotherhood and masculine bonding, Newman questioned accepted norms of gender for both men and women in the trade union movement. She bonded with hard-boiled male unionists, who accepted her as one of their own, even as she helped to create and sustain a woman-centered trade union federation through the New York and National Women's Trade Union Leagues (NYWTUL and WTUL). Throughout her 80 years in the labor movement, she pursued a difficult balancing act—negotiating with male unionists, middle- and upper-class women reformers, and government officials to improve the lives of working women. She left a lasting imprint on each of these very different worlds.

Newman was born into a world in transition, that of poverty-stricken but deeply religious Jews in Kovno, Lithuania, around 1890. (The exact date of her birth was lost with the family bible when she emigrated.) The youngest of four children, three girls and a boy, Newman was launched on her activist career at a tender age when she demanded to know why girls did not receive the same religious education as Jewish boys. Her father, a Talmud teacher, accommodated her desire to learn, teaching her to read Hebrew and Yiddish. (She taught herself Russian and, later, English.) Newman would later claim that her childhood resentment at the privileges accorded men and boys in Jewish education and worship sparked a lifelong commitment to fight sex discrimination wherever she found it.

When her father died in 1901, Newman, her sisters, and her mother left Kovno for New York, where her brother had settled a few years earlier. There Newman began work at a hairbrush factory and moved soon to the infamous "kindergarten" at the Triangle Shirtwaist Factory in Greenwich Village. She found herself powerfully drawn to the labor socialism espoused by older workers in her shop and by the Yiddish language *Jewish Daily Forward*—the most popular Jewish immigrant newspaper of her day. Ever hungry for education, Newman organized reading groups for the teenage girls among whom she worked. Teaching themselves English by reading Dickens, Thomas Hood, and other literary exposés of nineteenth-century English industry, Newman and her friends soon felt "ready to rise up" against the long hours, low pay, and miserable conditions in which they lived and worked. These young immigrant girls sparked a series of strikes and walkouts. Then, in 1907, they planned and organized a rent strike on Manhattan's Lower East Side that involved more than 10,000 families. It was the largest rent strike

New York had yet seen and began decades of tenant activism in the city.

Hailed by newspapers as the Lower East Side Joan of Arc, the young Newman came to the attention of the Socialist Party, which nominated her for New York secretary of state. She campaigned along the leader of American Socialists, Eugene Victor Debs, and used the election season as a time to proselytize for woman suffrage. At the same time, she was organizing young women garment workers, paving the way for the 1909 general strike that came to be known as the "Uprising of the 20,000." During the long, cold months of the strike, Newman played two important roles. Through inspiring speeches at street corner rallies and in the union halls of Lower Manhattan, she kept up the spirits of the strikers. She also fund-raised among New York's wealthiest women, drawing upon her readings of English literature to win their support for the strike. Newman was even able to draw some of these women out onto picket lines, hoping by their presence to diminish police brutality against the strikers. These "mink brigades" won the strike its first positive press in the city's mainstream newspapers.

In recognition for all she had done, the ILGWU appointed the 18-year-old as its first female general organizer. She spent the next four years traveling the country, organizing garment strikes in Philadelphia, Cleveland, Boston, and Kalamazoo, Michigan. By decade's end, these strikes would bring upwards of 40% of all women garment workers into trade unions, a remarkable percentage for workers in any trade and a clear refutation of union leaders' oft-repeated assertions that women could not be organized.

Still, the years on the road were lonely for Newman as one of the only women in a male world of labor organizers, and deeply frustrating since she felt that the male union leadership undermined and undervalued her work. Seeking other avenues for her activism, she also stumped for the Socialist Party in the bleak, freezing coal-mining camps of southern Illinois. And everywhere she went, she preached the gospel of woman suffrage, for she saw women's right to vote as an essential part of the working-class struggle.

Newman nearly collapsed under the weight of her grief when the Triangle Shirtwaist Factory burned on March 25, 1911, in which 146 young workers lost their lives, most of them Jewish and Italian women, and many of them friends Newman had come to cherish in her years at Triangle. Desperate to do whatever she could to prevent such disasters in the future, Newman accepted a post in 1913 inspecting industrial shops for the Joint Board of Sanitary Control—established by New York State in the aftermath of the fire to improve factory safety. At the same time, Newman worked as a lobbyist for the New York Women's Trade Union League, pushing for passage of wage, hour, and safety legislation for women workers. Through this work, she met Frances Perkins, then an activist for the Consumers League, later to become Franklin Roosevelt's secretary of labor. She also met the future New York governor, Al Smith, and the future senator, Robert Wagner. These friendships convinced Newman that working through government was as important to the future of working women as grassroots organizing. She never abandoned union work, but she now divided her energies between organizing, education, and lobbying.

In 1917, the Women's Trade Union League dispatched Newman to Philadelphia, to build a new branch of the League. There she met a young Bryn Mawr economics instructor named Frieda Miller, who enthusiastically left academia to join Newman in "the movement." The two were soon living together. It was the beginning of a turbulent relationship that would last until Miller's death in 1974. In 1923, the two women moved to New York's Greenwich Village where, as part of a community of politically active female couples, they raised Miller's daughter, Elisabeth. Happy to take a job that would allow her to stay close to New York after more than a decade of traveling, Newman became educational director for the ILGWU Union Health Center, the first comprehensive medical program created by a union for its members. Newman would retain that position for the next six decades, using it to promote worker health care, adult education, and greater visibility for the concerns and needs of women workers.

Newman continued to organize into the 1930s, reaching out to African-American and Afro-Caribbean women through NYWTUL campaigns to unionize laundry, hotel, and domestic workers. She also continued her government work, consulting for New York State on minimum wage and safety standards and serving as a member of the U.S. Women's Bureau Labor Advisory Board, the United Nations Subcommittee on the Status of Women, and the International Labor Organization Subcommittee on the Status of Domestic Workers.

Through the WTUL, Newman was part of a community of women that sustained her, providing essential support for a working-class immigrant who had chosen to forgo the traditional protections of marriage and family. Theirs was a multi-ethnic and cross-class circle. It included the Irish-Catholic labor activists Maud Swartz and Leonora O'Reilly; the Jewish immigrant garment organizer Rose Schneiderman; and affluent native-born Protestant reformers, among them Eleanor Roosevelt and Newman's partner of 56 years, Miller. (Miller served in the 1930s as industrial commissioner for New York State and in the 1940s as director of the U.S. Women's Bureau.)

These women were regular guests at Val-Kill, the home that Franklin Roosevelt built for Eleanor near the family mansion at Hyde Park. And during the Roosevelt presidency, Newman visited the White House with some regularity, making national headlines in 1936 when she accompanied a delegation of young garment and textile workers invited by the First Lady for a weeklong stay. After World War II, Newman and Miller were called on by President Truman to investigate postwar factory conditions in Europe. Newman also addressed the White House Conference on the Child and consulted regularly on labor safety issues for the U.S. Public Health Service. During the early decades of the twentieth century, Newman and her WTUL circle had played a vital role in sparking and sustaining women's labor uprisings across the country. During the 1920s, 1930s, and 1940s, they shaped new government agencies and labor laws that guaranteed a minimum wage and minimum standards of safety for all American workers.

Newman continued to work for the ILGWU into the 1980s, writing, lecturing, and advising younger women trade unionists. In the 1970s, Newman was hailed by the feminist labor federation, the Coalition of Labor Union Women, as a foremother of the women's liberation movement. Newman spoke regularly through the 1970s and 1980s, to historians, reporters, and groups of young women workers.

Newman also left an important legacy through her writings as one of the few working-class women of her generation to chronicle the political activism of immigrant and native-born workingwomen. Labor journalist, essayist, and poet, Newman contributed to the *New York Call*, *Progressive Woman*, the WTUL magazine *Life and Labor*, the *Ladies Garment Worker*, and the ILGWU newspaper, *Justice*.

Newman died in 1986, at approximately 96 years of age.

ANNELISE ORLECK

References and Further Reading

Kessler-Harris, Alice. "Organizing the Unorganizable: Three Jewish Women and Their Union." *Labor History* 17, no. 1 (Winter 1976): 5–25.

Morrison, Joan, and Charlotte Fox Zabusky, eds. *American Mosaic*. New York: E. P. Dutton, 1982.

Orleck, Annelise. *Common Sense and a Little Fire: Women and Working-Class Politics in the United States, 1900–1965*. Chapel Hill: University of North Carolina Press, 1995.

Schofield, Ann. *"To Do and To Be ": Portraits of Four Women Activists, 1893–1986*. Boston: Northeastern University Press, 1997.

See also **Debs, Eugene V.; International Ladies' Garment Workers' Union (ILGWU) (1900–1995); Jews; Perkins, Frances; Schneiderman, Rose; Women's Trade Union League**

NIXON, EDGAR DANIEL (1899–1987)
African-American Labor Organizer

Edgar Daniel Nixon, a civil rights activist, was born in Robinson Springs, Alabama, near Montgomery. His father was a tenant farmer and Primitive Baptist preacher. His mother died when Nixon was nine, and he was brought up in Montgomery by a paternal aunt. With little formal education, Nixon possessed an inquiring mind and a strong personality. After leaving school at the age of 13, he took a variety of menial jobs and then became a baggage handler at the Montgomery railroad station. In 1923, he became a Pullman porter, making regular trips outside the South. These journeys widened Nixon's horizons and stimulated his developing class and race consciousness. Although Pullman porters were considered as the elite of the African-American working class, Nixon resented the degrading treatment they received from the Pullman Company and white passengers. Impressed by the oratory and social vision of A. Philip Randolph, the organizer of the Brotherhood of Sleeping Car Porters (BSCP), Nixon joined the union, became president of the Montgomery chapter in 1938, and served until 1964. When the union finally secured a contract with the Pullman Company in 1937, Nixon memorized every section of the personnel rules and used them to advantage. Active involvement in the BSCP increased Nixon's standing in the city's black (and white) communities.

Nixon first became engaged in community action in 1925. When two black children drowned while swimming in a drainage ditch, he organized an unsuccessful petition to build a swimming pool for Montgomery's black residents. In 1934, he founded the Montgomery Welfare League, which attempted to secure access for African-Americans to assistance from the federal government. During the 1930s, Nixon worked with Myles Horton of the Highlander Folk School in Tennessee to organize Alabama's cucumber pickers. During World War II, Nixon supported A. P. Randolph's March on Washington Movement (MOWM), a threatened mass march on the nation's capital by 100,000 African-Americans that forced President Franklin D. Roosevelt to issue an executive order banning discrimination based on color, creed, or national origin in the federal government and defense industries. Following a meeting with Eleanor Roosevelt while she was a passenger on his train, Nixon secured the construction of a United Services Organizations Club (USO) for black military personnel stationed near Montgomery. Always sensitive to the practices of racial discrimination, during the 1950s, Nixon went for three years without a telephone in Montgomery rather than accept one on a four-party "all colored" line.

Nixon also became prominent in the Montgomery chapter of the National Association for the Advancement of Colored People (NAACP) and was elected its president in 1945 and 1946. In 1947, he became president of the state organization and successfully protested against segregated admission to the "Freedom Train"—a touring exhibition of such notable historical documents as the Declaration of Independence and the original manuscript of the "Star Spangled Banner"—when it visited Montgomery. The national leadership of the NAACP, embarrassed by Nixon's radicalism and bluntness, engineered his re-election defeat in 1949. In 1950, he also lost the presidency of the Montgomery chapter.

During the 1940s, Nixon also headed voter registration and school desegregation campaigns in Montgomery and pursued many cases involving the rape of African-American women, police brutality, murders, and lynchings. He organized the Montgomery Voters League in 1940, and in June 1944, he led 750 African-Americans to the board of registrars, demanding to be registered to vote. At this time fewer than 50 Montgomery blacks were on the electoral rolls. Nixon himself had paid the $36 poll tax in Montgomery and tried to register to vote for 10 years. Only after filing one lawsuit and threatening another was he finally registered in 1945. Nixon became the first African-American candidate to seek public office in Alabama since Reconstruction, when he ran (unsuccessfully) in 1954 for election to the Montgomery County Democratic Party Executive Committee.

A leading figure and tactician in several protests against Montgomery's segregated public transportation system, Nixon, through his friendships with Rosa Parks, the liberal white attorney Clifford Durr, and Jo Ann Gibson Robinson, an English professor at Alabama State College and a leading activist in the Women's Political Council (WPC), was instrumental in planning and sustaining the 381-day Montgomery Bus Boycott (1955–1956). This grassroots protest against segregation on the city's buses was sparked off by Mrs. Parks's refusal to relinquish her seat to a white passenger. Nixon secured her bail and urged Parks to use her arrest as a test case for the city's segregation laws. It was Nixon who forcefully persuaded the city's African-American ministers to lend their support to the protest after it was decided to extend the one-day bus boycott indefinitely. He also acted as the treasurer of the Montgomery Improvement Association (MIA). Through his contacts with organized labor, Nixon disseminated the MIA's objectives at union meetings and conventions across the country and raised thousands of dollars for the protest—notably from southern branches of the BSCP. According to his own account, Nixon quickly perceived the worth and potential of a young African-American Baptist minister newly arrived in Montgomery, who was to assume leadership of the MIA: Martin Luther King Jr.

A lifelong spokesman for the working class, Nixon criticized the influence and conservatism of Montgomery's African-American, college-educated elite. He also resented their failure to accord him proper recognition for his role in the boycott and the subsequent inflation of King's leadership role. Following his resignation as MIA treasurer in 1957, an embittered Nixon remained active in the Alabama Democratic Party and worked for better facilities for Montgomery's African-American children and the elderly. An uncompromising advocate of racial integration, Nixon rejected the separatism of the Black Power ideology of the 1960s. To the end of his life, Nixon asserted that the BSCP, under the leadership of A. P. Randolph, had not only empowered black workers but also inspired his own resolve to remain in the South and challenge the degradations and lunacies of racial discrimination and segregation.

In 1986, the Alabama Historical Commission—with the endorsement of Governor George Wallace, no longer a symbol of southern white resistance to desegregation—registered Nixon's modest home on Clinton Street as "a significant landmark."

JOHN WHITE

References and Further Reading

Baldwin, Lewis V., and Aprille V. Woodson. *Freedom Is Never Free: A Biographical Portrait of E. D. Nixon, Sr.* Atlanta: United Parcel Service, 1992.

White, John. "E. D. Nixon (1889–1987): A Founding Father of the Civil Rights Movement." In *Portraits of African American Life since 1865*, edited by Nina Mjagkij. Wilmington DE: Scholarly Resources, Inc., 2003, pp. 199–217.

———. "Nixon *Was* the One: E. D. Nixon, the MIA, and the Montgomery Bus Boycott." In *The Making of Martin Luther King and the Civil Rights Movement*, edited by Anthony J. Badger and Brian Ward. Washington Square: New York University Press, 1996, pp. 45–63.

NORRIS-LAGUARDIA FEDERAL ANTI-INJUNCTION ACT

The Norris LaGuardia Act, passed by the U.S. Congress in 1932, represented the culmination of a decades-long struggle by American labor organizations to prevent federal courts from issuing injunctions against strikes, boycotts, and other labor actions. In the late 1870s, federal equity courts began the practice of issuing injunctions against unions engaging in strikes and boycotts against railroads in federal receivership. Federal judges then used the Sherman Antitrust Act of 1890, conceived as a means of controlling predatory business monopolies, instead as a means to issue injunctions against striking labor unions, whom judges found to be restraining commerce by monopolizing the supply of labor, deemed to be a commodity.

The Norris-LaGuardia Act was conceived as a replacement for the Clayton Act of 1914. The Clayton Act, which Samuel Gompers had proclaimed to be labor's "Magna Carta," was the first attempt by the U.S. Congress to prevent federal courts from issuing injunctions in labor disputes. But federal courts themselves largely gutted the law. The U.S. Supreme Court, in the 1921 *American Steel Foundries* case, held that courts could lawfully limit labor unions to one picket per plant entrance during a strike, effectively making picketing useless. The court also ruled in the *Truax* case in 1921 that a strike could be enjoined if it interfered with the ability of an owner to operate a business at a profit. Essentially, the courts ruled that the judiciary had the power to enjoin strikes, as owners were deemed to be deprived of their property rights; owners were deemed to have a property right in the labor of their employees. The Court's decision gave federal courts broad powers to enjoin strikes, which they did with alarming regularity in the 1920s.

The judicial destruction of the Clayton Act outraged the labor movement, and labor leaders once again threw themselves into organizing political power to write a new law that would prevent the courts from intervening in strikes. By 1932, the cause had gained significant support from others as well, including many reformers, who had come to believe that the system of labor injunctions clearly turned the federal courts into an ally of management during strikes and had actually contributed to increased labor unrest. The spectacle of the Great Depression also convinced many lawmakers that reform was needed in the nation's economy and that a revitalized labor movement might be a necessary stimulus for recovery. Thus, George Norris of Nebraska and Fiorello LaGuardia of New York introduced a bill, authored by Felix Frankfurter and Donald Richberg, reforming the federal judiciary's role in labor disputes. The Norris-LaGuardia Act received bipartisan support, passed a Republican legislature by a massive majority, and Herbert Hoover approved the Act.

Norris-LaGuardia accomplished several tasks that were critical to the success of labor unions in the United States. First, it was the first act that stated that collective bargaining was necessary in a modern industrial economy. The Act stated that freedom of contract was meaningless to an individual worker in a modern corporate economy and that collective bargaining was a way for workers to achieve a real parity in bargaining with an employer. This did not amount to a federal guarantee of the right to unionize—this would not be suggested until Section 7a of the National Industrial Recovery Act and not firmly established until the National Labor Relations Act (Wagner Act). The most important part of Norris-LaGuardia decreed that federal courts could not issue injunctions in labor disputes. The only exception allowed by the law was if a strike could be determined to promote violence or property damage. Even in these circumstances, the law limited courts to issuing a temporary restraining order. The law also granted unions the right to employ picketing as a means of publicizing a strike, as well as to convince workers to join a strike or not cross a picket line. Picketing also could be used to encourage consumers to boycott a business. Norris-LaGuardia also put an end to baseless conspiracy charges against unions, establishing that workers could not be charged for doing in combination things that would be legal for a single worker to do. Minor rights granted to unions by the legislation included the right to a jury trial for workers charged with violating an injunction, a guarantee that unions could provide strike benefits to workers, and the right of workers to pool resources to defend members of the union charged with a crime during a strike. Finally, Norris-LaGuardia prevented the federal judiciary from enforcing yellow-dog contracts—a critical section, since employers had used the yellow-dog contract as one of the most effective anti-union measures of the 1920s.

Norris-LaGuardia gave the labor movement its first impetus to the massive organizing successes that it achieved in the 1930s. Free of the labor injunction, unions and workers undertook a massive grassroots organizing campaign throughout the 1930s and 1940s. The U.S. Supreme Court, after the Roosevelt administration had appointed several new liberal members, upheld Norris-LaGuardia in 1938.

The Taft-Hartley Act, passed in 1947, restored some limited injunction powers to federal courts. Taft-Hartley allowed that the president could order a 60-day halt to a strike if it were determined that the strike constituted a threat to national security or well-being. The new law also allowed the National Labor Relations Board to order a cooling-off period for both sides of a dispute. But Taft-Hartley fell far short of overturning Norris-LaGuardia; Taft-Hartley allowed the issuance of an injunction only in a narrow range of circumstances, and employers could not individually petition courts.

Norris-LaGuardia remains more or less intact today. Because Norris-LaGuardia removed the power of the federal judiciary to break strikes and boycotts by fiat, it allowed unions to operate for the first time without fear of legal retribution. This, as much as later laws that established a federal presence in collective bargaining, made possible the development of the modern labor movement in the 1930s. In this regard, Norris-LaGuardia can arguably be called the most important piece of labor legislation in United States history.

STEVEN DIKE-WILHELM

References and Further Reading

Forbath, William. *Law and the Shaping of the American Labor Movement*. Cambridge, MA: Harvard University Press, 1991.

Greene, Julie. *Pure and Simple Politics: The American Federation of Labor and Political Activism, 1881–1917*. New York: Cambridge University Press, 1998.

Taylor, Benjamin, and Fred Witney. *U.S. Labor Relations Law: Historical Development*. Englewood Cliffs, NJ: Prentice Hall, 1992.

Tomlins, Christopher. *The State and the Unions: Labor Relations, Law, and the Organized Labor Movement in America, 1880–1960*. New York: Cambridge University Press, 1985.

NORTH AMERICAN FREE TRADE AGREEMENT

The political battle over the North American Free Trade Agreement (NAFTA), which entered into effect on January 1, 1994, brought U.S. organized labor from the political drift of the Reagan-Bush years (1980–1992) to the center of a nationwide debate about the U.S. role in the global economy. On June 11, 1990, the opening of negotiations for a Mexican-U.S. free trade agreement was announced by the U.S. president, George Bush, and the Mexican president, Carlos Salinas Gotari, and joined by Canada in February 1991. After a contested May 23, 1991, congressional vote on "Fast Track" negotiating authority, NAFTA emerged as a defining issue in the 1992 presidential election between the Republican George Bush, the critical but supportive Democratic

candidate Bill Clinton, and a strongly anti-NAFTA third-party candidate, H. Ross Perot. Despite the addition of side accords on labor and the environment under Clinton, NAFTA's fate was uncertain until the eve of the November 17, 1993, vote in the House of Representatives, where Clinton prevailed by 34 votes, with 132 GOP representatives in favor to 43 opposed, while losing the vote of his party by 156 to 102.

NAFTA's near defeat required an unusual degree of unity among the member unions of the AFL-CIO, a weak confederative apparatus. Not only did the AFL-CIO successfully focus the energies of diverse organizations of workers on NAFTA, but its anti-NAFTA campaign did not remain solely at the level of paper resolutions and backroom arm-twisting by professional labor lobbyists in Washington, DC. Instead, leaders of national unions mobilized the lower ranks of their organizations, including many members, while reaching out to potential allies. At local and regional levels, this popular mobilization found an outlet in innovative forms of grassroots activism that opened outward toward allies on the left that, less than a decade earlier, would have been suspect to the long-standing Cold War leadership of the AFL-CIO president, Lane Kirkland.

As its opponents were quick to point out, the 2,000-page NAFTA treaty was far from being a "free trade agreement," since trade barriers between the three countries had already been largely dropped—through the Canada-U.S. Free Trade Agreement of 1989 and by Mexico unilaterally. As much an investment as a trading agreement, NAFTA codified a common set of rules, especially in Mexico and Canada, that liberalized access for foreign financial, service, agricultural, and industrial investors and producers—primarily to the benefit of U.S.-based capital. NAFTA sought to achieve a *de jure* and not just a *de facto* integration of North American markets, but only for trade and investment since it accelerated capital mobility while leaving the free movement of labor untouched. In the end, the inclusion of labor and environmental side accords, however inadequate, did symbolically point toward a different future path in an increasingly globalized world.

Labor's Anti-NAFTA Strategy: "NAFTA Math" and "Job Body Counts"

The fate of a proposed bilateral and eventually continental free trade agreement depended upon the extension of Fast Track negotiating authority by the U.S. Congress, which was scheduled to expire in June

1991. Fast Track allowed the U.S. president to submit implementing legislation, such as a trade pact or treaty, leaving Congress 90 days to vote it up or down with no possibility of amendments. In January 1991, the AFL-CIO formally demanded "Full Debate: No Fast Track: Fair Trade," although even the House Democratic leader Richard Gephardt, one of labor's most articulate congressional supporters, in the end sided with the Bush administration. Although 170 Democrats broke with their leadership, the final vote in favor of Fast Track on May 23, 1991, was 231 to 192.

With Fast Track approved, organized labor's job became clear: defeat NAFTA. At its November 1991 convention, NAFTA was denounced as "an agreement based solely on exploitation," and the AFL-CIO declared "that a new trade agreement with Mexico, unless carefully structured, will only encourage greater capital outflows from the United States, bring about an increase in imports from Mexico, and reduce domestic employment as the United States remains mired in a recession. . . . A bad trade agreement for the United States would result in less job creation, less productivity increases, and regression in environmental and other social standards. For Mexico, it could well reduce that country's comparative advantage to simply cheap labor, turning Mexico's economy into one large export platform, sacrificing balanced and equitable economic development" (AFL-CIO, "North American Free Trade Agreement," *Proceedings of the 1991 Convention,* Detroit: AFL-CIO, 1991, p. 145).

The touchstone of the unfolding NAFTA controversy was potential job losses to Mexico, the single most potent political obstacle to congressional approval. With even President Bush's Secretary of Labor Lynn Martin conceding 150,000 U.S. jobs would likely be eliminated, pro-NAFTA analysts and policy makers sought to diffuse the issue by aggressively trumpeting statistical studies that claimed that U.S. exports to Mexico post-NAFTA would produce a net gain of 175,000 to 200,000 U.S. jobs. Speaking at the 1992 Republican National Convention, the U.S. special trade representative, Carla Hills, would hail NAFTA as above all else a jobs agreement. Moreover, the creation of better-paying jobs in Mexico, it was said, would reduce the number of Mexicans illegally seeking jobs in the United States. "Create jobs there," it was said, "so they won't come here," a claim echoed by the Mexican president, Carlos Salinas, who told a U.S. newsweekly, "we want to export goods and not people" ("Mexico according to Carlos Salinas," *U.S. News & World Report,* July 8, 1991, p. 41). If this "NAFTA

math," as it was dubbed by the U.S. senator Carl Levin, simply did not add up, due to the arbitrary nature of the modeling exercises, this did not diminish the ubiquitous circulation of such claims, especially once the Business Roundtable had launched an active and well-financed lobbying campaign through USA*-NAFTA.

With NAFTA supporters on the defensive, U.S. organized labor sensibly placed the intensely emotional issue of job "losses" at the center of its anti-NAFTA campaign. In doing so, it successfully moved the insecurity of the U.S. worker to the forefront of domestic political debate. In touching a nerve in mass public opinion, jobs gave substance and resonance to the anti-NAFTA campaign by pointing effectively toward the suffering, uncertainty, and anxiety of U.S. working people over the previous two decades. While pro-NAFTA forces had difficulty crafting convincing images of U.S. workers who, were it not for exports to Mexico, would otherwise have been unemployed, there was no shortage of workers who could personally relate the negative impact of plant flight to Mexico. Interviewed by the *Wall Street Journal,* Bernie Leonka explained that the workforce at his General Electric plant had shrunk to 450. "We've lost 1,200 jobs," the union official said, because "they're going to Mexico for cheap labor." With unionized workers making an average $12.67 an hour, "at 50 cents and 60 cents an hour down there, we can't compete." (Jackie Calmes, *Wall Street Journal,* May 22, 1991, p. A16).

For workers, residents, and local politicians from traditional manufacturing regions, now dubbed the "rust belt," the most potent anti-NAFTA image was the shuttered factory, the "runaway shop" of labor and community lore. The emphasis on jobs also rallied some who were unsympathetic to organized labor, while blunting the charge that a privileged minority, the unionized 11% of the private-sector workforce, was seeking to protect itself from a salutary global competition that would reduce consumer prices for all. The contrasting anti-NAFTA image was one of trade unionists who stood up to defend their families and communities from harm, in the form of imports and capital mobility, and thus championed the very living standards that made mass consumption for all possible in the United States.

The jobs argument advanced by the AFL-CIO operated on several interconnected levels that paralleled the tactics of pro-NAFTA forces. It argued that liberalized trade, foreign imports, and the lack of controls over capital investment had already produced a significant loss of U.S. jobs. It also used academic and legislative analyses that attempted to predict, in quantitative terms, the heightened negative impact that NAFTA would have on gross and net U.S. employment. In disputing the job gains trumpeted by NAFTA supporters, the AFL-CIO cited studies that projected 130,000 to 550,000 in net job losses (AFL-CIO Task Force on Trade, "North American Free Trade Negotiations, The Jobs Debate: Fiction and Reality," no. 21, 1992; "North American Free Trade Agreement, The Jobs Debate: Part II," no. 22, 1993). Others invoked the dramatically higher estimate of 5.9 million U.S. manufacturing jobs at risk of being moved to Mexico as a consequence of NAFTA. Drawn from a study conducted by the Manufacturing Policy Project, this figure was based on tallying all U.S. manufacturers in the low- to mid-technology range with a labor content equivalent to 20% to 30% of sales (Pat Choate, "Jobs at Risk: Vulnerable U.S. Industries and Jobs under NAFTA," Amherst: The Manufacturing Policy Project, April 1993).

The economic frustration that fed the revitalization of labor's public role was equally conducive to other NAFTA opponents, including the billionaire Republican H. Ross Perot, who made NAFTA the defining issue of his 1992 third-party presidential campaign. Author of *Save Your Job, Save Our Country: Why NAFTA Must Be Stopped Now* (New York: Hyperion, 1993), Perot was also responsible for the single most memorable NAFTA sound bite, "Let's go to the center of the bull's eye—the core problem," he said during the third presidential debate. "And believe me, everybody on the factory floor all over the country knows this. You implement that NAFTA—the Mexican trade agreement where they pay people $1 an hour, have no health care, no retirement, no pollution controls, etc., etc., etc.—and you are going to hear a giant sucking sound of jobs being pulled out of this country" (Frederick Mayer, *Interpreting NAFTA: The Science and Art of Political Analysis*, New York: Columbia University Press, 1998, p. 229).

In opposing NAFTA , Perot was joined by a minority of other conservatives, including the Republican Pat Buchanan, who combined an anti-NAFTA stance with a heightened defense of national sovereignty, which they identified with restrictions upon immigration, especially the "illegal alien" problem posed by undocumented Mexicans in the United States. Yet, such anti-immigrant and anti-Mexican arguments were rejected by labor and its allies in the Afro-North American community, a powerfully anti-NAFTA constituency of the Democratic Party (Latinos were more divided). In his testimony before Congress, the prominent civil rights leader Jesse Jackson observed that "right now many Americans are screaming that Mexicans are taking our jobs, which is not true. And the more they say it, the more racist it sounds. Racist. Mexicans are not taking jobs from us. United States corporations are taking jobs to Mexico to exploit them and undercut our own workers. . . .We have a point of view different than Mr. Perot's point of view, different than Pat Buchanan's point of view. And ours is not narrowly nationalistic. It is not building a wall. It is not racist. It is not protectionist. . . . That is why, when people start talking . . . some narrow nationalism, about America first and isolation, we are not talking about the same thing" (Jesse Jackson, testimony transcribed in *NAFTA: A Negative Impact on Blue Collar, Minority, and Female Employment?* Hearing before the Employment, Housing, and Aviation Subcommittee of the Committee on Government Operations, U.S. House of Representatives, 103rd Congress, First Session, November 10, 1993, Washington, DC: GPO, 1994, pp. 61, 64).

In deploying its own NAFTA math in leaflets, articles, speeches, and testimony, the labor movement faced certain fundamental difficulties. The "job loss" argument was fundamentally defensive in nature and operated on the unfavorable terrain defined by its pro-employer opponents. The anti-NAFTA jobs argument was not, after all, about creating needed new jobs, but about preserving those that still existed. Moreover, the "jobs body count" approach had difficulty grappling effectively with the overwhelming global trend toward international capital mobility and further reduction of barriers to trade, both of which negatively impacted the bargaining power of nation-specific labor relative to transnational capital. As pro-NAFTA analysts were quick to point out, the hypothetical jobs "lost" or "gained" through NAFTA were insignificant given total U.S. employment, with its enormous fluctuations given the weakness of job security guarantees. "With almost 120 million people currently employed" in the United States, noted the Congressional Budget Office, the expected contributions of NAFTA to total employment either way was "negligible," and the *New York Times* noted that an estimated 20 million U.S. workers would suffer future displacement, for various reasons, even without NAFTA (Congress of the United States Congressional Budget Office, *A Budgetary and Economic Analysis of the North American Free Trade Agreement*, Washington: July 1993, p. 84; "Demythologizing the Trade Pact," *New York Times*, July 25, 1993). Finally, voting down NAFTA would not, in and of itself, prevent a single "runaway shop," restore a single job, or raise the wages of a single worker in the United States.

Electoral Politics, Bill Clinton, and NAFTA's Environmental and Labor Side Accords

The groundswell of debate about NAFTA showed deep concerns within the U.S. public about the place of their country in the global economy. "To those who believe that average Americans don't know their own interests, or fail to appreciate the benefits of free trade theory, you are wrong," declared the House Democratic leader Dick Gephardt in September 1992. "The American people get it, this issue resonates with them, and the NAFTA agreement is rapidly becoming, substantively and symbolically, representative of everything that is wrong in their lives economically" ("North American Free Trade Agreement [NAFTA]: Update on Recent Developments," SourceMex, September 16, 1992). Given these political realities, congressional Democrats inclined to vote in favor of NAFTA believed that the only way they could explain a "yes" vote to their troubled constituents would be if the "Bush NAFTA" was reshaped to include labor and environmental concerns.

The Democratic presidential candidate, Bill Clinton, who backed Fast Track in 1991, delayed taking a clear position on NAFTA until a month before the November 1992 elections. Speaking in Raleigh, North Carolina, Clinton declared NAFTA to be beneficial for all three countries, but pledged *not* to sign it "until we have reached additional agreements to protect America's vital interests." While disclaiming any intention to renegotiate the basic agreement, Clinton said we must "reaffirm our right to insist that the Mexicans follow their own labor standards, now frequently violated, and that they do not aggravate the wage differentials which already exist." We need an agreement, he said, "that permits citizens of each country to bring suit in their own courts when they believe their domestic environmental protections and worker standards aren't being enforced."

In publicly backing the highly controversial NAFTA, Clinton broke ranks with many of his fellow Democrats, as well as important Democratic constituencies such as labor, the African-American community, and the environmentalists (who would later split on the final vote in 1993). To mollify criticism from these groups, which were campaigning vigorously for him, the candidate had pledged that, if elected, NAFTA would go into effect only if accompanied by strong side agreements to protect labor rights and environmental standards. In doing so, he also suggested that the unfettered "free market" was not enough to protect workers and the environment from potential abuses or to equitably distribute the fruits of North American trade.

Bill Clinton's strategy for converting NAFTA into a politically palatable trade policy led organized labor to hold back from overt anti-NAFTA mobilization in early 1993. Although facing some internal dissent, the decision by the AFL-CIO leadership reflected its strong ties to the Democratic Party, as well as the belief that its access to the White House might secure strong enough side agreements and other changes in the basic pact as to be opposed by Canada, Mexico, or the congressional Republicans. While labor called for a side accord "with teeth," the Clinton administration had opted by March 1993 for the weakest of three policy options: national enforcement of national laws, exclusion of important labor rights from effective coverage, and weak oversight and enforcement mechanisms. Finalized on August 13, 1993, and released one month later, the "North American Agreement on Labor Cooperation" did little to assuage the opposition to NAFTA. The AFL-CIO judgment was emphatic: "Because our trade negotiators have produced labor and environmental standards that are just political window-dressing on a bad agreement, we will vigorously oppose NAFTA before Congress," the AFL-CIO president Lane Kirkland pronounced ("AFL-CIO News: AFL-CIO Finds NAFTA Terms Unacceptable," August 13, 1993). Labor's negative reaction was re-assuring to NAFTA's vigorous and mobilized business supporters, who were opposed, in principle, to legitimizing any linkage between workers' rights and trade.

Seeds of the New

Labor's response to the changed circumstances of the United States—as they came to be symbolized by NAFTA—was necessarily multiform and heterogeneous. "Old" approaches and mind-sets were changing, but slowly and unevenly, within the mental universe of U.S. trade unionists. If anything, the U.S. labor movement was less monolithic in the early 1990s than it has been at any point since the AFL-CIO was created in 1955. Even the right and center-right forces that controlled the AFL-CIO apparatus had moved, if only grudgingly, somewhat to the left. There was also much that was "new" within the ranks of U.S. labor, although its contours were still foggy, as generational shifts and the harsh attacks of the 1980s created a groundswell of change that began to blossom in the freer ideological atmosphere of the post-Cold War era. The fight against NAFTA from 1990 to 1993 united both old and new, traditionalists and reformists, the more conservative and the more radical. The fight against NAFTA proved a period of rich experimentation and learning as the U.S. labor movement and its allies grappled with how to confront the problem of transnational capital. It also marked the beginning of a new era of grassroots mobilization and cross-border coalition building with a transnational flavor. Direct forms of labor transnationalism, such as transnational coalition building, cross-border solidarity actions, and grassroots union linkages grew in number and frequency. Among the more exciting were cross-border tours of Mexican *maquiladoras* sponsored by unions whose companies had plants in the border zone. These forms of grassroots mobilization stimulated new reflection on the differences and similarities across the divide between NAFTA North (the United States and Canada) and NAFTA South (Mexico). These bold and exciting initiatives inspired activists as they worked to build a common terrain beyond the narrowly restrictive conceptual space of national identity and interests. Most significant, work was begun on carefully constructing transnational arguments against NAFTA, all of which went beyond U.S. protectionist paradigms and inherited nationalist reactions to the encroaching global economy.

While seeking allies across borders was symbolically important, the search for domestic alliances was an equally significant dimension of the anti-NAFTA fight. Significant segments of U.S. organized labor reached out toward other nonlabor coalitions, such as the Alliance for Responsible Trade (ART, formerly MODTLE), the Citizens' Trade Campaign, and the Coalition for Justice in the Maquiladoras (CJM). These groups brought together religious organizations, environmental groups, consumer advocates, and policy research organizations to develop sophisticated critiques of and alternatives to NAFTA and, in the case of CJM, to perform important community work and watchdog functions directly at the U.S.-Mexican border. Organized labor's role in these groups—with the exception of the CJM, which received official support from the AFL-CIO—was largely limited to a small number of committed individual union leaders, staff, and activists, but it represented a step forward.

The 1995 election of the "New Directions" leadership of Sweeney was one legacy of the fight against NAFTA, as was organized labor's presence in the tens of thousands at the 1999 protests against the ministerial conference of the World Trade Organization in Seattle. The subsequent years of economic globalization have also weakened the illusions of labor leaders, still vibrant in 1993, about a golden age of capital, labor, and government cooperation. And the existence of the North American Agreement on Labor Cooperation, although deeply flawed, left an institutional space through which to denounce violations of labor rights, however fruitlessly. By injecting the issue of labor rights into a trade agreement, the NAFTA labor side accord embodies a hope for future progress in the fight for a meaningful social dimension for an increasingly integrated global economy.

JOHN D. FRENCH

References and Further Reading

Ayres, Jeffrey M. *Defying Conventional Wisdom: Political Movements and Popular Contention against North American Free Trade.* Toronto: University of Toronto Press, 1998.

Bacon, David. *The Children of NAFTA: Labor Wars on the U.S./Mexico Border.* Berkeley: University of California Press, 2004.

Bandy, Joe, and Jackie Smith, eds. *Coalitions across Borders: Transnational Protest and the Neoliberal Order.* Lanham, MD: Rowman & Littlefield, 2005.

Carr, Barry. "Crossing Borders: Labor Internationalism in the Era of NAFTA." In *Neoliberalism Revisited: Economic Restructuring and Mexico's Political Future*, edited by Gerardo Otero. Boulder, CO: Westview, 1996, pp. 209–232.

Compa, Lance. "The First NAFTA Labor Cases: A New International Labor Rights Regime Takes Shape." *US-Mexico Law Journal*, no. 3 (1995): 159–181.

Cowie, Jefferson R. "National Struggles in a Transnational Economy: A Critical Analysis of U.S. Labor's Campaign against NAFTA." *Labor Studies Journal* 21, no. 4 (1997): 3–32.

Cowie, Jefferson R., and John D. French. *NAFTA's Labor Side Accord: A Textual Analysis.* Durham, NC: The Duke-UNC Program in Latin American Studies, 1994.

Dreiling, Michael C. *Solidarity and Contention: The Politics of Security and Sustainability in the NAFTA Conflict.* New York: Garland Publishing, 2001.

Folsom, Ralph H., Michael Wallace Gordon, and David A. Gantz. *NAFTA and Free Trade in the Americas: A Problem-Oriented Coursebook.* 2 vols. Vol. 1. St. Paul, MN: West, 2005.

French, John D. "From the Suites to the Streets: The Unexpected Re-emergence of the 'Labor Question,' 1994–1999." *Labor History* 43, no. 3 (2002): 285–304.

———. "Labor and NAFTA: Nationalist Reflexes and Transnational Imperatives in North America." In *Labour and Globalisation: Results and Prospects*, edited by Ronaldo Munck. Liverpool: University of Liverpool Press, 2004, pp. 149–165.

French, John D., Jefferson R. Cowie, and Scott Littlehale. *Labor and NAFTA: A Briefing Book.* Durham, NC: The Duke-UNC Program in Latin American Studies, 1995.

Kingsolver, Ann. *NAFTA Stories: Fears and Hopes in Mexico and the United States.* Boulder, CO: Lynne Rienner Publishers, 2001.

MacArthur, John R. *The Selling of "Free Trade": NAFTA, Washington, and the Subversion of American Democracy.* Berkeley: University of California Press, 2000.

Mayer, Frederick. *Interpreting NAFTA: The Science and Art of Political Analysis.* New York: Columbia University Press, 1998.

Robinson, Ian. *North American Trade as if Democracy Mattered: What's Wrong with NAFTA and What Are the Alternatives?* Ottawa/Washington: Canadian Centre for Policy Alternatives, International Labor Rights Education and Research Fund, 1993.

Smith, Russell E., and John D. French. "Labor, Free Trade, and Economic Integration in the Americas: A Conference Report." *Latin American Labor News*, nos. 12–13 (1995): 3–4.

NO-STRIKE PLEDGE

Few moments reveal the gap between union leadership and rank-and-file workers more than national mobilization for war. Historically, wartime has brought enhanced bargaining power for labor as both production and labor demand increased; yet it also has brought patriotic appeals for organized labor and workers to set aside their narrow interests on behalf of the nation. During U.S. involvement in World War I and World War II, union leaders agreed to suspend all strike activity in exchange for basic concessions by employers, guaranteed by the enhanced power of the wartime state.

This no-strike pledge, however, did not always prove popular with rank-and-file workers, who feared they had abandoned the one tool they had to win concessions from employers. During both wars, the result was turmoil on the shop floor and unauthorized wildcat strikes. Organized labor itself often had to step in to discipline rank-and-file workers when they violated the no-strike pledge, exacerbating tensions between union leadership and members.

When the United States entered World War I in 1917, the labor committee of the Council on National Defense, chaired by the American Federation of Labor (AFL) president, Samuel Gompers, proclaimed that "neither employers nor employees shall endeavor to take advantage of the country's necessity to change existing standards." Met by a deluge of complaints from workers about this apparent binding of the AFL by a no-strike pledge, Gompers insisted that unions could still continue to use strikes as a last resort. Nevertheless, World War I proved a strike-prone era, with over 1,100 breaking out in the first five months of the conflict alone. Not only did AFL unions like the International Association of Machinists engage in strike action, but of course Socialist and Industrial Workers of the World (IWW) unionists had no interest in setting aside labor militancy on behalf of a war they opposed. Individual organizations, however, like the Stockyards Labor Council in Chicago, agreed to suspend strike action during the war in exchange for government mediation that would help labor win some major concessions on hours and wages from employers. Finally, in March 1918, a year after American entry into the war, the War Labor Conference Board (the predecessor to the War Labor Board) secured an agreement from the AFL leadership that "there should be no strikes or lockouts during the war" in exchange for the right to collective bargaining, protection of existing union shops, the eight-hour day, and a "living wage."

Twenty-five years later, World War II brought an even more forthcoming, if just as weakly honored, no-strike pledge on the part of organized labor, which now represented many more workers than it had in 1918. One week after U.S. entry into the war in December 1941, the AFL president, William Green, promised that, for the duration, "labor will produce, and produce without interruption." The AFL executive board immediately embraced a no-strike pledge, as did its counterparts in the Congress of Industrial Organizations (CIO). Although these decisions reflected widespread patriotic sentiment among workers, they also represented a pre-emptive effort to forestall any restrictive legislation and a desire to secure beneficial arbitration on issues of wages and union security from the National War Labor Board (NWLB).

Since the no-strike pledge was a "pledge" rather than a formally binding agreement, the NWLB devised nonjudicial sanctions with which to enforce adherence to it. By threatening to withdraw the benefits it had granted in arbitrated union contracts, such as protection of the closed shop, the NWLB effectively recruited unions to police the widespread wildcat strikes of their own members. In the last two years of the war, union leaders proved especially anxious to enforce the no-strike pledge to defend against growing antilabor sentiment embodied in the Smith-Connally Act of 1943 and the danger that Roosevelt would enact a national service program, or "labor draft," to discipline unruly workers and shore up a chaotic labor market. The necessity of disciplining wildcat strikers enhanced bureaucratic tendencies in large industrial unions, strengthening the hands of centralized leadership at the expense of a less tractable rank and file. By 1944, the CIO president, Philip Murray, complained that a large portion of his union's treasury was "being used to enforce the WLB directives...which in the first instance we do not believe in."

Historians disagree about the relative gains and losses of wartime no-strike pledges. In both conflicts, organized labor made significant organizational and contractual gains by agreeing to suspend strike activity in exchange for increased federal intervention in labor-management relations. Patriotic allegiance to national war aims gained legitimacy for the trade unions that supported the war effort, and destroyed those, like the IWW, that did not. At the same time, the no-strike pledge relinquished the one coercive mechanism available to unions, made workers' organizations dependent on the government, and put labor leaders in the uncomfortable position of having to quash, on behalf of the state, their members' grievances and strike actions.

ALEX LICHTENSTEIN

References and Further Reading

Dubofsky, Melvyn. *The State and Labor in Modern America*. Chapel Hill and London: University of North Carolina Press, 1994.

Lichtenstein, Nelson. *Labor's War at Home: The CIO in World War II*. Philadelphia: Temple University Press, 2004.

McCartin, Joseph A. *Labor's Great War: The Struggle for Industrial Democracy and the Origins of Modern American Labor Relations, 1912–1921*. Chapel Hill: University of North Carolina Press, 1997.

See also **American Federation of Labor; Congress of Industrial Organizations; Gompers, Samuel; Industrial Workers of the World; International Association of Machinists and Aerospace Workers; National War Labor Board (WWI); National War Labor Board (WWII); Smith-Connally Act; World War I; World War II**

NOVELS, POETRY, DRAMA

From the days of America's rural, agricultural economy to the current postindustrial period of service-sector work, American writers have chronicled the struggles of the nation's workforce with varying success. Much of a considerable body of novels, poetry, and drama plays that focused on work and labor struggles failed to attract a wide audience and fell into neglect. Still, several works successfully integrate the conditions of workers and strikes, providing important literary contributions and bringing inspiration to the American labor movement.

Novels

The novel emerged as a venue for working-class themes very slowly in the United States. Before the Civil War, most novelists had genteel backgrounds and produced texts with a middle-class readership in mind. Most plots featured characters struggling with questions surrounding property, inheritance, and Puritan virtues. If writers described the working class, they emphasized the nation's rural, small-town society and depicted workers as self-employed

craftsmen, shopkeepers, professionals, or farmers. In the 1840s, however, more novelists began using the city as a background for their narratives, calling attention to urban poverty and offering hints of the world of work as they described the streets of the city. By the next decade, some novels included more detailed descriptions of workers on the job. For example, Day Kellogg Lee's *The Master Builder; or Life at a Trade* (1853) features a protagonist who works as a sawmill operator. His next novel, *Merrimack; or Life at the Loom* (1854), depicts young women laboring in the textile mills of Lowell, Massachusetts.

The dramatic rise of industrialization in the middle of the nineteenth century coincided with the literary shift to realism. As writers strove for greater verisimilitude, it was inevitable that works would begin to include more specific information about the difficult workplace conditions faced by many workers. Rebecca Harding Davis produced what many consider the first full-scale industrial narrative when her *Life in the Iron Mills* appeared in the *Atlantic Monthly* in 1861. The novella focuses on a young immigrant ironworker, Hugh Wolfe, and the dangerous working conditions he faces as he stirs molten iron inside the choking atmosphere of the plant. More and more writers in the Gilded Age would follow this precedent and offer more detailed treatments of the American working class. Eventually, the rising labor movement and its struggles would work its way into fiction.

One of the earliest depictions of a strike in American fiction appeared in 1871 in Elizabeth Stuart Phelps's *The Silent Partner*. Significantly, the heroine of the novel is not a worker but a "silent partner" in the New England textile mill she inherited. Similarly, labor struggles play a significant role in the plot of the most influential novel of the period, Edward Bellamy's utopian novel *Looking Backward, 2000–1887* (1888). The novel's protagonist, the Bostonian Julian West, is frustrated that strikes have delayed the construction of his new home. In the utopian society of the year 2000, however, the elimination of classes has made strikes and labor unions obsolete. *Looking Backward* influenced subsequent generations of writers as it introduced the theme of socialism into American fiction. But as the nineteenth century drew to a close, it remained clear that the novelists addressing working-class life wrote from a middle-class perspective and drew a great deal of their information from secondhand sources. For the most part, industrialists were depicted admirably, the trade union organizer was the subject of suspicion, and foreign-born workers were the source of most problems.

The industrial scene and union activity were eventually drawn with greater insight as the Gilded Age waned and the nation moved deeper into the Progressive Era. Many writers, either through their own work experiences or their investigations of labor struggles as journalists, developed deeper insight and understanding of the workers' perspective. For example, Upton Sinclair's investigation of conditions in the Chicago stockyards and events during the Chicago Stockyard Strike of 1904 led to his landmark novel of industrialization, *The Jungle* (1906). The Russian immigrant Theresa Serber Malkiel toiled in New York City's garment industry when she first arrived in the United States. She later became a labor activist, and the New York Shirtwaist Makers' Strike of 1909–1910 inspired Theresa Serber Malkiel to produce a highly detailed fictional treatment of the labor struggle, *The Diary of a Shirtwaist Striker* (1910). The gains made by the Industrial Workers of the World (IWW) and the Socialist Party also inspired many writers. The novelist Ernest Poole, for example, personally witnessed the IWW in action during the Lawrence Textile Strike of 1912 and the Paterson Silk Strike of 1913 and was moved to fictionalize the labor struggles in what would become one of the most popular books of 1915, *The Harbor*. The novel is notable for the insight it provides into the gains made by the Socialist Party and the IWW prior to World War I.

In the 1920s, the seeds of the proletarian novel and "strike" novel were sown as more writers attacked the idea of economic mobility and voiced a general repugnance for the state of American life. More novels featured worker-protagonists. In Elias Tobenkin's *The Road* (1922), the heroine works in the New York garment industry to support herself and her illegitimate son. She later becomes an effective trade union organizer. Occasionally, novels question the impact of the American business ethic on immigrants. *Haunch, Paunch, and Jowl* (1923) by Samuel Ornitz depicts an immigrant garment worker who eventually becomes an attorney for the textile industry. He abandons his family, friends, and fellow workers as he become more affluent and is lonely and unhappy by the close of the novel.

As the nation moved deeper into the Great Depression, the worker-writer began to emerge. Many workers in factories, mines, and farms were moved to record their experiences during their time away from their jobs. Firsthand experience led to highly detailed descriptions of the workplace and union operations. Because many of these writers participated in strikes, labor struggles in the novels are often developed through the eyes of the workers. The strike is also used symbolically to represent the struggles and the victories of the working class. Key proletarian and strike novels of the 1930s include Jack Conroy's *The Disinherited* (1933), Mary Heaton Vorse's *Strike!*

(1930), Thomas Tippett's *Horse Shoe Bottoms* (1935), and John Steinbeck's *In Dubious Battle* (1936). Fictional treatments of the struggles of African-American workers and their experiences during the Great Migration were also developed at around this time in such works as William Attaway's *Blood on the Forge* (1941) and Alden Bland's *Behold a Cry* (1947).

In the last decades of the twentieth century, plant-closing recessions, the loss of millions of manufacturing jobs, a steady decline in union membership, and an economy increasingly dependent on service-sector work led to a resurgence in working-class themes in literature. Writers with worker roots such as Raymond Carver, Joyce Carol Oates, Tillie Olsen, James Dickey, and Carolyn Chute often depict the problems, apathy, and discontent of workers, both working-class and blue-collar. The closing decades of the twentieth century also led to a resurgence in the theme of ethnicity, race, and working-class oppression. Chicano labor is fictionalized in works such as Raymond Barrio's *The Plum Plum Pickers* (1972) and Ernesto Galarza's *Barrio Boy* (1971). Similarly, the work situations faced by African-American women are addressed in works such as Gloria Naylor's *The Women of Brewster Place* (1988), Toni Cade Bambara's *The Salt Eaters* (1980), and Ramona Lofton's *Push* (1997).

Poetry

Working-class life has been a very significant subject for American poets, and many poetic texts provide important inspiration to the labor movement. Poets in the Early Republic often emphasized the American work ethic and the nation's rural, small-town society. For example, Henry Wadsworth Longfellow, in poems such as "The Village Blacksmith" (1841), presented the workingman as industrious, skillful, sober, and independent:

> Under a spreading chestnut tree
> The village smithy stands;
> The smith, a mighty man is he,
> With large and sinewy hands;
> And the muscles of his brawny arms
> Are strong as iron bands

In the age of Manifest Destiny, workers were celebrated as the builders of the expanding nation in poems such as Walt Whitman's "A Song for Occupations" (1855). Later, the Yiddish poet Morris Rosenfeld developed a reputation as the "poet laureate of labor" as his experiences as a presser and baster in New York's Lower East sweatshops inspired him to put pen to paper. Poems such as "In the Factory" were noted for their realistic description of sweatshop life:

Oh, here in the shop the machines roar so wildly
That oft, unaware that I am, or have been.
I sink and am lost in the terrible tumult
And void is my soul . . . I am but a machine!

In many cases, many of labor's successes, defeats, or tragedies prompted poets to express their emotions. Rosenfeld, for example, wrote a requiem for the victims of the Triangle Shirtwaist Company Fire of March 25, 1911. Due to blocked exits and faulty fire escapes in the factory, a total of 146 workers, mostly young immigrant women, perished in the flames or jumped 10 stories to their deaths. Rosenfeld's poem, written four days after the fire and published in the *Jewish Daily Forward*, mixes fury and sorrow over the tragedy:

And Mammon devours our sons and daughters
Wrapt in scarlet flames, they drop to death from this
  maw
And death receives them all.
Sisters mine, oh my sisters; brethren
Hear my sorrow:
See where the dead are hidden in dark corners,
Where life is choked from those who labor.
Oh, woe is me, and woe to the world.

As unionization increased, more labor journals and newspapers were founded and became outlets for aspiring poets. Journals such as Edward Bellamy's *The New Nation*, Horace Traubel's *Conservator*, the *International Socialist Review*, *Il Proletario*, the *Masses*, and the *Liberator* published verse. Noteworthy poets during this period who protested the struggles of the exploited laborer in the United States include Charlotte Perkins Gilman, Rose Pastor Stokes, Edwin Markham, Arturo Giovannitti, and the author considered the most active of the socialist poets, Carl Sandburg. In many of his poems, Sandburg expressed admiration for the toughness of the working class, as these lines from "Chicago" indicate:

Under the smoke, dust all over his mouth, laughing with
  white teeth,
Under the terrible burden of destiny laughing as a young
  man laughs,
Laughing even as an ignorant fighter laughs who has
  never lost a battle,
Bragging and laughing that under his wrist is the pulse,
  and under his ribs the heart of the people,
Laughing!

Most poetry dealing with working-class themes has been sung, and as labor organizations grew, the song continued to be a popular form for rallying workers. The genre of the union song probably reached its height in the early twentieth century under the organization described as the "singingest union"—the Industrial Workers of the World (IWW). The IWW's leading troubadours were Joe Hill (1879–1915) and another IWW poet and artist, Ralph H. Chaplin (1887–1961). The union's songbook, *IWW Songs: To Fan the Flames of Discontent* (also known as the *Little Red Songbook*), was distributed, along with a membership card, to all who joined the organization. The songs could be heard at union meetings, on picket lines, and in jails, and they often parodied the popular songs and hymns of the period. Hill's "Pie in the Sky" is a cutting parody of the hymn "Sweet By-and-By":

Long-haired preachers come out every night,
Try to tell you what's wrong and what's right;
But when asked how 'bout something to eat
They will answer with voices so sweet:

CHORUS:

You will eat, bye and bye,
In that glorious land above the sky;
Work and pray, live on hay,
You'll get pie in the sky when you die.

With government crackdown on communist and socialist activities at the close of the Progressive Era and nationalistic sentiment on the rise as America entered World War I, the Wobblies and their music were largely silenced by repression. Persistent low wages and poor working conditions in the 1920s, however, continued to spur unionization and strikes. As the problems facing the working class intensified with the onset of the Great Depression, it once again became clear that songs were an effective tool for calling workers back into the labor movement. Labor militancy rose in the 1930s thanks to musicians such as Woody Guthrie, Huddie Leadbetter (Leadbelly), and Aunt Molly Jackson. In the 1940s, groups such as the Almanac Singers and the People's Songs formed in support of CIO organizing campaigns. "Talking Union," by the Almanac Singers, provides instructions about how to form a union local:

Now, you know you're underpaid, but the boss says you ain't;

He speeds up the work till you're about to faint.
You may be down and out, but you're not beaten
You can pass out a leaflet and call a meetin'
Talk it over—speak your mind—
Decide to do something about it.

Folk groups produced a virtual library of protest songs that stressed unity and mutual assistance among the working class. In the 1950s, groups such as the Weavers, who continued to perform despite political pressure to disband, kept the tradition alive. Later, the popularization of folk groups led to music styles that played a significant role in the Civil Rights Movement and the protest against the Vietnam War. Artists who successfully bridged the gap between folk music and popular taste include Bob Dylan, Joan Baez, the Byrds, and Peter, Paul, and Mary.

Contemporary poets explore the need for satisfying work and attempts to avoid dead-end jobs and alienating labor. For example, works such as Barbara Smith's "The Bowl" and Marge Piercy's "To Be of Use" give insight into the joy that can be found in physical labor. Social class, most notably immigrant labor, is the focus of poems such as Benjamin Aliere Saenz's "Journeys" and Jimmy Santiago Baca's "So Mexicans Are Taking Jobs from Americans." Some entire books of poetry are focused on workers in particular industries. For example, the poet Jim Daniels' book *Punching Out* focuses on the activities of workers on the assembly line of a Detroit auto manufacturer.

Drama

Theater for working-class audiences has a long history, and several productions have an important place in labor culture. Even in the formative years of the labor movement in the antebellum period, plays appealed to the spreading discontent among workers. In the 1830s and 1840s, some productions were blamed for the spreading of mob violence in major cities. *The Carpenter of Rouen* played in New York City's Bowery Theatre and dramatized the successful revolt against autocratic repression in the French Revolution. Eventually, as the shift from an agricultural to an industrial society continued, working-class culture grew and the local theater played an important place in meeting the entertainment needs of laborers who had free time on Saturday afternoons. Regional subjects and working-class themes were popular, and playwrights worked to adapt well-known dramatic formulas to local tastes. As more immigrants arrived in the United States in search of work in the mines, mills, and factories, ethnic characterizations also enjoyed tremendous appeal. A significant example of drama aimed at local audiences is found among the ironworkers and glass craftsmen in Pittsburgh in 1878 when a play, *The Lower Million*, proved to be extremely successful. The lavish production dramatized the Great Railroad Strike of 1877 and carried an increasingly popular theme: the skilled craftsman is the hero of the industrial system.

In the late nineteenth century, workers became more involved in theater productions. A key example is the development of workers' theater by German socialists in the 1880s. Socialists often wrote their own festival plays to celebrate events significant to the working class. A leading figure in German-American socialist workers' theater was the anarchist Johann Most (1846–1906), who acted and produced successful versions of Gerhard Hauptman's naturalistic drama, *Die Weber* (*The Weavers*) in San Francisco, New York, and Chicago. At about the same time, there was an increase in the number of plays produced for immigrant, working-class audiences. Classical and foreign language plays were revised to fit into the urban, industrial setting of the Gilded Age. In New York's Lower East Side, for example, popular commercial productions used garment factories and sweatshops as settings.

In the opening decades of the twentieth century, radical organizations saw an opportunity in dramatizing labor struggles. The most significant example occurred during the Paterson Silk Strike of 1913. Strike organizers and the IWW hoped to rally workers and raise much-needed strike funds. Approximately 1,000 striking workers were part of the cast in the dramatization of the labor struggle. The production was mainly orchestrated by John Reed, the writer for the *Masses*, who experienced the strike firsthand and was jailed with the immigrant laborers. "The Pageant of the Paterson Strike" was divided into six major episodes from the strike. The mass actions by strikers were re-enacted, accompanied by excerpts from the stirring speeches made by strike leaders during the labor struggle. The cast also sang songs such as "The Marseillaise" and "The International." Prepared in only three weeks, the play was performed on June 7, 1913, before an audience of approximately 15,000 at New York's Madison Square Garden. The play won critical praise and by several accounts moved the audience deeply; it failed, however, to generate the desperately needed strike funds.

During the Progressive Era and into the late 1920s, companies expanded the use of theater as a venue to indoctrinate their workers with company ideology. Large corporations financed company auditoriums and subsidized company drama clubs and vaudeville acts. The productions not only entertained the workers but also limited outside influences such as saloons and dance halls. Company shows often involved workers and their families. Examples include the Goodyear Greater Minstrels and the *Hawthorne Follies* held at the Western Electric Company's Hawthorne Works in Chicago. Entertainers glorified hard work, exemplified the idea of positive relations among employees, or showed proper methods for selling merchandise.

Workers' education leaders and labor colleges also recognized theater's ability to instruct and inspire. Due to the unemployment, evictions, speedups, and wage cuts brought on by the Great Depression, amateur workers' theater grew into a full movement as hundreds of troupes and tens of thousands of workers wrote, directed, and performed theatrical pieces. Notable examples include participation of members of the International Ladies' Garment Workers' Union (ILGWU) in the play *Pins and Needles*. Similarly, Local 65 of the United Wholesale and Warehouse Employees produced shows such as *Sing While You Fight*. In this play, the two main characters—Jean and Bill—find meaningful activities once they become union members. Jean enjoys duties with the union newspaper. Bill participates in union athletic teams. Ultimately, the two characters find each other at a Saturday night social sponsored by the union. They also find romantic bliss.

The 1930s produced very powerful protest dramas, due in large measure to the agitational performances produced by the Workers' Laboratory Theater (WLT) of New York. The most successful "agitprop" play of the period was the one-act *Waiting for Lefty*, which was written in three days by one of the left's most successful playwrights, Clifford Odets (1906–1963). The play was inspired by the New York taxi strike of 1934 and is set in a union hall where members of the taxicab drivers' union are waiting for the arrival of the popular committeeman, Lefty Costello. The progress of the drivers' union meeting is alternated with flashbacks of the frustrated lives of various workers and their financial difficulties. At the close of the play, a messenger arrives to report the news to the labor leader Agate Keller that Lefty has been murdered:

Man: They found Lefty . . .
Agate: Where?
Man: Behind the car barns with a bullet in his head!
Agate (crying): Hear it boys, hear it? Hell, listen to me! Coast to coast! HELLO AMERICA! WE'RE THE STORMBIRDS OF THE WORKING-CLASS. WORKERS OF THE WORLD . . . OUR BONES AND BLOOD . . . [To audience] Well, what's the answer?
All: Strike!
Agate: Louder!
All: Strike!
Agate and others on stage: AGAIN!
All: Strike! Strike! Strike!!!

Waiting for Lefty was widely performed by theater groups and amateur performers in union locals. The short play won Odets tremendous acclaim and is considered one of the most powerful protest dramas of the 1930s.

The counterculture movement beginning in the 1960s brought new theatrical forms that were suitable for outdoor demonstrations. Theater companies such as the Bread and Puppet Theatre, San Francisco Mime Troupe, and Pageant Players in New York performed on city street corners, parks, parking lots, and inside businesses to rally opposition to the Vietnam War, the nuclear arms race, and homelessness. Labor organizations worked for support through theater productions. Unstable Coffeehouse Productions in Detroit, for example, presented an original play, *Sitdown '37*, to an audience of United Auto Workers members as part of the twenty-fifth anniversary of the major labor struggle that helped unionize General Motors. In addition, the San Francisco General Strike of 1934 inspired the playwright Jack Rasmus to write "1934: The Musical." The major non-English theater of the 1960s was El Teatro Campesino (Farm Workers' Theater). The group's productions aimed at recruiting farmworkers and promoting union activities.

MARK A. NOON

References and Further Reading

Aaron, Daniel. *Writers on the Left*. New York: Harcourt, Brace, and World, 1961.
Blake, Fay. *The Strike in the American Novel*. Metuchen, NJ: Scarecrow, 1972.
Bromell, Nicholas. *By the Sweat of the Brow: Literature and Labor in Antebellum America*. Chicago: University of Chicago Press, 1993.
Dietrich, Julia. *The Old Left in History and Literature*. New York: Twayne, 1996.
Denisoff, R. Serge. *Great Day Coming: Folk Music and the American Left*. Urbana: University of Illinois Press, 1971.
Foner, Philip. *American Labor Songs of the Nineteenth Century*. Urbana: University of Illinois Press, 1975.
Halker, Clark D. *For Democracy, Workers, and God: Labor Song-poems and Labor Protest, 1865–95*. Urbana: University of Illinois Press, 1991.
Hapke, Laura. *Labor's Text: The Worker in American Fiction*. New Brunswick, NJ: Rutgers University Press, 2001.
Hyman, Colette. *Staging Strikes: Workers' Theatre and the American Labor Movement*. Philadelphia: Temple University Press, 1997.
McConachie, Bruce, and Daniel Friedman. *Theatre for Working-Class Audiences in the United States, 1830–1980*. Westport, CT: Greenwood, 1985.
Oresick, Peter, and Nicolas Coles, eds. *Working Classics: Poems of Industrial Life*. Urbana: University of Illinois Press, 1990.
Prestridge, Virginia. *The Worker in American Fiction: An Annotated Bibliography*. Champaign: University of Illinois Institute for Industrial and Labor Relations, 1954.
Reuss, Richard. *American Folk Music and Left-Wing Politics*. Lanham, MD: Scarecrow, 2000.
Rideout, Walter. *The Radical Novel in the United States, 1900–1954*. Cambridge, MA: Harvard University Press, 1965.
Taylor, Walter Fuller. *The Economic Novel in America*. Chapel Hill: University of North Carolina Press, 1942.

NURSING AND HEALTH CARE

In the mid-nineteenth century, women reformers took a long-accepted female duty, nursing the sick, and fashioned it into paid women's work. One impetus for this came from England's indignation at the treatment of its wounded soldiers in the Crimea. The public outcry resulted in a group of religious sisters and lay women, led by Florence Nightingale, being sent to organize nursing care for these men. After the war, Nightingale led the incipient drive for formal nursing education. Whereas care for family members was an accepted province for women, institutionalized care in the battlefield and in hospitals was considered suitable only for the meanest levels of society. Progressive Era reformers, such as Nightingale and her U.S. counterparts, sought to impose order and moral discipline in hospital wards through their innovation of trained nurses. Indeed, with increasingly complex care following the introduction of anesthesia in the 1840s and the emerging scientific base of medicine, skilled nursing was essential.

Yet there were inherent barriers to instituting an educated nursing workforce, and these barriers have persisted to this day. Care by educated nurses is expensive and constitutes a more protracted expense for patients than physicians' isolated charges. In addition, society typically undervalues and underrewards caring. Nursing care ranges from relatively unskilled domestic work to complex and specialized interventions, yet a clear line of differentiation is impossible to draw. Furthermore, nursing was initiated as a women's field—indeed, Nightingale introduced her 1860 *Notes on Nursing* with "Nursing is women's work." Women were considered subordinate to men, and their occupations carried less esteem. Female nurses worked alongside male physicians within the paternalistic hospital environment, where physicians were positioned to demand medical authority over nursing practice, which was professionally inhibited because of its very femaleness. Addressing these difficult issues resulted in compromises in nursing education, conflicts among nurses, and conflicts between nursing leaders and physicians.

This essay opens with a description of hospital-based nursing training and the characteristics of the worker-students from the 1870s through to the post-WWII decline in the number of hospital training schools. The graduates of these schools, who initially worked as independent contractors for individual patients and later as hospital employees, will then be described. The education and work opportunities for nurses over the following decades of the twentieth century will be followed by a discussion of the American Nurses Association's (ANA) involvement in shaping working conditions for nurses.

Setting the Stage

Florence Nightingale asserted that prior to trained nursing, hospital nurses were generally "those who were too old, too weak, too drunken, too stolid, or too bad to do anything else." Her disparagement merits discussion. Hospitals were charitable institutions for the very poor, the dregs of Victorian society, who presented with noxious diseases and intimate needs. Their nurses were from similarly unfortunate backgrounds, often former patients themselves, who needed steady employment and a place to live. There is much evidence to show that many of these women and men were hardworking and caring of their charges.

With Nightingale's example from overseas, the first U.S. educational programs to train nurses and reform hospital nursing were opened in the early 1870s. These schools, like the hundreds that followed, sought to engender moral training as well as nursing techniques. The nurse historian Carol Helmstadter notes that moral discipline was the overarching concern of the Victorian age, particularly in relation to women. Additionally, the growth of women's wage labor threatened traditional patriarchal authority among all classes. Nurses were to express the Victorian concept of ideal womanhood—moral, submissive, and obedient. Student nurses were subjected to strict discipline within a hierarchical system that oversaw every aspect of their lives for their two or three years of training. Unquestioning obedience and deference were demanded. Helmstadter claims that the new trained nurse was subservient, dependent, and exploited.

Nurses' Training: 1880–1950

After the first handful of prestigious nursing schools opened, modeled after Nightingale's and with their own governing boards, the benefits that this hardworking, disciplined corps of young women could bring to hospitals became readily apparent. Scores of schools opened that were operated and controlled by hospitals. Hospital administrators appreciated that their own nursing schools could provide essentially free nursing care. To hospital management, it

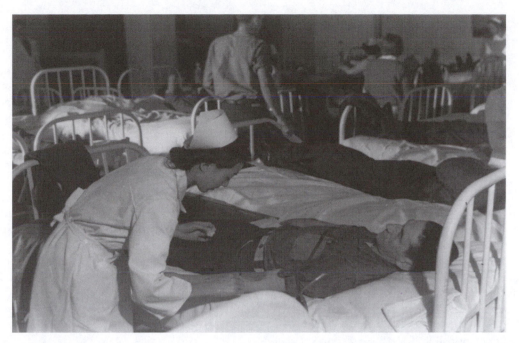

Nurse preparing arm of prisoner, possibly for blood donation to aid the armed forces during World War II, San Quentin prison, California. Library of Congress, Prints & Photographs Division [LC-USZ62-97127].

constituted an astoundingly fortunate development, and they began to develop business strategies and court both patients and physicians to their facilities, based on provision of free nursing labor. Schools were essentially organized as nursing service departments within the hospitals and were governed by the hospital administration. Predictably, the number of nurse training schools mushroomed; in 1880, 15 were in operation, and in 1910, there were 1,129. The number of hospitals likewise increased rapidly along with the number of nurse training schools. In 1873, there were 178 hospitals in the United States; 50 years later, there were 6,830 and every fourth one had a nursing school. Most were small community hospitals, open to paying patients, usually admitted for a surgical procedure, who expected efficient and competent nursing care. Some of these hospitals were specialized, and their student nurses were exposed only to that specialty, while others were small with highly limited experiences for their students. Yet they still maintained their profitable schools. Instruction in many of these schools, particularly the smaller ones, was certainly poor. In 1932, 23% of schools did not have even one full-time instructor, while only 25% had two or more. In the mid-1930s, about 30% of the instructors had not themselves finished high school, while only 20% had as much as one year of college.

Yet it may be argued that this arrangement was not totally unfair to the student nurses. In return for two or three years of physical work, which was usually supported with a stipend and always included room and board, graduating nurses received a diploma that offered, at minimum, the prospect of a career.

The lives of nursing students from the 1880s through to the 1940s and beyond were ones of unrelenting control and discipline. Every aspect of work, study, and recreation was subject to the authority of the nursing school. Nursing superintendents and hospital managers demanded total loyalty and obedience from the nurses and tolerated no infractions of their rules. Some students rebelled and left while many others found fulfillment in the total relinquishment of independent thinking and the boarding school-like environment that was demonstrated in their yearbooks and alumnae association activities. Inexpensive rewards for length of service, such as different-colored belts and stripes on caps, were coveted and worn proudly. Some writers have commented that students entered training as women and left as girls, while others discuss the subjugation of independent thinking and inquiry to the unquestioning obedience demanded.

Trained nurses were expected to belong to a superior social class, although the hard work and menial connotations associated with nursing made this type of applicant elusive. Most students came from farms or small towns. Those who were from socially higher families were targeted to become directors of training schools or hospital administrators—opportunities open to few women in the late nineteenth century. However, all students in the early public hospitals were expected to be of a higher social class than their patients and were also counted upon to be pleasing to look at and to have appropriate social skills. By the 1920s, however, admission standards were lower. Concerns were raised about the inferior women entering nursing in the report of a major study of nurses commissioned by the American Nurses Association. Writing in 1928, the author (Burgess) voiced concern over the undereducated women entering nursing, who were of "inadequate social and academic background" and should really be kept out of the profession.

Nursing training has been likened to an apprenticeship system, since students essentially worked with patients for three years, gaining experience through work. However, the historian Barbara Melosh has argued that a true apprenticeship requires the presence of experts—in this case, graduate nurses—who were lacking in the hospital schools of this period. Student nurses in the 1890s were predominantly responsible for domestic chores as well as rapidly becoming totally responsible for the care of very ill patients, particularly when on night duty. There were few graduate nurses, and those were in a supervisory role. Students swept, dusted, and cleaned the lavatories, made the beds, and cleaned the bedpans. Yet they also assisted with dressing wounds and dispensed medications. In 1896, a survey of three hundred nurse training schools revealed that students typically worked 60 to 105 hours a week, with typical workdays or nights of eight to 15 hours. Many days after work, students were obliged to listen to lectures from physicians or nursing supervisors. At most hospital training schools, students were also sent out on private duty, to nurse patients in their homes. Students might stay on the case for days or weeks. The patients' fees were pocketed by the hospital and were regarded as a major part of the income for many of the smaller schools. Students in 1934 worked more than 48 hours a week, working every day with two half days off a week. Yet this work could not be called an apprenticeship. In 1932, two thirds of the schools did not have even one graduate nurse employed for bedside work. In most schools, students received a small monthly allowance, although the more prestigious schools did not do this—wanting to maintain the image that their nurses were students rather than workers.

Training lasted three years in most schools, and a standardization of the curriculum was attempted through the first edition of the *Standard Curriculum* published in 1917. There were successful efforts throughout the country to mandate state registration of nurses, and nurses' living conditions and hours of work eased considerably compared with earlier years. The quality of nursing education was also changing.

Ninety-nine percent of all nurse training schools required graduation from high school by 1935, and in 1937, the *Curriculum Guide for Schools of Nursing* recommended an increase in nurses' theoretical education. The number of schools giving a university degree in addition to a nursing diploma was also growing; in 1935, there were over 70 such programs. These combined two or three years in the hospital with two years of college courses. There were also three nursing programs within universities, with school or department status.

This type of practical education rendered nursing students, and not graduate nurses, a valuable commodity. At graduation, following presentation of the school's pin and laudatory speeches, the newly minted nurses were dismissed from the hospital and a new crop of students took their place. Most of these young women tried to find work as private-duty nurses, either in private homes or working for individual patients in hospitals.

Nurses' Work: 1880–1950

Nursing rapidly became the second largest female-dominated profession, after teaching. In 1920, there were 635,000 school teachers and 144,000 nurses. Most nurses worked in private duty during the early decades of the century and typically connected with prospective private patients through registries—often operated by their hospital or its alumnae association. Registering on the hospital list sometimes meant competing with the hospital's current nursing students for positions, and certainly placements were at the whim of the hospital's nursing supervisors. By 1896, approximately 40 alumnae associations existed, and several of them operated registries. During the early years of the twentieth century, commercial employment agencies and some medical organizations operated nurses' registries. For physicians, medical registries generated a convenient method of contacting nurses for their patients. Nurses paid a registration fee to be placed on a list of available nurses. A typical large agency, Chicago's Nurses' Professional Registry, was formed in 1913 by several local alumnae associations. By 1923, the Chicago registry was well established with around 950 members and annually received more than 11,000 requests for private-duty nurses.

Even with registries, private-duty nursing was an insecure means of earning a living. Private-duty nurses were isolated and unorganized and vulnerable to the idiosyncrasies of their patients and the market. Additionally, by the 1920s, there was not nearly enough work for the numbers of nurses being produced by the nurse training schools. The private-duty fees barely generated enough to cover periods of unemployment, while saving for retirement was next to impossible. Unlike hospital nurses, who lived rent free in nurses' "homes," private-duty nurses needed their own place to live as well as a telephone for the registry to contact them. Following a period of employment, most registries ruled that nurses who had worked three or more days would move to the end of the list. The work, too, could generate different stressors from hospital nursing, as private-duty nurses worked in a social limbo, not at one with their patient's family or the servants. The hours of private-duty nurses were longer than for any other group of nurses; some nurses worked 24-hour shifts even as late as 1937. Also, the close and unremitting patient contact was difficult. Patients' illnesses also affected nurses' earning ability. If they nursed patients suffering from contagious diseases—including cancer, which for many years was considered contagious—they were barred from taking surgical or maternity cases for the following several weeks.

By the mid-1920s, the already limited market for private-duty nursing was saturated. When the Great Depression effectively crushed most opportunities for such nursing, nurses had been teetering on the brink of severe unemployment for years. In addition to diminishing work prospects, the number of nurses produced continued to increase. Nurse training schools had increased from 1,775 in 1920 to 2,286 just eight years later, and the number of nurses had doubled from 104,000 in 1920 to 214,000 in 1930. In 1920, the percentage of nurses who entered private-duty nursing was 80% but declined to about 55% in 1930. At the end of 1930, the registries reported that 25% to 40% of graduate nurses were unemployed.

This unemployment for private-duty nurses sparked a transition from private-duty to hospital nursing for the nation's trained nurses. This transition also significantly impacted nursing education. Hospitals, in desperate financial straits, capitalized on the nurses' unemployment and financial distress by hiring them for far lower wages than the usual rates or even paying them for merely room and board. By the late 1920s, most private-duty nurses worked as bedside—or staff—nurses in acute-care hospitals rather than for private patients. Restrictions on graduate nurses working in hospitals imitated the restrictions of student life. Hospitals routinely required graduate nurses to live in the nurses' dormitory, and they were subject to the same discipline and regimentation that had characterized their student life. They were hired for general ward work and dismissed or re-appointed based upon patient occupancy.

The rationale for operating schools of nursing faded in the face of this newly available and inexpensive corps of graduate nurses generated by the Depression, and many schools closed. This school closure was supported by the state nurses' associations and the American Nurses Association. Some members even donated one month's free nursing service to compensate the schools for the loss of student work. In 1936, there were 1,381 schools, compared with 2,296 just eight years earlier. The number of graduate nurses employed by hospitals rose dramatically from about 4,000 in 1929 to over 100,000 in 1941, about 46% of all practicing nurses. Graduate nurses became accepted as hospital nurses during this decade, and the importance of student nurses as primary caregivers receded. Although many schools of nursing closed during this period, the enrollment of those that remained went up, resulting in a net increase in the number of students and thus graduates. Yearly salaries were $1,000 plus room and board for institutional work.

Nurses' work in hospitals in the 1930s was labor intensive. Nurses were involved extensively with caring for patients confined to bed and with preparing diets and pharmaceutical solutions. There were dozens of solutions to be prepared as well as different prescriptions for baby formula. Medications too were sometimes prepared by nurses, weighing drugs such as quinine and salicylates and making them into capsules. Complex diets were prepared, such as diets low in ions or high in alkalinity, diets low in bulk or high in fat. Remedies using applications of heat or cold, with their inherent danger of tissue damage, were frequently ordered although the temperatures were only vaguely prescribed. For example, vaginal douches to stop bleeding were ordered "as hot as the patient can stand," while stupes, poultices, and electric light baths all relied on indeterminate amounts of heat to generate the desired effect. Nurses were trusted with procedures that had previously been in the domain of physicians, such as blood pressure measurement. Enemas and laxatives stand out as frequent nursing activities of this period—cleansing enemas; carminative (gas-reducing) enemas; sedative and stimulating enemas; oil and nutrient, antithelmintic (antiworm), antiseptic, astringent, and saline enemas. In one public hospital, enemas were part of the standard care for patients with pneumonia.

Although most nurses found work as private-duty and then as hospital bedside nurses, there were other less common career opportunities. Nurses working in the community, known as public health nurses, experienced more autonomy and prestige than individual patient or hospital-based nurses. The first quarter of the twentieth century saw increasing numbers of nurses enter this field. In 1926, at the height of public health nursing, nearly a fifth of all nurses were in public health. The maternity and child health programs of the 1921 Sheppard-Towner Act supported an increased role for these nurses.

Wars and other disasters provided more scope for the varied work of nurses and proved appealing for many with an adventurous, patriotic, and/or charitable bent. Twenty-four thousand nurses served in the First World War, 25% of all graduate nurses in the United States, and nearly three hundred nurses died. This effort severely taxed civilian nursing, which was exacerbated by the 1918 and 1919 flu pandemic. The nursing shortage prompted an Army School of Nursing, which was opened in May 1918. The Second World War saw about 74,000 nurses join the military services. Following the oversupply of the 1920s and 1930s, the 1940s was a time of nursing shortage. The return of peace enabled nurses to leave work for marriage and families, and younger women had an array of work options not available to the previous generation.

Nursing Education and Work after Mid-Century

Nursing education slowly shifted away from hospital training schools during the second half of the twentieth century, largely due to the use of trained nurses rather than students at the hospital bedside. The 1948 Brown Report, *Nursing for the Future*, also served as a catalyst for change.

Esther Lucile Brown, a researcher with the Russell Sage Foundation, had been charged with studying nursing education and nurses' work in the face of the critical postwar nursing shortage. The essence of her influential report was that nurses' training should move away from the confines of individual hospitals and into mainstream higher education. States and communities, Brown reasoned, supported the education of other professional occupations, while a non-educational entity—hospitals—provided for nursing training. Brown's report was derided by hospital administrators and the American Medical Association (AMA), both groups being apprehensive about loss of control over nursing education. The AMA had long held a paternalistic interest in nursing education. Many members were anxious that nurses' knowledge be strictly contained and not usurp any medical prerogative.

The ANA, however, fully supported Brown's findings, and some insurance companies and hospitals were also concerned with the inappropriateness of patients' hospital fees also supporting charges for nurses' education. In the late 1940s, federal aid for nursing programs, through the Emergency Professional Health Training Act, was proposed but was defeated partially through the efforts of the AMA as well as a newly formed association, the National Organization of Hospital Schools of Nursing. A few years later, in 1956, the Health Amendment Act, which supported further education for graduate nurses, was signed into law. In 1964, the landmark Nurse Training Act was passed. This bill provided federal aid for nursing education through school construction grants and student loans and scholarships.

The few baccalaureate programs that were in existence at mid-century did not offer a typical degree but were essentially a regular diploma program coupled with additional college courses. These programs typically lasted five years. In contrast, associate degree nursing programs, which first appeared in 1952, took just two years. These programs rapidly expanded in number. The associate degree program was seen as a way to relieve the critical nursing shortage as well as moving nursing education into the mainstream. The programs were highly successful. There were 16 community colleges offering associate degrees in nursing in 1955, and by 1964, there were 130. Graduates from all types of nursing programs, diploma, associate degree, and baccalaureate, sat for the same nurse licensure examination. In 1965, the ANA produced a position paper on nursing education that mandated a baccalaureate degree for nursing practice, but this apparently did not impact nursing education. The following decades witnessed the number of associate degree programs increase with a commensurate decline in hospital diploma programs, but the number of baccalaureate programs remained modest.

The postwar years saw tremendous growth in the hospital industry, which exacerbated the nursing shortage. Hospital building was largely financed by the Hospital Survey and Reconstruction (known as the Hill-Burton) Act of 1946. In the first six years following the Act, about 88,000 new hospital beds were created. Meanwhile, technological and scientific medical innovations generated increased patient demand, and private insurance plans supported more patient business. Employer-provided insurance plans were in place for about 75% of the civilian population by 1960, up from 33% in 1946. As the nurse historian Victoria Grando notes, care of acute illness, surgery, the baby boom, a growing elderly population, and care of the war-injured all increased the demand for hospital nursing care. Hospital admissions rose by 25% between 1946 and 1952. The loss of nurses to industry and public health exacerbated the shortage.

The critical postwar nursing shortage continued. Nursing continued to struggle for students while competing with other employment opportunities. There were several reasons for this. Nurses returning from the autonomy of war service braced at the authoritarian restrictions prevailing in civilian hospital nursing. In addition, the 48-hour workweeks, the assignment of split shifts—where nurses worked the busy morning and evening hours with their time off during the slow afternoons—and mandatory unpaid "on call" hours were unappealing. Additionally, most nurses did not receive medical care or insurance benefits. The persistence of low pay, compared with other female professionals and office and industrial workers, coupled with more and more responsibility as the science of health care rapidly developed, all combined to keep women and men out of nursing. At the same time, many women who had nursed during the war years now left nursing for marriage and raising a family.

The low pay was in part due to hospital administrators and the public continuing to see hospitals as charitable institutions rather than businesses and nurses as having a vocation rather than needing to work for a wage. The need to adequately compensate nurses could be conveniently disregarded because of this excuse. More pragmatically, hospitals were hard pressed to internally justify paying nurses comparably with other female workers when for years they had enjoyed the benefits of cheap student labor. To the chagrin of nursing leadership, buildings and technologies were afforded but not attractive nursing salaries.

The nurse shortage created a unique situation for female workers in the immediate postwar years. Married and older nurses were asked to stay at work in nursing although they were not tempted with increased salaries, in contrast to other women who were encouraged to leave their jobs for the returning men. The nurse shortage was partially addressed through hiring untrained aides or lesser-trained "practical nurses." Thus, the cheap nursing care formerly provided by students was now carried on by a second tier of lesser-educated nurses who were directed by licensed registered nurses. These nursing teams cared for groups of 15 to 20 patients. The nurse historians Joan Lynaugh and Barbara Brush have argued that nurses were unable to define their unique work, which led to the situation of low pay and substitution of lesser-prepared nurses.

In the 1960s and 1970s, sicker patients were admitted for shorter hospital stays. With Medicare and Medicaid legislation of 1965, there were increased pressures placed on hospitals and nursing services.

Nursing practice became more complex and diverse. To use nurses most effectively, the sickest patients were grouped together, under nurses experienced in their special needs—evolving into early intensive and coronary care units.

Nursing Organizations

Nursing leaders established four national organizations within a few decades of the inception of trained nursing in the 1870s. The first of these, the American Society of Superintendents of Training Schools for Nurses, was created in the wake of Chicago's 1893 World Fair. The new society was seen by its founders as a vehicle to organize and professionalize nursing. In 1912, the name was changed to the National League of Nursing Education. In 1896, this group founded a second professional organization, the Nurses' Associated Alumnae Association of the United States and Canada, later the American Nurses Association. The ANA was open to all graduate nurses, regardless of specialty, through their alumnae associations. The other nursing organizations were the National Organization for Public Health Nursing, founded in 1912, and the National Association of Colored Graduate Nurses, founded in 1908. The latter was instituted when some African-American nurses were essentially denied membership in the ANA because some state associations barred African-American nurses because of race. (See also the entry "National Association of Colored Graduate Nurses.") This section deals primarily with the ANA as the dominant organization, as well as the group charged with being nursing's collective bargaining representative at mid-century.

The first state associations of the ANA were formed in 1901 when the national body saw a need for more local organizations to co-ordinate activities within the state. By 1907, 28 state associations had been formed, although alumnae associations remained the primary basis for membership in the national organization. However, over the following years, membership in state associations became the only method of joining the national organization.

The ANA, through its state organizations, was early on involved in obtaining registration for nurses and in the formulation of acts to define nursing practice. Having invested three years in laborious hospital training, nurses were fierce in defending the title of "nurse" and restricting its use to themselves, both for their job security and for the protection of consumers. State registration of nurses was one way of achieving this. North Carolina was the first state to pass such a bill, although it was weaker than the nurses wanted due to opposition from the state medical society. Later state acts included educational requirements as well as a licensure examination. Another early activity of the ANA was the publication of the first American journal owned by nurses, the *American Journal of Nursing*, which began publication in 1900.

The contact of the hospital nurse with the ANA, whether hospital or private-duty, was greatest through the nurse's alumnae association. Members of alumnae associations held regular meetings, usually in the nurses' residence where they had lived during training. The meetings kept nurses abreast of patient care advances or were of general interest. Care of sick and needy members was another traditional focus of alumnae associations. Many associations funded an endowed hospital bed for their members, which allowed a nurse needing hospital care to use the "alumnae bed" free of charge. Some associations made special arrangements for their members stricken with tuberculosis—an occupational hazard. In Chicago, the First District of the Illinois State Nurses' Association sponsored a six-room cottage for its members with the disease on the grounds of a suburban sanatorium. The ANA also served to identify employment opportunities for nurses through operation of nurses' registries. Probably because membership in the ANA registry was necessary to obtain work as a private-duty nurse, the ANA was the largest professional organization of women in the world in 1930, with 100,000 members.

During the late 1930s, the issue of whether the ANA should serve as nurses' collective bargaining agent was discussed. Economic conditions for nurses continued to be poor in the postwar years. In 1941, the California Nurses' Association successfully represented its members before the War Labor Board. Its success prompted the ANA to adopt a more extensive national program for nurses. In 1946, the ANA adopted an economic security program, which allowed state nursing associations to act as representatives for their members in employment concerns and as their collective bargaining agents. The ANA wanted a 40-hour workweek with no decrease in salary. Yet the ANA's efforts became moot for many nurses when the Taft-Hartley Act was passed in 1947. The bill exempted nonprofit hospitals from the 1935 Labor Relations Act, which obligated employers to bargain collectively with their employees. The ANA immediately worked to get this Act repealed, but was not successful. In 1974, an amendment was finally signed into law permitting nurses in nonprofit hospitals to engage in collective bargaining.

Leadership in the ANA came from a group of women who wanted nursing to be recognized as a profession, with professional education and professional commitment to practice. This was frequently at odds with the nurses, who were frequently lesser-educated private-duty nurses whose livelihood would be affected by nursing leadership's professional aspirations. Many activities of the ANA at this time were concerned with nursing issues at the national and legislative level, sometimes leading to professional status at the price of longer hours and lower pay.

In 1950, the ANA and the National Association of Colored Graduate Nurses began a process of merger, while the National League of Nursing Education, the National Organization of Public Health Nurses, and the more recently formed Association of Collegiate Schools of Nursing formed the National League for Nursing.

Nursing contributes several unique attributes to an examination of labor history. Nurses' professional aspirations were impacted and hindered by gender and class. Nurses' work ranged from providing comfort measures to instituting life-threatening interventions. Nurses, predominantly women, were not, historically, associated with women's suffrage, yet they represented a significant group of this country's workingwomen. Thus, a study of nursing may inform labor, medical, social, women's, and political historical analysis.

BRIGID LUSK

References and Further Reading

Ashley, Jo Ann. *Hospitals, Paternalism, and the Role of the Nurse.* New York: Columbia University, 1976.

Brown, Esther Lucile. *Nursing for the Future.* New York: Russell Sage Foundation, 1948.

Burgess, May Ayres. *Nurses, Patients, and Pocketbooks: A Study of the Economics of Nursing by the Committee on the Grading of Nursing Schools.* History of American Nursing. New York: Garland, 1984.

Committee on the Grading of Nursing Schools. *Nursing Schools Today and Tomorrow.* New York: The Committee, 1934.

Grando, Victoria T. "A Hard Day's Work: Institutional Nursing in the Post-World War II Era." *Nursing History Review* 8 (2000): 169–184.

Hampton, Isabel Adams. *Nursing: Its Principles and Practice.* Philadelphia: Saunders, 1893.

Helmstadter, Carol. "Old Nurses and New: Nursing in the London Teaching Hospitals before and after the Mid-Nineteenth-Century Reforms." *Nursing History Review* 1 (1993): 43–70.

Kalisch, Philip A., and Beatrice J. Kalisch. *Advance of American Nursing*, 3rd ed. Philadelphia: Lippincott, 1995.

Lusk, Brigid. "Professional Strategies and Attributes of Chicago Hospital Nurses during the Great Depression." Ph.D. diss., University of Illinois at Chicago, 1995.

Lynaugh, Joan E., and Barbara L. Brush. *American Nursing: From Hospitals to Health Systems*. Cambridge, MA: Blackwell, 1996.

Melosh, Barbara. *"The Physician's Hand": Work Culture and Conflict in American Nursing*. Philadelphia: Temple University Press, 1982.

Nightingale, Florence. *Notes on Nursing: What It Is and What It Is Not*. New York: Dover, 1969.

Reverby, Susan M. *Ordered to Care: The Dilemma of American Nursing*. Cambridge: Cambridge University Press, 1987.

———. "The Search for the Hospital Yardstick: Nursing and the Rationalization of Hospital Work." In *Sickness and Health in America: Readings in the History of Medicine and Public Health*, 2nd ed., edited by Judith Walzer Leavitt and Ronald L. Numbers. Madison: University of Wisconsin Press, 1985, pp. 206–216.

Whalen, Jean C. "'A Necessity in the Nursing World': The Chicago Nurses Professional Registry, 1913–1950." *Nursing History Review* 13 (2005): 49–75.

INDEX